EQ

Encyclopaedia of the Qurʾān

VOLUME ONE

A–D

Jane Dammen McAuliffe, *General Editor*

Brill, Leiden–Boston–Köln

2001

ISBN 90 04 11465 3

Printed in The Netherlands on acid-free paper.

PREFACE

For more than a billion Muslims around the globe, the Qur'ān reproduces God's very own words. To hear its verses chanted, to see its words written large on mosque walls, to touch the pages of its inscribed text creates a sense of sacred presence in Muslim minds and hearts. For countless generations, Muslim families have greeted a newborn baby by whispering words from the Qur'ān in the infant's ear. For centuries, small children have begun their formal education with the Qur'ān. Seated around the teacher, they have learned to form the letters of the Arabic alphabet and to repeat the words and phrases from which their own recitation of the Qur'ān will develop. In a religious culture that extols learning, those individuals who acquire an advanced knowledge of the Qur'ān are accorded profound respect. People who commit all of the text to memory are treated with reverence. In fact, reverence marks most Muslim interaction with the Qur'ān, whether that be in silent prayer, public proclamation or serious study.

A description of the Qur'ān

For those with little previous exposure to the Qur'ān it may be helpful simply to describe this book. In the library of world scriptures, the Qur'ān stands as one of the shorter entries. When a textual tradition like the Buddhist canon of Pali, Sanskrit and Chinese scriptures is compared to the Qur'ān, the size differences are significant. Even the Hebrew Bible or the Christian canon of Old and New Testaments comprise much larger collections. In contrast, the Qur'ān is a fairly compact text of 114 sections. These sections or chapters, virtually all of which begin with the introductory formula "In the name of God, the Merciful, the Compassionate," are called *sūras*. The sūras, in turn, are composed of verses or, in Arabic, *āyāt* (sing. *āya*). Individual sūras can contain just a few verses or a few hundred. This variation in length is noteworthy because the Qur'ān uses length as an organizing principle. The canonical text is arranged by roughly descending order of sūra length. In other words, the longer sūras appear earlier in the text, the very shortest ones toward the end.

The contents of the Qur'ān are varied and not easily categorized. Nor are they ordered in a manner that systematic modern minds might prefer. You will not, for example, find separate sūras devoted to theological pronouncements, to rules for social and personal behavior, to prayers and liturgical specifications, to narratives about past prophets, to warnings about the last judgment and descriptions of heaven and hell or to polemical challenges directed toward those with other beliefs. You will, however, find all of these themes, as well as others, woven through the various sūras of the qur'ānic text. In fact, the thematic complexity of the Qur'ān has spawned a genre of Islamic literature that seeks to extract and to categorize. Some of these works attempt a comprehensive classification of qur'ānic material under numerous headings and subheadings while others concentrate upon a particular topic. In Muslim bookstores, therefore, one finds books such as "What the Qur'ān says about women" or "What the Qur'ān says about a just society."

Just as there is thematic variation within the Qur'ān, there is also stylistic diversity. While the Qur'ān contains relatively little sustained narrative of the sort to which readers of the Hebrew Bible or Christian New Testament would be accustomed — the twelfth sūra being the principal exception — the language of the Qur'ān is frequently strong and dramatic. Vivid imagery and evocative similes abound. Oaths and dialogues combine with divine direct address, whether to the prophet Muḥammad, to those who believe his message or to those who reject it. Terse, elliptical language alternates with more prolonged, prosaic passages. Prayers and prophecy intermix with the proscriptions and prescriptions that must guide human action.

The full force of this rhetorical diversity, however, may not be available to those who read the Qur'ān in translation. It is an article of Muslim faith and belief that the Qur'ān is the Qur'ān only in Arabic. When translated it ceases to be "God's very own words" and becomes simply an interpretation of the Arabic original. For this reason, whenever Muslims recite the Qur'ān in ritual prayer or other liturgical formats, they always recite it in Arabic. Nevertheless, there are numerous translations of the Qur'ān in most of the major languages of the world, including English.

The study of the Qur'ān

The long tradition of scholarship that the Qur'ān has generated provides another indication of the reverence that surrounds this text. Although the history of the text's pronouncement and transmission, as well as the relation of this history to that of its earliest phases of interpretation, remain matters of scholarly controversy, there is no doubt that questions about the text itself and reflections upon its meaning were a part of the qur'ānic environment from its inception. Not unexpectedly, matters of language took precedence, and the first efforts at interpretation or exegesis involved providing synonyms and explanations for unfamiliar words. As would be the case with a recited text, variant vocalizations appeared and the increasing number and variety of these eventually prompted steps toward regularization. Not all earlier listeners were equally prepared to understand the sometimes elliptical nature of qur'ānic discourse. Individual phrases required exegetical interpolation as did narrative passages of a more allusive nature.

Other questions quickly arose: When, and in what circumstances, were certain verses revealed? Who or what is intended by an ambiguous term or phrase? To whom or to what does a particular pronoun refer? Who is being addressed by a specific passage and to whom should it apply: to all believers, present and future, or to a restricted set of individuals? Is the intended sense metaphorical or should the verse be understood literally? Are all parts of the Qur'ān equally comprehensible or are some parts more inherently obscure or problematic? Are there connections between verses, either within a sūra or across various parts of the Qur'ān? Can a passage elsewhere in the text help to explain the one under present examination? Are there levels or layers of meaning in the text and are these accessible only to individuals with special intellectual or spiritual training?

Clearly what motivated this multiplicity of interpretive inquiries was more than a scholarly interest in the scripture. Those with a thorough or intimate knowledge of the text were pressed to provide answers to crucial questions about individual and group behavior. The words of the Qur᾽ān, understood as coming directly from God, guided social and religious practices within the nascent Muslim community, so an adequate comprehension of the text was seen as essential to its correct application. But even the outlines of this early history remain a matter of scholarly controversy. The question of "Islamic origins," understood to include the first two centuries of this new religious movement, is the most contentious topic within the field of Islamic studies. Scholars, both Muslim and non-Muslim, debate over matters of chronology, geography and source reliability. Assertions and counter-assertions about the Qur᾽ān stand at the center of these contentions.

A brief sketch of the earliest stages of both the promulgation and interpretation of the Qur᾽ān can only allude to these debates, rather than engage them directly. Many scholars feel that the initial stages of both promulgation and interpretation of the Qur᾽ān were oral. And they were connected. In the midst of reciting a portion of the text, the reciter might stop to provide synonyms for terms unfamiliar to his audience. He might also make associations between one part of the Qur᾽ān and another or offer short explanatory glosses for passages that seemed allusive and elliptical. Storytelling was another activity of the first generations and apparently qur᾽ānic recitation was frequently supplemented with associated narratives that drew upon a common store of biblical, hagiographical and legendary material.

Seeking the connection between this oral-performative period and its written conveyance, asking whether it was simultaneous or subsequent, raises all of the historiographical concerns just mentioned. Much of the traditional scholarship about this era is drawn from sources that postdate it by several generations. The paucity of extant textual and epigraphic material that can be incontestably ascribed to much of the first Islamic century exacerbates the situation. What some scholars see as an exciting era of rapid religio-political change that has been adequately and reliably described by later Muslim historians, other scholars view as a period of intense sectarian strife whose chronological and geographical specifics can only be dimly glimpsed. And there are a range of scholarly perspectives that lie between these two extremes.

By the late ninth century, however, Muslim understanding of the Qur᾽ān had reached a stage of doctrinal and exegetical stabilization and the tendency in academic study of the Qur᾽ān has been to view this as a pivotal moment. Theological debates about the nature of the Qur᾽ān, about whether it was "created" or "uncreated," had been sustained and surmounted. Generations of qur᾽ānic interpretation, both oral and written, had produced a massive accumulation of exegetical data, an accumulation captured in the key work that defines this moment. "The compendium of explanations for the interpretation of the verses of the Qur᾽ān" *(Jāmiʿ al-bayān ʿan ta᾽wīl āy al-Qur᾽ān)* was composed by the Baghdādī scholar Abū Jaʿfar b. Jarīr al-Ṭabarī (d. 310/923) and its most widely-available edition — it is still being reprinted — runs to thirty volumes. Al-Ṭabarī's commentary on the Qur᾽ān represents itself as the summation of all previous exegetical activity. From the vantage point of this commentary and similar works that followed it, later Muslim scholarship on the Qur᾽ān looks back to the first centuries of its history and tracks this history in a generational schema.

Within this schema, the prophet Muḥammad himself assumes pride of place as the Qur᾽ān's first interpreter. After his death, this primacy is passed to his closest followers, whom Islamic history calls his Companions. Among the most prominent names of this exegetical generation are: Ibn ʿAbbās, Ibn Masʿūd, Ubayy b. Kaʿb and the fourth caliph, ʿAlī b. Abī Ṭālib. Qur᾽ānic interpretation attributed to this period is also associated with the Prophet's youngest widow, ʿĀʾisha. The next generation, that of the Followers according to traditional Muslim terminology, includes names like Mujāhid b. Jabr, ʿIkrima, Saʿīd b. Jubayr, al-Ḍaḥḥāk, Qatāda b. Diʿāma and ʿAlī b. Abī Ṭalḥa. Later sources list all of these figures as students of Ibn ʿAbbās, a Companion whom the tradition has honored as being "the Ocean" of exegetical knowledge.

Between these very early names and the compendium work of al-Ṭabarī other important figures entered the landscape of qurʾānic interpretation: al-Ḥasan al-Baṣrī (d. 110/728), Muqātil b. Sulaymān (d. 150/767), Sufyān al-Thawrī (d. 161/778), Sufyān b. ʿUyayna (d. 196/811), ʿAbd al-Razzāq (d. 211/827), Sahl al-Tustarī (d. 238/896) and Hūd b. Muḥakkim (d. ca. 290/903). During the last several decades printed editions have appeared whose attribution to these, and other, early scholars raises all the questions of redaction history and authorial retrojection that continue to preoccupy the study of Islamic origins. Nevertheless, continuing source-critical work on this period should provide both greater security in the accuracy of attribution and a more refined understanding of the lines of exegetical influence.

While al-Ṭabarī's commentary remains a fundamental source, the library of qurʾānic interpretation grew steadily in the centuries following its early tenth-century appearance. Both Muslim and non-Muslim surveys of exegetical history tend to classify these works by doctrinal or ideological orientation. Without attempting to be exhaustive I will group some of the major names in this fashion to help orient readers of this encyclopaedia who are less familiar with the field of qurʾānic studies. Most closely associated with the approach of al-Ṭabarī are: Abū l-Layth al-Samarqandī (d. 375/985), Abū Isḥāq al-Thaʿlabī (d. 427/1035), al-Baghawī (d. 516/1122), Ibn ʿAṭiyya (d. 541/1147), Ibn al-Jawzī (d. 597/1200), Ibn Kathīr (d. 774/1373) and al-Suyūṭī (d. 911/1505).

A more fluid categorization is that which identifies certain forms of interpretation as being less concerned with conveying the exegetical *dicta* of the earliest Islamic centuries and more interested in expressing particular theological or philosophical orientations. Muslim exegetical history records a more mixed reception to this kind of interpretation. While the works of interpreters such as al-Qāḍī ʿAbd al-Jabbār (d. 415/1025), al-Zamakhsharī (d. 538/1144) and Fakhr al-Dīn al-Rāzī (d. 606/1210) have been questioned or condemned, those of Ibn Ḥabīb al-Nīsābūrī (d. 406/1015), al-Bayḍāwī (d. ca. 700/1301), al-Nasafī (d. 710/1310) and al-Khāzin al-Baghdādī (d. 742/1341) have received a generally favorable response.

Lists of the most famous Shīʿī commentators usually include al-ʿAyyāshī (d. ca. 320/932), al-Qummī (fl. mid 4th/10th), al-Ṭūsī (d. 460/1067) and al-Ṭabarsī (d. 548/1153). While these works do not represent an exegetical tradition that is completely divorced from that of Sunnī commentary, they do mark their distinctiveness through reference to certain early authorities, such as Jaʿfar al-Ṣādiq (d. 148/765) and other Shīʿī imāms, and through attention to particular topics and modes of interpretation. Shīʿī Islam is, of course, no more monolithic than its Sunnī counterpart and there are important groups within Shīʿism, such as the Ismāʿīlīs and the Zaydīs, who cherish a lineage of commentators within their own intellectual communities.

A far more diverse form of qurʾānic commentary is that associated with "mystical" Islam or Ṣūfism. A very early figure in this tradition, Sahl al-Tustarī, has already been mentioned. Other important Ṣūfī commentaries are those of al-Sulamī (d. 412/1021), al-Qushayrī (d. 465/1072) and Rūzbihān al-Baqlī (d. 606/1209), as well as that published under the name of Ibn al-ʿArabī (d. 638/1240) but actually the work of a successor. Ṣūfī commentary is less likely to attempt comprehensive exegetical coverage of the qurʾānic text than the other works that have been mentioned. Often it records the spiritual insights and mystical illuminations that a particular word or phrase of the Qurʾān has generated, either in the author's mind or in the minds of those whose thoughts he seeks to convey.

The selective nature of Ṣūfī commentary finds its counterpart in another exegetical genre that also focuses chiefly upon only certain parts of the qurʾānic text. Legal commentaries on the Qurʾān concern themselves primarily with those verses that have behavioral implications, that mandate or prohibit various kinds of human activity. The principal works in this category are those of al-Jaṣṣāṣ (d. 370/981), Ilkiyā al-Harrāsī (d. 504/1110), Muḥammad b. ʿAbdallāh b. al-ʿArabī (d. 543/1148) and al-Qurṭubī (d. 671/1272). Mention of the two last-named scholars on this list allows me to note the geographic and linguistic spread of qurʾānic exegesis.

Both Ibn al-ʿArabī and al-Qurṭubī are from Andalusia, an area of the medieval Muslim world that produced a rich intellectual heritage. They wrote in Arabic, as did all of the commentators whose names have been mentioned thus far. But important exegetical work on the Qurʾān has certainly not been limited to Arabic. Persian and Turkish contributions are complemented by those in the languages of south and southeast Asia and of sub-Saharan Africa. Especially in more recent centuries the linguistic spread of this interpretive tradition has become more pronounced. While the twentieth century witnessed the publication of major commentaries in Arabic, such as those of Muḥammad ʿAbduh and Rashīd Riḍā, of Sayyid Quṭb, of al-Ṭabāṭabāʾī — a Persian who wrote in Arabic — of Bint al-Shāṭiʾ and of Muḥammad Mutawallī al-Shaʿrāwī, it also welcomed Urdu contributions by Abū l-Aʿlā al-Mawdūdī and Amīn Aḥsan Iṣlāḥī, as well as a thirty-volume work by Hamka (Haji Abdul Malik Karim Amrullah) in Bahasa Indonesian.

Southeast Asia, which is home to about one quarter of the world's Muslim population, has witnessed a contemporary resurgence of all forms of qurʾānic studies. Recitation of the Qurʾān, for instance, takes the form of local, regional and national competitions for both men and women, with qurʾānic quiz shows as a popular part of these events. While quiz shows may be a decidedly modern way to display expertise in qurʾānic studies, the desire for comprehensive attention to all aspects of the text and its conveyance has a very long history within Islamic intellectual life. Although sequential commentary on the Qurʾān constitutes an important part of that history and is a major element of what Muslims like to call the "qurʾānic sciences," it is by no means the only element.

Recitation itself has evolved into an elaborate set of disciplines that must be mastered in order to insure the accurate and euphonious reproduction of the text. Students wishing to develop this skill, whether native speakers of Arabic or not, spend years learning how to pronounce every phonological element perfectly, how to pace the recitation properly and to pause where required or suggested, how to render particular combinations of letters and to elongate, with some syllables, the sound production for a precise duration. Along with assimilating the rules of recitation, students also begin to memorize the Qurʾān and many eventually can recite all 114 sūras from memory, as have generations of their predecessors.

At advanced levels, recitation of the Qurʾān includes the acquisition of a thorough knowledge of the various "readings" of the Qurʾān. These represent yet another realm of the qurʾānic sciences and one with very ancient roots. According to traditional accounts of the Qurʾān's textual canonization, an acceptable range of variability eventually emerged and was ratified by the scholarly community. While most printed texts of the Qurʾān that are in circulation today draw upon only one of these textual traditions, others remain alive and are sustained by varying numbers of adherents.

As the qurʾānic text continued to attract scrutiny from successive generations of scholars, other categories within the broad range of the qur'ānic sciences became more standardized and generated their own subgenres of scholarly literature. Attempts to provide historical contextualization for specific qur'ānic passages created the "occasions of revelation" literature, exemplified in a noted work by al-Wāḥidī (d. 468/1076). The belief that the Qur'ān contained elements of its own abrogation, that some verses nullified the prescriptive force of others, gave rise to an extensive interpretive and cataloguing effort that found expression in the works of scholars like al-Zuhrī (d. 124/742), al-Naḥḥās (d. 338/949), Hibat Allāh b. Salāma (d. 410/1020) and Ibn al-ʿAtāʾiqī (d. ca. 790/1020).

Lexical examination led to yet further forms of categorization: qur'ānic vocabulary deemed "difficult" or "unusual" by virtue of its derivation or dialectical connection was collected in works by Ibn Qutayba (d. 276/889), al-Sijistānī (d. 330/942) and al-Rāghib al-Isbahānī (d. 502/1108). Words with multiple meanings and words that function as synonyms are also treated by Ibn Qutayba as well as by al-Damaghānī (d. 478/1085) and Ibn al-Jawzī. The more vexing problem of semantic ambiguity prompted additional works of classification and textual cross-referencing. Taken as a whole this exacting lexical scrutiny demonstrates a profound and reverential engagement with the text, a reverence that is also evident in the rhetorical engrossment that characterizes the developed qur'ānic sciences.

From a very early period it has been a point of Muslim doctrine that the religious and rhetorical power of the Qur'ān could never be replicated: the Qur'ān, in the belief of Muslims, is inimitable. Traditional literary criticism of the text concentrates upon elaborating the grounds for this doctrinal declaration. As developed by classical scholars such as al-Rummānī (d. 386/996), al-Khaṭṭābī (d. 388/998), al-Bāqillānī (d. 403/1013) and al-Jurjānī (d. 470/1078), these grounds are both substantive and stylistic. Muslims hold the Qur'ān to be the ratifying miracle of Muḥammad's prophethood because it contains information about the past and the future and about God's relations with the world that no human being could attain unaided. The Muslim belief that Muḥammad was illiterate adds additional force to this sense of suprahuman origin and content. But beyond such matters of content lies the emphasis upon the aesthetic effectiveness of the Qur'ān. Careful and painstaking analysis of the text isolated relevant examples of genre forms and literary figures; it scrutinized patterns of rhyme and assonance; it catalogued specific instances of word choice and arrangement. This scrutiny and analysis intermingled with praise of the Qur'ān's overpowering eloquence. In fact, much of the intricate dissection of the qur'ānic text to be found in works on the "sciences of the Qur'ān" could be viewed as an effort to explain the effect of qur'ānic recitation upon the believer. The rhetorical experience finds written manifestation in the extraordinarily detailed classifications produced by scholars such as al-Zarkashī (d. 794/1392) and al-Suyūṭī. Surveying the eighty chapters of al-Suyūṭī's monumental synthesis of the qur'ānic sciences gives one a good sense of textual scholarship as an act of abiding reverential attention.

Scholarship on the Qur'ān was also produced by non-Muslims. Just as Muslim authors have attended to the scriptural heritage of other religions, particularly Judaism and Christianity, non-Muslim scholars have interested themselves in the Qur'ān. Of course, much of this interest was fostered by polemical concerns, a "know the enemy" mentality that became particularly acute during periods of military hostility and intense economic competition. Even from a very early period, verses or passages from the Qur'ān were used by non-Muslims, in the time-honored tradition of religious polemic, in an attempt to discredit its status as divine revelation and to demonstrate internal inconsistencies. Even without direct quotation, polemical arguments against the Qur'ān became a commonplace of medieval Jewish and Christian religious discourse. Such noted figures as John of Damascus (d. 749) al-Qirqisānī (mid 10th cent.), Maimonides (d. 1204) and Thomas Aquinas (d. 1274) may be mentioned in this regard.

The later medieval period, however, brought a new approach, one associated with the renowned Abbot of Cluny, Peter the Venerable (d. 1156). While certainly not divorced from polemical motives, Peter's initiative broadened the active translation movement that was producing Latin versions of important Arabic scientific and medical works to include the Qurʾān and other works of a religious nature. To do this, Peter assembled a team of translators including the Englishman Robert of Ketton (fl. 1136-57) who is credited with creating the first full translation of the Qurʾān into any Western language. Despite criticisms of its accuracy and arrangement, Robert's rendering remained the standard Latin version of the Qurʾān for several centuries.

It was soon joined, however, by that of Mark of Toledo (fl. 1193-1216) and recent scholarship has demonstrated that both of these translators did not restrict themselves to the qurʾānic text alone but clearly had access to a number of major commentaries, either directly or through a scholarly Muslim informant, and made skillful use of them. Much later translation also followed this procedure, including that of the eighteenth-century English Orientalist George Sale and his compatriot, the twentieth-century convert, Mohammed Marmaduke Pickthall.

Robert of Ketton's translation, via its Italian rendering by Andrea Arrivabene published in 1547, influenced the first German and then Dutch translations. Extant manuscripts of Hebrew translations of the Qurʾān, such as that of Yaʿaqov b. Israel ha-Levi which too appeared in Venice in 1547, apparently draw upon this same lineage. During this same period French versions were also being produced and in 1698 Ludovico Marraci published another Latin translation that soon saw replication in various European languages. George Sale's 1734 combined publication of both a translation of the Qurʾān and a "Preliminary Discourse" that drew upon earlier prolegomena served as the principle English-language primer on Islam for more than a century.

Translation is, of course, not the only form of non-Muslim qurʾānic studies that the medieval and early modern Europe generated. Access to the Qurʾān via such translations provoked responses from Jewish and Christian authors. The interests of both polemic and apologetic were served by a closer knowledge of the qurʾānic text, prompting scholars such as Ricoldo da Montecroce (d. 1320) and Nicholas of Cusa (d. 1464) to pen refutations. Reference to the Qurʾān and the citation of specific passages can be found in many works of Jewish and Christian scholarship from these periods. Fragments of transcriptions of the Qurʾān into Hebrew characters, including some from the Genizah materials, provide additional indication of non-Muslim study of the text. Then, of course, there has been the post-Enlightenment emergence of "oriental" studies as a distinct academic discipline. Much of what is to be found in the *Encyclopaedia of the Qurʾān* builds upon the work begun in those academic centers that undertook the "scientific" study of non-Western cultures and religions.

Even before this, faculties devoted to such studies had been founded in places like Leiden (1593), Rome (1627) and Oxford (1638). Later they opened at other major European universities and, eventually, at certain North American ones, as well. Arabic and other Islamic languages, such as Persian and Turkish, were a primary focus of instruction because language competency was the indispensable prerequisite to the study of texts and other historical sources. In this regard the emerging discipline of Islamic studies modeled itself upon classical studies as these had developed during the Renaissance and after. Philology, understood as the study of a culture through the lens of the texts that it produced, became the dominant methodology.

Because the Qurʾān was recognized as central to the identity and historical development of Islam, close attention was given to it, and qurʾānic studies emerged as a major subfield within the study of Islam.

In its development, non-Muslim (or "Western") qurʾānic studies was profoundly influenced by its sibling discipline of biblical studies. Eighteenth- and nineteenth-century biblical criticism, at least that part of it which had migrated from a rabbinic or monastic setting to a university one, bracketed belief in the divine character of the Jewish and Christian scriptures. The Renaissance willingness to apply principles of literary and historical criticism to ancient Greek and Latin texts was adopted for another ancient text, the Bible. Taking a rationalist perspective, some scholars sought to reconcile biblical teaching with the mandates of reason while others concentrated upon the contradictions between the Bible and the canons of scientific orthodoxy. Contextual investigations multiplied as scholars probed the cultural and historical background of the biblical texts and pursued the literary heritage out of which these grew, as well as the redactional process which created their final form.

As scholars schooled in Semitic philology and conversant with the historical-critical study of the Hebrew Bible and the New Testament turned their attention to another ancient text, the Qurʾān, they brought with them this same disregard of dogmatic assumptions as irrelevant to the tasks of scholarship. The Qurʾān, like the Bible, was subjected to textual and philological analysis and in the second half of the nineteenth century some of the seminal works that still guide the field today were written. The names of Gustav Weil, Theodor Nöldeke, Abraham Geiger and Hartwig Hirschfeld were soon joined by their twentieth-century counterparts, such as Ignaz Goldziher, Gotthelf Bergsträsse, Otto Pretzl, Richard Bell, Arthur Jeffery and Rudi Paret. From a related perspective, some of these scholars and others approached the Qurʾān as the most reliable source for reconstruction of the life of Muḥammad and the history of the early Muslim community.

New factors in the study of the Qurʾān

As this very brief sketch indicates, the history of Muslim and non-Muslim study of the Qurʾān could be characterized as two parallel conversations. Ordinarily these conversations proceeded in relative isolation from each other except for those times when polemical salvos were exchanged. The long trajectory of Muslim study and interpretation of the Qurʾān has been a largely self-contained exercise. Similarly, the more recently established field of qurʾānic studies within European and American institutes of higher education has certainly drawn upon the centuries-long results of Muslim scholarship but has rarely established sustained, collaborative conversation with contemporary scholars of the qurʾānic sciences.

But the "two solitudes" of Muslim and non-Muslim qurʾānic studies are beginning to break open, at least on some occasions and within some contexts. Increasingly, international conferences devoted to the academic study of the Qurʾān attract scholars from both groups. Journals that were formally quite segregated now show a greater diversity of authors' names and institutional identifications. Opportunities to lecture at universities in the Muslim world are being offered to non-Muslim scholars and the reverse of such invitations bring scholars from these universities to European and North American institutions.

Perhaps the most significant point of confluence, however, is graduate training and the production of new generations of doctoral degrees in the field of qurʾānic studies. Increasingly, students pursuing graduate work in qurʾānic studies, as well as other subfields of Islamic studies, in major universities in Europe, the United States, Canada and elsewhere are coming from immigrant Muslim families. Many of these are second or third generation products of post-colonial patterns of Muslim migration to Great Britain, France, Germany and North America. Consequently, most of these students enter graduate programs with an educational background and a set of academic assumptions that are indistinguishable from those of their non-Muslim peers. The present mix of academic publication in the field already reflects this dynamic and future productivity will surely manifest its amplification.

The vastly increased rate of scholarly exchange facilitated by electronic communication, including the Internet, further accelerates the opportunities for scholarly interaction within the field of qurʾānic studies. And it enhances another form of availability that will surely affect the future of the field. It is worth noting that, until quite recently, the Qurʾān as a written text was available to a relatively small proportion of Muslims worldwide. Most Muslims for most of Islam's long history have experienced the Qurʾān orally. Literacy rates in pre-modern populations generally were far lower than they are today. In the last century, particularly with the withdrawal of colonial domination in the Muslim world and the subsequent development of systems of public education, there has been great change in mass literacy. The nineteenth- and twentieth-century growth in book production has created the concomitant phenomenon of textual accessibility.

Vast print runs, often subsidized by governmental agencies of religious affairs, have made the Qurʾān available to large segments of the Muslim population worldwide. Multiple translations into virtually all of the world's languages have brought qurʾānic teaching directly to the individual without the necessary mediation of a religious scholar. Although translations do not have the same status as the Arabic text, they have allowed many more Muslims to become students of qurʾānic meaning than was ever possible before. One area where such changes in literacy and textual accessibility are proving transformative is that of Muslim women. Currently Muslim women are achieving secondary and post-secondary degrees in far greater numbers than in any previous generation. And these educated women are reading the Qurʾān. Within its pages they are finding resources for religious and social renewal and they are forging forms of leadership with which to effect these changes.

Easily-available printed versions are but one aspect of the contemporary textual accessibility of the Qurʾān. Television and radio broadcasts of qurʾānic recitation are frequent. Audio cassette or CD ROM recordings of the most famous reciters can be purchased in any town with a substantial Muslim population, whether in the Middle East, Asia or North America. And, of course, the Qurʾān is on the Internet. Thousands of web sites offer the Arabic text, translations into European, Asian and African languages, synchronized recitation of all or part of the text and countless pages of introduction, explanation and commentary. Some versions are searchable, whether by keyword, word segment or chapter and verse number. In fact, some of the editorial accuracy checking for the qurʾānic citations in this encyclopaedia was done with a searchable, web-based text.

Creating the EQ

Planning for the *Encyclopaedia of the Qurʾān (EQ)* began in 1993 when I met in Leiden with a senior Brill editor, Peri Bearman, to explore the possibility of initiating such a project. Very quickly, four superb scholars, Wadad Kadi, Claude Gilliot, William Graham and Andrew Rippin, agreed to join the editorial team. Both the desire to take stock of the field of qurʾānic studies at the turn of the century and an interest in seeing this field flourish in the new millennium prompted our initial conversations. From its inception, then, the *EQ* has gazed both backwards and forwards and this dual visioning has shaped the structuring of this encyclopaedia. As the associate editors and I proceeded with the planning, we were determined to create a reference work that would capture this century's best achievements in qurʾānic studies. But we also wanted the EQ to stimulate even more extensive scholarship on the Qurʾān in the decades to come. In the service of this dual ambition, it was decided to expand the expected alphabetical format of an encyclopaedia to include a series of longer, more comprehensive articles. The associate editors and I envisioned these as synoptic statements of the present state of reflection and research on major topics within the purview of qurʾānic studies. The combination of encyclopaedia entries, of varying length, and of essay-length overviews of major research areas within the field of qurʾānic studies seemed to us the best way both to honor the accomplishments of the last century and to foster the achievements of this one.

But as important as this retrospective and prospective vision was to the creation of the EQ, yet more important was the desire to make the world of qurʾānic studies accessible to a very broad range of academic scholars and educated readers. The various fields of literary studies have produced countless dictionaries, encyclopaedias, commentaries and concordances dedicated to the study of particular periods, areas, authors and works. Similarly, religious literature, especially the Bible, has been the subject of hundreds of such works, with new ones being produced at an ever-increasing rate. This scholarly abundance stands in stark contrast to the situation in qurʾānic studies. The number of reference works for the Qurʾān that are accessible in European languages remains quite small; much of the available information is partial and incomplete or hidden in difficult-to-secure sources.

Of course, scholars who can command classical Arabic can avail themselves of thousands of works on the Qurʾān, including concordances, dictionaries and commentaries, but those without this linguistic access have very little. For example, the last English dictionary of qurʾānic Arabic was published in 1873 and the only widely-available English concordance is keyed to a translation of the Qurʾān that used a nineteenth-century numbering system for the verses now rarely encountered in printed versions. English-speaking scholars from fields other than Islamic studies, therefore, are poorly served when they attempt to learn anything about the Qurʾān, either for their own research purposes or to introduce it to their students. It is with this need in mind that the associate editors and I made the decision to use English-language entry-words for this encyclopaedia. Our colleagues in the field of Islamic studies will appreciate that this was neither an easy nor an uncontroversial decision. The *Encyclopaedia of Islam (EI)*, which has long been the most widely-used general reference work in the field, employs transliterated Arabic entry-words or lemmata and this has come to be regarded as the scholarly norm. Such a system allows a precision that is lost with the move to English-language lemmata. To take but one example: There is no exact Arabic equivalent for the word "prayer." *Ṣalāt* refers to the ritual worship that observant Muslims perform five times a day, while *duʿāʾ* connotes less formalized, intercessory prayer. *Dhikr* is the term used for a very broad range of Ṣūfī practices and both classical and contemporary Arabic contain other relevant vocabulary items, as well. The EI has articles on each of these three but nothing under the single entry-word, "Prayer." Consequently the non-Arabist scholar or student who wants to know something about this more general topic has a difficult time using the EI but will not encounter such hurdles with the EQ.

Yet another, much-debated decision was that concerning the scope of this encyclopaedia. The Qurʾān, as a major piece of world literature, and as the primary scripture of a world-wide religious tradition, has generated a huge exegetical corpus. As I have already noted, multivolume commentaries on the Qurʾān have been produced by virtually every generation of Muslim scholars and, while most of these are written in Arabic, the languages of other Islamic populations are well represented. The continuing popularity of this genre, in both its classical and its contemporary productions, is manifest through sustained publication and sales. The works of major classical commentators like al-Ṭabarī, al-Zamakhsharī, Ibn Kathīr and al-Suyūṭī can be found on the shelves of any good-sized bookstore in the Muslim world, alongside such contemporary standards as the commentaries of al-Mawdūdī, Sayyid Quṭb and al-Ṭabāṭabāʾī.

Consequently, the question had to be considered: Should this be an encyclopaedia of the Qurʾān or should it be an encyclopaedia of the Qurʾān and its interpretation? There is, of course, no clear division between these two categories. Virtually every article in this encyclopaedia draws, directly or indirectly, upon the corpus of qurʾānic exegesis. Nevertheless, project containment demanded that the focus of concentration remain the Qurʾān itself. Therefore, readers of the EQ will not find a separate article on al-Ṭabarī or Fakhr al-Dīn al-Rāzī, but they will find frequent reference to the works of these commentators and the EQ's cumulative index will allow users to track these references through all of its volumes. This, too, was a tough editorial choice and one that I hope can be reconsidered if this encyclopaedia eventually generates a second, expanded edition.

Along with the desire to create a reference work that would be accessible to scholars and students from a broad range of humanistic and social scientific disciplines, the associate editors and I shared a desire to include rigorous, academic scholarship on the Qurʾān, scholarship that grows from a plurality of perspectives and presuppositions. The key words in the preceding sentence are "rigorous" and "academic." There is, as I have just recounted, no single academic tradition of qurʾānic scholarship. Centuries of Muslim scholarship on the Qurʾān constitutes a time line that overlaps with that of generations of Western scholarship on the text. And neither of these categories, inexact as they are, represents a single, monolithic approach or a unique, overriding methodology. Both between and within the worlds of Muslim and Western qurʾānic scholarship one finds vigorous and contentious debate. Increasingly these worlds overlap, both geographically and intellectually. With the rapid growth of Muslim populations in Europe, North America and other parts of the world, the rough polarity of "Muslim" and "Western" becomes ever more blurred. The internationalization of scholarship and of academic life accelerates this trend. As mentioned above, Muslim and non-Muslim scholars interact freely at conferences on the Qurʾān, whether these be in Leiden or Lahore. Academic journals are much less self-segregated than they were a generation ago and the number of Muslim scholars who have taken advanced degrees in Euro-American institutions in some field of Islamic studies has increased exponentially. Scholarly perspective can no longer be neatly pinned to religious identification and good scholarship is flourishing in this richly plural environment. The editors of the EQ have striven to capture that plurality within the pages of this encyclopaedia, wanting this work to represent the widest possible range of rigorous, academic scholarship on the Qurʾān.

Using the EQ

Entries in the *Encyclopaedia of the Qurʾān* appear in the customary alphabetical order but are of two kinds. By far the majority are articles of varying lengths that treat important figures, concepts, places, values, actions and events to be found within the text of the Qurʾān or which have an important relationship with the text. For example, the entry on "Abraham" deals with a figure found in the text while that on "African Literature" discusses a literary relationship. The second category of articles that have been commissioned for the EQ are essay-length treatments of important topics within the field of qur'ānic studies. Again to take examples from the first volume, I would point to the entries "Art and Architecture" and "Chronology and the Qur'ān." Here scholars were asked to let their writing reflect the past and present "state of the question" on these significant topics.

As noted above, the decision to use English-language lemmata in the EQ has both advantages and disadvantages. While it makes the work much more widely accessible to scholars in cognate fields, it does not afford Arabists and Islamicists the familiar starting point of transliterated terminology. To solve this, a very thorough indexing of both English words and transliterated Arabic terminology is planned for the EQ's final volume. Within the body of the encyclopaedia, however, readers will find extensive use of transliteration, both in identification of the lemmata and in the articles themselves, so that specialists in this field can have the precision that is important to them.

Of course, in planning the list of entries the decision about what constitutes an English word could never be entirely straightforward. In general, our editorial policy has been guided by current English usage as reflected in contemporary dictionaries and works of general reference. Where an Arabic proper name has a clear English cognate, that has been used. Where it does not, the Arabic form has been retained. Relevant examples would be "Adam and Eve" as opposed to "Dhū l-Kifl."

Because the EQ has been created both to present scholarly understanding of the Qur'ān and to promote it, all authors have been urged to provide relevant and representative bibliography for their articles. Readers will find these a helpful entry into further study of a particular topic. In addition, in-text citation of both primary and secondary literature should assist scholars in the field of Islamic studies as they develop more detailed studies of the topics treated in this work. Citations of the Qur'ān are given by chapter (sūra) number, followed by verse (āya) number, e.g. Q 30:46. This represents a departure from the more common Muslim practice of identifying sūras by name rather than number — the previous example would thus be Sūrat al-Rūm, 46 — but it makes it much easier for those unfamiliar with sūra titles to find a passage in a translated text of the Qur'ān. The verse numbering itself follows the now-standard 1924 Cairo edition. Most of the English versions of the Qur'ān that are commonly available follow this numbering. The one significant exception is the translation of A.J. Arberry which follows the verse numbering of Gustav Flugel's edition (1834), a numbering that can have a negative or positive variance of several verses from the Cairo edition.

Although every effort has been made to assure accuracy of qur'ānic citation in the articles of the EQ, no particular translation was mandated by the project's style sheet. Authors were free to use available translations or to make their own translations of the passages quoted in their entries. Similarly, there was no way to insure absolute standardization of reference to primary sources in classical Arabic, such as ḥadīth collections or commentaries on the Qur'ān. While the EQ style sheet, its "Instructions for Authors," listed preferred editions of many such works, these were not always the ones available in the university or private libraries of individual authors. Although I wish it had been possible to standardize all such references, the editorial time required would have postponed the publication of the EQ considerably.

At the risk of repeating myself, I would like to underscore that the *Encyclopaedia of the Qur'ān* is an inaugural effort. It is a first attempt to create a substantial work of reference in a field that has relatively few such resources. From its inception as a scholarly project, the editors of the EQ knew that they could never claim consummate thoroughness for this first edition. Many readers and reviewers will have additional subjects and themes to suggest and both the editors and the publisher welcome these proposals. If the *EQ* serves the purpose intended by those who have shepherded it to publication, there will eventually be another, expanded edition enhanced by the suggestions.

A concluding comment on controversy

As a concluding remark, I will broach a topic that may seem odd coming from the pen of a general editor. (But perhaps it is but another form of the "situated scholarship" that has become so prevalent in the last two decades.) That topic is this project's potential for controversy. Many times since undertaking the responsibility of the *EQ* I have been asked by journalists, colleagues and acquaintances whether I feel uneasy or at risk with such an involvement. My answer is always "no" and it is usually accompanied by some expression of regret that the frequent misrepresentation of Muslim sensibilities could even prompt such a question. Yet the study of a text that millions of people hold sacred is a sensitive task. Some Muslims feel strongly that no non-Muslim should even touch the Qurʾān, to say nothing of reading and commenting upon it. Yet most Muslims do not feel this way. While there are those who choose to ignore non-Muslim scholarship on the Qurʾān as irrelevant or inherently flawed and misinformed, others welcome the contributions that non-Muslim scholars have made to this field.

Conversely, there are non-Muslim scholars who have attempted to write about the Qurʾān in a manner that is not immediately offensive to the theological sensibilities of Muslims. Others have operated with the assumption that such considerations have no place in the realm of academic discourse. Personalities differ, ideological orientations differ and scholarly practices differ on both sides of the dividing line. I have deliberately embraced a plurality of method and perspective within the pages of the *EQ*, but I have done so conscious of the fact that not all scholars, whether non-Muslim or Muslim, agree with this approach. There are Muslim colleagues who have preferred not to participate out of fear that association with the *EQ* would compromise their scholarly integrity. There are non-Muslim colleagues who have demurred for exactly the same reason. Nevertheless, these are very much the exceptions. Most scholars who were invited to contribute accepted with enthusiasm and alacrity, pleased to see the appearance of a reference work that would foster continued development within the field of qurʾānic studies. It is my sincere hope, and that of the associate editors, that the *EQ* will do precisely that.

Jane Dammen McAuliffe
Georgetown University

ABBREVIATIONS

AI = *Annales islamologiques*
AIUON = *Annali dell' Istituto Universitario Orientale di Napoli*
AO = *Acta orientalia*
AO-H = *Acta orientalia (Academiae Scientiarum Hungaricae)*
Arabica = *Arabica. Revue d'études arabes*
ARW = *Archiv für Religionswissenschaft*
AUU = *Acta Universitatis Upsaliensis*
BASOR = *Bulletin of the American Schools of Oriental Research*
BEO = *Bulletin d'études orientales de l'Institut Français de Damas*
BGA = *Bibliotheca geographorum arabicorum*
BIFAO = *Bulletin de l'Institut Français d'Archéologie Orientale du Caire*
BO = *Bibliotheca orientalis*
BSA = *Budapest studies in Arabic*
BSOAS = *Bulletin of the School of Oriental and African Studies*
Der Islam = *Der Islam. Zeitschrift für Geschichte und Kultur des islamischen Orients*
EI[1] = *Encyclopaedia of Islam,* 1st ed., Leiden 1913-38
EI[2] = *Encyclopaedia of Islam,* new ed., Leiden 1954-
ER = *Encyclopedia of religion,* ed. M. Eliade, New York 1986
ERE = *Encyclopaedia of religions and ethics*
GMS = *Gibb memorial series*
HO = *Handbuch der Orientalistik*
IA = *Islâm ansiklopedisi*
IBLA = *Revue de l'Institut des Belles Lettres Arabes, Tunis*
IC = *Islamic culture*
IJMES = *International journal of Middle East studies*
IOS = *Israel oriental studies*
IQ = *The Islamic quarterly*
Iran = *Iran. Journal of the British Institute of Persian Studies*
JA = *Journal asiatique*
JAL = *Journal of Arabic literature*
JAOS = *Journal of the American Oriental Society*
JE = *Jewish encyclopaedia*
JESHO = *Journal of the economic and social history of the Orient*
JIS = *Journal of Islamic studies*
JNES = *Journal of Near Eastern studies*
JRAS = *Journal of the Royal Asiatic Society*
JSAI = *Jerusalem studies in Arabic and Islam*
JSS = *Journal of Semitic studies*
MFOB = *Mélanges de la Faculté Orientale de l'Université St. Joseph de Beyrouth*
MIDEO = *Mélanges de l'Institut Dominicain d'études orientales du Caire*
MO = *Le monde oriental*
MSOS = *Mitteilungen des Seminars für orientalische Sprachen, westasiatische Studien*
Muséon = *Le Muséon. Revue des études orientales*
MW = *The Muslim world*
OC = *Oriens christianus*

OLZ = *Orientalistische Literaturzeitung*
Orientalia = *Orientalia. Commentarii periodici Pontificii Instituti Biblici*
Qanṭara = *al-Qanṭara. Revista de estudios arabes*
QSA = *Quaderni de studi arabi*
RCEA = *Répertoire chronologique d'épigraphie arabe*
REI = *Revue des études islamiques*
REJ = *Revue des études juives*
REMMM = *Revue du monde musulman et de la Méditerranée*
RHR = *Revue de l'histoire des religions*
RIMA = *Revue du l'Institut des Manuscrits Arabes*
RMM = *Revue du monde musulman*
RO = *Rocznik Orientalistyczny*
ROC = *Revue de l'orient chrétien*
RSO = *Rivista degli studi orientali*
SIr = *Studia iranica*
SI = *Studia islamica*
WI = *Die Welt des Islams*
WKAS = *Wörterbuch der klassischen arabischen Sprache*
WO = *Welt des Orients*
WZKM = *Wiener Zeitschrift für die Kunde des Morgenlandes*
ZAL = *Zeitschrift für arabische Linguistik*
ZDMG = *Zeitschrift der Deutschen Morgenländischen Gesellschaft*
ZGAIW = *Zeitschrift für Geschichte der arabisch-islamischen Wissenschaften*
ZS = *Zeitschrift für Semitistik*

AUTHORS OF ARTICLES

VOLUME I

Nadia Abu-Zahra, Oxford University
Nasr Hamid Abu Zayd, University of Leiden
Camilla P. Adang, Tel-Aviv University
Mohammad Ali Amir-Moezzi, École Pratique des Hautes Études, Paris
Mohammed Arkoun, Sorbonne University, Paris
Ali S.A. Asani, Harvard University
Ahmad M. al-Baghdadi, Kuwait University
Julian Baldick, University of London
Shahzad Bashir, College of the Holy Cross, Worcester, MA
Doris Behrens-Abouseif, University of London
Herbert Berg, University of North Carolina at Wilmington
Khalid Y. Blankinship, Temple University, Philadelphia
Michael Bonner, University of Michigan, Ann Arbor
Maurice Borrmans, Pontificio Istituto di Studi Arabi e d'Islamistica, Rome
Donna Lee Bowen, Brigham Young University
Gerhard Böwering, Yale University
William M. Brinner, University of California, Berkeley
Jonathan E. Brockopp, Bard College, Annandale, NY
Christopher George Buck, Michigan State University, East Lansing
John Burton, University of St. Andrews (retired)
Heribert Busse, Mühlheim/Main
Juan Eduardo Campo, University of California, Santa Barbara
Ahmad Salim Dallal, Stanford University
Frederick Mathewson Denny, University of Colorado, Boulder
Eerik Dickinson, Washington, DC
Abul Fadl Mohsin Ebrahim, University of Durban Westville
Herbert Eisenstein, University of Vienna
Nadia Maria El Cheikh, American University of Beirut
Mohammad Fadel, Augusta, GA
Toufic Fahd, University of Strasbourg
Reuven Firestone, Hebrew Union College, Los Angeles
Kais M. Firro, University of Haifa
Yohanan Friedmann, Hebrew University, Jerusalem
Dmitry V. Frolov, Moscow University
Avner Giladi, University of Haifa
Hugh Philip Goddard, University of Nottingham

Oleg Grabar, Princeton University, Institute for Advanced Studies
William A. Graham, Harvard University
Sidney H. Griffith, Catholic University of America, Washington, DC
Beatrice Gruendler, Yale University
Sebastian Günther, University of Toronto
Rosalind W. Gwynne, University of Tennessee, Knoxville
Wael B. Hallaq, McGill University, Montreal
Isaac Hasson, Hebrew University, Jerusalem
Gerald R. Hawting, University of London
Thomas Emil Homerin, University of Rochester
Qamar-ul Huda, Boston College
John O. Hunwick, Northwestern University, Evanston, IL
Sherman A. Jackson, University of Michigan, Ann Arbor
Herbjorn Jenssen, University of Oslo
Anthony Hearle Johns, Australian National University, Canberra
Nola J. Johnson, University of Toronto
Wadad Kadi (al-Qadi), University of Chicago
Ahmet T. Karamustafa, Washington University, St. Louis
Marion H. Katz, Mount Holyoke College, South Hadley, MA
Linda L. Kern, St. John's College, Annapolis, MD
Tarif Khalidi, Cambridge University
Raif Georges Khoury, University of Heidelberg
Richard Kimber, University of St. Andrews
Leah Kinberg, Tel-Aviv University
Alexander D. Knysh, University of Michigan, Ann Arbor
Jacob Lassner, Northwestern University, Evanston, IL
Frederik Leemhuis, University of Groningen
Keith Lewinstein, Smith College, Northampton, MA
Daniel A. Madigan, Pontifical Gregorian University, Rome
Fedwa Malti-Douglas, Indiana University, Bloomington
Richard C. Martin, Emory University
Jane Dammen McAuliffe, Georgetown University, Washington DC
Sheila McDonough, Concordia University, Montreal
Barbara D. Metcalf, University of California, Davis
Mustansir Mir, Youngstown State University
Roy P. Mottahedeh, Harvard University
Harald Motzki, University of Nijmegen
Azim Nanji, The Institute of Ismaili Studies, London
John A. Nawas, Université Catholique de Louvain, Belgium
Angelika Neuwirth, Free University of Berlin
Gordon Darnell Newby, Emory University
Kathleen M. O'Connor, University of California, Davis
Solange Ory, University of Aix-Marseille
Rudolph Peters, University of Amsterdam
Daniel C. Peterson, Brigham Young University
Ute Pietruschka, Philipps University, Marburg
Nasser O. Rabbat, Massachusetts Institute of Technology
A. Kevin Reinhart, Dartmouth College, Hanover, NH
G. John Renard, St. Louis University
Andrew Rippin, University of Victoria, BC
Chase F. Robinson, University of Oxford
Neal S. Robinson, University of Wales
Uri Rubin, Tel-Aviv University
Abdulaziz Sachedina, University of Virginia
Usha Sanyal, Charlotte, NC

Robert Schick, Henry Martyn Institute of Islamic Studies, Hyderabad
Sabine Schmidtke, Free University of Berlin
Cornelia Schöck, University of Kiel
Hannelore Schönig, Martin Luther University, Halle-Wittenberg
Michael A. Sells, Haverford College
William E. Shepard, University of Canterbury, Christchurch, New Zealand
Denise A. Spellberg, University of Texas, Austin
Devin J. Stewart, Emory University
Rafael Talmon, University of Haifa
David Thomas, Selly Oak Colleges, Birmingham
Shawkat M. Toorawa, Cornell University
James A. Toronto, Brigham Young University
Roberto Tottoli, University of Turin
Jacques D.J. Waardenburg, University of Lausanne
David Waines, Lancaster University
Earle H. Waugh, University of Alberta
Gisela Webb, Seton Hall University
Alford T. Welch, Michigan State University, East Lansing
Brannon M. Wheeler, University of Washington
A.H. Mathias Zahniser, Asbury Theological Seminary, Wilmore, KY
Mohsen Zakeri, University of Frankfurt am Main
Mona M. Zaki, Princeton University

SHORT TITLES

Abbott, *Studies II*
N. Abbott, *Studies in Arabic literary papyri. II. Qurʾānic commentary and tradition*, Chicago 1967

ʿAbd al-Bāqī
Muḥammad Fuʾād ʿAbd al-Bāqī, *al-Muʿjam al-mufahras li-alfāẓ al-Qurʾān al-karīm*, Cairo 1945

ʿAbd al-Jabbār, *Mutashābih*
ʿAbd al-Jabbār b. Aḥmad al-Asadābādī al-Qāḍī al-Hamadhānī, *Mutashābih al-Qurʾān*, ed. ʿAdnān M. Zarzūr, 2 vols., Cairo 1969

ʿAbd al-Jabbār, *Tanzīh*
ʿAbd al-Jabbār b. Aḥmad al-Asadābādī al-Qāḍī al-Hamadhānī, *Tanzīh al-Qurʾān ʿan al-maṭāʿin*, Beirut 1966

ʿAbd al-Raḥmān, *Tafsīr*
ʿĀʾisha ʿAbd al-Raḥmān, *al-Tafsīr al-bayānī lil-Qurʾān al-karīm*, 3rd ed., Cairo 1968

ʿAbd al-Raḥmān, *ʿAṣrī*
ʿĀʾisha ʿAbd al-Raḥmān, *al-Qurʾān wa-l-tafsīr al-ʿaṣrī*, Cairo 1970

ʿAbd al-Razzāq, *Muṣannaf*
ʿAbd al-Razzāq b. Hammām al-Ṣanʿānī, *al-Muṣannaf*, ed. Ḥabīb al-Raḥmān al-Aʿẓamī, 11 vols., Beirut 1390/1970; 2nd ed. Johannesburg 1983; ed. Muḥammad Sālim Samāra, 4 vols. (with indices of ḥadīth), Beirut 1408/1988

ʿAbd al-Razzāq, *Tafsīr*
ʿAbd al-Razzāq b. Hammām al-Ṣanʿānī, *al-Tafsīr*, ed. Muṣṭafā Muslim Muḥammad, 3 vols. in 4, Riyadh 1410/1989; ed. ʿAbd al-Muʿṭī Amīn Qalʿajī, 2 vols., Beirut 1411/1991; ed. Maḥmūd Muḥammad ʿAbduh, 3 vols., Beirut 1419/1999.

Abū Dāwūd
Abū Dāwūd Sulaymān b. al-Ashʿath al-Sijistānī, *Sunan*, ed. Muḥammad Muḥyī l-Dīn ʿAbd al-Ḥamīd, 4 vols., Cairo 1339/1920; ed. Kamāl Yūsuf al-Ḥūt, 2 vols., Beirut 1988

Abū l-Futūḥ Rāzi, *Rawḥ*
Abū l-Futūḥ Ḥusayn b. ʿAlī Rāzī, *Rawḥ al-jinān wa-rūḥ al-janān*, 12 vols., Tehran 1282-7/ 1962-5; 5 vols., Qumm n.d.

Abū Ḥayyān, *Baḥr*
Abū Ḥayyān al-Gharnāṭī, *Tafsīr al-baḥr al-muḥīṭ*, 8 vols., Cairo 1328-9/1911; repr. Beirut 1983; ed. ʿĀdil Aḥmad ʿAbd al-Mawjūd and ʿAlī Muḥammad Muʿawwad, 8 vols., Beirut 1993

Abū l-Layth al-Samarqandī, *Tafsīr*
Abū l-Layth Naṣr b. Muḥammad b. Aḥmad al-Samarqandī, *Baḥr al-ʿulūm*, ed. ʿAbd al-Raḥīm Aḥmad al-Zaqqa, 3 vols., Baghdad 1985-6; ed. ʿAlī Muḥammad Muʿawwaḍ et al., 3 vols., Beirut 1413/1993

Abū Shāma, *Murshid*
ʿAbd al-Raḥmān b. Ismāʿīl Abū Shāma, *Kitāb al-Murshid al-wajīz ilā ʿulūm tataʿallaq bi-l-kitāb al-ʿazīz,* ed. Ṭayyar Altikulaç, Istanbul 1968

Abū ʿUbayd, *Faḍāʾil*
Abū ʿUbayd al-Qāsim b. Sallām, *Faḍāʾil al-Qurʾān,* ed. Wahbī Sulaymān Khāwajī, Beirut 1411/1991

Abū ʿUbayd, *Gharīb*
Abū ʿUbayd al-Qāsim b. Sallām, *Gharīb al-ḥadīth,* ed. Muḥammad ʿAbd al-Muʿīd Khān, 4 vols., Hyderabad 1384-7/1964-7; 2 vols., Beirut 1406/1986; ed. Ḥusayn Muḥammad M. Sharaf et al., 4 vols., Cairo 1404-15/1984-94; ed. Masʿūd Ḥijāzī et al., Cairo 1419/1999

Abū ʿUbayd, *Nāsikh*
Abū ʿUbayd al-Qāsim b. Sallām, *Kitāb al-Nāsikh wa-l-mansūkh,* ed. J. Burton, Cambridge 1987

Abū ʿUbayda, *Majāz*
Abū ʿUbayda Maʿmar b. al-Muthannā al-Taymī, *Majāz al-Qurʾān,* ed. F. Sezgin, 2 vols., Cairo 1954-62

Akhfash, *Maʿānī*
Abū l-Ḥasan Saʿīd b. Masʿada al-Akhfash al-Awsaṭ, *Maʿānī l-Qurʾān,* ed. Fāʾiz Fāris al-Ḥamad, 2nd ed., 2 vols., Kuwait 1981; ed. ʿAbd al-Amīr Muḥammad Amīn al-Ward, Beirut 1405/1985; ed. Hudā Maḥmūd Qurrāʿa, Cairo 1990

Allard, *Analyse*
M. Allard, *Analyse conceptuelle du Coran sur cartes perforées,* Paris 1963

Ālūsī, *Rūḥ*
Maḥmūd b. ʿAbdallāh al-Ālūsī, *Rūḥ al-maʿānī fī tafsīr al-Qurʾān al-ʿaẓīm wa-l-sabʿ al-mathānī,* 30 vols. in 15, Cairo 1345/1926; repr. Beirut n.d.

ʿĀmilī, *Aʿyān*
Muḥsin al-Amīn al-ʿĀmilī, *Aʿyān al-shīʿa,* 56 parts, Damascus 1935-63; 11 vols., Beirut 1986

Anbārī, *Bayān*
Abū l-Barakāt ʿAbd al-Raḥmān b. Muḥammad b. al-Anbārī, *al-Bayān fī gharīb iʿrāb al-Qurʾān,* ed. Ṭāhā ʿAbd al-Ḥamīd and Muṣṭafā al-Saqqā, 2 vols., Cairo 1969-70

Anbārī, *Nuzha*
Abū l-Barakāt ʿAbd al-Raḥmān b. Muḥammad al-Anbārī, *Nuzhat al-alibbāʾ fī ṭabaqāt al-udabāʾ,* Cairo 1294; Stockholm 1963; ed. Ibrāhīm al-Sāmarrāʾī, Baghdad 1970

Arberry
A.J. Arberry, *The Koran interpreted,* London 1955

Arkoun, *Lectures*
M. Arkoun, *Lectures du Coran,* Paris 1982

ʿAyyāshī, *Tafsīr*
Muḥammad b. Masʿūd al-ʿAyyāshī, *Tafsīr,* 2 vols., Tehran 1380/1961

Baghawī, *Maʿālim*
al-Ḥusayn b. Masʿūd al-Shāfiʿī al-Baghawī, *Tafsīr al-Baghawī al-musammā bi-Maʿālim al-tanzīl,* ed. Khālid ʿAbd al-Raḥmān al-ʿAkk and Marwān Sawār, 4 vols., Beirut 1983

Baghdādī, *Farq*
Abū Manṣūr ʿAbd al-Qāhir b. Ṭāhir al-Baghdādī, *al-Farq bayna l-firāq,* ed. Muḥammad Badr, Cairo 1328/1910; ed. Muḥammad Muḥyī l-Dīn ʿAbd al-Ḥamīd, Cairo n.d.

Baghdādī, *Taʾrīkh Baghdād*
Abū Bakr Aḥmad b. ʿAlī al-Khaṭīb al-Baghdādī, *Taʾrīkh Baghdād,* 14 vols., Cairo 1349/1931

Baḥrānī, *Burhān*
Hāshim b. Sulaymān al-Baḥrānī, *Kitāb al-Burhān fī tafsīr al-Qurʾān,* ed. Maḥmūd b. Jaʿfar al-Mūsawī al-Zarandī et al., 4 vols., Tehran 1375/1995; repr. Beirut 1403/1983

Baljon, *Modern*
I.M.S. Baljon, *Modern Muslim Koran interpretation (1880-1960),* Leiden 1961, 1968

Bāqillānī, *Iʿjāz*
al-Qāḍī Abū Bakr Muḥammad b. al-Ṭayyib al-Bāqillānī, *Iʿjāz al-Qurʾān,* ed. al-Sayyid Aḥmad Ṣaqr, Cairo 1954

Bāqillānī, *Intiṣār*
al-Qāḍī Abū Bakr Muḥammad b. al-Ṭayyib al-Bāqillānī, *Nukat al-intiṣār li-naql al-Qurʾān,* ed. Muḥammad Zaghlūl Salām, Alexandria 1971

Bayḍāwī, *Anwār*
ʿAbdallāh b. ʿUmar al-Bayḍāwī, *Anwār al-tanzīl wa-asrār al-taʾwīl,* ed. H.O. Fleischer, 2 vols., Leipzig 1846; Beirut 1988

Beeston, *CHAL*
A.F.L. Beeston et al., eds., *The Cambridge history of Arabic literature,* 4 vols. to date, Cambridge 1983-

Bell, *Commentary*
R. Bell, *A commentary on the Qurʾān,* ed. C.E. Bosworth and M.E.J. Richardson, 2 vols., Manchester 1991

Bell, *Qurʾān*
R. Bell, *The Qurʾān. Translated, with a critical re-arrangement of the sūras,* 2 vols., Edinburgh 1939; repr. 1960

Beltz, *Mythen*
W. Beltz, *Die Mythen des Koran. Der Schlüssel zum Islam,* Düsseldorf 1980

Bergsträsser, *Verneinungs*
G. Bergsträsser, *Verneinungs- und Fragepartikeln und Verwandtes im Ḳurʾān,* Leipzig 1914

Biqāʿī, *Naẓm*
Burhān al-Dīn Ibrāhīm b. ʿUmar al-Biqāʿī, *Naẓm al-durar fī tanāsub al-āyāt wa-l-suwar,* 22 vols., Hyderabad 1969-84; repr. Cairo 1992

Birkeland, *Lord*
H. Birkeland, *The Lord guideth. Studies on primitive Islam,* Oslo 1956

Birkeland, *Opposition*
H. Birkeland, *Old Muslim opposition against interpretation of the Koran,* Oslo 1955

Blachère
R. Blachère, *Le Coran. Traduit de l'arabe,* Paris 1966

Blachère, *Introduction*
R. Blachère, *Introduction au Coran,* Paris 1947

Bobzin, *Koran*
H. Bobzin, *Der Koran. Eine Einführung,* Munich 1999

Bobzin, *Reformation*
H. Bobzin, *Der Koran im Zeitalter der Reformation. Studien zur Frühgeschichte der Arabistik und Islamkunde in Europa,* Beirut/Stuttgart 1995

Bouman, *Conflit*
J. Bouman, *Le conflit autour du Coran et la solution d'al-Bāqillānī,* Amsterdam 1959

Bouman, *Gott und Mensch*
J. Bouman, *Gott und Mensch im Koran. Eine Strukturform religiöser Anthropologie anhand des Beispiels Allāh und Muḥammad,* Darmstadt 1977

Böwering, *Mystical*
G. Böwering, *The mystical vision of existence in classical Islam. The qurʾānic hermeneutics of the Ṣūfī Sahl at-Tustarī (d. 283/896),* Berlin 1980

Brockelmann, *GAL*
C. Brockelmann, *Geschichte der arabischen Litteratur,* 2nd ed., 2 vols. and 3 vols. suppl., Leiden 1943-9; with new introduction, Leiden 1996

Buhl, *Das Leben*
F. Buhl, *Das Leben Muhammeds,* trans. H.H. Schaeder, Leipzig 1930; 1931 (3rd ed.)

Bukhārī, *Ṣaḥīḥ*
Abū ʿAbdallāh Muḥammad b. Ismāʿīl al-Bukhārī, *Kitāb al-Jāmiʿ al-ṣaḥīḥ,* ed. L. Krehl and T.W. Juynboll, 4 vols., Leiden 1862-1908; 9 vols., Cairo 1958

Burton, *Collection*
J. Burton, *The collection of the Qurʾān,* Cambridge 1977

Chabbi, *Seigneur*
J. Chabbi, *Le seigneur des tribus. L'islam de Mahomet,* Paris 1997

Creswell, *EMA*
K.A.C. Creswell, *Early Muslim architecture,* 2 vols., Oxford 1932-40; 2nd ed., London 1969

Dāmaghānī, *Wujūh*
al-Ḥusayn b. Muḥammad al-Dāmaghānī, *al-Wujūh wa-l-naẓāʾir li-alfāẓ Kitāb Allāh al-ʿazīz,* ed. Muḥammad Ḥasan Abū l-ʿAẓm al-Zafītī, 3 vols., Cairo 1412-16/

1992-5; ed. ʿAbd al-ʿAzīz Sayyid al-Ahl (as *Qāmūs al-Qurʾān*), Beirut 1970

Damīrī, *Ḥayāt*
Muḥammad b. Mūsā al-Damīrī, *Ḥayāt al-ḥayawān al-kubrā,* 2 vols., Cairo 1956

Dānī, *Muqniʿ*
Abū ʿAmr ʿUthmān b. Saʿīd al-Dānī, *al-Muqniʿ fī rasm maṣāḥif al-amṣār maʿa Kitāb al-Naqṭ = Orthographie und Punktierung des Koran,* ed. O. Pretzl, Leipzig/Istanbul 1932; ed. Muḥammad al-Ṣadīq Qamḥawī, Cairo n.d.

Dānī, *Naqṭ*
Abū ʿAmr ʿUthmān b. Saʿīd al-Dānī, *al-Muḥkam fī naqṭ al-maṣāḥif,* ed. ʿIzzat Ḥasan, Damascus 1379/1960

Dānī, *Taysīr*
Abū ʿAmr ʿUthmān b. Saʿīd al-Dānī, *Kitāb al-Taysīr fī l-qirāʾāt al-sabʿ = Das Lehrbuch der sieben Koranlesungen,* ed. O. Pretzl, Leipzig/Istanbul 1930

Dāraquṭnī, *Muʾtalif*
Abū l-Ḥasan ʿAlī b. ʿUmar al-Dāraquṭnī, *al-Muʾtalif wa-l-mukhtalif,* ed. Muwaffaq b. ʿAbdallāh b. ʿAbd al-Qādir, 5 vols., Beirut 1986

Dārimī, *Sunan*
ʿAbdallāh b. ʿAbd al-Rāḥmān al-Dārimī, *Sunan,* Cairo 1966

Darwaza, *Tafsīr*
Muḥammad ʿIzzat Darwaza, *al-Tafsir al-ḥadīth,* 12 vols., Cairo 1381-3/1962-4

Dāwūdī, *Ṭabaqāt*
Muḥammad b. ʿAlī al-Dāwūdī, *Ṭabaqāt al-mufassirīn,* ed. ʿAlī Muḥammad ʿUmar, 2 vols., Beirut 1983

Dhahabī, *Mufassirūn*
Muḥammad Ḥusayn al-Dhahabī, *al-Tafsīr wa-l-mufassirūn,* 2 vols., Cairo 1976

Dhahabī, *Qurrāʾ*
Shams al-Dīn Muḥammad b. Aḥmad al-Dhahabī, *Maʿrifat al-qurrāʾ al-kibār ʿalā l-ṭabaqāt wa-l-aʿṣār,* ed. Sayyid Jad al-Ḥaqq, n.p. 1969

Dhahabī, *Siyar*
Shams al-Dīn Muḥammad b. Aḥmad al-Dhahabī, *Siyar aʿlām al-nubalāʾ,* ed. Shuʿayb al-Arnaʾūṭ et al., 25 vols., Beirut 1981-8

Dhahabī, *Tadhkira*
Shams al-Dīn Muḥammad b. Aḥmad al-Dhahabī, *Tadhkirat al-ḥuffāẓ,* 4 vols., Hyderabad 1375/1955

Dhahabī, *Taʾrīkh*
Shams al-Dīn Muḥammad b. Aḥmad al-Dhahabī, *Taʾrīkh al-Islām,* ed. ʿUmar ʿAbd al-Salām Tadmurī, 52 vols. to date, Beirut 1989-; 4 vols. (years 601-640), ed. Bashshār ʿAwwād Maʿrūf et al., Beirut 1408/1988

van Ess, *TG*
J. van Ess, *Theologie und Gesellschaft im 2. und 3. Jahrhundert Hidschra. Eine Geschichte des religiösen Denkens im frühen Islam,* 6 vols., Berlin/New York 1991-7

Fārisī, *Ḥujja*
Abū ʿAlī al-Ḥasan b. ʿAlī al-Fārisī, *al-Ḥujja lil-qurrāʾ al-sabʿa,* ed. Badr al-Dīn al-Qahwajī et al., 4 vols., Damascus 1985-91

Farrāʾ, *Maʿānī*
Abū Zakariyyāʾ Yaḥyā b. Ziyād al-Farrāʾ, *Maʿānī l-Qurʾān,* ed. Aḥmad Yūsuf Najātī and Muḥammad ʿAlī al-Najjār, 3 vols., Cairo 1955-72

Fīrūzābādī, *Baṣāʾir*
Majd al-Dīn Muḥammad b. Yaʿqūb al-Fīrūzābādī *Baṣāʾir dhawī l-tamyīz fī laṭāʾif al-kitāb al-ʿazīz,* ed. Muḥammad ʿAlī l-Najjār, 4 vols., Cairo 1964; repr. Beirut n.d.

GAP
W. Fischer and H. Gätje, eds., *Grundriss der arabischen Philologie,* 3 vols., Wiesbaden 1982-92

Gardet and Anawati, *Introduction*
L. Gardet and M.M. Anawati, *Introduction à la théologie musulmane,* Paris 1948, 3rd ed., 1981

Gilliot, *Elt*
C. Gilliot, *Exégèse, langue, et théologie en Islam. L'exégèse coranique de Ṭabarī (m. 310/923),* Paris 1990

Gimaret, *Jubbāʾī*
D. Gimaret, *Une lecture muʿtazilite du Coran. Le tafsīr d'Abū ʿAlī al-Djubbāʾī (m. 303/915) partiellement reconstitué à partir de ses citateurs,* Louvain/Paris 1994
Goldziher, *GS*
I. Goldziher, *Gesammelte Schriften,* ed. J. Desomogyi, 6 vols., Hildesheim 1967-73
Goldziher, *MS*
I. Goldziher, *Muhammedanische Studien,* 2 vols., Halle 1888-90; trans., C.R. Barber and S.M. Stern, *Muslim studies,* London 1967-72
Goldziher, *Richtungen*
I. Goldziher, *Die Richtungen der islamischen Koranauslegung,* Leiden 1920; repr. 1970
Graham, *Beyond*
W.A. Graham, *Beyond the written word. Oral aspects of scripture in the history of religion,* Cambridge and New York 1989
Grimme, *Mohammed, I-II*
H. Grimme, *Mohammed. I, Das Leben nach den Quellen. II, Einleitung in den Koran. System der koranischen Theologie,* Münster 1892-5
Grünbaum, *Beiträge*
M. Grünbaum, *Beiträge zur semitischen Sagenkunde,* Leiden 1893
Ḥājjī Khalīfa, *Kashf*
Muṣṭafā ʿAbdallāh Ḥājjī Khalīfa, *Kashf al-ẓunūn,* ed. and trans. G. Flügel, 7 vols., Leipzig 1835-58; ed. Şerefettin Yaltkaya and Kilisli Rifat Bilge, 2 vols., Istanbul 1941-3; repr. Beirut 1992-3
Hawting and Shareef, *Approaches*
G.R. Hawting and A.A. Shareef (eds.), *Approaches to the Qurʾān,* London 1993
Hawting, *Idolatry*
G.R. Hawting, *The idea of idolatry and the emergence of Islam. From polemic to history,* Cambridge 1999
Ḥawwā, *Tafsīr*
Saʿīd Ḥawwā, *al-Asās fī l-tafsīr,* 11 vols., Cairo 1405/1985
Horovitz, *KU*
J. Horovitz, *Koranische Untersuchungen,* Berlin/Leipzig 1926
Hūd b. Muḥakkam, *Tafsīr*
Hūd b. Muḥakkam/Muḥkim al-Huwwārī, *Tafsīr,* ed. Balḥājj Saʿīd Sharīfī, 4 vols., Beirut 1990
Ibn ʿAbbās, *Gharīb*
ʿAbdallāh b. ʿAbbās (attributed to), *Gharīb al-Qurʾān,* ed. Muḥammad ʿAbd al-Raḥīm, Beirut 1993
Ibn Abī l-Iṣbaʿ, *Badīʿ*
Ibn Abī l-Iṣbaʿ al-Miṣrī, *Badīʿ al-Qurʾān,* ed. Ḥifnī Muḥammad Sharaf, Cairo n.d.
Ibn Abī Uṣaybiʿa, *ʿUyūn*
Aḥmad b. al-Qāsim b. Abī Uṣaybiʿa, *ʿUyūn al-anbāʾ fī ṭabaqāt al-aṭibbāʾ,* ed. A. Müller, 2 vols., Cairo 1299/1882; 3 vols., Beirut 1957
Ibn al-Anbārī, *Īḍāḥ*
Abū Bakr Muḥammad b. al-Qāsim b. al-Anbārī, *Īḍāḥ al-waqf wa-l-ibtidāʾ fī Kitāb Allāh,* ed. Muḥyī l-Dīn ʿAbd al-Raḥmān Ramaḍān, 2 vols., Damascus 1391/1971
Ibn al-ʿArabī, *Aḥkām*
Muḥammad b. ʿAbdallāh Abū Bakr b. al-ʿArabī, *Aḥkām al-Qurʾān,* 2nd ed., Cairo 1392/1972
Ibn al-ʿArabī, *Tafsīr*
Muḥammad b. ʿAbdallāh Abū Bakr b. al-ʿArabī, *Tafsīr al-Qurʾān,* 2 vols., Beirut 1968 (see Qāshānī)
Ibn ʿAsākir, *Taʾrīkh*
ʿAlī b. al-Ḥasan b. ʿAsākir, *Taʾrīkh madīnat Dimashq,* abridged ed. ʿAbd al-Qādir Bardān and Aḥmad ʿUbayd, 7 vols., Damascus 1329-51/1911-31; facsimile ed., 19 vols., Amman n.d.; 29 vols., Damascus 1404-8/1984-8; ed. Muḥyī l-Dīn ʿUmar b. Gharāma al-Amrāwī, 70 vols. to date, Beirut 1995-98
Ibn ʿĀshūr, *Tafsīr*
Muḥammad al-Ṭāhir b. ʿĀshūr, *al-Tafsīr al-taḥrīrī wa-l-tanwīrī,* 30 vols., Tunis 1984
Ibn ʿAskar, *Takmīl*
Muḥammad b. ʿAlī al-Ghassānī b. ʿAskar, *al-Takmīl wa-l-itmām li-Kitāb al-Taʿrīf wa-l-iʿlām,* ed. Ḥasan Ismāʿīl Marwa, Beirut/Damascus 1418/1997 (see Suhaylī)

Ibn al-Athīr, *Kāmil*
ʿIzz al-Dīn ʿAlī b. al-Athīr, *al-Kāmil fī l-taʾrīkh,* ed. C.J. Tornberg, 14 vols., Leiden 1851-76; corrected repr. 13 vols., Beirut 1385-7/1965-7

Ibn al-Athīr, *Nihāya*
Majd al-Dīn al-Mubārak b. al-Athīr, *al-Nihāya fī gharīb al-ḥadīth wa-l-athar,* ed. Ṭāhir Aḥmad al-Zāwī and Maḥmūd al-Ṭanāḥī, 5 vols., Cairo 1963-6

Ibn ʿAṭiyya, *Muḥarrar*
Abū Muḥammad ʿAbd al-Ḥaqq b. Ghālib b. ʿAṭiyya al-Gharnāṭī, *al-Muḥarrar al-wajīz,* ed. ʿAbd al-Salām ʿAbd al-Shāfī Muḥammad, 5 vols., Beirut 1413/1993

Ibn Ḍurays, *Faḍāʾil*
Muḥammad b. Ayyūb b. Ḍurays, *Faḍāʾil al-Qurʾān,* ed. Ghazwa Budayr, Damascus 1988

Ibn Ḥajar, *Tahdhīb*
Ibn Ḥajar al-ʿAsqalānī, *Tahdhīb al-tahdhīb,* 12 vols., Hyderabad 1325-7/1907-9; Beirut 1968

Ibn Ḥanbal, *Musnad*
Aḥmad b. Ḥanbal, *Musnad,* ed. Muḥammad al-Zuhrī al-Ghamrāwī, 6 vols., Cairo 1313/1895; repr. Beirut 1978; ed. Aḥmad Muḥammad Shākir et al., 20 vols., Cairo 1416/1995

Ibn Ḥazm, *Milal*
ʿAlī b. Aḥmad b. Saʿīd b. Ḥazm, *al-Fiṣal fī l-milal wa-l-aḥwāʾ wa-l-niḥal,* ed. Muḥammad Ibrāhīm Naṣr and ʿAbd al-Raḥmān ʿUmayra, 5 vols., Beirut 1995

Ibn al-ʿImād, *Shadharāt*
ʿAbd al-Ḥayy b. Aḥmad b. al-ʿImād, *Shadharāt al-dhahab fī akhbār man dhahab,* 8 vols., Cairo 1350-1/1931-2; repr. Beirut n.d.

Ibn Isḥāq, *Sīra*
Muḥammad b. Isḥāq, *Sīrat rasūl Allāh* (recension of ʿAbd al-Malik b. Hishām), ed. F. Wüstenfeld, Göttingen 1858-60; repr. Beirut n.d.; ed. Muṣṭafā al-Ṣaqqā et al., 4 vols. in 2, 2nd ed., Cairo 1955

Ibn Isḥāq-Guillaume
The life of Muhammad. A translation of Ibn Isḥāq's Sīrat rasūl Allāh, trans. A. Guillaume, Oxford 1955; repr. Karachi 1967

Ibn al-Jawzī, *Funūn*
Abū l-Faraj ʿAbd al-Raḥmān b. ʿAlī b. al-Jawzī, *Funūn al-afnān fī ʿajāʾib ʿulūm al-Qurʾān,* ed. Rashīd ʿAbd al-Raḥmān al-ʿUbaydī, Baghdad 1408/1988

Ibn al-Jawzī, *Muntaẓam*
Abū l-Faraj ʿAbd al-Raḥmān b. ʿAlī b. al-Jawzī, *al-Muntaẓam fī taʾrīkh al-mulūk wa-l-umam,* ed. Muḥammad and Muṣṭafā ʿAbd al-Qādir ʿAṭā, 19 vols., Beirut 1412/1922; ed. Suhayl Zakkār, 11 vols. in 13, Beirut 1995-6

Ibn al-Jawzī, *Nuzha*
Abū l-Faraj ʿAbd al-Raḥmān b. ʿAlī b. al-Jawzī, *Nuzhat al-aʿyun al-nawāẓir fī ʿilm al-wujūh wa-l-naẓāʾir,* ed. Muḥammad ʿAbd al-Karīm Kāẓim al-Rāḍī, Beirut 1404/1984

Ibn al-Jawzī, *Zād*
Abū l-Faraj ʿAbd al-Raḥmān b. Alī b. al-Jawzī, *Zād al-masīr fī ʿilm al-tafsīr,* intr. Muḥammad Zuhayr al-Shāwīsh, 9 vols., Damascus 1384-5/1964-5; annot. Aḥmad Shams al-Dīn, 8 vols., Beirut 1414/1994

Ibn al-Jazarī, *Ghāya*
Shams al-Dīn Abū l-Khayr Muḥammad b. Muḥammad b. al-Jazarī, *Ghāyat al-nihāya fī ṭabaqāt al-qurrāʾ = Das biographische Lexikon der Koranleser,* 3 vols. in 2, ed. G. Bergsträsser and O. Pretzl, Leipzig/Cairo 1933-5

Ibn al-Jazarī, *Munjid*
Shams al-Dīn Abū l-Khayr Muḥammad b. Muḥammad b. al-Jazarī, *Munjid al-muqriʾīn wa-murshid al-ṭālibīn,* ed. Muḥammad Ḥabīb Allāh al-Shanqīṭī et al., Cairo 1350/1931; Beirut 1980

Ibn al-Jazarī, *Nashr*
Shams al-Dīn Abū l-Khayr Muḥammad b. Muḥammad b. al-Jazarī, *Kitāb al-Nashr fī l-qirāʾāt al-ʿashr,* ed. ʿAlī Muḥammad al-Ḍabbāʿ, 2 vols., Cairo 1940; repr. Beirut n.d.

Ibn Jinnī, *Muḥtasab*
Abū l-Fatḥ ʿUthmān b. Jinnī, *al-Muḥtasab fī*

tabyīn wujūh shawādhdh al-qirāʾāt wa-l-īḍāḥ ʿanhā, 2 vols., ed. ʿAlī al-Najdī Nāṣif et al., Cairo 1386-9/1966-9; repr. 1994

Ibn Kathīr, *Bidāya*
ʿImād al-Dīn Ismāʿīl b. ʿUmar b. Kathīr, *al-Bidāya wa-l-nihāya,* 14 vols., Beirut/Riyadh 1966; repr. Beirut 1988

Ibn Kathīr, *Faḍāʾil*
ʿImād al-Dīn Ismāʿīl b. ʿUmar b. Kathīr, *Faḍāʾil al-Qurʾān,* Beirut 1979

Ibn Kathīr, *Tafsīr*
ʿImād al-Dīn Ismāʿīl b. ʿUmar b. Kathīr, *Tafsīr al-Qurʾān al-ʿaẓīm,* ed. ʿAbd al-ʿAzīz Ghunaym et al., 8 vols., Cairo 1390/1971; 4 vols., Cairo n.d.; repr. Beirut 1980

Ibn Khālawayh, *Ḥujja*
Abū ʿAbdallāh al-Ḥusayn b. Aḥmad b. Khālawayh, *al-Ḥujja fī l-qirāʾāt al-sabʿ,* ed. ʿAbd al-ʿĀl Salīm Mukarram, Beirut 1971

Ibn Khālawayh, *Iʿrāb*
Abū ʿAbdallāh al-Ḥusayn b. Aḥmad b. Khālawayh, *Iʿrāb thalāthīn sūra min al-Qurʾān al-karīm,* Baghdad 1967

Ibn Khālawayh, *Iʿrāb al-qirāʾāt*
Abū ʿAbdallāh al-Ḥusayn b. Aḥmad b. Khālawayh, *Iʿrāb al-qirāʾāt al-sabʿ wa-ʿilaluhā,* ed. ʿAbd al-Raḥmān b. Sulaymān al-Uthaymīn, 2 vols., Cairo 1413/1992

Ibn Khaldūn, *ʿIbar*
ʿAbd al-Raḥmān b. Khaldūn, *Kitāb al-ʿIbar,* ed. Naṣr al-Ḥūrīnī, 7 vols., Būlāq 1284/1867

Ibn Khaldūn-Rosenthal
ʿAbd al-Raḥmān b. Khaldūn, *The Muqaddimah,* trans. F. Rosenthal, 3 vols., New York 1958; 2nd rev. ed., Princeton 1967

Ibn Khallikān, *Wafayāt*
Shams al-Dīn b. Khallikān, *Wafayāt al-aʿyān wa-anbāʾ al-zamān,* ed. F. Wüstenfeld, 4 vols., Göttingen 1835-50; ed. Iḥsān ʿAbbās, 8 vols., Beirut 1968-72; trans. M. De Slane, *Ibn Khallikān's biographical dictionary,* 4 vols., Paris 1842-71; repr. New York 1961

Ibn Māja
Muḥammad b. Yazīd b. Māja, *Sunan,* ed. Muḥammad Fuʾād ʿAbd al-Bāqī, 2 vols., Cairo 1952-3

Ibn Mujāhid, *Sabʿa*
Abū Bakr Aḥmad b. Mūsā b. Mujāhid, *Kitāb al-Sabʿa fī l-qirāʾāt,* ed. Shawqī Ḍayf, Cairo 1979

Ibn al-Nadīm, *Fihrist*
Muḥammad b. Isḥāq b. al-Nadīm, *Kitāb al-Fihrist,* ed. G. Flügel, 2 vols., Leipzig 1871-2; ed. Riḍā Tajaddud, Tehran 1971; 2nd ed., Beirut 1988

Ibn al-Nadīm-Dodge
Muḥammad b. Isḥāq b. al-Nadīm, *The Fihrist of al-Nadīm,* trans. B. Dodge, 2 vols., New York/London 1970

Ibn al-Naqīb, *Muqaddima*
Abū ʿAbdallāh Muḥammad b. Sulaymān al-Naqīb, *Muqaddimat al-tafsīr fī ʿulūm al-bayān wa-l-maʿānī wa-l-badīʿ wa-iʿjāz al-Qurʾān,* ed. Zakariyyāʾ Saʿīd ʿAlī, Cairo 1415/1995

Ibn Qayyim al-Jawziyya, *Tibyān*
Muḥammad b. Abī Bakr b. Qayyim al-Jawziyya, *al-Tibyān fī aqsām al-Qurʾān,* Beirut 1982

Ibn al-Qifṭī, *Ḥukamāʾ*
Abū l-Ḥasan ʿAlī b. Yūsuf b. al-Qifṭī, *Taʾrīkh al-ḥukamāʾ,* ed. J. Lippert, Leipzig 1903; repr. Baghdad 1967

Ibn Qutayba, *Gharīb*
Abū Muḥammad ʿAbdallāh b. Muslim al-Dīnawarī b. Qutayba, *Tafsīr gharīb al-Qurʾān,* ed. al-Sayyid Aḥmad Ṣaqr, Cairo 1958; Beirut 1978

Ibn Qutayba, *al-Shiʿr*
Abū Muḥammad ʿAbdallāh b. Muslim al-Dīnawarī b. Qutayba, *Kitāb al-Shiʿr wa-l-shuʿarāʾ,* ed. M.J. de Goeje, Leiden 1900

Ibn Qutayba, *Taʾwīl*
Abū Muḥammad ʿAbdallāh b. Muslim al-Dīnawarī b. Qutayba, *Taʾwīl mushkil al-Qurʾān,* ed. al-Sayyid Aḥmad Ṣaqr, Cairo 1954; Cairo 1973; Medina 1981

Ibn Qutayba-Lecomte
G. Lecomte, *Le traité des divergences du ḥadīṯ d'Ibn Qutayba,* Damascus 1962

Ibn Saʿd, *Ṭabaqāt*
Muḥammad b. Saʿd, *al-Ṭabaqāt al-kubrā,* ed. H. Sachau et al., 9 vols., Leiden 1905-40; ed. Iḥsān ʿAbbās, 9 vols., Beirut 1957-8
Ibn Taymiyya, *Daqāʾiq*
Taqī l-Dīn Aḥmad b. ʿAbd al-Ḥalīm b. Taymiyya, *Daqāʾiq al-tafsīr. al-Jāmiʿ li-tafsīr al-Imām Ibn Taymiyya,* ed. Muḥammad al-Sayyid al-Julaynid, 6 vols. in 3, Jedda/Beirut/Damascus 1986
Ibn Taymiyya, *Muqaddima*
Taqī l-Dīn Aḥmad b. ʿAbd al-Ḥalīm b. Taymiyya, *Muqaddima fī uṣūl al-tafsīr,* Beirut 1392/1972; Riyadh 1382/1962
Ibn Wahb, *al-Jāmiʿ*
ʿAbdallāh b. Wahb, *al-Ǧāmiʿ. Die Koranswissenschaften,* ed. M. Muranyi, Wiesbaden 1992
Ibyārī, *Mawsūʿa*
Ibrāhīm al-Ibyārī and ʿAbd al-Ṣabūr Marzūq, *al-Mawsūʿa al-qurʾāniyya,* 6 vols., Cairo 1388/1969; 11 vols., Cairo 1405/1984
Ihsanoglu, *Translations*
E. İhsanoğlu, ed., *World bibliography of translations of the meanings of the holy Qurʾān. Printed translations* 1515-1980, Istanbul 1406/1986
Iṣfahānī, *Aghānī*
Abū l-Faraj al-Iṣfahānī, *Kitāb al-Aghānī,* 21 vols. in 7, Cairo 1323/1905; 25 vols., Beirut 1955-62
Iṣfahānī, *Muqaddima*
Abū l-Ḥasan al-ʿĀmilī al-Iṣfahānī, *Muqaddimat tafsīr mirʾāt al-anwār wa-mishkāt al-asrār,* ed. Maḥmūd b. Jaʿfar al-Mūsawī al-Zarandī, Tehran 1374/1954
Iṣlāḥī, *Tadabbur*
Amīn Aḥsan Iṣlāḥī, *Tadabbur-i Qurʾān,* 8 vols., Lahore 1967-80
ʿIyāḍ b. Mūsā, *Shifāʾ*
al-Qāḍī Abū l-Faḍl ʿIyāḍ b. Mūsā, *al-Shifāʾ bi-taʿrīf ḥuqūq al-muṣṭafā,* 2 vols. in 1, Damascus 1978; ed. Muḥammad Amīn Qara et al., Amman 1407/1986
Izutsu, *Concepts*
Toshihiko Izutsu, *Ethico-religious concepts in the Qurʾān,* Montreal 1966
Izutsu, *God*
Toshihiko Izutsu, *God and man in the Koran,* New York 1964; repr. 1980
Jāḥiẓ, *Bayān*
ʿAmr b. Baḥr al-Jāḥiẓ, *al-Bayān wa-l-tabyīn,* ed. ʿAbd al-Salām Muḥammad Hārūn, 4 vols., Cairo 1948-50; repr. Beirut n.d.
Jalālayn
Jalāl al-Din Muḥammad b. Aḥmad al-Maḥallī and Jalāl al-Dīn al-Suyūṭī, *Tafsīr al-Jalālayn,* Damascus 1385/1965
Jansen, *Egypt*
J.J.G. Jansen, *The interpretation of the Koran in modern Egypt,* Leiden 1974, 1980
Jaṣṣāṣ, *Aḥkām*
Abū Bakr Aḥmad b. ʿAbdallāh al-Jaṣṣās al-Rāzī, *Aḥkām al-Qurʾān,* 3 vols., Istanbul 1335-8/1916-19
Jawālīqī, *Muʿarrab*
Abū Manṣūr Mawhūb b. Aḥmad al-Jawālīqī, *al-Muʿarrab min al-kalām al-ʿajamī ʿalā ḥurūf al-muʿjam,* ed. Aḥmad Muḥammad Shākir, Cairo 1361/1942
Jeffery, *For. vocab.*
A. Jeffery, *Foreign vocabulary of the Qurʾān,* Baroda 1938
Jeffery, *Materials*
A. Jeffery, *Materials for the history of the text of the Qurʾān. The Kitāb al-Maṣāhif of Ibn Abī Dāwūd together with a collection of the variant readings from the codices of Ibn Masʿūd, etc.,* Leiden 1937
Jeffery, *Muqaddimas*
A. Jeffery, *Two muqaddimas to the Qurʾānic sciences. The muqaddima to the* Kitab al-Mabani *and the muqaddima of Ibn ʿAtiyya to his* Tafsir, Cairo 1954
Jurjānī, *Asrār*
ʿAbd al-Qāhir al-Jurjāni, *Asrār al-balāgha,* ed. H. Ritter, Istanbul 1954
Jurjānī, *Dalāʾil*
ʿAbd al-Qāhir al-Jurjānī, *Dalāʾil iʿjāz al-*

Qurʾān, Cairo 1372; ed. Maḥmūd Muḥammad Shākir, Cairo 1404/1984

Justi, *Namenbuch*
F. Justi, *Iranisches Namenbuch,* Marburg 1895

Kaḥḥāla, *Muʿjam*
ʿUmar Riḍā Kaḥḥāla, *Muʿjam al-muʾallifīn,* 15 vols. in 8, Beirut n.d.; Damascus 1957-61

Kaḥḥāla, *Nisāʾ*
ʿUmar Riḍā Kaḥḥāla, *Aʿlām al-nisāʾ fī ʿālamay l-ʿarab wa-l-Islām,* 5 vols., Damascus 1379/1959

Kāshānī, *Minhaj*
Mullā Fatḥ Allāh Kāshānī, *Minhaj al-ṣādiqīn fī ilzām al-mukhālifīn,* 10 vols., Tehran 1347[solar]/1969

Kāshānī, *Ṣāfī*
Mullā Muḥsin Fayd Kāshānī, *al-Ṣāfī fī tafsīr kalām Allāh al-wāfī,* ed. Ḥusayn al-Aʿlamī, 5 vols., Beirut 1399/1979

Khāzin, *Lubāb*
ʿAlāʾ al-Dīn al-Khāzin, *Lubāb al-taʾwīl fī maʿānī l-tanzīl,* Cairo 1381/1961

Khwānsārī, *Rawdāt*
Muḥammad Bāqir al-Mūsawī al-Khwānsārī, *Rawdāt al-jannāt,* ed. Asad Allāh Ismāʿīlīyān, 8 vols., Tehran 1392/1972

Kisāʾī, *Mutashābih*
ʿAlī b. Hamza al-Kisāʾī, *Kitāb Mutashābih al-Qurʾān,* ed. Ṣabīḥ al-Tamīmī, Tripoli 1994

Kisāʾī, *Qiṣaṣ*
Muḥammad b. ʿAbdallāh al-Kisāʾī, *Vita prophetarum auctore Muḥammed ben ʿAbdallāh al-Kisāʾī,* ed. I. Eisenberg, 2 vols., Leiden 1922-3

Kulaynī, *Kāfī*
Abū Jaʿfar Muḥammad b. Yaʿqūb al-Kulayn, *Rawḍat al-kāfī,* ed. ʿAlī Akbar al-Ghifārī, Najaf 1395/1966; repr. Beirut n.d.

Kutubī, *Fawāt*
Ibn Shākir al-Kutubī, *Fawāt al-wafayāt,* 2 vols., Cairo 1299/1882; ed. Iḥsān ʿAbbās, 5 vols., Beirut 1973-4

Lane
E.W. Lane, *An Arabic-English lexicon,* 1 vol. in 8 parts., London 1863-93; New York 1955-6; repr. 2 vols., Cambridge 1984

Lecker, *Muslims*
M. Lecker, *Muslims, Jews and pagans. Studies on early Islamic Medina,* Leiden 1995

Le Strange, *Lands*
G. Le Strange, *The lands of the eastern caliphate,* 2nd ed., Cambridge 1930

Lisān al-ʿArab
Muḥammad b. al-Mukarram b. Manẓūr, *Lisān al-ʿArab,* 15 vols., Beirut 1955-6; ed. ʿAlī Shīrī, 18 vols., Beirut 1988

Lüling, *Ur-Qurʾān*
G. Lüling, *Über den Ur-Qurʾān. Ansätze zur Rekonstruktion der vorislamisch-christlicher Strophenlieder im Qurʾān,* Erlangen 1972; 2nd ed. 1993

Makkī, *Ibāna*
Makkī b. Abī Ṭālib al-Qaysī, *Kitāb al-Ibāna ʿan maʿānī l-qirāʾāt,* ed. Muḥyī l-Dīn Ramaḍān, Damascus 1979

Makkī, *Kashf*
Makkī b. Abī Ṭālib al-Qaysī, *al-Kashf ʿan wujūh al-qirāʾāt al-sabʿ wa-ʿilalihā wa-ḥujajihā,* ed. Muḥyī l-Dīn Ramaḍān, 2 vols., Damascus 1974

Makkī, *Mushkil*
Makkī b. Abī Ṭālib al-Qaysī, *Mushkil iʿrāb al-Qurʾan,* ed. Yāsīn M. al-Sawwās, Damascus 1974

Mālik, *Muwaṭṭaʾ*
Mālik b. Anas, *al-Muwaṭṭaʾ,* ed. Muḥammad Fuʾād ʿAbd al-Bāqī, Cairo 1952-3; Beirut 1985; ed. ʿAbd al-Majīd Turkī, Beirut 1994

Masʿūdī, *Murūj*
Abū ʿAlī b. al-Ḥusayn al-Masʿūdī, *Murūj al-dhahab,* ed. C. Barbier de Meynard and Pavet de Courteille, 9 vols., Paris 1861-77; ed. and trans. Ch. Pellat, *Les prairies d'or,* 7 vols. text and 4 vols. translation, Paris-Beirut 1962-89; ed. Qāsim al-Shamāʿī al-Rifāʿī, 4 vols., Beirut 1989

Māturīdī, *Ta'wīlāt*
Abū Manṣūr Muḥammad b. Muḥammad al-Māturīdī, *Ta'wīlāt ahl al-sunna,* ed. Ibrāhīm and al-Sayyid ʿAwadayn, Cairo 1391/1971; ed. Jāsim Muḥammad al-Jubūrī, Baghdad 1404/1983
Māwardī, *Nukat*
ʿAlī b. Muḥammad al-Māwardī, *al-Nukat wa-l-ʿuyūn fī l-tafsīr,* ed. al-Sayyid b. ʿAbd al-Maqṣūd b. ʿAbd al-Raḥīm, 6 vols., Beirut 1412/1992
McAuliffe, *Qur'ānic*
J.D. McAuliffe, *Qur'ānic Christians. An analysis of classical and modern exegesis,* Cambridge 1991
Mir, *Dictionary*
M. Mir, *Dictionary of Qur'ānic terms and concepts,* New York 1987
Mir, *Verbal*
M. Mir, *Verbal idioms of the Qur'ān,* Ann Arbor, MI 1989
Mufaḍḍaliyyāt
al-Mufaḍḍal b. Muḥammad al-Ḍabbī, *al-Mufaḍḍaliyyāt,* ed. Aḥmad Muḥammad Shākir and ʿAbd al-Salām Muḥammad Hārūn, Cairo 1942
Muir, *Mahomet*
W. Muir, *The life of Mahomet. With introductory chapters on the original sources of the biography of Mahomet, I-IV,* London 1858-61
Mujāhid, *Tafsīr*
Abū l-Ḥajjāj Mujāhid b. Jabr, *al-Tafsīr,* ed. ʿAbd al-Raḥmān b. Ṭāhir b. Muḥammad al-Suwartī, Qatar 1976; ed. Muḥammad ʿAbd al-Salām Abū l-Nīl, Cairo 1989
Mukarram, *Muʿjam al-qirā'āt*
ʿAbd al-ʿĀl Salīm Mukarram, *Muʿjam al-qirā'āt al-qur'āniyya,* 8 vols. to date, Kuwait 1982-
Muqātil, *Ashbāh*
Abū l-Ḥasan Muqātil b. Sulaymān al-Balkhī, *al-Ashbāh wa-l-naẓā'ir fī l-Qur'ān al-karīm,* ed. ʿAbdallāh Maḥmūd Shiḥāta, Cairo 1975
Muqātil, *Khams mi'at*
Abū l-Ḥasan Muqātil b. Sulaymān al-Balkhī, *Tafsīr al-khams mi'at āya min al-Qur'ān,* ed. I. Goldfeld, Shfaram 1980
Muqātil, *Tafsīr*
Abū l-Ḥasan Muqātil b. Sulaymān al-Balkhī, *al-Tafsīr,* ed. ʿAbdallāh Maḥmūd Shiḥāta, 5 vols., Cairo 1980-7
Muslim, *Ṣaḥīḥ*
Muslim b. al-Ḥajjāj, *Ṣaḥīḥ,* ed. Muḥammad Fu'ād ʿAbd al-Bāqī, 5 vols., Cairo 1955-6
Nāfiʿ, *Masā'il*
Masā'il al-Imām ʿan as'ilat Nafiʿ b. al-Azraq wa-ajwibat ʿAbd Allah b. ʿAbbas, ed. ʿAbd al-Raḥmān ʿUmayra, Cairo 1413/1994
Nagel, *Einschübe*
T. Nagel, *Medinensische Einschübe in mekkanischen Suren,* Göttingen 1995
Nagel, *Koran*
T. Nagel, *Der Koran. Einführung-Texte-Erläuterungen,* Munich 1983
Naḥḥās, *Iʿrāb*
Abū Jaʿfar Aḥmad b. Muḥammad al-Naḥḥās, *Iʿrāb al-Qur'ān,* ed. Zuhayr Ghāzī Zāhid, 2nd ed., 5 vols., Beirut 1985, 1988
Nasafī, *Tafsīr*
ʿAbdallāh b. Aḥmad b. Maḥmūd al-Nasafī, *Madārik al-tanzil wa-ḥaqā'iq al-ta'wīl,* ed. Zakariyyā' ʿUmayrāt, 2 vols. Beirut 1415/1995
Nasā'ī, *Faḍā'il*
Aḥmad b. Shuʿayb al-Nasā'ī, *Faḍā'il al-Qur'ān,* ed. Samīr al-Khūlī, Beirut 1985
Nasā'ī, *Sunan*
Aḥmad b. Shuʿayb al-Nasā'ī, *al-Sunan al-kubrā,* ed. ʿAbd al-Ghaffār Sulaymān al-Bundārī and al-Sayyid Kisrawī Ḥasan, 6 vols., Beirut 1411/1991
Nawawī, *Sharḥ*
Abū Zakariyyā' Yaḥyā b. Sharaf al-Nawawī, *Sharḥ Ṣaḥīḥ Muslim,* 18 vols. in 9, Cairo 1349/1929-30; ed. Khalīl Muḥammad Shīḥā, 19 vols. in 10, Beirut 1995
Neuwirth, *Studien*
A. Neuwirth, *Studien zur Komposition der mekkanischen Suren,* Berlin 1981
Nīsābūrī, *Tafsīr*
Abū l-Qāsim al-Ḥasan b. Muḥammad b.

Ḥabīb al-Nīsābūrī, *Tafsīr gharāʾib al-Qurʾān wa-raghāʾib al-furqān,* on the margin of Ṭabarī, *Jāmiʿ al-bayān,* 30 vols., Cairo 1323-9/1905-11; repr. Beirut 1392/1972; ed. Ibrāhīm ʿAṭwa ʿAwaḍ, 13 vols., Cairo 1962-4

Nöldeke, *GQ*
T. Nöldeke, *Geschichte des Qorāns,* new edition by F. Schwally, G. Bergsträsser and O. Pretzl, 3 vols., Leipzig 1909-38

Nwyia, *Exégèse*
P. Nwyia, *Exégèse coranique et langage mystique. Nouvel essai sur le lexique technique des mystiques musulmans,* Beirut 1970

Paret, *Kommentar*
R. Paret, *Der Koran. Kommentar und Konkordanz,* Stuttgart 1971; 1977; Kohlhammer 1980

Paret, *Koran*
R. Paret, *Der Koran. Übersetzung,* Stuttgart 1962

Paret (ed.), *Koran*
R. Paret (ed.) *Der Koran,* Darmstadt 1975

Penrice, *Dictionary*
J. Penrice, *A dictionary and glossary of the Koran,* London 1873; repr. 1971

Pickthall, *Koran*
M.M. Pickthall, *The meaning of the glorious Koran,* London 1930; New York 1976

Qāshāni, *Taʾwīl*
ʿAbd al-Razzāq al-Qāshānī, *Taʾwīl al-Qurʾān,* 2 vols., Beirut 1968. See Ibn al-ʿArabī

Qāsimī, *Tafsīr*
Muḥammad Jamāl al-Dīn al-Qāsimī, *Maḥāsin al-taʾwīl,* 18 vols., Cairo 1957-70

Qasṭallānī, *Laṭāʾif*
Aḥmad b. Muḥammad b. Abī Bakr al-Qasṭallānī, *Laṭāʾif al-ishārāt li-funūn al-qirāʾāt,* ed. ʿĀmir al-Sayyid ʿUthmān and ʿAbd al-Ṣabūr Shāhīn, Cairo 1972

Qasṭallānī, *Mawāhib*
Aḥmad b. Muḥammad b. Abī Bakr al-Qasṭallānī, *al-Mawāhib al-laduniyya bi-l-minaḥ al-muḥammadiyya,* ed. Ṣāliḥ Aḥmad al-Shāmī, 4 vols., Beirut/Damascus/Amman 1412/1991

Qummī, *Tafsīr*
Abū l-Ḥasan ʿAlī b. Ibrāhīm al-Qummī, *Tafsīr,* ed. Ṭayyib al-Mūsāwī al-Jazāʾirī, 2 vols., Najaf 1387/1967; Beirut 1991

Qurṭubī, *Jāmiʿ*
Abū ʿAbdallāh Muḥammad b. Aḥmad al-Qurṭubī, *al-Jāmiʿ li-aḥkām al-Qurʾān,* ed. Aḥmad ʿAbd al-ʿAlīm al-Bardūnī et al., 20 vols., Cairo 1952-67; Beirut 1965-7

Qushayrī, *Laṭāʾif*
Abū l-Qāsim ʿAbd al-Karīm b. Hawāzin al-Qushayrī, *Laṭāʾif al-ishārāt,* ed. Ibrāḥim Basyūnī, 6 vols., Cairo 1968-71

Quṭb, *Ẓilāl*
Sayyid Quṭb Ibrāhīm Ḥusayn Shādhilī, *Fī ẓilāl al-Qurʾān,* 6 vols., Beirut 1393-4/1973-4; rev. 11th ed., Cairo 1993

al-Rāghib al-Iṣfahānī, *Mufradāt*
Abū l-Qāsim al-Ḥusayn al-Rāghib al-Iṣfahānī, *Muʿjam mufradāt alfāẓ al-Qurʾān,* Beirut 1392/1972

Rashīd Riḍā, *Manār*
Muḥammad Rashīd Riḍā and Muḥammad ʿAbduh, *Tafsīr al-Qurʾān al-ḥakīm al-shahīr bi-Tafsīr al-Manār,* 12 vols., Beirut n.d.

Rāzī, *Tafsīr*
Fakhr al-Dīn al-Rāzī, *al-Tafsīr al-kabīr (Mafātīḥ al-ghayb),* ed. Muḥammad Muḥyī l-Dīn Abd al-Ḥamīd, 32 vols. in 16, Cairo 1352/1933; Tehran n.d.; Beirut 1981

Rippin, *Approaches*
Andrew Rippin (ed.), *Approaches to the history of the interpretation of the Qurʾān,* Oxford 1988

Rummānī et al., *Rasāʾil*
ʿAlī b. ʿĪsā al-Rummānī, Ḥamd b. Muḥammad al-Khaṭṭābī and ʿAbd al-Qāhir al-Jurjānī, *Thalāth rasāʾil fī iʿjāz al-Qurʾān,* ed. Muḥammad Khalaf Allāh Aḥmad and Muḥammad Zaghlūl Sallām, Cairo 1976

Rūzbihān al-Baqlī, *ʿArāʾis*
Rūzbihān b. Abī Naṣr al-Baqlī, *ʿArāʾis al-bayān fī ḥaqāʾiq al-Qurʾān,* 2 vols., Cawnpore 1301/1884

Ṣābūnī, *Tafsīr*
Muḥammad ʿAlī Ṣābūnī, *Ṣafwat al-tafāsīr. Tafsīr lil-Qurʾān al-karīm,* 3 vols., Beirut 1981
Ṣafadī, *Wāfī*
Khalīl b. Aybak al-Ṣafadī, *al-Wāfī bi-l-wafayāt. Das biographische Lexikon des Ṣalāḥaddīn Ḫalīl ibn Aibak aṣ-Ṣafadī,* ed. H. Ritter et al., 24 vols. to date, Wiesbaden-Beirut-Damascus 1962-
Sakhāwī, *Jamāl*
ʿAlam al-Dīn ʿAlī b. Muḥammad al-Sakhāwi, *Jamāl al-qurrāʾ wa-kamāl al-iqrāʾ,* ed. ʿAlī Ḥusayn al-Bawwāb, 2 vols., Mecca 1408/1987
Ṣaliḥī, *Subul*
Shams al-Dīn Muḥammad b. Yūsuf al-Ṣāliḥī, *Subul al-hudā wa-l-rashād,* ed. ʿĀdil Aḥmad ʿAbd al-Mawjūd and ʿAlī Muḥammad Muʿawwad, 12 vols., Beirut 1414/1993
Samʿānī, *Ansāb*
ʿAbd al-Karīm b. Muḥammad al-Samʿānī, *Kitāb al-Ansāb,* facsimile ed., D.S. Margoliouth, Leiden 1912; ed. Muḥammad ʿAbd al-Muʿīd Khān et al., 13 vols., Hyderabad 1382-1402/1962-82
Schawāhid-Indices
A. Fischer and E. Bräunlich, eds., *Indices der Reimwörter und der Dichter der in den arabischen Schawāhid-Kommentaren und in verwandten Werken erläuterten Belegverse,* Leipzig 1934-45
Schwarzbaum, *Legends*
H. Schwarzbaum, *Biblical and extra-biblical legends in Islamic folk-literature,* Wallford-Hessen 1982
Sezgin, GAS
F. Sezgin, *Geschichte des arabischen Schrifttums,* 9 vols., Leiden 1967-84
Shāfiʿī, *Aḥkām*
Muḥammad b. Idrīs al-Shāfiʿī, *Aḥkām al-Qurʾān,* 2 vols. in 1, Beirut 1980
Shāfiʿī, *Mufassirān*
Muḥammad Shāfiʿī, *Mufassirān-i shīʿah,* Shiraz 1349[solar]/1970
Shahrastānī, *Milal*
Abū l-Fatḥ Muḥammad al-Shahrastānī, *al-Milal wa-l-niḥal,* ed. W. Cureton, 2 vols., London 1846; ed. Muḥammad Fatḥ Allāh Badrān, 2 vols., Cairo 1947-55; ed. Fahmī Muḥammad, Beirut 1992
Shawkānī, *Tafsīr*
Abū ʿAbdallāh Muḥammad b. ʿAlī al-Shawkānī, *Fatḥ al-qadīr al-jāmiʿ bayna fannay l-riwāya wa-l-dirāya fī ʿilm al-tafsīr,* 5 vols., Cairo 1349/1930; repr. Beirut 1973
Sibṭ Ibn al-Jawzī, *Mirʾāt*
Shams al-Dīn Abū l-Muẓaffar Yūsuf b. Qizoğlu Sibṭ Ibn al-Jawzī, *Mirʾāt al-zamān fī taʾrīkh al-aʿyān,* ed. Iḥsān ʿAbbās, Beirut 1405/1985
Speyer, *Erzählungen*
Heinrich Speyer, *Die biblischen Erzählungen im Qoran,* Gräfenhainich 1931; repr. Hildesheim 1961
Sprenger, *Moḥammad*
A. Sprenger, *Das Leben und die Lehre des Mohammad,* 3 vols., 2nd ed., Berlin 1869
Storey, PL
C.A. Storey, *Persian literature. A bio-bibliographical survey,* 2 vols. in 5, London 1927
Sufyān al-Thawrī, *Tafsīr*
Abū ʿAbdallāh Sufyān al-Thawrī, *al-Tafsīr,* ed. Imtiyāz ʿAlī ʿArshī, Beirut 1403/1983
Suhaylī, *Taʿrīf*
Abū l-Qāsim ʿAbd al-Raḥmān b. ʿAbdallāh al-Suhaylī, *al-Taʿrīf wa-l-iʿlām fī mā ubhima fī l-Qurʾān min al-asmāʾ wa-l-aʿlām,* ed. ʿAbdallāh Muḥammad ʿAlī al-Naqrāt, Tripoli 1401/1992
Sulamī, *Ziyādāt*
Abū ʿAbd al-Raḥmān Muḥammad b. al-Ḥusayn al-Sulamī, *Ziyādāt ḥaqāʾiq al-tafsīr,* ed. G. Böwering, Beirut 1995
Suyūṭī, *Durr*
Jalāl al-Dīn al-Suyūṭī, *al-Durr al-manthūr fī l-tafsīr bi-l-maʾthūr,* 6 vols., Beirut 1990
Suyūṭī, *Ḥuffāẓ*
Jalāl al-Dīn al-Suyūṭī, *Ṭabaqāt al-ḥuffāẓ,* ed. ʿAlī Muḥammad ʿUmar, Cairo 1973

Suyūṭī, *Itqān*
Jalāl al-Dīn al-Suyūṭī, *al-Itqān fī ʿulūm al-Qurʾān,* ed. Muḥammad Abū l-Faḍl Ibrāhīm, 4 vols. in 2, Cairo 1967

Suyūṭī, *Khaṣāʾiṣ*
Jalāl al-Dīn al-Suyūṭī, *al-Khaṣāʾiṣ al-kubrā,* Hyderabad 1320/1902; repr. Beirut n.d.

Suyūṭī, *Mufḥamāt*
Jalāl al-Dīn al-Suyūṭī, *al-Mufḥamāt al-aqrān fī mubhamāt al-Qurʾān,* ed. Muṣṭafā Dīb al-Bughā, Damascus and Beirut 1403/1982

Suyūṭī, *Muhadhdhab*
Jalāl al-Dīn al-Suyūṭī, *al-Muhadhdhab fī mā waqaʿa fī l-Qurʿān min al-muʿarrab,* ed. al-Tihāmī al-Rājī al-Hāshimī, Rabat n.d.; in *Rasāʾil fī l-fiqh wa-l-lugha,* ed. ʿAbdallāh al-Jubūrī, Beirut 1982, pp. 179-235

Suyūṭī, *Ṭabaqāt*
Jalāl al-Dīn al-Suyūṭī, *Ṭabaqāt al-mufassirīn,* ed. ʿAlī Muḥammad ʿUmar, Cairo 1976

Suyūṭī, *Taḥbīr*
Jalāl al-Dīn al-Suyūṭī, *al-Taḥbīr fī ʿilm al-tafsīr,* ed. Fatḥī ʿAbd al-Qādir Farīd, Cairo 1406/1986

Suyūṭī, *Tanāsuq*
Jalāl al-Dīn al-Suyūṭī, *Tanāsuq al-durar fī tanāsub al-suwar,* ed. ʿAbd al-Qādir Aḥmad ʿAṭā, Beirut 1406/1986

Ṭabarānī, *Awsaṭ*
Abū l-Qāsim Sulaymān b. Aḥmad al-Ṭabarānī, *al-Muʿjam al-awsaṭ,* ed. Ṭāriq b. ʿAwaḍ Allāh b. Muḥammad and ʿAbd al-Muḥsin Ibrāhīm al-Ḥusaynī, 10 vols., Cairo 1415/1995

Ṭabarānī, *Kabīr*
Abū l-Qāsim Sulaymān b. Aḥmad al-Ṭabarānī, *al-Muʿjam al-kabīr,* ed. Ḥamdī ʿAbd al-Majīd al-Salafī, vols. i-xii, xvii-xx and xxii-xxv, Baghdad 1398-1404/1977-83; Mosul 1401/1983

Ṭabarī, *Tafsīr*
Abū Jaʿfar Muḥammad b. Jarīr al-Ṭabarī, *Jāmiʿ al-bayān ʿan taʾwīl āy al-Qurʾān* [up to Q 14:27], ed. Maḥmūd Muḥammad Shākir and Aḥmad Muḥammad Shākir, 16 vols., Cairo 1954-68; 2nd ed. for some vols., Cairo 1969; ed. Aḥmad Saʿīd ʿAlī et al., 30 vols., Cairo 1373-77/1954-7; repr. Beirut 1984

Ṭabarī, *Taʾrīkh*
Abū Jaʿfar Muḥammad b. Jarīr al-Ṭabarī, *Taʾrīkh al-rusul wa-l-mulūk,* ed. M.J. de Goeje et al., 15 vols., Leiden 1879-1901; ed. Muḥammad Abū l-Faḍl Ibrāhīm, 10 vols., Cairo 1960-9

Ṭabarsī, *Majmaʿ*
Abū ʿAlī l-Faḍl b. al-Ḥasan al-Ṭabarsī, *Majmaʿ al-bayān fī tafsīr al-Qurʾān,* intr. Muḥsin al-Amīn al-Ḥusaynī al-ʿĀmilī, 30 vols. in 6, Beirut 1380/1961

Ṭabāṭabāʾī, *Mīzān*
Muḥammad Ḥusayn Ṭabāṭabāʾī, *al-Mīzān fī tafsīr al-Qurʾān,* 20 vols., Beirut 1393-4/1973-4; vol. xxi, Beirut 1985

Tāj al-ʿarūs
Muḥibb al-Dīn al-Sayyid Muḥammad Murtaḍā al-Zabīdī, *Sharḥ al-qāmūs al-musammā Tāj al-ʿarūs min jawāhir al-Qāmūs,* 10 vols., Cairo 1306-7; ed. ʿAbd al-Sattār Aḥmad Faraj et al., 20 vols. to date, Kuwait 1965-

Thaʿālibī, *Iʿjāz*
ʿAbd al-Malik b. Muḥammad al-Thaʿālibī, *al-Iʿjāz wa-l-ījāz,* ed. Iskandar Āṣāt, Constantinople 1897; Beirut 1983

Thaʿālibī, *Iqtibās*
ʿAbd al-Malik b. Muḥammad al-Thaʿālibī, *al-Iqtibās min al-Qurʾān al-karīm,* ed. Ibtisām Marhūn al-Ṣaffār and Mujāhid Muṣṭafā Bahjat, 2 vols. in 1, Cairo 1412/1992

Thaʿālibī, *Yatīma*
ʿAbd al-Malik b. Muḥammad al-Thaʿālibī, *Yatīma al-dahr fī maḥāsin ahl al-ʿaṣr,* 4 vols., Damascus 1304/1886-7; ed. Muḥammad Muḥyī l-Dīn ʿAbd al-Ḥamīd, 4 vols., Cairo 1375-7/1956-8

Thaʿlabī, *Qiṣaṣ*
Aḥmad b. Muḥammad b. Ibrāhīm al-Thaʿlabī, *Qiṣaṣ al-anbiyāʾ al-musammā bi-ʿArāʾis al-majālis,* Cairo 1322; repr. Beirut 1980

Thaʿlabī-Goldfeld
I. Goldfeld, *Qurʾānic commentary in the eastern Islamic tradition of the first four centuries of the hijra. An annotated edition of the preface to al-Thaʿlabī's "Kitāb al-Kashf wa-l-bayān ʿan Tafsīr al-Qurʾān,"* Acre 1984

Tirmidhī, *Ṣaḥīḥ*
Abū ʿĪsā Muḥammad b. ʿĪsā al-Tirmidhī, *al-Jāmiʿ al-ṣaḥīḥ,* ed. Aḥmad Muḥammad Shākir et al., 5 vols., Cairo 1937-65

Ṭūsī, *Fihrist*
Muḥammad b. al-Ḥasan al-Ṭūsī, *al-Fihrist,* Najaf 1356/1937; Beirut 1983

Ṭūsī, *Tibyān*
Muḥammad b. al-Ḥasan al-Ṭūsī, *al-Tibyān fī tafsīr al-Qurʾān,* intr. Āghā Buzurk al-Ṭihrānī, 10 vols., Najaf 1376-83/1957-63

Tustarī, *Tafsīr*
Sahl b. ʿAbdallāh al-Tustarī, *Tafsīr al-Qurʾān al-ʿaẓīm,* Cairo 1329/1911

ʿUkbarī, *Tibyān*
Abū l-Baqāʾ ʿAbdallāh b. al-Ḥusayn al-ʿUkbarī, *al-Tibyān fī iʿrāb al-Qurʾān,* ed. ʿAlī Muḥammad al-Bajāwī, 2 vols., Cairo 1396/1976

Wagtendonk, *Fasting*
K. Wagtendonk, *Fasting in the Koran,* Leiden 1968

Wāḥidī, *Asbāb*
Abū l-Ḥasan ʿAlī b. Aḥmad al-Nīsābūrī al-Wāḥidī, *Asbāb al-nuzūl,* Cairo 1968

Wāḥidī, *Wasīṭ*
Abū l-Ḥasan ʿAlī b. Aḥmad al-Nīsābūrī al-Wāḥidī, *al-Wasīṭ fī tafsīr al-Qurʾān,* ed. ʿĀdil Aḥmad ʿAbd al-Mawjūd et al., 4 vols., Beirut 1415/1994

Wansbrough, *QS*
J. Wansbrough, *Quranic studies. Sources and methods of scriptural interpretation,* Oxford 1977

Wāqidī, *Maghāzī*
Muḥammad b. ʿUmar al-Wāqidī, *Kitāb al-Maghāzī,* ed. M. Jones, 3 vols., London 1966

Watt-Bell, *Introduction*
W.M. Watt, *Bell's introduction to the Qurʾān,* Edinburgh 1970, 1991

Wensinck, *Concordance*
A.J. Wensinck et al., *Concordance et indices de la tradition musulmane,* 8 vols., Leiden 1936-79; repr. 8 vols. in 4, 1992

Wensinck, *Handbook*
A.J. Wensinck, *A handbook of early Muhammadan tradition,* Leiden 1927

Wild, *Text*
S. Wild, ed., *The Qurʾān as text,* Leiden 1996

Yaḥyā b. Sallām, *Tafsīr*
Yaḥyā b. Sallām al-Baṣrī, *al-Taṣārīf. Tafsīr al-Qurʾān mimmā shtabahat asmāʾuhu wa-taṣarrafat maʿānīhi,* ed. Hind Shalabī, Tunis 1979

Yaʿqūbī, *Buldān*
Aḥmad b. Abī Yaʿqūb b. Wāḍiḍ al-Yaʿqūbī, *Kitāb al-Buldān,* ed. M.J. de Goeje, Leiden 1892, 1967

Yaʿqūbī, *Taʾrīkh*
Aḥmad b. Abī Yaʿqūb b. Wāḍiḥ al-Yaʿqūbī, *Ibn Wādhih qui dicitur al-Jaʿqubi historiae,* ed. M.T. Houtsma, 2 vols., Leiden 1883; repr. 1969

Yāqūt, *Buldān*
Yāqūt b. ʿAbdallāh al-Ḥamawī, *Muʿjam al-buldān,* ed. F. Wüstenfeld, 6 vols., Leipzig 1863-6; 5 vols., Beirut 1374-6/1955-7; ed. Farīd ʿAbd al-ʿAzīz al-Jundī, 7 vols., Beirut 1990

Yāqūt, *Irshād*
Yāqūt b. ʿAbdallāh al-Ḥamawī, *Irshād al-arīb ilā maʿrifat al-adīb. Muʿjam al-udabāʾ,* ed. D.S. Margoliouth, 7 vols., London and Leiden 1923-6; ed. Iḥsān ʿAbbās, 7 vols., Beirut 1993

Zajjāj, *Maʿānī*
Abū Isḥāq Ibrāhīm b. Muḥammad b. al-Sarī l-Zajjāj, *Maʿānī l-Qurʾān wa-iʿrābuhu,* ed. ʿAbd al-Jalīl ʿAbduh Shalabī, 5 vols., Beirut 1408/1988

Zamakhsharī, *Asās*
Maḥmūd b. ʿUmar al-Zamakhsharī, *Asās al-balāgha,* Beirut 1979

Zamakhsharī, *Kashshāf*
Maḥmūd b. ʿUmar al-Zamakhsharī, *al-*

Kashshāf ʿan ḥaqāʾiq ghawāmiḍ al-tanzīl wa-ʿuyūn al-aqāwīl fī wujūh al-taʾwīl, 4 vols., Beirut 1366/1947; ed. Muḥammad ʿAbd al-Salām Shāhīn, 4 vols., Beirut 1995

Zambaur, *Manuel*
E. de Zambaur, *Manuel de généalogie et de chronologie pour l'histoire de l'Islam,* Hanover 1927; repr. Bad Pyrmont 1955

Zarkashī, *Burhān*
Badr al-Dīn al-Zarkashī, *al-Burhān fī ʿulūm al-Qurʾān,* ed. Muḥammad Abū l-Faḍl Ibrāhīm, 4 vols., Cairo 1957; Beirut 1972; ed. Yūsuf ʿAbd al-Raḥmān al-Marʿashlī et al., 4 vols., Beirut 1994

Zayd b. ʿAlī, *Musnad*
Zayd b. ʿAlī Zayn al-ʿĀbidīn, *Musnad,* ed. Bakr b. Muḥammad ʿĀshūr, 1328/1910; Beirut 1983

Ziriklī, *Aʿlām*
Khayr al-Dīn al-Ziriklī, *al-Aʿlām. Qāmūs tarājim li-ashhar al-rijāl wa-l-nisāʾ min al-ʿArab wa-l-mustaʿribīn wa-l- mustashriqīn,* 10 vols., Damascus 1373-8/1954-9; 8 vols., Beirut 1979

Zubaydī, *Ṭabaqāt*
Abū Bakr Muḥammad b. al-Ḥasan al-Zubaydī, *Ṭabaqāt al-naḥwiyyīn wa-l-lughawiyyīn,* ed. Muḥammad Abū l-Faḍl Ibrāhīm, Cairo 1373/1954

Zubayrī, *Nasab*
Muṣʿab al-Zubayrī, *Nasab Quraysh,* ed. E. Lévi-Provençal, Cairo 1953

Zurqānī, *Sharḥ*
Muḥammad b. ʿAbd al-Bāqī al-Miṣrī al-Mālik, *Sharḥ al-mawāhib al-laduniyya,* ed. Muḥammad ʿAbd al-ʿAzīz al-Khālidī, 12 vols., Beirut 1417/1996

A

Aaron

The brother and companion of Moses (q.v.). Aaron (Hārūn b. ʿImrān) is mentioned by name twenty times in the Qurʾān. He is given prophetic status alongside Moses, having received the criterion (q.v.) of revelation (*furqān*, Q 21:48-9; cf. 19:53; 7:122; 23:45; 37:114-20; and 20:70 and 26:48, containing the phrase, "We believe in the Lord of Moses and Aaron"; see REVELATION AND INSPIRATION), and is listed with a number of other prophets (Q 4:163; 6:84). Moses asked God to make Aaron his partner *(wazīr)* in his affairs when he was commanded to go before Pharaoh (q.v.; Q 25:35; cf. 10:75; 20:29-36; 26:13; 28:35). Moses also asked God to let Aaron be his spokesman because he was so eloquent (Q 28:34-5). The form of the name "Hārūn" is also known from early Arabic poetry and entered Arabic from Hebrew, likely via Syriac (see FOREIGN VOCABULARY).

A focus of attention regarding Aaron in the Qurʾān is the worship of the calf of gold (q.v.). The incident is mentioned twice. In the first account (Q 7:148-57), the story is told as in Exodus 32, with the anger of Moses toward Aaron quite apparent even though his role was just that of an onlooker. In the second version, (Q 20:83-98) a Samaritan (see SAMARITANS) is presented as the tempter of Israel (q.v.). He urged the people to throw their ornaments in the fire and he made the calf that was worshipped by the people, despite Aaron's advising them not to do so. Again, Moses' anger toward Aaron is apparent. Thus, it may be said that the Qurʾān agrees with the Jewish biblical commentary *(midrash)* in reducing the blame upon Aaron, although that innocence is not connected, as it is in Jewish commentary, to Aaron's status as high priest, an idea not mentioned in the Qurʾān (see IDOLATRY AND IDOLATERS).

Later Islamic tradition has paid a good deal of attention to the death of Aaron. When Aaron died, the people accused Moses of having murdered him, but angels (q.v.) appeared — or other divine interventions took place — in order to alleviate their suspicions. According to Muslim legend, a similar accusation was lodged against Joshua in the death of Moses.

An issue related to Aaron which has proven to be subject to dispute since the early days of Islam is Q 19:28, in which Mary (q.v.), the mother of Jesus (q.v.), is called "the sister of Aaron" (see also Q 3:35, "a woman of ʿImrān (q.v.)" and 66:12, "Mary, the daughter of ʿImrān, who guarded her chastity"). In Muslim's *Ṣaḥīḥ, K. al-Adab,* for example, there is a ḥadīth from al-Mughīra b. Shuʿba (d. 50/670) which indicates that the polemical nature of the charge of "errors" in the Qurʾān existed from the earliest period of Muslim-Christian relations.

Al-Mughīra said, "When I came to Najrān (q.v.), the Christians asked me, 'You read, "O sister of Aaron," in the Qurʾān, whereas Moses was born much before Jesus.' When I came back to the messenger of God, I asked him about that, whereupon he said, 'People used to give [to their children] the names of the messengers and [other] pious persons who had gone before them.' "

According to the biblical story, Aaron did have a sister called Miriam (who watched over the baby Moses in the bulrushes according to Exodus 2:4-7; see Exodus 15:20-1 for her name), but she was not, of course, the same as Mary, the mother of Jesus, and the Muslim tradition has never taken that to be the case. Al-Ṭabarī (d. 310/923), for example, in speaking of Mary, says that people reacted to her presentation of the baby Jesus by saying, "Sister of Aaron, your father was not a wicked man and your mother was not unchaste. So what is your case, sister of Aaron?" This al-Ṭabarī explains as follows: "[Mary] was descended from Aaron, the brother of Moses, so that this expression is the equivalent of saying, 'O brother of such-and-such tribe'; i.e. it indicates a familial relationship [but not necessarily the exact one indicated]" (*Taʾrīkh,* i, 734; M. Perlmann (trans.), *History,* iv, 120). Other exegetes suggest that the Aaron referred to here is an otherwise unknown brother of Mary, the mother of Jesus, and of Elizabeth, the mother of John the Baptist (q.v.), who were related through their father ʿImrān b. Matthān (see Bayḍāwī, *Anwār,* ad Q 3:30-1). See also PROPHETS AND PROPHETHOOD.

Andrew Rippin

Bibliography

Primary: Kisāʾī, *Qiṣaṣ,* 222-3, 238; Ṭabarī, *Taʾrīkh,* i, 471-81 (Aaron in Egypt), 489-98 (Aaron and the calf), 502-5 (Aaron's death), trans. W.M. Brinner, *History of al-Ṭabarī, iii. The children of Israel,* Albany 1991, 55-65, 72-80, 85-8; and M. Perlmann, *History of al-Ṭabarī, iv. The ancient kingdoms,* Albany 1987; Thaʿlabī, *Qiṣaṣ,* Cairo n.d., 163-5, 184-8, 218.

Secondary: A. Geiger, *Was hat Mohammed aus dem Judenthume aufgenommen?* Baden 1833, trans. *Judaism and Islam,* Madras 1898, 130-2; B. Heller, Sāmirī, in *EI²,* viii, 1046; Horovitz, *KU,* 128 (Imran), 138-40 (Mary), 148-9 (Aaron); Jeffery, *For. vocab.,* 283-4; H. Schwarzbaum, *Biblical and extra-biblical legends in Islamic folk-literature,* Walldorf-Hessen 1982, 13-5; id., Jewish, Christian, Muslim and Falasha legends of the death of Aaron, the high priest, in *Fabula* 5 (1962), 185-227; H. Speyer, *Erzählungen,* 242-3, 260-2, 323-33; A.J. Wensinck, Maryam, in *EI²,* vi, 628-32.

ʿAbd see SERVANT; SLAVES AND SLAVERY

Ablution see CLEANLINESS AND ABLUTION

Abortion

The premature expulsion of a fetus. Classical Muslim jurists applied a number of terms to abortion, including *ijhāḍ, isqāṭ, ṭarḥ, ilqāʾ* and *imlāṣ.* The Qurʾān makes no reference to abortion as the term is commonly understood, although it upholds the sanctity of human life in general (e.g. Q 5:32) and forbids the killing of children (Q 17:31) and female infants (Q 81:8-9) in particular (see CHILDREN; INFANTICIDE; MURDER). The restrictive view of abortion commonly held by jurists was based on the general qurʾānic interdiction of unlawfully taking human life.

The qurʾānic descriptions of the development of the human embryo (see BIOLOGY AS THE CREATION AND STAGES OF LIFE) led scholars to differentiate between an initial soulless and unformed biological entity and the human being into which it developed: "We created man from an extraction of clay (q.v.), then we set him as a drop *(nuṭfa)* [of sperm] in a safe lodging. Then we created from the drop a clot of blood (*ʿalaqa,* see BLOOD AND BLOOD CLOT); then we created from the clot a small piece of tissue *(muḍgha),* subsequently creating from the tissue bones and covering the bones in flesh; and then we produced it as another creature" (Q 23:12-14). With the exception of the reference to creation from "an extraction of clay," which was believed to apply only to the special case of the first man, Adam, this passage was held to represent the normal development of the human fetus. Some scholars interpreted "and then we produced it as another creature" as indicating that the infant was given a soul some time after conception (Qurṭubī, *Jāmiʿ,* xii, 5-14; Rāzī, *Tafsīr,* xxiii, 84-7; Ṭabarsī, *Majmaʿ,* vii, 101; Ṭabāṭabāʾī, *Mīzān,* xv, 20-4). Well-known ḥadīth, recorded in both Sunnī and Shīʿī collections, provided further justification for this view. Some of these set the duration of the first three stages of the fetus, namely drop, clot and tissue, at forty days each. After the completion of this cycle, God dispatched an angel to breathe the soul *(rūḥ)* into the fetus at which point its fate on earth and in the hereafter was ordained (Bukhārī, *Ṣaḥīḥ, K. al-Qadar;* Muslim, *Ṣaḥīḥ, K. al-Qadar;* al-Ḥurr al-ʿĀmilī, *Wasāʾil, K. al-Diyāt,* no. 35652).

For this reason, all Muslim jurists forbade abortion after the fetus had been in the womb for 120 days, although the legal schools and individual scholars differed over the permissibility of abortion before this point (Qurṭubī, *Jāmiʿ,* xii, 8; Nawawī, *Sharḥ,* xvi, 191). The majority of the members of the Mālikī law school prohibited abortion at any time on the basis that once conception took place the fetus was destined for animation. Some individual Mālikīs and the majority of the adherents of the other legal schools did allow abortions, but they disagreed over whether the period of permissibility extended forty, eighty or 120 days after conception. These thresholds determined whether a person who caused a woman to miscarry or a woman who caused herself to abort, either deliberately or through negligence, was liable for the full compensation stipulated for the killing of a human being (*diya kāmila,* see BLOOD MONEY) or a lesser penalty. In practice, the status of the expelled fetus was determined by examining its apparent state of development, i.e. whether it was "formed" or "unformed," a distinction having its roots in the other qurʾānic account of fetal development (Q 22:5).

The justification for an abortion most commonly cited in the classical legal literature was the threat posed to a nursing infant by the cessation of the flow of its mother's milk due to another pregnancy. In the case of a pregnancy which threatened the mother's life, a majority of jurists gave priority to preserving the life of the fetus, if it was believed that it had already acquired a soul (Ibn ʿĀbidīn, *Ḥāshiya,* i, 602; vi, 591; al-Ghazālī, *Iḥyāʾ,* ii, 53; Ibn Rajab, *Jāmiʿ al-ʿulūm,* 46). More recently, some thinkers have come to advocate saving the mother's life in such cases. Rape and incest have also been recognized as suitable justifications for abortion. See also BIRTH CONTROL.

Abdulaziz Sachedina

Bibliography
Primary: Bukhārī, *Ṣaḥīḥ;* al-Ghazālī, Abū Ḥāmid Muḥammad, *Iḥyā' 'ulūm al-dīn,* 4 vols., Cairo 1312/1894; al-Ḥurr al-ʿĀmilī, *Wasā'il al-Shīʿa,* ed. Muḥammad al-Rāzī, 20 vols., Beirut 1389/1969; Ibn ʿĀbidīn, *Ḥāshiya;* Ibn Qudāma, *al-Mughnī,* ed. Ṭ.M. al-Zaynī et al., 10 vols., Cairo 1968-70; Ibn Rajab, *Jāmiʿ al-ʿulūm wa-l-ḥikam,* Cairo 1970; Muslim, *Ṣaḥīḥ;* Nawawī, *Sharḥ;* Qurṭubī, *Jāmiʿ;* Rāzī, *Tafsīr;* Ṭabarsī, *Majmaʿ;* Ṭabāṭabāʾī, *Mīzān.*
Secondary: M.A. Anees, *Islam and biological futures,* London 1989, 164-87; M.ʿA. al-Barr, *Khalq al-insān bayna l-ṭibb wa-l-Qurʾān,* Jeddah 1995[10]; A.F.M. Ebrahim, *Abortion, birth control and surrogate parenting. An Islamic perspective,* Indianapolis 1991; M.S. Makdur, Sterilization and abortion from the point of view of Islam, in I.R. Nazer et al. (eds.), *Islam and family planning,* 2 vols., Beirut 1972, ii, 263-85 (extensive references); B.F. Musallam, *Sex and society in Islam. Birth control before the nineteenth century,* Cambridge 1983, 53-9.

Abraha

The Christian ruler of a south Arabian kingdom founded by the Abyssinians (see ABYSSINIA), whose name is traditionally associated with the interpretation of Q 105, where there is a description of God smiting the People of the Elephant (q.v.). Although he is not mentioned in the qurʾānic text, his name is regularly given in the commentary literature. Epigraphic evidence, the writings of the Byzantine military historian Procopius as well as ecclesiastical sources provide independent historical attestation for this figure, but his association with the sūra is limited to Muslim sources, especially historical and exegetical texts.

The standard account of the Islamic Abraha may be found in the early pages of Ibn Isḥāq's *Sīra,* the most commonly cited biography of the Prophet. It is repeated or summarized in many subsequent commentaries (cf. Ṭabarī, *Tafsīr,* xxx, 299-303; Ṭūsī, *Tibyān,* x, 409-11; Rāzī, *Tafsīr,* xxxii, 96). Read as an extended commentary on Q 105, the story forms part of a larger account of Yemeni history in the generations immediately preceding the birth of Muḥammad (see SĪRA AND THE QURʾĀN). Its earliest segment is clearly framed as the annunciation of "an apostle who will bring truth and justice among men of religion and virtue" (Ibn Isḥāq-Guillaume, 6). As his portion of the story unfolds, Abraha is presented as seizing power of the Abyssinian-controlled territory in the Yemen (q.v.) by a coup and then cleverly defusing the sworn revenge of the Abyssinian ruler, the Negus *(al-Najāshī).* To mollify him further, Abraha builds a magnificent church in Sanʿāʾ and then pledges to divert Arab pilgrimages to this new sanctuary. Angered by a Meccan of the tribe of the Banū Kināna who defiles the church — by defecating in it, according to some exegetes (cf. Rāzī, *Tafsīr,* xxxii, 96; Qurṭubī, *Jāmiʿ,* xx, 188) — to prevent its use as a pilgrimage site, Abraha, in turn, vows revenge on the Meccan sanctuary and marches toward the Kaʿba (q.v.) at the head of a vast army. Abraha's defeat involves miraculous animals, including an Abyssinian battle elephant that kneels before the Kaʿba and refuses to fight and flocks of birds who rain stones down upon his assembled troops. Variants of this narrative abound, some offering as an additional explanation for Abraha's advance upon Mecca the destruction of a Christian church in Abyssinia by a cooking fire carelessly abandoned by some Arab traders (Muqātil, *Tafsīr,* iv, 847; Qummī, *Tafsīr,* ii, 442-3; Ibn al-Jawzī, *Zād,* ix, 232; Qurṭubī, *Jāmiʿ,* xx, 192-5).

Abraha's advance upon Mecca acquired additional importance in the Muslim sources as a point of chronological calculation for the birth of Muḥammad. Dates in pre-Islamic Meccan history were reckoned from the Year of the Elephant *(ʿām al-fīl)* and the key dates in the life of the Prophet were coordinated with this year. Although Abraha's invasion and Muḥammad's birth are often dated to a year equivalent to 570 C.E., the commentators record no unanimity on this matter. Qurṭubī (*Jāmi'*, xx, 194) is representative in presenting sources that equate the Year of the Elephant with that of Muḥammad's birth as well as those that place Abraha's attack 23 or 40 years earlier. Western scholars have also long questioned the accuracy and historical reliability of these chronologies. Those of previous generations, such as T. Nöldeke, H. Lammens and R. Blachère, pointed out the inconsistencies within the early Arabic sources and the contradictions between them and evidence from extra-Islamic traditions. More recent work, such as that of L. Conrad and U. Rubin, has investigated the symbolic and topological significance of the dates and periodization of Muḥammad's career in traditional biographies. See also PRE-ISLAMIC ARABIA AND THE QUR'ĀN.

Jane Dammen McAuliffe

Bibliography
Primary: Ibn Isḥāq, *Sīra*, ed. M. al-Saqqā, i, 43-62, Ibn Isḥāq-Guillaume, 20-30; Ibn al-Jawzī, *Zād*, ix, 231-37; Muqātil, *Tafsīr*, iv, 847-54; Qummī, *Tafsīr*, ii, 442-4; Qurṭubī, *Jāmi'*, xx, 187-200; Rāzī, *Tafsīr*, xxxii, 96-102; Ṭabarī, *Tafsīr*, xxx, 296-304; Ṭusī, *Tibyān*, x, 409-11.
Secondary: M.J. Kister, The campaign of Ḥulubān. New light on the expedition of Abraha, in *Le Muséon* 78 (1965), 425-36; G. Newby, Abraha and Sennacherib. A talmudic parallel to the *tafsīr* on *Sūrat al-Fīl*, in *JAOS* 94 (1974), 431-7; L. Conrad, Abraha and Muḥammad. Some observations apropos of chronology and literary *topoi* in the early Arabic historical tradition, in *BSOAS* 50 (1987), 225-40; U. Rubin, *The eye of the beholder. The life of Muḥammad as viewed by the early Muslims*, Princeton 1995, 199-203; I. Shahid, Two qur'ānic sūras: *al-Fīl* and *Qurayš*, in W. al-Qāḍī (ed.), *Studia Arabica et Islamica. Festschrift for Iḥsān 'Abbās*, Beirut 1981, 429-36.

Abraham

Some two hundred and forty-five verses in twenty-five sūras of the Qur'ān make reference to Abraham (Ibrāhīm), the progenitor of the nation of Israel (q.v.). Among biblical figures, only Moses (q.v.) receives more attention and in the Qur'ān Abraham and Moses are the sole prophets explicitly identified as bearers of scriptures (Q 53:36-7; 87:18-9; see BOOK; SCRIPTURE AND THE QUR'ĀN). Although the Islamic Abraham shares many characteristics with the figure in the Bible and later Jewish exegetical literature, the Qur'ān especially emphasizes his role as a precursor of Muḥammad and the establisher of the pilgrimage rites in Mecca (see PILGRIMAGE).

Abraham in the Qur'ān

The references to Abraham in the Qur'ān take a number of different forms and appear in a wide variety of contexts. Several descriptive appellations are applied to him. He is deemed "very truthful" (*ṣiddīq*, Q 19:41) and "kind and gracious" (*ḥalīm*, Q 9:114; 11:75). He is one who "paid his debt in full" (*alladhī waffā*, Q 53:37). His qur'ānic appellation as [God's] friend (*khalīl*) in Q 4:125 formed the basis of his honorific title "Friend of God" (*khalīl Allāh*) in the Islamic tradition. (The city of Hebron, traditionally regarded as the site of his grave, takes its Arabic name *"al-Khalīl"* from this honorific). Abraham is also called *"ḥanīf"* (q.v.), usually translated as "upright" or "pure of faith," in eight places (Q 2:135; 3:67, 95; 4:125; 6:79, 161; 16:120, 123). The term appears elsewhere only twice, in both cases referring to Muḥammad (Q 10:105; 30:30), and in the first of these he is called "*ḥanīf* and not a polytheist," a phrase also several times applied to Abraham. It is to be assumed that Muḥammad's connection to this respected figure served to enhance his religious authority and prestige among those Arabs familiar with the Bible. The depiction of Abraham as *ḥanīf,* frequently in association with the phrase "religion of Abraham" (*millat Ibrāhīm,* Q 2:130, 135; 3:95; 4:125; 6:161; 12:38; 16:123; 22:78), has suggested to Muslim believers and Western scholars alike that an indigenous Abrahamic monotheism may have existed in Arabia prior to Muḥammad's mission.

Many Abrahamic references in the Qurʾān parallel biblical material. Abraham leaves his father and people and encounters God in a new land where he will raise his family (Q 19:48-9; 21:71; 29:26; 37:83-101; cf. *Gen* 12:1-5). He establishes a sacred shrine, the House of God (Q 2:125-7; cf. *Gen* 12:6-8, 13:18). He mildly challenges God and is then told to cut open or divide birds (Q 2:260; cf. *Gen* 15:1-10). He is associated with a covenant (q.v.) with God (Q 2:124-5; 33:7; cf. *Gen* 17:1-14). He is visited by divine messengers who announce the forthcoming birth of a son to him and his wife, and who then proceed to destroy the people of Lot (q.v.; Q 11:69-76; 15:51-9; 29:31; 51:24-30; cf. *Gen* 18:1-20). He argues with God over the fate of the people of Lot (Q 11:74-6; cf. *Gen* 18:20-33). He takes his son and attempts to offer him as a sacrifice, but is released from the task by God (Q 37:99-111; cf. *Gen* 22:1-19). He is God's friend (Q 4:126; cf. *Is* 41:8; *2 Ch* 20:7).

Two of these parallels find expression in sustained narrative form. The visit of the divine messengers is mentioned in four qurʾānic loci, a repetition which attests to its importance. The messengers — or a guest — come to Abraham and he hospitably offers them a calf to eat. Yet Abraham fears these strangers because, according to Q 11:70, they eat nothing. In some earlier Jewish interpretive literature, the messengers also do not eat — despite the statement in *Gen* 18:8 that they did — because angels (q.v.) were believed neither to eat nor to have any other human bodily functions (*TB Ḥagigah* 16a; *Targum Yerushalmi, Gen* 18:8; *Genesis Rabba* 48:14). The post-biblical Jewish motif of these guests not eating Abraham's food was retained in the qurʾānic version, but the Jewish explanation for this was not. The qurʾānic Abraham therefore interprets their refusal to eat as a sign of hostility, causing him to fear for his safety until he is assured by them that they have come to announce the happy news of a future son (Ṭabarī, *Tafsīr,* xiv, 70-1). His unnamed wife laughs (*ḍaḥikat,* Q 11:71) or strikes her head in unbelief (Q 51:29), but since the Hebrew play on words between laugh (*ṣaḥoq*) and Isaac (Yiṣḥāq, see ISAAC) is not retained in Arabic, Muslim commentators offer a series of alternative explanations for her behavior (Firestone, *Journeys,* 52-9).

Many motifs in the qurʾānic account (Q 37:99-111) and Islamic exegesis of Abraham's attempted sacrifice of his son (*dhabīḥ*) find parallels in Jewish tradition (Firestone, *Journeys,* 105-34), although in the Qurʾān the son knows beforehand of his father's intention and actually encourages him to perform the deed. Of greatest interest to the Muslim commentators was the identity of the son, who is not named in the Qurʾān. Some identified him, as the Bible does, as Isaac, Abraham's son by his wife Sarah; although others wished to cast the progenitor of the Arabs, Ishmael (q.v.), his son by Sarah's handmaiden Hagar, in this central role. Muslim interpreters read the explicit reference to Isaac in Q 37:112 in ways that support Ishmael as well as Isaac as the intended sacrifice.

The most oft-repeated Abrahamic narrative in the Qurʾān, the story of his smashing the pagan idols (Q 6:74-84; 19:41-50; 21:51-73; 26:69-86; 29:16-27; 37:83-98; 43:26-7; 60:4), has no biblical parallel, but is well known in Jewish exegetical literature (e.g. *Genesis Rabba* 38:13; *TB Pesaḥim* 118a,

ʿ*Eruvin* 53a; *PRE* 26). The various qurʾānic versions tend to emphasize different issues for which parallels can be found in Jewish sources. In Q 6:74, Abraham calls his father by the name Āzar (q.v.). Q 6:75-9 describes Abraham's discovery of monotheism through logical reflection and the empirical observation of nature, a story of great antiquity (Ginzberg, *Legends,* v, 210, n. 16). Despite his father's hostility towards him (Q 19:46), Abraham prays that he be forgiven for his sin of worshipping idols (Q 9:113-4; 14:41; 19:47; 26:86; 60:4). This aspect of the legend may have held particular poignancy for Muḥammad, who, according to tradition, wished to do the same for his idolatrous ancestors (Ṭabarī, *Tafsīr,* xiii, 40-53). Abraham destroys his father's idols and those of his compatriots (Q 21:57-8; 37:93; see IDOLATRY AND IDOLATERS). For this he is sentenced to be burnt alive, but God rescues him (Q 21:68-9; 29:24; 37:97-8). He also endures further trials in which he prevails (Q 2:124; 37:106; cf. *Avot* 5:3, with details provided in the *midrash* and elsewhere).

One series of Abrahamic references in the Qurʾān finds no parallel in either the Bible or later Jewish traditions. These associate Abraham, and often Ishmael, with the building of the Kaʿba (q.v.), with Arabian cultic practice and with terminology of Islamic religious conceptions. Abraham and Ishmael raise up the foundations of the House and entreat God to keep them and their descendants forever a "nation in submission to You" and to show them the proper pilgrimage rituals (*manāsik,* Q 2:127-8). Elsewhere, Abraham prays for the safety of the territory around the Kaʿba and prays for those of his descendants whom he settled in Mecca to engage in regular prayers and remain secure (Q 14:35-7). God settles Abraham at the House or makes the area habitable and enjoins him (or, perhaps, Muḥammad) to announce officially the pilgrimage to Mecca (Q 22:26-7). Abraham and Ishmael are ordered to render the Kaʿba pure for the proper monotheistic pilgrimage ritual of circumambulation and for kneeling and prostration there in prayer (Q 2:125). The famous place of prayer, the Place of Abraham (q.v.; Q 2:125; 3:96-7), is situated near the Kaʿba.

For Jews Abraham's special covenantal relationship with God established him as the authenticator and founder of Judaism. It was natural that when Christianity established itself as related to but independent of Judaism, Christians appropriated the figure of Abraham as a means of legitimating their religion (*Rom* 4:9-25; 9:7-9; *Ga* 4:21-31). Similarly, Abraham's role in the Qurʾān includes a related but more polemical aspect as he appears as neither a Jew nor a Christian but as a *ḥanīf muslim* (Q 3:65-70; cf. 2:140). Like the New Testament citations, the Qurʾān stipulates that the divine covenant established with Abraham does not automatically include all of his progeny (Q 2:124; 4:54-5; 37:113; 57:26). Inasmuch as the religion of Muḥammad is the religion of Abraham (Q 22:78), those Jews who reject Muḥammad and the religion he brings are, in fact, rejecting their own religion. The Jews further deny the religious sanctity of Mecca, despite Abraham's intimate association with it (Q 3:95-8).

It is worth noting that the inconsistent qurʾānic references to Abraham's descendants have been an issue of some interest to Western scholars. Abraham is told by God's messengers that he will be the father of an unnamed son in Q 15:53; 37:101; 51:28. In Q 37:112 the son is named Isaac. A number of verses list Isaac and Isaac's son Jacob (q.v.) together as if they were both sons of Abraham (Q 6:84; 11:71; 19:49; 21:72; 29:27). In a series of quite different passages, Ishmael is listed as if he had no familial connection to Abraham (Q 6:86; 19:54-5; 21:85; 38:48). The idiomatic phrase, "Abraham, Isaac and Jacob," is employed in two passages (Q 12:38; 38:45; cf. Q 2:132), while in yet another idiom, "Abraham, Ishmael, Isaac, Jacob and the tribes," is used (Q 2:136, 140; 3:84; 4:163). Already in the nineteenth century C.S. Hurgronje *(Het Mekkaansche Feest)* theorized that this material reflects some confusion over the exact relationship between Abraham and his descendants, claiming that these verses date from the Meccan period of revelations, i.e. before Muḥammad came into regular contact with Jews or Christians. The verses that reproduce the biblical genealogy were held to date from Muḥammad's days in Medina, when he apparently had ongoing contact with the local Jewish community.

The narrative Abraham cycle

Reports from the genres of ḥadīth, prophetic biography, qurʾānic exegesis and universal histories expand the spare qurʾānic material on Abraham. Linked together, this interpretive literature forms a full narrative cycle in three parts. The first takes place in Mesopotamia, the land of Abraham's birth; the second in the vicinity of Jerusalem (q.v.) and the third in Mecca (q.v.) and its environs. These three lands represent a hierarchy of sanctity culminating with the most sacred place and its holy sites. All of this material can properly be considered scriptural exegesis, although some of it indirectly interprets biblical scripture in addition to the Qurʾān by supplementing the qurʾānic revelation with material deriving from a biblicist milieu ("biblicist" referring to Jewish or Christian, whether "orthodox" or syncretistic in practice and belief). Given the great variety in the literature, only a representative account can be given here.

Part one begins with the astrological portents of Abraham's impending birth in Mesopotamia, often associated with Kūthā in southern Iraq. Nimrod (q.v.) is the king and he attempts to prevent the birth of his nemesis through a variety of stratagems, all of which fail. Abraham's infancy and youth are marked by miraculous signs (q.v.) and events. While still a boy, he determines through his natural intelligence and perspicacity that neither idols nor even the sun or moon could possibly be divine (Q 6:75-9). Soon after, he argues against the idolatry of his father and his people and a variety of traditions weave together one or more of the qurʾānic renderings of Abraham destroying his father's idols. In some versions of the story, Abraham destroys the idols of king Nimrod as well. Consequently, he is to be burned alive but instead is miraculously saved from the flames. The extra-qurʾānic sources add many details. Nimrod, for instance, dies when God causes a gnat to fly through his nose into his head and torture him to death. Meanwhile, Abraham marries Sarah who is sometimes described as the daughter of the king of Haran (thus explaining the Hebrew meaning of *sārāh*, "princess").

While traveling, Abraham encounters a tyrant, king or pharaoh who becomes enamored of Sarah's stunning beauty. Asked about her, Abraham informs him that she is his sister and she is taken from him. The tyrant reaches for her when they are in his chambers, but his hand, or entire body, is miraculously stricken, sometimes repeatedly as he continually attempts to touch her. He returns her to Abraham, along with Hagar, who according to some accounts had been given to him as compensation. Hagar later gives birth to Ishmael, but the references to Ishmael's birth are inconsistent and do not seem to reflect a coherent narrative tradition. Abraham settles in Sabaʿ near Jerusalem where he digs a well (see WELL AND SPRINGS) and establishes a place of prayer. The people in the area wrong him, so he moves away and the well immediately dries up. After this the people pursue him to beg forgiveness. Abraham gives them seven goats and tells them that when they are brought to the well it will provide water, thus providing a narrative explanation for the etiology of the name of the place Beer-Sheba (*biʾr sabaʿ* or "well of the seven [goats]").

After these events, the scene is transferred to Mecca. Sarah's jealousy toward Hagar after the birth of Ishmael forces Abraham to separate the two women. He personally brings Hagar and Ishmael to Mecca, where he places them in the shade of a thorn tree and entrusts them to God's mercy. Afterwards he returns to his family in Syria/Palestine. With no water in Mecca, Hagar cannot provide for her infant son, who begins to show signs of distress. She leaves him and desperately searches for water by running between the nearby hills of al-Ṣafā (q.v.) and al-Marwa (q.v.), an action that sets the precedent for the "running ritual" *(saʿy)* of the pilgrimage. When all hope seems lost, they are rescued by an angel, sometimes identified as Gabriel, who scratches the ground to bring forth water from what would become the famous Zamzam spring in Mecca. Abraham does not neglect his son in Mecca, but comes to see him three times, although Ishmael is away during the first two visits. On his first attempt to see his son, Abraham encounters Ishmael's inhospitable and unfriendly wife. He gives her a coded message to pass on to his son to the effect that she is not acceptable. Ishmael dutifully divorces her and remarries. On Abraham's second visit he finds a hospitable and respectful wife. With another coded message, he lets his son know he approves of her. During this visit, according to some accounts, Abraham stands on a rock which would become known as the Place of Abraham, leaving his footprint. On his third visit, Abraham finds Ishmael at home and together, in response to God's command, they build the Kaʿba. Abraham then calls all humanity to perform the pilgrimage to God's House.

In a distinctly different version of the Meccan sequence attributed to the Prophet's son-in-law and the eventual caliph ʿAlī b. Abī Ṭālib (q.v.; d. 40/661), Abraham travels to Mecca with Hagar and Ishmael in response to God's command to establish the Kaʿba. They are guided by a supernatural being called the "sechina" (q.v.) or by a magic cloud that leads them to the exact location for the structure. In some accounts, Abraham and Ishmael discover the ancient foundations of a Kaʿba originally established for Adam which God had removed so as to prevent its desecration by the great Noachian flood. In a series of traditions without any consistent attribution or sequence of events, Abraham makes the first paradigmatic pilgrimage.

The qurʾānic rendering of Abraham's attempted sacrifice of his son is embellished considerably in the exegetical literature. Its relative placement within the full Abraham cycle varies in the different versions, as does the scene of the action, in some accounts occurring in Syria and in others in Arabia. In some renderings of the legend, Abraham and his family are confronted by Satan or a devil (q.v.), occasionally in the form of an old man. He attempts to convince them through appeals to logic and mercy to refrain from carrying out God's command. In some versions, Satan appears to Abraham at the location of various ritual stops of the Meccan pilgrimage and Abraham finally drives him away by casting stones at him near the three stone pillars (sing. *jamra*) where to this day stones are thrown as part of the pilgrimage.

Abraham's son — whose identity is contested by the qur'ānic commentators — is informed that he will be sacrificed. In a touching response, he asks his father to tie him tightly so that he will not squirm, to draw back his clothes so they will not be soiled by his blood and to return his shirt to his mother so as to offer her comfort. Abraham kisses his son and they soak the ground with their tears. Abraham actually draws the knife across his son's throat, but discovers that it will not cut because it has miraculously reversed in his hand to its dull side. Or he finds that an impenetrable sheet of copper has suddenly formed around his son's neck. In some versions, Abraham tries repeatedly to fulfill the divine command, but is thwarted each time by these miracles. He finally redeems his son by sacrificing a ram, sometimes identified as the very one that was successfully offered to God in sacrifice by Abel (see CAIN AND ABEL) and kept in heaven for this purpose.

The Muslim exegetes of the first two Islamic centuries differed about which of his sons Abraham was commanded to sacrifice. They approached the question in different ways and no consensus prevailed. The historian al-Mas'ūdī (d. 345/956) succinctly stated the geographical argument: "If the sacrifice occurred in the Hejaz, it was Ishmael, because Isaac never entered the Hejaz. If the sacrifice took place in Syria [i.e. Jerusalem], then it was Isaac because Ishmael did not enter Syria after he was taken from there" (*Murūj*, i, 58). Nevertheless, some Shī'ī commentators claimed that Abraham attempted to sacrifice Isaac in Mecca while on the pilgrimage. Muslim thinkers, like their Jewish and Christian counterparts, came to believe that Abraham's willingness and that of his son to undergo the sacrifice brought blessings on them and their descendants. If Isaac were the intended victim, the merit would naturally accrue to his progeny, the Jews or Christians; if Ishmael, then to the Arabs. Those arguing in favor of Ishmael suggest that Isaac is an interpolation of the Jews and Christians: "[The People of the Book (q.v.)] forced this understanding because Isaac is their father while Ishmael is the father of the Arabs" (Ibn Kathīr, *Tafsīr*, ad Q 37:101). A quantitative study of the early exegetical literature suggests that most qur'ānic exegetes until about the middle of the second/ninth century, regarded Isaac as the intended victim, but later the choice of Ishmael gained favor and this has prevailed until the present day (R. Firestone, Abraham's son). See also PROPHETS AND PROPHETHOOD.

Reuven Firestone

Bibliography

Primary: *Babylonian Talmud* (TB); *Genesis Rabba*, traditional ed., chaps. 39-56, trans. H. Freedman, *Genesis Rabba*, London 1983, i, 313-503; L. Ginzberg, *Legends of the Jews*, 7 vols., Philadelphia 1968, i, 185-286; v, 207-55; Ibn Kathīr, *Tafsīr;* Ibn Qutayba, *Ma'ārif*, 19-20; Kisā'ī, *Qiṣaṣ*, 124-47, trans. W. Thackston, *The tales of the prophets of al-Kisa'i*, Boston 1978, 131-57; Mas'ūdī, *Murūj*, 4 vols., Beirut 1385/1965-1385/1966; *Pirqey Rabbi Eli'ezer* (PRE), traditional ed., chaps. 24-31, trans. G. Friedlander, *Pirke de Rabbi Eliezer*, New York 1916, 174-230; Ṭabarī, *Tafsīr*, ed. A.S. 'Alī et al.; id., *Ta'rīkh*, i, 253-325, trans. W. Brinner, *History of al-Ṭabarī, ii. Prophets and patriarchs*, Albany 1987, ii, 49-111; *Targum Yerushalmi.*

Secondary: R. Dagorn, *La geste d'Ismael*, Paris 1981; R. Dozy, *Die Israeliten zu Mekka*, Leipzig 1864; R. Firestone, Abraham's association with the Meccan sanctuary and the pilgrimage in the pre-Islamic and early Islamic periods, in *Museon* 104 (1991), 365-93; id., Abraham's son as the intended sacrifice, in *JSS* 89 (1989), 95-131; id., *Journeys in holy lands. The evolution of the Abraham-Ishmael legends*, Albany 1990; G.R. Hawting, The origins of the Muslim sanctuary at Mecca, in G.H.A. Juynboll (ed.), *Studies on the first century of Islamic society*, Carbondale 1982, 23-47; C.S. Hurgronje, *Het Mekkaansche feest*, Leiden 1880; M.J. Kister, A bag of meat, in *BSOAS* 33 (1970), 267-75; id., Call yourselves by graceful names, in M.J. Kister, *Lectures in memory of Professor Martin*

M. Plessner, Jerusalem 1975, 3-25; id., al-Ḥīra, in *Arabica* 15 (1968), 143-69; Y. Moubarac, *Abraham dans le Coran*, Paris 1958; R. Paret, Ibrāhīm, in *EI²*, iii, 980-1; A. Rippin, Raḥmān and the Ḥanīfs, in W.B. Hallaq and D.P. Little (eds.), *Islamic studies presented to Charles J. Adams*, Leiden 1991; U. Rubin, Ḥanīfiyya and Kaʿba, in *JSAI* 13 (1990), 85-112; id., The Kaʿba, in *JSAI* 8 (1986), 97-131; J. Wansbrough, *QS*.

Abrogation

A prominent concept in the fields of qurʾānic commentary and Islamic law which allowed the harmonization of apparent contradictions in legal rulings. Despite the voluminous literature Muslims have produced on this topic over the centuries, Western scholars have historically evinced little interest in analyzing the details of "abrogation." Although aware of these details, T. Nöldeke and F. Schwally, for example, failed to probe adequately the significant distinction made in applying theories of abrogation to the Qurʾān. To understand this application, it is important to distinguish the difference between the Qurʾān as a source and the Qurʾān as a text, the difference being the verses removed from the text, the substance of which remains a probative source for doctrine (J. Burton, *Collection*, 233). On the question of the relation between the Qurʾān and sunna (q.v.) — the customary practice of the Prophet Muḥammad as documented in the ḥadīth — inadequate information betrayed I. Goldziher (*Muhammedanische Studien*, ii, 20) into inadvertently misrepresenting the importance of the stance adopted by the classical jurist al-Shāfiʿī (d. 204/820). More recently, J. Schacht's concentration on "contradiction" *(ikhtilāf)* as an acknowledged category in the ḥadīth and sunna as well as his speculation on the origin and nature of ḥadīth led him to minimize the role of the Qurʾān, its interpretation and its perceived relation to the sunna as factors important to the evolution of jurisprudence (*Origins*, 95-7).

Classical Islamic jurisprudence recognizes two primary sources of legal rulings: the Qurʾān and the sunna. In addition, two secondary post-prophetic sources were acknowledged: analogy *(qiyās)* derived from one or other of the primary sources, and the consensus of qualified legal experts *(ijmāʿ)*. Abrogation is applicable to neither of the subsidiary sources, but only to the documents on which they are based. Since abrogation is solely the prerogative of the lawgiver, it may be argued that it must be indicated before the death of the Prophet who mediated the laws supplied in the Qurʾān and sunna.

"The cancellation of a legal enactment" is an inadequate translation of the Arabic term *naskh* which includes, when applied to the Qurʾān, reference to "omission," although it more commonly signifies "substitution." Abrogation may be external to Islam or internal. On its appearance, Christianity deemed itself to have replaced Judaism, while with its revelation, Islam saw itself as dislodging both of its predecessors as an expression of the divine will (al-Ghazālī, *al-Mustaṣfā*, i, 111). For each of the historical revelations, there was a preordained duration (Q 13:38), although Islam, intended to be the last of the series, will endure until judgment day (Q 33:40). Like Christ, Muḥammad came to confirm the Torah (q.v.) and also to declare lawful some of what had been previously declared unlawful (Q 2:286; 3:50). For example, the Prophet was instructed to declare the food of Muslims lawful to the Jews (Q 5:5). Indeed, some elements of Jewish law had been intended as punishment, imposed on account of their wrongdoing (Q 4:160; 6:146).

To Muslim scholars, the abrogation of

Judaism and Christianity by Islam was obvious, although internal abrogation remained less so. The latter had to be vigorously defended by appeal to the analogy of external abrogation, to verses in the Qurʾān and by reference to alleged instances of abrogation. For example, the Companion Salama b. al-Akwaʿ (d. 74/693) is reported to have said, "When 'and those who can shall feed one of the poor (Q 2:184)' was revealed, those who chose to break their fast [during the month of Ramaḍān, q.v.] fed the poor until the verse was abrogated by 'Whoever is present during the month shall fast (Q 2:185)' " (Muslim, *Ṣaḥīḥ, K. al-Ṣiyām*). In another instance, when a man inquired about the night prayer, the Prophet's widow ʿĀʾisha (q.v.) asked him, "Do you not recite Q 73? The Prophet and his Companions (see COMPANIONS OF THE PROPHETS) observed the night prayer for a whole year during which God retained in Heaven the closing of the sūra, revealing the alleviation only twelve months later, whereupon the night prayer became optional from being obligatory" (Muslim, *Ṣaḥīḥ*). In these two instances of alleged abrogation, it is claimed that one regulation was withdrawn and replaced with a later one, although the replaced verses remained in the text.

Q 2:180 requires Muslims to make testamentary provision for their parents and other close kin, while another passage (Q 4:11-12) stipulates the shares in an estate which must pass automatically to a Muslim's heirs (see INHERITANCE). In deference to the legal principle that no one may benefit twice from a single estate, parents and other close family members now lost the right to the benefit stipulated in Q 2:180. Widows, being named in Q 4:12, lost the maintenance and accommodation for twelve months granted in Q 2:240 (see MAINTENANCE AND UPKEEP). For some classical jurists, one verse of the Qurʾān here abrogated another. Others argue that the provisions of Q 2:180 and Q 4:11-12 were by no means irreconcilable, but that the exclusion of parents and widows from their dual entitlement had been settled by the Prophet's announcement, "There shall be no testament in favor of an heir." Here the Prophet's practice was seen as abrogating the Qurʾān.

The words and actions of the Prophet came to be regarded by many as a second source of Islamic regulation which, like the Qurʾān, was subject to the same process of change (al-Ḥāzimī, *Iʿtibār,* 23). For example, Muḥammad announced, "I prohibited the visiting of graves, but now you may visit them. I had prohibited storing the meat of your sacrifices for more than three nights, but now you may store it as long as you see fit. I had prohibited the keeping of liquor in anything but skin containers, but now you may use any type of container, so long as you drink no intoxicant" (Muslim, *Ṣaḥīḥ, K. al-Janāʾiz*).

The qurʾānic passages concerning the change of the direction of prayer (*qibla,* q.v.) leave unclear which type of abrogation has taken place (Q 2:142-50). Some scholars argued that the change of direction indicated was a case of external abrogation. They held that the Prophet was bound by God's command to the Jews to face Jerusalem when praying, until this was abrogated by the qurʾānic verse. Others, interpreting the words "We appointed the direction of prayer which you formerly faced" (Q 2:143) as a reference to turning to Jerusalem, saw the change as internal abrogation, with one qurʾānic ruling abrogating the other (al-Naḥḥās, *al-Nāsikh,* 15). Noting the silence of the Qurʾān on the earlier direction of prayer, some other scholars presumed that praying toward Jerusalem had been introduced by the Prophet and later changed by the Qurʾān.

Al-Shāfiʿī's theory of abrogation

The Prophet's mission extended over twenty years. There was therefore nothing surprising in the idea that his instructions to his community should show signs of development. Little resistance was expressed to the notion that one of the Prophet's practices could abrogate another. Indeed, for scholars who undertook the derivation of the law from its sources in the Qurʾān and sunna, the simplest means of disposing of an opponent's view was the blunt assertion that, although it had been correct at one time, it has since been abrogated. It was the need to regularize appeals to the sources and especially to the principle of abrogation that led the scholar al-Shāfiʿī (d. 204/820) to compose his *Contradictory ḥadīth (Ikhtilāf al-ḥadīth)* and *Treatise [on Jurisprudence] (al-Risāla),* the earliest surviving statements on jurisprudential method.

A key feature of al-Shāfiʿī's work is the emphasis on redefining the term "sunna" to restrict it to the words and actions reported from the Prophet alone. Others had interpreted the term in the older, broader sense to include the practice of other authorities, in addition to the Prophet. Al-Shāfiʿī sought to convince them that God had singled out the Prophet as alone qualified to pronounce on the law. He amassed from the Qurʾān evidence that God insisted on unquestioning obedience to his Prophet (e.g. Q 4:13, 65). Appealing to a series of verses linking Muḥammad's commands and prohibitions to the divine will, and culminating in a verse which identified Muḥammad's will with the divine will (Q 4:80), al-Shāfiʿī succeeded in recovering the unique prophet-figure central to and partner in the processes of divine revelation.

Those who denied the sunna any role in the construction of the law did so on the basis that the Qurʾān contains everything that is needed and that many reports about the Prophet's behavior were forged. Al-Shāfiʿī sought to convince these scholars that it was the Qurʾān itself that enjoined appeal to the prophetic sunna (*al-Risāla,* 79-105). The result was not merely his assertion that the Qurʾān required adherence to the sunna of the Prophet, but also the elevation of the sunna to the status of another form of revelation (*Umm,* vii, 271), elucidating, supplementing and never contradicting the Qurʾān. Only a verse of the Qurʾān could abrogate another verse of the Qurʾān and these verses could only abrogate other qurʾānic verses. By the same token, a prescriptive practice of the Prophet could only be abrogated by his adoption of another practice. Contrary to the practice of earlier generations of scholars who were willing to believe that their doctrines abrogated those of their foes without any evidence to support the claim, al-Shāfiʿī asserted that the ḥadīth documenting every actual instance of abrogation have survived. Therefore, one had to show that one sunna followed the other chronologically in order to determine which was abrogated. Although al-Shāfiʿī defined "abrogation" as "to abandon" (*taraka, al-Risāla,* 122), he added that no ruling is abrogated without a replacement ruling being promulgated in its stead, as had occurred in the case of the change of the direction of prayer (*al-Risāla,* 106-13). Thus, for him, "abrogation" actually meant "substitution."

Abrogation and divine knowledge

To some minds, the idea that one verse from the Qurʾān abrogated another suggested that divine will changes and divine knowledge develops and this was held to contravene basic theological tenets. Those who allowed that some verses of the Qurʾān abrogated others, responded that no Muslim ever objected to the notion that Islam had abrogated Christianity and

Judaism. External abrogation of this type was an acknowledged reality, one to which the Qur'ān referred and consequently one that could be accepted. If God adapts his regulations to the different circumstances prevailing in different ages, as is apparent in the alteration of laws revealed to the different prophets, he may equally adapt regulations appropriate to the initial stages of one revelation to meet the changes wrought in the course of the revelation (al-Ghazālī, *al-Mustaṣfā,* i, 111). Moreover, there was historical evidence of this having happened. For example, the Muslims at Mecca were bidden to be patient under the verbal and physical assaults of their enemies. When the Muslim community emigrated to Medina, they were ordered to answer violence with violence. The weakness of Meccan Islam was replaced by the numerical and economic strength of Medinan Islam. Given these changed conditions, patient forbearance could be replaced by defiant retaliation (Q 2:191, 216; 20:130; 30:60; 73:10).

Muslim theologians maintained that divine will is sovereign and limited by no power in the universe. God may command or forbid whatever he wants. In the same way, divine knowledge is infinite and instantaneous. From all eternity, God has known what he proposed to command, when he would command it, the precise duration intended for each command and the exact moment when he proposed to countermand it. There is perfect harmony between divine will and divine knowledge. Perfect will does not alter and perfect knowledge does not develop. In the case of fasting during the month of Ramaḍān, the earlier option of fasting was subsequently made obligatory. In the case of the night prayer, an obligation was reduced to an option. In the case of the change in the direction of prayer, the Muslims were required to face Mecca after having been required to turn to Jerusalem. In each instance, the earlier ruling was viewed to be proper for its time and the later abrogation was also viewed to be proper in its time (al-Shāfiʿī, *al-Risāla,* 117-37).

Human circumstances, however, do change and human knowledge does develop. When humans command one another and subsequently become aware of unforeseen consequences, they are obliged to withdraw a command. Their lack of perfect foresight often obliges them to have second thoughts (*badā',* Qurṭubī, *Jāmiʿ,* ii, 64), which according to classical Sunnī theology, may never by posited of the divine being.

When abrogation occurs people may perceive a change, but this is only a change from the human perspective. God sends his prophets with his commands and the true believer is the one who obeys (Q 4:65). Muslims should emulate the ideal attitude adopted by Abraham and his son, when both of them with full knowledge — in the Islamic tradition — were willing to proceed with the sacrifice.

The qur'ānic evidence

The claim that abrogation, understood as the cancellation of a legal ordinance, was solidly rooted in the revelation was connected with the appropriation of the qur'ānic root *n-s-kh* as a technical term. The root occurs in no fewer than four verses which the classical exegetes treated as circumstantially unrelated contexts to be interpreted independently. That prevented scholars from agreeing on an unequivocal etymology and definition of *"naskh"* and led to the consequent emergence of a host of irreconcilable theories of abrogation. Q 7:154 *(nuskha)* and Q 45:29 *(nastansikhu),* the first referring to tablets *(alwāḥ)* and the second to a book *(kitāb),* united with the everyday usage, *"nasakha l-kitāb"* (copied a book), to produce the concept of "duplication." The essence of this understanding is a plurality of texts. This secular usage was said to be a synonym for *"naqala l-kitāb"* (transcribed the book) which, however, bears the added sense of "removal" hence "transfer" or "replace," as in the phrase *nasakhat al-shams al-ẓill,* "the sunlight replaced the shadow" (an etymology that is rejected by some, see Qurṭubī, *Jāmiʿ,* ii, 61). "God abrogates *(yansakhu)* whatever Satan brings forth" (Q 22:52) could yield only the sense of "suppression." This paralleled the secular usage *"nasakhat al-rīḥ al-āthār"* (The wind obliterated the traces [of an encampment, etc.]; cf. Qurṭubī, *Jāmiʿ,* ii, 61; al-Ghazālī, *al-Mustaṣfā,* i, 107). In this usage, abrogation as "removal" carries the connotation of "withdrawal."

"We will make you recite so you will not forget except what God wills" (Q 87:6-7) and "We do not abrogate *(nansakh)* a verse or cause it to be forgotten without bringing a better one or one like it" (Q 2:106) introduced the idea that God might cause his Prophet to forget materials not intended to appear in the final form of the text (J. Burton, *Collection,* 64). This interpretation could be reinforced by reference to "We substitute *(baddalnā)* one verse in the place of another" (Q 16:101). The concept of "omission" was added to the growing list of meanings assigned to abrogation (Qurṭubī, *Jāmiʿ,* ii, 62). According to one report, one night two men wished to incorporate into their prayer a verse which they had learned and had already used, but they found that they could not recall a syllable. The next day they reported this to the Prophet, who replied that the passage had been withdrawn overnight and they should put it out of their minds (Qurṭubī, *Jāmiʿ,* ii, 63). In another report, the Companion Ibn Masʿūd decided to recite in his prayers one night a verse he had been taught, had memorized and had written into his own copy of the revelations. Failing to recall a syllable of it, he checked his notes only to find the page blank. He reported this to the Prophet who told him that that passage had been withdrawn overnight (Nöldeke, *GQ,* i, 47, ii, 44).

Irrecoverable forgetting was thus formalized as "withdrawal," a more satisfactory explanation for the disappearance of revealed material. Although the majority of scholars viewed forgetting as one of the mechanisms of abrogation affecting the Qurʾān, there were those who strove to keep it separate from abrogation. According to one report, the Prophet omitted a verse in a prayer and asked one of his Companions why he had failed to prompt him. The Companion replied that he thought the verse had been withdrawn. "It was not withdrawn," declared the Prophet, "I merely forgot it" (Saḥnūn, *al-Mudawwana al-kubrā,* i, 107).

Theological objections to the interpretation

Still some scholars had difficulty in accepting the mechanism of abrogation as worthy of God. Some went so far as to provide variant readings for the references to abrogation in the holy text (Ṭabarī, *Tafsīr,* ii, 478). One particular difficulty was "We do not abrogate a verse or cause it to be forgotten without bringing a better one or one like it" (Q 2:106). Some objected that no part of the holy text could be said to be superior to another so "without bringing a better one" could not be a reference to the Qurʾān. The same consideration applies to the Prophet's sunna abrogating the Qurʾān since no ḥadīth could be thought superior or even similar to a divine verse. The proponents of abrogation claimed that God was not referring to the text of the Qurʾān, but to the rulings conveyed by the text (al-Ghazālī, *al-Mustaṣfā,* i, 125; cf. Ṭabarī, *Tafsīr,* ii, 471-2). While in terms of beauty, no qurʾānic verse can be considered superior to another and certainly no ḥadīth is more beautiful than a verse from the

Qurʾān, the legal content of one verse — or even of a ḥadīth — could be considered superior to the ruling contained in another verse. Less easy to explain was the reason that in these cases God did not suppress the abrogated texts to avoid confusion (Ṭabarī, *Tafsīr*, ii, 472).

Variant readings

That the notion of portions of the holy text being forgotten was repugnant to some is shown in two procedures adopted to avoid that interpretation. As an exegetical alternative, a number of different readings (see READINGS OF THE QURʾĀN) were proposed for the troublesome passages. In the passage "We do not abrogate a verse or cause it to be forgotten *(nunsihā)* without supplying a similar or better one" (Q 2:106) attention focused on the word which the majority of scholars read as *nunsi* (cause to forget). This reading was supported by "You will not forget *(tansā)*, except what God wills" (Q 87:6-7). Also suggested were "You are caused to forget" *(tunsa)* which is to be preferred to "You forget" (*tansa*, Ṭabarī, *Tafsīr*, ii, 474-5). Both of the problems, Muḥammad forgetting on his own and God making him forget, could be circumvented by reading *nansaʾ*, "We defer" (Ṭabarī, *Tafsīr*, ii, 476-8). Q 2:106 would then be mentioning two revelatory processes, *naskh* and deferment. The deferment of *naskh*, in the sense of "copying," could mean "the deferring of revelation from the heavenly original (see PRESERVED TABLET) to its earthly representation in the Qurʾān," said to have occurred in the case of the night prayer which the revelation of Q 73:6 changed from obligatory to optional (al-Shāfiʿī, *al-Risāla*, 108). Or it could mean deferring the removal of a passage from the Qurʾān, by leaving the passage in the text despite suppression of the ruling it contained (Ṭabarī, *Tafsīr*, ii, 478). Generally, the sense of the verb *nasaʾa* (to defer) is held to be temporal, although it has also been said to have a physical connotation, "driving away," as men drive strange animals away from the cistern intended for their own beasts (Zamakhsharī, *Kashshāf*, ad Q 2:106; cf. Ṭūsī, *Tibyān*, i, 395). Transferred to the qurʾānic context, verses might be driven away from a text, even from human memory. Men may be caused to forget. In support of this interpretation, reports were cited which claimed that certain sūras were originally longer than they are in the present-day text of the Qurʾān. Even verses which had allegedly been revealed and failed to find a place in the final text — such as the Ibn Ādam and Biʾr Maʿūna verses (see J. Burton, *Sources*, 49-53) — were cited, supposedly from the few Companions who had not quite forgotten them (Ṭabarī, *Tafsīr*, ii, 479-80). Through another approach it is not even necessary to resort to variant readings because the Arabic word for "to forget" *(nasiya)* could be construed to mean "to remove something" or its opposite, "to leave something where it is" (Ṭabarī, *Tafsīr*, ii, 476). This could mean that the verses were in the heavenly original, but not revealed, or the verses were left in the text of the Qurʾān and were neither repealed nor removed. Once replacement is ascertained to have occurred, it is immaterial whether the wording of an abandoned ruling is expunged or whether it is left to stand in the Qurʾān. The passages whose rulings have been replaced become inoperative or effectively removed (Ṭabarī, *Tafsīr*, ii, 472).

Abrogation and the law

Legal scholars appealed to the principle of abrogation continually to resolve the apparent contradictions between the legal practice of the various regions of the Islamic world and between all of these and their putative sources in the revelation. "Forgetting" and "omission" were of no interest to the legal scholars who concentrated on "substitution" derived from "We substitute one verse in the place of another" (Q 16:101) and imposed by them on "We do not abrogate a verse or cause it to be forgotten without bringing a better one or one like it" (Q 2:106). The difficulties which beset the exegetes and theologians were of little concern to legal scholars, who declared that "abrogation" *(naskh)* was a technical term with a meaning now clear to all (al-Jaṣṣāṣ, *Aḥkām,* ad Q 2:106). Most cited "We substitute one verse in the place of another" (Q 16:101) as evidence that abrogation in the form of "substitution" had occurred, an interpretation already mentioned by the oldest exegetes (e.g. al-Farrāʾ, *Maʿānī,* i, 64-5). In fact, abrogation as substitution became the theater of the liveliest development of the theories of abrogation.

The third type of abrogation

To the jurisprudent's interpretation of abrogation as "the replacement of the ruling but not of the text in which it appears" and to the exegete's "the withdrawal of both the ruling and its wording," a third type was added. Q 5:89 mentions "a fast of three days" as one way to atone for breaking an oath. The Companion Ibn Masʿūd (d. ca. 33/653) was said to have preserved in his personal notes the original reading of "a fast of three *consecutive* days." His anomalous reading was still referred to in the time of the legal expert Abū Ḥanīfa (d. ca. 150/767). Although the word "consecutive" was not found in the text of the Qurʾān that was in general use, the ruling was adopted into Ḥanafī doctrine (al-Sarakhsī, *Uṣūl,* ii, 81). This exemplifies the third type of abrogation in which the text, but not the ruling, of a qurʾānic revelation was cancelled.

Q 4:15-16 introduces a penalty for illicit sexual behavior (see ADULTERY AND FORNICATION). Both partners are to be punished with unspecified violence and the female held under house arrest for life or "until God makes a way for them." The promised way was thought to have been provided in Q 24:2, which imposed a penalty of one hundred lashes for male and female fornicators. Nevertheless, a Companion reported that the Prophet had announced, "Take it from me! Take it from me! God has now made the way for women. Virgin with virgin, one hundred lashes and banishment for twelve months. Non-virgin with non-virgin, one hundred lashes and death by stoning" (al-Shāfiʿī, *al-Risāla,* 129). Reports from other Companions show the Prophet extending the dual penalties to males while a number state that he stoned some offenders without flogging them (Mālik, *al-Muwaṭṭaʾ, Ḥudūd, Ḥadd al-zinā*). On the basis of this material, some concluded that this was a case of the Prophet's practice abrogating the Qurʾān.

The vast majority of scholars, however, regarded the imposition of stoning as the penalty for adultery as an instance of a verse from the holy text being eliminated, although the ruling it contained remained in effect. The Medinan scholar Mālik b. Anas (d. 179/795), for instance, had heard that the penalty of stoning had originated in "the book of God," which in this case he understood to be the Torah. He reported that the Prophet had consulted the rabbis and the stoning ruling was indeed found in the Torah. With explicit reference to "the book of God," Muḥammad imposed the ruling. Other scholars interpreted the term "the book of God" as a reference to the Qurʾān and were puzzled that they could not find such a ruling within its pages. The Prophet's second successor ʿUmar (r. 12/634-22/644) gravely urged the Muslims not to overlook "the stoning verse" which, he maintained, had been revealed to Muḥammad, taught by him to his Companions and recited in his company in the ritual prayers: "The mature male and female, stone them outright." ʿUmar insisted that the Prophet, his immediate successor Abū Bakr (r. 11/632-13/634) and he himself had put this ruling into practice and claimed that fear of being accused of adding to the holy text was the only reason that he did not actually write the "verse" in the Qurʾān. Countless scholars in succeeding centuries have stated with assurance that a verse with the same or similar wording had once stood in the qurʾānic text. From this, they concluded that a verse could be removed from the Qurʾān without this vitiating the validity of the ruling it contained (al-Ghazālī, *al-Mustaṣfā*, ii, 124).

Al-Shāfiʿī did not analyze these materials from the standpoint of those who saw here the abrogation of the Qurʾān by the sunna, a claim which he at all times studiously avoided. Rather he preferred to review the case on the basis of his theory of exclusion *(takhṣīṣ)*. By imposing on slave women half the penalty of the free, Q 4:25 excluded slaves from the full brunt of Q 24:2 — which ordered a flogging of one hundred lashes for male and female adulterers — and from the stoning penalty, since death has no definable half. Therefore certain classes of free Muslims may also be exempt from some of the penalties. The Prophet's practice indicated that married offenders were not covered by Q 24:2 or, if they had originally been covered by that provision, they were subsequently excluded. Their penalty was to be stoning. The sunna of stoning had replaced the earlier sunna of flogging and stoning. In his analysis, al-Shāfiʿī maintained that the Prophet's words, "God has now made a way for women," showed that the qurʾānic ruling "confine [the women] in their home until they die or until God makes a way for them" (Q 4:15) had been abrogated (J. Burton, *Sources*, 143-56). He asserted that the Prophet had dispensed with flogging those who were to be stoned, although earlier he had applied both penalties. Because flogging was undeniably a qurʾānic ruling, some have mistakenly assumed that al-Shāfiʿī believed that stoning was a qurʾānic ruling as well.

Al-Shāfiʿī did acknowledge a third type of abrogation in his discussion of a different question, that of the withdrawal of a qurʾānic verse while the ruling it contained remained in effect. Q 4:23 lists the women whom a Muslim male is forbidden to marry, including his wet-nurse and any female to whom she has given suck. Scholars disputed the number of times a child had to be suckled by a woman to establish this ban to marriage. For Mālik, a single suckling in infancy sufficed to create a barrier to marriage (Mālik, *al-Muwaṭṭaʾ*, *al-Raḍāʿa*, *Raḍāʿat al-ṣaghīr*). For others even a single drop of breast-milk initiated the ban. Al-Shāfiʿī fastened on one report in which the Prophet's widow ʿĀʾisha was said to have claimed that a verse imposing ten suckling sessions had been revealed to the Prophet and it was replaced by a second verse reducing the number of sessions to five, which was also subsequently lost. Earlier Mālik had curtly dismissed this report *(al-Muwaṭṭaʾ, al-Raḍāʿ, al-Raḍāʿa baʿd al-kibar)*, but al-Shāfiʿī made it central to his conclusions. He accepted this as the one undoubted instance of the withdrawal of a qurʾānic verse while the ruling it expressed remained valid (*Ikhtilāf al-ḥadīth*, vii, 208 margin; see also J. Burton, *Sources*, 156-8).

Conclusion

It is clear that the theory of abrogation developed its own internal dynamic. Al-Shāfiʿī's theory that the abrogating verses of the Qurʾān had once existed was not accepted by all of his contemporaries, but it later gained widespread support. Mālikīs and Ḥanafīs had no general need of this principle while Shāfiʿīs had no need whatever to posit that the sunna abrogated the Qurʾān or vice-versa. One nevertheless finds Mālikī and Ḥanafī scholars claiming that three forms of abrogation are documented (al-Sarakhsī, *Uṣūl,* ii, 81; Qurṭubī, *Jāmiʿ,* ii, 66), just as one also finds Shāfiʿīs adducing occurrences of the sunna abrogating the Qurʾān and the reverse which, they claimed, their eponym had overlooked (al-Ghazālī, *al-Mustaṣfā,* i, 124). See also TRADITIONAL DISCIPLINES OF QURʾĀNIC STUDY.

John Burton

Bibliography

Primary: Farrāʾ, *Maʿānī;* al-Ghazālī, Abū Ḥāmid Muḥammad, *al-Mustaṣfā min ʿilm al-uṣūl,* 2 vols., Cairo 1322/1904; al-Ḥāzimī, Muḥammad b. Mūsā, *Kitāb al-Iʿtibār,* Hyderabad 1319/1901; Hibat Allāh Ibn Salāma, *Kitāb al-Nāsikh wa-l-mansūkh,* Cairo 1379/1960; Jaṣṣāṣ, *Aḥkām;* Mālik, *Muwaṭṭaʾ,* 3 vols., Cairo 1303/1885; Muslim, *Ṣaḥīḥ;* Naḥḥās, *Kitāb al-Nāsikh wa-l-mansūkh fī l-Qurʾān al-karīm,* Cairo n.d.; Qaysī, Makkī b. Hammūsh, *Kitāb al-Īḍāḥ li-nāsikh al-Qurʾān wa-mansūkhihi,* ed. A.Ḥ. Farḥat, Riyadh 1976; Qurṭubī, *Jāmiʿ;* Rāzī, *Tafsīr;* Saḥnūn b. Saʿīd, *al-Mudawwana l-kubrā,* 16 vols., Baghdad 1970; al-Sarakhsī, Shams al-Aʾimma, *al-Uṣūl,* 2 vols., Hyderabad 1372/1952; al-Shāfiʿī, *Kitāb Ikhtilāf al-ḥadīth,* on margin of *Kitāb al-Umm,* vol. 7, Cairo 1322/1904-1324/1906; id., *al-Risāla,* ed. A.M. Shākir, Cairo 1358/1940; Ṭabarī, *Tafsīr;* Ṭūsī, *Tibyān;* Zamakhsharī, *Kashshāf.*

Secondary: J. Burton, The exegesis of Q 2:106, in BSOAS 48 (1985), 452-69; id., *Collection;* id., The interpretation of Q 87:6-7, in *Der Islam* 62 (1985), 5-19; id., *The sources of Islamic law,* Edinburgh 1990; Goldhizer, *MS;* Nöldeke, *GQ;* J. Schacht, *Origins of Muhammadam jurisprudence,* Oxford 1950; M. Zayd, *al-Naskh fī l-Qurʾān al-karīm,* 2 vols., Cairo 1383/1963.

Abstinence

In the Qurʾān abstinence in the sense of "restraint in or refraining from the indulgence of human appetites and impulses" is connected with words deriving from four different Arabic roots, namely *ʾ-l-w, ʿ-ṣ-m, ʿ-f-f* and *h-j-r.*

The paradigmatic event for the qurʾānic notion of abstinence is Q 74:2-5, which recounts one of the early examples of Muḥammad's experience of coming close to God as the revelation descends on him. God commands, "Arise and warn, your Lord magnify, your robes purify, and defilement flee *(fa-hjur).*" Drawing close to God requires abandoning or fleeing from all that might inhibit the human response to the divine initiative. This interpretation of an experience in the life of Muḥammad is supported by a later qurʾānic reference — following the chronology of T. Nöldeke (see CHRONOLOGY AND THE QURʾĀN) — to an event in the story of Joseph (q.v.). Potiphar's wife admits that she tried to seduce Joseph, saying, "Yes, I attempted to seduce him, but he abstained *(fa-staʿṣama)*" (Q 12:32).

Humans are continually in need of rejecting or fleeing from anything that interferes with the on-going movement of the spirit in response to God. For instance, Q 4:6 states, "If any man be rich, let him be abstinent *(fal-yastaʿfif),*" in reference to the use of the property of orphans (q.v.) by their guardians, who are enjoined to abstain from misusing their power to exploit their vulnerable charges.

Abstinence also means refraining from illicit sexual activity, as in Q 24:33: "And let those who find not the means to marry be abstinent *(wal-yastaʿfif)* till God enriches them of his bounty." On the other hand, marriage entails responsibilities. Q 2:226 forbids a man to carry out an oath of sexual abstinence *(īlāʾ)* from his wife for longer than four months: "For those who swear to abstain *(yuʾlūna)* from their women, a wait of four months." After that, he must break his oath or she is divorced. See also FASTING.

Sheila McDonough

Bibliography
Bell, *Commentary;* Izutsu, *Concepts;* Mir, *Dictionary;* Paret, *Kommentar.*

Abū Bakr

A prosperous merchant in Mecca who was an early convert to Islam (see Ṭabarī, *Ta'rīkh,* ed. M.J. de Goeje et al., i, 1165-6) and the first caliph of the community. Abū Bakr (d. 13/634) is often thought to be referred to in the Qur'ān, for example, in Q 39:33, where he is considered to be the one who "confirms the truth" of Muḥammad's message.

See also COMPANIONS OF THE PROPHET.

Andrew Rippin

Abū Lahab

An individual named once in the Qur'ān at Q 111:1. The name literally means "father of the flame," that is of hell. "Abū Lahab" was the nickname of an uncle of Muḥammad by the name of ʿAbd al-ʿUzzā b. ʿAbd al-Muṭṭalib who was a major opponent of the Prophet. See also OPPOSITION TO MUḤAMMAD.

Andrew Rippin

Bibliography
Ibn Isḥāq, *Sīra,* i, 231; U. Rubin, Abū Lahab and sūra CXI, in *BSOAS* 42 (1979), 13-28.

Abū Ṭālib see FAMILY OF THE PROPHET

Abyssinia

Abyssinia *(al-Ḥabash* or *al-Ḥabasha)* does not appear in the Qur'ān, although the Christian Abyssinian state of Axum exerted a powerful influence on Arabia in the sixth century. Separated from the Yemen by only the narrow Bab al-Mandab Strait, Abyssinia controlled southern Arabia for some time and Christianity spread in the region. One sūra is ordinarily interpreted to allude to an Abyssinian military incursion that reached Mecca and it is said that some of the early Meccan converts to Islam took refuge in Abyssinia. Ethiopic languages influenced the dialects of southern Arabia and words of Ethiopian-derivation are found in the Qur'ān (see FOREIGN VOCABULARY). According to the exegete and historian al-Ṭabarī (d. 310/923), the Meccan tribe of Quraysh (q.v.) traded in Abyssinia.

Sūra 105 (Sūrat al-Fīl) mentions God's destruction of the People of the Elephant (q.v.). According to the classical commentators, this is a reference to an Abyssinian incursion from the Yemen to Mecca in 570 C.E., which, some reports claim, was the year Muḥammad was born. Islamic references to this military campaign are largely folkloristic and find no corroboration from south Arabian inscriptions or other sources. The expedition made an impression on the local population because of the use of one or more elephants in the campaign. Abraha (q.v.), who was said to have been the leader of the expedition, was known to the Byzantine historian Procopius as a former slave who had seized control of the Abyssinian forces in the Yemen.

According to some Islamic sources, a group of Muḥammad's followers left Mecca for Abyssinia around the year 615. The authority on the life of the Prophet, Ibn Isḥāq (ca. 85/704-150/767), names eighty-three adult male participants and claims that this first emigration (*hijra,* see EMIGRATION) in Islam occurred as a result of pagan Meccan persecution, although other possible reasons have also been suggested (Watt, *Muhammad at Mecca*, 113-6). The ruler of Abyssinia, the Negus *(al-Najāshī)*, is said to have granted them refuge, despite the fact that the pagan Meccans sent representatives who tried to convince him to deny them protection. In recognition of this, Muḥammad mourned the Negus at his death and led public prayers in his honor.

In the Arabic genealogical tradition, the Abyssinians — along with the Egyptians, Sudanese and most other black African peoples — descended from Ham, the son of Noah (q.v.). The scholar Ibn Hishām (d. 218/834) in his *Kitāb al-Tījān* (p. 55), an early work on south Arabian history, claims that the south Arabian descendant of Shem, Ḥaḍramawt b. Qaḥṭān, inherited Abyssinia, creating by this claim a connection which draws attention to the close geographical and cultural ties between southern Arabia and Abyssinia. According to one tradition, the biblical Esau married the daughter of an Abyssinian king and eventually came to rule his kingdom (Kisāʾī, *Qiṣaṣ*, 154). In light of the Jewish association of Esau with Christianity, this explained the Christian presence in Abyssinia. See also PRE-ISLAMIC ARABIA AND THE QURʾĀN.

Reuven Firestone

Bibliography

Primary: Bukhārī, *Ṣaḥīḥ*, *K. Manāqib al-anṣār;* Ibn Hishām, ʿAbd al-Malik, *Kitāb al-Tījān fī mulūk Ḥimyar*, Sanʿa n.d., 55; Ibn Isḥāq, *Sīra*, ed. M. al-Saqqā et al., i, 41-56, 322-38; Ibn Isḥāq-Guillaume, 20-7, 146-53; Ibn Saʿd, *Ṭabaqāt*, ed. H. Sachau, i, 136-7.

Secondary: A.F.L. Beeston, Abraha, in *EI²*, i, 102-3; id., al-Fīl, in *EI²*, ii, 895; Jeffery, *For. vocab.*, 305-7; W.M. Watt, *Muhammad at Mecca*, Oxford 1953.

Accident see GOD AND HIS ATTRIBUTES; EXEGESIS OF THE QURʾĀN: CLASSICAL AND MEDIEVAL

ʿĀd

An ancient tribe to whom the prophet Hūd (q.v.; Q 7:65; 11:50; cf. 46:21) was sent. They are mentioned twenty-four times in the Qurʾān.

The ʿĀd are described as a powerful tribe which existed after the people of Noah (q.v.; Q 7:69). They were mighty and proud of their strength (Q 41:15; cf. 26:128-9) as well as very tall of stature (Q 7:69). The prophet Hūd was sent to the ʿĀd, but his preaching was largely unsuccessful (Q 7:70-1; 11:53-4; 46:22). Other messengers were also sent to the ʿĀd, but they too were rejected (Q 26:123). Hūd tried to convince his people to invoke God's intervention after a period of drought (Q 11:52) and God punished them. The ʿĀd were devastated by a violent wind (Q 41:16; 46:24; 51:41; 54:19; 69:6; see AIR AND WIND), "the chastisement of a dreadful day" (Q 26:135), which blasted for a week (Q 69:7) and left only their dwelling-places standing (Q 46:25). Only those who believed Hūd were saved (Q 7:72; 11:58; 26:139). Some other references are unclear. It is said that God caused the death of the "first ʿĀd" (Q 53:50). The ʿĀd were summoned to faith in a place called al-Aḥqāf (Q 46:21). Another verse connects the ʿĀd with the mysterious Iram Dhāt al-ʿImād (Q 89:6-7; see IRAM). In other verses the ʿĀd are briefly mentioned with Noah (q.v.), the Thamūd (q.v.) and others (Q 9:70; 14:9; 22:42; 29:38; 38:12; 40:31; 50:13).

Frequent references in pre-Islamic poetry show that legends about the tribe of ʿĀd were well known among Arabs before the time of the Prophet (Horovitz, *KU*, 126-7) and the qurʾānic versions of these stories apparently belong to this cycle of genuinely Arabian traditions. Qurʾānic exegesis and works on the early prophets created a complete and coherent narrative of the vicissitudes of the ʿĀd, adding many remarkable details (see PUNISHMENT

STORIES). According to differing interpretations, Iram was either the name of a place associated with the ʿĀd or the name of the most representative subtribe of the ʿĀd. The ʿĀd were originally a nation of ten or thirteen subtribes and one of the first Arab tribes. Al-Aḥqāf, which literally means "the sand dunes," was identified as a place called al-Shiḥr, located between Oman and Hadramawt. An utterance attributed to Muḥammad specifies that the wind which killed the ʿĀdites was a western one. The ʿĀd were giants between ten and five hundred cubits in height and on one occasion they sent a delegation to Mecca to ask for rain. Stories are told about the tribe's legendary eponym ʿĀd and his powerful sons Shaddād and Shadīd. According to some reports, the sage Luqmān (q.v.) belonged to the ʿĀd. The surviving ʿĀdites sought refuge in Mecca according to some stories while others place them in the mythical towns of Jābalqā and Jābarsā.

Roberto Tottoli

Bibliography
Primary: ʿAbd al-Malik b. Ḥabīb, *Kitāb al-Taʾrīkh,* ed. J. Aguadé, Madrid 1991, 40-3; ʿAbd al-Razzāq, *Tafsīr,* ii, 217, 370; Bukhārī, *Ṣaḥīḥ,* Beirut 1992, ii, 384; Isḥāq b. Bishr, *Mubtadaʾ al-dunyā wa-qiṣaṣ al-anbiyāʾ,* Bodleian Library, MS Huntingdon 388, 116a-139b; Kisāʾī, *Qiṣaṣ,* 103-10; al-Majlisī, M. Bāqir, *Biḥār al-anwār,* 105 vols., Beirut 1983, xi, 343-70; Māwardī, *Nukat,* v, 282; Muḥammad b. Ḥabīb, *Kitāb al-muḥabbar,* ed. I. Lichtenstädter, Hyderabad 1942; Muqātil, *Tafsīr,* iv, 23-6, 687-8; Muṭahhar b. Ṭāhir al-Maqdisī, *al-Badʾ wa-l-taʾrīkh,* ed. C. Huart, 6 vols., Paris 1899-1919, iii, 31-7; Sibṭ Ibn al-Jawzī, *Mirʾāt,* i, 253-62; Ṭabarī, *Tafsīr,* Cairo 1968, viii, 216-22; xxvi, 22-4; xxvii, 78; xxx, 175-7; id., *Taʾrīkh,* Leiden, i (1), 68, 231-44; Thaʿlabī, *Qiṣaṣ,* 53-7; Tirmidhī, *Ṣaḥīḥ,* v, 391-2.
Secondary: J.E. Bencheikh, Iram ou le clameur de Dieu, in *REMMM* 58 (1990), 70-81; F. Buhl, ʿĀd, in *EI²,* i, 169; Horovitz, *KU,* 125-7; G.D. Newby, *The making of the last prophet,* Columbia, SC 1989, 50-7; Speyer, *Erzählungen,* 118-9.

Adam and Eve

Adam is the first human being *(bashar)* and the father of humankind in the Pentateuch and the Qurʾān. "Adam" (Ādam) as an individual person occurs eighteen times in the Qurʾān. In addition, the phrase "the sons of Adam" *(banū Ādam)* in the sense of "humankind" is attested seven times. The qurʾānic commentators derive the name "Ādam" from *adīm al-arḍ* (ʿAbd al-Razzāq, *Tafsīr,* i, 43; ii, 20; Ibn Saʿd, *Ṭabaqāt,* i, 26; Ṭabarī, *Tafsīr,* i, 214-5) or from *adamat al-arḍ* (Ṭabarī, *Tafsīr,* i, 208), because he was created from "the surface of the earth." The name of Adam's wife Eve, in the Islamic tradition "Ḥawwāʾ," is not qurʾānic, although she figures in the Qurʾān as Adam's counterpart and complement. "Ḥawwāʾ" is said to be derived from *ḥayy,* because she is the mother of everything "living" (Ibn Saʿd, *Ṭabaqāt,* i, 39-40) or because she was created from something "living" (Ṭabarī, *Tafsīr,* i, 229). The qurʾānic material on Adam and Eve addresses a number of basic topics.

The announcement of the creation of man
Q 2:30 reports the announcement of the creation of man: "And when your lord said to the angels (q.v.), 'I am about to place a vice-regent (*khalīfa,* see CALIPH) on earth,' they said, 'Will you place thereon one who will work corruption (q.v.) there and shed blood, while we proclaim your praise and call you holy?' He said, 'I know what you do not know.'" Like the Talmudic explanation of Genesis 1:26 (Speyer, *Erzählungen,* 52-3; C. Schöck, *Adam,* 97; cf. Ṭabarī, *Tafsīr,* xiv, 31; Rāzī, *Tafsīr,* ii, 154), God's announcement (*innī jāʿil,* Q 2:30; *innī khāliq,* Q 15:28; 38:71) is given before the council of angels (*al-malaʾ al-aʿlā,* Q 38:69), who argue against the creation of man (Ṭabarī, *Tafsīr,* xxiii, 183-4). The commentaries on the

Qurʾān discuss the meaning of *"khalīfa,"* his identity and the identity of "the one who will work corruption there and shed blood." The term *"khalīfa"* denotes a person who takes the place of someone else and most commentators agree that it refers to Adam. This raised the question of whom Adam replaced on earth. Early commentary assumes that Adam was the successor of the angels or jinn (q.v.) who dwelled on earth before him and who were replaced because they became corrupt and shed blood. The famous early religious scholar al-Ḥasan al-Baṣrī (d. 110/728) identified the *"khalīfa"* as the offspring of Adam who succeed their father, generation after generation. Others take Adam for the *khalīfa* of God on earth in exercising judgment with justice (*al-ḥukm bi-l-ʿadl,* cf. Q 38:26). The commentators attribute the corruption and bloodshed (q.v.) to those descendants of Adam who do not follow the law of God (Ṭabarī, *Tafsīr,* i, 199-201). There is general agreement that Adam was not the one causing corruption and shedding blood. This interpretation reflects the understanding of Adam as the first prophet and messenger, because these actions were deemed to be a great sin *(kabīra)* and thus inappropriate for a prophet (see IMPECCABILITY AND INFALLIBILITY). Modern commentators tend not to accept the early ḥadīth reporting that a rational species *(al-ṣinf al-ʿāqil)* resided on the earth before mankind (e.g. Rashīd Riḍā, *Manār,* i, 258). Some combine this view with their refutation of Darwin's theory of the evolution of man (ʿA.W. al-Najjār, *Qaṣaṣ,* 31; see also M.J. Kister, Legends, 84-100; id., Ādam, 115-32; C. Schöck, *Adam,* 97-102).

Learning all of the names

The announcement of the creation of man (Q 2:30) is followed by the verses "And [God] taught Adam the names, all of them *(al-asmāʾ kullahā).* Then he presented them to the angels, and said, 'Tell me the names of these, if you speak the truth!' They said, 'Glory be to you! We know only what you have taught us....' He said, 'Adam, tell them their names!' When he had told them their names, [God] said, 'Did I not tell you that I know the hidden things of the heavens and the earth?'" (Q 2:31-2). The Qurʾān does not mention how God taught Adam all the names nor does it refer explicitly to what God presented to the angels. Early commentaries on these verses presuppose that God showed Adam all the things while teaching him their names. In this case, "the names, all of them" means "the name of everything" *(kullu shayʾ)* for which the commentators give examples such as "man, animal, earth, plain, sea, mountain, donkey." Already al-Ḥasan al-Baṣrī and his pupil Qatāda (d. ca. 116/734) understand God's teaching as a demonstration of the connection between names and things, the signifier and signified (cf. Rashīd Riḍā, *Manār,* i, 262). They add the deictic "this is" *(hādhā/hādhihi),* explaining that God said, "This is a sea. This is a mountain," etc. (ʿAbd al-Razzāq, *Tafsīr,* i, 42-3; Ṭabarī, *Tafsīr,* i, 216). Adam's knowledge of "all the names" was later interpreted as a general knowledge of all languages and through man's gift of language it was understood as a knowledge of the entire animate and inanimate world. Q 2:31 provided the starting point for the traditional Muslim discussion of the origin of language (cf. Speyer, *Erzählungen,* 51-4; Kister, in Rippen, *Approaches,* 107-9; id., in *IOS* (1993, 140f.; Schöck, *Adam,* 79f., 87).

The prostration of the angels before Adam

God's teaching of "the names" is followed by the qurʾānic verse: "And when We said to the angels, 'Bow down before Adam!' they bowed down, except Iblīs (q.v.). He refused and behaved proudly. He was one of the unbelievers" (Q 2:34; cf. 7:11-2; 15:29-33; 17:61; 18:50; 20:116; 38:72-6). The early commentators discussed the reason Iblīs refused, reasoning that the bowing was primarily intended as an act of obedience to God and secondarily as a display of respect for Adam (see BOWING AND PROSTRATION). In other words, the angels bowed down before Adam out of deference to Adam and obedience to God, not in worship of Adam (Ṭabarī, *Tafsīr*, i, 227; see ADORATION). Later scholars examined the question of whether Adam's knowledge *(ʿilm)* was cause for the prostration of the angels and whether it was the reason for Adam's superiority to the angels (Rāzī, *Tafsīr*, ii, 212-4). They also debate whether Adam's knowledge, when demonstrated to the angels, might be understood as a miracle *(muʿjiza,* e.g. Rāzī, *Tafsīr*, ii, 163-5, 169).

The creation of Adam

The Qurʾān mentions several materials from which Adam was created, i.e. earth or dust (*turāb*, Q 3:59), clay (*ṭīn*, Q 7:12; see CLAY), and sticky clay or mud *(ṭīn lāzib)*. More specifically, it is described as "clay from fetid foul mud" *(ṣalṣāl min ḥamaʾ masnūn)* and "clay like earthenware," i.e. baked or dry clay *(ṣalṣāl ka-l-fakhkhār)*. These terms are commonly interpreted as describing the different states of a single material. Commentators insist that Adam's clay *(ṣalṣāl)* was not baked, but was dried *(ṭīn yābis/turāb yābis)* without the use of fire, for Q 15:26-7 and Q 55:14-5 report that the jinn, unlike man, were created from fire. Narrative commentary and prophetic ḥadīth specify the places from which the earth was taken and provide various etiological explanations. According to some commentators, different kinds of dust were taken from the four corners of the earth so that the offspring of Adam would vary in color and quality. Others held that the dust was taken from different regions of the world, so that every part of Adam's body corresponded to an area. Others speculated that Adam's clay was taken from the seven earths (cf. Q 65:12) or the four elements so that his body combines the four temperaments. One view held that the material for creating his body was taken from the entire universe so that he became the microcosm *(al-ʿālam al-aṣghar)* corresponding to the macrocosm.

God himself formed the material of which Adam is made and breathed his spirit (q.v.; see also AIR AND WIND) into him (Q 15:29; 38:72). God says, "I created [Adam] with my own hands" (Q 38:75). In some commentaries God acts as a potter. He left the clay until it became good *(khammara)* and then kneaded *(ʿajana)* it. The question of the proper interpretation of God's "hand" or "hands" held a central place in the debates over corporealism *(tajsīm)* and anthropomorphism (*tashbīh*, Speyer, *Erzählungen*, 43-6; M.J. Kister, Legends, 100-5; id., Ādam, 135-7; C. Schöck, *Adam*, 67-8, 74-8, 82-6; J. van Ess, *TG*, iv, 399-400; Gimaret, Dieu à l'image de l'homme, 190-8).

The creation of Eve

The Qurʾān speaks of the creation of the second human being with the words: "People!... Your lord who created you from a single person and created from him his wife *(zawjahā)*" (Q 4:1). This "single person" *(nafs wāḥida)* is interpreted as Adam and "his wife" as Eve (Ṭabarī, *Tafsīr*, iv, 224). The early commentators report that she was created from the lowest of Adam's ribs *(quṣayrā)* — which is sometimes also understood as the shortest rib *(al-ḍilʿ al-aqṣar)* — or from a rib on his left side. This was done while he was sleeping with the aim "that he might dwell with her" (Q 7:189). The Qurʾān does not report when she was created, although some ḥadīth recount that she was created while Adam was dwelling in the garden of paradise (q.v.), where he had roamed alone (Ibn Saʿd, *Ṭabaqāt,* i, 39; Ṭabarī, *Tafsīr,* iv, 224-5). According to other reports, she was created before Adam entered the garden (q.v.; Ṭabarī, *Tafsīr,* i, 229-30). After describing the creation of Eve, Q 7:189 continues: "Then, when he covered her, she became pregnant with a light burden." The Qurʾān is not clear about where this happened, but most of the commentators situate Eve's pregnancy after their fall from paradise (Ṭabarī, *Tafsīr,* ix, 145).

The sojourn in paradise, the offense against God's command and the descent to earth

God commanded Adam and Eve to enjoy paradise with only a single restriction: "Adam, dwell you and your wife in the garden *(al-janna)* and eat freely of it wherever you desire, but do not go near this tree, lest you become wrong-doers!" (Q 2:35; cf. 7:19). This was a contract God made with Adam (*ʿahidnā ilā Ādam,* Q 20:115). Most commentators interpret the forbidden tree as an ear of grain *(sunbula),* wheat *(burr, ḥinṭa),* a vine *(karma, shajarat al-ʿinab, shajarat al-khamr)* or a fig tree (*tīna,* Ṭabarī, *Tafsīr,* i, 231-3). Other explanations mention trees with delicious and fragrant fruits. It is also called the "tree of knowledge *(ʿilm)*" or "tree of eternity *(khuld)*" (Q 20:120). The angels eat its fruit because they are immortal (ʿAbd al-Razzāq, *Tafsīr,* ii, 226; cf. Q 7:20).

Upon Satan's prompting, Adam and Eve ate from the forbidden tree (Q 7:20-2; 20:121) and descended from the garden to the earth (Q 2:36; 7:24-5; 20:123). The early commentators do not question that Adam sinned, although his sin was viewed as predetermined (J. van Ess, *Zwischen Ḥadīṯ und Theologie,* 161-8). The later commentaries, influenced by the dogma of the prophetic impeccability *(ʿiṣma),* emphasize that Adam and Eve were made to "slip" by Satan (*azallahumā,* Q 2:36) and Adam forgot (*nasiya,* Q 20:115); or they characterize the disobedience (q.v.) as an error in judgment *(khaṭaʾ fī l-ijtihād)* since Adam had assumed a single tree *(shakhṣ)* to be forbidden rather than the species *(nawʿ)*. He did not eat from the particular tree God showed him, but from another one of the same species. Tradition reports that from paradise Adam was made to descend to India and Eve to Jeddah. They re-united in ʿArafāt (q.v.) near Mecca (q.v.; Speyer, *Erzählungen,* 61-73; M.J. Kister, Ādam, 146-55; C. Schöck, *Adam,* 89-96, 106-32, 185). See FALL OF MAN.

God's forgiveness and guidance

After his "slip," "Adam received words *(kalimāt)* from his Lord and He forgave him *(tāba ʿalayhi)*.... We [viz. God] said, 'Get down from [the garden of paradise], all together! If guidance comes to you from me, whoever follows my guidance will experience no fear and will suffer no sorrow.'" (Q 2:37-8). Most commentators explain the "words" which "Adam received" as his speech: "Our Lord, we have wronged ourselves. If you do not forgive us and have mercy on us, we shall surely be among the lost" (Q 7:23). The key element of these verses is God's forgiveness of man and man's repentance. Together with God's "guidance" (*hudā,* cf. Q 20:122) and repentance *(tauba),* they will lead to man's return to paradise (Ṭabarī, *Tafsīr,* i, 242-5). For Muslim orthodoxy, repentance became the first step toward a religious life (al-Ghazālī, *Iḥyāʾ,* iv, 2-4).

The election of Adam

Muslims consider Adam a prophet, although this is not explicitely stated in the Qurʾān. God elected *(iṣṭafā)* Adam as he did the prophets and prophetic families, e.g. Noah (q.v.); Abraham (q.v.) and his family; the family of the father of Moses (q.v.), ʿImrān (q.v.); Isaac (q.v.); Jacob (q.v.); and Moses. The earliest testimony for Adam's status as a prophet is a ḥadīth narrated by Abū Dharr al-Ghifārī (d. 32/653), in which he asks Muḥammad who was the first prophet and he replies Adam. Q 20:122 reports that God "chose" *(ijtabā)* Adam, when he forgave him and guided him after his disobedience. Sunnī theology reconciled Adam's sin with the dogma of prophetic impeccability by arguing that his vocation began *after* his sin and his descent from paradise and thus he did not sin as a prophet.

The covenant

Prior to creation, "Your lord took from the backs of the children of Adam their offspring and made them testify against themselves. [God said,] 'Am I not your lord?' They said, 'Yes, we bear witness [to this]' " (Q 7:172). Early commentators interpreted this verse as a covenant (*mīthāq*, see COVENANT) between God and humankind, which committed men to monotheism. Although the Qurʾān states that the offspring were taken from "the children of Adam," most early scholars interpreted this to mean that God took from Adam's loins all of his progeny until the day of resurrection (e.g. ʿAbd al-Razzāq, *Tafsīr*, ii, 242). Although not all of the religious schools within Islam accepted this interpretation, the idea of the innate monotheistic nature of man (*fiṭra*, Q 30:30) was derived from this verse (cf. Ṭabarī, *Tafsīr*, xix, 40-1; Rashīd Riḍā, *Manār*, ix, 386-8; R. Gramlich, Der Urvertrag, 205-30).

The two sons of Adam

The Qurʾān reports the story of the two sons of Adam, one of whom murders the other because his sacrifice was not accepted while his brother's was (Q 5:27-32; see CAIN AND ABEL). In commentary the brothers are identified as Cain (Qābīl) and Abel (Hābīl). In the Islamic tradition, Cain is the prototypical murderer and the two brothers are seen as exemplars of good and evil (M.J. Kister, Ādam, 145-6; W. Bork-Qaysieh, *Kain und Abel*, 19-21). See also PROPHETS AND PROPHETHOOD.

Cornelia Schöck

Bibliography

Primary: ʿAbd al-Razzāq, *Tafsīr;* al-Ghazālī, Abū Ḥāmid Muḥammad, *Iḥyāʾ ʿulūm al-dīn,* 4 vols. in 2, Cairo 1927; Ibn Saʿd, *Ṭabaqāt;* Rashīd Riḍā, *Manār;* Rāzī, *Tafsīr;* Ṭabarī, *Tafsīr.*

Secondary: H.M.-D. al-Alousī, *The problem of creation in Islamic thought,* Ph.D. diss., Cambridge 1965; W. Bork-Qaysieh, *Die Geschichte von Kain und Abel (Hābīl wa-Qābīl) in der sunnitisch-islamischen Überlieferung,* Berlin 1993; J. van Ess, *TG;* id., *Zwischen Ḥadīṯ und Theologie. Studien zum Entstehen prädestinatianischer Überlieferung,* Berlin 1975; D. Gimaret, Dieu à l'image de l'homme, Paris 1997; R. Gramlich, Der Urvertrag in der Koranauslegung (zu Sure 7, 172-173), in *Der Islam* 60 (1983), 205-30; M.J. Kister, Legends in *tafsīr* and *ḥadīth* literature. The creation of Ādam and related stories, in A. Rippin, *Approaches,* 82-114; id., Ādam. A study of some legends in *tafsīr* and *ḥadīṯ* literature, in *IOS* (1993), 113-174; ʿA.W. al-Najjār, *Qaṣaṣ [sic] al-anbiyā,* Beirut 1405/1985; W. al-Qāḍī, The term "Khalīfa" in early exegetical literature, in *WI* 28 (1988), 392-411; C. Schöck, *Adam im Islam. Ein Beitrag zur Ideengeschichte der Sunna,* Berlin 1993; Speyer, *Erzählungen.*

Adoption see CHILDREN; FAMILY

Adoration

The acts and attitudes of praise and honor accorded to God. The standard English renderings of the Qurʾān typically use "adoration" and its cognates to translate *sajada* (to prostrate oneself; see BOWING AND PROSTRATION), the quintessential Islamic ritual of adoration (see PRAYER). There is, however, a great deal more to adoration than a physical gesture. A variety of qurʾānic terms vividly communicate the sense of "adoration" as a response to the divine being, including various forms of the roots *ḥ-m-d* (praise), *s-b-ḥ* (glorify), *m-j-d* (exalt) and *ʿ-ẓ-m* (magnify). Certain verses combine two or more of these terms (especially the first two, e.g. Q 2:30; 20:130; 39:75) to intensify the meaning, sometimes explicitly associating praise and glorification of God with prostration (Q 15:98; 32:15; 50:39-40). One widely-used Arabic-language concordance glosses the word *ḥamd* in Q 15:98 with all of the above-mentioned roots, adding *thanāʾ* (lauding), which is not used in the Qurʾān, but found in the ḥadīth, "I cannot adore you adequately" (Haykal, *Muʿjam*, i, 309).

More attitude than action, adoration encompasses various aspects of the orientation of creation toward the creator. All created things naturally adore God (Q 13:13: "the thunder adores by praising him"), but human beings need constant reminders. Adoration is thus an integral part of *islām* (surrender, see ISLAM), representing its more spiritually advanced and active aspect.

The exclamation *subḥāna llāh* (Praise be to God!) is a widely-used expression of admiration. *Subḥāna* and its cognate *tasbīḥ* are from a root associated with "swimming" or "floating," which is applied metaphorically to the heavenly bodies (e.g. Q 21:33; 79:3). It is often linked in the Qurʾān with *ḥamd* (Dāmaghānī, *Wujūh*, i, 446-7; Mir, *Dictionary*, 84), which is in turn related to one of the divine names (see GOD AND HIS ATTRIBUTES), *al-Ḥamīd* (Worthy of Adoration), and typically paired with other names such as *al-ʿAzīz* (Mighty) and *al-Ghanī* (All-Sufficient). Many commentators (e.g. Ṭabarī, *Commentary*, i, 61-3; A. Rippin, Tafsīr Ibn ʿAbbās, 79, 81) gloss the word "adoration" *(ḥamd)* in the phrase with which the first sūra begins, *al-ḥamdu li-llāh* "Adoration belongs to God," as "thanks" (Dāmaghānī, *Wujūh*, i, 263-4; Mir, *Dictionary*, 86), underscoring an understanding of adoration as the natural response of all creation to the source of all blessings.

Mystical exegesis often draws out more personal implications of adoration, emphasizing, for example, that bridging the infinite gap between the adorer and the one being adored implies annihilation of the one adoring (Nwyia, *Exégèse*, 284-5). Shīʿī commentators (see SHĪʿISM AND THE QURʾĀN), many of whom also have been mystically inclined, sometimes attached a significance to each of the letters of a word. For example, the imam Jaʿfar al-Ṣādiq (ca. 80/699-148/765) identified the root letters of *ḥamd (ḥ-m-d)* with divine unity *(waḥdaniyya)*, kingdom *(mulk)* and divine immutability *(daymūmiyya)*, respectively (Nwyia, *Exégèse*, 166). Ayatollah Khomeini (1902-1989), commenting on the meaning of *ḥamd*, emphasizes the impossibility of directing adoration to any other than God, for all that is not God lacks truly adorable qualities. Picking up a theme important in some medieval mystical exegesis such as that of al-Qūnawī (d. 673/1274, *Iʿjāz*, 271-5), Khomeini explores the metaphysical intricacies of adoration.

John Renard

Bibliography

Primary: Dāmaghānī, *Wujūh*, ed. M.Ḥ.A. al-Zafītī, 2 vols., Cairo 1992; R. Khomeini, Lectures on sūrat al-fātiḥa, in *Islam and revolution. Writings and declarations of Imam Khomeini*, trans. H. Algar, Berkeley 1981, 365-434; Ṣadr al-Dīn al-Qūnawī, *Iʿjāz al-bayān fī taʾwīl umm al-Qurʾān*, ed. ʿA.Q.A. ʿAṭā, Cairo 1969; Ṭabarī, *The commentary on the Qurʾān*, ed. and trans. J. Cooper et al., Oxford 1989.
Secondary: M. Ayoub, Thanksgiving and praise in the Qurʾān and in Muslim piety, in *Islamochristiana* 15 (1989), 1-10; M.H. Haykal et al., *Muʿjam al-alfāẓ al-Qurʾān al-karīm*, 2 vols., Cairo 1970²; Mir, *Dictionary*; Nwyia, *Exégèse*; A. Rippin, Tafsīr Ibn ʿAbbās and criteria for dating

early tafsīr texts, in *JSAI* 18 (1994), 38-83, esp. 79-83.

Adultery and Fornication

The qurʾānic word *zinā* (elsewhere more commonly *zināʾ*) means sexual intercourse outside the institutions of marriage and concubinage. Q 17:32 characterizes this behavior as a *fāḥisha,* i.e. an obscene act of transgression against God from which a Muslim should refrain (cf. Q 25:68). These transgressions together with their specified punishment are called *ḥudūd* (sing. *ḥadd,* lit. limit, boundary; see BOUNDARIES AND PRECEPTS) and also include associating others with God and homicide. The Ḥanafite jurist al-Jaṣṣāṣ (d. 370/981) explains that adultery and fornication are transgressions because of the social chaos they create. The patrilineal descent of the offspring of such unions is unidentified. Thus, his right to inherit from the father is denied and he cannot know his patrilineal *maḥārim,* i.e. the relatives with whom sexual intercourse is considered incest (*Aḥkām,* iii, 200; see FAMILY; INHERITANCE). It is God who guides people to avoid this sin, as in the story of Joseph (q.v.), where God's intervention saved him from giving in to Potiphar's wife (Q 12:24). Prayers also help people to refrain from committing such acts (Q 29:45).

Q 4:15 commands that women who commit an obscene act of transgression — understood here to be either adultery or fornication — witnessed by four witnesses, be confined in their home until death or until "God makes a way for them." Q 4:16 orders that both participants be lightly punished, but if they repent and reform, they are to be left alone. Most interpreters maintain that these two verses were later abrogated (see ABROGATION) by Q 24:2 (e.g. Jaṣṣāṣ, *Aḥkām* ii, 105-6), which stipulates that the punishment for adultery and fornication, if witnessed by four competent men (Q 24:4), is one hundred lashes. (On the other hand, some who did not acknowledge the existence of abrogation in the Qurʾān believed that Q 4:15-16 refer to homosexuality.) The flogging is to be administered in public and the spectators are warned against misplaced compassion. Q 34:3 stipulates that these individuals will be allowed to marry only those who have committed similar wrongs and polytheists. The punishment of an adulterous or fornicating slave is half of that of a free woman (Q 4:25). A divorced wife guilty of proven adultery may be turned out of her home during the three months during which she would otherwise be entitled to remain there (*ʿidda,* Q 65:1; see MAINTENANCE AND UPKEEP; WAITING PERIOD). The Qurʾān does not specify the marital status of the culprits eligible for flogging, but the jurists and interpreters (e.g. Ṭabarī, *Tafsīr,* xviii, 46-8) understood it to refer exclusively to non-*muḥsan* individuals — essentially adults who have never experienced sexual intercourse within a legitimate relationship. The practice of stoning (q.v.) *muḥsan* adulterers and fornicators is stipulated in the prophetic ḥadīth, but not in the Qurʾān. Schacht (Zināʾ, 1227-8) doubted that the Prophet ever ordered this punishment.

The qurʾānic teachings and the prophetic ḥadīth make it practically impossible to prove adultery. In the first place, in practice it would be difficult to procure the testimony of four men who witnessed the act of penetration. Furthermore, inquiry into the matter and questioning the culprits is forbidden because prying into people's concealed actions is unlawful. The word of a husband who accuses his spouse of adultery, but lacks the corroborating witnesses, is acceptable, provided that he swears four times that he is telling the truth. In the fifth oath (q.v.) he invokes God's curse on himself if he is lying (see CURSE). The wife averts the punishment if she swears to her innocence four times, followed by a solemn oath that her husband is telling a lie and invokes God's wrath (see ANGER) on herself if her husband is telling the truth (Q 24:6-10). This procedure is called *liʿān*, related to *laʿna*, "to curse." The person who voluntarily confesses adultery must repeat his confession four times and even then it may later be withdrawn. Persistent admission of sin and demand for punishment indicate a desire for atonement for the sin committed. Repentance exonerates the culprit from punishment. Inasmuch as adultery and fornication constitute serious offences, Q 24:4 prescribes eighty lashes for those who accuse women of adultery without the necessary proof and forbids that their testimony ever again be accepted. Some commentators believed that this revelation was occasioned by a false accusation lodged against ʿĀʾisha (q.v.), one of the Prophet's wives (see WIVES OF THE PROPHET).

It should be noted that qurʾānic teaching emphasizes that Muslims should refrain from abominable thoughts and desires (Q 6:151). However, if major sins are avoided, an adulterous thought *(lamam)* is not punishable (Q 53:32). The Prophet explained that these are the look in the eye, the desire within the heart and the verbal expressions which constitute the preliminaries for sexual intercourse. These are forgiven if they remain unacted upon (Bukhārī, book on social etiquette, see adultery of the senses: 5865).

The social development of Islamic teaching

It is a tradition of the Prophet that if adultery is discovered, the punishment is atonement for the sin committed. If it is divinely concealed, it is then left for God to punish the culprit or forgive him. This, together with the qurʾānic verses Q 24:10-18 (Quṭb, *Ẓilāl*, iv, 2494-505), which forbid slander are adapted to the social conditions and values of Muslim societies in various areas. In the coastal area of Tunisia, for instance, the concept of concealment is interwoven with the values of the power and wealth of a woman's agnates (father, sons, father's brothers and their sons). The wealth of the rich enables them to seclude their women and control their behavior. Furthermore, their influence and material power intimidate other men and deter them from approaching their women and also enable them to conceal any offences committed by their women. Such privileges are denied poorer men, who, together with their erring women, suffer social degradation which they consider "destined by God" *(maktūb)*. However, the punishment ordained by Islamic law is not inflicted (Abu-Zahra, *Social structure*).

In Egypt sexual offences committed by women also disgrace their agnates for it makes them appear unable to defend their honor or control their women. In the countryside adulterous women are drowned in the Nile. In Cairo people say, "If you disgrace yourselves, hide it" *(idhā bulītum fa-statirū)*. They may also say, "God commanded concealment." Both sayings are based on ḥadīth and the interpretation of Q 24:19. The principle that repentance exonerates one from punishment is also followed by authorities in the local mosques (Abu-Zahra, *Pure and powerful*, 197-9). The Azhar Fatāwā Committee *(Lajnat al-fatāwā)* also follows this Islamic teaching. In the case of a girl who contracted gonorrhea through adultery, the Committee was asked whether it would be lawful for her to conceal the illness from her fiancé. A judgment was issued that it would be a crime to do so (al-Ahrām, *Taqrīr*, 53).

In 1995, the Muftī of Egypt declared that it is necessary to integrate the qurʾānic *ḥudūd*, including those for adultery, in the state penal code, on condition that they are carried out with meticulous observance of the traditional Islamic safeguards (al-Ahrām, *Taqrīr,* 78). This recommendation, however, has not been implemented. See also LAW AND THE QURʾĀN; SIN, MAJOR AND MINOR.

Nadia Abu-Zahra

Bibliography

Primary: Bukhārī, *Ṣaḥīḥ, Kitāb al-Ḥudūd, Kitāb al-Muḥāribīn;* Jaṣṣāṣ, *Aḥkām;* Quṭb, *Ẓilāl;* Rāzī, *Tafsīr,* xii, 131-81.

Secondary: N. Abu-Zahra, *Social structure of the village of Sidi Ameur in the Sahel of Tunisia,* Ph.D. diss., Oxford 1968; id., *The pure and powerful. Studies in contemporary Muslim society,* Reading 1997; al-Ahrām, Markaz al-dirāsāt al-siyāsiyya wa-l-istrātījiyya, *Taqrīr fal-ḥāla al-dīniyya fī Miṣr,* vol. 3, Cairo 1996; J. Schacht, Liʿān, in *EI²,* v, 730-3; id., Zināʾ, in *EI¹,* iv, 1227-8; M. Shaltūt, *al-Islām. ʿAqīda wa-sharīʿa,* Cairo 1997[17].

African Americans

Historical information about individuals like Job ben Solomon (ca. 1700-73), Abd al-Rahman Ibrahima (1762-1829) and Omar ibn Said (ca. 1770-1864) demonstrates that some of the Africans brought to America as slaves were not only Muslim but well-versed in the Qurʾān as well. For example, the first-named, born Ayuba Suleiman Ibrahima Diallo, came from a family of religious leaders in Futa in present-day Senegal. After he was manumitted and taken to England, he wrote several copies of the Qurʾān from memory. These men, however, were exceptional. Enslavement eventually stripped nearly all Muslim Africans of their language, culture and religion.

Only considerably later did African Americans seek to reclaim their Islamic heritage. The foundation of the Moorish Science Temple in 1913 by Noble Drew Ali represents one of the first attempts. According to Drew Ali, true emancipation would come to African Americans through knowledge of their Moorish heritage and the return to their religion, Islam. Each racial group had its own religion. For Europeans it was Christianity and for Moors it was Islam. Although couched in Islamic phraseology, many of the practices and insignia of the Temple seem to have been derived from The Ancient Egyptian Arabic Order of Nobles of the Shrine (also known as the Black Shriners). This movement had adopted its practices and insignia from The Ancient Arabic Order of Nobles of the Mystic Shrine (originally a whites-only organization in the United States) which had acquired its "Islamic" elements through its Scottish Rite Mason founders. They claimed an initiation from a Grand Shaykh of Mecca, honors from the Ottoman Sultan Selim III, a charter from the Bavarian Illuminati and links with the Bektashi Sufi Order.

The pseudo-Islamic nature of the Moorish Science Temple is particularly evident in the sixty-four-page *The Holy Koran of the Moorish Science Temple of America,* also known as the *Circle Seven Koran.* About half of this *Koran* is taken from an earlier text which purports to provide an account of Jesus' adolescence and early adulthood in India. Another major section, entitled "Holy Instructions from the Prophet," is an adaptation of the Rosicrucian or Masonic *Unto Thee I Grant* (or *The Economy of Life* and *Infinite Wisdom*). Drew Ali's personal contribution consisted of replacing the word "God" with "Allāh" and removing the description of Jesus as blond and blue-eyed. Nothing in the *Circle Seven Koran* comes from the Qurʾān. Muḥammad, in fact, is mentioned only twice and then only as the fulfiller of the works of Jesus (Wilson, *Sacred Drift,* 19-26). Therefore the *Circle Seven Koran*'s significance to Islam lies mainly in the implicit challenge to the uniqueness and finality of the Qur'ān that the use of the title "Koran" represents.

The Nation of Islam represents another attempt to rediscover a Muslim heritage for African-Americans. Its founder, Wali Fard Muhammad (ca. 1877-1934?), is reported to have taught directly from an Arabic Qur'ān and to have consecrated it as the movement's primary scripture. When Fard Muhammad disappeared in 1934, his disciple Elijah Muhammad (1897-1975) became the movement's leader for the next four decades. Fundamental doctrines of the Nation of Islam included the belief that God had appeared in the person of Fard Muhammad; that Elijah Muhammad was his messenger; that the "devil" Christian white race was created by a renegade black scientist six thousand years ago; and that, although it had been prophesied that the white race would enslave the black race, the battle of Armageddon that would destroy the white race was imminent. Although these teachings appear to be unqur'ānic to most Muslims, Elijah Muhammad found qur'ānic support for them. For example, he interpreted qur'ānic passages about God, his messenger, Satan and the last day as references to Fard Muhammad, himself, the white race and contemporary America, respectively. His exegesis therefore consisted largely of reading the Qur'ān as a prophecy about peoples and events in the United States. This put him in conflict with the classical exegetical tradition, which relies heavily on lexical and grammatical explanations and particularly on the historicization of the Qur'ān through reference to the occasions of revelation (q.v.), abrogation (q.v.) and so forth. Elijah Muhammad's framework is not that provided by the biography of Muammad (see SĪRA AND THE QUR'ĀN), but by the doctrines of Fard Muhammad. It is noteworthy that Elijah Muhammad relied much more on the Christian Bible than the Qur'ān, even though he felt that the former was a "poison" book full of "slave teachings." The Qur'ān, in his mind, was a perfectly pure book of guidance, truth and wisdom. Therefore, he encouraged all African Americans to buy it and read it. Despite his heretical views, he is primarily responsible for introducing African Americans to the Qur'ān.

After his death in 1975, Elijah Muhammad was succeeded by his son Wallace D. Muhammad — now known as Warith Deen Muhammad — who led the movement in the direction of more traditional Islamic beliefs and practices and changed its name to "The World Community of al-Islam in the West" and later to "The American Muslim Mission." Louis Farrakhan (b. 1933), unhappy with these changes, reconstituted the Nation of Islam in 1977 under the original teachings of Fard Muhammad and Elijah Muhammad. In both present-day movements, the Qur'ān is the main scripture. Although the Moorish Science Temple, the Nation of Islam and the American Muslim Mission have been the most prominent African American Muslim movements, there are at least fifteen other groups of this type, each possessing its own understanding of the Qur'ān.

Herbert Berg

Bibliography
N. Drew Ali, *The holy Koran of the Moorish Science Temple of America,* Chicago 1927; Anon., *Unto thee I grant,* 1925; H. Berg, Elijah Muhammad. An African American Muslim *mufassir?* in *Arabica* 44 (1997), 1-27; E.D. Beynon, The voodoo cult among negro migrants in Detroit, in *The American journal of sociology* 43 (July 1937-May 1938), 894-907; C.A. Clegg III, *An original man. The life and times of Elijah Muhammad,* New York 1997; Levi [H. Dowling], *The aquarian Gospel of Jesus,* Bellville 1908; E. Muhammad, *The supreme wisdom. The solution to the so-called negroes' problem,* Chicago 1957; id., *Message to the blackman in America,* Chicago 1965; R.B. Turner, *Islam in the*

African-American experience, Bloomington 1997; P.L. Wilson, *Sacred drift. Essays on the margins of Islam,* San Francisco 1993.

African Literature

As is the case elsewhere in the world, the memorization of the Qurʾān, or at least a portion of it, is the starting point for a Muslim child's education in sub-Saharan Africa. For those whose education continues beyond this point, the Qurʾān plays a relatively small role in their studies. Nevertheless, the language of the Qurʾān remains the stylistic point of reference for everything they subsequently write in the Arabic language, especially among the majority for whom Arabic itself is not the mother tongue. Thus, in the seventeenth-century chronicle of Timbuktu, *Taʾrīkh al-sūdān* (ed. O. Houdas, Paris 1898) of ʿAbd al-Raḥmān al-Saʿdī, we find a large number of phrases which were either taken from the Qurʾān or inspired by it, e.g. *fī ḍalālin mubīn* (Q 3:164 et passim), *fataḥa lahu fatḥan mubīnan* (cf. Q 48:1), *al-fasād fī l-arḍ* (Q 11:116; cf. 2:205; 5:32), *al-taʿāwun ʿalā l-birr* (cf. Q 5:2), *yaqūlūna mā lā yafʿalūna* (Q 26:226), *lā tasmaʿū illā qīlan salāman* (cf. Q 56:25-6), *ẓulman wa-ʿudwānan* (cf. Q 4:30). Qurʾānic echoes are a marked feature of the prose writing of West African religious scholars *(ʿulamāʾ)* in particular, regardless of the topic they are treating.

Despite its mention in the study curricula of some scholars, qurʾānic exegesis *(tafsīr)* does not seem to have occupied a major place in African teaching traditions and few scholars wrote works in this field. An examination of the catalogs of public manuscript collections shows that *Tafsīr al-Jalālayn* of Jalāl al-Dīn al-Maḥallī (d. 864/1459) and Jalāl al-Dīn al-Suyūṭī (d. 911/1505) was, as in many parts of the Muslim world, the most popular commentary in West Africa. In fact, it is found in almost every collection. Al-Suyūṭī communicated with a number of West African scholars and his writings are still greatly admired in the region. Together with the prominent Malikite legal work, the *Muwaṭṭaʾ* by Mālik (d. 179/795), and a book on the miraculous nature of the Prophet, *Kitāb al-Shifāʾ* by al-Qāḍī ʿIyāḍ (d. 544/1149), this commentary forms the triad of fundamental texts for aspiring scholars of the clans of the Dyula. Other commentaries one finds in West African libraries are *Lubāb al-taʾwīl* of al-Khāzin (d. 741/1340), *Anwār al-tanzīl* of al-Bayḍāwī (d. ca. 700/1301) and *Maʿālim al-tanzīl* of al-Baghawī (d. 516/1122). Less commonly found are *al-Tashīl li-ʿulūm al-tanzīl* of Ibn Juzayy al-Kalbī (d. 741/1340), *Madārik al-tanzīl* of al-Nasafī (d. 710/1310), *al-Jawāhir al-ḥisān* of ʿAbd al-Raḥmān al-Thaʿālibī (d. 875/1471) and *al-Sirāj al-munīr* of al-Shirbīnī (d. 977/1576).

Local writing of qurʾānic commentaries is less common, except for brief treatises on specific verses or short sūras. The earliest complete commentary by an author from sub-Saharan Africa is that of the Mauritanian Muḥammad b. al-Mukhtār al-Daymānī, known as al-Walī al-Yadālī (d. 1168/1753), whose *al-Dhahab al-ibrīz* is a Ṣūfī exegesis (see ṢŪFISM AND THE QURʾĀN) which seems to be little known outside its land of origin. Much better known is *Ḍiyāʾ al-taʾwīl fī maʿānī al-tanzīl* (Cairo 1961) of ʿAbdallāh b. Muḥammad Fodiye (d. 1245/1829; see J. Hunwick (ed.), *Arabic literature,* ii, ch. 2, and esp. p. 93), brother of the celebrated Fulani warrior for the faith *(mujāhid)* and state founder ʿUthmān b. Muḥammad Fodiye. Copies of this commentary have been found in libraries in the Ivory Coast, Mali, Senegal, Mauritania and Morocco. The original work is in two volumes and its author later produced a one-volume abridgement, appropriately entitled *That which suffices for the weaklings of the Sudan (Kifāyat ḍuʿafāʾ al-Sūdān)*. The same author also wrote a versified introduction to the traditional disciplines of qurʾānic study (see EXEGESIS OF THE QURʾĀN), entitled *al-Miftāḥ lil-tafsīr,* based on two works by al-Suyūṭī, *al-Nuqāya* and *al-Itqān fī ʿulūm l-Qurʾān*. More recently from the same region, the former chief judge *(qāḍī)* of Northern Nigeria, Abū Bakr Gumi (d. 1992) wrote a simple commentary partially based on that of al-Bayḍāwī, entitled *Radd al-adhhān ilā maʿānī l-Qurʾān* (Beirut 1399/1979). Abū Bakr Gumi also published a Hausa translation of the Qurʾān (Beirut 1399/1979; see TRANSLATION OF THE QURʾĀN). A voluminous commentary entitled *Aḍwāʾ al-bayān fī īḍāḥ al-Qurʾān bi-l-Qurʾān* by the Mauritanian scholar Muḥammad al-Amīn b. Muḥammad al-Mukhtār al-Jakanī al-Shinqīṭī has also been published in ten volumes (Beirut n.d.).

If formal written exegesis in Arabic has not been such a widely practiced art, oral and hence unrecorded commentary in both Arabic and African languages has been more common. Nevertheless, to date little study of this form of exegesis has been done. However, a project of the Research Centre on Islamic History, Art and Culture in Istanbul — an organ of the Organisation of the Islamic Conference — aims to establish a library of recordings of the oral exegesis in the various African languages. At a more modest level, the practice of writing glosses in African languages seems to have some historical depth. An example of glossing in Kanembu, a language of Bornu, dating from ca. 1700, has been published by A.D.H. Bivar. At least one large written commentary exists in an African language. The manuscript collection of the Institut Fondamental d'Afrique Noire Cheikh Anta Diop has a work in Wolof by Mouhammadou Dème which runs 2,161 pages (see *Islam et Sociétés au Sud du Sahara,* vii [1994], 178, item 203). In the 1960s the Sudanese scholar, critic and poet ʿAbdallāh al-Ṭayyib undertook a bold experiment, offering on the radio a nightly commentary in colloquial Sudanese Arabic during the month of Ramaḍān (q.v.), which was an immediate success.

West African and Mauritanian scholars have also written works which deal with the Qurʾān in other ways. There is a literature on the "virtues of the Qurʾān" *(faḍāʾil al-Qurʾān)* and the virtues of particular sūras (see POPULAR AND TALISMANIC USES OF THE QURʾĀN). Asmāʾ bt. ʿUthmān b. Fodiye (d. 1280/1864), for example, wrote an Arabic treatise on the healing properties of certain sūras (see J. Hunwick [ed.], *Arabic literature,* ii, 164) and there is a poem in Fulfulde (also translated into Hausa) which consists in large part of the names of the various sūras to be recited to bring blessing (J. Hunwick [ed.], *Arabic literature,* ii, 168). The acrostic was a form of verse writing which found favor in West Africa. Although acrostics have been composed, for example, on the names of Shaykh Aḥmad al-Tijānī or Shaykh Ibrāhīm Niasse (and even on the names of the astronauts who landed on the moon in 1969), one of the more frequent choices is the first letters of one or more verses of the Qurʾān (see, for example, J. Hunwick (ed.), *Arabic literature,* ii, 348, 398). Additionally, there are a small number of works on the readings of the Qurʾān (q.v.) and on the orthography of the Qurʾān (q.v.). One example of the latter is Aḥmad Mālik Ḥammād al-Fūtīʿs *Miftāḥ al-amān fī rasm al-Qurʾān* (Dakar 1395/1975).

Africa has produced one true philosopher of the Qurʾān, who takes an approach to the text which has been considered by most Muslims to be errant if not heretical. Maḥmūd Muḥammad Ṭāhā was, in fact, hanged in the Sudan for apostasy in 1985. Born in 1909 (or 1911) in Rufa, he was graduated from Gordon Memorial College in Khartoum with a degree in Engineering in 1936. In 1948, after two years in jail for leading an anti-government demonstration, he spent a further three years in religious retreat *(khalwa)* in his home town, praying, fasting and meditating. This retreat was the breeding ground for the ideas expressed in his book *The second message of Islam* (*al-Risāla al-thāniya min al-Islām,* Khartoum 1967). While denying he had received a revelation as such, he did claim that human beings can receive an "enlightened understanding" of God's word directly from God. The Republicans, a political party which he had founded in 1945, was now transformed into a religious grouping known as the Republican Brothers.

According to Ṭāhā, society has gone through three stages: an initial stage in which people were Muslims in the simple sense of professing Islam; a second stage in which people have been believers *(muʾminūn)* practicing the Holy Law (*sharīʿa,* see LAW AND THE QURʾĀN); and a more advanced stage in which people are Muslims in the higher sense, submitters to God who practice a prophetic lifestyle. The guidance for this more advanced stage was revealed to Muḥammad in Mecca as a spiritual message for the moral uplift of humanity. But it was "abrogated" (see ABROGATION) in the sense of being "postponed" by the message of the Medinan period which was necessitated by the exigencies of the time (see CHRONOLOGY AND THE QURʾĀN). This interpretation of abrogation is premised on the adoption of an alternative reading of Q 2:106. The standard text reads: "Whatever message we abrogate or cause to be forgotten *(aw nunsihā),* We produce one better than it or equal to it." Ṭāhā adopted the reading *aw nansaʾhā* (see Ṭabarī, *Tafsīr,* i, 477), i.e. "or postpone," arguing that the "one better than it" is the Medinan message that was closer to the understanding of the people at the time of the Prophet. The original message that was "postponed" would only be reinstated when people were sufficiently advanced materially and intellectually to appreciate it.

During the second half of the Prophet's mission and thereafter up till the present-day, Muslims have continued to live in the "believer" stage, enacting the social teachings of the Medinan revelation which was revealed in accordance with the understanding of the people of the Prophet's day. But now after 1400 years, Ṭāhā claimed, Muslims have reached a stage of material and intellectual advancement that makes it possible for the third more advanced stage, that of the true Muslim, to come into being. We are now far from Muḥammad's epoch — which in Ṭāhā's view was not a perfect epoch because its manners and conceptions were very close to those of the Age of Ignorance (q.v.), the period prior to the qurʾānic revelation — hence we need to reinterpret the Holy Law. This law is perfect in its ability to assimilate and develop the capabilities of individuals and society and guide human life up the ladder of continuous development.

This daring interpretation of a single verse was the basis for a complete revaluation of the nature of the qurʾānic message. The legislative verses of the Medinan portions of the Qurʾān could now be regarded as being secondary to the original message of Mecca and no more than concessions to the social realities of the Prophet's day. In Ṭāhā's view, these verses have now outlived their usefulness and Muslims in the fifteenth/twentieth century should look to the Meccan verses of the Qurʾān and formulate new laws in accordance with the moral and ethical precepts found in them. Hence he could proclaim that *jihād* (q.v.), slavery (see SLAVES AND SLAVERY), polygamy, divorce (see MARRIAGE AND DIVORCE) and the seclusion of women (see VEIL; WOMEN AND THE QURʾĀN) are not the original precepts of Islam, but have been sanctioned simply because the early Muslims did not have the tools to build a social order based on the Meccan revelations. In a similar vein, he held that complete equality between men and women was an original precept of Islam, as were democracy, socialism, the eradication of social classes and even the social equality of non-Muslims in a Muslim state.

Ṭāhā's theory of a first and second message was a bold way of trying to establish a qurʾānic basis for genuine social and political reform. It must be viewed, however, within the context of present-day Sudanese society, where women are largely secluded and discriminated against, a long-drawn-out civil war rages over the status of the non-Muslim southerners, and there is constant pressure to "islamize" the law, i.e. to establish the traditional Holy Law. Ultimately, it was Ṭāhā's political and social views (especially as expressed in a 1984 pamphlet), rather than his theology, that turned the government of General Numeiri against him and his small band of Republican Brothers. His engagement with the Qurʾān, however, is symptomatic of the need felt by many modernist Muslims to find a way around the impasse formed by the doctrine of the undifferentiated eternal validity of the entire text.

John O. Hunwick

Bibliography

A.D.H. Bivar, A dated Kuran from Bornu, in *Nigeria magazine* 15 (1960), 199-205; L. Brenner and B. Sanankoua, *L'enseignement islamique au Mali*, Bamako 1991; M. Hassane, *La transmission du savoir religieux en Afrique sub-saharienne. Exemple du commentaire coranique à Saayi (Niger)*, Ph.D. diss., Paris 1995; J.O. Hunwick and R.S. O'Fahey (eds.), *Arabic literature of Africa*, ii. *The writings of central Sudanic Africa*, Leiden 1995; F. Leconte, *Une exegèse mystique du coran au xviii siècle dans le sud-ouest de la Mauritanie (al-gibla). al-Ḏāhab al-ibrīz fī tafsīr kitāb Allāh al-ʿAzīz de Muḥammad ibn al-Muḫtār al-Yadālī (1685-1753)*, Mémoire de 3e cycle, Université de Provence Aix-Marseille I 1994-5; A. An-naʾim (trans.), *The second message of Islam*, Syracuse 1987; R. Santerre, *Pédagogie musulmane d'Afrique noire. L'école coranique peule du Cameroun*, Montreal 1973; M.M. Ṭāhā, *al-Risāla al-thāniya min al-Islām*, Khartoum 1967, 1388/1968[3] (with new intro.), 1983[4] (with revised intro.); T. Tamari, L'exegèse coranique *(tafsīr)* en milieu mandingue, in *Islam et sociétés au sud du Sahara* 10 (1996), 43-80; I. Yusuf, An analysis of Swahili exegesis of *Sūrat al-shams* in Shaykh Abdallah Saleh Farsy's *Qurani Takafitu*, in *Journal of religion in Africa* 22 (1992), 350-66.

Afterlife

see RESURRECTION; PARADISE; HELL; FIRE

Afternoon

The time between noon and evening. The Qurʾān refers frequently to various times of the day, but does not explicitly mention the afternoon. In most cases this segment of the day appears simply in the context of instructions for Muḥammad's followers involving the Islamic rituals that were being established during his lifetime.

Several passages that address Muḥammad's situation in Mecca before his emigration to Medina command him to perform a ritual prayer (see PRAYER) twice daily: "at the two ends of the day" (Q 11:114), "at evening and at dawn" (Q 40:55), etc. (Welch, Muḥammad's understanding, 21-2). A third daily prayer, most likely instituted in Medina (Watt and Welch, *Der Koran*, 264-71), is mentioned in Q 2:238: "Remember the prayers, and [also] the middle prayer *(al-ṣalāt al-wusṭā)*, and stand reverently before God." This ritual was probably performed in the "middle" of the day, specifically in the early afternoon, thus being a precursor to "the noon prayer" (*ṣalāt al-ẓuhr,* Paret, *Kommentar,* 50-1). When, sometime after Muḥammad's death, the performance of the prayer ritual came to be required five times daily, Qurʾān commentators interpreted Q 2:238 as referring to the "middle" of the five, the *ṣalāt al-ʿaṣr.* Many ḥadīth in al-Bukhārī *(Ṣaḥīḥ, K. Mawāqīt al-ṣalāt),* Muslim *(Ṣaḥīḥ, K. al-Ṣalāt)* and the other major collections show that the times when the daily prayers were performed as well as their names were not set during Muḥammad's lifetime.

The term *ʿaṣr* occurs in the Qurʾān only once, in the oath *wa-l-ʿaṣr* in Q 103:1 (see OATHS). This oath form *wa-...* ("[I swear] by...") occurs at the beginning of eighteen sūras, half involving times of the day or celestial bodies: "the dawn" *(al-fajr,* Q 89:1), "the forenoon" *(al-ḍuḥā,* Q 93:1), "the night" *(al-layl,* Q 92:1), "the star" *(al-najm,* Q 53:1), "the sun" *(al-shams,* Q 91:1), etc. The basic meaning of *ʿaṣr* is "epoch" or "era" in the sense of passing time. The Shāfiʿite commentator al-Bayḍāwī (d. ca. 700/1300) in his commentary (*Tafsīr,* ii, 670) and Jalāl al-Dīn al-Maḥallī (d. 864/1459) and al-Suyūṭī (d. 911/1505) in theirs (*Jalālayn,* 810) summarize well the views of most classical commentators, saying *ʿaṣr* in Q 103:1 could refer to time *(al-dahr,* see TIME), the late afternoon, the *ṣalāt al-ʿaṣr,* the era of the prophets or the era of Muḥammad. Variant readings of this sūra (see READINGS OF THE QURʾĀN) provided by the Companions Ibn Masʿūd (d. 32/652) and ʿAlī (d. 40/660, see ʿALĪ B. ABĪ ṬĀLIB) add verses ending with *al-dahr* (Jeffery, *Materials,* III, 192), supporting the preference of many modern Muslim scholars for interpreting *ʿaṣr* in Q 103:1 simply as "time" (see Ibn al-Khaṭīb, *Awḍaḥ,* 761; Nadwī, *Qāmūs,* 418). The translation "afternoon" preferred by R. Bell, A.J. Arberry, R. Paret and other Europeans appears to derive from the association of this verse with *ṣalāt al-ʿaṣr.* M. Pickthall possibly best translates *ʿaṣr* in Q 103:1 as "the declining day" (Bell, 676; Paret, *Kommentar,* 521).

Unlike the Jewish Sabbath and the Christian Sunday, the Islamic weekly congregational service on Friday afternoon was set to occur during a busy day of commerce, as is seen in the Qurʾān's only explicit reference to it: "Believers, when the call is given for worship on the Day of Assembly, hasten to God's service and stop bar-gaining.... Then when the worship is finished, disperse and seek God's bounty" (Q 62:9-10). The Islamic weekly service appears to have been established to coincide with the Friday market day held by the Jewish clans in Medina before the beginning of their Sabbath at sundown (Goitein, Origin, 185; Watt and Welch, *Der Islam,* 296-7). See also DAY, TIMES OF.

Alford T. Welch

Bibliography
Primary: Bayḍāwī, *Anwār,* 2 vols., Istanbul 1296; *Jalālayn,* Beirut n.d.; Qurṭubī, *Tafsīr,* 20, 178-9; Rāzī, *Tafsīr,* 32, 84-6.
Secondary: S.D. Goitein, Origin and nature of the Muslim Friday worship, in *MW* 49 (1959), 183-95; M. Ibn al-Khaṭīb, *Awḍah al-tafsīr,* Cairo n.d. (represents the views of several al-Azhar scholars); Jeffery, *Materials;* ʿA.A.ʿA. Nadwī, *Qāmūs alfāẓ al-Qurʾān al-karīm,* Jiddah 1983; R. Paret, *Grenzen der Koranforschung,* Stuttgart 1950, 31-5; id., *Kommentar;* W.M. Watt and A.T. Welch, *Der Islam,* i. *Mohammed und die Frühzeit — Islamisches Recht — Religiöses Leben,* Stuttgart 1980, 262-347; A.T. Welch, Muḥammad's understanding of himself. The Koranic data, in R. Hovannisian and S. Vryonis (eds.), *Islam's understanding of itself,* Malibu 1983.

Age

see BIOLOGY AS THE CREATION AND STAGES OF LIFE

Age of Ignorance

This phrase is a common translation of the Arabic word *jāhiliyya* used by Muslims to refer to the historical period in west-central Arabia covering the centuries immediately prior to the mission of Muḥammad, a period characterized by ignorance of the divine truth. To the original audience of the Qurʾān, however, it almost certainly referred primarily to the moral condition of those individuals and their society which led them to oppose the mission of the Prophet (see OPPOSITION TO MUḤAMMAD) and only secondarily, if at all, to a defined historical epoch. It is also possible that the word was a kind of collective plural of "ignorant person" *(jāhil)*, as has been asserted by F. Rosenthal (*Knowledge triumphant*, 33-4). As to the nature of this moral condition, I. Goldziher and T. Izutsu have argued that the primary meaning of the root, *j-h-l*, from which *jāhiliyya* is derived, is not "ignorance" but "barbarism," especially the tendency to go to extremes of behavior. According to this view the original antonym was not *ʿilm* (knowledge) but *ḥilm* (moral reasonableness, self-control). I. Goldziher (*MS*, 201-8) has adduced considerable evidence for this from pre-Islamic Arabic poetry, while T. Izutsu (*Concepts*, 28-35) has examined key passages from the Qurʾān and the biography of the Prophet (see SĪRA AND THE QURʾĀN). The word *jāhiliyya* is often translated "pagandom" or "heathendom" and it may be argued that its effective antonym is *islām* (q.v.), as it certainly is for many later writers (see IGNORANCE).

The texts of the four passages where the word *jāhiliyya* occurs in the Qurʾān tend to bear these prints out, though not conclusively. The contrast between *jāhiliyya* and *ḥilm* seems particularly clear in Q 48:26: "When the unbelievers stirred up fierce arrogance in their hearts, the fierce arrogance of *jāhiliyya (ḥamiyyat al-jāhiliyya)*, God sent down his tranquility upon the messenger and the believers and imposed on them the command of self-restraint *(taqwā)*." T. Izutsu (*Concepts*, 31) interprets "the fierce arrogance of the *jāhiliyya*" as "the staunch pride so characteristic of the old pagan Arabs, the spirit of stubborn resistance against all that shows the slightest sign of injuring their sense of honor and destroying the traditional way of life." Q 3:154 speaks of "a band anxious for themselves, wrongly suspicious of God with a suspicion *(ẓann)* of the *jāhiliyya*." Here *jāhiliyya* may mean ignorance, but a lack of trust in God would seem more specific. Q 5:50 reads, "Do they seek a *jāhiliyya* judgment *(ḥukm jāhilī)*?" i.e. a judgment by pagan rather than divine standards. Here *islām* would seem the likely antonym. Finally, Q 33:33 admonishes the wives of the Prophet: "Stay in your homes and do not make a display of yourselves in the manner of the first [or old] *jāhiliyya (al-jāhiliyya al-ūlā)*." Only here does it seem plausible, though not necessary, to interpret "*jāhiliyya*" as an epoch.

These passages illustrate some but not all of the contrasts between the beliefs and values represented by *jāhiliyya* and those of the Qurʾān. The key difference is the attitude toward God. The Qurʾān insists that only God is to be obeyed and worshipped. The pagan Arabs did recognize God as creator of the world and as a kind of remote figure to be approached in certain crisis situations (Q 29:65), but they also recognized other deities closer at hand, such as the three Meccan deities, al-Lāt, al-ʿUzza and Manāt, who were thought to intercede with God (Q 53:19-20; see SATANIC VERSES). The Qurʾān calls this the association of other beings with God *(shirk)*, and treats it as the worst of sins, the one thing God will not forgive (Q 4:48; see BELIEF

AND UNBELIEF). While the Qurʾān inculcates an attitude of submission to God and dependence on him, the pagan Arabs were marked by a spirit of independence and self-sufficiency in relation both to God and to other deities, seeing themselves as subject only to a rather impersonal fate (q.v.). The ways of their ancestors had more authority than the commands of God. While the Qurʾān preaches universal values (Q 49:13), their highest loyalty was to the tribe and to tribal solidarity *(ʿaṣabiyya)* as illustrated by the words of the poet Durayd: "I am of Ghaziyya: if she be in error, then I will err; and if Ghaziyya be guided right, I go right with her" (R.A. Nicholson, *Literary history,* 83). Whereas the key motive for ethical action in the Qurʾān is the hope of reward and fear of punishment in the future life (see REWARD AND PUNISHMENT), for the pagan Arab there was no future life: "There is nothing but our present life. We die and we live. Nothing but time destroys us!" (Q 45:24). W.M. Watt has called these attitudes "tribal humanism" (*Muhammad at Mecca,* 24-5).

The Qurʾān, however, by no means rejects all the values of the pagan Arabs. At many points the concern is rather to redirect and moderate them. Nobility comes not from having noble ancestors whose deeds one emulates, but from deeds of piety as defined by God (Q 49:13). The loyalty, courage and fortitude that once served the tribe in battle and elsewhere are now meant to serve God and the Muslim community *(umma)*. Honor is a value, but not the sort of honor that leads to unending vendettas. The Qurʾān permits limited retribution, but encourages forgiveness (Q 2:178; 17:33). Generosity and hospitality are values, but not to the extent of Ḥātim of Tayy, who gained fame by giving away all his father's camels (R.A. Nicholson, *Literary history,* 85-6). The Qurʾān says, "Be neither miserly nor prodigal" (Q 17:29).

At other points, pagan values and practices are more completely rejected. The hard-drinking and womanizing admired by the pre-Islamic poets are rejected in favor of bans on alcohol (Q 5:90; see INTOXICANTS; GAMBLING) and on adultery (Q 17:32; see ADULTERY AND FORNICATION). In place of the class stratification of the *jāhiliyya* the Qurʾān supports human equality and encourages concern for the poor (Q 49:13; 80:1-16). In relations between the sexes, the Qurʾān seems, at least in some cases, to have limited women's freedom, as Q 33:33 suggests. On the other hand, it also appears to have given women greater security and greater recognition of their status as humans, as suggested by the ban on female infanticide (Q 16:58-9; see INFANTICIDE).

While the word *"jāhiliyya"* in the Qurʾān refers primarily to the moral condition of the pagan Arabs, it came later to refer primarily to the epoch in which they lived. The reasons for this are not hard to imagine. What was a living force when the first Muslims confronted their pagan neighbors became in time a matter of history, the characteristics of a past age. Thus in the ḥadīth collection of al-Bukhārī, *jāhiliyya* is almost always a past epoch. For example, we read "The tribe of the Quraysh (q.v.) used to fast on the day of Ashūrāʾ in the *jāhiliyya,*" and "The best people in the *jāhiliyya* are the best in Islam, if they have understanding" (*Ṣaḥīḥ,* iii, 65; iv, 461). The exact period of historical time covered by the term *"jāhiliyya"* was a matter of discussion among the early Muslims, as is reflected in the commentaries on Q 33:33. These suggest various time spans for the "first *jāhiliyya,*" such as the time between Adam (see ADAM AND EVE) and Noah (q.v.) or that between Idrīs (q.v.) and Noah, or the time when Abraham (q.v.) was born, with the implicit "later *jāhiliyya*" being the time between Jesus (q.v.) and Muḥammad.

Some also suggest that the first *jāhiliyya* was "the *jāhiliyya* of unbelief" *(jāhiliyyat al-kufr)* before Islam and the other is "the *jāhiliyya* of iniquity" *(jāhiliyyat al-fusūq)* after the coming of Islam. They illustrate this with a ḥadīth in which Muḥammad says to one of his followers, "Within you is *jāhiliyya,*" and when asked whether he meant the *jāhiliyya* of unbelief or the *jāhiliyya* of Islam (i.e. of iniquity), he said the *jāhiliyya* of unbelief (Ṭabarī, *Tafsīr;* Zamakhsharī, *Kashshāf;* Bayḍāwī, *Anwār;* Qurṭubī, *Jāmi;* Ibn Kathīr, *Tafsīr* ad Q 33:33.).

As these last examples illustrate, there has always been an awareness that *jāhiliyya* is not simply a past epoch but that the qualities that characterize *jāhiliyya* have continued to be present even after the coming of Islam. This also appears quite forcefully in the Shīʿī ḥadīth, "Whosoever of my community dies and does not have an imām (q.v.) from among them, has died the death of the *jāhiliyya*" (M. Momen, *Shiʿi Islam,* 158). Indeed, the early centuries of Islamic history may be interpreted as a struggle between the older *jāhiliyya* culture and the newer Islamic culture (e.g. A. Amīn, *Fajr,* 78-83) and some have seen *jāhiliyya* present in much later times. Ibn Taymiyya (d. 728/1328) wrote of "a *jāhiliyya* in a restricted sense" in reference to the pre-Islamic customs persisting among the Muslims of his time (M. Memon, *Ibn Taimiya's struggle,* 146). In recent centuries, the idea of a contemporary *jāhiliyya* has regained currency in some circles. Muḥammad b. ʿAbd al-Wahhāb, the twelfth/eighteenth-century Arabian reformer who began the Wahhābī movement, and his followers perceived their fellow Muslims, either throughout the world or in the Arabian peninsula, as living in a *jāhiliyya* (E. Peskes, *Muhammad b. ʿAbdalwahhab*) because of their adoption of practices and beliefs lacking scriptural support.

More recently reformers such as Muḥammad ʿAbduh (d. 1905) and Muḥammad Rashīd Riḍā (d. 1935), in their qurʾānic commentary entitled *al-Manār* (vi, 422), have compared the conservatism, injustice, superstition and secular tendencies found in their society with comparable aspects of the pre-Islamic *jāhiliyya* criticized by the Qurʾān. For example, their commentary on Q 5:50 (listed as Q 5:53 in the verse-numbering of *al-Manār*) identifies the "*jāhiliyya* judgment" as the favoring of the strong over the weak and argues that some geographical Muslims in this age are "more corrupt in their religion and morals than those concerning whom these verses were revealed." The idea of *jāhiliyya* as a contemporary reality has been more forcefully asserted, however, by the twentieth-century revivalists, Abū l-ʿAlāʾ Mawdūdī (d. 1979) in India and Pakistan and Sayyid Quṭb in Egypt. Mawdūdī (*Meaning of the Qurʾān,* x, 106) defined "*jāhiliyya*" as any conduct which goes against Islamic culture, morality and the Islamic way of thinking and behaving. He found it in both the West and the communist world. Sayyid Quṭb took a similar position but went further. In his best known book, *Maʿālim fī l-ṭarīq (Milestones on the way),* he said that a *jāhilī* society is any society that does not serve God by following his guidance in all areas of its life. Such societies serve human beings instead of God and thus are inevitably unjust, inhumane and backward. Only an Islamic society can be truly "civilized." In his view, contemporary *jāhiliyya* is at least as bad as that of Muḥammad's time. He further asserted that not only Western and communist societies were *jāhilī* at present but also all of the so-called Muslim societies. This idea, along with his apparent belief that the nature of *jāhilī* societies is such that they cannot be replaced without violence, led to his execution by the Egyptian government in 1966 and has inspired many militants since his death.

Although relatively few Muslims would take things this far, the idea of *jāhiliyya* as a contemporary moral and social reality seems to be quite widespread today. In this current usage the term refers not so much to the distinctive failings of the old pagan Arabs as to those of modern societies, such as materialism and secular ideologies. The notion of *jāhiliyya* has thus been effectively updated. See also IDOLATRY AND IDOLATERS; IDOLS AND IMAGES.

William E. Shepard

Bibliography
Primary: A. Amīn, *Fajr al-Islām,* Cairo 1929; Bayḍāwī, *Anwār,* 2 vols., Cairo 1388/1968²; Bukhārī, *Ṣaḥīḥ,* trans. M.M. Khan, 9 vols., Chicago 1976-9³ (revised); Ibn Kathīr, *Tafsīr,* Beirut 1385/1966; A.ʿA. Mawdūdī, *Tafhīm al-Qurʾān* [in Urdu], A.A. Kamal (trans.), *The meaning of the Qurʾān,* Lahore 1974-³; Qurṭubī, *Jāmi,* 18 vols., Cairo 1387/1967; S. Quṭb, *Maʿālim fī l-ṭarīq,* Cairo 1384/1964, trans. S. Badrul Hasan, *Milestones,* Kuwait 1398/1978; M. Rashīd Riḍā and M. ʿAbduh, *Manār,* 12 vols., Cairo 1346/1927-1354/1936; Ṭabarī, *Tafsīr;* Zamakhsharī, *Kashshāf.*
Secondary: Goldziher, *MS;* T. Izutsu, *Concepts;* M.U. Memon (trans.), *Ibn Taimiya's struggle against popular religion,* The Hague 1976; M. Momen, *An introduction to Shiʿi Islam. The history and doctrines of Twelver Shiʿism,* New Haven 1985; R.A. Nicholson, *A literary history of the Arabs,* Cambridge 1907; E. Peskes, *Muhammad b. ʿAbdalwahhab (1703-92) im Widerstreit. Untersuchungen zur Rekonstruktion der Frühgeschichte der Wahhabiya,* Beirut 1993; F. Rosenthal, *Knowledge triumphant. The concept of knowledge in medieval Islam,* Leiden 1970; W.M. Watt, *Muhammad at Mecca,* Oxford 1953.

Agriculture and Vegetation

The production of crops and plants in general. Agriculture and vegetation figure prominently in the Qurʾān, reflecting their significance in the environment in which the text was revealed. The Arabic root *f-l-ḥ* carries the basic meaning of "cleaving" or "splitting." When applied to the land, it carries the sense of "furrowing," "tilling" or "plowing." *"Filāḥa,"* therefore, is the art of plowing and cultivating and is the term used in the general sense of "agriculture" in the titles of medieval Arabic treatises on agronomy. The qurʾānic references to this root, however, all derive from the form *"aflaḥa,"* carrying the meaning "to prosper" and "to be in a fortunate, happy state." Other roots denoting cultivation in the Qurʾān are *z-r-ʿ* and *ḥ-r-th,* appearing together in Q 56:63-4. The verb *athāra,* "to till," occurs in Q 30:9. The most general term for "vegetation" is *nabāt,* which is found in Q 18:45 and 71:17. Edward Lane renders *nabāt* "whatever God causes to grow, vegetate or germinate, in the earth" (Lane, viii, 2754).

Agriculture and vegetation in the Qurʾān

There are frequent direct and indirect references to the general concepts of agriculture and vegetation in the Qurʾān, despite the mention in Q 14:37 of Abraham (q.v.) having settled his son Ishmael (q.v.), the traditional "father of the Arabs," in "an uncultivated valley" beside the sacred house of the Kaʿba (q.v.), and possible references to famine (q.v.). With regard to the latter, it is impossible to determine the degree of need Mecca and the surrounding areas experienced in seasonal or cyclical shortages of food. Although shortages were likely as much a part of the rhythm of daily life there as was the case in many other regions of the Middle East, the Qurʾān suggests less severe austerity. The storage of grain in anticipation of lean times, as exemplified in the story of Joseph (q.v., Q 12:47), was well known. Widely-grown hulled grains, such as emmer, spelt and barley could be stored in the spikelet stage, their hard outer glumes protecting them against insects and pests. Moreover, recent ethno-archaeological evidence suggests that storage decision-making in the ancient Mediterranean occurred at the level of the household or farm unit — rather than the community — amid a complex trade-off between environmental, political and economic factors (Forbes and Foxhall, Ethnoarchaeology and storage, 69-86); storage strategies, therefore, should be considered as part of the overall economic picture of sixth and seventh century Arabia. Grain was produced for animal as well as human consumption (Q 32:27). One verse (Q 6:136) mentions the practice of setting aside a portion of the cattle and seed produce *(ḥarth)* for God, which may be a reference to storage.

There were other crops as well, like date palms (q.v.), pomegranates, olives and grapes (Q 6:99, 141; 13:4; 16:11) and one qurʾānic passage (Q 18:32) depicts two gardens (sing. *janna*) of grape vines surrounded by palm trees with cultivated fields between them. Nouns referring to planted areas include *janna* (pl. *jannāt*) as already noted (also Q 6:99, 141; 17:91), not all of its very frequent occurrences being in reference to a heavenly paradise (see PARADISE; GARDEN). In one of these, however, the expression "gardens under which rivers flow" (Q 2:25) may conceivably be an allusion to the underground irrigation systems well-known in Arabia at the time. One of the signs of the divine economy was the revival of "dead land" with gardens of dates and vines watered from flowing springs, giving forth fruit *(thamar)* to feed humankind (Q 36:33-5). Luxuriant gardens *(ḥadāʾiq)* are also mentioned (Q 27:60; 80:30). Natural meadows (*rawḍa,* pl. *rawḍāt,* Q 30:15; 42:22) are noted as rewards in the afterlife while pastures *(marʿā)* were created on earth so that flocks may feed (Q 79:31; 87:4). One qurʾānic simile compares the self-inflicted harm in this life that is the consequence of improper behavior to a destructive glacial wind laying low the crops (*ḥarth,* Q 3:117; see also 3:14; 10:24). Similar to this is the moving parable of the owners of a garden or orchard who on discovering their possessions destroyed overnight (*ka-l-ṣarīm,* as though all the fruit had been severed from the trees) acknowledged their transgression against God (Q 68:17-33). The threat to or actual loss of what is precious yet familiar, as described in these passages, underlines the fine balance between sufficiency and want in Arabian material life. A passage promising cultivated fields in a future life (*ḥarth al-ākhira,* Q 42:20) has a similar import. In a long description of paradise, there is the single occurrence of a word, meaning "two well-watered and intensely green gardens" (*mudhāmmatān,* Q 55:64). This term was less commonly applied to cultivated gardens in this world, but the comparative intention of the expression would have been obvious to the Prophet's audience.

A notable aspect of the Qurʾān is the number of terms related to the date palm, possibly the single most important food crop throughout the pre-modern Middle East. A range of other words, often appearing only once, refers to vegetation in the broadest sense, dry or fresh, including leaves or stalks of corn (*ʿaṣf,* Q 55:12), trefoil or clover (*qaḍb,* Q 80:28), acacia (*ṭalḥ,* Q 56:29), a bunch of grapes (*quṭūf,* sing. *qiṭf,* Q 69:23), stubble (*hashīm,* Q 18:45; 54:31), plant stalk (*shaʾ,* Q 48:29), a handful of green or dry grass or husks (*ḍighth,* Q 38:44; pl. *aḍghāth,* Q 12:44; 21:5), gardens with thickly planted trees (*jannāt alfāf,* Q 78:16), leaves (*waraq,* Q 7:22; 20:121; *waraqa,* Q 6:59). *Ayka,* the word for "woods" or "thicket," occurring in the phrase "the people of the thicket" (q.v.; Q 15:78; 26:176; 38:13; 50:14), is said to refer to the people of Midian (q.v.). Two words *(sidr, ʾathl)* designate plants growing in hell. *Ḍarīʿ* (Q 88:6), a plant with large thorns which no animal would approach —

known to the people of the Hejaz in its dry form — is described as the sole nourishment of the inhabitants of the nether world. The tree of al-Zaqqūm (Q 37:62; 44:43; 56:52), the fruit of which was like the head of devils, is described as the fare of sinners and was evidently known in Arabia for its bitter taste.

Many of these terms and others to be noted now are used in contexts demonstrating the all-powerful nature of God. For example, the word *ḥaṣīd* (Q 10:24) is used in the sense of "stubble" to describe the formerly fertile fields destroyed by God to punish the owners' presumption that they had control. In Q 56:65 (also 57:20) the word *ḥuṭām,* "dried straw," describes what God could do to fields in a similar instance. Plants, including fruit *(fākiha),* herbage *(abb)* and seeds *(ḥabb),* exemplify the benefits of God's creation (Q 80:24-32). A person who expends his property for the sake of God is likened to a seed producing seven ears of corn *(sanābil,* sing. *sunbul)* each of which contains one hundred seeds (Q 2:261). Another passage describes how God revives "bare land" *(al-arḍ al-juruz,* Q 32:27) to produce cereals *(zarʿ).*

Several words and expressions referring to water, a necessity of life, should be mentioned. For water as rain, there are the terms *ghayth* (Q 31:34; 42:28; 57:20), *wābil* (Q 2:265, which also contains the word for dew, *ṭall*), and *wadq* (Q 24:43; 30:48). "The impregnating winds" *(al-riyāḥ lawāqiḥ,* Q 15:22) are so called because they are cloud-bearing winds which cause rain to fall. Underground water comes from springs (*yanbūʿ,* Q 17:90, pl. *yanābīʿ,* 39:21; *ʿayn,* 88:12, dual *ʿaynān,* 55:50, pl. *ʿuyūn,* 26:57) and appears in the phrase "water running underground" *(māʾuhā ghawran,* Q 18:41; cf. 67:30). By far the most common word is simply "water" *(māʾ)* employed in the frequent expression "[God] sent down water from the sky" *(anzala min al-samāʾ māʾ).* This expression occurs twenty-six times and in another nine instances the word "water" appears in a similar context. The following verse may be considered the key passage which captures both this expression and a number of the plant terms already noted:

God is the one who sent down water from the sky and with it we brought forth all manner of plants *(nabāt)* and foliage *(khaḍir)* from which we bring forth clustered seed *(ḥabb);* and from the flowering date palm *(al-nakhl min ṭalʿihā)* [come] accessible clusters of the fruit *(qinwān).* [We also brought forth] gardens *(jannāt)* planted with grapes *(aʿnāb),* olives *(zaytūn)* and pomegranates *(rummān),* in many similar and distinct varieties. When they blossom, look to the fruit *(thamar)* when they bear fruit and ripen. These are surely signs for people who believe (Q 6:99).

Drawing upon what has been already said, it is possible to correct an image which has been present in Western scholarship at least since C.C. Torrey submitted his doctoral dissertation, *The commercial-theological terms in the Koran* (published in Leiden in 1892), to the University of Strasburg at the end of the last century. In this brief work, Torrey asserted that, while in the Hebrew Bible and the New Testament commercial-theological terms are found only "as occasional figures of speech," in the Qurʾān they are not used to adorn certain facts, but rather are "terms regularly employed to state the bare and blunt facts themselves" (p. 7). These qurʾānic "facts" then produce a theology governed by the predominating "business atmosphere" (sic, p. 3) of the Qurʾān: "The mutual relations between God and man are of a strictly commercial nature. Allāh is the ideal merchant... Life is a business for gain and loss. He who does good or evil work ("earns" good or evil), receives his pay for it, even in this life. Some debts are forgiven, for Allāh is not a hard creditor...." (p. 48). The commercial background of the rise of Islam has been treated in the established biographies of the Prophet Muhammad by W.M. Watt and M. Rodinson and examined closely in the more recent rebuttal of Watt's argument by P. Crone in her *Meccan trade* (Princeton 1987). Whatever the actual complex of forces at work in the historical background of the Qurʾān, the text offers a dominant motif quite distinct from Torrey's "commercial theology." This motif, while addressed to actual human experience is at once rich in theological meaning and goes to the core of the qurʾānic message. The theological import of passages like the one cited above is that the life cycles of the natural world, of plants and animals, are governed by the divine gift of water which an equally dependent humankind should acknowledge with appropriate expressions of gratitude (Q 34:15). On the other hand, the secular significance of the numerous references to agriculture, vegetation and animal husbandry in the Qurʾān will be better understood as our knowledge of these subjects related to central Arabia in the early centuries of the common era is enriched. We turn now briefly to the background against which the qurʾānic text may be set.

The origins of agriculture

In the generations following the Prophet's death, Islam became the newly-established religion in the very lands where, as is now almost universally accepted, the origins of agriculture had begun several millennia earlier. The food-producing revolution of the post-Pleistocene era (from about 9,000 B.C.E.) occurred in the great arc of hills stretching from Palestine and western Jordan, through southeastern Turkey, northern Iraq and thence down through western Iran. The revolution was decisive for the subsequent emergence of urban civilization for "with the domestication of plants and animals... vast new dimensions for cultural evolution suddenly became possible" (Braidwood, The agricultural revolution, 71). The earlier hunting-gathering way of life slowly yielded to the development of settled villages, although this did not immediately entail the adoption of agriculture or the total abandonment of former ways of food collection. Sedentation, however, did lead to an increase in population, which caused an increased demand for food. This could not be met through hunting and gathering in a village and its immediate environs. At this time, the implements for reaping the grains of wild grasses, grinding stones for their preparation for cooking and storage facilities already existed. With the use of stored grain to raise cereal crops, the area given over to cultivated plants gradually increased and the time devoted to the older methods of food gathering decreased (Reed, *Origins*, 543-67, 941-4). The rise of towns and cities in the arid and semi-arid region of the Middle East was accompanied — in places, perhaps, preceded — by the emergence of new techniques for marshalling the water resources, of both river and rain, for more intensive and extensive cultivation of food crops. Irrigation took different forms in different areas, including the flood and natural flow methods of irrigation; the use of manual hydraulic devices *(shādūf, sāqiya)* and waterwheels *(nāʿūra, dūlāb)* and the construction of surface and underground water channels of Iran *(qanat, kārīz)* and the systems in Arabia *(ghayl, falaj)*. It is known that all of these hydraulic machines had long been in use before the rise of Islam, although the questions of their origin and diffusion have yet to be resolved.

Archeological knowledge of Arabia has

grown more slowly than that of the thoroughly-explored regions of Iraq, Egypt and Iran. The ancient hydrological systems of Arabia have only recently begun to be investigated. Nevertheless, it is now clear that early settled life differed considerably from the stereotype of the nomad and the desert tent-dweller. The Yemen, long regarded as the center of trade, possessed an agricultural system almost entirely dependent upon irrigation. Although there is only a single possible reference to the artificial control of water in the Qur'ān (Q 34:16, which may refer to the Mārib Dam, the remains of which lie approximately 135 km. east of San'a; see AL-'ARIM), it is evident that sophisticated systems for the catchment, storage and distribution of water existed from early times in other areas of the peninsula, suggesting that Arabia should also be considered a "hydrological society," like Iraq and Egypt, where settlement was dependent upon hydraulic constructions. "One of the most characteristic settlement patterns throughout Arabia is the concentration of the main built-up area on a rocky outcrop surrounded by a cultivated flood plain" (Costa, Notes on traditional hydraulics, 264). See ARCHAEOLOGY AND THE QUR'ĀN.

Commentary on selected passages

The prophetic ḥadīth, the qur'ānic commentaries and similar works assign secular and religious significance to many of the words and phrases noted above in the first section. Al-Bukhārī (d. 256/870), for example, in the section of his ḥadīth collection concerned with qur'ānic exegesis provides a lexicographical explanation for three terms in Q 55:12, *'aṣf, rayḥān* and *ḥabb*. He says *'aṣf* is the stem of cereal plants which have been cut before reaching full maturity and *rayḥān* is the residual product after the *ḥabb* (seed) has been extracted for consumption. Al-Bukhārī also adds other definitions from mainly unnamed sources which do not always prove helpful. Certain authors, he says, claim that the *'aṣf* is the consumable part of the cereal, another says it is the leaf of the plant and yet another that it is the straw. Further in the same sūra, Q 55:68 reads, "Therein are fruit *(fākiha)*, date palms *(nakhl)* and pomegranates *(rummān)*." Al-Bukhārī comments that the odd overlapping of "fruit" and "pomegranates" can be explained by reference to Q 2:238, which reads "observe the prayers and the middle prayer," the repetition of "prayer" being added for emphasis.The nearly-contemporary exegesis of al-Ṭabarī (d. 310/923) is much more extensive than that of al-Bukhārī. In dealing with the vocabulary of the plant kingdom, his approach is also lexicographical, citing ḥadīth as evidence in his own exposition. However, glossing the passage cited above (Q 6:99), beginning, "God is the one who sent down water from the sky," al-Ṭabarī writes, "With the water we sent down from the heavens, we produced nourishment for cattle, beasts, birds and wild animals and sustenance and food for human beings" (*Tafsīr*, vii, 292). He concludes that creation contains "proofs, a demonstration and an illustration" for "those who affirm the unity of God and rate him as all-powerful" (*Tafsīr*, vii, 296).

The eighth/fourteenth century commentator Ibn Kathīr (d. 774/1372) adds nothing of substance to al-Ṭabarī's discussion of this particular passage. He is, however, more expansive than al-Ṭābarī in his commentary on Q 2:21-2, where the divine gift of rain which brings forth fruits *(thamarāt)* as sustenance for humankind is also mentioned. God's unity, divine power and blessings, both manifest and hidden, are all expressed here and the meaning of the phrase "[Your Lord] is the one who made the earth a place of repose for you and the heavens a protecting edifice" (Q 2:22) is explained by reference to other qur'ānic passages (e.g. Q 21:32; 40:64). What particularly interests Ibn Kathīr in the passage is the command, "Do not set up rivals *(andād)* to God," for which he adduces a number of references in the ḥadīth collections supporting the prohibition. A man once said to the Prophet, "What God has willed, and what you have willed." The Prophet reproached him, saying, "Have you set me up as a rival to God? Say, 'What God wills,' and nothing else." Associating peers or rivals with God is pure polytheism (*shirk*, see BELIEF AND UNBELIEF). A tradition from Ibn ʿAbbās describes "polytheism" as undetectable "as an ant crawling over a black rock in the dead of night." Ibn Kathīr's exegesis stresses, on the one hand, the absolute singularity of God, a point Jews, Christians and even Muslims tended to forget in practice, despite the common acknowledgement in their scripture of one, sole divine being. On the other hand, using an earthy analogy that "droppings (in the desert) indicate the presence of a camel," Ibn Kathīr stresses how the divine existence and unity are mirrored in the multiplicity of God's creation (q.v.), that is the "signs (q.v.)," including the heavens, the earth and all that comes forth from them such as the life-giving rain which supports the plant kingdom upon which the existence of the humans and animals depends. It should be noted that, differences in presentation aside, al-Ṭabarī's commentary on Q 6:99 and that of Ibn Kathīr on Q 2:21 are in essential agreement in their view of the nature of God as demonstrated in creation.

Scriptural insistence, therefore, on observing God's signs in the natural world as proof of his existence, unity, power and beneficence, was seconded by the commentators who further affirmed the need to use the mind in pursuit of the truth. Al-Bayḍāwī (d. 685/1282), for example, commenting on Q 2:164, which concerns God's signs for people with understanding, adds that this verse provides instruction as well as a "stimulus for the pursuit of research and study." Developing John Burton's schema of the three broad sources of exegesis — tradition, reason and intuition — which illuminate the meaning of the qurʾānic text, a further indirect and pragmatic method of exegesis was the investigation of the "signs" which serve to confirm the truth of the text. In the early centuries of Islam, this stimulated an impulse toward the collection and dissemination of information on plants in general and agriculture in particular. This concern, traced in the following sections, is reflected in a rich agronomic literature and in the medieval "green revolution" which fostered the study and diffusion of new plants westward across the Islamic domains.

Ibn Waḥshiyya and al-Filāḥa al-Nabaṭiyya

During the vigorous translation movement of the early ʿAbbāsid period (late eighth to late tenth century C.E.), there was evident interest in agronomic, and indeed botanical, works. Among the ancient geoponic works known to the Arabs was one by Apollonius of Tyana (not Anatolius of Berytos as once thought), which was translated under the title *Kitāb al-Filāḥa* in 179/795. The *Georgica* of Cassianus Bassus was translated first into Pahlavi and then into Arabic in 212/827 as *al-Filāḥa al-Rūmiyya*. The most outstanding of these treatises, however, was *al-Filāḥa al-Nabaṭiyya*, "Nabatean [i.e. Syriac] Agriculture," attributed to Abū Bakr b. Waḥshiyya. The author — whose identity has been disputed — claims that he translated it from the "ancient Syriac," the Aramean dialect of the Kasdān community of Iraq, in 291/903 and then dictated the translation to a disciple in 318/930. If for no other reason, the work is remarkable for its sheer size, the author saying that the original ran to around fifteen hundred folios. The work appears to have been compiled in a milieu where Alexandrian Hellenism and gnosticism still survived and where neither Judaism nor Christianity had much influence, suggesting an era prior to the fifth century C.E. While the work reflects Hippocratic medical principles and certain aspects of Dioscorides' *Materia medica,* it may also represent a tradition independent of the latter. Furthermore, it seems to have no connection with the Arabic botanical writing which had already appeared prior to Ibn Waḥshiyya's translation. Indeed, it presents a far more varied range of plant life than that found in Akkadian sources: more than 360 plants, with special attention given to the olive tree, the vine and the date palm, indicating their essential place in the agricultural activities of the region. In comparison with known Greek geoponic works, *al-Filāḥa al-Nabaṭiyya* is more developed, dealing with matters both practical and theoretical. In short it represents a kind of "philosophy" of humankind's relationship with the soil. The text's editor Toufic Fahd has argued that *al-Filāḥa al-Nabaṭiyya* presents a picture of the state of knowledge of agriculture, botany and the rural and domestic economy in Iraq at the end of the Hellenistic era (Matériaux pour l'histoire, 276-379).

The opening chapters of *al-Filāḥa al-Nabaṭiyya* are dedicated to the olive tree, its benefits, the places where it best grows and the properties of its various components such as the leaves, roots, the oil and pits of the fruit. At one point the text says that "concerning all these matters, some [information] came to us by experience *(tajriba)* and some by revelation *(waḥy)* from the gods to our forefathers... some by inspiration *(ilhām)* to us and to the idols who in turn instructed us... all of which we put to the test and thus were able to judge the soundness of the best practice... for which we are grateful to [the gods]" (i, 49). The contrast with the monotheistic spirit of the Qurʾān is evident. It is similar, however, to the response of gratitude found in the qurʾānic verse, "Vegetation comes forth from good earth with the permission of its Lord, while from bad land it comes forth with difficulty; thus do we expound the signs to a people who are grateful" (Q 7:58). Indeed, the pagan Nabatean text translated well into the monotheistic Islamic context as it provided a rich catalog of the gifts of the divine economy. Inserted in a lengthy and largely theoretical discourse on how to manage an agricultural estate — complemented by a discussion of the principles of procreation and generation — is an agricultural calendar which lists the activities occurring each month of the year (i, 218-41). This is the earliest example of the genre in Arabic and may be compared with later works from al-Andalus and the Yemen.

As stated above, detailed attention is given to the olive tree, the vine and the date palm, the first and last of the trio forming the opening and closing sections of the work. The three plants are also grouped together in two qurʾānic passages, Q 16:11 and 80:28-9, signaling the importance of the triad. Apart from this, the bulk of the work is devoted to a wide range of other edible plants, the names for many of which the translator was obliged to leave in transliteration as he could find no Arabic equivalents.

Following the section on the olive, cereals are the next group of plants treated. Wheat and barley are discussed at greatest length, as both had played a major role in the Mesopotamian diet for several millennia. Rice and sorghum *(dhura)* are also noted among many other grains. Various aspects of cereal culture are discussed: the appropriate location for growing; the season and atmospheric conditions required for a good crop; the procedures for harvesting, threshing, winnowing and storing the grain and the means of testing whether the grain is beginning to deteriorate.

In sum, the spirit of *al-Filāḥa al-Nabaṭiyya* may be expressed in words not so distant from the qurʾānic passages cited earlier, save for the absence of the single divine agent:

> Agriculture is a source of plant life whose nutritional benefits are the very foundation of [human] life... Plants have also medicinal value, dispelling pains, ailments and illnesses... Furthermore, our clothes which conceal our nakedness and protect our bodies from the dangers of heat and cold also come from [cultivated] plants (i, 702).

Later agronomic works: Egypt, Yemen, Syria

No surviving agronomic work matches the encyclopedic breadth and detail of *al-Filāḥa al-Nabaṭiyya*. The manual of Ibn Mammātī (d. 606/1209), *Kitāb Qawānīn al-dawāwīn*, contains information on the farming practices in his native Egypt. In the beginning of the eighth/fourteenth century, the Egyptian Jamāl al-Dīn Muḥammad b. Yaḥyā al-Waṭwāṭ (d. 718/1318) produced another work on agriculture, in which he frequently cites Ibn Waḥshiyya. Later in the same century, the Yemeni Rasūlid sultans al-Malik al-Ashraf ʿUmar (d. 696/1296) and al-Malik al-Afḍal al-ʿAbbās b. ʿAlī (d. 778/1376) wrote agricultural treatises. To al-Ashraf's brother al-Malik al-Muʾayyad Dāwūd is attributed another book on agriculture now lost. These almanacs provide a basis for reconstructing the agricultural activities throughout the year. In the almanac of al-Malik al-Ashraf, it is clear that the dominant crop in the Yemen was sorghum, some twenty-two different varieties of which — distinguished chiefly by color — are listed. Indeed, the common term for sorghum was simply "food" *(ṭaʿām)*. There is evidence of Ibn Waḥshiyya's influence on this Yemeni "school," although its nature and degree have yet to be determined precisely. Although there is the eighth/fourteenth-century *Miftāḥ al-raḥā li-ahl al-filāḥa* (ed. M. Ṣāliḥiyya) by an unknown author, likely a Syrian, it is in the far west of the Islamic domains, in al-Andalus, that the tradition of agronomic writing continued with vigor and novel contributions of its own.

The agricultural revolution and the Andalusian "school" of agronomy

In the first half of the fourth/tenth century, Dioscorides' *Materia medica* became known in al-Andalus, stimulating an interest in botany and pharmacology, which were allied to the development of agronomy. The so-called *Calendar of Cordoba* of ʿArīb b. Saʿīd (d. 370/980) contains data on arboriculture and horticulture, reflecting local knowledge and custom. ʿArīb may have also written a treatise on agriculture and, if this is correct, it would have been the first of its kind in al-Andalus. From the end of the fourth/tenth century, an agronomic treatise of unknown authorship has survived entitled *Kitāb fī tartīb awqāt al-ghirāsa wa-l-maghrūsāt* (ed. A. Lopez) with contents similar to those of the *Calendar*, complementing that work with an important section on the cultivation of ornamental plants.

These activities were undoubtedly fostered by another factor, which A. Watson in 1983 called "the agricultural revolution" in his important and controversial book *Agricultural innovation in the early Islamic world*.

At the heart of this revolution was the diffusion of new crops westward from India and Persia through the Arab lands to the Iberian peninsula during the early centuries of Islamic expansion and consolidation. Watson examines in detail sixteen food crops and one fiber crop as part of this process of diffusion. In most cases, diffusion meant the acclimatization of plants native to a humid tropical environment to a Mediterranean climate. Diffusion was accompanied by changes in farming practices. The development of summer crops and more intensive and extensive land exploitation were made possible by a combination of the use of more varied types of soil, the more widespread application of a different kind of manure, improvements in irrigation and changes in landholding size and fallow practices. Watson's critics have challenged certain of his conclusions, while confirming others. The overall impression remains that during the first Islamic centuries there was indeed a greatly renewed interest in agriculture, including horticulture and arboriculture, with a corresponding rise in food production, which made possible the rise of new urban cultures throughout the Middle East. In al-Andalus, a concomitant development was the appearance of experimental botanical gardens, generally founded by rulers, where new plants were grown and old varieties improved. A more precise picture of the process and scope of this "green revolution" will be gained only when a thorough study of the agronomic treatises is closely integrated with an examination of works of the botanical, medical (especially dietetic) and culinary traditions.

By the fifth/eleventh century, *al-Filāḥa al-Nabaṭiyya* was not only known in al-Andalus, but was a factor in the emergence of what Garcia Sanchez has called the "Andalusian school of agronomy," which continued uninterrupted into the seventh/thirteenth century. Andalusian agronomic writing culminated in the works of several individuals in different cities spanning the fifth/eleventh century to the seventh/thirteenth. First are the Toledans Ibn Wāfid (d. 466/1074) and Ibn Baṣṣāl (d. 499/1105), the latter's treatise being based upon his personal experience. Ibn al-Ḥajjāj of Seville wrote his work in 466/1074. The work of the Granadan botanist al-Ṭighnarī (fl. fifth/eleventh-sixth/twelfth century) has yet to appear in a printed edition. A contemporary of al-Ṭighnarī and a personal acquaintance of Ibn Baṣṣāl, Abū l-Khayr of Seville, also made a significant contribution. The great successor and synthesizer of this "school" was the Sevillian Ibn al-ʿAwwām, who lived between 512/1118 and 663/1265. He left the most extensive of all the Andalusian works, *Kitāb al-Filāḥa*. Its contents, covering agriculture and animal husbandry, are selected from eastern and Andalusian texts, supplemented by the author's own experimental practice. Finally, the cycle ends with Ibn Luyūn (d. 750/1349) of Almeria, who wrote a lengthy poem *(urjūza)* on agronomy. The sources employed by these Andalusian scholars, the relationship between the authors and the precise nature of the influence of the classical geoponic tradition have been subject to much recent investigation and debate. Compared with certain classical works translated into Arabic — such as the one sometimes attributed to Anatolius of Berytos — the Andalusian texts appear far more developed and sophisticated. They frequently exhibit both a theoretical and practical outlook and project the authors' collective conviction that agriculture was "the basis of subsistence for men and animals... [allowing for] the preservation of life and the sustaining of the spirit" (al-Ṭighnarī) and that it was "a well-founded science, a divine gift and a great recompense" (Abū l-Khayr).

Conclusion

In the works of qurʾānic commentary, the significance of the plant kingdom within the natural world is explained as an aspect of the Creator's unique, all-powerful, beneficent nature. In their broadest sense, the "signs" of creation are the keys to the comprehension of the divine reality. The works dedicated to agriculture are by extension the exploration of the signs themselves, the types of land, plants, climatic conditions and the like, a proper understanding of which could maximize for human society the benefit of the divine gifts. The relationship between these two literatures is suggested by the stimulus to learning of the "green revolution" in the early Islamic centuries which gave scope for the practical examination of plants and agricultural techniques documented in the agronomic texts. Taken together in this way, the works of the commentators and agronomists are complementary and illustrate that the proposition that God's creatures are both determined and yet free (see FREEDOM AND PREDESTINATION) is only an apparent contradiction in the thought of medieval scholars such as al-Ghazālī (d. 505/1111). That is, humankind is determined by the divine nature's creative act, but free to explore and exploit the natural world for its own greater benefit. See also FOOD AND DRINKS.

David Waines

Bibliography

Primary: Abū l-Khayr, *Kitāb al-Filāḥa,* ed. and trans. J.M. Carabaza, *Tratado de agricultura,* Madrid 1991; Arīb b. Saʿīd, *Le calendrier de Cordoue de l'anné* 961, ed. and trans. C. Pellat, Leiden 1961; Ibn al-ʿAwwām, *Kitāb al-Filaḥā,* L.J.A. Banqueri (ed. and trans.), *Libro de agricultura,* 2 vols., Madrid 1802; Ibn Baṣṣāl, *Kitāb al-Qaṣd wa-l-bayān,* J.M. Millas Vallacrosa and M. Aziman (eds. and trans.), *Libro de Agricultura,* Tetuan 1955; Ibn al-Ḥajjāj, *al-Muqniʿ fī l-filāḥa,* ed. S. Jirār and J. Abū Ṣāfiyya, Amman 1402/1982; Ibn Luyūn, *Tratado de agricultura,* ed. and trans. J. Eguaras, Granada 1975; Ibn Mammātī, *Kitāb Qawānīn al-dawāwīn,* ed. ʿA.S. ʿAṭiyya, Cairo 1943, trans. D. Waines, *Ibn Mammātī's rules for the ministries. Translation with commentary of the Qawānīn al-dawāwīn,* Berkeley 1973; Ibn Wāfid, *al-Muqniʿ fī l-filāḥa,* trans. J.M. Millas Vallicrosa, La traduccion castellana del "Tratado de Agricultura" de Ibn Wāfid, in *Andalus* 8 (1943), 281-332; Ibn Waḥshiyya, *Al-Filāḥa al-Nabaṭiyya,* trans. T. Fahd, *L'agriculture nabateenne. Traduction en arabe attribuée à Abū Bakr Aḥmad b. ʿAlī al-Kasdānī, Ibn Waḥshiyya,* 2 vols., Damascus 1993-5; A.C. Lopez (ed. and trans.), *Kitāb fī tartīb awqāt al-ghirāsa wa-l-maghrūsāt. Un tratado agricola andalusi anónimo,* Granada 1990; M.ʿI. Ṣāliḥiyya and I.Ṣ. al-ʿAmad (eds.), *Miftāḥ al-raḥā li-ahl al-filāḥa,* Kuwait 1984; P. Sbat, L'ouvrage geoponic d'Antolius de Berytos (IVᵉ siècle), in *Bulletin de l'Institut d'Égypte* 13 (1931) 47-54; C. Vázquez de Benito (ed. and trans.), *El manuscrito no XXX de la Colección Gayangos,* Madrid 1974.

Secondary: R.M. Adams, *Land behind Baghdad,* Chicago 1965; L. Bolens, *Agronomes andalous du Moyen Âge,* Geneva 1981; R. Braidwood, The agricultural revolution, in C.C. Lamberg-Karlovsky (ed.), *Old world archaeology. foundations of civilization,* San Francisco 1972; C. Cahen, Le service de l'irrigation en Iraq au debout du XI siècle, in *BEO* 13 (1949-50); id., Notes pour une histoire de l'agriculture dans les pays musulmans, in *JESHO* 14 (1971), 63-8; R. Cooper, Agriculture in Egypt 640-1800, in M. Ulmann, *Handbuch der Orientalistik,* 6/6/1, 188-204; P.M. Costa, Notes on traditional hydraulics and agriculture in Oman, in *World archeology* 14 (1983), 273-95; F.M. Donner, Mecca's food supplies and Muhammad's boycott, in *JESHO* 20 (1977), 249-66; T. Fahd, Matériaux pour l'histoire de l'agriculture en Irak. Al-Filaha n-Nabatiyya, in M. Ulmann, *Handbuch der Orientalistik* 6/6/1, 276-37; id., Al-filāḥa al-nabaṭiyya et la science agronomique arabe, in *Proceedings of the First International Symposium for the History of Arabic Science,* Aleppo 1976; id., Retour à Ibn Waḥshiyya, in *Arabica* 16 (1969), 83-8; id., Conduite d'une exploitation agricole d'apres l'"Agriculture nabateene," in *SI* 32 (1970), 109-28; id., Un traite des eaux dans al-Filāḥa n-Nabaṭiyya, in *La Persia nel Medioeve,* Rome 1971, 277-326; id., Le calendrier des travaux agricoles d'apres al-Filāḥa n-nabaṭiyya, in *Orientalia hispanica,* Leiden 1974, i, 245-72; H. Forbes and L. Foxhall, Ethnoarchaeology and storage in the ancient Mediterranean. Beyond risk and survival, in J. Wilkins et al. (eds.), *Food in antiquity,* Exeter 1995; E. García Gomez, Sobre agricultura arábigoandaluza. Cuestiones bibliograficas, in *Andalus* 10 (1945), 127-46; E. García Sánchez (ed.), *Ciencias de la naturaleza en al-Andalus. Textos y estudios (CNA),* Granada 1990-4, i-iii; id., Agriculture in Muslim Spain, in S.K. Jayyusi (ed.), *The legacy of Muslim Spain,* Leiden 1992, 987-99; id., El tratado agrícola del granadino al-Tignarī, in *Quaderni di studi Arabi* 5-6 (1987-8), 278-91; A.K.S. Lambton, Reflections on the role of agriculture in Medieval Persia, in A.L. Udovitch (ed.), *The Islamic Middle East 700-1900,* Princeton 1981, 283-312; id., Aspects of agricultural organization and agrarian history in Persia, in M. Ulmann, *Handbuch der Orientalistik* 6/6/1, 160-87; D. Oates and J. Oates, Early irrigation agriculture in Mesopotamia, in G. de G. Sieveking et al. (eds.), *Problems in economic and social archaeology,* London 1976, 109-35; C. Reed (ed.), *Origins of agriculture,* The Hague 1977; H. Samarra'i, *Agriculture in Iraq during the 3rd century A.H.,* Beirut 1972; Sezgin, *GAS,* iv, 301-46; M. Ulmann, *Die Natur- und Geheimwissenschaften im Islam [Handbuch der Orientalistik, Suppl. 6/2],* Leiden 1972; D.M. Varisco, *Medieval agriculture and Islamic science. The almanac of a Yemeni sultan,* Seattle 1994; id., Medieval agricultural texts from Rasulid Yemen, in *Manuscripts of the Middle East* 4 (1989), 150-4; D. Waines, Cereals, bread and society: an essay on the staff of life in medieval Iraq, in *JESHO* 30/3 (1987), 255-85; A. Watson, *Agricultural innovation in the early Islamic world,* Cambridge 1983.

Ahl al-Bayt

see FAMILY OF THE PROPHET; PEOPLE OF THE HOUSE

Aḥmad

see MUḤAMMAD

Aḥmadiyya

The Aḥmadiyya Movement in Islam (Urdu *Jamāʿat-i Aḥmadiyya*) is a modern messianic movement. It was founded in 1889 in the Indian province of the Punjab by Mirzā Ghulām Aḥmad (1835-1908) and has become exceedingly controversial within contemporary Muslim circles. Claiming for its founder messianic and prophetic status of a certain kind, the Aḥmadī Movement aroused fierce opposition from the Muslim mainstream and was accused of rejecting the dogma that Muḥammad was the last prophet. Under British rule, the controversy was merely a doctrinal dispute between individuals or voluntary organizations, but when the movement's headquarters and many Aḥmadīs moved in 1947 to the professedly Islamic state of Pakistan, the issue was transformed into a major constitutional problem and the Muslim mainstream demanded the formal exclusion of the Aḥmadīs from the Muslim fold. This was attained in 1974, when the Pakistani parliament adopted a constitutional amendment declaring the Aḥmadīs to be non-Muslims.

Despite the impression which may be gained from anti-Aḥmadī polemical literature, the Aḥmadīs passionately attest that the Qurʾān is a heavenly book of unsurpassable beauty and unquestionable validity which will never be superseded (see INIMITABILITY). They initiated the translation of the Qurʾān into numerous languages and maintain that it is the only scripture (see SCRIPTURE AND THE QURʾĀN) which has suffered no interpolation or corruption (q.v.). Their profound veneration of the Qurʾān has led them to re-interpret the idea of abrogation (q.v.). They claim that whenever abrogation is mentioned in the Qurʾān, it denotes the abrogation of all other religions by Islam rather than the abrogation of early qurʾānic verses by later ones. This implies that all qurʾānic verses have the same validity, a position which undermines the exegetical principle according to which injunctions included in later verses cancel those included in earlier ones. Consequently, they deal in an alternative manner with inconsistencies in the Qurʾān. Instead of following injunctions set forth in "abrogating" verses, they maintain that where there are contradictory statements about a certain issue, one should abide by the verses revealed in circumstances more similar to one's own.

Ghulām Aḥmad used this exegetical method in his reinterpretation of the mandated holy struggle, *jihād* (q.v.). According to his exposition, the verses commanding military struggle were revealed when nascent Islam was in danger of destruction by force. In Ghulām Aḥmad's times, Islam was no longer in danger of military attack, but suffered from defamation by Christian missionaries. Military struggle is therefore unnecessary and Muslims should respond by verbal struggle: they should refute the defamatory statements of their opponents and propagate Islam by preaching.

Two qur'ānic verses are central to Aḥmadī theology. "Jesus, I cause you to die and raise you to myself" (Q 3:55) is taken to mean that Jesus' ascension took place after his death. Coupled with the qur'ānic denial of the crucifixion in Q 4:157, the verses are interpreted to mean that Jesus died a natural death and, contrary to numerous ḥadīths, there will be no second coming. Q 33:40 which describes Muḥammad as "the seal of the prophets" (*khātam al-nabiyyīn,* see PROPHETS AND PROPHETHOOD) is not understood as meaning that he was the last prophet, but that he was "the owner of the seal" without whose confirmation no other prophet may be accepted. The dogma asserting the finality of Muḥammad's prophethood refers, according to the Aḥmadiyya, only to legislative prophets who bring a divinely revealed book of law. Non-legislative prophets like Ghulām Aḥmad whom God sends to revive the law promulgated in the Qur'ān can appear in a Muslim community even after the completion of Muḥammad's mission. A similar idea can be found in the works of the famous Ṣūfī Ibn al-ʿArabī (d. 638/1240) and Ghulām Aḥmad's prophetology may have been inspired by his thought. See also ṢŪFISM AND THE QUR'ĀN.

Yohanan Friedmann

Bibliography

Ghulām Aḥmad, *Ḥaqīqat al-waḥy,* Lahore 1952; id., *Government-i angrēzī awr jihād* [in Urdu], Rabwa 1965; M.D. Ahmad, Die Stellung des Koran in der Ahmadiyya-Theologie (fully documented), in *ZDMG* Suppl. III, 1, Wiesbaden 1977, 319-30; Y. Friedmann, *Prophecy continuous. Aspects of Aḥmadī religious thought and its medieval background,* Berkeley 1989 (extensive bibliography).

Air and Wind

The gases which surround the earth and the motion within these gases. Air is mentioned only twice in the Qur'ān, once as *jaww* and once as *hawā'*. The general word for wind, *rīḥ* and its plural *riyāḥ,* occurs more than thirty times. It is supplemented by a number of terms with significantly fewer attestations denoting specific types of wind.

Air

Of the attestations of air, one is literal, Q 16:79: "Have you not reflected on the birds set in the air *(jaww)* of the firmament, none holds them there other than God. In that, indeed, is a sign for those who believe," referring to the region between heaven and earth where the birds have their place. The other is metaphorical, Q 14:43: "Their hearts are air *(hawā')*," where it is used to emphasize the terror felt by the wicked on judgment day that renders their minds insubstantial and incapable of thought.

Wind

Wind, like the other phenomena of nature, is a sign *(āya)* of God (see SIGNS). It can be either beneficent or destructive. The qur'ānic references to wind give an account of the diverse forms in which it may occur: in the relief it brings from drought by bearing clouds laden with rain to the pastoral steppes and agricultural centers, in blinding sandstorms, in torrential rain and in its benefits and dangers to shipping. Yet however varied and unpredictable it may appear to humankind, wind in the Qurʾān is never arbitrary. It and all its concomitants — whether for good or ill — are in the hands of God and occur as a direct act of his will, whether to reward or punish.

The grammatical structures in which wind occurs and the contexts in which it has a role illustrate this. On most occasions wind is the direct object of God's action: he/we send(s) it (*arsala, yursilūna, arsalnā* [passim]). He uses it to drive (*yuzjī*, Q 17:66; 24:43) clouds and ships (q.v.) and may grant control of it to whomever he wishes. On three occasions it is mentioned that God put it at the disposal of Solomon (q.v.; Q 21:81; 34:12; 38:36). It moves according to God's direction (*taṣrīf al-riyāḥ*, Q 2:164; 45:5). He may still it (*yuskin*, Q 42:33), if he wishes. Only on four occasions is it the subject of a verb: it blows (*tahwī*, Q 22:31), it comes (*jāʾat*, Q 10:22), it blows violently (*ishtaddat*, Q 14:18), it scatters (*tadhrū*, Q 18:45). Thus its role in qurʾānic discourse, in direct speech, narrative, parables, metaphors and oaths alike, is clearly defined as a part of nature under God's command.

Rīḥ may at times express meanings beyond those common in everyday usage of the word "wind" in English. On two occasions it occurs with an extended meaning as in the exclamation of Jacob (q.v.), "I sense the fragrance *(rīḥ)* of Joseph (q.v.)" (Q 12:94), and, "Do not quarrel one with another lest you lose heart and your spirit *(rīḥ)* [i.e. zeal] depart" (Q 8:46). *Rūḥ*, derived from the same root, sometimes expresses a specialized significance of breath considered as air in motion, i.e. the breath of life and spirit. Thus Adam (see ADAM AND EVE) is brought to life by the divine breath God blows into him (Q 15:29; 32:9; 38:72; 66:12) and Jesus (q.v.) is created by the breath or spirit God breathes into Mary (q.v.; Q 19:17; 21:91). In its other attestations, the meanings *rūḥ* bears are conceptually distinct from the English word "wind" and do not fall within the scope of this entry (see SPIRIT).

In addition to *rīḥ* there are a number of words in the Qurʾān indicating winds of various kinds: *ʿāṣif* (Q 10:22) or *ʿāṣifa* (Q 21:81), "a violent wind"; *ḥāṣib* (Q 54:34), "a sandstorm"; *qāṣif* (Q 17:69), "a violent gale"; and *rukhāʾ* (Q 38:36), "a gentle breeze." Moreover, there are a number of words which qualify it adjectivally: *ṣarṣar* (Q 41:16; 54:19; 69:6), meaning "searing cold," if the root is associated with *ṣirr* (Q 3:117), or "terrible clamor," if associated with *ṣarra* (Q 51:29); *ʿātiya* (Q 69:6), "violent"; and *ʿaqīm* (Q 51:41), "stifling." On one occasion the verb *tanaffasa* (Q 81:18), "to breathe," is used to designate the tremulous stirring of the air before dawn.

As a divine gift

Wind is a gift of God and an integral part of the interlocking complex of blessings (see BLESSING) he bestows on humankind by which he reveals himself as Lord and Benefactor. Above all, it is a bearer of God's mercy. Its role is epitomized in Q 7:57: "It is he who sends the winds as dispersers/heralds *(nashran* [or *nushuran* or *nushran*]*/bush*[*u*]*ran)* of his mercy until when they bear clouds heavy with rain, We guide them to a land dead [in drought]. By them do we send down water, and by them do we bring forth fruits of every kind. Just so do we bring forth the dead. On this then should you reflect." Attention should be drawn to the alternative readings of "dispersers" and "heralds" (see READINGS OF THE QURʾĀN). Modern commentators, like Rashīd Riḍā (1865-1935), prefer "heralds." This is now widely regarded as canonical thanks to the prominent status of the

"Egyptian" edition of the Qurʾān and tacitly accepted as such by most translators. Al-Ṭabarī (d. 310/923), however, states explicitly his dislike of this recitation, preferring "dispersers" *(nashran* or *nushuran)*. He says that the Bedouin use *"nashr"* (or its alleged dialectal variant *nushr*) for "the nice, soft, diminishing winds which spawn clouds." He accepts the same recitation in Q 25:48 and 27:63 (*Tafsīr,* viii, 209). In this he is followed by al-Zamakhsharī (d. 538/1144), al-Rāzī (d. 606/1209), al-Bayḍāwī (d. ca. 700/1301) and others for whom the verse is a *locus classicus* for excursuses on wind in the divine economy. For these exegetes, the winds are "dispersers" of God's mercy (q.v.). They gloss "mercy" as "rain." It is by the rain that God revives the dead earth, just as he will raise the dead on judgment day. It is not a coincidence that the word *"nashr"* also refers to the raising of the dead at the resurrection (q.v.). It must be noted, however, that in a similar context (Q 30:46) the winds are described as "heralds" *(mubashshirāt),* without any recorded variant recitation.

In addressing Q 7:57, al-Rāzī (*Tafsīr,* vii, 143-51) presents a number of excursuses which establish a frame of reference for discussion of wind in the Qurʾān. He quotes Ibn ʿUmar (d. 73/693) to the effect that there are eight terms for wind in the Qurʾān, four of them designating winds sent as punishment — *qāṣif,* "violent gale"; *ʿāṣif,* "violent wind"; *ṣarṣar,* "searingly cold"; and *ʿaqīm,* "stifling" — and four as tokens of mercy — *nāshirāt,* "restoring to life"; *mubashshirāt,* "heralding"; *mursalāt,* "sweeping in succession"; and *dhāriyāt,* "raising dust."

The exegetical tradition highlights various aspects of the character and function of the wind in the Qurʾān, which can be enumerated as follows: 1. It fecundates the clouds: "We send the fecund wind. We send water down from the sky and give it to you to drink. It is not you who store it" (Q 15:22). 2. God shows his power by directing it: "The alternation of night and day, the water God sends down from the sky by which he revives the earth after its death and the directing of the winds are signs for a people who understand" (Q 45:5). 3. It brings rain: "It is God who sends the winds, stirs up the clouds and extends them in the sky as he wills and sunders them. You see the rain pour down from within them. He makes it fall on whichever of his servants he wills" (Q 30:48). 4. It is one of the signs of the resurrection: "It is God who sends the winds and stirs up the clouds. We drive [the clouds] to a dead land, and by them we revive the earth after its death. Like this is the resurrection...." (Q 35:9). 5. It drives ships across the sea: "We have honored mankind and carried them on the land and sea" (Q 17:70).

Such images occur throughout the Qurʾān and a majestic array of God's signs is given in Q 2:164. They include creation (q.v.) itself, the alternation of night and day, the ships moving swiftly through the sea, the rain reviving the dead earth, the clouds poised between heaven and earth and the winds that bear them. Yet no matter how many blessings the wind is instrumental in bringing, there are many who do not believe (see BELIEF AND UNBELIEF). Q 30:51 states that, even if God were to send a wind to turn the greenery of the earth yellow, they still would not believe.

God's control over the wind

As stated above, God grants power over the wind to whomever he chooses. As a reward for Solomon's faithfulness, God gave him the wind to carry him wherever he wished: "[We disposed] the wind to Solomon, a violent one *(ʿāṣifa)*. It moved swiftly at his command to the land on which we had laid our blessing" (Q 21:81). In Q 38:36 we are told how it moved at

Solomon's command as "a gentle breeze" *(rukhā')* and in Q 34:12 how it could carry him a month's journey, every morning and evening. On the other hand, God may withhold it to indicate his displeasure, as in Q 42:32-3: "Among his signs are the ships on the sea like mountains. If he wishes, he stills the wind so the ships rest motionless on its surface. In this are signs for all who are steadfast and grateful."

Wind as a warning

Wind is not always a blessing. The Qur'ān warns: "Can you be sure that he who is in the heaven will not send upon you a sandstorm *(ḥāṣib)?*" (Q 67:17). In Q 17:66-70 sailors are threatened with punishing winds:

> It is your Lord who [by the wind] drives onward *(yujzī)* ships at sea for you, that you may seek of his bounty. He is merciful to you. Whenever harm threatens you at sea, apart from [God] whomever you call upon will be lost. Yet when [God] brings you safely to shore, you turn away. Man is ungrateful. Can you be sure that when you are ashore he will not make a part of the land swallow you up, or send upon you a sandstorm *(ḥāṣib)?* Then you will find none to protect you. Can you be sure that [while you are still at sea] he will not put you in peril yet again, and send upon you a violent gale *(qāṣif)* of wind and drown you because of your ingratitude. Then you will not find for yourselves any support against Us for it.

Similar ideas are developed in Q 10:22, which tells how sailors when in peril from a tempest pray desperately, but once safe on land revert to their evil ways. See also WARNING.

Wind as punishment

Q 33:9 records that a cold wind led to the disintegration of the army of the pagan Meccans who besieged Medina in the Battle of Uḥud (q.v.). Muḥammad and the Muslims are reminded: "When armies came upon you, we sent against them a wind, and armies you did not see." The people of Lot (q.v.) were destroyed by a sandstorm (*ḥāṣib,* Q 54:34) and the people of ʿĀd (q.v.) were annihilated by a searing cold wind *(ṣarṣar),* when they rejected their prophet Hūd (q.v.): "We sent upon them a searing cold wind on a doom-laden day" (Q 41:16; see also 54:19; 69:6). In Q 51:41 this wind is described as stifling *(ʿaqīm)* and in Q 69:6 is a vivid account of its destructive power. It obliterated the community utterly, leaving only the remnants of their dwellings. See also PUNISHMENT STORIES.

In parables

Wind is a component in a number of similes (q.v.) and parables often introduced by expressions such as *mathal* and *ka-annamā,* putting to didactic effect everyday experiences with wind. In Q 3:117 the effort the wicked expend in the life of this world "is like a wind *(rīḥ)* which is biting cold *(ṣirr)* which strikes the tillage of a people who harm themselves and destroys it." In Q 14:18 all the efforts of those who disbelieve are dismissed as nothing more than "ash (see ASHES) blown violently by the wind on a stormy day." Q 18:45 reiterates the point: "[The life of this world] becomes chaff and the wind scatters it." In Q 22:31 the wicked are warned that someone who disbelieves in God is like a person falling from a great height, caught by the wind, "and blown to a remote place."

In oaths

A striking feature of the Qur'ān are the oaths sworn by natural phenomena including the wind to draw attention to and heighten the impact of its message (see OATHS). Of particular beauty is Q 81:18 declaring that the qurʾānic revelations are indeed brought to the Prophet by Gabriel (q.v.): "I swear... by the dawn when it draws its breath *(tanaffasa)*."

The clusters of oaths opening sūras 51 and 77 are of special interest. All the topics of asseveration are suggestive of power and inevitability, like the coming of the judgment day, which they foreshadow. They have particular strength because, as al-Ṭabarī suggests, their meaning is multilayered, which heightens the role of the wind to create a breathtaking impact. Thus in Q 51:1 *dhāriyāt* means "winds raising the dust," but in other contexts can mean "women giving birth." *Ḥāmilāt* in Q 51:2 has the meaning of "winds bearing rain clouds," but it can also mean "pregnant women." *Jāriyāt* in Q 51:3 may be understood, perhaps simultaneously, as "swiftly-moving winds," "ships cutting through the sea" and "stars following their course." Likewise in Q 77:1 *mursalāt* may be "successive surges of wind," as well as "the continuing revelation of the pericopes of the Qurʾān to Muḥammad." *Nāshirāt* in Q 77:3 may be "winds dispersing the rain of God's mercy" (cf. Q 7:57) or "spreaders of the news of the qurʾānic revelation." Wind is inseparable from the layers of meaning discoverable within these words. As each cluster of oaths creates images of "well-arranged and continuous movement" so the wind, as a component of these images, is associated with the coming and violence of judgment day. The sublime pun on *nashr* (dispersing/resurrection) and its derivatives highlights the inevitability and drama of this event.

Conclusion

Wind is part of the great array of signs and gifts that demonstrates God's power and benevolence. It belongs to the regenerative cycle of events that fills the earth with plants that sustain life. It also enables human beings to trade and interact with each other across the earth and is highlighted as one of the signs of the resurrection. In the cosmological sense, air and wind lie between the heavens and the earth. To humankind, wind may be terrifying and uncontrollable. Like all else in nature control over it is in God's hands. It is a symbol of the helplessness of humankind and the power of God. Everything said about it relates directly to human experience and as everything else in nature the Qurʾān presents it in all its diversity as a teacher of ultimate truths to humankind. See also NATURAL WORLD AND THE QURʾĀN.

Anthony H. Johns

Bibliography

Primary: Bayḍāwī, *Anwār;* Rashīd Riḍā, *Manār;* Rāzī, *Tafsīr;* Ṭabarī, *Tafsīr,* ed. A.S. ʿAlī; Zamakhsharī, *Kashshāf.*

Secondary: W.A. Graham, "The winds to herald his mercy" and other "signs for those of certain faith." Nature as token of God's sovereignty and grace in the Qurʾān, in S.H. Lee, W. Proudfoot and A. Blackwell (eds.), *Faithful imagining essays in honor of Richard R. Niebuhr,* Atlanta 1995, 19-37; A. Neuwirth, Images and metaphors in the introductory sections of the Makkan suras, in Hawting and Shareef, *Approaches,* 3-36; F. Rahman, *Major themes of the Qurʾān,* Chicago 1980; Watt-Bell, *Introduction,* esp. chapter 8.

ʿĀʾisha bint Abī Bakr

The woman thought by the majority of Muslims to be the Prophet Muḥammad's favorite wife. Although ʿĀʾisha bint Abī Bakr (d. 58/678) is never explicitly named in the Qurʾān, she was consistently defined with reference to the sacred text in the formation of her historical and symbolic standing in Islamic history. Through ʿĀʾisha, Muslim scholars, who historically were almost exclusively men, struggled with questions central to the formation of communal identity and gender roles. Her persona focused debate and determined the nuances of the Islamic identity in its formative phase. These intertextual exchanges, particularly in the early and classical periods of Islamic history, allowed scholars to establish for Muslim women the parameters of their social behavior, political participation and the feminine models endorsed for them as ideals. In this process, ʿĀʾisha acted as a prism for the focus and refraction of shared and sharply divided Islamic interpretations. At the heart of these significant debates — prompted by her actions as an historically attested figure — was the Qurʾān, the verses of which would be used both to defend and criticize her.

Three pivotal themes invoked important sacred precedents in ʿĀʾisha's depiction: her vindication from adultery (see ADULTERY AND FORNICATION); her participation in the first civil war; and the attempt to idealize her as an exemplary female in relation to Mary (q.v.), the mother of Jesus (q.v.). ʿĀʾisha's role as the wife of the Prophet Muḥammad conferred upon her and her co-wives an exalted status, but also a heightened visibility in the realm of sacred praxis and symbol. These additional responsibilities were outlined in the Qurʾān, which implicitly defined ʿĀʾisha as one of the mothers of the believers: "The wives of [Muḥammad]are the mothers of [the believers]" (Q 33:6), a unique female élite unlike other women (Q 33:32). Special conditions applied exclusively to the wives of the Prophet, including the injunction in Q 33:53 that they stay behind a screen or curtain (*min warāʾi ḥijāb;* see VEIL). All women, including the Prophet's wives, were instructed to wear cloaks (Q 33:59), cover their bosoms and comport themselves with modesty in public (Q 24:31). Yet the Qurʾān makes explicit that the wives of the Prophet were also held to a higher moral standard than other women since the punishment and reward for their acts in this life would be doubled in the hereafter (Q 33:30-1; see REWARD AND PUNISHMENT). In Q 33:33 the wives of the Prophet are specifically enjoined to stay in their houses, a restriction that was ultimately interpreted by religious scholars to include all Muslim women. This verse of the Qurʾān was applied to ʿĀʾisha in her one foray into politics in 11/632, the year after the Prophet's death, and was ultimately extended to all Muslim women over time in order to insure their seclusion from male spheres of public activity.

The accusation of adultery

Sectarian division within the classical Islamic world is nowhere more evident than in the interpretation of the Qurʾān regarding the accusation of adultery made against ʿĀʾisha in 5/627. The most direct linkage of ʿĀʾisha with the Qurʾān, found in Q 24:11-20, does not refer to her directly by name or to the accusation of adultery made against her, historically referred to by Sunnī Muslims as the account of the lie or slander *(ifk)*. Rather, the revelation explicitly concerns the dire punishments for those who spread slander without the four male witnesses required by Q 24:13.

The affair of the lie was celebrated as an example of ʿĀʾisha's divine vindication from the charge of adultery. According to the earliest written Muslim accounts, ʿĀʾisha accompanied the Prophet on a raid against a tribe called the Banū l-Muṣṭaliq. During a rest stop on the journey home, she found that she had lost her necklace and left the encampment to retrieve it. It was assumed by the other members of the party that she had remained seated in her covered litter. So they lifted the howdah on to the back of her camel and left with it. Stranded and alone in the desert, she was eventually found by a young Muslim named Ṣafwān b. al-Muʿaṭṭal al-Sulamī who returned her safely to the Prophet's camp. The enemies of the Prophet claimed that in fact ʿĀʾisha had betrayed her husband with her rescuer before they rejoined the rest of the party, although there were no witnesses to this (Ibn Isḥāq-Guillaume, 493-9). This account — first recorded in written form one hundred and fifty to two hundred years after the events described — represents the narrative frame for the explication of Q 24:11-20, which the majority of Muslims regard as supporting ʿĀʾisha's exoneration from the charge of adultery.

The famed Sunnī exegete al-Ṭabarī (d. 310/923) declared in his qurʾānic commentary on these verses that the people of Islam as a religious community were unanimous on ʿĀʾisha's vindication (*Tafsīr*, xviii, 96). Even as he wrote these unqualified words about this position in his exegesis, he surely knew that Shīʿī commentators, like his fourth/tenth-century contemporary al-Qummī (fl. fourth/tenth century), explicated the same verses quite differently. Al-Qummī stated that they referred not to ʿĀʾisha but to when the Prophet's Egyptian concubine Maryam was slandered, an incident which the author dates to five years later (*Tafsīr*, ii, 99; cf. Majlisī, *Biḥār al-anwār*, xxii, 153-5; M.M. Bar-Asher, *Scripture*, 42-3). These contradictory interpretations reflect both the emergence of contested religio-political identities and the importance of interpretation in recreating the Islamic past. The same revelation might, through sectarian explication, render two quite different readings. The Sunnī majority supported and defended ʿĀʾisha not just as the Prophet's favorite wife but as the daughter of Abū Bakr (q.v.; r. 11/632-13/634), one of the Prophet's closest friends and his successor as head of the Islamic community. Conversely, Shīʿī Muslims rejected and reviled ʿĀʾisha as an enemy of their political and spiritual leader, ʿAlī b. Abī Ṭālib (q.v.; r. 35/656-40/661), in a discourse consistent with their own vision of past events. Indeed, Shīʿī interpretation of these qurʾānic verses opened the way for their designation of ʿĀʾisha as an adulteress, in sharp contrast to the majority Sunnī Muslim vindication and ultimate praise of her chastity.

The sectarian differences between the Sunnīs and Shīʿīs emerged through contested interpretations of the Qurʾān and captured contradictory visions of a shared past as refracted through female as well as male historical figures (see SHĪʿISM AND THE QURʾĀN). The dual interpretations work, in part, because ʿĀʾisha is not explicitly named in the Qurʾān in the verses in question and the name of Maryam, the Copt, is also not present in the sacred text. In interpretation, the commentators attempted to clarify to whom these verses refer and in interpretation there remained latitude for contradictory human readings of the divine revelation and its gendered import. Historicizing such internal debates undermined Islam's claim, articulated by Muslim scholars, to be a monolithic and static truth. Their divisive, co-existent religious interpretations may assume an exclusive right to clarify an eternal and timeless Islam, but these same assertions of exclusivity are undermined by their attachment to a time-bound, very human struggle for definitional control over a shared faith and its political applications. Such fissures, once found, suggest the possibility that the history of an ostensibly religious discourse may reveal precedents for a multiplicity of present-day ideological interpretations of Islam by Muslim women as well as men.

The anthropologist Erika Friedl more recently recorded the voice of one Shīʿī woman from an Iranian mountain village who tells a story of the charge of adultery made against one of the Prophet's wives. Although ʿĀʾisha is not named and the rescuer of the early Arabic account, Ṣafwān b. al-Muʿaṭṭal al-Sulamī, is replaced with an anonymous caravansary owner, the details of this accusation reveal an alternative sectarian reading which eliminates the very existence of the Sunnī heroine and the centrality of divine revelation. Instead, this probably illiterate female Shīʿī interpreter proposes a distinctly human and logical outcome of the tale, which emphasizes the power of rumor and the ever-present threat of divorce in the lives of women, whose chastity (q.v.) is the object of communal gossip.

Although E. Friedl's anthropological work is exemplary, in this instance the broader implications of the modern female narrative remain subsumed within the ethnography. By privileging the voice of her Shīʿī source, the anthropologist did not make the critical contextual connections that characterize this modern interpretation as the distinctive outcome of a contested, exclusively male, classical Sunnī and Shīʿī sacred commentary. The ahistorical presentation suggests an implicit timelessness which undermines the source's gendered distinction in the history of religion. It is not simply an Iranian folktale told to a foreign anthropologist, but rather a modern oral interpretation of the Qurʾān expressed by a Shīʿī Muslim female in a clearly demarcated continuum of Islamic interpretation of the sacred.

The battle of the camel

The battle of the camel in 36/656 was the first military conflict in the first Islamic civil war (Ṭabarī, *History,* xvi, 122-3). Both the Qurʾān and the ḥadīth recording the words and actions of the Prophet were used by authors who, hundreds of years after the bloody conflict, were still trying to make sense of the event. All histories, whether Sunnī or Shīʿī accounts, had to consider the central presence of ʿĀʾisha bint Abī Bakr in this conflict. Her opposition to ʿAlī b. Abī Ṭālib and his partisans *(shīʿa)* was personal, political and ultimately military. Her forces, led by her two allies, were defeated by ʿAlī in his successful bid to defend his position as the fourth leader of the Muslim community after Muḥammad's death.

The central presence of a woman in the struggle for political succession did not escape censure by either the Sunnī or Shīʿī Muslim community. Indeed, although both communities would read this event differently in retrospect, both shared common tactics in their condemnation of ʿĀʾisha. The Sunnī and Shīʿī sources alike utilized the same qurʾānic verses and ḥadīth to buttress their criticism. The verse central to their shared arguments is found in Q 33:33. Specifically directed to the Prophet's wives in the plural, the verse enjoins them: "Stay in your houses." There are no extant written sources contemporary with the first civil war, but ʿĀʾisha is reminded in a later biography that had she stayed at home the carnage of the battle of the camel might not have occurred. Ibn Saʿd (d. 230/845), an early Sunnī biographer, records that, when ʿĀʾisha recited these verses of the Qurʾān years after the event, she wept until she soaked her veil with tears (*Ṭabaqāt,* viii, 81). The Shīʿī chronicler al-Masʿūdī (d. 354/956) allows ʿAlī, his Shīʿī hero and the victor, to reproach ʿĀʾisha directly by reminding her that the Prophet had once revealed that she should stay in her house, a reference to Q 33:33 (*Murūj,* iv, 102-19, nos. 1628-57, esp. no. 1644). Actually, the Qurʾān emphasizes that all of the Prophet's wives should stay, using a plural verb, in their houses, which also appears as a plural, but al-Masʿūdī is not troubled by the grammatical exactitude of the sacred verse. Later Shīʿī sources utilize this same verse of the Qurʾān even more pointedly to condemn ʿĀʾisha's political motives (M.M. Bar-Asher, *Scripture,* 40-1).

Her symbolic presence at the first battle

of the civil war struck a negative universal point of accord between Sunnī and Shīʿī Muslim authors. Through ʿĀʾisha's example, all Muslim women were warned not to leave home or involve themselves in political matters. Traditional lessons derived from the first civil war and the example of the Prophet's wife ʿĀʾisha proved a memorable warning against the future participation of any Muslim woman in politics. Male religious authorities could not have attached such a potent precedent to ʿĀʾisha's actions without their shared citation of the Qurʾān.

The definition of Islamic female ideals

Mary, the mother of the Jesus, whom Muslims regard as a prophet, is the only explicitly named female figure in the Qurʾān. She is highly praised in Q 3:42 as chosen, pure and preferred above all other women of creation. In Q 66:11-2, Mary and the wife of Pharaoh (q.v.), named Āsiya in the Islamic tradition, represent behavioral exemplars for all Muslim believers. Mary's chastity and obedience (q.v.) are particularly extolled in the Qurʾān. In the ḥadīth and qurʾānic exegesis, ʿĀʾisha was often associated with Mary, but never with the latter's divine selection, obedience and chastity. Indeed, references to her tended to underscore the particularly vexed aspects of her historical persona especially those attached to the accusation of adultery and the first civil war. Although ultimately exonerated according to the Sunnī interpretation of the affair of the lie, ʿĀʾisha's chastity remained a point of sectarian confrontation. In this critical controversy over female sexuality, ʿĀʾisha's comparison to Mary implied the accusation of sexual impropriety also lodged in the Qurʾān against the mother of Jesus in Q 19:27-8. Such a parallel established a negative precedent for the idealization of ʿĀʾisha. Her perceived disobedience in the first civil war also allowed scholars to condemn her behavior with reference to the verse Q 33:33, as they were cited in both Sunnī and Shīʿī spheres. Such a political precedent definitively excluded ʿĀʾisha as a potential Muslim female ideal of the obedience extolled in the qurʾānic Mary. Finally, ʿĀʾisha alone would be compared to the most negative female figures in the Qurʾān, the wives of the prophets Lot (q.v.) and Noah (q.v.), who are characterized in Q 66:10 as examples for unbelievers. Their refusal to obey their husbands became a Shīʿī criticism directed at ʿĀʾisha, their disobedient equivalent in her refusal to follow the instructions of Q 33:33.

Ultimately, examining ʿĀʾisha's legacy, unlike that of the women chosen as the most exalted of the first Muslim community, reveals that her depiction consistently aroused conflicting responses within the Muslim community. In Sunnī support or Shīʿī criticism, the qurʾānic precedents of both positive and negative female figures were applied to ʿĀʾisha alone. Although praised by Sunnīs, ʿĀʾisha defied categorization as absolutely positive or negative in the Muslim search for her meaning. The interpretation of her active, controversial life revealed that the process of idealization in Islamic history would never admit her into the realm of perfection. Thus, while Islamic tradition asserted that there were no perfect women except Mary and the wife of Pharaoh in Q 3:42, these two in qurʾānic exegesis would ultimately be joined by the Prophet's first wife, Khadīja (q.v.) bint Khuwaylid (d. 619 C.E.) and their daughter Fāṭima (q.v.; d. 11/632). The consistently positive, unchallenged portrayals of these women established, through direct parallels to the qurʾānic Mary, their centrality as Islamic female models. Both Khadīja and Fāṭima represented an idealized vision of the feminine on which both Sunnī and Shīʿī Muslims ultimately agreed.

As further idealized within Shīʿī texts,

Fāṭima finally transcended the precedent of Mary in the Qurʾān and challenged the Sunnī majority to defend ʿĀʾisha, not as an ideal female figure, but as one whose reputation was diminished by contrast. The impact of the dichotomy depicted between ʿĀʾisha and Fāṭima ultimately raises questions about the reaction of Muslim women to male interpretations of the Qurʾān. Until recently, the reaction of Muslim women to these male constructed ideal females has been missing from the written record. Although it has been argued that real Shīʿī women cannot hope to emulate Fāṭima's sacred transcendence of her own sexuality in the matters of propriety and motherhood, it is no more certain that the precedent of ʿĀʾisha's persona will finally yield a more practical legacy for Sunnī women. Although ʿĀʾisha bint Abī Bakr remains a model for the Sunnī majority especially with regard to her intelligence and prodigious memory in the transmission of the reports about the life of her husband, her biography remains securely attached to the qurʾānic precedent. The control of such sacred interpretations will continue to pose a challenge for those Muslims, whether male or female, who attempt to define ʿĀʾisha's persona as a positive force in the present. See also WIVES OF THE PROPHET; WOMEN AND THE QURʾĀN.

Denise A. Spellberg

Bibliography
Primary: Bukhārī, *Ṣaḥīḥ;* Ibn Ḥanbal, *Musnad;* Ibn Isḥāq, *Sīra;* Ibn Māja, *Sunan;* Ibn Saʿd, *Ṭabaqāt,* ed. I. Abbās; al-Majlisī, M. Bāqir, *Biḥār al-anwār,* Beirut 1403/1983; Masʿūdī, *Murūj,* ed. Pellat; Muslim, *Ṣaḥīḥ;* Nasāʾī, *Sunan;* Qummī, *Tafsīr,* Ṭabarī, *Tafsīr;* id., *Taʾrīkh,* A. Brockett (trans.), *The history of al-Ṭabarī, xvi. The community divided,* Albany 1985-99; Tirmidhī, *Ṣaḥīḥ.*
Secondary: ʿĀʾisha ʿAbd al-Raḥmān, *Nisāʾ al-nabī,* Beirut 1983; N. Abbott, *ʿĀʾisha the beloved of Mohammed,* Chicago 1942; G. Ascha, *Le statut inférieur de la femme en Islam,* Paris 1981; M.M. Bar-Asher, *Scripture and exegesis in early Imāmī Shiism,* Leiden 1999; E.W. Fernea and B.W. Bezirgan (eds.) and S. Spectorsky (trans.), ʿĀʾisha bint Abī Bakr, wife of the Prophet Muhammad, in E. Fernea and B. Bezirgen (eds.), *The Middle Eastern Muslim women speak,* Austin 1977; J.D. McAuliffe, Chosen of all women. Mary and Fāṭima in qurʾānic exegesis, in *Islamochristiana* 7 (1981), 19-28; E. Friedl, *Women of Deh Koh. Lives in an Iranian village,* Washington, D.C. 1989; al-Ṣadda, Hudā, Siyar al-nisāʾ wa-l-humiyya al-thaqafiyya. Namūdhaj ʿĀʾisha bint Abī Bakr, in H. al-Ṣadda et al. (eds.), *Ẓaman al-nisāʾ wa-l-dhākira al-bādila. Majmūʿat abḥāth,* Cairo 1997; G. Schoeler, *Charakter und Authentie der muslimischen Überlieferung über das Leben Mohammeds,* Berlin 1996, 113-63; D.A. Spellberg, *Politics, gender and the Islamic past. The legacy of ʿĀʾisha bint Abī Bakr,* New York 1994; B.F. Stowasser, *Women in the Qurʾān, traditions, and interpretation,* New York 1994.

Ākhira see RESURRECTION; PARADISE; HELL; ESCHATOLOGY

Al-ʿAbbās see FAMILY OF THE PROPHET

ʿĀlamīn see WORLD

Al-ʿArim

The most popular interpretation was that *ʿarim (*sing. *ʿarima)* were dam-like structures designed to hold back flood waters. The words occurs only once in the Qurʾān: "They turned away [from God], so we sent upon them the flood of the dams *(sayl al-ʿarim)* and gave them, instead of their two gardens, two which produced bitter fruit, and tamarisks and a few lote trees" (Q 34:16). Citing other Muslim sources, al-Ṭabarī (d. 310/923) describes the construction of the dams and their destruction after the people of Sheba (Sabā, see SHEBA), who had enjoyed the easiest existence on earth, rejected the thirteen prophets sent to them. According to one account, the

Queen of Sheba, identified in the Islamic tradition as Bilqīs (q.v.), originally built the dams to ensure the fair apportioning of water among her subjects, who had constantly feuded over water rights. Ironically, the mighty structures were brought down by a mouse *(faʾra)* or large rat *(juradh)*. Soothsayers had predicted that the dams would be destroyed by a mouse, so the Shebans stationed cats all over them. When God decreed the destruction of this sinful people, he sent a ferocious mouse — or a large rat — which overpowered one of the cats and penetrated the dam, unbeknownst to the Shebans. When the floods came, the weakened dam was swept away along with the homes and property of the Shebans (*Tafsīr,* xxii, 78-83).

However, there were other interpretations (see, for example, Yāqūt, *Buldān,* iv, 110). According to some, *sayl al-ʿarim* means "a violent flood," while others held that *al-ʿarim* was the name of the valley containing the flood waters. Still others believed that it was the name of the great rat which gnawed through the dam. The famous ḥadīth-collector al-Bukhārī (d. 256/870) put forth an interesting theory. He argued that *ʿarim* was "red water" which was used on the gardens of the Shebans. To punish them, God caused this water to drain so far into the earth that the roots of the plants could no longer reach it. Consequently, the once fertile gardens withered and died. See also ARCHAEOLOGY AND THE QURʾĀN; PUNISHMENT STORIES.

R.G. Khoury

Bibliography
A. Th. Khoury, *Der Koran. Arabisch-Deutsch Übersetzung und wissenschaftlicher Kommentar,* Gütersloh 1991f.; Ṭabarī, *Tafsīr,* ed. A.S. ʿAlī; Yāqūt, *Buldān,* 5 vols., Beirut 1374/1955-1376/1957.

ʿAlawīs see SHĪʿISM AND THE QURʾĀN

Alcohol see INTOXICANTS

Alexander

The Macedonian conqueror who lived from 356 until 323 B.C.E. Traditional and modern scholars have identified the figure the Qurʾān refers to as the Possessor of the Two Horns (Dhū l-Qarnayn, Q 18:83, 86, 94) as Alexander the Great (al-Iskandar in Arabic). His "two horns" may be the east and the west, suggesting breadth of his dominion. Anomalously, some early scholars saw the epithet as reference to a pre-Islamic monarch of south Arabia or Persia. The famous mystic Ibn al-ʿArabī (d. 638/1240) interpreted the figure allegorically, identifying the "Possessor of the Two Horns" as the "heart" ruling the "earth" of the body through the "east" and "west" of its palpitations.

Alexander is the best known qurʾānic figure not actually named in the scripture. In the Islamic tradition, his major roles are those of sovereign, seeker, sage, prophet and "perfect person." By constructing an iron wall to contain Gog and Magog (q.v., Q 18:93-9), Alexander joins the company of both David (q.v.), who could melt iron, and Solomon (q.v.), the only other "Muslim" to rule the globe and who built his temple with the help of the jinn (q.v.). In addition, Alexander defended the world against apocalyptic chaos (cf. Q 21:96-7).

Alexander shares his mysterious notoriety with al-Khaḍir (see KHAḌIR/KHIḌR), whom tradition identifies as Moses' unnamed guide on his search for the confluence of the two seas (Q 18:60-82). Firdawsī's (d. 411/1020) *Shāhnāme* names al-Khaḍir as Alexander's guide in his quest for the fountain (or spring) of life in the Land of Darkness. In fact, Alexander's relationship to al-Khaḍir (also rendered Khiḍr) is strikingly similar to that of Moses to his unnamed guide in sūra 18. Alexander did not reach the fountain, because he became distracted, just as Moses failed in his quest because he asked too many questions. Alexander's other guides in lore are the sage Luqmān (q.v.) and the prophet Elijah (q.v.). The legend that Aristotle tutored Alexander in dream-interpretation further enhanced his status as sage, a theme fully developed in Niẓāmī's (d. early seventh/thirteenth century) Persian romance *Iskandarnāme*.

Alexander's place in the narratives (q.v.) on the prophets *(qiṣaṣ al-anbiyāʾ)* is significant. In commenting on Q 18:83, al-Thaʿlabī (d. 427/1035) allots more space to the "Possessor of the Two Horns" than he accords to at least five other prophets. He says that most authorities identify him as Alexander, who, it is said, descended from Abraham (q.v.) on his father's side. Restating the views recorded by many exegetes, al-Thaʿlabī observes that Alexander was called the "Possessor of the Two Horns" either because he ruled both Greece and Persia; or because, when the prophet summoned his people to belief in one God, they struck one side of his head and then the other in defiance; or because he had two attractive locks of hair that people called horns. Citing a report in which Muḥammad does not know whether the "Possessor of the Two Horns" was actually a prophet, al-Thaʿlabī notes that scholars disagree, some arguing that he was a prophet (*nabī*, see PROPHETS AND PROPHETHOOD) but not a messenger (*rasūl*, see MESSENGER). Al-Kisāʾī (fl. 597/1200) mentions the "Possessor of the Two Horns" only in Jacob's (q.v.) prophecy of a great future king, not identified as Alexander. Alexander reaches the pinnacle of mystical and cosmic apotheosis as the "perfect person" *(al-insān al-kāmil)* in his legendary journey to Mount Qāf, which recalls Muḥammad's ascension (q.v.) into heaven. Confronting his mortality, Alexander gains wisdom enough to spread God's word and become a model of spiritual perfection.

John Renard

Bibliography

Primary: Firdawsī, *The book of kings* (selections), trans. R. Levy, London 1967, 232-50; Ibn al-ʿArabī, *Tafsīr al-Qurʾān al-karīm*, 2 vols., Beirut 1978, i, 773-4; Ibn Kathīr, *Tafsīr*, iii, 163-7; Kisāʾī, *Qiṣaṣ*, trans. W.M. Thackston, *Tales of the prophets*, Boston 1978, 166; Niẓāmī, *Kulliyāt-i khamsa*, Tehran 1351/1972, 839-1338; Qurṭubī, *Jāmiʿ*, xi, 45-54; M. Southgate (trans.), *Iskandarnāmah. A Persian medieval Alexander-romance*, New York 1978; Ṭabarī, *Tafsīr*, xvi, 8-12; Thaʿlabī, *Qiṣaṣ*, 322-32.

Secondary: A. Abel, Dhū 'l-Qarnayn, prophète de l'universalité, in *Annuaire de l'institut de philologie et d'histoire Or. et Slaves* 11 (1951), 6-18; P. Grillon, Le mythe d'Alexandre à travers le roman grec et la tradition islamique, in *Revue historique et de civilization du Maghreb* 3 (1967), 7-28; W.L. Hanaway, *Persian popular romances before the Safavid period*, Ph.D. diss, Columbia 1970; T. Nagel, *Alexander der Grosse in der frühislamischen Volksliteratur*, Waldorf-Hessen 1978.

ʿAlī b. Abī Ṭālib

The cousin of the Prophet Muḥammad and husband of his daughter Fāṭima. ʿAlī b. Abī Ṭālib (d. 40/661) was among the first to embrace Islam and was renowned for his loyalty to the Prophet and his courageous role in a number of the military expeditions in the defense of the early Muslim community. Also known for his piety, his profound knowledge of the Qurʾān and the sunna (the exemplary practice of the Prophet; see SUNNA), he figures prominently in several esoteric traditions in Islam including Ṣūfism (see ṢŪFISM AND THE QURʾĀN).

Shīʿī Muslims — originally "the partisans of ʿAlī" (*shīʿat ʿAlī*, see SHĪʿA) — citing texts from the Qurʾān and the ḥadīth, maintain that on the Prophet's death the temporal and spiritual leadership of the Muslim community should have devolved to ʿAlī, but instead was usurped by other close Companions of the Prophet (q.v.). According to Shīʿī doctrine, ʿAlī as the divinely-designated imām (q.v.) also bore the responsibility for preserving the divine message of the Qurʾān after its revelation. Upon his passing, his direct descendants inherited the imamate, although few of them were able to exercise the powers of their position due to persecution by the rival Sunnī rulers as well as the Sunnī religious establishment.

Early Shīʿī tradition claims that ʿAlī had in his possession an authentic version of the Qurʾān which was rejected by his political opponents among the powerful Meccan tribe of the Quraysh (q.v.). Instead the vulgate commissioned by his rival, the caliph ʿUthmān (q.v.), and purged of the verses naming ʿAlī and the other members of the Prophet's family as the leaders of the community became canonical (see COLLECTION OF THE QURʾĀN). According to the lore of the Twelver (or Imāmī) Shīʿites, the succeeding imāms secretly passed down ʿAlī's copy of the Qurʾān, the contents of which will be revealed to the world by the messianic twelfth imām. Shīʿī views on the nature of ʿAlī's Qurʾān were gradually modified from the fourth/tenth century onwards, when the majority of Shīʿī scholars came to accept the accuracy of the official ʿUthmānic vulgate, disputing only the order of the chapters and verses. ʿAlī's Qurʾān, they believed, while not containing any additional revealed texts, presented the chapters and the verses in the original order of their revelation and held as well his personal notes. This original arrangement and ʿAlī's notes were what subsequent imāms passed on.

Nevertheless, ʿAlī in his capacity as the imām, was held to possess a special knowledge of the inner meaning of the Qurʾān and hence was in a position to engage in hermeneutic interpretation *(taʾwīl)* of the text (see EXEGESIS OF THE QURʾĀN: CLASSICAL AND MEDIEVAL). This divinely endowed knowledge which ʿAlī transmitted to his descendants provided the Shīʿī Imāms with insight into the esoteric aspect *(bāṭin)* of the revelation, thus enabling him to guide the faithful to a truer and more comprehensive understanding of God's guidance to humanity. The Shīʿī imām in the role of the supreme interpreter of God's revelation is often referred to as the "speaking Qurʾān *(al-Qurʾān al-nāṭiq)*, while the text itself is called "the silent leader" *(al-imām al-ṣāmit)*. See also FAMILY OF THE PROPHET; SHĪʿISM AND THE QURʾĀN.

Ali S. Asani

Bibliography
M. Amir-Moezzi, *The divine guide in early Shiʿism*, trans. D. Streight, Albany 1994; J. Eliash, The Šīʿite Qurʾān. A reconsideration of Goldziher's interpretation, in *Arabica* 16 (1969), 15-24; E. Kohlberg, Some notes on the Imamite attitude to the Qurʾān, in S. Stern, A. Hourani and V. Brown (eds.), *Islamic philosophy and the classical traditions*, Oxford 1972, 209-24.

Alif Lām Mīm
see LETTERS AND MYSTERIOUS LETTERS

Alif Lām Rā
see LETTERS AND MYSTERIOUS LETTERS

Allāh
see GOD AND HIS ATTRIBUTES

Al-Lāt
see IDOLS AND IMAGES

Allegiance
see OATHS; PLEDGE

Allegory
see LANGUAGE AND STYLE OF THE QURʾĀN

Alliances see CONTRACTS AND ALLIANCES

Almsgiving

Charitable gifts to relieve the poor. In common with the teachings of most other faiths and more particularly the biblical traditions, the Qurʾān repeatedly emphasizes the moral value of giving. While the term "almsgiving" may suggest a somewhat simple and unfocused act of charity directed at the poor and needy, the Qurʾān articulates through a variety of terms, especially *ṣadaqa* and *zakāt,* a very textured and multivalent conception of giving which draws upon the ideals of compassion, social justice, sharing and strengthening the community. As this act aims at being both a social corrective and a spiritual benefit, it reflects the ethical and spiritual values which are associated with wealth, property, resources and voluntary effort in personal as well as communal contexts. It is in this broader sense that Muslims understand almsgiving and apply it in their daily life.

The perspective of the Qurʾān on sharing wealth and individual resources through acts of giving is rooted in specific essential ideals: 1. the absence of a dichotomy between spiritual and material endeavors in human life, i.e. acts sanctioned as a part of faith are also linked to the daily conditions of life in this world; 2. the nature, purpose and function of the Muslim community as "the best of communities created to do good and to struggle against evil" (Q 3:110); 3. the trusteeship of wealth and property and hence accountability for the way in which they are expended. These ethical perspectives in the Qurʾān, among others, established the basis for what came to be understood as an Islamic form of giving and its moral significance. As the Muslim philosopher Fazlur Rahman (1919-1988) observed in addressing the key ethical concepts of the Qurʾān, "Islam aims necessarily (and not just peripherally or indirectly) at the creation of a world order wherein the imperatives and principles will be embodied in such a way that the "earth shall be reformed" (Some key ethical concepts of the Qurʾān, 182-3). In an essay exploring the use of the qurʾānic term *ḥaqq,* "real" or "true," Clifford Geertz remarks that one finds the identification of the right with the real at all levels of Islamic practice (*Local knowledge,* 189). Other Western scholars of Islamic civilization, including Marshall Hodgson, have made the same point.

Inasmuch as true sovereignty, according to the Qurʾān, belongs only to God, the Prophet, his successors, the members of the community and even the state acted as the instruments by which these ideals were to be translated into practice. Individuals within that society, whom God endowed with a capacity to acknowledge and respond to him were seen as trustees through whom the moral and spiritual vision of the Qurʾān was fulfilled in personal and communal life. They were thus accountable for the way in which they used their resources and their wealth, and they earned religious merit by expending them in a socially beneficial way. While recognizing that individuals were endowed with different abilities, resources and property, the Qurʾān emphasizes the ideal of social solidarity and enjoins justice and generosity (Q 16:90). In particular, it holds up as truly virtuous those who spend their resources to assist others (Q 57:18) and condemns the hoarders of wealth (Q 3:180).

The specific notions of setting aside a portion of one's wealth for others or of recognizing the necessity and value of giving are articulated in the Qurʾān through a number of terms that are often used interchangeably. The most significant of these are *ṣadaqa* and *zakāt*. There are a number of other terms that signify "giving" in the Qurʾān. Forms of the verb *nafaqa* (expend) occur primarily with the sense of expending one's wealth to please God (e.g. Q 2:265). *Khayr* (charity) is another qurʾānic term which describes beneficent and voluntary acts of giving. Individuals are also urged to offer God "a beautiful loan" *(qarḍ ḥasan),* the benefit of which will be multiplied many times over by God's bounty (Q 2:245). Since God is deemed to be the ultimate giver, such offerings are interpreted merely as acts of returning to him what is ultimately his.

Ṣadaqa

While the word *ṣadaqa* and its various forms came to be interpreted in later Muslim religious and legal texts to connote the restricted notion of voluntary — rather than obligatory — giving, *ṣadaqa* and *zakāt* are used interchangeably in a broader sense in the Qurʾān. In the Arabic lexicographical literature, the root *ṣ-d-q* sustains numerous meanings associated with ideas of righteousness and truth. Elsewhere in the Qurʾān, related words, such as *al-ṣiddīq* (truthful, Q 12:46), which is used to describe the prophet Joseph (q.v.), or *ṣadīq* (trusted friend, Q 24:61), reflect this notion of moral excellence. Modern critical scholarship has suggested that the word *ṣadaqa* is linked etymologically to the Hebrew *s^edāḳā* (almsgiving), leading some experts to conclude that it is a loanword (see FOREIGN VOCABULARY).

The application of the term in its various contexts in the Qurʾān develops some of the key themes of the ideal of giving. Q 9:104-5 links God's acceptance of repentance (see REPENTANCE AND PENANCE) with *ṣadaqa,* thus suggesting its value for the expiation of sins. This is further emphasized by the joining of fasting (q.v.) with *ṣadaqa* (Q 2:196), as ways of fulfilling the obligations of a pilgrimage (*ḥajj,* see PILGRIMAGE) not completed because of illness or other reasons. Giving also benefits the givers spiritually as part of their quest to seek the "face of God" (q.v.; Q 2:272). Such a quest is pursued out of love for God (Q 76:8) and may be public or private (Q 2:274). According to the Qurʾān, those who give because they seek the face of God will be truly fulfilled (Q 30:39). An interesting use of *ṣadaqa* occurs in what has come to be called in the exegetical literature *(tafsīr),* the "verse of the audience" (*āyat al-najwā,* Q 58:12), which enjoins the offering of alms before an audience with the Prophet. This suggests that giving alms was viewed as both a way to expiate past sins and display respect, as well as a gesture of recognition of the values embodied by the Prophet, whose own acts of generosity were looked upon as a model for the rest of the followers of Islam.

According to the Qurʾān, words of kindness and compassion are better than *ṣadaqa* coupled with insult (Q 2:263). The donation of alms need not be a gift of material value. It can also consist of voluntary effort (Q 9:79) or merely a kind word (Q 2:263). It is better to offer alms discreetly to those in need rather than for the purpose of public acknowledgement (Q 2:271). The Qurʾān is critical of those who give in order to appear generous or who compromise the value of the act by ostentatious public behavior that serves only to render a normally charitable act purely self-serving (Q 2:264).

It is clear from Q 58:12 that the Qurʾān envisaged a broad framework both for those who might benefit from the more formalized practice that was evolving in the early Muslim community and for the fiscal support of the community's needy. Almsgiving served to benefit the early Muslims who had migrated from Mecca with the Prophet (see EMIGRANTS AND HELPERS). It was also used to encourage others to join the Muslim community and to support the Muslims in the conflict against Mecca. Q 9:60 specifies the types of recipients who ought to benefit from it: those afflicted by poverty; those in need and incapable of assisting themselves; those who act, sometimes in a voluntary capacity, as stewards and custodians to ensure the collection and appropriate expenditure of funds; those whose hearts need to become favorably inclined towards Islam; captives who need to be ransomed; debtors; travelers; and finally those active for the sake of God. All of these categories came to be strictly defined in later legal and exegetical literature. Q 2:273 suggests that the broader uses of *ṣadaqa* were not only to assist the poor but also others who during this period of transition were not visibly in need and who nonetheless either required assistance to enhance their livelihood or needed to be directed towards new occupations and economic opportunities. While one aspect of almsgiving in the Qurʾān was clearly projected towards charitable acts for the poor and the needy, the practice also encompassed the wider goal of applying the donations to improve the general condition and economic well-being of other recipients and constituencies in the growing community *(umma)*.

Zakāt

The word *zakāt* is etymologically linked to *zakā* (to be pure). The Qurʾān joins explicitly the word *zakāt* to other primary acts of belief: "Piety does not consist of merely turning your face to the east or to the west. Rather, the pious person is someone who believes in God, the last day, the angels, the book and the prophets and who out of his love gives his property to his relatives, orphans, the needy, travelers, supplicants and slaves; and who performs the required prayers and pays the *zakāt*" (Q 2:177).

The verb *zakā* suggests the idea of growth to emphasize that the giving of one's resources is simultaneously an act which entails the cleansing of oneself and one's property and, through sharing, an enhancement of the capacity of others. More specifically, this kind of giving is considered in the Qurʾān to be analogous to a fertile garden whose yield is increased by abundant rain (Q 2:265). It is this multiple connotation of *zakāt* that is reflected in subsequent interpretations and in the institutionalization of the principle in Muslim thought and practice. The centrality of *zakāt* is underscored by the many times it is coupled with the commandment of ritual worship. Right religion is summed up as serving God, sincere obedience (q.v.), virtue (q.v.), worship (q.v.) and paying the *zakāt* (Q 98:5). Abraham (q.v.) and the other prophets, including Jesus (q.v.), enjoined their followers to pay the *zakāt* (Q 19:31; 21:73).

Since one purpose of ritual action in religion in general is to establish and display communal solidarity, the performance of the duty of paying the *zakāt* acted as a visible symbol of individual commitment to the religious and social values of the growing Muslim community. This significance was further stressed by the incorporation of this duty as part of the observance of the two major Muslim holidays established by the Prophet, the Festival of Fast Breaking *(ʿĪd al-Fiṭr)* marking the end of Ramaḍān (q.v.) and the Festival of the Sacrifice *(ʿĪd al-Aḍḥā)*, when Muslims celebrate the culmination of the pilgrimage. The acts of giving "purify" the individual's wealth just as the fasting and the pilgrimage purify the individual. (See FESTIVALS AND COMMEMORATIVE DAYS.)

The institutionalization of qurʾānic values

The Prophet's own behavior was perceived as exemplary in the matter of almsgiving and his generous and selfless behavior was a model to be emulated. Reports about the

Prophet's almsgiving counteracted the excessive dogmatism about religious practice that was to emerge later. For instance, *ṣadaqa* in some reports means every good deed, even removing an obstacle from the road and planting a tree. Some of the Prophet's statements emphasize that a poor man's small offering is more meritorious than a rich person's donation of a large sum.

The fact that the Prophet eventually organized the collection and distribution of alms suggests that the process was being cast into specific institutional forms even in his day. According to the Qurʾān, some of the Bedouin groups which had converted to Islam remonstrated about the paying of the obligatory alms tax (Q 9:54-9). Al-Bukhārī (d. 256/870), the compiler of the most respected collection of Sunnī prophetic ḥadīth, cites a report in which the Prophet sends a representative to the Yemen to invite the local tribes to convert to Islam and pay the alms tax. Upon Muḥammad's death, his close Companion Abū Bakr (q.v.; r. 11/632-13/63-4) assumed the leadership of the nascent community and a number of tribes refused to pay the alms tax because they felt that the death of the Prophet absolved them from the obligations contracted with him (see APOSTASY). Their actions were perceived as a rebellion against the new authority in Medina which suppressed the revolts and reimposed the payment of the alms tax. Abū Bakr clearly regarded the payment of the alms tax to be obligatory and its imposition necessary in order to honor the Prophet's practice and sustain the well-being of the community. Shīʿite sources attributed to ʿAlī and the early imāms, also emphasize the need to entrust *zakāt* to the rightful authorities since they held the custodial authority to disburse them appropriately.

As the community expanded, through conversion and conquest, Muslim rulers and scholars looked to these values of community maintenance for guidance. Though the world of Islam was to encompass in time considerable geographical and cultural diversity, a common pattern of thought developed and was articulated in theological and legal forms, translating such principles into social practice. The Muslim community was not perceived as a merely religious community in the strictest sense of the word, but also a political, moral and social order (see COMMUNITY AND SOCIETY IN THE QURʾĀN). It provided the context in which Muslim thinkers could develop formalized approaches to all spheres of human life, including the institutionalization of the procedures for the collection and distribution of what was offered as alms.

The juristic literature produced by succeeding generations of scholars further formalized the collection and disbursement of the alms tax. Writers attempted to justify the prevailing custom by linking it retrospectively to the practice of the Prophet and other early authorities. In these juristic elaborations, the distinction of *zakāt* as an obligatory contribution and *ṣadaqa* as supererogation finally solidifies. The obligatory alms tax was to be paid to the treasury *(bayt al-māl)*, an institution which was developed more fully under the early caliphs.

Nevertheless, legal scholars attempted to elaborate and codify norms and statutes that gave concrete form to the qurʾānic prescriptions associated with almsgiving and their distribution. The work of the Ḥanafī jurist Abū Yūsuf (d. 192/808) on taxes, *Kitāb al-Kharāj*, which was written during the reign of the ʿAbbasid caliph Hārūn al-Rashīd (r. 170/786-193/809), is an instructive example of the collaboration between jurists and rulers to appropriate and extend such practices as almsgiving as part of the fiscal working of the state. A jurist such as al-Shāfiʿī (d. 204/820) was able to systematize and rationalize prevailing practice in his work. Generally, such works built upon the references to *zakāt* and *ṣadaqa* in the Qurʾān, detailing the payments based on the ownership of property, possessions and money, including income generated from farming. They prescribed when an amount was to be paid and to whom, as well as what minimum amounts were due in each category. It is interesting to note that the obligatory alms tax was also extended to include underground resources, such as minerals and treasure troves. The pattern that emerges in these juristic works illustrates clearly that the earlier practices of almsgiving were now developing into a more formalized obligation presented as a religious duty. It is important to note that many of the sources that exemplify the evolution of these practices continued to emphasize the moral agency of the act, linking its obligatory character to religious merit and reward. Moreover, they often identified *ṣadaqa* and *zakāt* as a means of seeking God's pleasure and the reward of the afterlife (see REWARD AND PUNISHMENT).

In distinguishing between *zakāt* and *ṣadaqa,* jurists pointed out that *zakāt* had specific limits and usages attached to it while *ṣadaqa* was unlimited. The Shīʿī imām Jaʿfar al-Ṣādiq (d. 148/765) is said to have emphasized that *ṣadaqa* spent in the "way of God (see PATH OF WAY [OF GOD])" included a variety of good works and thus provided a broader context for the charitable use of collected funds. Moreover, there were no constraints in terms of recipients, which could include mosques, individuals in distress or needy individuals who were not impoverished. Jurists often cite the qurʾānic narrative of Joseph (q.v.) where his brothers, unaware of his true identity, ask him to help their family temporarily in distress (Q 12:88).

Developments in legal theory also reflect the way different groups in Islam interpreted almsgiving. Shīʿite sources, citing ʿAlī b. Abī Ṭālib (q.v.) and the other early imāms (q.v.), also emphasize the need to pay the alms tax to the rightful authorities. Among the Shīʿīs, alms were to be entrusted to the imām or those designated by him and disbursed in accordance with qurʾānic values. Among Shīʿī groups such as the Twelvers, who believe that the imām is in a state of physical absence from the world *(ghayba),* alms are to be given to those considered his trusted worldly representatives. Their role is to ensure that alms reach the appropriate recipients. The Ismāʿīlīs interpret almsgiving as both a formal act and a significant spiritual deed whereby individuals employ their resources, talents and knowledge to assist the imām, the legatee of the Prophet, and the community at large.

The Ṣūfīs emphasize the mystical connotation of almsgiving. In certain circles, individuals were known to distribute their entire possessions as alms. Some groups sanctioned the acceptance of alms as a gift emanating directly from God. Other Ṣūfī groups practiced almsgiving both among themselves and throughout the general community. Most Sunnī jurists, fearing that an unjust ruler or authority might abuse such dues, recommend that individuals give the obligatory alms directly to the intended recipients. In some cases they even suggest that if individuals are constrained to give the alms to authorities whom they regard with suspicion, they should distribute the alms a second time directly.

This turn towards systematization and formalization did not preclude acts of voluntary almsgiving outside of what was deemed obligatory. Based again on qurʾānic precedents and prophetic practice, almsgiving was also translated into endowments created in perpetuity. The juristic tradition specified in most instances the ways such gifts were to be regulated. One narrative recounts how the Prophet wished to purchase land from a group for the building of a mosque. Rather than agreeing to sell the land, they gave it to the Prophet for "the sake of God." These charitable trusts were used to endow mosques, schools, hospitals, water fountains and other useful public structures and they have played an important role throughout Islamic history. Notable Muslims, descendants of the Prophet and many women played noteworthy roles in generating such philanthropic works. These acts were not restricted to benefiting Muslims alone. The Prophet himself specified that non-Muslims could also be beneficiaries of charity and encouraged non-Muslims to establish charitable foundations for the benefit of their own coreligionists.

The qurʾānic obligations were elaborated and articulated parallel to other taxes imposed. Ibn Khaldūn (d. 808/1406) argues in his *Muqaddima* that in the early history of Islam only those dues stipulated by the law *(sharīʿa),* such as the alms tax, were levied and these, though they were assessed at a low rate, yielded large sums. In his view, however, as dynasties grew and the state's economy became more complex, additional burdens in the form of taxes were imposed beyond the limits of equity. These non-qurʾānic taxes penalized enterprise and made people lose hope, thus generating less revenue and causing the economy to shrink. Simplistic as this may sound to modern ears, Ibn Khaldūn's account does underscore the fact that the qurʾānic taxes, which possessed a spiritual and moral dimension, were eventually supplanted by heavier, secular taxes that undermined the spirit.

Modern almsgiving

As modern Muslim nation-states sought to address questions of identity and development, almsgiving afforded them the opportunity to rethink the relevance of charitable practices. A majority of Muslims live in areas of the world which are considered to be less-developed. Hence, issues of social justice and the equitable distribution of resources figure prominently in discussions of the present-day significance of the qurʾānic injunctions. Some Muslim theorists have advocated the re-introduction of the obligatory alms tax as one element of a general tax policy to add the moral aspect of almsgiving to a modern economic policy.

In recent times, some Muslim states have adopted specific policies to incorporate the payment of the obligatory alms tax into their fiscal framework rather than leave it as a private and personal, voluntary contribution. Sudan and Pakistan are two examples. In Pakistan an alms tax fund was created in 1979 and distributed through a centralized agency for a variety of causes, including feeding the poor and providing scholarships for needy students. However, various Muslim groups, including the Shīʿīs, have objected to these practices on the basis that it is detrimental to traditional almsgiving and to the diversity of practice among Muslims. Many of the more wealthy Muslim countries practice a form of almsgiving by providing assistance to poorer Muslim countries and Islamic causes.

It is, however, within the framework of voluntary giving that the most innovative and sustainable adaptations of the qurʾānic spirit of almsgiving have occurred. Many Muslims, individually or as a community, have developed extensive networks to translate the Qurʾān's philanthropic values into active vehicles of assistance to a wide variety of constituencies. In some cases, these efforts have taken the form of voluntary associations and charitable organizations to help the poor and the needy in many parts of the world. Historical insight into the way the qur'ānic ideals of almsgiving strengthened communities and ameliorated inequities might still serve to aid Muslims to move beyond mere rhetoric in their search for continuity. See also GIFT AND GIVING.

Azim Nanji

Bibliography

Primary: Abū Yūsuf Ya'qūb b. Ibrāhīm, *Kitāb al-Kharāj*, trans. E. Fagnan, Paris 1921; Bukhārī, *Ṣaḥīḥ*, trans. A. Houdas and W. Marçais, *Les traditions islamiques*, 4 vols., Paris 1903-14; al-Ghazālī, Abū Ḥāmid Muḥammad, *Iḥyā' 'ulūm al-dīn*, N.A. Faris (trans. [partial]), *The mysteries of almsgiving*, Beirut 1966; al-Māwardī, *al-Aḥkām al-sulṭāniyya*, Cairo 1966; al-Nu'mān, Abū Ḥanīfa (Qāḍī), *Da'ā'im al-Islām*, ed. A.'A.A. Fyzee, 2 vols., Cairo 1969; al-Shāfi'ī, *al-Risāla*, ed. A.M. Shākir, Cairo 1940, trans. M. Khadduri, *al-Shāfi'ī's* Risāla *Treatise on the foundations of Islamic jurisprudence*, Baltimore 1961; Ṭabarī, *Ta'rīkh*, trans. W.M. Watt and M.V. McDonald, *The history of al-Ṭabarī*, Albany 1988-90, vi, vii.

Secondary: M. Ayoub, *The Qur'ān and its interpreters*, 2 vols., Albany 1984-92; N. Calder, Zakāt in Imāmī Shī'ī jurisprudence from the tenth to the sixteenth centuries A.D., in *BSOAS* 44 (1981), 468-80; H. Dean and Z. Khan, Muslim perspectives on welfare, in *Journal of social policy* 26 (1997), 193-209; J. Esposito (ed.), *Oxford encyclopedia of the modern Islamic world*, 4 vols., New York 1995; C. Geertz, *Local knowledge. Further essays in interpretive anthropology*, New York 1983; M. Hodgson, *The venture of Islam*, 3 vols., Chicago 1974; A. Nanji, Ethics and taxation. The perspective of the Islamic tradition, in *Journal of religious ethics* 13 (1985), 161-78; F.E. Peters, *A reader on classical Islam*, Princeton 1994; A. Sachedina, *The just ruler in Shī'ite Islam*, New York 1988; F. Rahman, Some key ethical concepts of the Qur'ān, in *Journal of religous ethics* 2 (1983), 170-185; N.A. Stillman, Charity and social service in medieval Islam, in *Societas* 2 (1975), 105-15.

Alphabet see ARABIC SCRIPT; LETTERS AND MYSTERIOUS LETTERS

Altar see IDOLS AND IMAGES

Ambiguous

A concept in qur'ānic exegesis which bears upon the controversial issue of the amount of interpretive license which may be taken in commenting on God's word. The root *sh-b-h* is attested several times in the Qur'ān. In reference to the Qur'ān or its verses, the active participle *mutashābih* (or *mutashābihāt*) appears twice with the sense of "ambiguous" or "similar."

Q 3:7 states that the Qur'ān consists partly of *muḥkam* verses and partly of *mutashābih*: "It is he who sent down upon you the book (q.v.), wherein are verses clear *(āyāt muḥkamāt)* that are the essence of the book *(umm al-kitāb)*, and others ambiguous *(mutashābihāt)*." Numerous commentators, while examining Q 3:7, mention two other verses which seem to contradict it. They are Q 39:23, which states that all the verses of the Qur'ān are *mutashābih*: "God has sent down the fairest discourse as a book consimilar *(kitāban mutashābihan)*" and Q 11:1 in which all the verses of the Qur'ān are characterized as clear: "A book whose verses are set clear *(uḥkimat āyātuhu)*." Al-Zarkashī (d. 794/1392), on the authority of the commentator Ibn Ḥabīb al-Nīsābūrī (d. 406/1015), argues that these passages present three different statements on the nature of the Qur'ān: the Qur'ān as clear *(muḥkam)*, as ambiguous *(mutashābih)* and as a combination of the two. He characterizes the verse that supports the idea of the compound nature, a Qur'ān made up of clear verses and ambiguous ones (Q 3:7), as the "correct" one (*ṣaḥīḥ*, *Burhān*, ii, 68; cf. Suyūṭī, *Itqān*, iii, 30).

The relation between the two components of the Qur'ān is governed by the meaning ascribed to the word *mutashābih*, for which the exegetical literature offers a variety of definitions. The meaning of "similar" is used to document the miraculous nature of the Qurʾān. On the other hand, the term interpreted as "ambiguous" has wider implications and bears upon three central qurʾānic issues: 1. The juridical validity of the Qurʾān, where the ambiguous verses are contrasted with the clear ones. 2. The question of the validity of interpreting the Qurʾān, where the ambiguous verses are used to argue the cases for and against interpretation. 3. The inimitability (q.v.) of the Qurʾān *(iʿjāz al-Qurʾān)*.

Similar verses

Similarity between verses may manifest itself either in the wording *(lafẓ)* or in the meaning *(maʿnā)* of the verse. Accordingly, *mutashābihāt* are sometimes defined as verses in which the same words are used to mean different things (Ibn Qutayba, *Taʾwīl*, 74; Ṭabarī, *Tafsīr*, iii, 114, 116) or else as verses that use different words to express a similar sense (Ṭabarī, *Tafsīr*, iii, 115-6; see L. Kinberg, Muḥkamāt, 145). In a widely-repeated definition, wording and meaning appear together and the similar verses are presented as those that "resemble one another in rightness and truth *(al-ḥaqq wa-l-ṣidq)*, i.e. meaning, and in beauty *(al-ḥusn)*, i.e. wording" (Baghawī, *Maʿālim*, i, 426). Naturally, the resemblance of verses can occur only in cases of repetition. This explains why repetition is presented as one of the characteristic features of the *mutashābih* verses. The correlation between the repetition of the *mutashābih* verses and their resemblance is treated in one of the definitions adduced by al-Ṭabarī (d. 310/923) where *mutashābih* verses are those in which the words resemble one another when repeated in other qurʾānic chapters (*Tafsīr*, iii, 116).

Similar verses and the inimitability of the Qurʾān

Each of the definitions dealing with the resemblance and the repetition of the *mutashābih* verses touches upon the inimitability of the Qurʾān. The relation between the inimitability (q.v.) of the Qurʾān and the *mutashābih* verses can be understood through the dichotomy of wording and meaning mentioned above. In his commentary on "It is he who sent down upon you the book, wherein are verses clear that are the essence of the book, and others ambiguous" (Q 3:7), Fakhr al-Dīn al-Rāzī (d. 606/1210) combines the verse under discussion with two verses already mentioned, Q 11:1 and Q 39:23, as well as "If [the Qurʾān] had been from other than God, surely they would have found in it much inconsistency" (Q 4:82; see DIFFICULT PASSAGES). Based on the four verses, he concludes that the *mutashābih* verses are those which repeat, resemble and confirm each other, and they prove the miraculous nature of the text. There are no contradictions in the Qurʾān. Rather, its verses confirm and reinforce one another. Simultaneously, the Qurʾān is also defined as consisting of *muḥkam* verses, namely, verses written in an inimitable way. Thus these two features, i.e. noncontradictory confirmed messages and an inimitable style of language which cannot be produced by mortals, attest to the divine source of the Qurʾān (Rāzī, *Tafsīr*, vii, 180).

Ibn al-Jawzī (d. 597/1200) offers a different explanation for the correlation between the inimitabilty of the Qurʾān and the *mutashābih* verses. Trying to find a reason for the existence of the *mutashābih* verses in the Qurʾān, he argues that stylistically the *muḥkam* and the *mutashābih* verses represent the two major forms of expression used in the Arabic language, the concise *(mūjaz)* and the allusive *(majāz)*. God has included both styles in the Qurʾān to challenge mortals to choose either style should they attempt to produce a Qurʾān similar to that brought by Muḥammad. However, no one can ever meet this challenge and the Qurʾān therefore, with its two styles, the *muḥkam* and *mutashābih,* will forever remain inimitable (*Zād,* i, 350-1; cf. Ibn Qutayba, *Taʾwīl,* 86).

Mutashābih *meaning "ambiguous"*

A common way to treat the terms *muḥkam* and *mutashābih* is to contrast the clarity of the first with the ambiguity of the other. As was mentioned, this contrast bears upon some of the most prominent qurʾānic issues: the abrogating and abrogated verses (*al-nāsikh wa-l-mansūkh,* see ABROGATION), the authority to interpret the Qurʾān and the inimitability of the Qurʾān.

Ambiguous verses and the abrogating and abrogated verses

Among the definitions that contrast the *muḥkam* with the *mutashābih,* there is to be found the presentation of the *muḥkam* verses as abrogating ones *(nāsikhāt)* and the *mutashābih* as abrogated ones *(mansūkhāt)*. A widely-cited definition represents the *muḥkam* as the abrogating verses, the verses that clarify what is allowed *(ḥalāl),* the verses that clarify what is prohibited *(ḥarām),* the verses that define the punishments (*ḥudūd,* see BOUNDARIES AND PRECEPTS) for various offenses, the verses that define the duties *(farāʾiḍ)* and the verses that one should believe in and put into practice. Conversely, the *mutashābih* verses are the abrogated ones, the verses that cannot be understood without changing their word order *(muqaddamuhu wa-muʾakhkharuhu),* the parables *(amthāl),* the oaths (q.v.; *aqsām*) and the verses in which one should believe, but not put into practice (Ibn ʿAbbās, *Tafsīr,* 124; Abū ʿUbayd, *Nāsikh,* 4; Ibn Abī Ḥātim, *Tafsīr,* ii, 592-3; Ṭabarī, *Tafsīr,* iii, 115; Baghawī, *Maʿālim,* i, 426; Ibn ʿAṭiyya, *Muḥarrar,* i, 400; Qurṭubī, *Jāmiʿ,* iv, 10; Ibn Kathīr, *Tafsīr,* i, 345; Suyūṭī, *Durr,* ii, 5; Shawkānī, *Tafsīr,* i, 314). The *muḥkam* are presented here as the verses that deal with essential matters whereas the *mutashābih* verses are held to deal with secondary matters. This is the way to understand the comparison made in the qurʾānic text itself. Q 3:7 defines the *muḥkam* verses as "the essence of the book" and the *mutashābih* as the rest.

Another way to examine the juridical value of the terms is to consider them as two kinds of divine commandments (q.v.). In this case, the *muḥkam* verses contain the commands that are universal and never change, whereas the *mutashābih* verses contain the commands that are limited and do change. The *muḥkam* contain the basic commandments, shared by all religions, such as obeying God and avoiding injustice. The *mutashābih* verses, on the other hand, contain the practical aspects of these commandments and may vary from one religion to another, e.g. the number of required prayers and the regulations concerning almsgiving and marriage (Rāzī, *Tafsīr,* vii, 183; cf. Māwardī, *Nukat,* i, 380). In this interpretation, the distinction between abrogating and abrogated verses becomes meaningless because the chronological element is replaced by a question of universality. This means that the *muḥkam* verses are defined as those that are universal to all of the revealed religions and the *mutashābih* verses are those that contain what distinguishes Islam from the other revealed religions.

Ambiguous verses and the authority to interpret the Qurʾān

Several commentators recognize three kinds of *mutashābih* verses: those that cannot be understood, those that can be examined and understood by everyone and those that only "the experts" *(al-rāsikhūn fī l-ʿilm)* can comprehend (e.g. Fīrūzābādī, *Baṣāʾir,* iii, 296). The *muḥkam* are defined as clear verses that require nothing to be understood whereas the comprehension of the *mutashābih* requires explanation (Ṭabarī, *Tafsīr,* iii, 116-7; ʿAbd al-Jabbār, *Mutashābih,* i, 13; Māwardī, *Nukat,* i, 369; Baghawī, *Maʿālim,* i, 428; Ibn ʿAṭiyya, *Muḥarrar,* i, 401; Rāzī, *Tafsīr,* vii, 184; Qurṭubī, *Jāmiʿ,* iv, 9; Suyūṭī, *Itqān,* iii, 3; Shawkānī, *Tafsīr,* i, 314). A different set of definitions represents the *muḥkam* as verses that contain or permit only one interpretation whereas the *mutashābih* are those that may be interpreted in more than one way (Ṭabarī, *Tafsīr,* iii, 115-6; al-Jaṣṣāṣ, *Aḥkām,* ii, 281; Māwardī, *Nukat,* i, 369; Wāḥidī, *Wasīṭ,* i, 413-4; Baghawī, *Maʿālim,* i, 427; Ṭabarsī, *Majmaʿ,* ii, 15; Qurṭubī, *Jāmiʿ,* iv, 10; Suyūṭī, *Itqān,* iii, 4; Shawkānī *Tafsīr,* i, 314). While there is no room to doubt the instructions supplied by the *muḥkamāt,* the ambiguity of the *mutashābih* verses may create a situation in which the believers become confused, not knowing which direction to choose. They may then tendentiously interpret these verses in favor of their own personal interests.

This raises the question as to whether any exegetical effort should be made to eliminate the vagueness of the *mutashābih* verses and two contradictory attitudes developed. Some scholars claimed that the *mutashābih* verses are meant to remain ambiguous and any attempt to interpret them might lead the believers astray. Only God knows their true meaning and this is the way it should stay. Others maintained that the *mutashābih* are meant to be illuminated. Not only does God know the meaning of these verses, but the scholars of the Qurʾān also know it. Their duty is to supply the interpretation of them and this may vary among the different scholars since the *mutashābih* verses may be interpreted in a variety of ways. These two opposing views on the validity of interpreting the *mutashābih* verses parallel those on the interpretation of the Qurʾān as a whole.

Ambiguous verses as those that should not be interpreted

The basic argument against the interpretation of the *mutashābih* is that knowledge of these verses is limited to God (Ṭabarī, *Tafsīr,* iii, 116; Māwardī, *Nukat,* i, 369; Ibn ʿAṭiyya, *Muḥarrar,* i, 401; Qurṭubī, *Jāmiʿ,* iv, 9; Abū Ḥayyān, *Baḥr,* ii, 381; Ālūsī, *Rūḥ,* ii, 82). As such, they concern matters about which no mortal has clear knowledge. To show that the essence of the *mutashābihāt* cannot be grasped by human beings, several topics defined as *mutashābih* are mentioned: resurrection day (Māwardī, *Nukat,* i, 369; Baghawī, *Maʿālim,* i, 427; Rāzī, *Tafsīr,* vii, 184; Qurṭubī, *Jāmiʿ,* iv, 10; Abū Ḥayyān, *Baḥr,* ii, 381; Zarkashī, *Burhān,* ii, 70), the appearance of the Antichrist *(al-Dajjāl)* before the end of days, the return of Christ (Ṭabarī, *Tafsīr,* iii, 116) and the prophesied day the sun will rise in the west (Māwardī, *Nukat,* i, 369; Baghawī, *Maʿālim,* i, 427; Abū Ḥayyān, *Baḥr,* ii, 381), among others (see ANTICHRIST, APOCALYPSE, RESURRECTION; LAST JUDGMENT).

A different argument contends that the *mutashābih* are those verses whose meaning can be easily distorted (Ṭabarī, *Tafsīr,* iii, 116; Ibn ʿAṭiyya, *Muḥarrar,* i, 401; Qurṭubī, *Jāmiʿ,* iv, 9; Suyūṭī, *Durr,* ii, 5; Shawkānī, *Tafsīr,* i, 314). This should be understood in light of the second part of the key verse "As for those in whose hearts is swerving, they follow the ambiguous part, desiring dissension and desiring its interpretation" (Q 3:7). The commentators who correlate the *mutashābih* and dissension (q.v.) adduce a number of qurʾānic verses in support of their position. One such example is presented by al-Suyūṭī (d. 911/1505) on the authority of Saʿīd b. Jubayr (d. 95/714): To justify their ideas, the early sect of the Khārijīs (q.v.) employed "Whoever fails to judge according to what God has sent down is a wrongdoer" (Q 5:47) and "Then the unbelievers ascribe equals to their

Lord" (Q 6:1) to support their controversial doctrines. When the Khārijīs faced the injustice of a leader, they read these two verses together and, by assuming correlation between the two, they set forth the following argument: He who does not judge according to the principles of justice is an unbeliever. An unbeliever is a polytheist *(mushrik)* who ascribes equals to God. Thus a leader who acts in this manner can be deemed a polytheist (*Durr,* ii, 5). The technique used here joins two verses that were not necessarily meant to be combined and draws conclusions from this juxtaposition. By so doing, the Khārijīs were able to prove that their teachings — such as espousing that a caliph should be deprived of his position for acting improperly — are anchored in the Qurʾān and thus fully authorized.

Another example of the correlation between the *mutashābih* verses and dissension deals with the controversial issue of free will versus predestination (see FREEDOM AND PREDESTINATION). The rivals are the rationalist Muʿtazilīs (q.v.) and the conservative Sunnīs. Both sides refer to the same verse, Q 18:29 which states "Say, 'The truth is from your Lord.' So whoever wishes, let him believe and whoever wishes, let him disbelieve." The Muʿtazilīs define the verse as *muḥkam,* i.e. the kind of verse that should be followed since it favors the argument for free will. The Sunnīs, who do not accept the idea of free will, define this verse as *mutashābih,* i.e. the kind of verse that should not be followed. Q 76:30 presents the opposite view: "You cannot will [anything] unless God wills it." The Muʿtazilīs define this verse as *mutashābih* since it contradicts their view, but the Sunnīs define it as *muḥkam* because it favors the idea of predestination. By shifting the terms, it became possible to endorse or refute an idea according to one's needs (Rāzī, *Tafsīr,* vii, 182; Abū Ḥayyān, *Baḥr,* ii, 382). The same method was applied to other verses on topics such as the disagreements between the proponents of determinism (Jabriyya) and the proponents of indeterminism (Qadariyya), or the issue of whether believers will see God in the afterlife (Rāzī, *Tafsīr,* vii, 185; Abū Ḥayyān, *Baḥr,* ii, 382; cf. L. Kinberg, Muḥkamāt, 159).

The correlation between the *mutashābih* verses and dissension was also mentioned in the discussion of the reasons for the existence of the *mutashābih* in the Qurʾān: God revealed them to test the people. Those who do not follow the *mutashābih* will be rewarded as true believers, while those who follow them will go astray (Ibn al-Jawzī, *Zād,* i, 353). The same idea is mentioned along with the fact that the *mutashābih* can be easily distorted. Although established and profoundly elaborated, the negative approach to the interpretation of the *mutashābih* was not the only one adduced in the exegetical literature. No less detailed were the arguments favoring their interpretation (see EXEGESIS OF THE QURʾĀN: CLASSICAL AND MEDIEVAL).

Ambiguous verses as those that may be interpreted

The perception of the *mutashābih* as ambiguous verses was used to argue, as shown above, against their interpretation. The same perception, however, is also used to support and encourage their interpretation. Although contradictory, the two approaches had a common starting point: Ambiguous verses are dangerous in the sense that a wrong interpretation might mislead the believer. With this idea in mind, some scholars recommended avoiding any examination of these verses whereas others encouraged the interpretation of them, but prescribed caution with regard to the steps that need to be taken in this process. One precaution is to check the *mutashābih* against the *muḥkam.* This is expressed in a set of definitions which oppose the *muḥkam* and the *mutashābih* regarding the dependence of the latter. The *muḥkam* are defined as independent verses that need no explanation (Māwardī, *Nukat,* i, 369; Ibn al-Jawzī, *Zād,* i, 350; Abū Ḥayyān, *Baḥr,* ii, 381) nor reference to other verses to be understood (al-Naḥḥās, *Iʿrāb,* i, 355; Qurṭubī, *Jāmiʿ,* iv, 11; Shawkānī, *Tafsīr,* i, 314). Conversely, the *mutashābih* are dependent verses that cannot be understood without consulting or comparing them to other verses (Baghawī, *Maʿālim,* i, 427; Zarkashī, *Burhān,* ii, 68). The *mutashābih*'s dependence on the *muḥkam* derives from the clarity of the latter and the ambiguity of the former. The *muḥkam,* by interpreting the *mutashābih,* clears away any misunderstanding that might mislead the believer (Rāzī, *Tafsīr,* vii, 185). It thus can happen that when a believer consults a *muḥkam* to understand an ambiguous *mutashābih,* he finds his way to the true faith (Rāzī, *Tafsīr,* vii, 185; Ibn Kathīr, *Tafsīr,* i, 345). When a *mutashābih* is not interpreted in accordance with a *muḥkam,* those who rely on it will go astray (al-Jaṣṣāṣ, *Aḥkām,* ii, 281). In light of this argument, the *muḥkam* are regarded as "the essence of the book" (*umm al-kitāb,* Q 3:7) or "a source to which other verses are referred for interpretation" (Suyūṭī, *Itqān,* iii, 9).

Thus the ambiguity of the *mutashābih* verses creates the need to scrutinize them. Had the Qurʾān consisted only of *muḥkam* verses, there would have been no need for the science of the interpretation of the Qurʾān to develop (Rāzī, *Tafsīr,* vii, 185-6). Had every verse been clear to everyone, the difference in people's abilities would not come to the fore. The learned *(ʿālim)* and the ignorant *(jāhil)* would have been equal and intellectual endeavor would cease (Ibn Qutayba, *Taʾwīl,* 86; cf. Rāzī, *Tafsīr,* vii, 185). Behind this perception is the notion that the *mutashābih* are verses that make people think when they try to identify them and use their own judgment in interpreting them. Consequently, it can be said that they are presented as verses that stimulate people and put them on their guard. It seems that the *mutashābih* are perceived as the conscience of the believer and indicate the level of his religious knowledge. Due to their ambiguity, dealing with them requires a high degree of religious discernment. The more profound the person, the better his decisions and thus the more pleasant his condition in the next world. This issue is thoroughly discussed in the commentaries with regard to the status of "the experts in knowledge" *(rāsikhūn fī l-ʿilm)* mentioned in Q 3:7.

Ambiguous verses and the inimitability of the Qurʾān

As indicated above, the features of the *mutashābih* as "similar verses" are held to supply proof of the miraculous nature of the Qurʾān. Additional evidence of this was found in the features of the *mutashābih* in the sense of "ambiguous verses." This derives from two opposing attitudes toward the interpretation of these verses, opposition to interpreting the *mutashābih* and support for their interpretation.

Almost every commentator identifies the "mysterious letters" (*fawātiḥ* — or *awāʾil al-suwar,* see LETTERS AND MYSTERIOUS LETTERS) of the Qurʾān as *mutashābih* (e.g. Ṭabarī, *Tafsīr,* iii, 116-7). These are the letters that occur at the beginning of certain sūras and whose meaning is unclear. The significance of the mysterious letters, as well as the other *mutashābih* verses, is considered a divine secret known only to God himself. Both should be regarded as parts of the book that God has prevented his people from understanding. Their concealed meaning points to the divine source of the Qurʾān and thus attests to its miraculous nature (ʿAbd al-Jabbār, *Mutashābih,* i, 17).

The ambiguity of the *mutashābih* verses enables believers to interpret them in more than one way. This means that the Qur'ān accommodates more than one approach to a given issue and that different trends in Islam are likely to find their ideas reflected in the Qur'ān (ʿAbd al-Jabbār, *Mutashābih,* i, 26, 28. See also L. Kinberg, Muḥkamāt, 158, 168). This allows the holy text to serve as a source of answers and solutions to any problem at any time and represents one of the central aspects of the miraculous nature of the Qur'ān.

In examining the different attitudes toward the interpretation of the Qur'ān, H. Birkeland (*Opposition,* 9) states that the opposition to qur'ānic exegesis was never comprehensive and was aimed at the usage of human reasoning *(ra'y)*. The validity of *tafsīr bi-l-ʿilm,* i.e. exegesis based on ḥadīth (the records of the pronouncements and actions of the prophet Muḥammad, see ḤADĪTH AND THE QUR'ĀN) was, in H. Birkeland's view, never disputed. Support for this theory can be found in the way the term *mutashābih* is treated in the exegetical literature as well as in its relation to the term *muḥkam*. The prohibition of interpreting the *mutashābih* verses may be understood as a reflection of the opposition to the use of human reason. At the same time, allowing the interpretation of these verses seems to be conditional upon the usage of ḥadīth as a means of interpretation. Indeed, Muslim scholars have traditionally not regarded the employment of ḥadīth to illuminate a qur'ānic verse as interpretation, but rather as a means of confirming the message included in the verse. Consequently, a verse in harmony with a reliable ḥadīth may be relied upon as a source of guidance. Such a verse would be defined as *muḥkam*. The *mutashābih,* on the other hand, can never be regarded as authoritative. Both the need of various streams in Islam to have their distinctive ideas anchored in the Qur'ān and the injunction to follow only the *muḥkam* verses may explain the variance in the identity of the verses which different groups view as *muḥkam* and *mutashābih*. As shown above, a verse defined by one scholar as *mutashābih* may be characterized as *muḥkam* by another. The flexible way in which the two terms were used enabled the commentators to adapt a verse to their needs by defining it as *muḥkam*. In so doing they were actually using their own independent reasoning presented as ḥadīth. See also TRADITIONAL DISCIPLINES OF QUR'ĀNIC STUDY.

Leah Kinberg

Bibliography
Primary: ʿAbd al-Jabbār, *Mutashābih;* Abū Ḥayyān, *Baḥr;* Abū ʿUbayd, *Nāsikh;* Ālūsī, *Rūḥ;* Baghawī, *Maʿālim;* Fīrūzābādī, *Baṣā'ir;* Ibn ʿAbbās (attributed), *Tafsīr Ibn ʿAbbās al-musammā Ṣaḥīfat ʿAlī ibn Abī Ṭālib ʿan Ibn ʿAbbās,* Beirut 1991; Ibn Abī Ḥātim al-Rāzī, *Tafsīr al-Qur'ān al-ʿaẓīm,* 10 vols., Riyadh 1997; Ibn ʿAṭiyya, *Muḥarrar;* Ibn al-Jawzī, *Zād;* Ibn Kathīr, *Tafsīr;* Ibn Qutayba, *Ta'wīl;* al-Jaṣṣāṣ, *Aḥkām;* al-Naḥḥās, *Iʿrāb;* Qurṭubī, *Jāmiʿ;* Rāzī, *Tafsīr;* Shawkānī, *Tafsīr;* Suyūṭī, *Durr;* id., *Itqān;* Ṭabarī, *Tafsīr;* Ṭabarsī, *Majmaʿ;* Wāḥidī, *Wasīṭ;* Zarkashī, *Burhān.*
Secondary: M. Ben Milad, Ambiguïté et mathānī coraniques. Pour une théorie générale de la polarité dans la culture arabe, in J. Berque and J.P. Charnay (eds.), *L'ambivalence dans la culture arabe,* Paris 1967, 366-81; H. Birkeland, Old Muslim opposition against the interpretation of the Qur'ān, Oslo 1955; A. von Denffer, *ʿUlūm al-Qur'ān. An introduction to the sciences of the Qur'ān,* n.p. 1983; Y. Friedmann, *Shaykh Aḥmad Sirhindī. An outline of his thought and a study of his image in the eyes of posterity,* Montreal 1971; L. Kinberg, Muḥkamāt and mutashābihāt (Koran 3/7). Implication of a koranic pair of terms in medieval exegesis, in *Arabica* 35 (1988), 143-72; M. Lagarde, De l'ambiguité (mutashabih) dans le Coran, in *QSA* 3 (1985) 45-62; J. McAuliffe, Text and textuality. Q 3:7 as a point of intersection, in I. Boullata (ed.), *Literary structures of religious meaning in the Qur'ān,* London (2000, 56-76); Z. Muṣṭafā, *Dirāsāt fī l-tafsīr,* Cairo 1967-8; S. Syamsuddin, Muḥkam and mutashābih. "An analytical study of al-Ṭabarī's and

al-Zamakhsharī's interpretations of Q 3:7," in *Journal of Qur'ānic Studies* 1 (1999), 63-79; G. Sale, *The Korān,* London 1900; Ṣ. al-Ṣāliḥ, *Mabāḥith fī 'ulūm al-Qur'ān,* Beirut 1965; K. Versteegh, A dissenting grammarian. Quṭrub on declension, in K. Koerner, H.J. Niederehe and K. Versteegh (eds.), *The history of linguistics in the Near East,* Amsterdam 1983, 403-29; id., *Arabic grammar and qur'ānic exegesis in early Islam,* Leiden 1993; S. Wild, The self-referentiality of the Qur'ān. Sura 3,7 as an exegetical challenge, in J. McAuliffe et al. (eds.), *With reverence for the word. Medieval scriptural exegesis in Judaism, Christianity and Islam,* Oxford (forthcoming).

Amulets

Ornaments worn as charms against evil and sickness. Muslims have used amulets *(ruqā,* sing. *ruqya)* most often to cure spiritual or psychological conditions, including madness, spirit possession and the evil eye.

The Qur'ān may be recited in the form of a spell *(du'ā')* or worn in written form *(ṭilasm)* on the person or placed in the home. Among the Indonesian Gayo, spells, called *doa,* include the use of qur'ānic verses in Arabic for healing and other purposes accompanied by supplementary words in Gayo and visualizations (J.R. Bowen, *Muslims through discourse,* 77-105; J. Flueckiger, Vision, 271). Others employ a practice known as "erasure" *(maḥw),* whereby select verses, or the whole Qur'ān, are written out and water is poured over the paper. The water is then drunk (Ibn Qayyim al-Jawziyya, *Ṭibb,* 124; J. Robson, Magical uses, 40; A.O. El-Tom, Drinking the Koran, 414-8; J. Flueckiger, Vision, 258). Another way to tap the power of the Qur'ān has been to recite verses over water and to apply the water as an external wash (*nushra,* al-Suyūṭī, *Ṭibb,* 172; D. Owusu-Ansah, *Talismanic tradition,* 107-11). Other procedures include reciting the *mu'awwidhatān,* the last two sūras of the Qur'ān, and other verses and names of God, together with magical gestures such as spitting into the hands, blowing to the four winds and stroking the face or other parts of the body (Ibn Qayyim al-Jawziyya, *Ṭibb,* 11, 121-4, 139, 145-6; C. Padwick, *Muslim devotions,* 84-91, 104-7; J.C. Bürgel, Feather, 34-5). Ḥadīth mention written uses of the Qur'ān for healing, including talismans to be attached to clothing or animals or placed in the home (Ibn Qayyim al-Jawziyya, *Ṭibb,* 172-3; 'Abdallāh and al-Ḥusayn b. Bisṭām, *Ṭibb,* 125; J. Robson, Magical uses, 42; C. Padwick, *Muslim devotions,* 87; J. Campo, *Other side,* 104-5). Amulets bearing qur'ānic verses, numbers and geometric symbols, such as magical squares, were often carried or worn on the person (E. Westermarck, *Ritual and belief,* 144-6; A.O. Owusu-Ansah, *Talismanic tradition,* 96-100 and appendix; J. Robson, Magical uses, 35-7; J. Flueckiger, Vision, 251-7; V. Hoffman, *Sufism,* 154-5).

The essential qur'ānic justification for the use of the Qur'ān in amulets to transmit the divine blessing *(baraka)* of the text is its God-given characterization as "a healing and a mercy" (*shifā'un wa-raḥmatun,* Q 17:82; D. Owusu-Ansah, *Talismanic tradition,* 122). The words of the Prophet Muḥammad as recorded in the ḥadīth have also been used as support for the practice. In its chapter on medicine *(Kitāb al-Ṭibb),* the famous collection that is the *Ṣaḥīḥ* of al-Bukhārī (d. 256/870) contains a number of ḥadīth on the proper use of amulets bearing verses from the Qur'ān. Those who employed amulets could cite a range of positive juristic opinions which argue that amulet use cannot be an act of unbelief *(kufr),* if the process brings benefit and the contents of the amulet are from the Qur'ān (D. Owusu-Ansah, *Talismanic tradition,* 25-40). Nevertheless, the use of amulets was surrounded by continual legal debate.

Medieval sources for the making of qur'ānic amulets drew on the books of magical healing, such as the so-called "books tested by experience" *(mujarrabāt)* of Aḥmad al-Dayrabī and Abū ʿAbdallāh Muḥammad b. Yūsuf al-Sanūsī (d. 892/1486) and the magical texts like the *Sun of knowledge (Shams al-maʿārif)* by al-Būnī (d. 622/1225), *Strung pearls on the special properties of the Qurʾān (al-Durr al-naẓīm fī khawāṣṣ al-Qurʾān al-ʿaẓīm)* by al-Yāfiʿī (d. 768/1367), and *The brightest lights and the secret treasures (Shumūs al-anwār wa-kunūz al-asrār)* by Ibn al-Ḥājj al-Ṭilimsānī (d. 737/1336). These works were complemented by the various ḥadīth collections and the medical corpus devoted to "prophetic medicine" *(al-ṭibb al-nabawī),* the medical practices ascribed to the Prophet. Some notable works on prophetic medicine include Sunnī works by Abū Nuʿaym al-Iṣbahānī (d. 430/1038), al-Dhahabī (d. 748/1348), Ibn Qayyim al-Jawziyya (d. 751/1350), and al-Suyūṭī (d. 911/1505). There is as well a Shīʿī text known as the *Medicine of the imāms (Ṭibb al-aʾimma)* by ʿAbdallāh b. Bisṭām and his brother al-Ḥusayn (fl. 300/913) which collects the reports of the medical practices of the Shīʿī imāms (see IMĀM; SHĪʿISM AND THE QURʾĀN).

This higher literature on religious healing generated a large body of popular literature on folk religious healing in the form of chapbooks for amulet usage, usually bearing the title "a collection of cures" *(majmaʿ al-adwiya),* in manuscript form and later in print. Among these are *The gleanings of safety in medicine (Luqaṭ al-amān fī 'l-ṭibb)* by Ibn al-Jawzī (d. 597/1200) and *The benefits of medicine made easy (Kitāb Tashīl al-manāfiʿ fī l-ṭibb)* by Ibrāhīm b. ʿAbd al-Raḥmān al-Azraq (d. 815/1412). This testifies to the widespread popularity of employing amulets (F. Rahman, *Health and medicine,* 41-58). Such practical manuals become the guide for local handwritten copies used by adepts, e.g. the *umbatri* of the Sudanese Berti (A.O. El-Tom, Drinking the Koran, 416; see also D. Owusu-Ansah, *Talismanic tradition,* 44-91). Special editions of the Qurʾān were even published with marginal notation on the methods of divination and the apposite verses for magical spells or talismans. The talismanic manuals traditionally categorize the verses into various classes, e.g. verses for protection *(āyāt al-ḥifẓ),* for healing *(āyāt al-shifāʾ),* for victory *(futūḥ al-Qurʾān).* These verses, the divine names of God *(al-asmāʾ al-ḥusnā)* and qurʾānic formulae such as the *basmala* ("In the name of God, the merciful and compassionate," see BASMALA) and the repetition of the formulae of taking refuge *(istaʿādha)* became the *materia medica* of the makers of amulets (K. Opitz, *Medizin im Koran;* J. Robson, Magical uses; B.A. Donaldson, Koran as magic; C. Padwick, *Muslim devotions;* A.O. El-Tom, Drinking the Koran).

The belief in and use of qurʾānic amulets continues as living practice within the framework of Islamic religious healing and is documented in anthropological studies throughout the contemporary Muslim world, particularly in the Middle East (C. Padwick, *Muslim devotions,* pp. xi-xiv, 289-97; P. Antes, Medicine, 187-91), Africa (A.O. El-Tom, Drinking the Koran), south Asia (J. Flueckiger, The vision), and southeast Asia (J.R. Bowen, *Muslims through discourse*). Men and women still have recourse to qurʾānic amulets and other forms of religious healing, often for the sake of children. The amulets are carried on the person and placed in the home, vehicle and place of business. The male practitioner is more likely to be able to consult the amulet chapbooks and texts on "Prophetic medicine" or to be trained by someone expert in the use of amulets, e.g. a local Ṣūfī adept or a religiously learned person in the urban neighborhood or rural village (A.O. El-Tom, Drinking the Koran, 415-7). Women, especially older women, can also occupy a visible position in public ritual as charismatic healers and as spirit mediums and by employing the techniques of dream interpretation, divining and other folk religious healing techniques, such as amulets (J. Flueckiger, The vision, 261-80). Contemporary religious healers operate as alternatives or complements to the practitioners of western medicine, in both Muslim countries and among the emigrant Muslim communities in the West (P. Antes, Medicine, 181-91). The widespread production and use of qurʾānic healing images highlight the strong creative interaction of authoritative sources, the Qurʾān and ḥadīth, and actual belief and practice in medieval and modern Islam.

Kathleen Malone O'Connor

Bibliography
Primary: al-Ḥusayn and ʿAbdallāh b. Bisṭām, *Ṭibb al-aʾimma,* Beirut 1994; Ibn Qayyim al-Jawziyya, *al-Ṭibb al-nabawī,* Cairo 1978; al-Suyūṭī, *al-Ṭibb al-nabawī,* Beirut 1986.
Secondary: P. Antes, Medicine and the living tradition of Islam, in L.E. Sullivan (ed.), *Healing and restoring. Healing and medicine in the world's religious traditions,* New York 1989; J.R. Bowen, *Muslims through discourse. Religion and ritual in Gayo society,* Princeton 1993; J.C. Bürgel, *The feather of Simurgh. The "licit magic" of the arts in medieval Islam,* New York 1988; J. Campo, *The other side of paradise,* Columbia, SC 1991; B.A. Donaldson, The Koran as magic, in *MW* 27 (1937), 258-63; A.O. El-Tom, Drinking the Koran. The meaning of koranic verses in Berti erasure, in J.D.Y. Peel and C. Stuart (eds.), *Popular Islam south of the Sahara,* Manchester 1985; J. Flueckiger, The vision was of written words. Negotiating authority as a female Muslim healer in south India, in D. Shulman (ed.), *Syllables of sky. Studies in south Indian civilization,* Delhi 1995; V. Hoffman, *Sufism, mystics, and saints in modern Egypt,* Columbia, SC 1995; K. Opitz, *Die Medizin im Koran,* Stuttgart 1905; D. Owusu-Ansah, *Islamic talismanic tradition in nineteenth-century Asante,* Lewiston 1991. C. Padwick, *Muslim devotions. A study of prayer-manuals in common use,* London 1961; F. Rahman, *Health and medicine in the Islamic tradition,* New York 1988; J. Robson, The magical uses of the Koran, in *Transactions* 6 (1929-33), 53-60; id., Islamic cures in popular Islam, in *MW* 24 (1934), 34-43; E. Westermarck, *Ritual and belief in Morocco,* 2 vols., New York 1926, i, ch. 1.

Analogy

see LANGUAGE AND STYLE OF THE QURʾĀN; EXEGESIS OF THE QURʾĀN: CLASSICAL AND MEDIEVAL

Anatomy

References to the structure of the human body in the Qurʾān. The Qurʾān mentions body parts many times, but these are spread throughout the text and particular terms do not always convey the same meaning in different contexts. In some sections of the Qurʾān human anatomy is treated as a functional element, but most qurʾānic references to the human body are employed in metaphors (see METAPHOR) aimed at encouraging the pursuit of an ethical and pious life. Anatomy and body parts in the Qurʾān are cited in conjunction with the faith of believers to ensure that there is a complete understanding of the harmony between the workings of the body and the message of the Qurʾān. In the Qurʾān, human anatomy can be divided into two spheres. The first consists of the various physical elements, such as the flesh, fluids, eyes, ears, head, heart and backside. The second includes anatomical experience, such as speaking, weeping, eating, fasting, listening and dying, and what the body experiences in the light of religious faith.

While the Qurʾān does not have many references to the specific Arabic word for the human body, *jism,* one instance of its occurrence is when a prophet says to the Children of Israel (q.v.), "God chose [Saul, q.v.] above you and increased him vastly in knowledge and body *(jism)*" (Q 2:247). The Qurʾān mentions the body to support the validity of the Prophet Muḥammad's mission as well as that of the previous prophets, despite their lack of supernatural qualities. Q 21:8 affirms the ordinary humanity of prophets: "We did not endow them with a body *(jasad)* that could dispense with food and they were not immortal" as a defense against those who claimed that to be a messenger of God an individual should possess extraordinary human qualities. Q 23:12-13 explains that the original composition of the body is from organic and inorganic substances: "We create man out of the essence of clay (q.v.) and then made a drop of sperm in firm keeping."

Human flesh *(laḥm)* is referred to both literally and metaphorically in the Qurʾān. Q 23:14 describes the way that flesh protects the bones in the body: "Then we clothed the bones in flesh *(laḥm)*." The Qurʾān also characterizes activities such as gossiping, spreading rumors and second guessing one another as eating the flesh of an individual. Q 49:12 states, "Would any of you like to eat the flesh *(laḥm)* of his dead brother?" which Fakhr al-Dīn al-Rāzī (d. 606/1210) interprets as cautioning the believers to be conscious of their conversations with one another. Al-Rāzī also felt this passage was urging believers to preserve their dignity by not involving themselves in rumors (*Tafsīr*, ad loc.).

The Arabic word for backside *(dubur*, pl. *adbār)* is commonly applied in the Qurʾān to describe the times when unbelievers turn away from God's message, e.g. "When you invoke your Lord — and him alone — in the Qurʾān, they turn their backs *(adbār)*, fleeing" (Q 17:46) and "Those who turn their backs *(adbār)* in apostasy after the way of guidance was made clear to them are tempted by Satan" (q.v.; Q 47:25). Here, turning the backside symbolizes rejecting truth and being led astray (q.v.). The expression also may refer to cowardice and a lack of faithfulness: "If they do help them, they will turn their backs" (*adbār*, Q 59:12). Other examples of the word include, "How will it be when the angels draw out their soul, striking their face and their backs *(adbār)*?" (Q 47:27).

Additional qurʾānic references to turning the backside are not meant for unbelievers but are specifically directed at the believers who were preparing themselves to fight in a battle. Q 8:15-16 states, "When you meet those who disbelieve, never turn your backsides *(adbār)* to them. Whoever on that day turns his backside *(dubur)* on them — except as a battle maneuver or to join another unit — will have earned the wrath of God." The combat theme is continued in passages such as "If the unbelievers had fought you, they would have turned their backsides *(adbār)*" (Q 48:22) and "If you fight them, they will turn their backsides *(adbār)* to you" (Q 3:111).

The references to blood in the Qurʾān range from the blood on the shirt of Joseph (q.v.) to the blood of useless animal sacrifices (see ANIMAL LIFE; SACRIFICE). "They brought his shirt with false blood *(dam)* on it" (Q 12:18) occurs in the situation where brothers of Joseph go to their father to explain his disappearance. The Qurʾān emphasizes that wasting blood, either in animal offerings or physical self-sacrificing, is not acceptable and does not bring one closer to God. In passages such as "Their flesh *(luḥūm)* and blood *(dimāʾ)* will never reach God, but your reverence will reach him" (Q 22:37), the Qurʾān wants to make clear that blood is a precious element in the human body and should not be wasted out of negligence.

Blood and a blood clot (see BLOOD AND BLOOD CLOT) also figure as important features in human creation (see BIOLOGY AS THE CREATION AND STAGES OF LIFE), e.g. "[Your lord] created man from a blood-clot *(ʿalaq)*" (Q 96:2), "Then we created a clot *(ʿalaqa)* from the drop" (Q 23:14), "Then from a sperm-drop, then from a blood clot *(ʿalaqa)*" (Q 40:67; 22:5) and "Then he was a blood clot *(ʿalaqa)*" (Q 75:38). Al-Rāzī's commentary stresses both the divine origin of human life and the inconsequential material of this genesis (*Tafsīr*, ad loc.).

Blood as a source of impurity finds expression when the Qurʾān instructs male believers not to have intercourse when their spouses are menstruating *(ḥāʾiḍ)* or about to menstruate (see MENSTRUATION; PURITY AND IMPURITY). For example, Q 2:222 states, "They will question you concerning the monthly cycle *(maḥīḍ)*. Withdraw from women during the monthly cycle and do not approach them until they become ritually clean."

References to the eye and eyesight express not only physical vision but also spiritual enlightenment. "Did we not make two eyes *(ʿaynayn)* for him" (Q 90:8) is an affirmation that human beings were created with the faculty of sight. "You will see their eyes *(aʿyun)* overflow with tears" (Q 5:83) refers to an experience of spiritual sight. In various other verses, the Qurʾān asserts that eyes are meant both to see and understand, as in Q 16:78: "He appointed for you hearing and sight *(abṣār)*."

Negative references to eyes and sight sustain this usage as a metaphor for those who are unable to distinguish right from wrong. Q 6:46 warns, "If God seizes your hearing and sight *(abṣār)*." Q 7:179, "They have eyes *(aʿyun)*, but do not see with them," expresses the strong disapproval of those whose eyes have been sealed. The possibility of divine retribution occurs in Q 36:66: "We would have obliterated their eyes *(aʿyun)*," while Q 3:13: "In that is a lesson for men possessed of eyes *(abṣār)*," continues the theme of spiritual insight. Yet the limits of this metaphor are indicated in verses such as "It is not the eyes *(abṣār)* that are blind" (Q 22:46).

Literal and metaphoric usages also characterize the qurʾānic references to the head. Prior to performing the pilgrimage (q.v.), male pilgrims shave their head immediately before they don the customary garb. The prescriptive force of "You shall enter the holy mosque *(al-masjid al-ḥarām)*, if God wills, in security, your heads *(ruʾūs)* shaved" (Q 48:27) conveys this instruction. Additional reference to the ritual treatment of the head may be found in verses like "Wipe your heads *(ruʾūs)* and your feet" (Q 5:6), which underscores the importance of purifying the body before praying or even entering a sacred space like a mosque. "Do not shave your heads *(ruʾūs)* until the offering reaches the place of sacrifice" (Q 2:196) gives the pilgrim permission to shave his head at the conclusion of the pilgrimage. Metaphorical allusions to the head or to raising it occur in connection with the sinner who is incapable of understanding the message the Prophet brought because of his arrogance (q.v.). Al-Zamakhsharī (d. 538/1144) understood, "We have put shackles up to their chins, so that their heads are forced up" (Q 36:8) as an allegory for the deliberate refusal of the truth (*Kashshāf*, ad loc.). For him, the rejection of the truth results in total chaos in the afterworld, as in "[They will be] running in confusion with their heads *(ruʾūs)* raised" (Q 14:43). In the verses that have been interpreted both literally and metaphorically, the Qurʾān speaks about sinners whose heads will suffer from their punishment (see REWARDS AND PUNISHMENT), as in "Boiling water will be poured on their heads *(ruʾūs)*" (Q 22:19). More particularly, the forehead is specified in "On the day they will be heated in the fire of hell (q.v.) and their forehead *(jibāh)*, sides and back will be burnt" (Q 9:35) to warn those who mispend their wealth.

Reference to the heart (*qalb*, pl. *qulūb*, see HEART) functions repeatedly as a mark of distinction between believers and unbelievers (see BELIEF AND UNBELIEF). "God has not assigned to any man two hearts *(qalbayn)* within his breast" (Q 33:4) indicates the individual's free choice to believe or disbelieve. Heart terminology also captures images of divine immanence, as in "God knows what is in your hearts *(qulūb)*" (Q 33:51) and "Know that God stands between a man and his heart *(qalb)*" (Q 8:24). In passages like "There is no fault in you, if you make mistakes, but only in what your hearts *(qulūb)* did purposely" (Q 33:5), the heart operates as a metaphor for the will. In others like "Those, in whose hearts he has inscribed faith and whom he has strengthened with a spirit from him *(bi-rūḥin minhu)*" (Q 58:22), the heart represents the imaged reception of divine guidance. For al-Zamakhsharī, the phrase "with a spirit from him" meant both illumination from the divine and the ways one becomes spiritually strengthened from that inspiration (*Kashshāf*, ad loc.). For him, the heart is integrally linked to being faithful as well as to remembering God, as in, "Those who believe, their hearts *(qulūb)* being at rest in remembrance of God" (Q 13:28).

As an explanation for unbelief, the Qurʾān frequently uses the metaphor of the "sealed heart." For example one finds, "thus God seals the hearts *(qulūb)* of the unbelievers" (Q 7:101), "God set a seal on their hearts *(qulūb)* and hearing" (Q 2:7) and many similar phrases (e.g. Q 6:46; 9:87, 93; 10:74; 16:108; 30:59; 40:35; 42:24; 45:43; 47:16; 63:3). Other similar images include Q 6:25: "We laid veils upon their hearts *(qulūb)*, but they failed to understand it," and Q 3:167: "Saying with their mouths that which never was in their hearts *(qulūb)*," both of which depict hearts that were affected by the misguided actions performed by unbelievers (Zamakhsharī, *Kashshāf*, ad loc.).

Mentions of the mouth often focus on its ethical misuse. Sins of hatred and hypocrisy are cited in "Hatred has already shown itself from their mouths *(afwāh)*" (Q 3:118), "Such men say, 'We believe,' with their mouths *(afwāh)*" (Q 5:41) and "Saying with their mouths *(afwāh)* something which never was in their heart" (Q 3:167). Additional misuses of the mouth are indicated in verses such as "You were speaking with your mouths *(afwāh)* regarding something of which you have no knowledge" (Q 24:15) and "They desire to extinguish the light of God with their mouths *(afwāh)*" (Q 9:32; 61:8). Less usual than references to the mouth are specific reference to the lips, as in "Have we not given him two eyes, and a tongue and two lips *(shafatayn)*?" (Q 90:8-9).

From another angle, qurʾānic injunctions target the speaking voice, both in regard to its potential for misuse and in regard to the necessity for propriety and control. In describing the qualities of the unbelievers, Q 47:30 mentions the way they are evasive and convoluted in their speech, when it states, "You shall certainly recognize them by their faulty speech *(laḥn al-qawl)*." To counteract these unacceptable forms of speech, the Qurʾān instructs the believers in their tone and in the times when they should reduce their speech. Examples are "Be modest in you gait and lower your voice *(ṣawt)*" (Q 31:19) and "Believers raise not your voice *(aṣwāt)* above the voice *(ṣawt)* of the Prophet" (Q 49:2-3). Q 49:3 even refers to lowering one's voice in the presence of the Prophet "Those who lower their voices *(aṣwāt)* in the presence of God's messenger."

References to the tongue *(lisān*, pl. *alsina)* center on its use for speaking the truth and following the way of God, as in the previously mentioned "Have we not given him two eyes, a tongue *(lisān)* and two lips"

(Q 90:8-9) and "We appointed unto them a high tongue of truthfulness" (Q 19:50). "Move not your tongue *(lisān)* with it to hasten it" (Q 75:16) urges the believers to recite the revelation carefully and thoughtfully. The tongue also appeals to God for forgiveness and repents for its sins, as in "Appoint me a tongue of truthfulness among the others" (Q 26:84).

By extension, the word "tongue" *(lisān)* is used to refer to language and human speech. Several passages proclaim that the Qurʾān was revealed in the Arabic language, for example "In a clear Arabic tongue *(bi-lisānin ʿarabiyyin mubīnin)*" (Q 26:195), "We have made it easy in your tongue" (Q 44:58) and "This is a book confirming in the Arabic tongue" (Q 46:12). Another instance of this usage is "We never sent a messenger who did not speak the tongue *(lisān)* of his people so that he may explain to them" (Q 14:4).

As with other parts of the body, the misuse of the tongue receives attention in the qurʾānic text. Q 4:46 speaks of the Jews "twisting their tongues *(alsina)* and slandering religion." While "Their tongues *(alsina)* describe falsehood" (Q 16:62) and the previously cited "They say with their tongues *(alsina)* something which is not in their hearts" (Q 48:11) provide further reference to this, verses like "Do not utter the lies your tongues *(alsina)* make up: 'This is lawful and that is forbidden,' in order to attribute your own lying inventions to God" (Q 16:116) connect with those that have an eschatological significance, such as, "The day when their tongues *(alsina)*, their hands and their feet shall testify against them" (Q 24:24).

Many qurʾānic passages forge a particular connection between the function of hearing and the reception of revelation. The verb "to hear" *(samiʿa)* corresponds to the active process of learning from what was heard. "He appointed for you hearing *(samʿ)*, sight and a heart" (Q 16:78) connects hearing to seeing and feeling, and "So that they may have hearts to understand and ears to hear with" (Q 22:46) confirms the linkage with comprehension of the revelation. Some verses point to the believers' continuity with previous communities who heard the revelation, as in "You will hear from those who were given the book before you" (Q 3:186). As with eyes and eyesight, the ears and the function of hearing are used to convey conceptions of God's intimacy with his creation and the probative signs he provides for them. Examples include, "Surely I will be with you, hearing *(asmaʿu)* and seeing" (Q 20:46) and "In that are signs for a people who listen *(yasmaʿūna)*" (Q 10:67).

By the same token, the unbelievers are chastised for their refusals to hear or to let their ears comprehend. Q 2:93 states, "They said, 'We hear *(samiʿnā)* and we disobey'" and Q 41:4 claims, "Most of them have turned away and do not hear *(lā yasmaʿūna)*." Additional instances are, "They have ears *(ādhān)*, but they hear not with them *(lā yasmaʿūna bihā)*" (Q 7:179), "If you call them to the guidance, they do not hear *(lā yasmaʿū)*" (Q 7:198), "But the deaf do not hear *(lā yasmaʿu)* the call when they are warned" (Q 21:45) and "When they hear *(samiʿū)* the reminder and say, 'Surely he is possessed'" (Q 68:51). The image of "sealing" and of possible divine intervention also finds a place in the qurʾānic references to ears and hearing, as with "God set a seal on their hearts and on their hearing" (*khatama 'llāhu ʿalā qulūbihim wa-ʿalā samʿi-him,* Q 2:7) and "Had God willed, he would have taken away their hearing and sight *(la-dhahaba bi-samʿihim wa-abṣārihim)*" (Q 2:20).

Both the generative organs of the human body and its other sexually provocative parts are ordinarily referred to indirectly in qurʾānic allusions to modesty. The preservation of modesty is mandated in "The believers have prospered... who guard their private parts *(furūj)*" (Q 23:1-5). Q 33:35 announces forgiveness and rewards for "men and women who guard their private parts *(furūj),*" while Q 4:34 praises "women who guard the intimacy *(ghayb)* which God has guarded." References such as "Those who guard their private parts *(furūj)*" (Q 70:29) have been understood to mean wearing clothing that does not reveal the body and restricting one's sexual desires to one's lawful mate. Similarly, mention of nudity (q.v.) in the Qurʾān has been understood both figuratively and spiritually. Q 20:118 refers to the initial condition of Adam and Eve (q.v.): "There you will have no hunger and not be naked *(lā taʿrā),*" while Q 20:121 "Then they ate from [the tree] and thereupon became conscious of their private parts *(sawʾāt)* and began to hide themselves with leaves" records one consequence of their fall from grace and innocence (see FALL OF MAN). In the verses concerning social and sexual legislation, the Qurʾān speaks of the circumstances under which the body may be partially or completely unclothed. Q 24:58, for example, specifies, "Before the prayer of the daybreak, when you lay aside your garments from the heat of the middle of the day and after the prayer of nightfall: the three occasions on which your nakedness *(ʿawrāt)* is likely to be bared.

Qamar-ul Huda

Bibliography
Primary: Abū ʿUbayda, *Majāz,* ed. F. Sezgin, 2 vols., Cairo 1954-62; Darwaza, *Tafsīr;* Ibn al-ʿArabī, *Aḥkām,* Cairo 1972[2]; Rāzī, *Tafsīr,* Cairo 1352/1933; Zamakhsharī, *Kashshāf,* 4 vols., Beirut 1995.
Secondary: M.K. ʿAbd al-ʿAzīz, *Iʿjāz al-Qurʾān fī ḥawāss al-insān. Dirāsa fī l-anf wa-l-udhun wa-l-ḥanjara fī ḍawʾ al-ṭibb wa-ʿulūm al-Qurʾān wa-l-ḥadīth,* Cairo 1987; V.A. Aʾzami, *Bait-ul-hikmat kī tibbī khidmāt* [in Urdu], New Delhi, 1989; P. Biller and A.J. Minnis (eds.), *Medieval theology and the natural body,* Rochester 1997; A.-K. Chéhadé, *Ibn an-Nafis et la découverte de la circulation pulmonaire,* Damascus 1955; A. Cranny-Francis, *The body in the text,* Carlton South, Vic. 1995; G. Flugel, *Concordance of the Koran,* Lahore 1978; S.K. Hamarneh, *Health sciences in early Islam,* ed. M.A. Anees, San Antonio 1984; H. Kassis, *A concordance of the Qurʾān,* California 1983; D.P. MacDonald, *Transgressive corporeality. The body, poststructuralism, and the theological imagination,* Albany 1995; F. Malti-Douglas, *Woman's body, woman's word. Gender and discourse in Arabo-Islamic writing,* Princeton 1991; M.G. Muazzam, *Ramadan fasting and medical science,*Stockwell 1991; J.B. Nelson, *Body theology,* Louisville 1992; T. Persaud, *Early history of human anatomy. From antiquity to the beginning of the modern era,* Springfield 1984; A.N. Qāsimī, *Miftāḥ al-Qurʾān,* trans. A. Shah, 2 vols., Lahore 1900; F. Rahman, *Health and medicine in the Islamic tradition. Change and identity,* Chicago 1998; C.J. Singer, *Evolution of anatomy. A short history of anatomy from the Greeks to Harvey,* New York 1957; S. Tirmizi, *Ilm-i tashrih-i badan men Musalmanon ka hissah* [in Urdu], Tirmizi 1978.

Ancestors see KINSHIP AND FAMILY

Angel

Heavenly messenger. Like its Hebrew *(malʾak)* and Greek *(angelos)* counterparts, the Arabic term *malak* (pl. *malāʾika*) means "messenger." The Qurʾān uses the term about ninety times, with some angels designated by name, Gabriel (Jibrīl, see GABRIEL) and Michael (Mikāʾīl, Q 2:97-8; see MICHAEL) and others only by function, e.g. reciters, glorifiers, dividers, guardians, ascenders, warners, recorders. Reflection about the role of angels — as described in the Qurʾān and elaborated in ḥadīth and commentary — constitutes a fundamental aspect of Muslim theological contemplation and spirituality.

Historical sources of discussion on the role of the angel

Belief in angels as a tenet of Islamic faith, as well as the theological and philosophical discussions that emerged in the Islamic world as to the nature and function of angels, must be understood within the larger context of three issues: 1) the qurʾānic worldview which affirms many elements of the monotheistic faiths of Judaism and Christianity including the concepts of the one transcendent God, revelation (q.v.), prophets (see PROPHETS AND PROPHETHOOD), angels, an end time and divine justice (see APOCALYPSE; LAST JUDGMENT); 2) the intellectual and cultural flowering that began under ʿAbbāsid rule in the second/eighth century which put Islamic scholars in contact with past and current intellectual traditions including those of Greek, Iranian and Indian origin and 3) the development and reciprocal influence of emerging discourses within the Islamic world particularly between philosophy *(falsafa)* and theology (*kalām*, see S.H. Nasr, *al-Ḥikma*, 139-43). Thus, for example, the most important of Muslim philosophers, Avicenna (Ibn Sīnā, d. 428/1037), integrated Aristotelian and neo-Platonic views on knowledge and experience into a fundamentally Islamic monotheistic revelatory worldview. In his treatment of angels, Avicenna shows how the angelic hierarchy affirmed in Muslim faith corresponds to the gradation of intelligences discerned by the philosophers, providing a philosophical grounding for the canonical imagery and function of angels and a religious grounding for the ontological and cosmological theories of the philosophers. Avicenna's work in turn was read, critiqued and incorporated in the work of subsequent scholars and popular wisdom teachers, from al-Ghazālī (d. 505/1111) to Ibn al-ʿArabī (d. 638/1240). The most striking use of angelic imagery in Islamic philosophy and mysticism was that of Shihāb al-Dīn al-Suhrawardī (d. 578/1191), founder of Illuminationism *(ishrāq)*, which is a form of mysticism deriving from Neoplatonism and the divine wisdom *(al-ḥikma al-ilāhiyya)* school of thought in Islam, which integrated qurʾānic, Platonic, Zoroastrian (with its vivid angelology), and Hermetic elements into a view of the universe the reality of which consists wholly of gradations of light (q.v.) with God as pure "Light of lights" (based on Q 24:35, the Light Verse), source of all existents and all knowledge — the inner reality of a thing being its "angel." See G. Webb, *The human-angelic relation* for a summary of the intellectual currents important in the development of commentary and interpretation of angels in the Qurʾān.

Qurʾānic thematic sources on the angels

The role of the angel in classical Islamic thought may be understood by looking at three major themes of the Qurʾān: creation (q.v.), revelation, and eschatology (q.v.) — and the elaboration thereof in ḥadīth — the sayings and stories attributed to Muḥammad — and commentary. The nature and function of angels is clearly meant to be understood in relation to the nature and function of other orders of reality, especially the divine and the human orders. Creation stories point to the theme of the relation between human beings and angels in terms of their differing natures and functions as well as to the theme of a pre-existent covenant (q.v.) between humankind and God. Qurʾānic materials on the "descent" *(tanzīl)* of the revelation to the Prophet Muḥammad and the "ascent" (*miʿrāj*, see ASCENSION) of the Prophet become sources of reflection on the nature of prophecy and revelatory knowledge including the role of angels therein. Qurʾānic eschatological materials reveal the intermediary function of the angels, that is, the carrying out of the divine consequences of human accountability, but they also become sources in Islamic spirituality for psycho-spiritual interpretations of the tomb and the end time ("the hour," *al-sāʿa*, or "the resurrection," *al-qiyāma,* see RESURRECTION).

Angels and the creation accounts

The qur'ānic accounts of creation provide models for the distinct nature of the human and angelic species, as well as for the distinction of types of knowledge in the human and angel. God asks the angels and Adam to name things; the angels could not and Adam could (Q 2:31-3). Muslim commentators interpret this qur'ānic statement as a demonstration of a human capacity which the angels lacked, that of creative knowledge, the knowledge of the nature of things. By virtue of his knowledge of the names, Adam became master over created things. Some commentators see the story as implying that God had taught Adam all of the divine names reflected in creation; therefore the human being stands in the unique ontological position of — potentially — being a mirror of the totality of the names and qualities of God, which became a prominent theme in Ṣūfī (Islamic mystical; see ṢŪFISM AND THE QUR'ĀN) thought (see al-Rūmī, *Mathnawī,* i, 1234; Ibn al-ʿArabī, *The bezels of wisdom,* ch. 1). The story is also seen as an affirmation of man's vicegerency. God creates Adam as his vicegerent *(khalīfa,* see CALIPH) on earth (Q 2:30) and ordered the angels to prostrate before him (Q 2:34; see ADORATION; BOWING AND PROSTRATION); hence the view that the human being *(insān)* is superior to angels. The angels plead with God, "Why will you [create one] who will create mischief therein and shed blood while we celebrate thy praises?" to which God responds, "I know what you do not know." A traditional reading of the narrative is humankind's superiority over the angels because, whereas the angels' nature is to worship God in perfect obedience (q.v.), human beings suffer moral choice, the struggle between good and evil, the tendency toward forgetfulness and heedlessness. Furthermore, man was burdened with the trust *(amāna,* Q 33:72) which heaven and earth refused to undertake — the trust being interpreted variously as responsibility, free will or love. Only Satan does not prostrate himself before Adam; but as Satan in other accounts is described as "of the jinn" (q.v.) those who are made of fire, not clay (q.v.) as Adam or light as the angels (see ADAM AND EVE). Satan (Shayṭān) is less identified with the "fallen angel" and more with the force that strengthens the tendencies toward evil and forgetfulness in man which function in tension with the human qualities of goodness and knowledge of the real (see DEVIL; ANTICHRIST).

The primordial time envisioned in the creation narratives, where "we were the companion of angels" as the mystic al-Rūmī (d. 672/1273) describes it in his *Kullīyāt-i Shams yā Dīwān-i kabīr* becomes, particularly among Ṣūfī commentators, a source of reflection and of longing for that original time of unity between man and God, when human beings "knew their Lord." Commentators on the primordial experience in which the souls of all future humans are "pulled from the loins of Adam" and testify to God's sovereignty (Q 7:172), see these verses as describing an on-going possibility of such "intimate colloquy" *(munājāt)* between man and God. Al-Tustarī (d. 283/896) identifies the idea of (spiritual) genesis with the cognizing and re-cognizing of divine lordship. He describes the act of remembrance in prayer *(dhikr)* as the re-actualization of God's presence in his innermost being, comparing this state of recollection to the constant celestial celebration of God's commemoration *(tasbīḥ)* on the part of the angels, holding that this celebration is their mode of being, their very sustenance *(rizq).* Just as the angel's very life *(ḥayāt)* is by virtue of the commemoration of God, so prayer is the vital part of man's spiritual life, the provision for the spiritual self *(nafs al-rūḥ)*.

Angels and the revelatory experience

The role of angels is a prominent feature in the qurʾānic theme of the revelatory event itself and the prophetic function, for it is in passages dealing with the revelation of the Qurʾān that we see the close relationship between the holy spirit *(rūḥ al-qudus)* and angels (Q 16:102). "Spirit" (q.v.) is the agency of revelation "that came upon the Prophet's heart," and the spirit and the angels appear together in several sūras (Q 70:4; 97:4; 16:2). As F. Rahman points out (*Major themes*, 97), the figure of Gabriel in the Qurʾān, who is mentioned as having brought down the Qurʾān, is never given the appellation of "angel" and is always differentiated from "the angels" as if to signify a different rank or even species, a supra-angelic function. The qurʾānic identification of Gabriel with the "bringing down" *(nazzalahu)* of the very word of God (Q 2:97), along with ḥadīth, in which Gabriel is spoken of as an angel, albeit with a special function and rank, contributed to the theological, philosophical and mystical theories which identified these concepts with each other (Holy Spirit = Angel = Gabriel). Note, for example, the "annunciation of Mary (q.v.)" passages in Q 3:42-8 and Q 19:17. In the former, the angels are messengers announcing to Mary that "God has chosen you and purified you and chosen you above women of all nations." In the latter, the messenger is singular and has the appearance of a man: "Then we sent to her our spirit (*rūḥanā*, though some translations, e.g. A. Yūsuf ʿAlī, render the phrase "our angel") and he appeared before her as a man." Other related passages, e.g. "We breathed into her of our spirit" (Q 21:91) and "Into whose body we breathed of our spirit (Q 66:12)" engender a close association between the concepts of spirit, angel and Gabriel. Rahman argues therefore that strictly speaking the Qurʾān seems to make a distinction between the angels and the agent of revelation sent to Muḥammad. Yet the spirit and angels are not wholly different, "the spirit" being the highest form of angelic nature and closest to God (e.g. Q 81:19-21).

There is also a close connection between the qurʾānic "command" *(amr)*, spirit and angels. "The command" in the qurʾānic phrase, "The spirit is by the command of my lord" (Q 17:85), is identified with the Preserved Tablet (*al-lawḥ al-maḥfūẓ*, see PRESERVED TABLET), the source of all books — in fact, all reality — including the Qurʾān (Q 85:22). It is from thence that the spirit is brought by the angels to the heart of the Prophet and, as the source of all books, ranks "higher" than the angels. These images and associations become food for speculative thought on the nature of "logos," the generation of the cosmos and such cosmogonic metaphysical conceptions as the world of archetypal realities *(ʿālam al-mithāl)*. A common feature of both early and late speculation in Islamic thought — in consonance with numerous qurʾānic passages (e.g. Q 2:97; 97:4) — is that the spirit exists as a power, faculty or agency which descends from "above" *(nazzalahu)*, clearly emphasizing the dependency and origin of human knowledge — particularly prophetic and visionary — in God. This power, or faculty, of spirit/Gabriel is described as being located in the Prophet's heart and Islamic mystical exegesis as early as the third/ninth century develops the notion of the heart (*qalb*, see HEART) as the seat of spiritual vision and intuitive cognition.

Related to the conception of the descent of revelation on the Prophet's heart — and closely related to the development of eschatological notions, are commentaries and literature about the qurʾānic reference to God sending Muḥammad on a night journey *(asrā bi-ʿabdihi)* in Q 17:1, in which the Prophet travels from "the sacred mosque to the farthest mosque," from Mecca to Jerusalem (q.v.; see also AQṢĀ MOSQUE) in the usual interpretation and then in a vertical journey to the divine throne ("in order that we might show him some of our signs"). By the third/ninth century many of these narratives of the ascension *(miʿrāj)* had come into the form of ḥadīth, many of which are attributed to Ibn ʿAbbās, a contemporary of Muḥammad, but are more likely the work of the second/eighth-century Egyptian Ibn Wahb (d. 197/813) which in varying versions and degrees of detail describe the awakening of the Prophet by Gabriel followed by the preparation of Muḥammad for his ascent by two angels' washing his breast and filling it with faith and wisdom. Gabriel — in some versions accompanied by the angel Michael — then leads Muḥammad on a night journey from Mecca to Jerusalem, then through the heavens of the Ptolemaic universe to the gates of paradise and finally to the throne of God (q.v.). Muḥammad's journey always includes the vision of hell and the appropriate punishment experienced by sinners who have committed various kinds of evils as well as a vision of the paradisiacal garden (see REWARD AND PUNISHMENT; PARADISE; HELL; GARDEN). The paradisiacal scene contains the traditional image of the lotus tree of the boundary (Q 53:14) beyond which no human or angel may pass. There is a hierarchy of angels with varying functions, an allusion to Q 25:25, which implies descending ranks of angels and Q 35:1 whose discussion of the varying number of wings possessed by angels is usually interpreted as their functions, duties or errands. The angels of the heavenly spheres — the association made explicit by Avicenna — down through the sixth sphere are the guardians of the throne and singers of praise. Gabriel ranks above the guardians of the throne. Angels in the highest sphere under the throne are the cherubim whose light is so strong that no angel in the lower spheres may raise its eyes lest it be blinded. Gabriel, the guide of Muḥammad, acts as interpreter of the visions to which the Prophet is witness. Descriptions of the garden are based on the qurʾānic imagery of the fount of abundance (*kawthar,* Q 108:1) and of peace (Q 14:23). Angels in these traditions, which have been traced to the second/eighth-century Persian Maysara b. ʿAbd Rabbihi appear sometimes in human form, sometimes as huge and monstrous beings, always radiating dazzling light. At each stage of the journey, Muḥammad experiences fear of being blinded by the brilliant spectacle and Gabriel in many versions intercedes with God so that Muḥammad is granted new vision that allows him to look at the light that had heretofore blinded him. Gabriel furthermore acts as advisor and comforter. Although Gabriel acts as interpreter of the visions for the duration of the ascent, Muḥammad is left by the angel to accomplish the last stage alone.

The ascension *(miʿrāj)* literature developed alongside and fused with Muslim eschatological literature. What the angel reveals to Muḥammad in his journey becomes the prototype of the experience of the soul upon physical death and the angel functions both as part of the hierarchy of being and as revealer and interpreter of that hierarchy. Abū Yazīd al-Bisṭāmī (d. 261/874), who first formulated the Islamic notion of annihilation of the self in God *(fanāʾ),* appears also to have been the first to describe the inner transformative experience of the pious Muslim in terms of the ascension of the Prophet which thereafter becomes the prototype of the various stages and stations of the experience of the Ṣūfī in his experience of attaining the presence of God. Inasmuch as the qurʾānic verses on the nocturnal ascent (Q 17:1), Muḥammad's ecstatic vision of the two bows (Q 53:1-18) and the descent of the Qurʾān (Q 2:97) all became associated in tradition with an angelic event, the specific relation of the angel to the role of the Prophet — and angelic knowledge to human knowledge — becomes a source of speculation. In L. Massignon's remarks on the "two bows verse" he states, "In Surah 53, the culminating point of ecstasy is clearly marked by the sentence of verses 8-9: 'Then he went out, then he returned, near; it was a distance of two bow shots or a little closer (*thumma danā fa-tadallā; fakāna qāba qawsayni aw adnā, The passion of al-Hallaj,* trans. H. Mason, iii, 295-6). He points out that opinions have differed as to the subject of the sentence: some commentaries consider Gabriel as the one who draws near to Muḥammad who in turn sees him (e.g. Ibn Qayyim al-Jawziyya); some say it is God who draws near to Muḥammad (al-Ḥasan al-Baṣrī); some suggest Muḥammad as subject (Ibn ʿAbbās and al-Ḥallāj); others suggest two successive subjects, Muḥammad and Gabriel (Fakhr al-Dīn al-Rāzī); finally, others say it is a simultaneous mutual coming together of God and Muḥammad. However, in all cases Muḥammad's experience is seen as an ecstatic vision of "divine nature by man's spiritual nature, through the instrumentality of an illuminated angelic nature" (L. Massignon, *The passion of al-Hallāj,* iii, 298).

Angels in eschatological literature

Parallel to the development of the literature on Muḥammad's ascension are the traditions which discuss and interpret the process of death and the day of resurrection — eschatological themes — that is, themes referring to the "end time." Murata (Angels) and Smith and Haddad *(Islamic understanding)* detail the qurʾānic and subsequent interpretive traditions regarding angels in Islamic eschatology. Angels function in qurʾānic end-time — the cataclysmic end of the created order — sources in a number of ways. They usher in the day of resurrection: "The day when they see the angels. No good tidings that day for the sinners" (Q 25:22). "The day when the heavens and the clouds are split asunder and the angels are sent down in a great descent" (Q 25:25). They are gatherers of souls: "The angel of death, who has been charged with you, will gather you; then to your Lord you will be returned" (Q 32:11; cf. 6:93). They guard over hell: "Believers, guard yourselves and your families against a fire whose fuel is men and stones, and over which are harsh, terrible angels" (Q 66:6). They shall enter the eternal abode with those human souls who have shown devotion: "The angels shall enter unto them from every gate" (Q 13:23). The "Mālik" (Q 43:77) who rules over hell is traditionally thought to be an angel. Ḥadīth materials and traditional commentators give names to other angels whose functions are described in the Qurʾān: ʿIzrāʾīl is the angel of death that appears to the person at the cessation of life and Isrāfīl is the angel charged with the blowing of the trumpet at the arrival of "the hour" (*al-sāʿa,* Q 39:68; 69:13). Though not mentioned in the Qurʾān or early ḥadith, the angel Riḍwān became an accepted figure in Arabic literature from the time of al-Maʿarrī onwards, perhaps in relation to the word (*riḍwān,* Q 9:21) indicating God's favor, or sanction.

There are a number of manuals and teaching stories describing end-time events which became particularly important in popular piety with regard to issues of death: al-Ghazālī's *al-Durra al-fākhira* (fifth/eleventh century), Ibn Qayyim al-Jawziyya's *Kitāb al-Rūḥ* (an authoritative eighth/fourteenth century text on the life of the spirit after death), al-Suyūṭī's *Bushra al-ka'īb bi-liqā' al-ḥabīb* (ninth/fifteenth century), the anonymous *Kitāb Aḥwāl al-qiyāma* (ed. M. Wolff; most likely an adaptation of al-Qāḍī's work, probably fifth/eleventh century, *Daqā'iq al-akhbār fī dhikr al-janna wa-l-nār*). Contemporary manuals on death reflect these traditions, such as *To die before death* by the twentieth-century Sri Lankan Ṣūfī Shaykh, Bawa Muhaiyaddeen. It is clear that the theologians *(mutakallimūn)* and the Ṣūfī commentators were for the most part not interested — when it came to death themes — in determining a given sequence of events, but rather were concerned with using these traditions to illustrate specific points about the nature of God, the human being and ethics. Qur'ānic discussions on death and resurrection are aspects of the theme of the nature of divine justice; the symmetry of the heavens is a symmetry — a perfection — of justice and accountability for one's deeds. There is ultimately no evasion from acknowledging the shape that one's faith *(dīn)* and piety *(taqwā)* has taken during one's life. The *Durra* and the *Kitāb Aḥwāl* develop the theme of the death visit of the recording angels, Nakīr and Munkar, who in some narratives allow the deceased a glimpse of the gates of Eden; who question the deceased on their recitation of the Qur'ān, prayers and right conduct; who remove the soul from the body with ease, shock or pain depending on the quality of faithfulness in life, the latter, an extension of Q 79:1-5, "By the angels who tear out (the souls of the wicked)… by those who gently draw out (the souls of the blessed)…." The descriptions of the fate of the soul after death parallel the ascension imagery, the overarching theme being the soul's immediate tasting of the fruits of its religious duties as it ascends on a journey with Gabriel or the angels, sometimes mentioned as two or four, acting as guides through the successive heavens.

Al-Ghazālī's *Durra* describes the cosmological stages of the journey of the faithful soul through the seven levels of the heavens, through oceans of fire, light, darkness, water, ice and hail, the length of which is a thousand years and, finally, through the covering affixed to the throne of mercy. The fate of the impious soul is described as an attempted journey by the soul in the company of the angel Daqyā'īl, but he is thwarted in his attempt to lead the soul to the throne. The gates of heaven do not open up to the pair and Daqyā'īl flings the soul back into the body — even as the corpse is being washed. Thus, the traditions of the soul's peace or suffering at death as well as the discussions of the symmetry of the cosmological heavens as abodes for various categories of saints and sinners support qur'ānic and theological themes of divine justice and the variety of human responses to the call of faith. Al-Ghazālī also utilizes the figure of the angel Rūmān who visits each newly deceased person even prior to the questioning of Nakīr and Munkar and asks the deceased to write down the good and evil deeds he has done. The dead person protests that he or she has no pen, ink, or paper; Rūmān — or in some traditions, simply Munkar and Nakīr — orders the deceased to substitute his own finger, saliva and shroud. The tradition concludes with the deceased sealing the record and hanging it onto his neck until the day of resurrection, an allusion to Q 17:13, "We have fastened the fate of every man on his neck."

Little is said in the Qur'ān about the state between death and resurrection, the time of angelic visitation and instruction immediately after death. The term partition (*bar-*

zakh, q.v.) in the Qurʾān (Q 23:100) simply refers to the inability of the departed to return to earth — to do or to undo how one has lived his or her faith. The partition or barrier comes to denote, however, the time between death and resurrection and the place or abode wherein the waiting occurs. The imagery of the partition in death and resurrection literature is a further affirmation of the qurʾānic themes of divine justice and human accountability. Moreover, the traditions regarding the barrier emphasize the themes of conscious awareness of the configuration of the life of faith or lived religion *(dīn)* during one's earthly existence *(al-dunyā)* and the angel — mirroring the role of Gabriel in Muḥammad's ascension — as constant companion, guide and cognitive intermediary in the death process. These traditions regarding the barrier echo qurʾānic end-time themes, focusing on that moment: "When the great cataclysm comes, that day when man will recall what he had been striving for" (Q 79:34-5), "the hour" when every human being will be shaken into a unique and unprecedented self-awareness of his deeds in which "We have lifted your veil so your sight today is keen" (Q 50:22). The eschatological themes of the transparency of the heart as an ultimate aim of the human being and the questioning of the soul "immediately" after death by the angels and by the guards of the gates of hell (Q 39:71-4) — also identified with angels — signify key theological themes in Islam: while God is utterly transcendent, it is through the divine mercy and illumination that self-understanding takes place and this justice mandates that the human being experiences/knows the motivations and consequences of his deeds.

The mystical schools of thought in Islam in particular interpreted the qurʾānic day of resurrection *(yawm al-qiyāma),* "the day when the earth shall be transmuted into something else" (Q 14:48), when "we shall create you in [forms] you do not know" (Q 56:61) as referring not only to the end of the world and one's physical existence but also to an interior state of transformation *in this life*. The annihilation of all things at the end time, is seen as a spiritual state of having overcome the struggle in the human heart against the lower self *(nafs),* the world *(dunyā)* and Satan — a "dying before death." As Böwering describes in *The mystical vision of experience in classical Islam* (149-58), this experience is one of reintegration into the lasting presence of the one God in which one is granted the encounter with God *(liqāʾ al-ḥaqq),* the abiding in the divine truth *(al-baqāʾ maʿa al-ḥaqq)* and the visual perception of God *(al-naẓar ilā l-ḥaqq)*. The heart *(qalb)* becomes in mystical literature the seat of knowledge "through God's knowledge" and the angel becomes identified as the purifier of the heart, the spiritual cleansing of which is seen as a prerequisite for clear understanding of God, self and the world. Furthermore, the qurʾānic "expansion" of Muḥammad's breast: "Did we not expand your breast?" (Q 94:1) is read as a widening or opening of Muḥammad to the infusion of divine gifts and is described as being initiated "through the light of the prophetic mission" *(nūr al-risāla)* and through the "light of Islam" *(nūr al-islām)*. Thus, links are made in early Islamic mystical literature (e.g. Tustarī, *Tafsīr,* 123, in Böwering, *Mystical vision*) between the heart of Muḥammad — the essence or living reality of Muḥammad, which receives its pristine light from the divine substance, the light of prophecy — and the symbol of the angel as the agent of the initial expansion of Muḥammad's breast and, by extension, the expansion (the opening and receptivity) of "whomsoever God desires to guide" to spiritual realities. The early Islamic mystics speak of the peak of mystical experience as a prefiguring of the final day of resurrection in which all humankind will be exposed before God in order to account for their deeds as well as a prefiguring of that final annihilation of the created order (Q 28:88; 55:26-7). In the eschatological traditions, Isrāfīl (who is not named in the Qurʾān) is the angel who sounds the trumpet signaling the arrival of the hour, as stated above, and who reads from the Preserved Tablet (q.v.; *al-lawḥ al-maḥfūẓ*), the account of human creatures' deeds and motivations. In many traditions there is a second blast signaling the final cataclysm at which time all created order must lose itself, even the angels and archangels. We see, then, in classical mystical literature the development of the notion of the unveiling *(kashf)*, that is, the revealing of one's most secret motivations to oneself by the agency of the angel of God through the light of God himself and the notion of the ultimate goal and end of individual existence as the annihilation of the self *(nafs)*, the realization that all perishes but the "face of God" (Q 55:26-7).

Gisela Webb

Bibliography
Primary: ʿAbd al-Raḥīm b. Aḥmad al-Qāḍī, *Daqāʾiq al-akhbār fī dhikr al-janna wa-l-nār,* trans. ʿA. al-Raḥmān, *Islamic book of the dead,* Norwich 1977; al-Ghazālī, Abū Ḥāmid Muḥammad, *al-Durra al-fākhira,* ed. M. Gautier, Leipzig 1877, trans. J. Smith, *The precious pearl. A translation from the Arabic with notes of the* Kitāb al-durra al-fākhira fī kashf ʿulūm al-ākhira, Missoula 1979; Ibn al-ʿArabī, *Fuṣūṣ al-ḥikam,* ed. A.A. Affifi, Cairo 1946, trans. R.W.J. Austin, *Bezels of wisdom,* New York 1980; id., *al-Futūḥāt al-makkiyya,* 4 vols., Cairo 1911; Jalāl al-Dīn Rūmī, *Mathnawī-yi maʿnawī,* i, 1234; id., *Kullīyāt-i Shams yā Dīwān-i kabīr;* Muhaiyaddeen, M.R. Bawa, *To die before death,* Philadelphia 1997; al-Qazwīnī, Zakariyya, *Kitāb ʿAjāʾib al-makhlūqāt wa-gharīb al-mawjūdāt,* ed. F. Wüstenfeld, Gottingen 1849; al-Suhrawardī, Shihāb al-Dīn, *Oeuvres philosophiques et mystiques. Opera metaphysica et mystica II,* ed. H. Corbin, Teheran 1954; id., *Oeuvres philosophiques et mystiques. Opera metaphysica et mystica III,* ed. S.H. Nasr and H. Corbin, Teheran 1970, 1976 (rev. ed.), trans. W. Thackston, *The mystical and visionary treatises of Suhrawardi,* London 1982; al-Suyūṭī, *Bushrā al-kaʾīb bi-liqāʾ al-ḥabīb,* Cairo 1969; M. Wolff (ed.), *Kitāb Aḥwāl al-qiyāma,* Leipzig 1872.
Secondary: M. Asin Palacios, *La escatologia musulmana en la Divina Comedia,* Madrid 1919; G. Böwering, *The mystical vision of existence in classical Islam,* New York 1980; W. Chittick, *The Sufi path of knowledge,* New York 1989; id., *The Sufi path of love,* Albany 1983; H. Corbin, *Avicenna and the visionary recital,* Irving 1980; id., *Creative imagination in the Sufism of Ibn ʿArabi,* Princeton 1964; id., *The man of light in Iranian Sufism,* Boulder 1978; T. Izutsu, *A comparative study of key philosophical concepts in Sufism and Taoism,* Tokyo 1966; A. Jeffery, Ibn ʿArabi's *shajarat al-kawn* (trans. and comm.), in *SI* 10-11 (1959), 43-77, 113-60;L. Massignon, *The passion of al-Hallaj,* trans. H. Mason, 4 vols., Princeton 1982; J. Morris, The spiritual ascension. Ibn ʿArabī and the miʿrāj, in *JAOS* 107 (1987), 629-52; 108 (1988), 63-77; S. Murata, Angels, in S.H. Nasr (ed.), *Islamic spirituality foundations,* New York 1987, 324-44; S. Murata and W. Chittick, *The vision of Islam,* New York 1994; S.H. Nasr, *al-Ḥikmat al-ilāhiyyah* and *kalām,* in *SI* 33 (1971), 130-43; id., *Three Muslim sages,* Delmar 1976; id., Shihāb al-Din Yaḥyā Suhrawardī's *maqtūl,* in M.M. Sharif (ed.), *A history of Muslim philosophy,* 2 vols., Wiesbaden 1963-6; I. Netton, *Muslim neoplatonists. An introduction to the thought of the Brethren of Purity,* London 1982; F. Peters, Origins of Islamic Platonism. The school tradition, in P. Morewedge (ed.), *Islamic philosophical theology,* Albany 1979; F. Rahman, *Prophecy in Islam,* Chicago 1979; id., *Major themes in the Quran,* Minneapolis 1980; A. Schimmel, *Mystical dimensions of Islam,* Chapel Hill 1975; J. Smith and Y. Haddad, *The Islamic understanding of death and resurrection,* Albany 1981; G. Webb, *The human-angelic relation in the philosophies of Suhrawardi and Ibn Arabi,* Ph.D. diss., Temple 1989.

Anger

A manifestation of God's opprobrium mentioned numerous times in the Qurʾān in the context of his censure of unbelievers, detractors of Muḥammad and those guilty of moral and material crimes and general wrongdoing. It is furthermore an emotion attributed to believers, Muḥammad's enemies and prophets, for instance Moses (q.v.) and Jonah (q.v.).

God's anger, paired occasionally with his curse (q.v.; Q 4:93; 5:60; 24:9; 48:6), symbolizes his negative opinion of certain human behavior. Among past nations, the pre-Islamic prophet Hūd (q.v.) informed the people of ʿĀd (q.v.) of God's anger against them (Q 7:71), while the People of the Book (q.v.) incurred God's anger by mistreating messengers sent to them (Q 3:112). Jews (see JEWS AND JUDAISM) in particular are chastised for disobeying their prophets' monotheistic injunctions (Q 2:61; 7:152; 20:86).

Polytheists, hypocrites and those who swear to falsehood knowingly are among those who provoke God's wrath (Q 48:6; 58:14; see BELIEF AND UNBELIEF; HYPOCRITES AND HYPOCRISY). Their lasting abode is a blazing fire that wants to consume them in its fury (Q 25:12). Jews and other People of the Book also continue to incur God's wrath by aligning themselves with the unbelievers (Q 5:59-60) and by "denying the revelation which God has sent down" (Q 2:90). See also OPPOSITION TO MUḤAMMAD.

Aside from the specifically named groups, those who are religiously and morally misdirected in a general sense are also subject to God's anger (Q 1:7; 3:162; 20:81; 47:28; 60:13). In addition, God's wrath falls on those miscreants who spread discontent among the believers by attempting to dissuade them from their faith (Q 42:16). The same fate is reserved for a believer who relinquishes his faith, unless under compulsion or torture (Q 16:106), for someone who murders a believer (Q 4:93) and for a believer who turns away from a righteous battle (Q 8:16). A woman accused of adultery by her husband may, in the absence of any evidence in support of the adultery such as other witnesses, refute the charge by professing her innocence and swearing that God's wrath be upon her if her accuser is telling the truth (Q 24:9). See also APOSTASY; MURDER; ADULTERY AND FORNICATION.

With respect to anger as a human emotion, the Qurʾān mentions Moses' outburst against his people for being led astray in worshipping a calf of gold (q.v.) during his absence (Q 7:150, 154; 20:86). The prophet Jonah was angry at God in a moment of unjustified frustration, but eventually realized his error and was saved (Q 21:87-8). When the time of fighting against those who oppose Muḥammad is over, the Qurʾān states that God improves the believers' hearts by removing their anger against their enemies and making them merciful (Q 9:15). Suppression of anger is generally deemed a praiseworthy quality (Q 3:134; 42:37). In contrast to the merciful believers, the unbelievers (Q 22:15; 33:25; 48:29), the hypocrites (Q 3:119) and those who criticize Muḥammad out of greed (Q 9:58) are said to be seething in anger because of his success and God's protection of him. See also PUNISHMENT STORIES.

Shahzad Bashir

Bibliography
Nwyia, *Exégèse*, 74-99; Watt-Bell, *Introduction*, 127-35.

Animal Life

The references to fauna in the Qurʾān. There are more than two hundred passages in the Qurʾān dealing with animals and six sūras bear the names of animals as titles (Q 2 The Cow [Sūrat al-Baqara]; Q 6 The Herding Animals [Sūrat al-Anʿām]; Q 16 The Bee [Sūrat al-Naḥl]; Q 27 The Ant [Sūrat al-Naml]; Q 29 The Spider [Sūrat al-ʿAnkabūt]; Q 105 The Elephant

[Sūrat al-Fīl]). Nevertheless, animal life is not a predominant theme in the Qurʾān.

Animal species

The common Arabic word for "animal" *ḥayawān* (lit. life) occurs only once in the Qurʾān (Q 29:64) and actually does not refer to an animal, but rather to life in the next world. Arabic authors of the Middle Ages commonly classified animals into four basic categories on the basis of their habitat. They separated animals living on dry land from those living in the air, those living in dust and those living in water. We find no evidence of this classification in the Qurʾān, which only distinguishes between animals which creep on their belly, animals which walk on two legs and animals with four legs. Yet some other distinctions are also found, e.g. animals similar to men are of greater importance than others. Likewise, some kinds of animals, such as fish, are discussed less.

The qurʾānic term for animal in general and the land animal in particular is *dābba* with 18 occurrences (pl. *dawābb*), although this word is not typically used in this sense in medieval Arabic works on zoology. The most frequently-occurring animal name in the Qurʾān is *anʿām,* "gregarious or herding animals" (thirty-two occurrences) and there are three occurrences of its synonym *bahīmat al-anʿām,* referring to livestock and large domestic animals. The singular form *naʿam* only occurs once. The animals which live in herds include domestic animals as well as those driven to pasture, which represent the wealth of men. Q 6:143-4 identifies them as sheep, goats, camels — more precisely dromedaries — and cattle. There is also a certain number of specific references to each of these species. General terms for camel (q.v.) such as *ibil* (twice), *jamal/jimāla* (twice) and *nāqa* (seven times) occur alongside more specific terms. *ʿIshār* (a she-camel ten months with young), *ḍāmir* (the lean one, meaning a riding camel), *rikāb* (a generic term for "riding animal," which in the Qurʾānic passage [Q 59:6] is clearly not referring to a horse but to a camel), *budn* (sacrificial camels) and *hīm* (camels crazed with thirst) occur only once. In addition, there are two terms which probably also mean "camel," *ḥamūla* and *farsh* (Q 6:142), but the exact meaning and scope of these words was disputed. *Ḥamūla* was obviously connected with the root *ḥ-m-l,* bearing the basic sense of "to carry." Thus, according to the interpretation preferred by the famous exegete al-Ṭabarī (d. 310/923) and most others who have commented on this passage, *ḥamūla* are mature camels capable of carrying a load while *farsh* are camels too young to support any weight. Some commentators have speculated that *ḥamūla* are camels and cows while *farsh* are sheep or that *ḥamūla* are camels and cows while *farsh* are everything else. Others reasoned that *ḥamūla* are camels, horses, asses and other animals and *farsh* are sheep (*Tafsīr,* viii, 62-4). There are nineteen occurrences of terms for "cattle" and "cow" (*baqar/baqara/baqarāt,* and *ʿijl* for calf), eight occurrences of terms for "sheep" (*ḍaʾn, ghanam* and *naʿja/niʿāj,* "female sheep"), but only one occurrence of *maʿz* (goat).

The word *khayl* for "horse" occurs five times in the Qurʾān and we find once the word *muʿallaqa* used metaphorically for a "disregarded woman" (Q 4:129), a term with the original sense of a mare which is no longer ridden. The title and the first verse of sūras 79 (Those that Draw *[al-nāziʿāt]*) and 100 (The Runners *[al-ʿādiyāt]*) are probably further references to horses. The titles of sūras 37 (Those who Dress the Ranks *[al-ṣāffāt]*), 51 (Those that Scatter *[al-dhāriyāt]*) and 77 (Those that are Sent *[al-mursalāt]*) may also refer to them as well. We also find words denoting asses (*ḥimār/ḥumur/ḥamīr,* four occurrences) and mules (*bighāl*, a single occurrence). "Swine" *(khinzīr/khanāzīr)* and "dog" (*kalb*, see DOG) each occur five times in the Qurʾān.

Wild animals are also mentioned. We find four references to "quarry" *(ṣayd)*, i.e. an animal being hunted, and three references to "wolf" *(dhiʾb)*. Furthermore, there is one occurrence of a general term for "beast of prey" *(sabuʿ)*, one occurrence of "lion" (*qaswara*, a word for "lion" that is otherwise rarely encountered), three occurrences of "apes" *(qirada)* and one occurrence of "elephant" *(fīl)*.

With regard to flying animals or birds, there are twenty-four occurrences of the general terms *ṭayr* and *ṭāʾir* (*ṭayr* is also used for "omen"). A term of particular interest is *jawāriḥ* which in qurʾānic usage means "hunting animals," while later Arabic authors use this term exclusively for "birds of prey." There are only a few references to specific species of birds. We find one mention of "quail" *(salwā)*, one of "hoopoe" *(hudhud)* and two of "raven" *(ghurāb)*. Furthermore, mention is made of flocks of birds called *abābīl*, although the exact meaning of this word remains unclear. According to some commentators, there was a verse in the Qurʾān referring to the three pre-Islamic goddesses al-Lāt, al-ʿUzzā and Manāt, who were described as "cranes" (*gharānīq*, the qurʾānic usage of this word is connected to Q 53:19-20). However, it should be noted the question of whether this verse ever existed has been hotly debated (see SATANIC VERSES).

Although the Arabic language has a great number of words for reptiles and crawling and flying insects, very few of them are to be found in the Qurʾān. Only "snake" *(thuʿbān, ḥayya)*, "ant" (*naml/namla*, also *dharra*, "ant" being only one of several possible meanings of the last), "fly" *(dhubāb)*, "gnat" *(baʿūḍa)*, "lice" *(qummal)*, "locusts" *(jarād)*, "moths" (*farāsh*, also used for "butterflies"), "bees" *(naḥl)*, "spider" *(ʿankabūt)* and "termite" (*dābbat al-arḍ*, with *arḍ* understood to be "wood" and not "earth" in this usage. This term is not to be confused with the *dābba min al-arḍ* — beast coming from the earth — of the Apocalypse, q.v.). We find *ḥūt/ḥītān* used for "fish" in general in the Qurʾān and there is one special fish (*nūn*, a whale?) which swallowed Jonah. Frogs *(ḍafādiʿ)* are also mentioned. Several passages also make reference to body parts of animals, such as wings, claws and trunks, as well as to products from animals, such as eggs, feathers, fat, milk, meat and skin, and even musk, pearls and coral.

The creation of animals and their destiny

God cares for all his creatures and provides for them (Q 11:6; 29:60; see CREATION). The Qurʾān asserts that God is the creator of every living creature (Q 2:29). The beasts which God has dispersed in the heavens and the earth are given special mention in the Qurʾān as divine signs (Q 2:164; 31:10; 42:29; 45:4; cf. also Q 25:49). God created animals *(dābba)* from water (Q 24:45), just as he created every living thing (*shayʾ ḥayy*, Q 21:30). No further remarks about the origin of life are found in the Qurʾān. God created pairs of every living thing (Q 43:12 and 51:49 refer to couples and hence to the different species of living beings), which should be interpreted as a reference to males and females. Q 53:45 definitely makes a distinction between the two sexes. Herd animals close to man are explicitly emphasized (Q 16:5; 36:71). Four of the animals usually driven to pasture — sheep, goats, camels and cattle (Q 6:143-4; 39:6) — were said to have been created in pairs. Gregarious animals are of great importance. When Satan wanted to lead humankind astray, he planned to cut the ears of camels with the intention of changing an animal which God had created (Q 4:119). Furthermore, God instructed Noah (q.v.) to take two examples of all the animal species onto his ark to save them from drowning (Q 23:27). Just like men, animals *(dābba)* and birds form communities (*umam,* Q 6:38, a reference to groups of animals of the same species living together), which will be assembled before God (Q 42:29). The following passages seem to indicate that animals will be resurrected, although this is never explicitly stated.

God subjected his whole creation (q.v.), including animals, to men (Q 22:65; 45:13) and also provided men with cattle (Q 26:133). Therefore animals must have been created in order to serve men, especially the domestic animals and those driven to pasture. Q 16:5-8 refers to these two main uses for animals, to carry loads and to warm and feed men. Furthermore, horses, mules, asses and camels are to be ridden (Q 6:142; 22:27; 36:72; 40:79-80). Men regard horses as desirable property (Q 3:14), but they are only appurtenances of the life of this world and should not be esteemed too highly. There are also passages in the Qurʾān referring to animal products like pure milk from the belly of animals (Q 16:66; 23:21; 36:73), skins (Q 16:80) and the healing power of honey (Q 16:69). All of these benefits exemplify God's concern for humanity. Animals are of still further use for men as adornments. Q 16:8 refers explicitly to horses, mules and asses in this regard. Q 35:12, in an apparent reference to pearls, speaks of the wearing of adornments coming from the depths of the sea (Q 22:23; 35:33). Coral (q.v.) in particular is described as pleasing to look at (Q 55:58; 56:23; 76:19). Q 16:6 describes the pleasure one has in looking at cattle when they are brought home or driven out to pasture. Thus it seems to have also been God's intention to create animals for the aesthetic enjoyment of man.

Naturally, all of the animals are at God's disposal: "There is not a beast but he takes it by the forelock" (Q 11:56). God sends down rain to revive dead land and slake the thirst of his creation (Q 25:48-9; cf. 10:24; see AGRICULTURE AND VEGETATION). By his order, flocks are led to pasture (Q 20:54). The bee is following God's command when it makes its home in the mountains, trees and manmade structures and eats from the various fruits (Q 16:68-9). Animals benefit man in many ways and stand as proof of God's benevolence toward man, who, according to the Islamic viewpoint, stands in the center of creation and dominates the universe, having precedence over all other creatures (cf. Q 17:70). Even animal products coming out of the sea, such as pearls and corals, represent God's mercy (Q 55:22).

Animals in Islamic law

The Qurʾān includes many regulations for the use of animals and animal products, as well as for hunting. The quintessence of these regulations is that animals are a benefit to humankind, either as food or as sacrifices. Man is allowed to kill animals to keep himself alive. He may eat animals on condition that they are lawful *(ḥalāl)* and that they fall into the category of "good things" (*ṭayyibāt,* cf. Q 2:172; 7:157; 23:51). Furthermore, they must be slaughtered in accordance with the law, although the Qurʾān itself offers no information regarding the technical details of this operation (see CONSECRATION OF ANIMALS).

The Qurʾān provides the basic outline of Islamic dietary law, emphasizing the unlawful over the lawful foods. A number of verses (Q 2:173; 5:3, 145; 16:115; cf. 6:118-9, 121; 22:34) prohibit the consumption of carcasses, blood, and pork as well as any other meat over which any name other than God's has been invoked. The Qurʾān explicitly mentions what is unlawful while everything else is assumed to be lawful and permitted (cf. Q 5:1; 6:119) and even the forbidden foods are permitted in emergencies

(Q 2:173; 6:119; 16:115). The only foods explicitly characterized as lawful in the Qur'ān are animals taken from fresh or salt water (Q 16:14; 35:12). The consumption of poultry and veal are mentioned in contexts that indicate that they specifically are not forbidden. Poultry will be the food of the blessed in paradise (Q 56:21) and Abraham (q.v.) fed the flesh of a calf to his angelic guests (Q 11:69). Dishes eaten by Jews and Christians are also permitted to Muslims except for those which are specifically forbidden (q.v.), such as pork.

Islamic dietary restrictions are portrayed as a relaxation of both the customs observed by the pagan Arabs (Q 6:138) and the Jewish dietary law (Q 6:146, 4:160), which is described as prohibiting the eating of animals having claws and certain kinds of fat from cattle and small livestock. The Jewish prohibitions had already been partially abrogated by Jesus (q.v.; Q 3:50; see ABROGATION).

Q 22:36 refers to sacrificial camels *(budn)* as signs *(sha'ā'ir)* of God (see SIGNS). The sacrificial animals *(hady)* mentioned in Q 5:2 and 5:97 should probably be identified as camels and sheep. The Qur'ān prohibits the bloodless sacrifices or consecrations practiced in pre-Islamic times in which animals were set free and allowed to go wherever their impulses led them (Q 5:103). These animals are privileged creatures that were neither milked nor ridden. According to the most common interpretation of the relevant Arabic terms, the animals which could serve as a bloodless consecration in the past were a she-camel which has borne five young ones, the last one being male *(baḥīra);* a she-camel subject to the owner's vow *(sā'iba);* the only male descendant of a goat which had also given birth to three female kids *(waṣīla);* a camel having offspring old enough to be ridden; or a stallion which has sired ten foals *(ḥāmī).*

As for hunting, animals living within the sacred precincts (q.v.) around Mecca are taboo (Q 5:1). The prescription declares that the hunting of land animals within this area is forbidden, while aquatic animals remain lawful (Q 5:95). According to the Qur'ān, this prohibition is nothing less than a test God is imposing on man (Q 5:1, 94-6). It is interesting to note that all of the qur'ānic references to punishment and compensations having to do with animals concern the pilgrimage (q.v.) to the Ka'ba (q.v.) in Mecca (5:94-5).

The qur'ānic dietary regulations are neither completely nor systematically presented. The rules concerning slaughtering and hunting are also not very detailed. This situation may be a reflection of a debate or dialogue over dietary regulations occurring between the Muslims and the Jews of Medina (q.v.; see also JEWS AND JUDAISM), since the rules offered by the Qur'ān appear to be answers to particular questions raised in that environment and do not constitute a full-fledged dietary code. Thus, many vital questions awaited the attention of later scholars for answers. In order to elaborate and systematize the isolated qur'ānic injunctions, the experts in Islamic law turned to the practice of the Prophet as documented in the ḥadīth. Initially, the passages concerning animals in the ḥadīth received little attention, but when the jurists tried to draw up a complete dietary code, emphasis was also placed on what the Prophet himself had said about animals. It was then that the relevant and appropriate passages became of interest and hence of real importance.

Animals as signs of God's omnipotence and warnings of punishment

Animals were created because of God's benevolence and goodwill toward humankind. Moreover, their existence is proof of God's omnipotence and wisdom. He is the one who has the power to create life and to destroy it (cf. Q 3:27). The Qurʾān particularly emphasizes the marvelous flight of birds which are kept in the air by God (Q 16:79; 67:19). There are also tales about the events of the past which illustrate God's omnipotence and in which animals figure. Manna and quails were sent down to the Children of Israel (q.v.; Q 2:57; 7:160; 20:80). The dog of the Seven Sleepers is mentioned (Q 18:18; see MEN OF THE CAVE). There is also a similar story of a man who was brought back to life after one hundred years and instructed to look at his ass, among other things, so that he could appreciate how much time had passed (Q 2:259). God brought to life four dead birds before the eyes of Abraham (q.v.; Q 2:260). There has been only one living being who on one special occasion God permitted to create life and this was Jesus. He created figures like birds from clay and then breathed upon them, bringing them to life (Q 3:49; 5:110). Therefore, Jesus is privileged. Although not a part of the New Testament, in the apocrypha we do find a story about the young Jesus creating twelve sparrows from clay on the Sabbath.

Here, one may see a relation between animals which are signs of God's omnipotence and those which are symbols representing warnings and admonitions. Animals are frequently cited when humankind is commanded to fear God's punishment. God may let the animals needed by men perish in order to call them to account for their misdeeds (Q 16:61; 35:45; during the events of the Apocalypse (q.v.), even camels ten months with young will be untended, cf. Q 81:4). On the other hand, animals are powerful signs to convert the infidels and make them observe God's commands. In this connection, the unbeliever is instructed to examine a camel to realize God's greatness (Q 88:17) and we are warned that sinners "will not enter the Garden until a camel passes through the eye of a needle" (Q 7:40; cf. *Matt* 19:24, *Mark* 10:25, and also *Luke* 18:25, not referring to sinners but to the rich).

As for the warnings, the Qurʾān cites instances in history in which animals play different roles (see also PUNISHMENT STORIES; WARNING). The people of Thamūd (q.v.) were punished after they hamstrung a she-camel the prophet Ṣāliḥ (q.v.) had brought forth to demonstrate the power of God (Q 7:73-9). In this case, an animal led to God's intervention. There are many different occasions when God used animals as instruments to guide men toward the good or the bad. God sent plagues of locusts, lice and frogs to punish the sinful Egyptians who thought themselves mighty (Q 7:133). God also dispatched the raven which showed Cain how to hide the corpse of his brother Abel (Q 5:31; see CAIN AND ABEL). As a punishment for impiety, God transformed human beings into swine and apes for worshipping evil (Q 5:60) and some Jews were transformed into detestable apes as punishment for breaking the Sabbath (Q 2:65; 7:166). In reference to more recent times, Q 105 describes the military expedition of the Abyssinian general Abraha (q.v.) to Mecca (ca. 570 C.E.) on which occasion the Abyssinians were accompanied by at least one elephant. In their raid against the Meccans, the Muslims had horses at their disposal (Q 8:60). Flocks of birds attacked and destroyed the army of the people of the elephant (Q 105:3-4; see also ABYSSINIA). In another passage speaking of the successes of the early Muslims, God reminds them that he alone is responsible: "You spurred neither horse nor camel" (Q 59:6). Even Satan musters horses (Q 17:64).

Many of the animals found in the Bible are also mentioned in the Qurʾān to show God's authority, omnipotence and wisdom. The staff of Moses (q.v.) was turned into a snake as a divine sign. (The serpent is called *thuʿbān* in Q 7:107; 26:32, but *ḥayya* in Q 20:20. Minor differences in the versions of the story itself are neglected in this article.) Solomon (q.v.) understands the speech of an ant advising caution to his fellows (Q 27:18.) The jinn (q.v.) learned that Solomon had died when a termite *(dābbat al-arḍ)* ate away the staff his body had been leaning on (Q 34:14). A fish (a whale?, *ḥūt,* Q 21:87-8; 37:142-5; 68:48-9; *nūn,* Q 21:87-8) swallowed Jonah (q.v.) and then cast him in the desert.

In the Qurʾān, we find further references to legendary events dealing with animals. There are references to the cow being sacrificed by the Israelites by order of Moses (Q 2:67-71). The intended breakfast of Moses on his journey with the wise man to reach the junction of the two seas is a fish (Q 18:61-3; see KHAḌIR/KHIḌR). Birds are gathered as troops by Solomon, in addition to men and jinn (Q 27:17-20, followed by the story of the hoopoe). Birds are seen in a dream which Joseph (q.v.) interprets (Q 12:36, 41). The dog of the Seven Sleepers is mentioned four times but is never named (Q 18:18, 22). David (q.v.) and Solomon ruled in a case in which the sheep of one shepherd wandered into the field of someone else (Q 21:78). David also settled a dispute between two brothers over the ownership of another sheep (Q 38:23-4). In the narrative on Joseph, his brothers play on their father's fear that Joseph would be eaten by a wolf by claiming that a wolf had killed him (Q 12:13-7).

Nevertheless, God grants grace and possesses unlimited compassion, e.g. toward the Israelites who have taken as a god the golden calf (Q 2:521-4, 92-3; 7:148, 152; 20:88; see CALF OF GOLD). Humankind should not forget about the goodness of God. They should turn to him, praise him, adore and worship him and confess their dependence on him (see ADORATION; BOWING AND PROSTRATION; WORSHIP). This is the reason that the Qurʾān offers a number of arguments derived from history and from nature (Q 2:116, everything is submissive to God; 17:44; 24:41; 43:12; 59:24; 61:1; 62:1; 64:1, everyone in the heavens and on earth gives glory to God). The animals (every *dābba,* Q 16:49; 22:18) worship God by prostrating themselves, including the birds, which do so while flying (Q 24:41). The birds as well as mountains sing his praises (Q 34:10; cf. 38:19).

Animals as symbols and objects of comparisons

In certain cases, we find animals referred to in analogies. The flames of hell throw out sparks as large as castles the color of "yellow camels" (*jimāla ṣufr,* Q 77:32-3). The word *dharra* means a "tiny particle," an "atom," a "grain" or an "ant." God does not do an ant's weight of wrong (Q 4:40). Something as tiny as an ant does not escape God's attention (Q 10:61). Those who have done an ant's weight of good or evil (q.v.) will see it on the day of judgment (Q 99:7-8; see LAST JUDGMENT). Other small insects are symbols of the insignificant and trivial. The idols (see IDOLS AND IMAGES) people had formerly worshipped cannot create even a "fly" (*dhubāb,* Q 22:73). God "does not disdain to coin a simile (q.v.) from a gnat" (*baʿūḍa,* Q 2:26).

As for the comparison of men with animals or the metaphorical use of animals in the Qurʾān, it is worth noting that negativity and deprecation predominate. It is chiefly the sinners and infidels who are compared to animals. Those who have disbelieved and those who do not want to believe (Q 8:55) and the metaphorically deaf and dumb who do not understand (Q 8:22) are the worst of beasts *(dawābb).* In hell, the infidels will drink boiling water the way a camel crazy with thirst *(hīm)* drinks (Q 56:55). Unbelievers are more misguided and heedless than cattle *(anʿām)* and are even further astray than cattle (Q 7:179;

25:44). They even eat as cattle do, oblivious to anything else (Q 47:12). The Jews, who do not understand or adhere to the laws of the Torah (q.v.), are like an ass carrying books (Q 62:5). On the day of judgment, sinners will be like startled asses fleeing from a mighty lion (*qaswara,* Q 74:50-1). Those who choose for themselves benefactors other than God are to be likened to the spider (q.v.) because it chooses for itself the frailest of houses (Q 29:41). An unflattering comparison with animals also occurs in Q 2:171: "A simile of those who disbelieved is like someone calling to goats, something which hears nothing but a calling and a shouting [without comprehension]." In Q 7:176, one of the infidels is compared to a dog that lolls out its tongue "whether you attack him… or leave him alone." If anyone associates anything with God, it is as if he fell down from heaven and the birds snatched him away or the wind swept him to a remote place (Q 22:31). Furthermore, on the day of judgment, men will come forth from the tombs as if "they were locusts scattered abroad" (Q 54:7) and people will be "like moths scattered" (Q 101:4). Those who disbelieve and behave arrogantly will not enter the garden until "a camel passes through the eye of a needle" (Q 7:40).

The zoological elements of the Qurʾān

Very little zoological information is found in the Qurʾān. Zoological realities based on actual observation are not offered in the Qurʾān. The Qurʾān does not describe animals in any depth and only very few passages refer to animal behavior. Remarkably, where we do find zoological accounts is mainly in reference to insects. The spider chooses the frailest of houses (Q 29:41). God commanded the bee, in the sūra named after the insect: "Take as houses the mountains, the trees and the arbors men erect. Then eat all of the fruits" (Q 16:68-9). These verses show awareness of the natural environment spiders and bees inhabit. The mention of the termite *(dābbat al-arḍ)* gnawing Solomon's staff displays knowledge of its eating habits (Q 34:14). Locusts are described as "scattered abroad" (Q 54:7).

The qurʾānic descriptions of animal behavior are very basic and for the most part are confined to commonly-known matters. The Qurʾān also draws upon popular pseudo-zoological lore, e.g. some animals are able to talk. Three animals speak in the presence of Solomon, who understands their language (Q 27:16, 18, 22-6). As was mentioned above, Solomon understood the words of an ant advising the other ants to avoid being stepped on (Q 27:18). Solomon was said to know the speech of birds as well (Q 27:22-6). In fact, it is a hoopoe — an exotic looking bird indigenous to most of the old world — who informs Solomon about the Queen of Sheba, her magnificent trappings and her heathen ways (Q 27:22-6; see also SHEBA; BILQĪS). The bird then bore a letter from Solomon to the Queen. This story was a favorite of the commentators and was considerably elaborated in later literature. The fourth animal able to speak is the beast of the Apocalypse (*dābba min al-arḍ,* "the beast coming out of earth," Q 27:82) which has not yet spoken, but eventually will. There is no information in the Qurʾān about what this beast will look like or what it will do. Nevertheless, later commentators, basing their accounts on the prophetic ḥadīth, are able to provide a fairly detailed description of it. Apart from the beast of the Apocalypse (q.v.) and the aforementioned birds *(abābīl)* which destroyed the army of the People of the Elephant (q.v.), no other mythical and theriomorphic beings are mentioned in the Qurʾān. While the Qurʾān does not personify animals, in a very few instances animals appear as primary actors. The most notable exceptions are King Solomon's hoopoe (Q 22:28), Cain's raven (Q 5:31) and the flocks of birds which stymied the People of the Elephant (Q 105:3) and Solomon's ant and termite. However, these animals always act to benefit men and none actually possesses any individuality. Consequently, we cannot say that the Qurʾān offers much information about animal behavior.

The Qurʾān, like Arabic zoological literature of later centuries, contains no reflections on animals for their own sake or in connection to purely zoological aims. Animals are only examined in respect to humankind. The description of animals in classical Arabic literature centers on a few important points. Only one of these is treated in the Qurʾān and these are the practical components of the legal regulations. The Qurʾān clearly did not provide a framework for the zoological research of later authors. This fact is indeed striking, since the Qurʾān contrasts with pre-Islamic poetry which is full of descriptions of the appearance and behavior of a great number of wild and domestic animals.

Conclusion

Neither animals nor animal life are a principal theme in the Qurʾān. Though there are six sūras named after identifiable animals, animals are not described in any depth. They stand as signs of God's omnipotence and sometimes play a role in his attempts to warn sinful peoples. The Qurʾān, like later Islamic writing on animals, deals with them in relation to man and not their life in their natural surroundings. Animals were created to serve humankind. Nevertheless, the Qurʾān does not provide much information on how people should treat animals. Observation of animals in their natural surroundings is not a qurʾānic topic. If it had been, it may have led to the development of scientific zoology. There are certain passages in the Qurʾān which would make us expect far-reaching reflections on animals. But even in these passages, many details remain unexamined or not described. Reflections on folk and animal lore are lacking as well. Also, the few animals who are mentioned in more than a few passages in the Qurʾān are neither really informative nor detailed. Furthermore, the presentation of animals sometimes seems inconsistent. For instance, cattle adore the Lord, but when mentioned in analogies their description is negative. Apart from the power of speaking, animals are not personified and they never bear personal names. Animals have no individual existence in the Qurʾān. What is more, the Qurʾān displays a decidedly urban attitude towards animals. This attitude is also prominent in later Arabic prose writings on animals. Within this literature as well, numerous accounts of animals are collected without any real scientific research.

The qurʾānic view of animals created the Islamic tendency toward anthropocentrism. According to this viewpoint, animals are beholden to humankind in principle and must be seen in relation to men. Therefore, the animal's right to exist is based on its coexistence with men. As a consequence, pets were not considered fit companions for humans, and they were not portrayed as such in either the Qurʾān or in later Arabic literature.

Herbert Eisenstein

Bibliography

Primary: Ṭabarī, *Tafsīr*, ed. A.S. ʿAlī.
Secondary: A. Abel, Dābba, in *EI²*, i, 71; A.A. Ambros, Gestaltung und Funktionen der Biosphäre im Koran, in *ZDMG* 140 (1990), 290-325.; id., Mensch und Biosphäre im Koran, in B. Scholz (ed.), *Der orientalische Mensch und seine Beziehungen zur Umwelt. Beiträge zum 2. Grazer Morgenländischen Symposion (2.-5. März 1989)*, Graz 1989, 51-7; M. Bucaille, *The Bible, the Qurʾān and science. The holy scriptures examined in the light of*

modern knowledge, Tripoli 1987, esp. 197-210; J. Burton, Those are the high-flying cranes, in *JSS* 15 (1970), 246-65; H. Eisenstein, Bemerkungen zur *dābbat al-arḍ* in Koran 34, 13 (13), in *WZKM* 79 (1989), 131-7; id., *Einführung in die arabische Zoographie. Das tierkundliche Wissen in der arabisch-islamischen Literatur*, Berlin 1991, esp. 12-21; E. Gräf, *Jagdbeute und Schlachttier im islamischen Recht. Eine Untersuchung zur Entwicklung der islamischen Jurisprudenz*, Bonn 1959, 4-66; I. Lichtenstädter, A note on the *gharānīq* and related Qurʾānic problems, in *IOS* 5 (1975), 54-61; T. O'Shaughnessy, Creation from nothing and the teaching of the Qurʾān, in *ZDMG* 120 (1971), 274-80; C. Pellat, L.P. Elwell-Sutton and P.N. Boratav, Ḥayawān, in *EI²*, iii, 304-15; N. Robinson, Creating birds from clay. A miracle of Jesus in the Qurʾān and in classical Muslim exegesis, in *MW* 79 (1989), 1-13; T. Sabbagh, *La métaphore dans le Coran*, Paris 1943, esp. 100-7.

Anointing

The ritual practice of touching objects or persons with scented oils. A practice common to various cultures of the ancient Near East, anointing is typically done on festive occasions and avoided during periods of fasting and mourning, although it is used in burials. It has also been a ritual act of the dedication of an individual to the deity. In the ancient Near East, kingship especially was conferred formally through anointing rather than through a crown or other fabricated symbols. The practice of anointing was then extended to the priesthood in the person of the high priest who adopted many of the roles of the king. It is in that context that the anointing of David (q.v.) in ancient Israel and the image of Jesus (q.v.) as the anointed one — in Greek, the "Christ", and Hebrew, the "Messiah" — were developed. The Christian usage carries a deeper sense than that of the simple act of being anointed. It conveys also the eschatological idea of the promised redeemer.

In Arabic, *duhn* can be used in the sense of anointing oil and that may be the meaning reflected in Q 23:20, "a tree issuing from the Mount of Sinai that bears oil *(duhn)* and flavoring for foods." In the common use of the word *duhn*, however, there appears to be no particular religious significance. It is used in connection with the anointing of one's moustache, face or hair with oil, perhaps specifically sesame oil, or an ointment. *Zayt*, another word for oil, perhaps specifically olive oil, has the sense of an oil for burning, certainly when used in Q 24:35, "whose oil well-nigh would shine, even if no fire touched it."

It is in the word *masīḥ* in reference to Jesus, of course, that the prime interest in this concept arises. The word is used eleven times in the Qurʾān ("the Messiah, Jesus, son of Mary (q.v.)" in Q 3:45; 4:157; 4:171; "the Messiah, Mary's son" in Q 5:17, 72, 75; 9:31; "Messiah" in Q 4:172; 5:17, 72; 9:30) and is a loanword from the Aramaic *meshīḥā* (see FOREIGN VOCABULARY). The sense often attached to that word is "purified" or "filled with blessing," both fairly obvious attempts at isolating an appropriate meaning with little foundation in the language and mainly derived from exegesis (see Q 19:31 in which Jesus says of himself, "He has made me blessed *(mubārak)* wherever I be"). The idea of connecting the word to "touching," a root sense in Arabic, also produced the idea that Jesus' touch could heal; thus it was suggested that Jesus had this power because he had been "touched" himself as had the earlier prophets (see PROPHETS AND PROPHETHOOD). Al-Fīrūzābādī (*Baṣāʾir*, iv, 499-505) has been able to compile a list of forty-nine different meanings for the word *masīḥ*, indicating the extent to which the exegetes went in order to find an explanation for a word which would avoid the Christian connotations. In the use of *al-masīḥ* in reference to Jesus in the Qurʾān, there is little significance given to the sense of "anointing" as it had become connected to the

Redeemer in Christianity, who is known as *al-Masīḥ*. The common statement that *al-Masīḥ* is understood as a proper name or perhaps a title of honor — in the same way that "Christ" frequently is understood in popular Christianity — would appear to be the best conclusion about its occurrence in Q 3:45: "His name *(ism)* shall be the Messiah, Jesus, son of Mary," although the use of the proper article with a non-Arabic proper name is unknown in other instances.

The use of the word *al-masīḥ* in connection with the Antichrist (q.v.; see also APOCALYPSE), the one-eyed *al-Masīḥ al-Dajjāl*, follows the Syriac usage and does not alter the fundamental observation that the ancient idea of "anointed" is very remote from any Muslim use of the term *al-masīḥ*.

Andrew Rippin

Bibliography
Primary: Fīrūzābādī, *Baṣāʾir*, iv, 499-505.
Secondary: M. Hayek, L'origine des termes ʿIsā al-Masīḥ (Jésus-Christ) dans le Coran, in *Orient syrien* 7 (1992), 223-54, 365-82; Horovitz, *KU*, 129-30; Jeffery, *For. vocab.*, 765-6; H. Michaud, *Jésus selon le Coran*, Neuchatel 1960, 44-9; G. Parrinder, *Jesus in the Qurʾān*, London 1965, 30-4; A. Wensinck and C. Bosworth, al-Masīḥ, in *EI*[1], vi, 726.

Anṣār see EMIGRANTS AND HELPERS

Ant see ANIMAL LIFE

Anthropocentricity see CREATION

Anthropology see SOCIAL SCIENCES AND THE QURʾĀN

Anthropomorphism

Ascribing human attributes to God. *Tashbīh*, the term most commonly rendered in English as "anthropomorphism," does not appear in the Qurʾān with that meaning. The second form of the root *sh-b-h* appears only once, in the passive voice, in reference to Jesus' death: "They did not kill him nor did they crucify him, but it appeared to [Jesus' followers that they had]" (Q 4:157). The sixth form occurs nine times, predominantly denoting "likeness," as in Q 2:70: "To us all cows look alike." The form *tashābaha* also connotes ascribing associates to God (Q 13:16). It also appears in Q 3:7, which distinguishes between the ambiguous verses of the Qurʾān *(mutashābihāt)* and the clear verses (*muḥkamāt*, see AMBIGUOUS).

Another expression of anthropomorphism was found in the ontological claim by some Muslims that God has a physical body *(jism)*. Corporealism *(tajsīm)* was not based on any occurrence of the term with that sense in the Qurʾān but rather on literal understandings of qurʾānic descriptions of God as having a physical body and also on the ground that God exists and only that which has physical extension can exist. Nonetheless, references in the Qurʾān gave rise to the image of God having a human form. Often cited were such passages as the Throne Verse (Q 2:255; cf. 20:5; see THRONE OF GOD) which suggests that God is seated on a throne in heaven and the passages that suggest God has hands (e.g. Q 3:73; 5:64; 48:10) and eyes (e.g. Q 20:39; 52:48; 54:14). Quite early on, those who accepted literal meanings of passages in the Qurʾān that likened God to humans were labeled by their opponents as anthropomorphists *(mushabbihūn)*.

The background of Islamic anthropomorphism

The topic of likening God or gods to humans was already well-known in the Middle East prior to the rise of Islam, both in Christianity and in Judaism. It had been discussed much earlier by the Greeks. The poet Xenophanes (fl. ca. 570-470 B.C.E.), in his criticism of the anthropomorphism of Homer and Hesiod (fl. ca. 700 B.C.E.), claimed that God could in no way be like human beings. This led, as H. Wolfson has argued (*Philo,* i, 125), to a struggle between the popular conception of Olympic deities in human form on the one side and the abstract philosophical conceptions on the other. The latter came to be expressed through allegorical interpretations of the human representations of the gods, a solution not unlike the one argued by Muʿtazilite theologians in Islamic discussions of the question. In certain passages the Hebrew Bible portrays God in human terms, with hands (e.g. *Isa* 41:13) and feet (*Zech* 14:4) and so on; but Hebrew scripture in other passages distances God from human likeness (*Isa* 40:25, 46:5; *Ps* 89:7). As with the Greeks, opposition to anthropomorphic understandings of God in the Hebrew Bible was strongest among philosophers like Philo (d. ca. 50) and later Talmudic scholars. Among the Church Fathers, it was the less educated monks who asserted the anthropomorphic conceptions of God. Clement of Alexandria (d. ca. 215) and Origen (d. ca. 254), under the influence of Philo and perhaps the Greek philosophers, rejected anthropomorphism on theological grounds.

The formation of the discourse on anthropomorphism and corporealism in the first three centuries of Islam in many ways resembles the earlier discussions among the Christians, Jews and pagan Greeks. It was Plotinus (d. ca. 270) who said in the *Enneads,* "The One is, in truth, beyond all statement; whatever you say would limit it..." (5, iii, 1215). In the early second/eighth century, the church father John of Damascus (d. 749), under the employ of the Umayyad chancery, included in his *De fide orthodoxa* a chapter on the human need to conceive of God metaphorically in human terms (A.J. Wensinck, *Muslim creed,* 68). Although some Neoplatonic and Christian influence on Muslim thinking in this regard is possible, the earliest statements of the problem in Islam are clearly linked to disputes about how to interpret passages in the Qurʾān that ascribe, or seem to ascribe, human attributes to God. Moreover, since the great majority of Muslim speculative theologians *(mutakallimūn)* denied anthropomorphism, the textual record of this dispute is accordingly biased against those who held that God may be described literally in human terms. The critique of anthropomorphism among those who denied the anthropomorphic doctrine of God was expressed by the term *taʿṭīl* (divesting God of all human attributes). In point of fact, most of the speculative theologians and their opponents who disputed this doctrine found ways to hedge extreme positions of totally affirming or totally denying the human attributes of God. *Tashbīh* and *taʿṭīl* became terms of opprobrium used ascriptively, rather than descriptively, as accusations against theological opponents.

Anthropomorphism in early and medieval Islam

The context of the earliest expressions of anthropomorphic views of God is difficult to establish with precision. Although it is possible to speak in general terms of the way theological movements, such as Ashʿarī or Muʿtazilīs (q.v.) or the Ḥanbalī scholars of ḥadīth *(muḥaddithūn),* approached the problem of anthropomorphism, it is more accurate to analyze how individual theologians stated the problem and often that must be based on textual evidence as scant as one or more brief quotations preserved in later sources.

Muslim heresiographical sources locate the first arguments in favor of the position that God lacks human attributes, that is, denying anthropomorphic views of God, in the tumultuous final decade of the civil war during the second quarter of the second/eighth century that brought the Umayyad Arab kingdom down and ushered in the ʿAbbāsid age. Two rather shadowy figures among the earliest theologians were said to have advanced arguments against anthropomorphism: Jaʿd b. Dirham, who was put to death for his heterodox religious views around the year 126/744, and Jahm b. Ṣafwān, who also was executed in 128/745 for his religious teachings. The theological views of Jahm are better attested by later heresiographers. According to the heresiographer al-Shahrastānī (d. 548/1153), Jahm said it is not possible to describe the Creator by an attribute by which his creatures are described because this would entail likening God to his creatures (*Milal*, i, 86). Abū l-Ḥasan al-Ashʿarī (d. 324/936) quotes Jahm and some of the Zaydī Shīʿīs as saying that God cannot be described as a thing *(shayʾ)* because a created thing has a likeness to other created things (*Maqālāt*, 181). Al-Ashʿarī quotes an argument from Jahm that identifies him also as an anti-corporealist: God cannot be a thing because a thing, according to Jahm, is an existent body and God cannot be so described (*Maqālāt*, 494). Modern scholars have suspected that Jahm was influenced by the Neoplatonic doctrine of the unique Transcendent One (R.M. Frank, Neoplatonism, 399-402; B. Abrahamov, *Anthropomorphism*, 12). One can infer from the later association of the attack against anthropomorphism with such heterodox figures as Jaʿd and Jahm that in the emerging orthodoxy of the late Umayyad period anthropomorphic conceptions of God must have been well established. Denying that God had human attributes entailed more than mere theological conflict. R. Strothmann has pointed out that third/ninth-century Muʿtazilīs in Baghdad accused the pro-ʿUthmān party, known as the "rising generation" *(nābita)* among the speculative theologians, of professing anthropomorphic views of God. Political conflict played a role that one can identify in these early theological conflicts but not always describe in much depth or detail.

Those often accused of anthropomorphism, the collectors and teachers of the prophetic ḥadīth, were known as the "adherents of ḥadīth" *(aṣḥāb al-ḥadīth, ahl al-ḥadīth)*. The extreme literalists were often referred to contemptuously by Muʿtazilī and Ashʿarī theologians as *ḥashwiyya* (derived from *ḥashwa*, forcemeat) because they accepted anthropomorphic descriptions of God in the Qurʾān "without [asking] how" *(bi-lā kayf)*. The defense of their views regarding anthropomorphism is often traced to Aḥmad b. Ḥanbal (d. 241/855) whose statements on anthropomorphism were described in the next generation by al-Ashʿarī (d. 324/935) in his *Maqālāt* (pp. 290-7). There al-Ashʿarī reports that the "adherents of the ḥadīth and sunna (q.v.)" — referring in this context to the followers of Ibn Ḥanbal — confess "without [asking] how, that God is on his throne, just as He said [in the Qurʾān] — 'The Beneficent One, who is seated on his throne' [Q 20:5] — and that he has two hands" (*Maqālāt*, 290). Although Ibn Ḥanbal and the adherents of ḥadīth generally rejected the Muʿtazilī doctrine of purifying God of all human attributes, he is also counted among those who rejected the doctrine of anthropomorphism. Indeed, the Ḥanbalī method of dealing with troublesome theological claims by not attempting to explain them rationally often led to the stance of affirming neither of two conflicting views. Al-Shahrastānī tells us that Aḥmad b. Ḥanbal and other adherents of ḥadīth took a more moderate position, affirming their belief in everything revealed in the Qurʾān and authentic ḥadīth while at the same time asserting that God is not like any of his creatures (*Milal*, i, 104). Some of the early Imāmī (Twelver) Shīʿīs — referred to by Muʿtazilīs, Ashʿarīs and others as "turncoats" *(rāfiḍa)* — on the other side, asserted both corporealism, i.e. God has a physical body, and anthropomorphism, i.e. God's body is like a human body. The later Imāmī Shīʿīs who studied theology *(kalām)* with Muʿtazilī teachers did not affirm anthropomorphism (al-Ashʿarī, *Maqālāt*, 34-5). Another early Muslim sect accused of anthropomorphism and corporealism was the Karrāmiyya, a group that began in Khurāsān in the first half of the third/ninth century and continued to attract followers until the Mongol devastation of the seventh/thirteenth century.

Beyond the ascription of anthropomorphism to these sects, certain individuals among the early theologians were also accused of holding and defending such views. Opposing such views were the majority of the theologians of the Muʿtazilī, Ashʿarī and Māturīdī schools. Also, the second/eighth-century Qurʾān exegete, Muqātil b. Sulaymān, was accused by later Muslims of holding anthropomorphic views of God, but the recent publication of his qurʾānic commentary *(tafsīr)* indicates that he understood some of the seemingly anthropomorphic passages in the Qurʾān figuratively (B. Abrahamov, *Anthropomorphism*, 4-6).

The problems of anthropomorphism and corporealism lay at the heart of the disputes about God in Islamic theology. For some, such as the more extreme Imāmī Shīʿīs, anthropomorphic and corporealistic notions of God were necessary ontologically; for they believed that God could not be said to exist unless he had physical extension in space and time. Yet, as the Muʿtazilites and other theologians argued, a God limited by a body could not be omnipresent. For the extremists among the Sunnī adherents of ḥadīth, asserting anthropomorphic views of God seems to have been more a matter of fideism based on scriptural literalism *(tamthīl)*. Such crude literalism could be attacked by reference to the Qurʾān itself. Q 42:11, for example, says of God: "nothing is like him" *(laysa ka-mithlihi shayʾun)*. For the theologians who attacked anthropomorphism, the discourse became more abstract and specialized over the problem of divine attributes. The Muʿtazilī and Ashʿarī theologians generally disagreed with each other as to why anthropomorphism was a matter of theological error. Inasmuch as they denied that it was possible for God to possess human or any attributes, the majority of the Muʿtazilīs adopted a doctrine of God *via negativa*. Al-Ashʿarī described the Muʿtazilī view in the third/ninth century as God "is not comparable with humans and does not resemble creatures in any respect" (*Maqālāt*, 155). The Muʿtazilīs also advanced the concept of *tanzīh*, the declaration that God is free of any impurities such as the ascription of human attributes to him. Al-Ashʿarī himself, following scholars of ḥadīth *(muḥaddithūn)* like Aḥmad b. Ḥanbal, argued that what the Qurʾān states about God — such as passages referring to God's eyes, feet, hands, face and seated body — should be accepted as true "without [asking] how," thus neither affirming the anthropomorphic or non-anthropomorphic interpretations (B. Abrahamov, *Anthropomorphism*, 6).

Anthropomorphic passages in the Qurʾān basically posed a problem in hermeneutics, for the question that remained for all but the most crude literalists *(mumaththilūn)* was how these qurʾānic passages could be interpreted without violating the divine nature. The Muʿtazilīs took the position that God's word, i.e. the Qurʾān, must be rational and therefore the rational, i.e. true, meaning of the anthropomorphic and ambiguous *(mutashābihāt)* passages must be determined allegorically or figuratively. This is the hermeneutical principle behind allegorical interpretation *(taʾwīl)*. Eventually Ashʿarī and Shīʿī exegetes came to prefer allegorical over literal methods of interpreting the Qurʾān (S. Wasserstrom, *Between Muslim and Jew*, 136-53). Like Ibn Ḥanbal, al-Ashʿarī also claimed that the anthropomorphic passages in the Qurʾān must be accepted "without asking how." Yet, in the *Book of the sparkle* (*Kitāb al-Lumaʿ*, 9) he offers a rationale for rejecting the claim that God is like his creatures: If he were like them in any or all respects, he would be, like creatures, temporally produced in those respects and it is impossible to say this about the eternal, uncreated God (*Lumaʿ*, 9).

In contemporary Islamic theology, the position usually found is the Ashʿarite melding of literalist and rationalist treatments of the anthropomorphic passages in the Qurʾān. Among many modernist thinkers, the more stringent Muʿtazilī denial of anthropomorphism is even argued, though it is seldom identified as such. See also GOD AND HIS ATTRIBUTES; EXEGESIS OF THE QURʾĀN: CLASSICAL AND MEDIEVAL.

Richard C. Martin

Bibliography

Primary: al-Ashʿarī, Abū l-Ḥasan, *Maqālāt al-islāmiyyīn*, ed. H. Ritter, Wiesbaden 1963; al-Qāsim b. Ibrāhīm, *Kitāb al-Mustarshid*, ed. and trans. B. Abrahamov, *Anthropomorphism and the interpretation of the Qurʾān in the theology of al-Qāsim ibn Ibrāhīm*, Leiden 1996; al-Shahrastānī, *al-Milal wa-l-niḥal*, ed. M.S. Kīlānī, 2 vols., Beirut 1406/1986; G. Turnbull (comp.), *The essence of Plotinus*, New York 1934.

Secondary: van Ess, *TG*, ii, 206-15; R. Frank, The Neoplatonism of Ǧahm ibn Ṣafwān, in *Le muséon* 78 (1965), 395-424; W. Kadi, The earliest "Nābita" and the paradigmatic "Nawābit," in *SI* 78 (1993), 27-61; R. Strothmann, Tashbīh, in *EI¹*, iv, 685-7; S. Wasserstrom, *Between Muslim and Jew. The problem of symbiosis under early Islam*, New York 1995; A.J. Wensinck, *The Muslim creed. Its genesis and historical development*, London 1965; H. Wolfson, *Philo. Foundations of religion and philosophy in Judaism, Christianity and Islam*, 2 vols., Cambridge, Mass. 1947.

Antichrist

In the Islamic tradition, an evil figure who will lead people astray (q.v.) in the last days and whose advent will be one of the signs of the approaching "hour." The Antichrist *(al-Dajjāl, al-Masīḥ al-Dajjāl)* is not mentioned in the Qurʾān, but he figures in numerous ḥadīth that are cited by the classical commentators. Although many Jews expected an eschatological conflict between God's agents and the forces of evil (see ESCHATOLOGY), the belief that those forces would be concentrated in a specific individual called the Antichrist seems first to have arisen in Christian circles shortly before the destruction of the temple in 70 C.E. During that period, there were rumors that the Roman emperor Nero (r. 54-68 C.E.) who had committed suicide in 68 C.E. was not dead but had escaped to the East and was about to return to recapture the Roman empire. As Nero was a notoriously cruel man who had instigated the persecution of Christians, it is possible that this rumor gave rise to the specifically Christian belief in the Antichrist (cf. *Ascension of Isaiah* 4:2; *Sibylline oracles* 4:121; *Rv* 13:3; 17:8).

Etymology

It is likely that the Muslims learned about the Antichrist from Syriac-speaking Christians as the Arabic *dajjāl* almost certainly comes from the Syriac *daggāl* which means "a liar" or "lying" (see FOREIGN VOCABULARY). Hence, *al-dajjāl* literally means "the liar" and *al-masīḥ al-dajjāl* "the lying Messiah." However, medieval lexicographers attempted to derive *dajjāl* from an Arabic root (Lane, iii, 853). One fanciful suggestion is that it comes from the verb *dajala*, "to cover [a mangy camel] with tar," because the *dajjāl* will in like manner cover the earth with his adherents. The claim that it comes from a homonym of the same verb meaning "to have one eye and one eyebrow" is equally implausible, for when *dajala* is used in this sense it is clearly denominal and means "to resemble the Antichrist." A third suggestion is that *dajjāl* is derived from *dajala* meaning "to gild," because the Antichrist will deceive humankind by covering up the truth, which has the merit of giving a sense not far removed from that of the original Syriac term.

Jewish background

The English word "Antichrist" comes from the Greek *antichristos*, which is composed of two elements: the preposition *anti*, "in place of," and the noun *christos*, "Messiah" or "anointed one." However, as in other compound words of this sort, the prepositional element implies that the substitute is a counterfeit and that his relationship with the real person is antagonistic. Thus the Antichrist is not simply a substitute Messiah, he is a false Messiah, the opponent of the genuine one.

Although the Jews looked for the coming of a Messiah, there is no specific mention of an Antimessiah in the Hebrew Bible or intertestamental Jewish writings. Nevertheless, there are several Old Testament types which set a precedent for a belief in this figure: 1) Sea monster. Together with the ancient Babylonians and Canaanites, the Jews believed that before creating the world God had vanquished a sea monster (e.g. *Isa* 51:9; *Ps* 74:13f.). According to some authors, the monster still lies dormant (*Amos* 9:3; *Job* 7:12) and will eventually be slain in an eschatological struggle (*Isa* 27:1). 2) Angelic adversary. Probably through contact with the Persians, the Jews came to believe in Satan (*Shayṭān*, lit. the Adversary), a member of the heavenly court whose role is to accuse human beings (*Jb* 1:6; *Zech* 3:1). As the devil (q.v.), Satan was subsequently identified with the serpent who brought death into the world (*Wisd of Solomon* 2:24; cf. *Gen* 3:1-15) and Belial, who gains power over all human beings (*Jub* 1:20). According to some authors, Belial will be the eschatological enemy who will perform signs and wonders and deceive many before he is finally destroyed (*Sibylline oracles* 3:63-74). 3) Evil human ruler. From the sixth century B.C.E. onwards, when Jerusalem was conquered by Nebuchadnezzar of Babylon (r. ca. 605-561 B.C.E.), the Jews were increasingly oppressed by foreign rulers. Matters came to a head in 168 B.C.E., when the Hellenistic king of Syria, Antiochus IV (r. 175-164 B.C.E.), erected a statue of the Greek god Zeus in the Jewish temple in Jerusalem (1 *Macc* 1:54). The Book of Daniel refers to this as "the abomination of desolation" (*Dan* 8:13) and fictionally projects the incident into the future so that it marks the last of the seventy weeks of years before the restoration of God's people (*Dan* 9:1-2, 20-7). 4) False prophet. The Book of Deuteronomy contrasts "the prophet like Moses (q.v.)" who must be obeyed (*Deut* 18:15-9) with the "false prophet" who will lead people astray by performing signs and wonders (*Deut* 13:2-6; 18:20). Originally, both descriptions were generic. By the time of the New Testament, however, some groups, including the Qumran sectaries, expected the advent of a specific prophet-like-Moses (1*QS* 9:11). A corollary to this was the belief that one or more false prophets would be active in the last times.

Christian background

The New Testament writers assume that Jesus (q.v.) is the Messiah and often refer to him as Christ Jesus or Jesus the Christ. However, they differ over the nature of the eschatological conflict in which he and the

Christians will be involved. Features of all of the four types from the Old Testament are combined in the Johannine apocalypse, which purports to be a revelation of those things which must soon take place (*Rev* 1:1). It includes a vision of a sea monster (*Rev* 13:1-10) which is clearly an allegorical description of the Roman empire and the emperors who persecuted Christians. There is also a reference to Satan who will lead the whole world astray and who is identified with the devil and the serpent of old (*Rev* 12:9). Finally, there are three references to the "false prophet" (*Rev* 16:13; 19:20; 20:10).

Mark's gospel, which portrays the eschatological conflict as having already begun during Jesus' ministry, depicts Jesus' adult life as coinciding with the fulfillment of time and the approach of God's kingdom (*Mark* 1:15). Because of this, it portrays the eschatological conflict as having already begun during his ministry. Thus, the Markan Jesus quells a storm on the Sea of Galilee, addressing it as if it were a sea monster (*Mark* 4:39), and presents his healings and exorcisms as the binding of Satan (*Mark* 3:23-7). Nevertheless, Mark holds that there will be other developments in the future. When the disciples see "the abomination of desolation standing where he ought not to be," they will know that the days of tribulation have arrived (*Mark* 13:14-20). The disciples are warned that in those days there will be "false Christs" *(pseudochristoi)* and "false prophets" who will perform signs and wonders and seek to lead people astray (*Mark* 13:21f.) before Jesus finally returns on the clouds as the Son of Man (*Mark* 13:26).

Although Mark does not use the term Antichrist, he probably has the Antichrist in mind when he employs the Danielic expression "the abomination of desolation." In this context, the term can be understood as a reference to a human embodiment of evil who will make his stand in the Jerusalem temple as the eschatological adversary of God. In a similar vein, the author of 2 *Thess* insists that Jesus will not return until "the man of lawlessness is revealed, the son of perdition who opposes and exalts himself against every so-called god or object of worship, so that he takes his seat in God's temple proclaiming himself to be God" (2 *Thess* 2:3f.). He further states that Jesus will slay him by the breath of his mouth (2 *Thess* 2:8). Some scholars still defend the Pauline authorship of this letter, but it is probably a pseudonymous work written like Mark in the turbulent period immediately before the destruction of the temple in 70 C.E. At that time, as mentioned above, there were rumors that Nero was about to return and this may have catalyzed the Christian formulation of the figure of the Antichrist.

The only New Testament writer to employ the actual word *antichristos* is the author of the first and second letters of John, which were probably written some thirty years after the destruction of the Temple:

> Children it is the last hour. You heard that the Antichrist is to come. Well now many Antichrists have come.... (1 *John* 2:18)
>
> Who then is the liar? None other than the person who denies that Jesus is the Christ. Such is the Antichrist.... (1 *John* 2:22).
>
> Every spirit which does not profess Jesus is not from God. It is rather of the Antichrist (1 *John* 4:3).
>
> For many deceivers have gone out into the world, those who do not confess that Christ has come in the flesh. This is the Deceiver and the Antichrist. (2 *John* 7).

These passages are striking in the extent to which they demythologize the notion of the Antichrist. The recipients of the letters had been led to await his coming as that of a distinct eschatological figure, but the author urges them instead to recognize him in the false teachers who have broken with the community and who fail to acknowledge the full humanity of Jesus.

With some justification, the Fathers of the Church assumed that the Markan "abomination of desolation" and the Pauline "man of lawlessness" were alternative names for the Antichrist. Hence, they inferred that the Antichrist would come to the temple; that he would rule for three and a half years (Irenaeus, *Against the heresies,* 5:1-3; cf. *Dan* 7:25); and that Jesus, upon his own return, would dispatch him (e.g. Cyril of Jerusalem, *Catechetical lectures,* 15:12). Ephraem Syrus (ca. 306-373 C.E.) added the interesting detail that the Antichrist will come from Khurāsān *(Sermo II de fine extremo)*. Some of these features recur in the Islamic tradition. Moreover, in the *Peshitta* — the standard Syriac translation of the New Testament — the Greek words for "the liar" and "the Antichrist" (in 1 *Jn* 2:22) are rendered as *daggālā* and *mashīḥā daggālā* respectively, furnishing a precedent for the two ways of rendering "the Antichrist" in Arabic.

The Antichrist in Islamic tradition and qurʾānic exegesis

The Sunnī collections of ḥadīth contain numerous traditions about the Antichrist. When these are pieced together, the following picture is obtained. He was born to parents who waited thirty years to have a son. He is a thick-set man with a ruddy face and a mass of very curly hair. He is blind in his right eye, which swims in its orbit like a swollen grape. He also has the word "unbeliever" *(kāfir)* written on his forehead. He is currently chained up on an island in the East, where a Companion of the Prophet (see COMPANIONS OF THE PROPHET) called "Tamīm al-Dārī" claimed to have seen him. The Prophet himself dreamed that he saw him circling the Kaʿba (q.v.) and he was shown him again on the night of his ascension (q.v.). The Antichrist will be released after a six- or seven-year war between the Arabs and the Byzantines (q.v.) which will culminate in the capture of Constantinople. His coming will be one of the ten signs (q.v.) which will precede the last hour. The signs usually listed are smoke; the Antichrist; the beast; the rising of the sun from the West; the descent of Jesus; Gog and Magog (q.v.); a landslide in the East; a landslide in the West; a landslide in Arabia; and fire burning forth from the Yemen. However, some reports substitute a violent gale for the descent of Jesus and others make his descent the tenth and final sign. The Antichrist will come from the East via Khurāsān. He will ride a white donkey and will be followed by seventy thousand hooded Jews from Isfahan. He will not be able to enter Mecca or Medina. He will set out to attack the latter but, when he reaches the mountain of Uḥud (q.v.) outside of Medina, the angels will turn his face towards Syria. He will have two canals with him, one flowing with water and the other with fire. The people will believe in him because he will work miracles and will bring an abundant supply of water, bread and mutton. He will be at large for forty days or forty years. Jesus will descend in Damascus and will catch up with him at the port of Lydda in Palestine, where he will kill him with a lance. In addition, there are ḥadīth that the Prophet said that the person who most resembled the Antichrist was a pagan Arab called ʿAbd al-ʿUzza b. Qaṭan. It is also reported that he suspected a Medinese Jew named Ibn Ṣayyād (or Ibn Ṣāʿid) of being the Antichrist. Muḥammad is said to have loved the tribe of Banū Tamīm because they would put up the staunchest resistance to the Antichrist. He also prayed for refuge from the trial of the Antichrist and urged his Companions to do the same; and he promised that reciting the first (or last) ten verses of sūra 18 would offer protection against the Antichrist. Many of these details are also reported in Shīʿī ḥadīth but the Shīʿī belief is that the Antichrist will be dispatched by the Mahdī and not by Jesus (see SHĪʿISM AND THE QURʾĀN).

The folkloric character of much of this material suggests that it may have originated with Muslim story-tellers long after the rise of Islam. However, there is little doubt that the Prophet and his Companions were concerned about the Antichrist. Proof that this must have been an interest of theirs may be gleaned particularly from the authentic ring of the extensive traditions about Ibn Ṣayyād, a Jew who apparently indulged in *merkavah* mysticism. Moreover, the difficulty of reconciling these traditions with some of the other reports tells against their having been invented.

The classical commentators make reference to the Antichrist principally in the following contexts: 1) Traditional accounts of the Prophet's description of the Antichrist are mentioned in their commentaries on the allusion to Muḥammad's night journey in Q 17:1. 2) Traditions that indicate that Jesus is alive and will return to kill the Antichrist are cited as evidence that the phrase "before his death" in Q 4:159 means before Jesus' death. 3) They use the same traditions in connection with Q 3:55 as evidence that this verse refers to Jesus' rapture rather than his death. 4) Traditions which list all the signs that will precede the final hour are contained in their comments on the references to Gog and Magog in Q 18:94 and Q 21:96, to the beast in Q 27:82, and to smoke in Q 44:10. 5) They cite the same traditions in connection with the references to the hour in Q 7:187 and Q 79:42. 6) They cite these same traditions of the signs preceding the final hour together with those which relate that Jesus will kill the Antichrist as evidence that Q 43:61 alludes to Jesus' final descent. 7) In their introduction to sūra 18, they cite traditions, as mentioned above, about the merits of reciting its first (or last) ten verses. See also APOCALYPSE; RESURRECTION.

Neal Robinson

Bibliography
Primary: R.H. Charles, *The apocrypha and pseudepigrapha of the Old Testament in English*, 2 vols., Oxford 1913; S. Cyril, Archbishop of Jerusalem, *The catechetical lectures*, Oxford 1839; Irenaeus, *Against the heresies*, ed. D.J. Unger, New York 1992; A. Roberts and J. Donaldson (eds.), *The ante-Nicene Christian library*, vol. ix (Irenaeus, ii, etc.) Edinburgh 1868; J. Robson, *Mishkāt al-maṣābīḥ. English translation with explanatory notes*, repr. Lahore 1990 (most of the relevant ḥadīth are in iii.xvi.1, viii.i, x.vii.1, and xxvi.iii-vii); G. Vermes, *The Dead Sea scrolls in English*, Harmondsworth 1975.
Secondary: W. Bousset, *The Antichrist legend*, London 1896; R. Brown, *The epistles of John*, London 1983; D.J. Halperin, The Ibn Ṣayyād traditions and the legend of al-Dajjāl, in *JAOS* 16 (1976), 213-25; N. Robinson, *Christ in Islam and Christianity. The representation of Jesus in the Qurʾān and the classical Muslim commentaries*, London 1991.

Apocalypse

Revelation of things to come, especially at the end of times, and a religiously-motivated form of eschatology (q.v.) with an emphasis upon the cosmic events which will occur at the end of the world. Since most of the apocalyptic events mentioned in the Qurʾān are connected with the resurrection (q.v.) of the dead, they are called by Fakhr al-Dīn al-Rāzī (d. 606/1210) "the portents of the day of resurrection" (*muqaddimāt yawm al-qiyāma, Tafsīr*, ad Q 39:68).

In the Qurʾān

As a prophetic, revealed message, the Qurʾān is to a large extent apocalyptic yet there are parts of it that carry this theme in a more intense manner. For example, Q 81 The Overthrowing (Sūrat al-Takwīr), Q 82 The Cleaving (Sūrat al-Infiṭār) and Q 99 The Earthquake (Sūrat al-Zilzāl) are accurately termed "apocalyptic sūras," inasmuch as they are entirely devoted to the portrayal of the upset in the natural order of things that will occur at the end of times. A good example of this is Q 81:1-14, which is considered one of the earliest passages with an apocalyptic theme to have been revealed: "When the sun will be darkened, when the stars will be thrown down, when the mountains will be set moving, when the ten-month pregnant camels will be neglected... then will a soul know what it has produced." Nevertheless, other parts of the Qurʾān are not necessarily less apocalyptic. In the earlier sūras in particular, the theme of the end of the world and its accompanying terrifying phenomena is often repeated. Although Muslim and non-Muslim qurʾānic scholarship — notwithstanding their interdependency — do not always agree on the order of the revelation of these segments of the qurʾānic text, there is a general consensus that the following apocalyptic passages: Q 56:1-56; 75:7-15; 80:33-42; 81:1-14; 82; 83; 84; 89:21-30; 99; 101 are to be dated to the earlier period of revelation (see CHRONOLOGY AND THE QURʾĀN). Western scholarship, when using the classification of T. Nöldeke and R. Blachère, considers the most picturesque apocalyptic parts to be from the latter part of the first Meccan period and from the second Meccan period. In R. Bell's schema, they are attributed to the "early Qurʾān period."

Images of the end of the world in these early sūras are often quite vivid and contain colorful descriptions of cosmic events. However, given the variety of images depicted in the various sūras, one cannot form an exact picture of the events which will occur at the end of times. As R. Paret states, on the last day "the earth begins to move violently. It staggers, quakes and is crushed and flattened. It brings forth what is inside of it and empties itself. Like a mirage the mountains assume variable forms. They collapse, are like teased wool and disintegrate into sand and dust. Heaven will be like molten metal and be rent asunder, split open and full of gaping holes. The sun will be coiled up. The moon will darken. The sun and moon will be brought together. The stars will go out and tumble down (or become dull), etc. It would be pointless to try to patch together a coherent and comprehensive account of the events on the last day from the different statements. The individual sūras must be taken separately, just as they originally were recited. Indeed, the images of the events on the last day are not intended to, as it were, depict objective reality or to foretell the future exactly in all its details. They have been designed and formulated with the intention to shock the audience, to foreshadow the terror that, at some time in the future, on the last day, will seize all of creation" (*Mohammed,* 64-5). In addition to these cosmic events, there are other signs which will signal the end, e.g. the breaking loose of Gog and Magog (q.v.; Q 18:94, 21:96). God will bring forth from the earth a beast that will speak (Q 27:82) and the trumpet or horn (*ṣūr,* e.g. Q 27:87; 36:51; 39:68; 69:13; 78:18; *nāqūr,* Q 74:8) will be blown to summon every creature.

Interestingly, the early apocalyptic passages do not explicitly mention the end of the world, refer directly to the resurrection of the dead or give much detail about the day of judgment (see LAST JUDGMENT). Much is implicit, although the final result is clear: the unbelievers (or ungrateful, *kuffār*) and the evildoers *(alladhīna ajramū)* will receive their punishment in hell *(al-*

jahīm or *al-jahannam)* and the reward of the believers *(alladhīna āmanū)* who do righteous deeds *(ʿamilū al-ṣāliḥāt)* will be paradise (*al-janna,* see HELL; PARADISE; GARDEN; BELIEF AND UNBELIEF; REWARD AND PUNISHMENT). The fact that much is implicit in these early apocalyptic passages suggests that in the Mecca of the early qurʾānic revelations at least part of Muḥammad's audience must have been familiar with some of this apocalyptic imagery. Scholars have noted that it calls to mind many parallels with Jewish and Christian, canonical and apocryphal apocalyptic literature, although Arabian features, such as the neglect of ten-month pregnant camels (Q 81:4) are unique to the Qurʾān.

Some of the expressions used to indicate apocalyptic phenomena occur only once in the Qurʾān, e.g. "when the earth shall be rocked and the mountains crumbled" *(idhā rujjati l-arḍu rajjan wa-bussati l-jibālu bassan,* Q 56:4-5). One conspicuous characteristic of the descriptions of the apocalyptic events is that there is no mention of who or what brings them about (ʿĀ. ʿAbd al-Raḥmān, *Tafsīr,* i, 80). Often the meaning of the apocalyptic terms is not straightforward, as in the case of "the great catastrophe" (*al-ṭāmma al-kubrā,* Q 79:34) and "the blast" (*al-ṣākhkha,* Q 80:33) and traditional exegesis does not offer much more than to say that they are names for the day of resurrection (e.g. Ṭabarī, *Tafsīr*). The same is said about "the calamity" (*al-qāriʿa,* Q 101:1-3) but this term is also used to denote the catastrophe that overtakes unbelieving communities in the punishment stories (q.v.; Q 13:31; 69:4). Likewise, the root *r-j-f* — basically "to tremble" — is used both in apocalyptic passages and in punishment stories (q.v.; Q 7:78, 91, 155; 29:37; 73:14; 79:6). The apocalyptic passages in combination with the announcement of the final judgment belong to the earliest themes of the qurʾānic message. As in Christianity and Judaism, the theme of punishment has raised the question of compatibility with the idea of a good creator God (see Watt-Bell, *Introduction,* 158-62; R. Paret, *Mohammed und der Koran,* 62-71).

Just as the identity of the author and the precise nature of the events of the last day are ambiguous, so too is the time when it will occur. Not even the Prophet himself was able to tell when the apocalyptic end of the world and the subsequent resurrection and judgment will come (Q 79:43), but that they are sure to happen and nearly at hand is stated more than once (e.g. Q 51:5-6; 52:7; 53:57; 78:40). According to Q 47:18, its tokens or portents *(ashrāṭ)* have already come, but the hour itself will arrive suddenly.

In exegesis and ḥadīth

The fact that the Qurʾān mentions that even the Prophet cannot foretell the coming of the hour is probably one of the reasons why the exegetical works generally do not elaborate on the apocalyptic phenomena or try to determine when the end of the world will come. Referring to Q 3:7 and Q 7:187, al-Ṭabarī (d. 310/923), for instance, mentions in his introduction that God has reserved the knowledge and the interpretation of the future apocalyptic events for himself (*Tafsīr,* i, 74).

Nevertheless, one can find some additional and traditionally accepted details in the exegetical works. For instance, it is commonly stated that an angel (q.v.), Israfel (Isrāfīl) or Gabriel (Jibrīl; see GABRIEL), will blow the trumpet and that he is also the "caller" *(al-munādī)* of Q 50:41. The commentaries elaborate upon the two blasts of the trumpet of Q 39:68. At the first blast everybody will die except for a few chosen by God (the archangels and/or the martyrs, cf. Q 3:169) and the resurrection of the dead will occur forty years later at the second blast (Muqātil, *Tafsīr;* Ṭabarī, *Tafsīr;* Qurṭubī, *Jāmiʿ;* Bayḍāwī, *Anwār* ad loc.). In an apparent attempt to harmonize Q 39:68 and Q 27:87 (cf. Rāzī, *Tafsīr,* ad Q 39:68), Abū l-Layth al-Samarqandī (d. ca. 375/985), in his commentary mentions a variant given on the authority of the Prophet: The first blast of the trumpet or horn — which has a circumference as great as the distance between heaven and earth — frightens all of creation. At the second blast, the inhabitants of heaven and earth die. At the time of the third blast, all the souls or spirits *(arwāḥ)* are gathered in the horn and then blown into their respective bodies for the resurrection (*Tafsīr,* ad Q 39:68). The famous commentator al-Ṭabarī (d. 310/923) mentions the tradition of the Companion Abū Hurayra about the three blasts (*Tafsīr,* ad Q 27:87 and 39:68), without any further comments and al-Qurṭubī (d. 671/1272), after having mentioned the three, explicitly states that there will only be two blasts (*Jāmiʿ,* ad Q 27:87). Ibn Kathīr (d. 774/1373) in his commentary on Q 27:87 and 39:68 also mentions three blasts (*Tafsīr,* ad loc.). Another accepted detail of the end of times is that Jesus (q.v.) will defeat the Antichrist (*al-dajjāl,* see ANTICHRIST). Ibn Kathīr, in keeping with his penchant for providing very detailed information on the events at the end of times, says (quoting, among other sources, the ḥadīth contained in the *Ṣaḥīḥ* [*Fitan,* 117] of Muslim, d. 261/875) that the period of peace after this defeat will extend seven years. Usually in connection with the "near place" *(makān qarīb)* of Q 50:41, "the rock of Jerusalem" *(ṣakhr bayt al-maqdis)* is identified as the place where the trumpet shall sound. Often this is rationalized on the grounds that it is the place on earth nearest to heaven (e.g. Muqātil, *Tafsīr;* Ṭabarī, *Tafsīr;* Abū l-Layth al-Samarqandī, *Tafsīr;* Māwardī, *Nukat;* Zamakhsharī, *Kashshāf;* Qurṭubī, *Jāmiʿ;* Ibn Kathīr, *Tafsīr;* al-Maḥallī and al-Suyūṭī, *Jalālayn* ad loc.). Muqātil (d. 150/767) suggests that the end of times will not witness the end of the earth, but rather the world "will become empty with nothing in it. It will be laid out new and white, as if it were silver or as if it were unwrought. It will have rays like the rays of the sun. There will be no sin committed on it and no blood shed" (*Tafsīr,* ad Q 99:2).

The ḥadīth literature — such as the chapter of Muslim's *Ṣaḥīḥ* entitled *Kitāb al-Fitan wa-ashrāṭ al-sāʿa,* which contains 143 ḥadīth on the subject — gives much more detailed and precise accounts of the apocalyptic events than is found in the Qurʾān and the commentaries (see ḤADĪTH AND THE QURʾĀN). In Western qurʾānic scholarship the study of the apocalypse in the Qurʾān and its commentaries is somewhat underdeveloped, especially when compared with the recent upsurge of attention given to Jewish and Christian apocalyptic literature.

Frederik Leemhuis

Bibliography
Primary: ʿAbd al-Raḥmān, *Tafsīr,* Cairo 1966²; Abū l-Layth al-Samarqandī, *Tafsīr,* Beirut 1413/1993; Bayḍāwī, *Anwār;* Ibn Kathīr, *Tafsīr; Jalālayn;* Māwardī, *Nukat;* Muqātil, *Tafsīr;* Muslim, *Ṣaḥīḥ;* Qurṭubī, *Jāmiʿ;* Ṭabarī, *Tafsīr;* Zamakhsharī, *Kashshāf.*
Secondary: R. Blachère, *Le Coran,* Paris 1966, 1980⁶, 32-7; M. Cook, *Muhammad,* Oxford 1983; R. Paret, *Mohammed und der Koran. Geschichte und Verkündigung des arabischen Propheten,* Stuttgart 1957, 62-71; U. Rubin, Apocalypse and authority in Islamic tradition. The emergence of the twelve leaders, in *al-Qanṭara* 18 (1997), 1-42; P. Ryan, The descending scroll. A study of the notion of revelation as apocalypse in the Bible and in the Qurʾān, in *Ghana Bulletin of Theology* 4 (1975), 24-39; Watt-Bell, *Introduction,* 1970, 1977, 158-62; V.P. Zimbaro, *Encyclopedia of apocalyptic literature,* Santa Barbara 1996, 12-4, 134.

Apocalyptic Sūras see SŪRA

Apologetics

A systematic argumentative discourse in defense of a religion or doctrine. In the history of encounters between Muslims of differing opinions and between Muslims and members of other faiths, the Qurʾān has usually been central as a guide and source in debates and has often been a significant topic in these discussions.

Within the Qurʾān itself there are arguments defending both its proclamations and its own status. Its fundamental emphasis that God is one and distinct from all other beings is most emphatically asserted in Q 112, which is generally thought to have been delivered in the context of debates with polytheists, Jews or Christians (e.g. Rāzī, *Tafsīr,* ad loc.). The Qurʾān argues generally against anyone who thinks of God as a creature (Q 2:255; 43:81, etc.); against those, including the Jews and Christians, who implicate him in human-like relationships (Q 5:116; 6:100-1; 9:30; see ANTHROPOMORPHISM) or suggest he is Trinitarian (see TRINITY; cf. Q 4:171; 5:73); and against the notion that anyone else is capable of creating anything without his aid (Q 6:1). Likewise, Muḥammad's activity as God's messenger is distinguished from the actions of soothsayers and people possessed by the jinn (q.v.; Q 52:29-31; 68:2), authenticated (Q 53:10-1) and supported by God against opponents (Q 108:3; see OPPOSITION TO MUḤAMMAD) and defined as a continuation of the work of previous messengers (Q 4:163; 33:40; 37:37; 61:6; see MESSENGER; PROPHETS AND PROPHETHOOD). With equal emphasis, the divine origin of the Qurʾān is defended against its detractors (Q 46:7-8) by reference to its inimitability (q.v.; Q 2:23-4; 10:38; 11:13-4; 17:88).

On the whole, the Qurʾān counsels against involvement in pointless disputes about matters of faith (Q 4:140; 6:68-70). The appropriate course of action is to point out true belief politely and tactfully (Q 16:125; 29:46). It does, however, explicitly sanction confronting those who deny the plainly revealed truth, as is indicated by the injunction given in Q 3:61 that the opposing parties should meet and ritually invoke a curse (q.v.) on the liars among them. This verse is connected with the mutual cursing *(mubāhala)* that was arranged to decide the outcome of the meeting between Muḥammad and the Christians, who are said to have come from Najrān (q.v.) in 10/631 to put questions to him (Ibn Isḥāq-Guillaume, 277). It is the first intimation of the long history of debate between Muslims and Christians in which the Qurʾān was nearly always crucial.

Among some Muslims the status of the Qurʾān was a matter of dispute from an early date. In the second/eighth century, Muʿtazilī (see MUʿTAZILĪS) theologians *(mutakallimūn,* sing. *mutakallim)* rejected the Qurʾān's uncreatedness as part of their perception of the strict unity and uniqueness of God (see CREATEDNESS OF THE QURʾĀN). At the same time scholars of a more independent frame of mind have openly rejected the notion that its miraculous nature could be readily proven (al-Qāḍī ʿAbd al-Jabbār, *Tathbīt,* 412-3). The fragmentary form in which their views have come down to us makes it difficult to appreciate the real intention behind them, but if the early third/ninth-century Muslim Abū ʿĪsā l-Warrāq, who will be discussed further below, is in any way typical of them, it appears that they were rebutting apologetic arguments based upon the Qurʾān's literary qualities. Remarkably, he denigrates the notion that the Qurʾān represents an inimitable literary achievement.

Among the points he makes is that the Qur'ān stands out only because literary ability was lacking at the time it appeared, that Muḥammad's opponents were too occupied with resisting him to meet the challenge to produce passages comparable to the Qur'ān and, maybe most telling, that literary abilities can be acquired naturally and are not necessarily indications of divine endowments (al-Māturīdī, *Tawḥīd,* 191; see also D. Thomas, *Anti-Christian polemic,* 28). These particularly provocative criticisms presuppose a lively and developed debate about the claims made within the Qur'ān itself for its distinctiveness and suggest that the opposition to which the text itself attests was by no means silenced in every quarter by the defensive responses it contains.

If such radical criticisms were relatively rare among Muslims themselves and leveled by marginal figures, they persisted among Christians who expressed views about the Qur'ān throughout much of the shared history of the two faiths. The first major figure whose opinions are clearly known is John of Damascus (d. ca. 132/750) who accuses Muḥammad of writing a work on his own on the basis of what an Arian monk had told him about the Bible (q.v.; J.-P. Migne, *Patrologia graeca,* xciv, col. 765; see INFORMANTS). Here there is a clear allusion to the story of the monk who recognized Muḥammad as a prophet, which the classical biographies of Muḥammad (see SĪRA AND THE QUR'ĀN) relate (e.g. Ibn Isḥāq-Guillaume, 79-81). However, the Christian apologists identify him as a heretic who was consciously exploited by Muḥammad. The accusation that the Qur'ān springs from Muḥammad's own authorship became commonplace in the Christian anti-Muslim polemic in the Middle Ages, when it was generally accepted unquestioningly that he was driven by selfish ambition in composing it (N. Daniel, *Islam and the West,* 47-99). Some modern scholars have substantially reversed this received verdict. Their views concerning the sincerity of Muḥammad's sense of vocation may suggest that Muslims and Christians can move closer together with regard to their view of the status of the Qur'ān in the light of present-day understandings about the incidence of inspiration (see REVELATION AND INSPIRATION).

Undoubtedly, the Qur'ān has been the most important single influence upon Muslim thinking about other faiths. This is attributable to the explicit teachings it contains concerning the leading figures and beliefs of Judaism and Christianity, and even more importantly to the relationship it asserts both between itself and previous revelations and between the faith it proclaims and earlier beliefs. Among the most detailed, though nevertheless incomplete, teachings in the Qur'ān are the explanations about the person of Jesus (q.v.), the Messiah, and the community who claimed to follow him. Muslims who were involved in encounters with Christians in the early centuries of Islam often made these teachings the basis of arguments with which they attempted to show that Jesus was only human, that God was one and not triune, and that Christians had been misled in a number of their beliefs. One of the earliest surviving, though incomplete, examples of this demonstrative literature, perhaps dating from as early as 210/825, is the now incomplete *Response to the Christians (al-Radd ʿalā l-naṣārā)* of the Zaydī imām al-Qāsim b. Ibrāhīm (d. 246/860). This relatively short tract contains full and accurate information about Christian doctrines and beliefs. Nevertheless, its author remains loyal to what he understands to be the qur'ānic view of Christianity. Thus his main argument that Christianity is wrong about the divinity of Christ, which he adduces Gospel texts to support, is essentially a vindication of the teaching on this point given in the Qurʾān (see JEWS AND JUDAISM; CHRISTIANS AND CHRISTIANITY; SCRIPTURE AND THE QURʾĀN).

It might be assumed that polemical literature of this type runs the risk of failing to carry its arguments home to Christians for the reason that it was not addressing their understanding of the doctrines but rather the qurʾānic interpretation of them. Nevertheless, in numerous later instances it is still evident that Muslim authors were guided primarily by the teachings of the Qurʾān. Even when they took Christian doctrinal explanations into account, they still generally conformed to the tendency to follow the Qurʾān's guidelines in their approach. The most striking exception to this general trend appears to be the independent thinker Abū ʿĪsā al-Warrāq, from the early third/ninth century, one of the most intense periods of intellectual encounter between Muslims and Christians. His long and concentrated refutation of the doctrines of the Trinity and Christ's divine and human nature is based upon exhaustive research into the teachings of the major Christian denominations. It relies for its effect entirely upon stringent logical reasoning, which reveals the inconsistencies and contradictions in the doctrines he examines. Thus, his arguments stem from the structure of Christian thought itself. It is little wonder that within a few decades Christians recognized the cogency of his attack and saw the need to marshal responses. Nonetheless, the work tacitly acknowledges the pervasive influence of the Qurʾān, since its twin attacks are effectively amplifications of the qurʾānic denial of the Christian assertion of the Trinity (*tathlīth*, cf. Q 4:171; 5:73) and the divine sonship of Jesus (Q 9:30; 19:34-5). Therefore, despite its stance of rational impartiality, the attack is as much a defense of absolute unity *(tawḥīd)* as a refutation of Christian doctrines. In this respect it conforms to the typical model of Muslim anti-Christian polemic.

The general stance of Muslim polemicists may be linked to the attitude expressed in the Qurʾān itself that it was revealed to confirm the earlier revelations (Q 3:3-4; 5:48; 6:92; 10:37; 46:12) and that it should be taken as the complete guide to the truth (Q 9:33; 25:1). Believing that the Qurʾān was the source of the truth and that Islam was the authentic expression of this truth, polemicists viewed other religions as either incomplete or incorrect forms of Islam (q.v.; see also BELIEF AND UNBELIEF). It followed that one main purpose of their arguments was to show where the inadequacies of the other faiths were to be found. Another was to establish the truth of Islam by demonstrating that other attempted versions of the truth did not have the inner consistency or comprehensiveness of their own. Some of the fullest examples of this approach are to be found in the theological compendiums of the two leading fourth/tenth century theologians, the *Book of preparation (Kitāb al-Tamhīd)* of the Ashʿarī theologian al-Bāqillānī (d. 403/1013) and the *Only work necessary on the various aspects of [divine] unity and justice (al-Mughnī fī abwāb al-tawḥīd wa-l-ʿadl)* of the Muʿtazilī al-Qāḍī ʿAbd al-Jabbār al-Hamadhānī (d. 415/1025). In both of these works a refutation of the main doctrines of other religions as understood by Islam follows the exposition of the corresponding Islamic doctrine. A refutation of the Christian doctrines of the Trinity and Incarnation follows the exposition of the Muslim doctrine of God's unity. In the same way, Jews are criticized for their rejection of prophets who succeeded Moses and this is combined with an exposition of Muḥammad's authenticity as a prophet. In such cases the refutations of the rival doctrines serve to adumbrate the soundness of the Islamic formulation. This is a large-scale expression of the way in which qur'ānically-inspired religious thinking in Islam gives arguments against the validity of other religions a character which is both instructive and apologetic. Again, this approach accords with the qur'ānic injunction to desist from unedifying discussions about matters of faith (Q 4:140; 6:68-9) and to use the best means when arguing with the other so-called "People of the Book" (q.v.; Q 29:46).

A last feature of Muslim apologetics worth noting is the manner in which the scattered remarks given in the Qur'ān regarding the concealment and corruption of earlier revelations (Q 2:75, 140; 3:78; 4:46; 5:15, 41) are systematized into the general principle that the Torah (q.v.) and Gospels (q.v.) are unreliable. Some authors proceeded on the assumption that, while the actual text of the biblical books was more or less sound, the Jewish and Christian interpretations of them were confused. Among these were the aforementioned al-Qāsim b. Ibrāhīm, who adduces long quotations from the Gospels to support his argument that Jesus was only human. Another was the Christian convert to Islam ʿAlī b. Rabbān al-Ṭabarī (d. ca. 250/864), whose *Book of religion and empire (Kitāb al-Dīn wa-l-dawla)* contains about 150 verses translated from throughout the Bible together with ingenious and sometimes tortuous interpretations to show the ways in which they foretell the coming of Muḥammad and Islam. The author of *The beautiful response (al-Radd al-jamīl)*, which has often been attributed to al-Ghazālī (d. 505/1111), also followed this course. Other scholars adopted the position that the texts themselves had been corrupted. They postulated that this came about when the early Christians attempted to reconstruct the original Gospels, which they had lost, or when the apostle Paul introduced extraneous material into the sacred text. The anti-Christian polemic of the famous littérateur al-Jāḥiẓ (d. 255/869) implies that the evangelists have lied (*al-Radd ʿalā l-naṣārā*, 24). Al-Qāḍī ʿAbd al-Jabbār argued at length that Paul corrupted the original purity of Jesus' message *(Tathbīt dalāʾil al-nubuwwa)*. The Andalusian theologian and littérateur Ibn Ḥazm (d. 458/1065) composed one of the most searching critiques of the biblical texts *(Milal)*. Al-Juwaynī (d. 478/1085) attempted to show that textual corruption had taken place *(Shifāʾ al-ghalīl)*. Whether exposing misinterpretations or misrepresentations of the original texts, Muslim authors produced their arguments in conformity with the belief that the Qur'ān itself provided unimpeachable guidance.

A small but instructive indication of the trust placed in sacred text by Muslim polemicists is that for many of them a proof verse against the divinity of Jesus was *John* 20:17, where Jesus says to Mary Magdalene, "Do not touch me, for I have not yet ascended to my father, but go to my brethren and say to them, 'I ascend to my father and your father, to my God and your God.'" They could presumably feel confident in citing this because it was close enough to Jesus' words to the people of Israel in the Qur'ān, "It is God who is my lord and your lord. So worship him" (Q 3:51), for them to consider it authentic. See DEBATE AND DISPUTATION.

David Thomas

Bibliography
Primary: ʿAbd al-Jabbār b. Aḥmad, *al-Mughnī fī abwāb al-tawḥīd wa-l-ʿadl*, various eds., Cairo 1958-65; id., *Tathbīt dalāʾil al-nubuwwa*, ed. ʿA.-K. ʿUthmān, Beirut 1966; Abū ʿĪsā al-Warrāq, *Kitāb al-Radd ʿalā l-thalāth firaq min al-naṣārā*, ed. and trans. D. Thomas, *Anti-Christian polemic in early Islam. Abū ʿĪsā al-Warrāq's* "Against the Trinity," Cambridge 1992; al-Bāqillānī, *Kitāb al-Tamhīd*, ed. R.J. McCarthy, Beirut 1957; al-Ghazālī (attributed), *al-Radd al-jamīl li-ilāhiyyat ʿĪsā bi-ṣarīḥ al-injīl*, ed. and trans. R. Chidiac, *Réfutation*

excellente de la divinité de Jésus Christ d'après les evangiles, Paris 1939; al-Jāḥiẓ, *al-Radd ʿalā l-naṣārā,* in *Thalāth rasāʾil li-Abī ʿUthmān ʿAmr b. Baḥr al-Jāḥiẓ,* ed. J. Finkel, Cairo 1926; al-Juwaynī, *Shifāʾ al-ghalīl fī bayān mā waqaʿa fī l-tawrāh wa-l-injīl min al-tabdīl,* ed. M. Allard, *Textes apologétiques de Ǧuwaynī,* Beirut 1968; al-Māturīdī, *Kitāb al-Tawḥīd,* ed. F. Kholeif, Beirut 1970; J.-P. Migne, *Patrologia graeca,* xciv, col. 765; al-Qāsim b. Ibrāhīm, *al-Radd ʿalā l-naṣārā,* ed. and trans. I. di Matteo, Confutazione contro i Cristiani dello zaydita al-Qāsim b. Ibrāhīm, in *RSO* 9 (1921-2), 301-64; al-Ṭabarī, ʿAlī b. Rabbān, *Kitāb al-Dīn wa-l-dawla,* ed. A. Mingana, Manchester 1923. Secondary: N. Daniel, *Islam and the West. The making of an image,* Oxford 1960, 1993²; D. Kerr, "He walked in the path of the prophets." Toward Christian theological recognition of the Prophet Muḥammad, in Y.Y. Haddad and W.Z. Haddad (eds.), *Christian-Muslim encounters,* Gainsville 1995; H. Lazarus-Yafeh, *Intertwined worlds. Medieval Islam and biblical criticism,* Princeton 1992; I. Shahīd, *The martyrs of Najrān. New documents,* Bruxelles 1971; W.M. Watt, *Muslim-Christian encounters. Perceptions and misperceptions,* London 1991.

Apostasy

Turning away from or rejecting one's religion. The qurʾānic notion of apostasy is functionally represented by two main concepts, *kufr* and *irtidād,* the latter bearing more directly than the former upon notions of apostasy. Beginning sometime during the second/eighth century, *irtidād* came to be used in legal and other discourses to speak exclusively of apostasy. In the Qurʾān, however, the semantic and conceptual connection between the terms *irtidād* and *kufr* seems to have already been made, albeit tenuously, before the emigration to Medina, as evidenced in the verse: "Those who come to disbelieve *(kafara)* after believing" (Q 16:106). In the Medinan period of the Qurʾān, the connection became more pronounced and in some instances the terms were used synonymously.

The meaning embedded in the qurʾānic concept of disbelief *(kufr)* assumes God to be infinitely merciful, generous, compassionate, and beneficent. Being directed towards human beings, these qualities dictate that humans, in turn, should be grateful to God for his goodness. Disbelief, then, is the act of failing to acknowledge, even of rejecting, God's benevolence, and together with this ingratitude and rejection comes, in a more developed sense of the term, the renunciation of God himself (see BELIEF AND UNBELIEF). In this respect, the Qurʾān distinguishes between two types of disbelief: that of the person who could never see God's goodness and thus remains in his original state of disbelief and that of someone who did acknowledge God, but subsequently turned his back upon his benevolence and finally upon God himself. This latter type becomes the exact equivalent of the apostate *(murtadd),* one who commits apostasy *(irtidād).* Derivatives of the root *k-f-r* occur some 482 times in the Qurʾān. When verbal variations of *kafara* are used, it is not always clear which of the two types is meant. In at least nineteen verses, *kufr* is unmistakably used in the sense of apostasy. A small number of other verses may arguably be interpreted as carrying this sense, but such interpretations remain shrouded in uncertainty.

Yet another central qurʾānic term conceptually associated with apostasy is *fisq,* a stage beyond that of *kufr,* when the person stubbornly persists not only in turning away from God but also in deliberately disobeying his commands. Q 24:55 reads: "God has promised to appoint those of you who believe and perform honorable deeds as [his] representatives on earth, just as he made those before them into such overlords, and to establish their religion for them which he has approved for them, and to change their fear into confidence. They serve me [alone] and do not associate anything else with me. Those who disbelieve *(kafara)* henceforth are the miscreants *(fāsiqūn).*" Abandoning the religion of Islam is therefore not only *irtidād* but also *kufr* and *fisq*. It is through the juxtaposition of this terminological triad that the Qurʾān articulates the idea of apostasy.

The characterization and fate of those who commit apostasy vary in the Qurʾān. What is striking, especially in light of later juristic developments, is that although apostates are usually assigned a place in hell, there is no mention of any specific corporeal punishment to which they are to be subjected in this world. In certain chapters of the Qurʾān, the apostates are described merely as "having strayed from the right path" (Q 2:108; also 4:167), while in others they are threatened with a severe yet unspecified punishment in this world and in the hereafter (Q 9:74). They are ignorant and "their punishment is that upon them is heaped the curse of God, of angels and of people in their entirety" (Q 3:87). In fact, in Q 2:109, the believers are even asked to forgive them: "Many People of the Book (q.v.) would like to turn you back *(yaruddūnakum)* into unbelievers *(kuffār,* sing. *kāfir)* after you have professed the faith, out of envy of their own, even though the truth has been manifested unto them. Pardon and forgive them till God brings his commands." The relatively lenient position of the Qurʾān toward apostates is also betrayed by the self-reassurance expressed in such verses as Q 3:176-7: "Let not their conduct grieve you, who rush into disbelief, for lo! they injure God not at all. It is God's will to assign them no portion in the hereafter, and theirs will be an awful doom. Those who purchase disbelief at the price of faith harm God not at all, but theirs will be a painful torment." It is quite plausible that the various types of reaction to apostasy, from the near oblivion to the angry chastisement (see CHASTISEMENT AND PUNISHMENT), may be a reflection of the changing circumstances with which the Qurʾān had to deal as its mission evolved. At the early stages, the Prophet did not have the effective power to deal with the apostates and thus the Qurʾān adopted a considerably more lenient attitude. With the growing strength of the new religion that attitude changed into a confident and less compromising one.

Despite the apostates' fate (q.v.) in the hereafter and their awful doom, they can always return to Islam, for God is "forgiving and merciful." This is especially true in the case of those who were coerced to apostatize (Q 16:106). But the repentance of those who persisted in and cherished apostasy and heresy (q.v.), and who remained for long obdurate in their antagonism toward Islam, shall never be accepted (Q 3:90). The Qurʾān frequently reminds the apostate who is not long persistent in his heresy and disbelief to re-embrace the faith soon while he still has the opportunity to do so. For death can come stealthily and seal the fate of the apostate into an eternal and irreversible doom. Q 47:34 is quite clear and sums up the qurʾānic position on the matter: "Those who disbelieve *(kafarū)* and turn from the way of God (see PATH OR WAY [OF GOD]) and then die unbelievers, God surely will not pardon them" (see also Q 2:161, 217; 3:91).

Upon the Prophet's death and until the early months of 13/634, Muslim armies engaged in a number of battles that came later to be known as the wars of apostasy *(ḥurūb al-ridda)*. Except for Medina, Mecca and the immediately surrounding regions, nearly all the rest of Arabia rose up against Muslim rule. Scholars disagree as to the causes of resistance, some arguing that it was provoked by a rejection of the taxes the Prophet imposed on the Islamicized tribes together with what that clearly implied in terms of political domination. Others have seen it as expressing a religious revolt, challenging the religion of the new state at Medina. A more convincing view, however, is that each of the revolts against the new order had its own causes. Of the six major centers of uprising, four had a religious color, each led by a so-called prophet, prophetess or soothsayer: al-Aswad al-ʿAnsī in Yemen, Musaylima (q.v.) in Yamāma, Ṭulayḥa b. Khuwaylid of the tribes of Banū Asad and Banū Ghaṭafān and Sajāḥ of the tribe of Tamīm. The resistance in the two other centers — east and southeast of the Arabian peninsula — seems to have been caused by a refusal to submit to the political authority of Medina including the payment of taxes imposed upon them by the Prophet in 9/630.

Following classical Islamic sources, much of modern scholarship tends to see all these wars and battles that took place within the boundaries of Arabia — before the conquests in Syria and Ḥīra began — as falling into the category of the wars of apostasy. In point of fact, of all the centers of revolt only Najd qualifies, strictly speaking, for classification as a center of apostate rebellion. The Banū Ḥanīfa, led by Musaylima in Yamāma, had never been subject to Medinan domination nor did they sign any treaty either with Muḥammad or with his successor Abū Bakr (11/632-13/634). It was only when the military commander Khālid b. al-Walīd (d. 21/642) defeated them in 12/633 that they came, for the first time, under Medinan domination. In other words, they never converted to Islam in the first place so that they cannot correctly be labeled as apostates. A similar situation existed in ʿUmān, al-Baḥrayn, al-Yaman, and Ḥaḍramawt. There, Muḥammad concluded treaties with military leaders — some of whom were Persian agents — who were quickly ousted by the local tribes. Thus, the tribes' resistance to Medina did not presuppose a particular relationship in which they paid allegiance to the Muslim state. Again, their uprising does not constitute apostasy, properly speaking. The tribes of Najd, on the other hand, were their own masters and signed treaties with Muḥammad, the terms of which required them to adopt Islam and to pay homage as well as taxes to Medina. Their revolt, thus, constituted a clear case of apostasy. In the other cases it was not exactly apostasy on the part of the tribes which prompted the wars but rather the Medinan religious, political and territorial ambitions.

It is highly probable that the events making up the so-called wars of apostasy, together with their fundamental impact upon the collective Muslim psyche, generated a new element in the attitude toward apostasy. Being largely a reflection of the post-Prophetic experience, ḥadīth — the reports that are believed to document the words and deeds of the Prophet — stipulate, at variance with the Qurʾān, that the apostate should be punished by death. To be sure, this stipulation reflects a later reality and does not stand in accord with the deeds of the Prophet. In fact, if we go by what seems to be reliable information about Muḥammad, the Qurʾān emerges as a more accurate representation of his attitude toward apostasy. It is more likely that Abū Bakr was the first to be involved in putting to death a number of apostates, an action which was in the course of time perceived as the practice (sunna, q.v.) of the Prophet. Later sources sanctioned this penalty and made a point in mentioning that the other Companions approved of Abū Bakr's action.

On the authority of the Companion Ibn ʿAbbās (d. 68/688), the Prophet is reported to have said, "He who changes his religion, kill him." Another ḥadīth from Ibn ʿAbbās and the Prophet's wife ʿĀʾisha (see ʿĀʾISHA

BINT ABĪ BAKR) states that the Prophet allowed the execution of anyone who abandoned Islam and dissented with the community. The Prophet is also reported to have given Muʿādh b. Jabal the following order when he dispatched him to govern in the Yemen: "Any man who turns away from Islam, invite him [to return to it]; if he does not return, cut off his neck." The second half of the ḥadīth occurs also in a virtually identical formulation, but applies to women. A more categorical, yet valueless, ḥadīth specifies that "He whose religion differs from that of Islam, behead him." The means of implementing capital punishment so stated in ḥadīth did vary. One ḥadīth, reported by ʿĀʾisha, specifies that beheading, crucifixion or banishment are acceptable, but burning at the stake is not. Another ḥadīth — used by Ibn ʿAbbās in criticism of the fourth caliph ʿAlī (r. 35/ 656-40/661), who burned some unbelievers or heretics *(zanādiqa,* sing. *zindīq)* — declares that: "He who abandons his religion (variant: "turns back on his own religion") kill him, but do not punish anyone by means of God's punishment," i.e. fire.

Within Islamic law, apostasy is defined as releasing oneself from Islam *(qaṭʿ al-Islām)* by means of saying or doing something heretical, even in jest. Upholding a theological doctrine which negates the existence of God; rejecting the Prophets; mocking or cursing God or the Prophet; kneeling down in prayer to an idol, the moon or the sun (see IDOLS AND IMAGES); dumping a copy of the Qurʾān in a waste basket; declaring legal what is otherwise strictly illegal, such as adultery (see ADULTERY AND FORNICATION), all constitute apostasy.

The apostate who is *compos mentis (mukallaf),* is given a three-day grace period to reconsider his decision. If he repents, there are to be no legal consequences. If he does not, then he is by juristic consensus *(ijmāʿ)* to be executed by the sword. The female apostate receives the same punishment according to all the schools except the Ḥanafīs and Twelver Shīʿīs (Jaʿfarīs), who waive this punishment and replace it by imprisonment. If the apostate is killed during the grace period, his killer is not prosecuted nor under the obligation to pay blood money *(diya,* see BLOOD MONEY). Some of the civil consequences of apostasy are that the property of the apostate is appropriated by the state treasury and all his transactions are considered null and void. If the person repents, he is given what is left of his property. This precept was formulated in a context where apostates had escaped to non-Muslim territory and returned much later to repent and reclaim their property. Legally speaking, minors, madmen and fully capacitated persons coerced into apostasy are not considered apostates. The foregoing discussion of the Qurʾān makes it clear that nothing in the law governing apostates and apostasy derives from the letter of the holy text. See also FAITH.

Wael Hallaq

Bibliography
Primary: al-Balādhurī, *Futūḥ al-buldān,* Hyderabad 1932; al-Ghunaymī, *al-Lubāb fī sharḥ al-kitāb,* 4 vols., Cairo 1963, iv, 148-53; Ibn Ḥajar, *Fatḥ al-bārī bi-sharḥ Ṣaḥīḥ al-Bukhārī,* ed. ʿA.ʿA. al-Bāz et al., 13 vols., Beirut 1980, xii, 264-75; Ibn Isḥāq-Guillaume; Ibn Kathīr, *Tafsīr;* Ibn Qudāma, *al-Kāfī fī fiqh al-imām Aḥmad b. Ḥanbal,* ed. S. Yūsuf et al., 4 vols., Cairo 1994, iv, 73-9; M. al-Khaṭṭāb, *Mawāhib al-jalīl li-sharḥ Mukhtaṣar al-Khalīl,* 6 vols., Tripoli (Libya) 1969, vi, 279-90; Nawawī, *Minhāj al-ṭālibīn,* trans. E.C. Howard, London 1914, 436-8; Qasṭallānī, *Irshād al-sārī li-sharḥ Ṣaḥīḥ al-Bukhārī,* 15 vols., Beirut 1990, xiv, 392-8; Ṭabarī, *Taʾrīkh,* repr. Karachi 1967, iii, 223-342.
Secondary: W. Heffening, Murtadd, in *EI*[2], vii, 635-6; Izutsu, *Concepts,* 119-33, 156-9; E. Shoufani; *al-Ridda and the Muslim conquest of Arabia,* Toronto 1972.

Apostle

The disciples of Jesus (q.v.). The word for the apostles, *ḥawāriyūn (*sing. *ḥawārī),* occurs four times in the Qurʾān (Q 3:52; 5:111, 112; 61:14) and only in the plural. Most Muslim commentators (cf. M. Ayoub, *The Qurʾān,* 158-62) regard *ḥawārī* as a pure Arabic word derived from the verb *ḥāra,* meaning "to return," or from *ḥawira,* "to be glistening white." The first derivation yields the meaning "disciples," since a prophet *turns* to a disciple for help. This understanding would also be compatible with another tradition that the apostles are "helpers" *(anṣār).* This reflects Jesus' question in the Qurʾān, "Who will be my helpers to God?" (*man anṣārī ilā llāh,* Q 3:52). Some reports indicate that apostles are, in a general sense, the "special companions of the prophets" *(khāṣṣat al-anbiyāʾ wa-ṣafwatuhum),* as in the statement of Muḥammad, "[The Companion al-Zubayr b. al-ʿAwwām]... is my apostle from my community" (cf. M. Ayoub, *The Qurʾān,* 159; Ibn Kathīr, *Tafsīr,* ii, 42-3). The most popular etymology derives the meaning of *ḥawārī* from *ḥawar,* meaning "intense whiteness." Some report that the apostles wore pure white garments. Others make them fullers (sing. *qaṣṣār*). Still others hold that the name refers to the purity of the apostles' hearts.

Interpretations closer to the witness of the Christian gospels frequently mention that Jesus' apostles, corresponding to the twelve tribes of Israel, were twelve in number; they were fishermen and his first loyal followers *(khulaṣāʾ* or *talāmīdh),* even leaving their families and homes to follow Jesus. Others say *ḥawāriyūn* means "strivers" (sing. *mujāhid*) because in Q 61:14 believers are being asked to fight for Muḥammad in a spirit of obedience like that of Jesus' apostles. The most difficult interpretation to justify with reference to a specific Qurʾānic passage is that the apostles were "kings" (sing. *malik*).

Most Western interpreters trace the origin of *ḥawārī* to the Ethiopic word *ḥawāryā,* meaning "messenger." In the Ethiopic translation of the New Testament this word is used for the twelve apostles of Jesus (see FOREIGN VOCABULARY).

The Qurʾān mentions only two events involving the apostles of Jesus. In Q 5:112 the apostles ask Jesus to have God send down a table of food to satisfy their hunger and strengthen their faith. Jesus agrees to do so, but warns them that, because they have witnessed such a confirmation of faith, God will tolerate no future deviation from faith on their part. The second instance takes place at the end of Jesus' mission. When he is under attack from unbelievers, his apostles testify to the constancy of their faith in him. Jesus asks, "Who will be my helpers to God?" His apostles answer, "We are God's helpers! We believe in God and do you bear witness that we are Muslims. Our lord! We believe in what you have revealed and we follow the messenger. Then write us down among those who bear witness (Q 3:52-3)." One final passage probably refers to the apostles of Jesus and his other followers: "We sent... Jesus the son of Mary (q.v.), and bestowed on him the Gospel (q.v.); and We ordained in the hearts of those who followed him compassion and mercy" (Q 57:27). See also CHRISTIANS AND CHRISTIANITY.

A.H. Mathias Zahniser

Bibliography
Primary: Ibn Kathīr, *Tafsīr,* 7 vols., Beirut 1389/1970, ii, 42-3; Ṭabarī, *Tafsīr,* 16 vols., Cairo 1961-9, vi, 442-52.
Secondary: M. Ayoub, *The Qurʾān and its interpreters,* 2 vols., Albany 1992, ii. *The House of Imran,* 154-69; Jeffery, *For. vocab.,* 115-6; McAuliffe, *Qurʾānic,* 260-6; N. Robinson,

Christ in Islam and Christianity, Albany 1991, 31-8; A.J. Wensinck, "Ḥawārī," in *EI²*, iii, 285.

Apparition

The preternatural appearance of a specter or vision. There is no specific qur'ānic term for apparition, and qur'ānic words which in some contexts may be taken to indicate an apparition, such as *burhān* (proof) and *āya* (sign), have different meanings in other verses. For example, Joseph (q.v.) "saw the proof of his Lord," while being seduced by his master's wife. The qur'ānic verse reads "For she desired him and he would have taken her but that he saw the proof *(burhān)* of his Lord" (Q 12:24). "Proof" in this verse has been interpreted in a variety of ways. Most commonly exegetes claim that Joseph saw a vision of his father Jacob (q.v.), from which he came to understand that he was acting improperly (e.g. Muqātil, *Ashbāh,* ii, 329; Ṭabarī, *Tafsīr,* xii, 110-3; Wāḥidī, *Wasīṭ,* ii, 608; Rāzī, *Tafsīr,* ix, 122; Qurṭubī, *Jāmiʿ,* ix, 169-80; Ibn Kathīr, *Tafsīr,* ii, 474; see also *The Babylonian Talmud,* Tractate *Sota,* ii, 36b). Others claimed that he saw a vision of something that appeared through the roof of the house which reminded him that he was one of the prophets of God and therefore infallible (Ṭabarī, *Tafsīr,* xii, 113; Suyūṭī, *Durr,* iv, 15; Shawkānī, *Tafsīr,* iii, 18; see IMPECCABILITY AND INFALLIBILITY). The commentaries give different form to this vision, e.g. the palm of a hand, a note of warning, certain verses read or heard by Joseph (Ṭabarī, *Tafsīr,* xii, 113; Ibn Abī Ḥātim, *Tafsīr,* xii, 2124-6; Qurṭubī, *Jāmiʿ,* ix, 169; Ibn Kathīr, *Tafsīr,* ii, 475). In each of these cases, the "proof" is interpreted as an apparition.

If "apparition" is understood to include visual illusions or optical errors, we may cite other examples. For instance, the commentators regarded "There was already a sign *(āya)* for you in the two companies which met, one company fighting in the way of God and the other unbelieving. Their eyes saw them to be twice their number" (Q 3:13) as dealing with the battle of Badr (q.v.). However, they differed as to whether it was the infidels who saw the believers in this fashion or vice versa. One view is that the infidels were made to see the believers as being twice as many in number as themselves. Another holds that the believers saw the infidels as being twice their own number while in reality the Meccan force was three times as large as theirs (Ṭabarsī, *Majmaʿ,* i, 7-28). Whichever interpretation is adopted, the victory of the believers is attributed to a divine sign in the form of the apparent change in number.

In the case of "and for [the Jews] saying, 'We slew the Messiah, Jesus (q.v.), the son of Mary (q.v.), the Messenger of God,' yet they did not slay him or crucify him. It only appeared like that to them *(wa-lākin shubbiha lahum)*" (Q 4:157), we are dealing here with something else which was perceived differently from its actual state (for the way in which the change became possible, see Ṭabarsī, *Majmaʿ,* i, 282-3). The illusion was created by God to mislead the Jews.

Another apparition of a different nature is implied in Q 7:148: "And the people of Moses took to them, after him, a calf [made] of their jewelry, a mere body that lowed *(jasadan lahu khuwār)*" (see CALF OF GOLD). The commentators had to answer two questions: How did the idol produce the sound and why? The last question is more relevant to our topic. Most commentators argue that God turned the golden calf into flesh and blood and enabled it to low, with the intention of putting the people to a test (Qurṭubī, *Jāmiʿ,* vii, 284-5, see esp. the secret conversation between God and Moses). This means that the people who melted the gold and created the calf witnessed an apparition: They saw their idol as a living creature and took it to be God, failing the test. All of these apparitions originate in the divine will and demonstrate the divine plan. In this sense, the apparitions in the Qurʾān may be viewed as a particularly edifying means for God to communicate with mankind. See also SIGNS; VISIONS.

Leah Kinberg

Bibliography
The Babylonian Talmud, Jerusalem 1979; C.M. Horowitz (ed.), *Pirke de Rabbi Eliezer,* Jerusalem 1972 (critical edition of codex); Ibn Abī Ḥātim al-Rāzī, *Tafsīr al-Qurʾān al-ʿaẓīm,* 10 vols., Riyad 1997; Ibn Kathīr, *Tafsīr; Midrash Tankhuma,* Jerusalem 1927; Muqātil, *Ashbāh;* Qurṭubī, *Jāmiʿ;* Rāzī, *Tafsīr;* Shawkānī, *Tafsīr;* Suyūṭī, *Durr;* Ṭabarī, *Tafsīr;* Ṭabarsī, *Majmaʿ;* Wāḥidī, *Wasīṭ.*

Appointed Time see FREEDOM AND PREDESTINATION; TIME

Aqṣā Mosque

An early mosque located in Jerusalem on what is called in Islam "The Noble Sanctuary" (*al-Ḥaram al-Sharīf,* see ARCHAEOLOGY AND THE QURʾĀN). "The farthest place of prayer" *(al-masjid al-aqṣā)* is attested once in the Qurʾān, in Q 17:1 (see ASCENSION): "Glory be to he who transported his servant by night from the sacred place of prayer *(al-masjid al-ḥarām)* to the farthest place of prayer *(al-masjid al-aqṣā).*" Within Muḥammad's life-time "the sacred place of prayer" (*al-masjid,* the place of prayer, mosque; *al-ḥarām,* the sacred) was recognized as the sacred mosque at Mecca (q.v.) while "the farthest *(al-aqṣā)* place of prayer" might have been in heaven, in Jerusalem (q.v.) or perhaps in a locale near Mecca. Only at a later, unknown time did the topographical attribution become the proper name of the Aqṣā Mosque. In the earliest associations of *al-masjid al-aqṣā* with Jerusalem, it is likely that the whole of the Ḥaram was thought to be a place of prayer.

There was no mosque on al-Ḥaram al-Sharīf before Muḥammad's death; the Herodian platform was used then as a refuse dump and it is said that the second Caliph (q.v.), ʿUmar b. al-Khaṭṭāb, who accepted the surrender of Jerusalem in about 17/638, commenced clearing away the rubbish. No Muslim source records the Ḥaram's first mosque but, in the reign of Caliph Muʿāwiya I (41/661-60/680), the Gallic pilgrim Arculf saw that the "Saracens" had a rough prayer house, unnamed, in its eastern part, built on what he understood to be the remains of the Jewish Temple. That mosque has been attributed to ʿUmar b. al-Khaṭṭāb.

The Aqṣā Mosque is situated in the southwest corner of the Ḥaram and during the repairs of 1938-42, five previous major (Aqṣā I-V), and several lesser, structural periods were identified. In period V (746-7/1345-751/1350), associated with the Mamlūk ʿIzz al-Dīn Aybak al-Miṣrī, the western vaulted aisles and the outer western porch bays were constructed. Period IV was the work of the Knights Templar who occupied the mosque (492/1099-582/1187), when some of the eastern aisles were demolished and replaced with vaulted galleries and the central porch bays built. Literary evidence credits two Umayyad caliphs, ʿAbd al-Malik (65/685-86/705) and al-Walīd I (86/705-96/715) and two ʿAbbāsids, al-Manṣūr (136/754-158/775) and al-Mahdī (158/775-169/785) with the building or restoration of the first three archaeologically distinguishable structures, which will now be discussed.

Al-Muqaddasī, who saw the Aqṣā

Mosque in 374/985, Nāṣir-i Khusraw who saw it in 438-9/1047 and the eighth/fourteenth century author of *Muthīr al-gharām* quoted by al-Suyūṭī all say that ʿAbd al-Malik built the mosque. Remains of Aqṣā I were found in the mosque's southern part and nineteen meters short of its present northern wall (Hamilton, *Structural history,* fig. 30). Archaeological evidence for Aqṣā II, which had a wide central nave, a dome before the *miḥrāb* (see ART AND ARCHITECTURE AND THE QURʾĀN) and the nineteen meter extension of its northern wall, included Greek graffiti found on and deemed to be contemporary with the nave timbers. On epigraphic grounds, these carpenters' notes have been given a date range from the end of the sixth century C.E. to the beginning of the second/eighth century.

For Aqṣā III the nave and aisles north of the dome were demolished and new columns installed. Al-Muqaddasī wrote of these "marbled" columns which, Hamilton determined, had been specially prepared for the mosque and which remained in place until the 1938-42 repairs, when they were transferred to the Ḥaram museum. The *Muthīr,* written at Jerusalem in 752/1351, states that the Aqṣā Mosque was rebuilt by al-Manṣūr after the earthquake of 130/747-8, and built again by al-Mahdī after a second earthquake; this second quake is unrecorded and is generally thought to duplicate the earlier one.

No contemporary Muslim reports of the building of the Aqṣā Mosque exist. Its most detailed, sometimes contradictory, descriptions are those of al-Muqaddasī, Nāṣir-i Khusraw and the author of the *Muthīr al-gharām* as repeated by al-Suyūṭī, while Hamilton's study provides the most complete archaeological record. Greek papyri of ca. 90/708-96/714 found at the Egyptian village of Aphrodito mention workmen and materials having been requisitioned for construction of a mosque and palace at Jerusalem, but it cannot be determined if the reference is to a new mosque or to an ongoing project.

According to Creswell's interpretation of all of the evidence, al-Walīd I built Aqṣā I, al-Mahdī Aqṣā II, and, after the 424/1033 earthquake, the Fāṭimid Caliph al-Ẓāhir constructed Aqṣā III. He believed that the Aphrodito papyri confirmed al-Walīd I as the mosque's originator and inferred from al-Ẓāhir's mosaic inscription (see below) that, in addition to his renovation of the dome and its supports, al-Ẓāhir rebuilt the nave and aisles. Stern understood the evidence to mean Aqṣā I and II were Umayyad and Aqṣā III ʿAbbāsid; furthermore, he believed that the Fāṭimid mosaics on the dome were modeled after those of the original Umayyad building, pointing out their resemblance to those found in the Dome of the Rock. In more recent evaluations of the literary and archaeological record summarized by Hamilton (Creswell and Allan, *A short account,* 79-82), Aqṣā I is credited to ʿAbd al-Malik, Aqṣā II to al-Walīd I and Aqṣā III to al-Manṣūr and al-Mahdī after the earthquake of 130/748-9. It is surmised that Aqṣā II was enlarged considerably because the original building was too small.

An extant mosaic inscription at the base of the dome recording al-Ẓāhir's repairs of 426/1034-6 contains Q 17:1 immediately following the *basmala* (q.v.). A second inscription of al-Ẓāhir, in the dome and now lost but recorded by ʿAlī al-Harawī in 568-9/1173, also contained Q 17:1 immediately after the *basmala.* An inscription of part of Q 17:1, dating from 583-4/1187, appears on the wall east of the *miḥrāb,* while the inscription of Q 17:1-6 which is found at the eastern end of the transept is dated 731-2/1331.

N.J. Johnson

Bibliography
Primary: Adamnan, *De locis sanctis*, ed. D. Meehan, Dublin 1958; H.I. Bell (ed.), *Greek papyri in the British Museum*. iv. *The Aphrodito papyri*, London 1910; G. Le Strange (ed.), Description of the noble sanctuary at Jerusalem in 1470 A.D., by Kamāl (or Shams) ad-Dīn as-Suyūṭī, in *JRAS* 19 (1887), 247-305; al-Maqdisī al-Shāfiʿī, Shihāb al-Dīn Abū Maḥmūd Aḥmad b. Muḥammad, *Muthīr al-gharām*, ed. Aḥmad al-Khuṭaymī, Beirut 1994; al-Muqaddasī, Shams al-Dīn Abū ʿAbdallāh Muḥammad, *Aḥsan al-taqāsīm fī maʿrifat al-aqālīm*, ed. M.J. de Goeje, Leiden 1906; Nāṣir-i Khusraw, *Sefer Nameh. Relation du voyage en Syrie, en Palestine, en Égypte, en Arabie et en Perse, pendant les années de l'Hégire* 437-444 (1035-1042), trans. C. Schefer, Paris 1881.
Secondary: H.I. Bell, The Aphrodito papyri, in *The journal of Hellenic studies* 28 (1908), 97-120; R. Bell, Muhammad's visions, in *MW* 24 (1934), 145-54; M. van Berchem, *Matériaux pour un corpus inscriptionum arabicarum*, II part 2, nos. 275, 284 and p. 407, Cairo 1927; A.A. Bevan, Mohammed's ascension to heaven, in *Zeitschrift für Alttestamentliche Wissenschaft* 27 (1914), 51-61; Brockelmann, *GAL*; H. Busse, Tempel, Grabeskirche und Ḥaram aš-šarīf. Drei Heiligtümer und ihre gegenseitigen Beziehungen in Legende und Wirklichkeit, in H. Busse and G. Kretschmar, *Jerusalemer Heiligtumstraditionen in altkirchlicher und frühislamischer Zeit*, Wiesbaden 1987, 1-27; Creswell, *EMA*; id., *A short account of early Muslim architecture*, 1958, rev. and suppl. J.W. Allan, Aldershot 1989; E.C. Dodd and S. Khairallah, *The image of the word. A study of quranic verses in Islamic architecture*, 2 vols., Beirut 1981; M. Gil, *A history of Palestine*, 634-1099, trans. E. Broido, Cambridge 1992; O. Grabar, al-Ḥaram al-Sharīf, in *EI²*, iii, 173-5; id., al-Masdjid al-Akṣā, in *EI²*, vi, 707-8; A. Guillaume, Where was al-Masŷid al-Aqṣà? in *al-Andalus* 18 (1953), 323-36; R.W. Hamilton, *The structural history of the Aqsa mosque. A record of archaeological gleanings from the repairs of 1938-1942*, Oxford 1949; id., Once again the Aqṣā, in J. Raby and J. Johns (eds.), *Bayt al-Maqdis. ʿAbd al-Malik's Jerusalem, Part One*, Oxford 1992, 141-4; M.J. Kister, You shall only set out for three mosques. A study of an early tradition, reprinted in M.J. Kister, *Studies in jāhiliyya and early Islam*, London 1980, 173-96 and extra notes 1-8; G. Le Strange, *Palestine under the Moslems*, London 1890; R. Paret, Die "ferne Gebetsstätte" in Sūre 17,1, in *Der Islam* 34 (1959), 150-2; *RCEA*, VII, no. 2410, Cairo 1937; M. Rosen-Ayalon, *The early Islamic monuments of al-Ḥaram al-Sharīf*, Jerusalem 1989; H. Stern, Recherches sur la mosquée al-Aqṣā et sur ses mosaïques, in *Ars orientalis* 5 (1963), 27-47; M. de Vogüé, *Le temple de Jérusalem*, Paris 1864; J. Wilkinson, *Jerusalem pilgrims before the Crusades*, Warminster 1977; C.W. Wilson, *Ordinance survey of Jerusalem*, 1865, facsimile Jerusalem 1980.

Arabic Language

The language codified by the grammarians of al-Baṣra and al-Kūfa in the second/eighth century as representing the speech of the pre-Islamic Arabs and the language of the Qurʾān. Ever since, this language has been the one in which most of the Islamic cultural and religious heritage has found expression. Historical, geographical and social varieties closely related to this language exist or have existed and a number of linguistic communities currently use variants of this language.

Considerable controversy surrounds such questions as the status of Arabic *(al-ʿarabiyya, lisān al-ʿarab)* before and at the time of codification, the status of the variety of Arabic used in the Qurʾān at the time of revelation (see DIALECTS), the nature of the relationship between Arabic and the colloquials spoken in the various parts of the Arab world as well as the nature of the relationship between this "classical" Arabic language and that used for written and formal spoken communication in the Arab world today. This article will outline current terminology relating to the varieties of the language and then address these questions. (For an outline of the structure of Arabic, the reader is referred to works such as M.C. Bateson's *Handbook* and C. Holes' *Modern Arabic*.)

Varieties of Arabic

Twenty modern states use Arabic as an official language: Algeria, Bahrayn, Djibouti, Egypt, Iraq, Jordan, Kuwait, Lebanon, Libya, Mauritania, Morocco, Oman, Qatar, Saudi Arabia, Somalia, the Sudan, Syria, Tunisia, the United Arab Emirates and the Yemen. To this list should be added the Palestinian Authority/State and Israel, where Arabic is not the principal language, but is nevertheless widely used. The language used in all of these states, and taught in their schools, is said to be structurally identical to the classical Arabic language and the language of the Qurʾān (*al-fuṣḥā* or "classical Arabic"). It is, however, freely admitted that both its vocabulary and idiomatic usage have developed considerably. One, therefore, frequently finds a distinction being made between classical Arabic, on the one hand, and contemporary Arabic *(al-lugha al-ʿarabiyya al-ḥadītha* or *al-muʿāṣira),* on the other. Contemporary Arabic, which in Western studies is frequently referred to as Modern Standard Arabic (MSA) or, mainly in textbooks, as Modern Literary Arabic, is not a variety used for everyday, informal speech by any community, even if certain groups would like to see it become one. Nor is it a purely written language. It is, perhaps, best described as a formal language, used for all types of formal communication, both written in most contemporary literature and in the press and spoken on all formal occasions, including "serious" programs on radio and television as well as in most educational contexts. Its use is acquired mainly through formal education and only a relatively small group within the communities which it serves as an official language can be said to have mastered it.

For informal communication, regional dialects, referred to as *al-lahjāt* or as *al-ʿāmmiyya,* the language of the commonality, or sometimes as *al-dārija,* the popular language, is used. In Western research, they are commonly called "colloquials." The various dialects all belong to the same recognizable type of Arabic, sometimes called neo-Arabic, but show a great deal of divergence among themselves, increasing according to geographical distance. The dialects of the extreme west and those of the eastern parts of the Arabic world are thus almost mutually incomprehensible. Dialects are normally referred to by names derived from the geographical area in which they are used, qualified, at times, with a reference to the religious status of the users. For purposes of classification, a distinction is made between sedentary *(ḥaḍarī)* and Bedouin *(badawī)* dialects, the Bedouin dialects being those descended from the varieties used by tribal groups that migrated from the Arabian peninsula well after the original conquests. These groups may later have settled so that one encounters places where the sedentary population speak Bedouin dialects (see BEDOUIN). The sedentary dialects are again subdivided into town *(madanī)* and village *(qarawī)* dialects.

The term "Proto-Arabic" has frequently been used for the language in which the Thamūdic, Liḥyānic, Ṣafāʾitic and Ḥaṣāʾitic inscriptions were written (see ARABIC SCRIPT). This language may be an early stage of the later Arabic language. K. Versteegh suggests that it be called Early North Arabic to distinguish it from the language of Arabic inscriptions (Proto-Arabic) and that the language of the Islamic papyri pre-dating the codification of Arabic be called Early Arabic (*Arabic language,* 26). It is to be hoped that this distinction will be adopted.

Classical Arabic is the language which was defined at the beginning of this article. The term is, however, used for a wide range of purposes. It is thus commonly used for the formal language as opposed to the colloquials throughout all periods of the development of Arabic but also for a specific period in the history of this development. Sometimes this period is narrowly defined — for instance, classical as opposed to medieval — while at other times it is defined more broadly — the classical language as opposed to the modern. It is also ordinarily used to designate a style of language, that of literature and religious learning as opposed to the "modern standard" of the press. In short, readers of works where this term is used would do well to look for clues as to its exact meaning in the specific text in which it is encountered. In this article, it is used as a translation of the Arabic term *fuṣḥā* for all of the varieties of the formal language irrespective of the period from which they stem.

Old Arabic is a term sometimes used for the tribal dialects which are supposed to have co-existed with classical Arabic as vernaculars from pre-Islamic times onwards. The use of this term signals a belief in an essentially diglossic relationship between these dialects and classical Arabic. Most Arabs, and certain Western researchers, prefer to see these dialects as local variations of the classical language. Evidence as to the nature of the dialects is limited to a few scattered remarks in the works of the philologists regarding the forms they perceived to be unusual.

From Old Arabic, or from the dialects of the classical Arabic if one subscribes to this view, developed the medieval vernaculars collectively known as Middle Arabic. Much can be inferred about this stage of development from various kinds of text produced in circumstances where the normative influence of classical Arabic was not too strongly felt, either for religious reasons (Jewish and Christian Arabic) or because the purpose of the text was simply too mundane to warrant the effort entailed in attempting to produce correct classical Arabic. It is generally recognized that the modern colloquials developed from Middle Arabic vernaculars.

The impression of diversity — which the plethora of terms used above must necessarily create — should not be left unqualified. The Arabs will insist on the essential unity of their language and are right in doing so. Anyone with an educated person's command of Modern Standard Arabic finds it easy to acquire the knowledge necessary to read classical or medieval Arabic texts and the divergence between the various dialects is, on the whole, small, considering the distances and geographical obstacles which separate their users.

Classification and early history

Arabic is usually classified as belonging, alongside the south Arabian and Ethiopian languages, to the southwestern branch of the Semitic family of the Afro-Asiatic phylum. The classification as such is relatively undisputed, yet a number of points pertaining to its meaning deserves special consideration. Firstly, the group of languages referred to as the Semitic family is not such a widely divergent and heterogeneous one as, for instance, the Indo-European family, and a comparison to one of the smaller branches of the latter, such as the Romance languages, would provide a truer picture of the facts. Secondly, the varieties within the Semitic family tend to show continuous rather than discrete variation among themselves. This family of languages should therefore be seen as a large and varied continuum, specific segments of which have, at specific points of time, been liberalized and codified, becoming, through this process, the individual Semitic languages of antiquity and modern times.

The early history of the Arabic language cannot at present be satisfactorily established. This is mainly due to the lack of sources or to the unreliable nature of those sources which do exist. At the time of the revelation of the Qurʾān, Arabic had long been the bearer of a literary, mainly poetic, tradition. Yet the development of the Arabic script (see CALLIGRAPHY), and hence of Arabic as a written language, is almost entirely connected to the transmission of the text of the Qurʾān. The process was a long one and the Arabic script was not fully developed until the end of the third/ninth century. Epigraphic evidence of Arabic predating the revelation of the Qurʾān is mainly limited to five brief inscriptions the oldest of which is the five-line Namāra inscription from 328 C.E., written in Nabatean characters, but in a language which is essentially identical to Classical Arabic. Then follows the Zebed inscription dated to 512 C.E., the Jabal Usays inscription dated to 528 C.E., the Ḥarrān inscription dated to 568 C.E., and the Umm al-Jimāl inscription, also from the sixth century C.E. All of these are brief inscriptions representing an early stage of the Arabic script. All these inscriptions tell us, however, that for some time before the Arabic language emerges into the light of history with the mission of the prophet Muḥammad, a language very similar to classical Arabic was in use on the peninsula and in neighboring areas, and that some of the users of this language had mastered the art of writing (see EPIGRAPHY AND THE QURʾĀN).

The poetic literature of the pre-Islamic Arabs was committed to writing only through the efforts of the Muslim philologists towards the middle of the second/eighth century. The earliest preserved specimens of the tradition would seem to date from the beginning of the sixth century C.E., so that the time span in which oral transmission was unsupported by writing was quite considerable. This has made several researchers doubt the validity of the poetic evidence for purposes of research on the linguistic situation prior to the codification of Arabic. In addition, there is evidence indicating that the philologists collecting the poems may have corrected them a bit during the process. To rely on the poetic corpus as evidence for the linguistic situation prior to the codification of Arabic is therefore to rely on the work of early Muslim philologists. Another matter is that the very nature of poetry, and the specific use to which poetry was put in the pre-Islamic society of Arabia, makes it likely that the language of the poetic corpus may not directly represent the linguistic varieties used for purposes of everyday communication within the tribes of the peninsula. The question which arises at this point, to wit, that of how great the differences between the language of the poetry and the vernaculars were in pre-Islamic times, has been a matter of contention throughout the twentieth century. Currently, the proponents of the view that the "poetic koine" existed in a diglossic relationship with the vernaculars would seem to outnumber those who think that the "poetic register" and the vernaculars essentially represented one and the same language. The latter view, which is represented mainly in the writings of K. Versteegh, does, however, have the considerable weight of the Islamic scholarly tradition to recommend it. See POETRY AND POETS.

To sum up, of the very little that can be known about Arabic before the dawn of Islam, we know that varieties very similar to classical Arabic were used for several hundred years before, extending over an area encompassing not only the Arabian peninsula but also parts of the Fertile Crescent. We also know that some of these varieties had sufficient prestige to be used for inscriptions and poetic composition. We do not, however, know who the users of these varieties were, what name they gave to their language, or for what other purposes, besides inscriptions and poetry, they may have used them. Nor do we know how great were the differences between the varieties in question since only one of them, classical Arabic, has been preserved for us in the form of a corpus of text and a systematic description.

Codification

The actual codification of Arabic took place, as has already been stated, in the second/eighth century. The first dictionary was compiled — but never completed — by al-Khalīl b. Aḥmad (d. 175/791), who also codified Arabic prosody. The first grammar is the famous *Kitāb* of al-Khalīl's student Sībawayhi (d. 177/793), which was completed and transmitted after the author's death by his student al-Akhfash al-Awsaṭ (d. 221/835).

Among the factors usually mentioned to explain the process of codification, the most important are, on the one hand, the needs of non-Arab citizens of the empire to master Arabic as well as the linguistic corruption which supposedly came about as a result of the uprooting of Bedouin tribesmen from their natural environment and, on the other hand, the decision taken during the reign of the Umayyad caliph ʿAbd al-Malik b. Marwān (r. 65/685-86/705) to make Arabic the language of the public registers. It should, however, be noted that the early works on grammar are not elementary textbooks for teaching language to beginners. On the contrary, a work such as the *Kitāb* is concerned mainly with explanation and the systemization of the hierarchical ordering of facts with which the student is assumed to be familiar into a coherent whole. It is, in short, a treatise on grammar. Yet, the object of this systematization is definitely not Arabic as it was spoken in the time and place of the actual codification. Sībawayhi aims at an ideal which M. Carter terms "good old Arabic" (Sībawayhi, 526). The data of which Sībawayhi makes use include passages from the Qurʾān and verses of poetry, but also data obtained from contemporary Bedouin. This indicates that "good old Arabic" was a living language among the Bedouin at the time, in the sense that they could produce it upon demand, but not necessarily that it was a common medium of day-to-day communication. It should be noted that although as a totality the three groups of data are seen as embodying "good old Arabic," no individual group is given priority or accepted uncritically. The variety among the "readings" (*qirāʾāt*, see READINGS OF THE QURʾĀN) of the Qurʾān sometimes makes it possible to reject certain readings. Poetic usage is in some cases seen as differing from prose and certain Bedouin usages are dismissed as incorrect.

M. Carter has argued convincingly that Sībawayhi's system of grammar was, on the whole, inspired by the science of "law" (*fiqh*) as it was taught at that time. This implies a wholly pragmatic view of language: A language is not a system — though its grammar is — but rather a type of behavior, the individual acts of which are to be judged "by motive, structure and communicative effectiveness" (M. Carter, Sībawayhi, 526). Communicative effectiveness is the absolute. Speech is right *(mustaqīm)* if it conveys meaning, but wrong *(muḥāl)* if it does not. Structural correctness, on the other hand, is relative and speech may be *mustaqīm qabīḥ*, that is, make sense and thus be right, but still be structurally incorrect and hence "ugly." This implies that the codification of Arabic was neither a prescriptive project, aimed at teaching a forgotten language — or a language rapidly becoming forgotten — nor a descriptive one, aimed at setting down the facts of acknowledged contemporary usage. Rather it was a conservative effort, intended to keep linguistic behavior from straying too far from what was the "way" of the Arabs (q.v.) and, more importantly, of the Qurʾān.

The Qurʾān

The Qurʾān is somewhat self-conscious with respect to its language. Generally speaking it identifies the language (the word used is *lisān*, "tongue"), in which it is revealed as that of the Prophet (Q 19:97; 44:58), as that of the Prophet's people (*bi-lisni qawmihi*, Q 14:4) and as Arabic (Q 26:195; 46:12). The epithet "Arabic" is also given to the Qurʾān itself (Q 12:2) and to its function as a decisive utterance (*ḥukm*, Q 13:37).

As was recently pointed out by Jan Retsö, the Qurʾān, which is the oldest source in Arabic which actually talks about a language named after the Arabs, does not contrast the Arabic language to any other languages identified by name. Throughout, the epithet *ʿarabī*, "Arab" or "Arabic," is contrasted to *aʿjamī*, "non-Arab" or "non-Arabic," but it is never stated that the Arabic tongue is not understood by non-Arabic speakers. Indeed, verses such as Q 26:199 seem to indicate that the Qurʾān would be understood by non-Arabs should it be recited to them. However, it is also clear, from e.g. Q 16:103, that one whose tongue is *aʿjamī* cannot be expected to produce Arabic.

In order for the Qurʾān to be able to declare itself Arabic, there had to exist some sort of criteria for what is Arabic and what is not. Such criteria may, of course, be very loose, but if one assumes that the *aʿjām* were foreigners in the sense of people speaking languages entirely different from Arabic and maybe even incomprehensible to an Arab the qurʾānic argumentation loses much of its force. For the argument "this is Arabic and hence divine" to have any noticeable force, the criteria for what is Arabic have to be quite narrow, to amount, in fact, to a standard of language recognizably out of reach of the ordinary member of society. In the words of J. Wansbrough: "The linguistic tradition to which reformers and prophets, as well as poets, turn may be ancient. What it must be, is other than the current *usus loquendi*..." (*QS*, 103).

The philologists' choice of the poetic corpus as the second source for the codification of Arabic has been taken to indicate what the tradition to which Muḥammad turned was. Their use of contemporary Bedouin informers demonstrates that this tradition was, at least in some areas, still alive at the time of codification. What is important to note is that the tradition is presented neither as a language nor as a literature but as a way of life, an ideal of culture. Even in works specifically devoted to the language itself, it is the "speech of the Arabs" *(kalām al-ʿarab)* which is presented and it is presented as a "way," a set of manners and customs. Equally important is the fact that both the Qurʾān and the philologists present the tradition as essentially somebody else's. Whether the "way" of the Arabs consisted in the active use of case and mode endings *(iʿrāb)* no longer in use in the vernaculars, as the proponents of the "poetic koine" hypothesis would have it or merely in the deliberate use of an archaic tradition of poetic diction and eloquent speech encompassing such features as the careful pronunciation of the glottal stop (a phoneme not realized in the Meccan dialect), use of the elevated register of poetry, the use of rhymed prose and the deliberate creation of parallelism, the effect would be much the same. The point, in both cases, is the appeal to a tradition which is both an essential part of the community's heritage and at the same time definitely not a "natural" part of the community's everyday language. Whoever coined the translation "classical" for *fuṣḥā* knew what he was doing.

The current situation: diglossia

The concept central to most descriptions of the linguistic situation of the Arab world today is that of diglossia. In Ferguson's classic paper from 1959, diglossia is defined as "a relatively stable language situation in which, in addition to the primary dialects of the language (which may include a standard or regional standards), there is a very divergent, highly codified (often grammatically more complex) superimposed variety, the vehicle of a large and respected body of written literature, either of an earlier period or in another speech community, which is learned largely by formal education and is used for most written or formal spoken purposes, but is not used by any sector of the community for ordinary conversation" (Diglossia, 336). To Ferguson, this definition is an attempt to outline one specific type of language situation, in the hope that other contributions, outlining other types of language situations, would in the end lead to the establishment of a viable taxonomy. However, much of the discussion relevant to Arabic pivoted on the validity of the concept itself, with alternatives such as pluriglossia and multiglossia competing with models employing the concept of variation along a continuum.

The crux of the problem lies in the fact that Ferguson's original article outlined the properties and areas of use of two "varieties" of language as if these varieties — which Ferguson later identified as cases of register variation — were linguistic (sub-) systems in normal and frequent use. As is shown by D.B. Parkinson's attempts to have Egyptians produce classical Arabic, at least this high variety is used very seldom by most members of the Egyptian speech community in any kind of pure form. Though I do not know of any published investigations of the problem, I would predict that "pure" Egyptian colloquial, without the slightest admixture of classical forms, is not very common either. In most cases of actual conversation, elements of the high variety and elements of the low variety are mixed in such a manner that it is frequently difficult to identify both the underlying matrix on which the specific instance of usage builds and the target at which the user aims. Actual usage is normally neither "high" nor "low" but somewhere in between.

S. Badawi's very influential *Levels of contemporary Arabic in Egypt* recognizes this problem. For him, modern Egyptian Arabic exhibits a continuum of socio-linguistic variety which he illustrates through the identification of five imaginary levels: "the classical of the heritage" *(fuṣḥā al-turāth),* "contemporary classical" *(fuṣḥā al-ʿaṣr),* "the colloquial of the cultured" *(ʿāmmiyyat al-muthaqqafīn),* "the colloquial of the enlightened" *(ʿāmmiyyat al-mutanawwirīn)* and "the colloquial of the illiterate" *(ʿāmmiyyat al-ummiyyīn).* Although Badawi stresses that the levels are imaginary points of reference on a scale of free variation, he does assign specific linguistic features to the different levels. However, analysis of actual speech will show that there is normally a mixture of elements from various places on such a scale, operating on all levels of analysis. Not only may a sentence contain some words that are markedly classical side by side with some that are markedly colloquial but a single word marked as one variety may take an ending marked as another. The varieties, seen as levels on a scale, are therefore not discrete systems. The study of this phenomenon, called code-switching, has currently not reached the point where any decisive results can be established but a considerable amount of research is at present being carried out.

If Ferguson's original term diglossia still remains the most frequently used description of the current linguistic situation in Arab societies, it is because, as he himself points out, the type of variation which he calls diglossic is just that and not pluriglossic because there are only two identifiable poles or ends to the scale of variation (Epilogue, 59). Furthermore, these poles are identifiable in the sense that systematic descriptions do exist, based, for the classical end of the scale, on the Arabic linguistic tradition and for the colloquial end, mostly on textbooks aimed at foreign students.

Attitudes

As K. Versteegh recently pointed out, languages are surprisingly often discussed as if they were some kind of living organisms, capable of birth, growth, change and decline. Yet they are not. They are patterns of human behavior, conventions acquired and manipulated by individuals. The attitude which the individual user of a language takes towards that language is therefore a matter of some importance. Of even greater importance are the attitudes which researchers take towards the object of their research.

Classical Arabic is, throughout the Arab world, seen as the Arabic language *par excellence*. Correspondingly, the colloquials are often seen as not being languages at all, but rather as chaotic, unsystematic and lacking in grammar. Yet a certain ambivalence of feeling towards the use of the classical language is often reported. D.B. Parkinson relates how users with an active command of the classical language are often constrained to deliberately employ a certain admixture of colloquial forms, even when speaking from rather formal platforms like that of the university lecture theatre (Variability, 92). On the other hand, suggestions for linguistic reform involving modification of the classical language or letting the colloquials take over some of its functions are either met with hostility or ignored. Classical Arabic remains the language in which the religion of Islam finds expression throughout an area considerably greater than that of the Arabic-speaking countries. It remains the language in which the cultural and political life of the Arab world is conducted and the language used by most mass media in the Arab world. It may be that the percentage of speakers who can claim an active command of the language is rather small, but there is no sign that this will seriously affect its position.

Classical Arabic is often treated as something of a special case in modern linguistics. Dominant trends, such as generative grammar, have assigned a somewhat important place among their data to the "intuition" of "native speakers" about their "first language." Classical Arabic does not quite fit in here since there is no one who has it as a first language. This may, unless due care is taken, lead to a view of classical Arabic as somehow "artificial" or "congealed" or as a "dead language" artificially kept alive by the conservatism of certain elites. The feeling that the "real" or "living" Arabic language is represented by the colloquials is quite widespread. This has the laudatory effect of drawing attention to the actual colloquial usage in which most communication within the Arab world takes place, a field which is seriously understudied. It is, however, also an attitude which an Arab may regard as offensive. Not only is this person denied the status of a "native speaker" of his own language, he is also being told that he may not really master it (Parkinson, Variability), and that it is a foreign language, or at least a strange dialect, even to the great linguists from whom he inherited its rules (Owens, *Foundations*, 8). One cannot help but feel that this is quite unnecessary and certainly counterproductive.

In the end, classical Arabic is much more

than a language. A ḥadīth of the Prophet, related in the *History of Damascus (Ta'rīkh madīnat Dimashq)* of Ibn ʿAsākir (d. 571/1176) illustrates this point: "Oh my people! God is one and the same. Our father [i.e. Adam, (see ADAM AND EVE)] is the same. No one amongst you inherits Arabic from his father or mother. Arabic is a habit of the tongue, so whoever speaks Arabic is an Arab" (Y. Suleiman, *Nationalism*, 22). Classical Arabic is thus the heritage of all Arabs, though it may not be the heritage of any individual Arab. It is the primary indicator of the Arab identity, though individual Arabs may partake of it in varying degrees. In most cases it is, and as far as we know it may always have been, more of an ideal to be striven for through painstaking effort, than an actual habit of everyday life, but this does not diminish its reality nor its status. As a matter of fact, it enhances it, for such strife is the theme around which the entire religion of Islam revolves. Thus, Arabic is more than the language of Islam, it is part of Islam. It is, as indeed are all languages, a phenomenon of culture, not one of nature, and changes as does the culture for which it is a medium changes but at the core it is unchanging, just as the document which is at the core of the culture of Islam, the Qurʾān, is unchanging.

Herbjørn Jenssen

Bibliography
S. Badawī, *Mustawayāt al-ʿarabiyya l-muʿāṣira fī Miṣr,* Cairo 1973; M.C. Bateson, *Arabic language handbook,* Washington, D.C. 1967; J. Blau, *Studies in middle Arabic and its Judaeo-Arabic variety,* Jerusalem 1988; G. Bohas, J.-P. Guillaume and D.E. Kouloughli, *The Arabic linguistic tradition,* London 1990; M.G. Carter, *Arab linguistics. An introductory classical text with translation and notes,* Amsterdam 1981; id., Language control as people control in medieval Islam. The aims of the grammarians and their cultural context, in *al-Abḥāth* 31 (1983), 65-84; id., Writing the history of Arabic grammar, in *Historigraphia linguistica* 21 (1994), 385-414; id., Sībawayhi, in *EI²*, ix, 524-31; M. Eid, The non-randomness of diglossic variation, in *Glossa* 16 (1982), 54-84; C.A. Ferguson, Diglossia, in *Word* 15 (1959), 325-40; id., Epilogue. Diglossia revisited, in Alaa Elgibali (ed.), *Understanding Arabic. Essays in contemporary Arabic linguistics in honor of El-Said Badawi,* Cairo 1996; W. Fischer and H. Gätje (eds.), *Grundriss der arabischen Philologie,* 3 vols. to date, Wiesbaden 1982; B. Hary, The importance of the language continuum in Arabic multiglossia, in Alaa Elgibali (ed.), *Understanding Arabic. Essays in contemporary Arabic linguistics in honor of El-Said Badawi,* Cairo 1996; C. Holes, *Modern Arabic. Structures, functions and varieties,* London 1995; J. Owens, *The foundations of grammar. An introduction to medieval Arabic grammatical theory,* Amsterdam 1988; D.B. Parkinson, Variability in standard Arabic grammar skills, in Alaa Elgibali (ed.), *Understanding Arabic. Essays in contemporary Arabic linguistics in honor of El-Said Badawi,* Cairo 1996; Y. Suleiman, Nationalism and the Arabic language. A historical overview, in Y. Suleiman (ed.), *Arabic sociolinguistics. Issues and perspectives,* Richmond/Surrey 1994; K. Versteegh, *The Arabic language,* Edinburgh 1997; J. Wansbrough, *QS.*

Arabic Literature and the Qurʾān

see LITERATURE AND THE QURʾĀN

Arabic Script

Arabic script *(al-khaṭṭ al-ʿarabī)* refers to 1) a set of characters and their sequential and spatial arrangement, 2) their forms and media and 3) the typology of a consonant-only system *(abjad)* denoting utterances in an abbreviated manner with linguistic and sociological implications (P. Daniels, Fundamentals, 730). Arabic script also forms part of the broader concept of Arabic writing which usually defines one Arabic variant (classical, Modern Standard or "written") within a multiglossic environment (see ARABIC LANGUAGE). The significant role of Arabic writing in religion, art, administration and scholarship, as well as in public and private life, characterizes the Arabic-Islamic world as a literate culture, albeit one in which the written and oral transmission of knowledge were continuous and complementary (F. Rosenthal, Many books, 46-7). The impact of Arabic script throughout the multilingual Muslim world far surpassed that of Arabic language (F. Rosenthal, Significant uses, 53-4). As the Islamic script par excellence, Arabic was adapted by many non-Semitic Muslim languages, notably Berber, Persian, Pashto, Kurdish, Urdu, Sindhi, Kashmiri and Uyghur. In the past, languages as diverse as Medieval Spanish (Aljamiado), Ottoman Turkish, Azeri, Serbo-Croatian, Malay (Jawi), Sulu, Malagasy (Sorabe), Swahili, Hausa, Fulani and Afrikaans were periodically spelled with Arabic characters. Conversely, Christian Arabic was also recorded in Syriac (Karshūnī) and Judeo-Arabic in Hebrew characters. Today, the Arabic *abjad* is, next to the Latin alphabet, the most widely employed segmental script in the world.

Sources and methods

Arabic paleography, i.e. the history of Arabic script and its emerging styles, is based both on medieval Muslim accounts and preserved written specimens. In addition, it draws on the disciplines of papyrology, codicology, numismatics and art history (see EPIGRAPHY AND THE QUR'ĀN).

Medieval accounts of Arabic script and penmanship appear in over forty literary sources, notably Ibn al-Nadīm's (d. 385/995 or 388/998) *Fihrist* and the extensive treatment by al-Qalqashandī (d. 821/1418) in *Ṣubḥ al-aʿshā* (ii, 440-88; iii, 1-226/ii², 440-88; iii², 1-222; cf. G. Endress, Arabische Schrift, 190-1; A. Gacek, al-Nuwayrī's classification, 129-30). Some of these accounts claim that the Arabic script originated in al-Anbār or al-Ḥīra in Iraq, against the mainly Syrian epigraphic evidence, a conflict N. Abbott attempts to reconcile (*Rise*, 3-12). But G. Endress (Arabische Schrift, 169-70) interprets the accounts as a retrospective construction by Muslim scholars to place the inception of writing at the point of the encounter between Aramaic-Hellenistic culture and a pre-Islamic Arab culture as exemplified by the person of ʿAdī b. Zayd (d. ca. 600 C.E.). The literary accounts of this early stage, generally composed after the time of the scribal practices they discuss, lack complete descriptions of graphemes. Ibn al-Nadīm defines one letter *(alif)* of the early Meccan script, allowing its identification in actual specimens (N. Abbott, *Rise*, 18-9, pls. 8-13). The terms *māʾil* and *mashq*, often understood as names of scripts today, may not have meant that originally (F. Déroche, Écritures coraniques, 213-21). Nonetheless scholars have ventured to identify scripts listed in the sources. J.G. Adler first applied the term *kūfic* in 1780 to qur'ānic material and J. von Karabacek did the same with *māʾil* and *ʿirāqī* (F. Déroche, Écritures coraniques, 209-12). Others identified *badīʿ* (Schroeder, *Badīʿ* script, 234-48), *ghubār* (N. Abbott, *Rise*, 37-8), *musalsal* (N. Abbott, Arabic paleography, 98-9), *jalīl* (A. Grohmann, *From the world*, 75-7), *thuluth rayḥān* (A. Grohmann, *From the world*, 81), and *qarmaṭa* (A. Dietrich, *Arabische Briefe*, 46, 67). Some medieval terms became too vague, so the *kūfī* of early Qurʾāns has been split into six groups of scripts by Déroche (*Abbasid tradition*, 34-47), and *naskhī* should no longer be used in reference to early papyri, according to G. Khan (*Arabic papyri*, 45-6). In short, the use of medieval terminology in paleographic study can be treacherous, and one should, according to Déroche, rely instead on datable specimens (Paléographie des écritures livresques, 3-5). Irrespective of their often dubious factual accuracy for the early period, the rich literary sources underscore the interest of Arabic-Islamic culture in the history of its script (see ART AND ARCHI-

TECTURE AND THE QUR'ĀN). Later, Mamlūk secretarial manuals described and even illustrated chancellery scripts which were also partially used for calligraphy. By the seventh/thirteenth century, five or, more frequently, six scripts (later called *al-aqlām al-sitta*) had established themselves in chancellery and popular practice. They fell into a "moist" *(murattab)* subgroup which emphasized the curvilinear elements and consisted of *thuluth, tawqīʿ, riqāʿ* and a "dry" *(yābis)* subgroup that tended towards the rectilinear and included *muḥaqqaq, rayḥān* and *naskh*. Scripts were further classified by size — the extremes being the gigantic *ṭumār* and the tiny *ghubār* used for pigeon post — or by the presence of serifs *(tarwīs)* or closed loops (*ṭams*, A. Gacek, Arabic scripts, 144-5). The literary sources also recorded pioneering calligraphers: Ibn Muqla (d. 328/940), who codified *naskh*, elevating it to a qurʾānic script; Ibn al-Bawwāb (d. 413/1022), who further refined it; and Yāqūt al-Mustaʿṣimī (d. ca. 697/1298), who invented a new way of trimming the pen and excelled in the six scripts. Ibn al-Bawwāb left us the first Qurʾān in *naskh*, dated 391/1001 (D. Rice, *Ibn al-Bawwāb*, 13 and pl. 7) and Yāqūt's name appears on several (partly forged) Qurʾāns (D. James, *Master scribes*, 58-74).

The second type of source, groups of dated or datable specimens, provides a more reliable basis for early paleographic study. Even so, this research remains in a preliminary state with a vast amount of yet uncharted material in Eastern and Western libraries including that from recent finds, such as the one in the Great Mosque of Sanʿāʾ in 1971-2. The latter discovery not only offers new material for the paleography of the Qurʾān but also for the history of its codification (G. Puin, *Maṣāḥif Ṣanʿāʾ*, 11-14; id., Observations, 110-1; E. Whelan, Forgotten witness, 13). During the first three centuries of Islam, scripts diverged among four more or less homogenous groups of texts with distinct functions: memorial and votive inscriptions, Qurʾāns, papyrus documents and letters, and scholarly and literary manuscripts. To apply one script terminology derived from secretarial manuals to these various groupings is problematic. Some scholars prefer a careful analysis of all, or a significant sample, of a script's graphemes in order to build a typology, yet the conclusions drawn from small samples are limited (S. Flury, *Islamische Schriftbänder*, 8-21; F. Déroche, Écritures coraniques, 213). Different concepts have been introduced to grasp the level of execution in a piece of writing. For example, a cluster of scripts can be viewed as a circle with the specimen closest to the "ideal" at its center and the loosest reproduction at the periphery (F. Déroche, *Abbasid tradition*, 16). Similarly, N. Chomsky's syntactical notion of competence versus performance serves to distinguish a writer's ideal form, "competence," from the actual result, "performance" (G. Khan, *Arabic papyri*, 39, n. 53).

The formation of Arabic script before Islam

Prior to the (north) Arabic script, inhabitants of the Arabian desert wrote graffiti — short informal texts on rocks and the like — using the Dedānic, Liḥyānic, Ṣafāʾitic, Thamūdic and Ḥasaean (also called Ḥasāʾitic), derivatives of South Arabian script. In Tell el-Maskhūṭa near Ismailiyya in Lower Egypt, Arabs used Imperial Aramaic as early as the fifth century B.C.E. but, four centuries later, the Arab satellite states of the Seleucid and Roman empires developed their own branches of Aramaic script, including Nabatean and Palmyrenian. The script of the Nabateans continued to be used after the Romans defeated them in 106 C.E. for inscriptions made by Arabs throughout the Provincia Arabia until the fourth century C.E. Two such inscriptions (ʿEn Avdat, between 88-9 and 125-6 C.E.; al-Namāra, 328 C.E.) employ Nabatean characters for writing Arabic while others (e.g. Umm al-Jimāl, ca. 250 C.E.; Madāʾin Ṣāliḥ, 267/268 C.E.) show a linguistic admixture of Arabic (A. Negev, Obodas, 48; K. Versteegh, *Arabic language,* 30-6 with further bibliography).

The characteristic basic forms of later Arabic

The characteristic basic forms of later Arabic (the Arabic *abjad*) first materialized in five brief pre-Islamic inscriptions from Syria and northwest Arabia. They display a clearly Arabic *ductus* — general shape and formation of letters and their combinations — though their language is controversial and their writing unhomogeneous. Except for the graffito in a Nabatean sanctuary in Jabal Ramm near Aqaba, datable to the first half of the fourth century C.E., they all belong to the sixth century C.E. They include a trilingual inscription in Greek, Syriac and Arabic on a Christian martyry in Zabad southeast of Aleppo (512 C.E.), a historical inscription in Jabal Usays (Sēs) on the Syrian-Roman border about 100 kilometers southeast of Damascus (528 C.E.), a graffito in the double church of Umm al-Jimāl southwest of Bosra (ca. sixth century C.E.) and a Greek and Arabic bilingual inscription on a martyry in Ḥarrān in the Lejāʾ (586 C.E.; see A. Grohmann, *Arabische Paläographie,* ii, 14-5; B. Gruendler, *Development,* 13-4.). The general proportions of this pre-Islamic Arabic script suggest Syriac calligraphic influence (N. Abbott, *Rise,* 19-20; F. Briquel-Chatonnet, De l'araméen, 143-4; J.F. Healey, Nabatean, 41-3). Yet the individual Arabic graphemes descend through Nabatean from the west Semitic alphabet. T. Nöldeke first established this link in 1865, later to be confirmed against J. Starcky's Syriac thesis (Pétra, 932-4) by A. Grohmann (*Arabische Paläographie,* ii, 13, 17-21).

This affiliation is now fully documented (J.F. Healey, Nabatean, 44-5 and tables; B. Gruendler, *Development,* 123-30 and charts). The shift from Nabatean to Arabic was complex, for the Nabatean script combined epigraphic, formal and free cursive variants, developing at different rates. At the end of the first century C.E. the formal cursive of the Engaddi papyrus (J. Starcky, Contrat, 162, pls. 1-3) and the free cursive of the Nessana ostraca (F. Rosenthal, Nabatean, 200) already include shapes which the epigraphic script only achieves two centuries later. But few cursive documents have been preserved and supplementary evidence must be gleaned from late epigraphic Nabatean (J. Naveh, *Early history,* 156; J.F. Healey, Nabatean, 43-4, 50-2 with further bibliography, 156).

The five constitutive trends of Arabic script articulated themselves very early: 1) positional variants (allographs) emerged in the Aramaic cursive of the fourth century B.C.E., 2) letters became fully connected in cursive Nabatean of the first century C.E., 3) the *lām-alif* ligature appeared in the Namāra inscription (328 C.E.), 4) the "ceiling-line" limiting the height of most letters yielded to a baseline for free cursive in the first century C.E. (and for graffiti the third century C.E.), 5) the bars of letters were integrated into continuous strokes and formerly distinct letters merged *(bēṯ/nūn, gīmel/ḥēṯ, zayin/rēš, yōḏ/tāw, pēh/qōp̄)* in the cursive of Naḥal Ḥever. (In this article, a letter's name, e.g. *zayin* or *zāy,* is a reference to its *shape;* and one mentioned by its phonetic symbol, e.g. *z,* is a reference to its *sound*). These mergers are the only ways to account for the Arabic homographs *jīm/ḥāʾ, rāʾ/zāy,* medial *bāʾ/nūn, yāʾ/tāʾ,* and medial *fāʾ/qāf* and by themselves preclude a provenance from Syriac, where these graphemes stay distinct. Cursive Nabatean graphemes most closely approximate those of pre-Islamic Arabic: straight (Nabatean)

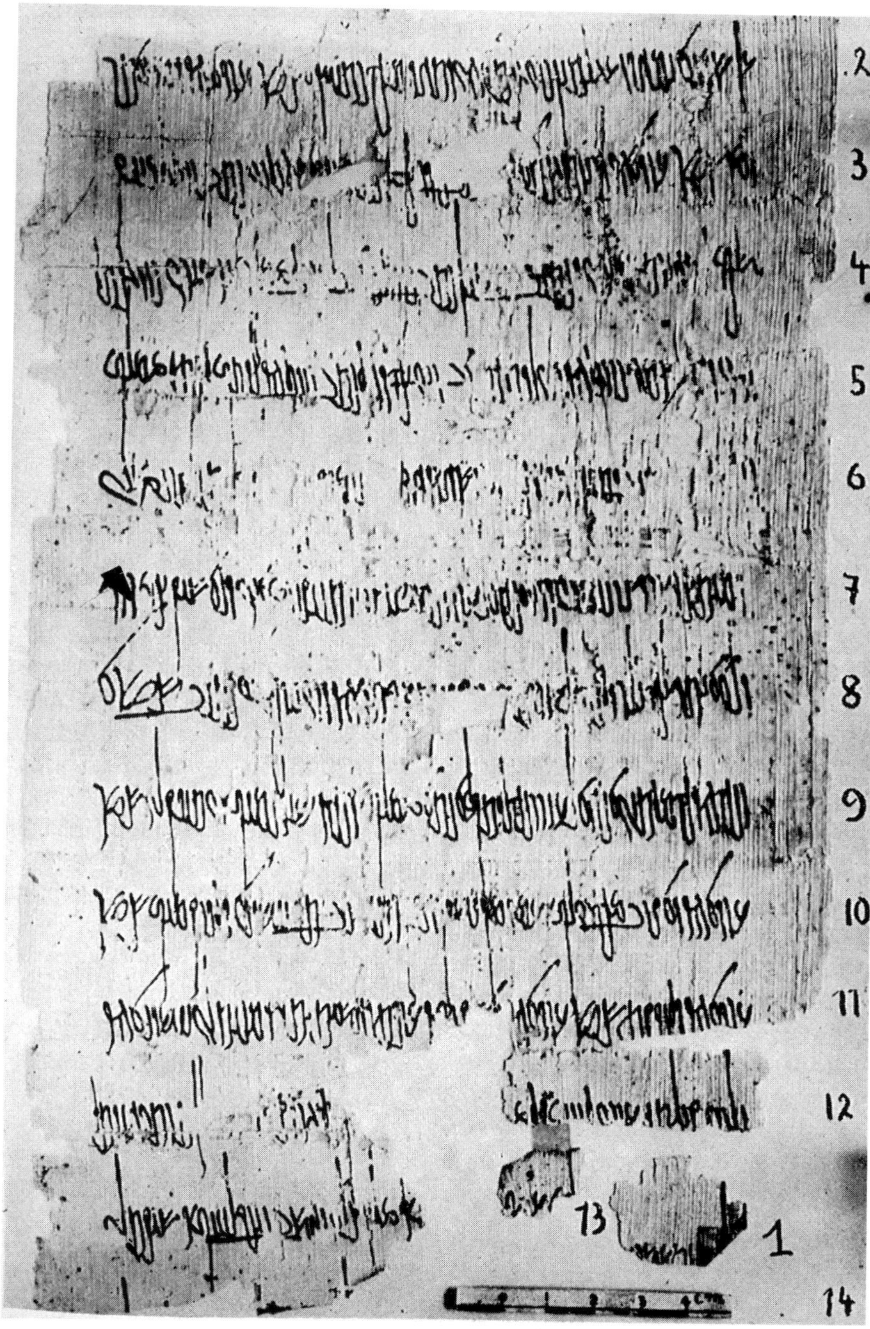

[1] Nabatean cursive, datable to 40–71 CE, from J. Starcky, Contrat, 169.

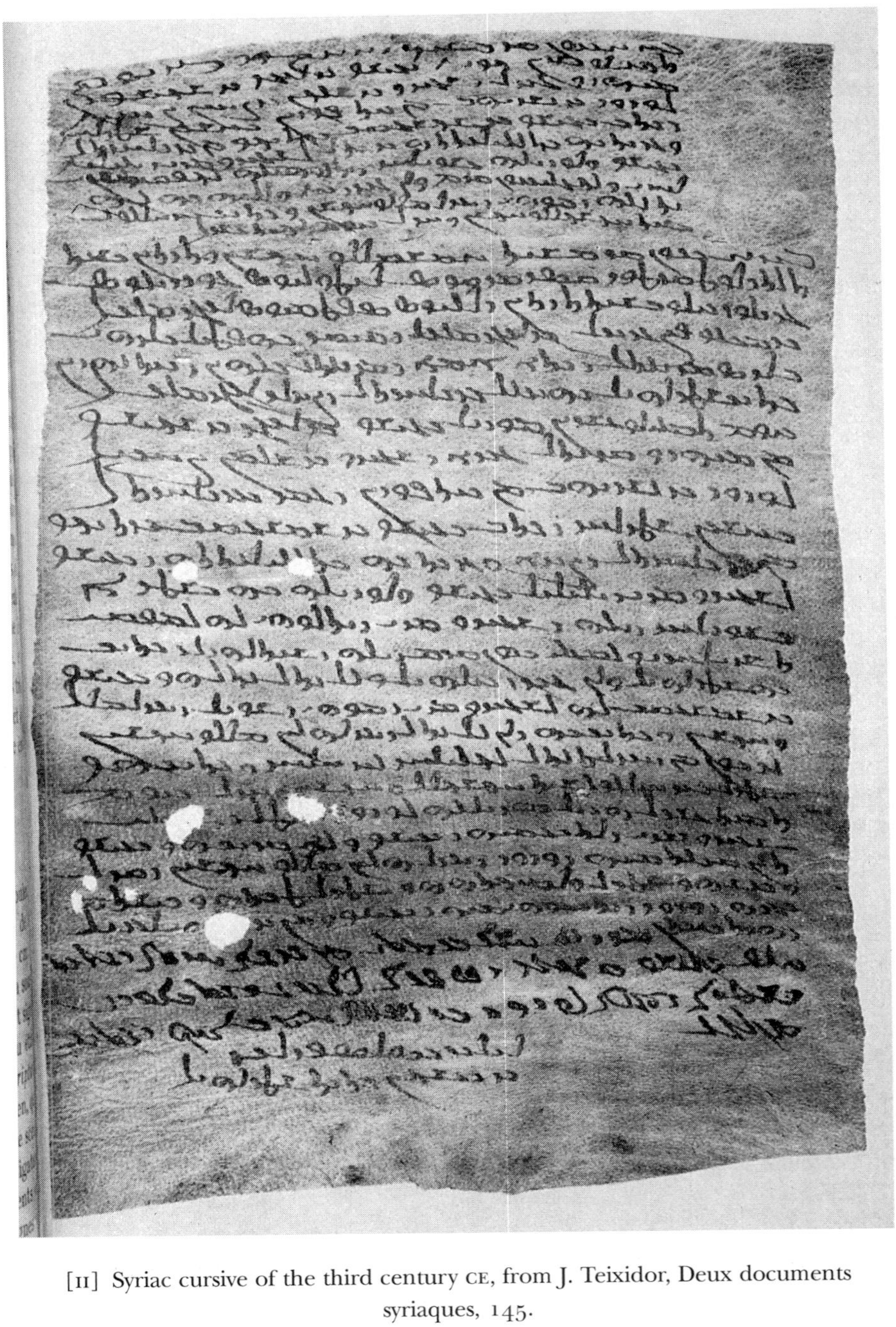

[11] Syriac cursive of the third century CE, from J. Teixidor, Deux documents syriaques, 145.

III
Dates A.D.
A-B Monumental 1st. cent.
C-E Cursive 1st/2nd cent.
11 211/2
16 265/6
17-18 266/8
21-22 305/7
23 328/9
’
h
w
ṭ
y
m
‘
p
š
t

[III] Cursive Nabatean chart, from J. Healey, Nabatean to Arabic, 51.

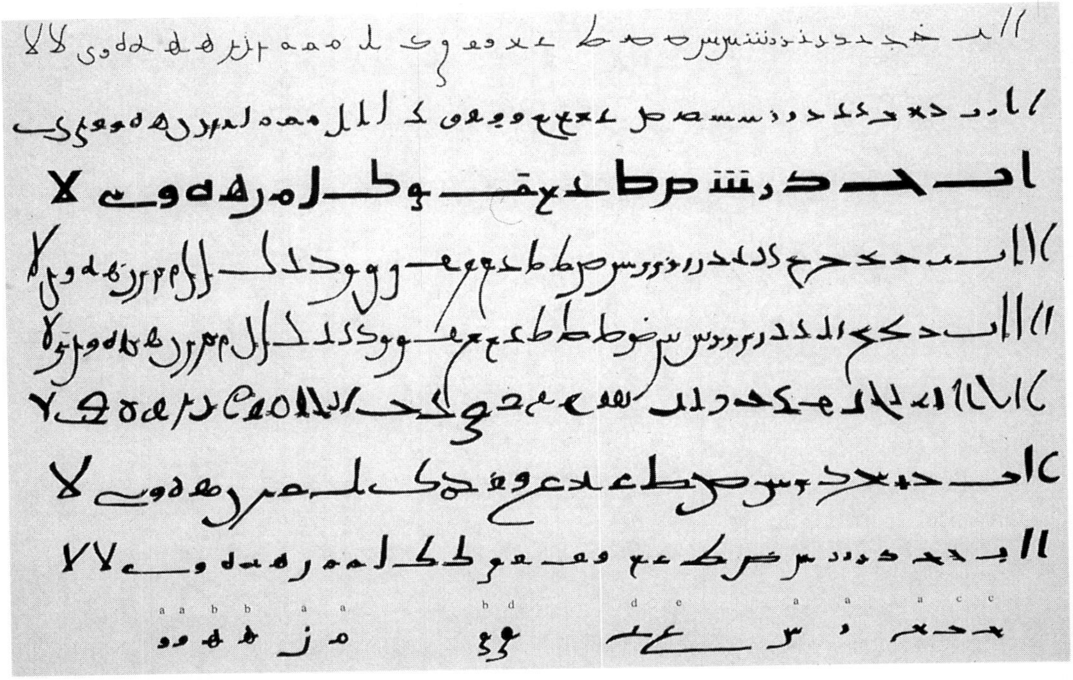

[IV] Arabic scripts of the first/seventh century: early cursive (ll. 1–2), epigraphic script (l.3), chancellery cursive (l.4), entagia cursive (l.5), protocol cursive (l.6), cursive of palimpsest PSI 1272^{v} (l.7), and slanting qurʾānic script (8–9), from B. Gruendler, *Development*, 141.

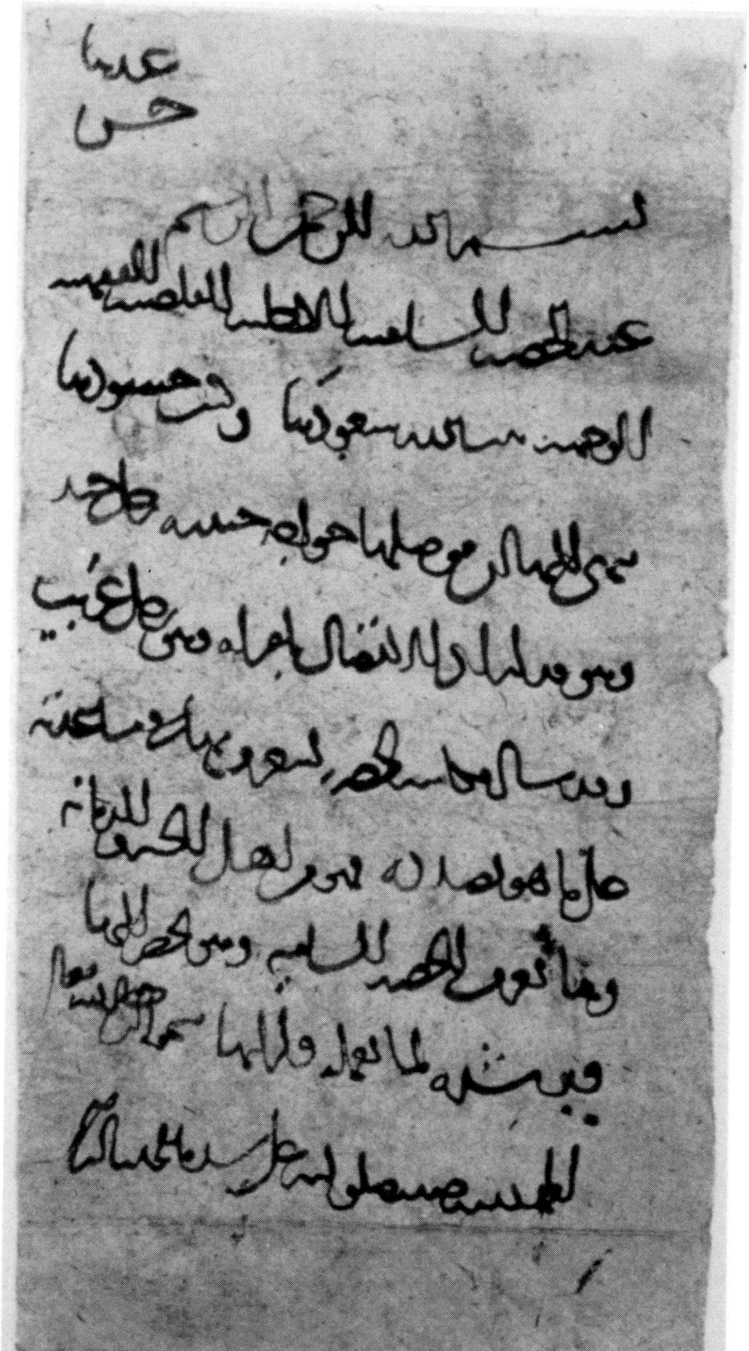

بسم الله الرحمن الرحيم

[v] Letter, datable to the sixth/twelfth century, from W. Diem, *Arabische Briefe*, no. 48.

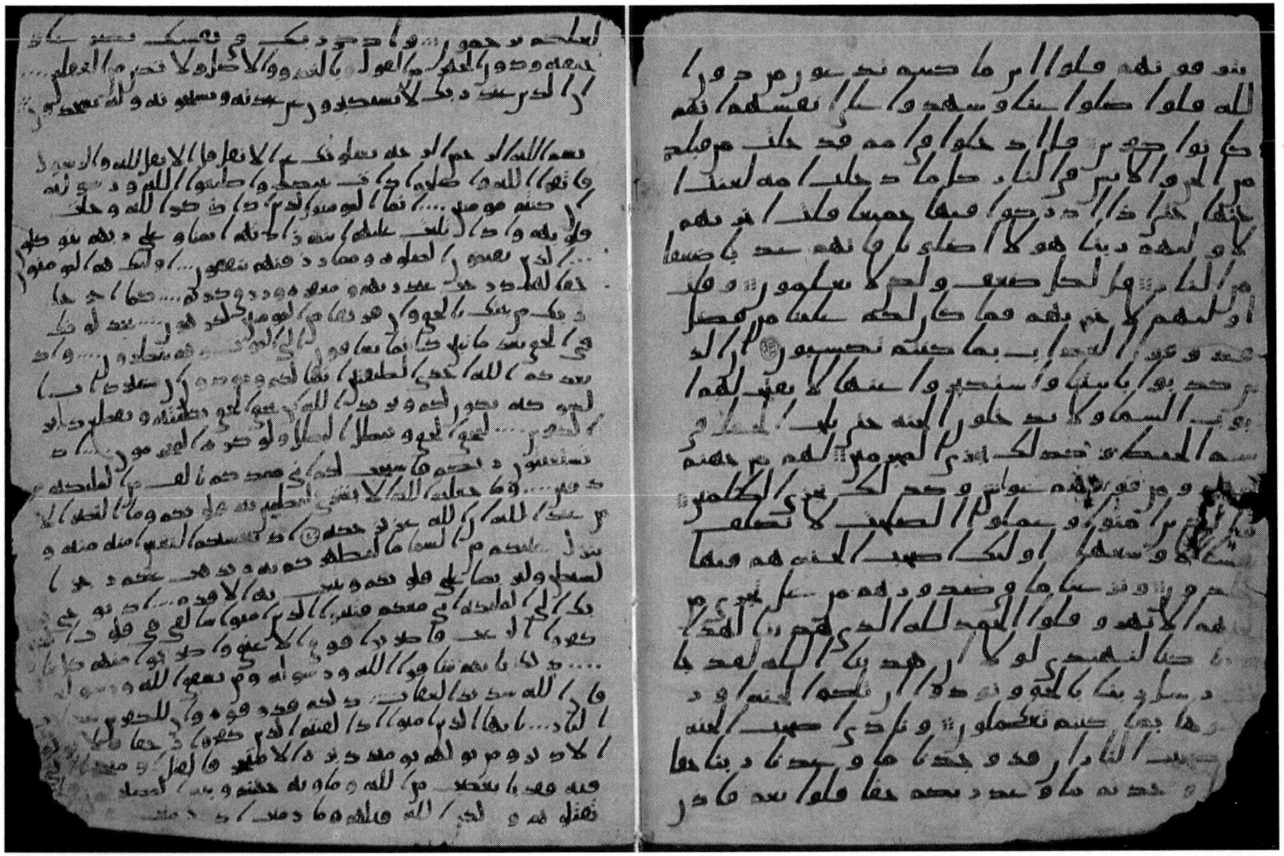

[VI] Qurʾān in *ḥijāzī* script, datable to the first/seventh century, from *Maṣāḥif Ṣanʿāʾ*, 60–61.

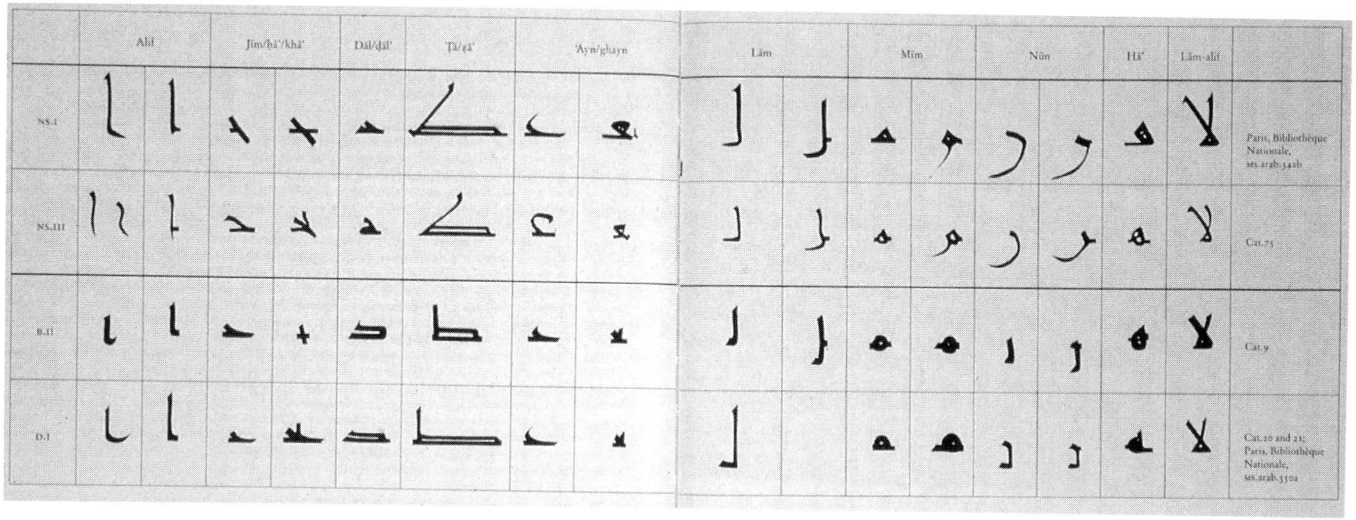

[VII] ʿAbbāsid Styles B, D and New Style, from F. Déroche, *Abbasid tradition*, 136.

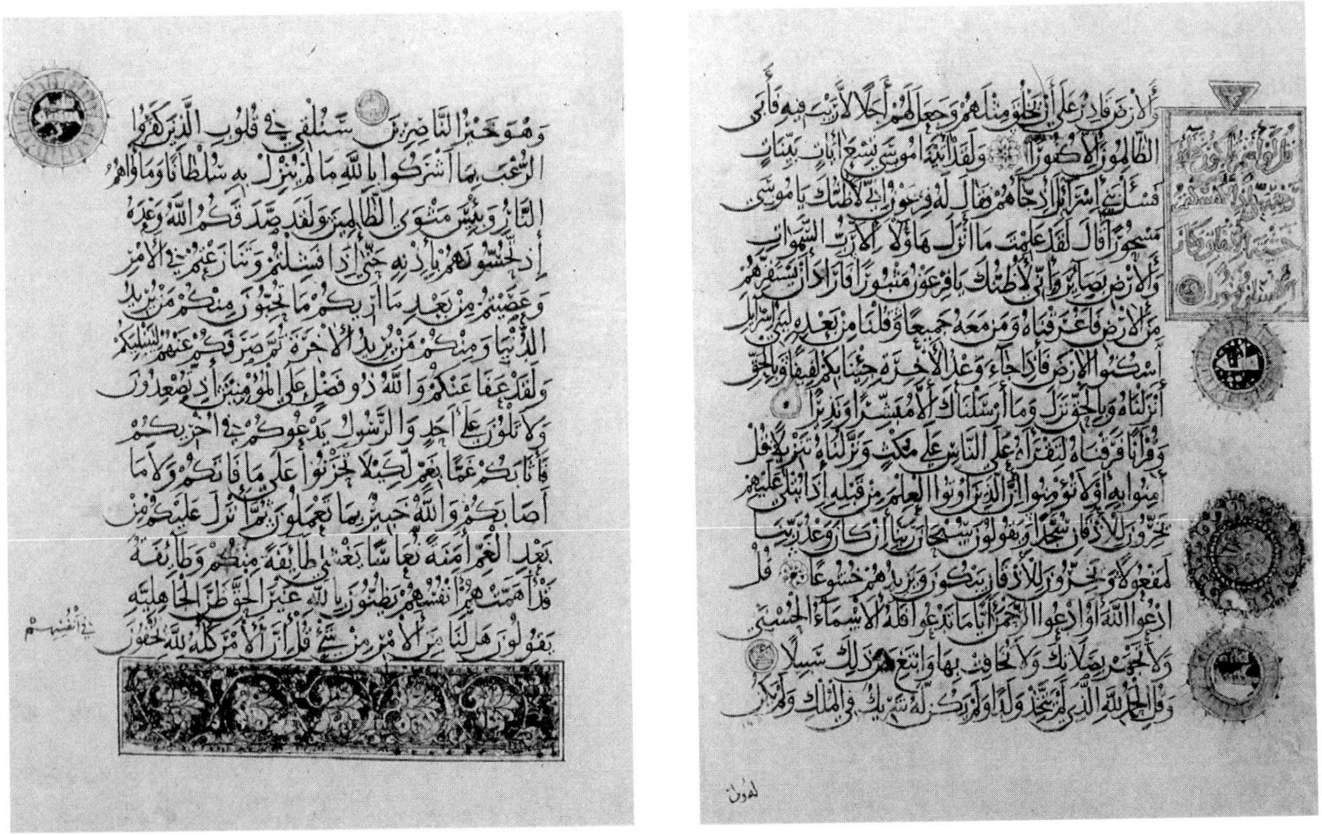

[VIII] Qurʾān in *naskh*, dated 391/1000, from D.S. Rice, *Ibn al-Bawwāb manuscript*, pl. VIII.

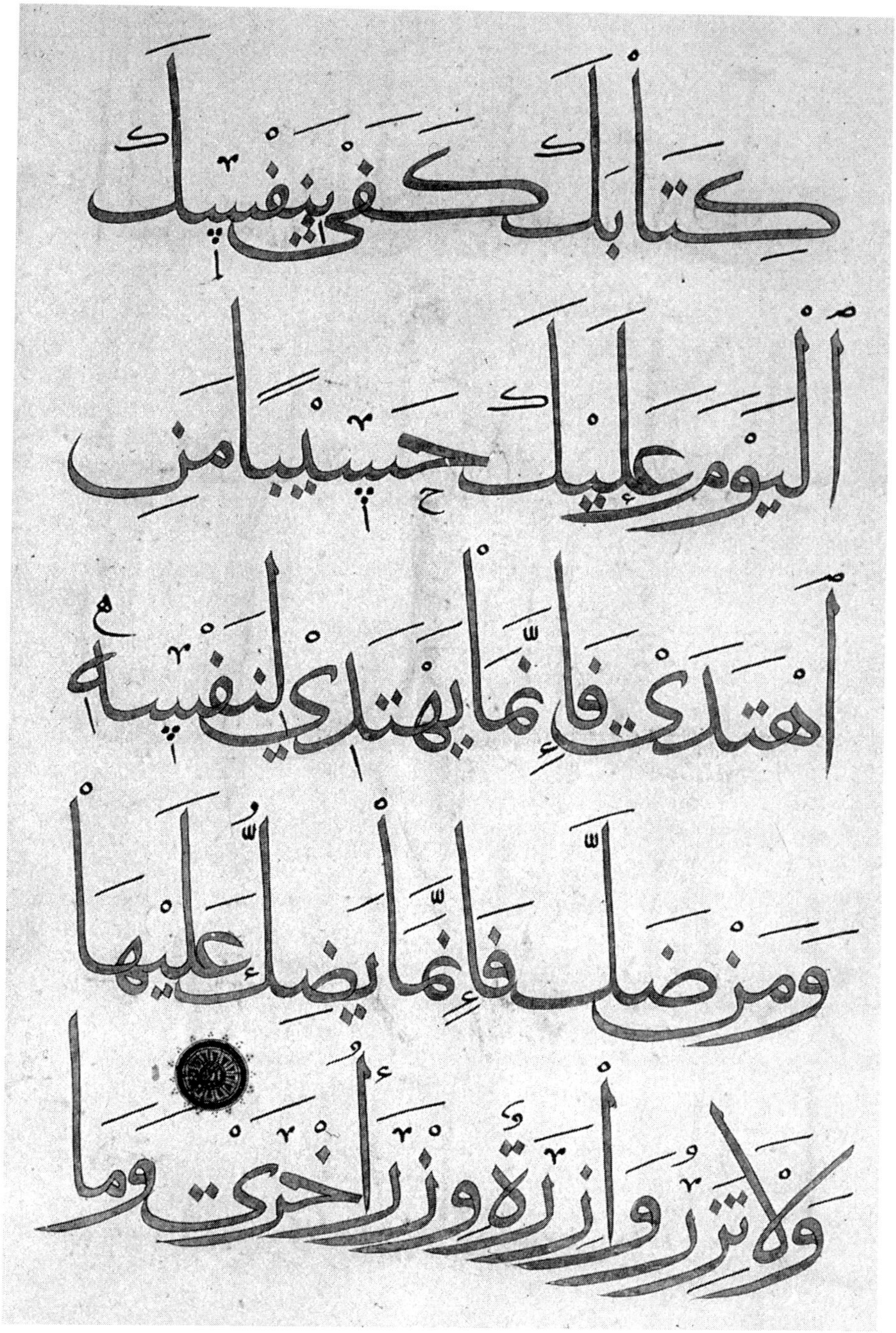
كتابك كفى بنفسك
اليوم عليك حسيبا من
اهتدى فانما يهتدي لنفسه
ومن ضل فانما يضل عليها
ولا تزر وازرة وزر اخرى وما

[IX] Mosul Qurʾān of Öljaytü, in *muḥaqqaq*, dated 706/1306–7, from D. James, *Qurʾāns*, 99.

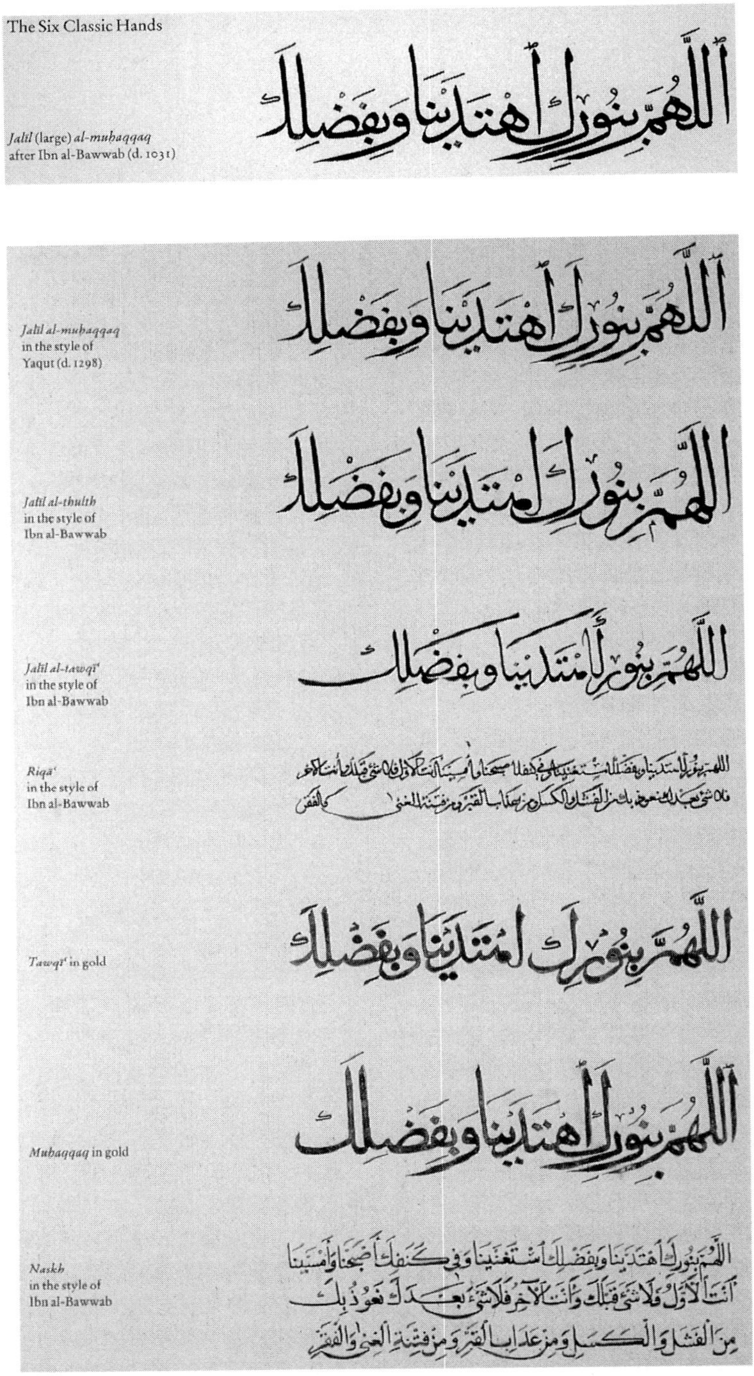

[x] The Six Pens interpreted by M. Zakariya, from N. Safwat, *Art of the pen*, 230–32.

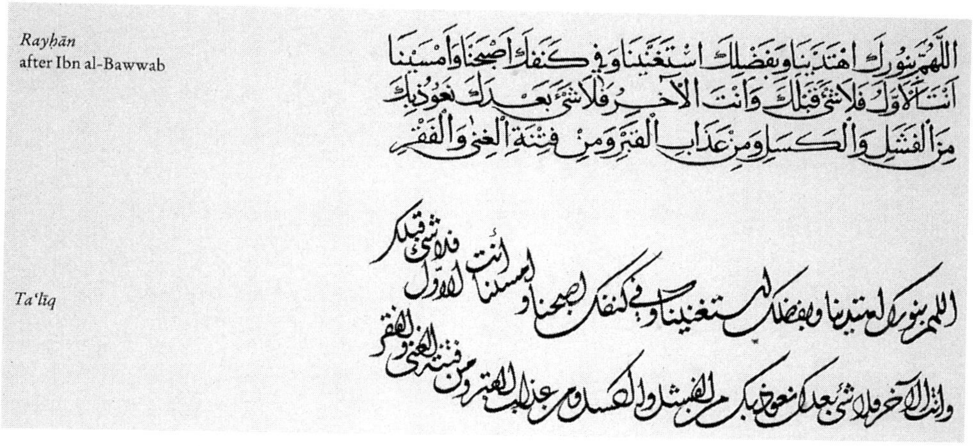

[x] The Six Pens interpreted by M. Zakariya, from N. Safwat, *Art of the pen*, 230–32. Cont.

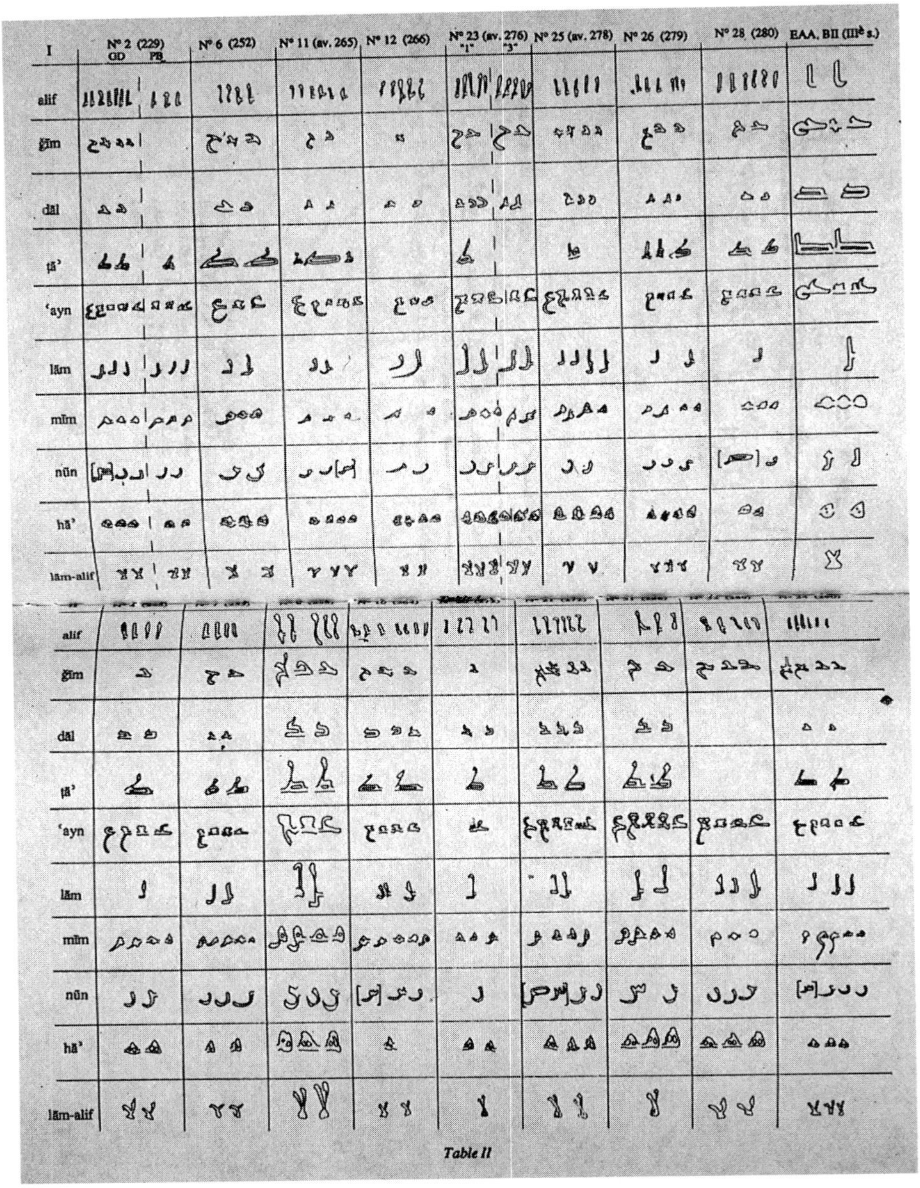
I
N° 2 (229)
GD PB
N° 6 (252)
N° 11 (av. 265)
N° 12 (266)
N° 23 (av. 276)
"1" "3"
N° 25 (av. 278)
N° 26 (279)
N° 28 (280)
EAA. BII (IIIe s.)
alif
ǧīm
dāl
ṭā'
'ayn
lām
mīm
nūn
hā'
lām-alif
alif
ǧīm
dāl
ṭā'
'ayn
lām
mīm
nūn
hā'
lām-alif
Table II

[XI] Scripts of Muslim and Christian Arabic manuscripts from the third/ninth century, from F. Déroche, *Manuscrits arabes*, pls. I–II.

alep̄/(Arabic) *alif,* short hooked *tāw/tāʾ,* three parallel teeth for *shīn/shīn,* integrated *ṭēṯ/ṭāʾ,* hooked *ʿayin/ʿayn,* a closed loop without stem for *pēh/fāʾ,* rounded *mēm/mīm,* looped *hēh/hāʾ,* lowered curved *wāw/wāw,* and s-shaped left-turning final *yōḏ/yāʾ*. At the present state of paleographic evidence, the emergence of the Arabic *abjad* must be assigned to the late second or third century C.E., between the latest cursive Nabatean and the earliest attested Arabic script.

In the Arabic *abjad,* two formative trends (1 and 2 above) were harmonized into a coherent system, each shape corresponding to a specific (initial, medial, final or isolated) position, excepting the six letters *alif, dāl/dhāl, rāʾ/zāy* and *wāw,* which formed no connection to the left. In addition to the above-mentioned mergers (5), homographs had been imported with the West Semitic *abjad* based on its reduced inventory of twenty-two Phoenician sounds. In Arabic most proto-Semitic sounds (except ś) had been preserved and had to be recorded by an extant grapheme. This explains the presence of multiple homographs. The Nabatean letters *tāw, ḥēṯ, dāleṯ, ṣādeh, ṭēṯ* and *ʿayin* denoted additionally the sounds *th, kh, dh, ḍ, ẓ* and *gh,* and Nabatean *shīn* denoted both Arabic *s* and *sh.* The spelling of a given Arabic word followed its (Imperial Aramaic or Nabatean) etymological cognate (W. Diem, Hauptentwicklungsstadien, 102-3). Combined graphic and sound mergers reduced the Arabic graphemes to eighteen *(alif, bāʾ, jīm, dāl, rāʾ, sīn, ṣād, ṭāʾ, ʿayn, fāʾ, qāf, kāf, lām, mīm, nūn, hāʾ, wāw, yāʾ),* or fifteen in non-final position (identical *bāʾ/nūn/yāʾ* and *fāʾ/qāf*) expressing a total of twenty-eight sounds. This homogeneity became an asset for Arabic calligraphy, but it also hampered the legibility of texts.

The development of Arabic script in early Islam

The pre-Islamic formation and early Islamic documentation of Arabic script suggest that it was readily available at the time of the Prophet. Some qurʾānic fragments on papyrus have indeed been attributed to the first/seventh century, though a more precise dating remains impossible. As the medium recording the Qurʾān and the official script of the Umayyad caliphate since ʿAbd al-Malik's (d. 86/705) reforms, the Arabic script thrived and spread from Upper Egypt to Sogdiana within a century. In this time, five distinct scripts emerged: 1) An angular epigraphic script, first attested in a clumsily carved Egyptian tombstone (31/652), reached a regular *ductus* in milestone inscriptions (65/685-86/705) and the mosaic band and copper plate of the Dome of the Rock (both 72/691; see ARCHAEOLOGY AND THE QURʾĀN). Arabic rounded cursive, first attested in a requisition of sheep on papyrus (22/643), diversified into 2) a routinized ligatured protocol script, 3) a wide-spaced slender chancellery hand, preserved in the gubernatorial correspondence of Qurra b. Sharīk (r. 90/709-96/714), including 4) a denser and squatter variant for bilingual tax notifications *(entagie)* and 5) a slanting script of qurʾānic fragments, now referred to as *ḥijāzī* (B. Gruendler, *Development,* 131-41).

Diacritical marks *(iʿjām, naqṭ)* were possibly inspired by pre-Islamic Nabatean or Syriac examples (G. Endress, Arabische Schrift, 175, n. 82 with further bibliography). They appear as a full system, though used selectively, on the earliest dated documents: the aforementioned requisition and a building inscription (58/678) on a dam of the first Umayyad caliph Muʿāwiya (r. 41/661-60/680). During the next two centuries diacritics were generalized in Qurʾāns and difficult texts. As points or strokes — the former predominate in Qurʾāns, the latter in papyri and manuscripts — they marked either several meanings of a homograph *(<bāʾ/tāʾ/thāʾ/nūn/yāʾ>, <jīm/ḥāʾ/khāʾ>, <fāʾ/qāf>)* or only one of a pair

(<dāl/dhāl>, <ṭāʾ/ẓāʾ>, <ʿayn/ghayn>, <sīn/shīn>). In the second/eighth century, *qāf* alone was distinguished by a dot above or below. Only later did *fāʾ* receive the respective opposite diacritic. This method was preserved in *maghribī* script, while a single dot on *fāʾ* and a double dot on *qāf* spread in the East from the third/ninth century onwards. The early fluidity of the system articulated itself in further alternate diacritics. A qurʾānic manuscript (Paris Ar. 376 b) distinguishes *zāy* from *rāʾ* and *ʿayn* from *ghayn* with a dot beneath and *sīn* from *shīn* with three dots beneath. In the second/eighth century, the feminine ending written in pausal form as *hāʾ* received two dots, forming the *tāʾ marbūṭa,* and a century later, a miniature *kāf* was placed inside the final *kāf* to prevent confusion with *lām*. *Muhmal* signs indicated unmarked letters in the form of dots, tilted small *lā* or miniatures of the letters themselves. In modern print, diacritics have become part of the letters, yet in pre-modern writing, their presence varied greatly. Business and private correspondence largely dispensed with them, and an entirely unmarked epistle conveyed a writer's respect for the learning of the addressee.

The Arabic script is an *abjad* (or consonantal) system, with the added obligatory notation of long vowels. It abbreviates words by omitting the short vowels, doubled consonants and inflectional endings. Thus it can be read faster than alphabetic script, denoting both consonants and vowels, but it requires simultaneous linguistic reconstruction. This is done for each word theoretically by paradigmatic-etymological analysis and practically by lexical recognition. Many words, however, are ambiguous, *<ktʾb>* for instance, stands for *kitāb,* "book," and *kuttāb,* "scribes," the correct reading depending on the syntactic and semantic context. Such reconstruction requires competence in the classical language *(ʿarabiyya),* and Arabic-Islamic society is unique in the precedence it assigns this knowledge as the foundation of general culture. The same graphic economy safeguards the inclusiveness of Arabic script, for it tends to veil the mistakes and hypercorrections of uneducated writers. This feature also permits written texts to be read as colloquial, a capacity the renowned Egyptian writer Tawfīq al-Ḥakīm (1898-1987) exploited in his play *al-Ṣafqa,* "The Deal."

Most medieval Arabic sources ascribe the invention of qurʾānic vocalization to Abū l-Aswad al-Duʾalī (d. 69/688) or his disciple Naṣr b. ʿĀṣim (d. 89/707), but they trace the impulse back to an Umayyad governor, Ziyād b. Abīhi (r. 45/665-53/673) or al-Ḥajjāj (r. 75/694-95/714). Evidence of the actual use of vowel signs in the mid-second/eighth century can be gathered from the theological dispute about them, as well as from contemporary qurʾānic fragments (N. Abbott, *Rise,* nos. 9-13, 15). There, a colored dot above a consonant indicates the following short vowel /a/ *(fatḥ),* beneath it /i/ *(kasr),* at the letter's base /u/ *(ḍamm)* and a double dot in these positions signifies indeterminacy *(tanwīn).* Further orthographic signs — an inverted half-circle or hook for a double consonant and a line above *alif* for its zero-value *(waṣl)* — were ascribed to al-Khalīl b. Aḥmad (d. 175/791) though attested only in the third/ninth century. Since the orthography of the consonantal text reflected the dialect of the Quraysh, it did not indicate the glottal stop *(hamz)* unless an otiose *alif* had been kept or a glide had replaced it. *Hamz* was reinstated as a supplemental sign to an existing letter *(alif, wāw* or *yāʾ)* or placed on the line. The marker was a colored dot, a semi-circle or a miniature *ʿayn*. In the same century, papyri began to display the use of short strokes for the vowels /a/ and /i/, a small *wāw* for /u/ and a double stroke (or a double *wāw*) for indeterminacy. Further miniature letters were introduced: to indicate the absence of vowels *(sukūn)*, a small *mīm* standing for the word for "apocopation," *jazm;* a small *shīn* derived from the word *shadd* or *tashdīd,* "strengthening," for a double consonant; a small *ṣād* standing for either *waṣl* or *ṣila,* "connection," for *alif* with zero-value, and small *mīm-dāl* derived from the word *madd,* "extension," for word-initial /ʾā/ or word-final /āʾ/. These orthographic signs became fully used a century later in Qurʾāns and difficult texts. Qurʾānic verse markers (dots, strokes, circles or rosettes) remained the only punctuation. Occasionally, non-qurʾānic texts were subdivided with dotted circles or extended words *(mashq)*.

Papyri, Qurʾāns, and manuscripts

Ibn Durustawayh's (d. 346/957) thesis that script varies by profession, that there are, for example, differences between a copier of Qurʾān codices *(maṣāḥif)*, a bookseller-copyist *(warrāq)* and a chancellery scribe *(kātib)*, is supported by the fact that three functionally distinct groups of texts — letters and documents on papyrus or paper, Qurʾāns, and literary and scholarly manuscripts — have warranted their own subdisciplines (Ibn Durustawayh, *Kuttāb,* 113-27; E. Whelan, Early Islam, 49-53).

Papyrus remained in use until the cheaper and smoother rag paper replaced it in the middle of the fourth/tenth century. In addition to governmental use, papyrus was (re)used for legal documents as well as commercial and private letters, which were written in a careless non-official style *(muṭlaq)*, governed by common use rather than formal rules *(muḥaqqaq)*. The writing can be divided into two phases dominated by "tendencies" rather than discrete scripts, as a piece of writing depended not only on date, but also on purpose and addressee. For example, a later text might revert to archaic graphic features, an earlier text might anticipate new developments or different stages of development could coincide (W. Diem, *Arabische Briefe,* nos. 24/25). 1) The script of the first two Islamic centuries was angular with mostly open loops, well-separated letters and extended connecting strokes. Typical letter shapes recall the epigraphic script, e.g. isolated *alif* with a bent foot and extending high above other letters; medial/final *alif* extending below the connecting stroke; *dāl* bending rightward at its top; and medial/final *ʿayn* made up of two oblique strokes (G. Khan, *Arabic papyri,* 27-39; id., *Bills,* 19-21). 2) With the third Islamic century, letters grew rounded, most loops were filled in, and four cursive tendencies dominated the performance: Angular forms became rounded, rounded forms, straightened, the nib no longer left the writing surface between letters and the pen covered a shorter distance. New homographs ensued, such as *dāl/rāʾ* and final *nūn/yāʾ*. Unusual ligatures abounded to the point of connecting most letters of a given line. This, as well as the papyri's laconic formulation, complicates their decipherment. A comprehensive assessment of the papyri's scripts is still needed; nonetheless, recent publications by W. Diem, R. Khoury, G. Khan and others have rendered much material accessible.

As is the case with the Yemeni find, Qurʾāns offer cohesive groups of scripts, conducive to establishing script families. For some areas and periods they also provide the only illuminated specimens. Qurʾānic fragments prior to the third/ninth century, however, lack dates, leaving their dating to paleographic considerations (A. Grohmann, Problem, 225). The production of Qurʾāns falls into two larger phases, using very different scripts. From the beginning of Islam until the fourth/

tenth century, Qurʾāns were written on vellum and more rarely on papyrus. During the earliest period, usually limited to the first/seventh century, Qurʾāns were written in high format in various styles of slanted *ḥijāzī* script. From the second/eighth century onwards, broad format fragments exhibit six "ʿAbbāsid styles" (F. Déroche's term replacing *kūfī*), each of which is defined by a significant sample of letters. During the third/ninth century, "new styles" (F. Déroche's term replacing "eastern" or "broken *kūfī*") emerge with oblique letter shapes and a changing thickness of the line, resembling contemporary book script (F. Déroche, Collection, 157-60). Meanwhile, the western part of the Arab-Islamic world developed the "new style" into *maghribī* and *andalusī*, written on vellum in a square format. These western scripts persisted, unaffected by the eastern emergence of *naskh* script. Ibn al-Bawwāb's *naskh* codex dated 391/1001 heralds the second phase of Qurʾān production in rounded scripts written in high format and on paper. An early *muḥaqqaq* Qurʾān is attested in 555/1160 (M. Lings and Y. Safadi, *Qurʾān*, no. 60). Rounded scripts soon reached calligraphic perfection. *Naskh, muḥaqqaq* and *rayḥān* formed the Qurʾān's main text and *thuluth* adorned headings as did ornamental *kūfī*. The Saljūq and Ayyūbid dynasties commissioned magnificent Qurʾāns, celebrating the return to Sunnī orthodoxy. Yet the earliest fully preserved (single or multiple-volume) Qurʾāns belong to the Mamlūk and Īlkhānid periods. Under Tīmūrid, Ṣafavid, Mughal and Ottoman patronage, the qurʾānic scripts themselves hardly changed, but were creatively adorned and framed with exquisite illuminations.

The scripts of scholarly and literary manuscripts and codices are the least studied to date and pose the greatest problems for classification. The scholars, literati and copyists were not committed to formal scribal criteria and their hands diverged substantially. Systematic paleographic study has been almost nonexistent up to the present and is urgently needed. Much material must still be consulted in the albums collected around the turn of the last century. However, a preliminary survey based on dated specimens suggests five styles (G. Endress, Handschriftenkunde, 282-4), the first two of which, dating mostly to the third/ninth century, overlap with a style defined in another study as "ʿAbbāsid book script" (F. Déroche, Manuscrits arabes, 356-63, tables i-ii).

Calligraphy

Arabic script also served as a highly refined artistic medium on buildings, objects, paper and other supports. Calligraphy flourished in the post-Mongolic period, particularly under Ṣafavid, Mughal and Ottoman patronage. The Ottoman *dīwānī* script emerged and scripts of the oblique *ductus, taʿlīq, nastaʿlīq* and the "broken" *shikasta* found application in illuminated pages and albums, mostly in Persian. New calligraphic genres were invented, among them the *tughrā* (originally a sultan's stylized signature, later any pious name or formula shaped into a graphic), pages of single letter exercises, mirrored writing, the verbal image of the prophet *(ḥilya)*, miniature script inside larger letters *(ghubār)*, decoupage and the gilt leaf. Arabic or pseudo-Arabic script was also adopted as an ornamental feature in European medieval and Renaissance art. See also CALLIGRAPHY AND THE QURʾĀN.

Beatrice Gruendler

Bibliography
Primary: Ibn Durustawayh, *Kitāb al-Kuttāb al-mutammam fī l-khaṭṭ wa-l-hijāʾ*, ed. I. al-Samarrāʾī and A. Fatlī, Kuwait 1977; Ibn al-Nadīm, *Fihrist,*

ed. Riḍā Tajaddud, Teheran 1971; al-Qalqashandī, *Ṣubḥ al-aʿshā fī ṣināʿat al-inshā'*, 14 vols., Cairo 1913-20, 1357/1938^{2}, repr. 1383/1963. Secondary (arranged by topic): *Script and literality:* J. Brockmeier, *Literales Bewußtsein. Schriftlichkeit und das Verhältnis von Sprache und Kultur,* München 1997; P. Daniels, Fundamentals of grammatology, in *JAOS* 110 (1990), 727-30; P. Daniels and W. Bright (eds.), *The world's writing systems,* New York 1996 (esp. secs. 5, 47, 50 and 62, by M. O'Connor, P. Daniels, T. Bauer and A. Kaye); Fichier des manuscrits moyen-orientaux datés (Fi.M.M.O.D.), published as insert of *Nouvelles des manuscrits du Moyen-Orient,* Paris 1992-; W. Graham, *Beyond the written word. Oral aspects of scripture in the history of religion,* Cambridge 1989; H. Günther and O. Ludwig (eds.), *Schrift und Schriftlichkeit. Writing and its use,* 2 vols., Berlin 1994-96 (esp. secs. by C. Scheffler, V. Wilbertz, A. Schimmel, H. Biesterfeldt and T. Bauer); H. Jensen, *Sign, symbol and script. An account of man's efforts to write,* trans. G. Unwin, New York 1969^{3} (rev. and enlarged); J. Naveh, *Early history of the alphabet,* Leiden 1982; F. Rosenthal, "Of making many books there is no end." The classical Muslim view, in G. Atiyeh (ed.), *The book in the Islamic world,* Albany 1995, 33-55. — *Formation and early development:* N. Abbott, *The rise of the north Arabic script and its Kur'ānic development,* Chicago 1939; id., Arabic paleography, in *Ars Islamica* 8 (1941), 65-104; F. Briquel-Chatonnet, De l'araméen à l'arabe. Quelques réflexions sur la genèse de l'écriture arabe, in F. Déroche and F. Richard (eds.), *Scribes et manuscrits du Moyen-Orient,* Paris 1997, 135-49; J. Cantineau, *Le Nabatéen,* Paris 1930, repr. Osnabrück 1978; W. Diem, Some glimpses at the rise and early development of the Arabic orthography, in *Orientalia* 45 (1976), 251-61; id., Die Hauptentwicklungsstadien der arabischen Orthographie, in *Akten des VII. Kongresses für Arabistik und Islamwissenschaft,* Göttingen 1976, 101-7; id., Untersuchungen zur frühen Geschichte der arabischen Orthographie. i. Die Schreibung der Vokale, in *Orientalia* 48 (1979), 207-57; ii. Die Schreibung der Konsonanten, in *Orientalia* 49 (1980), 67-106; iii. Endungen und Endschreibungen, in *Orientalia* 50 (1981), 332-80; iv. Die Schreibung der zusammenhängenden Rede. Zusammenfassung, in *Orientalia* 52 (1983), 357-404; G. Endress, Die arabische Schrift, in *GAP* i, 165-83, 190-97; A. Grohmann, *Arabische Paläographie,* 2 vols., Vienna 1967-71; B. Gruendler, *The development of the Arabic scripts. From the Nabatean era to the first Islamic century according to dated texts,* Atlanta 1993; J. Healey, Nabatean to Arabic. Calligraphy and script development among the pre-Islamic Arabs, in *Manuscripts of the Middle East* 5 (1990-1, publ. 1993), 41-52; B. Levine and A. Yardeni, *The documents from the Barkokhba period in the cave of letters, iii. Hebrew Aramaic and Nabatean documents* (forthcoming); Ṣ. al-Munajjid, *Dirāsāt fī ta'rīkh al-khaṭṭ al-ʿarabī mundhu bidāyatihī ilā nihāyat al-ʿaṣr al-Umawī,* Beirut 1972; A. Negev, Obodas the god, in *Israel exploration journal* 36 (1986), 56-60; E. Revell, The diacritical dots and the development of the Arabic alphabet, in *JSS* 20 (1975), 178-90; F. Rosenthal, Nabatean and related inscriptions, in H.P. Colt (ed.), *Excavations at Nessana,* 3 vols., London 1962, i, 198-210, pls. 34-35 (cf. J. Naveh, Arabic Nabatean incantation text, in *Israel exploration journal* 29 [1979], 111 n. 4); E. Schroeder, What was the badīʿ script?, in *Ars Islamica* 4 (1937), 232-48; J. Segal, *The diacritical point and the accents in Syriac,* London 1953; J. Sourdel-Thomine, Khaṭṭ, in *EI*^{2}, iv, 1113-22; J. Starcky, Un contrat nabatéen sur papyrus, in *Revue biblique* 61 (1954), 161-81; id., Pétra et la Nabatène, in *Dictionnaire de la Bible. Supplément,* Paris 1966, vii, 886-1017; J. Teixidor, Deux documents syriaques du IIIe siècle après J.C. provenant du Moyen-Euphrate, in *Comptes rendus de l'académie des inscriptions et belles-lettres* (1990), 144-66; K. Versteegh, *The Arabic language,* Edinburgh 1997. — *Papyrus and paper:* N. Abbott, *The Ḳurrah papyri from Aphrodito in the Oriental Institute,* Chicago 1938; id., *Studies in Arabic literary papyri,* 3 vols., Chicago 1957-72; W. Diem, *Arabische Briefe auf Papyrus und Papier aus der Heidelberger Papyrus-Sammlung,* 2 vols., Wiesbaden 1991; id., *Arabische Geschäftsbriefe des 10. bis 14. Jahrhunderts aus der Österreichischen Nationalbibliothek in Wien,* 2 vols., Wiesbaden 1995; id., *Arabische Privatbriefe des 9. bis 15. Jahrhunderts aus der Österreichischen Nationalbibliothek in Wien,* 2 vols., Wiesbaden 1996 (excellent glossary and indices); A. Dietrich, *Arabische Briefe aus der Papyrussammlung der Hamburger Staats- und Universitäts-Bibliothek,* Hamburg 1955; A. Grohmann, *From the world of Arabic papyri,* Cairo 1952; id., *Einführung und Chrestomathie zur arabischen Papyruskunde. i. Einführung,* Prague 1954; id., *Arabic papyri from Ḫirbet el-Mird,* Louvain 1963; id., *Arabische Chronologie. Arabische Papyruskunde* (HO 1. Abt. Ergbd. II, 1. Halbbd.), Leiden 1966; G. Khan, *Arabic papyri. Selected material from the Khalili collection,* London 1992 (cf. W. Diem, Philologisches zu den Khalili-Papyri, in *WZKM* 83 [1993], 39-81); id., *Bills, letters and deeds. Arabic papyri of the 7th to 11th centuries,* London 1993; id., *Arabic legal and administrative documents in the Cambridge Genizah collections,* Cambridge 1993; R. Khoury, Papyruskunde, in *GAP,* i, 251-70; id., *Chrestomathie de papyrologie arabe. Documents relatifs à la vie privée, sociale et administrative dans les premiers siècles islamiques* (HO 1. Abt. Ergbd. II,

2. Halbbd.), Leiden 1993; id., *Papyrologische Studien. Zum privaten und gesellschaftlichen Leben in den ersten islamischen Jahrhunderten,* Wiesbaden 1995. — *Qurʾān:* A. Arberry, *The Koran illuminated. A handlist of the Korans in the Chester Beatty Library,* Dublin 1967; F. Déroche, Les écritures coraniques anciennes. Bilan et perspectives, in *REI* 48 (1980), 207-24; id., Collection de manuscrits anciens du Coran à Istanbul. Rapport préliminaire, in J. Sourdel-Thomine (ed.), *Études médiévales et patrimoine turc. Cultures et civilisations médiévales no. 1,* Paris 1983, 145-65; id., *Catalogue des manuscrits arabes. 2. partie. Manuscrits musulmans. i. Les manuscrits du Coran. Bibliothèque Nationale. Département des manuscrits,* 2 vols., Paris 1983-85; id., *The Abbasid tradition. Qurʾans of the 8th to the 10th centuries A.D.,* London 1992 (detailed script charts); id., The Qurʾān of Amāǧūr, in *Manuscripts of the Middle East* 5 (1990-1, publ. 1993), 59-66; id., *Catalogue des manuscrits de Coran damascènes au Musée des arts turc et islamique* (forthcoming); id., and S. Noja Noseda, *Sources de la transmission manuscrite du texte coranique. I. Manuscrits de style hijazi. i. Ms. arabe 328 (a)* (forthcoming); A. Grohmann, The problem of dating ancient Qurʾans, in *Der Islam* 33 (1958), 213-33; D. James, *Qurʾāns of the Mamlūks,* London 1988; id., *The master scribes. Qurʾans of the 10th to 14th centuries A.D.,* London 1992; id., *After Timur. Qurʾans of the 15th and 16th centuries,* London 1992; M. Lings, *The quranic art of calligraphy and illumination,* London 1976; M. Lings and Y. Safadi, *The Qurʾān. Catalogue of an exhibition of Qurʾān manuscripts at the British Library,* London 1976; N. al-Naqshbandī, al-Maṣāḥif al-karīma fī ṣadr al-Islām, in *Sūmar* 12 (1956), 33-37 (pls.); Nöldeke, *GQ;* G. Puin, Methods of research on Qurʾānic manuscripts — a few ideas, in *Maṣāḥif Ṣanʿāʾ. 19 March — 19 May 1985,* Kuwait n.d., 9-17; id., Observations on early Qurʾān manuscripts in Ṣanʿāʾ, in Wild, *Text,* 107-11; D. Rice, *The unique Ibn al-Bawwāb manuscript in the Chester Beatty Library,* Dublin 1955; E. Whelan, Forgotten witness. Evidence for the early codification of the Qurʾān, in *JAOS* 118 (1998), 1-14; id., Writing the word of God. Some early Qurʾān manuscripts and their milieux, Part I, in *Ars orientalis* 20 (1990), 113-47 (with 22 pls.). — *Manuscripts and codices:* G. ʿAwwād, *Aqdam al-makhṭūṭāt al-ʿarabiyya fī maktabāt al-ʿālam,* Baghdad 1982; F. Déroche, Les manuscrits arabes datés du IIIe/IXe siècle, in *REI* 55-7 (1987-9), 343-79 (ills. and script charts); id., La paléographie des écritures livresques dans le domaine arabe, in *Gazette du livre médiéval* 28 (1996), 1-8; G. Endress, Handschriftenkunde, in *GAP,* i, 271-96; B. Moritz, *Arabic paleography,* Cairo 1905, repr. Osnabrück 1986, pls. 117-88; Ṣ. al-Munajjid, *al-Kitāb al-ʿarabī al-makhṭūṭ ilā l-qarn al-ʿāshir al-hijrī, i. al-Namādhij,* Cairo 1960; R. Sellheim, *Materialien zur arabischen Literaturgeschichte,* 2 vols., Stuttgart 1976-87; E. Tisserant, *Specimina codicum orientalium,* Bonn 1914, pls. 45-61; G. Vajda, *Album de paléographie arabe,* Paris 1958; E. Wagner, G. Schoeler and R. Quiring-Zoche, *Arabische Handschriften,* 3 vols., Stuttgart 1967-94. — *Calligraphy:* S. Flury, *Islamische Schriftbänder. Amida-Diarbekr. XI Jahrhundert,* Basel 1920; A. Gacek, al-Nuwayrī's classification of Arabic scripts, in *Manuscripts of the Middle East* 2 (1987), 126-30; id., Arabic scripts and their characteristics as seen through the eyes of Mamluk authors, in *Manuscripts of the Middle East* 4 (1989), 144-49; C. Huart, *Les calligraphes et les miniaturistes de l'Orient musulman,* Paris 1908, repr. Osnabrück 1972; E. Kühnel, *Islamische Schriftkunst,* Berlin 1942, repr. Graz 1972; H. Massoudy, *Calligraphie arabe vivante,* Paris 1981; F. Rosenthal, *Four essays on art and literature in Islam,* Leiden 1971 (esp. Significant uses of Arabic writing, pp. 50-62 and Abū Ḥayyān at-Tawḥīdī on penmanship, pp. 20-49); Y. Safadi, *Islamic calligraphy,* London 1978; N. Safwat, *The art of the pen. Calligraphy of the 14th to 20th centuries,* London 1996; A. Schimmel, *Islamic calligraphy,* Leiden 1970; id., *Calligraphy and Islamic culture,* New York 1984; D. Sourdel, Ibn Muqla, in *EI²,* iii, 886-7; J. Sourdel-Thomine, Ibn al-Bawwāb, in *EI²,* iii, 736-7; E. Whelan, Early Islam. Emerging patterns (622-1050), in E. Atıl (ed.), *Islamic art and patronage. Treasures from Kuwait,* New York 1990, 41-96; N. Zaynaddin, *Muṣawwar al-khaṭṭ al-ʿarabī,* Baghdad 1388/1968.

Arabs

The native inhabitants of the Arabian peninsula and their descendants. The Qurʾān refers repeatedly to what may loosely be called peoples, communities, tribes and nations (see TRIBES AND CLANS). Most belong to the past but a few are contemporaneous, e.g. the Byzantines (al-Rūm, see BYZANTINES) and the Quraysh (q.v.). However, the Arabs *(al-ʿarab)* are not among these groups, either of the past or of the present. Instead, the Qurʾān employs the adjective *ʿarabī* (Arab, Arabic) to qualify a number of substantives such as the Qurʾān itself (six times) and the language in which it is revealed (three times). In one instance only, Q 13:37, the expression "an Arab(ic) judgment" *(ḥukm ʿarabī)* is used in a context which may suggest a contrast between two ethnic groups but may equally be interpreted linguistically. Finally, there is another phrase in Q 41:44, which contrasts *ʿarabī* (Arab, Arabic) to *aʿjamī* (non-Arab) but here, too, the linguistic interpretation is as likely as the ethnic. From this brief portrait of the term "Arab(ic)," one might conclude that the Qurʾān does not employ this term to refer to a distinct ethnic group. This impression is fortified by the fact that in pre-Islamic (*jāhilī,* see AGE OF IGNORANCE) poetry, the terms *ʿarab* and *ʿarabī* are hardly ever encountered as an ethnic designation.

Yet the issue appears to be more complex than this. To begin with, it is not entirely legitimate to conclude from the absence of ethnic designators the absence of any concept of an Arab *ethnos*. Secondly, the Qurʾān insists upon its own manifest clarity and derives this clarity from its use of the Arabic language (q.v.; e.g. Q 16:103; 26:195). In this, one may well detect an appeal to Arabism as a form of collective consciousness. Thirdly, the ten references in the Qurʾān to a group called *al-aʿrāb* (nomadic Arabs; see BEDOUIN; NOMADS) — a term that has preserved the same meaning up to the present day in many Arab countries and has been consistently applied by urban Arabs to nomads — suggests a contrast of group identities that is not far from the ethnic. "You call us *aʿrāb* but our name is the Arabs," sings a poet of the Umayyad pe-riod (41/661-132/750), not too many years after the revelation of the Qurʾān.

Examined from this or a similar perspective, it appears that the term "Arab" in the Qurʾān should be contextualized within a broad array of kindred terms. One such that should be singled out here is the term *umma* (group, community, religious following; see COMMUNITY AND SOCIETY IN THE QURʾĀN). The *umma* of Muslims is what the Qurʾān proposes as the new collective identity of the faithful: "You are the best *umma* that ever was delegated to mankind" (Q 3:110). If we now reintroduce the emphasis by the Qurʾān on its Arabic speech, it would be possible to argue that this new *umma,* this new collective identifier, is to be coupled with Arabic, which is, as it were, its banner of clarity. Thus, although a community of the faithful strictly defined by religion is put forward as the ideal, this is nevertheless combined with a particular cultural expression. In short, while the term "Arab" may not have been used in a strictly ethnic sense in the Qurʾān, a quality of Arabness is attached to the concept of *umma,* rendering it an essential aspect of the earliest self-definition of the new faith. See also PRE-ISLAMIC ARABIA AND THE QURʾĀN.

Tarif Khalidi

Bibliography
J. ʿAlī, *Taʾrīkh al-ʿarab qabla l-islām,* Baghdad 1950; S. Bashear, *Arabs and others in early Islam,* Princeton 1997; A.A. Duri, *The historical formation of the Arab nation,* London 1987; I. Goldziher, *Muslim studies,* 2 vols., London 1967-72; T. Khalidi, Aspects of communal identity in Umayyad poetry, paper presented to Workshop IV of Late Antiquity and Early Islam, The Wellcome Institute, London, May 1994 (publication forthcoming); N. Naṣṣār, *Mafhūm al-umma bayna l-dīn wa-l-taʾrīkh,* Beirut 1978.

ʿArafāt

A plain extending about six and a half km in breadth from east to west and about twelve km in length, lying twenty-one km to the east of Mecca (q.v.). The grammarians agree that the word ʿArafāt is a singular noun in the form of a plural. Although the plain is also referred to by the singular form ʿArafa, this is regarded by some experts as a later-day corruption (Yāqūt, *Buldān,* iv, 104). The name, according to the classical scholars, is derived from the verbs based on the root *ʿ-r-f*. According to one account, Gabriel (q.v.) is said to have taught *(ʿarrafa)* the rites of the pilgrimage to Abraham (q.v.). When Gabriel made the prophet stand *(waqqafahu)* on the plain, he asked him "Do you know? *(ʿarafta)*" and he replied, "yes." Other discussions of the etymology claim that the plain was where Adam and Eve (q.v.) encountered each other *(taʿārafā)* after the fall. The sole mention of this place in the Qurʾān is in Q 2:198: "There is no fault in you that you seek bounty from your Lord. So when you pour out from ʿArafāt, remember God at the sacred monument. Remember him as he has guided you, though formerly you had gone astray (q.v.)."

The plain of ʿArafāt plays an important role in the rites of the pilgrimage. According to a famous ḥadīth of the Prophet, the ritual at ʿArafāt *is* the pilgrimage. On the ninth day of the month of Dhū l-Ḥijja, the pilgrim must stand *(waqafa)* before God from shortly after midday until sunset. Most of this time is occupied by two long sermons (sing. *khuṭba*), which are usually delivered by a local dignitary. The preacher sits astride a camel on the side of a low hill known as the Mountain of Mercy (Jabal al-Raḥma), also sometimes called ʿArafāt or ʿArafa, which lies in the northeastern corner of the plain.

At one time, the plain was fertile. It is described as containing fields, meadows and fine dwellings which the inhabitants of Mecca occupied during the pilgrimage. Indeed, the area produced a number of notable transmitters of ḥadīth and poetry (Yāqūt, *Buldān,* iv, 104-5). Today, little remains but a few stunted mimosas and the plain is uninhabited with the exception of one day of the year. See also PILGRIMAGE.

R.G. Khoury

Bibliography
Primary: Ṭabarī, *Tafsīr,* ii, 166-7; A.J. Wensinck and H.A.R. Gibb, ʿArafa, in *EI²*, i, 604; Yāqūt, *Buldān,* 5 vols., Beirut 1374/1955-1376/1957, iv, 104-5.
Secondary: G.E. von Grunebaum, *Muhammadan festivals,* London 1951, A. Th. Khoury, *Der Koran. Arabisch-Deutsch Übersetzung und wissenschaftlicher Kommentar,* Gütersloh 1991-, ii, 308.

Ararat

The tallest of two peaks of a group of mountains, actually an extinct volcanic range, in the northeast of modern Turkey, south of present-day Armenia. Mount Ararat is identified by Jews and Christians with the biblical story of the flood and the ark (q.v.) of Noah (q.v.) in *Gen* 6-9. This peak is known by the Arabs as Jabal al-Ḥārith, by the Turks as Büyük Ağrı Dağ, by the Iranians as Kūh-i Nūḥ (Mountain of Noah) and as Mount Masis (or Masik) by the Armenians, who view the mountain as their national symbol, but did not come to consider it to be the resting-place of Noah's ark until about the twelfth century C.E.

Islamic tradition makes no mention of Ararat, for Q 11:44 states that "[Noah's] ship came to rest on Mount Jūdī," present-day Cudi Dağ. This mountain lies some forty km northeast of Jazīrat Ibn ʿUmar (now Cizre) in Turkey, just north of the Iraqi border, and some three hundred km southwest of Ararat. Nearby lies the town of Thamānīn (Arabic for "eighty"), supposedly named for the eighty passengers of the ark who survived the flood.

Attempts at locating the biblical Ararat are complicated by the names and locations given to the resting-place of the ark in other languages and traditions. It is often overlooked that the biblical text, which has inspired repeated searches of remnants of the ark, actually states (*Gen* 8:4) that "the ark [of Noah] rested on the mountains of Ararat" as the flood waters subsided. In the Jewish Aramaic Targum and in Syriac "mountains of Ararat" is translated "turē Qardū." The latter appears as Qardā in the famous geographical dictionary of Yāqūt (d. 626/1229), *Muʿjām al-buldān* (iv, 56), which locates it south of the present day Ararat. Yāqūt states that "[al-Jūdī]... is a mountain overlooking Jazīrat Ibn ʿUmar, on the east side of the Tigris, in the district of Mosul" (ii, 144, s.v. al-Jūdī), hence in the territory of ancient Qardū. Some scholars have linked this name with Gordyene, the Greek appellation for the entire area and generally connected with the Kurds, whose ancient presence in this area seems to be attested by Xenophon (d. ca. 350 B.C.E.). The q/k of Qardū/Kurd, however, presents a problem and scholars are now of the opinion that an earlier people in this area, named Qardū were succeeded by the Kurds coming from the east.

The location of Ararat is undoubtedly connected with the ancient kingdom of Urarṭu (Araraṭ in ancient Hebrew). Urarṭu ruled much of the area of today's eastern Turkey from about the ninth to the seventh century B.C.E., vying for control of the region with the Assyrians until, weakened by constant warfare with its neighbors, it was finally conquered by the Medes in 612 B.C.E. A current view is, therefore, that the biblical phrase "the mountains of Ararat" actually refers to the entire area of mountain ranges of the kingdom of Urarṭu which includes both Mount Jūdī and Mount Ararat. See also JŪDĪ.

William M. Brinner

Bibliography
A. Heidel, *The Gilgamesh epic and Old Testament parallels,* Chicago 1946, 250-1; G. LeStrange, *Lands of the eastern caliphate,* Cambridge 1905, 93 (Mount Judi), 182-3 (Ararat); V. Minorsky, Kurds, Kurdistān, in *EI²*, v, 447-9; B.B. Piotrovskii, *Urartu. The kingdom of Van and its art,* trans. and ed. P.S. Gelling, New York 1967; M. Streck and F. Taeschner, Aghri Dagh, in *EI²*, i, 251-2; M. Streck, Djūdī, in *EI²*, ii, 573-4; Ṭabarī, *Taʾrīkh,* trans. F. Rosenthal, *The history of al-Ṭabarī. i. From the creation to the flood,* Albany 1989, 366, n. 1137.

Arbitration

An arrangement by which two or more persons, having a difference, appoint someone to hear and settle their dispute and to abide by that decision. Arbitration appears in the Qurʾān several times. The Arabic equivalent, used only in the singular, is *ḥukm,* a verbal noun of *ḥakama*. The root *ḥ-k-m,* which is said to be of non-Arabic origin (Jeffery, *For. vocab.,* 111), has a number of meanings (see FOREIGN VOCABULARY). The principal meanings of the simple verbal form *ḥakama* are "to govern," "to restrain," "to pass judgment" and "to be sage." From these original meanings *ḥākim,* "he who decides, the authority, governor, judge, wise," and *ḥukm,* "order, rule, sentence, judgment, wisdom," are derived (Q 5:46-9; 6:56; 12:39; 18:25; 26:82). *Ḥakam,* "arbiter," appears twice in the Qurʾān. One verse enjoins the appointment of an arbiter in the case of marital disputes: "If you fear a split between a man and his wife, send for an arbiter from his family and an arbiter from her family. If both want to be reconciled, God will adjust things between them. For God has full knowledge, and is acquainted with all things" (Q 4:35). The other is "Shall I seek an arbiter other than God, when he it is who has sent you the book, explained in detail?" (Q 6:114).

The appointment of arbiters, like a number of other practices of the Islamic community, is of pre-Islamic origin. In the Mecca of Muḥammad's day, it was customary for the parties in a dispute to select their own arbiter, usually a man noted for his tact, wisdom and knowledge of ancestral custom. Very often the disputing parties referred their case to a soothsayer (*kāhin,* see SOOTHSAYERS), a practice the Qur'ān specifically denounces (Q 52:29; 69:42).

Ultimately, the Qur'ān stresses that final judgment belongs to God alone (Q 6:57, 62; 12:40; see LAST JUDGMENT) and "the Arbiter" *(al-ḥakam)* is one of his titles (see GOD AND HIS ATTRIBUTES). It is he who conferred the authority to make decisions on his prophets (Q 21:78-9). As long as Muḥammad was alive, he was naturally regarded as the ideal person to settle disputes and was elevated to the position of judge supreme. His functions and responsibilities in Medina are defined in terms of qur'ānic decrees: "We have sent down to you the Book (q.v.) with the truth in order that you may judge *(li-taḥkuma)* between the people on the basis of what God has shown you" (Q 4:105). Muḥammad distinguished himself from soothsayers by basing his judgments upon scripture.

Muḥammad is told that if Jews come to him seeking arbitration and he accepts, "Judge *(faḥkum)* between them fairly" (Q 5:42; see Watt-Bell, *Introduction,* 29). The Prophet left Mecca for the purpose of acting as an arbiter between the feuding tribes in Medina (see EMIGRATION). His role as the messenger (q.v.) of God apparently suggested that he was a man of superior wisdom (Watt, *Islamic political thought,* 21). Later generations ascribed to Muḥammad a great number of legal decisions which, coupled with the existing customary law, formed the basis of Islamic law. See also JUDGMENT; LAW AND THE QUR'ĀN.

Mohsen Zakeri

Bibliography
W.M. Bell, *Introduction to the Qur'ān,* Edinburgh 1953; N. Coulson, *A history of Islamic law,* Edinburgh 1964, 11, 26; L. Gauthier, La racine arabe *ḥukm* et ses dérivés, in *Homenaje a Don Francisco Codera,* Saragossa 1904, 435-54; A.-M. Goichon, Ḥukm, in *EI²,* iii, 549; J. Horovitz, *KU* 71-3; A. Jeffery, *For. vocab.,* 111; id., The Qur'ān as scripture, in *MW* 40 (1950), 121-2; J. Schacht, *An introduction to Islamic law,* Oxford 1964, 10-1; W.M. Watt, *Islamic political thought,* Edinburgh 1968, 20-1, 24, 26, 40-1; T.H. Weir, Ḥukm, in *EI¹,* ii, 332.

Archaeology and the Qur'ān

At present the field of archaeology has little to contribute to an understanding of the Qur'ān and the milieu in which Islam arose. Archaeological excavations are taboo in Mecca (q.v.) and Medina (q.v.) and only a few other excavations or surveys have yet taken place in the Arabian peninsula that shed much light on the topic.

The pioneering work on historical geography and on the initial survey and collections of inscriptions in the Arabian peninsula began at the end of the nineteenth century with such explorers as Alois Musil in northern Arabia and Eduard Glaser in the Yemen, but only a limited number of archaeological surveys or excavations were carried out prior to the second World War. Substantial archaeological work has been underway since the 1950s in the Yemen (see B. Doe, *Monuments,* for a summary) and in the Arabian Gulf states (conveniently synthesized by D. Potts, *Arabian Gulf*). Archaeology in Saudi Arabia, beginning with the excavation at Qaryat al-Fā'w in 1972 and regional surveys since 1976 (published in the first issues of *Aṭlāl*), is less advanced than in those two areas.

Yet some information has become available. Among the principal journals devoted to the archaeology of the Arabian peninsula are *Aṭlāl,* published by the Department of Antiquities in Saudi Arabia since 1977, the *Proceedings of the seminar for Arabian stud-*

ies, held annually in Great Britain since 1971, and *Arabian archaeology and epigraphy* since 1990. One should also note in general the several volumes of the *Studies in the history of Arabia* published in Riyadh between 1979 and 1989. While few articles in those journals examine the physical remains of the cultural milieu of early Islam, there are two articles — S. Rashīd, Āthār Islāmiyya and G. King, Settlements — that summarize the state of knowledge about the archaeology of Arabia around the rise of Islam. One should also note numerous short entries of relevance in the *Oxford encyclopedia of archaeology in the Near East* (1997).

The light that archaeology can shed on the Qurʾān falls into two categories: 1) the physical remains from the distant pre-Islamic past that can be associated with earlier biblical and Arabian prophets and peoples (see SCRIPTURE AND THE QURʾĀN; PUNISHMENT STORIES), 2) the physical remains that can be informative for the lifetime of Muḥammad. Concerning the distant pre-Islamic past, the archaeological remains in Palestine that can be associated with the Israelites and other peoples also recorded in the Bible have been receiving intensive attention for over a century and little need be said here. But one should note that there is no recorded physical trace of the destruction of the people of Lot (q.v.; Q 15:76; 25:40; 37:137; 15:73; 37:136) other than the general God-forsaken barrenness of the Dead Sea region.

A number of qurʾānic verses relate to events that took place in Jerusalem (q.v.) in the pre-Islamic periods. Likewise, the Muslims early on localized there the *miḥrāb* of Mary (q.v.; Q 3:37), the *miḥrāb* of Zechariah (q.v.; Q 3:39; 19:11), the cradle of Jesus (q.v.; Q 3:46; 5:110; 19.29), the *miḥrāb* of David (q.v.; Q 38:21) and the gate where the Children of Israel (q.v.) were to enter and say "Repentance" (Q 2:58; 7:161; cf. A. Elad, *Medieval Jerusalem;* A. Kaplony, Die fatimidische Moschee). The Islamic tradition has also associated eschatological traditions with the double-door golden gate on the east enclosure wall of the Ḥaram (the Arabic-Islamic designation of the Temple Mount), called the "gate of mercy and repentance" (localizing Q 57:13). Yet the development of the architectural manifestations associated with those qurʾānic allusions, which have no claim to preserving any pre-Islamic features, falls within the purview of later Islamic art and architectural history rather than archaeology. No trace of the palace of Solomon (q.v.; Q 27:44) or the first temple has been identified nor would they have survived the neo-Babylonian destruction of the city in 586 B.C.E. and subsequent rebuildings.

The people of Midian (q.v.), to whom the prophet Shuʿayb (q.v.) was sent (Q 7:85; 11:84; 26:176), are also known from the Bible and can be identified with the population of northwest Arabia in the northern Hejaz and Gulf of Aqaba coast during the late second millennium B.C.E. in the Late Bronze Age (G. Mendenhall, Qurayya). But only limited survey work has been done in the area, notably at the major site of Qurayya, which consists of a citadel, a walled sedentary village and irrigated fields. Such clearly important sites like al-Badʾ, the probable city of Midian itself, and Maghāʾir Shuʿayb await careful examination.

To turn to the non-biblical, pre-Islamic peoples, the Thamūd (q.v.), the people to whom the prophet Ṣāliḥ (q.v.) was sent (e.g. Q 7:73-9; 11:61-8; 26:141-58; 27:45-52; 54:23-31), are a historically well-documented tribal group in northwest Arabia. The Thamūd first appear in Assyrian texts in the eighth century B.C.E. as tribal enemies of the Assyrians (I. Ephʿal, *The ancient Arabs*); the name also appears in a variety of Greek and Roman written sources. Most interestingly, a bilingual Greek-Nabataean dedicatory inscription records the erection of a temple dedicated to the god Ilāhā between 166 and 169 C.E. in the reign of the Roman emperors Marcus Aurelius and Lucius Verus at Ruwwāfa in northwest Saudi Arabia by the confederation of the Thamūd (*Thamudênôn ethnos* in Greek; *ŜRKTH TMWDW* in Nabataean), by the heads of the confederation and by the efforts of the Roman governor who had made peace among them (D. Graf, The Saracens; M. O'Connor, Etymology of Saracen). The term *ŜRKTH* for confederation is a possible etymology for the term "Saracen" that the Romans used to identify the Arabs in general. The architectural style of the temple is typical Nabataean and along with the use of Nabataean for the dedicatory inscriptions reflects the acculturation of the Thamūd to their Nabataean rulers. One assumes that the temple functioned as a central shrine for the Thamūdic confederation along the major caravan route. The Thamūd became federate allies of the Romans and served as auxiliaries in the Roman army. For example, there were cavalry units in the fourth century C.E. identified as "Thamudeni" stationed in Palestine in the Negev, and as "Saraceni Thamudeni" stationed in Egypt in the Nile Delta.

The name Thamūd, however, only occurs a very few times in pre-Islamic Arabian inscriptions themselves. The inscriptions found by the thousands throughout northern Arabia and southern Syria and Jordan of uncertain date and debated classification, which modern scholars have attributed to nomads in the pre-Islamic centuries and have labeled as "Thamūdic" for the sake of convenience, need not have had anything to do with the Thamūd themselves. The "Thamūdic" inscriptions, mostly short graffiti recording personal names, may have been written by a number of diverse tribes with no necessary connection with the Thamūdic confederation. See also ARABIC SCRIPT.

The place where the Thamūd cut the mountains into dwellings (Q 7:74; 89:9) has commonly been identified with Ḥijr/Madā'in Ṣāliḥ in northwest Arabia where in the first century C.E. the Nabataean rulers, generals and other central government authorities, rather than the locals, cut numerous tombs for themselves into the mountain sides, similar to their more famous tombs in Petra. Architectural studies were carried out there in an earlier period (A. Jaussen and F. Savignac, *Mission archeologique*) and archaeological excavations began in 1986 (see the preliminary reports in *Aṭlāl* since 1988). The area of Ḥijr (*Hegra* in Nabataean) marked the southern limit of Nabataean territory and the Nabataeans established Ḥijr along the caravan route as their military and government center in the south in preference to nearby Dedān/al-ʿUlā. The earliest pottery found there is Nabataean, leaving open the question of whether there was substantial pre-Nabataean occupation at the site. The site continued as a government center after the Roman annexation of the Nabataean kingdom in 106 C.E. Some Latin inscriptions at Madā'in Ṣāliḥ and at al-ʿUlā from the second century C.E. provide slight evidence for a Roman military presence, although the area was always outside the frontier of the Roman empire (D. Graf, The Saracens). There is no trace of occupation at the site after the second or third century C.E.

The other peoples that were destroyed after they rejected the prophets who were sent to them are not readily identifiable as any archaeological remains. They include the ʿĀd (q.v.) who built monuments and strongholds on every high place (Q 26:128-9) and whose fate, according to the Qur'ān, is manifest from the remains of their dwellings (Q 29:38; 46:25). Likewise remains have not been found which could be associated with the dwellers in al-Rass

(Q 25:38, see also PEOPLE OF THE DITCH; RASS).

The site of Mārib, capital of the Sabean kingdom in southwest Arabia, and its irrigation dam (Q 34:15-6) have been investigated intensively, especially by German scholars (B. Doe, *Monuments,* 189-202; W. Daum, *Yemen,* 55-62; and the several volumes of the *Archäologische Berichte aus dem Yemen* of the *Deutsches Archäologisches Institut* Ṣanʿāʾ). The Mārib dam was the largest and most technologically sophisticated of the numerous other dams in southwest Arabia. While the Mārib oasis was being irrigated as early as the third millennium B.C.E., the oldest extant inscription that refers to separate irrigation works for the north and south halves of the Mārib oasis (Q 34:15) dates to 685 B.C.E. The extant single large dam, eight kilometers from the city, was first constructed after the date of these inscriptions, in ca. 528 B.C.E. Like the other dams, its function was not to store water long term but rather to reduce the velocity of the twice yearly flood waters and to raise the water level so that the water could be diverted through two sluices and distributed through a complex system of canals onto a wide cultivated area. The area irrigated by the dams was some 9,600 hectares along a distance of some eleven kilometers for the northern oasis and twenty-one kilometers for the southern oasis. The dam would have required frequent maintenance, and dam bursts necessitating repairs are recorded numerous times in inscriptions in the first centuries C.E., and for the last time in 553 C.E. Another dam burst occurred some thirty-five years later and it was repaired. The final, unrepaired burst caused by the qurʾānic flood of al-ʿArim (q.v.; Q 34:16; *ʿ-r-m* is the Sabean word for "dam") would have occurred in the early years of the first/seventh century.

The principal difficulty with such flood diversion irrigation is the gradual accumulation over time of deposits of silt that continuously raise the ground level of the irrigated fields. This necessitates the periodic raising of the water channels and the dams or relocating them so that they remain higher than the fields. Such maintenance to keep the system in operation becomes increasingly difficult and eventually becomes uneconomical and results in the abandonment of the irrigation works. The ultimate abandonment of the Mārib dam was, however, not due to questions of the technical feasibility of repairing it, but rather due to the political and social conditions of decline, culminating in the Sasanian Persian occupation of southern Arabia in 575 C.E., that broke down the public institutions needed to maintain such large projects as the dam.

Various locations have been proposed for the cave referred to in the qurʾānic passage on the Men of the Cave (q.v.; Q 18:9-27). One such possible location is at an excavated rock-cut Roman-Byzantine tomb at al-Raqīm, just south of Amman in Jordan (R. al-Dajānī, *Iktishāf kahf*).

To turn to more general topics, in south Arabia the Kingdom of Sheba (q.v.), with its capital at Mārib, was the leading state in the first millennium B.C.E. It was formed as a tribal confederation headed by a ruler who was given the title of "Mukarrib." The early chronology of the Sabean state is obscure due to the lack of early datable inscriptions or links with events outside southern Arabia. A Solomon and Queen of Sheba (see BILQĪS; Q 22:15-44) synchronism would need to be in the tenth century B.C.E. (see J. Pritchard, *Solomon and Sheba*), but the Queen is not an otherwise attested historical figure. There is no reference to a queen in any Sabean inscriptions, although queens of the Arabs are cited in several eighth-century B.C.E. Assyrian inscriptions recording the Assyrian military campaigns into the northern Arabian peninsula (I. Ephʿal, *Ancient Arabs*). These obscurities have led to two competing scholarly reconstructions of Sabean history, one dating the origins of the state to the eighth century B.C.E., based on synchronisms, which are not definite, of names of Sabean rulers appearing in the Assyrian annals. The other reconstruction locates the start of the monumental cultures of south Arabia hundreds of years later, around the fifth century B.C.E. For the second view of Sabean history, that of the shorter chronology, the Solomon and Queen of Sheba incident becomes more legendary than historical.

The other independent states in southern Arabia, Maʿīn, Qatabān and Ḥaḍramawt also arose by the fifth and fourth centuries B.C.E. In the first centuries C.E. the political situation changed with the emergence of the state of Ḥimyar. Tubbaʿ (q.v.) was the title used by the Ḥimyarite rulers, thus localizing the people of Tubbaʿ (Q 44:37; 50:14) in southwest Arabia. By the mid-first millennium B.C.E. the south Arabians certainly were building monumental stone architecture, including city walls and temples, characterized by a distinctive style of square-sectioned monolithic pillars, perhaps evocative of the multi-columned Iram (q.v.; Q 89:7). There are any number of major surviving monumental temples in southwest Arabia (see B. Doe, *Monuments*). The temples are often identified with the term *maḥram* in the south Arabian dedicatory inscriptions. Those temples typically are rectangular columned structures without any direct influence on later mosque design. The ʿAwwam temple of the god Ilmuqah at Mārib is unique in having a large oval enclosure wall (100 X 75 m), delineating a sacred space *(ḥawṭa)* with a rectangular entrance hall on one side.

The caravan trade linking the incense-producing areas in southern Arabia and the Mediterranean was of major importance and was facilitated by the domestication of the camel (q.v.). While the first use of camels may have been as early as the fourth or third millennium B.C.E., and camels were certainly being used as pack animals by the second millennium B.C.E., it was the development of a suitable camel saddle by the early first millennium B.C.E. that enabled nomadism to develop fully (see BEDOUIN; NOMADS). At first the Sabeans were in control of most of the caravan route north to the Mediterranean but in the last centuries B.C.E., the Minaeans controlled the route, and they established a trading colony in the oasis at Dedān/al-ʿUlā in northwest Arabia. The site of Dedān is known to have been occupied previously and the kingdom of Liḥyān was centered there by around 400 B.C.E., about the time that the colony of traders from Maʿīn was established. Dedān continued in the Hellenistic period until the Nabataeans took over in the second or first century B.C.E. and moved their center to Ḥijr/Madāʾin Ṣāliḥ to the north. The connection between the Liḥyāns and the Thamūd, discussed earlier, is obscure. The archaeological site of al-Khurayba, ancient Dedān, has been surveyed and the water supply system has received focused attention (A. Nasif, *ʿal-ʿUlā*).

A few excavation projects at other sites from the distant pre-Islamic past took place in Saudi Arabia in the 1980's. Accompanying these projects were brief preliminary reports published in *Aṭlāl*, such as the excavation at Taym at the sixth or fifth century B.C.E. palace of Qaṣr al-Ḥamrāʾ, and at tombs dating from 1450-750 B.C.E. and excavations at the multi-period site of Dūmat al-Jandal/al-Jawf (K. al-Muaikel, *Study of the archaeology;* A. al-Sudayri, *The desert frontier*). Of greater interest here is the excavated site of Qaryat al-Fāʾw, the thriving capital of the pre-Islamic state of Kinda in southwest Arabia, occupied between the second century B.C.E. and the fifth century C.E. (A. al-Anṣārī, *Qaryat al-Fā'w*). The ancient name of the site was Dhāt Kahl, named after their chief god. Although there was some limited agricultural potential at the site, trade was important for the city. It was a large town with its buildings constructed of mud bricks on stone foundations. The excavations uncovered remains of a walled, two-storied market, with further open markets surrounding it; a palace; a temple; a residential area and a number of tombs, including one of the king, Muʿāwiya b. Rabīʿa, and tombs of nobles and commoners. Among the striking finds were a collection of bronze statues from the temple, some with Hellenistic features; painted wall plaster depicting people and animals from the palace; coins minted at the site; and numerous inscriptions in south Arabian *musnad* script.

There are large numbers of rock drawings throughout the Arabian peninsula spanning a wide range of time, both pre-Islamic and Islamic. They frequently depict hunting and pastoral scenes (E. Anati, *Rock art*, M. Khan, *Prehistoric rock art;* and issues of *Aṭlāl* since 1985).

Inscriptions from the pre-Islamic period in the Arabian peninsula number in the tens of thousands. H. Abū l-Ḥasan's 1997 study of Liḥyānic inscriptions is only the most recent of a number of publications of inscriptions by King Saʿūd University in Riyadh; one should also note a growing number of masters theses by the students of Yarmouk University in Jordan. There are many different types of inscriptions, ranging from dedicatory inscriptions to graffiti. Some of these are the monumental dedicatory inscriptions in southwest Arabia written in the *musnad* script. Others include the thousands of graffiti written in a variety of scripts labeled, as stated above, by scholars for convenience as Thamūdic. Another group includes over fourteen thousand north Arabian inscriptions whose sites are concentrated in southern Syria and northeastern Jordan, labeled by scholars as "Ṣāfā'itic", again for convenience, after the Ṣafā' basalt region of southern Syria, regardless of the fact that few such Ṣafā'itic texts have been found there specifically. The Ṣafā'itic texts are rarely dated but range from the first century B.C.E. and seem to end by the fourth century C.E. because there is no hint of any Christian influence in them (M. Rūsān, *al-Qabā'il al-Thamūdiyya*). The evolution of the Nabataean script into the Arabic script has been well established (B. Gruendler, *The development*).

Of special note is a south Arabian inscription from the second century B.C.E. that decrees a ban on the practice of killing (new-born?) girls (C. Robin, *L'Arabie antique*, 141-3; see Q 16:58-9; 81:8-9; see INFANTICIDE). It is noteworthy that around the fourth century C.E. pagan formulas in the south Arabian inscriptions are replaced by monotheistic expressions, using the term *raḥmān* (C. Robin, *L'Arabie antique*, 144-6; see GOD AND HIS ATTRIBUTES). The term *miḥrāb* — later used to indicate the direction of prayer (*qibla*, q.v.) in mosques — is used in the south Arabian inscriptions to mean a structure, along the lines of an audience chamber, or the title of a government official, along the lines of chancellor (C. Robin, *L'Arabie antique*, 152-5). There are some surviving papyrus documents and inscriptions that shed light on the period of the Rightly-Guided Caliphs (11/632-40/661; see F. Donner, The formation), but not on the lifetime of the Prophet.

Turning to the time period of Muḥammad himself, very little can be said about the physical remains of pre-modern Mecca and Medina, although much can be known from the historical sources which have been repeatedly analyzed. Nothing remains of the original architectural features of the sanctuary in Mecca except for the Kaʿba (q.v.) itself nor of the sanctuary in Medina due to the repeated rebuilding and expansions over the centuries. Little of the pre-modern cities in general has survived massive modern development, although there are a number of pre-modern historic mosques in the two cities and elsewhere in Saudi Arabia (G. King, Historical mosques). A few stone defensive towers *(uṭūm)* from the pre-Islamic period are known around Medina (A. Anṣarī, *Āthār al-Madīna,* 72-4; G. King, Settlements in Arabia, 189-91). There are, of course, many place names recorded in the biographies of the prophet Muḥammad (see SĪRA AND THE QURʾĀN), such as battle sites or places where Muḥammad built mosques, but archaeological inquiry, as opposed to the study of historical geography, has little to offer. A number of places known to have been major settlements at the time of Muḥammad, such as Khaybar (q.v.) or ʿUkāẓ, remain essentially uninvestigated beyond basic identification in the course of surveys. Nothing is known about al-Ṭāʾif beyond several dams and other irrigation works, one of which was constructed in 58/678 under the Umayyad caliph Muʿāwiya (M. Khan and A. al-Mughannam, Ancient dams).

However, a few excavated sites are worth mentioning here. The major site of Najrān (q.v.) in southwest Arabia is well known historically from the sixth century C.E. as a center of Christianity. The persecution of the Christians there by the Jewish ruler around 520 C.E. is one candidate for the incident of the People of the Ditch (q.v.; Q 85:4-9). Ukhdūd, the archaeological site of Najrān, received some attention in 1967 and the early 1980s (J. Zahrins et al., Second preliminary report, 23-4; G. King, Settlements, 201-5). It had a stone-walled citadel within which possible remains were found of the Kaʿba of the Banū l-Ḥārith b. Kaʿb, mentioned by Ibn al-Kalbī (d. 204/819). During the late pre-Islamic period continuing into the Islamic period, the principal settlement in the area of al-ʿUlā shifted to Qurḥ or Wādī al-Qurā. Qurā is identifiable with the archaeological site of al-Mābiyāt, where two seasons of excavations were carried out in 1984 and 1985 (M. Gilmore et al., Preliminary report; A. Nasif, *al-ʿUlā*). The site of Jurash was excavated, but few details beyond a pottery analysis are available (A. al-Ghamedi, *The influence,* 176-220). The port of Ayla, modern-day Aqaba in Jordan, which some commentators have identified as the Sabbath-breaking town on the sea (Q 7:163), has received intensive attention in the last decade. Work has been done excavating at the early Islamic settlement, founded perhaps as early as the reign of the third caliph ʿUthmān (r. 23/644-35/656; D. Whitcomb, *Ayla*) as well as at the Roman-Byzantine site nearby (T. Parker, Roman ʿAqaba project), whose surrender on terms to Muḥammad in 630 C.E. is prominently recorded in the Islamic sources.

Of particular note is the excavated site of al-Rabadha, a settlement east of Medina along the caravan route between the Hejaz and al-Kūfa. Al-Rabadha experienced a continuity of settlement in the pre-Islamic and early Islamic periods, although the excavation report (A. al-Rashīd, *al-Rabadhah*) makes little mention of the pre-Islamic and pre-ʿAbbāsid remains there. The second caliph ʿUmar b. al-Khaṭṭāb (r. 13/634-23/644) set aside the area around the site as a state pasturage *(ḥimā)*. Reservoirs and wells were studied there, along with a western mosque and a second mosque in the residential area; a fortress or palace; several residential units; industrial installations; and a portion of the town enclosed by a wall with towers.

P. Crone and M. Cook's idea (*Hagarism,*

22-4) that the original pre-Islamic shrine of Bakka (Q 3:96) was located in northwest Arabia has no remaining physical support. The orientation of some early mosques that are well off the true direction of prayer can be explained as the result of inaccurate measurement rather than as a deliberate orientation to a shrine in northwest Arabia. One should also note that Y. Nevo and J. Koren's (Origins of Muslim descriptions) discussions of the pre-Islamic cultic practices in Mecca are based on fundamental misidentifications as cultic of the non-cultic sites that Y. Nevo excavated in the Negev area of southern Palestine.

The diffusion of Christianity in the Arabian peninsula was limited (see CHRISTIANS AND CHRISTIANITY). J. Beaucamp and C. Robin (Le Christianisme) summarize the evidence, to which should be added more recent archaeological discoveries along the Persian Gulf. These include churches (see CHURCH) in Jubayl, Saudi Arabia and elsewhere (J. Langfeldt, Early Christian monuments). An example of one of these is the church at Failaka, Kuwait dating from the end of the fourth century C.E. with later non-church occupation starting in the seventh century C.E. (V. Bernard et al., L'église d'al-Qousour). Another of these is the Nestorian monastery at Ṣīr Banī Yās in Abu Dhabi, dating around the sixth to seventh century C.E. (G. King, A Nestorian monastic settlement). One may also note the isolated hermitage at Kilwa in extreme northwest Saudi Arabia; one cell has a cross and a Christian Arabic inscription on its lintel (N. Glueck, Christian Kilwa). In South Arabia, a few columns remain of the famous al-Qalīs church built by Abraha (q.v.) in the middle of the sixth century C.E. to surpass the sanctuary of Mecca (R. Serjeant and R. Lewcock, *Ṣanʿā*, 44-8). These columns can now be found appropriated for use in the main mosque of Sanʿa. There seems to be no identified physical trace of the Jewish presence, known from historical sources, which existed in Medina and northern and central Arabia in the pre-Islamic period (see JEWS AND JUDAISM; KHAYBAR; NAḌĪR; QAYNUQAʿ; QURAYẒA).

Several aspects of archaeological inquiry, such as palaeo-botanical and faunal analyses, and environmental studies, have not yet been fully integrated into archaeological projects, so the contribution that they could make for understanding the milieu of early Islam remains mostly a potential for the future. There are no physical anthropological studies of human skeletal remains particularly close to the time of Muḥammad, although one can note the Bedouin cemetery excavated at the Queen Alia International Airport south of Amman in Jordan dating to the first and second centuries C.E. (M. Ibrahim and R. Gordon, *A cemetery*). The issue of possible climate changes remains open (J. Dayton, The problem of climatic change).

No examples are known to have survived of divining arrows (Q 5:3, 90), and one would have to move beyond the close cultural milieu of the Hejaz in Muḥammad's day to find surviving examples of jewelry (Q 24:31). There are no surviving early examples of armor (Q 21:80). The first Islamic artistic depictions are the stucco statues of soldiers from the eighth-century C.E. Umayyad palace at Khirbat al-Mafjar (R. Hamilton, *Khirbat al-Mafjar*). Just what distinguished the famous sword of Muḥammad and ʿAlī (see ʿALĪ B. ABĪ ṬĀLIB) to warrant its special name Dhū al-Faqār (sword with grooves) is not clear, but it may have been a straight-bladed, double-edged sword with two grooves as known from the Yemen (W. Daum, *Yemen 3000 years*, 15-6, 24); it would scarcely have had the impractical bifurcated tip so often described. The swords attributed to Muḥammad and other early figures in the Topkapı Museum in Istanbul are of dubious authenticity (A.

Zaky, Medieval Arab arms, 203-6).

In addition to the major settlements that they passed through, the various trade routes throughout the peninsula were provided with numerous way stations. Such facilities for travelers were expanded along the routes that were used by the pilgrims to Mecca (see PILGRIMAGE). The way stations, reservoirs and wells along the main pilgimage route from Kufa to Mecca have been well-documented. That route is known as the Darb Zubaydah, named after the wife of the ʿAbbāsid caliph Hārūn al-Rashīd (r. 170/786-193/809), who expanded the route's facilities. The Egyptian and Syrian pilgrimage routes in the northwest Arabian peninsula have also been studied (A. Hamed, *Introduction*). Some fragments of stone figures (see IDOLS AND IMAGES), seemingly deliberately destroyed at the onset of Islam, are at Qaryat al-Fāʾw and al-ʿUlā (G. King, Settlements, 211-2). The Nabataeans had often depicted their gods in a non-figurative manner (J. Patrich, *The formation*).

Concerning Jerusalem, the early Islamic tradition quickly identified it as the location of the Aqṣā Mosque (al-Masjid al-Aqṣā, Q 17:1; see AQṢĀ MOSQUE) which is associated with Muḥammad's night journey and ascension (q.v.) to heaven (q.v.). The use of the term "al-Ḥaram al-Sharīf" to identify the area of the former Jewish Temple Mount in Jerusalem, as well as the identification of the tomb of Abraham (q.v.) in Hebron as a *ḥaram,* has no explicit qurʾānic authority and only came into general use in the Mamluk and Ottoman periods. Prior to that period, the term "al-Masjid al-Aqṣā" was used to refer both to the entire Ḥaram area as well as to the roofed structure in the south edge of the Ḥaram, the Aqṣā mosque in the narrower sense. The Dome of the Rock in Jerusalem, the oldest surviving Islamic monument, contains the earliest extant extensive portions of the qurʾānic text, datable by ʿAbd al-Malik's dedicatory inscription to 72/692 C.E. (see EPIGRAPHY AND THE QURʾĀN; ART AND ARCHITECTURE AND THE QURʾĀN). The qurʾānic passages vary slightly from the standard text with changes from the first to the third person and are interspersed with other non-qurʾānic pious phrases (see most recently O. Grabar, *The shape of the holy*). The Aqṣā Mosque was first built as a monumental stone structure by the Umayyad caliph al-Walīd (r. 86/705-96/715), replacing a wooden structure noted by the Christian pilgrim Arculf around 675 C.E. But al-Ḥaram al-Sharīf, where both the Aqṣā Mosque and the Dome of the Rock are located, is off limits for excavations, while the results of the excavations of the Umayyad palaces just to the south and southwest of the Ḥaram await substantive publication. See also MATERIAL CULTURE AND THE QURʾĀN; PRE-ISLAMIC ARABIA AND THE QURʾĀN.

Robert Schick

Bibliography

H. Abū l-Ḥasan, *Qirāʾa li-kitābāt liḥyāniyya min jabal ʿAkma bi-minṭaqat al-ʿUlā,* Riyadh 1997; E. Anati, *Rock art in central Arabia,* Louvain 1968-74; A. al-Anṣārī, *Āthār al-Madīna al-munawarra,* Medina 1973; id., *Qaryat al-Fāʾw,* Riyadh 1981; J. Beaucamp and C. Robin, Le Christianisme dans le péninsule arabique d'après l'épigraphie et l'archéologie, in *Hommage à Paul Lemerle. Travaux et mémoire,* Paris 1981, 45-61; V. Bernard, O. Callot and J.-F. Sales, L'église d'al-Qousour Failaka, Etat de Koweit, in *Arabian archaeology and epigraphy* 2 (1991), 145-81; P. Crone and M. Cook, *Hagarism,* Cambridge 1977; R. al-Dajānī, *Iktishāf kahf ahl al-kahf,* Beirut 1964; W. Daum (ed.), *Yemen. 3000 years of art and civilization in Arabia Felix,* Innsbruck 1988; J. Dayton, The problem of climatic change in the Arabian peninsula, in *Proceedings of the seminar for Arabian studies* 5 (1975), 33-60; B. Doe, *Monuments of south Arabia,* New York 1983; F. Donner, The formation of the Islamic state, in *JAOS* 106 (1986), 283-96; A. Elad, *Medieval Jerusalem and Islamic worship,* Leiden 1995; I. Ephʿal, *The ancient Arabs,* Leiden 1982; A. al-Ghamedi, *The influence of the environment on pre-Islamic socio-economic organization in southwestern Arabia*, Ph.D. diss., Arizona State 1983; M. Gilmore et al., A preliminary report on the first season of excavations at al-Mabiyat, an early Islamic site in the northern Hijaz, in *Aṭlāl* 9 (1985), 109-2; N. Glueck, Christian Kilwa, in *Journal of the Palestine Oriental Society* 16 (1936), 9-1; O. Grabar, *The shape of the holy. Early Islamic Jerusalem*, Princeton 1996; D. Graf, The Saracens and the defense of the Arabian frontier, in *BASOR* 229 (1978), 1-26; B. Gruendler, *The development of the Arabic scripts. From the Nabatean era to the first Islamic century according to dated texts*, Atlanta 1993; A. Hamed, *Introduction à l'étude archeologique des deux routes syrienne et égyptienne de pèlerinage au nord-ouest de l'Arabie Saoudite*, Ph.D. diss., Université de Provence aix Marseille 1988; R. Hamilton, *Khirbat al-Mafjar*, Oxford 1959; M. Ibrahim and R. Gordon, *A cemetery at Queen Alia International Airport*, Wiesbaden 1987; A. Jaussen and F. Savignac, *Mission archéologique en Arabie*, Paris 1909-14; A. Kaplony, Die fatimidische "Moschee der Wiege Jesu" in Jerusalem, in *Zeitschrift des deutschen Palästina-Vereins* 113 (1997), 123-32; M. Khan, *Prehistoric rock art of northern Saudi Arabia*, Riyadh 1993; M. Khan and A. al-Mughannam, Ancient dams in the Ṭāʾif area 1981 (1401), in *Aṭlāl* 6 (1982), 125-3; G. King, *The historical mosques of Saudi Arabia*, London 1986; id., Settlement in western and central Arabia and the Gulf in the sixth-eighth centuries A.D., in G. King and A. Cameron (eds.), *The Byzantine and early Islamic Near East ii. Land use and settlement patterns*, Princeton 1994, 181-212; id., A Nestorian monastic settlement on the island of Ṣīr Banī Yās, Abu Dhabi. A preliminary report, in *BSOAS* 60 (1997), 221-35; J. Langfeldt, Recently discovered early Christian monuments in northeastern Arabia, in *Arabian archaeology and epigraphy* 5 (1994), 32-60; G. Mendenhall, Qurayya and the Midianites, in *Studies in the history of Arabia 2. Pre-Islamic Arabia*, Riyadh 1984, 137-45; K. al-Muaikel, *Study of the archaeology of the Jawf region, Saudi Arabia*, Riyadh 1994; A. Nasif, *al-ʿUlā. An historical and archaeological survey with special reference to its irrigation system*, Riyadh 1988; Y. Nevo and J. Koren, The origins of the Muslim descriptions of the Jâhilî Meccan sanctuary, in *JNES* 49 (1990), 23-44; M. O'Connor, The etymology of Saracen in Aramaic and pre-Islamic Arabic contexts, in P. Freeman and D. Kennedy (eds.), *The defense of the Roman and Byzantine East*, Oxford 1986, 603-32; T. Parker, The Roman ʿAqaba project. The 1994 campaign, in *Annual of the Department of Antiquities of Jordan* 40 (1996), 231-57; J. Patrich, *The formation of Nabataean art*, Leiden 1990; D. Potts, *The Arabian Gulf in antiquity*, Oxford 1990; J. Pritchard, *Solomon and Sheba*, London 1974; S. al-Rashīd, *al-Rabadhah. A portrait of early Islamic civilization in Saudi Arabia*, Riyadh 1986; id., *al-Āthār al-islāmiyya fī l-jazīra l-ʿarabiyya fī aṣr al-rasūl wa-l-khulafāʾ al-rāshidīn*, in *Studies in the history of Arabia, iii. Arabia in the age of the Prophet and the four caliphs, part 2*, Riyadh 1989, 145-99; C. Robin, L'Arabie antique de Kariba'il à Mahomet. Nouvelles données sur l'histoire des Arabes grâce aux inscriptions, in *REMMM* 61 (1991-93); M. al-Rūsān, *al-Qabāʾil al-thamūdiyya wa-l-ṣafawiyya. Dirāsa muqārana*, Riyadh 1992; R. Serjeant and R. Lewcock, *Ṣanʿā. An Arabian Islamic city*, London 1983; A. al-Sudayri, *The desert frontier of Arabia. al-Jawf through the ages*, London 1995; D. Whitcomb, *Ayla. Art and industry in the Islamic port of Aqaba*, Chicago 1994; J. Zahrins, A. Murad and Kh. al-Yaish, The second preliminary report on the southwestern province, in *Aṭlāl* 5 (1981), 9-42; A. Zaky, Medieval Arab arms, in R. Elgood (ed.), *Islamic arms and armour*, London 1979, 202-12.

ʿArim see AL-ʿĀRIM

Ark

The English term most frequently used in reference to the vessel that bore Noah (q.v.) and his family during the flood, it also denotes (2) the sacred chest that, for the Israelites, represented God's presence among them known as the ark of the covenant, and (3) the raft that carried the infant Moses (q.v.).

The ark of Noah

The ark or vessel that bore Noah, his family and two of every kind of animal is referred to in the Qurʾān by two separate Arabic words, *fulk* and *safīna*, both meaning "boat," as well as one circumlocution, "a thing of planks and nails" *(dhāti alwāḥin wa-dusur)*. The last, found in Q 54:13, is the only qurʾānic reference to the composition of the vessel. In extra-qurʾānic legends, which are generally derived from haggadic sources, the early Muslim commentators elaborated on the materials and method of the ark's construction, the number of its levels, the types and location of the animals and the sundry difficulties that Noah faced when loading and unloading it. In accordance with the Qurʾān's general tendency to present a more abstract and paradigmatic representation of themes paralleled in the Jewish and Christian scriptures (see SCRIPTURE AND THE QURʾĀN), the ark is a sign both of God's punishment and of his willingness to save believers. When the Qurʾān is read in Arabic, the words referring to Noah's ark resonate with the more general uses of the words, usually translated as "ship" or "boat," reinforcing the sense of the ark as one of God's portents and providing a connection to the story of Jonah (q.v.; Q 37:140) and to that of Moses and God's servant in Q 18:71 (see KHĀḌIR/KHIḌR).

The ark of the covenant

In Q 2:248, the ark *(tābūt)* of the covenant (q.v.) is mentioned as a sign of God's sovereignty. In that verse, it is said to contain the divine presence (*sakīna*, see SECHINA). Extra-qurʾānic commentaries on this verse identify the ark of the covenant with the same cultic object mentioned in the Hebrew scriptures (see *Exod* 25:10-22).

The ark of Moses

The ark *(tābūt)* in which the infant Moses floated down the Nile is mentioned in Q 20:39. The qurʾānic account follows the biblical and extra-biblical stories of Moses being set adrift during the time Pharaoh (q.v.) was killing the first-born sons of the Israelites. Moses was found by a sister of Pharaoh and was given, by divine intervention, to a wet nurse who was Moses' actual mother. The Islamic tradition understands the ark as a small chest rather than the pitch-covered reed vessel in the biblical account. See also SHIPS.

Gordon D. Newby

Bibliography
Primary: Ṭabarī, *Tafsīr;* Thaʿlabī, *Qiṣaṣ*.
Secondary: G.D. Newby, *The making of the last prophet,* Columbia, SC 1989.

Army see EXPEDITIONS AND BATTLES

Arrogance

A sense of superiority which manifests itself in an overbearing manner. Acting arrogantly or insolently has different connotations in reference to God and his creatures. In the case of God, the creator of the whole universe and the supreme authority on heaven and earth, his expression of his superiority is devoid of any negative connotation. "The Great" *(al-kabīr)* is mentioned six times in the Qurʾān as one of God's attributes; five times in association with "the Supreme" (*al-ʿalī*, Q 4:34; 22:62; 31:30; 34:23; 40:12) and once with "the Exalted" (*al-mutaʿāl*, Q 13:9). The Qurʾān specifies, "God possesses greatness *(kibriyāʾ)* in the heavens and on earth" (Q 45:37). As a divine attribute, "exalting in his greatness" *(al-mutakabbir)* means that God exalts himself over his creation (q.v.) and transcends the characteristics of his creation.

Humans who claim to be great are guilty of an unwarranted assumption of dignity, authority (q.v.) and knowledge. A human who claims any of these attributes is to be considered an infidel *(kāfir)* and should be punished as a polytheist. In fact unbelief *(kufr)*, "as man's denial of the Creator, manifests itself most characteristically in various acts of insolence, haughtiness, and presumptuousness" (Izutsu, *Concepts,* 120;

see BELIEF AND UNBELIEF). The basic difference between God and his creatures is that "whereas God is infinite and absolute, every creature is finite. All things have potentialities but no amount of potentiality may allow what is finite to transcend its finitude and pass into infinity. This is what the Qur'ān means when it says that everything except God is 'measured out' (*qadar* or *qadr, taqdīr,* etc.) and is hence *dependent upon* God, and that whenever a creature claims complete self-sufficiency or independence (*istighnā', istikbār*), it thus claims infinitude and a share in divinity (*shirk*)" (F. Rahman, *Major themes,* 67). Human arrogance is a form of injustice (*ẓulm*) against God and the self (Q 6:93), as well as against other people. "Those regarded as weak" (*mustaḍʿafūn*) are a category of people mentioned in the Qur'ān as subjugated by the arrogant (*alladhīna stakbarū,* Q 7:75; 34:31-3). The Qur'ān urges Muslims to fight for the weak (Q 4:75).

The common word for "arrogance" (*kibr*) occurs only once with this sense in the Qur'ān: "Those who dispute about the signs of God without any authority, there is nothing in their hearts but an [unfounded] sense of greatness (*kibr*) that they will never [actually] attain" (Q 40:56). Related to *kibr* is the verbal noun *kibriyā'* (greatness) which occurs twice in the Qur'ān, once as one of God's attributes, "To him be greatness throughout the heavens and the earth: and he is exalted in power full of wisdom" (Q 45:37). The second occurrence is associated with the allegation made by Pharaoh (q.v.) and his people against Moses (q.v.) and Aaron (q.v.) that they wanted to turn the people of Pharaoh away from their traditions in order for Moses and his people to gain greatness, *al-kibriyā',* in the land of Egypt (Q 10:78). Moses' prayer, on the other hand, asks God to provide protection for him and his people against every arrogant one (*mutakabbir,* Q 40:27). Conceiving of oneself as great and superior is considered by the Qur'ān to be claiming one of God's attributes, because only he is great (*al-kabīr*). Thus, arrogance in man is a grievous sin (*kabīra,* see SIN, MAJOR AND MINOR). Acting insolently or behaving arrogantly is to claim God's position (Q 59:23). It is reported in one of the pronouncements of God preserved as a ḥadīth and not found in the Qur'ān (*ḥadīth qudsī,* see ḤADĪTH AND THE QUR'ĀN) that God said, "Magnificence (*al-ʿaẓama*) is my garment and greatness (*al-kibriyā'*) is my covering. Whoever claims them surely will be thrown into hell." A well-known ḥadīth of Muḥammad reads, "Whoever has in his heart the smallest portion of arrogance (*kibr*) will never enter paradise."

Al-Ghazālī (d. 505/1111) explains that the arrogant person (*al-mutakabbir*) is one who considers the position of every one else to be inconsiderable. He looks down on others and treats them like slaves. If arrogance manifests itself as mere insolence, it is wicked behavior. Whoever claims absolute greatness is nothing but a liar, because this position is absolutely inconceivable for anyone but God. Al-Ghazālī concedes that some individuals who enjoy higher positions or authority in society have the right to be somewhat arrogant. He explains that, according to mystical terminology, "arrogant" (*mutakabbir*) also may refer to the ascetic gnostic, i.e. one who renounces whatever keeps him from serving and communicating with God (*al-Maqṣad al-asnā,* 75).

Takabbur and *istikbār,* acting insolently or behaving arrogantly have different connotations in reference to God and to his creatures. For humans, acting arrogantly is a form of behavior directed towards other people on the grounds that they are inferior. It has been defined as undue assumption of dignity, authority, or knowledge, aggressive conceit, presumption or haughtiness. In the case of God, understood as the creator of the whole universe and the supreme authority on heaven and earth, arrogance is devoid of such a connotation. As a divine attribute *al-mutakabbir* means that he exalts himself over doing injustice to his creation, or that he transcends the characteristics of his creation. Besides being great, high and self-exalted, he is also exalted in might *(jabbār)*. Whoever acquires or claims any of these attributes is to be considered *kāfir* and should be punished as a polytheist. In fact *kufr,* "as man's denial of the Creator, manifests itself most characteristically in various acts of insolence, haughtiness, and presumptuousness" (Izutsu, *Concepts,* 120).

The first act of arrogance was committed by Satan when he refused the command of God to prostrate before Adam (see ADAM AND EVE). For this he was condemned as an infidel. Although Satan represents the most wicked example of arrogance (Q 7:13; 38:74, 75), Pharaoh became the human reflection of Satan when he rejected the message God revealed to Moses (Q 28:39) and misled his people into acting arrogantly (Q 7:133; 10:75; 23:46; 29:39). Thus Satan and Pharaoh became the two representative symbols for the disastrous consequences of arrogance and insolence *(takabbur* and *istikbār)*. The majority of Muslim theologians and jurists consider Satan's arrogance, and to a great extent Pharaoh's, to be the act of disobedience that led to the existence of the devil (q.v.) on earth. The jurist and theologian Ibn Ḥazm (d. 456/1064), with the obvious intention of condemning speculative theology *(kalām)*, considers Satan the first one to employ analogy *(qiyās)* in religious matters.

The view of the famous mystic al-Ḥallāj (d. 309/940) regarding Satan and Pharoah was exceptional. He saw their arrogance as a manifestation of their awareness of the divine nature of all creatures. Their apparent disobedience was thus in consonance with their real inner nature. Though Satan was cursed and expelled from God's presence, his loyalty and sincerity did not change. For his part, Pharaoh was drowned, but he did not betray himself. Al-Ḥallāj considered them his true models (*Ṭawāsīn,* 16-20). As is to be expected, this view was totally rejected by the mainstream of Islamic thought (see ṢŪFISM AND THE QURʾĀN).

There are many references in the Qurʾān to communities, groups and individuals who insolently and arrogantly rejected the word of God. In addition to the subjects of Pharaoh, the Qurʾān mentions the neighbors of Noah (q.v.; Q 71:7), the people of ʿĀd (q.v.; Q 41:15), the people of Thamūd (q.v.; Q 7:75-6), the people of Midian (q.v.; Q 7:88) and the pagan Meccans (passim). Apart from these specific groups, a number of general classes of people are portrayed as arrogant, including those in defiance of right (Q 7:146); those who dispute about the signs of God (Q 40:35; see SIGNS); those who refuse to serve God (Q 4:172); those who tell lies about God, scornfully rejecting his revelation (Q 6:93; see REVELATION AND INSPIRATION); those who turn away from listening to the Qurʾān and prefer frivolous tales (*lahw al-ḥadīth,* Q 31:6); those who ignore the revelations of God completely (Q 45:8); those who do not believe in the afterlife (Q 16:22); and the hypocrites (*munāfiqūn,* see HYPOCRITES AND HYPOCRISY) of Medina (Q 63:1,7-9). Hell will be the final dwelling place of all of these arrogant people (Q 16:29; 39:60, 72; 40:76).

Those who are not arrogant, but rather are humble, unconditionally obey God and willingly accept his revelation. The Qurʾān several times refers to those who do not disdain to be God's servants (*lā yastakbirūna ʿan ʿibādatihi,* Q 7:206), e.g. the followers of Jesus (q.v.; Q 5:83), the angels (q.v.) and all of creation (Q 16:48-9; 21:19) and those who believe in the Qurʾān (Q 32:15). In contrast with the arrogant disobedience of Satan and Pharaoh, Jesus, who is described as a servant of God (Q 19:30-2), was neither overbearing *(jabbār)* nor miserable *(shaqī)*. He will never disdain *(lan yastankifa)* to serve and worship God (Q 4:172). The believers are those who accept the Qurʾān. When the verses are recited to them, they fall down in adoration (q.v.), praising their Lord. They are never puffed up with pride (*lā yastakbirūna,* Q 32:15). The ideal behavior expected from Muslims that makes them worthy of the title "servants of God most gracious" *(ʿibād al-raḥmān)* is, among other things, that they walk on the earth in humility (Q 25:63). The advice of the sage Luqmān (q.v.) to his son was "Do not put on a contemptuous mien toward people and do not walk on the earth exuberantly, for God does not like any self-important boaster" (Q 31:18). All those who disdain his worship and are arrogant (*man yastankif ʿan ʿibādatihī wayastakbir,* Q 4:172) will be gathered together to be questioned and punished grievously, while those who believe and perform righteous deeds will be given their just rewards and more from God's bounty (Q 4:173). The *mustaḍʿafūn,* the ill-treated or the disinherited, is a category of people mentioned in the Qurʾān as oppressed by the *mustakbirūn* (Q 7:75; 34:31-3). The Qurʾān urges Muslims to fight for the liberation of the *mustaḍʿafūn* (Q 4:75) and encourages them in the meantime to resist such oppression even by emigrating to another land (Q 4:97). *Istikbār* thus leads to oppression which is a grievous form of *ẓulm,* injustice against others.

It is worthwhile to refer briefly to the recent political manipulation of the notion of arrogance. The old slogan of the national movements in the Arab and Muslim countries through the sixties was commonly "The struggle against international imperialism" *(al-kifāḥ ḍidda l-istiʿmār al-ʿālamī)*. The increasing power of the Islamic movements in the seventies led to the replacement of the non-qurʾānic concept of "imperialism" with "arrogance" *(istikbār)*. Before the Islamic revolution in Iran, Ayatollah Khomeini (d. 1989) started using the concept in reference to the Shah's regime. "The *mustakbirūn* were those who supported the regime of the Shah. After the revolution, *mustakbirūn* was used in a broader sense to describe also external enemies of the Islamic Republic" (Gieling, *Sacralization,* 100). The same negative connotation was applied to "the industrialized world, with the United States as its major representative. In this sense, *istikbār* was synonymous with other concepts with a negative connotation like colonialism and imperialism" (Gieling, *Sacralization,* 100). During the Iran-Iraq War (1980-88), the concept was used to condemn Saddam Hussain and other enemies. See also GOD AND HIS ATTRIBUTES.

Nasr Abu Zayd

Bibliography
Primary: Bukhārī, *Ṣaḥīḥ;* al-Ghazālī, Abū Ḥāmid Muḥammad, *al-Maqṣad al-asnā fī sharḥ maʿānī asmāʾ Allāh al-ḥusnā,* Cyprus 1987; id., *Kitāb al-Tawba (*from *Iḥyāʾ ʿulūm al-dīn),* ed. R. al-Sayyid, Beirut 1403/1983; al-Ḥallāj, *Kitāb al-Ṭawāsīn,* ed. P. Nwyia, Beirut 1972.
Secondary: S. Gieling, *The sacralization of war in the Islamic republic of Iran,* Ph.D. diss., Nijmegen 1998; Izutsu, *Concepts;* F. Rahman, *Major themes of the Qurʾān,* Chicago 1980.

Art and Architecture and the Qurʾān

The relationship between the revealed scripture of Islam and attitudes towards art and architecture and the practice thereof will be discussed under three headings:
1. Qurʾānic references or allusions to art and architecture, including passages later

cited with respect to artistic creativity, even if they were not initially so intended; 2. The uses of the Qurʾān as a source for citations in the making and decorating of works of art; and 3. The enhancement of the Qurʾān itself through art.

Art and architecture in the Qurʾān

It must be stated at the outset that, with the partial exception of Q 27:44, which will be discussed later, the Qurʾān does not contain any statement which may be construed as a description of manufactured things or as a doctrinal guide for making or evaluating visually perceptible forms. The world in which the revelation of the Qurʾān was made was not one which knew or particularly prized works of art and later ḥadīth — the reports recording the Prophet's words and deeds — only briefly mention a few fancy textiles owned by the members of the entourage of the Prophet. Furthermore, although ḥadīth do attribute to the Prophet theoretical positions or practical opinions on the making of works of art, none is directly asserted in the Qurʾān itself, but only deduced from various passages. Finally, while the Qurʾān is quite explicit about such practices as prayer (q.v.) or pilgrimage (q.v.) being specifically restricted to Muslims, it provides no direct or implied definition or even a requirement for a particular locale for the accomplishment of these practices. For all these reasons, the consideration of art and architecture in the Qurʾān does not lead to a coherent whole, but to a series of disjointed observations which may be divided into two groups: the direct references to things made or to spaces built; and the indirect implications for the making of things and the design of spaces.

Direct references

There are, first of all, references to categories of manufacture and especially of construction. One rather striking set of examples involves concrete items which are mentioned only once. All of them are described as being in the possession of Solomon (q.v.), the prophet-king whose patronage for works of art was legendary and whose artisans were usually the no less legendary jinn (q.v.). In Q 34:12 he ordered the making of a fountain of molten brass, a Muslim adaptation of the celebrated brazen sea in Solomon's temple in Jerusalem (q.v.) as it is described in *2 Kings* 25:13 and *1 Chron* 18:8. Then in Q 34:13, the jinn manufacture for him *maḥārīb, tamāthīl, jifān* of enormous size and *qudūr* which were anchored down so that they could not easily be removed. The meaning of the word *miḥrāb* (sing. of *maḥārīb*), which will be discussed later, appears in other contexts as well. *Jifān* — meaning some sort of receptacle, usually translated as "porringer," a term of sufficiently vague significance to hide our uncertainty as to what was really involved — and *qudūr*, "cooking-pots" are only mentioned in this particular passage. The exact meaning and function of these two items are somewhat mysterious. *Timthāl*, also in the plural, appears again in Q 21:52, where it clearly refers to the idols worshiped by the father of Abraham (q.v.). These idols would have been sculptures of humans or of animals and it is probably sculptures in general rather than idols in particular that must be understood in Q 34:13 (see IDOLS AND IMAGES).

The association of Solomon with unusual buildings is confirmed by Q 27:44, where, in order to test the Queen of Sheba (q.v.) and ultimately to demonstrate his superiority to her, Solomon orders the construction of a *ṣarḥ* covered or paved with slabs of glass (*mumarrad min qawārīr*). Usually translated as "pavilion" or "palace," the word *ṣarḥ* occurs also in Q 28:38 and Q 40:36. Both times it is modified by the adjective "high" and refers to a construction ordered by Pharaoh (q.v.). Since all these passages deal with mythical buildings and because the root of the word implies purity and clarity, the term may reflect the attribute of transparency in a building, rather than its form. It would then be a pavilion comparable to the elaborate construction alleged to have existed on top of pre-Islamic Yemeni palaces. Generally speaking, it seems preferable to understand the term as a "constructed space of considerable merit and attractiveness," without being more specific, though the matter remains open to debate. What is of import here is not the exact meaning of the term but the presence within the qurʾānic images of works of art that have not been seen, but only imagined. Further on it will be seen that the story of Solomon and the Queen of Sheba (see BILQĪS), as told in the Qurʾān, has many additional implications for the arts.

A second category of qurʾānic terms dealing with or applicable to the arts consists of much more ordinary words. There is a series of terms for settlements, such as *qarya* (Q 25:51), usually the term for a city as well as for smaller settlements; *madīna,* a word used only twice (Q 28:18, 20), possessing very broad connotations; *masākin* "[ruined] dwellings" (Q 29:38), which often occurs in poetry; and a more abstract term like *balad* in *al-balad al-amīn,* "the place of security" (Q 95:3), which is probably a reference to Mecca (q.v.). *Bayt* is the common word for a house and it is supposed to be a place of privacy (Q 3:49; 4:100; 24:27-9), a quality which has been sought until today by architects building in what they assume to be an Islamic tradition. The word was used for the dwellings of the wives of the Prophet (q.v.; Q 33:33-4), for whom privacy was an essential criterion, and also for the presumably fancy abode of Zuleika, the wife of Potiphar (Q 12:23; see JOSEPH). When it is mentioned as adorned with gold (q.v.; Q 17:93), it is meant pejoratively as an expression of vainglorious wealth. *Dār* occurs occasionally (e.g. Q 17:5; 59:2) with no clear distinction from *bayt* except insofar as it implies some broader function as in *al-dār al-ākhira* in Q 28:83 indicating "the space of thereafter." The rather common word *qaṣr* (castle, palace) occurs only four times, twice metaphorically, once in a well-known cliché referring to the destroyed "palaces" of old and once with reference to paradise (q.v.) in a passage which will be examined later. Other terms for something built or at least identified spatially are rarer, like *mathwā* (dwelling, Q 47:19) or *maṣāniʿ* (buildings, Q 26:129). There are a few instances when techniques of construction are indicated, often in a metaphorical way as in Q 13:2, where the heavens are depicted as a miraculous, divine creation built without columns.

A third category of terms consists of words which, whatever their original meaning, acquired a specifically Muslim connotation at the time of the Prophet or later. The two most important ones are *masjid* and *miḥrāb*. *Masjid* (place of prostration, see MOSQUE) occurs twenty-eight times in the Qurʾān. In fifteen instances it is modified by *al-ḥarām,* a reference to the Meccan sanctuary whose pre-Islamic holiness was preserved and transformed by the Muslim revelation, i.e. the Kaʿba (q.v.), the holy house (*al-bayt al-ḥarām* in Q 53:97) which Abraham and Ishmael (q.v.) built (Q 2:125). It is mentioned as the *qibla* (q.v.) or direction of prayer (Q 2:142-7) and as the aim of the pilgrimage (Q 5:96-7). However, nothing is said about its form or about the space around it and there is only a vague reference to the importance of its proper maintenance (Q 9:19). Even this action is not as important as professing the faith in all of its truth. In Q 17:1, the word is once used for the Meccan sanctuary while in Q 17:7 it refers to the Jewish temple in Jerusalem (q.v.). The word is used a second time in Q 17:1 in the expression "the farthest mosque" *(al-masjid al-aqṣā),* the exact identification of which has been the subject of much debate (see AQṢĀ MOSQUE). There is no doubt that, at some point in history and possibly as early as the mid-second/eighth century, it became generally understood as a reference to Jerusalem. This, however, was not the case during the first century after Muḥammad's emigration to Medina (*hijra,* see EMIGRATION), when it was identified by many as a place in the neighborhood of Mecca or as a symbolic space in a miraculous event (see ASCENSION).

The remaining ten occurrences of *masjid* do not form a coherent whole except insofar as they all mention a place where God is worshiped (Q 7:29). It literally belongs to God (Q 72:18, a passage often used in mosque inscriptions, see below) and unbelievers are banned from it (Q 9:17). "Those who believe in God and his last day, practice regular prayer and give to charity, and fear none but God must maintain and frequent [the verb *ʿamara* has a complex range of meanings] the mosques of God" (Q 9:18, another passage frequently used in inscriptions). In recounting the story of the seven sleepers of Ephesus (see MEN OF THE CAVE), the Qurʾān asserts that God built a *masjid* over them (Q 18:21). A most curious and somewhat obscure passage is Q 22:40, which contains a list of sanctuaries that would have been destroyed had God not interfered to save them. The list includes *ṣawāmiʿ, biyaʿ, ṣalawāt* and *masājid,* usually — but there are variants — translated as "monasteries [or cloisters], churches, synagogues and mosques." The first two words are never again used in the Qurʾān. The third term, *ṣalawāt,* is the plural of *ṣalāt,* the word commonly used for the Muslim ritual prayer. Here it seems to mean a place rather than the act of prayer. But the sequence itself suggests four different kinds of sacred spaces, probably representing four different religious traditions. If there are four religious groups implied, Islam, Judaism and Christianity are easy to propose — even if one does not quite know which term goes with which system of faith —, what is the fourth religion? It is, in fact, with some skepticism that the word *masājid* is translated as "mosques" since nowhere else in the Qurʾān is the word *masjid* used alone to be understood correctly as a place of prayer restricted to Muslims. It always means a generally holy space which could be used by Muslims. This verse must, therefore, be connected to some particular event or story whose specific connotations are unknown.

In short, the proper conclusion to draw from the evidence is that, while the Qurʾān clearly demonstrates the notion of a sacred or sanctified space, it does not identify a specifically Muslim space as a *masjid.* The only specifically Muslim space mentioned in the Qurʾān is the *masjid* of Mecca and its sacred enclosure. The vagueness of nearly all references to it may explain some of the later problems in actually defining the exact direction of prayer *(qibla).* Was it toward the city of Mecca (q.v.), a large enclosure, the Kaʿba, one of its sides or the black stone in its corner? In short, the word *masjid* — destined for a long and rich history in Arabic and in many other languages — soon after the death of the Prophet in 11/632 came to mean a special type of building restricted to Muslims. In the Qurʾān it appears to have a very broad significance with a very uncertain relationship to exclusively Islamic worship.

Matters are almost as complicated with the word *miḥrāb,* which also possesses a range of practical and symbolic meanings. It too was destined for a long and distinguished history as the name for the niche indicating the direction of prayer on the wall of all Muslim sanctuaries. The term *miḥrāb* also refers to a type of decorative recess found on tombstones, faience panels and rugs. As has been shown in a recent article (N. Khoury, Mihrab), the word originally designated elevated structures which had acquired some sort of honorary significance, although the element of height is only clearly present in one qurʾānic verse. In Q 38:21 the disputants go *up* to the *miḥrāb* where David (q.v.) is. The honorific quality applies to this particular place by inference as it does in the three instances (Q 3:37, 39; 19:11) where the term is used for Zechariah (q.v.), the servant of God and the father of John the Baptist (q.v.). When used in the plural *maḥārīb* (Q 34:13), it has usually been interpreted as "places of worship," but, even if consecrated by tradition, this interpretation does not seem necessary since the other terms listed in this passage — the *maḥārīb, tamāthīl, jifān* and *qudūr* (see above) that the jinn manufactured for Solomon — are mostly exemplars of power and wealth rather than of religious, though pagan, needs. Altogether, the exact meaning of this word in the Qurʾān seems to be more secular than pious and bears no direct relationship to the word's later uses in mosques and as a theme of design.

While *masjid* and *miḥrāb* became terms to define major elements of Islamic architecture and while other terms dealing with created forms remained consistent and relatively clear *(bayt* or *dār)* or rare and fairly obscure *(ṣarḥ),* there is a category of qurʾānic references to visually-perceived matters which have not been seen, but which nonetheless are held to exist. The numerous accounts of paradise include a great number of references which fall into the category of architecture and planning. These accounts may have had an impact on the design of gardens, most particularly in Mughal India as with the tomb of Akbar in Sikandara near Agra and with the Taj Mahal in Agra itself (see W. Begley and Z.A. Desai, *Taj Mahal,* although their arguments are not universally accepted). It has also been argued that these qurʾānic passages were literally illustrated in the decoration of mosques, most specifically in the early second/eighth century mosaics of the Great Mosque of Damascus, also known as the Umayyad Mosque (B. Finster, Die Mosaiken; C. Brisch, Observations) although others (O. Grabar, *The formation*) have remained more skeptical. Whatever turns out to be appropriate to explain later developments in decoration and in design, an architectural and decorative imagery pervades most of the Qurʾān's vision of paradise and even, at times, of hell (q.v.).

Both paradise and hell are entered through fancy gates, green being the color of the ones for paradise (Q 39:72). Rivers and formal — as opposed to natural — gardens abound (Q 43:70-3; 44:51; 47:15; 76:12, among many places; see GARDEN) in paradise. There are also fountains (Q 76:6). In a celebrated passage (Q 61:12) gardens are described above underground rivers and beautiful dwellings (*masākin* in Q 61:12 or *quṣūr* in Q 25:10) are erected in the gardens. In five passages (Q 25:75; 29:58; 34:37; 39:20-1), these dwellings are called *ghuraf (*sing. *ghurfa),* in all cases but one modified by the adjective "lofty" with apparently the same equation between height and importance as in the instance of the word *miḥrāb*. It is difficult to know what was meant or imagined by the term in its singular occurrence in a strange passage (Q 25:75), which seems to state that there is only one *ghurfa* in paradise. Were these meant to be whole architectural establishments or simple pavilions? Inasmuch as we have no means to enter the imaginary world of qurʾānic sensitivity, the question cannot be answered in historical terms, although it possibly, as will be seen, may be entered in the fiction of later art.

The same difficulty appears when we try to imagine the *khiyām,* "tents or pavilions" (Q 55:72) in which houris (*ḥūr,* see HOURIS) are found, the *surur* (sing. *sarīr,* one of the several words for "throne," [q.v.]) with perpetually youthful companions (Q 56:15) and especially the throne of God himself. The word for God's throne is *ʿarsh,* as in Q 40:7, only one of its twenty-nine occurrences in the Qurʾān. Most of the time the word is used in the singular and refers to the throne as the place of divine presence (see SECHINA). The word *ʿarsh* is also used once in the story of Solomon and the Queen of Sheba (Q 27:41-2). When used in the plural (*ʿurūsh,* Q 2:259; 18:42; 22:45), it refers to some part of a larger architectural composition. Here it is usually translated as "turrets" or "trellis," which reflects the uncertainty of the translators and commentators about a feature which is always shown as destroyed by divine wrath.

One last visually significant qurʾānic reference dealing with paradise and with visually-perceived matters is that the elect are beautifully dressed (Q 35:33; 76:21) and the companions they find there (Q 76:15-7) carry vessels *(āniya),* cups *(akwāb)* and goblets *(kaʾs)* polished to look like crystal or silver (this seems to be the correct interpretation of *qawārīra min fiḍḍa,* Q 76:16). Their clothes are of silk (q.v.), the most precious metals are silver and crystal and polished glass is the model for the expected visual effect. These images are important in suggesting the materials and objects which were considered luxurious in early first/seventh century Arabia and also serve as inspiration for later Persian painting, where the association between paradise and luxury through expensive clothes and other objects was fully exploited.

Implications for art

Quite early passages from the Qurʾān came to be used to justify and explain Muslim attitudes toward the arts in general and the representation of living beings in particular. This last topic has been and will continue to be the subject of much debate and discussion because it reflects the ever-changing needs and concerns of the prevailing culture and society as much as the actual positions apparent in the Qurʾān. The latter is, on the whole, quite clear. Unlike the second commandment of the Old Testament, there is no opposition to art or to representation, just as there is no call for the creation of works of art or of a material culture that would be distinctly Muslim. Thus terms like "iconoclasm" (a call for the destruction of images) or even the German *Bilderverbot* (forbidding the making of images) are inappropriate to define any part of the message of the Qurʾān. The term "aniconism," meaning simply "the absence of a doctrine or even of much thought about representational imagery," has found favor among some scholars and is more accurate in reflecting the attitude of the Qurʾān.

On the other hand, once a broad Muslim culture had been established over vast territories, it was compelled to deal with the rich and varied artistic traditions of the alien cultures it encountered and it sought in the Qurʾān either direct answers to its own questions about the validity of artistic activities or, at the very least, references that could lead to such answers. In the absence of direct statements, three kinds of arguments could be, and were, derived from the Qurʾān.

One is based on a few passages which may be construed as dealing with representations. The "statues" made for Solomon (Q 34:12-3) have already been mentioned. A more frequently used passage to uphold a prohibition of images is Q 6:74, where Abraham, a far more saintly figure than Solomon in the Islamic tradition, says to his father Āzar (q.v.): "Do you take idols *(aṣnām)* as gods? Indeed, I see that you and your people are in manifest error." This passage must be connected with Q 5:90, where idols *(anṣāb)* are also mentioned, together with wine and games of chance (see INTOXICANTS; GAMBLING), as "abominations of Satan's handiwork." Both words mean "idols," which usually have the shape of men or animals, or "statues" of figures that could be used as idols. The two passages are usually seen as expressing an objection to images, but they are more appropriately construed as being in opposition to idols regardless of their shape. A third passage is more specific and, therefore, more pertinent. In Q 3:47-9, God says to Mary (q.v.), "God creates what he wills. When he decrees something, he only says to it 'be' and it is." An example is the case of Jesus (q.v.), who comes with the following message: "I have come to you with a sign from your lord. I will make for you out of clay the figure of a bird. I will breathe into it and it will become a [real] bird by God's leave." Here it is clear that the making of a representation is only meaningful if life is given to that representation. Since the giving of life is reserved to God alone, it is only with his permission that the creation of a three-dimensional and lifelike bird can occur.

These few specific passages dealing with representations are not conclusive in themselves, but they served as important points of reference in the later development of the opposition to the making of images. They acquired their particular importance when put next to a second type of argument based less on specific passages than on two themes which pervade the Qurʾān: the absolute opposition to idolatry and God's uniqueness as creator. These two Islamic doctrines were used as arguments against the legitimacy of images as long as images were indeed worshiped and the belief existed that they partook of the spirit of what was represented. It may also be argued that they lost their pertinence once the old equation no longer held. Over the years, much has been written arguing that abstraction, visual distortion and ornamentation occur with such frequency in Islamic art because mainstream Muslim patrons and artists sought to conform to a doctrine that always aimed at the equation of the representation and the represented. According to this view, alternate modes of expression had to be found in order to avoid criticism or even condemnation for vying with God, as a result of such an alleged doctrine.

Another doctrine alleged to have been derived from the Qurʾān has been that of opposition to luxury, what may be called an ideal of reasonable asceticism in private and public life. Its premise is that art is a luxury, a point which certainly has been argued forcefully by fundamentalist groups and more moderately by moralists down through the centuries. Although common enough in any religious movement with a populist base, as Islam was certainly at the beginning, such a doctrine is difficult to represent as one which has maintained itself on a significant scale throughout time and even its qurʾānic basis is somewhat uncertain.

In spite of a number of contrary arguments, on the whole it is difficult to explain the development of an Islamic art through doctrines derived from the Qurʾān. This view may only appear to be correct, because too many problems have not received the proper attention. Instead, it would seem to have its roots in the complex contingencies of a new ethic encountering the well-developed cultures of the world with their rich visual heritage There is a need for a careful investigation of the terminology dealing, directly or potentially, with the arts. Words like *aṣnām* (idols), *anṣāb* (idols), *tamāthīl* (statues), *ṣūra* (shape, Q 82:8), *hayʾa* (form, Q 3:49; 5:110) are all terms which actually refer to or imply a likeness or copy and suggest some sort of relationship to a previously existing original. The full investigation of the occurrences of these terms in the Qurʾān and in early Arabic poetry, as well as later usage both among *littérateurs* and in technical philosophical thought, may well provide a sketch of the conceptual framework implied by the revelation and give some idea of what the arts may have meant at the time. An interesting beginning in that direction occurred in a recent article by Muhammad Qlaaji published in a Saudi Arabian legal journal which argues, on the basis of a set of qurʾānic citations, for the canonical value of ornament in Islamic art. A much more imaginative work by the young French esthetician Valérie Gonzalez *(Piège de crystal)* will soon demonstrate the deep philosophical problems behind the qurʾānic passage mentioned earlier (Q 27:44) in which Solomon creates an object, the mysterious *ṣarḥ*, which is supposed to appear real and to be understood as such, without in fact being what it appears to be. The implications are striking not only for Islamic art, but for the very nature of art in general. Comparable statements have been made by twentieth-century surrealists like René Magritte. Yet such efforts at an interpretation adapted to the needs, tastes and paradigms of our own century are rare. Also they may well go against an interpretative current which asserts that only in its historical truth can the divine message be accepted.

Altogether, there is no doubt that the Qurʾān will continue to be mined for answers to the esthetic and social needs of Muslim societies and cultures as they evolve with time. It is also fairly clear, however, that the arts were not a significant concern of the revelation nor did they play a large role in the modes of life prevalent in the Arabian peninsula during the first decades of the first/seventh century. Fancy and elaborate objects were largely absent in the surroundings of Mecca and Medina and the vision of architecture was limited to the simple Kaʿba. There was a vision of art and architecture based on the legends of Solomon and memories of the ancient Arabian kingdoms. Ruins in the desert or in the steppe could then, as they do now, be transfigured into mirages of a lost man-made world of awesome proportions. It does not, however, seem that the milieu in which the Qurʾān appeared was truly aware of the great artistic traditions of the Mediterranean, Mesopotamia, Iran, India, or even of the Yemen and Ethiopia. Furthermore, the Qurʾān contains no trace of the neoplatonic debates about the nature of art. The emerging universal Muslim culture had to seek in the Qurʾān answers to questions which were only later formulated.

Uses of the Qurʾān in later art

It is well known that script played an important part in the arts of all Muslim lands, regardless of whether that art was primarily secular or religious (see ARABIC SCRIPT). Large inscriptions are a common part of the decoration of buildings and many objects have long bands or short cartouches with writing, at times even with imitations of writing. These inscriptions often used to be identified in older catalogs and descriptions as "Koranic" without proper concern for what they really say. It is, of course, true that there is an ornamental or esthetic value to these inscriptions which is independent of whatever meaning they convey. In order to organize a subject, which heretofore has received little attention, it has been broken into two headings: iconographic uses of the Qurʾān and formal uses of qurʾānic scripts.

Iconographic uses

The founder of the systematic study of Arabic epigraphy (see EPIGRAPHY AND THE QURʾĀN), Max van Berchem, was the first scholar to establish that most formal inscriptions in monumental architecture consist of citations from the Qurʾān which bear or may bear a relationship to the function of the buildings on which they were found. He initiated the systematic publication with commentary of all Arabic inscriptions. Beginning in 1931 these were published under the title *Matériaux pour un corpus inscriptionum arabicarum* as part of the *Mémoires* of the Institut Français d'Archéologie Orientale in Cairo. M. van Berchem himself published the volumes on Cairo (with a supplementary volume by G. Wiet), Jerusalem and Anatolia, while E. Herzfeld produced the volumes on Aleppo. A similar survey, although less elaborate in its commentaries, was made by Muhammad Husain for the Archaeological Survey of India. In recent years, G. Wiet and M. Hawary, using almost exclusively secondary sources, produced collections of the inscriptions of Mecca. In addition, S. Blair recently collected the inscriptions of pre-Mongol Iran and M. Sharon published those of Palestine. Unfortunately, M. van Berchem adopted the practice of providing only the sūra and verse numbers of the qurʾānic quotations, usually according to the verse division of the G. Flügel edition, which does not always agree with the now-standard Egyptian edition. Therefore, there are problems whenever one tries to identify the exact wording of an inscription. Although most recent publications have abandoned this practice, it is still found in the most important corpus of Arabic epigraphy, the eighteen volumes published so far of the *Matériaux pour un corpus inscriptionum arabicarum*.

A particularly important tool has been derived from all these efforts. Erica Dodd and Shereen Khairallah produced the work *The image of the word*, the first volume of which contains a list of all of the qurʾānic passages cited in inscriptions and where they have been used, thus allowing one to study the frequency of use of certain passages and the temporal or geographical variations in their use. The second volume is comprised of a series of essays on individual monuments and on questions which grow out of these catalogs, for example why certain inscriptions were placed in different places on different monuments. All of the essays show the influence of a major article written by E. Dodd in 1969 entitled "The image of the word," outlining the historical and psychological premises behind the existence of an iconography of the Qurʾān. She argues that in trying to avoid or even reject the religious imagery of Christianity and paganism, the mainstream of Islamic culture replaced images with words whenever it wished to make some pious, ideological or other point. Within this scheme, the Qurʾān was pre-eminent both because of its sacredness and because most Muslims were familiar with it. Therefore, the viewer appreciates the significance of the selection of the particular passages from the Qurʾān and interprets them in accordance with the expectations of the patron. It may be noted that Buddhism and Hinduism do not appear to have been pertinent to the formation of Islamic culture, even though this assertion may be modified by future research.

Though never established as a formal doctrine, this "iconography" of the divine word developed quite early in Islamic times, under Umayyad rule (r. 41/661-132/750). It might even be proper to associate its appearance with the caliph ʿAbd al-Malik (r. 65/685-86/705), who made the language of administration Arabic and introduced Arabic inscriptions on the coinage. For the latter, the so-called "mission verse," "It is [God] who sent his messenger with guidance and the religion of truth to proclaim it over all religion, even though the pagans may detest it" (Q 9:33; see VERSES) became the standard formula for thousands and thousands of coins. It is, in fact, rather remarkable how rarely alternate passages were used. Even if there are sixty-one qur'ānic citations identified in North African coinage (H.W. Hazard, *Numismatic history*), many are only pious statements rather than fuller citations and should not be considered as iconographically or semantically significant quotations.

The ideological and political assertion of truth made by the passage chosen for coins is easy to explain for a coinage that was used all over the world and which, quite specifically, competed in its inscriptions with Byzantine gold and silver. It is also quite early that the glass weights and stamps used for internal consumption received as decoration "Give just measure and be not among the defrauders" (Q 26:181; G.C. Miles, *Early Arabic glass weights*). This selection demonstrates a considerable and very early sophistication in the manipulation of qur'ānic passages for pious as well as practical purposes.

The most spectacular early use of qur'ānic quotations on a building occurs in the Dome of the Rock (dated 71/691) in Jerusalem, where 240 meters of Umayyad inscriptions running below on either side of the dome octagon are divided into seven unequal sections, each of which begins with the phrase known as the *basmala* (q.v.), "In the name of God, the merciful and the compassionate." The first five sections contain standard proclamations of the Muslim faith. "There is no god but God, one, without associate" is the most common of these. There is also a series of short passages which are probably excerpted from the Qur'ān (Q 112; 35:36; 17:111, 64:1 combined with 57:2), but which might also be merely pious statements not taken from the Qur'ān. The sixth section contains historical data while the seventh, occupying half of the space, repeats a few of the formulas or citations from the first half and then creates a composite of Q 4:171-2; 19:33-6 and 3:18-19 with only one minor addition in the middle. This statement exposes the main lines of the Christology of the Qur'ān (see CHRISTIANS AND CHRISTIANITY; SCRIPTURE AND THE QUR'ĀN), which makes sense in a city which was at that time a major ecclesiastical and devotional center of Christianity. Other inscriptions in the Dome of the Rock use various combinations of Q 2:255 and 2:112 (or 3:1 and 6:106); 3:26; 6:12 and 7:156, 9:33, 2:139 or 3:78 (slightly modified) in order to make clear the eschatological and missionary purpose of the building. Although the matter is still under much discussion, it is possible that the transmission of the qur'ānic text used for the decoration of the Dome of the Rock was done orally rather than through written copies of the text. This would seem to account for the fact that many of the inscriptions do not exactly agree in wording with the most common version of the Qur'ān in circulation.

While the use of the qur'ānic passage Q 9:33 on coins remained a standard procedure throughout Islamic history and the selection of verses made for the Dome of the Rock remained unique, other citations appear in several early Islamic inscriptions and deserve to be studied in detail. Such is the case with the series, known from later texts, of inscriptions from Mecca and Medina (see *RCEA*, nos. 38, 40, 46-52; G. Wiet and H. Harawy, *Matériaux*) with a primarily religious content. A curious painted graffito in Medina dated 117/735 contains a long citation dealing with faith (*RCEA*, no.

30), but its context is unclear and slightly troubling. There are no such concerns about the fragment of an inscription found on a floor mosaic in a private house, probably from the Umayyad period, excavated in Ramallah in Palestine. It contains a fragment of Q 7:205 "Do not be among the unheedful" next to the representation of an arch which may or may not be a *miḥrāb* (Rosen-Ayalon, The first mosaic). The actual point of the inscription and the reason this particular citation was chosen are still difficult to explain.

These early examples all suggest a considerable amount of experimentation in the use of qurʾānic citations during the first two centuries of Muslim rule. A certain norm became established from the third/ninth century onward. Epitaphs will almost always contain the Throne Verse Q 2:255, sūra 112 in its entirety, or both. These verses proclaim the overwhelming and unique power of God. Often these passages are accompanied by Q 9:33 with its missionary universality. Mosques will have the throne verse and Q 9:18 beginning with "the *masājid* of God will be visited and maintained by such as believe in God and the last day." *Miḥrāb*s have their own qurʾānic iconography with the beautiful Q 24:35: "God is the light of the heavens and of the earth, the parable of his light (q.v.) is as if there was a niche [*mishkāt*, another mysterious architectural term] and within it a lamp, the lamp enclosed in glass, the glass like a brilliant star, lit from a blessed tree, an olive neither of the East nor of the West, whose oil is luminous, although fire hardly touches it. Light upon light, God guides whom he wills to his light." There is little wonder that the decoration of *miḥrāb*s and of tombstones often included lamps hanging in a niche and tree-like vegetal ornaments.

The history of this iconography is still in its infancy but almost every major monument of Islamic architecture bears, in addition to the common and frequently repeated passages, citations expressing some special function or purpose or references to events which have been mostly forgotten. Examples include the great mosque of Isfahan (O. Grabar, *The great mosque*); the minarets of Iran (J. Sourdel-Thomine, *Deux minarets* and S. Blair, *Monumental inscriptions*); the striking minaret at Jām in Afghanistan (A. Maricq and G. Wiet, *Le minaret* and J. Moline, The minaret); the inscriptions of the small al-Aqmar mosque in Cairo, which expresses Shīʿī aspirations through qurʾānic citations (C. Williams, The cult); the Ghaznavid palace of Lashkar-i Bāzār in Afghanistan, which is the only building known so far to have used the Solomonic reference of Q 27:44 (J. Sourdel-Thomine, *Lashkar-i bazar*); the Firdaws law school *(madrasa)* in Aleppo, where a relatively unusual qurʾānic passage (Q 43:68-72) is found together with an extraordinary mystical text made to look like a qurʾānic inscription (Y. Tabbaa, *Constructions of power*). In the great mausoleums of the Mughal emperors of India (r. 932/1526-1274/1858), a wealth of qurʾānic inscriptions have allowed some scholars (W. Begley and Z.A. Desai, *Taj Mahal*) to interpret the buildings themselves in an unusual way as slightly blasphemous attempts to create on earth God's own paradise. These interpretations have not convinced all historians, but the point still remains that the choice of inscriptions and of qurʾānic citations is not accidental and reflects precise concerns on the part of patrons and constitutes a powerful message to the outside world.

In general, it is proper to conclude that qurʾānic citations were important signifying components of Islamic art, especially of architecture. They became part of the monument and served as guarantors or witnesses of its function and of the reasons for its creation. They could be highly personalized, as in the epitaphs filling graveyards, where endlessly repeated statements are attached to individuals or more general proclamations of power, glory or good deeds projected to the whole of humankind and especially to the faithful. What is, however, less clear is the extent to which these messages were actually understood and absorbed. It is, in part, a matter of evaluating the level of literacy which existed over the centuries or at the time of a building's construction. It is also a matter of seeking in the chronicles and other sources describing cities and buildings actual discussions of the choice of inscriptions made. These descriptions, however, are surprisingly rare. Often it seems as though this powerful visual instrument, from which modern scholars have derived so many interpretations, was hardly noticed in its own time. Much remains to be done, therefore, in studying the response of a culture to its own practice, if one is to accept the position that the use of the qur'ānic word can be equated with the use of images in other religious systems. It is just possible that modern, primarily Western, scholarship misunderstood the meaning of these citations by arbitrarily establishing such an equation.

In a fascinating way, the contemporary scene has witnessed rather interesting transformations of this iconographic practice. A recently-erected mosque in Tehran, the al-Ghadir Mosque designed by the architect Jahangir Mazlum and completed in 1987, is covered with large written statements, for the most part in glazed or unglazed bricks. Some of these calligraphic panels are indeed placed like icons or images in a church and contain qur'ānic passages. Others are pious statements or prayers, for example the ninety-nine names of God on the ceiling and the endlessly repeated profession of faith (see CONFESSION OF FAITH). While the esthetic success of the structure is debatable, the building itself is impressive for its use of writing so well-blended into the fabric of the wall that its legibility is diminished and its value as a written statement difficult to perceive. It is almost as if the difficulty of reading the words contributes to their esthetic and pious values (M. Falamaki, al-Ghadir mosque). Many other contemporary mosques, especially the monumental ones, provide examples of the same difficulties (R. Holod and H. Khan, *The mosque*).

A particularly spectacular use of the Qur'ān has been proposed by the architect Basil al-Bayati for the city of Riyadh in Saudi Arabia. He envisioned huge arches in the shape of open books of the Qur'ān along the main highway leading into the city as a sort of processional alley greeting the visitor. The project, however, has not been executed. Yet an open book appears as the façade of a mosque designed by the same architect in Aleppo and the Pakistani sculptor Gulgee created a stunning free-standing *miḥrāb* in the shape of two leaves from an open Qur'ān for the King Faisal Mosque in Islamabad. The effect is striking, if unsettling for those who are used to traditional forms, but it demonstrates the contemporary extension of an iconography taken from the Qur'ān to one that uses the book itself as a model. Whether successful or not as works of art, these recent developments clearly indicate that the future will witness further experiments in the use of the Qur'ān, as a book or as a source of citations, to enhance architecture, especially that of mosques, and to send religious and ideological messages. Thus, shortly after the end of the Cultural Revolution in the primarily Muslim Chinese province of Sinkiang, a modest plaque at the entrance of a refurbished mosque in the small town of Turfan (Tufu in Chinese) on the edge of the Tarim Basin quoted in

Arabic script, which presumably was inaccessible to the secret police, Q 9:17: "It is not for idolaters to inhabit God's places of worship *(masājid),* witnessing unbelief against themselves. Their work has failed and in fire they will forever dwell." Thus, the Qur'ān continues to reflect the passions, needs, and aspirations of Muslims everywhere.

The forms of the Qur'ān

Thanks to important recent studies in the paleography of early Arabic (F. Déroche, *Les manuscrits du Coran;* Y. Tabbaa, The transformation; E. Whelan, Writing the word) and to the stunning discovery of some forty thousand parchment pages of early Islamic manuscripts of the Qur'ān in the Yemen, we are beginning to understand the evolution of the Arabic script used in manuscripts of the Qur'ān in spite of the total absence of properly-dated examples before the third/ninth century. The variety of early scripts was already recognized by the bibliographer Ibn al-Nadīm (d. ca. 385/995) and modern collectors have transformed early pages of what is known in the trade as "Kūfic" writing into works of art which frequently fetch high prices on the market.

It is much more difficult to decide whether these early manuscripts were indeed meant to have a formal esthetic value independent of their sacred content. Some of them acquired many forms of ornamental detail, which will be examined in the following section of this entry. It is also difficult to evaluate whether they or the many styles of angular writing discovered in the Ṣanʿāʾ trove or elsewhere were meant primarily for the pleasure of the beholder. Matters changed considerably after the introduction of a proportioned script *(al-khaṭṭ al-mansūb)* by the ʿAbbāsid vizier Ibn Muqla (d. 328/940) in the fourth/tenth century. The establishment of a modular system of writing made it possible to create canons for scripts and variations of these scripts around well-defined norms. As a result, from the time of the small Qur'ān of Ibn al-Bawwāb (d. 413/1022) in the Chester Beatty Library dated to 391/1001 (D.S. Rice, *The unique Ibn al-Bawwāb*) until today, thousands of professional scribes and artists have sought to create variations on the conventional scripts which would attract and please the eyes of buyers. These scripts were not restricted to the text of the Qur'ān but, with the major exception of manuscripts of Persian poetry, the holy book was the text on which the most effort was lavished. This is demonstrated by the magnificent Qur'āns of the Mamlūks (r. 648/1250-922/1517) in Egypt, Syria and Palestine and those of the Īlkhānids (r. 654/1256-754/1353) in Persia (D. James, *Qur'ans* and *After Timur*). It is also for the accurate reading of the qur'ānic text that diacritical marks and other identifying signs were carefully integrated into the composition of words and of letters without detracting from the availability of the text. Already with the celebrated "Qarmatian" Qur'ān of the fifth/eleventh or sixth/twelfth centuries, the leaves of which are spread all over the world (B. St. Laurent, The identification), each page became a composed entity to be seen and appreciated in its own right and in which writing and ornament are set in an even balance. A potential conflict between form and content has begun, with the former of greater importance to the ordinary faithful and the latter more important to the collectors of artistic writing or calligraphy.

Enhancement of the Qur'ān through art

Two aspects of the enhancement of the Qur'ān have already been mentioned: the varieties of styles of writing and the addition of small, ornamental, usually abstract or floral, features in the midst of the text itself or in the margins. At some point, large headings were introduced between sūras and some of these acquired decorative designs. A group of pages, presumably in the Egyptian National Library in Cairo but not seen since their publication by B. Moritz almost a century ago, uses arcades and other architectural features, perhaps representing or symbolizing places of prayer, as well as geometric and floral designs. Large floral compositions project into the margins and the design of these headings has been compared to the *tabulae ansatae* of classical antiquity. In Mamlūk, Īlkhānid or later manuscripts, the cartouches with the titles of each sūra are often dramatically separated from the text proper, while in earlier manuscripts they are more closely imbricated with each other. Enhancement could also be provided by variations in size. There are minuscule copies of the Qurʾān and gigantic ones, like the Tīmūrid one which requires a special stand to be used and whose pages cannot be read and turned simultaneously. Accounts of calligraphers, especially in Iran, often boast of such feats of marvelous transformations of the holy book, thereby illustrating the major traditional esthetic value of being "astonishing" *(ʿajīb)*. Qurʾāns were also honored with fancy and expensive bindings. Especially valued copies were even kept in special boxes. When the Almohad ruler ʿAbd al-Muʾmin (r. 524/1130-558/1163) received from the people of Cordoba the copy of the Qurʾān which had allegedly belonged to the caliph ʿUthmān (r. 23/644-35/656) and preserved traces of his blood, he hired jewelers, metalworkers, painters and leather workers to embellish it. In Ottoman times (r. 680/1281-1342/1924) particularly beautiful cabinets were made for keeping pages and manuscripts of the holy book.

It is, on the whole, clear and not particularly surprising that many techniques were used to honor manuscripts of the Qurʾān by making them more attractive and more exciting than other books and by treating them like precious items, if not literally like works of art. What is more difficult to decide is whether certain styles of writing, certain techniques of binding, certain ways of ornamenting pages and certain motifs were, generally and exclusively, restricted to the Qurʾān. The argument may be made for the composition of pages after the fifth/eleventh century and for scripts which, angular or cursive, were written with particular care when used for the holy text. More tentatively, it may be argued that certain types of decorative feature like the marginal ornaments — which also served to signal divisions within the text — were exclusively restricted to the Qurʾān. All these hypotheses, however, still await investigation and discussion. The difficulty they present is well illustrated by two hitherto unique pages from the trove in Yemen which were published by H.C. von Bothmer (Architekturbilder) and discussed by O. Grabar *(The mediation)*. They illustrate large architectural ensembles, which have been interpreted as mosques shown in a curious but not unique mix of plans and elevations. Are they really images of mosques? If so, are they representations of specific buildings or evocations of generic types? Could they be illustrations of passages in the Qurʾān describing buildings in paradise? There are as yet no firm answers to these questions, but it may be suggested that there was a complex vocabulary of forms more or less restricted to the enhancement of the Qurʾān. These forms did indeed create an art. See also MATERIAL CULTURE AND THE QURʾĀN.

Oleg Grabar

Bibliography

M. Aga-Oglu, Remarks on the character of Islamic art, in *The art bulletin* 36 (1954), 175-202;

W. Begley, The myth of the Taj Mahal, in *The art bulletin* 61 (1979), 7-37; W. Begley and Z.A. Desai, *Taj Mahal,* Seattle 1989; M. van Berchem, *Matériaux pour un corpus inscriptionem arabicarum, Jérusalem,* Cairo 1922-7; M. Bernhard, *Arabic palaeography,* Cairo 1904; repr. Cairo 1974; S. Blair, *The monumental inscriptions from early Islamic Iran and Transoxiana,* Leiden 1992; H.C. von Bothmer, Architekturbilder im Koran. Eine Prachthandschrift der Umayyadenzeit aus dem Yemen, in *Pantheon* 45 (1987), 4-20; C. Brisch, Observations on the iconography of the mosaics in the Great Mosque at Damascus, in P. Soucek (ed.), *Content and context of visual arts in the Islamic world,* University Park, PA 1988; Dār al-Āthār al-Islāmiyya, *Maṣāḥif Ṣanʿāʾ,* Kuwait 1985; F. Déroche, *The Abbasid tradition. The Nasser D. Khalili collection of Islamic art,* Oxford 1992, i; id., Les écritures coraniques anciennes, in *REI* 48 (1980), 207-24; id., *Les manuscrits du Coran. Catalogue des manuscrits arabes de la Bibliothèque Nationale,* 2 vols., Paris 1983-5; E. Dodd, The image of the word, in *Berytus* 18 (1969), 35-62; E. Dodd and S. Khairallah, *The image of the word,* Beirut 1981; R. Ettinghausen, The character of Islamic art, in Nabih A. Faris (ed.), *The Arab heritage,* Princeton 1948, 251-67; id., Arabic epigraphy, in D. Kouymijian (ed.), *Near Eastern numismatics, iconography, epigraphy and history in honor of George C. Miles,* Beirut 1974, 297-317; M. Falamaki, al-Ghadir mosque, Tehran, in *Mimar* 29 (1988), 24-9; B. Farès, *Essai sur l'esprit de la décoration islamique,* Cairo 1952; B. Finster, Die Mosaiken der Umayyadenmoschee von Damaskus, in *Kunst des Orients* 7 (1970-1), 83-141; V. Gonzalez, *Piège de crystal en palais de Solomon,* Paris forthcoming; O. Grabar, *The formation of Islamic art,* New Haven 1983²; id., The mihrab in the mosque of Cordova, in A. Papadopoulo (ed.), *Le mihrāb dans l'architecture et la religion musulmanes. Actes du colloque international tenu a Paris en Mai 1980,* Leiden 1988; id., *The great mosque of Isfahan,* New York 1990; id., *The mediation of ornament,* Princeton 1993; id., *The shape of the holy,* Princeton 1996; H.W. Hazard, *The numismatic history of North Africa,* New York 1952; E. Herzfeld, *Matériaux pour un corpus inscriptionem arabicarum, Alep,* Cairo 1954-6; R. Holod and H. Khan, *The mosque and the modern world,* London 1997; M.A. Husain, *Quranic epigraphy in Delhi province,* Calcutta 1936; D. James, *Qurʾāns of the Mamluks,* London 1988; id., *After Timur. Qurʾāns of the 15th and 16th centuries,* New York 1992; N. Khoury, The mihrab. From text to form, in *IJMES* 30 (1998), 1-27 with a good bibliography; A. Maricq and G. Wiet, *Le minaret de Djam,* Paris 1959; G.C. Miles, *Early Arabic glass weights and stamps,* New York 1946; J. Moline, The minaret of Ṭam, in *Kunst des Orients* 9 (1973-4), 131-48; I.A. Muhammad, Muslims and *taṣwīr,* in *MW* 45 (1955), 250-68; M.R. Qlaaji, Decoration and the position of Islam, in *Majallat al-buḥūth al-fiqhiyya al-muʿāṣira (Contemporary jurisprudence research journal)* 8 (1991); D. van Reenen, The Bilderverbot, a new survey, in *Der Islam* 67 (1990), 27-77 (the latest survey of the subject); D.S. Rice, *The unique Ibn al-Bawwāb manuscript in the Chester Beatty Library,* Dublin 1955; M. Rosen-Ayalon, The first mosaic discovered in Ramleh, in *Israel exploration journal* 26 (1976); M. Sharon, *Corpus inscriptionum arabicarum palaestinae,* Leiden 1997f.; id., Deux minarets d'époque seljoukide, in *Syria* 30 (1953), 108-36; J. Sourdel-Thomine, *Lashkari Bazar IB. Le décor non-figuratif et les inscriptions,* vol. 18 of the *Mémoires de la délégation archéolo-gique française en Afghanistan,* Paris 1978; B.St. Laurent, The identification of a magnificent Koran manuscript, in F. Déroche (ed.), *Les manuscrits du Moyen-Orient,* Istan-bul 1989, the whole volume contains many pertinent contributions; Y. Tabbaa, The transformation of Arabic writing. Qurʾānic calligraphy, in *Ars orientalis* 21 (1991); id., *Constructions of power and piety in medieval Aleppo,* Uni-versity Park, PA 1997, ii; E. Whelan, Writing the word of God, in *Ars orientalis* 20 (1990), 113-47 with 22 pls.; G. Wiet and H. al-Hawary, *Matériaux pour un CIA. IV Arabie,* ed. N. Elisséeff, Cairo 1985 (rev. ed.); C. Williams, The cult of Alid saints, in *Muqarnas* 3 (1985), 39-60.

Artery and Vein

The only qurʾānic reference to these vessels which carry blood away from and to the heart is the word *warīd,* usually translated as "jugular vein:" "We are nearer to him than his jugular vein" (Q 50:16). The critical nature of the jugular heightens the import of the message: Just as human life is dependent upon this vein, so human existence is dependent upon God. Exegetes have observed four constellations of meaning in the verse: the closeness of God to the believer, the protection afforded the believer by God, God's control of and oversight of the individual and the profound relationship which demands caution in all of one's activities. Al-Bayḍāwī (d. ca. 716/1317) stresses that God knows everything about humans and this knowledge encompasses all details about the individual. Thus, God is closer to the individual than even the most intimate living person. This knowledge has immediate spiritual benefit because the believer can thus be assured that he is "closer to God because of his knowledge of humans." Al-Qurṭubī (d. 671/1272), on the other hand, finds significance in the blood flowing through the vein and sees this as symbolizing that God is "in control of and oversees everything the individual does or thinks." Hence, one becomes aware of God's closeness and lives in cautious awareness. He concludes that if one "knew the meaning of the verse, one would never do anything against God" (*Jāmiʿ*, iv, 4, no. 3362). For Ṣūfī commentators (see ṢŪFISM AND THE QURʾĀN), the divine watchfulness is a key factor in interpreting this verse. They see it as indicating a spiritual relationship between God and the believer that transcends ordinary language. They hold that this closeness is the confirmation of the special spiritual states, namely "intimacy" *(uns)* and "nearness" *(qurb)*, that a true believer moves through in his spiritual quest. Thus, these words are held to denote experiential levels of religious attainment and the verse is a scriptural validation of the metaphysical system that the Ṣūfīs practice in their spiritual exercises. The Ṣūfī commentator al-Qushayrī (d. 465/1072), for example, elaborates a complex system of meanings based on nearness to God that ends with an exploration of self-identity. The Pakistani savant ʿAbdullāh Yūsuf ʿAlī (1872-1948), in the commentary on his translation of the Qurʾān, combines these notions when he argues that just as the blood vessel is the vehicle of life and consciousness, so God "knows more truly the innermost state of our feeling and consciousness than does our own ego" (The holy Qurʾān, 1412 n. 4952). In short, the word is universally interpreted by commentators to indicate the depth of God's relationship with human beings.

Earle H. Waugh

Bibliography

ʿA. Yūsuf ʿAlī, *The holy Qurʾān. Text, translation and com-mentary*, Qatar 1934; Bayḍāwī, *Anwār*, ii, 422; Qurṭubī, *Jāmiʿ*, Beirut 1988; Qushayrī, *al-Risāla al-qushayriyya*, ed. ʿA. Maḥmūd and M. al-Sharīf, Cairo 1966.

Asbāb al-Nuzūl see OCCASIONS OF REVELATION

Ascension

Muḥammad's night journey. The qurʾānic grounding of the ascent *(miʿrāj)* of Muḥammad is tenuous in two ways. In the first place, the ascent is not described and the term *miʿrāj* is not used in the Qurʾān. Secondly, the Qurʾān stresses that Muḥammad brings no miracle (q.v.) other than the divinely-wrought miracle of the Qurʾān itself (see INIMITABILITY). Even so, key qurʾānic passages are woven through the post-qurʾānic narrative of Muḥammad's ascent.

The qurʾānic evidence for the tradition of the ascension is the first verse of Q 17, "The Night Journey" (Sūrat al-Isrāʾ): "Glory to the one who took his servant on a night journey from the sacred place of prayer *(al-masjid al-ḥarām)* to the furthest place of prayer (*al-masjid al-aqṣā*, see AQṢĀ MOSQUE) upon which we have sent down our blessing, that we might show him some of our signs (q.v.). He is the all-hearing, the all-seeing." The tradition has understood "the sacred place of prayer" either as the sacred enclosure at Mecca (q.v.) or the Kaʿba (q.v.)

itself. However, the identity of "the furthest place of prayer" has been disputed, leading to several traditions about the ascension. One modern scholarly view holds that the oldest tradition identified "the furthest place of prayer" with the heavenly prototype of the Kaʿba. The night journey *(isrāʾ)* was then a night journey from Mecca through the heavens to the celestial Kaʿba. A later tradition identified "the furthest place of prayer" as the abode of sanctuary *(bayt al-maqdis),* which is considered to be in Jerusalem (q.v.). Finally, the two journeys, the vertical and horizontal, were harmonized as Muḥammad was portrayed on a night journey to Jerusalem and from there on an ascension from Jerusalem through the heavens (see B. Schrieke and J. Horovitz, Miʿrādj).

The debate over the layers of tradition and the goal of the journey is largely based upon extra-qurʾānic evidence. There is little further information to be found in sūra 17. Verse 60 does mention a vision *(ruʾyā)* but within a hypothetical framework not tied clearly to Q 17:1. Verses 90-3 offer a list of proofs that the opponents of Muḥammad demand from him to validate his prophecy: a spring that bursts forth from the earth; a garden of date palms and grape vines among which rivers are gushing; the ability to bring down the sky or to summon God and the angels (see ANGEL); possession of an ornamented abode *(bayt);* and the ability of the prophet to "rise *(ruqī)* into the sky." These challenges are answered not by the claim that Muḥammad has carried out or could carry out such wonders, but rather by the repetition that he is merely a mortal messenger (q.v.).

Yet the challenges of Q 17:90-3 could have been an impetus for later storytellers who, qurʾānic statements to the contrary notwithstanding, began elaborating the miracles of Muḥammad in competition with miracle stories from other religious traditions. In such a spirit, storytellers may have been provoked by Q 17:90-3 into vindicating Muḥammad more literally in the face of such challenges. According to some ascension accounts, Muḥammad indeed attains a garden with gushing rivers — often named and specified as four — and a spring *(zamzam)* that bursts from the ground (see WELLS AND SPRINGS).

In the ascension stories, Q 17:1 is collated with the depiction of Muḥammad's prophetic vision or visions in Q 53, "The Star" (Sūrat al-Najm). Verses 1-12 begin with an oath, "By the star as it falls," then explain that "your companion" is not deluded and does not speak out of desire *(hawā)* but that the vision is a revelation given to him by one of great power. What was seen is described as being on the uppermost horizon, and then coming within a distance of "two bows' length" *(kāna qāba qawsayn).* Some consider Q 53:13-8 to be another description of the same vision, while others maintain that it is a description of a separate vi-sion. Here, there is another descent *(nazla ukhrā)* at the lote tree of the furthest boundary *(sidrat al-muntahā)* when the tree was enshrouded. In a phrase that would be key to the ascension tradition, the gaze of the Prophet neither exceeded its bounds nor strayed *(mā zāgha l-baṣaru wa-mā ṭaghā).* The passage ends with a statement that the Prophet had seen one or more of the greater signs of his Lord *(min āyāti l-rabbihi l-kubrā).*

The opening verses of sūra 53, especially Q 53:12-8, serve as a constant subtext for the ascension stories. The lote tree and the garden of sanctuary *(jannat al-maʾwā)* are not constants; that is, they appear at different stages in different accounts of the ascent. However, Q 53:1-18 was used as a subtext by commentators not only for Q 17:1, but also for the depiction of the descent of revelation on the night of destiny *(laylat al-qadr)* in Q 97:1-5: "We sent him/it down on the night of destiny (see NIGHT OF POWER). What could tell you of the night of destiny? The night of destiny is better than a thousand months. The angels come down — and the spirit among them/it/her — by permission of their lord from every decree. Peace she/it is until the rising of the dawn." Qurʾānic commentators disagree on whether what is sent down on the night of destiny is Gabriel (q.v.; "We sent him down") or the qurʾānic revelation ("We sent it down"). The angels that are said to come down in Q 97:4 are said, in some ḥadīth, to have been sent down from the lote tree of the furthest boundary (cf. Qurṭubī, *Jāmiʿ*, xx, 133-4). The fact that the visions of Q 53 serve as a subtext for both the ascension and the night of destiny sets up a tension between the sending down of revelation to Muḥammad and his rising up to receive it in the heavens. These two paradigms — the sending down of the revelation and the rising up to receive it — were in tension throughout the late antique era and they are clearly in tension in the tradition surrounding Muḥammad's prophetic call. As the tradition holds that the night of destiny and the night of the ascension are separate events, some commentators associate the first vision passage (Q 53:1-12) with the night of destiny and the second vision passage (Q 53:13-18) with the ascension. The tension is not easily resolved, however, and recurs throughout the exegetical tradition (see EXEGESIS OF THE QURʾĀN: CLASSICAL AND MEDIEVAL). A particularly revealing and brilliantly illustrated example of this tension occurs in the commentary of al-Qurṭubī (*Jāmiʿ*, xvii, 81-103).

Further heightening the tension between the ascent and descent paradigms is the intertextual connection between Q 97 and Q 70:1-9, which begins with a question about the "pain that would fall" *(ʿadhāb wāqiʿ)*: "From God, Master of the ascending stairways *(al-maʿārij)*, angels and the spirit (q.v.) ascend to Him on a day whose span is fifty thousand years. Patience, patience most fair. They see it from afar, we see it near. A day the sky will be like molten copper and the mountains like fluffs of wool." These verses depict the day of reckoning (*yawm al-dīn;* see LAST JUDGMENT) in terms that resonate directly with other day-of-reckoning passages such as Q 101:4-5, which also refers to a time when the mountains are like fluffs of wool *(al-ʿihn al-manfūsh)*.

A reference to stairways in a passage concerning the rising of the angels at the end of time would seem at first an unlikely proof for the ascent of Muḥammad during his lifetime. However, the intertextual link of Q 97 and Q 70:1-9 may have facilitated the use of the term *miʿrāj* and variations on the *ʿ-r-j* radical in traditional accounts of Muḥammad's ascent. In Q 70, the angels rise; in Q 97, the angels descend during the night of destiny or upon the night of destiny. The night of destiny is "better than a thousand months." Similarly, the day of reckoning is "a day whose span is fifty thousand years." These parallels in imagery are strengthened by sound and syntax parallels:

70:4	*taʿruju*	*l-malāʾikatu*	*wa-l-rūḥu*	*ilayhi*
	there rise	the angels	and the spirit	in/upon him/it
97:4	*tanazzalu*	*l-malāʾikatu*	*wa-l-rūḥu*	*fīhā*
	there descend	the angels	and the spirit	in/upon/among it/them/her

Both the night of prophetic revelation and the day of reckoning are boundary moments, moments in which the eternal realm comes into contact with the temporal realm. Although discrete in narrative sequence, they are nevertheless linguistically embedded within one another. The intertextual link between these two sūras accentuates further the tension between the ascent and descent models of revelation even as it binds the two models together.

Another day-of-reckoning passage critical to the ascension accounts is in Q 52:1-10: "By the Mount [i.e. Mount Sinai]. By the book inscribed on rolls of parchment most fine. By the enlivened house *(al-bayt al-maʿmūr)*. By the roof raised high. By the sea boiled over. The pain of your lord will fall *(inna ʿadhāba rabbika la-wāqiʿ)*. None can ward it off. On a day the sky will sway and the mountains will slide." These verses are bound to the opening verses of Q 70 in that both contain a warning of the pain that will fall *(ʿadhāb wāqiʿ)* and cannot be kept away, and by their depiction of the mountains sliding on the day of reckoning. Such intertextual connections cluster around the term *al-bayt al-maʿmūr,* a term difficult to translate but which means the abode that is inhabited and, as such, enlivened. The two major uses of the term *bayt* in the Qurʾān are with little ambiguity attributed to the Kaʿba: *al-bayt al-ʿatīq* (the ancient abode) and *al-bayt al-ḥarām* (the sacred abode). The identity of "the enlivened house," mentioned only this one time in the Qurʾān, is not specified.

The commentary of al-Qurṭubī on "the enlivened house" (*Jāmiʿ*, xvii, 59-61) elaborates on the controversy among various exegetes over which heavenly sphere contains the house. The region above the seventh sphere just before the divine throne, the sixth sphere, the fourth sphere, and lowest sphere are among the candidates (see COSMOLOGY IN THE QURʾĀN). In each case, the enlivened house would be a celestial abode that corresponds to the Kaʿba, although some others claim that the term refers to the Kaʿba itself. For those who put the enlivened house in the world of the celestial spheres, the way is paved for a connection between the apocalypse (q.v.) — in which the house will be encountered on the day of reckoning — and Muḥammad's ascent, a preview of what is revealed on the day of reckoning. Once Muḥammad's ascent is accepted, then it would be as natural to find him encountering the enlivened house as it would be to find him encountering the lote tree or the rivers of paradise (al-Qurṭubī cites the proof par excellence for such an encounter from Muslim's *Ṣaḥīḥ*). Given the association of "the sacred place of prayer" with the origin of Muḥammad's journey, the links between sūras 52, 70 and 97 facilitate the identification of "the enlivened house" as its goal, particularly when the journey is seen as one of heavenly ascent, and provide a matrix of qurʾānic subtexts for the development and differing versions of the traditions about the ascension.

Finally, Q 94:1, "Did We not open your breast?" becomes the evidence for stories of the extraction of Muḥammad's heart and its purification in the waters of *zamzam* that parallel accounts of shaman-like preparatory practices in other cultures. Eventually, almost any aspect of qurʾānic language can be incorporated into the ascension tradition but the passages above form its core.

A passage from Muslim's *Ṣaḥīḥ* concerning the Prophet near the culmination of his ascent offers an example of how these passages are incorporated into the ascent narrative: "He [Abraham] was resting his back against the enlivened house (*al-bayt al-maʿmūr,* Q 52:4) into which seventy thousand angels would disappear each day, not to return. Then I was taken to the 'lote tree of the furthest boundary' (Q 53:14, *sidrat al-muntahā*). Its leaves were like the ears of elephants and its fruits were as large as jugs of clay. He said, When by the command of its lord 'the tree was enfolded' (Q 53:16) it was transformed. None of the creatures of God could describe its beauty. 'Then God revealed to me what he revealed'" (Q 53:10).

The ascension traditions expanded in length, complexity and cultural accretions throughout the medieval world in which traditions of heavenly ascent abounded. The number seventy thousand was standard in the ascent of Enoch stories, for example. In other cases, features of cosmology, both qurʾānic and extra-qurʾānic, associated with the creation were woven into the story of the ascension.

Muḥammad's ascent brought together the imagery of creation, revelation and the reckoning, the three major boundary moments of qurʾānic and extra-qurʾānic tradition. Examination of the relation of the ascension to extra-qurʾānic sources must be left to another occasion. Once the notion of the physical ascent was established, qurʾānic subtexts with strong intertextual bonds became a vehicle for exploring the tensions between the this-worldly vision and the end-of-time vision. Within the individual religions, the interreligiously symbolic cosmos of successive spheres or heavens became the site of contest among differing religions. The ascension was Islam's principle vehicle for expressing such a contest.

Within the Islamic tradition, these heavens also became the site of exploring the tension between revelation as sent down to earth and its retrieval by a prophet rising through the heavens. Both sets of tensions were at the core of the apocalyptic traditions that surrounded Islam and with which Islamic traditions of ascent were in increasing competition. They were adapted into the Ṣūfī tradition, both in the forms of paradigms of Ṣūfī experience and in Ṣūfī accounts of their own personal ascents. (For Bisṭāmī's ascent, see M. Sells, *Early Islamic mysticism*, 121-231, 242-50; for that of Ibn al-ʿArabī, see his *al-Futūḥāt al-makkiyya*, trans. M. Chodkiewicz, *Les illuminations*, 350-81.)

Just as the mosque retains its basic elements but reflects the culture in which it is built, the ascent traditions reflect the historical and cultural diversity, tensions and interactions of the classical Islamic world. A late pictoral representation of the ascension offers an example. Among the angels encountered by Muḥammad is an angel half of fire and half of ice, reflecting a dichotomy and experience that can be traced back to the world of 1 Enoch (Séguy, plate 10). The angels recite the *tasbīḥ* (Praise be to God!) in the same place that the angels in the Jewish Merkevah tradition recite the *qedusha*. Yet this angel in full lotus position reflects the cultural sphere of Buddhism, even as the facial features, dress and the bearing of this and other angels are Mongolian.

Michael Sells

Bibliography
Primary: al-Ghayṭī, Muḥammad b. Aḥmad, *Qiṣṣat al-isrāʾ wa-l-miʿrāj*, Cairo 1974, trans. A. Pavet de Courteille, *Miʿrāj-Nameh*, Paris 1882; Ibn ʿAbbās (attr.), *al-Isrāʾ wa-l-miʿrāj*, n.p. 1957; Ibn al-ʿArabī, *al-Futūḥāt al-makkiyya*, trans. M. Chodkiewicz et al., *Les illuminations de la Mecque*, Paris 1988, 350-81; id., *Kitāb al-Miʿrāj*, trans. R. Rossi Testa, *Il libro de la scala de Mahoma*, Milan 1991; Qushayrī, *Kitāb al-Miʿrāj*, ed. A. ʿAbd al-Qādir, Cairo 1994; Suyūṭī, *al-Āya al-kubrā fī sharḥ qiṣṣat al-isrāʾ*, Beirut 1985.
Secondary: M. Amir-Meozzi (ed.), *Le voyage initiatique en terre d'islam*, Louvain 1996; M. Asín Palacios, *La escatología musulmana en la Divina Comedia. Seguida de historia y crítica de una polémica*, Madrid 1919, 1961[3]; J. Bencheikh, *Le voyage nocturne de Mahomet*, Paris 1988; G. Böwering,

Miʿrāj, in *ER* ix, 552-6; H. Busse, Jerusalem in the story of Muhammad's night journey and ascension, in *JSAI* 14 (1991), 1-40; B. Schrieke et al., Miʿrādj, in *EI*², vii, 97-105; M.-R. Séguy, *The miraculous journey of Mahomet*, New York 1977; M. Sells, Sound, spirit, and gender in *sūrat al-qadr*, in *JAOS* 111 (1991), 239-59; id., *Early Islamic mysticism*, New York 1996.

Asceticism

The principles or practice of people who engage in rigorous self-discipline, abstinence and austerity for the sake of spiritual or intellectual discipline. The Arabic term *zuhd* — not found in the Qurʾān — has usually been translated as "asceticism" but would be better rendered as "renunciation of the world." Another Arabic word that does not appear in the Qurʾān, *nask* (also vocalized as *nusk* and *nusuk*), which designates the pious lifestyle of the hermit, is a closer equivalent of "asceticism." There is not much about asceticism in the Qurʾān, but a certain amount of attention is given to two key elements of the ascetic lifestyle, vigils (q.v.) and fasting (q.v.), while there are also brief mentions of a third, weeping (q.v.), and of monasticism (*rahbāniyya*, see MONASTICISM AND MONKS), which asceticism overlaps. By contrast, the Qurʾān does not advocate celibacy (see SEX AND SEXUALITY; ABSTINENCE), another key element of asceticism, but enjoins marriage (see MARRIAGE AND DIVORCE). Men are permitted the pleasures of sex with wives and slave-girls. The Qurʾān also rejects the idea that one should give all one's wealth away (Q 17:26-9). While almsgiving (q.v.) is enjoined, the absolute and voluntary poverty which is characteristic of asceticism is not recommended. However, the presence of Christian — and especially Syrian — asceticism in the historical background to the Qurʾān is undoubtedly important as are the vigils apparently observed by Muḥammad himself.

Background

In eastern Christianity, in the centuries before Muḥammad, one finds an extremely strong ascetic tradition. Notably, one encounters the "Sons of the Covenant," who were neither priests nor monks but pursued mortification of the flesh and devotional exercises. Celibacy, even within marriage, was particularly venerated. Although Egypt is supposedly the birthplace of Christian monasticism, abstention from food does not seem to have been more than moderate amongst Egyptian monastics. In Syria, however, the mortification of the flesh was more extreme: There were "browsers" who ate nothing but plants and wearers of heavy iron chains, alongside the celebrated "stylites," ascetics who lived on the tops of pillars for decades. Here laymen often retired into solitude to live like hermits for a time, and nightly vigils for prayer and recitation were particularly prominent. It is not clear how all of this would have had an influence on the Qurʾān. According to Christian sources, a large number of Arabs from northern Arabia came to the most famous of the stylites, St. Simeon Stylites (ca. 390-459 C.E.) and were converted by him (A. Vööbus, *History*, ii, 253-4). T. Andrae (*Mohammed*, 83-8) insists that Syrian Christian asceticism lies at the root of the Qurʾān's piety but K. Wagtendonk (*Fasting*, 129) sees this view as "certainly one-sided."

Muḥammad outside the Qurʾān

In assessing extra-qurʾānic materials that attribute ascetic practices or teachings to Muḥammad one comes up against the problems of the authenticity, historicity and reliability of the ḥadīth. Muḥammad is credited with advocating poverty and weeping (Wensinck, *Handbook*, q.v. "Poor" and "Weeping"). In general, however, the ḥadīths which have been collected that favor a renunciation of the world are often vague exhortations to a life of piety as opposed to specific recommendations of ascetic practices. By contrast, Muḥammad is said to have rejected both monasticism and the "wandering" *(siyāḥa)* characteristic of the Syrian anchorites (Wagtendonk, *Fasting*, 129-30). As regards Muḥammad's own practices, we are told that before his mission he would spend one month a year in seclusion on mount Ḥirāʾ (ibid., *Fasting*, 32-3). There he would engage in "the holding of pious exercises" (*taḥannuth*, a word again not found in the Qurʾān, and the exact meaning of which is not clear). Apparently asceticism as such did not exist as an indigenous Arabian phenomenon; fasting and other forms of abstinence existed only in particular rituals and as penance or as the result of specific vows but not as part of asceticism in the sense of a permanent way of life (cf. Wagtendonk, *Fasting*, 8, 31-40; and G. Hawting, Taḥannuth).

Muḥammad and vigils in the Qurʾān

In the Qurʾān itself Muḥammad is shown as engaging in vigils (Q 73:1-4, 20). Here the injunction to Muḥammad to keep awake for half the night is an echo of eastern Christian teachings. Similarly, the qurʾānic injunction for Muḥammad and his followers to recite the Qurʾān (see RECITATION OF THE QURʾĀN) during vigils also echoes Christian practices in which the recitation of the scriptures formed an important part of the vigil along with constant prostration. Here again, the Qurʾān's assertion that Muḥammad's true followers have marks on their faces as a result of their constant prostrating (Q 48:29) is an echo of a classic eastern Christian topos. The actual term for "keeping a vigil," *tahajjud*, occurs only once in the Qurʾān (Q 17:79). In Q 73:1-4 the command to keep a vigil and to recite the Qurʾān for about half the night is addressed to Muḥammad alone. In the same sūra (Q 73:20) we are informed that Muḥammad and some of his followers keep vigils for two-thirds, half or a third of the night. As there then ensues an obscure continuation, generally considered to be God's abrogation (q.v.) of his earlier command at the beginning of Q 73, this verse is said to have been revealed much later. God now gives a collective command to Muḥammad's followers to recite as much of the Qurʾān as they can easily manage, given their various difficulties (cf. Wensinck, Tahadjdjud). It is not clear, however, whether this collective command also includes Muḥammad himself; if it does not, then it does not require the hypothesis of abrogation and subsequent revelation since there is no contradiction with the initial individual command addressed to Muḥammad. In Q 76:26 Muḥammad is again told to prostrate himself to God and praise him through the night (see ADORATION; BOWING AND PROSTRATION). In Q 25:64 we are told that God's servants are those who spend the night prostrating themselves and standing in worship (q.v.) of him. In Q 17:79 the command to keep a vigil is again addressed to Muḥammad alone and it is explained that this is a "work of supererogation" *(nāfila)* for which Muḥammad may be rewarded with a glorious position in the hereafter (see REWARD AND PUNISHMENT). In Q 39:9 a rhetorical question asks whether someone who spends the night in worship, prostrating himself and standing up, in wariness as regards his fate in the next world and in hope of God's benevolence, is equal with someone who does not. In Q 3:113 we are told that among the People of the Book (q.v.) there are some good people who recite the scriptures and prostrate themselves all night long (see SCRIPTURE AND THE QURʾĀN). In Q 51:15-8 the righteous are depicted as being rewarded in heaven for having slept little at night and for praying at dawn and in Q 32:16 they are shown as forsaking their beds in order to pray in fear and in hope.

Fasting

Alongside the obligatory fast in the month of Ramaḍān (q.v.) and the examples of fasting prescribed as penance and acts of reparation or compensation (see ATONEMENT), supererogatory pious fasting is also mentioned in the Qurʾān (Q 9:112; 33:35; 66:5). In Q 9:112 and 66:5 the verb *sāḥa* is used to mean "fast" and here there is certainly an echo of the "wandering" *(siyāḥa)* of the Syrian Christian anchorites. As Wagtendonk observes, this verb is never used to designate the fast of Ramaḍān and it must designate supererogatory pious fasting as must the verb *ṣāma* in the comparable passage Q 33:35. In all three passages the context is that of the behavior of pious Muslims (see PIETY): They are obedient (see OBEDIENCE), persevering, humble, givers of alms, chaste (see CHASTITY), penitent, worshipping and also fasting (men and women in Q 33:35, potential wives of Muḥammad in Q 66:5 and fighters in the holy war in Q 9:112). However, this context cannot be seen as that of asceticism and the extreme fasting of ascetics cannot be intended. Thus *sāḥa,* in spite of its Syrian ascetic connotations, must here be used in a weaker sense of "supererogatory pious fasting" or "voluntary religious fasting" on a more moderate scale. As for the fast of Ramaḍān itself, it has its roots in Judaic penitential fasting but in the Qurʾān is associated with gratitude (Q 2:185; see GRATITUDE AND INGRATITUDE): it is a thank-offering (Wagtendonk, *Fasting,* 128-43).

Weeping

Weeping is an important aspect of both Christian and Islamic asceticism and, as F. Meier has pointed out (Bakkāʾ, 960), there is clear evidence of historical continuity between the two traditions, from the Coptic and Syrian monks, with Isaac of Nineveh in the seventh century C.E., to the "weepers" of early Islam. In the Qurʾān there are explicit references to weeping: The recitation of the Qurʾān itself causes people to weep (Q 17:109) and in the past the recitation of God's previous signs (q.v.) to true believers had the same effect (Q 19:58).

Monasticism

The Qurʾān's attitude to asceticism is probably best expressed in its specific mention of Christian monasticism (Q 57:27). Unfortunately, this verse is unclear and has been interpreted in different ways. It reads, "And in the hearts of those who followed him [i.e. Jesus], we put kindness and benevolence, and monasticism *(rahbāniyya)* — they instituted it — we did not prescribe it for them — out of desire to please God. But they did not observe it as they ought." Some exegetes take the view that here *rahbāniyya* is not one of the objects of God's "putting:" thus it would be of purely human origin. Other exegetes do see *rahbāniyya* as put in the hearts of Christians by God, and, thus, of divine origin but not prescribed for everyone and later perverted (cf. A.J. Wensinck, Rahbāniyya; McAuliffe, *Qurʾānic,* 263-81). The idea, in any case, seems to be that the extreme asceticism of Christian monasticism, however well-intentioned, is an unrealistic and impractical ideal and the monks have not lived up to it. This interpretation is supported by the Qurʾān's brief references to the Christian monks themselves: On the one hand, the Christians are closest to the Muslims because they have priests and monks (Q 5:82) but, on the other hand, the monks have become objects of worship and have amassed riches (Q 9:31-4).

Julian Baldick

Bibliography
T. Andrae, *Mohammed. The man and his faith*, London 1936; repr. London 1956; G.R. Hawting, Taḥannuth, in *EI*², x, 98-9; L. Massignon, Zuhd, in *EI*¹, iv, 1239-40; McAuliffe, *Qurʾānic;* F. Meier, Bakkāʾ, in *EI*², i, 959-61; A. Vööbus, *History of asceticism in the Syrian orient*, 3 vols., Louvain 1958-88; K. Wagtendonk, *Fasting in the Koran*, Leiden 1968; Wensinck, *Concordance*, q.v. *Bakā, Faqr, Faqīr, Ṣāma, Tahajjada, Taḥannatha;* id., *Handbook*, q.v. Fast, Fasting, Poor, Vigils, Weeping; id., Rahbāniyya, in *EI*¹, iii, 1103; repr. in *EI*², viii, 396-7; id., Tahadjdjud, in *EI*¹, iv, 607-8; repr. in *EI*², x, 97-8.

Ashes

The solid residue left when a material is burnt. The word "ashes" *(ramād)* occurs only once in the Qurʾān, in 14:18: "A similitude of those who have disbelieved in their Lord: Their actions will be like ashes swept away by a severe wind on a stormy day. They have no power over what they earned; it is this that is extreme misguidance." As the phrase "swept away by a severe wind on a stormy day" qualifies the ashes, it will be discussed here as well (see also AIR AND WIND). The point of the simile is that on the day of resurrection the disbelievers who had hoped to be saved on the strength of their supposedly good actions will be disappointed because these deeds will not avail them "just as no one can control ashes when [God] sends a wind against them on a blustery day" (Ṭabarī, *Tafsīr*, xiii, 198). The verse thus emphasizes the importance of grounding actions in faith and the utter futility of actions not so grounded, for the latter will not only be reduced to ashes, but these ashes themselves will be blown away and no trace of them will be left behind (Zamakhsharī, *Kashshāf*, ii, 298; Rāzī, *Tafsīr*, xix, 105; Quṭb, *Ẓilāl*, iv, 2094).

The qurʾānic use of the word *ramād* in the sense of wasted effort represents an older usage most likely derived from a nomadic lifestyle. The wind blowing away the ashes left by a campfire must have been a familiar sight to the dwellers of the desert (cf. Quṭb, *Ẓilāl*, iv, 2094). A proverb such as "Your brother roasted [meat] until it was cooked, but then threw ashes over it *(rammada)*" means that he spoiled the good he had done (cf. *Lisān al-ʿArab*, q.v. *r-m-d*, and Zamakhsharī, *Asās*, q.v. *r-m-d*). This particular usage appears to antedate the Qurʾān, as does this expression for destruction: "We arrived in this town and were reduced to ashes *(ramadnā)* in it" (Zamakhsharī, *Asās*, q.v. *r-m-d*). From a literary viewpoint, the Qurʾān's comparison of certain kinds of human actions to ashes is an instance of what the twentieth-century Egyptian theologian Sayyid Quṭb represents as the characteristic qurʾānic technique, corporealizing *(tajsīm)* abstractions *(al-Taṣwīr al-fannī fī l-Qurʾān)*.

Although the word "ashes" occurs only once in the Qurʾān and expresses wasted efforts, there are several instances in which other words and images are used to represent utter destruction in a similar eschatological context (see ESCHATOLOGY). God will turn the actions of the disbelievers into scattered dust motes (*habāʾan manthūran*, Q 25:23); the disbelievers will realize that their actions have been nullified. What they had regarded as water will turn out to be a mirage (Q 24:39). The wealth such people might have spent on good causes will become like a crop hit by a freezing cold wind (Q 3:117). The actions of someone who does somebody a favor and then reminds him of it will be washed away like the layer of dust on a rock (Q 2:264). Thus it may be seen that Q 14:18, with its mention of ashes, belongs to a larger category of verses. Indeed the concept of nullification of deeds is stated and explained in many places in the Qurʾān and all the above-mentioned verses and many others may be subsumed under that general concept. See also APOCALYPSE; RESURRECTION.

Mustansir Mir

Bibliography
Mir, *Dictionary;* Quṭb, *Ẓilāl;* id., *al-Taṣwīr al-fannī fī l-Qurʾān,* Cairo 1963; Rāzī, *Tafsīr;* Ṭabarī, *Tafsīr,* ed. A.S. ʿAlī, 30 vols., Cairo 1373/1954-1377/1957; Zamakhsharī, *Asās;* id., *Kashshāf.*

Ass see ANIMAL LIFE

Association see POLITICS AND THE QURʾĀN

Astray

To wander from a set path. *Ḍalla,* the root of which *(ḍ-l-l)* means "to err," "to go astray," "to lose one's way," is a ubiquitous and fundamental qurʾānic concept that appears 191 times in forty-seven derivatives of the Arabic verb. The best-known example is *al-ḍāllīn* "those who go astray," the final word in the opening sūra of the Qurʾān (Sūrat al-Fātiḥa, see FĀTIḤA). It is linked in the same sūra to a central qurʾānic theme "the straight way" *(al-ṣirāṭ al-mustaqīm).*

In pre-Islamic sources, the word *ḍalla* is employed primarily in discourse on mundane matters related to travel in the desert. With the advent of Islam and the growing influence of the Qurʾān on the Arabic language (q.v.), *ḍalla* assumed an array of moral and spiritual meanings related to the straight way. This concept, first encountered in Q 1:6, forms the basis of one of several religious dichotomies that characterize the qurʾānic worldview: the distinction between belief *(īmān)* and unbelief (*kufr,* see BELIEF AND UNBELIEF). In Sunnī sources, the straight way is interpreted as God's guidance *(hudā)* consisting of the Qurʾān and the exemplary words and practices of Muḥammad (q.v.). Humans respond to God's guidance either with belief — demonstrated by accepting God's guidance and adhering to the way *(ihtidāʾ)* — or with unbelief characterized by straying *(ḍalāl* or *ḍalāla),* the rejection of guidance and right conduct. Thus straying came to represent the harmful, base inclinations of human nature in the Qurʾān's dualistic moral conception.

The synonyms, correlatives and derivatives of *ḍalla* reflect its variant but related qurʾānic meanings. Synonyms include *ighwāʾ* (temptation, enticement to evil), *khusrān,* (spiritual deterioration, moral depravity) and *shaqāʾ* (misery, suffering). Among the chief causes of a person's going astray are Satan's desire to lead people astray (Q 4:60) and the natural, destructive appetites and passions of human nature (*ahwāʾ,* sing. *hawā,* Q 5:77; 6:56). The most prominent and exhaustively interpreted derivative is *al-ḍāllīn.* Classical Sunnī exegesis regularly identifies "those who have gone astray" *(al-ḍāllīn)* as the Christians who once possessed but subsequently lost true knowledge of the way. The famous commentator al-Ṭabarī (d. 310/923), however, points out that both Jews and Christians have incurred God's wrath and have gone astray in the same manner (*Tafsīr,* i, 189-95; see JEWS AND JUDAISM; CHRISTIANS AND CHRISTIANITY). Modern Sunnī commentators tend to interpret "those who have gone astray" more broadly, given the absence in the Qurʾān of specific reference to any particular religious group. For example, M. al-Shaʿrāwī, a famous contemporary Egyptian shaykh, states that *al-ḍāllīn* are people who do not know the way to where they want to go, who adopt any way of life other than God's and who thus become Satan's associate (*Tafsīr*, i, 90). Predictably, Shīʿī commentators identify "those who have gone astray" as those who do not recognize the spiritual primacy of the imām (q.v.). In mystical exegesis, spiritual seekers go astray if they fail to see the beauty and love of God in all things. See also ṢŪFISM AND THE QURʾĀN; SHĪʿISM AND THE QURʾĀN; EXEGESIS OF THE QURʾĀN.

Exegetical differences concerning going astray fueled debate in early Islamic theology on the question of indeterminism versus determinism (see FREEDOM AND PREDESTINATION). Some verses seem to affirm the principle of free will: "Those who receive guidance, do so for the good of their own souls. Those who stray, do so to their own loss" (Q 10:108); "Let him who will, believe. Let him who will, reject" (Q 18:29). Other verses appear to support the doctrine of God's causality: "For those whom God has led astray *(man yuḍlili llāh)*, never will you find the way" (Q 4:88); "God leads astray *(yuḍillu)* those whom he pleases and guides whom he pleases" (Q 14:4). Al-Ṭabarī deals with this controversy in his commentary on "those who have gone astray" in Q 1:7, first dismissing the conclusion that humans are free to choose their spiritual destiny and then affirming the traditional view that God is the cause of human action (*Tafsīr*, i, 195-7). The trend in modern commentary is to reconcile the apparent contradictions. ʿA. Yūsuf ʿAlī's commentary on Q 81:28-9 argues for a compromise position: "Both extremes, viz., cast-iron Determinism and an idea of Chaotic Free-will, are condemned" (*The holy Qurʾān*, ad loc.). M. Mir avers that according to Q 92:5-10 "God facilitates *(taysīr)* the doing of good actions for those who would perform them, and... he facilitates the doing of evil actions for those who would do such actions" (*Dictionary*, 79-80). M. Ṭanṭawī, the Shaykh of Sunnī Islam's al-Azhar University, holds that God gives humans only what they first choose for themselves: guidance for those who seek the straight path through God and misguidance for those who opt to go astray.

James A. Toronto

Bibliography
ʿA. Yūsuf ʿAlī (trans.), *The holy Qurʾān. English translation of the meanings and commentary*, Medina 1413/1992-3; A. ʿAṭiyyatullah, *al-Qāmūs al-Islāmī*, 5 vols., Cairo 1976; Mir, *Dictionary;* M. al-Shaʿrāwī, *Tafsīr al-Shaʿrāwī*, 10 vols., Cairo 1991; Ṭabarī, *Tafsīr*, 30 vols., Cairo 1954-7; M. Ṭanṭawī, interview with author, Cairo 1998.

Astronomy see COSMOLOGY IN THE QURʾĀN

Asylum see PROTECTION; OATHS

Atheism see POLYTHEISM AND ATHEISM

Atmospheric Phenomena see NATURAL WORLD AND THE QURʾĀN

Atom see SCIENCE AND THE QURʾĀN

Atonement

The act of making amends for an injury or an offense. The idea that acts, whether moral or ritual lapses, can be atoned or compensated for by other acts occurs on a number of occasions in the Qurʾān, but it does not seem possible to construct either a clear or complete doctrine of atonement on the basis of the qurʾānic references alone. In three passages, the act which atones, expiates or compensates is called a *kaffāra* (cf. the cognates in the other Semitic languages; see FOREIGN VOCABULARY), but there are other words used as well which are not easy to distinguish in sense.

Q 5:45 says that waiving, as an act of charity, one's right to retaliate for an injury or a death suffered is an atonement *(kaffāra)*. In this instance the idea seems to be that a voluntary meritorious act can atone for past sin. Here the commentators discuss whether the sin in question is that of the perpetrator or that of the one who waives his right to retaliate. In other passages the act of atonement appears to be undertood more as a compulsory consequence of a specified act or lapse.

Q 5:89 — where the word *kaffāra* occurs twice — sets out a choice of atonements in connection with oaths (q.v.): feeding ten poor people according to the normal level of the provision for one's own family, clothing them, emancipating a slave or fasting (q.v.) for three days. Commentators disagree whether the selected act atones for an oath which, for one reason or another, was not properly made *(al-laghw fī aymānikum)* or for an oath which was binding *(mā ʿaqqadtumu l-aymān)* but broken. In this connection it is questionable whether the idea of atonement for a sin (see SIN, MAJOR AND MINOR) or lapse actually applies since release from oaths which it was not desirable or possible to keep was a frequent and normal procedure.

Q 5:95 sets out three possible courses of action for someone who infringes the law by killing game *(ṣayd*, see HUNTING AND FISHING) while in the state of ritual consecration *(iḥrām)* of the pilgrim (see PILGRIMAGE). Such a person should provide a "compensation" *(jazāʾ*, see RECOMPENSE) in the form of a domestic animal comparable to the animal killed, to be brought as an offering *(hady*, see SACRIFICE) at the Kaʿba (q.v.); or he should make an "atonement" *(kaffāra)* by feeding an unspecified number of the poor or fasting for an unspecified period of time. These requirements are interpreted in qurʾānic commentary in ways which suggest no clear distinction between the idea of compensation and that of atonement. Some regard all three courses of action as equal in value so that the one who has killed an animal in a consecrated state may choose freely from among them (see CONSECRATION OF ANIMALS). Others regard the offering of an animal in compensation as preferable to the other two possibilities and thus perhaps see compensation as different in nature from atonement.

One possible distinction is that the compensation involves doing something comparable in kind to the sin: "As for [God's] saying, 'a compensation of livestock similar to what he killed,' he is saying that [the hunter] owes the equivalent and the reimbursement" *(wa-ammā qawluhu "fa-jazāʾun mithlu mā qatala min al-naʿami"* [Q 5:95] *fa-innahu yaqūlu wa-ʿalayhi kifāʾun wa-badalun*, Ṭabarī, *Tafsīr*, xi, 13). The idea that one can make up for having missed a duty by performing something similar in different circumstances occurs too without the word compensation *(jazāʾ)*. For example, in Q 2:184 it is said that someone who does not fast because he is sick or travelling might make up the missed days at a later time.

Another concept which seems to carry connotations of atonement is that of "ransom" *(fidya)*. Q 2:184 prescribes the feeding of a poor person or something more than that as a ransom *(fidya)* for someone who has failed to fast, and Q 2:196 asks for a ransom of fasting, charity or sacrifice from someone who has had to interrupt his pilgrimage.

Q 58:3-4 sets out a choice of acts required from a man who renounces sexual relations with his wife *(yuẓāhirūna min nisāʾihim)* by an oath known as *ẓihār* but then wished to retract it and resume sexual relations (see ABSTENTION). It is not clear whether the acts set out are a consequence of having made such an oath in the first place or are a condition of release from it. They are arranged not as equal alternatives but in descending order of acceptability: freeing a slave, fasting for two consecutive months, or feeding sixty poor people. Though the word "atonement" *(kaffāra)* is not used here, a connection with Q 5:89 seems obvious. Commentaries and works of Islamic law freely use "atonement" *(kaffāra)* when discussing the case.

The idea of atonement also occurs in Q 2:54 in connection with the story of the worship of the calf of gold (q.v.) by the Children of Israel (q.v.). The words of Moses (q.v.), "Kill yourselves," are understood as a command to the Israelites to atone to God for their sin. In commentary we are frequently told that the Israelites' subsequent fighting and killing one another was an atonement *(kaffāra)*. See also LAW AND THE QURʾĀN; REPENTANCE AND PENANCE.

Gerald R. Hawting

Bibliography
J. Chelhod, Kaffāra, in *EI*², iv, 406-7; D.S. Margoliouth, Expiation and atonement (Muslim), in *ERE*, v, 664; S.M. Zwemer, Atonement by blood sacrifice in Islam, in *MW* 36 (1946), 189-92.

Attributes of God see GOD AND HIS ATTRIBUTES

Augury see POPULAR AND TALISMANIC USES OF THE QURʾĀN

Authority

The right to act or command. The concept of authority is clearly attested in the Qurʾān but is not imparted by a single term or expression. The most common modern Arabic word for "authority," *sulṭa*, does not occur in the Qurʾān. Its cognate, *sulṭān*, does indeed occur there frequently, although solely as a verbal noun with an abstract sense. *Sulṭān* denotes mainly, according to the classical exegetes, "proof" or "argument"; it only occasionally seems to mean "authority," and even then mostly in association with "proof." Other terms which denote some form of authority are *quwwa* (power), *amr* (command), *ḥukm* (judgment or decision) and *mulk* (sovereignty, possession or power). With the exception of Q 4:59, which might hint at political authority, the authority with which the Qurʾān is concerned is essentially religious with credal, theological, legal, eschatological and moral implications.

There is no ambiguity whatsoever in the Qurʾān that all, full and absolute authority in the entire universe belongs to God and God alone. The Qurʾān thus keeps repeating: "To [God] belongs the sovereignty *(mulk)* of the heavens and the earth" (e.g. Q 5:40; 9:116). Although this authority does derive from God's singular and unique omnipotence, omnipresence and omniscience, it is essentially based on his being the creator of all things and on his holding supreme sway over their affairs in all matters, including the day of judgment (see LAST JUDGMENT). Thus one finds the strikingly simple "verily His is the creation and the command." (*a-lā lahu l-khalqu wa-l-amr*, Q 7:54). This makes God's relationship to his creatures one of sovereignty and ownership *(mulk)*, where he is "the lord of all being" (*rabb al-ʿālamīn*, e.g. Q 1:2) and his creatures are his servants and worshippers (*ʿibād, ʿabīd*, sing. *ʿabd*, e.g. Q 39:10). This relationship is one which all human beings accepted collectively before creation (q.v.) and which constituted the primordial and binding covenant (*mīthāq*, see COVENANT) between humankind and God (see ADAM AND EVE). It is binding for man until the day of judgment and man cannot deny being aware of it (Q 7:172). Accordingly, the Qurʾān emphasizes repeatedly the fundamental importance of man's obedience (*ṭāʿa*, see OBEDIENCE) to God (e.g. Q 3:50).

While the Qurʾān presents God as empowering both individuals and groups to perform extraordinary acts — e.g. Dhū l-Qarnayn (Q 18:83-98), Moses' (q.v.) companion (Q 18:60-82; see KHAḌIR/KHIḌR) and the people of ʿĀd (q.v.; Q 7:74) — such acts do not necessarily provide them with authority. In one case only does a verse come close to associating empowerment with authority. When God created Adam, he made him a vice-regent (*khalīfa,* see CALIPH) on earth, asked the angels to prostrate before him (Q 2:30-4; see ADORATION; ANGEL; BOWING AND PROSTRATION) and put the fruits of the earth at his service (e.g. Q 55:1-27). Nevertheless, in the Qurʾān the only area where God's authority is unambiguously and actually delegated to any creature is prophecy (see PROPHETS AND PROPHETHOOD).

According to the Qurʾān, God selected from among humankind a number of prophets and messengers (see MESSENGER) as guides to his way and warners against deviating from it (see WARNING). These messengers are provided by God, among other things, with power and authority supported by proof (*sulṭān,* Q 11:96; 4:144). The most paramount of these is a scripture (*kitāb,* see BOOK; SCRIPTURE AND THE QURʾĀN) which carries God's authoritative message (e.g. Q 2:29; 4:54, 113). Hence belief in it is a requirement of faith (q.v.; e.g. Q 2:177, 285; 3:84; see also BELIEF AND UNBELIEF). Most importantly, though, these prophets are fundamentally aware that their authority is not independently acquired, but is derived from God (e.g. Q 14:11). It is precisely because of this that they can demand obedience from others: "We sent no messenger save that he be obeyed by God's leave" (*wa-mā arsalnā min rasūlin illā li-yuṭāʿa bi-idhni llāh,* Q 4:64). This obedience to the prophets is given an elevated position in the Qurʾān and in the case of the Prophet Muḥammad it is coupled frequently with obedience to God, as in the repeated statement "Obey God and the messenger" (*aṭīʿū llāha wa-l-rasūl,* e.g. Q 3:32, 132). Indeed, obedience to the Prophet is equated once with obedience to God: "Whoever obeys the messenger obeys God" (*man yuṭiʿ al-rasūla fa-qad aṭāʿa llāh,* Q 4:80). In another significant verse (Q 4:59), the Qurʾān commands people to obey "those in charge among you" *(ulī l-amr minkum),* in addition to God and the Prophet.

Due to the nature of the topic and its manifestation in many contexts in the Qurʾān, the qurʾānic commentaries are of limited use, except where a particular verse (such as Q 4:59) is of direct relevance. The ambiguity of Q 4:59, as well as its potential political significance, made it subject to numerous interpretations, most of which reflect the opinions of the various theological and political groups in early Islamic society. The Sunnī groups identified "those in charge among you" variously as the Prophet's military commanders *(umarāʾ),* religious scholars *(ʿulamāʾ, fuqahāʾ),* the Prophet's Companions (see COMPANIONS OF THE PROPHET) or more specifically the Prophet's close associates and future caliphs Abū Bakr (q.v.; r. 11/632-13/634) and ʿUmar (q.v.; r. 13/634-23/644; see Ṭabarī, *Tafsīr,* viii, 495-502; Ibn al-Jawzī, *Zād,* ii, 116-7). The view that became prevalent, however, is that they are the actual rulers of the Muslim community *(al-umarāʾ wa-l-wulāt),* as al-Ṭabarī (d. 310/923) himself concludes (*Tafsīr,* viii, 502-5). The Shīʿīs, on the other hand, believe that "those in charge among you" are the infallible imāms (q.v.; *al-aʾimma min āl Muḥammad,* Ṭabarsī, *Tafsīr,* v, 138-9). Ṣūfīs tended to identify them as the Sufi saints (e.g.

Qu-shayrī, *Laṭāʾif,* ii, 36-7). See also IMĀM; SHĪʿISM AND THE QURʾĀN; ḤADĪTH AND THE QURʾĀN; ṢŪFISM AND THE QURʾĀN.

While divinely sanctioned authority is considered legitimate in the Qurʾān, authority unauthorized by God is not (Q 55:33). Accordingly seven out of the thirty-six verses containing the word *sulṭān* assert the falsehood of idols and other "gods," calling them merely "names" devised by people without God's proof, authority or authorization (e.g. Q 7:71), a matter which has credal implications (see IDOLS AND IMAGES; IDOLATRY AND IDOLATERS). Seven others decry the machinations of the devil (q.v.), declaring that he has authority only over the non-believers (e.g. Q 14:22), an issue which has some bearing on the theological question of indeterminism or determinism (*qadar,* see FREEDOM AND PREDESTINATION). On the moral level, the worldly authority of Korah (Qārūn, see KORAH) derived from his wealth (Q 28:76-82), that of Hāmān (q.v.) was due to his ambitious constructions (Q 28:38-9; 40:36-7); and that of Pharaoh (q.v.) was because of his powerful kingship (e.g. Q 7:75-92). All of these figures are condemned for the fault of arrogance (q.v.; cf. Q 7:146; 10:75). This authority is in any case ephemeral and these figures are eventually destroyed by God. In contrast, the right or authority *(sulṭān)* of an heir to retaliate when his relative is wrongfully slain is confirmed (Q 17:33; see BLOODSHED). This produced a legal rule that had political and ideological implications in early Islamic history.

Although obedience to God and his messengers is obligatory upon people, due to their original and derived sovereignty, respectively, history, according to the Qurʾān, is replete with instances of unlawful and hence sinful disobedience to them (see PUNISHMENT STORIES). The arch-disobedient figure in the Qurʾān is the devil, who first refused to prostrate himself before Adam (Q 2:34) and then pledged — and implemented his pledge — to lead humanity astray (q.v.; e.g. Q 7:16-22). The various peoples who refuse to heed and obey God's messengers are sometimes considered to have been led astray by the devil (e.g. Q 6:121), although more frequently no mention of the devil's machinations is made. In any case, those people are held accountable for their transgressions. Some are severely punished, as human history has repeatedly shown, and all are to be subject to eternal punishment on the day of judgment (e.g. Q 7:59-136).

Wadad Kadi (al-Qāḍī)

Bibliography

P. Crone and M. Hinds, *God's caliph,* Cambridge 1986 (concerned more with the title of the Muslim rulers and the nature of their power than with the original, qurʾānic concept); H. Dabashi, *Authority in Islam,* New Brunswick 1989, 8-9, 60; J. van Ess, L'autorité de la tradition prophétique dans la théologie muʿtazilite, in G. Makdisi et al. (eds.), *La notion d'autorité au moyen age,* Paris 1982, 211-26; J. Jomier, L'autorité de la révélation et la raison dans le commentaire du Coran de Faḫr al-Dīn al-Rāzī, in G. Makdisi et al. (eds.), *La notion d'autorité au moyen age,* Paris 1982, 243-61; M.J. Kister, Social and religious concepts of authority in Islam, in *JSAI* 18 (1994), 84-127, esp. 98-9 (also discusses the occurrences of the concept in the ḥadīth); J.H. Kramer and C.E. Bosworth, Sulṭān, in *EI²*, ix, 849f. (the first part is particularly informative of the developments of the term in classical Muslim society and history); C. Lindholm, *The Islamic Middle East. An historical anthropology,* Oxford 1996 (see particularly 139-50. Like many modern studies on authority in Islam, it sidesteps the qurʾānic conception of authority, being more interested in authority as a political or anthropological concept in Islamic history.); W. Madelung, Authority in Twelver Shiism in the absence of the imam, in G. Makdisi et al. (eds.), *La notion d'autorité au moyen age,* Paris 1982, 163-73; M. Plessner, Mulk, in *EI²*, viii, 546-7; U. Rubin, Apocalypse and authority in Islamic tradition, in *al-Qanṭara* 18 (1997), 11-33 (analyzes the structure of reports and their reference to the twelve imāms).

Avarice

Greed or cupidity. Avarice is a multifaceted vice that plays an important role in the Islamic assessment of human nature and behavior. Despite the existence of synonyms, the primary term for the vice is *bukhl*. The miser is a *bakhīl* (with the rare form of *bākhil*), plural *bukhalāʾ* (and more rarely *bukhkhāl*).

The pre-eminent role that avarice holds is but a counterpart to the importance of generosity, long considered a primary social virtue by the Arabs, even before the advent of Islam. Both the Qurʾān and the ḥadīth have much to say about avarice. Qurʾānic verses, both Meccan and Medinan (see CHRONOLOGY AND THE QURʾĀN), argue in favor of generosity and the giving of alms as well (see ALMSGIVING) and oppose the notion that one should accumulate one's wealth. Two examples will suffice. Q 3:180 lays this out clearly: "But as for those who are niggardly *(alladhīna yabkhalūna)* with the bounty God has given them, do not let them suppose it is better for them; rather it is worse for them; that which they were niggardly with *(mā bakhilū bihi)* they will have hung about their necks on the resurrection day" (see LAST JUDGMENT). Q 92:5-11 also says, "As for him who gives, is god-fearing and testifies to the best; we will certainly make the path to bliss smooth for him. But as for him who is a miser *(man bakhila),* and self sufficient and denies what is good, we will certainly ease his way to misery. His wealth will not avail him when he perishes."

Qurʾānic exhortations must be seen alongside the numerous ḥadīth of the Prophet in which avarice plays an important role. There, avarice takes its place in the garden of vices, sitting side by side with, among others, laziness and cowardice. The Prophet sought God's protection from these vices, carefully enumerating them one after another. Avarice is also transformed into a tool that can permit the elaboration of proverbial constructions. It becomes, for example, one of the trees of hell (q.v.), the branches of which hang over the world and whoever grabs one of the branches will be led by this branch to hellfire. The Prophet even asked if there was a disease worse than avarice. It should not be a surprise then that he declared, "An ignorant (*jāhil,* a loaded word implying ignorance of Islam; see AGE OF IGNORANCE) generous man is more beloved to God than an avaricious worshipper."

Despite these various denunciations, the miser has a special place in the Arab-Islamic cultural sphere. Anecdotal works — like the much-beloved *Kitāb al-Bukhalāʾ* of al-Jāḥiẓ (d. 255/869) or the work of the same title by al-Khaṭīb al-Baghdādī (d. 463/1071) — testify to the fact that the miser is a character type who can become the subject of anecdotes. As such he or she (there are female misers) testifies to an aspect of avarice that is almost denuded of any religious significance. Here, avarice becomes a major player in a cultural game of hospitality in which the guest reigns supreme. Nevertheless, the religious injunctions with their concomitant moral repugnance mean that the miser as anecdotal type is not as ludic as his anecdotal cousins, such as uninvited guests. The synonyms for avarice *(bukhl)* play an important role here, directing the concept towards the area of covetousness *(ḥirṣ)* or a more intense and generalized state of avarice *(shuḥḥ),* as well as lowness or meanness *(luʾm)*. See also VIRTUES AND VICES.

Fedwa Malti-Douglas

Bibliography
Jāḥiẓ, *Kitāb al-Bukhalāʾ*, ed. Ṭ. al-Ḥājirī, Cairo 1971; al-Khaṭīb al-Baghdādī, *Kitāb al-Bukhalāʾ*, ed. A. Maṭlūb, K. al-Ḥadīthī and A. al-Qaysī,

Baghdad 1964; F. Malti-Douglas, *Structures of avarice. The bukhalāʾ in medieval Arabic literature,* Leiden 1985; id., Structure and organization in a monographic *adab* work. *al-Taṭfīl* of al-Khaṭīb al-Baghdādī, in *JNES* 40 (1981), 227-45.

Āya see VERSES; SIGNS; FORM AND STRUCTURE OF THE QURʾĀN

Ayyūb see JOB

Āzar

Generally considered to be a name for the father of Abraham (q.v.) in the Qurʾān, the word *"āzar"* appears only in Q 6:74: "[Remember] when Abraham said to his father, Āzar, do you take idols as gods? I most certainly see you and your people clearly in error." Early commentators know the biblical name of Abraham's father, Teraḥ (Arabic Tāriḥ or Tārakh; cf. *Gen* 11:24-32) and therefore suggest three interpretations to reconcile the difference. The most widely cited considers the name Āzar as a second name for Abraham's father, but only a few explanations are provided: one suggests that Teraḥ's name in Arabic is Āzar, another that it was a title given to him after he became responsible for Nimrod's (q.v.) idols. A second interpretation is that Āzar is the name of an idol (see IDOLATRY AND IDOLATERS; IDOLS AND IMAGES), with the verse therefore meaning: "... Abraham said to his father: "do you take 'Āzar' as idols for gods?" (cf. N. Calder, Tafsīr from Ṭabarī to Ibn Kathīr, 102). A third explanation is that *āzar* is a disparaging epithet with which Abraham insults his father for remaining idolatrous even after having been warned by Abraham.

There is no evidence in early Arabic literature for the name Āzar, either applied to humans or gods, although the names al-ʿAyzār and al-ʿAyzāra (both with the letter *ʿayn*) are attested (cf. J. Horovitz, Jewish proper names, 157). Moreover, there is no evidence that the word *āzar* was considered an insult outside of the commentaries on this verse. It therefore appears that in this as in many other cases in the Qurʾān, the name is borrowed from a non-Arabic source and this has been the approach of orientalist scholarship (see FOREIGN VOCABULARY). One school (Jeffery, *For. vocab.,* 53-5) suggests that it derives from Eusebius' error of metathesis when, in writing the Septuagint, he wrote Thara (for Teraḥ) as Athar, in which form it entered the Islamic corpus (but with an unlikely phonetic switch from *th* to *z*). Another proposes that the word derives from the old Persian *ātar* (modern Persian *ādhar*) associated with the fire demon. The most widely-accepted view (J. Horovitz, Jewish proper names, 157; cf. S. Fraenkel, Miscellen, 72) is that the name derives from the Hebrew *Eliʿezer,* the name of Abraham's servant in *Gen* 15:2, with the eventual omission of the *el* after it was construed as the Arabic article *al* and with a lengthening of the vowel of the first syllable according to the Arabic pattern *afʿal* (likewise with Ādam). This, however, does not adequately explain the problem of the dropping of the *ʿayn* in the Arabic form, and it also suggests an inability among early Muslims to differentiate Abraham's father from his servant in the biblical account. Another possibility derives from a rabbinical homiletic interpretation of *Ps* 89:20: "I have conferred help upon a warrior (Heb. *shūwwītī ʿēzer ʿal gibbōr*)..." The Psalm references David but the rabbis also associate it with Abraham (M. Margalioth (ed.), *Midrash va-yikra rabah,* 1:4). Although not now attested, a typical rabbinical interpretive hermeneutic would easily render the verse: "I have made ʿĒzer (i.e. Teraḥ) [the father] of warrior Abraham," a fitting reference to *Gen* 14, with which the *midrash* associates the verse. By the period of late antiquity, the rabbis had lost the phonetic distinction between the Hebrew *ʿayin* and *aleph* and would easily have rendered *ēzer* as *ʾēzer* which, in Arabic, would become *āzar*.

Abraham's father is referenced elsewhere in the Qurʾān, although never by name. Although Abraham later disowned his father, in Q 9:114 (and again in 26:86), he is noted to have prayed for his idolatrous father's forgiveness. In Q 19:42-9, Abraham tries to dissuade his father from idolatry but to no avail and, even after being banished by his father, tells him that he will ask God's forgiveness on his behalf. In Q 21:51-71, Abraham rejects his father's and his people's idols and is punished with burning, but is saved by God. These themes are repeated in Q 11:69-104; 37:85-99; 43:26-8; and 60:4.

Reuven Firestone

Bibliography

Primary: Bukhārī, *Ṣaḥīḥ*, *Anbiyāʾ*, 8; Ibn Qutayba, *Kitāb al-Maʿārif*, Cairo n.d., 19-22; Ibn Saʿd, *Ṭabaqāt*, i, 21, 27; *Lisān al-ʿArab*, 15 vols., Beirut 1955-6, iv, 18-9; M. Margalioth (ed.), *Midrash va-yikra rabah*, 2 vols., New York/Jerusalem 1993; Māwardī, *Nukat*, ii, 134 (q.v. Q 6:74); Ṭabarī, *Tafsīr*, ad Q 6:74; id., *Taʾrīkh*, i, 217-25, 253-60; ʿUlaymī, *al-Uns al-jalīl bi-taʾrīkh al-Quds wa-l-Khalīl*, ed. Abū al-Yaman Mujīr al-Dīn al-Ḥanbalī, 2 vols., Amman 1973, i, 24; Zamakhsharī, *Kashshāf*, ii, 29-30 (q.v. Q 6:74).

Secondary: N. Calder, Tafsīr from Ṭabarī to Ibn Kathīr. Problems with the description of a genre, in Hawting and Shareef, *Approaches*, 102-3; S. Fraenkel, Miscellen zum Koran, in ZDMG 56 (1902), 72; J. Horovitz, Jewish proper names and derivatives in the Koran, in *Hebrew Union College Annual* 2 (1925), 157; id., KU 85-6; A. Jeffery, Āzar, in EI^2, i, 810; id., *For. vocab.*, 53-5.

B

Baal

Baal *(baʿl)* is both a proper name of a pre-Islamic pagan deity worshipped by the people to whom the messenger Elijah (q.v.) was sent (Q 37:125) and a common noun meaning "husband" (Q 2:228; 4:128; 11:72; 24:31).

Baal as a pagan deity

The biblical prophet Elijah (*1 Kings* 17-22; *2 Kings* 1-2) is mentioned two times in the Qurʾān (Q 6:85; 37:123-30). He was sent to turn his people from the worship of the deity Baal. Commentary elaborates on the brief qurʾānic passages. It is said that, during the reign of the Israelite king Ahab (r. ca. 873-851 B.C.E.), Elijah attempted to turn the Children of Israel (q.v.) away from the false worship of Baal and asked God to give him power over the rain. That granted, Elijah caused a three-year drought during which time he concealed himself. This torment failed to divert the Israelites from their paganism, so Elijah prayed to be taken into heaven. There he was transformed into a heavenly being made up of light. The story of Elijah's control over the rain may possibly survive in the common modern use of the Arabic word *baʿl* in the sense of unirrigated land and plants relying exclusively on natural water. Some scholars see a parallel to the ancient Mesopotamian god Baal and his three daughters in the Meccan belief that the goddesses al-Lāt, Manāt, and al-ʿUzzāʾ were the daughters of God (Q 53:19-23). See also IDOLS AND IMAGES; PRE-ISLAMIC ARABIA AND THE QURʾĀN.

Baal as a common noun

The word *baʿl* is used four times in the Qurʾān as a common noun meaning husband, twice in the singular (Q 4:128; 11:72) and twice in the plural (*buʿūla,* Q 2:228; 24:31). In this sense, the word finds parallels in the northwest Semitic languages, in which the root bears the basic sense of "owner," one of the characteristics of the deity with that name in Canaanite mythology.

Gordon Darnell Newby

Bibliography

C.H. Gordon, The daughters of Baal and Allah, in *MW* 33 (1943), 50-1; G.D. Newby, *The making of the last prophet,* Columbia, SC 1989; A.J. Wensinck, Ilyās, in *EI²,* iii, 1156.

Bābil see BABYLON

Babylon

The renowned ancient Mesopotamian city. Babylon *(Bābil)* is mentioned once in the Qurʾān: "And follow what the devils used to recite in the reign of Solomon (q.v.). Solomon did not disbelieve, but the devils disbelieved, teaching the people magic and what had been sent down to the two angels, Hārūt and Mārūt (q.v.), in Babylon. They do not teach anyone without first saying, 'We are only a temptation, so do not disbelieve'" (Q 2:102).

According to the geographer and biographer Yāqūt (d. 626/1228), Babylon constituted an entire region famed for its magic and wine (*Buldān,* i, 309-11). The commentators are unanimous in their agreement that Babylon is a place in Mesopotamia, although they do not identify it as an ancient Akkadian city. Islamic tradition states that Noah (q.v.) settled in Babylon after the deluge and expanded it and that the Chaldeans served him as soldiers there. According to some commentators, Hārūt and Mārūt were two fallen angels (see ANGEL) condemned to live in Babylon as prisoners, where they devoted themselves to magic. Many legends about these angels are found in the classical qurʾānic commentaries (summarized in A. Khoury, *Der Koran,* ii, 77-9; Horovitz, *KU,* 146-8; M. Ayoub, *The Qurʾān,* i, 130-6; see also MAGIC, PROHIBITION OF).

Relying on the Qurʾān, the Muslim storytellers familiar with biblical lore connected Babylon and the Bible. Of special interest are the tales concerning Babylon in the oldest collections (see R. Khoury, Babylon, 123f.; id., *Les légendes,* 223-84). These contain a description of the prophet Jonah's (q.v.) encounter with the whale, his return to his people and the designation of Isaiah (q.v.) as his successor (R. Khoury, *Les légendes,* 223-37). The main Babylonian kings are then treated. Sennacherib (ibid., 237-50), ruling from Nineveh, is the first king of Babylon to be mentioned. He led into Palestine an army of "six hundred thousand banners," each representing a thousand warriors, which was defeated as the prophet Isaiah had prophesied. The story of Nebuchadnezzar is of more interest because it covers the fall of Jerusalem and the deportation of Daniel with the other Jewish captives. They are liberated when Daniel interprets the king's dream (ibid., 250-79).

Such early tales circulated first orally and were gradually written down in the second/eighth century. They may be viewed as elaborate commentaries on the qurʾānic material, taken primarily from Jewish and Christian converts — who knew more about this subject than the pagan Arab converts did — to explain the biblical elements in the Qurʾān. The historian and philosopher Ibn Khaldūn (d. 808/1406) mentions the necessity of relying on these sources, while condemning their overuse in the commentaries (see R. Khoury, Ibn Khaldūn, 197-8; id., Babylon, 142f.). In any case, the tales about Babylon belong to a common historical tradition and stories of this sort should be considered important sources for ancient history, especially when other information is lacking. The work of H. Schwarzbaum illustrates how useful such material can be in elucidating certain aspects of the biblical tradition (*Biblical legends,* 10f., 21f.; for the present topic, see 46f., esp. 57f.; see also SCRIPTURE AND THE QURʾĀN).

R.G. Khoury

Bibliography

Primary: R.G. Khoury (ed.), *Wahb B. Munabbih. 1. Der Heidelberger Papyrus PSR Heid Arab 23,* Wiesbaden 1972; Ṭabarī, *Tafsīr,* i, 359-66; Yāqūt, *Buldān.*

Secondary: G. Awad, Bābil, in *EI²,* i, 846; M. Ayoub, *The Qurʾān and its interpreters,* 2 vols., i,

130-6; Horowitz, *KU*; Jeffery, *For. vocab.*, 74-5; A.Th. Khoury, *Der Koran. Arabisch-Deutsch Übersetzung und wissenschaftlicher Kommentar*, Gütersloh 1991f., ii, 76-79; R.G. Khoury, Babylon in der ältesten Version über die Geschichte der Propheten im Islam, in G. Mauer and U. Magen (eds.), *Ad bene et fideliter seminandum. Festgabe für K. Deller zum 21. Februar 1987*, Neukirchen-Vluyn 1988, 123-44; id., *Les légendes prophétiques dans l'Islam depuis le Ier jusqu' au IIIe siècle de l'Hégire*, Wiesbaden 1978, 237-43; id., Ibn Khaldūn et quelques savants des deux premiers siècles islamiques, in *JSAI* 10 (1987), 192-204; H. Schwarzbaum, *Biblical and extra-biblical legends in Islamic folk-literature*, Walldorf-Hessen 1982.

Badr

The site of Islam's first major military victory which occurred in the month of Ramaḍān (q.v.) in the second year after Muḥammad emigrated from Mecca to Medina (March 624, see EMIGRATION). Badr is mentioned explicitly only a single time in the Qur'ān (Q 3:123), but there are allusions to it in at least thirty-two other verses. Almost all of these references are found in the eighth sūra, "The Spoils" (Sūrat al-Anfāl), which addresses the issues that arose as a direct consequence of this Muslim victory and stresses above all the spiritual gains that gave Islam its firm foundations.

Badr, also known as Badr Ḥunayn, was at the time a small settlement with water wells on the Arabian peninsula near the Red Sea coast, lying some one hundred and fifty kilometers southwest of Medina and more than three hundred kilometers northwest of Mecca. The encounter between the Muslims from Medina and their pagan Meccan foes was occasioned by the return of a Meccan caravan. One of the Prophet's archenemies, Abū Jahl, led the Meccan forces sent to defend the caravan. At Badr, the Prophet together with little over three hundred of his followers met Abū Jahl and his army of approximately one thousand. Despite the disparity in numbers, the Muslim force emerged victorious over the Meccans, who reportedly had not known defeat for generations. Abū Jahl and a number of other prominent Meccan leaders lost their life and many prisoners and the caravan's cargo were captured as well.

The basic theme of the qur'ānic allusions to the victory of Badr is God's unmistakable vindication of Islam. The Prophet prayed for deliverance and received clear signs of God's grace (Q 8:7, 9), causing the Muslims to fight with even greater conviction. God himself aided the Prophet's forces (Q 8:17), sending a thousand angels to help (Q 8:9, 12). God's direct intervention signified his confirmation of Islam and set the Islamic community (see COMMUNITY AND SOCIETY IN THE QUR'ĀN) apart from all others. In particular, the identification of the battle with the "Day of the Criterion" (*yawm al-furqān*, Q 8:41; see CRITERION) signaled the distinction between right and wrong which the battle of Badr had wrought.

Badr reflects other motifs as well. God tested his servants (Q 8:17; 33:11). Humankind must fear God and be grateful to him since, in spite of the small size of the Muslim force, he gave them victory (Q 3:123; see GRATITUDE AND INGRATITUDE). God also provided clear insight — i.e. the distinction between truth and falsehood — when he caused it to rain before the battle (Q 8:11), thereby aiding the Muslims (see HIDDEN AND THE HIDDEN).

The battle of Badr took place just after Muḥammad had broken with the Jewish tribes in Medina and the direction of the ritual prayers had been changed from Jerusalem to Mecca (see QIBLA). Thanks primarily to this triumph, the Prophet and his followers became even more assured of the righteousness of their cause. Furthermore, it consolidated their break with the pagan Meccans and their creation of an independent community of believers. Later generations viewed the Muslims who fought in this battle with special reverence. See also EXPEDITIONS AND BATTLES.

John Nawas

Bibliography
Primary: Ibn Isḥāq, *Sīra*, ii, 606-iii, 43, Ibn Isḥāq-Guillaume, 289-360; Ṭabarī, *Taʾrīkh*, i, 1281-1359, trans. M.V. McDonald, *History of al-Ṭabarī, vii. The foundation of the community*, 25-85 (with annot. by W.M. Watt).
Secondary: G.H.A. Juynboll, Fighting angels, in *Ohio journal of religious studies* 2 (1974), 85-7; A. Kherie, *Index-cum-concordance for the holy Qurʾān*, Delhi 1992, 986-7; A.D. al-ʿUmari, *Madinan society at the time of the Prophet*, 2 vols., Herndon 1991, ii, 31-47; W.M. Watt, Badr, in *EI*², i, 867-8; id., *Muhammad at Medina*, Oxford 1956, 10-6; Watt-Bell, 145-7.

Bahāʾīs

The adherents of Bahāʾism *(ahl al-Bahāʾ)*, widely recognized as the "Bahāʾī Faith," an independent world religion with Islamic origins. The Bahāʾī movement, a universalization of Bābism, was founded by Mīrzā Ḥusayn ʿAlī Nūrī (1817-92), known as Bahāʾullāh (Splendor of God; standardized Bahāʾī spelling, Bahāʾullāh), in Baghdad in the year 1863. In 1866, it emerged as a distinct faith-community in Adrianople (Edirne). Bahāʾism underwent transformations in ethos and organization throughout three missionary phases: the Islamic context (1844-92), the international missions (1892-1963) and global diffusion (1963-present). The Islamic context was co-extensive with the combined ministries of Bahāʾullāh and his precursor, Sayyid ʿAlī Muḥammad Shīrāzī (1819-50), known as the Bāb (Gate), the prophet-martyr of the Bābī movement.

The year 1260/1844 marked the Shīʿī millennium, a thousand lunar years since the occultation of the twelfth imām (see IMĀM; SHĪʿISM AND THE QURʾĀN). On 22 May 1844 the Bāb effected a decisive, eschatological break from Islam by means of an exegetical work entitled *The immortal renovator of the divine names (Qayyūm al-asmāʾ*, often referred to as *The commentary on the Joseph sūra)*, an audacious and revolutionary commentary on the twelfth sūra of the Qurʾān (see JOSEPH). In this work he "proclaimed himself the focus of an Islamic apocalypse" (T. Lawson, Structure, 8). One of his most distinctive exegetical techniques is his "exploded commentary." In works on Q 108 and Q 103, the exegesis proceeds "not only verse by verse, or even word by word, but also letter by letter" (T. Lawson, Dangers, 179). The Bāb's commentaries on the Qur-ʾān are remarkable in that, by force of his prophetic authority, "interpretation became revelation" (T. Lawson, Interpretation, 253). In 1848, he revealed a new law code *(bayān-i fārsī)*, paradoxically super-Islamic in piety, yet supra-Islamic in principle.

After the Bāb's execution (1850) by the Persian authorities, Bahāʾullāh revitalized the Bābī community by employing symbolic interpretation as strategy to abolish the Bābī antinomianism. In the Arabic *Tablet of "all food"* (*Lawḥ-i kull al-ṭaʿām*, 1854 — note that the titles of Bahāʾi works written in Arabic are conventionally given in Persianized form), Bahāʾullāh related the abolishment of the Jewish dietary restrictions in Q 3:93 to the mystical and cosmological realms. While the Baghdad period (1853-63) was eschatologically charged with his own messianic secrecy *(ayyām-i buṭūn)*, Bahāʾullāh, in his pre-eminent doctrinal work, the *Book of certitude* (*Kitāb-i Mustaṭāb-i īqān*, Jan. 1861), advanced an extended qurʾānic and biblical argument to authenticate the Bāb's prophetic credentials. Bahāʾullāh's repertoire of exegetical techniques includes most of the twelve "procedural devices" attested in the classical commentaries (Wansbrough, *QS*, part ii) as well as others. Bahāʾullāh's style of discourse is itself exegetical, with frequent pairings, linked by the Persian metaphorical genitive *(iḍāfa-yi majāzī)*, of qurʾānic symbols and referents. Hermeneutically, *Certitude* resonates with five Islamic orientations to symbolism: 1. the semanticism of rhetoric, especially the science of tropes *(ʿilm al-bayān)*; 2. the dialectic of theology *(kalām)*; 3. reason *(ʿaql)* and analogy *(qiyās)* as a reflex of philosophy *(falsafa)* and jurisprudence *(fiqh)*; 4. the use of allusion *(ishāra)* and gnosis *(maʿrifa qalbiyya)* in Ṣūfī/Ishrāqī mysticism (see ṢŪFISM AND THE QURʾĀN); 5. recourse to apocalyptic presentism, adducing prophetic prooftexts to instantiate a realized eschatology, a common characteristic of millenarian sectarianism. In his *Commentary on the sūra "By the sun" (Tafsīr sūrat wa-l-shams)*, while critical of rhetoric *(ʿilm al-balāgha)* and the cognate qurʾānic sciences, Bahāʾullāh echoes al-Ghazālī (d. 505/1111) and al-Taftazānī (d. 791/1389) in stressing the need to harmonize literal and figurative interpretations (C. Buck, *Symbol*, 91-2, 104). In his *Tablet on esoteric interpretation (Lawḥ-i taʾwīl)*, citing Q 3:5, he states that eschatological verses are properly susceptible to esoteric interpretation *(taʾwīl)* whereas qurʾānic laws are to be understood by their obvious sense (*tafsīr*, see EXEGESIS OF THE QURʾĀN: CLASSICAL AND MEDIEVAL).

Islamic prophetology is anchored in the received interpretation of Q 33:40, which is widely believed to establish Muḥammad as the final prophet (see PROPHETS AND PROPHETHOOD). In what is perhaps his most significant exegetical maneuver, Bahāʾullāh relativizes that claim in order to supersede it, refocusing the reader's attention a mere four verses later (Q 33:44) on the eschatological attainment to the presence of God *(liqāʾ Allāh)* on the last day (see ESCHATOLOGY). Arguing that direct beatific vision of God is impossible, Bahāʾullāh reasons that Q 33:44 anticipates a future theophany who, as *deus revelatus* and divine vicegerent, is symbolically God by proxy.

By force of explicative logic, *Certitude* — arguably the world's most-widely-read non-Muslim qurʾānic commentary — served as an advance prophetic warrant for Bahāʾullāh, who on 22 April 1863 declared himself "He whom God shall manifest" *(man yuẓhiruhu llāh)*, the messianic theophany foretold by ʿAlī Muḥammad. In public epistles to Queen Victoria, Napoleon III, Pope Pius IX and other world leaders during the Adrianople and ʿAkkā (Haifa) periods (1864-92), Bahāʾullāh proclaimed himself the advent of the millenarian "Promised One" of all religions — a "multiple-messiahship" (C. Buck, *Unique*, 158), i.e. the Zoroastrian Shāh Bahrām Varjāvand, the Jewish Everlasting Father (*Isa* 9:6)/Lord of Hosts, the Christian Spirit of Truth, the Shīʿī al-Ḥusayn *redivivus* and the Sunnī return of Christ (see APOCALYPSE).

As "the world-reformer," Bahāʾullāh advocated world peace, parliamentary democracy, disarmament, an international language, the harmony of science and religion, interfaith concord as well as gender and racial equality. From a historicist perspective, Bahāʾī principles represent modernist universalizations of Islamic canons, transcending the traditional believer/infidel dichotomy (see BELIEF AND UNBELIEF). In precocious religious preparation for a global society, Bahāʾullāh's signal contribution was to sacralize certain secular modernist reforms within an irreducibly original paradigm of world unity in which peace is made sacred. By designating his son ʿAbdu l-Bahāʾ (Servant of the Bahāʾ, d. 1921) as interpreter, exemplar and successor and by establishing elected councils, Bahāʾullāh instituted his Covenant, symbolized as "the Crimson Ark" (C. Buck, *Paradise,* ch. 5). This is the organizing principle of the Bahāʾī community and the means to safeguard its integrity against major schism. Succeeding ʿAbdu l-Bahāʾ in 1921 as "Guardian" of the Bahāʾī faith, Shoghi Effendi (d. 1957) globalized and evolved the Bahāʾī administration as a system of local and national Spiritual Assemblies. This led in 1963 to the establishment of the Universal House of Justice, the international Bahāʾī governing body, on Mount Carmel in Haifa, Israel.

While granting the Bible's divine inspiration, Bahāʾīs regard the Qurʾān as the sole world scripture which, apart from the Bahāʾī canon, qualifies as pure revelation. Sacred, but not central, the Qurʾān nonetheless profoundly enriches the Bahāʾī scripture as a revelation within a revelation and is essential to its study. Qurʾānic vocabulary, ideology and motifs, as well as a plethora of citations and allusions and even the use of rhymed prose similar to that in the Qurʾān (see RHYMED PROSE), inform and suffuse the other Bahāʾī scriptures. ʿAlī Muḥammad's earliest works exhibit a conscious effort to extend and amplify a qurʾānic voice, a crucial warrant of revelation. Bahāʾullāh's commentaries include *Commentary on the mysterious letters* (*Tafsīr-i ḥurūfāt-i muqaṭṭaʿa;* see LETTERS AND MYSTERIOUS LETTERS), which incorporates a discourse on the Light Verse (Q 24:35); *Commentary on "He is" (Tafsīr-i Hū[wa])* and *Essences of the mysteries (Jawāhir al-asrār).*

Christopher George Buck

Bibliography

Primary: ʿAlī Muḥammad, *Tafsīr sūrat al-ʿaṣr,* Cambridge, Browne Or. Ms. F. 9 (6); id., *Tafsīr sūrat al-kawthar,* Cambridge, Browne Or. Ms. F. 10 (19); id., *Tafsīr sūrat Yūsuf (Qayyūm al-asmāʾ),* Cambridge 1891; Mīrzā Nūrī, *Alvāḥ-i mubāraka-yi ḥaḍrat-i Bahāʾ Allāh,* ed. Mishkīn-Qalam, Bombay 1310; id., *Kitāb-i Mustaṭāb-i īqān* [in Persian], Hofheim-Langenhain 1980, trans. S. Effendi, *The book of certitude,* Wilmette 1931; id., *Lawḥ-i kull al-ṭaʿām,* in *Iran national Bahāʾī archives,* xxxvi (private printing), 268-77; id., *Tafsīr-i ḥurūfāt-i muqaṭṭaʿa* (also known as *Lawḥ-i āya-yi nūr*), in ʿA.H. Ishraq-Khavari (ed.), *Māʾida-yi āsamānī,* Tehran 1973, iv, 49-86 (unreliable); id., *Tafsīr sūrat wa-l-shams* [in Arabic], in M.D. Ṣabrī (ed.), *Majmūʿa-yi alvāḥ-i mubāraka-yi ḥaḍrat-i Bahāʾullāh,* Cairo 1920, 2-17.

Secondary: A. Amanat, *Resurrection and renewal. The making of the Bābī movement in Iran,* 1844-1850, Ithaca 1989; C. Buck, A brief description of the *Kitāb-i Īqān,* in *Occasional papers in Shaykhī, Bābī and Bahāʾī studies* 2 (1998); id., *Paradise and paradigm. Key symbols in Persian Christianity and the Bahāʾī faith,* Albany 1999; id., *Symbol and secret. Qurʾān commentary in Bahāʾullāh's Kitāb-i Īqān,* Los Angeles 1995; id., A unique eschatological interface. Bahāʾullāh and cross-cultural messianism, in *Studies in Bābī and Bahāʾī history* 3 (1986), 156-79; J. Cole, *Bahāʾullāh's commentary on the sūra of the sun,* in *Bahāʾī studies bulletin* 4 (1990), 4-27; id., A tablet by Bahāʾullāh on the figurative interpretation of scripture *(Lawḥ-i Taʾwīl),* in *Translations of Shaykhī, Bābī and Bahāʾī texts* 1 (1997); id., *Modernity and the millennium. The genesis of the Bahāʾī faith in the nineteenth century Middle East,* New York 1998; S. Lambden, A tablet of Mīrzā Ḥusayn ʿAlī Bahāʾullāh, in *Bahāʾī studies bulletin* 3 (1984), 4-67; T. Lawson, Interpretation as revelation. The Qurʾān commentary of Sayyid ʿAlī Muḥammad Shīrāzī, in Rippin, *Approaches,* 223-5; id., The terms "remembrance" *(dhikr)* and "gate" *(bāb)* in the Bāb's commentary on the sūra of Joseph, in *Studies in Bābī and Bahāʾī religions* 5 (1988), 1-63; id., The structure of existence in the Bāb's *tafsīr* and the Perfect Man motif, in *Bahāʾī studies bulletin* 6 (1992), 4-25; id., The dangers of reading, in M. Momen (ed.), *Scripture and revelation,* Oxford 1997; id., Reading reading itself. The Bāb's "Sūra of the bees," in *Occasional papers in Shaykhī, Bābī and Bahāʾī studies* 1 (1997); D. MacEoin, *The sources for early Bābī doctrine and history,* Leiden 1992; P. Smith, *The Babi and Bahaʾi religions,* Cambridge 1987; H. Taherzadeh, *Selections from the writings of the Bāb,* Haifa 1978; Wansbrough, *QS.*

Baḥīra see IDOLS AND IMAGES

Balance see ESCHATOLOGY

Banū Isrāʾīl see CHILDREN OF ISRAEL

Baptism

The practice of using water for religious purification, while a ritual feature in a number of religions, is often most closely identified with Christianity. There is one possible reference in the Qurʾān to baptism, Q 2:138: "The baptism *(ṣibgha)* of God and who is better than God in terms of baptizing *(ṣibghatan)?*" The term *ṣibgha*, however, usually refers to "color" or "dye" and it is not absolutely clear how the word has come to be understood as a reference to baptism. English translations of the Qurʾān reflect this ambiguity, with G. Sale, J.M. Rodwell, A.J. Arberry, K. Cragg and ʿA. Yūsuf ʿAlī rendering *ṣibgha* as "baptism." Preferring some reference to color or dye (see COLORS), M. Pickthall and A. Mawdudi translate it as "color," N.J. Dawood as "dye" and M. Asad as "hue." R. Bell gives "savour," focusing on a slightly different metaphor, that of taste. Bell comments that "the exact meaning of the word is uncertain" (Bell, i, 18).

Muslim commentaries on the Qurʾān display a similar range of understanding. Al-Ṭabarī (d. 310/923) takes *ṣibgha* as a synonym for *milla*, which occurs three verses earlier with the sense of "religion:" "Follow the religion of God, which is the best religion" (*Tafsīr*, iii, 18). For his part, al-Ṭabarsī (d. 548/1153) interprets it as the faith which is inculcated into children, so that the Jews give their children the *ṣibgha* of Judaism and the Christians give their children the *ṣibgha* of Christianity, the true *ṣibgha* being Islam (*Majmaʿ*, i, 492-3; cf. Q 3:19). Al-Wāḥidī (d. 468/1076), by contrast, takes the verse to be an explicit reference to the Christian custom of immersing a child in water seven days after its birth in order to purify it, a replacement for circumcision (*Asbāb*, 38). Similarly, al-Qurṭubī (d. 671/1273) suggests that *ṣibgha* refers to the ritual bath which must be taken by those who wish to enter into Islam, equating it with the major ablution (*ghusl*, *Jāmiʿ*, ii, 144-5; see CLEANLINESS AND ABLUTION; RITUAL PURITY). Among the modern commentators, Asad (*Message*, 28), following al-Ṭabarī, takes the term as referring to "creed" in general, while Mawdudi (*Towards understanding*, i, 117-8) sees the verse as commending the adoption of the color of God which comes from service and devotion to God rather than from any bathing or immersion: "Of what use is this formal baptism?"

Perhaps the most plausible explanation for the double meaning of the term comes from ʿA. Yūsuf ʿAlī who, building upon al-Bayḍāwī (d. ca. 700/1300) and al-Suyūṭī (d. 911/1505), speculates in a footnote to his translation that "apparently the Arab Christians mixed a dye or colour in the baptismal water, signifying that the baptized person got a new colour in life" (*Holy Qurʾān*, 56, n. 137). Bell, on the other hand, notes that *ṣibgha* has frequently been derived from the Syriac *ṣbaʿ*, meaning "to baptize" (see FOREIGN VOCABULARY), but comments that this is not the usual word for "to baptize" in Syriac and suggests that an Arabic usage referred to by E. Lane, i.e. a girl who is brought into the household of someone, is preferable (*Commentary*, i, 27). Perhaps M. Watt's careful conclusion is therefore best: "While the verse could possibly mean that God gives a man a certain colour when he serves him, it is better to regard its interpretation as uncertain." He adds, "It is doubtful if there is any reference to Christian baptism" (*Companion*, 31). See also CHRISTIANS AND CHRISTIANITY.

Hugh Goddard

Bibliography
Primary: Qurṭubī, *Jāmiʿ*; Ṭabarī, *Tafsīr*; Ṭabarsī, *Majmaʿ*; Wāḥidī, *Asbāb*.

Secondary: ʿA. Yūsuf ʿAlī, *The meaning of the holy Qurʾān*, Leicester 1975; M. Asad, *The message of the Qurʾān*, Gibralter 1980; Bell, *Commentary*; A. Mawdudi, *Towards understanding the Qurʾān*, i, ed. Z.I. Ansari, Leicester 1988; W.M. Watt, *Companion to the Qurʾān*, London 1967.

Barēlwīs

A group of religious scholars *(ʿulamāʾ)* and their followers, originally of South Asia, who trace their worldview to the teachings of Aḥmad Riḍā Khān Barēlwī (d. 1921). The Barēlwīs call themselves the "People of the [Prophet's] sunna (q.v.) and the majority community" *(Ahl-i sunnat wa-jamāʿat)* and reject the name "Barēlwī" as derogatory, because of its implication that their beliefs are local and deviant rather than universalistic and mainstream. Nevertheless, the term "Barēlwī" is widely current wherever the movement exists, which today includes not only South Asia but also Britain, continental Europe and South Africa, among other places.

The Barēlwīs emerged as a cohesive movement in the 1880s under the leadership of Aḥmad Riḍā Khān. He strongly opposed interpretations of Islam articulated by the leading contemporary figures. These included Mirza Ghulām Aḥmad (d. 1908), the founder of the Aḥmadiyya (q.v.); the Deobandīs (q.v.); the *Ahl-i ḥadīth* and *Nadwat al-ʿulamāʾ*; as well as modernist Muslim intellectuals such as Sayyid Aḥmad Khān (d. 1898) of Aligarh and Mawlānā Abū l-Kalām Āzād (d. 1958). In the twentieth century, the Barēlwīs have also opposed the interpretations of al-Mawdūdī (d. 1979) and his movement, the *Jamāʿat-i Islāmī*.

What was in dispute between the Barēlwīs and the nineteenth-century groups mentioned above related primarily to beliefs about the Prophet Muḥammad. The Barēlwīs' strong belief in the Prophet as intercessor with God on behalf of the faithful at all times contrasted particularly with the *Ahl-i ḥadīth* who denied the importance of prophetic intercession (see INTERCESSION). It also conflicted with the position taken by Sayyid Aḥmad Barēlwī (d. 1831) and Muḥammad Ismāʿīl (d. 1831), leaders of the Delhi-based *Ṭarīqa-i Muḥammadiyya* movement. Aḥmad Riḍā Khān referred to these and other like-minded religious groups as "Wahhābīs," a reference to the austere religious movement prevalent in the Arabian peninsula which has the unity of God as its central theme. The Barēlwīs also opposed these groups on questions related to Ṣūfism (see ṢŪFISM AND THE QURʾĀN). The *Ahl-i ḥadīth* and others were hostile to the idea of saintly intermediaries, while the Barēlwīs regard saints as an essential means to having a loving relationship with the Prophet and ultimately with God.

The sources for the Barēlwī interpretation of Islam and more particularly of its prophetology (see PROPHETS AND PROPHETHOOD) are the classic ones of Qurʾān, ḥadīth (see ḤADĪTH AND THE QURʾĀN) and Islamic law *(fiqh)*. It is noteworthy that Aḥmad Riḍā Khān was primarily a jurist *(faqīh)* and a religious scholar *(ʿālim)* rather than a Ṣūfī. He supported his positions regarding the Prophet primarily with textual citations from legal sources rather than Ṣūfī writings. In qurʾānic exegesis, Aḥmad Riḍā Khān employed the concept of abrogation (q.v.) to support his arguments. An illustration of this may be seen in his views regarding the question of the Prophet's knowledge of the unseen (*ʿilm al-ghayb*, see HIDDEN AND THE HIDDEN), which he addressed in numerous writings. Briefly, Aḥmad Riḍā Khān's position was that God gave the Prophet knowledge of the unseen, including the five items mentioned in Q 31:34 as known to God alone: "God has knowledge of the hour and he sends the rain. He knows what is in the womb. No one knows what he will gain tomorrow and no one knows where he will die." Aḥmad Riḍā Khān asserted that these five items were actually a small fraction of the Prophet's total knowledge, which encompassed knowledge of heaven (q.v.) and hell (q.v.), the resurrection (q.v.), the angels (see ANGEL), the nature and attributes of God (see GOD AND HIS ATTRIBUTES) and much else besides. Central to his argument is both "[God] will not disclose to you the secrets of the unseen, but he chooses of his messengers whom he pleases" (Q 3:179) as well as "He knows the unseen. He does not make any one acquainted with his mysteries, except a messenger whom he has chosen" (Q 72:26-7).

In Aḥmad Riḍā Khān's formal legal judgment *(fatwā)* written in Mecca in 1905 entitled *"al-Dawla al-makkiyya bi-māddat al-ghaybiyya,"* he argued that each time a verse *(āya)* or chapter *(sūra)* was revealed, the Prophet's knowledge increased further. Although some qurʾānic verses refer to Muḥammad's lack of knowledge of the prophets and of those to whom the Qurʾān refers as the hypocrites, for instance, this was only because the Qurʾān had not yet been fully revealed to him. Thus, these verses were abrogated by later ones, such as those quoted above. By the time the revelation was complete, the Prophet had detailed *(mufaṣṣal)* and clear knowledge of everything (Aḥmad Riḍā Khān, *al-Dawla,* 105). Elsewhere in the same document (175-91), he wrote that sometimes the Prophet was silent about certain things such as when judgment day (see LAST JUDGMENT) would come, for he had been ordered not to reveal them. Also he sometimes temporarily forgot something because his mind was preoccupied with other important matters. Aḥmad Riḍā Khān argued that "forgetting something is not a negation of knowledge [of that thing], rather it requires that one have known it first" (ibid., 110-12).

The concept of abrogation (q.v.) was again employed in the context of arguments made in 1919-20, when the Indian religious scholars were debating whether to support the Congress Party's Non-Cooperation Movement — which was largely Hindu — and whether to invite Congress to support their own Khilāfat Movement. In qurʾānic exegesis undertaken to oppose the above movements, Aḥmad Riḍā Khān used the exegetical principle that some earlier qurʾānic verses are abrogated by later ones to argue that Q 60:8-9, in which Muslims were told they could enter into friendly relations with non-Muslims as long as they were not fighting them, had been abrogated by Q 9:73, which advocated taking stern measures against "unbelievers" and "hypocrites" (see BELIEF AND UNBELIEF; HYPOCRITES AND HYPOCRISY).

Aḥmad Riḍā Khān relied heavily on quotations from the ḥadīth and Islamic legal texts, as well as the Qurʾān. He even accepted weak ḥadīths that elevate the Prophet's stature. It is interesting to note that on several issues concerning the Prophet he reached a position that resembles Shīʿī beliefs even though his arguments were based on Sunnī sources and not Shīʿī ones. Such issues include the concept of the pre-eminence of the Prophet's light (q.v.), which was created before God created the spiritual or material universe and before the creation of the first prophet Adam (see ADAM AND EVE); the belief that God created the world for the Prophet's sake; the belief that the Prophet's ancestors were believers; and the belief that the Prophet, being made of light, had no shadow (see SHĪʿISM AND THE QURʾĀN).

Aḥmad Riḍā Khān's translation of the Qurʾān, entitled *Kanz al-Īmān fī tarjumat al-Qurʾān*, published in Muradabad, India 1911, has recently been translated into English by Ḥ.A. Faṭmī and published by the Islamic World Mission, U.K. It is in current use among English-speaking followers of the Barēlwī movement, although it awaits scholarly attention. See also EXEGESIS OF THE QUR'ĀN: EARLY MODERN AND CONTEMPORARY.

Usha Sanyal

Bibliography
Primary: Aḥmad Riḍā Khān, *al-ʿAṭāyā l-nabawiyya fī fatāwā l-riḍawiyya* [in Urdu], vols. i-vii, x-xi, Saudagaran, Bareilly 1981-7; id., *al-Dawla al-makkiyya bi-māddat al-ghaybiyya* [in Urdu], Karachi n.d.; id., *Kanz al-Īmān fī tarjumat al-Qurʾān,* Muradabad 1911; id., *Holy Qurʾān,* trans. Ḥ.A. Faṭmī, London n.d.; Ẓ.D. Biḥārī, *Ḥayat-i aʿlā hazrat* [in Urdu], Karachi 1938, i.
Secondary: M.A. Masʿūd, *Neglected genius of the East. An introduction to the life and works of Mawlana Ahmad Rida Khan of Bareilly (India) 1272/1856-1340/1921,* Lahore 1987; B.D. Metcalf, *Islamic revival in British India. Deoband 1860-1900,* Princeton 1982; U. Sanyal, *Devotional Islam and politics in British India. Ahmad Riza Khan Barelwi and his movement, 1870-1920,* Delhi 1996.

Barrier

An obstacle; anything that hinders approach or attack. Both *ḥijāb* and *barzakh* (q.v.) are used to denote "barrier" in the Qurʾān. Under this general category of barrier, Ibn al-Jawzī (d. 597/1200) in two cases understands the word *ḥijāb* to mean a concrete division: he interprets "between the two is a *ḥijāb*" (*baynahum ḥijābun,* Q 7:46) as a bridge *(sūr)* between heaven (q.v.) and hell (q.v.); while he considers the *ḥijāb* that obstructs Solomon's (q.v.) view (*tawārat bi-l-ḥijāb,* Q 38:32) to be a mountain (*Nuzha,* 246). Other qurʾānic citations of *ḥijāb* are used to connote a covering *(satr),* such as a curtain or a veil (q.v.): Believers are instructed to speak with the wives of the Prophet from behind a *ḥijāb* (Q 33:53; see WIVES OF THE PROPHET); *ḥijāb* also appears in reference to Mary's (q.v.) seclusion from her people (Q 19:17); when Muḥammad recites the Qurʾān, God places between him and "those who do not believe in the hereafter a hidden *ḥijāb*" (*ḥijāban mastūran,* Q 17:45; cf. 83:15). However, the focus of this article is on barrier in its sense as an actual physical barrier.

Barzakh *as barrier*

Although *barzakh* is most commonly understood as the barrier that separates this world from the next, in Q 25:53 and 55:20 *barzakh* connotes a barrier, partition or separation between two oceans (see GEOGRAPHY IN THE QURʾĀN). Ibn Qutayba (d. 276/889) defines *barzakh* as a partition between two entities (*kullu shayʾ bayna shayʾayn fa-huwa barzakh, Gharīb,* 438). The *Lisān* (i, 193) describes *barzakh* as an obstacle or partition *(ḥājiz),* a term found in the exegetical works of Muqātil (d. 150/767; cf. *Tafsīr,* iv, 197), al-Ṭabarī (d. 310/923; cf. *Tafsīr,* xix, 16; xviii, 41), al-Qurṭubī (d. 671/1272; cf. *Jāmiʿ,* xiii, 59; xvi, 162-3), Ibn Kathīr (d. 774/1373; cf. *Tafsīr,* v, 158; vi, 488), al-Bayḍāwī (d. ca. 716/1316-7; cf. *Anwār,* ii, 167, 484), al-Rāzī (d. 606/1210; cf. *Tafsīr,* vi, 300-3), and Ṭabāṭabāʾī (d. 1403/1982; cf. *Mīzān,* xv, 229; xix, 99-100) — whereas al-Zamakhsharī (d. 538/1144) refers to *barzakh* as a hindrance of divine will *(ḥāʾil min qudratihi)* that bars the merging of the two oceans (*Kashshāf,* iii, 286-7; iv, 445). Al-Nasafī (d. 710/1310) uses both terms *(ḥājiz* and *ḥāʾil)* interchangeably (*Tafsīr,* ii, 548; iii, 455).

The two oceans

The interpretation about what the *barzakh* separates has been subject to varied interpretations. Al-Ṭabarī (*Tafsīr,* xix, 16) and al-Bayḍāwī (*Anwār,* ii, 167) interpret the fresh water as that of rain and rivers and the salt waters as that of the ocean. Al-Qurṭubī (*Jāmiʿ,* xvii, 162-3) lists other possibilities: the Persian Gulf *(baḥr fāris)* and the Mediterranean *(baḥr al-rūm);* the oceans of heaven and earth; or, metaphorically, the paths of good and evil (q.v.). The point of contact between the two seas *(majmaʿ al-baḥrayn)* has been somewhat mysterious. Al-Qurṭubī considers the destruction of the *barzakh* as one of the eschatological signs (see APOCALYPSE; COSMOLOGY IN THE QURʾĀN; ESCHATOLOGY). The two oceans are separated for the duration of this earth. The overflowing oceans of the earth (Q 82:3) herald the end (Qurṭubī, *Jāmiʿ*, xvii, 162-3). Ibn Kathīr, on the other hand, strongly objects to the notion of cosmological oceans. The barrier is concrete *(yābis min al-arḍ)* and maintains the separation of the distinct characteristics of salt and sweet waters (Ibn Kathīr, *Tafsīr*, v, 158). In describing the cyclical pattern of water, Ṭabāṭabāʾī infers that the barrier, though not visible, does exist nonetheless. The oceans help form clouds that fill the wells and rivers with sweet water through rain. These rivers, in turn, lead to the sea (Ṭabāṭabāʾī, *Mīzān*, xix, 99-100).

Cosmography

A.J. Wensinck (*The ocean*, 37-8) suggests that the isthmus and the dual form of ocean is part of a cosmographic story that is now lost. Within western Semitic cosmology the meeting of the oceans *(majmaʿ al-baḥrayn)* marks the end of the world. This *majmaʿ* was incorporated in legends of al-Khāḍir and the Alexander (q.v.) romance (see also KHĀḌIR/KHIḌR). In the latter, it is given as the goal of the journey. Al-Khāḍir is sometimes depicted as sitting on a pulpit *(minbar)* of light between the upper and lower oceans. Ibn al-Wardī (d. 749/1349; *Kharīda*, 6) identifies the *barzakh* as the four stages of the journey *(marāḥil)* separating the Mediterranean *(baḥr al-rūm)* and the Red Sea *(baḥr al-qalzam)*.

Mona M. Zaki

Bibliography

Primary: Bayḍāwī, *Anwār;* Ibn Ḥajar, *al-Zahr al-nāḍir fī nabaʾ al-Khāḍir*, Beirut 1988; Ibn Kathīr, *Tafsīr;* Ibn Qutayba, *Gharīb;* Ibn al-Wardī, Abū Ḥafṣ ʿUmar b. al-Muẓaffar, *Kharīdat al-ʿajāʾib wa-farīdat al-gharāʾib*, Cairo 1303/1885; *Lisān al-ʿArab;* Muqātil, *Tafsīr;* Nasafī, *Tafsīr;* Qurṭubī, *Jāmiʿ;* Rāzī, *Tafsīr;* Ṭabarī, *Tafsīr;* Ṭabāṭabāʾī, *Mīzān;* Zamakhsharī, *Kashshāf.*

Secondary: A.J. Wensinck, al-Khaḍir, in *EI²*, iv, 902-5; id., *The ocean in the literature of the western Semites*, Amsterdam 1918.

Barzakh

The term *barzakh* occurs three times in the Qurʾān; in Q 25:53 and 55:20, *barzakh* is a partition between two seas, a barrier that could be an allusion to a cosmic myth (see BARRIER; COSMOLOGY IN THE QURʾĀN). The third reference, which is the focus of this article, occurs in Q 23:100: "And behind them is a barrier until the day they are raised." This verse applies the concept of partition to the eschatological scene and death (see ESCHATOLOGY; DEATH AND THE DEAD). A. Jeffery (*For. vocab.*, 77) suggests Persian as a possible source for this loan word — *farsakh, parasang*, a measure of land that fits the description of a physical barrier (see FOREIGN VOCABULARY).

Barzakh *and the day of resurrection*

One interpretation places *barzakh* as a time barrier, a stated time or life span *(ajal)* in the momentous day of resurrection (*qiyāma*, see RESURRECTION). *Barzakh* is the time gap between the first and the second blowing of the trumpet (see APOCALYPSE). It lasts forty years and constitutes the only respite *(khumūd)* that the tormented sinners will ever experience (Ibn Ḥabīb, *Firdaws*, 105; Ghazālī, *Iḥyāʾ*, iv, 512-3; Qurṭubī, *Jāmiʿ*, xii, 150).

A second interpretation brings *barzakh* closer to home. Mujāhid (d. ca. 104/722) describes the *barzakh* as the grave that separates us from the hereafter (*al-barzakh hiya hādhihi l-qubūr allatī baynakum wa-bayna l-ākhira, Tafsīr,* 488). The term becomes central to belief in life after death and, thus, co-opts a range of issues related to the continual existence of the soul (q.v.). By the third/ninth century al-Ṭabarī (d. 310/923) defines *barzakh* as life span *(ajal);* as a veil *(ḥijāb)* between the dead and their return *(rujūʿ)* to this world; as what is between death *(mawt)* and resurrection *(baʿth);* and, spatially, as what separates this world *(al-dunyā)* from the hereafter (*al-ākhira,* Ṭabarī, *Tafsīr,* xii, 150). Al-Qurṭubī's (d. 671/1272) list is similar. Parsing these definitions in light of texts on the afterlife reveals how the temporal concept acquired a spatial concreteness that makes *barzakh* an indispensable phase in what happens after death (Qurṭubī, *Jāmiʿ,* xii, 150).

Ajal, which literally means a "stated time" or "life span," when used as a meaning for *barzakh* testifies to existence in the grave, a view adopted early by Muqātil (d. 150/767; *Tafsīr,* iii, 165-6). A later fourth/tenth century Ismāʿīlī text refers to *barzakh* as man's second *ajal* — a continuation of his time on earth. The author draws the conclusion that whoever has a long life on this earth has a shorter span in the *barzakh* and vice versa (Jaʿfar b. Manṣūr al-Yaman, *Sarāʾir,* 110).

Barzakh acts as an obstacle *(ḥājiz)* that prevents the dead from returning *(rujūʿ)* to this world. This is also an early idea suggested by Mujāhid (*Tafsīr,* 488). Al-Bayḍāwī (d. ca. 716/1316-7; *Anwār,* ii, 128) and al-Nasafī (d. 710/1310; *Tafsīr,* ii, 438) prefer the term *ḥāʾil.* Exegetes emphasize here the definitive aspect of *barzakh* that is applicable to sinners who, at the moment of death or in the process of eyeing the torments awaiting them in hell (q.v.), request a second chance. Death heralds the *barzakh* from which there is no return; the despair of the doomed is total.

Ibn Qutayba (d. 276/889) defines the *barzakh* as what lies between this world and the next. It acquires a life of its own. It is an interregnum *(mutawassiṭ)* between death and resurrection (Kāfiyajī, *Manāzil,* 72-3). Ibn Qayyim al-Jawziyya (d. 751/1350) refers to *dār al-barzakh* as the intermediary of three stages, which are this world *(dunyā), barzakh* and the hereafter *(ākhira);* in this schema, *barzakh* is seen as a partition through which the dead can look onto this world and the next. Each of the three stages is governed by its own rules (*aḥkām,* Ibn Qayyim al-Jawziyya, *Rūḥ,* 92-3, 105-6). Al-Suyuṭī (d. 911/1505) is more precise, interpreting *barzakh* as threefold: place, time and condition. The place is the grave from which the soul (q.v.) traverses either to the uppermost heaven (*ʿilliyūn,* see PARADISE; HEAVEN) or to the depths of hell *(sijjīn);* the time is that between death and resurrection; and the condition is that of pain, pleasure or incarceration — the last being a reference to the interrogation of the grave that should be over in seven days (Suyūṭī, *Ḥāwī,* ii, 185). Ibn Taymiyya (d. 728/1328) maintains that these conditions are experienced by both body and soul. The soul is free to roam and connect with other souls. It is God's will that permits it full or partial contact with its body. The soul has the full capacity of hearing and responding (Ibn Taymiyya, *ʿAdhāb,* 92-3).

Barzakh *as repository of souls*

The association of *barzakh* with souls was not limited to the dead. There is also a tendency to expand it so that it would incorporate all souls including the unborn. In rejecting the doctrine of the Ashʿariyya of the continual recreation of the soul, Ibn Ḥazm (d. 456/1064) asserts that the *barzakh* is the repository of all the spirits of Adam's progeny (see ADAM AND EVE). It exists in the lowest heaven where an angel (q.v.) blows these souls into wombs (see BIRTH). This doctrine is strongly rejected by Ibn Qayyim al-Jawziyya (Ibn Qayyim al-Jawziyya, *Rūḥ,* 158-9; see also I. Netton, Nafs).

Punishment in the barzakh

The interrogation by the angels Munkar and Nakīr and the punishment of the grave become central to the *barzakh* experience (see REWARD AND PUNISHMENT). The vision of Muḥammad during an eclipse and his ascension (q.v.; *miʿrāj*) were evidence that certain punishments are ongoing (Bayhaqī, *Ithbāt,* 76-9; Ibn Ṭulūn, *Barzakh,* 222-8; and for an analytical version, see Suyūṭī, *Āya,* 3-29). The Muʿtazilīs (q.v.) acknowledge *barzakh* as a stage but strongly object to the idea of punishment, maintaining that the soul does not reside in the grave and that the body would be incapable of experiencing pleasure or pain. Ibn Kathīr (d. 774/1373; *Tafsīr,* v, 38-9) emphasizes that Q 23:100 is primarily a warning (q.v.) and a threat *(tahdīd)* to tyrants *(ẓālimūn)* who will be punished in their graves until their resurrection. In more general terms, this punishment is treated as a preliminary penance prior to the reckoning *(ḥisāb)* of the resurrection *(qiyāma)*. There is no doubt that the punishment of the *barzakh* endorsed the legitimacy of the idea of a reckoning in the afterlife. The corporeality attributed to the dead in their graves has at times been exaggerated. Ibn al-Jawzī (d. 597/1200) alludes to and rebukes the credulity of the masses who believe the dead are currently partaking in carnal pleasures, such as food and sex, in their graves (*Ṣayd,* 40).

Relationship of the living to the barzakh

The deeds of the dead affect the conditions of the *barzakh*. These conditions are ameliorated further through the prayers of the living. Shīʿīs, who emphasize the concept of the return *(rajʿa)* as part of their millenarian thought, list among their criteria for good deeds that the rewards are reaped in this world, the *barzakh* and the afterlife. Good deeds performed in ignorance *(ghafla)* are rewarded in the *barzakh* by preventing the punishment of the grave or opening the gate of heaven to the grave so that the soul can enjoy respite (Aḥsāʾī, *Rajʿa,* 197). Later Ṣūfīs such as al-Shaʿrānī (d. 973/1565) describe the spatial dimensions and the quality of light and visibility in the *barzakh* as defined by the deeds of the dead. Unpaid debt can incarcerate the soul. The *barzakh* is portrayed as a cosmology of consecutive circles *(al-barzakh al-muṭlaq)* where every prophet resides with his own constituents in separate spheres (Shaʿrānī, *Durar,* 60-1; see also SHĪʿISM AND THE QURʾĀN; ṢŪFISM AND THE QURʾĀN).

Ibn al-ʿArabī and the barzakh

Ibn al-ʿArabī (d. 638/1240) expands the spatial idea of *barzakh* beyond the definition found in relation to death (cf. S. al-Ḥakīm, *al-Muʿjam al-ṣūfī*). Man himself is an intermediate creation, a *barzakh* between God and the world. The *barzakh* is also the beyond; Ibn al-ʿArabī coins the term *al-nubuwwa al-barzakhiyya* in the case of Khālid b. Sinān who promised to tell his sons what happens after death if they exhumed his body. Death signals the birth of man into the first stage of the afterlife, the *barzakh,* during which he continues to mature until resurrection. The soul could travel to *barzakh* in its dream-state thus making it an accessible realm to living humans. In Ibn al-ʿArabī's definition of imagination as a creative energy that is capable of touching the eternal, knowledge gained through dreams *(ʿilm al-khayāl)* is synonymous with that gained through the *barzakh* *(ʿilm al-barzakh),* a divine emanation where meanings manifest themselves without the need of form.

Conclusion

R. Eklund maintains that *barzakh* emerges on the eschatological scene free of any influence from the People of the Book (*ahl al-kitāb*, see PEOPLE OF THE BOOK; SCRIPTURE AND THE QURʾĀN) and represents a "genuine Islamic product, a rare phenomenon on the eschatological market" (*Life*, 82). Most scholars hesitate to label it as purgatory, preferring the term limbo. *Barzakh* as a barrier between this world and the next acquires a life of its own. The expanded sphere of the *barzakh* is exemplified in later works, like that of al-Shaʿrānī, where the dead are depicted as conducting an active afterlife allowing for a more dynamic interaction with the living. Here *barzakh* stops short of being the passive barrier to the afterlife.

Mona M. Zaki

Bibliography

Primary: Aḥsāʾī, Aḥmad b. Zayn al-Dīn, *Kitāb al-Rajʿa*, Beirut 1993; Bayḍāwī, *Anwār;* al-Bayhaqī, Abū Bakr Aḥmad, *Ithbāt ʿadhāb al-qabr*, ed. S. Qudā, Amman 1983; al-Ghazālī, Abū Ḥāmid Muḥammad, *Iḥyāʾ ʿulūm al-dīn*, Cairo 1965; Ibn Ḥabīb, Abū Marwān ʿAbd al-Malik al-Sulamī, *Waṣf al-firdaws*, Beirut 1987; Ibn al-Jawzī, *Ṣayd al-khāṭir*, ed. A. Abū Sunayna, Amman 1987; Ibn Kathīr, *Tafsīr;* Ibn Qayyim al-Jawziyya, *Kitāb al-Rūḥ*, ed. ʿAbd al-Fattāḥ Maḥmūd ʿUmar, Amman 1985; Ibn Qutayba, *Gharīb;* Ibn Rajab, ʿAbd al-Raḥmān, *Aḥwāl al-qubūr*, ed. Kh. ʿAlamī, Beirut 1990; Ibn Taymiyya, *Fatāwī ʿadhāb al-qabr*, ed. Abū Bakr al-Rāziq, Beirut 1992; Ibn Ṭūlūn, Shams al-Dīn, *Kitāb al-Barzakh*, ed. A. al-Atharī, Tanta 1991; Jaʿfar b. Manṣūr al-Yaman, *Sarāʾir wa-asrār al-nuṭaqāʾ*, ed. M. Ghālib, Beirut 1984; al-Kāfiyajī, Abū ʿAlī Muḥammad b. Sulaymān, *Manāzil al-arwāḥ*, ed. M. al-Sayyid, Cairo 1991; *Lisān al-ʿArab;* Mujāhid, *Tafsīr*, ed. M. Abū l-Nīl, Cairo 1989; Muqātil, *Tafsīr;* Nasafī, *Tafsīr;* Qurṭubī, *Jāmiʿ;* id., *al-Tadhkira fī aḥwāl al-mawtā wa-umūr al-ākhira*, ed. A. Saqqā, 2 vols. in 1, Cairo 1980; al-Shaʿrānī, ʿAbd al-Wahhāb, *Durar al-ghawwāṣ ʿalā fatāwī l-Khawwāṣ*, ed. M. Ismāʿīl, Cairo 1985; al-Suyūṭī, Jalāl al-Dīn, *al-Āya al-kubrā fī sharḥ qiṣṣat al-isrāʾ*, M. Mastu, Damascus 1985; id., *al-Ḥāwī lil-fatwā fī l-fiqh wa-ʿulūm al-tafsīr wa-l-ḥadīth wa-l-naḥw wa-l-iʿrāb wa-sāʾir al-funūn*, 2 vols., Cairo 1352/1933-4; Ṭabarī, *Tafsīr;* Zamakhsharī, *Kashshāf*.

Secondary: B. Carra de Vaux, Barzakh, in *EI²*, i, 1071-2; R. Eklund, *Life between death and resurrection according to Islam*, Uppsala 1941; S. al-Ḥakīm, *al-Muʿjam al-ṣūfī. al-Ḥikma fī ḥudūd al-kalima*, Beirut 1981 (see entries under *barzakh, khayāl*, and *al-nubuwwa al-barzakhiyya*); L. Kinberg, Interaction between this world and the afterworld in early Islamic tradition, in *Oriens* 29-30 (1986), 285-308; I.R. Netton, Nafs, in *EI²*, vii, 880-4; J.I. Smith, Concourse between the living and the dead in Islamic eschatological literature, in *History of religions* 19 (1980), 224-36; J.I. Smith and Y. Haddad, *The Islamic understanding of death*, Albany 1981.

Bashīr see PROPHETS AND PROPHETHOOD; GOOD NEWS

Basmala

The invocation *bi-smi llāhi l-raḥmāni l-raḥīm(i)*, "In the name of God, the Merciful, the Compassionate," also known as the *tasmiya*, "naming/uttering (God's name)," occurs 114 times in the Qurʾān: at the head of every sūra except the ninth, which is entitled "Repentance" (Sūrat al-Tawba or Sūrat al-Barāʾa), and also in Q 27:30 as the opening of Solomon's (q.v.) letter to the queen of Sheba (see BILQĪS). Of the 113 occurrences at the head of a sūra, only the first, that before the opening sūra, Sūrat al-Fātiḥa (see FĀTIḤA), is commonly reckoned as an *āya*, i.e. as Q 1:1, although the other 112 unnumbered prefatory occurrences are still considered part of the sacred text (Rāzī, *Aḥkām al-basmala*, 21; Suyūṭī, *Durr*, i, 20).

Precedents for and parallels to the basmala

The *basmala* has various historical precedents among invocational formulae in other traditions. Al-Zamakhsharī (d. 538/1144) long ago noted the pre-Islamic Arab use of parallel formulae such as "in the name of al-Lāt [or] al-ʿUzzā" (*Kashshāf,* i, 29; see IDOLS AND IMAGES; PRE-ISLAMIC ARABIA AND THE QURʾĀN). T. Nöldeke points out Jewish and Christian parallels to *bi-smi llāhi* in the recurrence of "in the name of the Lord" (*GQ,* i, 112, 116-7; cf. ii, 42; see JEWS AND JUDAISM; CHRISTIANS AND CHRISTIANITY) in the Hebrew and Christian bibles. Y. Moubarac suggests a coalescence of Jewish, Christian and pagan south Arabian influences behind the tripartite *Allāh al-raḥmān al-raḥīm* (Les études d'épigraphie, 58-61). There is also a parallel in the Mazdean formula *pad nām ī yazdān,* "in the name of (the) god(s)," attested as early as the third century at Paikuli (P. Gignoux, Pad Nām, 162).

Meaning of the basmala *in the Qurʾān*

Grammatically *bi-smi llāhi* has the form of an oath (see OATHS) introduced by *bi-* but traditionally it has been construed as an invocation, as opposed to an oath such as *bi-llāhi,* "by God!" The *bi-* is held to require an implied verb expressing the intention of the one uttering the *basmala* to act or begin an action "with the naming [glossing *ism* as *tasmiya*] of God." Thus al-Ṭabarī (d. 310/923) cites Ibn ʿAbbās as saying that an action following utterance of the *basmala* — be it reciting, standing or sitting down — implies intent to perform the act "in the name of" or "by naming" God, not "through" God (as agent; *Tafsīr,* i, 114-8). On the other hand, a modern interpreter, Rashīd Riḍā, says that to recite a sūra "in the name of God..." means to "recite it as a sūra coming from him, not from you" (*Tafsīr al-manār,* i, 44; A. Khoury, *Koran,* 147).

There are frequent invocations of God's name in the Qurʾān apart from the *basmala.* The short formula, "in the name of God," occurs only in Q 11:41: "[Noah (q.v.)] said, 'Embark in it [the ark (q.v.)]! In the name of God be its sailing and its mooring!...'" However, *bi-smi rabbikā,* "in the name of your Lord," occurs four times, after the command to "glorify" (Q 56:74, 96; 69:52; cf. 87:1) or to "recite" (Q 96:1) expressing similarly the invoking of God's name in performing an action. "Mentioning" or "remembering" *(dh-k-r)* God's name occurs 13 times and Q 55:78 speaks of blessing God's name *(tabāraka smu rabbika).* These passages have been interpreted specifically as exhortations to repeat the *basmala* to declare one's righteous intention and to bless and consecrate any act, from drinking water to ritual ablution to marital intercourse (see BLESSING).

There are two possible grammatical readings of the final three words of the *basmala:* (i) with *al-raḥmān* and *al-raḥīm* taken as parallel attributive epithets of *Allāh,* seen in modern translations that replicate the Arabic word order (e.g. M. Henning [1901], "Allah, der Erbarmer, der Barmherzige;" R. Bell [1937], "Allah, the Merciful, the Compassionate") or that emphasize the emphatic force of two cognate attributives (e.g. G. Sale [1734], "the most merciful God"; E.H. Palmer [1880], "the merciful and compassionate God"; R. Paret [1962], "der barmherzige und gütige Gott");
(ii) with *al-raḥmān* construed as a name of God in apposition to *Allāh,* modified by the attributive *al-raḥīm,* (e.g. R. Blachère [1949], "Allah, le Bienfaiteur miséricordieux"; K. Cragg [1988], "God, the merciful Lord of mercy"). Al-Ṭabarī's discussion (*Tafsīr,* i, 55f.) supports the former, which became the standard reading. Most commentators focus on distinguishing the meanings of *raḥmān* and *raḥīm,* taking the intensive *raḥmān* to refer to God's mercy (q.v.) generally either (a) in this world and the next or (b) to all creatures; and *raḥīm* for God's mercy more specifically, limited

either (a) to the next world only or (b) to the faithful only. The commentators note also that *raḥmān* can only be used of God while *raḥīm* can be applied to humans (Ṭabarī, *Tafsīr,* i, 55f.; Ibn al-ʿArabī [attr.], *Tafsīr,* i, 7; Zamakhsharī, *Kashshāf,* i, 41-5; M. al-Gharawī, *Ism,* 148-50).

While Muslim and non-Muslim scholars have preferred to read *al-raḥmān al-raḥīm* as paired attributive epithets (see GOD AND HIS ATTRIBUTES), the other instances of *raḥmān* and *raḥīm* in the Qurʾān could support reading *raḥmān* as an appositive modified by *raḥīm.* The two words are paired only four times (Q 1:3; 2:163; 41:2; 59:22) apart from the *basmala* and can in each case be cogently construed as a substantive *(al-raḥmān)* with a following adjective *(al-raḥīm),* "the compassionate Merciful [One]." *Raḥmān* occurs in the Qurʾān only with the definite article *al-* (57 instances in numbered *āyas*). *Raḥīm* occurs 81 times without the definite article as an adjectival predicate of God, most often paired with and following *ghafūr,* "forgiving." *Al-raḥīm* is found 32 times (including four occurrences apart from the *basmala* with *al-raḥmān*), all but once (Q 34:2: *al-raḥīm al-ghafūr*) as an attribute following other divine names or attributes: *al-ʿazīz* ("the Mighty"), *al-ghafūr* ("the Forgiving"), *al-tawwāb* ("the Relenting") and *al-birr* ("the Beneficent"). Thus the qurʾānic evidence could support the translation, "God, the compassionate *(al-raḥīm)* Merciful One *(al-raḥmān).*" This would accord also with pre-Islamic use of *al-raḥmān* as the name of God in south Arabia (see ARCHAEOLOGY AND THE QURʾĀN), the pagan Meccans' aversion to using it instead of *Allāh* (G. Ryckmans, *Les religions arabes,* 47-8; cf. J. Jomier, Le nom divin, 2; Y. Moubarac, Les études d'épigraphie, 58-9) and its use as God's name by Muḥammad's contemporary, the "Arabian prophet" Musaylima (Ṭabarī, *Taʾrīkh,* iii, 245-6; Zamakhsharī, *Kashshāf,* i, 42; cf. Nöldeke, *GQ,* i, 112-3; see MUSAYLIMA AND PSEUDO-PROPHETS).

Place of the basmala *in the Qurʾān*

The question as to whether the *basmala* is to be counted as the first *āya* in the Fātiḥa (Q 1) and the remaining 112 sūras it precedes has been discussed by Muslim and non-Muslim scholars alike. The Muslim consensus is represented in the modern Cairo text, which counts it as an *āya* only in the Fātiḥa, otherwise as an unnumbered line of text *(saṭr)* that separates the first *āya* of every sūra (except Q 9, "Repentance" [Sūrat al-Tawba]) from the last *āya* of the preceding sūra (cf. Suyūṭī, *Durr,* i, 20). The exception of Sūrat al-Tawba is held traditionally to stem from either (i) its being originally joined with Q 8, "The Spoils of War" (Sūrat al-Anfāl), as a single unit later divided in two before the word *barāʾa,* which thus became the first word of Q 9 (Suyūṭī, *Itqān,* i, 60, 65; Tirmidhī, 48:10.1; cf. Ibn al-ʿArabī, *Futuḥāt,* 4, 211-3, 355-6, who says the *basmala* of Q 27:30 is the one missing at the head of Q 9) or (ii) its having as a main theme God's threats against the idolaters which makes the *basmala* inappropriate for it (Rāzī, *Tafsīr,* vii, 225; M. al-Gharawī, *Ism,* 77; see IDOLATRY AND IDOLATERS; POLYTHEISM AND ATHEISM).

Whether the *basmala* even belongs to the Qurʾān at all has been a live question for Muslims (cf. M. b. ʿAlī al-Shawkānī, *Fatḥ al-qadīr,* i, 64-5). According to most reports, neither Ibn Masʿūd's nor Ubayy b. Kaʿb's Qurʾān copy (*muṣḥaf,* see CODICES OF THE QURʾĀN) included Sūrat al-Fātiḥa. Further, Anas is reported as saying, "I performed the ritual prayer *(ṣalāt)* with God's apostle, Abū Bakr (q.v.), ʿUmar (q.v.) and ʿUthmān (q.v.) and I did not hear any of them recite *'bi-smi llāh...'*" (Muslim, *Ṣaḥīḥ,* 4:50; cf. 4:52; see PRAYER). However, Anas is also said to have reported that Muḥammad recited Q 108, "Abundance" (Sūrat al-Kawthar), with the *basmala* (Muslim, *Ṣaḥīḥ*, 4:53) and al-Suyūṭī (d. 911/1505) cites traditions that the *basmala* belonged to the revelations from the beginning or sometime during the Prophet's mission (e.g. it "was sent down with every sūra"); however, he also cites traditions that the *basmala* was an opening or closing benediction given Muḥammad at the institution of the ritual prayer (*ṣalāt*, Suyūṭī, *Durr*, i, 20-3; cf. A. Spitaler, *Verszählung*, 31-2). The reciters (see RECITERS OF THE QUR'ĀN) and jurists of Medina, Basra and Syria did not consider it an *āya* at the beginning of a sūra, but a sūra-divider and a blessing that one would use to begin any important act. Abū Ḥa-nīfa (d. 150/767) agreed, and the Ḥanafīs do not recite it audibly in the ritual prayer. However, the Meccan, Kufan and most Iraqi reciters and jurists recognized it as an *āya* whenever it begins a sūra, as did al-Shāfiʿī (d. 204/820) and his followers who recite it aloud in the ritual prayer (*ṣalāt*) and likewise the Shīʿīs who recite it silently (Zamakhsharī, *Kashshāf*, i, 24-5; Rāzī, *Aḥkām al-basmala*, 20; Shawkānī, *Fatḥ al-qadīr*, i, 64-5; H. Algar, Besmellāh, 172). The division of the law schools over the audible reciting of the *basmala* likely reflects the early tradition's ambivalence about both the *basmala* and the Fātiḥa: Are they part of the Word of God (see BOOK) or only invocations used by Muḥammad? (cf. Nöldeke, *GQ*, ii, 79). It would also appear from the earliest extant Qur'ān pages that the *basmala* is almost always orthographically integral to the subsequent sūra's text and not set apart visually in any way (Dār al-Āthār al-Islāmiyya, *Maṣāḥif Sanʿāʾ*, 36-61).

Western scholars have also examined the question of the *basmala*'s relationship to the qurʾānic text (see COLLECTION OF THE QUR'ĀN). Nöldeke suggests that at least as early as the Qur'ān copy (*muṣḥaf*, q.v.) of Ḥafṣa the *basmala* was used to separate sūras (*GQ*, ii, 46). R. Blachère sees the *basmala* as a formula used by Muḥammad to introduce letters and pacts which was inaugurated at some point to mark the beginning of a sūra (*Introduction*, 143-4). R. Paret says it was likely added later as a seventh verse to Q 1 to allow "the seven oft-repeated [verses]" (*sabʿan mina l-mathānī*, Q 15:87) to apply to the Fātiḥa (*Kommentar*, 11). A. Neuwirth argues from Christian and Jewish liturgical formulae and the Fātiḥa's internal structure and content (e.g. repetition of part of the *basmala* in Q 1:3) that the *basmala* of Q 1:1 did not belong originally to the Fātiḥa (cf. Nöldeke, *GQ*, i, 116-7; ii, 41-2).

Place of the basmala *in Muslim life and tradition*

The *basmala* has been arguably the most-repeated sentence in Muslim usage. It is axiomatic that a Muslim should begin every act of any importance with the *basmala* (Zamakhsharī, *Kashshāf*, i, 26; Bājūrī, *Tuḥfat al-murīd*, 3; Rāzī, *Aḥkām al-basmala*, 19; M. al-Gharawī, *Ism*, 91; see RITUAL AND THE QUR'ĀN). Muḥammad is quoted as saying that "every important affair that one does not begin with 'in the name of God' is void" (Zamakhsharī, *Kashshāf*, i, 31; M. al-Gharawī, *Ism*, 13; Ṣabbān, *Risāla*, 21). Scriptural support is found in Q 6:119 which begins, "Why do you not eat that over which the name of God has been mentioned?" Various traditions stress the *basmala*'s great power and blessing, e.g. "Whoever recites *bi-smi llāh al-raḥmān al-raḥīm* enters paradise (*al-janna* [see PARADISE; GARDEN])" (A. Ghaylān, *Daʿwa*, 37; cf. M. b. ʿAlī al-Shawkānī, *Fatḥ al-qadīr*, i, 67-8).

The use of the *basmala* is often a legal and sometimes even political matter of importance. The divergence of the law schools concerning the audible recitation of the *basmala* in worship (q.v.), based on its status as an *āya* in the Fātiḥa and elsewhere, has

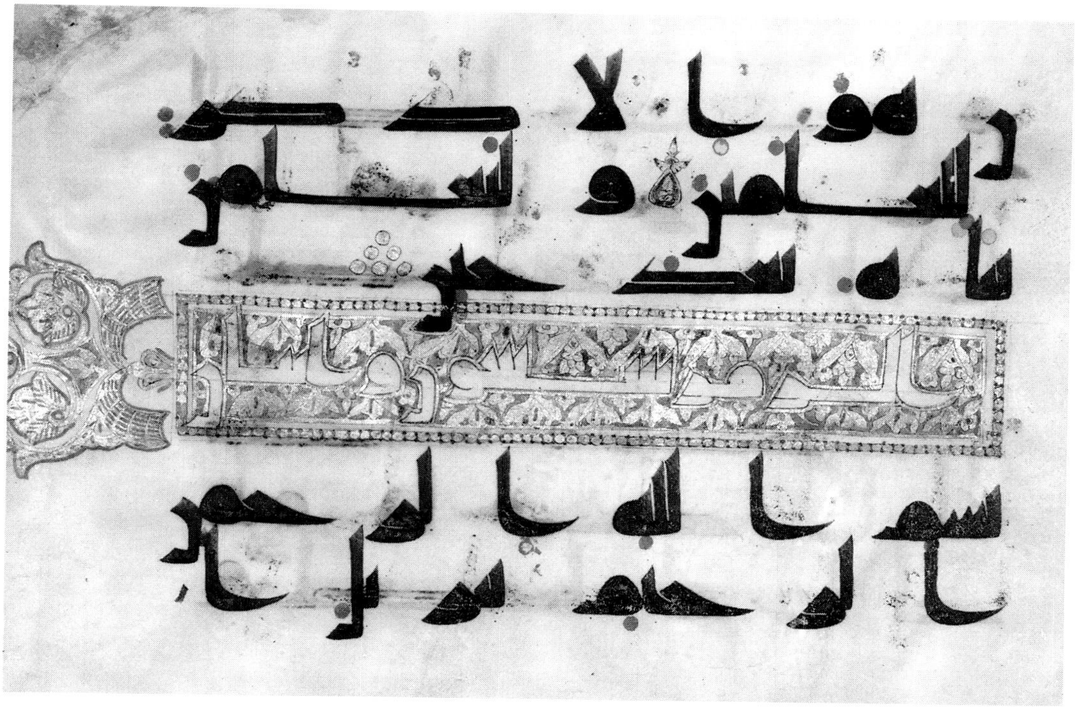

[1] End of Q 38 (Sūrat Ṣād) and initial *basmala* of Q 39 (Sūrat al-Zumar). Early Egyptian Kufic. Courtesy of the Freer and Sackler Gallery of Art, Smithsonian Institution, Washington, DC, F 1930.60-1.

[II] Opening page of Ibn al-Bawwāb's (d. 413/1022) copy of the Qurʾān, dated 391/1000. Q 1 (Sūrat al-Fātiḥa) and the beginning of Q 2 (Sūrat al-Baqara). Courtesy of the Trustees of the Chester Beatty Library, Dublin.

[III] Opening page of Q 86 (Sūrat al-Ṭāriq) with initial *basmala*. Eastern Kufic script copied in the fifth/eleventh century in Iraq or Persia. Courtesy of the Prince and Princess Sadruddin Aga Khan Collection, Geneva.

[IV] *Basmala* in upper façade of Imāmzāda Jaʿfar's tomb tower, 726/1325 (restored), Isfahan. Courtesy of Jonathan Bloom and Sheila Blair.

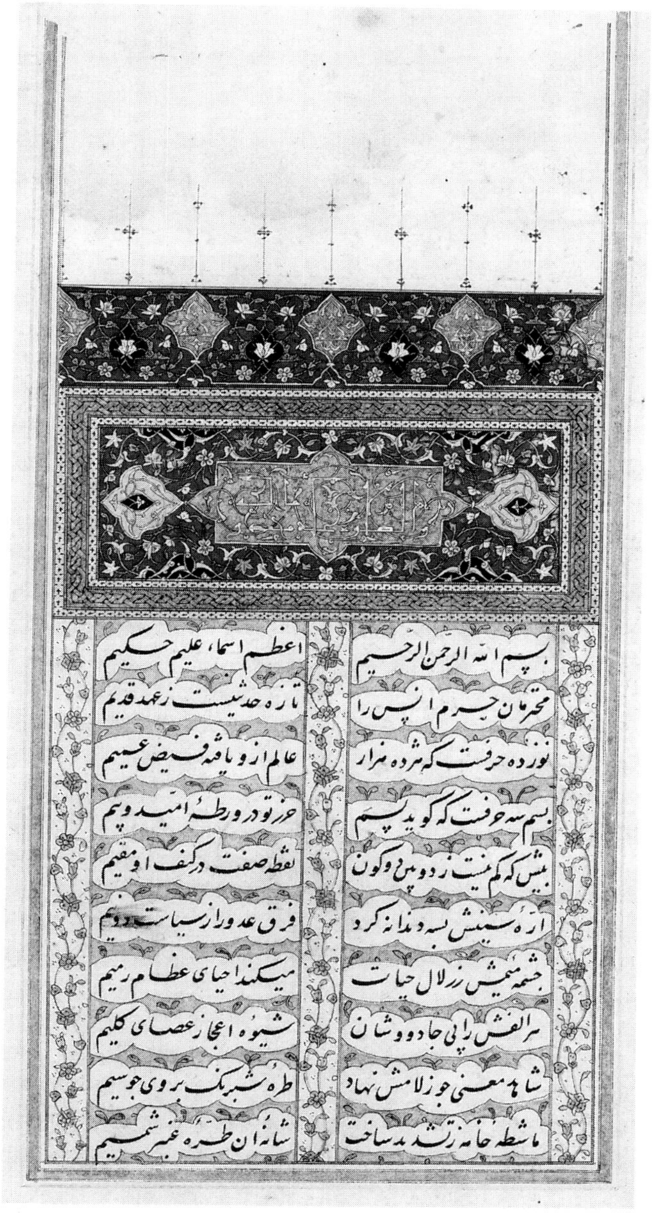

[v] Beginning of poem by Jāmī (d. 899/1492) on the secrets of the letters of the *basmala*. In *nastaʿlīq*, ca. 906/1500. Courtesy of the Metropolitan Museum of Art, New York.

[VI] Frontispiece of album of calligraphy by Aḥmad Karāḥiṣārī, showing the *basmala* in both chain and square Kufic scripts. Istanbul, ca. 957/1550. Courtesy of the Museum of Turkish and Islamic Art, Istanbul.

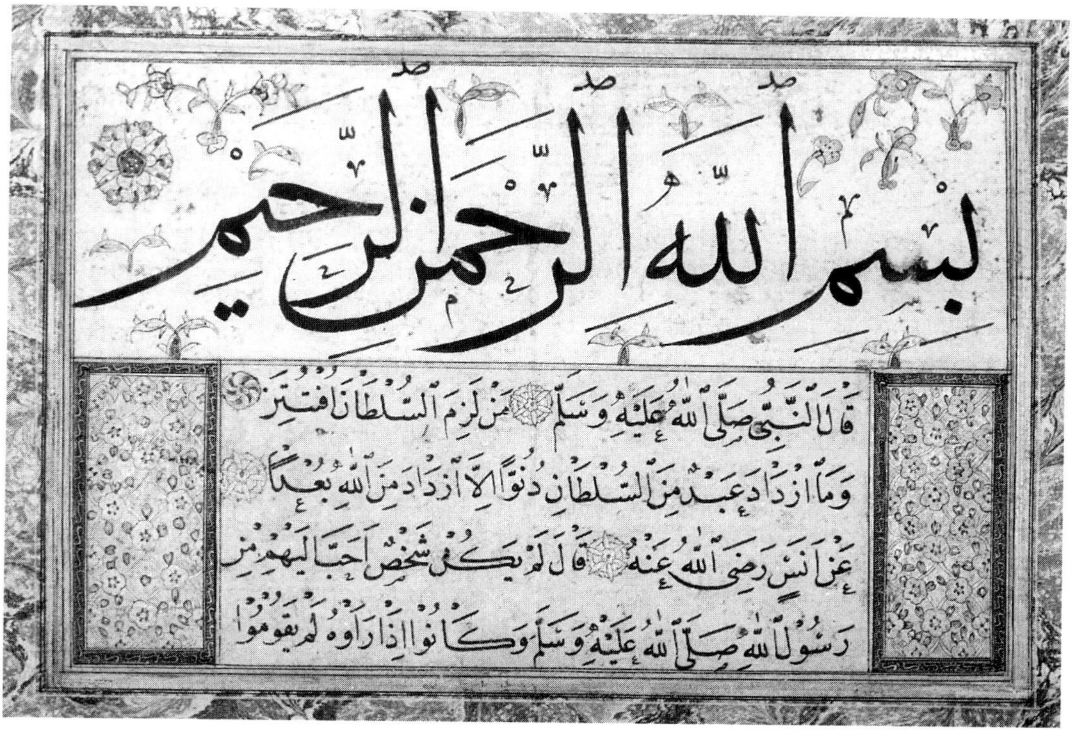

[VII] Leaf from an album of calligraphy by Ḥāfiẓ ʿUthmān, Istanbul, 1105/1693. Courtesy of the Staatliche Museen zu Berlin – Preußischer Kulturbesitz, Museum für Islamische Kunst, Berlin.

a By Aḥmed Ḳaraḥiṣārī, Turkey, 16th cty

b In oval shape, 19th cty (a)

c In Taʿlīq, by ʿAbdulqādir 1351/1932

e In a stork's shape, Turkey, 19th cty

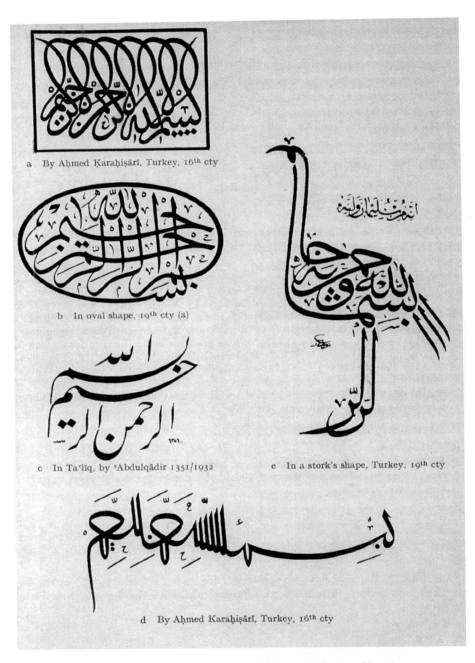

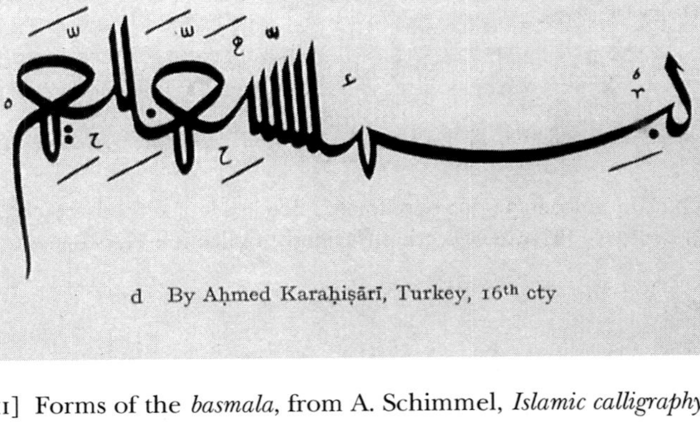

d By Aḥmed Karaḥiṣārī, Turkey, 16th cty

[VIII] Forms of the *basmala*, from A. Schimmel, *Islamic calligraphy*, 19.

been especially subject to considerable Muslim debate and discussion (e.g. Rāzī, *Aḥkām al-basmala,* 38-78; Murtaḍā al-Zabīdī, *Radd;* cf. Bājūrī, *Tuḥfat al-murīd,* 3-4). This question has even become the key issue for differing local interpretations of Islam as in the case of modernists and traditionalists in Gayo society in Acheh (J. Bowen, *Muslims,* 306-9).

Traditionally, the *basmala* carries special blessings and power (cf. I. al-Basyūnī, *Basmala,* 19-20; Ṭabarsī, *Majmaʿ,* i, 26-7) and is used as a talisman in popular magic (see AMULETS). One tradition claims it is "... an *āya* of God's scripture not revealed to anyone other than the Prophet save for Solomon (q.v.) the son of David (q.v.)" (Suyūṭī, *Durr,* i, 20). Especially in mystical thought it is considered the quintessence of the Qurʾān: According to Ibn al-ʿArabī (d. 638/1240) "the *basmala* is the key to every sūra" and God says that uttering the *basmala* is remembering *(dhikr)* him (*Futuḥāt,* viii, 343; vii, 274-5). An early Ismāʿīlī work studied by W. Ivanov explains its esoteric meaning in cosmological terms (W. Ivanov, *Studies,* 68). The mysteries of the letters of the *basmala* are many, e.g. the popular tradition that all of the scriptures are contained in the dot of the Arabic letter *bāʾ* in the *bi-* of the *basmala* (ʿAbd al-Karīm al-Jīlī, *Kahf,* 4-5; see LETTERS AND MYSTERIOUS LETTERS). Shīʿī sources develop a similar interpretation: According to Jaʿfar al-Ṣādiq (d. 148/765) and others, the greatest *āya* in the Qurʾān is the *basmala* (M. al-Gharawī, *Ism,* 77); all the areas of knowledge *(ʿulūm)* are contained in "the four [Shīʿī ḥadīth] books" and their *ʿulūm* in the Qurʾān and the *ʿulūm* of the Qurʾān in the Fātiḥa and the *ʿulūm* of the Fātiḥa in the *basmala* and the *ʿulūm* of the *basmala* in the *bāʾ* of the *basmala* (M. al-Gharawī, *Ism,* 64, 98). In a variation on this theme, Mir Dard (d. 1199/1785) cites ʿAlī b. Abī Ṭālib (q.v.) as saying all mysteries are contained in the dot beneath the *bāʾ* of the *basmala* and he, ʿAlī, is that dot (A. Schimmel, *Pain,* 90).

Orthographically, the *basmala* is set apart by the traditional but grammatically exceptional omission of the prosthetic *alif* of *ism (<s-m-w)* connecting the *bāʾ* directly to the *sīn*. One attestation of this is the absence of mention of the *alif* from the tradition that ʿUmar said "Lengthen the *bāʾ*, show clearly the teeth [of the *sīn*] and make round the *mīm*" (Zamakhsharī, *Kashshāf,* i, 35).

The calligraphic embellishment of the *basmala* has always been a favorite artistic undertaking in Islam, whether executed in formal script styles, zoomorphic (bird, lion, etc.) designs, stylized calligraphic shapes *(tughra)* or decorative calligrams (see ART AND ARCHITECTURE AND THE QURʾĀN; ARABIC SCRIPT; CALLIGRAPHY). The culmination of the calligrapher's art is often considered to be the famous *basmala* of the Ottoman artist Aḥmad Qarāḥiṣārī (d. 963/1520) in which extreme application of the principle of assimilation of letters (the letters *rāʾ* and *yāʾ* disappear, *lām* is shortened and "Allāh" becomes symbolic vertical strokes) leads to a *basmala* crafted into a single sweeping line of script without lifting the pen.

William A. Graham

Bibliography
Primary: Ālūsī, *Rūḥ;* Bājūrī, Ibrāhīm b. Muḥammad, *Tuḥfat al-murīd ʿalā jawharat al-tawḥīd,* Cairo 1939; Ibn al-ʿArabī, Muḥyī l-Dīn Abū ʿAbdallāh Muḥammad b. ʿAlī, *al-Futūḥāt al-makkiyya,* ed. Uthmān Yaḥyā, 14 vols. to date, Cairo 1972-; id. (attr.; actual author is ʿAbd al-Razzāq al-Kāshānī), *Tafsīr al-Qurʾān al-karīm,* ed. M. Ghālib, 2 vols., Beirut 1978; al-Jīlī, ʿAbd al-Karīm, *al-Kahf wa-l-raqīm fī sharḥ bi-smi llāh al-raḥmān al-raḥīm,* Hyderabad 1340/1922; Muḥammad b. ʿAlī al-Shawkānī, *Fatḥ al-qadīr. al-Jāmiʿ bayna fannay al-riwāya wa-l-dirāya min ʿilm al-tafsīr,* ed. ʿAbd al-Raḥmān ʿUmayrah, 6 vols., Cairo 1994; Murtaḍā al-Zabīdī, *al-Radd ʿalā man*

abā l-ḥaqq wa-iddaʿā anna l-jahr bi-l-basmala min sunnat Sayyid al-Khalq, ed. A. al-Kuwaytī, Riyadh 1991; Muslim, *Ṣaḥīḥ;* Rashīd Riḍā, *Manār;* Rāzī, *Aḥkām al-basmala,* ed. Majdī l-Sayyid Ibrāhīm, Cairo n.d.; id., *Tafsīr;* al-Ṣabbān, Muḥammad b. ʿAlī Abū l-ʿIrfān, *al-Risāla l-kubrā fī l-basmala,* ed. F. al-Zamrī and Ḥ. al-Mīr, Beirut 1995; Suyūṭī, *Durr;* id. *Itqān;* Ṭabarī, *Tafsīr;* id., *Taʾrīkh;* Ṭabarsī, *Majmaʿ;* Zamakhsharī, *Kashshāf.*
Secondary: H. Algar, Besmellāh. In exegesis, jurisprudence and cultural life, in E. Yarshater (ed.), *Encyclopaedia Iranica,* 7 vols. to date, London 1982-, iv, 172-4; M. Ayoub, *The Qurʾān and its interpreters,* 2 vols., Albany 1984, i; I. al-Basyūnī, *al-Basmala bayna ahl al-ʿibāra wa-ahl al-ishāra,* Cairo 1972; Blachère, *Introduction;* J. Bowen, *Muslims through discourse,* Princeton 1993; B. Carra de Vaux (rev. L. Gardet), Basmala, in *EI²*, i, 1084-5; Dār al-Āthār al-Islāmiyya, Kuwait National Museum, *Maṣāḥif Ṣanʿāʾ,* Kuwait 1985; M. al-Gharawī, *al-Ism al-aʿẓam aw al-basmala wa-l-ḥamdala,* Beirut 1982; ʿA.S. Ghaylān, *al-Daʿwa ilā llāh bi-afḍāl bi-smi llāh,* Rabat 1994; P. Gignoux, Besmellah. Origin of the Formula, in E. Yarshater (ed.), *Encyclopaedia Iranica,* 7 vols. to date, 1982-, iv, 172; id., Pad Nām i Yazdān. Pour une origine iranienne du bi'smillah, in *Travaux de l'Institut d'Études Iraniennes* (Sorbonne Nouvelle), Paris n.d., 159-63; W. Ivanov, *Studies in early Persian Ismailism,* Bombay 1955; J. Jomier, Le nom divin "al-Raḥmān" dans le Coran, in L'Institut Français de Damas, *Mélanges Louis Massignon,* 3 vols., Damascus 1956, ii, 361-81; A.T. Khoury, *Der Koran. Arabisch-Deutsch Übersetzung und wissenschaftlicher Kommentar,* 9 vols. to date, Gütersloh 1990-; K. Kufralı, Besmele, in *İslâm Ansiklopedisi,* 16 vols., Istanbul 1988-97, ii, 568-70; Y. Moubarac, Les études d'épigraphie sud-sémitique et la naissance de l'Islam, in *REI* 25 (1957), 13-68; A. Neuwirth, Sūrat al-Fātiḥa — "Eröffnung" des Text-Corpus Koran oder "Introitus" der Gebetsliturgie? in W. Gross, H. Irsigler and T. Seidl (eds.), *Text, Methode und Grammatik,* St. Ottilien 1991, 331-57; Nöldecke, *GQ;* Paret, *Kommentar;* G. Ryckmans, *Les religions arabes préislamiques,* Louvain 1951; Y. Safadi, *Islamic calligraphy,* Boulder 1979, 32-9; A. Schimmel, *Islamic calligraphy,* Leiden 1970, 3, 16-19; id., *Pain and grace,* Leiden 1976, 90; A. Spitaler, *Die Verszählung des Koran nach islamischer Überlieferung,* Munich 1935; M. Uzun, Besmele (Hat), in *Türkiye Diyanet Vakfi İslâm Ansiklopedisi,* 16 vols., Istanbul 1988-97, v, 532-40; S. Yıldırım, Besmele, in *Türkiye Diyanet Vakfi İslâm Ansiklopedisi,* 16 vols., Istanbul 1988-97, v, 529-32; M. Zakariya, *The calligraphy of Islam,* Georgetown 1979, 34-7.

Bāṭin and Ẓāhir

see EXEGESIS OF THE QURʾĀN: CLASSICAL AND MEDIEVAL

Battles/Warfare

see EXPEDITIONS AND BATTLES

Be

see CREATION; JESUS

Beast of Prey

see ANIMAL LIFE; LAWFUL AND UNLAWFUL

Beating

see CHASTISEMENT AND PUNISHMENT

Beauty

A quality in persons or objects that appeals to the human senses and exalts the spirit. At least a dozen terms describe beauty in the Qurʾān, which is more often understood as a moral quality than an aesthetic one. It is a quality defined by its deep effects upon the beholder rather than by its own properties. Aesthetic terms (e.g. the various terms related to *jamāl, iʿjāb, zīna, ḥilya, zukhruf, ṭayyib, alwān, qurrat ʿayn, bahīj*) signal moral choices to be made or divine grace rendered (see CONSOLATION), while moral terms (e.g. the various terms related to *ḥusn, itqān, fitna, karīm*) signal either beauty or the appropriate response to it. Reference to three kinds of beauty is discernible in the Qurʾān. The first characterizes the signs (q.v.) of God in creation (q.v.): awesome, delightful, instructive or useful, but ultimately transitory. The second describes the ornaments produced by human beings: attractive and enticing but also meaningless and even deceptive. This, too, is transitory. The third kind of beauty is not of this world but rather is sublime and eternal. Each of these three categories will be discussed in sequence.

The Arabic word most often translated as

"beauty" *(jamāl)* occurs only once in the Qurʾān and in that instance it has an aesthetic denotation: "And livestock… you find beauty in them when you bring them home in the evening and when you put them out to pasture" (Q 16:5-6). Yet other forms and effects of beauty are frequently cited. Humans delight in their children (q.v.; Q 28:13); fair winds (Q 10:22; 30:46; see AIR AND WIND); rain (Q 30:48) and the earth (q.v.) afterward (Q 57:20) and seed that grows (Q 48:29); fine animals (Q 2:69) and fertile pairs (Q 22:5; 26:7-8); and nice clothes and pure things (Q 7:31-2; see BLESSING). God has made things beautiful on purpose, as seen in the phrase "the creation of God, who has perfected *(atqana)* all things" (Q 27:88; cf. 22:6; 95:4). "We placed constellations in heaven and made them beautiful *(zayyannāhā)* to the beholders" (Q 15:16; cf. 37:6-7; 50:6; 67:3-5). "It is God… who has formed you and made your forms beautiful *(aḥsana ṣuwarakum)*" (Q 40:64).

Earthly beauty, however, can be a temptation and a test. Q 18:7 asserts: "What is on earth we have made a [mere] decoration for it *(zīnatan lahā)*, so that we might test which of them is best in his actions" (cf. Q 57:20). Q 2:221 notes that beauty must not be the overriding criterion: "A believing slave-woman is better than an unbeliever, however much the latter pleases you *(aʿjabatkum)*." Other verses remark that humans deceive themselves and others with superficialities *(zīna)*. Significantly, the calf of gold (q.v.) is made from "the people's ornaments" (*zīnat al-qawm*, Q 20:87). We hear of unbelievers dazzled by their own stratagems (Q 13:33) and of him "whose evil act is made to seem fine to him *(zuyyina lahu sūʾu ʿamalihi)*" (Q 35:8; cf. 9:37; 10:12; 47:14). Forms of natural and man-made ornamentation *(zukhruf)* can be assessed as both positive and negative: "The earth takes on its ornament *(akhadhat al-arḍu zukhrufahā)* and is adorned *(azzayyanat)*" (Q 10:24) but humans deceive each other with "fancy talk *(zukhruf al-qawl)*" (Q 6:112).

The delights of paradise (q.v.) are sometimes evoked by the mention of beautiful objects, e.g. luxuries such as gold (q.v.) and silk (q.v.; e.g. Q 35:33) or couches and rich drinking cups (e.g. Q 56:12-18 ; see CUPS AND VESSELS). More often, however, the pleasures of paradise are described in terms that would appeal particularly to desert dwellers: trees, gardens, shade, and water (q.v.; see GARDEN). The Qurʾān itself is more often described in terms that mark its connection to the divine. The jinn (q.v.) who hear the Qurʾān do not call it "beautiful" but "a wonder" (*Qurʾānan ʿajaban*, Q 72:1), while humans break out in gooseflesh (Q 39:23). God himself is the subject of an extended metaphor in the Light Verse (Q 24:35; see VERSES) from which the listener infers his beauty, though he is never called "beautiful." Aspects of divinity are awesome rather than beautiful (see GOD AND HIS ATTRIBUTES). Yet a ḥadīth says what the many qurʾānic references to beauty seem to imply: "God is beautiful and loves beauty" (Muslim, *Ṣaḥīḥ*). Beauty was certainly a factor in the later theological concept of the "miraculous inimitability" *(iʿjāz)* of the Qurʾan (see INIMITABILITY). See also ART AND ARCHITECTURE AND THE QURʾĀN.

Rosalind Ward Gwynne

Bibliography
Primary: al-Ghazālī, Abū Ḥāmid Muḥammad, *al-Ḥikma fī makhlūqāt Allāh*, Beirut 1398/1978; Muslim, *Ṣaḥīḥ;* Rāzī, *Tafsīr*, ed. M. Muḥyī l-Dīn; Suyūṭī, *Itqān*, ed. M.A.F. Ibrāhīm, 4 vols. in 2, Cairo 1967, esp. chaps. 64 and 73; Ṭabarī, *Tafsīr*, ed. Shākir; Ṭabarsī, *Majmaʿ*, 5 vols., Sidon 1333/1915.
Secondary: K. Cragg, *The mind of the Qurʾān*, London 1973; H. Kassis, *A concordance to the*

Qurʾān, Berkeley 1983; Nwyia, *Exégèse;* F. Rahman, *Major themes of the Qurʾān,* Minneapolis 1980.

Bedouin

The Arabic term for "desert-dweller" *(badawī)* is a derivation from the root *b-d-w.* Arabic lexicographers use the term *badw/badawī* as an antonym for "sedentary people" *(ḥāḍir),* and the expression "people became Bedouin" *(badā l-qawm badwan)* means that they went out to the desert (Ibn Sīda in *Lisān al-ʿArab,* xiv, 67). The cognate term *bādiya* refers to the sand-desert as opposed to the settled lands. The terms *badw, badawī* or the active participle *bādī* signify one who pursues a certain way of life, i.e. people of the desert or nomads as distinct from settled people. *Bādī* is used twice in the Qurʾān; of more frequent occurrence is another term for Bedouin, the plural form *aʿrāb* (sing. *ʿarab,* see ARABS).

Words derived from the root *ʿ-r-b* were used in pre-Islamic times in different Semitic languages as appellations for the inhabitants of the desert, whether for sand-dwellers or oasis dwellers. In the biblical context *ʿarab* is a term for a particular mode of life (*Isa* 13:20; *Jer* 3:2) and not the name of a particular people. The Old Testament locates the Arabs as nomads in the neighborhood of Israel (*Jer* 25:24; *Ezek* 27:21; 2 *Chron* 9:14). Assyrian documents of the second half of the eighth century B.C.E. frequently mention the *aribi/aribu* as referring to nomadic tribes in the deserts around Palestine and northern Sinai.

In south Arabian inscriptions from the third century C.E. onwards the term *ʿarab* (pl. *aʿrāb*) designates the Bedouin inhabitants of the Arabian peninsula as distinct from its sedentary people. From the mention of *aʿrāb* in Sabaic inscriptions in connection with accounts of armed conflicts between Sabaʾ and Ḥimyar, the conclusion can be drawn that Ḥimyar recruited some of its soldiers from the Bedouin. In a late Sabaic inscription (516 C.E.) the *aʿrāb* occur as soldiers too. An inscription from the late third century B.C.E. mentions the *aʿrāb* of Mārib and it is not clear whether they are part of a south Arabian tribe or serve as auxiliaries in armed conflicts. After the year 400 C.E. the royal title also includes the *aʿrāb* of the peninsula highlands and the Tihāma without precise definition.

Before Islam, the use of the term *ʿarab* was restricted and appears rarely in pre-Islamic poetry though it is seen more frequently in pre-Islamic prose (for examples see G. von Grunebaum, Nature of Arab unity, 21-2). In pre-Islamic times, the inhabitants of the Arabian peninsula did not know the term *ʿarab* as a name for themselves. Use of this word for the whole peninsula and its population was adopted from the Greeks who first described the inhabitants of the northern part of the peninsula with this term and applied it later to the whole peninsula. The close relationship between the word *ʿarab* and the meaning "Bedouin," especially in the sense that the Bedouin preserve the pure Arabic speech, is a later development. To date there has been no complete study of the development of the term *ʿarab* and its derivatives in early Islamic times.

Modern ethnology distinguishes between so-called full Bedouin and non-sedentary agriculturists and pastoralists. Yet these categories are frequently blurred because the main characteristic of both is nomadism or a non-sedentary life. There are many intermediate and transitional stages between a sedentary life and that of the full Bedouin (cf. M. von Oppenheim, *Beduinen,* i, 22-36). In addition to the transition of the breeders of sheep, goats and cattle from a non-sedentary life with occasional farming to a fully settled life, there is also evidence of the reverse development. Arabic lexicographical works that draw upon classical sources, however, do not reflect such ethnographic refinements. The appellation *aʿrāb* is given to those who dwell in the desert and move about in search of grazing and water (Lane, 1993). Such a definition presents no distinction between the above-mentioned different types of nomadic life nor does it permit a strict differentiation between the terms *aʿrāb* and *bādī* (e.g. *Lisān al-ʿArab,* i, 586; *Tāj al-ʿarūs,* iii, 333). In light of this, the translation of the term *bādī* as it occurs in the Qurʾān presents something of a problem. In Q 22:25 *bādī* is in contrast with *ʿākif,* a word that signifies someone who is remaining or staying in a place (Lane, 2122). In this verse, *bādī* can thus be interpreted as strangers or as visitors who are not permanent residents of Mecca (q.v.). It need not necessarily refer to non-sedentary people. The passage *bādūna fī l-aʿrāb* in Q 33:20 (translation by Arberry: "desert-dwellers among the Bedouins," Blachère: "au désert, parmi les Bédouins," Paret: "unter den Beduinen in der Steppe") gives the impression that a particular group of Bedouin is meant and *aʿrāb* functions as a generic term for different types of nomadic people. There is, however, no hint in pre-Islamic literature of a similar use.

The Qurʾān and later classical sources of Islamic literature present a composite picture of Bedouin lifestyles. The Bedouin are pastoralists specialized in camel breeding. Unlike pastoralists who specialize in the breeding and raising of other domesticated animals, such as cattle, sheep and goats, the Bedouin are almost self-sufficient. Nevertheless they are, to some extent, dependent on the settled lands. The existence of the Bedouin depends in great measure on the dromedary camel that supplies them with milk, meat (on festive occasions), leather, hair and dung (as fuel) and is used as both a means of transportation and a pack-animal (cf. Q 16:5; 40:79-80; 43:12-3; see CAMEL). The life of the Bedouin differs from that of the settled Arab despite the ties and relations between them. Summers are spent near permanent wells or other water-sources. With the beginning of the winter rains, animals are moved away from the exhausted summer pasture and are driven out to graze on the new grasses of the more arid steppes and deserts, a process called *tabaddī.* In spring the Bedouin return to their permanent wells to await the dry season. These places are called *ḥaḍar,* i.e. a fixed place. Q 16:6 refers to this periodic wandering of the Bedouin and the daily driving of their animals to pasture: "When you bring them home to rest and when you drive them forth to pasture" (see also early reports in Marzūqī, *Azmina,* ii, 119-23, 125-32). Of course, tent-dwelling is a feature of this nomadic existence and Q 16:80 mentions the tents or round huts *(buyūt)* made of leather *(min julūdi l-anʿāmi).*

Unlike the Bedouin, the population in urban and oasis settlements earned their livelihood from agriculture or from trade and pilgrimage income. Yet the development of trade in Arabia, especially on the incense route, was closely connected with camel nomadism. The Bedouin were certainly involved in conducting caravans of merchandise and in guaranteeing the safe transit of these caravans, although the details of that have not yet been closely studied. Because a Bedouin lifestyle also included raiding and plundering, people of the settled areas always strove for effective control of the Bedouin. Not only the trader had to come to an agreement with the Bedouin for guaranteeing him safe transit but also the oasis dweller often had to pay a so-called *khūwa* as protection money against raids on the settled population. Arab historiographers mention continual diplomatic conflicts in pre-Islamic times between the settled population and its nomadic neighbors (see the examples in R. Simon, Ḥums et īlāf, 217-20.)

In the Qurʾān, remarks about the Bedouin are not extensive and they testify to problems that emerged from forming alliances (see CONTRACTS AND ALLIANCES) with the Bedouin and to Muḥammad's suspicions about the existence or sincerity of their belief in God. In the years after the emigration from Mecca to Medina (the *hijra*, see EMIGRATION) the armed conflicts of the newly established Muslim community with the Bedouin were of great historical importance for Medina's development and independence. As we know from Arab historiography, raids *(ghazw)* against the Bedouin were more numerous than the armed conflicts with the Meccans (al-Wāqidī mentions 74 raids in his *Kitāb al-Maghāzī*); and problems that emerged from contracting alliances with Bedouin tribes came into focus in this period. One of the most important efforts to consolidate Muḥammad's own strength in Medina was the formation of alliances with nomadic tribes in the surrounding area of the town.

Some verses in the Qurʾān indicate that Muḥammad had enormous difficulties in controlling and using the Bedouin for his own ends. Q 9:90, 33:20, 48:11 and 48:16 refer to different expeditions (see EXPEDITIONS AND BATTLES) that depended upon the support of Bedouin on both sides, the Muslim and the Meccan. During the siege of Medina in the year 5/627, known to Muslims as the Expedition of the Trench (*khandaq*, see PEOPLE OF THE DITCH), the Meccans were supported by a vast confederacy, including some of the nomadic tribes. In Q 33:20 Muḥammad mentions the groups *(aḥzāb)* of Bedouin who joined the Meccans in this siege and criticizes the vacillation of some of his own Bedouin allies. In Q 48:11 and 16 — obviously revealed after the expedition of al-Ḥudaybiya (6/628; see ḤUDAYBIYA) — Muḥammad rebukes the Bedouin who were left behind (*mukhallafūn*, for an explanation see Paret, *Kommentar*, 208-9). The Bedouin *(al-aʿrāb)* mentioned in these verses did not join the expedition to al-Ḥudaybiya and made flimsy excuses for their absence. In Q 9:90 Muḥammad threatens the Bedouin with dire punishment in the afterlife (see REWARD AND PUNISHMENT) for absenting themselves from an expedition, probably that to Tabūk in the summer of the year 9/630. These verses show how deeply Muḥammad had been disappointed when some of the nomads refused to join the expedition. Apparently the Bedouin had seen no prospect of booty (q.v.) and therefore had rejected Muḥammad's appeal to them.

Q 9:97-9, 101, 120 and 49:14 offer indications of the fact that Muḥammad held the religious zeal of the Bedouin in low regard. He charges that some of the nomadic people pretend to be faithful simply in order to derive material advantage. These are described as more stubborn in unbelief (*ashaddu kufran wa-nifāqan*, Q 9:97) and as hypocrites (*munāfiqūn*, Q 9:101; see BELIEF AND UNBELIEF; HYPOCRITES AND HYPOCRISY). In the early Medinan years Muḥammad contracted alliances with nomadic tribes in the neighborhood on a secular basis, i.e. without demanding religious affiliation. After the treaty of al-Ḥudaybiya, however, the position of Muḥammad and the Muslims in Medina grew stronger and he began to demand acceptance of Islam and recognition of himself as Prophet. In letters and treaties concerning alliances with different tribes there are statements that, if the persons fulfil their obligations (performing the ritual prayer [*ṣalāt*, see PRAYER] and paying the communal alms [*ṣadaqa*, see ALMSGIVING]), they have a guarantee of security *(dhimma)*, meaning security for their lives, goods and rights to use the land (Ibn Isḥāq, *Sīra,* 963f.; Ibn Saʿd, *Ṭabaqāt,* i, 2, passim). Bedouin acceptance of these obligations does not appear to have modified their religious practices significantly nor could their degree of compliance be presumed to match that of those who had migrated from Mecca to Medina with Muḥammad (cf. Hamdānī, *Iklīl,* i, 167 for an account that there existed a special pledge made by the Bedouin to Muḥammad, *bayʿa aʿrābiyya* as against a pledge of migration, *bayʿa hijriyya*). In pre-Islamic times the religious life of the Bedouin consisted largely of periodic visits to holy places (q.v.), various forms of ritual sacrifice (q.v.) and the consultation of diviners (see PRE-ISLAMIC ARABIA AND THE QURʾĀN; DIVINATION). It is likely that most Bedouin managed with even less than that. Therefore the Bedouin considered the daily prayers *(ṣalāt)* and also the communal alms *(ṣadaqa),* which were two of the most important religious duties for a Muslim, as an unreasonable demand.

Later Muslim sources elaborated upon such differences of religious adherence and observance. Al-Marzūqī (*Azmina,* ii, 330-1) differentiates between those who emigrated from Mecca to Medina (*muhājirūn,* see EMIGRANTS AND HELPERS) and nomadic peoples who neither took part in the migration *(hijra)* nor submitted themselves to Muslim sovereignty. About the difference between Arabs *(ʿarab)* and Bedouin *(aʿrāb)* the philologist al-Azharī wrote that the *muhājirūn* and the residents of Medina who allied themselves with Muḥammad — the Helpers *(anṣār)* — are not Bedouin but Arabs because they live in settlements *(qurā ʿarabiyya)* and towns. Those who reverted to a nomadic lifestyle *(ahl al-badw)* after the migration to Medina became Bedouin again *(taʿarraba).* As indicated by passages such as Q 4:31 and Q 42:37, such reversion constitutes one of the "great sins" (*kabāʾir,* see SIN, MAJOR AND MINOR) for which an individual can be held accountable on the day of judgment (cf. Azharī in *Lisān al-ʿArab,* i, 586-7; *Tāj al-ʿarūs,* iii, 334; see LAST JUDGMENT). Only the Bedouin who performed the migration were considered to be full Muslims and this included the obligation of military service. From the last-mentioned remark of al-Azharī the conclusion can be drawn that, after the migration to Medina, many of the Bedouin returned to their tribes and refused to perform the military service (see TRIBES AND CLANS). This situation changed after the defeat of the *ridda,* the "defection" of some tribes that occurred after the death of the Prophet (see APOSTASY). Eventually nomadic units developed into important auxiliary troops and were brought together in garrison towns *(amṣār).* Nevertheless, the integration of the nomadic population into the Islamic state remained a source of social and political tension for centuries.

Ute Pietruschka

Bibliography

Primary: Hamdānī, Abū Muḥammad al-Ḥasan b. Aḥmad, *Kitāb al-Iklīl,* ed. M. al-Aqwaʿ al-Ḥiwālī, 2 vols., Cairo 1383-6/1963-6; Ibn Isḥāq, *Sīra;* Ibn Saʿd, *Ṭabaqāt;* al-Marzūqī, Abū ʿAlī Aḥmad b. Muḥammad b. al-Ḥasan, *Kitāb al-Azmina wa-l-amkina,* 2 vols., Hyderabad 1332/1914; *Tāj al-ʿarūs.*

Secondary: R.W. Bulliet, *The camel and the wheel,* Cambridge, MA 1975; W. Dostal, The development of Bedouin life in Arabia seen from archaeological material, in The International Symposium on Studies in the History of Arabia, *al-Jazīra al-ʿarabiyya qabla l-Islām,* 2 vols., Riyadh 1979, i, 125-44; id., The evolution of Bedouin life, in S. Moscati and F. Gabrieli (eds.), *L'antica società beduina,* Rome 1959, 11-34; I. Ephʿal, *The ancient Arabs. Nomads on the borders of the fertile crescent. 9th-5th centuries B.C.,* Jerusalem/Leiden 1982; G.E. von Grunebaum, The nature of Arab unity before Islam, in *Arabica* 10 (1963), 5-23; J. Henninger, La religion bédouine préislamique, in S. Moscati and F. Gabrieli (eds.), *L'antica società beduina,* Rome 1959, 115-40; J. Jabbur, *The Bedouins and the desert. Aspects of nomadic life in the Arab east,* New York 1995; Lane; A. Musil,

Northern Neǧd, New York 1928; T. Nagel, *Staat und Glaubensgemeinschaft im Islam,* 2 vols., Zürich 1981, i; M. von Oppenheim, *Die Beduinen,* 4 vols., Leipzig 1939-1968, i, 22-36; Paret, *Kommentar,* 208-9; C. Robin, La pénétration des Arabes nomades au Yémen, in *REMMM* 61 (1991-3); id., *L'Arabie antique de Karib'îl à Mahomet. Nouvelles données sur l'histoire des Arabes grâce aux inscriptions,* 71-88; R. Simon, Ḥums et īlāf, ou commerce sans guerre (Sur la genèse et le charactère du commerce de la Mecque), in *AO-H* 23 (1970), 205-32; J. Wagstaff, *The evolution of Middle Eastern landscapes. An outline to A.D. 1840,* London 1985; W.M. Watt, *Muhammad at Medina,* Oxford 1956; T. Weiss Rosmarin, Aribi und Arabien in den babylonisch-assyrischen Quellen, in *Journal of the Society of Oriental Research* 16 (1932), 1-37.

Bee see ANIMAL LIFE

Beguiling/Bewitching see MAGIC, PROHIBITION OF

Belief see BELIEF AND UNBELIEF

Belief and Unbelief

The fundamental attitudes to the divine being, to the prophethood of Muḥammad and to the message of the Qurʾān. The paired terms "belief and unbelief" *(īmān, kufr)* and their correlates "believer and unbeliever" *(muʾmin, kāfir)* represent the central antithesis of the qurʾānic discourse. The root *ʾ-m-n* in the sense of "believing" and its most common, though by no means only, antonym, *k-f-r* (see GRATITUDE AND INGRATITUDE), are among the most frequently attested roots in the Qurʾān with close to 500 cases of each. They appear, either separately or in combination, in most qurʾānic sūras, often more than once in a single verse. This in itself shows the central importance of these two pivotal concepts in the Qurʾān.

Belief and the believers

The term used most frequently in the Qurʾān to denote belief or faith (q.v.) is *īmān.* It is closely related to the term *islām* (q.v.) which is usually translated as "submission" or "the act of submitting." Although these two closely-related concepts seem at times to be near-synonymous (Q 10:84; 51:35-6), their difference is emphasized in Q 49:14: "The wandering Arabs (q.v.; see also BEDOUIN) say: We believe *(āmannā).* Say: You believe not, but rather say 'We submit' *(aslamnā),* for the faith has not yet entered into your hearts...."

Īmān is the verbal noun of the fourth form of the root *ʾ-m-n.* The active participle, *muʾmin,* is usually translated as "believer" (its plural, *muʾminūn,* is sometimes rendered "the faithful"), the only exception being Q 59:23 where it is God who is described as *muʾmin* but in the sense of a protector or guarantor of security (cf. also Q 106:3-4). According to M. Mir (Īmān), the root *ʾ-m-n,* especially in its fourth form, does indeed connote security since the one who believes becomes secure against untruth and misguidance in this world and against punishment in the next (cf. Ṭūsī, *Tibyān,* i, 54; Ṭabāṭabāʾī, *Mīzān,* i, 45). Muslim commentators usually provide an explanation of what is to be understood by the term *īmān* at its first occurrence in the Qurʾān (Q 2:3), glossing it as affirmation or attestation of the truth of something *(taṣdīq).*

Even though the term *muʾmin,* in an absolute sense, is primarily used to describe an adherent of the religion founded by Muḥammad — in other words, a Muslim — it should be emphasized at the outset that in the Qurʾān *muʾmin* does not have this exclusive meaning. It also covers the pre-Muḥammadan believers, i.e. those who believed in the messengers (see MESSENGER; PROPHETS AND PROPHETHOOD) that were sent by God before the appearance of Muḥammad, the most obvious example being the *muʾmin* mentioned in Q 40:28-45 who was a supporter of Moses (q.v.) at the court of Pharaoh (q.v.). A second group of non-Muslim *muʾminūn* consists of individuals among the People of the Book (q.v.; see below) who are described in the Qurʾān (Q 2:62; 3:110, 113-5, 199; 5:66, 83; 28:52-4; 57:27) as believers although most commentators regard them as converts to Islam. Strictly speaking, then, *muʾmin* and Muslim are not synonymous. However, in the following, *muʾmin* will be used primarily in the sense of an adherent to the religion of Muḥammad. The formula "O you who believe" *(yā ayyuhā lladhī āmanū),* which appears frequently in sūras from the Medinan period introducing a precept (see BOUNDARIES AND PRECEPTS) or an admonition, invariably addresses this class of believers. At times, female believers *(muʾmināt)* are explicitly addressed or mentioned, e.g. Q 9:71-2.

The objects of belief

What distinguishes true believers from polytheists (see POLYTHEISM AND ATHEISM) is the belief in one God, whereas what sets them apart from the earlier monotheists is the belief that Muḥammad is the messenger of God. This is reflected in the *shahāda,* the Muslim profession of faith (q.v.), which constitutes one of the five pillars of Islam and to which the Shīʿīs add the affirmation that ʿAlī (see ʿALĪ B. ABĪ ṬĀLIB; SHĪʿISM AND THE QURʾĀN) is the friend of God. But there is more to belief than that. In order to qualify as a *muʾmin,* one must furthermore believe in God's earlier messengers, his revealed books (see BOOK), his angels (see ANGEL) and the hereafter (see HEAVEN; HELL; Q 2:177, 285; 4:136). A separate article of faith is belief in *al-ghayb* (Q 2:3, see HIDDEN AND THE HIDDEN), which is given various glosses by the commentators (see Ibn al-Jawzī, *Zād,* i, 24-5). The commonly accepted view is that it refers to "unseen things," knowledge of which is hidden from humankind. Examples of "unseen things" that commentators on the Qurʾān frequently mention include the destiny (q.v.; see also FATE) of an individual human being, the events of the last day (see APOCALYPSE), the resurrection (q.v.), and the last judgment (q.v.; Ibn Kathīr, *Tafsīr,* i, 41; *Jalālayn,* 7; Qurṭubī, *Jāmiʿ,* i, 159). For a Shīʿī exegete like al-Ṭūsī (d. 460/1067; *Tibyān,* i, 55), *al-ghayb* includes the (unknown) duration of the occultation of the awaited Imām (q.v.) and the coming of the Mahdī. Only God has the keys to the unseen things *(mafātīḥ al-ghayb,* Q 6:59, also the title of the commentary by Fakhr al-Dīn al-Rāzī) but man must believe in their existence. Moreover, some commentators state that in order for *īmān* to be valid, it should be a genuine affirmation and not merely an attitude acquired by imitation *(taqlīd,* Rashīd Riḍā, *Manār,* ii, 111f., 145f. and cf. Ibn al-ʿArabī [attributed], *Tafsīr,* i, 16-7, who distinguishes between *īmān taqlīdī* and *īmān taḥqīqī).*

Belief and works

According to the Qurʾān, the attitude of true believers towards God is characterized by gratitude, awe, repentance, and submission. In their attitude to their fellow humans, they are distinguished by their chastity, modesty, humility, forgiveness, and truthfulness. They respect their contracts and covenants (see Q 8:2-4, 74; 9:112; 13:20-3; 23:1-6, 8-11, 57-61; 24:36-9; 25:63-8, 72-4; 28:54-5; 32:15-7; 33:35-6; 42:36-43; 48:29; 70:22-35; 76:7-10; see CONTRACTS AND ALLIANCES; COVENANT; BREAKING TRUSTS AND CONTRACTS). The sūras from the Medinan period emphasize the importance of the coherence of the

Muslim community (see COMMUNITY AND SOCIETY IN THE QUR'ĀN). Believers are brothers (Q 49:10; see BROTHERS AND BROTHERHOOD) and should assist and protect each other (Q 8:72, 74; 9:71). Peace must be established between them in case they should fight (Q 49:9-10) and they should show each other mercy (Q 48:29). Offending another believer is a sin (Q 48:29; see SIN, MAJOR AND MINOR). These passages, incidentally, show that all was not well and harmonious among the believers in Medina; there were even special rules governing their proper conduct towards the Prophet and his wives (e.g. Q 33:53; 49:2-5; 58:12-3; see WIVES OF THE PROPHET).

Belief should ideally be accompanied by and expressed in pious deeds (*ʿamal al-ṣāliḥāt*) such as worship (q.v.), charity and striving for the cause of God in different ways. Belief and works frequently appear together in the Qurʾān which suggests that *ʿamal* (see WORK) is an integral part of *īmān* (Q 2:82, 277; 3:57; 4:57, 122, 173; 5:9, 93; 7:42). However, post-qurʾānic literature reveals a tendency to separate *īmān* and *ʿamal*, often equating the latter with *islām* in the sense of an outward expression of the faith whose interior location is the heart (q.v.). This tendency can already be observed in certain traditions on *īmān* in the canonical collections of ḥadīth where Muḥammad is asked by the angel Gabriel (Jibrīl, see GABRIEL) about the essence of *islām, īmān* and *iḥsān* (which latter stands for supererogatory acts of worship; see Bukhārī, *Ṣaḥīḥ, K. al-Īmān*, 38, 50; cf. Muslim, *Ṣaḥīḥ, K. al-Īmān*). Compendiums of theology and heresiographical tracts invariably include discussions about the relationship between faith and works and the nature of belief. They raise such questions as whether someone who professes faith but does not observe the corresponding precepts can be considered a *muʾmin* and whether he or she is entitled to a reward (see REWARD AND PUNISHMENT) in the hereafter. (For a survey of theological positions held by different groups and individuals, see Rāzī, *Tafsīr*, ad Q 2:6.) Another much-debated question is whether belief can increase or decrease (based on Q 3:173; 8:2; 48:4).

For their belief and their righteous deeds, believers will be the recipients of God's favor and enjoy preferential treatment. Although they will be subjected to trials in this world (Q 2:214; 3:186; 47:31; see TRIAL), they also prosper and God makes their works succeed (e.g. Q 2:5; 3:104; 23:1; 33:71). He strengthens the believers and defends, saves and protects them (Q 58:22; 22:38; 39:61; 40:9). Ultimately, they will be admitted to paradise (q.v.) — described in vivid detail throughout the Qurʾān — where they will remain in eternal bliss (e.g. Q 2:25; 3:15; 9:72; 13:23; 18:31; 22:23; 23:19; 35:33; 55:54; see also GARDEN).

Unbelief and unbelievers

The most frequent, though not the only, Arabic term denoting unbelief, disbelief or misbelief is *kufr* but the Qurʾān contains a series of related and to some extent synonymous concepts. These include iniquity (*ẓulm*), sinfulness (*fisq*), arrogance (q.v.) or haughtiness (*istikbār*) and denial (*takdhīb*), each of which expresses an aspect of the unbeliever's attitude (for a detailed analysis, see Izutsu, *Concepts*, 105-77).

The basic meaning of *k-f-r* is to cover, to hide, to conceal, e.g. the truth. By extension, *kufr* came to mean to ignore or fail to acknowledge (Q 30:13; 35:14; 46:6; 3:115), to reject, to spurn, to be thankless or ungrateful (Q 2:152; 16:55, 83, 122-4; 17:27; 26:18-19; 29:66; 30:24; 43:15). Finally, mention must be made of the meaning which today is regarded as the primary one, to disbelieve. This signification of *kufr* retains all the connotations of the above-mentioned verbs. It was not so much transformed as extended in the course of the revelation of the Qurʾān (see M. Waldman, Development). According to classical sources of Arabic lexicography, such as the *Lisān al-ʿArab* (v. 144), the fundamental meaning of *kufr* is ingratitude for benefits received *(kufr al-niʿma)*.

Someone accused of *kufr* is called a *kāfir* (pl. *kāfirūn, kuffār, alladhīna kafarū,* and *kafara,* which latter occurs only once in the Qurʾān; often, however, the Qurʾān simply calls them *alladhīna lā yuʾminūna,* "those who do not believe"). The older English translation "infidel" is now used less frequently. The intensive forms, *kafūr* and *kaffār,* describe someone whose *kufr* takes extreme forms (Q 2:276; 11:9; 14:34; 22:38; 31:32; 35:36; 39:3; 42:48; 50:24). The derived form *takfīr,* not found in the Qurʾān, means branding someone, especially a fellow-Muslim, as a *kāfir*. This is condemned in ḥadīth but nonetheless *takfīr* became an effective instrument of excluding someone from the Muslim community. In the formative period of Islam the first ones to make this accusation were the Khārijīs (q.v.) who reserved for themselves the qualification *muʾminūn* while applying the term *kuffār* to all others. Their example has been followed by many others. Similarly, accusations of ascribing partners to God or of making anything else equal to him *(shirk)* have been used by Muslims in both medieval and modern times to challenge those whose views are deemed to be deviant.

The Qurʾān distinguishes two main groups of unbelievers. Although at first sight these two appear very different, they actually have much in common, not least being the fact that both rejected the message of Muḥammad. The idolaters (*mushrikūn,* see IDOLATRY AND IDOLATERS) were by far the most numerous for they constituted the majority among the Arabs, both sedentary and nomadic. The second group is that of the People of the Book *(ahl al-kitāb)*. A third group, to be discussed separately, is formed by the so-called hypocrites (*munāfiqūn,* see HYPOCRITES AND HYPOCRISY) who first appear in the Medinan period. Though outwardly professing belief, they are not truly committed to faith. This attitude is referred to in the *Lisān al-ʿArab* (v. 144) as *kufr al-nifāq,* to be distinguished from *kufr al-inkār* (failure to acknowledge the oneness of God either in the heart or in speech), *kufr al-juḥūd* (refusal to affirm in speech what the heart acknowledges as true), and *kufr al-muʿānada* (to acknowledge God in the heart and in speech but to refuse to act accordingly; cf. Lane, vii, 2621).

Idolaters, idol-worshippers, polytheists, pagans

The term *mushrik* is derived from *shirk,* i.e. associating, in the sense of ascribing partners to God, which is described in the Qurʾān as the only sin for which no forgiveness is possible (Q 4:48). Another common qurʾānic expression for this is "those who associate" *(alladhīna ashrakū)*. At first, Muḥammad's preaching was addressed almost entirely to the pagan Arabs whose attitude may be described as follows: Not believing in the existence of an afterlife, they are excessively attached to worldly goods and take great pride in their material possessions and in their sons (Q 19:77-80). But their enjoyment of this world will be brief (Q 2:126; 3:196-7; 31:24; 77:46) and their possessions and children will not avail them (Q 3:10, 116; 9:85; 34:35-7; 58:17; 60:3). Although they ascribe daughters to God (Q 16:57; 53:19-23), they themselves are aggrieved when female children are born to them (Q 16:58-9). God shows them his signs (q.v.), the wonders of nature, that they may believe and gives them of his bounties, that they may be grateful but they fail to acknowledge that the source of these favors is the one God, the creator of all things, who will resurrect and judge them on the last day. In their unbelief they follow the ways of their ancestors (Q 2:170;

37:69-70; 53:23) and are loath to give up their traditional beliefs and rites which are connected with idols (see IDOLS AND IMAGES) that will be of no help to them when the final hour comes. They ignore the warnings (q.v.) communicated to them by Muḥammad, just as earlier nations (the pre-Islamic unbelievers) had rejected the call of the messengers that God had sent, messengers such as Hūd (q.v.), Ṣāliḥ (q.v.), Noah (q.v.), Abraham (q.v.), Lot (q.v.), Moses (q.v.), and Jesus (q.v.; e.g. Q 6:34; 26:105, 123, 139, 141; 43:7; see also AGE OF IGNORANCE; PRE-ISLAMIC ARABIA AND THE QURʾĀN). They mock the believers (Q 83:29-32) and are not impressed by a message coming from someone who is a mere mortal like themselves, someone who fails to produce the miracles (see MIRACLE) that they demand as proof (q.v.; Q 17:90-3; cf. Q 74:52). Considering him possessed as had previous nations deemed the earlier warners, they call Muḥammad a liar who represents stories he received from outsiders as divine revelations. For their rejection, these nations had been severely punished (see PUNISHMENT STORIES) both in this life and in the hereafter, and this is what awaits the pagan Arabs unless they repent and turn to God and Muḥammad. However, most of the people to whom Muḥammad was sent will only recognize the truth of the warning and the reality of the punishment in the afterlife, when it is too late to mend their ways (e.g. Q 34:33; 39:56-8). Rather, they turned away when they were admonished (Q 21:2; 26:5; 74:49) or put their fingers in their ears (Q 71:7; see also BLASPHEMY). Theirs will be a painful doom in hell (graphic descriptions are found throughout the Qurʾān, e.g. Q 2:24; 4:56; 7:50; 8:50; 9:35; 21:39; 22:19; 23:104; 40:49, 72; 37:62-8; 44:43-8; 56:52-6). Criticism of the pagans continues into the Medinan period although there the focus shifts somewhat from the *mushrikūn* to the hypocrites and the People of the Book.

The People of the Book

This term (Q 2:105, 109; 3:64, 65, 69, 70, 71, 72, 75, 98, 99, 110, 113, 199; 4:123, 153, 159, 171; 5:15, 19, 59, 68, 77; 29:46; 33:26; 57:29; 59:2, 11; 98:1, 6), along with phrases like "those who were given the book" (*alladhīna ūtū l-kitāb,* Q 2:144, 145; 3:19, 20, 100, 186, 187; 4:47, 131; 5:5; 9:29; 74:31; 98:4, and cf. 2:213; 4:44, 51) and "those to whom we gave the book" (*alladhīna ātaynāhum al-kitāb,* Q 2:146; 6:20, 89, 114; 28:52; 29:47), is commonly taken to refer to the Jews and the Christians (see CHRISTIANS AND CHRISTIANITY; JEWS AND JUDAISM). In some verses that allude to the Jews and Christians, the Qurʾān mentions a third group: the enigmatic Sabians (*Ṣābiʾūn,* Q 2:62; 5:69; 22:17) but whether they and the Magians (*Majūs,* Q 22:17) are to be considered as "People of the Book" is disputed among commentators and legal scholars (see SABIANS AND MAGIANS).

The Meccan sūras contain little direct polemic against Judaism or Christianity. On the contrary, the Israelites or Jews and the Christians are presented as an example to be followed. This is because they acknowledge that there is only one God, the creator of the universe, who makes himself known to humankind through revelations (see REVELATION AND INSPIRATION) brought by prophets and messengers and who rewards obedience (q.v.) and severely punishes rejection and unbelief. In the Meccan period, the believers are still encouraged to seek the advice of the People of the Book who, having been steeped in monotheistic tradition, may be able to clarify for them issues that they do not understand (Q 10:94).

This initially benevolent attitude changes after Muḥammad moves to Medina (q.v.)

where he becomes closely acquainted with adherents of other monotheistic religions, especially with Jews. Although some of the Jews converted to the new religion, the majority rejected Muḥammad's claim to prophethood. This, combined with political factors, led to the deterioration of relations between Muḥammad and the Jews of Medina as is reflected in many of the sūras from the Medinan period. Jews are now grouped together with the idolaters as those who are the most inimical towards the believers. Christians, on the other hand, who constituted a less immediate threat, are presented as sympathetic to the believers (Q 5:82-3; see McAuliffe, *Qurʾānic*, chap. 7). Even though Christians themselves — although, according to certain commentators, only a portion of them — are judged more favorably than are the Jews, Christian teachings such as the Trinity (q.v.) and Jesus as the son of God, which are considered by Muslims to be distortions of true Christianity, are severely condemned in the Qurʾān as being in contradiction with the doctrine of the absolute oneness of God (Q 4:171; 5:75, 116; 9:30).

The unbelief of which the majority among the People of the Book are accused is of a different kind than that of the pagans. The stubborn rejection of Muḥammad's message by the People of the Book is simply incomprehensible because they had received revelations before and should therefore have been the first to believe in Muḥammad, whose coming was foretold in their scriptures (Q 7:157; 61:6; see SCRIPTURE AND THE QURʾĀN). Moreover, they shared with Muḥammad and his followers a number of essential truths. But, they refused to accept that Muḥammad had brought a new (or rather renewed) dispensation and are accused of having obscured scriptural references to him. In addition, they constituted a threat to the believers, whom they tried to lead astray (q.v.), seducing them back to their former unbelief (Q 2:109; 3:98-199).

The People of the Book, however, are not all alike. According to the Qurʾān, there are some among them who believe (Q 3:110, 113, 199; 28:52-4, and cf. 5:66, analyzed in detail in McAuliffe, *Qurʾānic*, chaps. 5, 6, 8). According to most commentators, this refers to those Jews and Christians who embraced Islam, such as the Jew ʿAbdallāh b. Salām and certain Christians from amongst the Abyssinians and others (e.g. Ṭabarī, *Tafsīr*, vii, 107; Ṭūsī, *Tibyān*, ii, 54; Ṭabarsī, *Majmaʿ*, iv, 170; Qurṭubī, *Jāmiʿ*, ii, 166; Ibn Kathīr, *Tafsīr*, i, 397; *Jalālayn*, 69-70; see also ABYSSINIA). They are, in other words, Muslims. Another view is that the reference is to people who did not formally convert to Islam but whose loyalty to the true interpretation of their scriptures impelled them to profess belief in Muḥammad as the one who was announced therein. Unlike their coreligionists, they were not dismayed by the fact that he was not from among their own people. The ones who are described in Q 28:52-4 as stating that they submitted before "it," i.e. before the coming of Muḥammad or the revelation of the Qurʾān *(innā kunnā min qablihi muslimīn)*, are seen as Jews and Christians who understood from their scriptures that a new prophet was to be sent and who recognized Muḥammad as that prophet when he appeared. They are promised a double reward because of their loyalty to two books, the earlier revelation and the Qurʾān.

Despite the potentially higher status of the earlier monotheists, those among them who are guilty of unbelief will share a painful doom with the pagans unless they mend their ways. Q 98, taken by most commentators to be Medinan, places the unbelievers amongst the People of the Book on the same level as idolaters *(mushrikūn),* calling them "the worst of created beings," as opposed to the believers, who are the best of them (Q 98:6-7).

The People of the Book were offered the choice of joining the new religion or of maintaining their own religious identity, but at the price of a poll-tax (*jizya,* q.v.), payment of which expressed submission to the Muslim community (Q 9:29). This arrangement was to become the basis for the *dhimma*-system which guaranteed the People of the Book protection (q.v.) of their lives and goods and which dates from the period following the death of Muḥammad (see A. Fattal, *Le statut légal;* C. Cahen, Dhimma; id., Djizya). The tolerance that was sometimes accorded to the People of the Book was not granted to the idolaters *(mushrikūn).* For them, the choice was between Islam and death. Q 2:256, which reads "there is no compulsion in religion" *(lā ikrāha fī l-dīn)* and which in modern times is often adduced as proof of Muslim tolerance of other religions, is considered by most exegetes to have been abrogated by the so-called sword-verse (Q 9:5; see ABROGATION) and other passages that call for an all-out war against the unbelievers (Q 2:216; 8:39; 47:4). Another passage which is often considered as proof of tolerance is "To you your *dīn,* to me mine" (Q 109:6) where *dīn* is interpreted either as religion or as the recompense for one's beliefs. Most commentators interpret this verse as a radical break with the pagans by those who had accepted the prophethood of Muḥammad (see Ibn al-Jawzī, *Zād,* ix, 252).

Relations between believers and unbelievers

Various passages in the Qurʾān speak of the attitude to be adopted by the believers towards the unbelievers, warning them against close contacts with others who are not of their own rank. Whoever associates with them is one of them (Q 3:28; 118; 4:144; 5:51; 9:23-4; 13:1; 60:1; and cf. 58:22). The unbelievers are each other's allies (Q 8:73). Sitting with the unbelievers who mock the Qurʾān is forbidden (Q 4:140); the contributions from unbelievers may not be accepted (Q 9:54) and praying at their graves is prohibited (Q 9:84). Some passages explicitly forbid relations with pagan Arabs even if these are one's own relatives. The reason for the passage's revelation (*sabab al-nuzūl,* see OCCASIONS OF REVELATION) is not clear in every case, nor is the category of unbelievers to which reference is being made: the pagans, the People of the Book or perhaps the hypocrites. Not surprisingly, then, the exegetical literature also presents many different solutions. The unbelievers in Q 3:28, for example, are identified once as Jews and then again as pagan Meccans (Ibn al-Jawzī, *Zād,* i, 371).

The unbelievers will only mock the believers (Q 83:29-32) and try to corrupt them (Q 3:99-100). One should, therefore, avoid and ignore them and pay no attention to their idle talk. Only in cases of fear for one's life may one associate with unbelievers (Q 3:28; cf. 16:106). In this context, the term *taqiyya* — dissimulation (q.v.) — is mentioned. Whereas Sunnī commentators tend to see *taqiyya* as an option, their Shīʿī counterparts consider it a duty when faced with a threat to one's life (Ṭūsī, *Tibyān,* ii, 435; Mufīd, quoted in Ṭabarsī, *Majmaʿ,* iii, 56; Ṭabāṭabāʾī, *Mīzān,* iii, 153, 162-3). More recently, a very negative attitude was adopted toward the unbelievers, i.e. non-Muslims, by the twentieth century Egyptian thinker Sayyid Quṭb (*Ẓilāl,* i, 568) who was executed in 1966.

The passages listed so far suggest that a passive attitude be adopted towards the unbelievers. Other verses, however, which may be encountered in any discussion of *jihād* (q.v.), stress that believers should exert themselves in the way of God (see PATH OR WAY [OF GOD]) in the struggle against unbelief or prescribe fighting against the unbelievers (e.g. Q 2:190-3, 218, 244; 4:74-6, 84, 95; 8:15-6, 45-6, 57, 65; 9:20, 81). Under certain circumstances, however, it is possible to make peace with them (Q 4:90-1; 8:61). Not surprisingly, all these verses are from the Medinan period when Muḥammad was in a position of power and no longer the persecuted preacher that he had been in Mecca.

The impurity of the unbeliever

Although at first Muḥammad tried to maintain amicable relations with the unbelievers, this attitude changed after the conquest of Mecca. Q 9:28 declares the *mushrikūn* to be impure (*najas,* see PURITY AND IMPURITY) and forbids them to come near the Meccan sanctuary *(al-masjid al-ḥarām).* This verse came to be interpreted in the Mālikī and Jaʿfarī schools of law as prohibiting all non-Muslims from entering Muslim places of worship and led to discussions about the nature of the unbeliever's impurity: Were they literally filthy or ritually impure because they did not perform ablutions (see CLEANLINESS AND ABLUTION; RITUAL PURITY)? Is their impurity a judgment or conception in the minds of the believers? Or are they intrinsically impure and contaminating (see CONTAMINATION) (Ibn al-Jawzī, *Zād,* iii, 417; Rashīd Riḍā, *Manār,* x, 417; and see A.J. Wensinck, Nadjis)? Shīʿīs like al-Ṭūsī *(Tibyān)* and al-Ṭabarsī (d. 518/1153; *Majmaʿ,* 43) subscribe to the latter view and declare that contact with the unbelievers should be limited. If one has shaken hands with an unbeliever and the hand of either party was moist one should wash one's hand. Ibn Ḥazm (d. 456/1064), representing a Ẓāhirī viewpoint, maintains the essential impurity of all unbelievers but, unlike the Shīʿīs, does not prohibit their access to mosques (*Muḥallā,* iii, 162). The Qurʾān does not demand that the unbelievers live in segregation from the believers or that they distinguish themselves from the believers in their outward appearance; this was a later development of Islamic jurisprudence (see A. Fattal, *Le statut légal;* M. Perlmann, Ghiyār).

Belief and unbelief: choice or destiny?

According to the Qurʾān, humankind can be divided into two basic categories, those who believe and those who do not believe. Yet to what extent are people free to choose between belief and unbelief? While several passages in the Qurʾān suggest that people are given the option to choose whether or not to respond to the call of God's messenger(s) and that in the final analysis a person's fate in the afterlife depends on that person alone (Q 17:15, 54; 18:29; 20:82; 27:92; 34:50; 39:41), a larger number of verses give the impression or leave no doubt that it is God who decides who will be guided and who will be led astray. In other words, it is he who decides the fate of man (Q 6:125; 7:178, 186; 10:96-7, 99; 13:33; 28:50; 39:23, 36, 37; 45:23; 74:31). This apparent contradiction has given rise to much theological debate in later Islam about the question of indeterminism ("free will") or determinism ("predestination"). The members of the Muʿtazila school (see MUʿTAZILĪS) and the Shīʿīs, who were influenced by them, felt that predestination *(qaḍāʾ wa-qadar)* was incompatible with the idea of God's absolute justice (see JUSTICE AND INJUSTICE). Exegetes like the Muʿtazilī al-Zamakhsharī (d. 538/1144) and the Shīʿī al-Ṭūsī (d. 460/1067) devote much effort to proving that the Qurʾān supports their claim that man creates his own actions. On the other hand, the Ashʿarī, Fakhr al-Dīn al-Rāzī (d. 606/1210) expends much effort in refuting this view. The Qurʾān describes the unbelievers as people in whose ears there is a deafness (Q 41:5, 44; cf. 16:108), whose hearts and hearing have been sealed by God (Q 45:23; 63:3) or covered with a veil (Q 6:25; 17:46; 18:57; 41:5). Their hearts have been made hard or have rusted (Q 39:22; 83:14, and cf. 47:24). The unbelievers are compared with people who are deaf, dumb and blind (Q 2:18, 171; 6:39; 8:22) and God put fetters on their necks (Q 36:8). Whether this should be seen as the cause or as the result of unbelief is a disputed question among commentators, their answers depending upon their theological orientations. See also FREEDOM AND PREDESTINATION.

Camilla Adang

Bibliography

Primary: Bukhārī, *Ṣaḥīḥ*, ed. ʿAbd al-ʿAzīz b. ʿAbdallāh b. Bāz, 8 vols. (and *fihrist*), Beirut 1411/1991; Ibn al-ʿArabī, Muḥyī al-Dīn (attributed), *Tafsīr al-Qurʾān al-karīm*, 2 vols., Beirut 1387/1968; Ibn Ḥazm, *al-Muḥallā bi-l-āthār*, ed. ʿA.S. al-Bandārī, 12 vols., Beirut 1408/1988; Ibn al-Jawzī, *Zād;* Ibn Kathīr, *Tafsīr; Jalālayn*, Beirut 1407/1987; Muslim, *Ṣaḥīḥ*, ed. M.J. al-ʿAṭṭār, 9 vols., Beirut 1415/1995; Qurṭubī, *Jāmiʿ*, ed. M.J. al-ʿAshā, 10 vols., Beirut 1414/1993; Quṭb, *Ẓilāl*, 8 vols., Cairo n.d; Rashīd Riḍā, *Manār;* Rāzī, *Tafsīr;* Ṭabarī, *Tafsīr*, ed. Shākir; Ṭabarsī, *Majmaʿ;* Ṭabāṭabāʾī, *Mīzān;* Ṭūsī, *Tibyān*, ed. A.Ḥ.Q. al-ʿĀmilī, 10 vols., Beirut n.d.

Secondary: *(General background)*: C. Adams, Kufr, in J. Esposito (ed.), *The Oxford encyclopedia of the modern Islamic world*, 4 vols., New York 1995; P. Antes, Relations with unbelievers in Islamic theology, in A. Schimmel and A. Falatūri (eds.), *We believe in one God. The experience of God in Christianity and Islam*, London 1979, 101-11; W. Björkman, Shirk, in EI[1], iv, 378-80 (still worthwhile); id., Kāfir, in EI[2], iv, 407-9; Cl. Cahen, Dhimma, in EI[2], ii, 227-31; id., Djizya, in EI[2], ii, 559-62; L. Gardet, Īmān, in EI[2], iii, 1170-4; id., Islām, in EI[2], iv, 171-4; D. Gimaret, Shirk, in EI[2], ix, 484-6; J.J.G. Jansen, Muʾmin, in EI[2], vii, 554-5; Lane; *Lisān al-ʿArab;* M. Mir, *Dictionary of qurʾānic terms and concepts*, New York 1987; id., Īmān, in J. Esposito (ed.), *The Oxford encyclopedia of the modern Islamic world*, 4 vols., New York 1995; M. Perlmann, Ghiyār, in EI[2], ii, 1075-6; F. Sherif, *A guide to the contents of the Qurʾān*, London 1985, 81-95; G. Vajda, Ahl al-kitāb, in EI[2], i, 264-6; A.J. Wensinck, Nadjis, in EI[2], vii, 870. *(Belief and unbelief):* M.M. Bravmann, *The spiritual background of early Islam. Studies in ancient Arab concepts*, Leiden 1972, 26-31; J. van Ess, TG, with full bibliography; L. Gardet, *Dieu et la destinée de l'homme*, Paris 1967, 353-99; Gardet and Anawati, *Introduction*, Paris 1970[2], 330-45; Izutsu, *Concepts;* id., *The concept of belief in Islamic theology. A semantic analysis of īmān and islām*, Tokyo 1965, repr. New York 1980; H. Ringgren, The conception of faith in the Koran, in *Oriens* 4 (1951), 1-20 (a critique of M. Bravmann's views); J.I. Smith, *An historical and semantic study of the term "islām" as seen in a sequence of Qurʾān commentaries*, Missoula 1975; W.C. Smith, Faith in the Qurʾān and its relation to belief, in id., *On understanding Islam. Selected studies*, New York 1981, 110-134; M. Waldman, The development of the concept of *kufr*, in JAOS 88 (1968), 442-455 (a critique of Izutsu's method). *(People of the Book):* W.A. Bijlefeld, Some recent contributions to qurʾānic studies. Selected publications in English, French, and German, 1964-1973, in MW 64 (1974), 79-102, esp. 89-95; J. Bouman, *Der Koran und die Juden*, Darmstadt 1990; H. Busse, *Die theologischen Beziehungen des Islams zu Judentum und Christentum. Grundlagen des Dialogs im Koran und die gegenwärtige Situation*, Darmstadt 1988; A. Fattal, *Le statut légal des non-musulmans en pays d'Islam*, Beirut 1958; McAuliffe, *Qurʾānic;* Kh. Samir, Le commentaire de Ṭabarī sur Coran 2/62 et la question du salut des non-musulmans, in AIUON 40 (1980), 555-617.

Believers and Unbelievers see BELIEF AND UNBELIEF

Bekka see MECCA

Benjamin

The brother of Joseph (Yūsuf, see JOSEPH). Identified in the Bible as the son of Jacob (q.v.) and Rachel, Benjamin (Binyamīn) is not mentioned by name in Q 12, the sūra which tells the story of Joseph. Of the eighteen dramatis personae of this sūra, only Joseph is named directly. Nevertheless the identity of Benjamin is clear and his presence in the story exemplifies the effectiveness of the referential character of qurʾānic rhetoric.

Benjamin is referred to on the following occasions: When the brothers complain "Joseph and his brother [i.e. Benjamin] are dearer to our father than are we" (Q 12:8); when they plot to rid themselves of him; when Joseph, while giving his brothers corn after having been established in Egypt, orders them, "Bring me another brother of yours by your father" (Q 12:59); when they say to Jacob on their return to Canaan, "Father, we are not to be given any more corn! So send our brother with us" (Q 12:63); when Jacob responds to them, "Shall I entrust him to you other than as I entrusted to you his brother long ago?" (Q 12:64); and in Jacob's reluctant words of consent, "I will not send him with you unless you make a pledge before God that you will bring him back to me" (Q 12:66).

Additionally, back in Egypt there are qurʾānic references, when Joseph takes Benjamin aside and says to him, "Truly, I am your brother" (Q 12:69); when Joseph has his cup (see CUPS AND VESSELS) put in the saddle bag of his brother (Q 12:70) from which it is taken (Q 12:76); when the brothers make an excuse for him, saying, "If he has stolen something, he has a brother who also stole" (Q 12:77); when the brothers plead to Joseph to take one of them in Benjamin's place, since he "has an aged father" (Q 12:78); prompting Joseph's response, "God forbid that we should take other than the one on whom we found our property" (Q 12:79). Further, when they return to Canaan to tell their father, "Father, your son has stolen" (Q 12:81); and Jacob exclaims, "Perhaps God will bring them all back to me" (Q 12:83); and orders them, "Go, search for Joseph and his brother" (Q 12:87). Finally, after their return to Egypt and to Joseph's presence, he asks them, "Do you know what you did to Joseph and his brother?" (Q 12:89); and after their hesitant reply he declares, "I am Joseph, and this is my brother" (Q 12:90).

Every reference to Benjamin has a role in the development of the narrative (see NARRATIVES): not, paradoxically, because of anything he says or does, but simply through his rel ationship to Joseph. It is jealousy of Benjamin as well as of Joseph that precipitates the events of the story (Q 12:8). It is through Benjamin that Joseph first exercises power over his brethren (Q 12:59). It is through Benjamin that Jacob puts his other sons to the test, to discover whether they will be faithful to their pledge. The discovery of the cup in Benjamin's saddle bag in Q 12:76 plays a pivotal role. The brothers' response to his arrest shows that they are faithful to their pledge (Q 12:78, 80). Benjamin is the agent of their change of heart. Jacob's order to his sons to search for Joseph and his brother (Q 12:87) leads to the narrative's denouement when Joseph reveals his identity to them (Q 12:90). The tensions that generated the story at a literary level are thereby resolved and the moral lessons of the sūra thereby confirmed.

The close fraternal relationship between Benjamin and Joseph is a leitmotiv in the qurʾānic story (see BROTHER AND BROTHERHOOD). The brothers are envious of Joseph and his *brother;* Jacob asks the brothers whether he can trust Benjamin with them any more than he trusted them with Benjamin's *brother* Joseph (Q 12:64); when revealing himself to Benjamin, Joseph says to him, "I am your *brother*" (Q 12:69); Joseph's cup is placed and found "in his *brother's* saddle bag" (Q 12:70, 76); the brothers' excuse for Benjamin's supposed theft is that he also had a *brother* who stole; Jacob sends the sons back to Egypt to seek Joseph and his *brother;* upon their return, Joseph puts to them the question, "Do you know what you did to Joseph and his *brother?*" and in revealing himself, says, "I am Joseph and this is my *brother.*"

The Muslim exegetical tradition elaborates these elements in the story. Qurʾānic commentators had no problem in identifying Benjamin and in noting that his mother Rachel died giving birth to him. Both commentary literature on the Qurʾān as well as the Muslim literary genre known as the "tales of the prophets" *(qiṣaṣ al-anbiyāʾ)* elaborated the elements of the core qurʾānic narrative that emphasized the positive role of Benjamin and that showed the love between the two brothers. The later Islamic mystical tradition, inspired by their closeness, saw in Joseph's love for Benjamin a metaphor for God's primordial love of the sinner (see ṢŪFISM AND THE QURʾĀN). See also SCRIPTURE AND THE QURʾĀN.

A.H. Johns

Bibliography
Primary: Kisāʾī, *Qiṣaṣ,* trans. W.M. Thackston, *The tales of the prophets of al-Kisāʾī,* Boston 1978.
Secondary: M.A.S. Abdel Haleem, The story of Joseph in the Qurʾān and the Old Testament, in *Islam and Christian-Muslim relations* (1990), 171-91; L.Ginzberg, *Legends of the Jews,* Philadelphia 1909-36, v, 83-4 (for the Jewish background to some aspects of the story); A.H. Johns, Joseph in the Qurʾan. Dramatic dialogue, human emotion and prophetic wisdom, in *Islamochristiana* 7 (1981), 29-55; id., The qurʾānic presentation of the Joseph story. Naturalistic or formulaic language? in Rippin, *Approaches,* 37-70; M. Mir, The qurʾānic story of Joseph. Plot, themes, and characters, in *MW* 76 (1986), 1-15; A.L. Premare, Joseph dans le Coran. Lecture de la sourate 12, in *Foi et vie* 86 (1987), 36-59; H. Ritter, *Das Meer der Seele,* Leiden 1955, 255; M.R. Waldman, New approaches to "biblical" materials in the Qurʾān, in *Studies in Islamic and Judaic traditions presented at the Institute for Islamic-Judaic Studies, University of Denver* (1986), 47-64 (Joseph story, appendix).

Bequest see INHERITANCE

Berries see AGRICULTURE AND VEGETATION

Betrothal see MARRIAGE AND DIVORCE

Bible

While there is no qurʾānic equivalent of the term, the Qurʾān refers to certain elements of this scriptural composite. The most prominent of these are: Torah *(tawrāt),* Gospel *(injīl),* Psalms *(zabūr)* and more ambiguously scrolls or leaves *(ṣuḥuf).* See TORAH; GOSPEL; PSALMS; SCRIPTURE AND THE QURʾĀN.

Jane Dammen McAuliffe

Bilqīs

The name most frequently given by Islamic commentators to the anonymous queen of the land of Sheba (q.v.). Bilqīs is the powerful and intelligent ruler whose celebrated visit to the court of the prophet Solomon (q.v.; see also ART AND ARCHITECTURE AND THE QURʾĀN) is mentioned in Q 27:20-44. The etymology of the name is unknown. The view that "Bilqīs" is derived from the Hebrew *pilegesh* (concubine) or from *Naukalis,* the Greek name given her by Flavius Josephus, is not at all convincing (see E. Ullendorff, Bilḳīs). Muslim religious scholars also refer to the queen as Balʿama (cf. Thaʿlabī, *Qiṣaṣ,* 312 and other sources with variant readings), i.e. the female Balaam. The Balʿama-tradition features an extended genealogy, with minor variations, that projects the queen's ancestors back to Qaḥṭān, the progenitor of the southern Arabs (Thaʿlabī, *Qiṣaṣ,* 313 among others).

The queen's story in the Qurʾān (J. Lassner, *Demonizing the queen,* 36-48), while lacking a coherent narrative, has a clear message. The Sheban ruler, a woman who worships other than God (see IDOLATRY AND IDOLATERS; BELIEF AND UNBELIEF), must be brought to submission by the prophet Solomon once he is made aware of her unbelief by the hoopoe, a bird from his flying corps who discovered the queen and her kingdom in the Yemen (see ANIMAL LIFE). The prophet sends a threatening letter to the queen commanding her to submit. She attempts to deflect Solomon with various gifts, all of which are scornfully rejected. The queen, alarmed by Solomon's reaction to her initiative, journeys to visit him at his court, where she is twice tested. She passes the first test, but when she enters the prophet's pavilion, she thinks it to be a pool of water and so lifting her skirt, she uncovers her ankles. This forces her to acknowledge — although no reason is given — that she has wronged herself and she submits through Solomon to the lord of the universe.

The subsequent commentary and exegesis on the qurʾānic verses (J. Lassner, *Demonizing the queen,* 47-86) fill the interstices of the loosely formulated qurʾānic text. By providing a lengthy and sustained narrative, later Muslim writers also added an additional dimension to the account of the queen's visit. From their perspective, the queen must be brought in line, not only because she does not recognize God, but because she violates the nature of the universe, which is God's design. That is to say, the queen, who is half jinn (q.v.) and hence an unnatural creature, has no plans to fulfill the time-honored functions of women, namely, child bearing and nurturing (see WOMEN AND THE QURʾĀN). Instead she arrogates to herself the prerogatives of rule in a most defiant manner. She marries to unite a divided kingdom only to slay her husband on their wedding night (Thaʿlabī, *Qiṣaṣ,* 312-3; al-Dīnawarī, *Akhbār,* 22-5; Yaʿqūbī, *Taʾrīkh,* ii, 222; Ṭabarī, *Taʾrīkh,* i, 684; Masʿūdī, *Murūj,* iii, 173; and others). Faced with Solomon's call for her submission and the rejection of her initial diplomatic efforts to bribe him, she travels to Solomon's court to test him. Should he fail the tests, she will retain her kingdom and with that the natural order so carefully designed by God will be undone (J. Lassner, *Demonizing the queen,* 57-61). But Solomon with some help from the angel Gabriel (q.v.) overcomes her carefully crafted ploys and in the end the queen, unable to distinguish between a pool of water — God's design for nature — and an artificially created pool made from glass — representing her unnatural desire to rule — capitulates. These themes also appear in the Jewish lore of Solomon and the Queen of Sheba, a body of tradition that is seemingly linked, however loosely, with the Muslim scripture and its commentary (J. Lassner, *Demonizing the queen,* 88-132). See also MYTHIC AND LEGENDARY NARRATIVES AND THE QURʾĀN.

Jacob Lassner

Bibliography
Primary: al-Dīnawarī, *Kitāb al-Akhbār al-ṭiwāl,* ed. V. Guirgass, Leiden 1888 (indices by I. Kratchkovsky, 1912); Masʿūdī, *Murūj;* Ṭabarī, *Taʾrīkh;* Thaʿlabī, *Qiṣaṣ;* Yaʿqūbī, *Taʾrīkh.*
Secondary: J. Lassner, *Demonizing the queen of Sheba,* Chicago 1993 (contains extensive bibliography of primary and secondary sources); J. Pirenne, Bilqis et Salomon. La reine de Saba dans le Coran et la Bible, in *Dossiers de l'archeologie* 33 (1979), 6-10; B.F. Stowasser, *Women in the Qurʾān, traditions and interpretation,* New York 1994, 62-66; E. Ullendorf, Bilḳīs, in *EI²,* i, 1219-20; W.M. Watt, The queen of Sheba in Islamic tradition, in *Solomon and Sheba,* ed. J. Pritchard, London 1974, 85-103.

Biology as the Creation and Stages of Life

The Qurʾān depicts the creation of the universe and everything within it as a miracle (q.v.) of God and as proof of the existence of divine power (see POWER AND IMPOTENCE). According to the Qurʾān, human life began with the creation of Adam and Eve (q.v.). The qurʾānic account of the creation (q.v.) narrative affirms that everything has been created in pairs for reproduction and perpetuation of its own species. Modern Muslim commentators, particularly those who are devoted to "scientific" exegesis (*tafsīr ʿilmī*, see EXEGESIS OF THE QURʾĀN), have decided that since the Qurʾān makes no mention of the evolution of one species to another kind of species, the Darwinian theory of evolution is contrary to the teachings of the Qurʾān. Such contemporary Muslim exegesis also makes the claim that the qurʾānic description from over 1400 years ago, of the conception of the fetus and of its subsequent development and growth, contains details of which scientific observation has become aware only in relatively recent times. A consistent pattern of interpretation, both medieval and modern, is to read the references to conception, birth and human development as evidence of God's creative majesty and care for humankind. The early life stages and aspects of human biology mentioned in the Qurʾān include conception, fetal development and growth, childbirth, lactation and weaning. There is also abundant reference to the various aspects of adult life as well as to death and to life after death (see DEATH AND THE DEAD). There is no sequential treatment in the Qurʾān of the biology of human life and of the human life span. Rather, these are treated in many different sūras and verses but relevant verses have here been grouped for the purpose of thematic analysis. See also LIFE.

Creation

The creation of humans from dust *(turāb)* is mentioned six times in the Qurʾān, from clay *(ṭīn)* in eight places and from dry clay *(ṣalṣāl)* in four places (see CLAY). Qurʾānic commentators are of the opinion that *turāb, ṭīn* and *ṣalṣāl* complement rather than contradict each other, as they refer to the various stages through which Adam was formed (Ṭabarī, *Tafsīr;* Ibn Kathīr, *Tafsīr,* ii, 457). According to this interpretation, God created Adam from clay, which is a mixture of water and soil or dust and this was then turned into dark fetid mud and brought into shape. This inorganic matter was then transformed into organic material through the divine command of "Be!" *(kun)* after the soul *(rūḥ)* had been "breathed" into Adam (see SPIRIT; AIR AND WIND). Not only was Adam created from dust but the Qurʾān speaks of all men as being created in a similar fashion, thus signifying that the bodies of the progeny of Adam are composed of various organic and inorganic substances such as those found within the soil (M. Asad, *Message,* 520). An apt verse that summarizes the process of human creation is: "From the [earth] did we create you, and into it shall we return you, and from it shall we bring you out once again" (Q 20:55).

Stages and materials of human creation are mentioned in numerous qurʾānic sūras: Q 6 ("Cattle," Sūrat al-Anʿām), Q 22 ("The Pilgrimage," Sūrat al-Ḥajj), Q 23 ("The Believers," Sūrat al-Muʾminūn), Q 40 ("The Believer," Sūrat al-Muʾmin), Q 30 ("The Romans," Sūrat al-Rūm), Q 32 ("The Prostration," Sūrat al-Sajda), Q 55 ("The Beneficent," Sūrat al-Raḥmān), Q 77 ("The Emissaries," Sūrat al-Mursalāt), and Q 86 ("The Morning Star," Sūrat al-Ṭāriq). The qurʾānic vocabulary in each relevant passage, however, varies in both its mention and its ordering. For example, the stages of dust *(turāb)*, sperm *(nuṭfa)*, a material that clings (*ʿalaqa,* see BLOOD AND BLOOD CLOT; ANATOMY) and a lump of flesh *(muḍgha)* are mentioned in Q 22:5, while in

Q 23:12 clay *(ṭīn)* is mentioned instead of dust *(turāb)*. In Q 55:14 only the dry clay *(ṣalṣāl)* is mentioned while the materials and stages of dust *(turāb)*, clay *(ṭīn)*, sperm *(nuṭfa)*, blood clot *(ʿalaqa)* and chewed lump *(muḍgha)* are omitted. As with Q 6:2, which refers to clay *(ṭīn)*, Q 30:20 refers to dust *(turāb)* and to the fully formed human stage but none of the other materials or stages is mentioned.

Conception and fetal development

In Qurʾān 23:12-4 reference is made to fetal development and growth. There is again reaffirmation, at the beginning of this passage, of human origin from clay. Explanations of these verses express the view that "sperm" and "firm lodging" refer to sperm within the female reproductive tract, more specifically within the uterus. Prior to fertilization, sperm bind to the zona pellucida or outer covering of the ovum. Following such lines of interpretation, *ʿalaqa* could be a reference to this, i.e. to sperm "clinging" to the ovum. However, *ʿalaqa* is also interpreted by some exegetes as "blood clot" and taken to refer to "something that clings" to the uterus (M. Būṭī, *Taḥdīd al-nasl,* 69). For those modern commentators who then extrapolate this interpretation scientifically, the "blood clot" could be taken to represent the fertilized ovum or early embryo implanting itself in the endometrium or uterine lining. The "chewed lump" could then be reference to the cleaved embryo and organogenesis, the "fashioning of bones and flesh." Some exegetes and jurists *(fuqahāʾ)* are of the opinion that "another act of creation" signifies the fetus being imbued with a soul (q.v.; cf. M. Madkūr, *Janīn,* 84).

A second passage, Q 22:5, follows in much the same vein as the first except that early fetal development is further explained and specified with the phrase "formed and unformed" *(mukhallaqa wa-ghayr mukhallaqa)*. Furthermore, the statement that "We cause whom we will to rest in the wombs for an appointed term," is understood as a recognition that not all fertilized ova (or embryos) complete the full fetal cycle. Some are aborted and this citation exemplifies God's prerogative and power over birth, life and death (see ABORTION; BIRTH CONTROL).

A third passage, Q 32:7-9, makes clear reference to the creation of Adam from clay and to the conception of his progeny by natural reproductive process, i.e. "an extract of despised fluid." The paradox in this latter phrase is noteworthy in that a pure form, the human being, is created from impure fluid (ʿA.Y. ʿAlī, *The holy Qurʾān,* 1094). According to Islamic law, semen is a polluting substance, one of the bodily emissions that necessitates a major ablution before the ritual prayer (q.v.; see also RITUAL PURITY; PURITY AND IMPURITY). The comment by ʿAbdullāh Yūsuf ʿAlī, a well-known translator of the Qurʾān, connects this situation of legal impurity with its consequence in the act of conception. Finally, Q 39:6 points out that fetal development within the womb proceeds in three veils of darkness *(ẓulumāt thalāth)*. The three veils of darkness are, according to qurʾānic exegetes, the abdominal wall, the uterine wall and the embryonic sacs which surround the fetus (Ibn Kathīr, *Tafsīr,* iv, 46; Ṭabarī, *Tafsīr,* x, part 23:125-7; see also BLOOD AND BLOOD CLOT).

Birth

According to Q 80:20, God lets the birth (q.v.) of the baby take place through the birth canal. Embryological science explains this by the sequence of events which occur just before birth and that enable the baby to be born through the birth canal: The ovaries and placenta secrete a hormone which loosens the ligaments of the pelvic joints and softens the cervix. This is followed by uterine contractions, the rupture of the bag of water, which helps in providing a smooth and slippery surface for the fetus to glide down, and, finally, birth. Q 46:15 also makes reference to this process, including the pangs of pregnancy, the actual birth and the subsequent period of lactation and weaning. Commentaries on this verse explain that since the minimum period of pregnancy is six months and the maximum period for breast-feeding is two years, the qurʾānic reference to a thirty month "carrying period" is an allusion to this entire process (Ibn Kathīr, *Tafsīr,* iv, 157; Ālūsī, *Rūḥ,* ad loc.).

Growth and maturation

The full cycle of human creation and development is described thus in the Qurʾān: "It is God who created you in [a state of] weakness, then gave [you] strength after weakness, then after strength, gave [you] weakness and a hoary head. He creates as he wills, and it is he who has all knowledge and power" (Q 30:54). Qurʾānic commentary on this verse sees both a succinct expression of the human life cycle and an affirmation of divine power over all things. A baby is born weak and slowly begins to grow, becomes a youth and then an adult — this is what is meant by strength after weakness. Thereafter the human reaches middle-age, then old age and finally senility — this is what is meant by weakness after strength. In other words, during old age, one's determination, movement, courage and other faculties are weakened (Ṣābūnī, *Tafsīr,* ii, 531). Moreover, the Qurʾān mentions that it is within God's prerogative to allow some of his creation to undergo the entire cycle from birth to old age and to end the lives of others before old age is attained (ibid., i, 567). For example, according to Q 6:2, the duration of one's existence on this earth is decreed by God alone.

Death

According to the Qurʾān life does not end with death. Death is not the total annihilation of human life. The Qurʾān uses the word *barzakh* (q.v.; Q 23:100) to signify the state that human beings enter into upon death. *Barzakh* is a screen or partition which separates this world from the next until the day of resurrection (q.v.; cf. Ṭabarī, *Tafsīr,* ad Q 23:100). In affirming human resurrection, the Qurʾān asserts that all human beings will be brought back to life to stand in judgment before their Creator (see LAST JUDGMENT). The Qurʾān contains innumerable passages confirming the day of resurrection and the belief that humankind will be raised from the dead, e.g. Q 22:7. Further, at the time of resurrection, an individual's deeds will be assessed and judgment will be rendered about whether entrance will be to paradise (q.v.) or hell (q.v.) as a permanent abode. This would then be the final stage of life, i.e. life after death (Q 4:121-2 and 168-9).

Abul Fadl Mohsin Ebrahim

Bibliography

Primary: Ālūsī, *Rūḥ,* repr. Beirut n.d.; Būṭī, Muḥammad Saʿīd Ramaḍān, *Taḥdīd al-nasl,* Damascus 1976; Ibn Kathīr, *Tafsīr,* ed. ʿAbd al-ʿAzīz Ghunaym et al., 4 vols., Beirut 1388/1979; M.S. Madkūr, *al-Janīn wa-l-aḥkām al-mutaʿalliqa bihi fī l-fiqh al-islāmī,* Cairo 1969; Ṣābūnī, *Tafsīr;* Ṭabarī, *Tafsīr,* 12 vols., Beirut 1400/1980[4].

Secondary: M.A. Albar, *Human development as revealed in the holy Qurʾān and ḥadīth,* Jeddah 1992[3]; ʿA.Y. ʿAlī, *The holy Qurʾān. Text, translation and commentary,* Lahore 1969; M. Asad, *The message of the Qurʾān,* Gibraltar 1980; M. Bucaille, *The Bible, the Qurʾan and science,* Indianapolis 1978; A.F.M. Ebrahim, *Abortion, birth control and surrogate parenting. An Islamic perspective,* Indianapolis 1991; K.L. Moore, *The developing human,* Jeddah 1983[3].

Biosphere see ANIMAL LIFE

Birds see ANIMAL LIFE

Birth

The act of bringing forth new life from the womb of a mother. The Qurʾān details the process leading to birth in the conception of the fetus (see BIOLOGY AS THE CREATION AND STAGES OF LIFE). It emphasizes the sacrosanct nature of life (q.v.), God's knowledge of and willing of all new life, and it acknowledges the honorable role of mothers (see WOMEN AND THE QURʾĀN).

The topic of birth receives less specific attention in the Qurʾān than that of creation (*khalq*, see CREATION), a more inclusive term with a wider set of meanings. Life, granted by God (Q 29:27), is sacred (Q 17:31). When God wills the birth of a child, no human physical barriers can prevent the birth (Q 3:39; 19:3-8; see ABORTION; BIRTH CONTROL). God knows each person before birth when each is hidden in his mother's womb (Q 53:32). God created the first man, Adam and the first woman, Eve, and their progeny is countless (Q 4:1; see ADAM AND EVE). Humankind is enjoined to respect God's creative power: "Men have fear of your Lord, who created you from a single soul (q.v.). From that soul he created its mate and through them he disseminated a multitude of men and women" (Q 4:1). The process leading to an individual's birth, more specifically, the creation of the fetus and its being imbued with a soul, takes place in stages. Q 23:12-14 is one of several passages that explains this process: "We first created man from an essence of clay (q.v.): then placed him, a living germ (sperm), in a safe enclosure. The germ we made a clot of blood (see BLOOD AND BLOOD CLOT), and the clot a lump of flesh. This we fashioned into bones, then clothed the bones with flesh, thus bringing forth another creation. Blessed be God, the noblest of creators!" Qurʾānic references to the stages of conception, fetal development and birth imply that God creates individuals as male or female. As ʿImrān's (q.v.) wife delivers Mary (q.v.), she exclaims, "Lord, I have given birth to a daughter." The passage continues by relating that God knew the gender of the child: "God knew well of what she was delivered: The male is not like the female" (Q 3:36).

The role of mothers — women who conceive, give birth and sustain infants through the period of lactation — is noted with respect. Muslims are commanded to "honor the mothers that bore you" (Q 4:1) and to show kindness to parents for "with much pain his mother bears him and he is not weaned before he is two years of age" (Q 31:14; see FAMILY).

The births of Adam and Jesus (q.v.) are treated in more detail in the Qurʾān as each birth miraculously differed from those of other mortals. Adam, the first man, was created from clay (Q 23:12) or dust (Q 3:59). Then God said to him "Be!" and he was (Q 3:59). In the same verse, the creation of Jesus is likened to that of Adam, supporting the point that Jesus was a man like Adam. Among those who are venerated as prophets (see PROPHETS AND PROPHETHOOD) in the Muslim tradition, Jesus holds special status through the sign (see SIGNS) of his miraculous birth. Mary, his mother, was given special protection from the time of her birth (Q 3:35-6, 42). An angel (q.v.) tells her to rejoice in a Word from God, the Messiah, Jesus the son of Mary (Q 3:45; 19:17-22). Mary replies, "How can I bear a child... when I am a virgin, untouched by man?" (Q 19:20; 3:47). "Such is the will of your Lord, he replied. That is no difficult thing for him. He shall be a sign to mankind, says the Lord, and a blessing from ourself" (Q 19:21).

Donna Lee Bowen

Bibliography
Primary: Ibn Qayyim al-Jawziyya, *Tuḥfat al-mawdūd bi-aḥkām al-mawlūd*, ed. ʿA.S. al-Bundārī, Cairo 1986.
Secondary: N.J. Dawood, *The Koran*, New York 1974; A. Giladi, *Children of Islam. Concepts of childhood in medieval Muslim society*, Oxford 1992; J.D. McAuliffe, Chosen of all women. Mary and Fāṭima in qurʾānic exegesis, in *Islamochristiana* 7 (1981), 19-28; N. Robinson, Jesus and Mary in the Qurʾān. Some neglected affinities, in *Religion* 20 (1990), 161-75; J. Smith and Y. Haddad, The virgin Mary in Islamic tradition and commentary, in *MW* 79 (1989), 161-87; B. Stowasser, *Women in the Qurʾān, traditions and interpretation*, Oxford 1994.

Birth Control

Avoiding pregnancy to space or to limit childbirth. The subject of birth control in this sense is not discussed in the Qurʾān. Rather, the major sources that both medieval and modern Muslim jurisprudence has used to assess practices of controlling birth are those of the prophetic tradition (sunna, q.v.) and its expression in ḥadīth, specifically those accounts that speak of coitus interruptus or withdrawal *(ʿazl)*. Yet verses of the Qurʾān have been used to support the practice of contraception and to argue the contrary despite the fact that no qurʾānic references bear directly on the permissibility or impermissibility of birth control.

According to classical Muslim sources that describe the historical period prior to the birth and prophethood of Muḥammad (see AGE OF IGNORANCE; PRE-ISLAMIC ARABIA AND THE QURʾĀN), pre-Islamic Arabs employed infanticide (q.v.) or infant exposure *(waʾd)* as a means of ridding themselves of unwanted female children. As such, it could be understood as a method of birth control. The Qurʾān condemns this practice of female infanticide in strong terms: "Do not kill your children for fear of want. We provide for you and for them; the killing of them is a great sin" (Q 17:31; also 6:151; 81:8-9; 60:12). Later sources, however, seem to indicate that less extreme forms of population control were known in the formative period of Islam.

Numerous ḥadīth speak of the use of *ʿazl* during the Prophet's lifetime and note that it was considered permissible. "We [the Companions of the Prophet, q.v.] used to practice *ʿazl* during the time of the Prophet. The Prophet knew about it and did not forbid it" (Muslim, *Ṣaḥīḥ*, from Jābir b. ʿAbdallāh). Reasons mentioned in the ḥadīth texts for employing contraception center primarily on property rights, that is, not wanting to impregnate a slave or female prisoners captured in war. A prophetic tradition that is commonly credited to Abū Hurayra (d. ca. 58/678) has become the most frequently cited justification for the majority of classical jurisprudence *(fiqh)* texts and the contemporary opinions of *ʿulamāʾ* on the use of birth control pills, IUDs and other temporary forms of family planning. According to one version of this ḥadīth, the Prophet said, "Do not use *ʿazl* with your wife without her permission." Consequently, the prevailing opinion of Muslim authorities has been to permit contraception when used with the consent of both spouses.

Breast-feeding children can also provide a measure of contraceptive protection. Some authorities, therefore, consider the Qurʾān's recommendation to nurse children for two years to be an indirect support for contraception (Q 2:233; 31:14; see also BIRTH; BIOLOGY AS THE CREATION AND STAGES OF LIFE).

Within the Islamic tradition, however, the acceptance of methods to avoid pregnancy has not been universal. Arguments which have been constructed against birth control emphasize qurʾānic texts that affirm the importance of marriage (see MARRIAGE AND DIVORCE) and progeny (see CHILDREN). Frequent reference is made to Q 16:72: "And God has given you wives from yourselves and has given you, from your wives, children and grandchildren and has made provision of good things for you" (cf. Q 2:223; 4:1; 6:140; 7:86; 11:61; 13:38; 25:74; see BLESSING). Opponents of birth control also argue that contraception denies the will and power of God (Q 7:18; 81:29). The ḥadīth collections, too, provide support for this position of prohibition. According to a report from Anas b. Mālik (d. ca. 91-3/709-11), the Prophet said, "Even if you spill the seed from which a child was meant to be born upon a rock, God will bring forth from that rock a child." The use of birth control for economic reasons has been criticized as a denial of God's promise to sustain man and man's duty to rely upon God (Q 3:159; 11:6; 65:2-3). See also ABORTION.

Donna Lee Bowen

Bibliography
Primary: Muslim, *Saḥīḥ*.
Secondary: A. Ide, *The Qurʾān on woman, marriage, birth control, and divorce*, Las Colinas, TX 1996; International Islamic Conference, Rabat, Morocco, December 1971, *Islām wa-tanẓīm al-usra. Islam and family planning. A faithful translation of the Arabic edition of the proceedings of the conference*, Beirut 1974; M.S. Madkūr, *Naẓrat al-Islām li-tanẓīm al-nasl*, Cairo 1965; B. Musallam, *Sex and society in Islam*, Cambridge 1983; A. Omran, *Family planning in the legacy of Islam*, London 1992.

Blasphemy

Speech that is derogatory to God. The qurʾānic terms that correspond most closely to blasphemy are *takdhīb*, "giving the lie, denial" and *iftirāʾ*, "invention" (cf. Izutsu, *Concepts*, 40, 99-101, 169-70). Inasmuch as God and his messages represent the ultimate truth (q.v.), blasphemy is denial of that truth or propagation of a falsehood in its place.

Blasphemy by denial *(takdhīb)* is the outright rejection of revealed religious truths, such as the revelations and warnings of God's messengers (Q 54; see MESSENGER; REVELATION AND INSPIRATION; WARNING), and the announcements of the day of judgment and the meeting with God (Q 6:31; 10:45; 23:33; 25:11; 82:9; see LAST JUDGMENT). It can also include the refusal to recognize and acknowledge God's signs (q.v.), particularly the wonders of the natural world which serve as evidence of his omnipotence and unity (Q 6:21; 17:59; 55; see POWER AND IMPOTENCE; CREATION). According to passages such as Q 5:10, the refusal to recognize God's signs is associated with unbelief (*kufr*, see GRATITUDE AND INGRATITUDE; BELIEF AND UNBELIEF) and guarantees doom in the afterlife: "Those who reject faith and deny our signs will be the denizens of hell-fire."

Blasphemy by invention *(iftirāʾ)* is the declaration of a false belief of one's own contrivance. It most often occurs in the verbal idiom "to invent a lie against God" (*iftarā ʿalā llāhi kadhiban*, Q 11:18). Similar expressions that convey this signification are "to lie against God" (*kadhaba ʿalā llāh*, Q 39:32) and "to say a lie against God" (*qāla ʿalā llāhi al-kadhib*, Q 3:75, 78). This form of blasphemy calls down God's curse (q.v.; Q 11:18) and is equated with great sin or wrongdoing (see SIN, MAJOR AND MINOR), as apparent from the oft-repeated rhetorical question, "Who does greater wrong than he who invents a lie against God?" (e.g. Q 6:21). The gravest offense of this type is polytheism (*shirk*, see POLYTHEISM AND ATHEISM): the attribution of partners to God or the worship of other gods independent of, or as intercessors with, God

(Q 6:24, 137; 7:89; 10:18, 30; 16:56, 87; 18:15; 21:22; 28:75; 29:61-8). A prominent example of such an affront to God is the Hebrews' worship of the calf of gold (q.v.) under Moses (q.v.; Q 2:51-4; 7:152; see also IDOLS AND IMAGES; IDOLATRY AND IDOLATERS). The Qurʾān strongly denounces the claims that God engendered a son (Q 10:68-9; 19:88-92; see CHRISTIANS AND CHRISTIANITY; JESUS), that God produced son or daughter gods (Q 6:100; 16:57; 53:19-22) and that demons (*jinn*, q.v.) share in God's divine power (Q 6:100; 37:158). Blasphemy need not refer directly to God but may simply infringe on a divine prerogative. Thus, it is held to include false claims to prophecy or revelation (Q 6:93; 23:38; see PROPHETS AND PROPHETHOOD) and declaring things lawful or unlawful of one's own accord (see LAWFUL AND UNLAWFUL; JEWS AND JUDAISM). This latter is a charge made against Jewish dietary laws and the taboos of the pagan Arabs concerning cattle or crops dedicated to various gods (Q 5:103; 6:136-45; 10:59; 16:116; see CONSECRATION OF ANIMALS).

Devin J. Stewart

Bibliography
M. Ayoub, *The Qurʾān and its interpreters*, 2 vols., Albany 1984-92, ii, 225-8; R. Bell, *Commentary*, i, 80; Izutsu, *Concepts*.

Blessing

Prosperity or favor *(niʿma, baraka)* bestowed *(anʿama, bāraka)* by God; a wish, invocation or greeting asking for such a favor to be granted to someone else; or an expression of praise (q.v.) for God.

Blessings in the Qurʾān, as in the Hebrew Bible, partake in an ongoing, reciprocal covenant (q.v.) between humans and God (Q 5:7). God bestows blessings on humankind, including the creation and ordering of life and the universe, sustenance, progeny, material wealth (q.v.), protection (q.v.), deliverance from enemies, and so on (R. Darnell, 50-4; Q 16:66-83; 55; see CREATION; BIOLOGY AS THE CREATION AND STAGES OF LIFE).

According to the Qurʾān, expression of gratitude for God's blessings is a fundamental obligation and failure to do so is tantamount to unbelief (Q 14:28; 16:114; see BELIEF AND UNBELIEF; GRATITUDE AND INGRATITUDE). God has particularly blessed earlier cities or nations (Q 34:18), the Israelites (Q 2:40, 47, 122; see CHILDREN OF ISRAEL), his prophets or messengers including Moses (q.v.), Lot (q.v.), and Jesus (q.v.; Q 5:20, 110; 19:31, 58) as well as other biblical figures such as Solomon (q.v.) and Mary (q.v.; Q 5:110; 27:19; see also PROPHETS AND PROPHETHOOD; MESSENGER). Abraham (q.v.), Moses, and Solomon fulfilled their obligations to God by giving thanks for his blessings (Q 16:121; 27:19; 28:17). The Israelites are often reminded of the special favor God has bestowed upon them in the past, implying a duty to express gratitude in the present (Q 2:211; 14:28). God will only alter his blessings in response to some change in the recipients' behavior (Q 8:53). Forgetting God's blessings, expressing dissatisfaction or "exchanging God's blessings for thanklessness" leads to severe punishment (Q 2:211; 14:28; see PUNISHMENT STORIES; CHASTISEMENT AND PUNISHMENT). Gratitude for God's favor leads to renewed blessings, as when Lot (q.v.) was rescued from the destruction which befell his people (Q 54:35).

Blessings take place at critical junctures in religious history. Abraham blessed Mecca and its inhabitants when he was about to build God's temple, the Kaʿba (q.v.; Q 2:126), and Noah (q.v.) blessed the ark (q.v.) upon embarkation (Q 11:41). Blessings also reflect bonds with the historical religious community. It is a duty to bless one's parents, praying for God's mercy on their behalf (Q 17:24) and to bless the earlier prophets (Q 37:78-9, 108-9, 119-20, 129-130).

Thanking God involves expressions of praise which are also blessings. The most frequently occurring are "Praise be to God!" (*al-ḥamdu lillāh,* Q 1:1); "Glory be to God!" (*subḥāna llāh,* Q 12:108), "Blessed" (or hallowed, *tabāraka,* Q 25:1, 10, 61), [be God]!"; and "Exalted be God!" (*taʿālā llāh,* Q 7:190). The inhabitants of heaven will pray, "Glory be to you, oh God!" (*subḥānaka llāhumma)* and conclude their prayers with "Praise be to God, Lord of the worlds" (*al-ḥamdu lillāhi rabbi l-ʿālamīn,* Q 10:10).

An important sub-category of qurʾānic blessings are greetings, the most common of which is "Peace!" *(salām):* thus will the inhabitants of heaven greet each other (Q 10:10; 14:23; 33:44). Abraham exchanges this greeting with his guests, the angels (Q 11:69; see ANGEL), and the Prophet greets believers with "Peace be upon you!" (*salām ʿalaykum,* Q 6:54). Other blessings in the context of greeting are "May God's mercy and His blessings be upon you!" (*raḥmatu llāhi wa-barakātuhu ʿalaykum,* Q 11:73), and "May you be well!" (*ṭibtum,* Q 39:73).

Devin J. Stewart

Bibliography
M. Ayoub, Thanksgiving and praise in the Qurʾān and Muslim piety, in *Islamochristiana* 15 (1989), 1-10; G.S. Colin, Baraka, in *EI²*, i, 1032; R.C. Darnell, *The idea of divine covenant in the Qurʾān,* Ph.D. diss., Michigan 1970; L. Sanneh, Thanksgiving in the Qurʾān. The outlines of a theme, in J. Carman and F. Streng (eds.), *Spoken and unspoken thanks. Some comparative soundings. Papers, Seminar on acts of thanksgiving and the virtue of gratitude,* Dallas, 1983, Cambridge, MA 1989, 135-43.

Blood and Blood Clot

The fluid which circulates in the arteries and veins (see ARTERY AND VEIN) of animals and a coagulated mass of such fluid. In the Qurʾān, the terms blood and blood clot do not refer primarily to concrete, physical, internal aspects of the body as they do in contemporary western cultures. Indeed, the two terms function quite differently than one might expect.

Except for one verse (Q 16:66), blood *(dam,* pl. *dimāʾ)* is always laden with a significance beyond its identity as the essential ingredient of living creatures. Thus, blood is a metaphor for illicit killing (Q 2:30, 84; see BLOOD MONEY; MURDER), is forbidden to humans for ingesting (Q 2:173; 5:3; 6:145; 16:115), is the sign of a plague from God (Q 7:133) and is an indication of false evidence (Q 12:18). The first of these metaphors bears the message of God's designation of humans as vicegerents (sing. *khalīfa,* see CALIPH) on earth, the second affirms the rule of law (see LAWFUL AND UNLAWFUL; LAW AND THE QURʾĀN) over such domestic matters as dietary fare, the third reflects the Qurʾān's affirmation of ancient historical details about God's relationship with earlier prophets (see PROPHETS AND PROPHETHOOD), and the fourth similarly asserts God's guidance even against the wiles of evil people (see OBEDIENCE). In the main, then, these meanings reflect themes analagous to those in the Hebrew and Christian scriptures (see SCRIPTURE AND THE QURʾĀN). Noticeably different, however, is the lack of reference to blood for sacrificial purposes, a theme that dominates the earlier sacred writings, both the Hebrew Bible and the Christian New Testament. For example, the concept of sacrifice (q.v.) is central to biblical explanations of the death of Jesus (q.v.), such as that in Paul's *Letter to the Romans* (*Rom* 5:9). The lack of this elaborate superstructure of blood sacrifice in the Qurʾān has been viewed by some historians as a distinctive shift from the Semitic and Near Eastern religious past.

Also unique are references to blood clot (*ʿalaq*, pl. *ʿalaqāt*, see BIOLOGY AS THE CREATION AND STAGES OF LIFE; BIRTH) which, besides being the title of a sūra (Q 96, traditionally held to be the first sūra revealed to the Prophet) is found within a series of verses reflecting upon the omnipotence of God and the evidence of his creative powers in the world. Blood clot references encompass three distinctive nuances, all of them associated with what we might term biological processes: a stage in human embryonic development (Q 22:5); a gum-like character in clay (q.v.) which produces adhesion (Q 23:12-4); and an ingredient out of which God shapes humans (Q 96:2). Commentators have universally acknowledged the leech-like qualities implied by the mention of blood clot in these verses and have seen them connoting various religious meanings. These include the loftiness of God's creation of humans, given the lowly and worthless character of their beginnings and the social character of human life as metaphorically expressed in adhesion during the first stages of existence (see SOCIAL RELATIONS; SOCIAL INTERACTIONS). Such adhesion then becomes the grounds for the kindness and affection generated in human society. Finally, it is understood as emblematic of the male seed "attaching" itself to the female egg, implying human procreation. By fixing these meanings within a larger process, the Qurʾān has been understood to reflect an awareness of human biology and to present a somewhat sophisticated model of human generation. Some modern interpreters combine these verses with Q 39:6, seeing in the reference to the "three veils of darkness" a reflection of the three anatomical layers that protect the fetus — the abdominal wall, the uterus and the matter surrounding the child, i.e. placenta, embryonic membranes, amniotic fluid. Traditionally, such biological specificity was held to indicate the superiority of the Qurʾān to earlier scriptures but in recent years some forms of qurʾānic exegesis (see EXEGESIS OF THE QURʾĀN: EARLY MODERN AND CONTEMPORARY) have found in such passages an affirmation that modern science validates the Qurʾān. The intent of these interpretations is to highlight the Qurʾān's superior knowledge of the creative process and to indicate not only its ascendancy over any other scriptures but also its superior insights into scientific understanding. Hence a contemporary commentary by Iranian scholars on the verses that refer to the blood clot notes, "It is true that at the time of the appearance of Islam these problems were not known to Man, but the Holy Qurʾān, as a scientific miracle, unveiled the true meaning" (A. Sadr al-Ameli (trans.), *Enlightening commentary*, 125). Interpretations of this sort are characteristic of a form of modern qurʾānic commentary known as "scientific" exegesis *(tafsīr ʿilmī)*. See SCIENCE AND THE QURʾĀN.

E.H. Waugh

Bibliography

Primary: A. Sadr-al-ʿAmeli (trans.), *An enlightening commentary into the light of the holy Qurʾān*, ed. S. Berrigan, Esfahan 1994, 125; Ṭabarī, *Tafsīr*, trans. J. Cooper, *The commentary on the Qurʾān* (abridged translation), 1 vol. to date, London 1987-, i, 206-30.

Secondary: J. Bouman, *Gott und Mensch im Koran. Eine Strukturform religioser Anthropologie anhand des Beispiels Allah und Muhammad*, Darmstadt 1989[2]; M. Bucaille, *The Bible, the Qurʾān and science*, trans. M. Bucaille and A.D. Pannell, Indianapolis 1979, 205; S. Hussain, The clot *(al-ʿalaq)*, in *IQ* 24 (1980), 107-10; I. Khalīl, *al-Dam fī l-ʿilm wa-l-Tawrā wa-l-Injīl wa-l-Qurʾān*, Cairo 1996.

Blood Kinship see KINSHIP; FAMILY

Blood Money

Money obtained in compensation for life. The qur'ānic term commonly translated as "blood money" is *diya*. It is practically a *hapax legomenon,* occurring only in the phrase "blood money is to be paid to his kin" *(diyatun musallamatun ilā ahlihi),* which occurs twice in a single piece of legislation in Q 4:92. The verse lays down the law of accidental homicide for which the perpetrator must emancipate a slave or fast for two months (see ATONEMENT) and deliver a *diya* to the victim's family if the victim was a believer or protected by treaty (see CONTRACTS AND ALLIANCES). Both the term and the institution may well be of pre-Islamic Arabian origin (see PRE-ISLAMIC ARABIA AND THE QUR'ĀN). The verbal expression *wdy nfs (fulān),* apparently in the sense of "he paid the *diya* for the life of (so and so)," occurs in two Liḥyānic inscriptions from the valley of al-ʿUlā in northwest Arabia. Under Jewish law even accidental homicide renders the perpetrator liable to retaliation, unless he can escape to a city of refuge, and payment of a ransom *(kōfer)* is specifically prohibited (*Num* 35:26-7, 32; *Deut* 19:4-6). On the other hand, Q 4:92-3 make clear that only accidental homicide must be compounded with a *diya*. Q 4:93 condemns the murderer with intent and unlawful killing is formally prohibited in Q 6:151, 17:33 and 25:68 (see BLOODSHED; MURDER). Q 5:45 reaffirms the principle of "a life for a life" and Q 17:33 endorses the right of the murdered victim's kin or protector to take vengeance (see JUSTICE AND INJUSTICE). All this sits uneasily with Q 2:178, which endorses retaliation in kind (*qiṣāṣ,* see RETALIATION) in respect of those killed, "a free man for a free man, a slave for a slave, a female for a female." Unlike Q 4:92-3, this verse makes no distinction between deliberate and accidental killing and — despite the best efforts of the exegetes — suggests that the person liable to retaliation is not necessarily the killer but any appropriate person of the same status as his victim. It encourages the compounding of the offense but without either the systematic distinction or the technical term *diya* of Q 4:92-3. The use of *adā'* (payment, delivery) in Q 2:178 is suggestive of the *diya* of Q 4:92, though neither exegetes nor lexicographers make any explicit connection between the two terms.

Classical Islamic jurisprudence (*fiqh,* see LAW AND THE QUR'ĀN) has harmonized these somewhat disparate elements. It sets its face firmly against retaliation on the innocent and insists in principle that "a life for a life" means the life of the murderer for the life of the victim. It does, however, make exceptions. For example, when the victim is a slave and the perpetrator a free Muslim there can be no retaliation (see SLAVES AND SLAVERY). It also extends the legality of compounding the offense of homicide to that of murder with intent, for which a *diya* may be paid instead of lawful retaliation if the victim's next of kin or protector agrees (see KINSHIP; PROTECTION). The amount of the *diya* for a free male Muslim is set at 100 camels, perhaps a gesture to Arabian origins rather than an original statute that has survived the test of time. In settled lands, the *diya* is payable in cash.

Richard Kimber

Bibliography
R. Brunschvig, ʿĀḳila, in *EI²*, i, 337-40; W. Caskel, *Lihyan und Lihyanisch,* Cologne 1954, 91-2, 116-8; A. Jaussen and R. Savignac, *Mission archéologique en Arabie,* 3 vols. in 4, Paris 1909-22, ii, 369-70, 441-5; B. Johansen, Eigentum, Familie

und Obrigkeit im Hanafitischen Strafrecht, in *WI* 19 (1979), 38-46; J. Schacht, *An introduction to Islamic law*, Oxford 1964, chap. 24; id., Ḳatl, in *EI*², iv, 766-72; id., Ḳiṣāṣ, in *EI*², v, 177-80; E. Tyan, Diya, in *EI*², ii, 340-3.

Bloodshed

Killing or injuring human life (q.v.). The Qurʾān bans bloodshed *(safk al-dimāʾ)*, but it is specifically mentioned in the Qurʾān only twice (Q 2:30, 84). Nevertheless, there are numerous less-specific references to this concept, just as there are in its biblical antecedents (see the numerous and thematically diverse biblical references cited in A. Khoury, *Der Koran*, i, 223). Furthermore, the qurʾānic accounts of human creation use blood as a metaphor for life (see BLOOD AND BLOOD CLOT; BIOLOGY AS THE CREATION AND STAGES OF LIFE). God is said to have created man of a clay of molded mud (*ṣalṣāl min ḥamāʾ masnūn*, Q 15:26, 28, 33) and, in a further stage of the physical formation, of a blood clot (*ʿalaq*, Q 96:2). The latter conveys the ancient idea that life "is" blood and *vice versa*. When blood leaves the body, it carries life with it (H. Wheeler Robinson, Blood, 715; J.H. Waszink, Blut, 469).

According to the Qurʾān, "not to shed blood" is a divine command that the Israelites received in their holy scripture. The qurʾānic expression of this connection has given rise to different explanations by Muslim exegetes about the binding nature of the command. The idea of the creation of man (cf. Q 2:30-9) forms the context for the first qurʾānic mention of bloodshed. God speaks to the angels: "'I am setting in the earth a viceroy.' The angels ask, 'What, will you set therein one who will do corruption there, and shed blood *(yasfiku l-dimāʾ)*?' He said, 'I know that which you know not.' And he taught Adam [how to] name all things..." (Q 2:30-1). According to qurʾānic and biblical understanding, God handed over his creation (q.v.) to humankind despite the angels' warning (cf. Khoury, i, 222; see CALIPH; ANGEL). Therefore, some Muslim commentators felt themselves forced to rule out any connection of Adam and his descendants with bloodshed by insisting that the passage referred to another kind of human being or to jinn (q.v.) "who lived on earth, doing corruption and shedding blood" before the time of Adam (Ṭabarī, *Tafsīr*, i, 154-5, 170-1; Rāzī, *Tafsīr*, i, 265; see also ADAM AND EVE).

According to other sources, however, the ethical-religious evidence is unequivocal: Bloodshed is related to corruption (q.v.). What is meant by the latter term becomes clearer with the description of the "workers of corruption" in Q 2:8-18. Here it is associated with the unbelievers, the opponents of the Muslims among the Jews and with the hypocrites of Medina (cf. Khoury, i, 178, 192; see OPPOSITION TO MUḤAMMAD; HYPOCRITES AND HYPOCRISY). The "mischief-makers" (*mufsidūn*, see also W. Caskel, *Entdeckungen*, 11, 27, 32) and "their evil abettors" *(shayāṭīn)* are "sinners" who trick God and the true believers and have "a sickness in their hearts" so that they "blindly wander in their insolence."

The second qurʾānic mention of bloodshed is contained in those passages that enjoin Jews to convert to Islam or to become allies of the Muslims (cf. Q 2:40-74; see JEWS AND JUDAISM). Hostilities between two Jewish tribes in Medina (q.v.) at the time of Muḥammad are also of relevance since they temporarily led to the situation in which Jews were fighting and killing each other (Ibn Kathīr, *Tafsīr*, i, 189; also Khoury, *Der Koran*, ii, 42). In this context the Children of Israel (q.v.) are addressed directly: "And when we took compact (*mīthāq*, see Q 2:27, 63; see COVENANT) with you: 'You shall not shed your own blood *(lā tasfikūna dimāʾakum),* neither expel your own from your habitations,' then you confirmed it.... Then there you are killing one another..." (Q 2:84-5). The exegete Fakhr al-Dīn al-Rāzī (d. 606/1210; *Tafsīr,* i, 422) notes that it is "difficult" *(fa-fīhi ishkāl)* to ascertain the binding character of the qurʾānic command not to shed blood. Accordingly, the interpretations cited by commentators and their authorities are multiple: (a) the ban was issued only to Jews ("the Banū Isrāʾīl [see CHILDREN OF ISRAEL] and their descendants are meant," Qurṭubī, *Jāmiʿ,* ii, 18); therefore, they are strictly forbidden to kill each other, according to "their" belief and to the word of "their holy scripture" (Ibn Kathīr, *Tafsīr,* i, 189; Rāzī, *Tafsīr,* i, 422; Ṭabarī, *Tafsīr,* i, 297; see SCRIPTURE AND THE QURʾĀN); (b) the ban is indirectly extended to Muslims by referring to people of "the same descent and belief" (Rāzī, *Tafsīr,* i, 423; Ālūsī, *Rūḥ,* i, 490); (c) the ban is directly in force for Muslims due to their civil wars *(al-fitan fīnā,* Qurṭubī, *Jāmiʿ,* ii, 19); (d) "unjustified" *(bi-ghayr ḥaqq)* bloodshed is forbidden (Ṭabarī, *Tafsīr,* i, 298; see BLOOD MONEY; MURDER); (e) the ban on suicide (q.v.) is intended because an excessive devotion to secular matters is tantamount to suicide of the soul (Rāzī, *Tafsīr,* i, 422).

Sebastian Günther

Bibliography
Primary: Ālūsī, *Rūḥ,* ed. M. Ḥusayn al-ʿArab, 16 vols., Beirut 1414/1994; Ibn Kathīr, *Tafsīr;* Qurṭubī, *Jāmiʿ;* Rāzī, *Tafsīr;* Ṭabarī, *Tafsīr.*
Secondary: W. Caskel, *Entdeckungen in Arabien,* Köln 1954; A.Th. Khoury, *Der Koran. Arabisch-Deutsch Übersetzung und wissenschaftlicher Kommentar,* 9 vols. to date, Gütersloh 1990-, i, 218-29 (Q 2:30-4); ii, 36-45 (Q 2:83-86); H. Wheeler Robinson, Blood, in *ERE,* ii, 714-9; J.H. Waszink, Blut, in Th. Klauser (ed.), *Reallexikon für Antike und Christentum,* 10 vols., Stuttgart 1954, ii, 459-73.

Boast

To vaunt oneself or one's possessions. Several passages in the Qurʾān warn of the dangers of boasting. Boastfulness is contrasted with positive virtues that should be cultivated by the righteous. For example, Q 4:36 commands serving God alone, in part by doing good to others, and by being neither boastful *(fakhūran),* nor arrogant nor stingy. Q 11:10 tells of those who exult and boast *(innahu la-fariḥun fakhūrun)* after experiencing blessing (q.v.) in the wake of adversity. Q 31:17-8 admonishes people to "enjoin what is good and forbid what is wrong [i.e. *al-amr bi-l-maʿrūf*]; and bear patiently against whatever befalls you... and do not turn your cheek scornfully to people, nor walk in the earth with exultant insolence *(lā tamshi fī l-arḍ maraḥan),* for God loves not any arrogant boaster *(kulla mukhtālin fakhūrin).*" The Qurʾan, from the earlier revelations to the later ones, consistently warns against boastful people and their close companions: those who are disdainful *(alladhīna stankafū,* Q 4:173), those who are haughty *(al-mutakabbirīn,* Q 39:60), those who consider themselves to be self-sufficient *(an raʾāhu staghnā,* Q 96:7) and those who are conceited *(mukhtālan,* Q 4:36).

Q 57:20 presents a characterization of the life of this world *(al-ḥayāt al-dunyā)* as "play and amusement, pomp and boasting *(tafākhur)* among you, and rivalry in proliferation of wealth and offspring." Compare this with the early Meccan sūra, Q 102, which is entitled "Mutual Rivalry" (al-Takāthur): "Piling up of [good things] distracts you until you visit the graves. But no, you soon shall know the reality.... You shall certainly see hell-fire.... Then you shall be interrogated on that day concerning the comfort you indulged in" (Q 102:1-3, 6, 8). The obvious lesson is that at the point of death a person will perhaps look back on a life wasted in a quest for material possessions and satisfactions. But the specialist of pre-Islamic poetry, Muḥammad al-Nuwayhī, once (in a 1970 exegesis seminar at the American University in Cairo) interpreted this passage as containing insider information that would have caused the original listeners to nod in recognition. It seems that Meccans used to argue and boast about who had the largest, most illustrious family, clan and tribe (see TRIBES AND CLANS), to the point that in altercations, they would stagger from tavern to cemetery to tally the departed as well as the living members of a kinship (q.v.) group.

The Meccan army that attacked the Muslims at Badr (q.v.) in 2/624 is characterized most unflatteringly in Q 8:47: "And do not be like those who came out of their dwellings boastfully *(baṭaran)* and in order to be seen by people, and to divert [them] from the path of God." This and other passages teach, in one way or another, that "pride goes before destruction, and a haughty spirit before a fall" (*Prov* 16:18). In a similar vein, Q 28:58 declares that: "And how many a community that was exulting *(baṭirat)* in its [comfortable] way of living have We destroyed; now those dwellings of theirs, after them, except for a few, are deserted. And we are their heirs!"

Various ḥadīths continue the Qur'ān's condemnation of pride and boastfulness as is illustrated in the well-known saying from Muslim's *Ṣaḥīḥ:* "He who has in his heart the weight of a grain of mustard seed of pride *(kibriyā')* shall not enter paradise." See also ARROGANCE; PRIDE; VIRTUES AND VICES.

Frederick Mathewson Denny

Bibliography
Primary: al-Ghazālī, Abū Ḥāmid Muḥammad, *Iḥyā' 'ulūm al-dīn,* 4 vols., Būlāq 1289/1872, iii, 288-323 (bk. 29, *K. Ḍamm al-kibr wa-l-'ujb*); Muslim, *Ṣaḥīḥ, K. al-Īmān, B. taḥrīm al-kibr,* Eng. trans. A.H. Siddiqi, 4 vols., Lahore 1976, i, 53.
Secondary: F. Denny, Ethics and the Qur'ān. Community and world view, in R. Hovannisian (ed.), *Ethics in Islam,* Malibu 1985, 103-21; Izutsu, *Concepts.*

Body see ANATOMY; GOD AND HIS ATTRIBUTES; ANTHROPOMORPHISM

Body Fluids see BLOOD AND BLOOD CLOT; BIOLOGY AS THE CREATION AND STAGES OF LIFE

Bohorās see SHĪ'ISM AND THE QUR'ĀN

Bones see BIOLOGY AS THE CREATION AND STAGES OF LIFE; DEATH AND THE DEAD

Book

There is probably no word more important to the understanding of the Qur'ān than *kitāb* and yet its meaning is far more complex than the simple and almost universal translation "book" would seem to imply. The Qur'ān uses the word 261 times, not only in describing itself but also in referring to earlier scriptures and to various other means God employs in dealing with creation (q.v.). The noun comes from the verb *kataba* (to write) and thus can be applied to written material in any form — it is used for a letter in Q 27:28-9 and for a legal document in Q 24:33 — or to the act of writing itself. It also has extensive metaphorical uses which lead to the conclusion that in the Qur'ān the term *kitāb* operates on several levels at once. Since it also carries the force of a verbal noun, in order to understand *kitāb* it is necessary to examine it together with the verb from which it derives. In qur'ānic usage the word represents a quintessentially divine activity and applies only rarely to human writing. The translation "scripture" does some justice to the connotations of *kitāb* but runs the risk of reading Jewish and Christian understandings of scripture into the Qurʾān which has its own unique conception of the phenomenon of God's writing.

Kitāb *and divine knowledge*

It is a commonplace of Near Eastern religions that God keeps both an inventory of everything created as well as a detailed record of all human deeds. The Qurʾān addresses its hearers as though they are quite familiar with these ideas. "Did you not know that God knows all that is in heaven and on earth? Surely it is in a *kitāb*. That is easy for God" (Q 22:70). Nothing is too small or too great to be comprehended by God's knowledge (Q 10:61) and nothing of the unseen remains unaccounted for in the *kitāb* (Q 27:75). The birds and beasts, no less than humanity, have been recorded and nothing has been neglected in this inventory (Q 6:38), not even their sustenance or habitation (Q 11:6). The important thing to note in these verses about the inventory is the close connection between *kitāb* and knowledge. The *kitāb* represents what God alone knows: "And with him are the keys of the unseen (see HIDDEN AND THE HIDDEN). No one but he knows them, and he knows what is in the land and the sea. Not a leaf falls without his knowing it, not a grain in the darkness of the earth, nothing either wet or dry but it is in a *kitāb* that makes things clear" (Q 6:59). This inventory is characterized as *ḥafīẓ* (guarding, watchful, remembering, Q 50:4) like God (Q 11:57; 34:21; see GOD AND HIS ATTRIBUTES). It is also said to be *mubīn* (clear or clarifying, Q 6:59; 10:61; 11:6; 27:75; 34:3), echoing a term that the Qurʾān uses of itself (Q 12:1; 27:1). This adjective is not only very common (119 uses) but also very significant in the Qurʾān: true clarity is something only God is able to provide, since only God has full knowledge of all things.

Closely related to this inventory is the divine recording of human deeds and thoughts, both good (Q 3:53; 5:83; 9:120-1; 21:94) and bad (Q 3:181; 4:81; 10:21; 19:79; 43:19, 80; 78:29). Everything said and done by human beings is recorded (Q 10:61; 54:52; 82:11) in order that retribution and recompense may be made on the day of judgment (see LAST JUDGMENT): "And the *kitāb* is put in place, and you see the guilty fearful of what is in it. They say, 'What kind of a *kitāb* is this that passes over no matter either small or great without taking account of it?' And they find all that they did confronting them. Your Lord treats no one unjustly" (Q 18:49). "And each soul (q.v.) will be recompensed in full for what it has done" (Q 39:70). Good deeds are said to be written "to people's credit" (*lahum*, Q 9:121; 21:94). This register is sometimes referred to as an *imām* (leader, example, authority): "Surely it is we who bring the dead to life. We record *(naktub)* what they send before, and the traces [they leave behind]. And everything we have kept account of in an *imām* that makes things clear" (Q 36:12; see also Q 17:71; 36:12). On one occasion (Q 54:52) it is called *zubur*, a word often translated as "psalms" although it is actually a more general word for books, writings or scriptures. It is most often God who is depicted as recording (Q 3:181; 4:81; 19:79: 21:94; 36:12; 45:29), but there is also talk of "envoys" (*rusul*, Q 10:21; 43:80; see MESSENGER) who write and of "guardians, noble scribes" (*ḥāfiẓīn kirāman kātibīn*, Q 82:10-1) who know all that is done.

Although the record of deeds is often spoken of as a single entity, the final judgment is pictured as one in which each person will be handed the *kitāb* detailing his or her deeds. "On the day when we shall summon all people with their record *(imām),* whoever is given his *kitāb* in his right hand — those will read their *kitāb* and they will not be wronged a shred" (Q 17:71; see also 69:19; 84:7). Anyone to be punished will be given the *kitāb* in the left hand (Q 69:25) or behind the back (Q 84:10). In another place, there seems to be a separate *kitāb* for each nation (Q 45:29). The image of judgment is a commercial one — a final settling of accounts. Like the inventory of creation the record of deeds is characterized as *mubīn* (Q 10:61; 34:4; 36:12) in that it makes clear precisely the recompense or punishment to be apportioned (see REWARD AND PUNISHMENT). It is intimately related to God's knowledge in that it reflects the fact that God is "most aware *(aʿlam)* of what they have done" (Q 39:70) and is a witness *(shuhūd)* to all actions in which people are engaged (Q 10:61). Taken together, these two activities of recording represent the completeness of God's knowledge of all that exists and all that takes place.

Kitāb *and divine authority*

The idea of writing is also very much associated in qurʾānic usage with the exercise of divine authority (q.v.; see also FATE). The length of one's life is "in a *kitāb*" and can neither be shortened nor lengthened (Q 35:11). One can neither escape death when it has been "written" (Q 3:154) nor hasten it since it comes by God's permission "as a writ to be carried out later" (*kitāban muʾajjalan,* Q 3:145). No city (q.v.) is punished by destruction without there having been a "known decree" (*kitāb maʿlūm,* Q 15:4; see PUNISHMENT STORIES). Such sentences of punishment are said to be "in the *kitāb*" (Q 17:58), as are those meted out to individuals (*bi-imām mubīn,* Q 15:79). "No calamity strikes either on the earth or among yourselves which is not already in a *kitāb* before we bring it into being — surely that is easy for God" (Q 57:22; see also Q 9:51).

It might seem that the use of the word *kitāb* in connection with these acts of divine authority indicates that they are envisaged as being recorded in some kind of book of decrees. However, the word is also used to apply independently to the decrees themselves (Q 2:235; 4:103; 8:68; 13:38; 30:56) suggesting that the usage of the root *k-t-b* (to write) is largely metaphorical. The verb *kutiba* (it has been written) is used when speaking of various aspects of law (see LAW AND THE QURʾĀN): retaliation (q.v.; Q 2:178), inheritance (q.v.; Q 2:180), fasting (q.v.; Q 2:183) and warfare (Q 2:216, 246; see WAR). God writes to determine obligations on various individuals and groups (Q 4:24, 66, 77; 5:32, 45; 57:27). In an unusual construction God is also said to have written mercy (q.v.) as an obligation for himself (Q 6:12, 54); this in effect expresses an element of the divine nature. In several uses of the verb "to write" there is a very close relationship between the decree and the record of people's deeds. God writes punishments (Q 22:4; 59:3; see CHASTISEMENT AND PUNISHMENT), entitlements (Q 2:187; 4:127) and rewards (Q 5:21; 7:156; 21:105). Indeed, it is sometimes difficult to make any separation at all between the recording of deeds and the determination of judgment: "This *kitāb* of ours pronounces against you truly. Surely we caused to be recorded *(kunnā nastansikh)* whatever you used to do" (Q 45:29). The definitive divine judgment against evildoers is inseparable from God's knowledge of all that they have done. Similarly, the recording of the time of each person's death is presented both as a matter of knowledge and also as an act of determination — foreknowledge and foreordaining are somehow inseparable. This very ambiguity suggests that the Qurʾān does not so much contain a reference to a heavenly archive with separate registers and inventories as it does, in a more amorphous sense, to the overarching knowledge and authority of God.

It is common, of course, for qurʾānic commentators to gloss occurrences of the verb *kataba* with such verbs as *amara, ḥafiẓa, ḥasiba* or *faraḍa* and, similarly, for translators to render them "command," "remember," "keep account of," "enjoin," "prescribe" or "decree." They are surely right in detecting here a metaphorical usage of the verb "to write." The question then arises whether the use of the noun *kitāb* is not likewise more metaphorical than concrete. As long as the *kitāb* operates only in the heavenly realm it makes little difference. However, the issue becomes more acute when an effort is made to try to understand what the Qurʾān means when it refers to itself as *kitāb* and when it speaks of the *kitāb* being "sent down" and given to other peoples through the prophets (see PROPHETS AND PROPHETHOOD).

Kitāb *and revelation*

One of the most important concepts used in connection with revelation in the Qurʾān is *kitāb* (see REVELATION AND INSPIRATION). It is several times stated in general terms that whenever God sent prophets and messengers to give good tidings and to warn of judgment, he sent down with them the *kitāb* (Q 2:213; 3:81; 35:25; 40:70; 57:25). The *kitāb* comes with the truth so that the Prophet may judge according to it (Q 2:213). It is specifically mentioned as having been given to Moses (q.v.; Q 2:53, 87; 17:2; 23:49; 25:35), to Jesus (q.v.; Q 3:48; 5:110; 19:30) and most often, of course, to Muḥammad (e.g. Q 5:48; 7:2; 14:1) . The Qurʾān also mentions by name several of those to whom God has given revelation: "Indeed we communicate to you just as we communicated *(awḥaynā)* to Noah (q.v.) and the prophets after him, as we communicated to Abraham (q.v.) and Ishmael (q.v.) and Isaac (q.v.) and Jacob (q.v.) and the tribes, and Jesus and Job (q.v.) and Jonah (q.v.) and Aaron (q.v.) and Solomon (q.v.), and as we granted to David (q.v.) the *zabūr* (see PSALMS)" (Q 4:163). This listing marks out one feature of the Qurʾān's understanding of *kitāb:* It is thought to have a particularly close association with the lineage of Noah, Abraham and Israel (q.v.; Q 4:54; 40:53; 57:26; see also CHILDREN OF ISRAEL). Although attempts have sometimes been made to distinguish between messengers *(rusul)* and prophets *(anbiyāʾ)* on the basis of whether they were given a canonical text or merely an oral message, there appears to be no such consistent distinction in the Qurʾān itself. Some canons resulting from God's sending of the *kitāb* are mentioned by name: Torah (*tawrāt,* 18 times; see TORAH) and Gospel (*injīl,* twelve times; see GOSPEL); the generic *al-ṣuḥuf al-ūlā* ("the former pages," Q 20:133; 87:18) are specified as belonging to Moses and Abraham (Q 53:36-7; 87:19). It is not clear that Moses' "pages" are thought of as identical to the *tawrāt*. Although the Qurʾān understands *tawrāt* to be the revelation given to the Jews, it is most often paired with Injīl and mentioned in connection not with Moses but with Jesus.

The *kitāb* is said to come to the prophets by *waḥy* (inspiration, revelation or communication; e.g. Q 18:27; 29:45; 35:31). However, more commonly God is said to "send it down" (*nazzala, anzala,* e.g. Q 2:174, 176, 213, 231) or simply to "give" it (*atā,* e.g. Q 2:53, 87, 121, 146). God teaches the *kitāb* to Jesus (Q 3:48; 5:110), gives it as an inheritance to the Children of Israel (Q 40:53) and to some chosen servants (Q 35:32). The messenger who brings the *kitāb* (Q 3:184, 6:91) in his turn teaches it to the people (Q 2:129; 2:151; 3:164; 62:2). The people recite it (*qaraʾa,* Q 2:44, 113, 121; 10:94; 69:19), learn it (*ʿalima,* Q 2:78, 144, 146), study it (*darasa,* Q 3:79; 34:44; 68:37) and teach it (*ʿallama,* Q 3:79; see KNOWLEDGE AND LEARNING).

In order fully to understand what the Qurʾān means when it speaks of *kitāb* in the context of revelation, it is necessary to view the word within the whole field of vocabulary with which it is used. The word acts as the focus for some of the most significant concepts in the Qurʾān. Two key terms in this respect *(āya* and *ḥikma)* appear with *kitāb* in something like a credal formula that occurs four times (Q 2:129, 151; 3:164; 62:2). The role of the messenger *(rasūl)* is to recite to the people God's signs or revelations (*āyāt,* see SIGNS), to purify them and to make known to them the *kitāb* and the *ḥikma*. This latter term is often translated "wisdom" but such a rendering fails to take account of the origins of the word in the verb *ḥakama* (to judge, to rule, to decide). To the extent that *ḥikma* is wisdom at all, it is not to be mistaken for the esoteric wisdom of the gnostic but should be understood as the practical wisdom or the wise authority of the experienced ruler (see WISDOM; JUDGMENT). *Kitāb* and *ḥikma* appear ten times together and form a virtual hendiadys. The term *āya* (pl. *āyāt*) is used to refer to everything that reveals God's will and ways, whether in nature (e.g. Q 2:266; 16:11-3; 30:46; see ANIMAL LIFE), history (e.g. Q 46:27), legislation (e.g. Q 24:61) or in revelation (e.g. Q 24:1). The *āyāt* of God are intended to prompt people to reason *(ʿaqala),* to learn *(ʿalima),* to ponder *(tafakkara, tadhakkara)* and so to come to faith *(āmana)*. The coming of the *kitāb* with its *āyāt* provides insight into what God knows and what God commands. Therefore, far from being clearly distinguished from the above-mentioned registers, the *kitāb* of revelation is intimately linked with the same divine knowledge and authority that they symbolize. The fundamental pattern (with associated verbal roots) is this: (a) As creator God knows *(ʿ-l-m)* the truth *(ḥ-q-q)* of all things and is in command *(ḥ-k-m)* of all things. The symbol for this knowledge and authority is *kitāb*. (b) Given close attention and reflection (*ʿ-q-l, f-k-r,* etc.), it is possible for people to learn *(ʿ-l-m)* from the *āyāt* of nature and history much of the truth of what God knows and commands. Yet, they rarely do so. (c) In order to call humanity to such attentiveness and reflection, God sends prophetic messengers *(r-s-l, n-b-ʾ)* who bring their communities guidance *(h-d-y),* a privileged insight into God's knowledge and authoritative decree. They recite *(q-r-ʾ, t-l-w)* God's *āyāt* in order to remind *(dh-k-r)* the people of them, to make quite clear *(b-y-n, n-w-r, f-ṣ-l)* precisely what God requires *(ḥ-k-m)* and to warn (*n-dh-r,* see WARNING) of the coming judgment *(f-ṣ-l, ḥ-k-m, d-y-n)*. (d) The symbol of this guidance is the *kitāb* — God's sending down *(n-z-l)* through the Prophet of an authoritative word *(q-w-l, k-l-m)* to address the current situation and the prevailing issue. This divine/prophetic address bears the name *kitāb* not because of its form (which remains oral and responsive) but because of its origin and its nature as a communication *(n-z-l, w-ḥ-y)* of God's knowledge *(ʿ-l-m)* and a clear statement *(b-y-n)* of God's commands *(ḥ-k-m)*. (e) The community (see COMMUNITY AND SOCIETY IN THE QURʾĀN) addressed by God accepts the relationship of guidance first by accepting *(ʾ-m-n)* that what the Prophet recites has a divine origin, then by committing themselves *(s-l-m)* to following *(t-b-ʿ, ṭ-w-ʿ)* the divine will manifested in the prophetic word and, finally, by reciting *(q-r-ʾ)* it in their turn. In this way, they become a people who are identified and defined by their having been granted the *kitāb*.

It is the phenomenon of the *kitāb* that

unifies this whole schema while itself remaining somewhat elusive. It is often referred to in the plural, the indefinite or the partitive form so it remains unclear from the Qurʾān whether anyone can be understood to be fully in possession of the *kitāb*. In this respect, the Qurʾān does not present the *kitāb* as a closed and definable corpus of text, but rather as an ongoing relationship of guidance.

Ahl al-kitāb — *the people of the* kitāb

It is the *kitāb* relationship that defines the Christians *(naṣāra),* the Jews *(yahūd, Banū Isrāʾīl)* and the Sabians *(ṣābiʾūn).* All of these groups are referred to in the Qurʾān as *ahl al-kitāb* or *alladhīna ūtū l-kitāb* (those who have been granted the *kitāb;* see PEOPLE OF THE BOOK; CHRISTIANS AND CHRISTIANITY; JEWS AND JUDAISM; SABIANS; MAGIANS). The Qurʾān calls for belief not only in the *kitāb* sent down to Muḥammad but also in the *kitāb* (or the plural *kutub*) sent down before him (Q 2:285; 4:136). It is precisely because they have already been recipients of God's revelation that the *ahl al-kitāb* are expected to recognize in Muḥammad a genuine messenger of God and to acknowledge in what he brings the same *kitāb* (Q 5:83; 13:43; 29:47) — not precisely the same text but the same message of God, the same guidance to humankind.

It is recognized that the Jews put "the *kitāb* that Moses brought as a light and a guidance for humanity" on papyri (*qarāṭīs,* sing. *qirṭās,* Q 6:91) yet it is not their possession of physical books that constitutes the *ahl al-kitāb*. If it had been, one might have expected an earlier attempt to have a written version of the Qurʾān. As it was, a standardized written text was not produced, according to Muslim tradition, until perhaps as late as twenty years after the death of the Prophet during the caliphate of ʿUthmān (r. 23-35/644-56; see COLLECTION OF THE QURʾĀN). The *ahl al-kitāb* seem to be thought of primarily as — like Muslims — reciters of the word of God rather than as writers and readers of books (see RECITATION OF THE QURʾĀN; READINGS OF THE QURʾĀN). *Ahl al-kitāb* should probably be understood as those who have been given not *possession of* but rather *access to* and *insight into* the knowledge, wisdom and sovereignty of God for which the very fluid term *kitāb* serves as a symbol. "Those who have been given the *kitāb*" are also called "those who have been given knowledge" (*alladhīna ʾūtū l-ʿilm,* e.g. Q 16:27; 17:107; 22:54). They have learned to read the "signs" (cf. Q 45:2-7), yet it is clear that they do not actually possess *all* knowledge. They have rather been given access to the divine knowledge through God's initiative in addressing humanity through the prophets (cf. Q 20:110-114).

Umm al-kitāb — *the "mother" of the* kitāb

Three times the Qurʾān refers to the *umm* (literally "mother" hence "essence" or "source") of the *kitāb* (Q 3:7; 13:39; 43:4). The latter two cases are traditionally read as referring to a heavenly archetype of the *kitāb,* a text that constitutes the source of all the particular versions given through Muḥammad and the other prophets. The commentary literature has developed what might be termed a "topography" of revelation that begins with the archetypal *kitāb* on the Preserved Tablet (*lawḥ maḥfūẓ,* Q 85:22; see PRESERVED TABLET) and involves the noble scribes (*safarat kirām,* Q 80:15-6) who are said to have revealed the text to Gabriel (q.v.) over twenty nights and who, in his turn, revealed it to Muḥammad over twenty years. Yet the term *umm al-kitāb* can just as well be read in the symbolic way that has been suggested above. To God alone belongs the essence of authority and knowledge, so whatever authoritative guidance is given through God's messengers comes from that source. In Q 3:7 this term seems clearly to refer to part of the text of the Qurʾān: "It is he who has sent down to you the *kitāb,* some of whose verses are decisive — they are the essence (*umm,* lit. "mother") of the *kitāb* — and others that are ambiguous." In this famously controversial verse the Qurʾān distinguishes between those verses that are considered *muḥkamāt* (defined, fixed, firm, decisive, straightforward) and those that are *mutashābihāt* (lit. "resembling one another" possibly meaning "ambiguous" or "metaphorical"; see AMBIGUOUS). Since the Qurʾān does not specify which verses are which, this pair of terms has been interpreted in many different ways. It is the *muḥkamāt* that are said to constitute the essence or substance of the *kitāb*. Qurʾānic commentators often understand this to mean that such verses lay down the principles of Islam; they contain the basis of creed and law; they outline all the duties, punishments and commandments (q.v.) that are essential to Islam (see BOUNDARIES AND PRECEPTS). The *muḥkamāt* are sometimes thought to be the abrogating *(nāsikh)* verses because they remain firm and fixed whereas the *mutashābihāt,* although they *resemble* the others, are in fact without legal force due to their having been abrogated (*mansūkh,* see ABROGATION). Other commentators distinguish the *muḥkamāt,* those verses that can stand alone and so require little or no interpretation, from the *mutashābihāt,* those that can only be fully understood in relationship to other verses treating the same matter. The exegetical tradition has often identified the first sūra of the Qurʾān (Sūrat al-Fātiḥa; see FĀTIḤA) as *umm al-kitāb* since it is thought to contain the essential content of the Qurʾān. So also the so-called mysterious letters *(fawātiḥ)* at the beginning of some sūras have been thought to contain in some mystical way the essence of the Qurʾān. (See LETTERS AND MYSTERIOUS LETTERS.)

The Qurʾān as kitāb

One of the most complex questions about the Qurʾān is what it means when it refers to itself as *kitāb.* Western scholars have, by and large, taken the use of the word *kitāb* as an indication that Muḥammad intended to provide his community with a written canon of scripture parallel to those possessed by the Christians and the Jews. G. Widengren draws on Near Eastern religious history to propose that the Prophet saw himself primarily as the bringer of a written corpus. Nöldeke-Schwally (*GQ,* ii, 1-3) argue that, given Muḥammad's understanding that his revelations were to serve in place of the Bible as the definitive document of the divine will, he must also have intended to safeguard them in written form. R. Bell takes *al-kitāb* to refer to a document originally conceived of as distinct from *al-qurʾān* and which ultimately replaced it. He suggests that what the text calls *al-qurʾān* is a collection of recitations that was probably closed about the time of the battle of Badr (2/624; see BADR). The *kitāb* was never actually completed and if it ever had any logical framework its organization was constantly intruded upon by the vicissitudes, both internal and external, of communal life. Bell understands the *kitāb* to have been intended to be the complete record of revelation; it was to comprise, in a slightly re-worked form, all the elements Bell previously distinguished as characterizing the stages in the development of the Prophet's revelations: "signs" passages, stories of punishment, Qurʾān. It was also intended to include the material — the appeals, regulations and exhortations demanded of him as a leader — unsuitable for a collection meant for recitation. Bell is largely followed in this approach by W.M.

Watt and A.T. Welch. For A. Neuwirth, the term *kitāb* functions as a symbol of the shared prophetic heritage, the common memory of salvation history which Muslims now share with the Christians and Jews. Neuwirth believes that only certain parts of the Qurʾān are to be understood as belonging to the *kitāb* — the pericopes excerpted from the heavenly book, i.e. the *dhikr* or recalling of prophetic history.

Perhaps the weakest part of all these scenarios is the idea that the task of producing a book of scripture was left undone because of other responsibilities and demands which pressed upon Muḥammad. If one understands the verses about the *kitāb* to indicate that it was the Prophet's defining function to produce such a canonical text, then it becomes difficult to see how Muḥammad could have placed any duty above this one.

Muslim tradition has long understood that the Prophet intended the written codification of the Qurʾān; yet, the traditions about the collection and writing down of the text are at cross purposes (see CODICES OF THE QURʾĀN). On the one hand, some traditions seek to assure those who trust written texts that there exists an unbroken manuscript tradition, authenticated not only by the Prophet but by the angel Gabriel. On the other, many traditions represent the writing down of the text as an act of doubtful piety and they portray the manuscript tradition as in some respects deficient and as dependent on an oral tradition codified only after the Prophet's death. Neither strand of the tradition represents the text at the time of the Prophet's death as having existed in a physical form that would indicate that Muḥammad had all but finished preparing the definitive document of revelation. The scraps of wood, leather and pottery, the bones and the bark on which the revelations were apparently written down seem to indicate that the Prophet did not have in mind producing the kind of scroll or codex that was characteristic of Jewish and Christian use in other places. Furthermore, given the limitations of the Arabic script (q.v.) at the time, such written material as did exist could serve as not much more than an *aide-memoire* to those who knew that part of the text by heart.

Given all this, there remains considerable doubt as to whether the Prophet thought of the word *kitāb* as defining either the form in which the Qurʾān was revealed or the form in which it was to be propagated and perpetuated. Both Western and Muslim approaches seem to read into the Qurʾān what they know of the Christian and Jewish use of scripture in other contexts outside Arabia. However, in order to understand the meaning of the qurʾānic *kitāb* as fully as possible, such preconceptions must not become the sole basis for its interpretation.

At the beginning of what might be called the text proper (Q 2:1-2) the Qurʾān speaks of the *kitāb: "Alif. Lām. Mīm.* That is the *kitāb* about which there is no doubt, guidance for the God-fearing." Qurʾānic commentators were rather puzzled to find *dhālika* ("that") rather than *hādhā* ("this") in Q 2:2, but the majority of exegetical traditions opted to equate the two and in this they are generally followed by translators. Others, recognizing that *dhālika* logically refers to something absent or already complete, took it to refer variously to the mysterious letters of Q 2:1 or to the sūras of the Qurʾān that had thus far been revealed or even to the Gospel and the Torah. The issue was in effect side-stepped at this point yet the question remains: what is this *kitāb* that the *kitāb* is always talking about? What is the recitation (Qurʾān) about which verses are constantly being recited? The abiding enigma of the text is that, along with verses that are to be construed as timeless divine pronouncements, it also contains a large amount of commentary upon and analysis of the processes of its own revelation and the vicissitudes of its own reception in time. One wonders how the two genres can exist not just side by side but interwoven within a single document; how the Qurʾān can so constantly refer to itself in the third person and at the same time be considered a unity; how it can define and defend itself even as it is being revealed.

The Qurʾān is both itself and *about* itself; both *hādhā* and *dhālika*. Even in its final form it seems still a work-in-process, carefully observing and commenting upon itself. This is what makes it so enigmatic as a canonized, codified text. What is to be found "between the two covers" remains a surprise because it does not behave as though it were a completed volume nor, indeed, as the copy of a pre-existent heavenly document.

The Qurʾān actually rejects certain common conceptions of *kitāb*. It is reiterated several times that in the ministry of the Prophet there comes to the Arabs (q.v.) "a *kitāb* from God" (e.g. Q 6:19, 114). However, it is also clear that Muḥammad does not consider that the lack of any written text invalidates this claim in any way. When the Prophet is challenged to produce a writing from heaven as proof (q.v.) of his authenticity (Q 17:93; see BELIEF AND UNBELIEF), he is told to reply that he is merely a human messenger. In Q 6:7 God says, "Even if we had sent down a *kitāb* on papyrus and they were to touch it with their hands, those who disbelieve would have said, 'This is clearly nothing but sorcery.'" So when the Qurʾān speaks of itself as *kitāb,* it seems to be talking not about the form in which it is sent down but rather about the authority it carries as a manifestation of the knowledge and command of God.

This is borne out in another situation of challenge where the Prophet's critics demand to know why the recitation he claims is from God is being given to him only piecemeal rather than "as a single complete pronouncement" (*jumlatan wāḥidatan,* Q 25:32). To Muḥammad's interlocutors, a divine pronouncement must, almost by definition, be complete. Yet the Qurʾān comes only, as the commentators like to say, responsively *(jawāban li-qawlihim),* in installments *(munajjaman)* according to situations and events in order that the Prophet will be able to address God's response to whatever objection is being raised, whatever question is being asked (Q 25:33). In this context they quote Q 17:106: "... and in the form of a recitation that we have divided up *(faraqnāhu)* that you might recite it to the people at intervals *(ʿala mukthin),* and we have indeed sent it down." In rejecting the claim that it should be sent down "as a single complete pronouncement" the Qurʾān is asserting its fluidity and its responsiveness to situations. It is refusing to behave as an already closed and canonized text but insists on being the authoritative voice of God in the present.

This immediate and responsive quality of the Qurʾān is illustrated again and again in one of its most characteristic rhetorical devices: the imperative, "Say!" (*qul,* the singular addressed to the Prophet is used 323 times, and it appears in other forms 26 times). This is not merely one among several literary forms (see LANGUAGE AND STYLE OF THE QURʾĀN) but rather demonstrates the Qurʾān's fundamental sense of itself: it "comes down" as the divine response placed on the lips of God's Prophet. In the ministry of Muḥammad, the *kitāb* comes not as a finished tome in which to search for the divine wisdom and will but as a wise and commanding voice to be heeded.

The term *kitāb,* then, does not indicate that the Qurʾān is to be understood as a closed corpus of text, codified in writing; it used that language of itself long before it was either closed or written. The Muslim community used the same term while at the same time preserving the text primarily in oral form. The word *kitāb* rather expresses a claim as to the origin of the words on the Prophet's lips: they are *kitāb* because they come from God, from the realm of God's knowledge and authority, as these are symbolized by writing. Writing, of course, is a process of engagement with an audience. It involves re-writing and rephrasing, emendation and development. This is what the Muslim interpretative tradition has recognized in the phenomenon of abrogation *(naskh):* that elements of God's word are conditioned by time and circumstance and so God exercises the prerogative of amending the text, removing the force of some earlier pronouncements and perhaps even their wording as well. The Qurʾān is God's writing in the sense that it is God's definitive and authoritative word. Yet it is not the sum total of God's word but rather a token of it and a guarantee of continuing guidance. See also SCRIPTURE AND THE QURʾĀN.

Daniel Madigan

Bibliography

H. Berg, Ṭabarī's exegesis of the Qurʾānic term *al-kitāb,* in *JAAR* 63 (1995), 761-74. Burton, *Collection,* passim; Graham, *Beyond,* 79-115; id., "Book, writ, and word." Scripture and the history of religion, in *Bulletin of the Center for the Study of World Religions, Harvard University* 16 (1989-90), 2-15; id., The earliest meaning of "Qurʾān," in *WI* 23-4 (1984), 361-77; id., Qurʾān as spoken word: an Islamic contribution to the understanding of scripture, in R.C. Martin (ed.), *Approaches to Islam in religious studies,* Tucson 1985, 23-40; A. Jeffery, *The* Qurʾān *as scripture,* New York 1952; D. Künstlinger, "Kitāb" und "ahlu l-kitābi" im Kurān, in *Rocznik Orjentalistyczny* 4 (1926), 238-47; D.A. Madigan, *The Qurʾāns self-image: books, writing and authority in Muslim scripture,* Princeton 2001; T. Nagel, Vom "Qurʾān" zur "Schrift." Bells Hypothese aus religionsgeschichtlicher Sicht, in *Der Islam* 60 (1983), 143-65; A. Neuwirth, Vom Rezitationstext über die Liturgie zum Kanon: zu Entstehung und Wiederauflösung der Surenkomposition im Verlauf der Entwicklung eines islamischen Kultus, in Wild, *Text* 69-105; Nöldeke, *GQ;* J. Pedersen, Review of *Ursprung und Geschichte der Mormonen: mit Exkursen über die Anfänge des Islams und des Christentums* by Eduard Meyer, in *Der Islam* 5 (1914), 110-5; W.C. Smith, The true meaning of scripture. An empirical historian's nonreductionist interpretation of the Qurʾan, in *IJMES* 11 (1980), 487-505; id., *What is scripture? A comparative approach,* Minneapolis 1993; Watt-Bell, *Introduction,* 132-41; G. Widengren, *The ascension of the apostle and the heavenly book,* Uppsala 1950; id., Holy book and holy tradition in Islam, in F.F. Bruce and E.G. Rupp (eds.), *Holy book and holy tradition,* Manchester 1968, 210-36.

Book of David see PSALMS

Booty

Plunder taken in war (q.v.). The Qurʾān does not mention the words *ghanīma* or *fayʾ*, which became the technical terms for booty in Islamic law, but refers explicitly only to the plural noun *maghānim* (Q 4:94; 48:15, 19, 20); the verb *ghanima,* to take booty (Q 8:41, 69); and the verb *afāʾa* (from the same root as *fayʾ*), to give as booty (Q 33:50; 59:6-7). In pre-Islamic times the terms were synonymous. There are indications that in Q 59:6-7, referring to the surrender of the Banū l-Naḍīr, *afāʾa* denotes booty acquired not by actual fighting but as a result of the surrender of the enemy. Q 48:15, 19 and 20 suggest that taking booty is considered a normal element of warfare and Q 8:69 confirms that booty taken from the enemy is lawful property. A specific rule is given in Q 8:41 where the pre-Islamic custom of assigning one-fifth of the booty *(ghanīma)* to the leader is upheld. The verse mentions that this share belongs to God and is to be spent on the Messenger, i.e.

the prophet Muḥammad, (his) relatives, the orphans (q.v.), the needy and travelers. Regarding *fay'*, Q 59:7 stipulates that this type of booty is not to be distributed among the fighters but also belongs to God and his messenger and is to be spent on (his) relatives (see FAMILY OF THE PROPHET), the orphans (q.v.), the needy and travelers. F. Løkkegaard (*Islamic taxation*, 50), however, asserts that this constituted a breach with the established custom introduced by Muḥammad and was prompted by his lack of means. In Q 4:94 the rewards of paradise (q.v.) are com-pared to booty (see REWARD AND PUNISHMENT).

A great deal of controversy exists among Muslim legal scholars with regard to the rules about booty (see LAW AND THE QUR'ĀN). *Ghanīma*, i.e. movable goods taken by force from unbelievers during actual warfare, must be divided among the army and the imām (as head of state; see IMĀM) once the army has returned to Islamic territory. The head of state is entitled to one-fifth (to be distributed to the leader, the Prophet's relatives, the orphans, the needy and travelers) and the remainder is to be divided among the soldiers. Only free, adult, male Muslims who were present during the battle have a share, regardless of whether they actually fought or not. The Ḥanafī form of Islamic law assigns a share also to soldiers who joined the troops after the battle but before reaching Islamic territory. Mounted soldiers are entitled to a double or triple portion. The head of state may reward certain warriors by giving them larger shares (*nafl*, pl. *anfāl*, cf. Q 8:1). Opinions differ on whether this reward is to be paid from the one-fifth portion of the state or at the expense of the other soldiers. Some jurists hold that a soldier is entitled to appropriate the spoils *(salab)* of the enemy he has killed, whereas others are of the opinion that the consent of the head of state is needed in this instance.

Opinions also vary on the status of land acquired by force. The Mālikī form of Islamic law holds that it is state land whereas the Shāfiʿī view is that it must be divided among the army that has conquered the region. The Ḥanafīs left the matter to the discretion of the head of state: He could make it state land, divide it among the army or leave its ownership to its inhabitants, provided they pay the *kharāj* tax.

As to *fay'*, enemy property (including tributes, the *kharāj* tax and the *jizya*) acquired by Muslims as a result of the surrender of the enemy, jurists generally hold that it is not to be divided among the army but that all of it is at the disposition of the head of state. See also JIZYA; TAXATION; TRIBUTE; EXPEDITIONS AND BATTLES.

Rudolph Peters

Bibliography
Primary: Abū Yūsuf Yaʿqūb b. Ibrāhīm, *Kitāb al-Kharāj*, Cairo 1973⁴, trans. A. Ben-Shemesh, *Taxation in Islam, iii. Abū Yūsuf's Kitāb al-Kharāj*, Leiden 1969; Ibn Rushd (al-Ḥafīd), *Bidāyat al-mujtahid*, 2 vols., Cairo 1960, ii, 390-403; Māwardī, *al-Aḥkām al-sulṭāniyya*, ed. M.Ḥ. al-Fiqī, Cairo 1966, 136-53.
Secondary: N.P. Aghnides, *Mohammedan theories of finance*, Lahore 1961², 407-11, 461-80; F. Løkkegaard, *Islamic taxation in the classic period*, Copenhagen 1950.

Boundaries and Precepts

Prescribed rules guiding behavior, which one should not transgress. The phrase "God's boundaries" *(ḥudūd Allāh)* occurs twelve times in the Qurʾān. It is used mainly as an admonitory conclusion to a preceding passage of legislation, as in "These are God's boundaries, do not approach them" (Q 2:187) or "These are God's boundaries, do not transgress them. Whoever does transgress God's boundaries, those are the wrongdoers" (Q 2:229) and "These are God's boundaries, and the unbelievers shall have a painful torment" (Q 58:4). Q 4:13-4 balances reward with retribution (see REWARD AND PUNISHMENT): "These are God's boundaries. Whoever obeys God and his messenger, He will cause him to enter gardens below which rivers flow (...), but whoever disobeys God and his messenger, and transgresses his boundaries, He will cause him to enter a fire" (cf. Q 2:230; 65:1; cf. 9:112; see FIRE; HELL; GARDEN). Both the meaning and use of qur'ānic *ḥudūd* are similar to those of the biblical *ḥuqqīm/ḥuqqōt*, "boundaries, statutes (of God)" (e.g. *Lev* 18:4-5, 26; 19:19, 37; 26:3, 15; *Num* 30:17; *Deut* 5:1; 6:1, 24; 26:16-7; *ḥuqqei hā-elōhīm* occurs in *Exod* 18:16).

The legislation in these qur'ānic passages is always concerned in some way with marital or family relations (see MARRIAGE AND DIVORCE). Q 2:183-7 reminds the believers of their obligation to observe fast days but tends to alleviate the burdens that this imposes. In particular, Q 2:187 permits sexual intercourse with women as well as eating and drinking during the hours of darkness (q.v.) before the day of fasting. This is a departure from Jewish law as it relates to the Day of Atonement (see FASTING; ABSTINENCE; JEWS AND JUDAISM). Q 2:229-30 occur as part of a long passage of legislation on divorce and deal specifically with the divorced wife's right to retain property granted her by her husband and with the permissibility of the divorced couple's remarrying if the ex-wife marries a different husband and is then divorced by him. This latter is also a permissive variation from Jewish law. Q 58:3 outlines the standard means (i.e. the freeing of a slave, see SLAVES AND SLAVERY) by which a man may lawfully resume relations with his wife after *ẓihār*, a device by which a husband could deny his wife her right to sexual intercourse in the marriage. The following verse lays down an alternative expiatory procedure for annulling the device. Q 4:11-3 contain detailed rules for inheritance (q.v.), one of the most important qur'ānic legal reforms and a mainstay of qur'ānic family law. Q 65:1 is again concerned with divorce. Returning to Q 2:229-30, its somewhat different usage of the phrase "God's boundaries" strengthens the impression that his "boundaries" are invoked especially in connection with marital relations. According to Q 2:229, a wife may redeem herself from marriage in certain circumstances by surrendering to her husband at least part of the settlement she would normally retain on divorce. The circumstances are those of likely marital breakdown expressed as the couple's anticipated failure to "uphold God's boundaries." Q 2:230 lays down a corresponding expectation to "uphold God's boundaries" as a precondition for the remarriage of a previously divorced couple.

In Islamic jurisprudence the expression *ḥudūd Allāh* has become detached from civil law and serves instead as symbolic qur'ānic sanction for the classical theory of penal law. Here, in theory, "God's boundaries" are the deterrent corporal penalties of flogging (q.v.), amputation and execution as laid down in the "Book of God" (see BOOK) for the infringement of specific prohibitions (see ADULTERY AND FORNICATION; THEFT; HIGHWAY ROBBERY; INTOXICANTS). This classical doctrine, with its emphasis on scriptural sanction for judicial punishments, has a close parallel in Jewish law but requires some exegetical ingenuity to be wholly reconciled with the actual text of the Qur'ān. See also SIN AND CRIME; CHASTISEMENT AND PUNISHMENT; STONING; CRUCIFIXION; LAW AND THE QUR'ĀN.

Richard Kimber

Bibliography
D. Amram, Divorce, in *Encyclopaedia Judaica*, 17 vols., Jerusalem 1971-2, iv, 624-8; B. Carra de Vaux/J. Schacht and A.-M. Goichon, Ḥadd, in EI², iii, 20-2; L. Dembitz, Fines and forfeiture, in *Encyclopaedia Judaica*, 17 vols., Jerusalem 1971-2, v, 386-7; id., Punishment, in *Encyclopaedia Judaica*, 17 vols., Jerusalem 1971-2, x, 273; G.R. Hawting, The significance of the slogan *lā ḥukma illā lillāh* and the references to the *ḥudūd* in the traditions about the Fitna and the murder of ʿUthmān, in BSOAS 61 (1978), 453-63; H. Hirschfeld, Fasting and fast days, in *Encyclopaedia Judaica*, 17 vols., Jerusalem 1971-2, v, 347-9; B. Johansen, Eigentum, Familie und Obrigkeit im Hanafitischen Strafrecht, in WI 19 (1979), 38-46; R. Peters, The Islamization of criminal law. A comparative analysis, in WI 34 (1994), 246-53; F. Rahman, The concept of *ḥadd* in Islamic law, in *Islamic studies. Journal of the Central Institute of Islamic Research, Karachi*, 4 (1965), 237-51; J. Schacht, *An introduction to Islamic law*, Oxford 1964, chap. 24; id., *The origins of Muhammadan jurisprudence*, Oxford 1950, 191, 208-10; Wansborough, QS 177.

Bovines

see ANIMAL LIFE

Bowing and Prostration

Bowing, an inclination of the head or a bending of the body in reverence; prostration, reclining with the face on the ground in humble adoration (q.v.). The two fundamental gestures of the ritual prayer, bowing *(rukūʿ)* and the more frequent prostration *(sujūd)* are mentioned numerous times in the Qurʾān.

Many qurʾānic passages that refer to bowing (Q 2:43; 5:55; 77:48) and prostration (Q 4:102; 15:98; 25:64; 26:219; 50:40; 76:26; 96:19) allude to prayer (q.v.) and devotion in general. Other verses mention the two gestures together (Q 2:125; 3:43; 9:112; 22:26; 22:77; 48:29), again evidently referring to prayer. The Qurʾān does not always seem to make a clear distinction between the two terms. One such verse (Q 38:24) states that David (q.v.) fell down bowing *(rākiʿan)* in repentance but in this instance the act was actually a prostration. In contrast, in those verses describing the command given to the Israelites (see CHILDREN OF ISRAEL) to enter the door "prostrating themselves" (*sujjadan*, Q 2:58; 4:154; 7:161), the act was most probably a bow.

Prostration is much more frequently cited in the Qurʾān than bowing. The use of the root *sajada* in the Qurʾān underlines the relevance of prostration to God in Muslim devotion and at the same time reflects the reactions of people during the time of Muḥammad when this act was prescribed. The Qurʾān attests that prostration met strong opposition among Arabs (Q 25:60; cf. 68:42-3) and that pride (q.v.) was the cause of this opposition (Q 7:206; 16:49; 32:15; see ARROGANCE). Later traditions describe the haughty behavior of the pagans and their attempts to harass Muḥammad and the Muslims when they were prostrating themselves (see OPPOSITION TO MUḤAMMAD). On the other hand, various other verses stress the importance of prostration for the believer (Q 39:9; cf. 3:113) and that it should be addressed to God only and not to the sun (q.v.) or moon (q.v.; Q 41:37). The true believer should also prostrate himself at the recitation of the Qurʾān (q.v.; Q 17:107; 19:58; 32:15; 84:21). Moreover, all the creatures in heaven or on earth, as a sign of their devotion to the creator, perform this act directly or by means of their shadows (Q 7:206; 13:15; 16:48-9; 22:18; 55:6). Finally, another verse (Q 48:29) refers to the mark of prostration *(athar al-sujūd)* that in later traditions came to indicate the mark or callous left on the forehead of the believer who performs many prostrations.

Prostration also occurs in several other verses relating to the narrative parts of the Qurʾān. The people of Sheba (q.v.) used to prostrate themselves to the sun instead of to God (Q 27:24-5). The magicians gathered by Pharaoh (q.v.) fell down prostrate and proclaimed their faith in God when Moses (q.v.) defeated them (Q 7:120; 20:70; 26:46). Joseph's (q.v.) parents and brothers fell down prostrate before him in Egypt (Q 12:100; cf. 12:4) and the angels prostrated themselves to Adam after his creation whereas Iblīs (q.v.) refused to do so (Q 2:34; 7:11-2; 15:29-33; 17:61; 18:50; 20:116; 38:72-5; see ANGEL; ADAM AND EVE). Given the strict Muslim prohibition against prostration to anything other than God (see IDOLS AND IMAGES; IDOLATRY AND IDOLATERS; POLYTHEISM AND ATHEISM), these last two episodes were problematic for commentators on the Qurʾān and exegetes have written many pages trying to account for these prostrations. Both bowing and prostration were widely diffused acts throughout the Middle East, especially in Jewish and Christian communities (see JEWS AND JUDAISM; CHRISTIANS AND CHRISTIANITY). They were also well-known to Arabs (q.v.) prior to the preaching of Muḥammad, as is attested in pre-Islamic poetry (see PRE-ISLAMIC ARABIA AND THE QURʾĀN). The Qurʾān particularly establishes the centrality of prostration to Muslim devotion and displays various attitudes, which were later expanded in Muslim literature.

Roberto Tottoli

Bibliography
Primary: ʿAbd al-Razzāq, *Tafsīr*, i, 328; Ibn al-ʿArabī, *Aḥkām*, ii, 368-73; Ibn Kathīr, *Bidāya*, i, 196; Khāzin, *Lubāb*, vii, 137-40; Māturīdī, *Taʾwīlāt*, ed. M.M. al-Raḥmān, Baghdad 1983, 94-100; Muqātil, *Tafsīr*, ii, 351; iv, 640, 794; Ṭabarī, *Tafsīr*, Cairo 1968, xxvi, 110-1.
Secondary: M.J. Kister, Some reports concerning al-Ṭāʾif, in *JSAI* 1 (1979), 3-6; G. Monnot, Ṣalāt, in *EI²*, viii, 925-34; Speyer, *Erzählungen*, 54-8; R. Tottoli, Muslim attitudes towards prostration *(sujūd)*. I: Arabs and prostration at the beginning of Islam and in the Qurʾān, in *SI* 88 (1998), 5-34; id., Traditions and controversies concerning the *suǧūd al-Qurʾān* in *ḥadīṯ* literature, in *ZDMG* 147 (1997), 371-93; A.J. Wensinck, *Muḥammad and the Jews of Medina*, trans. and ed. W.H. Behn, Berlin 1982², 75-6; id., Ṣalāt, in *EI¹*, iv, 96-105.

Bread

An article of food made from flour or meal by moistening, kneading and baking. The word "bread" *(khubz)* occurs only once in the Qurʾān, in the story of the prophet Joseph (q.v.) in the twelfth sūra. The wife of Potiphar (in the Qurʾān Potiphar is called *ʿazīz*, "powerful," that is, one holding a powerful position [cf. Q 12:30, 51, 78, 88]), on failing to persuade Joseph to sleep with her, carries out her threat to him and he is thrown into prison. Two young fellow-prisoners ask Joseph to interpret their dreams. One of them (whom the commentators on the Qurʾān, accepting the Biblical account in *Gen* 40:2, identify as the Egyptian king's baker) relates his dream in these words: "I see myself carrying on my head bread, and birds are eating of it." Joseph interprets the dream by saying that the young man "will be crucified and birds will eat of his head" (Q 12:41; see CRUCIFIXION). In this interpretation, "bread" comes to have the ominous signification of "feed," the prisoner in question being fated to "play host" to predatory birds.

This use of the word "bread" in the verse carries ironic connotations. First, the same life-sustaining bread he used to bake becomes the bread of death, foreboding the death of none other than the baker himself. A second, related point may be made in light of al-Ṭabarī's (d. 310/923) suggestion (*Tafsīr*, xii, 129; also Qurṭubī, *Jāmiʿ*, ix, 191) that the Egyptian king (see PHARAOH), when he intended to kill someone, used to send him a certain kind of food, signifying death. This suggestion, if followed, means that the baker, instead of serving nourishing food to the king, will receive from him deadly food. Third, in the phrase "I see myself carrying on my head bread," the Arabic preposition used for "on" is *fawqa* which, strictly speaking, means "over" rather than "on," for which *ʿalā* would be more appropriate. It can be argued that *fawqa* has been used here in the sense of *ʿalā* (Ṭabarī, *Tafsīr*, xii, 128). It is, however, possible that it has been used in its literal sense, graphically portraying the baker as carrying a basket of bread "over" his head for this would enable him to move briskly in order to serve his master. If so, then the irony becomes sharper still: The baker is hastening to his own death.

The fact that the baker mentions "bread" in relating his dream signifies that the content of his dream reflects his occupation. This is also true of the dream of the second prisoner (whom the qurʾānic exegetes, again following the Bible, identify as the king's cupbearer) who reports having dreamt of pressing wine (Q 12:36; cf. Rāzī, *Tafsīr*, xviii, 134: "The dream of each [prisoner] conforms to his occupation"). This may have some bearing on the broader issue of the qurʾānic view of dreams and dream-interpretation (see DREAMS AND SLEEP).

As we have seen, the use of the word "bread" in the Qurʾān is significant in its context. Its use, however, is essentially literal, even when it is interpreted to mean food in general (as in Rāzī, *Tafsīr*, xviii, 134: "... as if there were, on my head, three baskets containing bread and all kinds of foods and meals and suddenly birds of prey started biting into them"). Nonetheless, in this interpretation, as in the identification of the prisoner as the king's baker, the influence of the biblical account is obvious (cf. *Gen* 40:16-7; see also SCRIPTURE AND THE QURʾĀN).

Mustansir Mir

Bibliography
Primary: Qurṭubī, *Jāmiʿ*; Rāzī, *Tafsīr*; Ṭabarī, *Tafsīr*.
Secondary: M. Mir, Irony in the Qurʾān. A study of the story of Joseph, in I. Boullata (ed.), *Literary structures of religious meaning in the Qurʾān*, Richmond/Surrey, 1999; D. Waines, Cereals, bread and society. An essay on the staff of life in medieval Iraq, in *JESHO* 30/3 (1987), 255-85.

Breaking Trusts and Contracts

Not honoring one's legally enforceable obligation to another. Muslim exegetes identify a number of qurʾānic verses which require that contracts (*ʿuqūd*, sing. *ʿaqd*, see CONTRACTS AND ALLIANCES) not be broken, the most general of which is Q 5:1. Other verses enjoin keeping covenants (*ʿuhūd*, sing. *ʿahd*, see COVENANT), trusts (*amānāt*, sing. *amāna*), oaths (*aymān*, sing. *yamīn*, see OATHS) and pacts (*mawāthīq*, sing. *mīthāq*). According to many qurʾānic exegetes, the meanings of these terms are closely related but each carries particular legal obligations.

Q 9:4 and Q 16:91, both of which warn against breaking covenants, are interpreted by many exegetes as referring to particular events in the life of the Prophet. According to Fakhr al-Dīn al-Rāzī (d. 606/1210; *Tafsīr*, ad loc.), Q 16:91 is related to Q 5:7 and the covenant made between the Prophet and the *anṣār* at ʿAqaba (see EMIGRANTS AND HELPERS). According to al-Zamakhsharī (d. 538/1144; *Kashshāf*, ad loc.), Q 9:4 refers to an incident in which the Quraysh (q.v.) broke their pact with the Prophet by backing their clients, the Banū Bakr, against the clients of the Prophet, the Banū Khuzāʿa (see CLIENTS AND CLIENTAGE; TRIBES AND CLANS). Qurʾānic exegetes ordinarily claim that the Prophet's breaking of his contract in this case is a justifiable exception because the unbelievers with whom he had contracted did not uphold their end of the contract.

Concerning the most general verse about breaking contracts, Q 5:1, there is exegetical disagreement. Some exegetes disagree concerning the scope of Q 5:1. Ibn al-ʿArabī (d. 543/1148; *Aḥkām*, ad loc.) mentions a number of different interpretations, each associated with the name of a particular early commentator: Ibn ʿAbbās (d. 68/686-8) says the injunction to fulfill all contracts is coterminous with that of fulfilling all covenants; Qatāda (d. 117/735) says it refers only to keeping alliances *(aḥlāf,* sing. *ḥilf)* made in the period before Islam. According to Zayd b. Aslam, Q 5:1 includes keeping all contracts of marriage, partnership, sales, oaths, covenants and treaties. Interpreting the verse as applying only to divine-human relations and not to agreements among people, al-Zajjāj (d. 311/923) says Q 5:1 commands keeping all contracts made between God and humanity. The most general opinion is that of al-Ṭabarī (d. 310/923), who reports (*Tafsīr,* ad loc.) that the order to fulfill all contracts entails fulfilling all obligations *(farāʾiḍ)* incumbent on Muslims.

In his exegesis of Q 23:8, al-Qurṭubī (d. 671/1272; *Jāmiʿ,* ad loc.) repeats this comprehensive understanding when he remarks that keeping trusts and covenants includes all that for which people are responsible in the matters of religion and in matters of this world, in both speech and deed. An inclusive understanding finds additional confirmation in the ḥadīth literature. It is reported in several of the standard collections of prophetic ḥadīth that all people who act treacherously, i.e. not keeping their agreements, will be held accountable for this on the day of judgment (see Bukhārī, *Ṣaḥīḥ,* 9:72; Ibn Ḥanbal, *Musnad,* 2:70; Tirmidhī, *Saḥīḥ,* 2191; Ibn Māja, 2872-2873; Nasāʾī, *Sunan,* 6:180; see LAST JUDGMENT).

Moving on to other relevant qurʾānic references, Q 13:20 and the verse repeated in Q 23:8 and 70:32 seem to contain a slight variation on the qurʾānic understanding of keeping covenants, which is in line with that of the ḥadīth collections. In Q 13:20 fulfilling the covenant of God and not breaking the pact are listed along with other attributes of the people who will enter the gardens of paradise (see GARDEN; PARADISE), thus providing a positive obverse to the judgment scenarios already mentioned. Keeping covenants and trusts is also listed in the context of the attributes given in Q 23:1-11 and Q 70:22-35 of those who will enter paradise. (See REWARD AND PUNISHMENT.)

Note also that there are structural parallels among the three lists in Q 13:19-23, 23:1-11, and 70:22-35. Each list includes a ritual obligation or contract with God such as the requirement to pray or give alms (Q 13:22; 23:2, 4, 9; 70:34; see ALMSGIVING; PRAYER). Each list includes marriage and family obligations including the restriction of sex to properly contracted contexts (Q 13:21-2; 23:5-7; 70:29-31; see ABSTINENCE; CHASTITY; SEX AND SEXUALITY; MARRIAGE AND DIVORCE). At least two of the lists have reference to giving upright testimony (Q 70:33) and not engaging in idle talk (Q 23:3). Q 13:22 mentions repelling evil with good in this context. In commenting upon these lists, Ibn Kathīr (d. 774/1373; *Tafsīr,* ad loc.) reports that the connection between these social and religious contracts and the requirement of keeping such obligations, reflects the obligation arising from the "trust" accepted by Adam (see ADAM AND EVE) from God in Q 33:72. This trust, rejected by the heavens, earth and mountains, signifies the obligation to serve God when given the freedom to choose between good and evil (q.v.).

Brannon M. Wheeler

Bibliography
Primary: Bukhārī, *Ṣaḥīḥ;* Ibn al-ʿArabī, *Aḥkām;* Ibn Ḥanbal, *Musnad;* Ibn Kathīr, *Tafsīr;* Ibn Māja; Nasāʾī, *Sunan;* Qurṭubī, *Jāmiʿ;* Rāzī, *Tafsīr;* Ṭabarī, *Tafsīr;* Tirmidhī, *Ṣaḥīḥ;* Zamakhsharī, *Kashshāf.*
Secondary: M. ʿAbd al-Qadīr, *Kitāb al-Aymān wa-l-nudhūr,* Amman 1988; M. Abū Zahra, *al-Milkiyya wa-naẓariyyat al-ʿaqd,* Cairo 1939; Ch. Chehata, *Essai d'use théorie générale de l'obligation en droit musulman,* Cairo 1936; N. Ḥammād, *al-Ḥiyāza fī l-ʿuqūd fī l-fiqh al-islāmī,* Damascus 1978; E. Tyan, *Institutions du droit public musulman,* Paris 1954; B. Weiss, Covenant and law in Islam, in E. Firmage, B. Weiss and J. Welch (eds.), *Religion and law. Biblical-Judaic and Islamic perspectives,* Winona Lake, IN 1990, 49-83.

Bridewealth

The obligatory payment of a sum of money by the groom to the bride as stipulated in the marriage contract, a sum which in turn becomes her property. Modern English usage has shown a preference for the term bridewealth or marriage payment over the earlier term "dowry" (cf. *Encyclopaedia Britannica* 1996, s.v. "bridewealth" and "dowry"). In the Qurʾān three different words are used for the concept: *ajr* (reward), *farīḍa* (legal obligation) and *ṣaduqa* (nuptial gift).

Several aspects of bridewealth are treated in the Qurʾān: (1) The payment of bridewealth is a prerequisite of marriage (the term used is *ajr* in Q 4:24, 25; 5:5; 33:50) In Q 60:10, for instance, it is stated that "There is no fault for you to marry them when you have given them their rewards." (2) The bridewealth becomes the property of the bride. This is an obvious conclusion from Q 4:4 where men are asked to "give the women their nuptial gifts *(ṣaduqāt)* as a present *(niḥlatan)*" to which they no longer have any rights except any portion voluntarily renounced by the woman (cf. also Q 4:20). Such possible post-marriage arrangements between spouses concerning the bridewealth are also mentioned in Q 4:24 and 2:237. (3) There is a relation between bridewealth and marital intercourse (Q 4:21 and 24). According to Q 2:236-7 the full amount of the bridewealth has to be given only when marital intercourse has occurred (see MARRIAGE AND DIVORCE).

The qurʾānic concept of bridewealth and the terms used for it differ substantially from pre-Islamic Arab custom (see PRE-ISLAMIC ARABIA AND THE QURʾĀN). In old Arabic poetry (see POETS AND POETRY) the bridewealth is called *mahr* and was given to the father or male relatives of the bride (cf. also Q 60:10 and Farrāʾ, *Maʿānī,* i, 256). The bride may also have received from the groom a gift called *ṣadāq* which was, however, of much lesser value. Similar customs were known in ancient Israel (cf. *Gen* 34:12; *Exod* 22:16; *1 Sam* 18:25). The Qurʾān, on the contrary, reserves the bridewealth for the married woman herself and gives her the sole right of disposal. This must have constituted an innovation in Arabic-Islamic society, as suggested by two facts: 1) the avoidance of the term *mahr* in the extensive terminology concerning bridewealth in the Qurʾān; and 2) the qurʾānic idea that the bridewealth is a compensation for the permission to have sexual intercourse (not a compensation for the loss of a potentially productive member of a clan as *mahr* was probably considered in pre-Islamic Arab tribal society) and, related to this idea, the choice of the term *ajr* (reward).

The amount to be given as bridewealth is not stipulated in the Qurʾān. In Arab society it depended on the bride's social status. It is unknown whether the *qinṭār* (of silver or gold?) mentioned in Q 4:20 should be considered as an average measure of bridewealth among the wealthier followers of Muḥammad or as a very large one (cf. ʿAbd al-Razzāq, *al-Muṣannaf*, vi, no. 10420).

In early Islamic legal discussion on bridewealth the qurʾānic discussion of the subject forms the point of departure (see LAW AND THE QURʾĀN). In this discussion, however, many questions left unanswered in the Qurʾān are also tackled, such as the lower and upper limits of bridewealth, the date of payment, the possibility of payment by installments and so on. It is remarkable that in early legal discussions the qurʾānic terms for bridewealth are not used at all. The most favored term is *ṣadāq* (bridewealth) with *mahr* as a synonym occurring less frequently.

Harald Motzki

Bibliography
Primary: ʿAbd al-Razzāq, *Muṣannaf*, vi, *K. al-Nikāḥ;* Farrāʾ, *Maʿānī;* Mālik, *Muwaṭṭaʾ*, chap. 28; Ṭabarī, *Tafsīr*, ad loc.
Secondary: A.M. al-Ḥūfī, *al-Marʾa fī l-shiʿr al-jāhilī*, Cairo, 2nd ed., n.d. [1964], i, 190-6; G. Jacob, *Altarabisches Beduinenleben*, Berlin 1897, 57, 213; H. Motzki, Geschlechtsreife und Legitimation zur Zeugung im frühen Islam, in E.W. Müller (ed.), *Geschlechtsreife und Legitimation zur Zeugung*, Freiburg/ München 1985, 527-30; W. Robertson Smith, *Kinship and marriage in early Arabia*, Boston 1885[1], 1903[2], 93, 96, 105-6, 111, 113, 119, 151 (cf. the review by Th. Nöldeke in *ZDMG* 40 [1886], 154); O. Spies, Mahr, in *EI*[2], vi, 78-80; J. Wellhausen, Die Ehe bei den Arabern, in *Nachrichten von der Königlichen Gesellschaft der Wissenschaften und der Georg-August-Universität zu Göttingen* 11 (1893), 431-6.

Brocade

see MATERIAL CULTURE AND THE QURʾĀN

Brother and Brotherhood

The term brother *(akh)* is used in the Qurʾān in several senses: in its strict biological sense; in several partly metaphorical senses, especially to indicate membership in a genealogical group; and, in a more extended metaphorical sense, to indicate membership in a group united by a shared belief. There are verses in the Qurʾān that indicate that the sense of community and mutual respect, concern and aid implied by brotherhood in this extended, metaphorical sense can unite not only Muslims but any humans who do virtuous acts in response to God's expectations of them (see COMMUNITY AND SOCIETY IN THE QURʾĀN; GRATITUDE AND INGRATITUDE).

Brother, in its literal sense, a male who shares one or both parents with another sibling, is the object of several verses with legal implications. A brother is within the closer degrees of kinship (q.v.) and therefore both forbidden to marry the daughter of his brother (Q 4:23) and allowed to see his sisters dressed less formally than would be proper before men not in close kin relation or considered likely to see them as sexually desirable (Q 24:31; compare Q 33:55 on the Prophet's wives; see WIVES OF THE PROPHET; SEX AND SEXUALITY; SOCIAL INTERACTIONS). Since Q 4:23 also forbids a "milk sister" to marry a biologically unrelated male suckled by the same mother, specialists in Islamic law have usually included the milk brother as well as the milk sister and milk mother in most of the legal rulings that regulate marriageability and acceptable private association. The brother also has a fixed position in entitlement to inheritance (q.v.; Q 4:176 and Q 4:11, in which "brothers" *(ikhwa)* is generally understood to mean both brothers and sisters; see SISTER). The brother is referred to as the archetype of the *walī l-dam*, the next of kin with the right to demand retaliation (q.v.) for a deliberately slain kinsman or to settle for blood money (Q 2:178; see BLOOD MONEY; MURDER).

The most important "blood" brothers who figure in the Qurʾān are Cain and Abel, (who are referred to, but not mentioned by name; see CAIN AND ABEL), the brothers of Joseph (q.v.; see also BENJAMIN), and Moses (q.v.) and Aaron (Hārūn, see AARON). It is interesting that a figure so centrally important as Moses has a brother who is specifically called both a "prophet" (*nabī*, Q 19:53) and a messenger (*rasūl*, Q 20:47; see MESSENGER) of the Lord and who could, like his brother, receive divine inspiration (*waḥy*, Q 10:87; see REVELATION AND INSPIRATION) as well as miraculous signs (*āyāt*, Q 23:45; 20:42; see SIGNS). Moses, whose speech is hard to understand, has asked God to give him Aaron, his brother, as a "helper" *(wazīr)* from his family (Q 20:29-30; 25:35; 28:35). Moreover, both Moses and Aaron are given *sulṭān*, a word usually understood to mean authority, power and authoritative proof (Q 28:35; and 23:45, in which the phrase is *sulṭān mubīn*, "clear authority").

The simultaneous appearance of two prophet brothers among one people raised, for later generations, questions about the nature of prophethood (see PROPHETS AND PROPHETHOOD). The Qurʾān seems to contain a two-fold explanation of the need for both prophets: namely, the rebelliousness of the Israelites towards Moses and his resultant need of Aaron's help, and the assistance Moses needs in circumventing his difficulty in speech. Thus when Moses orders them to enter the Holy Land and they refuse, Moses prays: "My Lord, I control only myself and my brother. Distinguish us (or "distance us") from such perverse people" (Q 5:25). Yet one might argue that God could have given Moses the gifts of speech and authority that would have freed him from the need of a prophet-brother.

A further problem is raised by Aaron's presence when the calf (see CALF OF GOLD) was made to be an object of worship while Moses was absent and receiving the law on Mount Sinai (q.v.), especially as Moses had told Aaron, "Be my deputy among my people, act righteously and do not follow the path of the perverse" (Q 7:142). That Moses on his return at least pretends to hold his brother responsible is shown by the words: "He [Moses] took his brother by the head, pulling him toward himself" (Q 7:150). Hence Aaron says in explanation: "O son of my mother, the people have humiliated me [or, "thought me to be weak"] and almost killed me. So do not let my enemies gloat over me nor place me among the wrongdoers" (Q 7:150). Moses then prays for both himself and his brother: "O Lord, forgive me and my brother and cause us to enter in your mercy" (Q 7:151). Alongside all of these problems was the problem of the apparent sin of Moses in killing a man (Q 20:40; 26:14; 26:19). These verses offered rich material for the speculation of later Muslim thinkers on the sinlessness, the degree of foreknowledge (or reasons for withholding foreknowledge) and the timing of divinely ordained persuasive miracles that God might grant his prophets (see IMPECCABILITY AND INFALLIBILITY; MIRACLE).

The commentators by and large avoid this discussion. Al-Ṭabarī (d. 310/923) explains that "From our mercy we gave [Moses] his brother Aaron as a prophet *(nabī)*" (Q 19:53) means: "We supported and helped him [Moses] through his [Aaron's] prophethood" (*Tafsīr*, xvi, 95). Al-Ṭabarī (*Tafsīr*, xvi, 160) also implies that Aaron's station is in answer to Moses' prayers (which, perhaps, God anticipated) when Moses asks God to give him his brother Aaron as a vizier *(wazīr)* and says: "Let him share in my mission *(amrī)*" (Q 20:32). Moses is saying, al-Ṭabarī explains, "Make him a prophet just as you made me a prophet." Al-Bayḍāwī (d. ca. 716/1316-7) seems to be explaining Aaron's inability to stop the worship of the calf — and also, perhaps, to be justifying Aaron as a second prophet — when he says that Aaron was three years older than Moses and was "a mild-tempered and tractable person, better loved by the people of Israel" (*Anwār,* i, 345). Yet often, even when the verse refers to prophetic traits possessed by both brothers, the commentators remain principally interested in Moses. Thus, in discussing the "miraculous signs" mentioned in Q 23:45, *Tafsīr al-Jalālayn* (450) only refers to the miracles of Moses since Aaron plays such a subordinate role in the narrative of their lives. Nevertheless, as al-Ṭūsī (d. 460/1067) explains (*Tibyān,* iv, 532), when Moses went up Mount Sinai he was able to order Aaron to be his deputy even though God had sent Aaron as a prophet with a mission *(nabī mursal)* because Moses had leadership *(riyāsa)* over Aaron as well as over all of the rest of the religious community *(umma)* to whom Moses brought revelation. Interestingly, the *sulṭān* given to Moses and Aaron is understood by several commentators to mean *ḥujja,* "argument (for a case)" (e.g. Ṭabarī, *Tafsīr,* xx, 76; see PROOF). Al-Bayḍāwī (d. ca. 716/1316-7) interprets *sulṭān mubīn* (Q 23:45), in which *mubīn* would ordinarily be understood to mean "manifestly clear," as "a manifestly clear argument, compelling to the one who opposes it" and says that it may mean such miraculous signs as Moses' staff which turned into a snake (*Anwār,* ad loc.). Incidentally, the use of terms such as *sulṭān* and *wazīr,* later to become political terms frequently used in the Islamic world, caused the verses on Moses and Aaron to be examined in the light of this use (see AUTHORITY). The example of Aaron as an "infallible" aide sent to help Moses was of importance to some Shīʿīs in understanding the role of ʿAlī (see ʿALĪ B. ABĪ ṬĀLIB) and other imāms (see SHĪʿISM AND THE QURʾĀN; IMĀM).

Very common in the Qurʾān is the largely metaphorical use of "brother" to mean members of a tribe or people (see TRIBES AND CLANS) especially (though not exclusively) in connection with three of the so-called "Arabian" prophets sent by God to their people. Hūd (q.v.) is the "brother" of the ʿĀd (q.v.; Q 7:65; 11:50; 26:124; 46:21), Ṣāliḥ (q.v.) is the brother of the Thamūd (q.v.; Q 7:73; 11:61; 26:142; 27:45) and Shuʿayb (q.v.) is the brother of Midian (q.v.; Q 7:85; 11:84; 29:36). Similarly, Noah (q.v.) is the brother of the "people" or "tribe" *(qawm)* of Noah (Q 26:105-6). Lot (q.v.) is the brother of the *qawm* of Lot (Q 26:160-1); and, correspondingly, "the brothers *(ikhwān)* of Lot" (meaning the people of Lot) are listed among those peoples who rejected messengers sent by God (Q 50:13). Al-Rāghib al-Iṣfahānī (d. early 5th/11th cent.; *Mufradāt,* 68, under the heading *"akh"*) says that brother is used in these verses to convey that the compassion that such a messenger has for his people is just as that which a brother has for his brother. In a parallel usage the kin of Mary (q.v.) address her as "sister of Aaron" (Q 19:28).

There are a few verses that bridge or partially indicate the transference of "brother" from its literal or partly metaphorical use (as when it means kinsman) to its full metaphorical sense. A striking example of the use of the emotional closeness implied by brotherhood is the simile which warns the believers to avoid suspicion, spying and speaking ill of each other, for: "Would one of you like to eat the flesh of his dead brother? For you would have a horror of such things" (Q 49:12). The believers are told if they "become mixed" with orphans (q.v.), "they become your brothers *(ikhwānukum)*" (Q 2:220). *Tafsīr al-Jalālayn* (46) echoes many commentaries in saying that "brothers" here means "brothers in religion"; but, like many other commentaries, it implies that such acceptance means acceptance in a quasi-familial relationship, "For it is customary for a brother to mingle his expenses with his brothers, so you should act in this way [with such orphans]." Similarly, it is said of adoptive children that they should keep the names of their fathers "but if you do not know their fathers, then they are your brothers *(ikhwānukum)* in religion *(dīn)* and your friends/clients/protegés *(mawālī)*" (Q 33:5; see CLIENTS AND CLIENTAGE).

While several verses attest that biological kinship, including brotherhood, is less important than spiritual kinship, the verse following the discussion of adoption shows that for legal purposes real brotherhood is still the measure relevant to inheritance and kindred matters: "Blood relatives are closer to each other in God's book than to the believers and the emigrants. If (nevertheless) you act with goodness toward those affiliated with you *(awliyāʾikum),* that is set down in the Book (q.v.)" (Q 33:6). This verse is said by virtually all the commentators to confirm the abrogation of the *muʾākhāt,* the adoption of each other as brothers by the Meccan Emigrants *(muhājirūn)* and certain members of the Helpers *(anṣār),* the sincere believers among the Medinans, at the time that the Prophet settled in Medina (see EMIGRANTS AND HELPERS).

Nevertheless, in the larger scheme of things, the ties created by religion are more meaningful in the eyes of God and should be a more significant source of motivation. If your kin and your wealth are dearer to you than the Prophet, God and the struggle in his path (see PATH OR WAY [OF GOD]), "then lie in wait until God brings his command to pass" (Q 9:24). "Those who believe in God and the last day (see LAST JUDGMENT) will not show love to those who oppose God and his Prophet whether they be fathers or sons or brothers or members of their clan *(ʿashīra)*" (Q 58:22). This sūra belongs to the Medinan period and may refer to the attempts by the Prophet to make the sincere converts among the Medinans place their loyalty to Islam above their feelings of kinship to their relatives who were not real converts, the "hypocrites" (see HYPOCRITES AND HYPOCRISY).

Several verses affirm the brotherhood of the believers (see BELIEF AND UNBELIEF). The Qurʾān reminds Muslims that before accepting Islam they were enemies, "then he unified your hearts so that through his bounty you became brothers *(ikhwān)*" (Q 3:103). The believers must take care to preserve this condition for they "are but brothers *(ikhwa);* therefore, make peace between (any) two of your brothers" (Q 49:10). Correspondingly, those who share in some form of sinful behavior can be considered members of a "brotherhood" so that "those who squander money [or are prodigal] are the brothers of the devils (*shayāṭīn,* see DEVIL)" (Q 17:27). Al-Ṭabarī (*Tafsīr,* xv, 74) adds: "In this way the Arabs (q.v.) speak of anyone who adheres to a habit of a people and follows their tradition: [he is] their brother."

Other verses show that the brotherhood of the believers entails a feeling of mutual affection and interdependence regardless of gender. Thus Q 3:195 reads: "And their Lord answers them, 'I do not/will not cause the action of anyone of you to be lost, whether male or female; you depend on/belong to/proceed from each other *(baʿḍukum min baʿḍin).*'" Similarly Q 9:71 reads: "The believers, male and female, are friends/guardians of each other *(baʿḍuhum awliyāʾ baʿḍin).*" Indeed, Q 59:9, which refers to the Emigrants from Mecca and the Helpers in Medina but may be generalized to indicate the degree to which all true believers prefer the interests of other believers to their own, reads: "They do not find envy in their hearts for that which has been given [to the emigrants] but prefer them to themselves even if there be poverty amongst themselves. Whoever guards himself from the avarice (q.v.) of his own soul, those are the truly fortunate." (See also the next verse, Q 59:10 and compare Q 64:16).

According to some modernists all humans are believers by nature, and only by willful commitment to evil leave that state. Some verses might be seen to support this view. There are those who associate others with God (*mushrikūn*, see IDOLATRY AND IDOLATERS); "but" — adds a verse which need not be read as exclusively designating Muslims — "if they repent and establish worship (q.v.) and pay the alms-tax (*zakāt*, see ALMSGIVING), they are your brothers (*ikhwān*) in religion" (Q 9:11). And in a verse which seems from its context to be addressed to the righteous (*al-muttaqīn*), they are promised that in heaven (q.v.): "We shall root out whatever [remains] of hatred in their hearts; [they shall be] as brothers (*ikhwān*) on raised couches, face to face" (Q 15:47). If this verse is addressed to the righteous, both Muslim and non-Muslim, it conceives of brotherhood as their universal reward and ideal condition in the future life.

Elaboration of the concept of brotherhood as a heightened form of religious identification became prominent in medieval Islam. Literary examples of this would include the writings of the Brotherhood of Purity (Ikhwān al-Ṣafāʾ) and of Ibn Abī l-Dunyā (d. 281/894), whose ideas on "brotherhood" in God are often quoted by al-Ghazālī (d. 505/1111) in book 15 of his *Iḥyāʾ ʿulūm al-dīn*. Historical formulations, especially those associated with Ṣūfism, are a prominent feature of religious life in virtually every Islamic century (see ṢŪFISM AND THE QURʾĀN).

Roy P. Mottahedeh

Bibliography
Bayḍāwī, *Anwār;* al-Ghazālī, Abū Ḥāmid Muḥammad, *Iḥyāʾ ʿulūm al-dīn*, 4 vols., Būlāq 1289/1872, ii, 138-97; Ibn Abī l-Dunyā, *Kitāb al-Ikhwān*, ed. M. Ṭawliba, Cairo 1988 (rev. by M. ʿAr Khalaf); *Jalālayn;* al-Rāghib al-Iṣfahānī, *Mufradāt*, Beirut 1412/1992; Ṭabarī, *Tafsīr;* Ṭūsī, *Tibyān*.

Buildings see HOUSE — DOMESTIC AND DIVINE; MOSQUE; MARKETS

Burial

The interment of the body after death and accompanying practices involving the preparation of the body, its transportation to a cemetery, mourning, and erection of tombstones and mortuary buildings. In Islam, burial and its attendant preparations are the method prescribed for disposing of the dead. Islamic burial rituals (*janāʾiz*) normally require four elements: washing the body, shrouding, funeral prayers, and prompt burial with the face oriented towards the Kaʿba (q.v.) in Mecca. They are discussed most fully in Islamic legal literature (*fiqh*) and in modern ethnographies. The Qurʾān itself deals substantively with eschatology (q.v.) but has little to say about burial per se. Muslims nonetheless use verses from the Qurʾān in burial rites, mourning and mortuary inscriptions.

The Qurʾān briefly addresses itself to the question of the origin of burial in two ways. It depicts burial as the closing stage in the course that God has set for humans to follow from conception until death (see BIOLOGY AS THE CREATION AND STAGES OF LIFE). At death, he causes them to be buried (*aqbarahu*) in anticipation of the resurrection (q.v.; Q 80:18-22) when they will come forth from their graves (*ajdāth, qubūr*) for the day of judgment (Q 36:51-64; 100:9; see LAST JUDGMENT; APOCALYPSE). The

Qurʾān also alludes to the origins of burial in the narrative of Adam's two sons (identified as Cain [Qābīl] and Abel [Ḥābīl] in the commentaries) where a raven sent by God shows the murderer how to bury his brother's body (Q 5:31; cf. Ṭabarī, *Tafsīr,* vi, 127-8; see CAIN AND ABEL). Unlike the Bible, the Qurʾān does not explicitly discuss burial procedures. It does, however, prohibit prayer over the graves of hypocrites and disbelievers (Q 9:84; see HYPOCRITES AND HYPOCRISY; BELIEF AND UNBELIEF).

Despite the dearth of information about burial in the Qurʾān itself, Muslims have ubiquitously employed the sacred text in their funerary rites. According to some ḥadīths, the recitation of specific chapters and verses can earn the deceased special rewards in the hereafter (see REWARD AND PUNISHMENT). Thus, reciting Q 36, the sūra entitled Yā Sīn and known as "the heart of the Qurʾān," will bring them forgiveness, even a martyr's blissful status. According to another tradition, whoever dies after reading the last verses of Q 59, which glorify God, will be rewarded with paradise (q.v.). Comparable blessings are attributed to reciting Q 1, 67, 112, 113, and 114. Moreover, some ḥadīths report that the faithful will continue to recite and study the Qurʾān in their graves until resurrection.

Fiqh manuals and ethnographic descriptions of Muslim burial practices in the Middle East, North Africa, south and southeast Asia, and North America compensate for the paucity of information in historical literature. Jurists commend the reading of Q 36 when death approaches. Though they deplore recitation of the Qurʾān in funeral processions, those who follow the Shāfiʿī and Ḥanbalī forms of Islamic law approve reading the first sūra, Sūrat al-Fātiḥa (see FĀTIḤA), during prescribed funerary prayers. Shāfiʿī and Ḥanafī jurists favor reciting "From it we created you, to it we will return you, and from it we will extract you a second time" (Q 20:55) when the bereaved throw dirt on the grave. Another practice, involving advising the soul of the deceased on how to answer the angels that interrogate it in the grave the night after burial, includes the admonition that it should confess that the Qurʾān is its guide *(imām)* or book. Known as the *talqīn,* this rite is endorsed by most of the Islamic legal schools.

Ethnographies, on the other hand, indicate that recitation of the Qurʾān (q.v.) is a *sine qua non* in funerary rites, though these vary according to circumstance and local custom. This can be done by trained reciters (see RECITATION, THE ART OF), by the religiously learned or by ordinary mourners at the homes of the deceased, as well as in mosques, assembly halls and cemeteries. Qurʾānic recitation characterizes multiple aspects of the full range of Islamic burial practices. Generally, it occurs when someone is in the throes of death, while the body is being washed and enshrouded, at funerary prayers, and on death anniversaries. During the mourning period (usually forty days), a complete reading of the Qurʾān *(khatma)* is conducted in many Muslim cultures.

The written Qurʾān has various uses in burial rites. Sometimes the whole book is placed on the breast of the deceased or carried in the funeral cortege. In some cultures, the outer shroud has qurʾānic verses written upon it. More commonly, verses about God's unity and permanence, intercession, the afterlife, the Prophet, and the inevitability of death are inscribed on tombstones and mausolea. Epigraphic surveys (see EPIGRAPHY AND THE QURʾĀN) in medieval cemeteries reveal that the Throne Verse (Q 2:255); Q 3:169, 185; 112; and 55:26-27 were among the most popular verses, but many others are also attested. Funerary shrines and mosques dedicated to rulers, saints and esteemed scholars often feature artistically rendered inscriptions from the Qurʾān. The Taj Mahal in Agra, India, wherein lie the tombs of Shāh Jāhān (1000/1592-1076/1666) and his wife Mumtāz (d. 1040/1631), is exquisitely inscribed with verses from 23 sūras, including Q 36 and 112. Muslim jurists periodically condemn such practices, however, and none more than the Ḥanbalīs. See also DEATH AND THE DEAD; RITUAL AND THE QURʾĀN.

Juan Eduardo Campo

Bibliography
Primary: ʿAbd al-Raḥmān al-Jazīrī, *Kitāb al-Fiqh ʿalā l-madhāhib al-arbaʿa,* 5 vols., Beirut 1990 (see i, 455-91); al-Ghazālī, Abū Ḥāmid Muḥammad, *Iḥyāʾ ʿulūm al-dīn, iv. Kitāb Dhikr al-mawt wa-mā baʿdahu,* Cairo n.d., trans. T.J. Winter, *The remembrance of death and the afterlife,* Cambridge, UK 1989; Ṣuyūṭi, *al-Fawz al-aẓīm fī liqāʾ al-karīm,* ed. M. ʿAbd al-Ḥamīd and M. Fāris, Beirut 1994; id., *Itqān,* 2 vols. in 1, Beirut n.d., ii. On the excellences of the Qurʾān, 192-8. Secondary: M. Abdul Rauf, *Islam. Creed and worship,* Washington 1974, 96-100; W. Begly, The myth of the Taj Mahal and a new theory of its symbolic meaning, in *Art bulletin* 61 (1979), 7-37; J.R. Bowen, Death and the history of Islam in Highland Aceh, in *Indonesia* 38 (1984), 21-38; B.A. Donaldson, *The wild rue. A study of Muhammadan magic and folklore in Iran,* London 1938; repr. New York 1973, 69-78; N. Khoury, The mihrab image. Commemorative themes in medieval Islamic architecture, in *Muqarnas* 9 (1992), 11-28; E.W. Lane, *Account of the manners and customs of the modern Egyptians,* London 1860; repr. New York 1973⁵, ch. 28; H. Massé, *Persian beliefs and customs,* trans. C.A. Messner, New Haven 1954, 80-104; S. Mehdi (comp.), *Death and death ceremonies,* Karachi 1972; Kh. Moaz and S. Ory, *Inscriptions arabes de Damas. Les stèles funéraires. I: Cimetière d'al-Bāb al-Ṣaghīr,* Damascus 1977; A.K. Reinhart and F.M. Denny, Funerary rites, in *The Oxford encyclopedia of the modern Islamic world,* ii, 34-7.

Byzantines

The inhabitants of the Eastern Roman Empire, which had its capital at Constantinople. The Byzantines (*al-Rūm,* lit. "the Romans") are named in the Qurʾān only in Sūrat al-Rūm, Q 30:1-5: "The Byzantines have been defeated *(ghulibati l-Rūm)* in a nearby land, but after their defeat they will prevail *(sa-yaghlibūna)* within a few years.... On that day the believers will rejoice." An alternate reading going back to several early authorities, including Ibn ʿUmar (d. 73/693), reverses the voice of the verbs: "The Byzantines have prevailed *(ghalabati l-Rūm)*... [but afterwards] will be defeated *(sa-yughlabūna).*" This reading has mostly been rejected (e.g. Ṭabarī, *Jāmiʿ,* xxi, 15-21).

Historical context

The apparent context of this qurʾānic reference is the war between the Byzantine and Sasanian (Persian) Empires which coincided with the earliest years of Islam. The deposition of the Byzantine Emperor Maurice in 602 and his replacement by Phocas provoked the Sasanian Emperor Khusraw II Parviz into reopening hostilities. Byzantine defenses crumbled and the widely-hated Phocas was deposed in turn by Heraclius in 610. In the following decade, the Persians conquered Byzantine Syria, Palestine and Egypt, as well as much of Anatolia. Byzantine prestige received a harsh blow with the loss of Jerusalem and the True Cross in 614. But in the 620s Heraclius turned the tables in a series of northern campaigns crushing the Sasanians decisively at Nineveh in 627. He returned the Cross in triumph to Jerusalem in 630. By then, however, Muslim fighters from the south were already probing Byzantine defenses; they became the real beneficiaries of this long, devastating Perso-Byzantine war about which little is known except from archaeological evidence (C. Foss, The Persians; W. Kaegi, *Byzantium*).

The opening verses of Q 30, Sūrat al-Rūm, thus refer to Persian successes in Syria in the 610s, although it is not clear precisely when and where. In biographical literature *(sīra)* about the Prophet and in exegetical literature, Muḥammad and the early Muslims favor the monotheistic Byzantines in this war while their Meccan enemies favor the "pagan" Persians. Alternatively, the largely rejected reading could refer to an early defeat of the Muslims at Byzantine hands as at Muʾta (629) and predict Muslim victories about to come (see the discussion in M. Götz, Historischen Hintergrund).

In the decades before these events, imperial power in northern Arabia had already declined and with it the fortunes of Arab imperial protégés (see I. Shahid, *Byzantium;* B. Isaac, *The limits;* A. Cameron, *Byzantine Near East,* see PRE-ISLAMIC ARABIA AND THE QURʾĀN). But with the disappearance of the Sasanian Empire and the rapid success of Muslim armies almost everywhere, the stubbornly surviving Byzantine empire became what it had not been during Muḥammad's lifetime, the paradigmatic enemy of the Islamic polity. Despite the varied exchanges which took place constantly and the admiration which Byzantines and Muslims often expressed for one another, true coexistence remained impossible as expressed by André Miquel: "Which of the two of us was created for the ruination of the other?" ("Lequel de nous deux fut créé pour la ruine de l'autre?" *La géographie,* ii, 384). The conquest of Constantinople appears as a cosmic event *(fitan)* in eschatological ḥadīth (see ESCHATOLOGY; ḤADĪTH AND THE QURʾĀN), while the long history of the wars between the two powers often evidences a ritual character.

Michael Bonner

Exegetical explanations

As noted above, several scholars have alluded to the difficulty to be found in reading and interpreting the first verses of Sūrat al-Rūm, Q 30:1-5, pointing to the problematic vocalization of these verses, a textual situation that carries the potential of changing the meaning and the dependent historical explanation (cf. R. Bell, *Origin of Islam,* 137-8; id., *Commentary,* ii, 69-70; E. Beck, Die Sure ar-Rūm, 336-9). The most important problem concerns the forms of the verb *ghalaba,* "to vanquish," and whether in its repeated usages it is understood as passive voice or active. For this passage the voweling of the verbs is crucial as it fundamentally changes the meaning and interpretation of the verses.

The early commentary of Muqātil b. Sulaymān (d. 150/767) states that "Persia had defeated the Rūm and the unbelievers *(kuffār)* of Mecca rejoiced saying that the Persians, like us, do not have a [holy] book (q.v.) and they have defeated the Rūm who are People of the Book (q.v.) like you and so we will defeat you the way the Persians defeated the Rūm... On the day of Badr, the Muslims triumphed over the unbelievers *(kuffār)* of Mecca and the news reached them that the Rūm triumphed over the Persians and the Muslims rejoiced for that" (*Tafsīr,* iii, 406-7). Although the early exegetical texts stress the main reading that favors Byzantine victory, the variant reading is found already in texts of the early second/eighth and early third/ninth century with chains of authorities going back to much earlier times. According to the grammarian al-Farrāʾ (d. 207/822), "The reciters (*qurrāʾ,* see RECITERS OF THE QURʾĀN) agree on *ghulibat* except for Ibn ʿUmar who read it *ghalabat.*" Al-Farrāʾ, however, states that the exegetical tradition rejects the saying of Ibn ʿUmar (*Maʿānī,* ii, 319).

Al-Ṭabarī (d. 310/923) cites the material of the standard authorities, noting even insignificant variants. The main traditional reading, which is the most prevalent in the commentaries is, according to al-Ṭabarī, *ghulibat... sa-yaghlibūn.* The basic explanation provided by al-Ṭabarī (*Tafsīr,* xxi, 15-21), which reiterates earlier exegetical works and is repeated by a majority of later commentaries, is the following: The Rūm were defeated by the Persians but they will soon be victorious and on that day, the day when the People of the Book defeat the pagan Persians, the believers will rejoice. This reading reflects a positive outlook towards the Byzantines in the expectation of a later Byzantine victory that will give the believers cause to celebrate. The believers' "rejoicing" at a Byzantine victory is explained by the commentators in religious terms that stress the importance of Byzantine monotheism as a determining factor in securing such Muslim approval: The "believers shall rejoice" for the victory of the Byzantines, a People of the Book, over the polytheist Persians (see BELIEF AND UNBELIEF; POLYTHEISM AND ATHEISM). This explanation is also found in the major work on the occasions of revelation (*asbāb al-nuzūl,* see OCCASIONS OF REVELATION) of al-Wāḥidī (d. 468/1075; *Asbāb,* 258-9; cf. id., *Wasīṭ,* iii, 462-3).

Another explanation provided by the commentators is that which attributes the believers' "rejoicing" to a Muslim victory which coincided with the predicted Byzantine victory. Al-Ṭabarī (*Tafsīr,* xxi, 16) states that the Muslims and the unbelievers *(mushrikīn)* met in battle on the same day the Byzantines and Persians were confronting each other; God let the Muslims triumph over the polytheists and he let the People of the Book vanquish the Persians. Most commentaries mention the battle of Badr (2/624; see BADR) or the treaty of Ḥudaybiya (q.v.) as coinciding with the Byzantine victory over the Persians (see EXPEDITIONS AND BATTLES). It is significant that the exact date for the promised future victory became an important subject of debate and led the Companion of the Prophet, Abū Bakr (q.v.), to engage in a wager *(murāhana)* with his enemies. The importance of the debate is linked in the commentaries with Muḥammad's ability to prophesy future events. The *murāhana,* discussed at length since such an action subsequently became forbidden, centered around the definition of the phrase "a few years" in Q 30:4. The commentators' identification of this time span generally places it between three and nine years or at the outset of the seventh year.

Al-Ṭabarī mentions the principal variant reading *ghalabat... sa-yughlabūn* on the authority of Ibn ʿUmar and Abū Saʿīd. This tradition has the potential of changing the meaning of these verses drastically. The Byzantines defeated the Persians but, later, the Byzantines will be defeated by the Muslims, the real cause for Muslim rejoicing. Al-Ṭabarī, however, states that "the only correct reading for us is *ghulibat al-Rūm* and no other reading is acceptable..." (*Jāmiʿ,* xxi, 16). Nevertheless, a large number of commentaries record this variant *(ghalabat... sa-yughlabūn)* that promises the ultimate defeat of the Byzantines by the Muslims. This negative interpretation attempts to circumvent the issue of the believers' rejoicing by denying any previous ideological affiliation between Islam and Byzantium, a perspective that assumed prominence in the course of the eleventh century. The Muʿtazilī ʿAbd al-Jabbār (d. 415/1025) explained the believers' joy in light of his own times: "Why is it that the believers shall rejoice for the polytheists' victory over one another... the answer is that God will bring victory upon the believers by bringing about the humiliation of a group of polytheists by another such group..." (*Tanzīh,* 399; see also MUʿTAZILĪS). Similarly, the Muʿtazilī al-Zamakhsharī's (d. 538/1144) interpretation is that the Rūm were victorious and they will be defeated by the Muslims in a few years. Al-Zamakhsharī proposes that the continuous weakening of the warring parties would strengthen Islam, hence the believers' rejoicing (*Kashshāf,* iii, 466-7). Abū Ḥayyān (d. 745/1344) also includes the variant reading of Ibn ʿUmar and explains that after a certain period, the Muslims will triumph over the Rūm, whereas al-Bayḍāwī (d. 685/1286) provides the variant reading along with the traditional interpretation, but without any further discussion as to its veracity. It is as if the two interpretations, the prevalent and the variant, are on a par. The Ṣūfī ʿAbd al-Karīm al-Qushayrī (d. 465/1072) adheres to the traditional reading but does not neglect to specify that "the Muslims rejoiced for the victory of the Rūm over the Persians, even though unbelief unites them"; the Rūm, however, are a little better off having singled out a number of prophets for devotion (*Laṭāʾif,* v, 107; see also ṢŪFISM AND THE QURʾĀN).

Al-Qurṭubī (d. 671/1273) includes a third reading that uses both verbs in the active voice and provides the following explanation: On the day of Badr, the Rūm were victorious over the Persians and the Muslims rejoiced and then God brought down the good news that the Rūm would be victorious once again in a few years" (*Jāmiʿ,* xiv, 4). This variant promising a double Byzantine victory is exceptional but is in line with the traditional positive reading that promises a future Byzantine victory. Another isolated reading is found in the Shīʿī *tafsīr* of al-Qummī (d. 328/939) who offers a unique interpretation: The Persians defeated the Byzantines and they (the Persians) will be defeated by the believers (the Muslims). Al-Qummī is perhaps alone in explaining these verses in terms of a later Persian defeat by the Muslims and with reference to the reception of the Prophet's letters by the great leaders of the Near East (cf. Qummī, *Tafsīr,* ii, 152-3).

But to return to the principal alternative interpretation, commentators of the fifth/eleventh to seventh/thirteenth centuries adopted a new exegetical emphasis attempting to circumvent the believers' rejoicing (see EXEGESIS OF THE QURʾĀN; CLASSICAL AND MEDIEVAL). This new line of explanation reflects the emergence of two cardinal differences in relation to the prior standpoint. First, the Byzantines who were traditionally viewed as monotheists are now depicted as polytheists. Second, the joy of the believers no longer stems from the knowledge of a future Byzantine victory. In the commentaries dating from the twelfth century on, the "rejoicing" arises from a combination of reasons: because the polytheists (Persians and Byzantines) were battling one another; because the Muslims were victorious over their enemies; because the Byzantine victory coincided with a Muslim victory; or because the victory, predicted by the Prophet, testified to his truthfulness. This new attitude represents an attempt at depreciating the traditional explanation of the believers' rejoicing with its main emphasis on the shared monotheism of the Muslims and Byzantines. This traditionally proclaimed reason becomes now only one among a variety of other reasons.

Another departure from the traditional explanation occurs in the Shīʿī commentary of al-Ṭabarsī (d. 548/1153), which states that "Jerusalem (q.v.) was for the Rūm, the equivalent of the Kaʿba (q.v.) for the Muslims." In explaining the believers' "rejoicing" he introduces a nuance: "The believers will rejoice for the expulsion of the Persians from Jerusalem and not for the Byzantines' victory because the latter are infidels *(kuffār);* the other reasons for rejoicing are due to the polytheists' distress, to the fulfillment of the prophecy and the heralding of the Muslims' own future victory" (Ṭabarsī, *Majmaʿ,* xx-xxv, 7). This rising motif of the Byzantines as infidels is coupled with a novel stress on the importance of Jerusalem. Abū Ḥayyān similarly introduces Jerusalem into the debate: In "a few years" the Muslims will conquer Jerusalem (*Baḥr,* 162, par. 9-12). The fact that such interpretations coincided with the period of the Crusades is not accidental.

The late fourth/tenth and early fifth/eleventh centuries had seen major Muslim defeats at the hands of the Byzantine emperors. The anti-Byzantine interpretation that was now emphasized must be linked to the new defensive position taken by the Muslims. The late fifth/eleventh century saw the arrival of the Crusades with their fresh religious message. From then on, a clear religious consciousness would develop in response to this specific crusading mentality, one that rejected any identification with the other monotheists and that placed Jerusalem at the top of its military and cultural agenda.

Consequently, the principal variant reading assumed a more prominent place in the commentaries, in particular in the more polemical commentaries. The variant reading sought to find different reasons for the believers' rejoicing in an attempt to distance the early Muslim community from Byzantium. The variant reading never, however, stands on its own. The traditionally more accepted reading is always juxtaposed side by side with the variant. Working as they were within a tradition, the commentators reiterated the traditional reading and interpretation. Ideology created a further problem for the commentators who were caught by having to re-interpret a series of verses that were originally used to establish the very foundation of prophecy in Islam (see PROPHETS AND PROPHETHOOD). The miraculous character of the Qurʾān, partly reflected in the prophecies of future events, was essential to the theory of the inimitability of the Qurʾān (*iʿjāz al-Qurʾān,* see INIMITABILITY). In his chapter explaining the Qurʾān's information about future events, al-Bāqillānī (d. 403/1013) cites the opening verses of Sūrat al-Rūm (Q 30) as a major example of this (*Iʿjāz,* 78). To save the "prophesying" aspect of these verses was one of the commentator's essential tasks. The fulfillment of the prophecy partially hinged on the explanation of the believers' "rejoicing." Thus those departing from the traditional interpretation made the fulfillment of the prophecy one of the basic explanations for this "rejoicing."

Nadia Maria El-Cheikh

Bibliography

Primary: Abū Ḥayyān, *Baḥr;* ʿAbd al-Jabbār, *Tanzīh;* Bāqillānī, *Iʿjāz;* Bayḍāwī, *Anwār;* Muqātil, *Tafsīr;* Qummī, *Tafsīr;* Qurṭubī, *Jāmiʿ;* Ṭabarī, *Tafsīr;* Ṭabarsī, *Majmaʿ;* Wāḥidī, *Asbāb;* Zamakhsharī, *Kashshāf.*

Secondary: E. Beck, Die Sure ar-Rūm (30), in *Orientalia MS* 13 (1944), 334-55; Bell, *Commentary;* id., *The origin of Islam in its Christian environment,* London 1926; A. Cameron (ed.), *The Byzantine and early Islamic Near East, iii. States, resources and armies,* Princeton 1995; J. Chabbi, Ribāṭ, in EI^2, viii, 493-506; N. El-Cheikh, Sūrat al-Rūm. A study of the exegetical literature, in *JAOS* 118/3 (1998), 356-64; N. El Cheikh and C.E. Bosworth, Rūm, in EI^2, viii, 601-6; C. Foss, The Persians in Asia Minor and the end of Antiquity, in *English historical review* 90 (1975), 721-47; M. Götz, Zum historischen Hintergrund von Sure 30, 1-5, in E. Gräf (ed.), *Festschrift Werner Caskel,* Leiden 1968, 111-20 (with bibliography); B. Isaac, *The limits of empire. The Roman army in the East,* Oxford 1990; W. Kaegi, *Byzantium and the early Islamic conquests,* Cambridge 1992; A. Miquel, *La géographie humaine du monde musulman jusqu'au milieu du XIe siècle,* Paris 1980; I. Shahid, *Byzantium and the Arabs in the sixth century,* Washington 1995; id., Ghassān, in EI^2, ii, 1020-1.

C

Cain and Abel

The sons of Adam and Eve (q.v.). The qur'ānic account of Cain and Abel (Q 5:27-32) closely follows the narrative in the Bible (*Gen* 4:1-16; see SCRIPTURE AND THE QUR'ĀN). Each of the two sons of Adam and Eve — whose names are not mentioned in the Qur'ān — offers a sacrifice (q.v.): Only Abel's was accepted while Cain's was rejected because he was not God-fearing. Upon Cain's threat to murder Abel, the latter remained passive, wishing only that Cain be held responsible for the sins of both (*innī urīdu an tabū'a bi-ithmī wa-ithmika,* Q 5:29) and punished accordingly (see CHASTISEMENT AND PUNISHMENT). Having followed the guidance of a raven about the burial of Abel's body, Cain repents. The story closes by directing the *Banū Isrā'īl* (see CHILDREN OF ISRAEL) that murder (q.v.) is unlawful (see LAWFUL AND UNLAWFUL). Whoever kills someone for a reason other than justified punishment (*man qatala nafsan bi-ghayri nafsin aw fasādin,* Q 5:32) should be viewed as though he has killed all humanity *(fa-ka'annamā qatala l-nāsa jamī'an);* the opposite applies to those who save human life *(man aḥyāhā).*

Since the *Banū Isrā'īl* are mentioned toward the end of the story, some qur'ānic exegetes have offered the opinion that by "the sons of Adam" is meant not Adam's own sons but the Israelites. Most exegetes, however, reject this view. That the story was addressed to the Jews of Medina (q.v.) can be concluded from its context (see OCCASIONS OF REVELATION; JEWS AND JUDAISM). On the other hand, the exegete Muqātil (d. 150/767; *Tafsīr,* i, 468) explains "recount to them" (*wa-tlu 'alayhim,* Q 5:27) at the beginning of the narrative to mean: "Oh Muḥammad! Recount to the people of Mecca." According to Nöldeke (*GQ,* i, 61, 229), Q 5:15-38 is a textual unit probably anteceding the conquest of Khaybar (q.v.) in 7/628. Bell (i, 154) proposed an earlier date because of Abel's inaction. In support of this suggestion, one can adduce that *wa-tlu 'alayhim* was used as an opening clause already in the late Meccan period.

The exegetes were acquainted with the biblical account. To this they added a variety of details drawn from relevant Jewish and Christian traditions, much of which goes back to old Oriental and/or Greco-Roman mythology and folklore including, for instance, the story of Cain's punishment which recalls the myth of Prometheus (see MYTHIC AND LEGENDARY NARRATIVES). To render many of these additions authoritative, they were couched in the shape of a ḥadīth (see ḤADĪTH AND THE QURʾĀN). It should also be remembered that the borrowing also went in the other direction: Islamic elements did ultimately find their way into Jewish folklore.

Different locations for the events have been suggested (see GEOGRAPHY IN THE QURʾĀN): The sacrifice took place on Jabal Nawdh in India or at Minā (near Mecca). The fratricide was committed on the "Holy Mountain" (al-Jabal al-Muqaddas) from which Cain is said to have descended to the Land of Nawdh; Jabal Qāsyūn near Damascus; Jabal Murrān in the Ghūṭa of Damascus; Jabal Thawr or ʿAqabat al-Ḥirāʾ near Mecca; and, finally, in the Friday Mosque of al-Baṣra.

The importance of the story for Muslim thinking is obvious and its moral and theological dimensions have been discussed in exegetical and other relevant literature. Most exegetes tell us that Cain was to marry Abel's twin sister on the order of Adam. Others, who consider this objectionable, opt for a variant tradition according to which God sent a virgin (*ḥūriyya*, see HOURIS) from paradise (q.v.) to Abel and a female demon (*jinniyya*, see JINN) in human form to Cain, an account apparently based on the biblical story of the sons of God who married the daughters of man (*Gen* 6:1-4).

Abel's inaction and passivity (cf. Q 5:28) is evidently a Christian element since, according to Christian tradition, the murder (q.v.) of Abel is considered a prefiguration of the crucifixion of Jesus. Traditional Muslim exegesis asserts that killing in self-defense was prohibited at the time of Cain and Abel but that this prohibition was later abolished. In support of this interpretation a ḥadīth is cited in which it is declared forbidden for a Muslim to kill another Muslim in self-defense. If he prefers to fight and dies, both he and his opponent will be condemned to the fire (q.v.) of hell (q.v.). Other ḥadīths recommend the abandonment of self-defense. In emulation of Abel, the caliph ʿUthmān (q.v.; d. 35/656) is said to have renounced self-defense when his murderers entered his house. According to other commentators, the issue of self-defense is of no relevance in this context because Abel was murdered treacherously.

The interpretation of Q 5:29, "Verily I wish you to become liable for my sin and for your own" *(innī urīdu an tabūʾa bi-ithmī wa-ithmika),* is problematic because the Qurʾān teaches that nobody can bear another's burden of guilt (Q 6:164, and parallels). Often "for my sin" *(bi-ithmī)* is said to refer to Cain's sin of murdering Abel and "for your sin" *(bi-ithmika)* to Cain's other sins. According to others, the point under discussion is the punishment, not the sin (see SIN, MAJOR AND MINOR). It is held that the phrase in Q 5:29 has to be explained by adding *lā* to *an (allā),* i.e. by supplying an implied negative, as is also the exegetical situation in Q 12:85 and Q 16:15. Another ḥadīth on the last judgment (q.v.) offers yet another explanation; the ḥadīth states that a murderer will be charged with the sins of his victim.

Many interpretations of "as though he has killed all humankind" *(kaʾannamā qatala l-nāsa jamīʿan)* have also been offered: The practice of blood revenge (see BLOOD MONEY; RETALIATION; VENGEANCE) must be applied in all cases regardless of whether the murdered victim was a single person or the whole of humankind; everyone is bound to avenge the blood of a victim; as the very first human being to have taken the life of another, Cain made killing customary *(sanna al-qatl).*

The quarrel between Cain and Abel has also been explained allegorically. In Sunnī tradition, "whoever kills someone" *(man qatala nafsan)* means he "who seduces somebody to polytheism" (*shirk*, see POLYTHEISM

AND ATHEISM) and "whoever revives or saves someone" *(man aḥyāhā)* refers to one "who invites somebody to the right belief." With appropriate modification, this interpretation was adopted by the Shīʿīs (see SHĪʿA; SHĪʿISM AND THE QURʾĀN); for them *man aḥyāhā* means he "who guides somebody from error to true religion" *(min al-ḍalāl ilā hudan),* or "who supports one of ʿAlī's family (see ʿALĪ B. ABĪ ṬALIB), helping him to gain the victory" (Furāt b. Ibrāhīm, *Tafsīr,* i, 122).

Heribert Busse

Bibliography
Primary: ʿAbd al-Jabbār, *Mutashābih,* i, 221; Furāt b. Ibrāhīm al-Kūfī, *Tafsīr,* ed. M. al-Kāẓim, Beirut 1412/1991, i, 122; Ibn al-ʿArabī, *Aḥkām,* ii, 88-90; Ibn Hishām, *al-Tījān fī mulūk Ḥimyar,* 17-8; Ibn Kathīr, *Mukhtaṣar tafsīr,* ed. M.ʿA. al-Ṣabūnī, 3 vols., Beirut 1399/1979, i, 507; Ibn Qutayba, *Kitāb al-Maʿārif,* ed. Th. ʿUkāsha, Cairo 1960, 17; Ibn Saʿd, *Ṭabaqāt,* i, 14; Jaṣṣāṣ, *Aḥkām,* ii, 502-3, 507; Qummī, *Tafsīr,* 155; Qurṭubī, *Jāmiʿ,* vi, 89-92; Rāzī, *Tafsīr,* vi, 11; Suyūṭī, *Durr,* ii, 488; Ṭabarī, *Tafsīr,* x, 221-2, 228, 230, ḥadīth nos. 11746, 11765, 11767-9; Thaʿlabī, *al-Kashf wa-l-bayān ʿan tafsīr al-Qurʾān,* ms. Ahmet III 76/2, fol. 17 b-20 a; id., *Qiṣaṣ,* 37-41; Yaʿqūbī, *Taʾrīkh,* i, 4.
Secondary: Bell; W. Bork-Qaysieh, *Die Geschichte von Kain und Abel (Hābīl wa-Qābīl) in der sunnitisch-islamischen Überlieferung. Untersuchung von Beispielen aus verschiedenen Literaturwerken unter Berücksichtigung ihres Einflusses auf den Volksglauben,* Berlin 1993 (exhaustive treatment of Sunnī sources, including the author's report of a visit to the "Cave of Blood" *[maghārat al-dam* or *maqām al-arbaʿīn]* on Jabal Qāsyūn); C. Böttrich, *Die Vögel des Himmels haben ihn begraben. Überlieferungen zu Abels Bestattung und zur Ätiologie des Grabes,* Göttingen 1995, 33-77 (German translation of selected texts dealing with burial in the rabbinical and Islamic traditions); S. Günther, Hostile brothers in transformation. An archetypical conflict figuring in classical and modern (Arabic) literature, in Angelica Neuwirth et al. (eds.), *Myths, historical archetypes and symbolic figures in Arabic literature,* Beirut 1999, 309-36 (includes a section on relevant writings by Najīb Maḥfūẓ and Saʿdallāh Wannūs); D. Masson, *Le Coran et la révélation judéo-chrétienne. Études comparées,* 2 vols., Paris 1958, 1976² (rev. ed.), i, 336 (juxtaposition of texts in two columns: Q 5:27-32, *Gen* 4:1-16, and rabbinical stories); Nöldeke, *GQ;* N.A. Stillman, The story of Cain and Abel in the Qurʾān and the Muslim commentators. Some observations, in *JSS* 19 (1974), 231-9 (treats mainly the Jewish and Christian traditions); Wensinck, *Handbook,* 172 (q.v. murder).

Calendar

System of fixing the divisions of time (q.v.), adapted to the purposes of communal life. References in the Qurʾān related to calendar include the terms *waqt/mīqāt* which mean, among other things, fixed or appointed time (e.g. Q 2:189; 4:103; 7:143; 44:40; 78:17); the computation of years and numbers (*li-taʿlamū ʿadad al-sinīn wa-l-ḥisāb,* Q 10:5; 17:12; see NUMBERS AND ENUMERATION); and the division of the year into twelve months (q.v.): "The number of months with God is twelve in accordance with God's decree on the day he created the heavens and the earth; of which four are holy months" (Q 9:36).

There is no reference in the Qurʾān to the pre-Islamic system of *anwāʾ* (see PRE-ISLAMIC ARABIA AND THE QURʾĀN), which was used by the Arabs to estimate the passage of time and to predict the state of the weather (q.v.). In this system, the year is divided into precise periods on the basis of the rising and setting of certain stars (see COSMOLOGY IN THE QURʾĀN). According to tradition, this system was considered anathema in Islam. The most relevant qurʾānic allusion to calendar-related computation is the phases of the moon (*manāzil al-qamar,* Q 10:5; 36:39). Q 10:5 reads: "It is he who gave the sun (q.v.) its radiance, the moon (q.v.) its luster, and determined its phases so that you may compute years and numbers…" Qurʾānic exegesis as well as the exact scientific computations of calendars identify 28 such phases. The definition of these phases, however, is based on a combination of the pre-Islamic system of *anwāʾ* with the system of lunar phases. Thus the solar zodiac is divided into 28 equal parts defined by the rising and setting of certain stars or constellations. Each of these parts is a station, or phase, and in rough measure the moon occupies one of these stations each day of the lunar month. At the end of a lunar month, the moon would have traveled through all 28 stations; in other words, the moon would have completed one revolution along the solar zodiac (Qurṭubī, *Jāmiʿ*, viii, 310; xv, 29-30).

The official Islamic calendar is lunar with year one coinciding with the year 622 C.E., the date of Muḥammad's emigration (*hijra*, q.v.) from Mecca (q.v.) to Medina (q.v.). This calendar was adopted during the reign of the second caliph ʿUmar (q.v.; r. 13-23/634-44). Later sources, however, suggest that the use of the lunar calendar is already prescribed in the qurʾānic references to the phases of the moon. For example, in the commentary on Q 10:5 mentioned above, al-Qurṭubī (d. 671/1272; *Jāmiʿ*, viii, 310) maintains that after mentioning the light of the sun and the moon, the Qurʾān uses the singular (*qaddarahu*, not *qaddarahumā*). This is taken to indicate that only the lunar calendar is meant to serve as the basis for computing the official months or "new moons" (*ahilla*, Q 2:189) and for determining the dates for important religious activities such as fasting (q.v.) and pilgrimage (q.v.). Unless otherwise specified, time stipulations in legal contracts and documents are based on the *hijra* lunar calendar (see LAW AND THE QURʾĀN).

On average, the lunar months alternate between 29 and 30 days. Although the beginning of the lunar month is determined by sighting the new moon, numerous methods were developed to compute the exact length of the lunar months, to determine the days of the lunar year in relation to the solar year and to perform calendar conversions between different eras. Tables of varying details were also compiled to facilitate this conversion. In fact, in contrast to earlier Greek sources, Islamic astronomical handbooks often started with discussions of calendar computations and conversions between different eras (for example, Persian, Coptic, Syriac, Chinese-Ughur, Jewish and Hindu calendars). In addition to the basic computational techniques, numerous works also provide additional information covering calendar-related subjects, such as the length of day and night (q.v.); patterns of weather and wind (see AIR AND WIND); dates and descriptions of Christian, Jewish and Indian festivals as well as agricultural practices (see AGRICULTURE AND VEGETATION) at various times of the year. See also DAY, TIMES OF.

A. Dallal

Bibliography
Primary: Qurṭubī, *Jāmiʿ*.
Secondary: E.S. Kennedy et al., Calendars, in D.A. King and M.H. Kennedy (eds.), *Studies in the Islamic exact sciences*, Beirut 1983, 652-709; D.A. King, *Astronomy in the service of Islam*, Aldershot 1993; id., *Islamic mathematical astronomy*, Hampshire 1993; id., Mīḳāt, in *EI²*, vii, 26-32; L. Nabiron, Notes on the Arab calendar before Islam [orig. pub. in *JA* (Apr. 1843)], trans. C. de Perceval, in *IC* 21 (1947), 135-53; C. Pellat, Anwāʾ, in *EI²*, i, 523-4; M. Rodinson, al-Ḳamar, in *EI²*, iv, 517-9; id., La lune chez les Arabes et dans l'Islam, in *La lune, mythes et rites*, Paris 1962.

Calf of Gold

The image of a calf worshipped by the Israelites while Moses (q.v.) was on the mountain receiving the tablets of the Law. Allusion to this story is made in five passages of the Qurʾān. There, as in the main biblical account (*Exod* 32), the object of worship is not explicitly called a "calf of gold" but simply a "calf" (*ʿijl*, Heb. *ʿēgel*).

The Qurʾān says that it was made from ornaments (*ḥulī,* Q 7:148; *zīna,* 20:87), Exodus 32:2-3 from golden rings *(nizmey ha-zāhāb).*

The qurʾānic allusions to the story (Q 2:51, 54, 92, 93; 4:153; 7:148-53; 20:83-98) display several verbal and conceptual parallels and similarities: the evil committed by those who worshipped the calf (e.g. Q 2:51, 54, 92; 7:148); their punishment in this world (Q 2:54, 93; 7:152; 20:97; see CHASTISEMENT AND PUNISHMENT); God's forgiveness (q.v.) and mercy (q.v.), sometimes specified for those who repent (Q 2:54; 7:153; see REPENTANCE AND PENANCE), sometimes applied generally (Q 2:52; 4:153; 7:149); and the role of Moses in obtaining God's mercy (Q 2:54; 7:151). Absent from the Qurʾān, but sometimes evident in the commentary, is any attempt to use the story as polemic against Judaism (cf. the speech of Stephen in the Acts of the Apostles, chapter 7).

Qurʾānic commentary

The qurʾānic allusions to the story of the calf suggested several questions to the traditional commentators. Unlike the Exodus narrative, the qurʾānic passages nowhere explicitly connect Aaron (q.v.) with the construction of the calf, although Q 7:150-1 and 20:90-4 could imply that Aaron had in some way erred and that Moses was angry with his brother. These passages proved problematic in relation to the doctrine of the impeccability (*ʿiṣma,* see IMPECCABILITY AND INFALLIBILITY) of the prophets — both Moses and Aaron being accepted as prophets — and gave rise to various suggestions about how they might be understood in ways compatible with this doctrine (see PROPHETS AND PROPHETHOOD).

At Q 20:85, 87 and 95-7, responsibility for making the calf is placed squarely with a figure called "the Samaritan" (al-Sāmirī). Various suggestions are made in the qurʾānic commentaries about his origins and identity and about the significance of the phrase "do not touch" *(lā misāsa)* which, it is said at Q 20:97, Moses told him he would have to utter during his lifetime. Especially notable are statements by some commentators that the name of the Samaritan was "Aaron" (see SAMARITANS).

The ornaments from which the calf was fashioned are frequently described in the extra-qurʾānic materials as having been taken from the people of Pharaoh (q.v.) whom God had drowned in the sea (see DROWNING). One explanation of why, at Q 7:148, they are described as "their" (i.e. the Israelites') ornaments is that the Israelites borrowed them from the Egyptians for a festival and they became the property of the Israelites once the Egyptians died in the sea.

Q 20:96 may seem obscure: When Moses asked the Samaritan to give an explanation for his role in the making of the calf, he replied that he had noticed something which they (the Israelites) had not, that he had seized a "handful from the traces of the messenger" and had thrown it in *(qāla baṣurtu bimā lam yabṣurū bihi fa-qabaḍtu qabḍatan min athari l-rasūli fa-nabadhtuhā wa-kadhālika sawwalat lī nafsī).* This phrase and the identity of the messenger are variously understood, a common explanation being that the Samaritan saw the angel Gabriel (q.v.) on a horse at the time when Pharaoh's people were drowned in the sea. He seized a handful of the dust which the horse had turned up and threw it into the fire in which the ornaments were melted. This often explains the ability of the calf to low, for both Q 7:148 and 20:88 say that it had a body and lowed *(ʿijlan jasadan lahu khuwārun).*

There are various views about the nature of the calf. Had it been transformed into flesh and blood so that it could really low or had it remained simply an image made from ornaments? The qurʾānic *jasad* is interpreted by some, particularly the rationalist sect of the Muʿtazila (see MUʿTAZILĪS), as applicable to any solid object and it was explained how a lowing sound could have been produced by mechanical devices or human trickery. The question of whether the calf had been changed into a real one also affected the understanding of Q 20:97, where Moses tells the Samaritan that he is going to burn the calf *(la-nuḥarriqannahu)* and scatter it upon the sea. Some commentators, noting that gold cannot be burned, argue that this was an indication that the calf had indeed become flesh and blood. Those who maintain that it had remained merely an image were able, by associating the verb *ḥarraqa* with a meaning of the root indicating "rubbing" or "grinding," to interpret it as "filing down with a rasp" *(la-nabrudannahu bi-l-mibrad),* thus making it possible that the calf could have been scattered upon the sea. Some read *nuḥarriq* as *naḥruq* in order to make that interpretation clearer.

Q 2:93, "they were made to drink the calf in their hearts with their unbelief" (see BELIEF AND UNBELIEF), is sometimes connected in the commentary with the destruction of the calf and the scattering of its ashes into water subsequently drunk by the Israelites (as at *Exod* 32:20). But it is frequently read metaphorically: They were made to imbibe the love of the calf. Supporters of the doctrine of human free will argue that it should not be taken to mean that God caused them to drink it (see FREEDOM AND PREDESTINATION).

At Q 2:54 it is said that, when Moses came down from the mountain and found his people worshipping the calf, he called upon them: "Turn in repentance to your Creator and kill yourselves" *(fa-tūbū ilā bāriʾikum fa-qtulū anfusakum)*. This injunction is generally understood literally and we find various accounts of how the Children of Israel (q.v.) fulfilled the command. It is reported, for example, that they divided themselves into two groups which fought one another, father fighting against son, son against father and brother against brother. This continued until a large number had been killed and God, moved by the appeals of Moses and Aaron, allowed them to desist.

The qurʾānic material in relation to the biblical and post-biblical material

Most non-Muslim scholars have assumed that the qurʾānic allusions to the story depend ultimately on the biblical account and are to be understood as drawing on and developing the interpretations and embellishments which had arisen about the biblical narrative in subsequent Jewish and Christian reworkings of it. In other words, the qurʾānic material has been itself understood as part of the midrashic tradition (see SCRIPTURE AND THE QURʾĀN).

Compared with the account in Exodus, the responsibility for making the calf had already been shifted from Aaron, as noted above, in Stephen's speech in the Acts of the Apostles (7:40-1) to the people themselves. This development is also evident in the explanation given in the Jewish *midrash* that Aaron called upon the people to give him their golden ornaments in the belief that they would not do so, i.e. it was only a delaying tactic.

The identity of "the Samaritan" and the source of the name have been much discussed by academic scholars and it may be that it combines ideas from various sources. The "handful" *(qabḍa)* from the "traces" *(athar)* of the messenger which, Q 20:96 tells us, the Samaritan cast in, has been suggested to relate to the midrashic story that Micah (associated in *Judg* 17:4 and 18:14f. with molten and graven images) threw a fragment containing the words "come up ox," *ʿaleh shōr* (cf. *Gen*

49:22, "Joseph [q.v.] is a fruitful bough... whose branches run over the wall" *[aley shūr])* into the fire melting down the ornaments. The words had been written on the fragment by Moses when he cast it into the Nile in order to cause the coffin of Joseph to come to the surface. It was this fragment which caused the calf to appear, alive and leaping. Other accounts attribute the fact that the calf was alive to the activity of two Egyptian magicians, Jannes and Mambres (see MAGIC, PROHIBITION OF).

Aaron's words at Q 7:150, "The people considered me weak and came near to killing me," have been associated with the story that Hur — named at Exodus 24:14 by Moses as his deputy along with Aaron but subsequently absent from the account — tried to dissuade the people from worshipping the calf but was killed by them and that Aaron was afraid of suffering the same fate. Aaron's words at Q 20:94, "I was afraid that you would say, 'You have caused division among the Children of Israel and have not paid attention to what I said,'" may relate to the traditional image of Aaron as a peacemaker and to the story that he had thought it better to agree to the people's demands than to cause them to sin further by killing him as well as Hur.

The preference of the Muslim tradition for seeing the ornaments from which the calf was made as coming from the Egyptians — in spite of the fact that Q 7:148 simply says, "their ornaments" — reflects the wording of Q 20:87, "We have been burdened with the weight of the ornaments of the people" *(ḥummilnā awzāran min zīnati l-qawm)*. A connection seems likely here to Exodus 12:35-6, where it is related that the Egyptians were so eager to let the Children of Israel finally go that they were ready to lend them anything they needed, including "jewels of silver and jewels of gold." In the *midrash* the Children of Israel sought to excuse themselves for making the calf by complaining that God had given them an abundance of gold and silver when they left Egypt.

The explanation by the commentators of Moses' words "kill yourselves" *(fa-qtulū anfusakum)* in Q 2:54 probably relates to the story in Exodus 32:25-9, which describes how Moses ordered the sons of Levi to "slay every man his brother, every man his companion and every man his neighbor." It may be, however, that the words attributed to Moses in the Qurʾān reflect Leviticus 16:29, which is understood as the ordinance for the Day of Atonement in Judaism: "Afflict yourselves" *(teʿannū et-nafshotēkem)*. The meaning of the Hebrew phrase was much debated among Jewish groups, some of whom understood it to demand mortification and penitential practices. See also IDOLS AND IMAGES.

Gerald R. Hawting

Bibliography
Primary: Ibn Ḥazm, *Milal,* Cairo 1317, i, 161-3; M.A. Palacios (trans.), *Abenházem de Córdoba,* Madrid 1928, ii, 304-6; Ibn Kathīr, *Qiṣaṣ al-anbiyāʾ,* ed. ʿA.Q.A. ʿAṭāʾ, Beirut n.d., ii, 111-17; Qurṭubī, *Jāmiʿ,* Cairo 1354/1935, i, 393-7, 400-3; ii, 30-32; vi, 6-7; vii, 284-92; xi, 232-43; Rāzī, *Tafsīr,* iii, 84-7, 200-2; xv, 6-15; xxii, 98-113; Ṭabarī, *Tafsīr,* Cairo 1954-68, ii, 63-8, 72-9, 354-61; ix, 356-60; xiii, 117-37 and Cairo 1373-77/1954-7, xvi, 145-54; Ṭūsī, *Tibyān,* i, 243-49, 352-6; ix, 577-91; xvi, 195-206.
Secondary: P. Crone and M. Cook, *Hagarism. The making of the Islamic world,* Cambridge 1977, 177, n. 60; A. Geiger, *Was hat Mohammed aus dem Judenthume aufgenommen?* Bonn 1833, 165-8; Gimaret, *Jubbāʾī,* 88, 365-6, 603-5; G.R. Hawting, The *tawwābūn,* atonement and *ʿāshūrāʾ,* in *JSAI* 17 (1994), 166-81; H. Lazarus-Yafeh, *Intertwined worlds. Medieval Islam and Bible criticism,* Princeton 1992, 63, n. 41; D. Sidersky, *Les origines des légendes musulmanes,* Paris 1933, 87-9; Speyer, *Erzählungen,* 323-33.

Caliph

In Arabic, *khalīfa* is the title adopted by the head of the Muslim polity (see COMMUNITY

AND SOCIETY IN THE QUR'ĀN) ever since the death of the prophet Muḥammad in 11/632. The term occurs in the Qur'ān twice in the singular and seven times in the plural, as *khalāʾif* or *khulafāʾ*, and some of its verbal occurrences (particularly *khalafa* and *istakhlafa*) are semantically very closely connected with it.

There is little in the qur'ānic occurrences of the term that prepares for its politically and theologically charged meaning. By far its most prevalent meaning in the Qur'ān is "successor, substitute, replacement, deputy" which is particularly clear in the verbal and nominal plural occurrences. The basic notion is that — as human history has repeatedly shown, and as it will show in the future — God warns a people (see WARNING) when they go astray (q.v.), God destroys them and replaces them with another people who obey God's messengers (see MESSENGER), worship (q.v.) him, act morally and are consequently rewarded by inheriting the land and the scripture of their predecessors (Q 6:133, 165; 7:69, 74, 129; 10:14, 73; 11:57; 24:55; 27:62; 35:39; see also PUNISHMENT STORIES; GENERATIONS). In this sense, the term is, understandably, closely associated with such terms as *adhhaba* (to destroy; e.g. Q 4:133), *awratha* (to bequeath; e.g. Q 33:27) and *istabdala* (to replace; e.g. Q 47:38). The second, rarer and philologically less obvious meaning of the term is "inhabitant, settler on earth." This meaning is most evident in Q 2:30 where God says to the angels (q.v.): "I am making/creating on earth a *khalīfa*...," clearly meaning Adam (see ADAM AND EVE); it is also implied in Q 14:14 where the verb *sakana*, to dwell, connects it with the first meaning of a believing nation replacing a non-believing one (see BELIEF AND UNBELIEF). The third meaning has some political and juridical implications; it is "one who exercises authority (q.v.)." It is clear in only one verse, Q 38:26, where the prophet David (q.v.) is addressed thus: "O David, we have made you a *khalīfa* on earth; so judge justly between people and follow not desires lest they should thwart you from God's path."

The early Muslim exegetes who were philologically oriented and had some access to Jewish and Christian lore, i.e. *Isrāʾīliyyāt*, considered "succession and substitution" the main meaning of the term *khalīfa* and its cognates, and applied it with varying degrees to almost all of its occurrences, an interpretation that led them into great difficulties with the exegesis of the Adam occurrence (see SCRIPTURE AND THE QUR'ĀN). On the other hand, they did indeed mention the other two meanings of the term although they seemed inclined to link them, sometimes artificially, with the main meaning: succession. With regard to the Adam verse, a general sense seems to have existed that the term refers not only to Adam but also to all humanity, i.e. the children of Adam. Conversely, most exegetes considered the David verse as referring to David alone and not to "people in authority" in general. It can therefore be said that during the Umayyad period, the exegetes made no connection between the qur'ānic term *khalīfa* and the politico-religious reality of the institution of the caliphate.

This tendency began to change about the middle of the second/eighth century when a more comprehensive interpretation started to appear. Beginning with a hint by al-Suddī (d. 128/745; cf. Ṭabarī, *Tafsīr*, xxiii, 151: "[God] made [David] king *(mallakahu)* on earth") this became more generalized in Sufyān al-Thawrī's (d. 161/778) commentary on Q 24:55: The believers who succeed others on earth are the governors/the people in charge (*al-wulāt*, see his *Tafsīr*, 185). By the time of the great synthesizer of Muslim exegesis al-Ṭabarī (d. 310/923), the standard Sunnī exegetical position had created a complete merger between the qur'ānic *khalīfa* and the head of the Islamic caliphate. Thus, at the first occurrence of the term, in the Adam verse, and after indicating the philological meaning of the term as successor or replacement, al-Ṭabarī adds, "hence the supreme authority *(al-sulṭān al-aʿẓam)* is called "khalīfa" for he succeeds the one who preceded him, replacing him in taking charge of matters, thereby being his substitute" (Ṭabarī, *Tafsīr,* i, 199). This standard Sunnī position insists that the title "khalīfa" for the head of the Muslim polity is an abbreviation of the longer (and eventually cumbersome) formula *khalīfat rasūl Allāh* (successor of the messenger of God) which the first Muslim Caliph, Abū Bakr (q.v.; r. 11-3/632-4) adopted, not of *khalīfat Allāh* (viceregent of God). Although this last formula was indeed used by most Umayyad and ʿAbbāsid caliphs, it never received legitimation in Islamic political theory.

Wadad Kadi

Bibliography
Primary: Muqātil, *Tafsīr;* Sufyān al-Thawrī, *Tafsīr;* Ṭabarī, *Tafsīr.*
Secondary: P. Crone and M. Hinds, *God's caliph,* Cambridge 1986 (a new interpretation of Tyan's thesis); R. Paret, Signification coranique de *ḫalīfa* et d'autres dérivés de la racine *ḫalafa,* in *SI* 31 (1970), 211-7; W. al-Qāḍī, The term "khalīfa" in early exegetical literature, in *WI* 28 (1988), 392-411 (esp. for the views of pre-ʿAbbāsid exegetes; with bibliography on p. 392, n. 1); E. Tyan, *Institutions du droit public musulman. i. Le califat,* Paris 1956 (history of the title itself and the development of the institution); W.M. Watt, God's caliph. Qurʾānic interpretations and Umayyad claims, in C.E. Bosworth (ed.), *Iran and Islam in memory of the late Vladimir Minorsky,* Edinburgh 1971, 565-74.

Calligraphy

The Arabic script *(khaṭṭ),* its development, and its formal use in manuscripts of the Qurʾān. Though initially presented as an oral recitation (see BOOK), the Qurʾān has played an essential role in the development of the Arabic script (q.v.). According to traditional accounts, certain fragments were committed to writing by some of the Companions of the Prophet (q.v.) on crude materials such as flat stones, veins of palm leaves, animal skins or ceramic shards (see TEXTUAL HISTORY OF THE QURʾĀN). The script was then still imperfect and its signs were little more than a mnemonic technique for fixing a text already committed to memory — a far cry from the Arabic script we know today.

This primitive script, which probably originated in Ḥīra, capital of the Christian Arab kingdom of the Lakhmids (see CHRISTIANS AND CHRISTIANITY), was an adaptation of the Syriac script and was not widespread at the time. With the passing of the generation of the Companions, the first to have heard the Qurʾān from Muḥammad and to have learned it by heart, it became necessary to fix the final text of the holy book and to perfect the system for recording it in written form. Most versions of the textual history of the Qurʾān state that an official text was imposed by the third caliph, ʿUthmān (q.v.; r. 23-35/644-56), and distributed to the main centers of early Islam. Copies of the sacred text thence multiplied in territories conquered by the Arab armies. In an era when reproduction of the Qurʾān depended totally on the scribal art, considerable praise and merit was attributed to the skill of writing and its use in recording the Qurʾān. To emphasize the worthiness and nobility of this task, some religious scholars *(ʿulamāʾ)* asserted that at the day of judgment (see LAST JUDGMENT), the ink of calligraphers, placed on one of the arms of the scale of justice (see JUSTICE AND INJUSTICE), would balance the blood of martyrs on the other (see BLOOD AND BLOOD CLOT; MARTYR).

During the first three centuries of Islam, calligraphy underwent considerable development. This was due first of all to the need to meet the demands of state administration (most of the great calligraphers began their careers as secretaries either of the chancellery or the land-tax, both of which required skill in writing). An equal factor was the multiplication and distribution of copies of the Qur'ān throughout the entire empire. Given this increase in written production, efforts were thus made to make the script more legible. Diacritic signs were added to characters with an identical form to prevent confusion. At first, these were very fine lines superimposed above the letters, but the lines were then replaced by small, more or less regular dots. Beginning with the caliphate of ʿAbd al-Malik (r. 65/685-86/705), relatively large red dots corresponding to the vowels were joined to the letters to facilitate the reading of the Qur'ān and to prevent any falsification of the text: A dot above the letter corresponded to a *fatḥa* (a), a dot under the letter to a *kasra* (i) and a dot on the base line to a *ḍamma* (u). This practice provoked opposition among certain scholars *(ʿulamā')* who considered it a human addition to an already perfect text given by God and thus a reprehensible innovation (q.v.). At the beginning of the fifth/eleventh century, the vowel signs currently in use replaced the red dots; it is this custom of vocalizing the qur'ānic text which persists today.

In addition to increasing precision of the script, manuscripts of the Qur'ān began to include additional textual specification. In former times (the dating of which is difficult to specify), small superimposed lines, drawn with the same ink as the text, separated one verse from another. The sūras were separated by a single blank line and had no title. Later, colored bands with a crude geometrical design were added to the empty space separating the sūras. In turn, three small dots in gold replaced the previous separation marks in ink. Small rosettes indicated groups of five verses while larger ones were used for groups of ten verses. Later, titles of sūras were inscribed in golden ink or placed in the centre of a painted band often illuminated with gold.

Centers for the instruction and production of the calligraphic art multiplied in the great urban milieux of the empire, in which various writing styles developed as may be observed in the qur'ānic material written on parchment and preserved in museums all over the world. The calligraphy of these old, handwritten Qur'āns can be divided into two main groups: The first and oldest is a more or less angular type called Kūfic. The second, which is more cursive, appeared in Baghdad at the end of the third/ninth century. These two groups are further divided into a plethora of scribal forms of which both place of origin and period are difficult to determine. In fact, the earliest qur'ānic material written on parchment is not dated at all. The first established reference (264/877-8) appears in the *waqf* of the Qur'ān of Amājūr (governor of Damascus). This date refers to its placement in the Umayyad mosque; it was probably copied a bit earlier. Resort must be had to palaeography when attempting to classify the many types of old, handwritten copies of the Qur'ān in order to date them and/or trace their origin. This is a particularly arduous enterprise which specialists have undertaken for more than two centuries without any fully satisfactory results. This continuing ambiguity can be attributed to the fact, on the one hand, that variations in the written form are innumerable and imprecisely named and, on the other, that copies of the Qur'ān were moved from one calligraphic center to another or given as gifts to sovereigns or other notables who subsequently moved them to mosques in their respective capitals or added them to their personal libraries.

The primary source consulted by palaeographers is the *Kitāb al-Fihrist*, the famous work of Ibn al-Nadīm (d. after 377/987-8) who includes an inventory of the styles of writing in use during his time. From this and with the help of commentaries by later Arab authors, specialists have tried to identify the types of script encountered in available collections of ancient copies of the Qurʾān on parchment. With a few, rare exceptions, this effort has been unsuccessful since the information provided by Ibn al-Nadīm has proven insufficient to establish secure identification. From this perspective, even a work as important as that of Nabia Abbott *(The rise of the north Arabian script)* which refers to Ibn al-Nadīm as well as al-Qalqashandī *(Ṣubḥ al-Aʿshāʾ)* has resulted in very little. In fact, al-Qalqashandī (d. 821/1418) himself used terminology borrowed from writers of different epochs without any regard for possible evolution in the meaning of these terms. Consequently, by classifying very diverse types of script under one single name borrowed from Arab authors, Nabia Abbott's attempt has only added to the confusion since these authors had not clearly identified the terms they used.

Recent studies have made use of a new methodology that consists in classifying — independently from their designation by classical Arab authors — copies of the Qurʾān with easily identifiable common features. Once the numerous collections discovered during the twentieth century have been studied, it should be possible to match different scripts selected on the basis of clearly defined criteria to rare examples lacking dates. Scholars will then be able to fit certain examples into a sequence of which the date and the provenance are easier to determine.

The most recent conclusions of this new methodology distinguish two main groups which allow classification of the first handwritten copies of the Qurʾān: *ḥijāzī* and "classical Kūfic." This latter term is preferred to "Kūfic" which is used widely as though covering a single entity; it actually includes many forms. A broad consensus exists for the identification of the *ḥijāzī* script as a result of the comparative studies undertaken by A. Grohman between this style of writing and the related script used in papyri. *Ḥijāzī* — referred to in some works, notably that of Nabia Abbott, as *māʾil* (slanted), a term presently in question since it groups together scripts too diverse to be characterized by a single term — was already in use at a very early stage in Mecca (q.v.) and Medina (q.v.). It is characterized by oblique strokes, generally oriented, more or less unvaryingly, from right to left; *alif*s ending in a short curved return; letters having a circular loop *(fāʾ, qāf, mīm, wāw)*; *ʿayn*s having the shape of a small *v* when in medial position; *nūn*s in the form of a wide and very open curve when in isolated or final positions; characters packed together on the line; short ligatures slightly curved; and a regular, sober rhythm of script which is sometimes interrupted by stretching out letters at the end of a line.

Considered Iraqi in origin, classical Kūfic displays considerable variety but also enough common features to be classified under one heading. At first glance classical Kūfic conveys a balanced and harmonious impression because of the equal space between the lines and the regular dimensions and geometry of the characters. This impression is reinforced by the rhythm created, firstly, by the alternation of short and long ligatures and, secondly, by the contrast of compact *(rāʾ, zayn, ḥāʾ, mīm, hāʾ,*

wāw) and stretched *(dāl, dhāl, ṣād, ḍād, ṭāʾ, ẓāʾ, kāf, yāʾ)* characters. This type of script has slender, vertical strokes with upper ends that have a beveled edge while the lower ones have either a large, tapering curve *(alif)* or a right angle descending well below the line *(lām* and *nūn)*. The tails of the letters *jīm, ḥāʾ, khāʾ, wāw* are short and compact and their end-point falls below the line whereas the tail of the *ʿayn* ends in a large curve with a tapered point reminiscent of the *alif*. The tail of the *mīm* is reduced to a small horizontal stroke.

Between these two main groupings, a whole range of types shows particularities of both the *ḥijāzī* group and the classical Kūfic. These are the types of script which specialists attempt to classify for the sake of defining them more precisely.

Several other scripts, related to classical Kūfic but with specific criteria, arose at the end of the fourth/tenth century and were used conjointly with cursive writing (see below). Among these is "oriental Kūfic" which owes its name to its appearance in the easternmost provinces of the Islamic empire (see the examples in the catalogue of M. Lings, pls. 11-21). This type of writing, while retaining the geometry of classical Kūfic, exhibits characters with radically different proportions. In oriental Kūfic, the ratio of the length of the low characters (teeth and loops) to that of the tall characters (down-strokes) is 1:8 whereas it varies from 1:3 to 1:2 in classical Kūfic. The common features of oriental Kūfic can be summarized as follows:

— a strictly horizontal base-line broken by small dots which serve as ligatures between characters closely packed together (letters with teeth and loops); in other cases, the ligatures are rather short but those of the *basmala* (q.v.) are sometimes thoroughly stretched out so that the phrase fills up the entire line.

— very slender strokes with upper extremities ending in a small triangle or bevel extended by a fine oblique segment. Sometimes the down-strokes of certain characters *(ṭāʾ, ẓāʾ, kāf)* display an obliquity of 45 degrees and end in a leftward pointed bulge. The strokes of the *lām-alif* are either very close parallel lines or two fairly thin symmetric curves with conjoined ends. The strokes of the two *lāms* in the word Allāh are sometimes reduced to two small and very oblique segments packed together, thus reducing the size of the word by half.

— the loss of the verticality known in classical Kūfic in characters with teeth which are oblique in oriental Kūfic. The rectangular bodies of the letters *dāl/dhāl, ṣād/ḍād, ṭāʾ/ẓāʾ, kāf* are thoroughly stretched out in length and small in height.

— the loss of the circular shape of the letters *fāʾ, qāf, mīm* and *wāw* as in classical Kūfic, which become either triangular or square or even an oblique trapezoid pointed forward. Only the medial *hāʾ* has a circular shape with two eyelets.

— the loss of the regular curve in the tails of characters, although still just as large. The tails descend obliquely below the line, then break off and end in a triangle, parallel to the line with the points below. It is perhaps this rupture of curves that provides the origin of the name of broken Kūfic, sometimes used to designate this script.

Many examples of this oriental Kūfic are adorned with illuminated bands in gold which frame the title of the sūra, the number of its verses and its Mekkan or Medinan origin. The rosettes marking the separation between verses or groups of verses are also written in golden ink. The diacritical dots are generally in the same ink as the text but the vowels are often in red.

Some of these qurʾānic manuscripts are signed and dated, for example that written and illuminated by ʿUthmān Ḥusayn

Warrāq (466/1073-4) from Iraq or Iran, that by Abū Bakr Aḥmad b. ʿAbdallāh al-Ghaznawī (573/1177-8) which was copied in Afghanistan and, finally, the one by ʿAlī b. Muḥammad b. Muḥammad (620/1223) copied in Iran.

The appearance of cursive writing, the second main category of qurʾānic scripts, coincided more or less with that of paper (the first attested copy of the Qurʾān in cursive dates from 361/971). The cursive script, quite ancient but reserved up to that time for daily use, owes its nobility to the vizier and famous calligrapher, Ibn Muqla (d. 328/940). Using a circle with a diameter corresponding to the height of an *alif,* he standardized the method of tracing the characters, all other characters being defined in accordance with this circle. A system of measures allowed the standardization of the characters' proportions, where the unit used for measuring was the dot, still in use today by calligraphers. This square-shaped dot, resting on its point, corresponds to the trace left on paper by the tip of the calligrapher's reed when applied to the sheet with a certain pressure. Ibn Muqla's innovative style of writing is called *al-khaṭṭ al-mansūb,* "the well-proportioned script," though its exact meaning is not known. Another great master of calligraphy, ʿAlī b. Hilāl, known as Ibn al-Bawwāb (d. 413/1022) improved Ibn Muqla's style by increasing its elegance. In charge of the library of the Buwayhid Bahāʾ al-Dawla in the city of Shīrāz, Ibn al-Bawwāb was very pious and could recite the Qurʾān by heart. He appears to have made sixty-four copies of the Qurʾān, one of which, signed by him, is still extant: Dated 391/1000-1, it is conserved in the Chester Beatty Library in Dublin where it is possible to admire the aesthetic quality of its letters as well as the beauty of its illumination. D.S. Rice has, in a detailed study of the manuscript, demonstrated its authenticity. The style Ibn al-Bawwāb created is known as *naskhī.*

More than two centuries later, another calligrapher succeeded in surpassing Ibn al-Bawwāb. Yāqūt al-Mustaʿṣimī (d. 697/1298), known as the "sultan of calligraphers," brought Ibn al-Bawwābs *naskhī* to its apogee. Several manuscripts by this great artist have survived, among them one dated 685/1285, which was written in Baghdad in *rayḥānī* (a variety of *naskhī*) and bears witness to the exactness of his skill, as well as the suppleness and lightness of his hand. To attain this quality of writing, al-Mustaʿṣimī cut the tip of his reed at an angle so that it barely touched the paper. In the ornamental band at the head of each sūra, the title — written in oriental Kūfic — is outlined. Thus it appears in white on a blue background adorned with golden arabesque. A flower with slightly gyron-like petals separates each verse.

Cursive scripts multiplied in centers of calligraphy attached to the courts of princes and sultans; these scripts apparently received their name according to their size. It should also be noted that all of these scripts are vocalized. Particular care has been given to the slope of the *fatḥa*s and *kasra*s which are slightly oblique and at the same angle. According to F. Déroche, the six most "fundamental" varieties are the following:

— *naskhī,* the most common and widely used style throughout the centuries, is a medium-sized cursive. The base line is always horizontal but sometimes broken to allow a new beginning at a slightly higher level for characters starting inside the tail of a preceding letter. This style is easily recognized by its *alif,* the shape of which is reduced to a simple, vertical segment with a beveled upper end and a pointed, slightly tapered lower end. The tails have fairly small curves protruding under the next character which thus must be written slightly higher. The longevity of this style explains the many varieties it has. A great number of qur'ānic manuscripts from the Ottoman era were written in *naskhī* as witnessed in the numerous examples of the Bibliothèque Nationale de Paris now conserved in the Grande Bibliothèque de France (see the examples in the Déroche catalogue, nos. 88-120).

— the *rayḥānī* and *muḥaqqaq* scripts seem to present only slight differences. Déroche reserves the term *muḥaqqaq* for larger scripts whereas M. Lings gives the name of *rayḥānī* to some large types (see no. 85 of his catalogue). In *rayḥānī*, the characters appear more packed together than in *muḥaqqaq*. In both styles, the *alif* has a small hook at the upper end and terminates in a slightly curved point below. The tails pointing leftwards have such slight curves that they sometimes convey the impression of being oblique, especially in the cases of the *mīm* and the *wāw*. Nevertheless, the tails pointing towards the right (like *jīm, ḥā', khā', 'ayn*) and dropping well below the line, have very ample curves. These two styles were in favor among the Ilkhānids and the Tīmūrids (see the superb examples of *muḥaqqaq* in Ling's catalogue [nos. 45-51] and *rayḥānī* [nos. 81-85]). For another example of *muḥaqqaq*, mention can be made of the manuscript copied in 707/1307 by the great master Muḥammad b. Aybak for the Ilkhānid sultan Ūljāytū (r. 703-16/1304-16), preserved in the library of the Top Kapı Sarayı in Istanbul (no. 46). It has a large format (72 x 50 cm) and one of the two pages reproduced has alternating lines of handwritten characters, one in gold ink with a black-ribboned edge and the other in black ink with a golden edge. The rosettes embellishing the margins of the pages are very delicate and quite beautiful.

For examples of *rayḥānī*, mention can be made of the qur'ānic manuscripts copied in 827/1424 and 834/1440 by the great calligrapher Ibrāhīm Sulṭān b. Shāhrūkh b. Tīmūr. Richly illuminated under the supervision of the grandson of Tīmūr Leng, they also offer pages entirely written in gold (those of the Fātiḥa [q.v.]) in an illuminated frame in which gold is matched with blue. A detail concerning sūra titles should be added: The type of script selected for these titles is generally oriental Kūfic. A cursive style has rarely been retained but when this is the case, *thuluth* was chosen (see below). Within the classification of these two scripts, one can include some Mamlūk manuscripts also written in gold ink with frontispieces richly illuminated with geometrical motifs and interlaces that encircle fine golden arabesque which stand out against a blue or red background (cf. M. Lings, nos. 52-59).

— *thuluth*, rather similar to *muḥaqqaq*, is easily recognized by the triangular profile of the upper ends of the *alif* and the very tapered, and sometimes curved, lower end. It is rarely used in the calligraphy of the Qur'ān except for sūra titles (see above). It is equally favored by artists who reproduce "mirrored" qur'ānic verses on mosque walls, thanks to the possibility of giving its tails a tapered curve that intertwines with the down-strokes of other characters (see examples in H. Massoudi, pp. 103 and 104).

— the last two styles considered fundamental by F. Déroche are *tawqī'* and *riq'a* (sometimes vocalized as *ruq'a*); he underlines the links between these two styles and *thuluth*. Few qur'ānic manuscripts have been calligraphed in these styles.

The qur'ānic script originating in the western provinces of the Islamicate should be classified separately. In fact, this script has features of both classical Kūfic and some clearly cursive characteristics. The designation as Andalusian Kūfic for manuscripts copied in Andalusia or North African Kūfic for those copied in Ifrīqiyya or the Maghrib bears witness to the links binding them to the classical Kūfic in spite of the suppleness of certain types of characters. Lings defines this style as the first which stems directly from Kūfic and qualifies it as occidental Kūfic, contrasting it with the earlier oriental Kūfic. This style was known in Ifrīqiyya from the time of the Qurʾān calligraphed by ʿAlī al-Warrāq in 410/1019-20 for the wet nurse of the Zīrid prince al-Muʿizz b. Bādis (r. 407-54/1016-62), which was doubtlessly copied in Qayrawān where it is still preserved in the new museum of Raqqāda. The alphabetic repertoire of this type of large and massive script resembles that of oriental Kūfic: the same ruptures in the horizontal base-line by ligatures in the shape of triangular dots, characters with oblique teeth, characters with non-circular curls varying from the triangle to the square pointed forwards and with small eyes. All these characteristics belong to oriental Kūfic but certain particularities distinguish the two styles: the slight bending of the small oblique teeth, the inflection of median *jīm* and *ḥāʾ*, intersecting curves of the *lām-alif* and the slender and disproportionate tail of the *nūn* with its broad, angular, lance-shaped end. Classical Kūfic was also known and used in Ifrīqiyya as witnessed by examples from the mosque of Qayrawān and, in particular, one superbly calligraphed Qurʾān in gold on parchment tinted in indigo.

A number of particularities of classical Kūfic are clearly perceptible in North African-Andalusian Kūfic: the horizontal and rigid writing line and the great number of ligatures, the verticality and fineness of the down-strokes of the *alif* and *lām*, the open rectangular shapes of *dāl/dhāl* and *kāf* along with the stretching out of the body of certain characters. On the other hand, some features clearly refer to cursive writing, like certain supple or slightly dented ligatures, the *rāʾ* with a very open curve, the rounded teeth of the *sīn/shīn*, the flattened ovals of the *ṣād/ḍād, ṭāʾ/ẓāʾ*, the large semi-circular and sometimes slightly broken tails surrounding several characters, which give a rhythm to the base-line. In other respects, an old writing practice remains in practice in the diacritics of this writing style: The dot of the *fāʾ* is always placed below the letter whereas the *qāf* has only one dot placed above the letter. Some of these manuscripts (e.g. nos. 95-98 in the collection published by Lings) are written in large characters and have only a few lines per page (5-9) while certain others (nos. 99, 102 and 103 of the same catalogue) are written in an extremely fine script and have up to 27 lines on a page for qurʾānic manuscripts of a similar size. Splendid frontispieces with richly ornate bands, titles written in gold, series of medallions or small rosettes embellished with fine arabesques in the margin contribute to the beauty and majesty of these manuscripts (see in particular the frontispieces of nos. 100 and 101 of the Qurʾān of Valencia, copied by ʿAbdallāh b. ʿAṭūs in 578/1182).

A few words must be said about the use of qurʾānic calligraphy in epigraphy (q.v.). Its function is both educational and ornamental. It is educational because the choice of reproduced verses reminds the believers of the great truths of the Islamic faith (q.v.); this choice is adapted to the type of education religious authorities want to further (see TRADITIONAL DISCIPLINES OF QURʾĀNIC STUDY). It is ornamental because it is linked to religious architecture where it constitutes one of the essential decorative elements (see ART AND ARCHITECTURE). The bands decorated with qurʾānic verses surround the upper part of the walls of prayer rooms in mosques, *madrasa*s and mausoleums, frame the *miḥrāb*s, crown the arcades of mosque courtyards and make the shafts of minarets more attractive; they generate the composition of stone rosettes that decorate some portals and, inscribed on funerary stelae (see BURIAL), they accompany the faithful to the gates of the hereafter.

From the very outset, calligraphed verses of the Qurʾān have contributed to the beauty of monuments, like the superb, 240 meter-long band decorating both sides of the arcade around the rock of the Qubbat al-Ṣakhra (the Dome of the Rock; see AQṢĀ MOSQUE) in Jerusalem. The style, a form of classical Kūfic adapted to the material (see MATERIAL CULTURE AND THE QURʾĀN), became the prototype of the Kūfic used in official Umayyad inscriptions. Executed in gold mosaic on a blue background, the angular *ductus* of the characters is naturally more accentuated than in manuscripts (see MANUSCRIPTS OF THE QURʾĀN), but the shape and proportions of the letters correspond generally to the same norms. Throughout the centuries, qurʾānic calligraphy on stone (q.v.) has followed, more or less, the development of manuscript calligraphy, though sometimes with a certain delay. It has, however, made its own contributions to the efflorescence of character ornamentation (see ORNAMENT AND ILLUMINATION): The down-strokes intersect, curve, turn over and are stretched to create interlaces that balance the empty spaces in the band. Their ends are enriched with leaves, flowers, palmettes or foliage; the bodies of the letters are adorned with indentations, knots, strapwork or vegetal elements; their tails go up in elegant curves and counter curves and their ornate ends add to the whole decorative impression of the band.

At the end of the fourth/tenth century, cursive qurʾānic calligraphy appeared in stone inscriptions in the eastern provinces during the same period in which it appeared in manuscripts; it was often found in combination with Kūfic script and then finally replaced it. Its development was rapid and it attained a degree of perfection comparable to that of manuscripts. Examples are the so-called throne verse (see THRONE OF GOD) that frames the *miḥrāb* of the Arslanhan mosque in Ankara (seventh/thirteenth century) in *thuluth* with characters that stand out against a background of arabesque and flowers (G. Akurga et al., *Trésors de Turquie,* 132); at the Sukulu mosque in Istanbul (tenth/sixteenth century), one can find the four verses of Sūrat al-Ikhlāṣ (Q 112) written in *thuluth* and arranged in a circle embellishing the rosette of the portal. The radiating strokes of the *alifs* and *lāms* are interlaced into strapwork and open out into a star-shaped composition at the center of the rosette (H. Massoudi, *La calligraphie,* 74 and 110).

Qurʾānic calligraphy remains the most specific expression of Islamic aesthetics. Taken in its entirety, it is an astounding combination that embraces the geometrical rigidity of the Kūfic characters, the fantasy in the rhythm of the inscribed lines, the contrastive sobriety of lines and lavishness of illuminations, the subtle harmony of proportions and supple elegance of the cursive characters; and the delicacy of foliages and arabesques that interlace with the letters. In the eyes of a Muslim, qurʾānic calligraphy is the visible form of the revealed word, an achievement in which artists and faithful are united in their search for the unspeakable and the ineffable.

Solange Ory

Bibliography

N. Abbott, *The rise of the north Arabian script and its ḳurʾānic development with a full description of the Ḳurʾān manuscripts in the Oriental Institute,* Chicago 1939; E. Akurga, C. Mango, and R. Ettinghausen, *Trésors de Turquie, Skira,* Geneva 1966; F. Déroche, Les écritures coraniques anciennes. Bilan et perspectives, in *REI* 48 (1980), 207-24 (its excellent bibliography is useful for earlier works); id., *Catalogue des manuscrits arabes. Deuxième partie, manuscrits musulmans. Tome I/1, Les manuscrits du Coran. Aux origines de la calligraphie coranique,* Paris 1983; *Tome I/2, Les manuscrits du Coran. Du Maghreb à l'Insulinde,* Paris 1985; id., L'écriture arabe dans le Grundriss der Arabischen Philologie, in *REI* 53 (1985), 325-9; id., Les premiers manuscrits, in *Le monde de la Bible — Le Coran et la Bible,* 115 (1998), 32-7; O. Grabar, *The mediation of ornament. The A.W. Mellon lectures in the fine arts,* 1989, Princeton/Washington 1992 (ch. ii, The intermediary of writing, 47-119); Institut du Monde Arabe/Bibliothèque Nationale, *Splendeur et majesté. Corans de la Bibliothèque Nationale,* Paris 1987; M. Lings, *The qur'ānic art of calligraphy and illumination,* Westerham, Kent 1976; H. Massoudi, *La calligraphie arabe vivante,* Paris 1981; Ṣ. al-Munajjid, *Tarīkh al-khaṭṭ al-ʿarabī mundhu l-bidāyat ilā nihāyat al-ʿaṣr al-umawī,* Beirut 1972; D.S. Rice, *The unique Ibn al-Bawwāb ms. in the Chester Beatty Library,* Dublin 1955; H.S.S. Sabah et al., *Maṣāḥif Ṣanʿāʾ, 19 March-19 May* 1985, Kuwait 1985; A.-M. Schimmel, *Islamic calligraphy,* Leiden 1970; N. Zayn al-Dīn, *Atlas of Arabic calligraphy,* Baghdad 1968.

Camel

A large, ruminant mammal used for carrying burdens and for riding in the desert regions of Asia and Africa. The central Asiatic species has two humps on its back, while the Arabian camel, or dromedary, has only one. The presence of this animal in the Near East and North Africa appears to date back to the third millennium B.C.E., although there is no evidence of the domesticated dromedary prior to the 11th century B.C.E. (cf. H. von Wissmann, Badw). The camel played an important role in sacrifices (see SACRIFICE; CONSECRATION OF ANIMALS): Before Muḥammad's time, they were ritually slaughtered at the time of the pilgrimage (q.v.) to Mecca (q.v.; see also PRE-ISLAMIC ARABIA AND THE QURʾĀN; cf. J. Chelhod, *Sacrifice*). As the camel was an integral part of the Arabs' (q.v.) daily life, not only as a means of transportation, but also as a source of food (see FOOD AND DRINK) and clothing (q.v.), they developed a rich vocabulary for this animal. Many of these terms are not solely proper designations for the animal *per se,* but rather describe aspects of its appearance or its various stages of growth. Although the numerous words for camel are preserved in Arabic poetry and lexicography, only four of the names appear in the Qurʾān (cf. C. Pellat, Ibil).

Baʿīr, the generic term for camel, male or female, is mentioned in the Qurʾān in the story of Joseph (q.v.), and solely in connection with a measure (see WEIGHTS AND MEASURES): "We have lost the king's cup, and whoever brings it shall have a camel-load *(ḥamlu baʿīrin)*..." (Q 12:72; cf. 12:65). The most common Arabic word for the male camel, *jamal,* is mentioned only once in the Qurʾān: "Verily for those who have counted our signs (q.v.) false and been too proud to receive them, the gates of heaven (q.v.) will not be opened, nor will they enter the garden (q.v.), until a camel *(jamal)* passes through the eye of a needle *(fī sammi l-khiyāt);* so do we recompense the sinners" (Q 7:40). In reference to this single occurrence, most qurʾānic commentators read the Arabic word as *jamal* (as in *Matt* 19:24; *Luke* 18:25, repeated here with other terms) while they vocalize the word for the "eye" of the needle *(samm)* either with *a* or with *u (summ)* as noted by the tenth-century exegete al-Ṭabarī (d. 310/923; *Tafsīr,* viii, 130-2). Another possible reading of the consonantal structure *j-m-l* is *jummal* (i.e. a thick cord) but this rendition is an isolated occurrence in the exegetical literature. As a consequence of the reading of *jamal,* commentators ordinarily provide extensive descriptions of the camel in their commentaries on this verse.

A female camel *(nāqa)* appears in the stories of the prophet Ṣāliḥ (q.v.) and the Thamūd (q.v.): "And to Thamūd [we sent] their brother Ṣāliḥ. He said, 'Oh people!

Worship God, for there is no other god for you. Evidence from your lord has come to you. This is the she-camel *(nāqa)* of God as a sign for you. Let her eat in the land of God, and do not molest her lest a painful retribution afflict you'" (Q 7:73). However, the Thamūd disregard their prophet's warning (q.v.) and hamstring the camel. For this violation of his commandment (see COMMANDMENTS), God destroys them with an earthquake (cf. Q 7:77-8; 11:64-8; 17:59; 26:155-8; 54:27-31; 91:11-4; see PUNISHMENT STORIES).

The exegesis of the fourth qur'ānic term for camel, *ibil* (cf. Q 6:144), demonstrates the elasticity of the Arabic language (q.v.). A feminine word, *ibil,* is used for the species and the group. However, Q 88:17, which alludes to the creation (q.v.) of the camel *(ibil),* is understood by some interpreters to be a reference to the creation of the clouds. One example of a qur'ānic designation of a camel, which does not allude so much to an image of the animal itself as to a condition of that animal, is the camel that is in the tenth month of her pregnancy (*'ishār,* Q 81:4). This image is often invoked in Islamic apocalyptic literature (see APOCALYPSE), recalling its Arabian origins.

Popular beliefs about the camel abounded and have survived in classical Islamic exegetical literature. Some examples of these beliefs, testified by Ibn Qutayba (d. 276/889) and al-Jāḥiẓ (d. 255/868-9), among others, are that the animal descended from demons and that the jinn (q.v.) could take on the form of a camel, which urinated backwards so as not to soil Abraham (q.v.).

The camel, often dubbed "the ship of the desert," is one of the most important animals for Bedouins (see BEDOUIN) and very early it captured the interest of ancient Arab poets (see POETRY AND POETS). They considered no other companion more trustworthy and persevering than the camel, both for their settled and for their nomadic life-styles (see NOMADS). For this reason the Arabs of antiquity accumulated particular designations and descriptions of the camel and poets surpassed themselves in characterizing this animal's attributes (see especially the *mu'allaqa* poem by Ṭarafa b. al-'Abd, fl. sixth century C.E.; see also LITERATURE AND THE QUR'ĀN).

R.G. Khoury

Bibliography
Primary: Ṭabarī, *Tafsīr,* i, 359-66.
Secondary: R. Bulliet, *The camel and the wheel,* Cambridge, MA 1975, repr. New York 1990; J. Chelhod, *Le sacrifice chez les Arabes,* Paris 1955; Horovitz, *KU,* 146-8; Jeffery, *For. vocab.,* 74-5; A.Th. Khoury, *Der Koran Arabisch-Deutsch Übersetzung und wissenschaftlicher Kommentar,* 9 vols. (to date), Gütersloh 1991-, vii, 73; R.G. Khoury, Babylon in der ältesten Version über die Geschichte der Propheten im Islam, in G. Mauer and U. Magen (eds.), *Alter Orient und Altes Testamen 220 (1988). Ad bene et fideliter seminandum. Festgabe für Karlheinz Deller zum 21 februar 1987,* Kevelaer 1988, 123-4; id., *'Umāra b. Waṯīma b. Mūsā al-Fārisī. Les légendes prophétiques dans l'Islam depuis le I. jusqu'au III. siècle de l'Hégire avec éd. critique du texte* Kitāb Bad' al-khalq wa-qiṣaṣ al-anbiyā', Wiesbaden 1978, 237-43; id., *Wahb b. Munabbih. 1. Der Heidelberger Papyrus PSR Heid Arab 23. Leben und Werk des Dichters. (Codices Arabici Antiqui 1),* Weisbaden 1972, 232; C. Pellat, Ḥayawān, in *EI²,* iii, 304-9; id., Ibil, in *EI²,* iii, 665-8; H. Schwarzbaum, *Biblical and extra-biblical legends in Islamic folk literature,* Walldorf-Hessen 1982; H. von Wissmann, Badw II. The history of the origin of nomadism in its geographical aspect. d. The appearance of camel nomadism in North Africa, in *EI²,* i, 887-9.

Camphor

A white, translucent substance distilled from the wood of the camphor tree *(Cinnamomum camphora,* family *Lauraceae)* which is indigenous to China, Taiwan and Japan. The term camphor *(kāfūr, qāfūr, qaf[f]ūr)* denotes the tree, its resin and its drug.

South and southeast Asian designations of these botanical products include Indian *karpūra, kappūra* or Malayan *kapur*. It is attested once in the Qurʾān at Q 76:5. Besides the qurʾānic *kāfūr* there are references to the spelling with *qāf* instead of *kāf* in works of qurʾānic commentary (Ālūsī, *Rūḥ*, xxix, 154; Qurṭubī, *Jāmiʿ*, xix, 124; for further variants see M. Ullmann, *Wörterbuch*, i, 10b).

The single relevant verse, Q 76:5, reads: "Surely the pious shall drink of a cup whose mixture *(mizāj)* is camphor *(kāfūr)*." Among the classical exegetes, Fakhr al-Dīn al-Rāzī (d. 606/1210) and al-Qurṭubī (d. 671/1272) explain that this verse cannot mean that the liquid really contains camphor because it would not have a good taste (*lā yakūnu ladhīdhan*, Rāzī, *Tafsīr*, xxx, 240) or, respectively, one does not drink this drug (*lā yushrabu*, Qurṭubī, *Jāmiʿ*, xix, 123). According to this and other classical exegesis on the verse, the liquid to which reference is made is only similar to camphor *(ka-kāfūr)*. It has some of the camphor qualities, i.e. its fragrance *(ṭīb)* and its scent *(rāʾiḥa)*, its whiteness and coolness (Ṭabarī, *Tafsīr*, xxviii, 112-3; Ibn Kathīr, *Tafsīr*, vii, 179-80; Qurṭubī, *Jāmiʿ*, xix, 123-4). It does not, however, have its harmful effect (*maḍarr*, Ṭabarī, *Tafsīr*, xxviii, 112; Rāzī, *Tafsīr*, xxx, 240). Again al-Rāzī (*Tafsīr*, xxx, 240) and al-Qurṭubī (*Jāmiʿ*, xix, 123) emphasize that it does not have its taste. Taking into consideration the beginning of the next verse, Q 76:6, "A fountain whereat drink the servants of God..." where the first word, "fountain" (*ʿaynan*, see FOUNTAINS), is in grammatical apposition to *kāfūran*, all the above-mentioned exegetes explain that there is a fountain in paradise (q.v.) called the camphor fountain. In his contemporary commentary the German scholar, R. Paret, like others, considers the drink mentioned in Q 76:5 to be wine (see INTOXICANTS) mixed with camphor-flavored water.

In the olfactory classification of the eight basic odors, camphor is qualified as spicy (G. Ohloff, *Düfte*, 14). According to the pharmacological humoral theory of the four elements (cold-warm, dry-moist) which should be in harmony in a healthy body, and the corresponding qualities of drugs, it is classified as cold and dry in the third degree (L. Leclerc, *Ibn el-Beïthar*, iii, no. 1868, 128). Camphor is often used as a metaphor for white. The Indian perfume-tradition obtained — already 5000 years ago by a primitive method of distillation — scented waters from camphor. At the same time in China, the wood of the tree was burnt with other incenses. There camphor has long been one of the most important scents, used not only as a remedy, but also in a ritual context, e.g. embalming. Within the Islamic tradition can be found ḥadīths which refer to the use of camphor to wash the corpse (Nasāʾī, *Sunan*, iv, no. 1890), a practice that can still be found in Muslim countries (see BURIAL; DEATH AND THE DEAD). Besides its use as an aromatic, camphor offers a wide range of medicinal qualities (cf. L. Leclerc, *Ibn el-Beïthar*, iii, no. 1868, 129-30). It remains an ingredient in cosmetic compounds, ointments and rubbing alcohol.

Hanne Schönig

Bibliography

Primary: Ālūsī, *Rūḥ;* Ibn Kathīr, *Tafsīr;* Nasāʾī, *Sunan;* Qurṭubī, *Jāmiʿ;* Rāzī, *Tafsīr;* Ṭabarī, *Tafsīr*.
Secondary: Arberry; A. Dietrich, Kāfūr, in *EI²*, iv, 417-8; L. Leclerc, *Traité des simples par Ibn el-Beïthar. Notices et extraits des manuscrits de la Bibliothèque Nationale et autres bibliothèques*, 3 vols., Paris 1877-83; G. Ohloff, *Irdische Düfte himmlische Lust. Eine Kulturgeschichte der Duftstoffe*, Frankfurt 1996; Paret; M. Ullmann and A. Spitaler (eds.), *Wörterbuch der Klassischen Arabischen Sprache*, Wiesbaden 1970.

Cape see CLOTHING

Capital Punishment see BOUNDARIES AND PRECEPTS

Captives

Persons who are captured in an act of war and whose lives are in the hands of the captor. According to Islamic law a captive may be killed, enslaved or returned for ransom. The Qurʾān refers to captives directly as *asīr* (pl. *asrā, asārā* or *usarāʾ*), the literal meaning of which is "one who is shackled" (cf. Q 2:185; 18:73; 94:5, 6). *Raqaba* (pl. *riqāb*), literally "nape of the neck," is used six times (cf. Q 2:177; 5:89; 9:60; 47:4; 58:3; 90:13) to refer to captives or slaves synecdochically; the verb *taʾsirūna*, "you make captive," is found in Q 33:26 (see SLAVES AND SLAVERY).

Pre-Islamic rules of warfare (see WAR; PRE-ISLAMIC ARABIA AND THE QURʾĀN) involved small raiding parties rather than full-scale battles. This practice was well-known to Muḥammad who used such raids to great effect in his campaigns (see EXPEDITIONS AND BATTLES) against the Meccans after his emigration to Medina (*hijra*, see EMIGRATION). References to captives from the Medinan period of the Qurʾān (see CHRONOLOGY AND THE QURʾĀN) are all in the context of such raids and some may be connected with specific events, such as Q 33:26, which commentators connect with the killing and enslaving of members of the Qurayẓa (q.v.) tribe in Medina (q.v.). Other references are more vague but seem to refer to a strategy of engaging in more violent raids before taking captives (see Q 8:67).

In the Meccan period, the only mention of *asīr* is in a list of actions undertaken by the "servants of God:" "For the love of [God], they give food to the poor, the orphan, and the *asīr*" (Q 76:8). There is some debate in the commentaries as to whether this verse refers to captives or prisoners, but compare similar lists at Q 2:177 and 9:60. The former reads: "The pious (see PIETY) is the one who believes in God, and the last day (see APOCALYPSE; ESCHATOLOGY; LAST JUDGMENT), the angels (q.v.), the book (q.v.), and the prophets (see PROPHETS AND PROPHETHOOD), and who shares wealth (q.v.), for the love of [God], with relatives (see KINSHIP), orphans (q.v.), the poor (see POVERTY AND THE POOR), the traveler, beggars, and with the *riqāb*." In this case, al-Zamakhsharī (d. 538/1144; *Kashshāf*, i, 217-8) and others gloss sharing wealth with the *riqāb* as "helping *mukātab* slaves... or ransoming captives *(fakka l-usarā)*." While the ransoming of captives of war (see HOSTAGES) seems reasonable for the qurʾānic period, recent scholarship has questioned the commentators' implicit assertion that the institution of *mukātab* slaves (i.e. slaves who have entered into a contract of emancipation with their masters) was already established (J. Brockopp, 183-221; P. Crone, 64-76). Further, scholars continue to debate the ways in which Meccan society distinguished among captives, slaves, clients *(mawālī)* and allies *(ḥulafāʾ)*, all of whom were in a dependent relationship with the tribal unit (see TRIBES AND CLANS; CLIENTS AND CLIENTAGE).

That captives were a known source for slaves is demonstrated by Joseph's (q.v.) capture and sale in the Joseph narrative (Q 12:19-20). Of the many Companions of the Prophet (q.v.) who were slaves, only Ṣuhayb b. Sinān (d. 38/659) appears to have been an actual captive, though the accounts are contradictory (see Ibn Isḥāq, *Sīra*, i, 488-9). During the conquests (q.v.) in the years following the death of Muḥammad, Medina and Damascus were flooded with thousands of captives, leading to significant slave markets in these and other cities. Since Islamic law forbids enslaving Muslims, capture from outlying, non-Muslim territories was essential to maintaining slave populations.

Jonathan E. Brockopp

Bibliography
Primary: Ibn Isḥāq, *Sīra;* Zamakhsharī, *Kashshāf.*
Secondary: J.E. Brockopp, *Early Mālikī law. Ibn ʿAbd al-Ḥakam and his* Major compendium of jurisprudence, Leiden 2000; id., *Slavery in Islamic law,* Ph.D. diss., Yale 1995; R. Brunschvig, ʿAbd, in *EI²*, i, 24-40; P. Crone, *Roman, provincial and Islamic law,* Cambridge 1987; M. Kister, The massacre of the Banū Qurayẓa. A re-examination of a tradition, in *JSAI* 8 (1986), 61-96; H. Müller, Sklaven, in *HO 6/6/1. Wirtschaftsgeschichte des Vorderen Orients in islamischer Zeit,* 53-83; D. Pipes, *Slave soldiers and Islam,* New Haven 1981; R. Roberts, *The social laws of the Qorân,* London 1925.

Caravan

A company of travelers on a journey through a desert or hostile region; also, the vehicles which transport the company. The most prominent qurʾānic word denoting a "caravan" is *ʿīr,* which occurs three times in Q 12, "Joseph" (Sūrat Yūsuf; Q 12:70, 82, 94). Arabic lexicographers say that originally this term denoted camels, asses or mules that carried provisions of corn but that it was later applied to any caravan (see CAMEL). Some say, however, that in the Qurʾān it signifies asses not camels (Lane, q.v. *ʿīr*) which does not comply with the biblical version of the story of Joseph (q.v.) where camels are mentioned explicitly (*Gen* 37:25). In the qurʾānic story of Joseph, a caravan is also called *sayyāra* (Q 12:10, 19) which recalls the Hebrew *shayyāra*. However, lexicographers explain this term as coming from the Arabic root *s-y-r* in the sense of *jamāʿa sayyāra:* "a company of persons journeying" (Lane, q.v. *s-y-r*).

Muslim commentators have also discovered an allusion to caravans in Q 106 (Sūrat Quraysh; Q 106:2), in which the "journey of the winter and the summer" is mentioned (see JOURNEY; TRIPS AND VOYAGES). In English translations of the Qurʾān, the "journey" *(riḥla)* is often rendered as "caravan" (e.g. Arberry). Commentators usually identify the journeys of the winter and the summer with the commercial caravans of pre-Islamic Meccan traders (see PRE-ISLAMIC ARABIA AND THE QURʾĀN). The winter journey is ordinarily said to have set out to Yemen (q.v.) and the summer journey to Syria (q.v.). Less current interpretations say that both journeys were to destinations in Syria. The leaders of Quraysh (q.v.), who are said to have initiated the journeys while obtaining pacts of security for their travels, were heads of prominent Meccan clans and mainly the sons of ʿAbd Manāf: Hāshim, al-Muṭṭalib, ʿAbd Shams and Nawfal (see TRIBES AND CLANS). The reports about them may reflect political tensions between their respective Muslim descendants (U. Rubin, Ilāf, 170-1; see POLITICS AND THE QURʾĀN). A less commercial perception of the winter and summer journey is reflected in interpretations to the effect that Quraysh carried them out not merely for trade but also for pleasure and recreation. In summer they reportedly used to travel to cool places in Yemen, Syria or al-Ṭāʾif and in winter they went to warmer places in Syria. Conversely, other interpretations hold that the journeys did not start from Mecca (q.v.) but rather ended there. These were journeys of pilgrims coming to Mecca from various zones twice a year to perform the *ʿumra* and the *ḥajj,* i.e. the lesser and the greater pilgrimage respectively (U. Rubin, Ilāf, 174, n. 59; see PILGRIMAGE). Implicit here is the notion that pilgrimage and commerce are closely associated.

Most modern scholars have tended to adopt the commercial interpretation of the winter and summer journey and infer from them that Mecca of the sixth century C.E. rose to the position of an important center of transit trade (e.g. M.J. Kister, Mecca and Tamīm, 120). This has been challenged by Patricia Crone who, relying on the variety of inner contradictions in the suggested interpretations, has observed that "the exegetes had no better knowledge of what this sura meant than we have today" (*Meccan trade,* 210).

Whatever the case may be, the Qurʾān mentions the winter and the summer caravan journey that Quraysh performed regularly in order to illustrate a divine benevolence that is consequent upon belief in God (see BLESSING; BELIEF AND UNBELIEF).

Uri Rubin

Bibliography
Primary: ʿAbd al-Raḥmān b. Muḥammad b. Abī ʿĀṣim, *Tafsīr al-Qurʾān al-ʿaẓīm,* ed. A.M. al-Ṭayyib, 10 vols., Riyadh 1997, x, no. 19491; Hūd b. Muḥakkam, *Tafsīr,* iv, 536; Māwardī, *Nukat,* vi, 347.
Secondary: H. Birkeland, *The Lord guideth,* Uppsala 1956, 102-30; P. Crone, *Meccan trade and the rise of Islam,* Princeton 1987, 205-9; M.J. Kister, Mecca and Tamīm, in *JESHO* 8 (1965), 329-56 (repr. in M.J. Kister, *Studies in Jāhiliyya and early Islam,* London 1980); Lane; I. Mahmood, Social and economic conditions in pre-Islamic Mecca, in *IJMES* 14 (1982), 343-58; F.E. Peters, The commerce of Mecca before Islam, in F. Kazemi and R.D. McChesney (eds.), *A way prepared. Essays on Islamic culture in honor of Richard Bayly Winder,* New York 1988, 3-26; id., *Muhammad and the origins of Islam,* Albany 1994, 68-75; U. Rubin, The *īlāf* of Quraysh. A study of sūra cvi, in *Arabica* 31 (1984), 165-88.

Carcass
see CARRION

Carpet
see MATERIAL CULTURE AND THE QURʾĀN

Carrion

The putrefying flesh of a carcass. The Arabic term is *mayta,* from the verbal root meaning "to die." Hence the word is used in an adjectival sense as in Q 36:33: "The dead earth *(al-arḍ al-mayta)* is a sign for them. We have brought it to life [i.e. by means of rain]..." In all other qurʾānic instances, the term refers specifically to carrion, one of the Islamic food taboos supported also in prophetic traditions (see FOOD AND DRINK; FORBIDDEN).

E. Lane's definition of *mayta* includes both animals which have died a natural death (explicitly *mayta,* as in Q 2:173; 5:3; 6:139, 145; 16:115) and those killed in a state or manner different from that prescribed by the religious law (see LAW AND THE QURʾĀN). In the latter situation the circumlocution is used, "over which has been invoked a name other than that of God" (as in all the above-mentioned references except Q 6:139; see CONSECRATION OF ANIMALS). Thus the term carrion may be applied where either the agent or the animal killed may not meet prescribed conditions, as for example, a person who slaughters an animal in a state of ritual purity (*iḥrām,* see RITUAL PURITY) or an animal sacrificed to an idol (see IDOLS AND IMAGES; SACRIFICE). The prohibition of carrion in these two senses (to which one could add the refinements of Q 5:3 that include animals who died from asphyxiation, a beating, a fall or being gored) is mentioned along with the religious taboos against eating blood and pork meat. An exception is made (Q 16:115; 6:145) when one might be forced to consume any of these prohibited substances under duress. Q 6:139 also suggests that a fetal or stillborn animal could be lawfully eaten (see LAWFUL AND UNLAWFUL).

The ḥadīth literature expanded upon these few and brief qurʾānic references. Fish (and, according to some authorities, by extension all sea animals and birds) and locusts were deemed lawful since they required no ritual slaughter. According to the caliph ʿUthmān (q.v.; r. 23-35/644-56), doves could be slaughtered and were therefore governed by the conditions of *mayta.*

Among the traditions recounted by al-Bukhārī (d. 256/870) a shepherd slaughtered one of his flock after noticing that it was on the verge of death. Following consultation (q.v.) with the Prophet, the meat was permitted for consumption as slaughtering the dying animal had prevented it from becoming carrion. In another tradition, al-Bukhārī cites an episode in which an expedition of the Prophet's troops began to suffer severe hunger. They discovered a huge fish cast upon the shore which provided nourishment for several days. Upon their return to Medina, the incident was related to the Prophet who replied, "Eat of those things which God sends you" (cf. Q 5:4). This tradition offered an implicit extension of the qur'ānic context (Q 16:115), which dealt only with prohibited foods, and the tradition may also have helped settle what was considered a problematic case of fish. Other traditions prohibit the sale of meat and by-products from such prohibited carcasses though there was exegetical and legal discussion about the permissibility of using the skin.

Islamic restrictions governing food preparation and consumption are fewer than in Judaism (see JEWS AND JUDAISM). However, the context of the verses cited here reflects close adherence to Jewish religious tradition. In both, the name of God has to be invoked when an animal is slaughtered and blood — the essential life force given by God (see BLOOD AND BLOOD CLOT; LIFE) — cannot be consumed but must be poured out, returned to the earth (q.v.) whence it came.

David Waines

Bibliography

M. Benkheira, Chairs illicites en Islam. Essai d'interpretation anthropologique de la notion de *mayta,* in *SI* 84 (1996), 5-33; M. Cook, Early Islamic dietary law, in *JSAI* 7 (1986), 217-77; F. Dachraoui, A propos de l'ethique alimentaire traditionelle. Preceptes islamiques, in *Revue d'études Andalouses* 18 (1997), 47-62; E. Gräf, *Jagdbeute und Schlachttier im islamischen Recht. Eine untersuchung zur Entwicklung der islamischen Jurisprudenz,* Bonn 1959; R. Lobban, Pigs and their prohibition, in *IJMES* 26 (1994), 57-75; J. Schacht, Mayta, in *EI²,* vi, 924-6; A. Sharma, Licit food in Hindu and Islamic mysticism, in *Bulletin of the Henry Martin Institute of Islamic Studies* 8.4 (1985), 127-30.

Cattle see ANIMAL LIFE

Cave

A hollow space in a mountain or hill. The term cave *(kahf, ghār, maghārāt)* is used in the Qur'ān to designate a place of refuge for the faithful or a locus of intimate contact with God. *Kahf* occurs six times (Q 18:9, 10, 11, 16, 17, 25). *Ghār* and *maghārāt* (sing. *maghāra*) each occur once (Q 9:40, 57); lexicographers consider these latter terms to be synonymous with *kahf* or to be designations for small caves.

"The Cave" (Sūrat al-Kahf) is the title of Q 18, which consists of 110 verses. It refers to the story of the Companions of the Cave (vv. 9-26), an Arabic version of widely-circulated Christian accounts about the Seven Sleepers of Ephesus (see MEN OF THE CAVE). This version tells of a group of youths who, fearing persecution or death for their faith, fled to a cave with their dog (q.v.). God sheltered them there in a slumberous state for perhaps 309 years. When they awoke, they were discovered by their townspeople who decided to build a mosque over them and their hiding place. Muslim commentators and traditionists (Ṭabarī, *Tafsīr,* xv, 130-54; Thaʿlabī, *Qiṣaṣ,* 370-86; Zamakhsharī, *Kashshāf,* ii, 473-81; for Fakhr al-Dīn al-Rāzī's commentary on Q 18: 9-12, see R. Gramlich, Faḫr ad-Dīn ar-Rāzī) debate the meaning of the ambiguous qur'ānic narrative and embellish it with details from Christian accounts (see CHRISTIANS AND CHRISTIANITY; NARRATIVES). According to these sources, after the youths discovered that their religion had finally prevailed in their homeland, they blessed Theodosius, the faithful ruler, and returned to their death-like sleep to await the final resurrection (q.v.).

In the Qurʾān and its subsequent interpretation, this cave was understood to be a sanctuary for the faithful and a place where they enjoyed God's mercy (q.v.). It also represents the tomb from which the dead were to be resurrected. Ibn Isḥāq (d. 150/767; *Sīra*, i-ii, 302-3), a biographer of the Prophet, said that this story was revealed in response to challenges to Muḥammad's authenticity as a prophet and to his growing persecution in Mecca (q.v.; see also OPPOSITION TO MUḤAMMAD). It functioned as a proof of God's ability to revive the dead (see DEATH AND THE DEAD) but it was also to portend the emigration (q.v.; *hijra*) to either Abyssinia (q.v.) or Medina (q.v.). The cave thus signified the goal of emigration. For Ṣūfī commentators, it came to represent a place for spiritual retreat for the worldly body awaiting illumination from the divine spirit (see ṢŪFISM AND THE QURʾĀN). The modern commentator Sayyid Quṭb (d. 1966) saw it as a metaphor for the heart (q.v.) filled with faith (q.v.). The story of the Companions is also the subject of a play by the Egyptian playwright Tawfīq al-Ḥakīm (d. 1987) and was used by the Egyptian media to describe anti-government Islamist groups such as that led by Shukrī Muṣṭafā in Egypt during the 1970s. Muslim exegetical and geographical literature ordinarily followed the Christian placement of the Companions of the Cave at Ephesus in present-day Turkey (see GEOGRAPHY IN THE QURʾĀN). In addition to Ephesus, however, Muslims fixed the geographical site of the cave in various locations including the Muqaṭṭam hills in Cairo, Mount Qāsyūn in Damascus and even Tuyuk in Chinese Turkestan.

Caves were also the locations of pivotal moments in the life of Muḥammad. After periods of spiritual retreat, Muḥammad received his first revelations (see REVELATION AND INSPIRATION) from the angel Gabriel (q.v.; Q 96:1-5) in a small cave *(ghār)* on Mount Ḥirāʾ, according to reports attributed to ʿĀʾisha (Bukhārī, *Ṣaḥīḥ, Badʾ al-waḥy* 3, *Tafsīr sūra* 96; Ibn Saʿd, *Ṭabaqāt*, i, 194; Ṭabarī, *Tafsīr* xxx, 161; see ʿĀʾISHA BINT ABĪ BAKR). Through the centuries this site, which is located five miles north of Mecca near Minā, was visited by pilgrims who came for the pilgrimage (q.v.; *ḥajj*). It is mentioned in medieval texts (Azraqī, *Akhbār Makka*, i-ii, 204; Yaqūt, *Buldān*, ii, 228; Ibn Jubayr, *Travels*, 160) and modern pilgrim narratives (M. Faraḥānī, Safarnāmeh, 235-6; M. Haykal, *Manzil*, 228-46). Tradition also maintains that Q 77 was revealed to Muḥammad in a cave at Minā itself (Bukhārī, *Ṣaḥīḥ, Tafsīr sūra* 77).

Another noteworthy cave in Islamic tradition is on Mount Thawr, south of Mecca on the road to Yemen (q.v.). It was there, according to early accounts (Ibn Isḥāq, *Sīra*, i-ii, 485-6; Ibn Saʿd, *Ṭabaqāt*, i, 228-9; Ṭabarī, *Tafsīr*, x, 95-6), that Muḥammad and Abū Bakr secluded themselves for three nights during their emigration *(hijra)* to Medina to avoid capture by their Quraysh (q.v.) opponents. According to commentaries, this event is addressed in a late Medinan sūra: "If you do not help him [Muḥammad], God certainly will, as he did when the disbelievers expelled him and the second man. When they were in the cave, he said to his companion (see COMPANIONS OF THE PROPHET), 'Grieve not, for God is with us'" (Q 9:40). The spider's web and the dove's nest that God used to conceal them in the cave (according to Ibn

Saʿd, d. 230/845) became popular symbols of the emigration.

A cave was not a shelter for disbelievers and hypocrites, however (see HYPOCRITES AND HYPOCRISY). The Qurʾān states that they would like to flee to caves (*maghārāt*, cf. Q 9:57) and other places of refuge to escape divine retribution but God has readied a harsher abode (i.e. hell [*jahannam*], cf. Q 9:63, 68, 73) for them in the hereafter (see HELL; LAST JUDGMENT).

Juan Eduardo Campo

Bibliography
Primary: al-Azraqī, *Akhbār Makka wa-mā jāʾa fīhā min al-āthār*, ed. R.Ṣ. Malḥas, 2 vols. in 1, Beirut 1969; Bukhārī, *Ṣaḥīḥ*, 9 vols. in 3, Cairo 1957-60; M.Ḥ Farahānī, *A Shiʿite pilgrimage to Mecca, (1885-1886). The* Safarnāmeh *of Mirza Mohammad Hosayn Farahani*, ed., trans. and annotated by H. Farmayan and E.L. Daniel, Austin 1990; T. al-Ḥakīm, *Ahl al-kahf*, Cairo 1933; M.Ḥ. Haykal, *Fī manzil al-waḥy*, Cairo 1937, repr. 1986; Ibn Isḥāq, *Sīra* (recension of ʿAbd al-Mālik b. Hishām), ed. M. al-Ṣaqqā et al., 4 vols. in 2, Cairo 1955²; Ibn Jubayr, *The travels of Ibn Jubayr*, ed. W. Wright, Leiden 1907² (rev. by M.J. de Goeje); Ibn Saʿd, *Ṭabaqāt*, ed. Iḥsān ʿAbbās, 9 vols., Beirut 1957-8; Qutb, *Ẓilāl;* Ṭabarī, *Tafsīr;* Thaʿlabī, *Qiṣaṣ*, Beirut n.d.; Yaqūt, *Buldān;* Zamakhsharī, *Kashshāf.*
Secondary: M. Campanini, La Sūrah della Caverna. Meditazione filosofica sull'unicità di Dio, in *Pubblicazioni della Facoltà di Lettere e Filosofia dell'Università di Milano* 125 (1986), sect. 13; P. Dall'Oglio, *Speranze nell'Islām. Interpretazione della prospettiva escatologica di Corano XVIII*, Genoa 1991; R. Gramlich, Faḫr ad-Dīn ar-Rāzīs Kommentar zu Sure 18, 9-12, in *Asiatische Studien/Études asiatiques* 33 (1979), 99-152; I. Guidi, Seven sleepers, in *ERE*, xi, 428-30; R. Kriss and H. Kriss-Heinrich, *Volksglaube im Bereich des Islam*, 2 vols, Wiesbaden 1960; L. Massignon, Les sept dormants d'Ephèse *(ahl al-kahf)* en Islam et en Chrétienté, in *REI* 22 (1954), 59-112; Nadwī, Abū l-Ḥasan ʿAlī, *Faith versus materialism.* (*The message of* Surat-ul-Kahf), Lucknow 1972; H. Nibley, Qumran and the Companions of the Cave, in *Revue de Qumran* 5 (April 1965), 177-98; R. Paret, Aṣḥāb al-kahf, in *EI²*, i, 691.

Cave, Men of the see MEN OF THE CAVE

Celibacy see ABSTINENCE; CHASTITY

Ceremony see FESTIVALS

Chair see THRONE OF GOD

Challenges of Modern Science see SCIENCE AND THE QURʾĀN

Chance and Coincidence see MARVELS; OMENS; SECRETS; HIDDEN AND THE HIDDEN; THEOLOGY AND THE QURʾĀN

Chapters see SŪRA(S)

Charity see ALMSGIVING

Charm see AMULETS

Chastisement and Punishment

To discipline, especially by corporal means, as retribution for a wrong and incidentally for correction and prevention. "Chastisement" and "punishment" correspond to several Arabic terms used in the Qurʾān, e.g. *ʿadhāb, nakāl, ʿiqāb, jazāʾ* and their cognates, although, in addition to these discrete terms, the Qurʾān does use other expressions to convey the same meaning. The word *ʿadhāb* and its cognates appear in the Qurʾān over 350 times; *jazāʾ* and its cognates over 100 times; *ʿiqāb* and its cognates 26 times; and *nakāl* and its cognates four times. Considering the numerous qurʾānic stories of divine punishment meted out to those who rejected God's prophets, it is clear that divine chastisement — in this world and the next — is one of the most important topics in the Qurʾān.

While these terms have shared meanings, it is useful to distinguish them carefully. The most general of these terms is *ʿadhāb*, which al-Zamakhsharī (d. 538/1144; *Kashshāf*, i, 164-5) defines as any type of burdensome pain. More specifically, *ʿiqāb* is used to mean various forms of punishment while *nakāl* is used to refer particularly to exemplary punishment. Therefore while every *ʿiqāb* and *nakāl* is also a type of *ʿadhāb*, the opposite is not true — one can suffer some type of *ʿadhāb* that is not a punishment. Finally, *jazāʾ* carries the signification of "just deserts," i.e. the deserved consequences of one's actions, and can therefore be found in the sense of either chastisement or reward. These terms and their cognates appear in a variety of contexts in the Qurʾān and are employed to describe events both in this world and the next (see REWARD AND PUNISHMENT). When their use is related to events in this world, moreover, they apply equally to both divine and human acts. Finally, *ʿadhāb* and *nakāl* are used to describe punishments required by law, e.g. flogging (q.v.), which in Q 24:2 is the prescribed punishment for adultery (see ADULTERY AND FORNICATION) and the amputation of the hand of the thief, the qurʾānic punishment for theft (q.v.; cf. Q 5:38), but the use of these terms in this sense is extremely limited in the Qurʾān (see BOUNDARIES AND PRECEPTS; LAW AND THE QURʾĀN; STONING).

According to the Qurʾān, both humans and God share in the capacity to administer punishment (see JUDGMENT). Further, there is an acknowledgement of the destructive power of some events and processes. Consequently, theological reflection takes up the question of the cause of human calamities, attributing them variously to natural explanations and acts of divine judgment. This question presents a tension that is central to the qurʾānic view of humankind's relationship to the divine.

Human acts of chastisement

The Qurʾān describes many instances where one human, typically a ruler or the equivalent, inflicts a terrible punishment upon another who is, predictably, powerless. Interestingly, the Qurʾān does not attach any independent ontological significance to the act of punishment itself. Thus, at times the wicked succeed in torturing the good, as in the story of Pharaoh's (q.v.) treatment of the Jews (Q 2:49), as well as that of Pharaoh's treatment of his magicians after they announced their faith in Islam (Q 20:71; see MAGIC, PROHIBITION OF); at other times, the good is empowered over the wicked and is able to punish accordingly, as in Dhū l-Qarnayn's (see ALEXANDER) punishment of the unjust whom he encountered in his travels and conquests (Q 18:86-7).

The central lesson of the Qurʾān regarding these events is that the ontological status of any human act of punishment is derivative, viz. a result not of the act itself but rather of the nature of the actor. For that reason, the qurʾānic view is that a naive "empiricism" is insufficient to grasp the moral reality behind actual exercises of power (see INTENTION), i.e. mere empiricism is unable to judge whether the exercise of power was just (see JUSTICE AND INJUSTICE). The Qurʾān presents a vivid example of the fallacy of confusing empirical manifestations of power with the moral judgment of truth (q.v.) and falsehood when it describes Abraham's (q.v.) encounter with a king who had fallaciously claimed to share in divine attributes (see GOD AND HIS ATTRIBUTES; KINGS AND RULERS) because he, just as God, could grant life and take it away (Q 2:258).

It is not just the powerful, however, who endow their acts with ontological significance. The powerless, according to the Qurʾān, also believe, on the basis of the power of their oppressors, that they must be right or, less drastically, that God has no concern for the believers' welfare (see BELIEF AND UNBELIEF). Thus, when Pharaoh began to slaughter the male offspring of the Jews in retaliation for their support of Moses (q.v.) and Moses urged the Jews to remain firm in their faith in God and to seek his help, their reply was simply: "Tortured were we *(ūdhīnā* from root, *ʾ-dh-y)* before you came to us, and [tortured are we] after you came to us" (Q 7:129; see JEWS AND JUDAISM). Likewise, the Qurʾān portrays the powerless' confusion of might with right as a failure to exercise their own judgment; they thus blindly follow the powerful to their own perdition:

Were you [O Muḥammad!] to see the moment when the unjust are brought standing before their Lord, as they exchange words, one with another, and the downtrodden say to the mighty, "But for you, we surely would have been believers!" And the mighty will say to the downtrodden "Did we keep you away from [God's] guidance after it came unto you? No, you indeed were wicked!" And the downtrodden will say to the mighty, "No, indeed, it was rather your plotting, day and night, commanding us to be ungrateful (see GRATITUDE AND INGRATITUDE) to God and to assign unto him peers" (Q 34:31-3; see POLYTHEISM AND ATHEISM).

Thus, despite the fact that punishment administered by humans — and the power that stands behind it — says nothing about the moral significance of that act, humans nevertheless tend erroneously to attribute moral value to the exercise of power. They presume to read moral meaning into punishment prescribed by the socially and politically powerful or they interpret it negatively as divine disinterest. Because of such human misapprehension, the qurʾānic demystification of the empirical phenomenon of power (see POWER AND IMPOTENCE) provides an answer to the question of how one is to differentiate good from evil (see GOOD AND EVIL), given that both will at times use the same means.

Divine chastisement in this world

Qurʾānic narrative repeatedly demonstrates the belief that God intervenes at least episodically in human history. In a frequently encountered qurʾānic pattern, the most spectacular of these interventions begins when God sends a prophet (see PROPHETS AND PROPHETHOOD) to a human group and ends when God destroys them for their rejection of this prophet (see PUNISHMENT STORIES). While these stories are mentioned throughout the Qurʾān, the seventh sūra, Sūrat al-Aʿrāf, narrates in succession the accounts of the major prophets whose peoples God had destroyed — Noah (q.v.), Hūd (q.v.), Ṣāliḥ (q.v.), Lot (q.v.), Shuʿayb (q.v.), and Moses (q.v.; Q 7:59-93, 103-37).

The Qurʾān concludes its narration of these events with some general observations: The missions of the prophets are simultaneously accompanied by some significant misfortune *(bi-l-baʾsāʾ wa-l-ḍarrāʾ)* inflicting the people to whom they are sent, so as to awaken them from their heedlessness (Q 7:94). But God does not allow their misery to continue unabated and eventually replaces their misfortune with good fortune leading to general prosperity (Q 7:95). Instead of responding to God with gratitude, however, the prophet's people *naturalize* the calamity, concluding that the cycle of misfortune followed by good fortune is natural, something which occurs at all times. They therefore conclude that what happened to them during the course of their prophet's preaching had no causal connection with the prophet's mission (Q 7:95). God then sends his chastisement at the moment when they convince themselves that their experience was simply natural, lulling themselves thereby into a false sense of security (Q 7:95; see NATURAL

WORLD AND THE QUR'ĀN). Apparently, it is their reckless disregard for the possibility that the prophet is telling the truth that warrants their punishment and by analogy the punishment of future sinners who fail to take heed of their predecessors' example (Q 7:97-100).

Although the Qur'ān creates the impression that the majority of the prophets' peoples rejected them, their leaders are singled out by the Qur'ān for particular blame. It is always the leading citizens such as the town or tribal assembly *(al-mala')* that constitutes the biggest obstacle to the success of the prophet's mission (Q 7:60, 66, 75-7). Such is the case with the story of Moses and Pharaoh where the conflict between prophets and wicked temporal authority reaches its apogee. Although there are a number of other versions of the conflict between prophets and the political power (see POLITICS AND THE QUR'ĀN), the story of Moses produced sign after sign of God's power — first miracles (Q 7:107-8; see MIRACLE) and the defeat of Pharaoh's magicians (Q 7:117-9); then after the request of Pharaoh and his people, Moses removed the plagues (q.v.) that God had sent upon Pharaoh's people (Q 7:133-4). Pharaoh and his people, however, insisted that Moses was a mere politician whose only goal was to drive the Egyptians from power (Q 7:109-10, 127). When Pharaoh and his people broke their promise to Moses to release the Children of Israel (q.v.) from captivity after Moses removed the plagues from Egypt (q.v.), God finally destroyed them because "they rejected our clear signs (q.v.) and were heedless of them" (Q 7:136; see also CAPTIVES; AUTHORITY).

According to the narrative in Q 7, the story of Moses and Pharaoh provides a more detailed demonstration of the dynamic relationship between the unacceptable status quo and the reforming prophet than is generally to be found in the stories of the other prophets. The common theme among all the punishment stories associated with prophets, however, is that human beings, due to their narrow self-interest, behave recklessly when God gives them an opportunity to reform themselves. It is their reckless disregard for God's teaching that constitutes ungrateful rejection of God *(kufr)* and justifies his intervention in the form of a terrible chastisement.

Yet given the indeterminacy of the means God chooses to punish the wicked, such as natural phenomena, the question facing human beings is how to distinguish a truly natural calamity from one that is an actual manifestation of divine judgment. The answer that the Qur'ān gives is the person of the prophet, and Q 17:15, "We never punish until we send a messenger (q.v.)," offers ratification of this. Thus when a prophet confronts evil and challenges his people with the consequences of sinful behavior (see SIN, MAJOR AND MINOR), human actions assume a moral dimension, thereby creating a solid basis for divine judgment. According to the Qur'ān, only when God sends a prophet, therefore, do humans become morally accountable to God for their actions. Otherwise, their injustice would be a result of mere negligence and, as discussed above, only reckless disregard for truth that has been conveyed by God through a prophet (see REVELATION AND INSPIRATION) creates, in the sight of the Qur'ān, a moral justification for punishment.

The nature of divine punishment in the next world

The Qur'ān is replete with descriptions of the torments of hell (q.v.) that await those whose deeds made them deserving objects of divine chastisement. Whether these vivid descriptions should be understood in a strictly literal manner is a question that has preoccupied Muslim theologians of both the medieval and the modern periods.

Even among the classical figures of Islamic thought there has been the recognition that this cannot be answered from the qurʾānic text itself (e.g. Rāzī, *Tafsīr,* ii, 54-8). Indeed, the language of the Qurʾān uses vivid, literal images of the chastisements of hell at the very least to create "literal *psycho-physical effects* of the Fire" (F. Rahman, *Major themes,* 112-3). According to some contemporary lines of interpretation, more interesting and more answerable is the Qurʾān's description of the psychological aspect of divine chastisement in the next world.

While the image of God sitting in judgment over humankind (see THRONE OF GOD; LAST JUDGMENT), separating the saved from the damned has been criticized as a gross oversimplification of qurʾānic eschatology (q.v.), it does have some basis in the qurʾānic text, e.g. Q 2:284. Although Muslim dogma certainly promotes this image of the day of judgment, some modern commentators understand the day of judgment to be more a moment of complete self-awareness than a trial before a judge. Within this perspective, punishment is as much a result of the guilty person's realization of his or her own guilt as something that God imposes upon the individual (Q 2:167; 17:14; 69:25-9; 78:40). As a result of their new-found self-awareness, the guilty accept the justice of their punishment in recognition of their own moral depravity. Thus "they say 'Had we listened or reasoned, we would not have been among the denizens of the flame.' Thus did they recognize their sin..." (Q 67:10-1). In support of such a view, these commentators note that the Qurʾān often describes punishment in the next world as a deprivation of divine blessings, the effect of which is the equivalent of a punishment (Q 2:174; 3:77; 83:14-5; see also SIN AND CRIME).

Moḥammad Hossam Fadel

Bibliography
Primary: Rāzī, *Tafsīr;* Ṭabarī, *Tafsīr;* Zamakhsharī, *Kashshāf.*
Secondary: M. Bravmann, Allāh's liberty to punish or forgive, in *Der Islam* 47 (1971), 236-7; R. Eklund, *Life between death and resurrection according to Islam,* Uppsala 1941; Izutsu, *Concepts;* id., *God;* T. Juynboll, ʿAdhāb, in *EI²,* i, 186; F. Rahman, *Major themes of the Qurʾān,* Chicago 1980; A.J. Wensinck/A.S. Tritton, ʿAdhāb al-ḳabr, in *EI²,* i, 186-7; A.J. Wensinck, *The Muslim creed,* Cambridge 1932 (see "punishment" in general index).

Chastisement and Sentences

see CHASTISEMENT AND PUNISHMENT; TRIAL; JUDGMENT

Chastity

Avoidance of illicit sexual intercourse. Within the Qurʾān, this concept is generally expressed by the Arabic verb *aḥṣana,* its participles and the verbal noun *taḥaṣṣun.* The original meaning of the fourth form of the verb is "to protect or preserve something or someone," in the fifth form "to protect oneself" (Lane, 586). Other verbs used to convey this idea are *ḥafiẓa* (to protect) and *istaʿaffa* (to abstain).

The special meaning of the concept can be discerned by a comparison of qurʾānic verses in which the word, its synonyms or antonyms occur. There are transitive and intransitive forms. The transitive ones have as their complement the word *farj* (vagina) or *furūj* (genitals). In Q 21:91 and 66:12, Mary (q.v.), the mother of Jesus (q.v.), is called a woman "who preserved her vagina" *(allatī aḥṣanat farjahā)* meaning that she had not had sexual intercourse before she became pregnant with Jesus (Q 19:19-20). In Q 33:35, 23:5 and 70:29 it is said that "preserving one's genitals" is a general virtue of Muslims, both males and females. This statement should not be taken as covering all connotations of the

English word "chaste," since the qurʾānic concept does not imply that it is a virtue to abstain completely from sexual intercourse and lead a celibate life (see ABSTINENCE). This is made clear by Q 23:5-7 and 70:29-30 where true Muslim men are described as "those who preserve their genitals except from their wives and slave women." Wives and concubines (q.v.) of a Muslim man are considered lawful sexual partners (see SEX AND SEXUALITY). The virtue of chastity is therefore limited to the abstention from sexual intercourse with all others who are by definition unlawful (see LAWFUL AND UNLAWFUL). In the case of a Muslim woman the only lawful partner is her husband. In the verses in which the term *aḥṣana* is used intransitively, the meaning is the same and can best be translated by "abstaining from unlawful sexual intercourse." This is obvious from the verses in which the term *muḥṣin* is contrasted with its opposites, namely people who have illicit sexual relations (men, *musāfiḥūn;* women, *musāfiḥāt*) and a man who takes mistresses (*muttakhidh akhdān,* cf. Q 5:5; 4:25). Other antonyms are *imrāʾ sawʾ, zānin* and *khabīth* for men, all of which are best rendered by "fornicator" (Q 19:28; 24:3, 26), and, for women, *baghī* (whore; cf. Q 19:28), and *zāniya* and *khabītha,* which are the feminine forms of terms for fornicator (cf. Q 19:20; 24:3, 26).

Free Muslims must be chaste. This is also assumed of Christians and Jews and therefore Muslim men may marry Christian and Jewish women (Q 5:5; see CHRISTIANS AND CHRISTIANITY; JEWS AND JUDAISM; PEOPLE OF THE BOOK). Heathens are regarded as unchaste and are — like Muslims, Jews or Christians who have fornicated — unacceptable marriage partners (Q 2:221; 24:3; 60:10). Slaves are generally not regarded as chaste (see SLAVES AND SLAVERY). The Qurʾān, however, prohibits forcing them into prostitution if they wish to live chaste lives (Q 24:33; in all likelihood this verse refers to Jews and Christians or to slaves who have converted to Islam). Free Muslims may even marry Muslim slaves who are then obliged by marriage to live chastely, i.e. to abjure illicit intercourse (Q 4:25; 24:33).

Although chastity was already considered a virtue (at least for women) among the heathen Arabs before Islam (see PRE-ISLAMIC ARABIA AND THE QURʾĀN), the qurʾānic ideal of chastity follows Jewish and Christian traditions. Besides the instances cited above, the example of Joseph (Yūsuf; see JOSEPH) who, as a slave in Egypt, had resisted with God's support the seduction of his master's wife (Q 12:22-34, 50-3) is a clear illustration of this continuity (see also SCRIPTURE AND THE QURʾĀN). In order to realize this ideal in the (early) Muslim community (see COMMUNITY AND SOCIETY IN THE QURʾĀN), the Qurʾān stipulates a special code of behavior among the sexes and prescribes severe sanctions for illicit sexual relations. The Qurʾān recommends that the sexes refrain from sexually provocative behavior and that people carefully veil their physical charms in front of the opposite sex (Q 24:30-1). People are warned by the Qurʾān not to enter other people's houses without asking permission to do so (Q 24:27-9, 58-9). If women have to leave the house, they are told to pull a piece of their clothes down (presumably over their heads) in order to be recognized as chaste women who do not want to be molested (Q 33:59; see VEIL). Unlawful sexual relations are condemned as sins (see SIN, MAJOR AND MINOR) and fornicators are threatened with severe punishment (Q 4:15-6, 19; 12:25; 17:32; 19:27; 23:5-7; 24:2; 65:1; see ADULTERY AND FORNICATION). For the wives of the Prophet even stricter standards of decent behavior are prescribed and their punishment in cases of adultery is doubled (Q 33:30, 32-3, 53;

see WIVES OF THE PROPHET; CHASTISEMENT AND PUNISHMENT). In Islamic jurisprudence the meaning of the word *iḥṣān* underwent a change and the measures to enforce chastity and to prevent illicit sexual intercourse became more severe over time. See also FAMILY; MARRIAGE AND DIVORCE; WOMEN AND THE QUR'ĀN.

Harald Motzki

Bibliography
J. Burton, The meaning of "iḥṣān," in *JSS* 19 (1974), 47-75; id., Muḥṣan, in *EI²*, vii, 474-5; H. Motzki, Geschlechtsreife und Legitimation zur Zeugung im frühen Islam, in E.W. Müller (ed.), *Geschlechtsreife und Legitimation zur Zeugung*, Munich 1985, 479-550; id., Wal-muḥṣanātu mina n-nisāʾi illā mā malakat aimānukum (Koran 4:24) und die koranische Sexualethik, in *Der Islam* 63 (1986), 192-218; id., Dann machte er daraus die beiden Geschlechter, das männliche und das weibliche... (Koran 75:39). Die historischen Wurzeln der islamischen Geschlechterrollen, in J. Martin and R. Zoepffel, *Aufgaben, Rollen und Räume von Frau und Mann*, Munich 1989, 607-41 (with full bibliography).

Cheating

Defrauding by deceit or trickery. Several qurʾānic expressions depict this vice (see VIRTUES AND VICES): *taṭfīf* (lit. making light of or slighting); *bakhs* (shortchanging); *akl amwāl al-nās bi-l-bāṭil* (devouring people's wealth on false pretext); *taghābun* (mutual fraud). Sūrat al-Muṭaffifūn, "The Slighters" (Q 83), is one of two sūras of the Qurʾān named for the actual practice of cheating. Its opening verses chide proprietors who manipulate the scales and measuring devices (see MEASUREMENT) in the market (see MARKETS) so that buyers receive less than the quantity for which they are paying. These same proprietors, meanwhile, go to market and demand full measure. This suggests some type of oligarchic conspiracy on the part of proprietors of which the general public was largely unaware (see COMMUNITY AND SOCIETY IN THE QURʾĀN). Muslim exegetes differ, however, over whether these verses were revealed in response to the actual situation at Mecca (q.v.) or Medina (q.v.). Lexicographically, the word *taṭfīf* implies that the gains it brings are trifling. *A fortiori*, its condemnation in the Qurʾān is seen to cover all measures of cheating, though no legal sanctions against *taṭfīf* are mentioned in the Qurʾān (see LAW AND THE QURʾĀN). The matter is referred, rather, to the *forum internum* as cheaters are reminded about the resurrection (q.v.) and the grievous penalty they will face on the day of judgment (see REWARD AND PUNISHMENT; LAST JUDGMENT). Later, Muslim society would entrust the regulation of proper weights and measures (q.v.) in the marketplace to a market inspector, the so-called *muḥtasib*.

Several verses (Q 2:282; 7:85; 11:85; 26:183) proscribe the practice of cheating in the form of *"bakhs"* or shortchanging people. The verses on *bakhs* are easily attributable to both the Meccan and Medinan periods. At Q 2:282, for example, the object is clearly the Muslim community at Medina. At Q 7:85 (a Meccan verse), meanwhile, the reference is to the pre-Islamic community of Midian (Madyan; see MIDIAN) to whom the prophet Shuʿayb (q.v.) was sent in order that, among other things, he might command his people to give just measure and not shortchange their countrymen *(lā tabkhasū l-nās ashyāʾahum)*. This same theme is repeated in the Meccan verses, Q 11:85 and 26:183. What can be found here is a type of intertextuality quite common in the Qurʾān, where the rhetoric serves as a form of warning (q.v.) by example. The people of Midian failed to heed the warnings of Shuʿayb and as a result suffered destruction, a fate that the Qurʾān describes in moving imagery (see PUNISH-

MENT STORIES). Muḥammad's condemnation of *bakhs* in his preaching to the early Muslim community could hardly fail to conjure up such images.

A number of verses (Q 2:188; 4:29; 9:34) condemn the practice of devouring people's wealth on false pretext *(akl amwāl al-nās bi-l-bāṭil)*. This is actually a general category of misappropriation of which cheating, including such activities as gambling (q.v.) and unlawful gain (*ribā*, see USURY), are a subset. In terms of psychological impact, the verses treating of *akl amwāl al-nās bi-l-bāṭil* constitute, in all likelihood, the most powerful condemnation of cheating since the word here translated as "false pretext" *(bāṭil)* is also used in some twenty other qur'ānic verses with the meaning of falsehood as the antithesis of divinely revealed truth (q.v.; see REVELATION AND INSPIRATION).

Sūrat al-Taghābun, "Mutual Fraud" (Q 64), also takes its title from the notion of cheating. Here, however, the reference is not to pecuniary cheating but to the self-deception of the unbelievers through which they "cheat" themselves (collectively) out of a place in paradise (q.v.). Judgment day is thus called *yawm al-taghābun*, "the day of mutual fraud," i.e. the time when the results of their mutual deception are brought to light (see also BELIEF AND UNBELIEF).

Sherman A. Jackson

Bibliography

ʿAbd al-Bāqī; Ibn Kathīr, *Mukhtaṣar tafsīr Ibn Kathīr*, 3 vols., Beirut 1402/1982; Ṣābūnī, *Tafsīr*; Shawkānī, *Tafsīr*; Ṭabarī, *Tafsīr*.

Children

Offspring; gender-inclusive term for young people, between infancy and youth. The Qur'ān contains a number of terms for "offspring" and "young people," (e.g. *dhurriyya; ghulām*, pl. *ghilmān; ibn*, pl. *banūn; walad*, pl. *awlād*), but it is only seldom clear from the context when these refer to the age group between birth (q.v.) and maturity (q.v.). More specific terms for infants and children are: *walīd*, "child" (pl. *wildān*, although in Q 56:17, *wildān* probably means "youths"); *mawlūd*, "born, child," *ṣabī*, "infant, boy," *ṭifl*, "infant" and *ṣaghīr*, "young." Generally the terms in this latter group do not distinguish between various stages or developments in childhood, whereas the transition from childhood to maturity *(balagha ashuddahu)* or to puberty *(balagha al-ḥulum)* is mentioned in a few places. Qur'ānic statements about children which convey a normative-ethical significance form the foundation for later Islamic legislation and are mainly concerned with infanticide, adoption, breast-feeding, and fatherless children (see FAMILY; MILK; ORPHANS).

Infanticide

Infanticide as a form of post-partum birth control in pre-Islamic Arab society was motivated either by want and destitution and therefore practiced on males and females alike (Q 6:151; 17:31), as in cases of sacrificing children to gods (Q 6:137, 140), or by the disappointment and fear of social disgrace felt by a father upon the birth of a daughter (Q 16:57-9; 81:8-9; see PRE-ISLAMIC ARABIA AND THE QUR'ĀN; COMMUNITY AND SOCIETY IN THE QUR'ĀN). Regarding it as a practice typical of the pagan social mores of the pre-Islamic period (*jāhiliyya*, see AGE OF IGNORANCE), the Qur'ān, already in Meccan sūras, defines infanticide as a grave sin (see SIN, MAJOR AND MINOR). Consequently, it totally forbids the practice, together with other grave sins such as polytheism (see POLYTHEISM AND ATHEISM) and homicide (see MURDER; cf. Q 6:151; see also Q 60:12 — the only reference to women committing infanticide). Infanticide is also implicitly denounced in the story of Pharaoh (q.v.) and the Children of Israel (q.v.; Q 2:49; 7:127, 141; 14:6; 28:4; 40:25). The case of an unbelieving young man, who is killed in order to preserve his parents from the disobedience (q.v.) to God which he is destined to bring to their life, appears in a legendary context (Q 18:74, 80; see MYTHIC AND LEGENDARY NARRATIVES) and is certainly not intended as an example to be followed. See BIRTH CONTROL.

Adoption

Adoption as a practice in which an adopted son would take the name of his adoptive parent was common in pre-Islamic Arabia. It was cancelled and forbidden, however, in the early years of Islam (Q 33:4-5). Thus, Muḥammad was able to marry Zaynab bt. Jaḥsh after his formerly adopted son Zayd had divorced her, confirming the rule that forbids father and son to marry the same woman (Q 33:37; see A. al-Azhary-Sonbol, Adoption, esp. 45-52; see also FAMILY OF THE PROPHET; WIVES OF THE PROPHET).

Breast-feeding

Two of the five (Medinan) verses which mention breast-feeding (Q 2:233; 65:6; see BIOLOGY AS THE CREATION AND STAGES OF LIFE) aim at protecting repudiated but still lactating women (see LACTATION) and their nurslings by guaranteeing them economic support from the father for at least two years and by sanctioning non-maternal nursing when needed (see MARRIAGE AND DIVORCE). A related verse, Q 4:23 forbids sexual relations between males and their milk-mothers as well as milk-sisters thereby extending the realm of incest as defined by Judaism and Christianity (see A. Giladi, *Infants*, chap. 1; see also LAWFUL AND UNLAWFUL). See WET NURSING.

Fatherless children

Qurʾānic sensitivity to society's weaker members finds its full expression in nineteen verses forbidding the harsh and oppressive treatment of fatherless children *(yatāmā,* sing. *yatīm)* while urging kindness and justice towards them. A passage from the first Meccan period (Q 93:6-8) celebrates God's providence towards the orphan Muḥammad (q.v.). The fatherless children mentioned in some of the Medinan verses (e.g. Q 8:41) are those of Muḥammad's followers who had fallen in battle (see T. O'Shaughnessy, Youth and old age, 35-8). See ORPHANS.

The many other qurʾānic references without any explicitly normative message reflect concepts of childhood and attitudes towards children that are, on the whole, typical of patrilineal societies (see PATRIARCHY; INHERITANCE): sons (and property) are signs of divine benevolence (e.g. Q 16:72; 17:6; 26:132-3; 71:12; see BLESSING) but can also be a temptation for the believers (Q 8:28) who, unlike pagans, are to rely on God, not on earthly power (e.g. Q 3:10, 116; 9:24; 18:46; 19:77; see ARROGANCE). Unlike daughters, whose birth evokes disappointment and protest against God's decree (Q 16:57-9; cf. 42:49-50), sons are much desired (cf. Q 7:189-90). Both parents invest much in their children, from the moment of conception through pregnancy and lactation to weaning and upbringing (Q 17:24; 31:14; 46:15) and hope to find comfort in them (Q 25:74). Mothers, particularly, love their children (Q 20:40; 28:7-13), with some indication of favoring sons. Children are sexually innocent and therefore may be in the company of adults of both sexes even when the latter are not completely dressed (Q 24:31, 58-9). See also KINSHIP; WOMEN AND THE QURʾĀN.

Avner Giladi

Bibliography
A. al-Azhary-Sonbol, Adoption in Islamic society. A historical survey, in E. Warnock Fernea (ed.), *Children in the Muslim Middle East,* Austin 1995, 45-67; A. Giladi, *Infants, parents and wet nurses. Islamic medieval views on breast-feeding and their social implications,* Leiden 1999, chap. 1; id., Ṣaghīr, in *EI²*, viii, 821-7; id., Some observations on infanticide in medieval Muslim society, in *IJMES* 22 (1990), 185-200; I. Lapidus, Adulthood in Islam. Religious maturity in the Islamic tradition, in E. Erikson (ed.), *Adulthood,* New York 1978, 97-112; R. Levy, *The social structure of Islam,* Cambridge 1969, 135-49; H. Motzki, Das Kind und seine Sozialisation in der islamischen Familie des Mittelalters, in J. Martin and A. Nitschke (eds.), *Zur Sozialgeschichte der Kindheit,* Munich 1986, 391-441; T. O'Shaughnessy, The qurʾānic view of youth and old age, in *ZDMG* 141 (1991), 33-51.

Children of Israel

One of the qurʾānic designations of Israelites as well as Jews (*yahūd,* see JEWS AND JUDAISM) and Christians (*naṣārā,* see CHRISTIANS AND CHRISTIANITY), in reference mainly to past generations (q.v.). The majority of the passages mentioning the Children of Israel *(Banū Isrāʾīl)* are dedicated to the Israelites of the time of Moses (q.v.), while references do exist to later stages of their history, such as the story of Saul (Ṭālūt; Q 2:246-52; see SAUL), the destruction of the Temple (Q 17:2-8) and the emergence of Jesus (q.v.) among them (Q 61:6). Sometimes, the label "Children of Israel" is interchangeable with the label "People of the Book" (*ahl al-kitāb,* see PEOPLE OF THE BOOK).

Biblical background

The qurʾānic treatment of the Children of Israel must be examined against the background of the biblical allusions to them. The labels "Israel," "House of Israel" and "Children of Israel" had already appeared in the Hebrew Bible as synonymous names for the Israelite nation, which is thus named after its genealogical father, Jacob (q.v.), whose name was changed to Israel (q.v.; cf. *Gen* 32:29). In the New Testament, "Israel" is retained as a name for the Jewish people (e.g. *Acts* 1:6; 2:22, 36; 3:12; 4:8).

In the Hebrew Bible, Israel is a holy community chosen by God to be his special people and ranks above all other nations that are upon the face of the earth (e.g. *Deut* 7:6). The election of Israel signifies a covenant (q.v.) between God and his chosen people whose duty it is to keep his laws (*Ps* 105:43-5), fight the idolaters (see IDOLATRY AND IDOLATERS) and avoid all kinds of sins (*Deut* 7:5-6; 14:1-2, etc.). This election signifies God's blessing (q.v.) of them; God did not choose the children of Israel because they deserved it, but merely because of God's love for Israel (*Deut* 7:7-8) and for the sake of His own name (*Isa* 48:9-11).

The historical evidence of the election of Israel is provided in the exodus, i.e. Israel's deliverance (q.v.) from slavery (see SLAVES AND SLAVERY) in Egypt (q.v.) "by signs (q.v.) and by wonders," which is followed by the conquest of the Promised Land. This represents the fulfillment of God's ancient promise to the fathers of Israel to bequeath the land of Canaan to their posterity (e.g. *Exod* 3:6-17; *Deut* 4:34; 7:8; *Jer* 11:4). Israel can remain a chosen community only as long as they obey God and keep his covenant (*Exod* 19:5), but when they stray (see ASTRAY) they are no longer regarded as God's people. Thus when the Israelites commit the sin of worshipping the golden calf (see CALF OF GOLD), God disclaims them, and refers to them as Moses' people whom Moses, not God, has brought out of Egypt (*Exod* 32:7). Due to their sin, the people of Israel have become *lo-ʿammī:* "not my people" (*Hos* 1:9). See SCRIPTURE AND THE QURʾĀN.

Qurʾānic Israelites as a chosen community

This set of ideas, which appears mainly in the *Book of Deuteronomy*, reappears almost intact in the Qurʾān. The qurʾānic allusions to the Children of Israel are focused on the election of Israel on the one hand, and on Israel's breaking of God's covenant on the other. Taken together, they convey the idea that Israel has betrayed God's love and lost the status of God's chosen community, which implies that the believers who follow the qurʾānic Prophet replace the Children of Israel as God's renewed chosen community (see COMMUNITY AND SOCIETY IN THE QURʾĀN). Most allusions are anchored in the story of the exodus, which exemplifies the election of Israel as well as their sin (see SIN, MAJOR AND MINOR).

The most explicit formulation of the idea of Israel's election is provided in Q 44:30-3 in which God announces that he has chosen them *(ikhtarnāhum)* above all beings. This statement is coupled with the story of Israel's deliverance from Pharaoh (q.v.), including the signs *(āyāt)* given to Israel during their deliverance. The signs are mentioned in additional passages presenting the Children of Israel as chosen by God, for example in Q 45:16-7, in which God gives them the book (i.e. the Torah [q.v.]; see also BOOK) as well as judgment (q.v.) and prophethood (see PROPHETS AND PROPHETHOOD), provides them with good things and "prefers" them *(wa-faḍḍalnāhum)* above all beings. Then the clear signs *(bayyināt)* that were given to them are mentioned. According to other passages (e.g. Q 5:32), the signs were brought to them by their prophets.

The election of Israel forms the essence of God's blessing *(niʿma)* unto them. Thus in Q 2:211, the "clear signs" given to Israel by God are mentioned within a warning (q.v.) against "changing" God's *niʿma*. God's *niʿma* features as something which the Children of Israel must remember; it consists not only of their preference above all beings (Q 2:47, 122) but also of their being given prophets and of their being made into kings (Q 5:20; see KINGS AND RULERS).

God's *niʿma* appears also in close association with God's covenant (*ʿahd*) which the Children of Israel must keep. Keeping the covenant means that they must believe in the Torah and observe God's laws (Q 2:40-3; see BOUNDARIES AND PRECEPTS). God's covenant with the Israelites is often called *mīthāq* (Q 2:63, 83-4, 93; 5:12, 70), which also applies to the obligation of keeping the sabbath (q.v.; Q 4:154). It is also a covenant with "those who have received the book" (Q 3:187).

The exodus from Egypt and the sins of Israel

Israel's deliverance from Pharaoh provides the clearest manifestation of God's *niʿma* (Q 14:6). This event, as well as the journey of the Israelites to the holy land, is recounted in the Qurʾān in several parallel passages of varying length. A detailed version is provided in Q 7 ("The Heights," Sūrat al-Aʿrāf) in verses 103-71. Here the story begins with Moses and Aaron (q.v.) and their encounters with Pharaoh, including the signs, i.e. the miracles they perform and the calamities they bring down upon Pharaoh (Q 7:103-33; see MIRACLE). This is followed by the departure of Israel from Egypt (q.v.) and the drowning (q.v.) of the troops of Pharaoh in the sea (Q 7:134-6). Then comes a short reference to Israelite settlement in the Promised Land (Q 7:137). This version of Pharaoh's story is one of a series of well-known qurʾānic punishment stories (q.v.) that deal with nations which have been destroyed because of their disobedience (q.v.). Sometimes Pharaoh's punishment story appears independently of the story of the Israelites (Q 26:10-68; 27:7-14; 28:3-47; 43:46-56; 51:38-40; 79:15-29). In Q 7 the story about Pharaoh's punishment is followed by an account of the events that take place after the Children of Israel cross the sea. The plot now focuses on their sins, mainly on their fashioning the calf of gold which results in the breaking of the Tablets (Q 7:138-51). Other sins mentioned in this sūra are the refusal to say *ḥiṭṭa* (a word, or profession, of repentance), for which they are destroyed in a disaster *(rijz)* sent from heaven (Q 7:161-2; see also Q 2:58-9) and the violation of the sabbath (q.v.), for which they are turned into apes (Q 2:65; cf. 7:163-7). Elsewhere (Q 5:20-6) the Qurʾān recounts the sin of the Israelites when refusing to wage war on the mighty inhabitants of the Promised Land. As punishment they must wander in the wilderness for 40 years (till they perish). This is based on the biblical affair of the spies (*Num* 13).

The Qurʾān is also aware of other Israelite sins, which are outside the scope of the exodus, for example, persecuting and killing their prophets (Q 2:61, 87, 91; 3:21, 112, 181; 4:155; 5:70). The Qurʾān also condemns the Children of Israel for inner conflicts *(ikhtilāf)* which divided them after they had been chosen by God (Q 45:16-7; see also Q 10:93). Elsewhere this divisiveness is attributed to the People of the Book (Q 3:19).

A major sin committed by the Children of Israel, one which signifies violation of God's covenant, is the distortion *(taḥrīf)* of the word of God, i.e. the Torah (Q 5:13; see CORRUPTION). The same is said of the Jews as well (Q 4:46; 5:41). The Qurʾān also mentions those of the People of the Book who conceal parts of the Book (Q 6:91; see also Q 2:159, 174; 3:187, etc.). The Qurʾān not only recounts the sins of the Children of Israel but states that some of their own prophets, namely David (q.v.) and Jesus have already cursed them for their deeds (Q 5:78).

The polemical purpose

The Qurʾān employs the theme of the Children of Israel for polemical reasons arising from tensions between Muslim believers and their contemporary Jews and Christians. The Qurʾān strives to prove that Islam provides the framework for God's newly chosen community and that the Children of Israel, i.e. the Jews and the Christians, are no longer a chosen community (see ELECTION). This is stated explicitly in Q 5:18, in which the Jews and the Christians are said to claim that they are "the sons of God and his beloved ones." To this the Qurʾān responds by asserting that they are no more than mortals *(bashar)* whom God punishes for having sinned (see CHASTISEMENT AND PUNISHMENT).

The elevation of the Muslims to the status of a chosen community destined to replace the Israelites is indicated in passages which shift to the believers various aspects of their share in God's blessing. Thus God's *niʿma* emerges as something equivalent to the religion given to the believers (Q 5:3) and is coupled with the divine covenant that is being made with them (Q 5:7). In this capacity, God's *niʿma* consists in giving the believers the book and the wisdom (q.v.; Q 2:231), in bringing their hearts together (Q 3:103; see HEART), in protecting them against the schemes of their enemies (Q 5:11; see PROTECTION) and in assisting them in battle (Q 33:9). See OPPOSITION TO MUḤAMMAD; POLEMIC AND POLEMICAL LANGUAGE; EXPEDITIONS AND BATTLES.

Righteous Israelites

On the other hand, the Qurʾān is also aware of a righteous Israelite group, consisting mainly of a minority who have remained faithful to the prophets. In Q 7:159 a group *(umma)* of the righteous living among the "people of Moses" *(qawm Mūsā)* is mentioned; they "guide by the truth and by it act with justice." Some early commentators on the Qurʾān (Muqātil, *Tafsīr,* ii, 553-4) identify them with the lost tribes of the Israelites who dwell beyond a river of running sand called *Ardaf* which "freezes" every Sabbath (i.e. the midrashic *Sambaṭyon*). More prevalent, however, are interpretations identifying them with contemporary Jews who have embraced Islam. Similarly, a righteous group of leaders (*aʾimma,* sing. *imām* [q.v.]) among the Children of Israel are mentioned in Q 32:24 (cf. Q 28:5). Mention is also made of a righteous group *(umma)* among the People of the Book (Q 5:65-6; 3:113-4; cf. Q 3:199). See OBEDIENCE; BELIEF AND UNBELIEF; GRATITUDE AND INGRATITUDE; JUSTICE AND INJUSTICE.

Qurʾānic Israelites and Muslims

Muslim historiographers used qurʾānic passages about the Children of Israel as an instrument to illuminate the relations between the prophet Muḥammad and the Jews of Medina (q.v.; see NAḌĪR; QAYNUQĀʿ; QURAYẒA). In the work of one of Muḥammad's earliest biographers, Ibn Isḥāq (d. 150/768), there is an early instance of regarding these passages as an attack on the Jews of Muḥammad's own times. He incorporated many of the verses recounting the sins of Israel — mainly from Q 2 ("The Cow," Sūrat al-Baqara) — in his description of conditions in Medina shortly after Muḥammad's emigration (q.v.; *hijra*) from Mecca (Ibn Isḥāq, *Sīra,* ii, 177f.). Most characteristic is his interpretation of Q 2:40 in which the Children of Israel are commanded by God to remain faithful to his covenant. For Ibn Isḥāq this verse is specifically addressed to the leaders of the Jews of Medina, requesting them to keep faithful to God's covenant, i.e. to believe in Aḥmad (cf. Q 61:6) when he comes to them (Ibn Isḥāq, *Sīra,* ii, 181).

However, qurʾānic models of Israelite sin, and particularly the making of the calf of gold, were also adduced to denounce objectionable phenomena within Islamic society itself, situations which were regarded as signaling the assimilation of Muslims to other communities. The sin of the making of the calf is mentioned, for example, in a story about Muḥammad in which he predicts that the Muslims will follow the evil ways (*sunan,* see SUNNA) of the Israelites. He declares this after being asked by the Muslims to establish for them a place of worship on the model of a nearby pagan sanctuary (see IDOLS AND IMAGES). The Prophet refuses and says that the Muslims have asked for the same thing that the people of Moses had previously requested, i.e. the calf (Ibn Isḥāq, *Sīra,* iv, 84-5). Qurʾānic models of Israelite punishment, especially transformation into apes and pigs (Q 2:65; 5:60; 7:166) were also employed as a warning against various phenomena of assimilation into Jewish and Christian beliefs and practices for which some heretical trends in Islam were held particularly responsible. Several traditions predict that heretics (such as Qadarīs, etc.) will suffer punitive transformation into apes or pigs. See RELIGIOUS PLURALISM AND THE QURʾĀN.

Qurʾānic Israelites and the Shīʿa

The qurʾānic Israelites play a key part in Shīʿī tradition where their history foreshadows the history of the Shīʿīs. The massacre of al-Ḥusayn and his following at Karbalāʾ by the hand of the Umayyads (61/680) is equated in Shīʿī tradition to the evil ways of the qurʾānic Israelites who killed their prophets (Furāt, *Tafsīr,* i, 136, no. 162). The Shīʿīs also applied to the Umayyads the qurʾānic model of Pharaoh who slew the sons of the Israelites (cf. Q 40:25), an interpretation which meant that the persecuted Shīʿīs were equal to the persecuted Israelites of Pharaoh's time (e.g. Ṭabarī, *Taʾrīkh,* ii, 711; Ibn Aʿtham, *Futūḥ*, vi, 281).

More frequently, however, the Shīʿa (q.v.) identify with the Children of Israel in their role as a chosen community. Shīʿī qurʾānic exegetes explain that the chosen Israelites mentioned in the Qurʾān (e.g. in Q 2:47) stand for the Shīʿīs. This is based on the notion that Isrāʾīl (see ISRAEL) is one of Muḥammad's own names (ʿAyyāshī, *Tafsīr*, i, 62-3) which, in turn, implies that the "Children of Israel" are Muḥammad's descendants, i.e. the *imāms*. Twelver Shīʿīs found the most suitable Israelite model for their *imāms* in the qurʾānic reference to the twelve "chieftains" *(nuqabāʾ*, sing. *naqīb)* whom, according to Q 5:12, Moses appointed to lead the Israelites. The twelve *imāms* were held to be analogous to them (Ibn Shahrāshūb, *Manāqib*, i, 258). See IMĀM; SHĪʿISM AND THE QURʾĀN.

Uri Rubin

Bibliography

Primary: ʿAyyāshī, *al-Tafsīr;* Ibn Aʿtham al-Kūfī, *Kitāb al-Futūḥ*, ed. ʿA. Shīrā, 8 vols., Beirut 1991; Ibn Furāt al-Kūfī, *Tafsīr Ibn Furāt al-Kūfī*, ed. M. al-Kāẓim, 2 vols., Beirut 1992; Ibn Hishām, *al-Sīra al-nabawiyya*, ed. M. al-Saqqā, I. al-Abyārī and ʿA.Ḥ. Shalabī, 4 vols., repr. Beirut 1971; Ibn Shahrāshūb, Abū Jaʿfar Muḥammad b. ʿAbdallāh, *Manāqib āl Abī Ṭālib*, 3 vols., Najaf 1956; Muqātil, *Tafsīr*.

Secondary: M.M. Bar-Asher, On Judaism and the Jews in early Shīʿī religious literature (in Hebrew), in *Peʿamim* 61 (1994), 16-36; A. Geiger, *Was hat Mohammed aus dem Judentum aufgenommen?* repr. Leipzig 1902, trans. F.M. Young, *Judaism and Islam*, New York 1970; M.J. Kister, *Ḥaddithū ʿan Banī Isrāʾīla wa-lā ḥaraja*, in *IOS* 2 (1972), 215-39, repr. in id., *Studies in* jāhiliyya *and early Islam*, London 1980; McAuliffe, *Qurʾānic;* U. Rubin, Apes, pigs, and the Islamic identity, in *IOS* 17 (1997), 89-105; id., *Between Bible and Qurʾān. The Children of Israel and the Islamic self-image*, Princeton 1999; W. Rudolph, *Die Abhängigkeit des Qorans von Judentum und Christentum*, Stuttgart 1922; H. Speyer, *Die biblischen Erzählungen im Qoran*, repr. Hildesheim 1961.

Christ *(masīḥ)* see JESUS

Christianity see CHRISTIANS AND CHRISTIANITY

Christians and Christianity

Evidence for the presence of Christians and currency of Christianity in the Arabian milieu in which Islam was born comes from the Qurʾān itself as well as from reports included in other documents of a similar date and provenance. From these texts it is clear that by the beginning of the first Islamic century, toward the end of the first quarter of the seventh century according to the common reckoning, the number of Christians in the territories frequented by the Arab tribes in the Middle East was on the increase (see TRIBES AND CLANS). Evidence of the Christian presence on the periphery of Arabia proper, in Syria/Palestine, in the Syrian desert, in southern Iraq, south Arabia and the coastal areas of the Red Sea as well as in Ethiopia (q.v.) is abundant and widely discussed in modern histories of Christianity in the Near East. Increasingly, there is further evidence of an important Christian presence in the first Islamic century within Arabia, in the territories of the central tribal confederations such as the Kinda, in the area of Najrān (q.v.), and even in the Ḥijāz, in Mecca (q.v.) and its surroundings, but the textual references are fragmentary, sometimes obviously legendary and often difficult to interpret. So far the published archaeological record is meager (see ARCHAEOLOGY AND THE QURʾĀN).

The province of Bostra/Būṣrā

Already in New Testament times a Christian presence existed in Arab territory. St. Paul reports that after his conversion, needing time away from Damascus to think about his experiences there, "I went off to Arabia" (*Gal* 1:17). While Paul's precise destination is unknown, it was in all probability in the territories controlled by the Nabateans, which in the year 106 C.E. were to be incorporated into the Roman Empire as the Province of Arabia. The capital of the former Nabatean kingdom, Bostra/Būṣrā in due course became the seat of a metropolitan bishop and by the first third of the third century, under bishop Beryllus (d. after 244 C.E.) the city was the scene of a theological controversy that drew into its affairs the intervention of no less an ecclesiastical figure than Origen of Alexandria (ca. 185-ca. 251 C.E.) who visited the locale at least three times over the course of almost thirty years for purposes of theological consultation. By the year 325 C.E. the Christian communities had grown so numerous in the region that there were five representatives of the province of Arabia at the council of Nicea. The churches in this Arab milieu had strong ties with the Syriac-speaking, Aramaean churches in Mesopotamia, especially Edessa and its environs. In Mesopotamia from the fourth century onward there was even a bishop for the nomad Arabs, whose see in later times was ʿAqūla, the site of Kūfa in the early Islamic period. Arab tribes associated with these areas, many of whom were at one time or another in alliance with the Byzantines (q.v.) or Sasanians, include Tanūkh, Ṣāliḥ, Judhām, Kalb, Ghassān, Lakhm, and al-Ṭayy. Syriac-speakers often used the name of the last-mentioned tribe to designate all Arabs and later the Muslims, viz., *Ṭayyāyê*.

Ghassānids and Lakhmids

It is reasonable to suppose that Christianity found its way into the Arab tribes on the periphery of desert Arabia through the ministrations of Greek and Aramaic-speaking monks in Sinai, Syria/Palestine, Mesopotamia and Iraq as well as through the attraction of pilgrimage centers (see PILGRIMAGE; HOLY PLACES) such as Jerusalem (q.v.) in the Holy Land, Qalʿat Simʿān and Ruṣāfa/Sergiopolis in Syria. What is more, the Byzantine practice of forging military alliances with Christianized Arab tribes on the Arabian frontier of the empire to counterbalance the comparable arrangement made by the Persians to the east, also encouraged the further spread of Christianity among the Arabs of the interior. In this connection the mention of the Ghassānid and Lakhmid confederations and their special relationships with the Romans and the Persians respectively highlights the situation in the fifth and sixth centuries C.E.

The Ghassānids became the principal group of Arab tribes who were the *foederati* of Byzantium on the Arabian frontier in the sixth century. The names of their leaders, Ḥārith (Arethas), Mundhir and Nuʿmān in particular, figure prominently in the accounts of the troubled relations between the Byzantines (q.v.) and the Persians in this period, in the annals of Byzantine political life more broadly as well as in the record of the current ecclesiastical controversies. As for the territories under the control of the Ghassānids, recent archaeological excavations in Transjordan have revealed the remains of extensive church and monastery building at this time along the whole extent of Rome's Arabian frontier (see CHURCH). Many of these installations include strikingly beautiful mosaic floors, some with Greek inscriptions, testifying to a certain level of material prosperity as well as cultural sophistication.

An important Christian center of influence among the Arab tribes in the territories under Persian influence in pre-Islamic times was the Lakhmid enclave of Ḥīra, on the lower Euphrates. Here, as was also the case further to the north in Syrian Mesopotamia, the dominant ecclesiastical language was Syriac but the predominant confessional allegiance was that of the so-called "Nestorians" or the "Assyrian Church of the East" whose principal hierarch occupied the see of Seleucia-Ctesiphon. The king of Ḥīra, Nuʿman b. Mundhir (583-ca. 602 C.E.), converted to this Christian allegiance toward the end of the sixth century but even prior to this development, the church had flourished in the area and its influence was felt in the associated Arab tribes. Archaeological investigations on the coast of southern Arabia (see SOUTH ARABIA), especially along the Persian Gulf, have uncovered a number of sites with extensive church remains typical of the Nestorians, particularly in the territory of modern Kuwait.

The movement of monks (see MONASTICISM AND MONKS), traders and caravans (see CARAVAN) from all these areas into central Arabia was unhindered as was the seasonal transhumance of the pastoral nomads (q.v.) from the heart of the desert to the pastures on the periphery at pilgrimage time in the spring of the year and at other times as well (see CALENDAR). These were the traditional routes of Christianity's spread eastward and southward from the beginning. By the time of Muḥammad's birth, in the late sixth century C.E., there is every reason to think that Christianity would have been well known, if not widely practiced, in the very heart of Arabia.

Arabia Deserta

From the fragmentary sources it is clear that already in the fifth century, the Arab tribal confederation of Kinda, whose leaders were originally from South Arabia (q.v.), had gained a strong political presence in the center and the northern reaches of the peninsula and had numerous contacts with both the Romans and the Persians on the borders of Arabia as well as with their Arab allies, the Ghassānids and the Lakhmids. Christianity, if not already present among them, probably came to the Kinda with the enlistment of the tribal leader, Ḥārith b. ʿAmr, as a Byzantine phylarch in the early sixth century.

Knowledge of the Christians of Najrān, who flourished in the sixth century as an enclave of the "Jacobite" church in the Arabic-speaking milieu of southwestern Arabia, is mostly preserved in the Syriac letters of Simeon of Bēth Arshām (fl. ca. 525 C.E.) and in the enigmatic *Book of the Ḥimyarites*. The texts tell of the martyrdom of some 300 Christians around the year 520 C.E. at the hands of Yūsuf Asʾar Yathʾar, the allegedly Jewish king of the Ḥimyarites. Their shrine in Najrān became a pilgrimage center. In later times, Islamic tradition passed on the account of a delegation of Christians from Najrān who are said to have visited Muḥammad (q.v.) at Medina (q.v.) and to have engaged in a debate with him about the true identity of the Messiah, Jesus (q.v.), "son of Mary (q.v.)." It ended, according to the Islamic exegetical tradition of a passage in the Qurʾān, when the Christian delegation withdrew at the threat of an ordeal to determine who was telling the truth about Jesus (Q 3:61-2), the Muslims or the Christians (see W. Schmucker, Mubāhala; see CURSE).

One finds in later Islamic traditions remarks which suggest that there was a cemetery in Mecca for Christians during Muḥammad's lifetime and a Christian group is mentioned who engaged in the water trade there (see WATER). But the most dramatic record of a Christian presence in Mecca is the claim voiced by al-Azraqī (d. 222/837), the early historian of the Muslim holy places, that among other images in the Kaʿba (q.v.) there was an icon of Mary and her son Jesus and that at the "cleansing of the Kaʿba" of its idols the Prophet himself forbade its effacement. While legendary reports such as this one, coming as they do from much later times in

Islamic history and normally rejected by Islamic tradition criticism, cannot be cited as convincing historical evidence, they do nevertheless testify to the sense among at least some early Muslim scholars of a more than casual Christian presence in the world of the Qurʾān at the very time of the birth of Islam. In the Islamic scripture itself a Christian presence among the Arabs who were its primary audience is openly mentioned and evidently taken for granted. The text refers to Christians, their beliefs and practices, both directly and indirectly.

Direct references to Christians in the Qurʾān

In most passages of the Qurʾān that directly concern Christians, they are included, along with Jews and others, under the general heading of "People of the Book" or "Scripture People" (*ahl al-kitāb,* see PEOPLE OF THE BOOK). This phrase occurs some 54 times in the Qurʾān, mostly in passages that reflect events in the last ten years of Muḥammad's prophetic career, when he governed the Muslim community in Medina. Christians and Jews together were among those who found some obstacles to the acceptance of the teachings of the new revelations (see REVELATION AND INSPIRATION; OPPOSITION TO MUḤAMMAD). The Qurʾān in turn observed faults and short-comings in both Jewish and Christian doctrines and practices. A major claim is that Jews and Christians both had fallen away from the faith of Abraham (q.v.), whom all the scriptures recognize as "God's friend" (*Isa* 41:8; *James* 2:23; Q 4:125). Whereas, according to the Qurʾān, "Abraham was neither a Jew nor a 'Nazarene,' but he was *"ḥanīfan, musliman"* (see ḤANĪF) and he was not one of the polytheists" (Q 3:67). The implied claim in this passage, that Abraham was a proto-Muslim, is reminiscent of the comparable early Christian claim, recorded in the *Ecclesiastical history* of Eusebius of Caesarea (ca. 260-ca. 340 C.E.) that Abraham could rightfully be considered a Christian "in fact if not in name" (i, 4).

Once in the Qurʾān Christians are called "Gospel People" (*ahl al-injīl,* Q 5:47; see INJĪL) and they are admonished to "judge by what God sent down in it." However, the Gospel (q.v.) is not what the Christians think it is. Rather, the Torah (q.v.), the Gospel and the Qurʾān are said to be on a par in terms of God's promise and covenant (q.v.; Q 9:111). In the form in which Jews and Christians have them, their scriptures are considered to be in some sense distorted (Q 2:75; see CORRUPTION). Jesus is presented as being but God's messenger (q.v.), like Abraham and Moses (q.v.) before him (Q 42:13) and like Muḥammad after him (Q 3:144).

Some 14 times in the Qurʾān Christians are named *al-naṣārā (*sing. *al-naṣrānī).* Interpreters of the text in western languages, both Muslims and non-Muslims, have customarily translated this term by substituting the noun "Christians" for it. Strictly speaking, this is not a correct rendering and the usage in fact obscures what the text actually says. The Arabic noun *Masīḥiyyūn,* which does properly mean "Christians," is never used in the Qurʾān.

The prevailing scholarly opinion is that the Arabic term *al-Naṣārā* is derived from the name of Jesus' home town of Nazareth in Galilee and that it literally means "Nazarenes," alternately "Nazoreans," that is to say, "people from Nazareth," echoing the Greek *nazôraioi* and the Syriac *naṣrāyê.* The Syriac name preserves the original Aramaic form, from which the Greek name was transcribed. This epithet is applied in the singular to Jesus himself in the Gospel (*Matt* 2:23; *John* 19:19) and in the plural in the Acts of the Apostles (24:5) to the associates of Paul who is himself described before the Roman governor Felix, by Tertullus, an attorney for the Jewish elders, as "a ringleader of the sect of Nazoreans." In later times the same Greek noun was used in the plural by Epiphanius of Salamis (ca. 315-403 C.E.) and other heresiographers of the established Church of the Roman empire, to designate a "Christian" community deemed heretical because of their Christological views. But in Greek the term was never used to designate "Christians" in general. However, the case was otherwise in Aramaic usage where the cognate noun in Syriac, *naṣrāyê*, was widely used in the early period to designate "Christians" in general, particularly in works by east Syrian writers living in the Persian empire.

Some early commentators on the Qurʾān, both Muslim and Arab Christian, seeking a properly Islamic sense for the term *al-naṣārā* have posited a linguistic connection in Arabic on the basis of the shared root consonants *n-ṣ-r* between the noun *al-naṣārā* and the expression *anṣār Allāh*, "God's helpers," as it is used in the Qurʾān to refer to Jesus' apostles *(al-ḥawāriyyūn)* in Q 61:14 (see APOSTLE). On this hypothesis, which is rejected by grammarians on philological grounds, the noun *al-naṣārā* as it is used in the Qurʾān would then be thought to indicate people in the Arabian milieu who were considered as in some way being "God's helpers" in the manner of Jesus' apostles, that is to say, those customarily called "Christians" elsewhere.

For the sake of completeness, one should note that some commentators have sought a connection between the *noṣrîm* of Jewish rabbinical literature and the *naṣārā* of the Qurʾān; both terms may be considered to have a similar etymology and to have been used to designate "Christians." And while there were certainly Jews in the environs of Mecca and Medina (see JEWS AND JUDAISM), it nevertheless seems most likely that the Arabic term *naṣārā* as it is used in the Qurʾān is a calque of the Syriac word *naṣrāyê*, meaning "Nazarenes" or "Nazoreans." It preserves an archaic usage current, though not dominant, in east Syrian circles, according to which "Christians" in general are called "Nazarenes," "Nazoreans," mostly by non-Christians. There are numerous other instances in the Qurʾān in which the Arabic religious vocabulary is used in accordance with the sense of the cognate words in Syriac. This is not surprising in contexts evoking Christian belief or practice since it is clear that the Christianity known in tribal Arabia during the time of the Qurʾān's appearance had its most immediate background in the Syriac-speaking communities of the desert's landward fringes.

The Qurʾān's posture towards Christians in the Arabian milieu is somewhat guarded. On the one hand, there are positive comments in the text about them but there are also sharp criticisms. In general, the Qurʾān says, the Christians (i.e. the "Nazarenes") will give Muslims a friendlier reception than will the Jews or the polytheists. And the text gives as the reason for this friendly attitude the fact that among the Christians "there are presbyters and monks, and the fact that they do not behave arrogantly" (Q 5:82). But in other passages there are strictures against monks. People in the past are said to have wrongly taken them as masters instead of God, and the monks themselves, the passage says, were among those who "would consume people's wealth (q.v.) for nought and turn them aside from God's way" (Q 9:31, 34). So it is not surprising in yet another passage to read that from the Qurʾān's viewpoint, the development of monasticism in the Christian community followed a path of unwarranted innovation (q.v.). The text says, "Monasticism they invented; we prescribed for them only to seek God's favor, but they did not keep its right observance" (Q 57:27).

Given this ambivalence about such a

typical ecclesiastical institution as monasticism, it is hardly surprising to read at another place in the Qurʾān about the Christian community at large that although they may give Muslims a friendlier reception than do most people of other religions, Muslims nevertheless should not, the text insists, take either Jews or "Nazarenes" as their friends (Q 5:51). For, as the scripture also says, "Neither the Jews nor the 'Nazarenes' will be pleased with you until you follow their religion" (Q 2:120). While listing the Christians (i.e. the "Nazarenes") among those who generally believe in God and the last day (see LAST JUDGMENT) and who do the works of righteousness (Q 2:62), the Qurʾān nonetheless also exhorts Muslims to fight against such "People of the Book" who do not uphold these truths until they pay the tribute (*al-jizya*, see TAXATION) and are humble (cf. Q 9:29).

The Qurʾān charges that the "People of the Book" exaggerate in their religion (Q 4:171; 5:77). The text in these passages clearly rejects the conventional Christian doctrines of the Trinity (q.v.) and the Incarnation (Q 4:171; 5:17, 72, 73, 116, 117), teaching to the contrary that Jesus, Mary's son, is but a man like Adam (see ADAM AND EVE) before him (Q 3:59) and that he is God's messenger (Q 5:75). The text also rejects the conventional Christian view of the crucifixion of Jesus in terms (*shubbiha lahum*, Q 4:157) that are reminiscent of certain issues in the Christological controversies in the churches of the time such as those of the so-called *Aphthartodocetists* and the followers of Julian of Halikarnassos (d. after 518 C.E.). They bedeviled the "Jacobite" followers of the teachings of Severus of Antioch (ca. 465-538 C.E.), who were prominent among the Christians of west Syrian theological heritage in the Arabian milieu of Muḥammad's day. On the face of it, the passage is addressed to Jews, as a reprimand for infidelity, for slander against Mary, the mother of Jesus, and for the claim that they killed Jesus by crucifixion. These are charges against Jews that are reflected in Syriac Christian texts as well.

Two things are very clear in the Qurʾān's assessment of conventional Christian teaching: the view that the doctrines of the Trinity and the Incarnation are wrong; and that in propounding them Christians go to an excess or they go beyond the bounds of scriptural truth in their religious confession. From the Qurʾān's perspective the exaggeration consists in saying more about God and about Jesus than the Torah and the Gospel warrant one to say. And the Qurʾān goes on to suggest that the exaggeration comes more proximately from the tendency on the part of Christian teachers "to follow the whims of a people who had earlier gone into error (q.v.), and had led many into error, and who had gone off the right path into error" (Q 5:77). The earlier people in question are the polytheists. Like the polytheists who also thought the one God had offspring, the Christians, according to the Qurʾān, have exposed themselves to the charge of infidelity and are liable to be branded as infidels. The text says, "They have become infidels who say that God is one of three" (Q 5:73).

The "one of three" with whom this verse (Q 5:73) claims the Christians wrongfully identify God is, as the text itself goes on to make clear, Jesus the Messiah (Q 5:75). In fact, the otherwise enigmatic epithet "one of three" sometimes translated "third of three" *(thālith al-thalātha)* finds its best explanation in the recognition that it reflects an epithet applied to Christ in Syriac Christian usage, the tradition most immediately available to Arab Christians. The epithet in Syriac is *thlîthāyă*, no easier to translate into a western language than the Qurʾān's reflection of it in Arabic. It means "third," "threefold," "treble" or "trine" and is sometimes used in the plural to refer to the three "persons" or "hypostases" of the Trinity. As an epithet of Christ it evoked for the liturgical poets in Syriac primarily the recollection of their belief in Christ's three-day stay in the tomb, after his passion and death on the cross, before his resurrection. That Jesus is "one of three" along with God and a Spirit from him, all three of whom are one God, is the Christian tenet the Qurʾān criticizes most explicitly in Q 4:171. In the Qurʾān's view the Christian doctrine of the Trinity thus involves an association of creatures with God the creator, an infidelity that participates in the pagan infidelity of polytheism (see POLYTHEISM AND ATHEISM). The basic problem with Christian teaching, according to the Qurʾān, is that "the 'Nazarenes' say that Christ is the Son of God… imitating the parlance of those who disbelieved before" (Q 9:30). It is for this reason that in another place the Qurʾān puts an emphasis on Jesus' full humanity by saying, "With God Jesus is as Adam; he created him from dust, then said to him 'Be,' and he was" (Q 3:59; see CREATION).

The Qurʾān often calls Jesus "Mary's son" as if to insist that he is in no strict sense God's son as the Christians say. The Qurʾān fully accepts Jesus' virgin birth from Mary, who became pregnant with him at the message of an angel (q.v.; Q 3:45-9; 19:1-22). But to say that Jesus the Messiah is God's son is to say that he is God or an associate of God in divinity, so the Qurʾān explicitly teaches, "They disbelieved who said God is the Messiah, Mary's son. Say, who could prevail with God in anything if he wanted to destroy the Messiah, Mary's son, and his mother" (Q 5:17). Furthermore, in a passage that pointedly criticizes the typical Christian veneration of Jesus and his mother Mary in both liturgy and icon (see IDOLS AND IMAGES), the Qurʾān envisions what God will ask Jesus at the end of time. He will say, "Jesus, son of Mary, did you say to mankind, 'Take me and my mother as two gods besides God?'" (Q 5:116).

Melkites, Jacobites and Nestorians

In its direct references to Christian beliefs and practices as well as in its judgments of them, the Qurʾān is reflecting its interaction with those main-line Christian communities whose Arabophone members owed their ecclesiastical formation to the monks and preachers whose languages were principally Syriac together with some Greek and Coptic. They were the "Melkites," "Jacobites" and "Nestorians" long familiar from the Christian history of the area; the progress of their teaching and preaching among the Arabs from the fifth century C.E. onward is demonstrable from a number of sources. The Qurʾān assumes that members of its audience are already familiar with the Bible stories and with many customary Christian interpretations of them. Too often in the past, Western scholars in particular have wrongly interpreted the rhetorical devices (see RHETORIC OF THE QURʾĀN) of the Qurʾān's criticism or rejection of conventional Christian doctrines as flawed reports of misunderstood teachings or as echoes of the doctrines of shadowy groups such as the "Nazarenes/Nazoreans" or the "Collyridians" of the Byzantine heresiographers or of "Jewish Christian" groups often mentioned by modern scholars, no historical trace of whom is otherwise to be found in the Arabian milieu in the time of Muḥammad and the Qurʾān. Such interpretations have themselves often been the product of a polemical or of an apologetic agenda in regard to the Qurʾān rather than the yield of a credible historical examination of the milieu in which the text appeared, and to which it spoke in the first instance. In light of the plentiful evidence of the presence of Christians in the world of earliest Islam, their several conventional denominations of that time and place, the most plausible interpretive stratagem is to relate the Qurʾān's statements about the "Nazarenes" and the "People of the Book," their beliefs and practices, to these known Christian groups with reference to the largely Syriac idiom in which modern scholars can find written expressions of their faith and works. On this reading of the evidence, the "Nazarenes" of whom the Qurʾān speaks were no other group than the "Melkites," "Jacobites" and "Nestorians" of ordinary church history, notwithstanding the fact that in earlier times there were some who were called "Nazarenes/Nazoreans" by the Byzantine heresiographers, whom they described as espousing views which, in hindsight, some modern scholars would regard as being compatible with views of Christ expressed in the Qurʾān. Rather, the term "Nazarenes" as it is used in the Qurʾān is taken to be a general one reflecting an archaic Syriac usage and indicating those "People of the Book" whom others customarily called "Christians." The Qurʾān would have had its own reasons for not using the more customary nomenclature and it is not inconceivable that these were polemical reasons comparable to the use of the cognate term *noṣrīm* by Jews as attested in some rabbinical texts and in accordance with the practice of non-Christians, as reported in Syriac texts, of calling Christians in Persia "Nazarenes/Nazoreans."

Indirect reference to Christians in the Qurʾān

Indirectly, the Qurʾān attests to the presence of Christianity and to Christians themselves in a number of passages that mention in passing such typical institutions and personages as monasteries and churches (Q 22:40), monks and monasticism (Q 57:27), people who argue with Muslims about religion (e.g. Q 3:61) or even to the troubles of the neighboring Byzantines (Q 30:2). Yet by far the most significant indirect evidence for the presence of Christians in the world of the Qurʾān is the sustained dialogue in the text about the proper understanding of the numerous biblical characters and events mentioned there as well as allusions to and comments on narratives that were widespread in the Christian communities of the day especially in the Syriac-speaking milieu such as the story of the "Companions of the Cave" (Q 18:9-26; see CAVE; MEN OF THE CAVE) or the memory of episodes in the apocryphal Gospels (Q 5:110). Biblical and literary echoes such as these evoke the realm of intertextuality in virtue of which the Qurʾān presumes in its audience a basic familiarity with narratives which are also to be found in the Bible and the lore of the churches. This textually-necessary presumption of familiarity with ecclesiastical lore is itself a testimony to the significant presence of Christians in the milieu of the Qurʾān and it demonstrates that from its origins, Islam has been in dialogue with Christianity as it has been with Judaism.

Sīra *and* ḥadīth

Other Islamic texts from the early period similarly document the ample presence of Christianity and Christians in the milieu of the Qurʾān. These include in particular the collections of pre-Islamic, Arabic poetry put together in the days of the early caliphs, which sometimes refer to Christians and their activities. In some instances the poets themselves were Christians but their poems did not on this account exhibit notably Christian themes. What is more to the point, Christians figure somewhat prominently in the numerous traditions assembled in the literature of the biography of the Prophet Muḥammad. Here the Christians portrayed as intimately involved with the Prophet range from monks like Baḥr, to the monotheist *(ḥanīf)* Waraqa b. Nawfal and the early Companion of the Prophet, Salmān the Persian. In the ḥadīth collections that came to govern religious practice in the Islamic community in later times there are also numerous evocations of Christianity. These and many other testimonies in Islam's foundational documents are, at the very least, literary intimations of the presence of Christianity, as the confessional "other" in the matrix of the delineation of the new community's distinctive religious profile.

Pre-Islamic, Arab Christian texts?

While there is thus abundant confirmation of Christianity among the Arabs in the world in which Islam was born, there is as yet no conclusive evidence of the existence of a pre-Islamic, Christian literature in Arabic. The patristic and liturgical heritage of the Arab Christians before the rise of Islam was predominantly Aramaic and Greek. As their own indigenous poetry was mostly oral, there is every reason to think that there would also have been among them a vibrant, oral Christian culture in Arabic reflecting in translation the religious diction of the Greek and especially the Syriac-speaking monks and preachers from whom the Arabs would have learned their Christian discourse. Traces of this diction seem to have survived even within the Qur'ān itself (see FOREIGN VOCABULARY). But as for the liturgy and the Bible or any other Christian text in the form of written translations into Arabic from the time before the rise of Islam, scholars have so far not been able to find any conclusive evidence of their existence. Perhaps this is not so surprising a fact; it was arguably the Qur'ān itself that gave the Arabic language a literary definition and provided a point of reference for the development of a classical language from a welter of previously current, tribal speech patterns. In this connection, one might think of the Qur'ān as having done for the Arabic language what the translations of the Bible did for the development of the Germanic and Slavonic languages in other parts of the world, just one or two centuries later. As for actual Christian texts in Arabic, the evidence in hand suggests that they were first produced in the eighth Christian century, in early ʿAbbāsid times, in monastic communities in the conquered territories outside of Arabia properly so-called. Typically, they exhibit a sometimes hypercorrect idiom that reflects the conventions of a developing Middle Arabic diction which had as its background the concurrent evolution of the classical form of the Arabic language. By the time of the appearance of these texts, the language of the Arab conquerors of the Middle East was fast becoming the *lingua franca* of all the peoples living in the burgeoning Islamic commonwealth and the principal carrier of their cultures, Christians included.

Sidney H. Griffith

Bibliography

T. Andrae, *Der Ursprung des Islams und das Christentum,* Uppsala 1926; R. Bell, *The origin of Islam in its Christian environment,* London 1926; W. Caskel, *Das altarabische Königreich,* Krefeld 1950; H. Charles, *Le christianisme des arabes nomades sur le limes et dans le désert syro-mésopotamien,* Paris 1936; L. Cheikho, *al-Naṣrāniyyatu wa-ādābuhā bayna ʿarab al-jāhiliyya,* 3 vols., Beirut 1913-23; R. Dussaud, *La pénétration des arabes en Syrie avant l'Islam,* Paris 1955; J.M. Fiey, Naṣārā, in *EI²,* vii, 970-3; S.H. Griffith, The Gospel in Arabic. An inquiry into its appearance in the first Abbasid century, in *OC* 69 (1985), 126-67; A. Havenith, *Les arabes chrétiens nomades au temps de Mohammed,* Louvain-La-Neuve 1988; C. Hechaïmé, *Louis Cheikho et son livre. Le christianisme et la littérature chrétienne en Arabie avant l'islam,* Beirut 1967; J. Henninger, Christentum im vorislamischen Arabien, in *Neue Zeitschrift für Missionswissenschaft* 4 (1948); R.G. Hoyland, *Seeing Islam as others saw it. A survey and evaluation of Christian, Jewish and Zoroastrian writings on early Islam,* Princeton 1997; M.J. Kister, *Concepts and ideas at the dawn of Islam,* Aldershot, Hampshire

1997; McAuliffe, *Qur᾿ānic;* A. Moberg, *Book of the Himyarites,* Lund 1920-1924; F. Nau, *Les arabes chrétiens de Mésopotamie et de Syrie du VIe au VIIe siècle,* Paris 1933; G. Olinder, *The kings of Kinda of the family of Akil al-Murār,* Lund 1927; R.A. Pritz, *Nazarene Jewish Christianity,* Leiden 1988; G. Rothstein, *Die Dynastie der Lahmiden in al-Ḥīra,* Berlin 1899; J. Sauvaget, Les Ghassanides et Sergiopolis, in *Byzantion* 14 (1939), 115-30; R. Schick, *The Christian communities of Palestine from Byzantine to Islamic rule,* Princeton 1995; W. Schmucker, Mubāhala, in *EI²,* vii, 276-7; I. Shahid, *The martyrs of Najran. New documents,* Brussels 1971; ibid., *Rome and the Arabs. A prolegomenon to the study of Byzantium and the Arabs,* Washington 1984; ibid., *Byzantium and the Arabs in the fourth century,* Washington 1984; ibid., *Byzantium and the Arabs in the fifth century,* Washington 1989; ibid., *Byzantium and the Arabs in the sixth century,* 2 vols., Washington 1995; J.S. Trimingham, *Christianity among the Arabs in pre-Islamic times,* London/New York 1979.

Chronological Sequence of the Qur᾿ān see CHRONOLOGY AND THE QUR᾿ĀN

Chronology and the Qur᾿ān

The Qur᾿ān is the most recent of the major sacred scriptures to have appeared in the chronology of human history. It originated at a crucial moment in time when Muḥammad proclaimed it in the northwestern half of the Arabian peninsula during the first quarter of the seventh century C.E. The Qur᾿ān exhibits a significant relationship to the biblical tradition, the scriptures of Judaism and Christianity, while it shows no literary affinity to the sacred literatures of Hinduism and Buddhism and little to Zoroastrian sacred writings (see SCRIPTURE AND THE QUR᾿ĀN). The elements of the biblical tradition included in the Qur᾿ān echo themes found in the apocryphal and midrashic writings of Judaism and Christianity more than those incorporated in their normative scriptures, the Hebrew Bible and the New Testament. No single collection of biblical writings, normative, apocryphal or midrashic, however, has been identified as the major source on which the Qur᾿ān might have depended directly. Nevertheless, as the last holy book in the historical sequence of the great world religions, the Qur᾿ān stands in a clear chronological relationship to the biblical tradition of Judaism and Christianity. There is no evidence that this tradition had been translated into Arabic by the time of Muḥammad, either as a whole corpus or in the form of single books. It is a widely shared view among historians of religion that Muḥammad's knowledge of the biblical tradition came principally, if not exclusively, from oral sources. This oral lore, enriched by extra-biblical additions and commentary, was communicated to Muḥammad in his mother tongue. It, however, ultimately originated in traditions recorded mainly in Syriac, Ethiopian, Aramaic and Hebrew, as evidenced by the vocabulary of foreign origin to be found in the Arabic Qur᾿ān (see FOREIGN VOCABULARY). In the main, this foreign vocabulary had already been assimilated, however, into the Arabic religious discourse of Muḥammad's native environment.

The Qur᾿ān is the first book-length production of Arabic literature and as such stands at the crossroads of the pre-Islamic oral, highly narrative and poetical tradition of the Arabic language (q.v.) and the written, increasingly scholarly prose tradition of the subsequently evolving civilization of Islam (see ORALITY AND WRITINGS IN ARABIA). The beginnings of this transition in the Arabic language from the oral to the written tradition can be pinpointed chronologically to the time and person of Muḥammad and can be seen as clearly reflected in the rhymed prose style of the Qur᾿ān. This rhymed prose (*saj῾,* see RHYMED PROSE), the mode of speech of the pre-Islamic soothsayer's oracles (see

DIVINATION), is a characteristic of the Qur'ān, the first sizeable Arabic document to exhibit this form of speech in written form. The roots of the Qur'ān as the first Arabic book can also be discovered in its content. In its verses (q.v.) the Qur'ān captured many topics that had formed an important part of the worship and cult of the non-scriptural tribal religion practiced in pre-Islamic Arabia (see SOUTH ARABIA, RELIGION IN PRE-ISLAMIC). Again, it is not possible to ascribe the origin of the Qur'ān to any single current of pre-Islamic tribal religion, though the religious practice of Mecca (q.v.) exerted the most influence on the vision of Arab tribal religion that Muḥammad had acquired in his early youth (see PRE-ISLAMIC ARABIA AND THE QUR'ĀN).

While the historian of religion classifies the Qur'ān as the last major scripture to appear in human history and the first actual book to be produced in the Arabic language, the Muslim believer views it as a text that in its essence fundamentally transcends all matters of chronology. For the believer the Qur'ān lies beyond the horizon of chronological analysis because it is the word of God, which is beyond all time, and the supreme book of divine revelation that derives its origin from God eternal (see REVELATION AND INSPIRATION). Since the dawn of creation (q.v.), God has manifested his will to humanity, revealing himself in his divine speech (q.v.). His word became book (q.v.) in the revealed scriptures that were communicated to the prophets throughout human history (see PROPHETS AND PROPHETHOOD). The Qur'ān is the most perfect and ultimate form of this divine revelation and represents the final stage of a process of "in-libration," the divine speech becoming holy book. In essence there is only one timeless revelation reiterated by the prophets, God's messengers (see MESSENGER) throughout the ages, without any contribution of their own. From Adam (q.v.) through Abraham (q.v.), Moses (q.v.), David (q.v.) and Jesus (q.v.) to Muḥammad, the messengers are human beings and divinely chosen mouthpieces of revelation through whom, in chronological succession, God speaks forth the primordial truth he wishes to reveal. God is the sole author of revealed scripture and his word passes untouched through the messenger whom it neither transforms nor divinizes. God is the speaker of the Qur'ān, Muḥammad its recipient; an angel of revelation, eventually identified as Gabriel (q.v.), its intermediary agent. Since the Qur'ān is and remains God's very own words, it includes only God's voice without any admixture of human speech. It literally *is* God's word, word for word. It holds nothing radically new because it brings the oldest thing of all, the first proclamation, unknown in the Arabic tongue prior to Muḥammad: God is one, creator of this world and judge in the world to come (see LAST JUDGMENT). Though clearly revealed at a definite point in time, in its essence the Qur'ān is rooted in the eternity of God (see CREATEDNESS OF THE QUR'ĀN).

The essential content of the divine revelation that would become the proclamation of the prophets is recorded in a heavenly book (q.v.), "the mother [i.e. essence] of the book," a qur'ānic phrase denoting the archetype of all divine revelation that is preserved in heaven and guarded by the angels (see PRESERVED TABLET). From this heavenly, a-temporal archetype the Qur'ān was revealed in clear Arabic to Muḥammad, the last prophet and messenger of God. Clearly understood, faithfully proclaimed and accurately recited by Muḥammad in historical time, the Qur'ān, according to the normative Muslim view, was memorized with exact precision and also collected in book-form by Muḥammad's followers after his death. Then it was recited and copied with infinite care in continuous transmission from generation to generation. Today, as in the past, the Qur'ān is copied and recited in Arabic, pronounced only in Arabic in Muslim ritual worship, by Arabs and non-Arabs alike (see RECITATION OF THE QUR'ĀN). It cannot be rendered adequately into any other tongue and, in the Muslim view, all translations are crutches, at best helpful explanations of its original intention and at worst doubtful makeshifts endangering its true meaning. Inasmuch as Muslims believe that the Qur'ān has been preserved unchanged through time in its pristine Arabic, it is superior to all other scriptures because of the faulty form in which these latter have been preserved by their respective communities. In particular, the revealed scripture given to Jesus, called the *injīl* (q.v.; see GOSPEL) and also the scripture given to Moses, called the *tawrāh* (see TORAH) have undergone alteration (*taḥrīf*, see CORRUPTION) at the hands of their followers through such modification of the original texts as insertions, omissions or falsifications (see POLEMIC AND POLEMICAL LANGUAGE). In Muslim eyes, the Qur'ān alone has remained unchanged over time in its divinely-willed form, transcending chronology both in its origin from God eternal and in its minutely faithful transmission through the centuries.

While respecting the faith perspective of Muslim believers about the Qur'ān, there have been since the middle of the last century philologists and orientalists and then in the present century islamicists and text-critical scholars of the history of religions who have tried to analyze the Qur'ān as a literary text and historical source. These scholarly approaches have focused principally on questions involving the "chronology" of the Qur'ān. What is the self-perception of time and history in the Qur'ān? What are the historical data in the Qur'ān that link it chronologically to Muḥammad's life and career? What differences exist between the chronological sequence of the revelation of individual qur'ānic passages and the actual order of the chapters *(suwar,* sing. *sūra)* and verses *(āyāt,* sing. *āya)* that appear in the final redaction of the Qur'ān as a book? What were the major stages of composition and redaction that were taken sequentially by the early Muslim community to produce the book of the Qur'ān in the form in which it appears today? These questions, focused on the chronology of the Qur'ān, were to become of central importance in any scholarly analysis of the text, its content, its style, its composition, its redaction and the history of its early transmission until the final fixation of the normative text of the Qur'ān. Due to the complexity of each of these questions, they shall be addressed separately below.

Qur'ānic perception of time

The qur'ānic text reflects an atomistic concept of time, while lacking a notion of time as divided into past, present and future. Chiefly this is because Arabic grammar knows only two aspects of time (q.v.), complete and incomplete, without distinguishing precisely between present and future. The Qur'ān also rejects the pre-Islamic fatalism of impersonal time (*dahr,* see FATE) which holds sway over everything and erases human works without hope for life beyond death (cf. Q 39:42; 45:24; 76:1). Affirming resurrection (q.v.) of the body and life in the world to come (see ESCHATOLOGY), the Qur'ān explains time from the perspective of a transcendent monotheism (see GOD AND HIS ATTRIBUTES) that promises paradise (q.v.) and threatens eternal damnation (see HELL). Obliterating the spell of fate and subduing the all-pervading power of time, God almighty made the heavens and the earth (Q 6:73; 7:54; 10:3; 11:7; 25:59;

32:4; 50:38; 57:4) and formed the first human being in an instant through his command, "Be!" (Q 3:59; for other references to God's creative ability, cf. Q 2:117; 3:47; 16:40; 19:35; 36:82; 40:68). He gives life and brings death according to his will and rules each moment of human existence (Q 53:44-54; cf. 35:12; 39:42; 40:69; 50:42): God is the Lord of each instant; what he has decreed happens. The most common term adopted in Arabic for time, *zamān*, does not appear in the Qur'ān, nor does *qidam*, its counterpart for eternity. The Qur'ān, however, has a great variety of terms for time understood as a moment or short duration (e.g. *waqt, ḥīn, ān, yawm, sāʿa*). These terms give expression to an atomism of time that includes a vision of God acting instantaneously in the world as the sole true cause. Of itself, creation (q.v.) is discontinuous. It appears to be continuous only because of God's compassionate consistency.

Qur'ānic perception of history

Bolstered by the lack of genuine verbs for "to be" and "to become" in the Arabic language, the atomism of time also underlies the qur'ānic vision of history, which is typological in nature and focused on the history of the prophets. In the Qur'ān, history is seen as the scenario of God's sending messengers as warners (see WARNING) and guides to successive generations (q.v.), each of whom rejects the monotheistic message that the prophets proclaim and is overtaken by a devastating divine punishment (see PUNISHMENT STORIES). Whether it refers to the legendary peoples of the ancient Arabs and their leaders or to biblical figures such as Noah (q.v.), Lot (q.v.) and their people, the same typology is repeated from messenger to messenger. Each of them comes with an essentially identical message and is himself saved, while his disobedient people are destroyed. History in the Qur'ān is principally portrayed as a series of such typological events, in which the features of similarity override the actual differences among individual stories of the prophets. The best explanation for this recurrent typological pattern is Muḥammad's ingenious interpretation of history in the light of his own life and time, which he took as the yardstick, projecting his own experience back onto all other messengers before him. Just as the qur'ānic emphasis on the atomism of time had frozen the flux of time into that of reiterated instants of God's action, so its typology of history had collapsed the rich variety of past events into a regularly recurring pattern. Not pretending to be a document of historical record, the Qur'ān simply represents the prophetic preaching of Muḥammad, making passing references to his personal situation, the opposition of his adversaries (see OPPOSITION TO MUḤAMMAD) and the questions of his followers. Consequently it often lacks precise historical information, mention of the specific dates of events and determination of detailed or approximate historical settings (see HISTORY AND THE QUR'ĀN).

Qur'ānic references to events contemporaneous with the lifetime of Muḥammad

There are certain allusions, however, which may be retrieved from the text of the Qur'ān as indicators of historical circumstances that relate to Muḥammad's life and times. These references are often obscure. They refer to Muḥammad's orphanage (see ORPHANS), his uncle Abū Lahab (see FAMILY OF THE PROPHET), his persecution at the hands of the Meccans, the tribal boycott of his clan at Mecca, the political rivalry of Mecca with Ṭā'if and the religious practices observed at the Meccan sanctuary of the Kaʿba (q.v.), the hills of Ṣafā (q.v.) and Marwa (q.v.), Mount ʿArafāt (see ʿARAFĀT) and the sanctuary in al-Muzdalifa. A somewhat cryptic reference to the military defeat of the Byzantine forces at the hands of their Persian enemies — probably leading to their loss of Jerusalem in 614 C.E. — is found in Q 30:2-5 (see BYZANTINES). The return to Mecca of some of Muḥammad's followers who had emigrated to Abyssinia (q.v.) — probably in 615 C.E. — and had recited Q 19 to the Negus, may be connected with Q 53:19-23 on the basis of references found in the traditional biography of Muḥammad (see SĪRA AND THE QURʾĀN). The conversion of ʿUmar (q.v.) — dated on the basis of extra-qurʾānic sources to the year 618 C.E. — occurred after the revelation of Q 20. The emigration *(hijra)* of Muḥammad and his followers from Mecca to Medina (see EMIGRATION), which is generally understood as the first firm date of the Islamic era (see CALENDAR), is implied in Q 2:218, although its actual dating to September, 622 can only be determined with the help of extra-qurʾānic sources. The change of the direction toward which ritual prayer must be performed *(qibla,* q.v.), which Muḥammad initiated more than a year after settling in Medina, is signaled in Q 2:142-4 in association with Q 2:150.

For the time after the emigration, there are explicit references to battles fought by Muḥammad at Badr (q.v.; 2/624) and Ḥunayn (q.v.; 8/630), and circumstantial references to the battle of Uḥud (q.v.; 3/625), the encounter at the Trench (5/627), and the expeditions to Khaybar (q.v.; 7/628) and Tabūk (9/630, see EXPEDITIONS AND BATTLES). We find as well implicit references to the pledges made by Muḥammad at ʿAqaba in the year prior to the emigration (cf. Q 40:12) and at al-Ḥudaybiya (q.v.) in 6/628 (cf. Q 48:27 in association with 48:18), the expulsion of the Jewish tribe of Banū l-Naḍīr from Medina (cf. Q 59:1-24; see NAḌĪR), an episode involving Muḥammad's adopted son Zayd b. Ḥāritha (q.v.; cf. Q 33:37) and a reference to Muḥammad's qurʾānic address at his farewell pilgrimage (cf. Q 5:3; see FAREWELL). The dates for these events, however, can only be supplied from extra-qurʾānic sources such as the biographical literature on the Prophet. Qurʾānic passages with chronological implications that are linked to the inner development of Muḥammad's prophetic career and religious experience are Q 96:1-5 and 74:1-7 (Muḥammad's call to prophethood), Q 53:1-18 and 81:15-29 (Muḥammad's visions, see VISIONS) and Q 17:1 (Muḥammad's night journey; see ASCENSION) among others. As is evident from all of these mainly circumstantial references, the framework for dating qurʾānic verses in relation to Muḥammad's life is rather tenuous. There are no reliable chronological references in the Qurʾān itself that could be matched with the period prior to the emigration and there are only a few firm dates concerning events of Muḥammad's biography after the emigration that can be coordinated chronologically with qurʾānic verses. Again, hardly any of the historical events in question can be established purely by reference to the Qurʾān without recourse to extra-qurʾānic sources.

Early Islamic methods for determining the order in which Muḥammad received the revelations

From the earliest centuries of Islam, the jurists and scholars of religious law *(fuqahāʾ)* developed a particular sensitivity for chronological inconsistencies affecting a variety of legal stipulations in the Qurʾān. Acknowledging the differences and variations of regulation found in disparate verses of the Qurʾān, they developed a theory of abrogation *(al-nāsikh wa-l-mansūkh,* see ABROGATION), which established lists of abrogating and abrogated verses on the basis of their chronological order. This analysis had its earliest example in the systematic work entitled *al-Nāsikh wa-l-mansūkh* of Abū ʿUbayd al-Qāsim b. Sallām (d. 224/838). For this theory — the qurʾānic basis for which is found in Q 2:106 and 16:101 — examples into the hundreds were cited. Q 5:90, prohibiting the drinking of wine, was understood as abrogating Q 2:219 and 4:43, which tolerated it (see INTOXICANTS). Q 4:10-1 on inheritance (q.v.), allotting to the relatives specific shares in a deceased's estate, were seen as revoking Q 2:180, which had instituted testamentary provisions for parents and nearest kin. Q 8:66 was taken to reduce from ten to two the number of unbelievers against whom the Muslims in Q 8:65 were required to fight. The "sword verse" (Q 9:5) alone was thought to have replaced 124 other verses. The "Ibn Adam verse" and verses praising the martyrs of Biʾr Maʿūna (see MARTYR) were claimed to have been lost altogether. The locus of the spurious "stone verse," mandating ritual stoning (q.v.) as a punishment for fornication, was believed to have been omitted from the qurʾānic text (see ADULTERY AND FORNICATION). The highly controversial and infamous "Satanic verses" (q.v.), cited in the extra-qurʾānic literature (e.g. Ṭabarī, *Taʾrīkh*, i, 1192-3), were understood as having been actually replaced by Q 53:19-23 with the significantly later Q 22:52-3 explaining the Satanic interference. (See also CHASTISEMENT AND PUNISHMENT; BOUNDARIES AND PRECEPTS).

Other Muslim scholars, especially the early works of qurʾānic exegetes *(mufassirūn)*, were fully aware of the scanty amount of chronological information that could be retrieved from the Qurʾān and hence turned to the Prophet's biography (*sīra*, see SĪRA AND THE QURʾĀN), the reports about his actions and words *(ḥadīth)* and the early historiography of Muḥammad's campaigns *(maghāzī)* for circumstances that might be seen as linked to individual passages of the Qurʾān. This led to the development of a separate genre of literature called "the occasions of the revelation" (*asbāb al-nuzūl*, exemplified by the work of al-Wāḥidī, d. 468/1075-6; see OCCASIONS OF REVELATION) that connected a small portion of qurʾānic verses with actual occurrences and with stories about Muḥammad's time and career, many of which were legendary. The method of the scholars dealing with the theory of abrogation was primarily intra-qurʾānic, i.e. replacing the legislative force of one qurʾānic verse with that of another. It, however, also made ample room for a ḥadīth to be abrogated by another ḥadīth and cited cases where a qurʾānic passage was abrogated by a ḥadīth or vice versa (see ḤADĪTH AND THE QURʾĀN). On the contrary, the method of the scholars dealing with the occasions of the revelation was primarily extra-qurʾānic, relating qurʾānic verses to circumstances that could be established through recourse to the extra-qurʾānic literature of the Islamic scholarly tradition. Both methods focused their chronological analysis on individual or isolated qurʾānic verses and small passages rather than on qurʾānic chapters and sūras as integral units of revelation. This approach, attentive to individual qurʾānic passages, was very much in step with the piecemeal character of the qurʾānic revelation itself.

Another group of Muslim scholars active in later medieval times based their analysis of qurʾānic chronology on the assumption that the individual sūras formed the original units of revelation and could best be divided into two sets, Meccan and Medinan, according to whether they were revealed before or after the emigration *(hijra)*. This division into Meccan and Medinan sūras became the most characteristic method of chronological analysis. The first attempt of this kind was the list of sūras attributed to Ibn ʿAbbās (d. 68/688), the traditional father of qurʾānic exegesis. Later scholars further elaborated this system until it achieved fixation in the qurʾānic commentary of al-Bayḍāwī (d. 716/1316) and the *Itqān* of al-Suyūṭī (d. 911/1505). Centuries later the latter became the principal starting point for Western scholarship on qurʾānic chronology. Muslim scholars, however, had to cope with the fact that the exact chronological listing of sūras had been in dispute since Qatāda (d. 112/730) and that qurʾānic scholars had not managed to agree on whether certain sūras were either Meccan or Medinan, and thus had furnished a list of 17 disputed sūras, namely Q 13; 47; 55; 57; 61; 64; 83; 95; 97; 98; 99; 100; 102; 107; 112; 113; 114). To these other scholars added six more (Q 49; 62; 63; 77; 89; 92). The traditional chronological order attributed to Ibn ʿAbbās, however, became widely accepted and was generally adopted by the Egyptian standard edition of the Qurʾān published in 1924. It enumerated 86 Meccan sūras and added headings to each sūra indicating its exact chronological locus in the traditional order of revelation established by Muslim scholarship. It also noted later Medinan verses which were inserted into a number of the earlier Meccan sūras and cited three Medinan sūras (Q 8; 47; 9) that incorporated earlier verses. This Muslim method of chronological analysis, separating Meccan from Medinan sūras, reflected two basic assumptions, namely that the sources of traditional Muslim scholarship provided a solidly reliable basis for the chronological ordering of the sūras and that the sūras could be treated and dated as integral units of revelation.

Western historical-critical qurʾānic analysis

From the mid-nineteenth century Western scholars began to engage in serious literary research on the Qurʾān linking the scholarly findings of traditional Muslim scholarship with the philological and text-critical methods that biblical scholarship was developing in Europe. An intensive scholarly attempt was made to arrive at a chronological order of qurʾānic chapters and passages that could be correlated with the development and varying circumstances of Muḥammad's religious career. Beginning with Gustav Weil (*Historisch-kritische Einleitung,* Bielefeld 1844), this Western chronological approach to the Qurʾān achieved its climax in the highly-acclaimed *Geschichte des Qorans* by Theodor Nöldeke (Göttingen 1860). It was later revised and expanded by Friedrich Schwally (Leipzig 1909-19) and later by Gotthelf Bergsträsser and Otto Pretzl (Leipzig 1938) into a three-volume work. This work became the classic of Western qurʾānic scholarship and the foundation of its widely-accepted framework of qurʾānic chronology, one to which Régis Blachère (*Introduction,* Paris 1947-50) added further refinements. The chronological sequencing of the sūras, elaborated by Western qurʾānic scholarship, largely adopted the distinction of traditional Muslim scholarship between Meccan and Medinan sūras. It further subdivided the Meccan phase of Muḥammad's proclamation of the Qurʾān into three distinct periods.

A different method leading to similar chronological results, however, was chosen by Hartwig Hirschfeld (*Composition and exegesis,* London 1902), who proposed an arrangement of the Meccan sūras into periods according to five literary criteria — confirmatory, declamatory, narrative, descriptive and legislative — followed by the group of Medinan sūras. Some years earlier (*The Corân. Its composition and teaching,* London 1875), William Muir made the innovative suggestion in his rearrangement of the sūras that eighteen short sūras, termed rhapsodies, dated from before Muḥammad's call (Q 103; 100; 99; 91; 106; 1; 101; 95; 102; 104; 82; 92; 105; 89; 90; 93; 94; 108). A drastically different approach was taken by Richard Bell (*The Qurʾān,* 2 vols., Edinburgh 1937-9 and posthumously

A commentary on the Qurʾān, 2 vols. Manchester 1991), who abandoned the chronological division into Meccan and Medinan periods and designed a highly subjective and disjointed dating system for individual verses in the Qurʾān taken as a whole. The two summary follow-up reactions to R. Bell in 1977 by John Wansbrough (*Quranic studies,* London 1977) and John Burton (*The collection of the Qurʾān,* Cambridge 1977) challenged the assumptions underlying the Western chronological approach from totally opposite sides. Rudi Paret (*Der Koran: Kommentar und Konkordanz,* Stuttgart 1971), on the other hand, integrated the major findings of Western scholarship on qurʾānic chronology with the principal ancillary studies authored in the West in his balanced manual of commentary and concordance to the Qurʾān.

The overriding goal of the chronological framework of the Qurʾān, elaborated in Western scholarship, was to divide the qurʾānic proclamation into four periods — Mecca i, Mecca ii, Mecca iii, and Medina — and to link these with a vision of the gradual inner development of Muḥammad's prophetic consciousness and political career that Western scholarship had determined through biographical research on the life of Muḥammad, worked out in lockstep with its research on the Qurʾān. This was initiated by Alois Sprenger (*Leben und Lehre,* 3 vols., 1861-5) and Hubert Grimme (*Mohammed,* 1892-5) and was later developed by Frants Buhl (*Das Leben Mohammeds,* 1934) and with certain modifications by W. Montgomery Watt (*Muhammad at Mecca,* 1953; *Muhammad at Medina,* 1956). Chronological research on the Qurʾān and biographical research on Muḥammad's career were closely dependent on each other. For this reason, the threat of a circular argument remained a constant danger for this approach because the subjective evaluation of Muḥammad's religious development had to be read back into a great variety of disparate qurʾānic verses from which it had been originally culled. Nevertheless, the division of the Meccan sūras into three sequential periods offered many new insights into Muḥammad's genesis as a prophet prior to the emigration and opened novel perspectives into significant stages of development in his early qurʾānic proclamation.

In general, the fourfold division of periods of the qurʾānic proclamation proceeded on the basis of two major principles. It related qurʾānic passages source-critically to historical events known from extra-qurʾānic literature and it systematically analyzed the philological and stylistic nature of the Arabic text of the Qurʾān passage by passage (see GRAMMAR AND THE QURʾĀN; FORM AND STRUCTURE OF THE QURʾĀN). It also placed clear markers between the Meccan periods at the approximate time of the emigration to Abyssinia (about 615 C.E.) and Muḥammad's disillusioned return from Ṭāʾif (about 620 C.E.) and retained the emigration in 622 C.E. as the divide between Meccan and Medinan sūras. An overview of major versions of the chronological re-arrangement of the sūras in comparison to their actual numbered order in the Qurʾān may be found in Watt-Bell, *Introduction,* 205-13.

The group of sūras classified as belonging to the first or early Meccan period — forty-eight sūras in T. Nöldeke's chronology — were identified by a similarity of style which gives expression to Muḥammad's initial enthusiasm in a language that is rich in images, powerful in passion, uttered in short and rhythmic verses, marked by a strong poetic coloring and with about thirty oaths or adjurations introducing individual sūras or passages. Most of these sūras, which are understood as a group rather than as standing in the exact chronological order of their revelation, are short.

Twenty-three of them have less than twenty and fourteen less than fifty verses. They are driven by a heightened awareness of the apocalyptic end of this world and God's final judgment of humanity (see APOCALYPSE). They include Muḥammad's vehement attacks against his Meccan opponents for adhering to the old Arab tribal religion and his vigorous rebuttals of their damaging accusations against his claim of divine inspiration, when they dismissively characterized him as a soothsayer (*kāhin,* see SOOTHSAYERS), poet (*shāʿir,* see POETRY AND POETS) and a man possessed (*majnūn,* see INSANITY).

The sūras of the second or middle Meccan period, twenty-one in number, have longer verses and longer units of revelation, which are more prosaic and do not exhibit a clearly distinct common character. They mark the transition from the excitement of the first phase to a Muḥammad of greater calm who aims to influence his audience by paranetic proofs selected from descriptions of natural phenomena, illustrations from human life and vivid depictions of paradise (q.v.) and hellfire (see FIRE; HELL; NATURAL WORLD AND THE QUR᾽ĀN). The stories of earlier prophets and elements from the story of Moses, in particular, are cited as admonitions for his enemies and as encouragement for himself and the small group of his followers. The place of the oaths (q.v.) is taken by introductory titles such as "This is the revelation of God" and by the frequently recurring, "Say!" *(qul),* the divine command for Muḥammad to proclaim a certain qur᾽ānic passage. The name *al-raḥmān* (the merciful), a name for God in use prior to Islam in southern and central Arabia, although rejected by the pre-Islamic Meccans, is frequently employed although it dies out in the third period (see below for a discussion on the names of God).

The sūras of the third or late Meccan period are also 21 in number but cannot be seen as standing in any kind of inner chronological order. They exhibit a broad, prosaic style with rhyme patterns that become more and more stereotyped, frequently ending in *-ūn* and *-īn*. The formula "You people" *(yā ayyuhā l-nās)* is frequently employed by Muḥammad in addressing his followers as a group. Muḥammad's imagination seems to be subdued, the revelations take on the form of sermons or speeches and the prophetic stories repeat earlier ideas. Overall, this group of sūras could be understood to reflect Muḥammad's exasperation at the stubborn resistance to his message on the part of his fellow Meccan tribesmen.

The sūras of the Medinan period, 24 in number, follow one another in a relatively certain chronological order and reflect Muḥammad's growing political power and his shaping of the social framework of the Muslim community (see COMMUNITY AND SOCIETY). As the acknowledged leader in spiritual and social affairs of the Medinan community, a community that had been torn by internal strife prior to his arrival, Muḥammad's qur᾽ānic proclamation becomes preoccupied with criminal legislation, civil matters such as laws of marriage, divorce (see MARRIAGE AND DIVORCE) and inheritance (q.v.), and with the summons to holy war (*jihād,* q.v.) "in the path of God" (*fī sabīl Allāh,* see PATH OR WAY [OF GOD]; LAW AND THE QUR᾽ĀN). Various groups of people are addressed separately by different epithets. The believers, the Meccan emigrants *(muhājirūn)* and their Medinan helpers (*anṣār,* see EMIGRANTS AND HELPERS), are addressed as "You who believe" *(yā ayyuhā lladhīna āmanū),* while the Medinans who distrusted Muḥammad and hesitated in converting to Islam are called "waverers" (*munāfiqūn,* see HYPOCRITES AND HYPOCRISY). The members of the Jewish tribes of the Qurayẓa (q.v.), Naḍīr (q.v.)

and Qaynuqāʿ (q.v.) are collectively called Jews (*yāhūd*, see JEWS AND JUDAISM) and the Christians are referred to by the group name of Nazarenes (*naṣārā*, see CHRISTIANS AND CHRISTIANITY). More than thirty times — and only in Medinan verses — the peoples who have been given a scripture in previous eras are identified collectively by the set phrase "the people of the book" (*ahl al-kitāb*, see PEOPLE OF THE BOOK). They are distinguished from the *ummiyyūn* (Q 2:78; 3:20, 75; 62:2), who have not been given the book previously but from among whom God selected Muḥammad, called *al-nabī al-ummī* in the late Meccan passage Q 7:157-8, as his messenger (see ILLITERACY). A significant group of qurʾānic passages from Medinan *sūra*s refers to Muḥammad's breach with the Jewish tribes and his subsequent interpretation of the figure of Abraham, supported by Ishmael (q.v.), as the founder of the Meccan sanctuary and the prototypical Muslim (*ḥanīf*, q.v.) who represents the original pure religion designated "the religion of Abraham" *(millat Ibrāhīm)* and now reinstated by Muḥammad.

The most radical chronological rearrangement of the sūras and verses of the Qurʾān was undertaken by R. Bell who concluded his elaborate hypothesis with many provisos. He suggested that the composition of the Qurʾān followed three main phases: a "Sign" phase, a "Qurʾān" phase and a "Book" phase. The earliest phase in R. Bell's view was that of "sign passages" *(āyāt)* and exhortations (q.v.) to worship God. These represent the major portion of Muḥammad's preaching at Mecca of which only an incomplete and partially fragmentary amount survive. The "Qurʾān" phase included the later stages of Muḥammad's Meccan career and about the first two years of his activity at Medina, a phase during which Muḥammad was faced with the task of producing a collection of liturgical recitals (sing. *qurʾān*). The Book phase belonged to his activity at Medina and began at the end of the second year after the emigration from which time Muḥammad set out to produce a written scripture *(kitāb)*. In the present Qurʾān, each of these three phases, however, cannot be separated precisely because sign passages came to be incorporated into the liturgical collection and earlier oral recitals were later revised to form part of the written book. In explaining his complex system of distinguishing criteria, Bell often remained rather general in his remarks. He dissected sūras on the basis of subjective impressions and suggested arbitrarily that certain passages had been discarded while the content of other "scraps of paper" that were meant to be discarded had been retained. He convincingly argued, however, that the original units of revelation were short, piecemeal passages which Muḥammad himself collected into sūras and that written documents were used in the process of redaction, a process undertaken with the help of scribes during Muḥammad's career in Medina. Regarding the redaction of the Qurʾān during Muḥammad's lifetime, the starting point for the Qurʾān as sacred scripture, in Bell's view, had to be related to the time of the battle of Badr (q.v.; 2/624). For Bell, this was the watershed event while the emigration *(hijra)* did not constitute a great divide for the periodization of the sūras.

None of the systems of chronological sequencing of qurʾānic chapters and verses has been accepted universally by contemporary scholarship. T. Nöldeke's sequencing and its refinements have established a rule of thumb for the approximate order of the sūras in their chronological sequence. Bell's hypothesis has established that the final redaction of the Qurʾān was a complex process of successive revisions of earlier material whether oral or already available in rudimentary written form. In many ways, Western qurʾānic scholarship reconfirmed the two pillars on which the traditional Muslim views of qurʾānic chronology were based. First, the Qurʾān was revealed piecemeal and, second, it was collected into book-form on the basis of both written documents prepared by scribes on Muḥammad's dictation and qurʾānic passages preserved in the collective memory of his circle of companions. All methods of chronological analysis, whether traditional Muslim or modern Western, agree that the order of the sūras in Muḥammad's proclamation was different from the order found in the written text we hold in hand today where, in general, the sūras are arranged according to the principle of decreasing length.

One consequence of the chronological periodization of sūras was the attention given to the first and last qurʾānic proclamations. There is a general consensus that either Q 96:1-5 or 74:1-7 represent the first proclamation of qurʾānic verses uttered by the Prophet. In particular Q 96:1-5 which includes the command, "Recite!" *(iqraʾ)*, derived from the same Arabic root as the word "Qurʾān" but also Q 74:1-7 which may refer to Muḥammad being raised from sleep at night, especially if seen in parallel to Q 73:1-5, are linked in ḥadīth literature with Muḥammad's call to prophethood. This call, the beginning of qurʾānic revelation, occurred according to Islamic tradition during the night of destiny (*laylat al-qadr*, Q 97:1-3; cf. 44:3; see NIGHT OF POWER), ordinarily identified as the twenty-seventh day of the month of Ramaḍān (q.v.). As is to be expected, the last passages of the Qurʾān were sought among the Medinan sūras and Muslim scholarship identified sūras 5, 9 or 110 as the last to be revealed. Some pointed to either Q 2:278 or 281 or Q 4:174 as the last verse of the Qurʾān, while others opted for Q 9:128-9, two verses said to have been finally found during the collection of the qurʾānic material into book-form. The most suitable candidate for the last verse, however, is Q 5:3 which includes Muḥammad's affirmation, "Today I have completed your religion," and one on which there is much agreement among Muslim and Western Qurʾān scholars.

Thematic manifestations of qurʾānic chronology

Qurʾānic chronology is also manifest in the development of inner-qurʾānic topics, four of which may be analysed as cases in point: disconnected letters, ritual prayer, the name for God and the figure of Abraham. From a stylistic perspective, a particular and characteristic phenomenon of the Qurʾān with chronological implications is the so-called mysterious or disconnected letters (*al-ḥurūf al-muqaṭṭaʿa*, see LETTERS AND MYSTERIOUS LETTERS) found immediately after the introductory *basmala* (q.v.; the formulaic saying "In the name of God, the merciful, the compassionate") of twenty-nine sūras. Muslim sources, which consider the disconnected letters an integral part of the qurʾānic revelation, record no recollection of their real significance as is shown by the great variety of explanations given for them. Many Muslim and Western scholars have attempted to interpret the function of the disconnected letters in the Qurʾān, but no satisfactory explanation has been found. Among the theories put forward are that the letters represent abbreviations of the divine names, the initials of the owners of manuscripts used in the redaction of the Qurʾān, numbers written in Arabic letters or simply letters possessing an inscrutable or mystical meaning known only by God. Three consistent factors, however, can be observed that may undergird a chronological explanation of their function in the Qurʾān. First, the disconnected letters at the beginning of the twenty-nine sūras belong to later Meccan and early Medinan sūras. The letters sometimes occur singly and sometimes in groups of two to five. Some of these occur only once while others are repeated before two, five or six sūras. Secondly, these letters are pronounced separately in recitation as the letters of the alphabet, and the literature on the variant readings of the Qurʾān reveals no differences regarding their recitation (see READINGS OF THE QURʾĀN). Thirdly, they represent every consonantal form of the Arabic alphabet in Kufic script, the earliest Arabic script (q.v.), namely fourteen forms, and no form is used for more than a single letter of the alphabet.

On the basis of these constant factors it may be argued that the disconnected letters are related to an ordering of sūras, using the letters of the Arabic alphabet in the time when Muḥammad collected sūras (q.v.) for liturgical purposes and began to take the first steps toward a written scripture. This rather general explanation of the function of the disconnected letters in the chronological genesis of the text of the Qurʾān could be confirmed by the fact that certain groups of sūras introduced by the same letters — especially those beginning with the letter patterns *alif - lām - mīm, alif - lām - rāʾ, ḥāʾ - mīm* and *ṭāʾ - sīn - [mīm]* — have been kept together in the actual order of the Qurʾān despite their sometimes widely varying lengths and by the fact that in almost all cases the disconnected letters are followed by a usually explicit or occasionally implicit reference to the revelation of scripture as a "Book" sent down or a "Qurʾān" made clear. Because the disconnected letters appear only at the beginning and never within the body of a sūra, such as at points of incision indicated by a change of style, rhyme or content, they belong to the initial phase of redaction by Muḥammad himself rather than to either the original proclamation of qurʾānic passages by Muḥammad or to the final redaction of the Qurʾān after his death. The insertion of the letters after Muḥammad's death would presuppose the sporadic introduction of letter patterns into the final text by a later hand. This general explanation favors the view that Muḥammad as redactor was the author of the disconnected letters affixed to the beginning of sūras and that he began quite early to produce his own scriptural text with the help of scribes, by piecing together passages of similar content in certain sūras. Some of these he then marked as a liturgical unit through the insertion of the disconnected letters, a marking scheme that the final redactors of the Qurʾān felt obliged to respect.

Yet another phenomenon that manifests significant chronological parameters is the genesis of central religious institutions introduced by Muḥammad such as the ritual prayer (*ṣalāt*, see PRAYER) of Islam. The institution of the ritual prayer cannot be traced to the earliest phase of Muḥammad's qurʾānic proclamation in which the root *ṣallā* is used in reference to the tribal practice of animal sacrifice (Q 108:2; see CONSECRATION OF ANIMALS; SACRIFICE) and the prayers of unbelieving Meccans (Q 107:4-7). At this stage the recitation of the Qurʾān is as yet not linked with ritual prayer but is connected with Muḥammad's labor in composing qurʾānic passages (Q 73:1-8). Somewhat later, about the middle of the Meccan period of his qurʾānic proclamation, Muḥammad began to observe a night vigil *(tahajjud)* which combined the recitation of the Qurʾān with the beginnings of a prayer practice called *ṣalāt* (Q 17:78-9; cf. 25:64; 51:17-8) that was performed both by day and by night (Q 76:25-6; 52:48-9). At first Muḥammad alone is called to perform the *ṣalāt* (Q 17:110; 20:130) but, then, in Q 20:132, he is clearly summoned to command his relatives or followers *(ahlaka)* to perform the *ṣalāt* together with him and to persevere with those who invoke God morning and evening (Q 18:28) or prostrate themselves in prayer at night (Q 39:9; see BOWING AND PROSTRATION). During this phase, Muḥammad also draws attention to the great qur᾽ānic models of prayer, Abraham (Q 26:83-9), Moses (Q 20:25-35) and Zechariah (q.v.; Q 19:3-6) and points to God's servant, Jesus, as a prophet divinely commissioned to practice *ṣalāt* (Q 19:30-1). Perhaps somewhat later in the Meccan phase of his proclamation Muḥammad is prompted, again in the singular, to perform the *ṣalāt* at three different times of day (see DAY, TIMES OF), in the morning and in the evening, and also during the night (Q 11:114-5; 50:39-40). His followers are admonished to join in the practice, which clearly includes the recitation of the Qur᾽ān and prostration in prayer (Q 7:204-6). The evolution of ritual prayer can also be traced in the varying yet vacillating qur᾽ānic vocabulary used in the late Meccan and early Medinan periods for the prayer times: in the morning (at the dawning of the day and before the rising of the sun), in the evening (at the declining of the day and before the setting of the sun) and during the night (*tahajjad,* Q 17:79; *zulafan min al-layl,* Q 11:114; *ānā᾽ al-layl,* Q 3:113).

After the emigration *(hijra),* qur᾽ānic chronology demonstrates that the *ṣalāt* becomes a firm institution of the individual and communal ritual prayer for Muslims. References to *ṣalāt* (generally used in the singular) occur with high frequency in the Medinan sūras (33 times in Q 2, 4, 5, 9 and 24 alone, representing half of all occurrences of this term in the entire Qur᾽ān) and are now frequently linked with its sister religious institution of almsgiving (*zakāt,* the development of which can itself be traced in the Qur᾽ān from an act of free giving to a religious duty and communal tax; see ALMSGIVING). The frequent reference to a normative obligation to perform *ṣalāt* is paralleled by the emphatic introduction of the obligatory direction of prayer *(qibla)*. At first this may have been observed in the direction of Jerusalem (q.v.), emulating Jewish-Christian custom, but then was changed toward the Kaʿba of Mecca by a qur᾽ānic command (Q 2:142-52). These particular early Medinan verses were proclaimed by Muḥammad at about the time of the battle of Badr in 2/624 although they may actually reflect a gradual process of change in the ritualization of the *ṣalāt* and the fixation of its *qibla*. Furthermore, in Medina, the specific prayer times are fixed for what has now clearly become a daily ritual prayer that is repeatedly enjoined in the plural *(aqīmū al-ṣalāt),* is performed standing upright (cf. Q 4:102) and includes the recitation of the Qur᾽ān (cf. Q 7:204-5). Finally, the Medinan verse Q 2:238 firmly establishes a ritual mid-day prayer *(al-ṣalāt al-wusṭā)* which may already have been introduced toward the end of Muḥammad's career in Mecca when he summoned his followers to praise God in the morning, the evening and during the middle of the day (*wa-ḥīna tuẓhirūn,* Q 30:17-8). From this point on, the *ṣalāt* is enjoined upon the believers at fixed times (*kitāban mawqūtan,* Q 4:103) and the communal prayer during the week is explicitly fixed on Friday *(yawm al-jumʿa),* the market day of Medina (Q 62:9). The believers are called to prayer (Q 5:58; 62:9) and ritual ablutions before prayer *(wuḍū᾽, ghusl)* are established in detail, including such specificity as the substitution of sand in the absence of water (*tayammum,* cf. Q 4:43; 5:6) and provisos for people who are traveling (see CLEANLINESS AND ABLUTION; RITUAL PURITY).

It is more difficult to trace stages of chronological development for the proper name for God in the Qur᾽ān, which relies principally on Allāh (*al-ilāh,* lit. the deity),

Lord *(rabb)* and the Merciful *(al-raḥmān)* but ultimately establishes Allāh as the predominant designation and the one adopted by Islam throughout the centuries. In what the Islamic tradition identifies as the first verses of qur'ānic revelation, Muḥammad is summoned to speak in the name of "your Lord" (*rabbika,* Q 96:1; *rabbaka,* 74:3). A non-secular usage of lord (q.v.) or master (*rabb,* never used with the definite article in the Qur'ān yet very often linked with a personal pronoun), was familiar to the Meccans from pre-Islamic times. This is demonstrated by the phrase "the lord of this house" (*rabba hādhā l-bayt,* Q 106:3), the house being the Ka'ba in Mecca. It is most frequently employed in the first Meccan period (e.g. "Extol the name of your lord the most high *[sabbiḥi sma rabbika l-a'lā]*" Q 87:1), less often in the second and third (as in Pharaoh's [q.v.] blasphemous utterance, "I am your lord the most high *[anā rabbukumu l-a'lā]*" Q 79:24; see also BLASPHEMY), and only rarely in Medinan verses. On the contrary, the term Allāh, known to the Meccans prior to Muḥammad as a proper name for God, is attested in pre-Islamic poetry and pre-Islamic personal names. In all probability it is a contraction of *al-ilāh* which, itself, is never used in the Qur'ān, though the form *ilāh,* without the definite article but in a genitive construction, is employed to denote a specific deity as in "the deity of the people," *ilāh al-nās,* Q 114:3, used interchangeably with "the lord of the people," *rabb al-nās,* Q 114:1). The term Allāh occurs very rarely in the first Meccan period, is still infrequent throughout the second and into the third Meccan periods but finally becomes so dominant that it appears on average about every five verses in the Medinan *sūras*. The Merciful (*al-raḥmān,* probably derived from the personal name for God in southern and central Arabian usage), makes a strong entry into the qur'ānic vocabulary for God in the second Meccan period but then is almost entirely subsumed by "Allāh," except for its inclusion (albeit in a subordinate position to *Allāh*) in the formula of the *basmala* (Q 27:30) that becomes the introductory verse to each qur'ānic chapter except Q 9.

One crucial stage of transition toward the breakthrough of the finally dominant "Allāh" may be traced in God's declaration of his unicity before Moses (Q 20:12-4; cf. 27:8-9). Immediately following the declaration, "I am your Lord" (*innanī anā rabbuka,* Q 20:12), the name Allāh is affirmed by the first form of the emphatic, "I, I am God *(innanī anā llāh),* there is no deity save me" (*lā ilāha illā anā,* Q 20:14) in a passage that belongs to the second Meccan period. This verse is chronologically later than sūra 79 including Pharaoh's blasphemous utterance, "I am your Lord the most high" (*anā rabbukum al-a'lā,* Q 79:24). After Q 20:12 the use of *rabb* decreases noticeably in frequency, while the affirmations, "there is no deity save me" (*lā ilāha illā anā,* in late Meccan verses, i.e. Q 16:2; 20:14; 21:25) and "there is no deity save him" (*lā ilāha illā huwa,* in late Meccan verses, i.e. Q 28:70, 88, and increasingly in Medinan verses, i.e. Q 2:163, 255; 3:6, 18) occur repeatedly. Since *rabb* was applied to a variety of deities in pre-Islamic Arabia, it proved less suitable to serve as the name for the one God of Muḥammad's monotheistic message than Allāh, a name that by its very nature is definite and unique. An explanation for the rare occurrence of Allāh in the early Meccan sūras may also be found in the possibility of Muḥammad's original reluctance to adopt any name associated with polytheistic practices as a proper name for a supreme God. For pre-Islamic Arabs swore solemn oaths "by Allāh" (*billāhi,* Q 6:109; 16:38; 35:42), worshipped Allāh as creator and supreme provider (Q 13:16-7; 29:60-3; 31:25; 39:38; 43:9, 87) and asserted Allāh to have a kinship with the jinn (cf. Q 6:100, 128; 37:158; 72:6) and a relationship to subordinate deities such as al-ʿUzzā, Manāt and al-Lāt, identified as his daughters (cf. Q 53:19-21; 16:57; 37:149), and others anonymously as his sons (*kharaqū la-hu banīna wa-banāt,* Q 6:100). The sheer amount of references to God in the Qur᾿ān, which number in the thousands, makes it difficult to develop a precise curve of chronological development. Nevertheless, the overwhelming inner-qur᾿ānic evidence suggests that Muḥammad moved from a forceful personal experience of God who could be addressed as "my Lord" *(rabbī),* to a conception of the unique godhead of Allāh, the one and only God of his message *(lā ilāha illā llāh),* to whom a great number of epithets and attributes *(al-asmā᾿ al-ḥusnā)* were applied in the Qur᾿ān (see GOD AND HIS ATTRIBUTES).

The figure of Abraham (q.v., Ibrāhīm), who appears with many details of his story in twenty-five sūras, also provides an important touchstone for inner-qur᾿ānic chronology. In the first Meccan period the "sheets" *(ṣuḥuf)* of Abraham are cited as previously revealed scriptures and Abraham stands as a prophetic figure next to Moses (Q 87:18-9). In the second and third Meccan periods Abraham is identified as "a prophet, speaking the truth" (*ṣiddīqan nabiyyan,* Q 19:41) and depicted in detail as a staunch monotheist who attacks the idol-worship of his father and his people (Q 37:83-98; 26:69-89; 19:41-50; 43:26-8; 21:51-73; 29:16-27; 6:74-84; see IDOLATRY AND IDOLATERS; POLYTHEISM AND ATHEISM). Next to many other details (e.g. Abraham's rescue from the fire and his intercession for his idolatrous father), the same periods also record men sent by God to visit Abraham and to announce the punishment imposed on Lot's people (Q 51:24-34; 15:51-60; 11:69-76; 29:31-2). They also refer to Abraham's near sacrifice of his son (Q 37:100-11), ordinarily understood to be Isaac (q.v.) on account of Q 37:112-3 and, anonymously, Q 51:28 and 15:53. In the Medinan sūras, Abraham, supported by his son Ishmael, erects the Kaʿba in Mecca as a place of pure monotheistic belief and as a center of pilgrimage (q.v.; cf. Q 2:124-41; 3:65-8, 95-7; 6:125; 22:26-9, 78). Called emphatically a "true monotheist" *(ḥanīf),* who did not belong to the idolaters (*mushrikūn,* cf. Q 2:135; 3:67, 95; 4:125; 22:31, 78) and mentioned once as God's friend (*khalīl,* Q 4:125), Abraham becomes the exemplary prototype for Muḥammad who identifies the religion he himself proclaims as "the religion of Abraham" (*millat Ibrāhīm,* Q 2:130, 135; 4:125; 6:161; 16:123).

The characteristic features of the qur᾿ānic story of Abraham have been the subject of much scholarly research by Snouck Hurgronje *(Mekkaansche feest),* A.J. Wensinck *(Muhammad and the Jews)* and Y. Moubarac *(Abraham),* and more recently R. Firestone *(Journeys).* These scholars have laid great stress on the re-interpretation of Abraham in the Medinan sūras as provoked by Muḥammad's break with the Jewish tribes of Medina. Muḥammad's reorientation to Mecca, linking the figure of Abraham with the change of the prayer-orientation *(qibla)* to Mecca, is most certainly a significant chronological incision in the interpretation of Abraham and in the thrust of the qur᾿ānic message. What tends to be de-emphasized in the chronological analysis, especially of the Meccan verses, however, is an indisputable fact analyzed by E. Beck (Die Gestalt des Abraham). According to Beck, Abraham was already understood in the Meccan verses as connected with Mecca, prior to his association with Ishmael in the Qur᾿ān, and Muḥammad had developed his idea of the *millat Ibrāhīm,* at least initially, already at Mecca prior to his break with the Jews of Medina. In this perspective, some of G. Lüling's observations about Muḥammad's "religion of Abraham" (pruned of their bitterly controversial aspects, cf. *Wiederentdeckung*, 213-303), call for a more substantive examination as to whether Muḥammad possessed a distinct knowledge of Hellenistic and Judaeo-Christian trends in Christianity that facilitated his turning to a pre-Islamic Arab tradition of Abraham, closer akin to the latter, while rejecting the icon-worship of the former.

These four examples of a detailed approach to inner-qurʾānic chronology that concentrates upon central themes — i.e. the literary phenomenon of the disconnected letters, the institutional genesis of the ritual prayer, the qurʾānic development of the proper name for God and the tradition of the prophetic figure of Abraham and his religion — may open ways to complement the standard approach to qurʾānic chronology based on the four-period classification advanced by T. Nöldeke or the three-phase hypothesis advocated by R. Bell. The mosaic stones of such inner-qurʾānic approaches, case by case and limited to a manageable amount of verse analysis, may help to fill the somewhat indistinct and conjectural framework of the chronological approach to the Qurʾān as a whole.

Compilation of the Qurʾān

As mentioned above, it is a well-known fact that in the "completed" Qurʾān, i.e. that finally produced as Islam's holy book, the sūras are generally arranged according to decreasing length. This order was established in the final redaction of the written text of the Qurʾān, which reached its canonical completion many years after Muḥammad's death in 11/632. This process of final redaction and canonical completion represents the history of the text from Muḥammad's last qurʾānic proclamation, shortly before his death, until the appearance of the final vocalized text of the Qurʾān in the fourth/tenth century. This history of the text moves the Qurʾān from the life of the Prophet into the life of the Muslim community and from the principal historical author of the qurʾānic message to the chief redactors who produced the final written version we hold in our hands today. Due to its very nature, the history of this process is a minefield of chronological problems that are deeply rooted in the highly complex and contradictory evidence included in the Islamic tradition, especially the ḥadīth.

After Muḥammad's death, the Muslim community faced three major tasks with regard to establishing the Qurʾān as canonical scripture: it had to collect the text from oral and written sources, establish the consonantal skeleton of the Arabic text (see ARABIC SCRIPT) and finalize the fully-vocalized text that came to be accepted as the canonical standard. The traditional view depicting the accomplishment of these tasks covers three centuries and telescopes the history of the text into a basic scheme (the principal objections to which are examined in volumes ii and iii of Nöldeke's revised *Geschichte des Qorans*). This scheme proceeded on the assumptions that Muḥammad did not leave a complete written text of the Qurʾān and that the Qurʾān was preserved primarily in oral form in the memory of a considerable number of Muḥammad's direct listeners with a sizeable amount of the text having been recorded in writing by scribes during Muḥammad's lifetime. A group of the Companions (see COMPANIONS OF THE PROPHET), led by Zayd b. Thābit (q.v.; d. 46/665), whom Muḥammad himself had employed as a scribe in Medina, collected and arranged the oral and written materials of the Qurʾān in a complete consonantal text during the second half of the caliphate of ʿUthmān (q.v.; r. 23/644-35/656; see COLLECTION OF THE

QUR'ĀN). The final fully-vocalized text of the Qur'ān was established and completed only in the first half of the fourth/tenth century after different ways of reading — either seven, ten or fourteen in number — displaying slight variations in vocalization, came to be tolerated and accepted as standard. In addition to these standardized variations of vocalization, however, thousands of other textual variants were recorded in the literatures of Islamic tradition and Qur'ān commentary *(tafsīr al-Qur'ān),* many of which cannot be found in the myriad, complete and fragmentary, manuscripts of the Qur'ān, extant in libraries all over the world (see CODICES OF THE QUR'ĀN).

It is unlikely, as is maintained in a number of early accounts, that the initial collection of the Qur'ān took place in the short reign of the first caliph Abū Bakr (11/632-13/634) at the instigation of ʿUmar. ʿUmar is supposed to have perceived a serious threat to the integrity of the transmission of the qur'ānic text in the many casualties at the battle of al-Yamāma because these included a number of reciters *(qurrā')* who knew the text by heart. According to this story, Abū Bakr, though hesitating for fear of overstepping Muḥammad's precedent, ordered Zayd b. Thābit to collect all of the qur'ānic fragments written on palm leaves, tablets of clay and flat stones and "preserved in the hearts of men" and to write them out on sheets *(ṣuḥuf)* of uniform size. These written sheets came into the possession of ʿUmar upon his accession to the caliphate in 13/634 and when he died in 23/644, his daughter Ḥafṣa, one of the Prophet's widows (see WIVES OF THE PROPHET), inherited them from him. Another account credits the creation of the first collected volume *(muṣḥaf)* to ʿUmar while yet another refutes this by asserting that ʿUmar did not live to see this collection completed. The historicity of these accounts, placing the collection of the Qur'ān within the caliphates of Abū Bakr and ʿUmar, has been challenged on the grounds that critical study shows only two of the dead at the battle of al-Yamāma actually qualified as reciters (see RECITERS OF THE QUR'ĀN), that ʿUthmān's widely-attested role in establishing the official text has been intentionally neglected and that Muḥammad's role in the preparation of the text and the scribal work done during his lifetime have been under-emphasized.

The most widely-accepted version of the traditional history of the Qur'ān places the collection of the final consonantal text in the caliphate of ʿUthmān about twenty years after Muḥammad's death. The occasion for the final collection of the Qur'ān, according to this account, was a military expedition to Azerbayjan and Armenia under the leadership of the general Ḥudhayfa. Apparently his Muslim contingents from Syria and those from Iraq fell into dispute about the correct way of reciting the Qur'ān during the communal prayers. Trying to establish order, ʿUthmān appointed a commission of four respected Meccans, presided over by Zayd b. Thābit, to copy the "sheets" that were in Ḥafṣa's personal possession. Where variant readings of words were encountered, they chose the one in the dialect of the Quraysh. When the scribes completed their assignment, ʿUthmān kept one copy in Medina and sent other copies to al-Kūfa, al-Baṣra and Damascus. He then commanded that all other extant versions be destroyed. His order, however, was not heeded in al-Kūfa by the Companion Ibn Masʿūd (d. 32/653) and his followers. The difficulties of this version of the story center on essential points, namely the doubt that accuracy in the recitation of the Qur'ān would have caused significant unrest in the military during the early conquests of

Islam, the widely-accepted view that the Qurʾān is not actually in the dialect of the Quraysh (q.v.) and the improbability that the caliph would have given an order to destroy the already existing copies of the Qurʾān. Further, the appearance of Ḥafṣa in this narrative probably functions simply as a mechanism to link the Abū Bakr/ ʿUmar and ʿUthmān versions together and to establish an unbroken chain of custody for an authoritative text that remained largely unnoticed in the community. Despite the difficulties in this version of the chronology of the collection of the Qurʾān, scholars generally accept that the official consonantal text of the Qurʾān was established in ʿUthmān's caliphate and that Zayd b. Thābit played a significant role in effecting it.

To gain a clearer picture of the collection of the standard consonantal text of the Qurʾān, one may have to consider the possibility of a number of factors, among them the following: 1) that Muḥammad himself had begun the work of establishing a written version of the Qurʾān without completing it; 2) that during the first two decades after his death, the Muslim community was focused on expansion and conquest rather than on standardizing the qurʾānic text; 3) that the need for a standardized text of the Qurʾān manifested itself only after local Muslim communities began to form in the newly established garrison cities *(amṣār)* such as al-Kūfa, al-Baṣra and Damascus; and 4) that the "ʿUthmānic text" established in Medina by the chief collector Zayd b. Thābit has to be seen as a parallel phenomenon to the codices containing textual variants — all of which are said to have been begun during Muḥammad's lifetime — the one attributed to ʿAbdāllah b. Masʿūd and accepted in al-Kūfa, the one attributed to Ubayy b. Kaʿb (d. ca. 29/649) and accepted in Syria, the one attributed to Abū Mūsā al-Ashʿarī (d. 42/662) and accepted in al-Baṣra as well as to other "primary" codices of individuals (see A. Jeffery, *Materials;* see also TEXTUAL HISTORY OF THE QURʾĀN). ʿAlī b. Abī Ṭālib (q.v.; d. 40/661), Muḥammad's cousin and son-in-law, is also cited in the early sources as the first to collect the Qurʾān after the Prophet's death. It is said that he arranged the sūras in some form of chronological order and that he allowed his codex to be burned when the "ʿUthmānic text" was promulgated.

While the establishment of the consonantal text of the Qurʾān, the "ʿUthmānic text," is intertwined with the question of the parallel personal or metropolitan codices (*maṣāḥif,* see MUṢHAF), the promulgation of the fully vocalized text involves the question of the various "readings" *(qirāʾāt)* of the Qurʾān (see READINGS OF THE QURʾĀN). Since the non-vowelized "ʿUthmānic text" was written in a "scriptio defectiva" that was merely a consonantal skeleton lacking diacritical marks that distinguish certain consonants from each other, oral recitation was needed to ascertain the intended pronunciation of the text. As the qurʾānic orthography developed step by step over more than two centuries and as the linkage between the consonantal skeleton and the oral recitation became more and more defined, the deficiencies of the Arabic script were gradually overcome. The variations of recitation, in the vast majority of a minor nature, were either reconciled or accommodated and the written text became increasingly independent of its linkage to oral pronunciation. This process culminated with the "scriptio plena," the fully-vocalized and pointed text of the Qurʾān.

This text may be considered as a "textus receptus, ne varietur" with the proviso that no single clearly identifiable textual specimen of the Qurʾān was ever established or accepted with absolute unanimity. Rather the final, fully-vowelized and pointed text of the Qur'ān, accepted as normative and canonical, may best be understood as a construct underlying the work of Abū Bakr b. Mujāhid (d. 324/936), who restricted the recitation of the Qur'ān to seven correct readings, termed *aḥruf* (lit. letters) on the basis of a popular ḥadīth. Ibn Mujāhid accepted the reading *(qirā'a)* of seven prominent Qur'ān scholars of the second/eighth century and declared them all as based on divine authority. In 322/934 the 'Abbāsid establishment promulgated the doctrine that these seven versions were the only forms of the text and all others were forbidden. Nevertheless, "three after the seven" and "four after the ten" ways of reading were added somewhat later to form, respectively, ten or fourteen variant readings. Finally, each of the ten ways of reading was eventually accepted in two slightly varying versions (sing. *riwāya*), all of which, at least theoretically, belong within the spectrum of the "textus receptus, ne varietur." For all practical purposes today, only two versions are in general use, that of Ḥafṣ (d. 190/805) from *('an)* 'Āṣim (d. 127/744), i.e. Ḥafṣ's version of 'Āṣim's way of reading, which received official sanction when it was adopted by the Egyptian standard edition of the Qur'ān in 1924; and that of Warsh (d. 197/812) from *('an)* Nāfi' (d. 169/785), i.e. Warsh's version of Nāfi''s way of reading, which is followed in North Africa, with the exception of Egypt.

The hypothetical nature of the scholarly arguments about the textual variants of the parallel codices ultimately led those scholars who most meticulously examined them (e.g. G. Bergsträsser, O. Pretzl, A. Jeffery, and A. Fischer) to pronounce a very guarded judgment about their authenticity. It became the increasingly accepted scholarly view that most of the allegedly pre-'Uthmānic variants could be interpreted as later attempts by Muslim philologists to emend the "'Uthmānic text." In the second half of this century two scholars came to the conclusion that these "codices" were virtual fabrications of early Muslim scholarship without offering, however, substantive and irrefutable proof for their claims. Arguing in opposite directions, J. Wansbrough *(QS)* concluded that the Qur'ān was not compiled until two to three hundred years after Muḥammad's death while J. Burton contended that Muḥammad himself had already established the final edition of the consonantal text of the Qur'ān. Such widely-differing hypotheses, as well as the fact that there is no single uniform text of the Qur'ān that would represent a text-critical edition composed on the basis of the essential extant manuscripts and the critically evaluated variant readings, demonstrate that much of the chronological reconstruction of the Qur'ān's fixation as a written text has reached an impasse. Only the future will tell whether a possible computer analysis (see COMPUTERS AND THE QUR'ĀN) of the sheer mass of textual material may enable scholarly research to develop a more consistent picture of the Qur'ān's textual chronology.

Certain breakthroughs with regard to qur'ānic chronology, however, may be achieved through a more systematic chronological analysis of the major themes within the Qur'ān such as the four examples cited in this survey. Another challenge might be a more consistent search for an Ur-Qur'ān, initiated by G. Lüling, that would reopen scholarly debate about the sources of Muḥammad's proclamation and whether he only began to produce religious rhymed prose after the defining religious experience that the sources identify as his call to prophethood, an event that took place when he was a man of about forty years of age. Searching the text for segments that could antedate this experience may reveal their roots in usages of religious worship and liturgy within the Arab environment in which Muḥammad grew up and reached his maturity. Finally, it may be necessary for scholarly research to espouse more unequivocally the view that Muḥammad was not the mere mouthpiece of the Qurʾān's proclamation but, as its actual historical human author, played a major role in its collection and compilation.

Gerhard Böwering

Bibliography
Primary: Ibn Isḥāq-Guillaume; Ṭabarī, *Taʾrīkh.*
Secondary: T. Andrae, *Mohammed, the man and his faith,* New York 1936; E. Beck, Der ʿuṯmānische Kodex in der Koranlesung des zweiten Jahrhunderts, in *Orientalia* 14 (1945), 355-73; id., Die Gestalt des Abraham am Wendepunkt der Entwicklung Muhammeds, in *Muséon* 65 (1952), 73-94; R. Bell, *The origin of Islam in its Christian environment,* London 1926; Blachère, *Introduction,* 1977²; F. Buhl, *Das Leben Mohammeds,* Heidelberg 1961; Burton, *Collection;* R. Firestone, *Journeys in holy lands,* New York 1990; Goldziher, *Richtungen;* H. Grimme, *Mohammed,* 2 vols., Aschendorff 1892-5; H. Hirschfeld, *New researches into the composition and exegesis of the Qoran,* London 1902; Horovitz, *KU;* Jeffery, *For. vocab.;* id., *Materials;* id., *The Qurʾān as scripture,* New York 1952; J. Jomier, Le nom divin al-Raḥmān dans le Coran, in Institut Français d'Études Arabes en Damas, *Mélanges Louis Massignon,* 3 vols., Damascus 1957, ii, 361-81; G. Lüling, *Über den Ur-Qurʾān,* Erlangen 1974; id., *Die Wiederentdeckung des Propheten Muhammad,* Erlangen 1981; Y. Moubarac, *Abraham dans le Coran,* Paris 1958; W. Muir, *The Corân. Its composition and teaching,* London 1878; Nagel; Nöldeke, *GQ;* Paret, *Kommentar;* id., *Der Koran,* Darmstadt 1975; id., *Mohammed und der Koran,* Stuttgart 1957; C. Snouck Hurgronje, *Het Mekkaansche feest,* Leiden 1880; Speyer, *Erzählungen,* repr. Hildesheim 1961; A. Sprenger, *Das Leben und die Lehre des Mohammed,* 3 vols., Berlin 1861-5; C.C. Torrey, *The Jewish foundation of Islam,* New York 1933; Wansbrough, *QS;* W.M. Watt, *Muhammad at Mecca,* Oxford 1953; id., *Muhammad at Medina,* Oxford 1956; Watt-Bell, *Introduction;* G. Weil, *Historisch-kritische Einleitung in den Koran,* Bielefeld 1844 ; A.J. Wensinck, *Muhammad and the Jews of Medina,* Freiburg 1975.

Church

Building in which public Christian religious services occur. Christian churches, shrines, monasteries and other institutions were common in the territories inhabited by Arabic-speaking peoples in the world in which Islam was born. In the early Islamic period both Muslims and Christians regularly used the word *kanīsa* to mean "church" and sometimes "synagogue." Although this conventional Arabic word for church does not appear in the Qurʾān, there is one verse that has been interpreted as referring to churches. In Q 22:40, churches *(biyaʿ)* are mentioned along with monasteries *(ṣawāmiʿ),* synagogues (*ṣalawāt,* see JEWS AND JUDAISM) and mosques (*masājid,* see MOSQUE) as places "in which God's name is mentioned frequently." The Arabic noun *bīʿa* (pl. *biyaʿ*) that appears in this verse very probably came into the language from Syriac where the cognate word, *bīʿtā,* means simply "egg." The egg-shaped dome found on many shrines and churches in the geographical milieu of early Islam is thought by many commentators to explain the appropriation of the word to mean "church" in Arabic already in pre-Islamic times. In the qurʾānic commentary *(tafsīr)* literature, the word *kanīsa* is used by the earliest exegetes to gloss the more obscure term *bīʿa.*

In addition to numerous references to churches in the documentary sources such as early Arabic poetry, inscriptions and the capitulation treaties of numerous cities at the time of the Islamic conquest, there is an increasingly abundant archaeological record of churches in the Arabian milieu well into early Islamic times (see SOUTH ARABIA, RELIGION IN PRE-ISLAMIC). Their ruins have been discovered in south Arabia, east of the Jordan river, in the modern Hashemite Kingdom of Jordan, in Syria and in Iraq as well as in Palestine and in the Sinai peninsula. Of particular significance are the shrine churches of Syria such as those at Qalʿat Simʿān and Ruṣāfa (Sergiopolis), the memorials of St. Simeon the Stylite the Elder and of St. Sergius the Martyr respectively where, according to the sources, in the sixth and seventh centuries Arab Christians were among the numerous pilgrims who thronged to these sites. Similarly important in early Islamic times would have been the smaller churches and chapels of the numerous monastic establishments that were located on the periphery of the Arabian desert (see MONASTICISM AND MONKS). Not only did Muslims and Christians sometimes both worship in them, but as a result of the practice of visiting monasteries for a measure of rest and recreation, a sub-genre of Arabic-Islamic poetry, "On Monasteries" *(al-diyārāt)*, soon developed. While these compositions had wine (see INTOXICANTS) and revelry as their principal themes, they did often mention in passing some aspects of the ecclesiastical structures in which they found their settings.

Churches also figured in early Islamic legal texts, particularly those concerned with spelling out the stipulations *(shurūṭ)* in the observance of which the subject Christian populations were allowed to live under the protection (*dhimma*, see PROTECTION) of the Islamic community in return for the payment of the capitation tax (*jizya*, see TAXATION) and the maintenance of a low social profile as the Qurʾān requires (cf. Q 9:29; see LAW AND THE QURʾĀN). Specifically, new church construction was often theoretically prohibited as were repairs to existing structures. Churches were required to be no taller or more sumptuous in presentation than neighboring mosques and they were not allowed to display crosses, icons or other troublesome decorations (see ICONOCLASM). They were forbidden to ring bells or to sponsor public parades or processions or in any other way to draw public attention to themselves. See also CHRISTIANS AND CHRISTIANITY.

Sidney H. Griffith

Bibliography
Primary: al-Shābushtī, *Kitāb al-Diyārāt*, ed. J. ʿAwwād, Baghdad 1966; al-Ṭabarī, *Tafsīr*, xvii, 112-5.
Secondary: Y. Calvet, Monuments paléo-chrétiens à Koweit et dans la région du Golfe, in R. Lavenant, *Symposium Syriacum VII, OCA*, 256, Rome 1998, 671-85; A. Fattal, *Le statut légal des non-musulmans en pays d'islam*, Beirut 1958; Jeffery, *For. vocab.*; R. Schick, *The Christian communities of Palestine from Byzantine to Islamic rule*, Princeton 1995; I. Shahid, Arab Christian pilgrimages in the proto-Byzantine period (v-vii centuries), in D. Frankfurter, *Pilgrimage and holy space in late antique Egypt*, Leiden 1998, 373-89; G. Troupeau, Kanīsa, in *EI²*, iv, 545-6; id., Les couvents chrétiens dans la littérature arabe, in *La nouvelle revue de Caire* 1 (1975), 265-79; Wensinck, *Concordance*, Leiden 1936-88.

Cinema and the Qurʾān see MEDIA AND THE QURʾĀN

Circumambulation see KAʿBA; PILGRIMAGE

Circumcision

The removal of the foreskin of the penis or, in the case of females, of the internal labia. Male circumcision is denoted in Arabic by the term *khitān*, and sometimes by *ṭahāra*, "purity." For female circumcision, the term usually employed is *khafḍ*, "reduction," i.e. of the clitoris. Circumcision of either type is nowhere mentioned in the Qurʾān but was practiced by pre-Islamic Arabs and is mentioned in poetry (see PRE-ISLAMIC ARABIA AND THE QURʾĀN; POETRY AND POETS).

There are two qurʾānic occurrences of the plural form of an Arabic term *(aghlaf*, pl. *ghulf)* that can mean uncircumcised. "They [the Jews] say: 'Our hearts are hardened *(qulūbunā ghulf)*.' Indeed, God has cursed them for their unbelief. Little is that which they believe" (Q 2:88; cf. 4:155). According to the qur'ānic exegete Ibn Kathīr (d. 774/1373; *Tafsīr,* ad loc.), the reference in Q 2:88 and 4:155 is to Jewish hearts as "wrappings" of God's word. Although ironic for its semantic relation to foreskin *(ghulfa),* the word probably does not intend the sense of uncircumcised in its qur'ānic occurrences (but cf. *Lev* 26:41, which refers to sinful Israelites with uncircumcised hearts and *Jer* 10:25-6, concerning "all those who are circumcised [i.e. in the flesh] but still uncircumcised [in the heart]").

To be uncircumcised *(aghral* or *aghlaf)* was considered a disgrace among pre-Islamic Arabs. According to the biographer of the Prophet, Ibn Isḥāq (d. ca. 150/767; *Sīra,* ii, 450; Ibn Isḥāq-Guillaume, 572), during the battle of Ḥunayn (q.v.) in the year 8/630, the corpse of a young enemy warrior was discovered by one of the Helpers (*anṣār,* those inhabitants of Medina who assisted Muḥammed as he emigrated from Mecca to Medina; see EMIGRANTS AND HELPERS) to be uncircumcised *(aghral)*. The discoverer of the dead man's anomalous condition "shouted at the top of his voice: 'O, fellow Arabs! God knows that Thaqīf are uncircumcised!'" Fearing that the report would spread among the Arabs, a comrade took the shouter's hand and said that the deceased was only a Christian slave. Upon examination, it was discovered that other slain soldiers were properly circumcised Arabs, albeit worshippers of al-Lāt (see IDOLS AND IMAGES) rather than of God.

The notion of *fiṭra,* which has the sense of humankind's natural disposition or character as created by God (mentioned once in the Qur'ān at Q 30:30), figures in later references to circumcision. The details of this disposition are given in the ḥadīth: "Five are the acts of *fiṭra:* circumcision *(khitān),* shaving the pubes, clipping the moustache, cutting the nails, plucking the hair under the armpits" (Abū Hurayra as reported by Muslim; cf. Nawawī, *Ṣaḥīḥ Muslim. K. al-Ṭahāra. B. Khiṣāl al-fiṭra,* iii, 146; Muslim, *Ṣaḥīḥ* [Eng. trans.], i, 159). Abraham's (q.v.) circumcision is also reported in the ḥadīth literature. Muslim (d. ca. 261/875) relates:... "Abraham circumcised himself *(ukhtatana)* by means of an adz *(bi-l-qadūm)* at the age of eighty" (Nawawī, *Ṣaḥīḥ Muslim. K. al-Faḍā'il,* xv, 122). Some scholars have attempted to discern circumcision in the Qur'ān by referring to Q 3:95 where Abraham is declared to have been a *ḥanīf* (q.v.) and not a polytheist (see POLYTHEISM AND ATHEISM), but D.S. Margoliouth (Circumcision) objects that the passage says nothing about any particular ritual obligations (see RITUAL PURITY).

The question of whether circumcision is absolutely required of Muslims was addressed by classical jurisconsults with varying opinions. For example, al-Shāfi'ī (d. ca. 204/820) considered it obligatory for both males and females (see al-Nawawī's commentary in Nawawī, *Ṣaḥīḥ Muslim. K. al-Ṭahāra,* iii, 148; for an English translation of the passage, see A.J. Wensinck, Khitān). Some jurists consider circumcision to be a recommended *(sunna)* rather than an obligatory *(wājib)* practice, although custom has usually supported it strongly, particularly in the case of males (see LAWFUL AND UNLAWFUL; LAW AND THE QUR'ĀN). Thus, while explicit qur'ānic support is lacking, the strong support for circumcision in the Islamic tradition suggests that it was simply assumed by Muḥammad and his community.

Frederick Mathewson Denny

Bibliography
Primary: Ibn Isḥāq, *Sīra,* Cairo 1955; Ibn Isḥāq-Guillaume; Ibn Kathīr, *Tafsīr;* Nawawī, *Ṣaḥīḥ Muslim bi-sharḥ al-Nawawī,* 18 vols., Cairo 1964; Muslim, *Ṣaḥīḥ,* A.H. Siddiqi (Eng. trans.), *Ṣaḥīḥ Muslim,* Lahore 1976.
Secondary: D.S. Margoliouth, Circumcision {Muhammadan}, in *ERE,* iii, 677; A.J. Wensinck, Khitān, in *EI²,* v, 20-2.

City

An inhabited place of greater size, population or importance than a town or a village. Although the construction of a monotheistic, just and ethical social order is a fundamental theme running throughout the Qurʾān, surprisingly little is said about the city, the most elaborate of human organizations (see COMMUNITY AND SOCIETY IN THE QURʾĀN; SOCIAL INTERACTIONS; SOCIAL RELATIONS). Even the city of Yathrib, which was at that time being refashioned as *madīnat rasūl Allāh,* the "city of the messenger of God" (i.e. Muḥammad), is mentioned only four times — at Q 9:101, 120; 33:60; 63:8 — and in each instance is termed al-Madīna, i.e. "the city" (see MEDINA). References to cities in the Qurʾān are typically laconic, non-specific and oblique. One of two terms — *qarya* and *madīna* — is always used to designate a city. A third term, *dār,* which generally means "abode," is ordinarily employed with a qualifier to designate the House of God (see HOUSE-DOMESTIC AND DIVINE) or the hereafter (see ESCHATOLOGY; RESURRECTION) but at least once (Q 59:9) it appears to indicate Yathrib at the time of the emigration from Mecca (*hijra,* see EMIGRATION; MECCA). *Qarya,* clearly the preferred term, occurs a total of 56 times. *Madīna* with its more meaningful etymological connections to religion *(dīn),* judge or governor *(dayyān)* and civilization *(madaniyya),* appears only 17 times. In two cases — Q 18:77, 82 and 36:13, 20 — *qarya* and *madīna* seem to have been used synonymously. This makes it difficult to assert that the Qurʾān originally drew the distinction that later developed in Islamic thought whereby *madīna* became the term for the city as the center of religiously and politically structured social life while *qarya* receded to mean a village or any small human agglomeration.

Madīna occurs 14 times in the singular form, four of which — Q 9:101, 120; 33:60; 63:8 — are in reference to *madīnat rasūl Allāh,* as Yathrib became known after the Prophet's emigration *(hijra).* It also appears three times in the plural *(madāʾin),* always in reference to a gathering of the sorcerers from the cities of Egypt (q.v.) in the context of the story of Moses (q.v.) and Pharaoh (q.v.). Of the 56 times that *qarya* appears, 37 are in the singular form, one followed by the second person masculine singular possessive, *"qaryataka,"* (in reference to Mecca), two by the second person masculine plural possessive, *"qaryatakum"* and one by the first person plural possessive *"qaryatanā."* It also occurs once in the dual form *"qaryatayn"* (Q 43:31), which seems to refer to the two cities of Mecca and Ṭāʾif and 18 times in the plural *"qurā,"* two of them (Q 6:92 and 42:7) in the form *umm al-qurā,* "the mother of cities." This epithet seems to have been applied to Mecca, although in one instance (Q 28:59) the expression refers to some other capital to which God sent a messenger (q.v.) to warn a group of cities (see also WARNING).

Most references to *qarya* and *madīna* occur in conjunction with the parables of past nations. In the majority of instances, the *qarya* is described as an insidious environment: Its people revel in excess and perversion, ignore their religious duties and chase out God's prophets (see PUNISHMENT STORIES; PROPHETS AND PROPHETHOOD). They therefore deserve God's fire and brimstone, not because of their status as cities, but because they usually reject God's warning delivered by his messengers (see CHAS-

TISEMENT AND PUNISHMENT). This negative impression of cities in the Qur'ān influenced many early Islamic views expressed in ḥadīth, exegesis *(tafsīr)* and belles-lettres *(adab)* and even found its way into later legal *(fiqh)* discourses, the main objective of which was to regulate the Islamic urban order (see LAW AND THE QUR'ĀN).

Nasser Rabbat

Bibliography
T. Khālidī, Some classical Islamic views of the city, in W. al-Qāḍī (ed.), *Studia Arabica et Islamica. Festschrift for Iḥsān ʿAbbās,* Beirut 1981, 265-76; J.M. Rogers, Innovation and continuity in Islamic urbanism, in I. Sarageldin and S. el-Sadek (eds.), *The Arab city. Its character and Islamic cultural heritage,* Medina 1982, 53-9; R. al-Sayyid, al-Madīna wa-l-dawla fī l-Islām. Dirāsa fī ruʾyatay al-Māwardī wa-Ibn Khaldūn, in *al-Abḥāth* 34 (1986), 67-85; J. Wellhausen, *Skizzen und Vorarbeiten,* 6 vols., Berlin 1889, iv (see Medina vor dem Islam and Die Gemeindeordnung Muhammeds).

Civil Society see POLITICS AND THE QUR'ĀN; COMMUNITY AND SOCIETY IN THE QUR'ĀN

Clans and Tribes see TRIBES AND CLANS

Clay

An earthy material, plastic when moist but hard when baked or fired. There are twelve references to clay *(ṭīn);* four to "resounding" clay *(ṣalṣāl);* three to petrified clay *(sijjīl);* and one to baked clay or earthenware *(fakhkhār)*. Whereas *ṣalṣāl* is pure Arabic, *ṭīn* and *fakhkhār* are probably Syriac loan words and *sijjīl* is almost certainly Persian (see FOREIGN VOCABULARY).

Etymology

Arabic lexicographers derive *ṭīn* from the verb *ṭāna,* "to plaster with clay" (said of a roof or wall) or "to seal with clay" (said of a written document). However, this verb, which is not found in the Qur'ān, is clearly denominal. Most European scholars assume that the substantive *ṭīn* is a loan word, although its occurrence in early poetry may indicate that it was already in circulation in pre-Islamic times (Jeffery, *For. vocab.,* 208). The most plausible derivation is from the Syriac *ṭīnā* which likewise means simply "clay." The noun *ṣalṣāl* is derived from the Arabic verb *ṣalṣala,* "to make repeated sounds." It denotes dry clay that has not been baked but which makes a sound when struck (Ṭabarī, *Tafsīr,* xxvii, 73). The noun *fakhkhār* cannot be derived from the Arabic verb *fakhara* which means "to boast." There is consensus among the classical commentators that the noun denotes baked clay or earthenware. It is probably derived from *paḥārā,* the Syriac term for potter. As *sijjīl* is used interchangeably with *ṭīn* (Q 11:82; 15:74; cf. 51:33), it must have a similar meaning. It is widely acknowledged that it is the Arabicized form of *säng-i gil,* a Persian expression denoting stones of clay or petrified clay.

The creation of humankind from clay

There are eight references to the creation of humankind from clay (Q 6:2; 7:12; 17:61; 23:12; 32:7; 37:11; 38:71, 76); three to their creation from "resounding" clay (Q 15:26, 28, 33) and one to their creation from "resounding clay like earthenware" (Q 55:14). Most of the passages refer to the creation of the first human being, although in Q 6:2, it is the Prophet's contemporaries who are envisaged (see BIOLOGY AS THE CREATION AND STAGES OF LIFE).

The ancient Egyptians depicted Knum, the ram-god of Elephantine, as fashioning man on a potter's wheel and the Bible, which speaks of God creating man from the earth (*Gen* 2:7), likens human beings to pots in his hands (e.g. *Jer* 18:6, *Rom* 9:21). In the Qur'ān, however, the emphasis is on humankind's base origins rather than their malleability or fragility. According to Ibn ʿAbbās (an early exegete to whom much material is ascribed, d. 68/688), Adam's body lay prostrate for 40 nights after God had fashioned it. Then Iblīs (the devil) came along and kicked it with his foot and it resounded (Ṭabarī, *Tafsīr*, xxvii, 73).

At Q 23:12, God says "We have created humankind from a *sulāla* of clay." A standard exegetical work glosses this as "He extracted him from it and it is his essence" (*Jalālayn*, 452). Hence most translators assume that *sulāla* means "an extract." However, the word occurs elsewhere in the Qurʾān only at Q 32:8 where it clearly means "semen." Bell therefore suggests that Q 23:12-4 was an early revelation which originally referred to natural procreation and that the words "of clay" *(min ṭīnin)* were added to make it rhyme when it was inserted in its present context (Watt-Bell, *Introduction*, 90-1; see BLOOD AND BLOOD CLOT).

Clay projectiles

God is said to have punished Lot's (q.v.) people by sending his angels to rain "pebbles of clay" (Q 51:33) or "pebbles of petrified clay" (Q 11:82; 15:74) upon them (see PUNISHMENT STORIES). This corresponds to the biblical account of their destruction by showers of brimstone (*Gen* 19:24). It is conceivable that the phenomenon in question was occasioned by a volcanic irruption but Aḥmad ʿAlī goes too far when he translates *sijjīl* as "hardened lava." God is also said to have sent flocks of birds to hurl "pebbles of petrified clay" at the owners of the elephant (Q 105:3-4; see ABRAHA). Some modernists have been reluctant to admit that the Qurʾān contains legends of this sort and have therefore attempted to interpret these verses in the light of modern science (see EXEGESIS OF THE QURʾĀN: EARLY MODERN AND CONTEMPORARY; MYTHIC AND LEGENDARY NARRATIVES). M. Asad, for example, notes correctly that the word which is usually translated "birds" simply means "flying creatures" and could therefore denote insects. As there is a tradition that smallpox first appeared in Mecca (q.v.) in the year of the expedition of the elephant (see MUḤAMMAD; EXPEDITIONS AND BATTLES; CHRONOLOGY AND THE QURʾĀN), he therefore argues that the Qurʾān is at this point referring to an insect-born disease. Then, ingeniously, but most implausibly, he connects *sijjīl* with *sijill*, a word which means a scroll (see SCROLLS) or written decree, and renders the passage "Thus, he let loose upon them great swarms of flying creatures which smote them with stone-hard blows of chastisement pre-ordained."

Other passages

Two Medinan verses relate how Jesus (q.v.) fashioned birds from clay (Q 3:49; 5:110). A similar miracle (q.v.) is attributed to him in an apocryphal gospel known as the *Infancy story of Thomas* (see CHRISTIANS AND CHRISTIANITY; SCRIPTURE AND THE QURʾĀN). Whereas Christians interpreted Jesus' action as proof of his divinity (Ibn Isḥāq-Guillaume, 271) because it resembled God's initial creation of humankind, the Qurʾān stresses that it was a sign which Jesus performed with God's permission (see CREATION; SIGNS). There is no justification for eliminating the supernatural element as M. Asad, Aḥmad ʿAlī and other modernist translators have done by giving the impression that Jesus, rather than fashioning birds from clay, moulded his disciples' destiny.

Finally, in one passage, Pharaoh (q.v.) is said to have ordered Hāmān to fire clay for him and build a lofty palace so that he could mount up to the God of Moses (q.v.; Q 28:38). This episode resembles the biblical story of the Tower of Babel (*Gen* 11), which contains a mocking allusion to the ziggurats of ancient Mesopotamia.

However, the pharaonic building projects were equally extravagant. According to the early exegete Qatāda (d. 117/735), Pharaoh was the first person to have bricks made in this way (Ṭabarī, *Tafsīr*, xx, 49).

Neal Robinson

Bibliography
Primary: Aḥmad ʿAlī, *al-Qurʾān. A contemporary translation*, Karachi 1984, Princeton 1988³; Ibn Isḥāq-Guillaume; *Jalālayn; Ṭabarī, Tafsīr*.
Secondary: M. Asad, *The message of the Qurʾān*, Gibraltar 1980; E. Hennecke, *New Testament Apocrypha*, 2 vols., London 1963, i; Jeffery, *For. vocab.;* T. O'Shaughnessy, Man's creation from clay and from seed in the Qurʾān, in *Boletin de la Asociation Española de Orientalistas* 7 (1971), 131-49; N. Robinson, Creating birds from clay. A miracle of Jesus in the Qurʾān and classical Muslim exegesis, in MW 79.1 (1989), 1-13; id., *Christ in Islam and Christianity. The representation of Jesus in the Qurʾān and the classical Muslim commentaries*, London 1991; id., Sectarian and ideological bias in English translations of the *Qurʾān* by Muslims, in *Islam and Christian-Muslim Relations* 8 (1997), 261-78; Watt-Bell, *Introduction*.

Cleanliness and Ablution

Cleanliness, the quality of keeping oneself free from defilement; ablution, an oftentimes ritual process by which one is purified. The concepts of cleanliness and ablution are represented in the Qurʾān both by a small set of specific injunctions regarding purity practices and by a vocabulary of purity with ethical and spiritual dimensions (see PURITY AND IMPURITY; RITUAL PURITY).

The Qurʾān's specific directions regarding ablutions and the occasions on which these must be performed are concentrated largely in two lengthy verses, Q 4:43 and Q 5:6. Q 4:43 opens by instructing the believers not to "approach" prayer when they are intoxicated *(sukārā)* or sexually polluted *(junub)*, a command that suggested to commentators an early date of revelation preceding the definitive proscription of wine (see INTOXICANTS; LAWFUL AND UNLAWFUL). Those who are intoxicated are to wait until they are cognizant of what they say, while those who are sexually polluted must wait until they have "washed" *(ḥattā taghtasilū)*, understood as a reference to the full-body ablutions known in the legal literature *(fiqh)* as *ghusl*. An exception to the requirement of washing is made for those who are "passing on the road" *(illā ʿābirī sabīl)*. This dispensation is commonly interpreted in two ways: Some commentators explain it as an allusion to the traveler's prerogative of performing substitute ablutions with dust *(tayammum)* when water is unavailable, while others argue that one does not "approach" the act of prayer (q.v.), thus inferring that one must not enter places of prayer (i.e. mosques, see MOSQUE) in a state of sexual pollution except when passing on a journey (q.v.).

Q 5:6 begins with a detailed description of the minor ablutions known to the juridical literature as *wuḍūʾ*: "O believers! When you rise to pray, wash your faces and your hands up to the elbows, and wipe your heads and your feet up to the ankles." It then instructs those who are in a state of sexual pollution *(junub)* to purify themselves *(iṭṭahharū)*. These apparently simple and explicit instructions contain several points which emerged as major interpretive controversy among jurists and writers of exegetical works *(tafsīr)*. These include the verse's opening injunction to perform *wuḍūʾ* when they rise to pray, which in its most literal meaning would contradict the almost universal understanding that one must perform *wuḍūʾ* only if in a state of minor impurity. Most commentators have understood this command to be qualified in light of the verse's later reference to "coming from the privy" and "touching women" while others have interpreted it as a reference to "rising" from sleep. Yet other interpreters accept a literal understanding of the verse's wording while rejecting its legal implications. Thus, some hold that the Prophet was originally enjoined to perform the minor ablutions before every prayer but that, this requirement proving onerous, it was abrogated *(mansūkh)* at the time of the conquest of Mecca (q.v.). Others argue that the directive to perform ablutions before every prayer was directed exclusively to the Prophet or that it is directed at all believers but represents a recommendation rather than a command (cf. J. Burton, The practice of *wuḍūʾ*, 32).

Questions have also been raised by the syntactical structure of the verse's instruction to "wash your faces and your hands up to the elbows and wipe your heads and your feet." The most obvious reading would place "feet" in apposition to "heads" and thus imply that the feet are to be wiped. This reading was early rejected by Sunnī commentators who believed that the feet were to be washed and accordingly read "feet" in apposition to "hands." Because Shīʿī interpretations rejected this understanding, the washing or wiping of the feet came to be among the most visible everyday ritual distinctions between Sunnīs and Shīʿīs, starting in the early Islamic period (see SHĪʿISM AND THE QURʾĀN).

Verses Q 4:43 and Q 5:6 then continue identically enumerating a series of situations understood to be the occasions of pollution ("coming from the privy," i.e. urination and defecation, and "touching women," variously understood as sexual intercourse or simple skin-to-skin contact) and the special circumstances (illness and travel) under which one is entitled to perform symbolic ablutions with dust *(tayammum)*. Each verse then ends with a reference to the clemency of God.

These two lengthy verses opened a number of questions debated by exegetes and jurists not only because of their syntactic and semantic complexity but because of their apparent interrelation. Some commentators argue that Q 4:43 was abrogated *(mansūkh)* by Q 5:6, a chronological sequence suggested by Q 4:43's apparent reference to the use of intoxicants (see ABROGATION). Further complication is introduced by a well-known tradition from the Prophet's wife ʿĀʾisha bint Abī Bakr (q.v.), in which her search for a misplaced necklace detains a caravan in a waterless spot and prompts the revelation of the "verse of *tayammum*" (see OCCASIONS OF REVELATION). Commentators are generally undecided about which of the two verses is intended since both contain the dispensation relating to *tayammum*. Perhaps the "verse of *tayammum*" of the tradition should in fact be understood as the segment on *tayammum* shared by Q 4:43 and Q 5:6.

Purity practices are also addressed in a small number of other verses. Q 2:222 instructs men to "avoid" (*iʿtazilū*, see ABSTINENCE) women during their menstrual periods, a command understood in the exegetical tradition to prohibit only sexual intercourse (in contrast with the comprehensive avoidance practiced by Zoroastrians and/or Jews). The praise of "those who purify themselves" *(al-muṭṭahhirīn)* in Q 9:108, although it seems to invite a metaphorical interpretation, is traditionally understood to refer to the practice of cleansing the affected parts with water after relieving oneself. A widespread ḥadīth identifies as the people of the Mosque of Qubāʾ the verse's "men who love to purify themselves" and who merit the right to stand in the "mosque founded upon piety." They are said to have learned this form of purification from neighboring Jews (see JEWS AND JUDAISM). Q 9:28, which identifies polytheists as "unclean" (*najas*, see CONTAMINATION) and bars them from the Sacred Mosque (i.e. that of Mecca), is understood in the Sunnī tradition either as a metaphorical reference to moral turpitude or as an allusion to chronic sexual pollution resulting from the failure to perform ablutions. The Twelver Shīʿī tradition, in contrast, has embraced a literal understanding that non-believers are substantively impure (see BELIEF AND UNBELIEF; POLYTHEISM AND ATHEISM).

The verses enjoining specific purity practices occur in Medinan chapters although the practice of ablution was traditionally understood to have been introduced to the Prophet by the angel Gabriel (q.v.), along with prayer, at the beginning of his mission (cf. Ibn Isḥāq-Guillaume, 112). In general, the qurʾānic chapters which contain the verses describing purity practices are sūras thematically concerned with the definition of community boundaries, containing a high proportion of references to defining ritual practices (prayer, pilgrimage [q.v.], fasting [q.v.], alms [see ALMSGIVING]) and to relations with non-believers and members of other religious communities (see COMMUNITY AND SOCIETY). The Qurʾān's provisions regarding ritual purity seem to be thematically linked with the concept of the covenant (q.v.) which is also strongly represented in the relevant chapters. This linkage is reflected in the end of Q 5:6 and the opening of Q 5:7 which conclude the instructions regarding ablutions by stating: "God does not wish to burden you, but to purify you and to complete his favor to you, so that you may give thanks. Remember God's favor to you, and his covenant which he concluded with you when you said 'We hear and we obey'…"

The relationship between the early study and interpretation of the qurʾānic text and the development of the Islamic law of ritual purity seems to have been a complex one. The centrality of qurʾānic exegesis to early legal discussion of purity practices is demonstrated by the fact that all important interpretive cruxes in the relevant qurʾānic verses generated juristic debates that can be traced in the early sources. However, the development of Islamic law *(fiqh)* does not merely represent unconstrained reflection on the qurʾānic text. Rather, as in the case of the washing or wiping of the feet, pre-existing understandings of right practice sometimes led to strained readings of the wording of the Qurʾān. The development of *fiqh* must be understood to represent a living tradition of normative practice as well as exegetical refinement (see LAW AND THE QURʾĀN).

In addition to providing instructions for the practice of ritual purity, the Qurʾān uses a terminology of purity in a number of different contexts. Notable among these are its description of paradise and its self-description as a revealed book (q.v.; see also REVELATION AND INSPIRATION). The blessed in paradise will enjoy pure drink (Q 47:15; 76:21) and consort with pure spouses (Q 2:25; 3:15; 4:57); the Qurʾān is a pure scripture (Q 80:14; 98:2) and is touched by none but the pure (Q 56:79), a statement interpreted either as a requirement of ritual purity for those who touch earthly copies of the Qurʾān or as a description of the heavenly exemplar of the Qurʾān touched only by the angels (see ANGEL). The term "pure" *(ṭ-h-r)* is also used in an ethical context referring to sexual and moral purity (Q 74:4, also sometimes interpreted in a physical sense; Q 2:232; 7:82; 11:78; 27:56; 33:53). The literal meaning of the word *zakāt,* "alms" (etymologically derived from the root *z-k-y,* "to be pure"), is reflected in verses describing almsgiving as purifying (Q 9:103; 58:12).

The strong connection between the Qurʾān's purity terminology and its moral vocabulary is exemplified by the antonyms *ṭayyib/khabīth* ("pure, pleasant, good"/"vile, evil") and the range of their usage extends from the purity status of foods (e.g. Q 5:4-5) to general moral censure and praise. These two contrasting roots are among the most frequently used in the purity terminology of ḥadīth and of opinions attributed to the earliest jurists. The antonyms *ḥalāl/ḥarām* ("licit"/"forbidden") cover a similar semantic range (cf. Q 5:1-5). Izutsu *(Concepts,* 237) suggests that these antonyms "go back to the old Semitic idea of ritual cleanness" with *ḥarām* denoting that which is taboo (i.e. both holy and polluted) and *ḥalāl* denoting that which is free from this ban. Significantly, the legal scholar al-Shāfiʿī (d. 204/820) uses *"ḥarām"* as a synonym of *"najis"* (i.e. substantively impure).

Marion Holmes Katz

Bibliography
Primary: Qurṭubī, *Jāmiʿ*; al-Shāfiʿī, *al-Umm*, 8 vols. in 4, Beirut n.d.; Ṭabarī, *Tafsīr*.
Secondary: ʿA. Abdel Kader, The concept of purity in Islam, in *Proceedings of the 11th international congress of the international association for the history of religions. ii. Guilt or pollution and rites of purification,* Leiden 1968, 104-7; G.H. Bousquet, Ghusl, in *EI²*, ii, 1104; J. Burton, The Qurʾān and the Islamic practice of *wuḍūʾ*, in *BSOAS* 51 (1988), 21-58; Izutsu, *Concepts,* 235-41; T. Juynboll, Djanba, in *EI²*, ii, 440-1; M. Katz, *Purified companions. The development of the Islamic law of ritual purity,* Ph.D. diss., Chicago 1997; C. Pellat, Djins, in *EI²*, ii, 550-3.

Clear and Unclear see AMBIGUOUS

Clients and Clientage

The legal attachment of a person or group to another person, family, clan or tribe (see FAMILY; TRIBES AND CLANS). The term "client" *(mawlā,* pl. *mawālī)* plays, along with "confederate, ally" *(ḥalīf)* and "protected neighbor, temporary protégé" *(jār),* a prominent role in pre-Islamic Arabia and in early Islamic society and law (see PRE-ISLAMIC ARABIA AND THE QURʾĀN; COMMUNITY AND SOCIETY; LAW AND THE QURʾĀN). A client was either under the protection of, or nominally equal to, those born into, and thus "full" member(s) of, a family, clan or tribe (Watt-Bell, *Introduction,* 6; see KINSHIP). The meanings of both *mawlā* (in the sense of client, protégé, affiliated free person or manumitted slave or a group of such individuals) and *walāʾ* (clientage, patronage) essentially vary according to their legal, historical or theological usage and according to the periods and the social contexts to which they were applied (A.J. Wensinck, Mawlā, in *EI¹*, iii, 417-8; J. De Bruijn, Iran, 44; Juda, *Mawālī,* 1-29; P. Crone, Mawlā, 874; and esp. id., *Roman law,* 43-4; 49-63; and W. Hallaq, Use and abuse, 84-7).

In the Qurʾān *mawlā* occurs 21 times (three of which are in the plural form, *mawālī*), predominantly with a signification antonymous to that of the English expression "client," i.e. with the meaning of master or patron. In the majority of the qurʾānic occurrences, *mawlā* is an epithet of God or a divine attribute with the meaning of Lord (synonymous with *al-sayyid*), Protector, Helper and Trustee (Q 2:286; 3:150; 6:62; 8:40; 9:51; 10:30; 19:5; twice in 22:78; 47:11; 66:2, 4). The term also indicates a master, a responsible person or thing (Q 16:76: "He is a burden upon his *mawlā*"; Q 57:15: "Your refuge is the fire (q.v.; see HELL), that is your *mawlā*"), a good protector (Q 47:11: "Unbelievers have no *mawlā*") or an evil protector (Q 22:13) and it occurs in the sense of heir (Q 4:33: "To everyone we have appointed *mawālī*") or kinsman (Q 19:5, where Zechariah [q.v.] prays: "Now I fear my kinsfolk *(mawālī)* behind me").

Only twice does *mawlā* occur in the Qurʾān with the common meaning of client. Q 33:5 from a Medinan sūra states: "They [i.e. the adopted sons] are your brothers in religion and your *mawālī*" (see CHILDREN). Q 44:41 from a Meccan sūra captures, in some interpretations, the term's antonymy: "the day a master *(mawlā)* shall be of no profit to a client *(mawlā)*." The basic meaning of the root *w-l-y*, "to be near or close to, to be connected with someone or something," is the linguistic explanation for this antonymy. *Mawlā* connotes primarily a person or party linked to another person or party by proximity *(walāʾ)*, and can thus, as attested in the Qurʾān, be a designation for both client and its counterpart lord (q.v.) or master (q.v.).

The qurʾānic use of client is explained by the exegetes as meaning close person or relative (*qarīb*, Ibn Kathīr, *Tafsīr*, iv, 233, ad Q 44:41) and, figuratively, fellow-tribesman *(ibn al-ʿamm)*, helper *(nāṣir)*, friend (*ṣadīq*, Qurṭubī, *Jāmiʿ*, xvi, 148, ad Q 44:41), the one to whom one feels connected by closeness or friendship (*bi-qarāba aw ṣadāqa*, *Jalālayn*, 377, ad Q 33:5), but also as protector (*walī*, Qurṭubī, *Jāmiʿ*, xvi, 148, ad Q 44:41) which again has a double meaning (see B. Carra de Vaux, Walī). However, on the day of judgment (see LAST JUDGMENT) no *mawlā* can protect another *mawlā* from punishment (*"lā yadfaʿ ʿanhu mina l-ʿadhāb,"* *Jalālayn* 457; cf. Qurṭubī, *Jāmiʿ*, xvi, 148, ad Q 44:41). Compared with the (also figuratively used) word, brother (*akh*, see BROTHER AND BROTHERHOOD), *mawlā* is the expression which describes a slightly firmer relationship to another person (Qurṭubī, *Jāmiʿ*, xiv, 119, ad Q 33:5). Both terms, however, can also be understood as synonyms (as exemplified by Ibn Kathīr, *Tafsīr*, iii, 772, citing the saying of the Prophet *"anta akhūnā wa-mawlānā,"* see Bukhārī, *Ṣaḥīḥ*, nos. 2700, 4251; Ibn Ḥanbal, *Musnad*, no. 933). It is important to note that the close relationship, which both client *(mawlā)* and brother *(akh)* commonly represent, seems to be specified and restricted in the Qurʾān to a relationship in terms of religion, as shown by the parenthetical usage of *"ikhwānukum fī l-dīn wa-mawālīkum"* (Q 33:5).

The qurʾānic conception of clientage, however, seems to reflect the old Arab pattern of collective, egalitarian social relationships of mutual assistance. This differs from Islamic patronage *(walāʾ)* in its institutionalized form, the latter's being individual and assimilative (P. Crone, *Roman law*, 35-42, 43). Furthermore, it is of theological relevance that the idea of God as the Lord and *mawlā* of believers not only indicates the one who has the authority (q.v.) over them but also implies that he is close to and, in a certain sense, in charge of them (while always protecting his "clients"). The qurʾānic notion of a certain kind of interrelation between the human and the divine spheres contributes to enabling Muslim believers to feel closer to God and to making the "All-Mighty" (e.g. Q 16:70) seem somewhat more approachable (see ṢŪFISM AND THE QURʾĀN).

Clientage of a slightly different nature is mentioned in Q 20:39-43. Here it is the word *iṣṭanaʿa* which signifies the patronage of God over a client: Moses (q.v.) is told by God when his mother puts him in the Nile: "And I laid upon you love from me, and to be formed in my sight" (*wa-li-tuṣnaʿa ʿalā ʿaynī*, Q 20:39). Moses grew up with the education and experience that God had desired for him, at which point God said to him: "I have bound you to myself" (*wa-ṣṭanaʿtuka li-nafsī*, Q 20:41) According to Muslim commentators, this phrase means that God had chosen, formed and educated Moses for himself in order that Moses might establish God's proof (q.v.) and serve as his spokesman, or that Moses might undertake a special task (see PROPHETS AND PROPHETHOOD). The idea of helping or promoting somebody as contained in the qurʾānic *iṣṭanaʿa*, seems to have gained a new importance in medieval Islamic society, as shown by its frequent appearance in texts of the fourth/tenth and fifth/eleventh centuries. Here it means "to foster someone's career" but connoting at the same time an almost parental connection of a master to his client or protégé *(muṣṭanaʿ, ṣanīʿ, ṣanīʿa)* who has been reared, educated and trained well by his master (cf. R. Mottahedeh, *Loyalty*, 82-3).

Sebastian Günther

Bibliography
Primary: Bukhārī = Ibn Ḥajar al-ʿAsqalānī, *Fatḥ al-Bārī bi-sharḥ Ṣaḥīḥ al-Bukhārī*, ed. M. Fuʾād ʿAbd al-Bāqī et al., 14 vols., Cairo 1407/1987; Ibn Kathīr, *Tafsīr*, ed. ʿA.Sh. al-Dimashqī, 4 vols., Beirut 1988; *Jalālayn*, ed. ʿA. Muḥammad, Cairo 1936; Qurṭubī, *Jāmiʿ*, 24 vols., Beirut 1985-93.
Secondary: J.T.P. de Bruijn et al., Iran, in *EI*², iv, 1-75; B. Carra de Vaux, Walī, in *EI*¹, viii, 1109-11; J. Juda, *Die sozialen und wirtschaftlichen Aspekte der Mawālī in frühislamischer Zeit*, Ph.D. diss., Tübingen 1983 (one of the most detailed studies on the social and economic aspects of the *mawālī* in ancient Arabia and early Islam), esp. pp. 1-51 (trans., *al-Awḍāʿ al-ijtimāʿiyya wa-l-iqtiṣadiyya lil-mawālī fī ṣadr al-Islām*, Amman 1989). P. Crone, Mawlā (in historical and legal usage), in *EI*², vi, 874-82; id., *Roman, provincial and Islamic law. The origins of the Islamic patronate*, Cambridge 1987; W.B. Hallaq, The use and abuse of evidence. The question of provincial and Roman influence on early Islamic law, in *JAOS* 110.1 (1990), 79-91; H.E. Kassis, *A concordance of the Qurʾān*, Berkeley 1983, 1276-7; R.O. Mottahedeh, *Loyalty and leadership in an early Islamic society*, Princeton 1980; A. Noth, *The early Arabic historical tradition. A source-critical study*, trans. M. Bonner, Princeton 1994 (see Mawlā in Index); A.J. Wensinck, Mawlā, in *EI*¹, iii, 417-8.

Clothing

Garments worn for modesty (q.v.), utility, protection and decoration. Explicit references to clothing appear 23 times in the Qurʾān. Qurʾānic terms for clothing are *libās* and *thiyāb* (clothing, garment), *zīna* (finery), *ḥilya* (ornament) and *rīsh* (attire). Only rarely are specific items mentioned: (mail) shirts *(sarābīl*, Q 16:81), sandals *(naʿl*, Q 20:12), robes *(jalābīb*, Q 33:59) and shirt *(qamīṣ*, Q 12:18, 25-8, 93). A wrap or cloak *(dithār)* is evoked in Q 74, which is entitled "The Cloaked One" (Sūrat al-Muddaththir). In the Qurʾān *ḥijāb* denotes a curtain or separation rather than a female head wrap or face-veil (see BARRIER; VEIL). As presented in the Qurʾān, clothing is made from various materials, including animal hides and furs (see CAMEL; ANIMAL LIFE). The making of coats of mail *(ṣanʿat labūs)* is alluded to in Q 21:80 (see SOLOMON); and mountains are likened to carded cotton *(al-ʿihn al-manfūsh)* in Q 101:5 (see APOCALYPSE).

On the whole, the Qurʾān provides little information regarding specific forms of dress, though it is categorical regarding women who should "draw their hooded robes *(jalābīb)* close around themselves" (Q 33:59; cf. 24:31; see WOMEN AND THE QURʾĀN). Yet the Qurʾān's use of clothing imagery in a metaphorical sense is noteworthy. The verse, "We have revealed *(anzalnā)* to you clothing *(libās)* to conceal your nudity/pudenda *(sawʾāt)*, and attire *(rīsh)*," for example, continues "but the garment *(libās)* of piety is superior" (Q 7:26; see NUDITY; PIETY). Indeed, the "first" garments were not Adam and Eve's "leaves of the garden" *(waraq al-janna)* but rather the "garment" of honor stripped away by Iblīs (Q 7:22; 20:121; see ADAM AND EVE; FALL OF MAN; DEVIL; GARDEN; PARADISE). And in Q 2:187 men and women are described as garments for one another (see MARRIAGE AND DIVORCE). The night (Q 25:47; 78:10) and hunger and fear (Q 16:112) are also described as garments.

The Qurʾān's most symbolic garment is the shirt *(qamīṣ)* of Joseph (Yūsuf; see JOSEPH). It is produced by Joseph's brothers as bloodstained proof of his death (Q 12:18; see BROTHER AND BROTHERHOOD); it is rent by Zulaykhā as she attempts to seduce him (Q 12:25-8) and is used to restore his father Jacob's (Yaʿqūb; see JACOB) sight (Q 12:93). The shirt, a synecdoche for Joseph, serves each time to establish truth (q.v.) or restore honor (q.v.). Q 12:18 explains that the shirt is in fact stained with false or lying blood *(dam kadhib)*. The discovery in Q 12:28 that it is torn from behind proves Joseph's innocence; and in Q 12:94, in proclaiming to Jacob that Joseph is still alive, prophecy and kingship are validated (see PROPHETS AND PROPHETHOOD). A similar validation is echoed in Q 27:44 where the Queen of Sheba (see BILQĪS; SHEBA), mistaking Solomon's crystal palace-floor for a deep pool, raises her garment and thus immodestly exposes her legs. On discovering her error, she is forced to acknowledge Solomon's superior knowledge. Her act of uncovering results in a validation of Solomon as prophet and ruler.

Shīʿī exegesis of Q 3:61-2 and Q 33:33 relates the tradition of Muḥammad's embracing his daughter Fāṭima (q.v.), his son-in-law ʿAlī b. Abī Ṭālib (q.v.) and their sons Ḥasan and Ḥusayn under his cloak, a group subsequently honored as the "people of the cloak" *(ahl al-kisāʾ*, cf. W. Schmucker, Mubāhala; A. Tritton, Ahl al-kisāʾ; see SHĪʿISM AND THE QURʾĀN). This bestowal of favor highlights a connection between clothing and reward (see REWARD AND PUNISHMENT; VIRTUES AND VICES). Indeed, the reward in heaven (q.v.) for the righteous includes garments of silk and brocade *(sundus, istabraq, ḥarīr)*. These luxurious fabrics are in contrast to the clothing of the inhabitants of this world — Muḥammad proscribed the wearing of silk for men — and in stark contrast to the fire-dwellers' garments of fire (Q 22:19; see HELL; FIRE).

Shawkat M. Toorawa

Bibliography
F. Altheim and R. Stiel, *Die Araber in der Alten Welt*, 5 vols. in 6, Berlin 1965, ii; H. Algar, Āl-e ʿAbā, in *Encyclopaedia Iranica*, London 1985, i, 742; R. Dozy, *Dictionnaire détaillé des noms des vêtements chez les Arabes. Ouvrage couronné et publié par la troisième classe de l'Institut Royal des Pays-Bas*, Amsterdam 1845; W. Schmucker, Mubāhala, in *EI*², vii, 276-7; Y.K. Stillman, *Arab dress. From the dawn of Islam to modern times*, Boston 2000; id., Libās, in *EI*², v, 732-50; Y.K. Stillman and N. Micklewright, Costume in the Middle East, in *Middle East Studies Association bulletin* 6 (1992), 13-38; S.M. Toorawa, Every robe he dons becomes him, in *Parabola* 19.3 (1994), 20-8; A. Tritton, Ahl al-Kisāʾ, in *EI*², i, 264.

Clouds see NATURAL WORLD AND THE QURʾĀN

Codes/Markings for Recitation see RECITATION, THE ART OF

Codices of the Qurʾān

A designation generally used to refer to the *maṣāḥif*, plural of *muṣḥaf*, meaning "a copy of the complete text of the Qurʾān" as these existed in the early period of Islam (see J. Burton, Muṣḥaf). These ancient codices, both extant and presumed, are important for the study of the history of the text of the Qurʾān. There are supposedly two categories of these early codices, the pre-ʿUthmānic codices and those with an ʿUthmānic text (see COLLECTION OF THE QURʾĀN; ʿUTHMĀN).

Until the present day, no pre-ʿUthmānic codices of the Qurʾān have been discovered and definitively identified, although possibly some extant palimpsest leaves may contain a non-ʿUthmānic text (Nöldeke, *GQ*, iii, 97-100, but also see W. Diem, Untersuchungen, 211 and 226-7). Nevertheless, many textual variants reported to have existed in these pre-ʿUthmānic codices are known from other sources such as exegetical works *(tafāsīr*, sing. *tafsīr)* and specialized works dealing with non-canonical readings *(al-qirāʾāt al-shādhdha)* like Ibn Jinnī's

(d. 392/1002) *Muḥtasab* and the much earlier *Maʿānī l-Qurʾān* works by al-Akhfash al-Awsaṭ (d. between 210-21/825-35) and al-Farrāʾ (d. 207/822). Or they are found in works dealing specifically with the non-ʿUthmānic codices as such, like the *Kitāb al-Maṣāḥif* of Ibn Abī Dāwūd al-Sijistānī (d. 316/929; Jeffery, *Materials*) which appears to be the only surviving example of this specialization in early qurʾānic studies.

Codices of the second category, however, those with an ʿUthmānic text, have been preserved. Yet the age of the oldest ones, written in the *māʾil* script, has still not been established beyond doubt (see ARABIC SCRIPT). Some of the codices that were discovered in the loft of the Great Mosque of Ṣanʿāʾ in 1972 appear to be of a very early date. However, very little of this material has become available for philological study and until now it is not clear to what extent these manuscripts deviate from the ʿUthmānic orthographic rendering (*rasm*, G.-R. Puin, Observations, 107-11). For a number of leaves from ancient codices that were originally preserved in the Umayyad Mosque in Damascus some scholars have suggested an Umayyad origin (Ṣ. al-Munajjid, *Dirāsāt*, 90-5; see also S. Ory, Nouveau type).

According to prevailing Islamic tradition, the members of a group led by Zayd b. Thābit (q.v.; d. ca. 34-5/655) discharged the task, assigned to them by the third caliph ʿUthmān (r. 23-35/644-56), of producing a complete codex of the Qurʾān. This became the master copy, usually referred to as *al-imām*. Copies of this codex were made and sent to the chief centers of the Muslim empire; all other codices were ordered to be destroyed. In Kufa, ʿAbdallāh b. Masʿūd (d. ca. 33/653) refused, however, to destroy his codex, and his reading apparently remained in use there for some time. Eventually, some seventy years later, the famous governor al-Ḥajjāj b. Yūsuf (d. 95/714) felt compelled to suppress it. Other codices, like those of Ubayy b. Kaʿb (d. 21/642), ʿAlī b. Abī Ṭālib (q.v.; d. 40/661), the Prophet's wife ʿĀʾisha bt. Abī Bakr (q.v.; d. 58/678) and Abū Mūsā al-Ashʿarī (d. ca. 42/662), are also reported to have been destroyed. Nevertheless, from these codices variant readings are reported in classical Islamic literature (see READINGS OF THE QURʾĀN).

The ʿUthmānic recension credited by Muslim tradition to the group led by Zayd b. Thābit only established the *rasm* of the text, i.e. the writing of the consonantal structure but without the diacritics and vowel signs incorporated at a later stage. Thus the reported variant readings of the ancient pre-ʿUthmānic codices — of which the Ibn Masʿūd codex appears to have been the most important — are of two kinds: those which do and those which do not presuppose a different *rasm* than that recorded in the ʿUthmānic master copy.

Variant readings of the first kind range from a difference of one Arabic character, like the reading of *sirāṭ* instead of *ṣirāṭ* in Q 1:6 and all subsequent occurrences in the Qurʾān as reported from a codex attributed to Ibn ʿAbbās (d. ca. 67-8/686-8), to the addition of whole verses or even sūras like "The Renunciation" (Sūrat al-Khalʿ) and "The Service" (Sūrat al-Ḥafd) in Ubayy's codex. Reported omissions fall within the same range: from *wa-nunsihā*, "and we cause to be forgotten," instead of *aw nunsihā*, "or we cause to be forgotten," in Q 2:106 as reported from ʿAlī and Ubayy, to the omission of the first and the two last sūras from the codex of Ibn Masʿūd.

The readings reported from Ibn Masʿūd of the kind which presupposes a different *rasm* may be characterized as follows: (a) They offer synonyms to the ʿUthmānic text like *irshadnā* for *ihdinā* in Q 1:6, both meaning "guide us." (b) They leave less room for ambiguity, as in *taʾwīluhu illā ʿinda llāhi*, "its interpretation is only with God," for *wa-mā ya'lamu ta'wīlahu illā llāhu,* "and none knows its interpretation, save only God," in Q 3:7, the frame of which excludes the possibility of the following phrase, *al-rāsikhūna fī l-'ilm,* "those firmly rooted in knowledge," being also "those who know." (c) They provide clarification, as in the addition of *fī mawāsim al-ḥajj,* "in the seasons of the pilgrimage (q.v.)," after *an tabtaghū faḍlan min rabbikum,* "if you seek bounty from your Lord," in Q 2:198. (d) They provide more easily understood alternatives like *mīthāq alladhīna ūtū l-kitāb,* "the covenant (q.v.) of those who were given the book" instead of *mīthāq al-nabiyyīn,* "the covenant of the prophets," in Q 3:81. It is thus no wonder that these readings continued to play a role in classical exegetical literature (*tafsīr,* see EXEGESIS OF THE QUR'ĀN: CLASSICAL AND MEDIEVAL). Indeed one often finds in early commentary *(tafsīr)* a qur'ānic term explained by a synonym or a phrase which elsewhere is mentioned as a variant reading. This is hardly surprising in view of the interdependence of early exegetical activity and the regular recitation of the Qur'ān (F. Leemhuis, Origins, 24 and 26-7; see RECITATION OF THE QUR'ĀN).

Sometimes non-'Uthmānic readings also occur among the ones which the commentators explain and 'Uthmānic readings are qualified as scribal errors. In Sufyān al-Thawrī's (d. 161/778) commentary on Q 24:27 (*Tafsīr,* ad loc.), Ibn 'Abbās is quoted as having said that *tasta'nisū,* "engaging in social talk," is a scribal error for *tasta'dhinū,* "asking for permission." In the *tafsīr* tradition of Mujāhid (d. 104/722) on Q 3:81 (both in al-Ṭabarī's *Tafsīr* and in the independently preserved recension of Mujāhid, ad loc.), the case is the same, the above-mentioned reading of Ibn Mas'ūd being presented as the correct one. In the manuscript of the commentary of Sufyān al-Thawrī the more than 60 variant readings transmitted are nearly always clustered together near the end of his treatment of each sūra. Most of these are attributed to Ibn Mas'ūd and his followers and the majority of them, but certainly not all, do not necessarily presuppose a non-'Uthmānic *rasm.* The same treatment of variant readings is found in the *Jāmi'* of the Mālikī traditionist of Egypt, Ibn Wahb (d. 197/813; cf. M. Muranyi, Materialien, 239-42). All of this suggests that in the first half of the second Islamic century (720-70 C.E.) variant readings were considered to fulfill a separate exegetical function and that the 'Uthmānic recension, apart from some exceptions, had been accepted as the textus receptus. About half a century later, al-Farrā' (*Ma'ānī,* i, 11) explicitly contrasts "the reading *(qirā'a)* of Ibn Mas'ūd" with "our reading." Nevertheless, these texts also make clear that the existence of variant readings which presupposed a non-'Uthmānic *rasm* was considered a matter of fact.

Apart from the connection with qur'ānic exegetical literature, there is also a connection with the corpus of ḥadīth as some additions from the non-'Uthmānic codices are also reported as sayings of the Prophet, whether inspired by God or not (see REVELATION AND INSPIRATION; ḤADĪTH AND THE QUR'ĀN). The verse about the greed of man (see AVARICE), "If man had two valleys of riches..." *(law [kāna] anna li-bni ādama wādiyāni min mālin...),* for instance, is reported both as an addition in Ubayy's codex at Q 10:24 and in all the six canonical ḥadīth collections as an utterance of the Prophet and sometimes as a non-'Uthmānic Qur'ān quotation as well. It also appears that, at least in some cases, the supposed existence of some verses in non-'Uthmānic codices functioned in the framework of the doctrine of the abrogation (q.v.) of the recited text but not of the divine directive contained therein (*naskh al-tilāwa dūna l-ḥukm*, cf. J. Burton, *Collection*, 68-86).

It is often asserted that Ibn Masʿūd's codex contained a number of Shīʿī readings which were omitted from the ʿUthmānic codex. Although some of these readings are reported to have also been present in other codices, like Ubayy's and ʿAlī's, a separate Shīʿī Qurʾān codex is not known (see SHĪʿISM AND THE QURʾĀN). It could be argued, however, that if there ever was a distinct Shīʿī codex of the Qurʾān it probably would have contained the explicit Shīʿī readings reported from Ibn Masʿūd's codex.

Eventually, the readings from the pre-ʿUthmānic codices which show a different *rasm* disappeared from the recitation of the Qurʾān. Those which did not, continued to play a role in the recitation systems of the Qurʾān as variant readings of the ʿUthmānic text. Parenthetically, it should be noted that al-Farrāʾ (*Maʿānī*, 95) suggests that in some cases a canonical reading may actually have its origin in a different *rasm*. Those non-ʿUthmānic readings which fitted in with the later systems of the seven, ten or fourteen accepted recitation systems *(qirāʾāt)* remained accepted, like the reading *ḥasanan* of Ibn Masʿūd in Q 2:83 which is also the reading of Ḥamza, al-Kisāʾī, Yaʿqūb, Khalaf and al-Aʿmash whereas the rest (of the fourteen) read *ḥusnan* (see RECITERS OF THE QURʾĀN). Those readings which did not fit acquired the qualification of "deviant readings" *(qirāʾāt shādhdha)* and became unfit for recitation, although they continued to play a role in the interpretation and linguistic explanation of the Qurʾān.

Alongside the different readings of these pre-ʿUthmānic codices, a variant order of sūras (q.v.) is frequently mentioned (see CHRONOLOGY AND THE QURʾĀN), the most plausible being the ones of Ibn Masʿūd and Ubayy. As in the case of the variant readings of the pre-ʿUthmānic codices, until recently there was no extant manuscript evidence to support this. In some early codices from Ṣanʿāʾ, however, such different arrangements are indeed found, agreeing or nearly agreeing with what is known from the Ibn Masʿūd and Ubayy arrangements (G.-R. Puin, Observations, 110-1).

Although the concept of the ʿUthmānic *rasm* suggests a uniform and invariable text, such uniformity is not presented by most of the oldest extant codices. Considerable variation in orthography is found especially in connection with long *ā* and words which in the later classical Arabic orthography required a *hamza*. Even the word *qurʾān* is found spelled as *qrn* (e.g. in Q 50:1 of the St. Petersburg fragment as reproduced in E. Rezwan, Frühe Abschriften, 120-1). In addition to their value for study of the Qurʾān's textual history such evidential examples are important for the history of Arabic orthography.

Before the second World War, two complementary projects for preparing a critical edition of the Qurʾān were initiated. A. Jeffery's aim was to present all variants of the ʿUthmānic text that could be collected from the Islamic literary tradition (see LITERATURE AND THE QURʾĀN), whereas G. Bergsträsser planned to collect variants from (photographs of) extant early manuscripts of the Qurʾān. Although neither project survived the war, Jeffery was able to publish his harvest of readings of the old codices together with his edition of the *Kitāb al-Maṣāḥif* of al-Sijistānī (d. 316/929), and at least part of Bergsträsser's work found its way into the third volume of *Geschichte des Qorāns* (Nöldeke, *GQ*), which was completed after his death in 1933 by O. Pretzl, T. Nöldeke having died in 1930.

According to the hypothesis of J. Wansbrough (*QS*, esp. 43-52), which asserts that the Qurʾān only reached its final, standard form during the formative process of the first two centuries of the Islamic community, the reports of the ʿUthmānic recension and of the existence of pre-ʿUthmānic codices, as well as accounts of their suppression must be regarded as fiction, probably patterned after Jewish views about the creation of the Hebrew scriptural canon. On the other hand, J. Burton's (*Collection*, esp. 160-89) thesis considers the collection and codification of the Qurʾān to have been the work of the prophet Muḥammed himself and the stories about its later collection and codification are therefore to be entirely distrusted since their function was probably only to provide a basis for the doctrine of abrogation *(naskh)*.

From these two contrasting views, it is apparent that the paleographical study of ancient codices has produced no clear, unambiguous and generally accepted results with respect to the dating of extant codices. Recent, new studies, however, do appear to be more promising in their attempts to develop a chronological framework based on an inductive approach or to apply classical, art-historical methods to the paleography of the early qurʾānic manuscripts. See also TEXTUAL HISTORY OF THE QURʾĀN; MUṢḤAF.

Frederik Leehmuis

Bibliography

Kh. Aḥmad Muftī, *Naḥw al-qurrāʾ al-kūfiyyīn*, Mecca 1985, (esp. 27-61); A. al-Baylī, *al-Ikhtilāf bayna l-qirāʾāt*, Beirut 1988, esp. 39-71; G. Bergsträsser, Plan eines Apparatus Criticus zum Koran, in *Sitzungsberichte der Bayerischen Akademie der Wissenschaften* 7 (1930); J. Burton, Muṣḥaf, in EI[2], vii, 668-9; S. Carboni, Die arabischen Handschriften, in J.A. Petrosjan et al. (eds.), *Von Bagdad bis Isfahan. Buchmalerei und Schriftkunst des Vorderen Orients (8.-18. Jh) aus dem Institut für Orientalistik, St. Petersburg*, Lugano 1995, 85-100; F. Déroche, Les manuscrits du Coran. Aux origines de la calligraphie coranique, in *Cataloque des manuscrits arabes, Bibliothèque Nationale. Pt. 2. Manuscrits musulmans*, Paris 1983; W. Diem, Untersuchungen zur frühen Geschichte der arabischen Orthographie, in *Orientalia* 48 (1979), 207-57; A. Jeffery, Progress in the study of the Qurʾān text, in *MW* 25 (1935), 4-16; F. Leemhuis, Origins and early development of the *tafsīr* tradition, in Rippin, *Approaches*, 24 and 26-7; Ṣ. al-Munajjid, *Dirāsāt fī taʾrīkh al-khaṭṭ al-ʿarabī*, Beirut 1972, 90-95; M. Muranyi, Neue Materialien zur *tafsīr*-Forschung in der Moscheebibliothek von Qairawān, in Wild, *Text*, 225-55; A. Neuwirth, Koran, in *GAP*, ii, 96-135, esp. 101-3 (with detailed bibliography); S. Ory, Un nouveau type de muṣḥaf, in *REI* 33 (1965), 87-149; G.-R. Puin, Observations on early Qurʾan manuscripts in Ṣanʿāʾ, in Wild, *Text*, 107-11; E.A. Rezwan, Frühe Abschriften des Korans, in J.A. Petrosjan et al. (eds.), *Von Bagdad bis Isfahan. Buchmalerei und Schriftkunst des Vorderen Orients (8.-18. Jh) aus dem Institut für Orientalistik, St. Petersburg*, Lugano 1995, 117-125; A. Spitaler, Die nicht-kanonischen Koranlesarten und ihre Bedeutung für die arabische Sprachwissenschaft, in R. Paret (ed.), *Der Koran*, Darmstadt 1995, 413-4; J.C. Vadet, Ibn Masʿūd, in EI[2], iii, 873-5; A.T. Welch, al-Ḳurʾān. History of the Ḳurʾān after 632, in EI[2], v, 404-9; E. Whelan, Forgotten witness. Evidence for the early codification of the Qurʾān, in *JAOS* 118 (1998), 1-14; id., Writing the word of God. Some early Qurʾān manuscripts and their milieux, in *Ars orientalis* 20 (1990), 113-47.

Coercion

see TOLERANCE AND COMPULSION

Collection of the Qurʾān

The assemblage, ordering and recording of the textual material of the Qurʾān. Muslim reports on the collection of the Qurʾān must, like any other ḥadīth, be tested by exposure to the wider background of Islamic definition from which they emerged. It was held by the most influential commentators and by a majority of the legal scholars that the entire Qurʾān was never collected. This view has been echoed by Western scholars following Nöldeke's *Geschichte* of 1860 (GQ[1], 43; GQ[2], i, 47; ii, 44). From this perspective it is important to note a basic verbal distinction: By Qurʾān was meant all that was ever revealed to the Prophet as "the Book of God." The word refers not to a physical object but to an idea. The inherited book or written manifestation, on the other hand, is called the *muṣḥaf* (q.v.) and the ḥadīths about the collection of the Qur᾿ān are concerned with its identity, provenance and completeness as a textual object (see BOOK).

Several members of the Prophet's circle (see COMPANIONS OF THE PROPHET) are said to have prepared during Muḥammad's lifetime personal copies of the qur᾿ānic revelations, the significance of which became apparent only after Muḥammad's death. These texts, also called *muṣḥaf*, exhibited mutual differences. They also differ from a definitive text, *muṣḥaf*, said to have been promulgated by official state action some dozen years after the Prophet's death. This last text, known as the ʿUthmānic *muṣḥaf* (see ʿUTHMĀN), shows three classes of "omission" relative to the Qur᾿ān and a fourth when compared to the *muṣḥaf*s of the Companions (see CODICES OF THE QUR᾿ĀN).

Legal rulings and the ʿUthmānic muṣḥaf

Islamic law (see LAW AND THE QUR᾿ĀN) is understood to have been derived primarily from two sources, the Qur᾿ān and the sunna (q.v.), the latter originally defined as reports on the words and actions of previous generations of Muslims but, as these reports showed wide differences by the late second century, redefined as reports on the words and actions of the Prophet specifically. These reports reach us through the Companions of the Prophet and their successors.

On certain topics the law exhibits rulings that are not mentioned in the ʿUthmānic *muṣḥaf* and are thought to derive from the sunna. Other rulings of the law clash with rulings mentioned in the *muṣḥaf*. Some scholars traced these discrepancies to the sunna as well, while others — impressed by their adoption in the law and by their certainty that the Prophet had constantly been directed by divine inspiration (see REVELATION AND INSPIRATION; PROPHETS AND PROPHETHOOD) — postulated texts (or pericopes) allegedly once revealed in the Qur᾿ān although omitted from all *muṣḥaf*s.

One finds, for instance, almost unanimous legal agreement in the early texts that for certain cases of adultery (see ADULTERY AND FORNICATION; CHASTISEMENT AND PUNISHMENT; FLOGGING) the penalty is death by stoning (q.v.), a ruling that cannot be reconciled with the penalty prescribed in Q 24:2, "Adulterers, male and female, flog each of them one hundred strokes." The law's stoning penalty had been rejected by some precisely because it was absent from the *muṣḥaf* (Mālik [d. 179/796], *Muwaṭṭa᾿, K. al-Ḥudūd*). But the majority accepted the penalty since it was present in the inherited law and argued that it demonstrated the repeal of the *muṣḥaf* penalty by the sunna penalty. Others, supposing that the words and actions of a human, however elevated, could never supersede the words of the divine lawgiver (see INIMITABILITY), were driven to argue that stoning "must" have originated in a further qur᾿ānic revelation, a stoning-verse that had simply been omitted from the *muṣḥaf* (Mālik, *Muwaṭṭa᾿, K. al-Ḥudūd*). Thus knowledge of the law indicated that the omission of a confirmatory text from the *muṣḥaf* carried no negative implication for the continuing validity of a revealed ruling. The inherited law also indicated that inclusion of a text in the *muṣḥaf* carried no positive implication for the continuing validity of a revealed ruling. As an example, Q 2:240 seemed to establish a period of twelve months during which a widow (q.v.), since she might not legally contract a fresh marriage, was entitled to accommodation and maintenance (see MARRIAGE AND DIVORCE). Q 2:234, it was argued, appears to reduce the period to four months and ten nights, the ruling adopted in the law. It was concluded that verse 234 had been revealed to repeal verse 240 although the wording of both verses survived in the *muṣḥaf* (Ṭabarī, *Tafsīr,* v, 250-62; J. Burton, *Sources,* 56-80). The two cases are said to represent partial omissions from the *muṣḥaf.* One involved the omission of a text but not its ruling; the other showed suppression of a ruling but not its text (see AMBIGUOUS).

Other cases involving omission of both text wording and ruling can with certainty be traced to old exegetical assertions about the implications of verses still present in the *muṣḥaf.* Q 87:6-7, for instance, "We shall instruct you to recite it and you will not forget — except what God wills," was held by commentators to mean, "except what God wills you, Muḥammad, to forget" (J. Burton, Interpretation; see ABROGATION). Ubayy b. Ka'b (d. 21/642) reports that Q 33 used to equal Q 2 in length "and we used to recite the stoning verse in Q 33." Abū Mūsā al-Ashʿarī (d. ca. 42/662) reported that Q 33 was once as long as Q 9 "but I have been caused to forget it — except one verse." Ḥudhayfa declared, "You do not recite today a quarter of Q 9" while ʿĀʾisha bint Abī Bakr (q.v.) stated that Q 33 had once consisted of two hundred verses (Burton, *Collection,* 80-2; Suyūṭī, *Itqān,* ii, 26f.). The *muṣḥaf*'s Q 33 consists of seventy-three verses. Such reports had convinced many that words and rulings together had been forgotten. The two kinds of omission, total and partial, are said to be the intended reference of the mention in Q 2:106 of the *āya* which was "abrogated" or "caused to be forgotten" *(mā nansakh min āya aw nunsihā)* and then replaced with a better or a similar one.

The muṣḥafs *of the Companions*

Following the Prophet's death, many of his Companions had dispersed to participate in the administration and islamization of newly conquered lands outside Arabia. Syrians and Iraqis, like the Arabians at Mecca and Medina, claimed to have acquired and preserved their stock of sunna and Qurʾān lore from these Companions. The surviving literature shows the use made of their names in disputes arising between regional coteries of scholars. The following will illustrate this trend: ʿUrwa was perplexed by the status of the *saʿy* or "running" between Ṣafā (q.v.) and Marwa (q.v.). Q 2:158, "There is no harm for him *(lā junāḥ ʿalayhi)* in moving about between the two of them" appears to suggest that it is optional — one Iraqi view — whereas the Medinan law assumes that it is a rite indispensable to the validity of the pilgrimage (q.v.). ʿUrwa consulted his aunt ʿĀʾisha, a widow of the Prophet, who replied that his view would call for a different reading, i.e. "There is no harm in not performing it." She explained that the obligatory status of this ritual derived not from the Qurʾān but from the sunna, which had cleared up the ambiguity of the text. The Medinese and other Iraqis agreed that the *saʿy* ritual was obligatory. One early Iraqi exegete reports an anonymous variant identical to ʿĀʾisha's hypothetical variant. Although convinced that the ritual is obligatory, he did not on that account reject the reading (see READINGS OF THE QURʾĀN). Comparing it with further qurʾānic usage, he neutralizes it. The variant incorporates a double negative and so just as Q 7:12 "What prevented you that you did not prostrate?" means "What prevented you from doing it?" Q 2:158 means "There is no harm in performing it." He can now accept the variant without having to accept the ruling it implies since the variant means the same as the *muṣḥaf* reading (Farrāʾ, *Maʿānī,* i, 95;

Burton, *Collection,* 12, 30-1). A century later, reporting that certain Companions and their successors had held this ritual to be optional, al-Ṭabarī (d. 310/923) states that their view was explicitly grounded in the *muṣḥafs* of Ibn Masʿūd (d. ca. 33/653) and Ibn ʿAbbās (d. ca. 67-8/686-8; Ṭabarī, *Tafsīr,* iii, 241-2). That discrete variants had logically evolved into discrete *muṣḥafs* was already a given for the earlier exegete mentioned above although, in this present instance, the variant he treated was still unattributed. One of two contending opinions had claimed support in Q 2:158. Its contrary, countering that such an understanding would necessitate a different text, had sought its evidence in the sunna. An understanding of this ritual as optional requires notional improvement of the text in the form of an interpolation. The interpolation is supplied, first as an anonymous reading, but one that can be linguistically neutralized. Persisting in its claim of qurʾānic support, the optional interpretation next acquires specific attribution to named Companion texts. The obligatory nature of the ritual finally claims support in the ʿUthmānic *muṣḥaf* as allegedly interpreted by the Prophet. The interpolation proved neither necessary nor effective.

Another example involves competing interpretations of a mandated expiation (see ATONEMENT). Ḥumayd and Mujāhid were circling the Kaʿba (q.v.) when a man approached and asked Mujāhid whether the days of fast in expiation of the breach of an oath (see OATHS) had to be consecutive (see FASTING). Ḥumayd said the matter was optional but Mujāhid disagreed. The fast must be consecutive since in the reading of Ubayy, "a fast of three consecutive days" was the wording that actually appeared. Non-committal as to the preferred reading, Mālik b. Anas (d. 179/796) expresses his own preference that all fasts imposed in the Qurʾān should be consecutive *(Muwaṭṭaʾ, Ṣiyām, al-nadhr fī l-ṣiyām)*. Al-Ghazālī's (d. 505/1111) much later view was that this fast need not be consecutive even if Ibn Masʿūd did read Q 5:89 as "three consecutive days" rather than the ʿUthmānic *muṣḥaf*'s reading of "three days." According to al-Ghazālī, since Ibn Masʿūd's interpolation was not universally acknowledged, it is not part of the Qurʾān. Possibly Ibn Masʿūd mentioned this restriction as his considered interpretation or he may have imported the wording from Q 58:4, where "consecutive" does occur, albeit in another context. Abū Ḥanīfa (d. 150/767), who conceded that the wording is not qurʾānic, had accepted Ibn Masʿūd's view — but as a ḥadīth. The practice, however, should be understood as based solely on what is reported from the Prophet (al-Ghazālī, *Mustasfā,* i, 102; Burton, *Collection,* 35, 128).

A Ḥanafī scholar argued that the principle of the omission of a qurʾānic wording with no negative implication for the continuing validity of its ruling is shown "by our doctrine that the fast in expiation of the breach of the oath must be consecutive on account of ʿAbdallāh's [i.e. Ibn Masʿūd] reading 'three consecutive days.'" That reading was still current in Abū Ḥanīfa's day but had not achieved the universal acknowledgment requisite to establish it as the definitive text of the Qurʾān. As nobody questions the integrity and trustworthiness of Ibn Masʿūd as transmitter, the early authorities had no alternative other than to presume that his reading had been the original text as preserved by him although omitted during the Prophet's lifetime by God's causing it to be forgotten — except by ʿAbdallāh b. Masʿūd whose reading was to be the means of preserving the ruling. Since the status of his ḥadīths is that they must be acted upon, his Qurʾān reading could not be held inferior to his ḥadīths as source (al-Sarakhsī, *Uṣūl,* ii, 81). Examples like these demonstrate that the

Companions were repositories of two classes of ḥadīths: Companion-sunna-ḥadīths and Companion-Qurʾān-ḥadīths (see ḤADĪTH AND THE QURʾĀN).

The collection of the muṣḥaf

Reports on the collection of the *muṣḥaf* reveal disparities as to its completeness or incompleteness, evincing pressure from some intepretations of Q 87 and from the condition of the law. To provide a summarized version of these reports: Muḥammad's death had been followed by the outbreak of civil wars, and al-Zuhrī (d. 124/741) reports that men who had memorized many Qurʾān passages fell in the fighting. Those passages had neither been written down nor had the Prophet's successors as yet collected the texts. Consequently, those passages had been lost. That impelled the Muslims to pursue the collection of the Qurʾān which, in the reign of Abū Bakr (r. 11-3/632-4), they assembled on sheets. They were motivated by fear that others who bore much of the Qurʾān in memory would perish and would take their memorized portions to their graves. Zayd b. Thābit (q.v.; d. ca. 34-5/655) states that he was reluctant to attempt what the Prophet had never undertaken but that he had agreed to do so at the urgent requests of Abū Bakr (q.v.) and ʿUmar (q.v.) who feared that much of the qurʾānic texts would perish. Little more than a year after the Prophet's death, Zayd collected the texts from the people's memories and their written memoranda. He found the final verse of Q 9 with Abū Khuzayma, having found it with no one else (Ibn Ḥajar, *Fatḥ,* ix, 9-12; Burton, *Collection,* 119, 128). It is also reported that Zayd and others collected the Qurʾān from the personal copy of Ubayy who dictated as they wrote (Jeffery, *Materials,* 9; Burton, *Collection,* 124). When they thought that they had completed the text of Q 9, Ubayy read to them two further verses which they recorded. Anas b. Mālik (d. ca. 91-93/709-711) claims to have been among those who dictated as this written record was being made (Ṭabarī, *Tafsīr,* i, 62). At a later date, when Zayd was editing the texts for ʿUthmān, he recovered from Khuzayma b. Thābit a verse missing from Q 33 (Jeffery, *Materials,* 18-9; Burton, *Collection,* 142). Others report that Khuzayma himself, noting the omission of the Q 9 verse, brought it to ʿUthmān, who accepted it (Jeffery, *Materials,* 11).

Additional reports provide amplification or variant scenarios. Adjudicating a legal case, ʿUmar inquired about the relevant verse. Informed that it had been known by a man who had fallen in battle, ʿUmar commanded that the Qurʾān be collected (Jeffery, *Materials,* 10; Burton, *Collection,* 120). On this occasion, al-Ḥārith b. Khuzayma brought the Q 9 verse to ʿUmar. Further, ʿUmar is said, before the Prophet's death, to have requested permission to record the stoning verse, but the request had been denied (Burton, *Collection,* 82; Suyūṭī, *Itqān,* ii, 26-7). ʿAlī said that the stoning verse had been revealed but that those who had memorized it and other revelations had perished in battle (Burton, *Collection,* 121). Questioned about his non-appearance at the inauguration of the Prophet's first successor, ʿAlī explained that he had solemnly sworn not to appear in public following the Prophet's death until he had first collected the Qurʾān. Having now done so, he was free to take the oath of allegiance to Abū Bakr (Jeffery, *Materials,* 10; Ibn Ḥajar, *Fatḥ,* ix, 9; Burton, *Collection,* 122).

In these and many similar reports, Western scholarship has traditionally detected competitive claims to primacy in the Qurʾān's collection on behalf of each of the Prophet's four immediate successors and sought to determine which was the one "true" version. It is, however, clear from the literature that this is not the usual Muslim duplication of attribution but an attempt to account for more than one aspect of the qur'ānic texts by assuming more than one phase in their collection. Abū Bakr assembled the text for fear of further loss as a result of the deaths of those who had memorized it (Jeffery, *Materials,* 23). The scrupulous care with which Zayd proceeded, taking account both of people's memories and of written records, is calculated to provide reassurance that nothing of what he could yet collect had been overlooked. The early date of the first collection initiative aims to provide similar reassurance. That is balanced by mention of loss through death but even more importantly by the placing of the first collection after the death of the Prophet. Some Muslim scholars suggested a cause for the Prophet's non-participation in the collection but none has explicitly questioned his exclusion.

The ʿUthmānic muṣḥaf

As the traditional reports proceed, they provide further elaboration: Scandalized by the beadle's separating those in the mosque who followed the Ibn Masʿūd *muṣḥaf* from those who adhered to that of Abū Mūsā, Ḥudhayfa counseled the ruler to take immediate action (Jeffery, *Materials,* 11; Burton, *Collection,* 142). ʿUthmān (r. 23-35/644-56) himself had been outraged by quarrels that broke out at Medina. He advised the other Companions that he proposed to unite the people on the basis of a single text. "Companions of Muḥammad! Act in unison to write out a definitive text for the Muslims that will unite them" (Jeffery, *Materials,* 21; Burton, *Collection,* 143). "Abū Bakr was the first to collect the Qur'ān into folios on the deaths of those slain in battle; ʿUthmān collated and published the folios to produce a single reading, he then commanded the destruction of all other texts" (Jeffery, *Materials,* 18-9; Burton, *Collection,* 141).

Inasmuch as reports about ʿUthmān's initiative are hostile to the Companion-*muṣḥaf*s, efforts were made to defend their legitimacy. A man complained to the Prophet, "Ibn Masʿūd taught me a Qur'ān passage; Zayd taught me the same passage and so also did Ubayy. The readings of all three are different, so whose reading ought I to adopt?" (Ṭabarī, *Tafsīr,* i, 24). The request received several replies in different versions of the report. "Recite as you were taught"; "their readings are all equally valid" (Ṭabarī, *Tafsīr,* i, 26, 30, 32); "only public contention over the Qur'ān amounts to apostasy (q.v.)" (Ṭabarī, *Tafsīr,* i, 44, 63; see RECITATION OF THE QUR'ĀN; RECITERS OF THE QUR'ĀN).

Arbitrating similar quarrels between ʿUmar and a fellow Meccan or between Ubayy and a fellow Muslim, the Prophet announced, "Each of your readings is correct. The Qur'ān was revealed in seven forms, so recite whichever is easiest" (Ṭabarī, *Tafsīr,* i, 24-5 [ʿUmar]; 32 [Ubayy]). Attempts to explain reading differences as being caused by their different local dialects (q.v.) foundered on the observation that ʿUmar's quarrel had been with a Meccan. Perhaps each had used different words. Reciting Q 73:6, *hiya ashaddu waṭ'an wa-aṣwabu qīlan,* Anas b. Mālik was corrected, "It is *aqwamu qīlan.*" He replied, "*Aqwamu, aṣwabu, ahya'u* — they all mean the same thing" (Ṭabarī, *Tafsīr,* i, 52). Even the synonym explanation had to be abandoned on the mature view that at no stage had the transmission of the Qur'ān according to the meaning only ever been countenanced. When the doctrine of the uniqueness *(i'jāz)* of the Qur'ān was being interpreted in the sense that the text was inimitable in the strict literary sense (see INIMITABILITY), it had to be agreed that the transmission of the early authorities had been rigorously verbatim. With the abandonment of the dialect and synonym explanations, a reserve rationalization was proffered. According to this interpretation, ʿUmar, an early convert, would have memorized the Qurʾān at an early date. His compatriot, Hishām, had converted only after the conquest of Mecca and had probably memorized later additions to the text which, at the time of their quarrel, ʿUmar had not yet heard (Ibn Ḥajar, *Fatḥ*, ix, 21).

The isnād *of the* muṣḥaf

ʿUthmān is said to have dispatched copies of his *muṣḥaf* to the metropolitan centers with the command that all other texts be shredded or burned. "When the copy arrived at Baṣra, Abū Mūsā declared that everything in ʿUthmān's text and lacking in his own should be added. Anything in his own but lacking in ʿUthmān's text should not be omitted. Ḥudhayfa exclaimed, 'What is the point of all our work? Nobody in this province will abandon ʿAbdallāh's [i.e. Ibn Masʿūd] reading, and nobody of Yemeni origin will abandon Abū Mūsā's'" (Jeffery, *Materials*, 35). ʿAbdallāh b. Masʿūd is projected as protesting, "How can I be ordered to conform to the reading of Zayd, when I recited seventy sūras from the very lips of the Prophet? Am I to be excluded from the collection and the task given to a man who was still an infidel in his father's loins when I first became a Muslim?" (Jeffery, *Materials*, 15, 17). Proponents of the Ibn Masʿūd *muṣḥaf* recruited the Prophet's authority in its defense. "Whoever wishes to recite the Qurʾān in its purest form, as it was revealed, should adopt the reading of ʿAbdallāh" (Ṭayālisī, *Musnad*, ii, 150-1). When ʿUthmān's order for the destruction of their copies reached Iraq, ʿAbdallāh b. Masʿūd is portrayed as advising his followers to conceal their *muṣḥaf* to preserve it from destruction (Ṭayālisī, *Musnad*, ii, 150-1; Jeffery, *Materials*, 15; Ṭabarī, *Tafsīr*, i, 28). Reading differences had thus allegedly evaded the supposed ʿUthmānic initiative to unite the Muslims on the basis of a single text.

The readings attributed to Companions are of two kinds: attempted interpolations into a universally acknowledged text or variations on the consonantal or vocalic values that may be assigned to the script used to record the *muṣḥaf*, a script which originally lacked both diacritics and short vowel markers (see ARABIC SCRIPT). The use of a denuded script has even been explained as a deliberate device to accommodate the "seven readings" which the Prophet was said to have sanctioned. A reading of the final verse which Zayd, or ʿUmar, or ʿUthmān had recovered, "There has now come to you a prophet from your own number *(anfusikum)*" was ascribed to ʿĀʾisha and Fāṭima (q.v.), respectively the Prophet's widow and daughter, and even to the Prophet himself, as *anfasikum*, "from the most noble among you" (Zamakhsharī, *Kashshāf*, ad Q 9:128).

At the time when irreconcilable doctrines were being attributed to the different past "authorities," to whom appeal was made in support of competing regional or school attitudes, the sunna showed bewildering contradictions and confusions. To control a growing accumulation of disparate source materials, scholars began to insist on the naming of those in each generation who transmitted relevant statements from their putative authors among the Companions. The lists could be compared and judgments made as to degrees of accurate memorization, *ḥifẓ*, and trustworthy transmission, *thiqa*. Al-Shāfiʿī (d. 204/820) sought to impose the solution of discounting all Companion information when reports from the Prophet himself were available. Reports from the Prophet continued to conflict, so al-Shāfiʿī insisted on closer scrutiny of the lists of transmitters (sing. *isnād*), applying the principle of abrogation. It is possible to date a shift in preference for reports from older to younger Companions. Invariably, where reports clash, the later are to be accepted. The application of this rule can already be seen in reference to the reported quarrel between ʿUmar and Hishām discussed above. In this light, the participation of Zayd in every phase of Qurʾān compilation becomes clearer. Addressing Zayd, Abū Bakr declared, "You are young, intelligent and we know nothing to your discredit. You served the Prophet by recording his revelations in writing, so now pursue the Qurʾān and bring it all together." Here, the moral uprightness *(ʿadāla)* of Zayd is assured, and the projection or "raising" *(rafʿ)* of the *isnād* of his *muṣḥaf* to the Prophet is established as against that of the older Companions. The ʿUthmān-Zayd label identifies the last historical link between the time of the Medinan caliphate (see CALIPH) and that of the Prophet. It was thus designed to supersede all other Qurʾān traditions.

As to the abrogation principle, two features can be observed when it is applied to the Qurʾān: alleged omissions from the Qurʾān and alleged omissions from the ʿUthmānic text. The latter are the Companions' "variants," actually attempted interpolations. Yet despite the near unanimity on the stoning penalty, for example, it is strikingly noteworthy that the wording of the stoning verse has never been attributed to any Companion-*muṣḥaf*. Thus it can be argued that it represents attempted interpolation into an ideal text.

In another example, Q 2:184 permits the sick and those who are travelling to breach the Ramaḍān (q.v.) fast on condition that, when they can, they will fast the precise number of days they had not fasted. The manner of this compensatory fast became the subject of dispute. ʿĀʾisha reports that the verse "was originally revealed: 'a number of alternative consecutive days.' Subsequently, the word 'consecutive' was dropped." One commentator explains "was dropped" to mean that the word was withdrawn by the divine author (Suyūṭī, *Durr*, i, 192). Elsewhere al-Suyūṭī (d. 911/1505) explains that "Abū Bakr's aim was seen to have been to collect the Qurʾān 'between two covers'; ʿUthmān's had been to collect those readings attested as coming from the Prophet and to reject all non-canonical readings. He sought to unite the Muslims on the basis of a single text containing no interpolations which still appeared in written documents alongside verses whose inclusion in the final version of the text had been endorsed" (Suyūṭī, *Itqān*, i, 60-1).

The extent of the Companion muṣḥafs

When isolated readings from Companions or their successors were discussed, the majority of scholars tended to mention them as curiosities and, apart from those who were dependent on them for their evidence, to view them as variants or as explanatory additions, hence as secondary to a generally recognized text. They were only prepared to acknowledge readings that conformed with the consonantal matrix of ʿUthmān's *muṣḥaf*, conformed with the rules of Arabic grammar (see GRAMMAR AND THE QURʾĀN) and were equipped with a sound *isnād*. Consonantal or vocalic readings can be indicated by symbols external to the core script, which thus remains unaltered. Given this limitation, these tolerated variants amounted to no more than the interpretation of a shared common text. Only in very rare cases was there potential for serious division of opinion. Such an instance occurred in the reading of Q 5:6, where the absence of short vowel markers raised the difficulty of deciding whether, in the ritual purification required for prayer (q.v.), the feet should be washed like the face and hands or merely wiped like the head (see RITUAL PURITY; CLEANLINESS AND ABLUTION).

When, to reinforce appeal to Companion readings, Companion *muṣḥaf*s began to be mentioned, they had to be differentiated from the ʿUthmānic *muṣḥaf*. The order of the sūras in Ibn Masʿūd's or Ubayy's *muṣḥaf* had, it was alleged, differed from that of the ʿUthmānic text (see SŪRA). Any sūra lists produced for these codices merely had to vary from the ʿUthmānic sequence. Adoption of the present order could have occurred, it was thought, when ʿUthmān arranged the sheets of Abū Bakr. Further reports state that annually during the Prophet's later years, in Ramaḍān, Gabriel (q.v.) reviewed the year's revelations. It was presumed that he would have fixed at least the order of the verses within their sūras. There has, in any event, been no recorded dispute over the internal arrangement of the individual sūras. Perhaps the order of the sūras themselves had also been fixed at the same time. The precise order of the sūras is, however, of no practical relevance. All classical Muslim scholars are agreed that the present order of the *muṣḥaf* bears no relation to the order in which the sūras were revealed. A chronological ordering of the revelations would have been of practical utility only in discussions on abrogation, the earlier being thereby more easily distinguished from the later revelation. Although ʿAlī is reputed to have collected his Qurʾān materials in chronological order and to have included notes on abrogation, no copy of his *muṣḥaf* has ever been located (Suyuṭī, *Itqān*, i, 58). A fourth/tenth century bibliographer claimed to have handled a number of *muṣḥaf*s, all of which were attributed to Ibn Masʿūd, but no two of them agreed in respect of sūra order (Ibn al-Nadīm, *Fihrist*, 46, on the arrangement of the Qurʾān in the *muṣḥaf* of ʿAbdallāh b. Masʿūd).

Both the ʿAbdallāh b. Masʿūd and the Ubayy *muṣḥaf*s were said to have varied from the ʿUthmānic *muṣḥaf* in length. Numerous reports relate ʿAbdallāh b. Masʿud's erasure of the first and the last two sūras on the grounds that "they were not part of the book of God." There was considerable speculation as to the implications of this procedure. In the end, it was concluded that, having seen the Prophet frequently employ the three short passages as charms (see AMULETS), ʿAbdallāh had supposed that they must be special prayers, as opposed to revealed passages. Others dismissed the reports outright as a pack of lies fathered upon a leading Companion of the Prophet who could not conceivably have entertained doubts about the revelation. ʿAbdallāh himself had characterized denial of any part of the Qurʾān as apostasy (Ṭabarī, *Tafsīr*, i, 38). Eventually it was settled that, because one may not simply dismiss reports of sound *isnād*, ʿAbdallāh had at first doubted whether the Companions were justified in their determination to include these passages and was only slowly won round to their view. It had to be presumed that by "book of God," ʿAbdallāh had meant only the *muṣḥaf* and not the Qurʾān. Further, he may have considered that the purpose of the collection was to obviate possible forgetting, loss or addition, dangers which would not arise with regard to the three sections. They were all extremely brief and one was repeated five times daily in the ritual prayers (Suyūṭī, *Itqān*, i, 79; Burton, *Collection*, 221-4; see PRAYER FORMULAS). Ubayy's *muṣḥaf* was said to have contained two sections absent from the ʿUthmānic *muṣḥaf*. It was similarly supposed that, having noted the frequency with which the Prophet had recited them in the ritual prayers, Ubayy had erroneously imagined that the formulae must have been part of the divine revelation since they were uttered in the ritual. Misapprehension had thus led him into admitting the two passages into his recension of the Qur'ān (Burton, *Collection,* 221).

The final review of the text

There are numerous reports that record what were understood to be the last stage of the Qur'ān's collection. The Prophet's daughter is reported as saying that her father told her that Gabriel, who checked the revelations with him once a year, had just checked them twice, from which Muḥammad inferred that his death must be imminent. According to another account when Ibn ʿAbbās asked, "Which of the two texts do you consider the later?" they said the Zayd text. "No," he replied, "the Prophet reviewed the texts annually with Gabriel, twice in his final year. The reading of Ibn Masʿūd is that of the later of the two final reviews" (Ibn Ḥajar, *Fatḥ,* ix, 35-6).

When a man referred to "the former reading," Ibn ʿAbbās asked what he meant. He said "When ʿUmar sent ʿAbdallāh [b. Masʿūd] to Kufa, the people there adopted his reading. Then when ʿUthmān changed the texts, they referred to the ʿAbdallāh reading as 'the former text.'" "But it is the later," insisted Ibn ʿAbbās, "based on the final review. Ibn Masʿūd attended the final review and learned what had been withdrawn and what had been altered" (Ibn Ḥajar, *Fatḥ,* ix, 35-6).

Two sets of ḥadiths involving ʿAbdallāh b. Masʿūd and Zayd concern the *isnād* of the texts. One stressed the early date of ʿAbdallāh's acceptance of Islam and claimed that his *muṣḥaf* had considerably predated that of Zayd. The second now seeks to claim that ʿAbdallāh's represents the most recent text. Appropriating this second ḥadīth motif, the proponents of the Zayd-ʿUthmān *muṣḥaf* insist that Zayd attended the final review, learning what had been withdrawn and what remained: "Zayd attended the final review in which he learned what had been removed and what remained. He wrote out this final review text and read it over to the Prophet for him to check once more. Thereafter Zayd taught that text to the Muslims. That explains why Abū Bakr and ʿUmar relied on Zayd to collect the texts and why ʿUthmān entrusted him with production of the copies" (Suyūṭī, *Itqān,* i, 51).

The ʿUthmān collection tradition was not opposed to the Abū Bakr-ʿUmar initiative. It was opposed to the "variant reading" and "variant *muṣḥaf*" tradition (Dānī, *Muqniʿ,* 7; Burton, *Collection,* 146). As noted earlier, the consolidation of the sunna involved the transition from the ḥadīths reported from the Companions to those reported from the Prophet and, as transmitters from the Prophet, younger Companions came to be preferred to older Companions in order to ensure reports from the Prophet's late period. *Muṣḥaf*s reported from the Companions, however, failed to complete the transition since no *muṣḥaf* has ever been attributed to the Prophet. The reason is clear and simple. No revealed verse still legally valid when the Prophet died could have been omitted from the *muṣḥaf* if the Prophet had been credited with its collection. To accommodate the concept of abrogation, the collection had logically to be consciously and deliberately placed in the period following the Prophet's death, a motif the scholars were keen to emphasize by repeating it in the collection ḥadīths. They knew why and they explained why: "It is probable that the Prophet did not himself collect the Qur'ān into a single volume, since he expected abrogation to affect either some of its legal provisions or certain of the wordings. Once revelation ceased absolutely on the Prophet's death, God inspired his Companions to the task of collecting the texts, in fulfillment of the divine promise (Q 15:9) to preserve them" (Ibn Ḥajar, *Fatḥ*, ix, 9).

Western scholarship has in the past century contributed considerably to the knowledge of the Qurʾān sciences (see EXEGESIS OF THE QURʾĀN: CLASSICAL AND MEDIEVAL; TRADITIONAL DISCIPLINES OF QURʾĀNIC STUDY) by discovering and publishing many works on the various aspects of the qurʾānic texts with particular emphasis on the structure of the composition, the periodization of the content and close examination of accumulated variants. Interest has focused principally on the Qurʾān as a literary monument and the labors of many outstanding experts might have resulted in a scholarly edition of the entire text. Such a project was, indeed, planned in the earlier years of the century by G. Bergsträsser, A. Jeffery and others but was frustrated by the outbreak of the second world war. It had probably, in any case, been rendered unnecessary by the excellent Royal Egyptian version of 1342/1923-4. It should also be remembered that to Muslims, the Qurʾān is both unparalleled literary document and legal source and it is this combined quality that has determined their view of its history. See also TEXTUAL HISTORY OF THE QURʾĀN; CHRONOLOGY AND THE QURʾĀN.

John Burton

Bibliography
Primary: Ibn Abī Dāwūd, *K. al-Maṣāḥif*, ed. Jeffery, Cairo 1936; Dānī, *Muqniʿ*; Farrāʾ, *Maʿānī*; al-Ghazālī, *Kitāb al-Mustaṣfā*, 2 vols., Būlāq 1322/1904; al-Ḥāzimī, Muḥammad b. Mūsā, *Kitāb al-Iʿtibār*, Hyderabad 1359/1940[2] (rev. ed.); Ibn Ḥajar, *Fatḥ al-bārī*, 12 vols., Cairo 1376/1957; Ibn al-Nadīm, *Fihrist*; Mālik, *Muwaṭṭaʾ*; Qurṭubī, *Jāmiʿ*; al-Sarakhsī, Shams al-Aʾimma, *al-Uṣūl*, 2 vols., Hyderabad 1372/1952; al-Shāfiʿī, *Kitāb Ikhtilāf al-ḥadīth*, on margin of id., *Kitāb al-Umm*, 7 vols., Būlāq 1322-4/1904-6, vii; id., *Kitāb al-Risāla*, Būlāq 1321/1904; Suyūṭī, *Durr*; id., *Itqān*; Ṭabarī, *Tafsīr*; al-Ṭayālisī, Abū Dāwūd, *Musnad*, Hyderabad 1321/1904 (an edition organised according to *abwāb al-fiqh* is found in A. Dimyati, *Minḥat al-maʿbūd*, 2 vols., Cairo 1372/1952-3); Zamakhsharī, *Kashshāf*.
Secondary: Burton, *Collection*; id., The interpretation of Q 87:6-7 and the theories of *naskh*, in *Der Islam* 62.1 (1985), 5-19; id., *The sources of Islamic law*, Edinburgh 1990; Goldziher, *Richtungen*; Jeffery, *Materials*; T. Nöldeke, *Geschichte des Qorans*, Göttingen 1860; id., *GQ*; ʿA.Ṣ. Shāhīn, *Taʾrīkh al-Qurʾān*, Cairo 1966.

Colors

The distinguishing hues and shades reflecting or emanating from a light source. The Qurʾān speaks of color generically as an attribute of God's creation: The fact of the existence of diverse hues, *alwān*, is mentioned nine times (twice in Q 2:69 and 35:27; also in Q 16:13, 69; 30:22; 35:28; and 39:21), most often connected to evidence for God's handiwork in creation (q.v.). As might be expected, then, a majority of the mentions of individual colors are connected to this same motif.

Before discussing the qurʾānic material, however, it is necessary to understand what is meant by color terminology. Linguists have established sets of criteria by which words for basic colors may be identified. The work of B. Berlin and P. Kay, *Basic color terms. Their universality and evolution* (Berkeley 1969) is the standard work in the field and the authors provide four such criteria for a word to be considered a "color term" (p. 6): (a) it is monolexemic (i.e. not predictable from the meaning of its parts); (b) its significance is not included in that of any other color term; (c) its application is not restricted to a limited class of objects; and (d) it is psychologically salient for informants, i.e. it appears at the beginning of elicited lists of color words, is stable across informants and is used in ideolects of all informants. Berlin and Kay have also made a significant contribution to the study of the historical development of color terms, but the limited corpus of early Arabic means that making suggestions about the emergence of color terms in that language is unlikely to be very profitable.

Using these criteria for the assessment of color terminology, then, certain words may be isolated in the Qur'ān as representing colors. White *(abyaḍ)*, black *(aswad)*, yellow *(aṣfar)*, red *(aḥmar)* and green *(akhḍar)* are all prominent; a number of other terms may also be suggested as conveying color perception, frequently with an ambiguous relationship to these primary terms.

Red *(aḥmar)* is used only once (in the plural form *ḥumr*) in the Qur'ān, in Q 35:27-8, a passage which speaks of the multi-colored nature of God's creation and which conveys the significance of most color references in the Qur'ān by indicating that they are a part of the way of appreciating God's creative work in the world (see NATURAL WORLD AND THE QUR'ĀN): "Have you not seen how God sends down water (q.v.) from heaven, and therewith we bring forth fruits of diverse hues *(alwān)*? And in the mountains are streaks white and red, of diverse hues *(alwān)*, and pitchy black; men too, and beasts and cattle — diverse are their hues." Another word for red (or crimson) is used in Q 55:37, in which the day of judgment (see LAST JUDGMENT; APOCALYPSE) is described: "And when heaven is split asunder, and turns crimson like [red] hide *(warda ka-l-dihān)*." The phrase *warda ka-l-dihān* apparently has an exact sense which, in this occurrence, is nonetheless unclear. *Dihān* is used only once (cf. Q 23:20 with its use of *duhn* in reference to the anointing oil flowing from a tree on Mount Sinai; see ANOINTING; SINAI) and some translations of the word suggest "ointment" or "grease" although the lexicographers certainly favor a meaning of "a red hide" (see Lane, ad loc.). *Warda,* likewise, is only used once in what appears to be a color reference (cf. *warīd* in Q 50:16 meaning "jugular vein"; see ARTERY AND VEIN) and the sense seems to flow from the context of a brilliant sky as being colored red, rosy or crimson. While the word red is commonly employed as a powerful image associated with blood and life (see BLOOD AND BLOOD CLOT; BIOLOGY AS THE CREATION AND STAGES OF LIFE), the Qur'ān does not follow that direction in its color language. Qur'ānic usage does, however, express the prominence or "strikingness" of this color.

Green is mentioned six times as an adjective (*khuḍr, akhḍar,* Q 12:43, 46; 18:31; 36:80; 55:76; 76:21) and once as a participle (Q 22:63), "to become green." The usage of *khaḍir* in Q 6:99 is a related nominal usage referring to a "green leaf" but is not, strictly speaking, a color word. Green conveys a sense of freshness and luxuriousness in the Qur'ān. It is likely that the connotation of vegetation (see AGRICULTURE AND VEGETATION) explicit in the reference to "green ears of corn" in Q 12:43 and 12:46, is the foundation for the associative senses of the color green, as in the green garments of silk (q.v.; Q 18:31; 76:21. Note may also be made of the connected uses of gold [q.v.] and silver here; see also CLOTHING) and of green cushions (Q 55:76) pictured within the comforts and lushness of the hereafter (see HEAVEN). The participial usage of *mukhḍarra* in Q 22:63 echoes the more general color connotation of the glories of God's creation manifested in the colors which result, in this instance, from rainfall. The word *mudhāmm* is commonly translated as green pastures but has more the sense of dark, tending towards black (which is the common meaning of the adjective *adham*). Its use in Q 55:64 in reference to the "two gardens" tends to demand a translation that stresses green; the lexicographers try to explain this as a shade of green so intense that it "appears black when viewed from a distance" (Lane, ad loc; see GARDEN).

The color yellow or golden, *aṣfar,* is used five times including three times in verbal form. The "golden cow" (see CALF OF GOLD) of the Moses (q.v.) story in Q 2:69 is understood as intense, bright or pure, *fāqiʿ,* a word associated with both yellow and white. In Q 77:33, the association of yellow is with hell fire (see HELL) in which sparks are spoken of "as if they were yellow camels." While it might be possible to suggest that there is an association of the quality of animals with brilliant yellowness, clearly the biblical story of the golden calf could very well have suggested the image as it is found in the Qurʾān. The three participial uses refer to a "yellow wind," perhaps of a sand storm (Q 30:51) and to the withering of vegetation after the rain has turned it green and it has grown (Q 39:21; 57:20). Reference to color is thus again evidence of God's work although notably in this instance not simply of a generative kind, but of involvement with the entire life cycle.

Absent in this list of colors thus far are brown and blue. The use of *zurq* (plural form of *azraq,* the common adjective for blue) in Q 20:102 denotes eyes (q.v.) specifically and cannot be considered truly a color word: "The day when the trumpet shall be sounded, at that time we will gather the sinful blue-eyed *(zurqan).*"

The fact that the adjective *azraq* is commonly associated with eyes (q.v.) that are blind and, as a color, is often seen to tend towards gray, makes it likely that the expression of the perception of the blue spectrum in Arabic is more closely aligned to that of green, as is common in many languages, despite the sense that blue is "one of the essential colors of nature" (A. Morabia, Lawn). There may also be a connection with the medical ailment of cataracts, which turns the eye blue or even grey or green. In contemporary Arabic dialects cataracts are called blue water *(al-māʾ* or *al-miya al-zarqa).* It is here that some of the dimensions of the cultural values which colors can convey may be perceived. The glorification of blue skies is perhaps something meaningful only to those who live in climates in which precipitation is an expected element in life (see WEATHER). It is more likely that the appearance of storm clouds is to be greeted with pleasure in areas where rain is not a predictable phenomenon. Thus the symbolic usages of the word — the praising of blue skies, blue waters, blue eyes — are more limited and, in fact, when used, tend towards the negative as indicated by the association of blue eyes with evil in Q 20:102. But even there, it should be noted that explicit development of the negative connotations of blue (the use of blue to ward off the evil eye, for example) is absent from the Qurʾān. According to A. Morabia, the color blue was so "magical, inauspicious and disturbing" that "the Arabs took pains to avoid mentioning this color" (Lawn). The overlap between brown and yellow and red makes the absence of the color brown from the Qurʾān perhaps less remarkable than the absence of blue.

White and black, often contrasted, constitute a substantial portion of the color references in the Qurʾān, as might be expected. *Abyaḍ,* "white," (including its feminine and plural forms) occurs eight times (the root is also used for eggs in Q 37:49) plus three times in a verbal conjugation. In Q 35:27, white is a color of creation, put alongside red, black and "many colors" as a description of colors in mountains, as mentioned above. Similar perhaps is Q 37:46 as a description of water in paradise (q.v.) but this may also be understood as the use of white as a symbol of purity, a notion conveyed in the contrast with black in Q 3:106 and 3:107 where the pure believers "glow in white" and the unbelievers "glow in black" (see BELIEF AND UNBELIEF; FAITH). Another sense here might be that to "glow in white" is to be filled with joy while "black" represents sadness (Mir, *Verbal,* 63-4). Likewise, Moses' hand being miraculously white when he withdraws it from his garments as an evidence to Pharaoh (q.v.) also conveys a sense of purity. Numerically, this is the most significant use of white, being mentioned in Q 7:108, 20:22, 26:33, 27:12 and 28:32. These passages have another interpretation, however, in precisely the inverse, emphasizing the miraculous element rather than the metaphoric. Developing a Rabbinic interpretation (*Pirke Rabbi Eliezer,* chapter 48, quoted in A. Geiger, *Judaism and Islam,* 125, n. 4), some Muslim commentators (e.g. Ṭarafī, *Qiṣaṣ,* p. 262) are aware of the version of the story in which Moses' hand was "white with leprosy *(baraṣ),*" thus white would mean impure (see PURITY AND IMPURITY). Finally, in a passage which must be understood as idiomatic, Jacob's (q.v.) grief over the loss of Joseph (q.v.) is described in Q 12:84 as causing his eyes (q.v.) to "become white with sorrow" *(ibyaḍḍat ʿaynāhu min al-ḥuzn),* sorrow causing blindness, which itself is characterized as showing the whites of one's eyes (see Mir, *Verbal,* 64).

The contrast between the "white thread (or streak)" and the "black thread" in Q 2:187, as this refers to daybreak and thus to the beginning of a day of fasting (q.v.; see also RAMAḌĀN), has been a locus of exegetical discussion about the meaning of the statement. Generally this contrastive terminology is understood to indicate the difference between dark and light (see DARKNESS) rather than the colors black and white *per se.* Clearly there is a relationship between these two pairs, especially on the metaphorical level in which God is seen as the source of light (q.v.) and of purity.

The color black is denoted primarily by *aswad* and its derivatives although several other terms apparently fall within the chromatic field. Of the seven uses of the root *s-w-d,* four (Q 2:187; twice in 3:106; 35:27) appear alongside white as detailed in the previous paragraph, suggesting not only the color black in nature but also its metaphorical usage as the opposite of white in the latter's sense of purity. The word *muswadd* is used in Q 16:58 and its parallel Q 43:17 to suggest the darkening of the face in the light of bad news as a reflection of grief, echoing the eschatological (see ESCHATOLOGY) usage in Q 39:60, as well as the previously-mentioned Q 3:106 (see Mir, *Verbal,* 177). Other words generally understood as the color black (or at least dark hues) include *aḥwā* in Q 87:5, where the contrast is between lush pasture land (i.e. green) and what becomes dark stubble *(ghuthāʾ aḥwā),* according to God's (i.e. nature's) laws. *Hāmida* in Q 22:5 means lifeless and is ordinarily taken as blackened, as though by fire (q.v.; an image sometimes connected to *aswad* as well, due to hell fire "blackening" the faces of its inhabitants). *Mudhāmm,* used in Q 55:64 in the sense of dark, sometimes seen as dark green (as mentioned in the discussion of "green") tending to black, is found as a description of lushness of the "two gardens." Several other terms related to darkness have a primary sense of cloud covering, shadows and the like and are not truly color terms.

Colors are present in the Qurʾān, therefore, in both descriptive and metaphoric usage. The most pervasive sense of color is detailed in God's creative power, which is witnessed in the presence and the changing of colors in the world. Cultural values, however, are also conveyed in the metaphorical instances, reflecting both common elements of the biblical Near Eastern tradition and the culture of Arabic speakers of the first/seventh century.

Andrew Rippin

Bibliography
Primary: al-Ṭarafī, Abū ʿAbdallāh Muḥammad b. Aḥmad, *Qiṣaṣ al-anbiyāʾ*, ed. and trans. R. Tottoli, *Storie dei profeti*, Genova 1997.
Secondary: B. Scarcia Amoretti, Lunar green and solar green. On the ambiguity of function of a colour in Islam, in AO-H 33 (1979), 337-43; A. Brenner, *Colour terms in the Old Testament*, Sheffield 1982 (contains a full bibliography on the study of color and color terms); W. Fischer, *Farb- und Formbezeichnungen in der Sprache der altarabischen Dichtung. Untersuchengen zur Wortbedeutung und zur Wortbildung*, Wiesbaden 1965 (the standard reference work on the subject in the field of Arabic); A. Geiger, *Judaism and Islam*, Madras 1898 (German original 1833); Lane; Mir, *Verbal;* A. Morabia, Lawn, in *EI²*, v, 698-707 (provides an excellent overview and extensive bibliography); A. Shivtiel, The semantic field of colours in Arabic, in *Proceedings of the colloquium on Arabic grammar. The Arabist* = BSA 3-4 (1991), 335-9.

Combat see WAR

Commandments

Moral regulations mandated by divine decree. The Qurʾān does not refer explicitly to the biblical Ten Commandments (see SCRIPTURE AND THE QURʾĀN) or "ten words," and Muslim exegetes have not generally tried to find either the Decalogue itself or a Muslim equivalent in the text. The Qurʾān does speak of tablets *(alwāḥ)* given to Moses (q.v.; Q 7:145f.) but alludes to their content only in general terms: "And we wrote for him on the tablets of everything an admonition *(mawʿiẓa)* and exposition *(tafṣīlān)* for everything." The tradition often seems as interested in what the tablets were made of (emerald with gold writing, according to Masʿūdī, *Murūj*, i, 49; other possibilities include ruby, chrysolite, wood, stone; see Qurṭubī, *Jāmiʿ*, vii, 179) as in what they contained. Otherwise, commentators generally see the tablets of Q 7:145 as containing a law code of sorts ("what [the Israelites, see CHILDREN OF ISRAEL] were commanded to do and forbidden from doing," Ṭabarī, *Tafsīr*, ix, 57). Some exegetes consider the tablets to have contained both statutory rules (*aḥkām*, see BOUNDARIES AND PRECEPTS) and narrative material intended to induce obedience (q.v.; e.g. Rāzī, *Tafsīr*, xiv, 193). Wahb b. Munabbih (d. 110/728 or 114/732), the Jewish convert and well-known transmitter of "Jewish lore" or *Isrāʾīliyyāt*, is said to have associated the tablets of Q 7:145 with the Ten Commandments and gives — without identifying it as such — a close paraphrase of some of the Decalogue: "[God] wrote: Do not associate with me anything of the heavens and the earth, for all of that is my creation (q.v.; cf. the wording of *Exod* 20:4, on graven images); Do not swear falsely in my name, for I will not cleanse the one who swears falsely (cf. *Exod* 20:7 and *Deut* 5:11, with the Hebrew *lō yənakkeh* [God will not acquit, or purify] semantically equivalent to the Arabic *lā uzakkī*, "I will not cleanse"); and honor your parents" (Ṭabarī, *Tafsīr*, ix, 57f.).

Apart from the tablets of Q 7:145, Moses (q.v.) also receives nine "clear signs" (*āyāt bayyināt*, see SIGNS) at Q 17:101. From the context, this must refer to something other than the Ten Commandments and most commentators have taken it to mean nine miracles performed for the benefit of Pharaoh (q.v.; see also EGYPT) and his people, spoken of elsewhere at Q 27:12. These are traditionally said to have included, among other things, the changing of the rod into a serpent, Moses' white hand and the plagues (q.v.) of locusts, lice, frogs and blood (Ṭabarī, *Tafsīr*, xv, 171; Bayḍāwī, *Anwār*, i, 583; Rāzī, *Tafsīr*, xxi, 54). However, one line of commentary takes these "nine clear signs" to refer to nine specific legal statutes, some of which are familiar from the biblical Decalogue while others are foreign to it: Do not associate anything with God; do not steal; do not kill anyone (whose blood) God has declared unlawful, except with just cause (see MURDER; BLOODSHED); do not use magic (see MAGIC, PROHIBITION OF); do not take unjust enrichment, i.e. usury (q.v.); do not bring an innocent person before the ruler (see KINGS AND RULERS) so that he may be killed; do not slander a chaste woman (see CHASTITY); do not flee on the day the army marches (see WAR); and — a matter specifically addressed to the Jews (see JEWS AND JUDAISM) — do not transgress the Sabbath (q.v.). Muḥammad's recitation of this list is supposed to have pleased the two Jews who had inquired about the meaning of Q 17:101 (Ṭabarī, *Tafsīr*, xv, 172; Tirmidhī, *Ṣaḥīḥ*, v, 286, no. 3144) and there are indications that Muḥammad's words were understood by some to recall the Decalogue. In a late collection of ḥadīths, one commentator remarks that the Prophet answered the question about the nine clear signs by reciting the Ten Commandments (Tabrīzī, *Mishkāt*, i, 62); moreover, the very next tradition in this collection gives ten commands which the Prophet is supposed to have made, some of which link up with the list of commandments Muḥammad recited to the two Jews. Finally, the presence of the Sabbath command in Muḥammad's list is a strong indication that reference to the Decalogue is being made here, as that particular command is frequently omitted in the few Muslim versions of the Ten Commandments we have. (The command has fallen out of Wahb's partial version noted above and it does not appear in Thaʿlabī, *Qiṣaṣ* 180-1; though glossed in a Muslim sense, it is present in Ibn Kathīr's version, *Bidāya*, i, 281. Both al-Thaʿlabī and Ibn Kathīr explicitly identify their text with the "ten words," *al-ʿashar al-kalimāt*, cf. the *ʿaseret haddevārīm* of *Deut* 10:4).

From the exegesis of Q 7:145 and 17:101, it would not seem that early Muslims had a precise notion of the biblical Decalogue or that they tried very hard to discern its presence in the Qurʾān, even if some did make that effort. Elsewhere, the Qurʾān offers a coherent list of precepts and prohibitions which a few Western scholars have taken to be an incomplete version of the Ten Commandments (M. Seale, *Qurʾān*, 74f.; T. Hughes, *Dictionary*, s.v. commandments). The list appears at Q 17:22-39 and an abbreviated version can be found at Q 6:151-3:

Set not up with God another god...
The Lord (q.v.) has decreed that you shall not serve any but him...
And [that you] be good to your parents...
Give the kinsman (see KINSHIP) his right, and the needy, and the wayfarer; and never squander...
Slay not your children (q.v.) for fear (q.v.) of poverty...
Approach not fornication *(zinā)*...
Slay not the soul (q.v.) God has forbidden, except by right....
Do not approach the property (q.v.) of the orphan (see ORPHANS) save in the fairest manner...
Fill up the measure when you measure, and weigh with the straight balance...
Pursue not what you have no knowledge of; the hearing, the sight, the heart (q.v.)...
Walk not in the earth (q.v.) exultantly...

Much of this does indeed parallel the biblical Decalogue. The first two echo Exodus 20:3f., where graven images and other gods are prohibited (see IDOLATRY AND IDOLATERS; IDOLS AND IMAGES); the third parallels Exodus 20:12; the sixth parallels, but is somewhat broader than, the biblical prohibition of adultery since the Arabic *zinā* is understood to apply to all kinds of sexual misconduct (see ADULTERY AND FORNICATION; SEX AND SEXUALITY); the seventh recalls the Decalogue's prohibition of murder (q.v.; *Exod* 20:13), although it is much less unequivocal, and goes on to allow the Arabian *lex talionis*. For other parts of this passage, parallels can be supplied from elsewhere in the Pentateuch: the ninth, for example, concerning weights and measures (q.v.), which echoes Leviticus 19:35. There are also divergences where biblical parallels are harder to find, as in the case of the fifth command prohibiting infanticide (q.v.).

None of this, however, amounts to very much: Commands such as these are the common stock of ethical monotheism and their collective grouping here need not suggest a failed qurʾānic attempt to appropriate the biblical Decalogue. It is not clear what particular importance the Qurʾān attaches to this list, although it is interesting to note that the abbreviated version in the sixth sūra is juxtaposed with a reference to Mosaic revelation. Although Muslim commentators have not generally connected the list with the Ten Commandments, Ibn ʿAbbās (d. ca. 67-8/686-8) is said to have referred to Q 6:151f. as the "essence of scripture" (*umm al-kitāb*, Ibn Kathīr, *Tafsīr*, ii, 178), and Ibn Kathīr (d. 774/1373) remarks, after giving a rare Muslim translation of much of the biblical Decalogue, that many consider the content of the "ten words" to be present in these verses from the sixth sūra (Ibn Kathīr, *Bidāya*, i, 281). W. Brinner has argued that Q 17:22-39 and 6:151-3 represent less an incomplete Decalogue than a uniquely Muslim code of ethics (see ETHICS IN THE QURʾĀN), albeit one perhaps shaped by a desire to rival Moses. The presence of this code in the seventeenth sūra may locate it, according to Brinner, in the context of Muḥammad's divine ascension (*miʿrāj*, see ASCENSION), traditionally associated with the first verse of this sūra if not explicitly mentioned in the Qurʾān. Just as Moses received the tablets while in the immediate presence of God, so too Muḥammad's commandments might be seen as the product of a similar experience, as the juxtaposition of Muḥammad's code with Mosaic revelation (Q 6:155) might suggest (W. Brinner, Islamic decalogue, 73-5, 81). Such a conclusion must remain speculative since neither the Qurʾān nor tradition unambiguously associates these verses with the Ten Commandments and the connection between the divine ascension and the seventeenth sūra is likely to be secondary. See also LAW AND THE QURʾĀN; LAWFUL AND UNLAWFUL.

Keith Lewinstein

Bibliography
Primary: Bayḍāwī, *Anwār;* Ibn Kathīr, *Tafsīr;* Qurṭubī, *Jāmiʿ;* Tabrīzī, Shams al-Dīn Muḥammad b. ʿAlī al-Khaṭīb, *Mishkāt al-maṣābīḥ*, 2 vols., n.p. 1961; Tirmidhī, *Ṣaḥīḥ*.
Secondary: W.M. Brinner, An Islamic decalogue, in W.M. Brinner and S.D. Ricks (eds.), *Studies in Islamic and Judaic traditions*, Atlanta 1986, 67-84; T.P. Hughes, *A dictionary of Islam*, London 1885; M.S. Seale, *Qurʾān and Bible*, London 1978; Speyer, *Erzählungen*.

Commentary and Commentaries

(tafsīr, tafāsīr; taʾwīl) see EXEGESIS OF THE QURʾĀN: CLASSICAL AND MEDIEVAL; EXEGESIS OF THE QURʾĀN: EARLY MODERN AND CONTEMPORARY

Commerce and Commercial Terminology

see SELLING AND BUYING

Community and Society in the Qurʾān

It is noteworthy that the Qurʾān, as Islam's preeminent source of information about God, is also the tradition's definitive guide to what constitutes a godly community and society, in both theory and practice. Although the Qurʾān's discourse on social dimensions of human existence is intended principally for guidance, inspiration and regulation of Muslims in the service of God, there is also an abundance of information on a diverse range of human groupings viewed from a religious perspective.

The Qurʾān is not a textbook that explicates the sociology of ancient Arabia (see PRE-ISLAMIC ARABIA AND THE QURʾĀN); that must be constructed from a wide variety of sources, including the Qurʾān. An extensive modern literature has been devoted to that task since the appearance of W. Robertson Smith's *Kinship and marriage in early Arabia* in 1885. Scholarship has ranged widely, embracing both ancient Arabia (e.g. H. Lammens, *L'Arabie occidentale* and B. Fares, *L'honneur chez les Arabes*) and more recent Middle Eastern tribal societies (e.g. T. Ashkenazi's analytical essay, La tribu arabe). For an extensive listing of sources and studies, see the articles "al-ʿArab," "Badāwī" (Bedouin, pastoral nomads),"Ḳabīla" (tribe), and "Nasab" (genealogy) in *EI²*. A relatively recent, comprehensive study, embracing the qurʾānic period and early Islamic history, is R. al-Sayyid, *Mafāhīm al-jamāʿāt fī l-Islām* (concepts of human groups in Islam). See also ARABS; BEDOUIN; KINSHIP; TRIBES AND CLANS.

The ancient Arabian context of qurʾānic religio-communal ideas and institutions

A stimulating and influential older study, with special reference to early Islam, is W.M. Watt's *Muhammad at Mecca* (1953) and a sequel *Muhammad at Medina* (1956) which provides detailed analyses of the Arabian tribes and clans that figured in the formative phases of the Muslim community's *(umma)* development. The birth of Islam as a new socio-religious system, unprecedented in some ways yet peculiarly and effectively adapted to the existing social and value system of the Ḥijāz, is addressed within the context of a theory of "tribal humanism" (*Muhammad at Mecca,* 24f.). This was, in Watt's view, the effective value system, really a functional religion, significantly advanced beyond the old cults of veneration of trees, sacred stones and springs, with an extensive and diverse pantheon (see SOUTH ARABIA, RELIGION IN PRE-ISLAMIC). Tribal humanism, focusing on social and economic matters far more than transcendent spiritual concerns, was itself also in decline by the time of Muḥammad. Its character can best be discerned in the poetry of those times which witnesses to a strong veneration of tribal heritages, a fiercely defended sense of honor, bravery in combat and generosity of a sometimes prodigal character. The tribe with its kinship subdivisions was the main focus of values rather than the individual, tribal unity and survival being the greatest good. There is little if any awareness of the possibility of a personal afterlife and this fact becomes a key element in the Qurʾān's challenge to the old Arabian worldview, with its fatalistic resignation (see FATE) and materialistic emphasis, denounced frequently by the Qurʾān as preferring the life of this world (*ḥayāt al-dunyā,* e.g. Q 2:86; 9:38; 16:107) over the afterlife (*al-ākhira,* see HEAVEN and HELL).

According to Watt (as summarized in his more recent work, *Muhammad's Mecca,* 1988, 15-25), the Arabian tribal system at the time of Muḥammad was organized principally in the male line (see PATRIARCHY). Kinship of a matrilineal type had earlier been known also in Medina (q.v.). Q 25:54 speaks of God having created humankind from water (q.v.; see CREATION), then establishing relationships both of consanguinity *(nasab)* and by marriage or affinity *(ṣihr)* which latter may possibly also refer to matrilineality, according to al-Bayḍāwī's commentary (*Anwār,* ad loc.). The Qurʾān also says (Q 49:13) that God created all humankind from one male and female couple and made them into nations *(shuʿūb)* and tribes *(qabāʾil)* so that they might know each other.

Tribes were subdivided into clans which contained families (see FAMILY), but according to Watt (*Muhammad's Mecca,* 16; also F. Donner, see below) the highly elaborated and differentiated definitions of ancient Arabian tribal kinship were largely a later development. During Muḥammad's time a kinship group was most often referred to as "the sons of" *(banū)* a certain tribal figure. The word *qawm* occurs very often in the Qurʾān with the general meaning of "people." Little can be learned from the Qurʾān about the specifics of tribal organization and structure. Watt points out the word *malaʾ,* a collective term for the leading males of a tribe and, in the Qurʾān, it sometimes connotes a council or assembly (e.g. Q 10:75 for Pharaoh's [q.v.] *malaʾ,* Q 27:29 for the Queen of Sheba's [see BILQĪS], Q 2:246 for the Children of Israel's [q.v.] "chiefs" as Yūsuf ʿAlī renders the term in his translation of the Qurʾān). The Qurʾān also speaks of *al-malaʾ al-aʿlā* (Q 37:8; 38:69), an "exalted assembly" of angels (see COURT). Mecca (q.v.) apparently had a *malaʾ* comprised of clan representatives, mentioned in Q 38:6 as Muḥammad's opposition (see OPPOSITION TO MUḤAMMAD).

Leadership of a tribe was in the hands of a *sayyid* or "chief," a term not found in the Qurʾān in this precise sense. A tribal chief was in no sense an autocratic ruler or hereditary monarch but a first among equals, respected for experience, character, good judgment, courage, hospitality and wisdom as well as the ability to provide protection. This last virtue Watt considers to be the most important aspect of pre-Islamic Arabian tribal life (*Muhammad's Mecca,* 17-20). Protection included the law of retaliation *(lex talionis),* where an injury or killing in one kinship group was answered in kind by the other group. This is supported by the Qurʾān, when it repeats the Mosaic law (Q 5:45) of "life for life, eye for eye, nose for nose, ear for ear, tooth for tooth and wounds equal for equal" and when it sets forth a guide for Muslims (Q 2:178f.) which is similar and also provides, as in ancient Israel, an opportunity for remission through a just compensation known as blood money (*diya,* see BLOOD MONEY). Killing people outside of one's group was not necessarily considered wrong per se but it could bring a most costly and bloody retaliation (q.v.; see MURDER; BLOODSHED). What is more, both warfare *(ḥarb)* and raiding *(ghazw)* had clearly understood rules and worked within the social system (see WAR; BATTLES AND EXPEDITIONS). War was the norm in pre-Islamic Arabia but it became unlawful under Islam for Muslims to shed their co-religionists' blood. Yet holy war (*jihād,* q.v.) was permitted, indeed encouraged under certain circumstances in order to defend the Muslims as well as to extend the territories to be governed by Islamic principles. War between Muslims and non-Muslims was to become a permanent state of affairs but governed by the principles and practices of Islamic law *(sharīʿa)* with respect to the treatment of prisoners (see CAPTIVES) and other matters (see M. Khadduri, *War and peace*).

People not belonging by blood to a protecting tribal structure could often find protection (q.v.) by attaching themselves to a powerful group in a protected neighbor *(jār)* relationship. The Qurʾān speaks of this arrangement in various ways: It regards good done toward both the distant and unknown as well as the near and intimate neighbor as meritorious (Q 4:36); it reveals that whereas God protects *(yujīru)* all things, he is himself unprotected (*lā yujāru ʿalayhi,* Q 23:88); and it advises that seeking protection from God is far more secure than relying on the material world even if there is no evidence beyond belief and trust in him (Q 67:28-9; see TRUST AND PATIENCE). Expressions in a new light of an old Arabian protection option did much to promote the idea of a Muslim community, an *umma,* that would far exceed tribal affiliation in benefits bestowed.

Watt adds (*Muhammad's Mecca,* 19) that a more common notion of protective affiliation was that of friend or protector *(walī,* pl. *awliyā),* terms that occur frequently in the Qurʾān. The word *walī* may apply to either the one protected or the protector as patron or guardian (see CLIENTS AND CLIENTAGE). Q 3:68 states that "God is the protector *(walī)* to those who believe" while Q 10:62-4 asserts "Truly, the friends *(awliyāʾ)* of God, no fear will be on them, nor shall they be sorrowful; those who believe and are god-fearing for them is good news, in the life of this world and in the hereafter." The helpless individual in ancient Arabian society could seek protection from a human group of higher status whereas Islam raised that paradigm to a theological level by providing membership in a community that itself received protection from the highest authority. Because the Qurʾān was able to express old ideas and to reformulate customs in new and appealing ways, Islam gained additional authenticity while preserving much of the old values and security. And, for example, the qurʾānic teaching on *walī*-hood would have far reaching effects in the elaboration of later Islamic ideas about human interpersonal and inter-group relations no less than divine-human relations, particularly in Ṣūfī confraternities (see ṢŪFISM AND THE QURʾĀN).

Yet even though Islam could claim a larger authority than the traditional tribal system for the ordering and regulation of community life, the old system was by no means simply abandoned. Rather it was incorporated into the larger complex of Muslim community life by means of what Fred M. Donner calls "genealogical legitimation" (*Narratives,* 104-11), an ancient practice in the Near East. And although the Qurʾān rejects claims that the superiority of people is based on their kinship affiliation, in post-qurʾānic times there developed a well-elaborated science of genealogy, as has been mentioned. Donner sees at the base of this a strong commitment by the dominant Arabs, however they were defined, to preserving hegemonic control in the early empire over the subject peoples of other ethnic-linguistic groups. Arab tribal legitimation became stronger, not weaker, as other peoples embraced Islam and questioned the Arab suzerainty. "Arabians were able to respond that their rule was legitimate because, as the people to whom the Prophet had been sent and in whose language the Qurʾān had been revealed, they were the rightful heirs of the Prophet, whose mission was, after all, universal" (ibid., 109). Further, Donner's analysis of the sources for early Islamic history includes attention to what he calls "themes of hegemony" (ibid., 174-82) whereby Muslim conquerors, leaders and claimants to leadership came to control not only non-Muslims but fellow Muslims as well. A major issue was *fitna,* variously translated as temptation or sedition, within the Muslim community itself and the ways in which various groups and interests justified themselves politically as fit to rule. In other words, war was not simply a matter of conflict between insiders and outsiders, Muslims and non-Muslims; increasingly, it became an intra-communal phenomenon with fateful consequences. Though the Qurʾān provides general principles for Islamic community life, history itself posed the greatest challenges to these ideals of harmony and cooperation. See POLITICS AND THE QURʾĀN.

Donner's contribution to our understanding of the beginnings of Islamic historical writing includes a useful treatment of "themes of community" (*Narratives,* ch. 6) in which he traces the *umma* idea from its qurʾānic context and relates it closely to another theme that he calls prophecy (*nubuwwa, Narratives,* ch. 5; see PROPHETS AND PROPHETHOOD). Although Donner sees the centrality of the qurʾānic message in the Prophet's development as both prophet and community leader or shaper, he also combines many other aspects of the complex history in a coherent manner. Thus, in addition to Muḥammad's establishment of social and ritual practices which were foundational, Donner includes consideration of how the cult of the community was routinized over time and administered in a larger context of government and taxation (q.v.). Donner's approach is important for its attention to the *diverse* historical sources, of which the Qurʾān is but one, however fundamental. He makes clear that one cannot arrive at a full understanding of community and society in the age of the Qurʾān and in the aftermath of the *umma*'s founding from the Qurʾān alone.

A richly documented study of the evolution of ideas about community and society since the pre-Islamic period in the Arabian peninsula is Riḍwān al-Sayyid's *al-Umma wa-l-jamāʿa wa-l-sulṭa. Dirāsāt fī l-fikr al-siyāsī l-ʿarabī l-islamī* (The *umma,* the community and political authority. Studies in Islamic Arab political thought). Drawing upon modern scholarship as well as traditional sources about Arabian religion and society before Islam, the author proceeds to demonstrate the novelty of the Islamic *umma* as a universal community intended to unite humankind in a system of common belief and action. The work is an absorbing example of a theologically informed sociology that utilizes not only the Qurʾān and other contemporary documents but also ḥadīth, qurʾānic interpretation *(tafsīr),* poetry (see POETRY AND POETS), history, prophetic biography (*sīra,* see SĪRA AND THE QURʾĀN) as well as qurʾānic sciences (see TRADITIONAL DISCIPLINES OF QURʾĀNIC STUDY) in addition to commentary (e.g. *asbāb al-nuzūl* and *nāsikh wa-mansūkh* discussions; see OCCASIONS OF REVELATION; ABROGATION) to show how the *umma* evolved over time into a multi-dimensional, charismatic community.

It has been important to situate the Qurʾān within its larger historical, social, cultural, linguistic and religious contexts — which can only be suggested here — before turning to an exploration and survey of its complex, evolving discourse on society and community throughout the period of Muḥammad's prophetic vocation. The remainder of this article focuses principally upon the contents of the Qurʾān itself with respect to this subject.

Religio-communal terms and ideas in the Qurʾān: umma

The idea of Islamic community is based definitively, if not exclusively, on the qurʾānic meanings of the ancient Semitic root that produced the Arabic word *umma* (pl. *umam*). *Umma* possibly derives ultimately from the Akkadian *ummatu* (Jeffery, *For. vocab.,* 69) or from the Hebrew *umma* or the Aramean *umetha* (Horovitz, Jewish proper names, 190). In the Qurʾān, *umma* most often means a human religious community although additional meanings include: any traditional value or belief system (Q 43:22, 23); a tribe or subgroup (Q 7:164; 28:32); a fixed term or time (Q 11:8; 12:45); a paragon or exemplar (see below in connection with Abraham in Q 16:20); and genera of animals (Q 6:38; see ANIMAL LIFE). This last is far-reaching in its moral and ecological implications, for animals and birds form "*umma*s like unto you" (see NATURAL WORLD AND THE QURʾĀN).

The term *umma* occurs in both Meccan and Medinan passages a total of 62 times (including 15 plurals). The term first occurs in Nöldeke's *(GQ)* second Meccan period where it refers to *ummas* either before or concurrent with the Qurʾān's revelation (see CHRONOLOGY AND THE QURʾĀN). The most numerous occurrences are in Nöldeke's third Meccan period. The term has a variety of references before it comes to designate, more or less exclusively by the Medinan period, a fledgling Muslim community under Muḥammad's guidance after the Muslim *umma* as both a religious and political entity had been established there (see MEDINA).

Q 2:128 speaks of an *umma muslima,* a community submitting to God; Q 2:213 refers to an *umma wāḥida,* meaning humankind as an archetypal "single community" or a specific unified community (Q 21:92); and 2:143 identifies the believers in the qurʾānic message as an *umma wasaṭan,* a "midmost community," properly balanced and standing as a kind of model among other communities in relation to God. To every *umma* has been given a prophetic messenger (Q 10:47; see MESSENGER) preaching both good news (q.v.) and warnings (see WARNING). And every *umma* has been provided by God with a ritual system *(mansak)* to observe (Q 22:67; see RITUAL AND THE QURʾĀN).

Although nowhere does the Qurʾān explicitly state this, it is not inaccurate to assert that the Muslim *umma* is seen in Islam's scripture as the "qurʾānic *umma.*" The word *al-kitāb,* meaning the scripture or book (q.v.), is frequently associated with religious communities such as the Jews, Christians and Muslims (see PEOPLE OF THE BOOK). When *kitāb* is used in connection with the Muslims it generally means the Qurʾān, as in Q 2:2-4: "This is the book *(kitāb);* in it is guidance sure, without doubt, to those who fear God... who believe in the revelation (see REVELATION AND INSPIRATION) sent to you [Muḥammad], and sent before your time, and they are certain of the hereafter." In Q 32:3 the book is designated as a message for those who had not previously received admonishment, namely the pagan Arabs (cf. Q 36:2-6 where *qurʾān* replaces *kitāb*). And in Q 42:7 an Arabic Qurʾān is declared to have been inspired in order to warn the "mother of cities," Mecca (q.v.). There have been and continue to be other entities known as *umma*s, but by the end of the Qurʾān's revelatory stages the term refers definitively, if not exclusively, to the Muslims as just stated. (Further consideration of *umma* will be given as it relates to other terms and concepts, but for a more extensive survey see F. Denny, The meaning of *ummah.*) Still, the qurʾānic concept of *umma* as it described the actual human groupings of the early Islamic generations should not be overemphasized. According to J. van Ess, "the *umma*-concept, which today has become so highly esteemed, hardly played a role"; tribal and partisan associations were far more prominent (*TG,* i, 17).

Other prominent religio-communal terms and concepts in the Qurʾān

Although the *umma* idea is the most fully developed qurʾānic concept of the community as applied to Muslims, other terms and concepts are also significant, both in themselves and as part of a comprehensive qurʾānic framework of socio-communal meaning. There seems to be a category for every type of individual and community in the Qurʾān's view and these categories present a broad range of values from exemplary religio-moral qualities to disapproved and condemned characteristics.

Ḥanīf (*pl.* ḥunafāʾ)

An example of the first is the type of generic monotheist — being neither Jew nor Christian — identified by the Qurʾān as *ḥanīf* (q.v.). Although there is considerable scholarly literature about the origins and meanings of the word *ḥanīf* in the Semitic languages (see F. Denny, Religio-communal), the Qurʾān employs the term twelve times in late Meccan and Medinan passages with distinctive emphases. Ten of the occurrences are in the singular, of which eight refer to Abraham (q.v.). Of these eight, five also contain the term *milla*, commonly translated as religion (Q 2:135; 3:95; 4:125; 6:161; 16:123) and one (Q 16:120) includes *umma*. All of the twelve passages but one (Q 4:125) directly contrast idolater *(mushrik)* and *ḥanīf* as opposites. So one finds in the Qurʾān, apart from the traditional monotheisms of Judaism and Christianity, an ideal of an Abrahamic *ur*-monotheism, as it were, that precedes them as a paradigm of what God intends as religion for his human creatures. Q 3:67 states: "Abraham was neither a Jew nor a Christian; but he was a *ḥanīf*, a *muslim* and was not of the *mushriks*"; (see IDOLATRY AND IDOLATERS; POLYTHEISM AND ATHEISM).

Ḥanīf is not strictly a term denoting community but it does stipulate what the Islamic *umma* is meant to embody and from where it should draw its inspiration: not from the older monotheistic siblings mentioned but from Abraham and his community at the beginning of authentic religion. Abraham was both a *ḥanīf* and an *umma*. The latter application seems somewhat strange so that instead of thinking of the patriarch as a community to himself, some have suggested that *umma* in Q 16:120 either has an eponymous meaning or means paragon of virtue as Fakhr al-Dīn al-Rāzī (d. 606/1210) speculated in his commentary (*Tafsīr*, ad loc.).

Milla (*pl.* milal)

This word is clearly a religio-communal term, most often related to Abraham, as in the phrase *millat Ibrāhīm* (e.g. Q 2:130; 3:95; 4:125; 6:161). *Milla* is a loan-word from Aramaic and in the Qurʾān a synonym for the Persian-derived *dīn* (Nöldeke, i, 20 n. 2). Although *milla* and *umma* overlap in their meanings to some extent, the former is a much more restricted term referring to any religion and, by extension, to its community but without defining or representing a tradition theologically or ethically. A *milla* simply *is* whereas the *umma*, in the sense of the Muslim community, *becomes* an historically particular community through faith (q.v.), responses to challenges (see TRIAL) and maturation. When the Qurʾān declares in Q 109 "The Unbelievers" (Sūrat al-Kāfirūn): "To you your religion and to me my religion," (*lakum dīnukum wa-liya dīn*, Q 109:6) it could just as well have used *milla* as *dīn*. W.C. Smith has wondered if *milla* "is not the only word in any language or culture that designates a specific and transferable religion, one as distinct from others, and nothing else" (*The meaning and end of religion*, 294). Of course, that the Qurʾān could employ terms such as *milla*, with the assumption that they would be understood by the first hearers, implies that the Ḥijāzī Arabs shared fully in the general Semitic worldview that featured close relations between religions and communities, between ethics and society in a pluralistic framework (see ETHICS IN THE QURʾĀN; THEOLOGY AND THE QURʾĀN). The qurʾānic message, though it sets forth absolute truth as it sees it, nevertheless also defines the rest of the world in terms of a range of options that assume close relationships between religious commitments — whether traditional and inherited or confessional (in the philosopher Karl Jaspers' sense) and thus changeable — and socio-communal groupings.

Submitters and believers constitute the Muslim umma

Arabic plural forms for human groups constitute much of the Qurʾān's categories of society and community. Two of the most frequently encountered terms also are pivotal for the Islamic religion: *muslimūn* and *muʾminūn,* submitters (i.e. Muslims) and believers, those who have faith *(īmān).* The two terms occur frequently, although perhaps surprisingly "believers" occurs five times as frequently (ca. 200 times) as "submitters" (ca. 40). Faith *(īmān)* is a weightier concept than submission *(islām)* both throughout the Qurʾān and in the developed Muslim theological tradition (see FAITH; ISLAM).

Only rarely does *umma* occur in close conjunction with *islām, īmān, muslim* or *muʾmin.* However, when it does it is a significant passage as in Q 3:110: "You are the best *umma* that has been raised up for humanity. You enjoin right conduct and forbid indecency; and you believe *(tuʾminūna)* in God. And if the People of the Book had believed *(law āmana),* it had been better for them. There are believers *(muʾminūn)* among them but most of them are wicked transgressors." This passage appears to say that being a nominal Jew or Christian is not sufficient to be acceptable to God; one must also be a believer. Q 3:113-4 states that "of the People of the Book there is an upright group *(umma qāʾima)*... [who] believe in God and the last day [see APOCALYPSE; LAST JUDGMENT]... they are in the ranks of the righteous *(wa-ulāʾika min al-ṣāliḥīn).*" This seems to be just as true of Muslims who without faith are understood to be merely submitters and at an inferior level of spiritual awareness and development.

The occurrences of *umma* along with references to faith and submission are generally found in the most highly developed instances of *umma,* those in Medinan passages when it refers to the Muslims exclusively. For example, Q 3:102-4 states, "O you who believe, fear God as he should be feared, and do not die except as *muslimūn.* And hold fast together to the rope of God *(ḥabl Allāh),* and do not become divided among yourselves.... Let there arise from you a community *(umma)* inviting to all that is good, enjoining what is right and forbidding what is wrong. Those, they are the prosperers." Islam's legendary sense of strong community loyalty and solidarity may be seen in its qurʾānic iteration in passages such as this. A similar passage (Q 2:256), that addresses the individual as much as the group, speaks of "the strongest handhold" *(al-ʿurwa al-wuthqā),* which is available to those who avoid evil and believe in God. It should be recalled that throughout the Qurʾān's discourse on community the emphasis is not on community as such; the ancient Arab world did not lack understanding and appreciation of strong social and communal networks. The important thing is the Qurʾān's consistent pattern of linking community with belief and morals within a monotheistic paradigm. This was one of the principal appeals of the new religion to tribal as well as town folk who already placed such a high value on kinship and covenants.

Watt has compared the Medinan Muslim *umma* to a kind of tribe that was based not on blood but on a common faith (*Muḥammad at Medina,* 239). The new order did not discard kinship relations; rather it placed them within the larger circle of loyalties and affiliations brought by Islam. Just as the Qurʾān appealed to its first hearers because of its excellence in Arabic expression so also there appears to have been an elective affinity between its socio-communal emphases and the Arabs' own strong community-mindedness, albeit at different levels. The "pattern-maintenance system," to borrow the sociologist Talcott Parsons' useful concept, of Arabian society and kinship was to be enhanced by that of the qurʾānic vision of submission, belief, obedience (q.v.) and solidarity within the *umma.* It is worth noting here that, according to Watt at least, the term *umma* apparently did not dominate the discourse on Muslim community to the end of the Medinan period for, after Mecca was incorporated, other terms, both non-qurʾānic and qurʾānic, such as, respectively, *jamāʿa* and *ḥizb Allāh* (party of God) took its place in extra-qurʾānic documents and treaties (*Muhammad at Medina,* 247).

The important contemporary, extra-qurʾānic document known as the Constitution of Medina uses the term *umma* but with a somewhat different meaning from that of the Qurʾān — moving in the direction of a political confederation more than a single community united by a common creed (see CREEDS). There is a diverse modern scholarly literature on this document that is fairly summarized by R. Stephen Humphreys in his *Islamic history. A framework for inquiry* (92-8).

Faith as a higher value than submission may also be seen in a dramatic passage (Q 49:14-5) where desert Bedouin declared to Muḥammad: "'We believe *(amannā).*' Say [Muḥammad], unto them, 'You do not believe yet.' Say rather, 'We have submitted *(aslamnā),* for faith *(īmān)* has not yet entered your hearts'... The believers *(muʾminūn)* are those who believe in God and his apostle [Muḥammad], and afterwards never doubt, but struggle with their wealth and their lives in the way of God, such are the sincere ones." Passages like this may mislead one into imagining that submission *(islām)* is not such a profound matter in the Qurʾān after all. It clearly is, but it must be understood in relation to other things. Submission is the crucial gateway to the service of God, without which faith would not be possible; humans themselves are capable of submitting according to their own will and power whereas faith is bestowed as a grace (q.v.) later on. As T. Izutsu has expressed the matter, "surrender, far from being, as is suggested by [Q 49:14]..., a lukewarm and superficial sort of belief, or the first stumbling step in the faith, is the very foundation on which the whole religion of Islam is based" (*Concepts,* 190-1). Faith and submission are often coupled and placed as opposites to other terms such as unbelievers *(kāfirūn),* idolaters *(mushrikūn)* and sinners *(mujrimūn).* The last group are often spoken of as a sinful people (*qawm,* e.g. Q 6:147; 15:58; see also BELIEF AND UNBELIEF; SIN AND CRIME).

Servants (ʿibād) *of God*

When the most important dimension of individual and group identity and values is religion, it is not surprising that fundamental distinctions will be made between insider and outsider, brother (see BROTHER AND BROTHERHOOD) and other. The striking early Meccan sūra, Q 109 "The Unbelievers" (Sūrat al-Kāfirūn) reveals the tension among Muḥammad's contemporaries that was brought by the preaching of Islamic monotheism. This brief, vital sūra is a tour-de-force focusing on the Arabic root letters *ʿ-b-d,* from which are derived the terms for worship of and service to God: *ʿabd,* slave or servant of God, *ʿibāda,* worship and *ʿibād,* servants, especially of God. The active verbal form of the root applies in the sūra both to Muslims and to disbelievers, as both are viewed as serving some superior power. The Muslims serve God whereas the disbelievers serve, according to classical commentary, idols and are thus *mushrik*s as well as disbelievers *(kāfirūn).* The terse ending of Q 109 sharply distinguishes the speaker's community, the Muslims, and the opposition's, which according to the commentaries, is devoted to disbelief *(kufr)* or idolatry *(shirk):* "Say: O unbelievers, I serve not what you serve and you are not serving what I serve, nor will I serve what you have served, neither will you serve what I serve. To you your religion *(dīn)* and to me my religion." Although the qur'ānic use of the *ʿ-b-d* root generally refers to worship of and service to God, this early sūra shows how it can be neutral as well, referring to the worship of anything.

The servant of God is not a passive adorer; active exertion is a key aspect of this status. There is a strong sense of work involved, in a manner that parallels the Jewish idea of worship *(avoda),* a Semitic parallel that also means service. A Christian parallel is the medieval Benedictine monastic expression, the work of God *(opus dei),* meaning the Divine Office of daily prayers and worship as the primary task of monks and nuns. The Qur'ān declares that the "servants of the Merciful are those who walk humbly on the earth, and when the ignorant address them say, 'Peace.' Who spend the night (in prayer), prostrate and standing" (Q 25:63-4; see BOWING AND PROSTRATION). Clearly, the qur'ānic idea of true religion is strongly invested in service, in "work" for God in ways parallel to Islam's older, cognate traditions of Judaism and Christianity (see WORK; SERVANT; WORSHIP; PRAYER).

Excursus: Concerning category formation in the Qur'ān

It is all too easy for western readers of the Qur'ān and other Arabic texts to fall into the practice of reifying dynamic, verbal expressions such as *islām, īmān, muslim, mu'min, shirk, mushrik* and their human plural forms. Stated differently, it would be a distortion to consider *muslimūn, mu'minūn, mushrikūn, mujrimūn* ("sinners") and so forth as rigid, unchangeable categories of human association based on this or that virtue or offense (see VIRTUES AND VICES; BOUNDARIES AND PRECEPTS). Nor do words like *islām, īmān, shirk* and *kufr* refer to static abstractions; they are essentially active and engaged.

Although it is true that the Qur'ān views human groups according to their degree of religion and/or impiety, generally the message also regards human beings as capable of repentance (see REPENTANCE AND PENANCE) and conversion (q.v.) to the "straight path" of Islam (see PATH OR WAY [OF GOD]). So, to denominate people as fated to sin or deceit or falsehood, at least in the present, is generally un-qur'ānic if it means there is no hope (q.v.) of deliverance (q.v.) or, to be more idiomatically qur'ānic, no hope of success or prosperity *(falāḥ).* Although the noun *falāḥ* does not occur in the Qur'ān, it appeared early on in Islamic history in the clause of the call to prayer: "Hasten to success" (*ḥayy ʿalā l-falāḥ,* see PRAYER FORMULAS). Verbal forms derived from the Arabic root letters *f-l-ḥ,* as well as the human plural *al-mufliḥūn,* the successful, do appear in strong ways, as in the frequently recalled Q 2:1-5, where those who fear God, believe in the unseen (see HIDDEN AND THE HIDDEN), persist in prayer, share their wealth (q.v.) with others, believe in divine revelation, and anticipate the hereafter will be considered to be "on true guidance from their Lord, and it is these who will be successful *(humu l-mufliḥūn).*"

Hence human groupings as described in ethical and spiritual terms are not rigid, unchanging realities in principal. Of course, the Qur'ān frequently presents its teachings through reference to historical groups whose fate was already sealed. Sometimes such groups saw the error of their ways, repented, and were forgiven and set on a new course (see FORGIVENESS). An example is when Moses' (q.v.) followers repented of their sin of creating and worshipping the graven image of a calf (Q 7:152-5; see CALF OF GOLD). At other times, groups fell into error (q.v.) from which they did not recover, as was the case of the people of certain unnamed towns in Q 7:94-102 who failed to heed God's wrath (see ANGER) after they were warned. "Did they feel secure against the trickery *(makr)* of God? But no one feels safe from God's stratagem *(makr)* except a people who have utterly lost their bearings *(al-qawm al-khāsirūn)*" (Q 7:99; see also PUNISHMENT STORIES).

Those who are saved and those who lose out from previous generations do not receive their recompenses because they are urban, or rural, or Jews, or Christians, or foreigners; they are judged according to their dispositions and behavior. The qur'ānic denomination of significant human groups, in the religious and moral senses, usually pertains to faith and righteousness or their absence. This universality of theological and moral vision has been fundamental in enabling Islam to be a world religion transcending social, cultural, political and regional boundaries. The *umma* ideal is thus global in both its intent and scope. (See F. Donner, *Narratives,* 141-6, for a classification of historiographical themes crucial for understanding the early Muslim community's "collective vision of the past" and how these enabled Muslims to make sense of their experience.)

The ideal of a unified umma *and the People of the Book*

Humankind were one *umma* but then they went in different directions and split up (Q 2:213). From a somewhat different slant, the Qur'ān states that God could have created a unified *umma* but declined that option so that people might be tested and find their own way as morally accountable beings (Q 5:48; see FREEDOM AND PREDESTINATION). A single *umma* of humankind would have included both unbelievers and believers, the bad and the righteous (Q 43:33). The Qur'ān does not equate humankind or the people *(al-nās)* with an *umma,* at least not descriptively. Ideally, it may turn out that all people will submit and follow God's teachings, but until then an *umma* will be a selective grouping drawn out from the larger human family to be a specially dedicated cohort.

Q 23:52-4 states, concerning the People of the Book: "Lo, this *umma* of yours is one *umma,* and I am your Lord so show piety (q.v.) towards me. But they cut their affairs into pieces amongst them in the matter of scripture, each sect *(ḥizb)* in what is with them rejoicing. Leave them in their confusion for a time." This passage is from the second Meccan period (according to Nöldeke, GQ), before *umma* came to refer more exclusively to the Muslims under Muḥammad's guidance. If the Nöldeke chronology is accepted, by the second Meccan period, *umma* in its true sense is a religious community, ideally unified in its beliefs, although not necessarily Muslim in the sense of Muḥammad's *umma.* During the Meccan periods of the Qur'ān's revelation, much attention is paid to Jews and Christians as fatefully important precursors of the Islamic venture between the archetypal era of Abraham who was neither a Jew nor Christian but a pure monotheist *(ḥanīf)* and the prophetic career of Muḥammad. Although the People of the Book had been called to serve God, many of them failed in their religion and fell astray (q.v.).

In addition to submission, belief, idolatry, and other frequently expressed qur'ānic ideas by which human groups are categorized, "brand name" communities are also identified. *Ahl al-kitāb,* the People of the Book, has already been mentioned as referring to the Jews and Christians, Islam's immediate precursors in scriptural monotheism. The phrase occurs about 30 times. Jews *(yahūd* or *hūd)* occurs some nine times (with *hūd* occurring three times; see JEWS AND JUDAISM). Christians *(naṣāra)* occurs 14 times and the adjective Christian *(naṣrānī)* once (with reference to Abraham's *not* being such, or Jewish, *yahūdī,* in Q 3:67; see CHRISTIANS AND CHRISTIANITY). The Sons of Israel *(Banū Isrāʾīl,* see CHILDREN OF ISRAEL) occurs some 40 times, whereas the Sons of Adam *(banū Ādam),* i.e. humanity, occurs seven times. *Ṣābiʾūn,* referring to the Sabians (q.v.; probably meaning Mandaeans, a Jewish-Christian sect in Iraq), occurs three times. Muslims, Jews, Christians, Sabeans, Magians (q.v.; i.e. Zoroastrians) and polytheists are all mentioned together in Q 22:17 as peoples among whom God will judge. In his commentary on this verse, al-Zamakhsharī (d. 538/1144) recalls the view that, according to the Qurʾān, there are five religions, four belonging to Satan (see DEVIL; IBLĪS) and one to God (Islam). In this schema, the Sabians are considered to be a branch of Christianity (Zamakhsharī, *Kashshāf,* ad loc.).

There are some very negative remarks directed at the Jews in the Qurʾān, much more so than against Christians (see POLEMIC AND POLEMICAL LANGUAGE). An example is Q 5:82: "The strongest among men in enmity to the believers are the Jews and idolaters; and the nearest to them in love are those who say, 'We are Christians.' Because among these are priests and monks (see MONASTICISM AND MONKS) and they are not arrogant." Al-Zamakhsharī comments that because the Jews are mentioned before the idolaters in the passage, they are at their head. The great rationalist commentator closes his interpretation of this passage by citing Q 2:96 wherein the Jews are portrayed as grasping for life as much as a thousand years; but God would still punish them at the end for "all that they do" (as translated in H. Gätje, *The Qurʾān,* 134). Al-Zamakhsharī declares: "The Jews are like this, and even worse!" Then he quotes a prophetic ḥadīth: "If a Muslim is alone with two Jews, they will try to kill him" (Gätje, *The Qurʾān,* 134). The Muslims had a great conflict with Jews in Medina and this is reflected in strongly critical qurʾānic passages such as Q 5:82 (quoted above). Nevertheless, the Jews were also considered, in the Constitution of Medina, to be an *umma* alongside the Muslim *umma.* And for a period Jews and Muslims worshipped together facing Jerusalem (q.v.) as their common prayer orientation (*qibla* [q.v.], see F. Denny, Umma, 44; also R. Humphreys, *Islamic history,* 92-8).

The Qurʾān's criticism of Jews and, to a lesser extent, Christians, exhibits early Islam's struggle to define itself over against the older siblings of the Abrahamic tradition. The disagreements between Islam and the other two religions are not like the fundamental controversy with the polytheists because there is a basic common foundation for the monotheistic traditions. The disagreements over actual behavior versus lofty ideals, as occurs in qurʾānic criticisms of Jews or over a doctrine regarded as heretical, such as the Christian Trinity (q.v.), are nevertheless disagreements among cognate systems. It is like a large, extended family with diverse branches: Their theological, scriptural and, with respect to Jews and Muslims, ritual, disagreements and conflicts only make sense within their common monotheistic framework, however generalized that may be. Religion is first of all an embodied and socially embedded reality in the Qurʾān's view, so it is individual Jews, Christians and others, as well as groups of them, that are the focus of criticism and occasional admiration (as in Q 5:82, quoted above) rather than Judaism and Christianity *per se.* From this perspective, it is hoped that the People of the Book will someday see the light and submit to God as proper Muslims; but meanwhile they are to be tolerated because they are not all astray and they do have a valid heritage in covenant (q.v.) with God. (For an extended qurʾānic discourse, see Q 3:64-115; covenant ideas are treated below).

Fred Donner (From Believers to Muslims,) hypothesizes that the Muslim followers of Muḥammad in the community's formative period did not necessarily make a strong distinction between themselves and other monotheists in their environment but viewed them as fellow believers *(muʾminūn)* before the term Muslim took on the increasingly political and exclusionary meanings of the caliphal era (see CALIPH). There is much to commend in Donner's carefully argued general thesis that the community of believers in the period of the Prophet and for a time thereafter did not constitute a distinct religious confession although such an argument certainly goes against the traditional Muslim view of the matter.

The Muslims as a covenant people and a people united by devotion to the Prophet of God

The Muslim *umma,* like its Jewish and Christian predecessors, is a covenant (*ʿahd* or *mīthāq*) community. Contracts, covenants and treaties were important factors in pre-Islamic Arabian society (see CONTRACTS AND ALLIANCES; BREAKING TRUSTS AND CONTRACTS). A key term was *wafāʾ,* "to fulfill, be faithful to." This idea was well established in pre-Islamic times as in the ode of Zuhayr: "Whoever keeps his word *(man yūfi)* goes unblamed; he whose heart is set on the sure path of piety (q.v.) needs not to fear or falter" (A.J. Arberry, *Seven odes,* 117; cf. Izutsu, *Concepts,* 87). This idea is clearly reflected in the following qurʾānic passage, which chides some People of the Book for not fulfilling concluded agreements with ignorant pagans *(ummiyyūn):* "No! The one who fulfills his promise *(ʿahd)* and is godfearing — truly God loves the godfearing (*al-muttaqīn,* Q 3:76).

The Muslim community came to view God as the guarantor of oaths (q.v.) and covenants. This belief in a divine witnessing of agreements contributed greatly to the establishment of an Islamic ideal of justice (see JUSTICE AND INJUSTICE; LAW AND THE QURʾĀN) that would be honored throughout an ever-increasing *umma.* In a way it reflects the notion that can be discerned in the Hebrew Bible, Genesis 31:49, the famous Mizpah Benediction, wherein Jacob and his uncle Laban, after much conflict and disagreement over property and relationships, solemnly declared together: "May the Lord watch between you and me when we are absent from one another." The core of this agreement is that God sees all and will judge any misdeeds accordingly. Q 16:91 reflects this idea: "Fulfill the covenant of God when you have entered into it, and do not break your oaths *(aymān)* after you have confirmed them; you have indeed made God your surety *(kafīlan),* for God knows what you do" (Q 16:91). Islam adopted this idea and applied it both to human social relations and to the divine-human relation of religion.

The establishment of the Muslim *umma* on the occasion of the emigration *(hijra)* of Muḥammad and his fellow Meccan Muslims (known henceforth as *al-muhājirūn,* the Emigrants) to Medina in 622 C.E. (see EMIGRATION) marked a definitive trend away from tribalism toward a supra-community knit together by faith more than by kinship, as was noted earlier. Before the *umma*'s founding, there had been an intertribal confederation for mutual defense known as *ḥilf al-fuḍūl,* which Muḥammad is said to have admired. Even so the Prophet reportedly declared that there was to be no *ḥilf* in Islam (see E. Tyan, Ḥilf, and C. Pellat, Ḥilf al-fuḍūl).

The Qurʾān frequently refers to the Mosaic covenant *(ʿahd)* as a paradigm of the divine-human relationship (e.g. Q 7:134). In the Bible, the covenant is not between God and Moses, but between God and the community of Israel. The Qurʾān, however, presents a covenant *(mīthāq)* that is first between God and his prophets — Noah (q.v.), Abraham (q.v.), Moses (q.v.), Jesus (q.v.) — and then through them to the Jews, Christians and Muslims (Q 33:7; cf. 3:81). There is, in the Qurʾān, a society of prophets, as it were, that will endure until judgment day and vindication, with their communities safeguarded by their faith. A vigorous declaration of these closely related convictions is the following passage from the Medinan period, Q 58:21-2: "God has decreed: 'Verily, I and my messengers shall prevail…' You will not find any people believing in God and the last day, loving those who resist God and his messenger, even though they were their fathers or their sons, or their brothers, or their kindred. For such he has written faith *(al-īmān)* in their hearts, and strengthened them with a spirit from himself. And he will admit them to gardens beneath which rivers flow, to dwell therein forever. God will be well pleased with them and they with him. They are the party of God *(ḥizb Allāh)*. Truly it is the party of God that will be successful *(al-mufliḥūn)*."

The word *ḥizb* (pl. *aḥzāb*) occurs a number of times and is pertinent to this discourse because it can mean sect, party or confederacy in the religious sense. A *ḥizb* of Satan is mentioned in Q 58:19 and shortly afterward countered by a *ḥizb Allāh* (Q 58:22). Q 33 takes its name, "The Confederates" (Sūrat al-Aḥzāb) from a grouping of clans opposed to Muḥammad at the Battle of the Ditch *(khandaq)* in 5/627. Earlier occurrences of *aḥzāb* refer to ancient peoples who had rejected their prophets (e.g. Q 38:11-3; discussed in F. Rahman, *Major themes*, 138-9). The idolaters are characterized in Q 30:32 as "Those who split up their religion *(dīn)*, and became sects *(shiyaʿ)* — each party *(ḥizb)* rejoicing in that which is with itself." Unlike *umma*, the term *ḥizb* does not come to refer to the Muslims exclusively. Even so, it does have a powerful rhetorical impact when conjoined with the divine name, as in *ḥizb Allāh*. The party of God trumps all other parties and is the opposite of sectarianism and division. The Qurʾān claims unity and communal coherence in belief and practice, and that not only for Islam as the religion established under the prophetic guidance of Muḥammad. The Qurʾān further insists that "the same religion *(dīn)* has he established for you [i.e. the Muslims under Muḥammad's leadership] as that which he enjoined upon Noah — that which we have sent by inspiration to you — and that which we enjoined on Abraham, Moses, and Jesus: Namely, that you should remain steadfast in religion and make no divisions therein" (Q 42:13). Passages such as this help us to understand better the direction and character of qurʾānic criticisms of Jews and Christians. The message is not denying the validity of those traditions' fundamental covenants and doctrines — indeed it is strongly affirming it; the problem is a perceived deviation from the primordial monotheism that the Qurʾān views as having been established by Abraham, Moses and Jesus preeminently. The quarrel is, as it were, a family affair. Inasmuch as the old-style "Muslims" have slipped and deviated as well as split up into sects, then the fresh Muslims of the Muḥammadan renewal movement — and such it is viewed to be — must fill the breach and constitute the party of God.

The principal covenant term in the Qurʾān is *mīthāq*, from *wathiqa*, meaning to place confidence in someone. In the third form the verb means to enter a compact or treaty. *Mīthāq* can have a secular sense, as in Q 4:21 where it concerns a marriage price compact. Most often, however, *mīthāq* in the Qurʾān refers to a religious agreement between God and humans or more specifically between God and his prophets, usually in the context of the People of the Book *(ahl al-kitāb)*. The term occurs 25 times, principally in Medinan passages.

Another important qurʾānic term for

covenants and contracts is *ʿahd,* whether with reference to the Children of Israel (e.g. Q 2:40) or to the Muslims. The root occurs more than 50 times, mostly in Medinan passages. (A valuable exploration and analysis of covenant ideas in the ancient Semitic world is J. Pedersen, *Der Eid bei den Semiten;* a review of selected theories concerning covenant in the Qurʾān is F. Denny, Religio-communal terms).

Some negative religio-communal terms

We have mostly considered positive communal terms and concepts such as *umma, milla, ḥanīf/ḥunafāʾ,* submitters, believers and the People of the Book. The strongly negative and accursed category of idolaters *(mushrikūn)* has also been included because of its frequent binary opposition with the various positive dimensions of monotheistic theology and ethics. Also, there are the so-called hypocrites (see HYPOCRITES AND HYPOCRISY), a category represented in the Qurʾān more than 25 times often in contrast to the believers. Although the historical Hypocrites *(al-munāfiqūn),* a disaffected Medinan community that, covertly, supported the Meccan Quraysh (q.v.), were nominally Muslim, they are consigned, together with the unbelievers, to hell (Q 9:68 with both masculine and feminine plural forms so as to specify equal accountability and treatment; cf. Q 4:140; Q 33:73 has the hypocrites and idolaters, male and female, paired for punishment; see REWARD AND PUNISHMENT).

Another strongly negative category centers upon *kufr,* which can be translated as unbelief, ingratitude or covering and concealing the truth (see GRATITUDE AND INGRATITUDE). The root occurs three times as often as the root *(s-l-m)* for Islam and Muslim. Only the root for faith *(ʾ-m-n)* occurs more frequently among the terms we are examining here. To disbelieve in or be ungrateful to God is not always considered to be as heinous as idolatry *(shirk)* but it is a grave offense and is sometimes understood as interchangeable with idolatry. So prevalent is the Muslim awareness of being a people strongly demarcated from other communities and so persistent is the Qurʾān's condemnation of unbelievers that Muslims have throughout history referred to non-Muslims as *kāfirūn,* "unbelievers, infidels," although the degree and type of unbelief has been a topic of reflection and mitigation (cf. Jewish characterizations of outsiders as Gentiles *(goyyim)* and Christian references to infidels and gentiles, whether Muslims or others). In this regard, recall Q 109, known as "The Unbelievers" (Sūrat al-Kāfirūn), quoted and discussed above.

Another frequent signifier for humans engaging in disapproved beliefs and behavior is the Arabic root *k-dh-b,* which occurs in the Qurʾān in active verbal forms as well as plural forms, e.g. *mukadhdhibūn,* "those who falsely accuse or deny." In Q 77, an early Meccan litany of punishments to come, the following phrase punctuates the building tempo ten times: "Ah woe, that day, to the rejecters of truth *(al-mukadhdhibīn)!*"

"Those who are astray, in error" are known in the Qurʾān as *ḍāllūn.* This term often implies a willful straying and not a haphazard mistake. An example is Q 3:90: "But those who disbelieve after they believed, and then go on adding to their disbelief — never will their repentance be accepted; for they are those who have [of set purpose] gone astray *(ūlāʾika humu l-ḍāllūn).*" The most frequently encountered example of this group term is in Q 1 "The Opening" (Sūrat al-Fātiḥa): "Show us the straight path, the path of those on whom you have bestowed your grace, not [the path of] those whose portion is wrath, nor of those who go astray *(al-ḍāllīn)*" (Q 1:6-7). One school of classical Qurʾān commentary *(tafsīr)* has interpreted this term in this particular passage to refer to the Christians, with the Jews being understood as the objects of the divine wrath. This is a questionable interpretation of the meaning of the references at the time of their revelation, however, because the sūra is universally regarded as very early and, thus, is more pertinent to the conflicts between Muḥammad and the polytheistic Qurayshīs of Mecca during a period when Muslim prayers at the Kaʿba (q.v.) sanctuary were a vexed issue. (But see F. Donner, *Narratives*, 162-3, for a discussion of the matter in the early Medinan context).

Another negative term applied to groups is *mutakabbirūn*, "arrogant ones" (e.g. Q 39:60 where hell is the "abode for the haughty"; see ARROGANCE). Although this category does not denote a moral meaning as such, the desert Arabs *(al-aʿrāb)* are viewed somewhat negatively in the Qurʾān, as in Q 9:97: "The Arabs of the desert are the worst in unbelief and hypocrisy, and most fitted to be in ignorance of the command which God has sent down to his messenger." But not all desert Arabs are considered wicked and, although some went to Muḥammad claiming to be believers, they had not quite reached that level yet (Q 49:14) as is described above. This survey has not been exhaustive but it does suggest the range of negative terms by which human groups or types are categorized.

Marriage and family

Marriage and domestic interrelations between the sexes figure fairly prominently in the Qurʾān. This is not surprising considering the importance of kinship in ancient Arabian society. Although before the founding of the Muslim *umma* there were no stable, large scale social groups, particularly of a political character, beyond the tribal level, kinship was a well delineated social reality with varied, complex levels. The Qurʾān does not explicate this topic although key terms and concepts occur here and there.

Perhaps the most explicit treatment of kinship relations in the Qurʾān in a sociological (as well as a legal and moral) sense involves the immediate family level in connection with what is permitted and forbidden with respect to marriage, family (q.v), sexual relations (see SEX AND SEXUALITY), women's rights, orphans (q.v.), inheritance (q.v.) and related matters (see SOCIAL RELATIONS). The fourth sūra, "Women" (Sūrat al-Nisāʾ), is in a way a parallel with the Jewish *mishna's* book on women. There is no sūra about men as such because the society into which the Qurʾān came was an increasingly patriarchal and patrilineal society albeit with some vestiges of matrilinearity (if not matriarchy), depending on how the sources are interpreted (see W.R. Smith, *Kinship and marriage*, ch. 3; W.M. Watt, *Muhammad at Medina*, 272-3; L. Ahmed, *Women and gender*, 41f.; A. Wadud-Muhsin, *Qurʾān and woman*, 1992; see WOMEN AND THE QURʾĀN).

Watt contends, as was noted earlier, that the pre-Islamic Arabian family tended most often towards a matrilineal type with both women and men "reckoned as belonging to their mother's groups. Tribes and individuals are known as sons of females." (*Muhammad at Medina*, 272). Marriage was uxorial and property was communally owned by the matrilineal group. Women in this system could have several husbands concurrently. But Watt finds evidence of patrilineal practices as well, strongest in Mecca. The Qurʾān favors patrilinealism and probably de-emphasized continuing evidence of matrilineal practices. By the time of the emigration *(hijra)* to Medina both systems existed side by side, according to Watt, and "often intermingled" (ibid., 273). Watt theorizes that the patrilineal system came to replace matrilineal tradition by the time Islam emerged and that it was based on increasing individualism. Males' interest in their own children went against the matrilineal tradition when it came to distributing inheritances. Under patrilineal authority a man could control the distribution of his wealth after his death and preserve it for his own sons especially, whereas under the matrilineal custom the inheritance would normally devolve to his sister's son. As patrilineal practices increased in influence men were much more interested in who was in fact father to sons while under a matrilineal system that was not deemed to be very important. Watt argues that the Qurʾān encourages patrilinearity, for example, in its legislation concerning the waiting period *(ʿidda)* between divorce and remarriage of a woman — to see if she were pregnant from her former husband. "In the case of divorce the man, if he was a 'gentleman,' would do nothing during the waiting period that would prevent cancellation of the divorce should his wife present him with a son" (ibid., 274).

The Qurʾān exhorts men to marry up to four wives (Q 4:3). In pre-Islamic Arabia men sometimes married more than four wives concurrently but the Qurʾān stipulates that if wives cannot be treated equally then only one woman should be married. There is much concerning marriage in Q 4. There is also a detailed listing of people whom it is forbidden for a male to wed (Q 4:22-4), namely his mother, daughter, sister, aunt (on either side), his brother's or sister's daughter, his wife's mother or daughter or his father's or son's wife, someone who has nursed the male, step-daughters (provided their mother and the male have consummated their marriage), women who have been married to one's sons or two sisters concurrently (see MARRIAGE AND DIVORCE).

The forbidden degrees of marriage just summarized are complemented by a listing of the legal bounds of consanguinity in Q 24:31. This regulation is situated in a discussion of personal and family privacy and propriety governing believers: They should not enter houses other than their own without gaining permission, and both men and women should be exceedingly modest in their relations with each other (see CHASTITY). Women, particularly, should draw their veils (see VEIL) over their bosoms and not display their beauty except to their husbands, their fathers, their husbands' fathers, their sons, their husbands' sons, their brothers or their brothers' sons or their sisters' sons or their women, or the slaves whom their right hands possess or male servants free of physical needs (see SLAVES AND SLAVERY) or small children who have no understanding of the nakedness of women (cf. Q 24:31).

Those enumerated in Q 4:22-4 are known in Islamic law as forbidden *(maḥram)* to marry because of being within the bounds of legal consanguinity (see LAWFUL AND UNLAWFUL). Until the present, Muslims have, more often than not, conducted their social lives strictly within these boundaries with the result that free mingling between the sexes, as is often found in the schools, workplaces, markets, entertainment centers and so forth of western societies, is severely censured by the traditionally-minded. Needless to say, strict interpretation of the qurʾānic teachings concerning social relations between the sexes is strongly challenging Muslim families and individuals now residing in western countries where such behavior is normal (see SOCIAL INTERACTIONS).

There is material in the Qurʾān pertaining to the prophet Muḥammad's marriages and family life (see FAMILY OF THE PROPHET). In Q 33:50 we read that, for a period, he was permitted by God to marry without limit, whereas other Muslims were limited to four wives concurrently. But this permission to Muḥammad was later withdrawn (Q 33:52) so that he ceased taking wives (except for Mary the Copt, but she was sometimes reported to have the status of concubine, not wife). One of the issues that loomed large in the Medinan period of Muḥammad's prophetic career was privacy and security for his family in a growing and sometimes unruly social milieu. The Prophet's family situation, with multiple wives and households beyond the four permitted to Muslims by the Qurʾān, required special attention and regulation. Watt characterizes Muḥammad's households as a "plural virilocal family" (*Muhammad at Medina*, 284), meaning that his residence was the base with close proximity of his wives' separate households. The Prophet visited his several wives in a scheduled manner and sought always to be equitable and just in his dealings with each of them. Muḥammad's wives had special status above other women in the early Islamic movement (see WIVES OF THE PROPHET). This is seen, for example, in the institution of veiling or covering *(ḥijāb)* addressed by the Qurʾān in Q 33:53: "O you who believe! Do not enter the Prophet's houses until leave is given to you, for a meal, but not so early as to await its preparation. But when you are invited, enter; and when you have taken your meal, disperse without small talk. Such behavior bothers the Prophet; he is ashamed to dismiss you, but God is not ashamed to tell the truth. And when you ask of the women of his household anything, do so from behind a screen *(ḥijāb):* That is more pure for their hearts and for yours." A bit farther in the same sūra, additional admonition is provided: "O Prophet, tell your wives and daughters, and the women of the believers, that they should draw their jilbabs [*jalābīb,* flowing garments covering the bosom and neck, or even the whole body] about themselves. That is better, that they be recognized [sc. as respectable women] and not bothered (Q 33:59)." Whatever the original reasons for such regulations, Muslims ever since have drawn on the above two passages for guidance in the conduct of their social relations, particularly regarding male-female contact, the presentation of the female self and proper deportment generally.

The original context for the revelations was clearly one of stressed conditions wherein the Prophet's family was subjected to more or less public display because of the proximity of their households to the center of power in Medina. People apparently attempted to access the Prophet by seeking the intervention of members of his household which in the case of his wives could lead to gossip and even scandal (see W.M. Watt, *Muhammad at Medina,* 285). There were also tensions and conflicts between the elements of Muḥammad's extended households.

There has been considerable discussion and debate over whether the passage about the screen, or curtain, namely the *ḥijāb,* applies only to the Prophet's wives in that context or more generally to Muslim women in all times and places. There is no consensus in a restricted sense although Muslims generally accept the passages as serious advice however the specifics are interpreted and emulated.

Society perfected

Although the Qurʾān's treatment of society and community is focused principally on the historical world, considerable attention is also given to the afterlife, whether in heaven or hell. The Companions of the Garden *(aṣḥāb al-janna),* those who believed and lived upright lives, will live an eternal existence of happiness in the company of God, the angels (see ANGEL), the lovely female denizens or houris (*ḥūr,* see HOURIS) and the community of the saved. As for this last grouping, believing husbands and wives will be together (Q 43:69-70) as will their pious parents and offspring (Q 13:23; cf. 52:21). Also in heaven will be those who fought in the way of God. The blessed of the garden will praise God (Q 10:10) and the angels in heaven will address the believers with: "Peace be unto you because you persevered patiently! How excellent is the final home!" (Q 13:24). Q 52 contains additional details about the heavenly society with its ranks of saved: persons reclining on couches (Q 52:20), the availability of good fruit and meat to eat (Q 52:22), the sharing of a convivial cup (Q 52:23; see CUP) and enjoyment of mutual inquiry and discussion without fear (Q 52:25; see GARDEN; PARADISE; BLESSING).

The damned, called Companions of the Fire *(aṣḥāb al-nār)* will suffer eternal woe and pain. The horrors of hell are described in various passages. The saved will be able to observe the damned and communicate with them in a limited way (Q 7:44). Some humans and jinn (q.v.; the creatures, made from fire, that have a moral nature similar to that of humans and include some converted by the Qurʾān; Q 72:1-19) will be consigned to hell (Q 7:179). Generally speaking, the saved in heaven will enjoy life in a society of purity, mutual respect and courtesy, and continued awareness of the blessings of God and his created order at an exalted level whereas the damned will suffer not only the literal pains of the fire (q.v.) but the alienation and meaninglessness that prevail when there is no meaningful social existence or community life. For the person who is consigned to hell, "therein shall he neither die nor live" (Q 20:74).

Conclusion

This article has covered the principle dimensions of the Qurʾān's views of society and community and it has attempted to place them in the social and cultural context of pre-Islamic Arabia. Although the material in the Qurʾān concerning more descriptive dimensions of our subject is limited, the doctrines and views contained there have nevertheless had the most important influences on the history, customs and attitudes of Muslim peoples everywhere. Even today we find Muslim countries aspiring to order their lives according to the Qurʾān, treating it as a charter and constitution for their societies.

Surely the most enduring and influential qurʾānic idea and ideal of community is that of *umma* and so flexible is it in specific social, religious, and political terms that it can be embraced across a wide range of concerns by Muslims without their losing a general sense of common cause and consensus concerning the big questions of belief and the proper conduct of life both individually and communally. Indeed, the *umma* idea has enabled Muslims to endure serious setbacks as in the times of western colonialism when political power was at a low point in many Muslim regions. What is more, the *umma* ideal does not require a unified political order among Muslims in order to be realized and activated. In America, for example, Muslim prison inmates constitute *umma*s in the facilities where they are incarcerated. And North America itself, as is often said, is a place where the *umma* is being established (see AFRICAN AMERICANS). There is one *umma* ideally but there are multiple instances of the *umma* being established, empowered and enjoyed as an enduring religio-moral community in touch with the Muslim mainstream.

Wherever one looks in the spreading Muslim populations of today — in the traditional centers of Muslim civilization and in new locales such as Europe, the Americas, Australia, New Zealand and the

Pacific — the qur'ānic foundations and models of social and communal life of Muslims predominate and provide an ever fresh and innovative approach to defining what it means to be Muslim and how to live in a pluralistic world alongside other communities and societies, whether religious or secular in nature. For an examination of the qur'ānic terminology relating to the commercial and economic aspects of communal life, see SELLING AND BUYING.

Frederick Mathewson Denny

Bibliography
Primary: Rāzī, *Tafsīr;* Zamakhsharī, *Kashshāf.*
Secondary: L. Ahmed, *Women and gender in Islam. Historical roots of a modern debate,* New Haven 1992; M.F. Ansari, *The qur'ānic foundations and structure of Muslim society,* 2 vols., Karachi 1973 (extensive applications of qur'ānic teachings for the contemporary Muslim world); A.J. Arberry, *Seven odes,* London 1957; T. Ashkenazi, La tribu arabe. Ses elements, in *Anthropos* 41-4 (1946-9), 657-72; D. Bakker, *Man in the Qur'ān,* Amsterdam 1965 (ch. 3 is a thorough summary of human groupings in the Qur'ān); J. Chelhod, Ḳabīla, in *EI²,* iv, 334-5; C.S. Coon et al., Badāwī, in *EI²,* i, 872-92; F.M. Denny, Ethics and the Qur'ān. Community and world view, in R.G. Hovannisian (ed.), *Ethics in Islam,* Malibu, CA 1985, 103-21; id., The meaning of *ummah* in the Qur'ān, in *History of religions* 15 (1975), 34-70; id., Some religio-communal terms and concepts in the Qur'ān, in *Numen* 24 (1977), 26-34; id., Umma in the Constitution of Medina, in *JNES* 36 (1977), 44; F. Donner, From believers to Muslims. Confessional self-identity in the early Islamic community, in L.I. Conrad (ed.), *The Byzantine and early Islamic Near East iv. Patterns of communal identity,* Princeton (forthcoming); id., *Narratives of Islamic origins. The beginnings of Islamic historical writings,* Princeton 1998; van Ess, *TG;* B. Fares, *L'honneur chez les Arabes avant l'Islam,* Paris 1932; L. Gardet, *La cité musulmane,* Paris 1969³; H. Gätje, *The Qur'ān and its exegesis,* London 1976; A. Grohmann et al., Arab, in *EI²,* i, 524-33; J. Horovitz, Jewish proper names and derivatives in the Koran, in *Hebrew Union College annual,* 2 (1925), 190; R.S. Humphreys, *Islamic history. A framework for inquiry,* Princeton 1991 (revised); H.E. Kassis, *A concordance of the Qur'ān,* Berkeley 1983 (an excellent reference work for readers without a knowledge of Arabic that includes topical headings in English with the original Arabic qur'ānic terms in Roman transliteration); M. Khadduri, *War and peace in the law of Islam,* Baltimore 1955; H. Lammens, *L'Arabie occidentale avant l'Hégire,* Beirut 1928; L. Massignon, L'umma et ses synonymes. Notion de "communauté sociale" en Islam, in *REI* (1947), 151-7; McAuliffe, *Qur'ānic;* C.A.O. van Niewenhuijze, The ummah. An analytic approach, in *SI* 10 (1959), 5-22; Nöldeke, *GQ;* J. Pedersen, *Der Eid bei den Semiten,* Strassburg 1914; C. Pellat, Ḥilf al-fuḍūl, in *EI²,* iii, 389; F.E. Peters, *Muhammad and the origins of Islam,* Albany 1994 (a clear, non-technical but sophisticated historical analysis of Islam's founding); F. Rahman, *Major themes of the Qur'ān,* Chicago 1980; G. Rentz, Djazīrat al-ʿarab, in *EI²,* i, 533-56; R. Roberts, *The social laws of the Qoran,* London 1925 (still a useful overview); F. Rosenthal, Nasab, in *EI²,* vii, 967-8; R. al-Sayyid, *Mafāhīm al-jamāʿāt fī l-islām,* Beirut 1984; id., *al-Umma wa-l-jamāʿa wa-l-sulṭān. Dirāsāt fī l-fikr al-siyāsī l-ʿarabī l-islāmī,* Beirut 1984; W.C. Smith, *The meaning and end of religion. A new approach to the religious traditions of mankind,* New York 1963; W. Robertson Smith, *Kinship and marriage in early Arabia,* Cambridge 1885; London 1903 (rev. ed.); B. Stowasser, *Women in the Qur'ān, traditions and interpretation,* New York 1994 (includes a review of modern interpretations); E. Tyan, Ḥilf, in *EI²,* iii, 388-9; A. Wadud-Muhsin, *Qur'ān and woman,* Kuala Lumpur 1992; W.M. Watt, *Islam and the integration of society,* Evanston 1961; id., *Muhammad at Mecca,* Oxford 1953; id., *Muhammad at Medina,* Oxford 1956; id., *Muḥammad's Mecca,* Edinburg 1988.

Companions of the Prophet

The body of people who had known or seen the Prophet Muḥammad during his lifetime. The plural "Companions of the Prophet" *(aṣḥāb al-nabī),* otherwise known simply as "the Companions" *(ṣaḥāba),* is derived from the root *ṣ-ḥ-b* and has referred, at least since the classical period, to this group. (On the question of whether a merely ocular encounter with the Prophet could be considered a sufficient criterion to render someone a Companion, cf. Goldziher, *MS,* ii, 240.) For Sunnī Muslims, a reference to the Companions serves not only to describe certain individuals as a collective entity but also carries with it an immense weight from a theologico-political prescriptive: Appeal is made to the sayings and deeds of the Prophet and his Companions, as recorded in the ḥadīth, in all matters of Islamic decision-making as well as for guidelines about personal piety and everyday conduct.

As explicitly articulated in al-Shāfiʿī's (d. 204/820) great legal treatise *al-Risāla*, the manner of conduct (*sunna*, q.v.) of the Prophet and his Companions is considered one of the four sources of the law *(uṣūl al-fiqh)* and commands an authority second only to that of the Qurʾān. Al-Shāfiʿī locates the authority for the prophetic sunna in the Qurʾān itself, insofar as the Qurʾān commands Muslims to obey the Prophet's orders. Although al-Shāfiʿī asserts that the Qurʾān "explains everything," he argues nonetheless that the sunna may clarify the general or particular meaning of a qurʾānic passage or supply an answer to an issue not treated in the book. In response to the question whether the Qurʾān can ever abrogate the sunna, al-Shāfiʿī replies that only another sunna can abrogate the sunna (see ABROGATION). This statement appears to be based on his explicit presumption that the sunna can never be in contradiction with the Qurʾān. He also avers that if there "is a contradiction [in the sunna], it is not a contradiction" (cf. *al-Risāla*, chapter ix, "On Traditions").

Qurʾānic references

Given the enormous religious significance later accorded the Companions of the Prophet by Sunnī Muslims, it is interesting to note that the phrase *aṣḥāb al-nabī* does not appear anywhere in the Qurʾān. Nor does the plural form *ṣaḥāba* occur there. Of the 94 times that the noun *ṣāḥib* and its plural *aṣḥāb* do appear in the Qurʾān, the vast majority of instances are found in the following phrases: companions of the fire (q.v.; or hell, q.v.) and companions of paradise (q.v.; 42 times), and companions of the right hand and companions of the left hand (14 times; see HANDS). The Companions of the fire (or hell) are also usually identified, in a nearly formulaic fashion, as "those who disbelieved [see BELIEF AND UNBELIEF; BLASPHEMY] and lied about our signs (q.v.)." It is emphasized that those people are not only "Companions" of the fire but also that they are most emphatically "dwelling in it."

The remaining instances of *ṣāḥib* carry a wide range of generic meanings including any fellow traveler, fellow dweller, friend or mate. In the three instances in which a verbal form of the root *ṣ-ḥ-b* occurs in the Qurʾān, the actions are predicated by Moses (q.v.; *lā tuṣāḥibnī*, Q 18:76), Luqmān (q.v.; *ṣāḥibhumā*, Q 31:15) and those who worship other gods (*yuṣḥabūna*, Q 21:43; see IDOLATRY AND IDOLATERS), respectively.

The Qurʾān qualifies the Prophet three times as "your [pl.] companion" and once as "their companion." However, in these four cases the Prophet is not being described as the companion of the faithful but rather as the companion of those who disbelieve. "Those who have lied about our signs" are addressed by the qurʾānic verse, "your companion is not possessed" (Q 81:22). The same group is urged to see that "there is no madness in their companion" (Q 7:184). After recalling those who have "lied about my messengers" (Q 34:45), the Qurʾān attests that "there is no madness in your companion" (Q 34:46). The Qurʾān also reminds that "your companion has not gone astray (q.v.), nor is he deluded" (Q 53:2; see IMPECCABILITY AND INFALLIBILITY). Q 9:40 is the only qurʾānic verse in which someone is designated as the "companion" of the Prophet. However, Abū Bakr appears to be designated as such only insofar as he is Muḥammad's "fellow dweller" in the cave (q.v.) where they were hiding (see EMIGRATION). The notion of the Companions of the Prophet as a defined body with a special theologico-political authority thus does not appear to be attested by the revelation.

The Companions in the ḥadīth and exegetical literature

While the Companions as a body as such are not mentioned in the Qurʾān, they, as well as their relations to the Qurʾān, are amply attested in the ḥadīth and exegetical literature. One finds ḥadīth collections in the form of short manuscripts or pamphlets dedicated to the sayings and deeds of a single companion, as well as larger anthologies that treat individual Companions in sub-chapters (*kutub*, literally "books"). The well known ḥadīth collections of the classical period gather stories about the virtues *(faḍāʾil* or *manāqib)* of the Companions, taken as a group, in discrete chapters. The remaining narratives about the sayings and deeds of the Prophet and his Companions in this literature are organized according to practically expedient themes such as prayer (q.v.), fasting (q.v.), alms (see ALMSGIVING) and so forth. Other compendia supply a list of the Companions with short biographical references along with some of the reports they handed down. (For some of the most famous collections of ḥadīth, *sīra* and *ṭabaqāt*, see bibliography below; see also SĪRA AND THE QURʾĀN).

For Muslims, it is the reputation of the men and women who handed down the stories about the sayings of the Companions that guarantees the veracity of these accounts rather than the content of the stories and sayings themselves. Accordingly, one finds prefixed to the text of each ḥadīth story *(matn)* a chain of transmitters *(isnād)* linking that particular account back to one of the Companions or to the Prophet himself (see ḤADĪTH AND THE QURʾĀN). According to al-Shāfiʿī, the minimum proof for the authenticity of a narrative about the Prophet is that the narrative must be "related by one person from another back to the Prophet or to one next to the Prophet." Ḥadīths are thus not only about the Prophet and his Companions but they are also recounted by them as well.

The ḥadīth narratives also address the question of their own authenticity internally. For example, one finds ḥadīths in which a Companion recounts that a ḥadīth about the Prophet and his Companions is to be considered sound only if two Companions can testify to it. In some story cycles, one finds the Companions openly discussing and then deciding upon the limits of their own authority. In the absence of a clear prophetic precedent, they are often called upon to make their own decisions on the basis of utility, which in turn may be further validated by God. One sees this, for example, in ʿUmar's and Abū Bakr's successful persuasion of Zayd b. Thābit to compile the revelation into one written book after the Prophet's death on the basis of God having "opened" their breasts to it and its being a "good" thing despite the fact that the Prophet himself had not done it (cf. Bukhārī, *Ṣaḥīḥ, Tafsīr al-Qurʾān,* 9, *Faḍāʾil al-Qurʾān,* 3 and *Aḥkām,* 37; see CODICES OF THE QURʾĀN; COLLECTION OF THE QURʾĀN).

Certain Companions enjoy a special distinction in ḥadīth literature. The first four caliphs (or successors to the Prophet; see CALIPH) are remembered by Sunnīs as the Rightly Guided Ones *(Rāshidūn)*. They are Abū Bakr (r. 11-3/632-4), ʿUmar b. al-Khaṭṭāb (r. 13-23/634-44), Uthmān b. ʿAffān (q.v.; r. 23-35/644-56) and ʿAlī b. Abī Ṭālib (q.v.; r. 35-40/656-61) respectively. Sunnīs recall the period of their political leadership as a golden age from which the Muslim community has devolved not only in time but also in righteousness. The caliph ʿUmar also appears to have predicted the revelation, verbatim, before it was announced by the Prophet on at least three different occasions. Accordingly, the narratives have him claim that "my lord agreed with me about three (things)" and that "I agreed with God about three (things)" (cf. Bukhārī, *Ṣaḥīḥ, Tafsīr al-Qurʾān*, 2 and *Ṣalāt*, 31). The Prophet's cousin Ibn ʿAbbās (d. ca. 67-8/686-8; see FAMILY OF THE PROPHET), as well as Muḥammad's youngest wife ʿĀʾisha bint Abī Bakr (q.v.; d. 58/678), are also frequently mentioned, among many others. Over 600 women are mentioned by name in the six canonical collections alone, either as transmitters or in the ḥadīth stories themselves.

The canonical ḥadīth also mention that "ten will be in paradise" although the ten names that comprise that list vary. According to Abū Dāwūd (d. 275/889) and Aḥmad b. Ḥanbal (d. 241/845), the ten include Muḥammad, Abū Bakr, ʿUmar, ʿUthmān, ʿAlī, Ṭalḥa, Zubayr, ʿAbd al-Raḥmān b. ʿAwf, Saʿd b. Abī Waqqāṣ and Saʿīd b. Zayd. According to al-Tirmidhī (d. ca. 270/883-4), Ibn Saʿd (d. 230/845) and Aḥmad b. Ḥanbal, on the other hand, the name of Abū ʿUbayda b. al-Jarrāḥ is substituted for that of Muḥammad in this list. The ten later came to be referred to as *al-ʿashara al-mubashshara*, although this term does not appear in the canonical ḥadīth collections themselves.

The Prophet's Companions were also commonly distinguished according to other categories such as whether they accompanied him as emigrants *(muhājirūn)* from Mecca to Medina (then known as Yathrib; see MEDINA), whether they were "helpers" (*anṣār;* see EMIGRANTS AND HELPERS) from Medina, whether they fought in certain battles (such as the battle of Badr, q.v.) and how early they converted to Islam. (Cf. Nawawī, *Sharḥ*, v, 161, for a collection of the differing views about the gradations attributed to the Companions).

Whereas the *muhājirūn* were largely pagan converts to Islam from Mecca, the *anṣār* were primarily converts from the Aws and Khazraj tribes of Medina (see TRIBES AND CLANS). Both categories are mentioned by name in Q 9:100 and 9:117. The term *anṣār* is related to the verb *naṣara*, in the sense of coming to the aid of someone who has been wronged by his enemy, which is found in Q 8:72, among other instances of its use. The word *anṣār* also bears some resemblance to the Arabic *naṣārā* or "Christians," as when Jesus (q.v.) asks in Q 3:52 "who will be my helpers in God's cause?" The more common exegetical etymology of *naṣārā*, however, connects it to the village of Jesus, i.e. Nazareth (al-Nāṣira; see CHRISTIANS AND CHRISTIANITY).

Another group of Companions is distinguished as the so-called "people of the bench" *(ahl al-ṣuffa)*. According to Lane, these were the people who reclined on the bench or banquette in a long, covered portico or vestibule attached to Muḥammad's home, part of the mosque complex in Medina. Later legend traces the origins of the mystical, ascetic Ṣūfī group to these Companions — based in part on the similarity between the Arabic words for bench *(ṣuffa)* and for the woolen *(ṣūfī)* garment the Ṣūfīs wore (see ṢŪFISM AND THE QURʾĀN). Some commentators, such as Muḥammad b. Kaʿb al-Quraẓī claim that qurʾānic passages such as Q 2:273-4, 6:52, 18:27-8 and 42:26-7 are intended to refer to the *ahl al-ṣuffa* even though they are not explicitly mentioned by name there. Other orthodox commentators, such as al-Bayḍāwī (d. ca. 716/1316-7), are more hesitant to make such assertions reporting only that "it is said" to be the case.

Although some of the stories in Shīʿī collections of ḥadīth overlap with those found in their Sunnī counterparts, they are read by the Shīʿa (q.v.) in different, and sometimes in directly opposite, ways. Most notably, the Shīʿa read the Prophet's sayings and deeds regarding ʿAlī b. Abī Ṭālib as an indication that the Prophet intended ʿAlī to succeed him following his death. Thus, in direct antithesis to the Sunnīs, the Shīʿa regard the rule of the first three caliphs not as a golden age but a period of unjust usurpation.

In many cases, this difference results in the paradoxical situation wherein Shīʿa may point to a ḥadīth about one of the first three caliphs as evidence of wickedness while Sunnīs may point to the very same story in their ḥadīth collection as evidence of that person's exemplary conduct. A classic example of this phenomenon would be their diametrically opposed readings of the second caliph ʿUmar. Shīʿa read these stories, such as the one where ʿUmar refuses to let the Prophet write something for his followers at the moment of his death, as evidence of ʿUmar's unsurpassed wickedness while Sunnīs interpret it as yet another example of ʿUmar's uncompromising defense of the Prophet's tradition (cf. Bukhārī, *Ṣaḥīḥ, Iʿtiṣām,* 28).

According to the tradition about the "people of the cloak" *(ahl al-kisāʾ)* the Shīʿa recount that Muḥammad went out one morning during the visit of the Najrān (q.v.) delegation and drew his daughter Fāṭima (q.v.), her husband ʿAlī and their sons al-Ḥasan and al-Ḥusayn under his cloak (see CLOTHING; CURSE). He then uttered the words in Q 33:33: "God only desires to put away filthiness from you as his household *(ahl al-bayt),* and with cleansing to clean you." While the Sunnīs interpret the "filthiness" in this verse as unbelief, the Shīʿa understand it as a concern with this impure world and in particular with the Sunnī caliphate. For the Shīʿa, the *ahl al-bayt,* or Family of the Prophet (q.v.), have a special salvational function (see SALVATION). Devotion to them is central to the religion and it has a redemptive quality. In one version of the Prophet's farewell (q.v.) sermon, Muḥammad proclaims that God has given two safeguards to the world, his book (q.v.) and the Prophet's sunna. In another version, however, Muḥammad describes the two safeguards God left the world as his book and the Prophet's family *(ʿitra).* The heads of the family are the infallible and sinless Imāms (see IMĀM). For Muslims in general and for Sunnīs in particular, the Companions of the Prophet, collectively, can also be said to have played a certain role in the work of salvation as the link between the Prophet and the transmission of the faith.

Linda L. Kern

Bibliography

Primary: Bukhārī, *Ṣaḥīḥ;* Ibn ʿAbd al-Barr, *Kitāb al-Istīʿāb fī maʿrifat al-aṣḥāb,* 4 vols., Hayderabad 1318/1900-1; Ibn al-Athīr, *Usd al-ghāba fī maʿrifat al-ṣaḥāba,* 5 vols., Cairo 1286/1869-70 (critical compilation of and supplement to Ibn Saʿd and Ibn ʿAbd al-Barr); Ibn Ḥajar, *al-Iṣāba fī tamyīz al-ṣaḥāba,* 4 vols., Calcutta 1853-94; 8 vols., Cairo 1323-5/1905-7 (in-depth treatment of works on the Companions); Ibn Kathīr, *Tafsīr;* Ibn Saʿd, *Ṭabaqāt* (contains short biographical references and excerpts from the narratives of the most famous authors of works on the Companions); Nawawī, *Sharḥ.*

Secondary: I. Goldziher, Aṣḥāb, in *EI*[1], i, 477-8; id., *MS;* L. Kern, *The riddle of ʿUmar b. al-Khaṭṭāb in Bukhārī's Kitāb al-Jāmiʿ al-saḥīḥ (and the question of the routinization of prophetic charisma),* Ph.D. diss., Harvard 1996; E. Kohlberg, Some Zaydi views on the Companions of the Prophet, in *BSOAS* 39 (1976), 91-8; W. Schmucker, Mubāhala, in *EI*[2], vii, 276-7; A. Tritton, Ahl al-kisāʾ, in *EI*[2], i, 264; L. Wiederhold, Blasphemy against the Prophet Muḥammad and his Companions *(sabb al-rasūl, sabb al-ṣaḥābah).* The introduction of the topic into Shafiʿī legal literature and its relevance for legal practice under Mamluk rule, in *JSS* 42 (1997), 39-70.

Compensation see RECOMPENSE

Compulsion see TOLERANCE AND COMPULSION

Computers and the Qurʾān

Electronic versions of the Qurʾān exist in two major forms: multimedia presentations of the Qurʾān on compact discs (CD-ROMs) and on the Internet, particularly on the World Wide Web (WWW). Each of these two forms has its own peculiarities and consequently they will be treated separately. The digitization of the Qurʾān also offers new but as yet relatively unexplored possibilities in computer-assisted textual analysis. Producing electronic versions of the Qurʾān presents no more of a technological difficulty than any other text, though the Arabic alphabet has several major encoding standards: ASMO 449, ISO 8859-6 and UNICODE. The pages of the Qurʾān need only be scanned and preserved as images or, alternatively, scanned and then encoded according to one of these standards using Optical Character Reader (OCR) software. Many such electronic versions of the Qurʾān already exist and most of the major translations of the Qurʾān have also been encoded. Nor does digitizing the Qurʾān present any significant theological difficulty. The importance of both qurʾānic recitation (see RECITATION OF THE QURʾĀN) and calligraphy (q.v.) demonstrates that Muslims accept the presentation of the Qurʾān in various media and even recitational requirements such as the *taʿawwudh* (a call for God's protection before reading the Qurʾān) can be incorporated digitally.

Multimedia presentations of the Qurʾān on CD-ROM

The storage capacity of compact discs not only allows the complete text of the Qurʾān to be preserved electronically in a relatively portable and inexpensive format but also permits it to be presented in a multimedia format. The description which follows is based upon the two most popular, currently available multimedia presentations on one or more CD-ROMs. Shared features of these presentations include: the fully vocalized text of the Qurʾān, a transliteration to aid pronunciation and as many as three English translations. The translations of ʿAbdallāh Yūsuf ʿAlī, Marmaduke M. Pickthall and Muḥammad Shākir are the most common. The ability to display these translations simultaneously along with the Arabic allows for easy comparison. One presentation also offers French, Spanish, German, Malay, Turkish, Indonesian, Chinese and Urdu translations as well as an Arabic exegetical commentary (*tafsīr;* see EXEGESIS OF THE QURʾĀN: CLASSICAL AND MEDIEVAL; EXEGESIS OF THE QURʾĀN: EARLY MODERN AND CONTEMPORARY). The other presentation has bundled a number of reference books with the Qurʾān. The most notable of these are English translations of selected sections of Mālik b. Anas' (d. 179/796) *Muwaṭṭaʾ*, al-Bukhārī's (d. 256/870) *Ṣaḥīḥ* and those traditions which Muslims believe convey God's very words as uttered by the Prophet (*ḥadīth qudsī*, see ḤADĪTH AND THE QURʾĀN). It also includes abridged versions of the ḥadīth collections *(Sunans)* of Muslim (d. ca. 261/875), al-Tirmidhī (d. ca. 270/883-4) and Abū Dāwūd al-Sijistānī (d. 275/889). None of these *ḥadīth*s are presented with their lines of transmission *(isnād*s). Additional bundled reference materials include English translations of Muḥammad's last sermon (see FAREWELL), a legal *(fiqh)* text, biographies of the Companions (see COMPANIONS OF THE PROPHET), various subject indices, concordances and dictionaries and the sūra introductions of the modern Pakistani exegete, Abū al-ʿAlāʾ al-Mawdūdī. Both of these multimedia presentations also provide audio recitations coordinated with the displayed text of the Qur'ān. Several recitation styles may be present (see RECITATION, THE ART OF), though at the time of writing these additional recitations require the use of more than one compact disc.

All of these features on one or even a few compact discs is certainly useful for a number of purposes. Pedagogically, they provide a means for more easily learning proper qur'ānic pronunciation and even the recitation(s) provided. The reference books included are also helpful for homiletic purposes. These multimedia presentations, however, are less useful as research tools. In one of the programs, searching can only be done with the English translation. In the other, searching is done with the Arabic text but only finds exact matches. Therefore, words that are vocalized or declined differently (for example, *al-kitābu* versus *al-kitābi*) are not found. As a result, no searching can be done according to the radical consonants alone. (For example, *kitāb* and its plural, *kutub* would have to be searched individually rather than by their three common consonants.)

The Qur'ān as hypertext on the World Wide Web

Electronic versions of the Qur'ān on the Internet predate those on CD-ROMs and can be downloaded to one's personal computer. Numerous sites on the WWW also contain electronic versions of the Qur'ān that can be viewed by browsers (front-end graphical interfaces) such as Netscape or Internet Explorer — though this normally requires that an Arabic font exist on the destination computer. Most of the popular translations of the Qur'ān are also readily available. The placing of the Qur'ān in this medium is not remarkable but it is the potential of this medium that may have an enormous impact on how the Qur'ān is used and understood.

The technology used for producing and preserving written documents whether inscriptions on stone, wood or clay, handwritten papyrus scrolls and codices or mechanically printed books, had a significant effect on the form and concept of scripture in two important ways (see CODICES OF THE QUR'ĀN; COLLECTION OF THE QUR'ĀN; TEXTUAL HISTORY OF THE QUR'ĀN). First, the prevalent technology determined who had access to the meaning of the texts and thus controlled that meaning. The scroll and the codex visibly fixed a text but left the interpretative authority in the hands of literate elites. This manuscript culture allowed the concept of canon — with its claims to unicity of authority, content and source — to develop. The printed book democratized direct access to scripture while largely retaining its stability. Second, the technology, particularly in the Islamic context, influenced the scripture's self-description. In the Qur'ān, God is even said to "teach by the pen" (Q 96:4). A sense of awe at the written word is also obvious in the use of the word *kitāb* for God's various revelations (see BOOK; REVELATION AND INSPIRATION), the records of deeds (*kitāb aʿmāl*, see RECORD OF HUMAN ACTIONS) and the knowledge and power of God (as in Q 34:3; see POWER AND IMPOTENCE; GOD AND HIS ATTRIBUTES). It is precisely in the areas of canonicity and respect for the written word, both products of a manuscript and print culture, that the reduction of God's speech to ones and zeroes may prove problematic.

Computers have introduced the use of hypertexts and hypermedia which represents a technological revolution as significant as the inventions of papyrus and the printing press. A printed book is a linear structure — the reader moves from beginning to end or in the case of the Qur'ān from one verse to the next sequentially. Cross references in footnotes, indices and concordances have adapted this linear retrieval system somewhat and are themselves a form of hypertext or "non-sequential writing." But such cross references are not problematic and in fact support theological claims for the unity of a text of scripture whereas hypertexts on the WWW may undermine such claims. More generally, hypertexts are texts with links to other texts. These information units are connected through linkages made by the author or by the reader using a browser. Instead of linear or sequential access required of the printed text, the author or reader can use the computer's ability to access a multitude of diverse texts, some or all of which are located on other computers connected by the Internet. The author of a particular text may be able to determine what links to other texts will be embedded in his or her own text, but cannot control which other texts will link themselves to his or her text. And since it is the reader who determines which links to follow, the text's context and meaning is also reader-dependent. In addition, these linked "texts" can include images, sounds, video and animation. Therefore it is more correct to speak of hypermedia or interactive multimedia. By its very nature hypermedia lends itself to multiple or even conflicting interpretations of these information units. They no longer speak with a single voice nor are they fixed and unified with a linear, hierarchical structure. Pundits predict that without this structure the binary opposites it produced such as central/marginal, top/bottom, first/last, orthodox/heretical, canonical/non-canonical will "vanish in the networked world of the hypertext" (R. Fowler, The fate of the notion of canon).

The doctrine of the Qurʾān's unicity of authority, content and source, a doctrine that has been so firmly established during the period of manuscript and print culture which produced concepts of "canon," is unlikely to be affected in a hypermedia culture. In other words, the content of the Qurʾān may not be as malleable or multilinear as other electronic texts and its status as the central authoritative text will probably survive the transition to the new technology. Where hypermedia is already affecting the Qurʾān is in its interpretation. Exegesis or interpretation of the Qurʾān *(tafsīr)* has been until now largely under the purview of scholars steeped in the classical tradition. Currently, a search of the WWW on the word "Qurʾān" will yield close to 10,000 "hits" with subjects that range from "how to become a Muslim" to "contradictions in the Qurʾān." Websites offering access to electronic versions of the Qurʾān or interpretation of the Qurʾān are as often those of the Nation of Islam, Aḥmadiyyas, Bahāʾīs as those of more "orthodox" groups and individuals (see AFRICAN AMERICANS; AḤMADIYYA; BAHĀʾĪS). While most do not present themselves as commentaries *(tafsīrs)*, clearly the context in which they are placed will affect how the reader interprets the Qurʾān. And on the WWW, there are no scholars or *ʿulamāʾ* to police or censor websites. Therefore, while the WWW and hypermedia are unlikely to make the qurʾānic canon more fluid, the democratization of *tafsīr* has already begun.

Although this development presents new possibilities for research about the popular understanding of the Qurʾān, it will unlikely become a significant new tool for scholars of the classical exegetical tradition. There are, however, far more practical research applications for the WWW. Digital libraries accessed through the WWW have obvious advantages. Ancient manuscripts of the Qurʾān, its commentaries or other early texts in museums and libraries around the world can easily be preserved electronically. Their copyrights or ownership can be protected by invisible electronic watermarks. As electronic images, these manuscripts would be far easier to protect from man-made and natural disasters and even the slow decay of time. Moreover, instead of relying on the expertise of one scholar to analyze the provenance and authenticity of a text, digital preservation and distribution allow anyone access to the "original" manuscript.

Computer assisted analysis of the Qurʾān

Computers have proven to be extremely useful and sophisticated tools for analysis of texts. Stylistic, grammatical and lexical features can be located and compared with relative ease using computers (see GRAMMAR AND THE QURʾĀN). Except for isolated efforts such as Rashad Khalifa's search for words and letters in the Qurʾān that occur in multiples of 19, little has been done with computer-assisted analysis of the text. For such analyses, the text of the Qurʾān and a complete index of all positions of the words (or words with the same roots) in the text are needed. At the very least, these two components would provide a simple computerized concordance — a useful project in itself. Automatic index and concordance software already exists: WordCruncher, Oxford Concordance Program, MacConcordance and TACT, for example. Each of these provides key-word-in-context (KWIC) concordances, meaning that these programs can generate a list of passages from the text in which a particular word occurs. Repetends, both fixed-order word sequences and collocations, can be discovered and even displayed using distributional graphs. Such software is not automatic — it still requires that the scholar produce some initial hypothesis.

Unfortunately, at the date of the writing of this article, the scholar must still work in translation. Such programs cannot be used with the Arabic text of the Qurʾān. Arabic, along with other Semitic languages, presents some unique morphological difficulties not present in most languages using Roman script (see ARABIC SCRIPT; ARABIC LANGUAGE). In order to search for a particular word in the Qurʾān, the software must be able to separate all the prefixes such as the definite article, conjunctions, prefixed prepositions, verbal prefixes and suffixes, nominal case suffixes and enclitic direct-object and possessive-pronoun suffixes. Only then could the root or stem of the word and its consonant-vowel pattern (both of which might be obscured by phonological and orthographic practices such as those associated with weak and hollow roots) be discerned. Such difficulties, though complex, are now being overcome. One new morphological analysis system includes a lexicon of 4,930 roots and a dictionary of 400 phonologically distinct patterns, many of which are obviously ambiguous (K. Beesley, Arabic morphological analysis). However, such a system has not yet been combined with KWIC software. Thus, for the present, computer-assisted analysis of the Qurʾān remains an intriguing but unexplored field. Nevertheless, given the speed of technological innovation the reader should remember that this article could capture only those advances available at the time of its authorship.

Herbert Berg

Bibliography
G. Armstrong, Computer-assisted literary analysis using the TACT text-retrieval program, in *Computers & Texts* 11 (1996), on *http://info.ox.ac.uk/ctitext/publish/comtxt/ct11/armstron.html;* K.R. Beesley, Arabic finite-state morphological analysis and generation, (1996), on *http://www.xrce.xerox.com/research.mltt/arabic;* id., Arabic morphological analysis on the Internet, (1997), on *http://www.xrce.xerox.com/research.mltt/arabic;* R.M. Fowler, The fate of the notion of canon in the Electronic Age, (1994) on *http://www2.bw.edu/*

~rfowler; R. Khalifa (trans.), *Quran. The final testament (authorized English version),* Tucson 1981; G.P. Landow and Paul Delany (eds.), *The digital word. Text-based computing in the humanities,* Cambridge 1993; P. Mullins, Sacred text in an electronic age, in *Biblical theology bulletin* 20 (1990), 99-106; A. Rippin, The study of *tafsīr* in the 21st century. E-texts and their scholarly use, (2000), on *http://www.lib.umich.edu/libhome/Area.Programs/Near.East/MELANotes6970/tafsir.pdf.*

Conceit

An exaggerated sense of one's own importance. The Qur'ān declares conceit and insolence toward others to be major human failings, especially when directed toward God and his prophets. Several qur'ānic terms elucidate the causes and consequences of conceit. *Mukhtāl* is a close Arabic equivalent to "self-conceit," and in the Qur'ān the three instances of the term are paired with the notion of boasting (*fakhūr,* see BOAST) as in Q 31:18: "Do not turn your cheek away from people in contempt, or strut about the earth (q.v.); God does not love any who are self-conceited and boastful!" This attitude of superiority stems from the mistaken belief that good and bad fortune are solely the product of one's own efforts whereas in fact they may be a test (see TRIAL) sent by God: "No disaster falls upon the earth or among yourselves, save that it is in a book (q.v.) before we cause it to appear — and that is easy for God — lest you should grieve for what has passed you by or be overjoyed by what has come to you. For God does not love any who are self-conceited *(mukhtāl)* and boastful *(fakhūr),* those who are stingy and encourage others to do likewise..." (Q 57:22-4; cf. 4:36).

While all humans are vulnerable to moments of smug self-satisfaction, according to the Qur'ān, persistent attitudes permeated with vanity and conceit have led many to think themselves self-sufficient and, so, they have scorned God's prophets and their calls for religious and social reform (see PROPHETS AND PROPHETHOOD; GRATITUDE AND INGRATITUDE; VIRTUES AND VICES). In this context the Qur'ān speaks of those who are insolent (verb: *'atā;* noun: *'utūw*): "Who is there to sustain you if he withholds his sustenance? Yet [the unbelievers] persist in insolence and aversion" (Q 67:21). Conceit and insolence, then, are directly opposed to belief which requires obedience (q.v.) and humility (see BELIEF AND UNBELIEF). "Those who do not hope to meet us say: 'Why have no angels descended to us?' or 'Why do we not see your Lord?' They are full of self-superiority *(istakbarū fī anfusihim)* and extremely insolent!" (Q 25:21).

This passage introduces a third related qur'ānic concept, that of being haughty, arrogant or proud *(kibr, takabbara, mutakabbir, istakbara, istikbār, mustakbir).* In over fifty verses (q.v.), the Qur'ān condemns arrogance and pride (q.v.) which were first manifest by Iblīs when he refused the divine command to bow before Adam (see ADAM AND EVE; BOWING AND PROSTRATION; DEVIL; ANGEL): "When we told the angels, 'Prostrate to Adam!' they did so save Iblīs; he scornfully refused and grew haughty, and so became an unbeliever!" (Q 2:34; cf. 38:74-5). Following in Satan's footsteps was Pharaoh (q.v.) and communities in the past including those of 'Ād (q.v.) and Thamūd (q.v.). In their arrogance, they denied God's message, persecuted his messengers and so earned God's wrath (e.g. Q 23:46; 7:73-84; see PUNISHMENT STORIES; CHASTISEMENT AND PUNISHMENT; ANGER). In response to such resistance "God seals up every haughty, pitiless heart!" (Q 40:35) and, as the Qur'ān declares on numerous occasions, damnation is the fate of all those who feel secure in their conceit and selfish ways: "And your Lord has said: 'Call to me, and I will answer you. Truly, those who are too proud to worship (q.v.) me will enter hell (q.v.), humbled!'" (Q 40:60; cf. 4:173; 7:36). See also ARROGANCE.

Th. Emil Homerin

Bibliography
Primary: *Lisān al-ʿArab*, v, 49-50, 125-31; xi, 199-200; xv, 27-8; Qushayrī, *Laṭāʾif*, i, 79; iii, 132, 311, 542-4; Quṭb, *Ẓilāl*, i, 58; v, 2558, 2790, 3081, 3089-91; vi, 3492-4, 3642-4; Rāzī, *Tafsīr*, ii, 235-6; xxiv, 68-70; xxv, 149; xxvii, 63; xxix, 238-9; xxx, 72; Ṭabarī, *Tafsīr*, i, 180-1; xx, 48; xxiv, 46, 52; xxvii, 134-6; xxix, 6-7.
Secondary: F. Rahman, *Major themes of the Qurʾān*, Chicago 1980.

Concordances of the Qurʾān see TOOLS FOR THE STUDY OF THE QURʾĀN; COMPUTERS AND THE QURʾĀN

Concubines

Female slaves who enter into a sexual relationship with their male master. In addition to four legal wives, Islamic law allows a Muslim man the right of sexual intercourse with his female slaves (see MARRIAGE AND DIVORCE; SEX AND SEXUALITY). This right is based on ancient Arab custom (see PRE-ISLAMIC ARABIA AND THE QURʾĀN) and on several verses of the Qurʾān which refer to "that which your [or their] right hands own *(mā malakat aymānukum,* variants: *aymānuhum, aymānuhunna, yamīnuka)*." The phrase occurs 15 times in the Qurʾān. Other qurʾānic terms for female slaves *(ama,* pl. *imāʾ, fatayāt)* do not refer to concubines but appear in the context of marriage (*ama*, pl. *imāʾ*, in Q 2:221 and 24:32; *fatayāt* in Q 4:25) or prostitution (*fatayāt* in Q 24:33). The classical Arabic word for concubine, *surriyya*, is unknown in the Qurʾān.

The circumlocution "that which your right hands own" appears as a generic term for slaves in several instances (e.g. Q 24:32, 58; 30:28; 33:55; 70:30) although elsewhere the subject of discussion appears to be marriage, not concubinage (Q 4:25; 33:50). For instance, Q 4:3, "Marry such women as please you — two, three or four — but if you fear that you will not be just, then only one, or those your right hands own," supports a reading of both marriage and concubinage, but al-Ṭabarī (d. 310/923; *Tafsīr*, ad loc.), *Jalālayn* (ninth/fifteenth century) and other exegetes gloss this verse as referring to concubines. Q 23:5-6 and 70:29-30 are more explicit in urging men to hide their private parts from all except their wives and "those their right hands own."

The vague qurʾānic pronouncements on concubines are matched by vigorous debates in the first few centuries over the status of children (q.v.) born to concubines. Although the Prophet is known to have had a child by his concubine Māriya, who was given to him by the Byzantine ruler of Alexandria (see FAMILY OF THE PROPHET; MUḤAMMAD; WIVES OF THE PROPHET), the rules on the *umm walad* (literally "mother of children") were not solidified until long after the Prophet's death. According to this law, the children born to a free man and his concubine are legitimate; further, the concubine is freed upon the master's death. As the Islamic empire grew, concubines were understood as a necessary part of a ruler's household and most of the ʿAbbāsid caliphs were sons of concubines, who were able to exert considerable influence at times on political and courtly affairs.

The right of intercourse with slaves is not unlimited in Islamic law. For instance, right of intercourse does not translate into license to sell that right, as the Qurʾān specifically forbids the prostitution of female slaves (Q 24:33); nonetheless, such prostitution appears to have existed in Islamic societies. Unlike ancient Roman law, Islamic law does not extend the right of concubinage to female masters of male slaves nor does it condone in any way homosexual intercourse. The Qurʾān also promotes marriage to slaves and abstinence (q.v.; see also CHASTITY) as alternatives to right of intercourse by possession. The marriage of free persons to slaves was unusual in other Near Eastern cultures and there appears to have been some problems with its incorporation into Islamic society. While al-Zamakhsharī (d. 538/1144; *Kashshāf*, i, 260) explains Q 2:221, "A believing female slave is better [to marry] than an idolatress," by stating that "all people are slaves of God *(al-nāsu kulluhum ʿabīdu llāhi wa-imāʾuhu),*" while the *Jalālayn* (ad loc.), on the other hand, regard marriage to slaves as shameful *(ʿayb)*. See also SLAVES AND SLAVERY.

Jonathan E. Brockopp

Bibliography
Primary: *Jalālayn; Ṭabarī, Tafsīr;* Zamakhsharī, *Kashshāf.*
Secondary: F-P. Blanc and A. Lourde, Les conditions juridiques de l'access au statut de concubine-mere en droit musulman malekite, in *Revue de l'Occident musulman et de la Mediterranee* 36 (1983), 163-75; J.E. Brockopp, *Early Mālikī law. Ibn ʿAbd al-Hakam and his* Major compendium of jurisprudence, Leiden 2000; id., *Slavery in Islamic law,* Ph.D. diss., Yale 1995; R. Brunschvig, ʿAbd, in *EI²*, i, 24-40; H. Müller, Sklaven, in *HO* 6.6.1, *Wirtschaftsgeschichte des vorderen Orients,* 53-83; R. Roberts, *The social laws of the Qorʾān,* London 1925; J. Schacht, *Origins of Muhammadan jurisprudence,* Oxford 1950, 264-6 and 277-8; id., Umm al-walad, in *EI¹*, iv, 1012-15.

Confession of Faith *(shahāda)* see WITNESS TESTIFYING

Conquest

Gain or acquisition by force of arms. In the Islamic context it is associated with the "opening" of a land to the message and rule of Islam. The Qurʾān, revealed as it was before the Islamic conquests had begun, does not possess a clear concept of conquest, but the Arabic root *f-t-ḥ* produced during the first Islamic century the technical term for the Muslims' conquests over the Byzantine and Sasanian empires *(fatḥ/futūḥ)* and is frequently translated as such in the Qurʾān.

The Qurʾān has much to say about warfare (see WAR). It is enjoined upon those able to do so (Q 48:17 exempts the blind, crippled and ill) at specific times, outside of specific places (Q 9:36; 2:217) and only within certain limits: "Fight in the way of God (see PATH OR WAY [OF GOD]) those who fight you, but do not aggress (or transgress)" (Q 2:190). Q 61:4 enjoins a formation, "God loves those who fight on his path in a rank," and Q 47:4 recommends a combat protocol, "when you meet the unbelievers, strike their necks until you have subdued them, then bind a bond" (cf. Q 8:12; see BELIEF AND UNBELIEF). In the next world, the reward for those who fight and die in battle is the pleasures of heaven (q.v.); in this world, it is the spoils of victory (q.v.), the distribution of booty (q.v.) figuring prominently — even producing the name of a sūra, Sūrat al-Anfāl (Q 8, "The Spoils of War"; see REWARD AND PUNISHMENT; BLESSING). The reason and purpose of warfare are less clear, perhaps because they were so clear to contemporaries; but they were probably religious. According to Q 9:33 and 61:9, Muḥammad had been sent by God to make his religion prevail over all others, "though the unbelievers loathe it." Q 2:193 and 8:39 instruct believers to fight until there is no *fitna*, a term usually understood to mean the Meccans' opposition to Muḥammad and his followers (see OPPOSITION TO MUḤAMMAD). According to Q 9:29, "those who have received the book (q.v.)" are to be fought until they pay the *jizya* (see TAXATION), an obscure verse that has inspired a small industry of scholarship.

For the historical context of these verses one conventionally turns to the historical and exegetical traditions. The Constitution of Medina, the series of documents understood to have been drafted by Muḥammad soon after his emigration (*hijra,* see EMIGRATION) from Mecca to Medina, makes it plain that he put his community on a war footing fairly soon after the *hijra* and indeed the first decade of the *hijra* was dominated by a string of campaigns, the most prominent being Badr (q.v.) in Ramaḍān (q.v.) of 2/624, Uḥud (q.v.), al-Khandaq ("The Ditch"; see PEOPLE OF THE DITCH), al- Ḥudaybiyya (q.v.), Khaybar (q.v.), Mecca (q.v.), Ḥunayn (q.v.), and Tabūk in Rajab of 9/630. The political context of this campaigning was tribal rather than imperial: Forces were small (tribesmen often numbering in the hundreds; see TRIBES AND CLANS), marches short and shows of strength more frequent than actual violence. The handling of captives (q.v.), one infers from Q 8:67, seems to have been *ad hoc*. The object of these campaigns, moreover, was not to acquire and control land so much as to secure the loyalty and obedience of the principal tribes, an object also achieved by negotiation and the promise of material blandishments of various sorts. That the tribesmen's loyalties had been committed to Muḥammad, rather than to his nascent polity, is made clear by the eruption of the so-called "Wars of Apostasy" that broke out upon his death (see APOSTASY). In the view of modern historians, Abū Bakr's (r. 11-3/632-4) campaigns to re-impose Islamic rule within the Arabian peninsula led directly to ʿUmar's (r. 13-23/634-44) campaigns beyond its borders.

The qurʾānic lexicon of warfare is dominated by the Arabic terms *qitāl* and *jihād* (q.v.), that of victory by *naṣr* and *fatḥ*. The first of this latter pair of terms, *naṣr,* poses fewer problems than the second, in part because its qurʾānic usage is so clearly mirrored by that in the Constitution of Medina where it, too, signifies "support" or "help" (either God's or the Believers'). As a first and second form verb, *f-t-ḥ* usually signifies the basic Semitic meaning "to open or loosen" (Hebrew *pātaḥ,* Aramaic and Syriac *pᵉtaḥ,* Ethiopic *fatḥa*). Qurʾānic usage correlates the verb with gates (usually of heaven [q.v.], sometimes of hell [q.v.], cf. Q 6:44; 7:40; 15:14; 23:77; 38:50; 39:71, 73; 54:11; 78:19), belongings or baggage (*matāʿahum,* Q 12:65; see JOSEPH), and Gog and Magog (q.v.; Q 21:96). Lexical authorities such as al-Rāghib al-Iṣfahānī (d. early fifth/eleventh cent.) not infrequently explain the Fātiḥa, the opening verses of the Qurʾān (see FĀTIḤA), as the "starting point, by which what follows is opened." The range of this verb also extends in several instances to the sense of revealing or delivering, e.g. "blessings from heaven and earth" and mercy (q.v.; Q 7:96 and 35:2, respectively) and in this sense it is echoed in Ḥassān b. Thābit's (d. ca. 40/659) verses as well as those of al-Farazdaq (d. ca. 110/728; *Sharḥ dīwān al-Farazdaq,* i, 375, line 6). In two instances of the imperative (Q 26:118 and 7:89; cf. the tenth forms in Q 2:89, 8:19 and 14:15), the root clearly has the narrower sense of to deliver, render or make a judgment. In Q 26:118, Noah asks God to "make a judgment between me and them" *(fa-ftaḥ baynī wa-baynahum fatḥan),* a translation that is indebted in the first instance to J. Horovitz ("Urteil," *KU* 18, n. 2) who is followed by A. Jeffery ("judgment, decision," *For. vocab.,* 221). Both adduce Ethiopic and Jeffery includes South Arabian as well (see J. Biella, *Dictionary,* 412f.; A. Beeston, *Dictionnaire,* 47; W. Leslau, *Comparative dictionary,* 170). Commentators suggest the same: R. Paret cites al-Farrāʾ (d. 207/822) *apud* al-Ṭabarī (d. 310/923) for his reading of Q 7:89 *(rabbanā ftaḥ baynanā wa-bayna qawminā bi-l-ḥaqq wa-anta khayru l-fātiḥīn),* to which can be added other authorities, both early and late. Thus Muqātil b. Sulaymān (d. 150/767; *Tafsīr,* ii, 49) glosses the imperative "make a judgment" *(ftaḥ)* as *iqḍi;* and Makkī b. Abī Ṭālib (d. 437/1045; *al-ʿUmda,* 136) and Abū Ḥayyān al-Andalusī (d. 745/1344; *Tuḥfat al-arīb,* 94) gloss it as *uḥkum,* the latter also glossing *al-fattāḥ* of Q 34:26 as the judge *(al-ḥākim).* Paret ("Bedeutungsentwicklung," *Kommentar,* 167) holds that this was the primary meaning *(Grundbedeutung)* of *f-t-ḥ,* translating it as *Entscheidung* (thus Q 8:19; 32:28, the latter perhaps best translated in English as reckoning). He further holds that it shifted towards success *(Erfolg),* which is how he suggests the noun and verb be read in a number of instances (Paret, Q 4:141; 5:52; 48:1, 18, 27; 57:10; 61:13; 110:1). Q 48:1, *innā fataḥnā laka fatḥan mubīnan,* which is said to have been revealed in connection with either Ḥudaybiyya or Khaybar, is translated by A.J. Arberry as "Surely we have given thee a manifest victory," and by Paret as "Wir haben dir einen offenkundigen Erfolg bescheiden." ʿAbd al-Razzāq al-Ṣanʿānī (d. 211/827; *Tafsīr,* ii, 225; see also Muqātil b. Sulaymān, *Tafsīr,* iv, 65) glosses this passage as "We have made a clear judgment for you" *(qaḍaynā laka qaḍāʾan mubīnan).*

For Paret, as for others (e.g. R. Bell, W.M. Watt), the fall of Mecca, particularly as mentioned in Q 57:10, probably explains the historians' use of *fatḥ* in the sense of conquer. In the words of Watt, "The meaning of conquest, however, is derived from this conception of the conquest of Mecca as a judgment or clearing up" (*Muhammad at Mecca,* 67). Certainly Mecca's capitulation hardly qualifies as conquest in any military sense. Only two Muslim fatalities are connected to the event, and these only tangentially. The city never really resisted, Abū Sufyān, the leader of pagan opposition, having been captured earlier. Even so, when medieval Muslims came across the term *al-fatḥ* in ḥadīth (e.g., *lā hijra baʿd al-fatḥ,* "there shall be no migration after the conquest") or in history in a more general context (e.g. *ʿām al-fatḥ,* "the year [A.H. 8] of the conquest"), they had no doubt which one was intended; indeed, according to some sources (e.g. Bukhārī, *Ṣaḥīḥ,* ii, 301), Muḥammad uttered a version of the *lā hijra* statement on the very day Mecca fell. Ibn Isḥāq (d. 150/767), as well as later authorities on the biography of the Prophet *(sīra),* describes any number of forays *(sariyyas)* and raids *(ghazwas),* but only one *fatḥ;* and it was the Prophet's campaigns (conventionally called *maghāzī*) that produced the normative form of prophetic biography in the first three centuries, alternative titles (e.g. al-Madāʾinī's putative *Kitāb Futūḥ al-nabī* cited by Ibn al-Nadīm, *Fihrist,* 113) being extremely rare.

That the fall of Mecca came to be called *"al-fatḥ" tout court* must therefore be explained in terms of salvation (q.v.) rather than military or legal history. For unlike the treaty of Najrān (q.v.) or especially Khaybar, the terms of Muḥammad's entrance into (pagan) Mecca seem to have played no important role in legal discussions about the conquest fate of the (mostly Christian and Jewish) communities of the Near East (see JEWS AND JUDAISM; CHRISTIANS AND CHRISTIANITY). It might be suggested that by labelling as *futūḥ* the Muslims' victories outside of Arabia, historians sought to reinforce a point made by Tabūk accounts and the modelling of Muḥammad's biography upon Moses', i.e. that warfare beyond both the Arabian peninsula and the Prophet's direct experience enjoyed his (and God's) sanction. The natural alternative, the Arabic root *gh-l-b* meaning to overcome, conquer or prevail, was perhaps too closely associated with the fate of the Byzantines (q.v.) in Q 30. Exactly when and how Mecca emerged as the definitive *fatḥ* is just as difficult to know, the evidence being so exiguous. For example, Q 110:1 (*idhā jā'a naṣru llāh wa-l-fatḥ,* see Nöldeke, *GQ*, ii, 219f.; followed by F. Buhl, *Leben,* 310) is variously held to be a Meccan or a Medinan verse. Adducing the Medinan-sounding second verse, Nöldeke opted for the latter categorization, connecting it, via the exegetical works, to the fall of Mecca. This does appear to have been the tradition's consensus, one attested already in the commentary attributed to Mujāhid b. Jabr (d. 104/722, *Tafsīr,* 792; cf. Ibn Ḥanbal, *Musnad,* v, no. 3127). But some authorities held that events at Ḥunayn gave rise to the verses (thus Wāḥidī, *Asbāb,* 506) or even that it was revealed after the Prophet's Farewell Pilgrimage some two years later (see FAREWELL; OCCASIONS OF REVELATION). Q 57:10 is sometimes taken to refer to Mecca but other times to the truce *(ṣulḥ)* of al-Ḥudaybiya. Al-Ṭabarī preferred the latter. In fact, G.R. Hawting has adduced some evidence suggesting that the association of *fatḥ* in the sense of conquest with Mecca is secondary on two counts: The opening of the sanctuary at al-Ḥudaybiya may be primary.

In any case, since the poetry of the early Islamic period betrays a clear debt to qur'ānic imagery, one can fairly infer that the infusion of the Arabic root *f-t-ḥ* with God's providential direction was indeed a qur'ānic innovation, albeit one with scriptural precedents (e.g. *Deut* 28:12 and *Ezek* 25:9, the latter closer to the classical notion of conquest than anything qur'ānic). The first instance of this connection is a verse attributed to Muḥammad's contemporary Ḥassān b. Thābit (*Dīwān,* i, 17, line 14) which is said to have been composed shortly before Mecca fell in Ramaḍān of 8/629. It already echoes Q 18:101 and 50:22, as well as prophetic ḥadīth (Wensinck, *Concordance,* v, 50). Similarly, al-Farazdaq's panegyric to the Muhallabids (*Sharḥ dīwān al-Farazdaq,* i, 375, lines 5-6) draws on Q 48:18 (*fa-anzala l-sakīnata ʿalayhim wa-athābahum fatḥan qarīban,* see SECHINA). Elsewhere (*Dīwān,* i, 330, line 1), we find the qur'ānic conjunction of *fatḥ* and *naṣr,* along with the familiar instrumentality of human agents (see also *Sharḥ dīwān Jarīr,* 218, line 31): God conquers through men. The poetry of this period now begins to exhibit signs of the conquest rhetoric that characterizes the historical prose of the second and third centuries, even producing one of its principal genres, the *futūḥ* works of Ibn Aʿtham al-Kūfī (fl. third/ninth century), al-Madā'inī (d. 225/840) and, most famously, al-Balādhurī (fl. third/ninth century), among others. When al-Farazdaq has strongholds *(maʿāqil)* defy the Sasanians, only to be conquered by the sword of the Muhallabids (*Dīwān,* i, 380, lines 5-6), the usage is identical to that found amongst the narrators of historical material *(akhbārīs)*. See also EXPEDITIONS AND BATTLES.

Chase F. Robinson

Bibliography

Primary: ʿAbd al-Razzāq, *Tafsīr;* Abū Ḥayyān al-Gharnāṭī, *Tuḥfat al-arīb bi-mā fī l-Qur'ān mina l-gharīb,* Ḥamāh 1926; Bukhārī, *Ṣaḥīḥ;* al-Farazdaq, *Sharḥ dīwān al-Farazdaq,* ed. M.I.ʿA. al-Ṣāwī, Cairo 1936; Ḥassān b. Thābit, *Dīwān,* ed. W. ʿArafāt, London 1971; Ibn Ḥanbal, *Musnad;* Ibn al-Nadīm, *Fihrist;* Jarīr b. ʿAṭiyya, *Sharḥ dīwān Jarīr,* ed. I. al-Ḥāwī, Beirut 1982; Makkī, *al-ʿUmda fī gharīb al-Qur'ān,* ed. Y.ʿA. al-Marʿashlī, Beirut 1981; Mujāhid, *Tafsīr;* Muqātil b. Sulaymān, *Tafsīr;* al-Rāghib al-Iṣfahānī, *al-Mufradāt fī gharīb al-Qur'ān,* Cairo 1906; Wāḥidī, *Asbāb.*
Secondary: E. Beck, Die Sure ar-Rūm, in *Orientalia* 13 (1944), 334-55 and 14 (1945), 118-42; A.F.L. Beeston et al., *Dictionnaire Sabéen,* Louvain-la-Neuve/Beirut 1982; J.C. Biella, *Dictionary of old south Arabian,* Chico, CA 1982; M. Bravmann, A propos de Qur'ān IX-29: *ḥatta yuʿṭū l-ǧizyata ʿan yadin wa-hum ṣāghirūna,* in *Arabica* 10 (1963), 94-5; repr. in Paret, 293-4; F. Buhl, *Das Leben Muhammads,* Leipzig 1930; H. Busse, The Arab conquest in revelation and politics, in *IOS*

10 (1980), 14-20; C. Cahen, Coran IX-29: *ḥatta yuʿṭū l-ǧizyata ʿan yadin wa-hum ṣāghirūna*, in *Arabica* 9 (1962), 76-9; repr. in Paret, 288-92; D.C. Dennett, *Conversion and the poll-tax in early Islam*, Cambridge 1950; F.M. Donner, *The early Islamic conquests*, Princeton 1981; id., Muḥammad's political consolidation in western Arabia up to the conquest of Mecca. A reassessment, in *MW* 69 (1979), 229-47; A. Fattal, *Le statut legal des non-musulmans en pays d'Islam*, Beirut 1958; G.R. Hawting, al-Ḥudaybiyya and the conquest of Mecca. A reconsideration of the tradition about the Muslim takeover of the sanctuary, in *JSAI* 8 (1986), 1-23; Horovitz, *KU*; Jeffery, *For. vocab.*; J.M.B. Jones, The chronology of the *maghāzī* — a textual survey, in *BSOAS* 19 (1957), 245-80. W. Leslau, *Comparative dictionary of Geʿez*, Wiesbaden 1987; Nöldeke, *GQ*; R. Paret, Die Bedeutungsentwicklung von arabisch *fatḥ*, in J.M. Barral (ed.), *Orientalia Hispanica sive studia F.M. Pareja octogenario dicata*, Leiden 1974, 537-41; id., *Kommentar*; R.B Serjeant, The *sunnah jāmiʿah*, pacts with the Yathrib Jews, and the *Taḥrīm* of Yathrib. Analysis and translation of the documents comprised in the so-called "Constitution of Medina," in *BSOAS* 41 (1978), 1-42; E.S. Shoufani, *al-Riddah and the Muslim conquest of Arabia*, Toronto 1972; M.W. Watt, *Muhammad at Mecca*, Oxford 1953; id., *Muhammad at Medina*, Oxford 1956; Wensinck, *Concordance*.

Consanguinity

see BLOOD AND BLOOD CLOT; KINSHIP

Consecration of Animals

The ritual reservation or segregation of animals for religiously mandated reasons. Some information about pre-Islamic practices of this sort can be gleaned from qurʾānic statements that proscribe them. Islamic forms of animal consecration and sacrifice (q.v.) present both continuities and discontinuities with earlier practice.

Consecration in pre-Islamic Arabia

Animal consecration in pre-Islamic Arabia can be conveniently divided into those forms that involve bloodshed (q.v.) and those that do not (see PRE-ISLAMIC ARABIA AND THE QURʾĀN). For the latter the locus of proscription is Q 5:103. Among ancestral customs *(ʿawāʾid)* that were considered sacred *(aḍḥā, ḍaḥāyā)* by pre-Islamic Arabs, the following were condemned by Q 5:103: (1) The consecration to the gods of any female camel with her female offspring after having given birth to the fifth. Such a camel (q.v.) was given the name of *baḥīra*, i.e. "with slit ear," because as a sign of her consecration her ear, as that of her female offspring, was slit; as a consequence, people refrained from mounting such an animal or cutting its hair. According to the biographer of the Prophet, Ibn Isḥāq (d. 150/767), however, her milk could be offered to a guest or to a person in need (*Sīra*, 57f.). Q 11:4 indicates that a camel consecrated in this manner *(nāqat Allāh)* was given by the prophet Ṣāliḥ as a "sign" *(āya)* of his mission and allowed to graze on the "land of Allah" without any harm being done to her. (2) The consecration of any she-camel (or he-camel) following an oath sworn for the purpose of healing an illness or ensuring the success of a business. No subsequent benefit was to be derived from this consecrated camel, and that is why it was called *sāʾiba*, "left in nature." Ibn Isḥāq records that a camel that has given birth to ten she-camels in five pregnancies with no intervening male offspring was also given this name (*Sīra*, 57-8). (3) The consecration of the fruit of the seventh pregnancy: If a he-camel, it was sacrificed, but if a she-camel, it was left in the herd; if twins were born, however, consisting of a male and a female, the male was not sacrificed. Hence the name of *waṣīla* was given to this she-camel whose birth spared the life of her brother. Although Ibn Isḥāq states that both the male and female were sacrificed, this contradicts the meaning of the name given to such a ewe. On the other hand, Ibn Hishām (d. 218/833), the redactor of Ibn Isḥāq's text, comments that this name is applied to the she-camel that gave birth to ten females in five pregnancies without any intervening male (*Sīra,* 57). (4) The consecration of a camel-bull that has become a great-grandfather. This animal was no longer mounted and it could graze and drink wherever it wanted. It was called a *ḥāmī,* or *ḥāmī ẓahrahu,* "protector of itself." Ibn Isḥāq (*Sīra,* 57) applied this term to a camel-bull that had fathered ten females in a row without a single intervening male. (5) The hundredth he-camel of the herd was added to these consecrated animals that had been dedicated to the gods. If the herd increased to one thousand animals, an eye of this camel-bull was pierced and, above this number, the second eye was torn out as well. (6) In addition to the customs just enumerated, the custom of tying the she-camel to the tomb of its master by pulling its head towards its tail and saddling it with its packsaddle should be mentioned. If the animal succeeded in escaping, it was given to the deity and could graze wherever it desired. In later heresiographical literature this custom was explained as the wish to provide the deceased with a mount on the day of universal resurrection (q.v.; Shahrastānī, *Milal,* 439-40; Fr. trans. ii, 513-4; Lammens, *Culte des Bétyles,* 99f.). Consecration of these animals to the gods is condemned by the Qurʾān together with the added stipulation that only males may benefit from them (i.e. eat the flesh of the sacrificed beast, Q 6:138-9), whereas both men and their wives might partake in the flesh of those animals which have died of natural causes. W.R. Smith (*Lectures,* 269) considered this common meal the most appropriate expression of the ancient ideal of religious life.

The sacred character of these animals is denoted by the term *ḥarām,* the primary meaning of which is "retrenchment, exclusion, prohibition" (see LAWFUL AND UNLAWFUL; FORBIDDEN). According to qurʾānic (as well as Mosaic) law, this designation precludes any secular use and sets aside a person, an animal, a place or a thing (the *ḥurumāt,* see SACRED PRECINCTS) from any common use as a result of its dedication to God, including the impossibility of repurchase or exchange (cf. *Lev* 27, 28). (This notion of taboo is also represented by the Sumerian *nig-nig.* The opposing notions of holiness and abomination, born out of the concept of inviolability, are also attested in other earlier Near Eastern Sources [W. Albright, *De l'âge de la pierre,* 128]).

Animal consecration that involved bloodshed also presents a specific vocabulary. Animals *(anʿām)* destined for sacrifice were called *farāʾiʿ* (also *faraʿ*) and *ʿatāʾir,* the first originally referring to the first-born she-camel and the second designating the sacrifices offered during the month of Rajab. Both were considered to be on the same level as the produce of the earth *(ḥarth),* of which the first fruit was offered to the gods (see AGRICULTURE AND VEGETATION). The Qurʾān expresses surprise that men dedicate to God a part of what he himself has given them and especially that they give another part to deities which are associated with him. In such dedications the deities will receive nothing nor will God receive his due (Q 6:136). Verses or verse segments of Q 6:138 elaborate the areas of contradiction and complexity: At the same time, men decide that such animals and produce are illicit *(ḥijr);* they determine to whom these can be given to eat (Q 6:138a); some animals are made sacred while others have their throats slit without the name of God spoken over them (Q 6:138b); people go even further by deciding that whatever is born from these animals is licit for their male children but illicit for their wives (Q 6:139a).

The Qurʾān raises the question of the

gender of the animal to be sacrificed. Of two sheep, goats, camels or cows, does God want the males or the females of the litter to be consecrated? Q 6:143-4 concludes with the accusation that lies are told in the name of God. Among animals are those created for carrying burdens while others are destined to be killed (Q 6:142)? Q 6:145 states: "Say: 'I do not find in what has been revealed to me anything which is forbidden to eat, except for dead animals, blood poured forth, and pig's meat.'" While the following verse explains what had been prohibited to the Jews: "We have forbidden to them all animals which have nails *(ẓufur)* and we have forbidden the fat of the cows and sheep, except that which covers their back or their intestines or their bones" (Q 6:146). This prohibition of fat is justified in Leviticus as follows: "All fat belongs to Yahweh. It is a perpetual law for your descendants, in whatever place you may live. You will eat neither fat nor blood" (*Lev* 3:14-5).

Q 6:143-4 refers to offerings of first-born animals which were made mainly during the month of Rajab and which included the firstborn animals of every herd (see Henninger, *Fêtes de Printemps*, 37-44). It is true that, according to these verses, the first-born animals were not explicitly the "actual object of sacrifice, as there is no other indication found that the Arabs felt obliged, as did the Hebrews, to sacrifice the firstborn animals" (J. Lagrange, *Étude*, 299). To be sure, *dhabḥ al-ʿatāʾir*, the sacrifice of small cattle, was practiced during Rajab but in reality the Arabs only carried out spontaneous sacrifices *(nadhr*, Heb. *nedharīm)* and Islam did not reject these sacrifices. During his farewell pilgrimage (see FAREWELL), the Prophet is said to have left everyone completely free to sacrifice the firstborn of the herd *(farāʾiʿ)* and to practice the sacrifices of the month of Rajab (*ʿatāʾir*, Ibn al-Athīr, *Usd*, i, 341) as he himself had carried out these sacrifices (Ibn Saʿd, *Ṭabaqāt*, i, 104; on this subject also see J. Chelhod, *Sacrifice*).

Consecration in Islam

It should be noted that the words *farāʾiʿ* and *ʿatīra* do not appear in the Qurʾān. Perhaps they are replaced by the term *manāsik* which refers to both sacrifices with and without bloodshed. The term *nusuk* consists of the cultic practice in general, including a sacrifice with bloodshed, there being no mention of *dhabḥ al-manāsik* during the month of Rajab. The Qurʾān considers *nusuk* to be at the same level as fasting (q.v.) and almsgiving (q.v.). Another term, *shaʿāʾir*, refers to the victims *(budn*, sing. *badana)*, destined for sacrifice which wear, as a distinctive mark, a silver or iron collar in the shape of a grain of barley (cf. T. Fahd, Shiʿār). Camels wore a garland *(qilāda*, pl. *qalāʾid)* of different materials. A practice called *ishʿār*, consisting of making incisions on one side of the bump of a camel or on its skin for the purpose of allowing its blood to be shed, is also mentioned. Such an animal often wore a special cover.

This ritually mandated sacrifice, called *hadī*, "oblation," is still practiced today in the entire Muslim world during the pilgrimage (q.v.) on the Day of Sacrifice *(yawm al-naḥr)* in Minā, in memory of the sacrifice of Ishmael (q.v.; see RITUAL AND THE QURʾĀN; FESTIVALS AND COMMEMORATIVE DAYS). In reference to the topic of almsgiving *(zakāt)* in the classical books about ritual obligations *(kutub al-ʿibādāt)*, one finds that pre-Islamic customs continued under Islam after being purified from any remains of paganism in accordance with the conditions set forth in the sunna (q.v.) of the Prophet. This is the case in particular for the *aḍāḥī l-naḥr*, i.e. sacrifices with bloodshed *(aḍḥā, ḍaḥāyā)*, just mentioned, and consecration of the *ʿaqīqa* of the newly born, i.e. the sacrifice of a sheep (cf. M. ʿAbduh, *ʿIbādāt,* 276ff.). These bloody sacrifices are optional, whereas consecration by invoking the name of God and by carrying out the *tazkiya* or by pouring out as much blood as possible from the animal slaughtered for eating, is obligatory (see PROHIBITED DEGREES).

Additionally, a temporary consecration of animals within the *ḥaram* (i.e. the sacred territory of Mecca) was in force during the sacred periods of the major pilgrimage *(ḥajj)* and the minor one *(ʿumra).* Whoever hunts while in the state of ritual purification *(iḥrām)* has to compensate for his yield by carrying out an equivalent number of bloody sacrifices *(hadī)* of camels, cows or sheep, by giving food to the poor, or by fasting (Q 5:94-5). Five harmful animals are exempted from this prohibition: crows, kites, scorpions, mice and mad dogs (Bukhārī, iii, *Bāb al-maḥṣar wa-jazāʾ al-ṣayd*) as well as animals that are similarly noxious, such as snakes, wolves or panthers (see ANIMAL LIFE).

In many ancient Near Eastern cultures, animals have been an object of worship and were thus included in the sacred, either through sacrifice or incarnation of a divinity, as in ancient Egypt, where they served as an omen for the divine (see OMENS). "The primitive belief that the god or demon comes to dwell in his statue, by virtue of the magic ritual of consecration, has, in ancient Egyptian religion, been raised to a real theological principle" (P. Kraus, *Jābir II,* 131-2; for more information, see H. Bonnet, Tierkult, 812-24). Giving a "soul" to the objects of worship has led to their sacralisation. Nothing similar is found in the cultic traditions of central Arabia, the cradle of Islam. The only known divinity in the shape of an animal is Nasr, the vulture god; but this god was part of the South Arabian pantheon where animal figures were numerous (Fahd, *Panthéon,* 132-4; see SOUTH ARABIA, RELIGION IN PRE-ISLAMIC). The sacred character of the animal dedicated to a divinity is reflected by the following rites: the use of its blood for the unction of the central pole of the tent or of an erect stone *(anṣāb),* the use of its flesh for a sacred meal and the prohibition of breaking its bones out of respect to the animal. This can be concluded from the book of Exodus (12:2-11); a text that is, in fact, a typical example of a sacrifice among nomads (Dhorme, *L'evolution,* 57f.; cf. Henninger, *Fêtes de prin-temps,* 58f.).

The main idea which emerges from sacrificing, among the ancient Arabs and in the Qurʾān, is that an animal is a gift (see GIFT AND GIVING) from the divinity to human beings as is the agricultural produce of the earth. To gain his favor, the human gives the divinity the blood, i.e. its life, so that his own life may be spared. It is at once an oblation (*hadī,* Q 5:95, 97) and a ransom (*fidāʾ,* Q 37:107) or a compensation, "because the soul of the flesh is in the blood" (*Lev* 17:11) and "it is by the soul that the blood atones" (*Lev* 27:9f.). To this, finally, should be added that the sacrifice of animals, common in Near Eastern religions since the third millennium before Christ, was meant to construct a dynamic bond between the divinity and the faithful who united with him in flesh and in spirit, by sharing the flesh of the sacrifice (Albright, *De l'âge de la pierre,* 195).

T. Fahd

Bibliography

Primary: Ibn al-Athīr, *Usd al-ghāba fī maʿrifat al-Ṣaḥāba,* 5 vols., Cairo 1869; Ibn Iṣḥāq, *Sīra,* ed. Wüstenfeld; Ibn Saʿd, *Ṭabaqāt;* Shahrastānī, *Milal,* D. Gimaret et al. (trans.), *Livre des religions et des sectes,* Paris 1986.
Secondary: M.M. Ismāʿīl ʿAbduh, *al-ʿIbādāt fī l-Islām,* Cairo 1954; W.F. Albright, *De l'âge de la pierre à la chrétienté. Le monothéisme et son évolution historique* (Fr. trans.), Paris 1951; H. Bonnet, Tierkult, in *Reallexicon d. aegupt. Religionsgesch.,*

Berlin 1952, 812-24; J. Chelhod, *Le sacrifice chez les Arabes,* Paris 1955 (with ample information on the subject); E. Dhorme, *L'évolution religieuse d'Israel,* Brussels 1937; T. Fahd, *Le panthéon de l'Arabie centrale à la veille de l'hégire,* Paris 1968, 4-6; id., Shiʿār, in *EI²,* ix, 424; J. Henninger, Fêtes de printemps chez les Arabes avant l'Islam, in *Les fêtes de printemps chez les Sémites et la pâque israélite,* Paris 1975, 37-50; P. Kraus, *Jābir ibn Ḥayyān. Contribution des idées scientifiques dans l'Islam. II Jābir et la science grecque,* Paris 1942, pp. 131-2; J.M. Lagrange, *Étude sur les religions semitiques,* Paris 1905² (rev. ed.); H. Lammens, Le culte des Bétyles et les processions religieuses chez les Arabes préislamites, in *BFIAO* 17 (1919-20), 39-101; W.R. Smith, *Lectures in the religions of the Semites,* London 1927 (1889¹); J. Wellhausen, *Reste arabischen Heidentums,* 2 vols., Berlin-Leipzig 1887-97.

Consolation

A form of divine beneficence bestowed upon the pious or those confronted with worldly misfortune despite their righteousness. The Qurʾān recalls instances of God or his agents consoling some pre-Islamic figures; in addition, a number of qurʾānic verses themselves constitute divine consolation for Muḥammad and his followers.

God strengthened the heart of Moses' (q.v.) mother *(rabaṭnā ʿalā qalbihā)* when she was told to cast him into the river to elude Pharaoh's (q.v.) soldiers (Q 28:10). She was comforted *(taqarra ʿaynuhā)* when Moses' life was spared and Pharaoh's wife selected her as his wet nurse (Q 20:40; 28:13). On her part, Pharaoh's wife urged him to adopt Moses rather than killing him so that he might be a comfort *(qurrat ʿayn)* for them (Q 28:9; Speyer, *Erzählungen,* 241-5; G. Newby, *Making,* 121-3; K. Prenner, *Muhammad und Musa,* 222-33). In another instance, God's messengers told Lot (q.v.) to "fear not, neither sorrow" *(lā takhaf wa-lā taḥzan)* when he felt himself unable to protect them from his people (Q 29:33; Speyer, *Erzählungen,* 147-58; G. Newby, *Making,* 83-5).

Muḥammad received God's consolation numerous times during periods of adversity or strife. After a discouraging period during which he feared that divine revelation (see REVELATION AND INSPIRATION) had lapsed *(fatrat al-waḥy),* Muḥammad was reminded how God sheltered *(āwā),* guided *(hadā)* and enriched *(aghnā)* him when he was a destitute orphan without direction (Q 93:6-8). God would not forsake him and would aid him further as long as he remained thankful and obedient despite hardships (cf. Q 93:3-5; 94:1-8; U. Rubin, *Eye,* 116-24, 250-2; see GRATITUDE AND INGRATITUDE; OBEDIENCE). He is advised to overlook the unbelievers' malicious words (Q 6:33-5; 10:65; 27:70; 36:76; 73:10; see BELIEF AND UNBELIEF; OPPOSITION TO MUḤAMMAD), not to regard their error as his failure (Q 31:23) and to elicit assurance from what God has revealed to him (Q 76:24). Similarly, he is to ignore the hypocrites and the Jews who twist his words in an attempt to manipulate potential believers (Q 5:41; see HYPOCRITES AND HYPOCRISY; JEWS AND JUDAISM). With respect to specific events, God's assurance *(sakīna,* see SECHINA) descended upon Muḥammad during his migration from Mecca to Yathrib (see MEDINA), giving him strength to console Abū Bakr (Q 9:40; M. Lings, *Muḥammad,* 118-9; see COMPANIONS OF THE PROPHET; EMIGRATION). He is told not to grieve over those who deserted him during the battle of Uḥud (q.v.; 3/625) since the weakness of their faith was a divine curse (q.v.) inflicted upon them (Q 3:175-7; Wāqidī, *Maghāzī,* i, 327; see FREEDOM AND PREDESTINATION). At Ḥunayn (q.v.; 8/630), it was God's assurance and unseen aid that enabled Muḥammad and his followers to win the battle after an initial retreat (Q 9:25-6; Wāqidī, *Maghāzī,* iii, 189-90; see EXPEDITIONS AND BATTLES). Muḥammad is counseled many times to be patient in affliction and await his due in both this world and the next (e.g. Q 11:115; 16:127; 40:77; 74:7).

Muslims as a group received the good news (*bushrā*, see GOOD NEWS) of victory from God when they feared a much stronger enemy at Badr (q.v.; 2/624; Q 8:10, 26; Wāqidī, *Maghāzī*, i, 131-8). His consoling words "fear not, nor sorrow" *(lā tahinū wa-lā taḥzanū)* comforted them after the retreat at Uḥud (Q 3:139-40; Wāqidī, *Maghāzī*, i, 320-1) and his assurance descended upon them at Ḥudaybiyya (q.v.; 6/628) as they negotiated a truce with the Meccans (Q 48:4, 18, 26; Wāqidī, *Maghāzī*, ii, 618-24). Their firm faith (q.v.) in God gained them blessedness (*ṭūbā*, Q 13:29), worldly refreshment *(qurrat aʿyun)* such as spouses and children (q.v.; Q 25:74-5), and it will secure them rewards in the hereafter (Q 32:17; 41:30; 78:31-6; 88:8-16; 95:6; 98:7-8). See also BLESSING; REWARD AND PUNISHMENT.

Shahzad Bashir

Bibliography
M. Lings, *Muḥammad. His life based on the earliest sources*, London 1983; Cambridge, UK 1991 (rev. ed.); G. Newby, *The making of the last prophet. A reconstruction of the earliest biography of Muhammad*, Columbia, SC 1989; K. Prenner, *Muhammad und Musa. Strukturanalytische und theologie-geschichtliche Untersuchungen zu den mekkanischen Musa-Perikopen des Qurʾān*, Altenberge 1986; U. Rubin, *The eye of the beholder. The life of Muḥammad as viewed by the early Muslims*, Princeton 1995; W.M. Watt, *Muhammad at Medina*, Oxford 1956.

Conspiracy see OPPOSITION TO MUḤAMMAD

Consultation

To confer with other individuals or a group. The term consultation *(shūrā)* does not appear to have been used in Arabic before Islam and the revelation of the Qurʾān and occurs only once in the text of the Qurʾān at Q 42:38. Yet, the term *shūrā* in the sense of "consultation" has important implications for social and political theory.

Etymology

The word *shūrā* is related to the verb *shāra*, meaning to remove something from its place. It can also refer to the display of a thing, showing the good qualities inherent in something. The term *al-shūrā* can thus connote a handsome outward appearance, while the linguistic usage of the term is also connected to removal and the appearance of the thing removed (*Lisān al-ʿArab*, iv, pp. 434-7). The term does not occur in pre-Islamic poetry (see AGE OF IGNORANCE; POETRY AND POETS) but is first found in the Qurʾān. There it is used to indicate or describe a consultation and deliberation, a practice which was known to the Arabs (q.v.) and other peoples before Islam. Given its pre-Islamic use the custom of consultation was not necessarily a religious impulse, but connected to a social or political impetus since consultation inevitably involves a social structure.

Consultation according to the Arabs before Islam

The Arabs before Islam engaged in practices of social and political deliberation and were considered to be knowledgeable and experienced in worldly affairs. The tribe of Quraysh (q.v.) had a meeting house *(dār al-nadwa* and sometimes *malaʾ)*, which was built by Quṣayy b. Kulāb and established southwest of the Kaʿba (q.v.). It was called this because the Quraysh used to convene there to deliberate on issues of social and political concern. Deliberative authority rested with the elders of the tribe (see TRIBES AND CLANS) as the Quraysh had stipulated that no one could enact legislation until reaching the age of 40. A number of different types of deliberations were conducted in this meeting house, including the consideration of issues related to marriage, matters of commerce, and war and peace (Shintināwī, *Dāʾirat al-Maʿārif,* ix, 92-3; Jawād ʿAlī, *Mifḍal,* ii, 109).

Among the Arabs who were familiar with consultation were the people of Yathrib (see MEDINA; CITY), the Aws and Khazraj, some of whom were among those who came to be known as the Helpers (*anṣār,* see EMIGRANTS AND HELPERS) for assisting the prophet Muḥammad after his emigration (q.v.; *hijra*) to Medina. Ibn Isḥāq (d. 150/767) mentions that they deliberated among themselves when they sent the delegation to negotiate the first pledge at ʿAqaba. This delegation consisted of twelve men representing different clans of the tribe of the prophet Muḥammad and the pledge itself has been called the "pledge of the women"; unlike the second pledge at ʿAqaba, this one did not stipulate fighting for the cause of the Prophet (Ibn Isḥāq, *Sīra,* 288-303).

Consultation in the Qurʾān

Because of the use of deliberation among the Arabs before Islam the mention of consultation in the Qurʾān need not be understood as the introduction of a new concept. As noted above, though the word consultation *(shūrā)* as such occurs only once in the Qurʾān, the word "consult" *(tashāwur)* occurs in Q 2:233 and the command "consult them" *(shāwirhum)* is found in Q 3:159. These three instances apply to different situation and categories of Muslims. Q 42:38 applies to all Muslims, Q 2:233 applies particularly to the potential controversy between two divorced partners (see MARRIAGE AND DIVORCE) concerning the matter of weaning an infant and Q 3:159 is a special text related to the prophet Muḥammad in the shadow of the occurrence of the battle of Uḥud (q.v.) in which the Muslims were defeated (see EXPEDITIONS AND BATTLES).

The three different significations of these verses can lead to the following conclusions. First, that consultation was originally understood in relation to the prophet Muḥammad and in connection with Uḥud as one of the most important early battles. Second, that consultation was connected to relations among Muslims in the establishment of an Islamic society (see COMMUNITY AND SOCIETY IN THE QURʾĀN). Third, that consultation was understood to be connected to situations of dispute (see DEBATE AND DISPUTATION) where a form of communal deliberation was required or recommended for the Muslim judge, a usage which continues to the modern period. A fuller consideration of the qurʾānic contexts of the three passages will elaborate these significations.

Sūrat al-Shūrā *(Q 42)*

According to traditional understandings, the 53 verses of this sūra were revealed in Mecca (q.v.), with the exception of four (Q 42:23-6) which were revealed in Medina (q.v.). This is also related to the fact that the sūra begins with the letters *ḥāʾ-mīm* and *ʿayn-sīn-qāf;* the other sūras (q.v.) which begin with *ḥāʾ-mīm* are all said to be revealed in Mecca (Q 41-46) with the exception of Q 42:23-6 and Q 45:14 which were revealed in Medina (see LETTERS AND MYSTERIOUS LETTERS).

It is not known with certainty why Q 42 was called al-Shūrā but it was well-known as *ḥāʾ-mīm-ʿayn-sīn-qāf* owing to the letters in the first two verses. According to al-Suyūṭī (d. 911/1505; *Itqān,* 148-57), other sūras derive their names from a word that is mentioned in one of the verses. It is possible that Q 42 derived its name from the mention of *shūrā* in verse 38. In the commentary known as *Jalalayn*, Q 42 is also called *Shūrā* but without the definite article.

Some scholars claim that an earlier verse in this sūra (Q 42:27) was revealed in reference to the *ahl al-ṣuffa*, a group of Muslims who emigrated to Medina with the Prophet but had no money or clothes with them (see ṢŪFISM AND THE QURʾĀN). They passed the night in the mosque of Medina and were fed there. The *Ahl al-Ṣuffa* include a number of prominent followers of the Prophet such as Abū Hurayra, Saʿd b. Abī Waqqāṣ and Abū Dhurr al-Ghafārī (Qurṭubī, *Jāmiʿ*, xvi, 27). The verse immediately preceding Q 42:37 is said to have been revealed in reference to the vilification of ʿUmar b. al-Khaṭṭāb (q.v.) at Mecca. It is also said that it was revealed concerning Abū Bakr al-Ṣiddīq (see ABŪ BAKR) when he was reproved by the people for giving his property for charity (Qurṭubī, *Jāmiʿ*, xvi, 35).

The expression "consultation" occurs in Q 42:38 and is understood in the context of verses 37-9 as one of a series of attributes of Muslims: They shun great sins (see SIN, MAJOR AND MINOR) and indecencies, forgive when angry, answer their Lord and persevere in prayer (q.v.). Their rule is to consult one another, spend out of what God provides and, when tyranny afflicts them, defend themselves. Exegetes agree that these verses were revealed in connection with the Helpers *(anṣār)* and that they were intended to order deliberation among them. It is also said that Q 42:38 refers to their deliberation when they heard about the appearance of the prophet Muḥammad (Qurṭubī, *Jāmiʿ*, xvi, 36-7; Ṭabarsī, *Majmaʿ*, xxv, 57-60). These interpretations are problematic, however, because the sūra is said to have been revealed in Mecca and so it would have to be supposed that the Helpers knew how to pray before they met with the Prophet. The interpretation of Sayyid Quṭb (d. 1966) resolves this problem by mentioning that the verse refers in general to all Muslims, requiring a new call to God, matters of prayer and faith (q.v.), consultation among themselves and charitable giving (see ALMSGIVING). It is also evident from the context of Q 42:37, that this refers to the Muslims of Mecca in particular, those who "respond to their Lord," i.e. through faith in the religion of Islam when the Prophet first began to call people to it. Then they persevere in their prayer, for they are the ones who were wronged by the unbelievers (see BELIEF AND UNBELIEF), such as what happened to Bilāl al-Ḥabashī, ʿAmmār b. Yāsir and his mother Samiyya (Ibn Isḥāq, *Sīra*, 205-7).

Sūrat al-Baqara *(Q 2)*

According to the exegetes, this sūra was the first to be revealed in Medina, except for v. 281 which is said to have been the last to be revealed. The verses on usury are also held to be among the last verses revealed in the Qurʾān (Qurṭūbī, *Jāmiʿ*, i, 152). Mention of consultation appears in Q 2:233. The verse is long and is said to contain 18 different legal rulings relative to nursing (see MILK; WET NURSING; LACTATION) and the occurrence of divorce between two parents (Qurṭubī, *Jāmiʿ*, iii, 160-73). If the two parents concur on weaning the child from the breast of its mother before the child is two and there is no obstacle to this, then it is legally permitted on condition of consultation and mutual satisfaction between the parents (Qurṭubi, iii, *Jāmiʿ*, 170-1). This is a separate instance of the use of consultation because it applies to the specific case of two divorced parents. The greater importance of this reference, however, lies in its allusion to the necessity of consultation in matters of the family (q.v.). In pre-Islamic tribal society, the man held complete control over family matters but with the revelation of this verse the extent of his control was modified and the role was given to the woman and the man jointly.

Sūrat Āl ʿImrān *(Q 3)*
This sūra contains the term "consultation" in the form of a command given directly to the prophet Muḥammad in the context of Medinese society. The term is found in Q 3:159 referring to the battle of Uḥud in which the Muslims experienced their first defeat after the battle of Badr (q.v.). This verse is not to be understood by itself or in isolation but is to be explained in the context of Q 3:118-74 and the picture of the relations among the Muslims in the earliest period of the Prophet's emigration to Medina. In Medina, social relations were organized according to different social groups, such as those who lived in Medina originally (the Helpers) and those who followed the Prophet to Medina from Mecca (the Emigrants). Likewise, there were divisions according to religion between Muslims and Jews (see JEWS AND JUDAISM). These groupings were further divided. To the Emigrants belonged the tribes of al-Aws and al-Khazraj, and the Jews were linked historically to the Helpers. There were also the so-called Hypocrites *(munāfiqūn)* under the leadership of ʿAbdallāh b. Ubayy, leader of an influential group in Medinese society. The relations between the Helpers and the Jews were based on long-standing connections between the Jews and the tribes of al-Aws and al-Khazraj. According to al-Qurṭubī (d. 671/1272) many of the offspring of the Helpers were among the Banū l-Naḍīr (Qurṭubī, *Jāmiʿ*, iii, 280; see NAḌĪR). The many affiliations between the people of Yathrib, al-Aws and al-Khazraj and the Jews is well-known from Ibn Isḥāq. The interactions among the Muslims, the Helpers and the Hypocrites headed by ʿAbdallāh b. Ubayy were also established according to tribal ties (see HYPOCRITES AND HYPOCRISY).

Q 3:118-74 must be understood in the context of these social relations. Verses 118-20 refer specifically to those among al-Aws, al-Khazraj and the Jews. Verses 121-2 refer to the fighting at the battle of Uḥud, verses 123-36 to the situation at the battle of Badr, verses 137-59 to the victory of the Muslims at the battle of Uḥud and verses 174-160 to what came after the battle of Uḥud.

Q 3:159 begins by indicating the tensions among the Muslims. The situation was not easy for the Prophet, who had to face the Muslims who had been insulted by the defeat and those who had left their position exposed to the enemy. This was compounded by other issues concerning patronage between the Helpers and the Jews, and the two groups of al-Aws and al-Khazraj who were upset about the failure of the call to fight after they themselves had been wounded (Qurṭubī, *Jāmiʿ*, iv, 185-6). After the events of this battle, the nascent Muslim community experienced a period of communal tension. This uncertain situation perhaps explains the recklessness of the Helpers in battle, seventy of whom were killed at Uḥud while only four Emigrants died in that engagement.
Q 3:159 addresses this situation: "This is due to mercy from God that you treat them lightly, for had you been heavy and hard-hearted, they would have left your side." The release of tension is attributed to God's mercy (q.v.). Then comes the divine command to pardon and forgive them (see FORGIVENESS), and consult with them in the matter. The sequence of these commands indicates that the command to Muḥammad to consult the people came after he had settled with them, pardoned them and forgiven them for their sins. It was only after these events, which assured him of the sincerity of his followers, that he established the process of consultation (Qurṭubī, *Jāmiʿ*, iv, 249).

Later theories concerning consultation

Based on these references in the Qurʾān, and particularly the command in Q 3:159, later Muslim thinkers have theorized about the social and political dimensions of consultation, including the scope and necessity of its application. Examination of prophetic ḥadīths related to these qurʾānic references also allowed for the extraction of more general principles about the application of consultation (Anṣārī, *Shūrā,* 65-9 and 113-222). The historical setting of Medina was generalized to allow the emergence of questions of political theory, such as the role of consultation in legislation, the installation of community leaders and the legitimacy of the state (see POLITICS AND THE QURʾĀN).

More recent theorists have sought to compare the qurʾānic concept of consultation with the modern western notion of democracy. Others have critiqued such a comparison, arguing that it often results in eschewing more felicitous explanations of "consultation" in its qurʾānic and classical exegetical contexts. According to these critics, a political system based on the consultation of a select group of religious scholars, whose status is founded upon their expertise in qurʾānic exegesis, is at odds with a number of the more normative understandings of broad-based and secular democracy.

Aḥmad Mubārak al-Baghdādī
(trans. Brannon M. Wheeler)

Bibliography
J. ʿAlī, *al-Mifḍal fī taʾrīkh al-ʿarab qabl al-Islām,* Beirut 1980; ʿAbd al-Ḥamīd al-Anṣārī, *al-Shūrā wa-atharuhā fī l-dīmuqrāṭiyya. Dirāsa muqārina,* Beirut n.d.; B.ʿA. Faraj, *al-Shūrā fī al-qurʾān wa-l-sunna. Dirāsa mawḍūʿiyya wa-taḥlīliyya,* Beirut 1996; A. al-Shintināwī et al., *Dāʾirat al-maʿārif al-islāmiyya,* Cairo 1933.

Consultative Assembly

see CONSULTATION

Consummation

see MARRIAGE AND DIVORCE

Contamination

Soiling or corrupting. It is perhaps surprising to find that the Qurʾān has no concept of contamination per se, in contrast, for example, to the Pentateuch which is very much concerned with the concept. There is no qurʾānic equivalent of Leviticus 15:19 which stipulates that "when a woman has a discharge of blood which is her regular discharge from her body, she shall be in her impurity for seven days, and whoever touches her shall be unclean until the evening." There are items to be avoided, events and substances that leave one ritually disabled, but in the qurʾānic text nothing suggests the transmission of impurity from one person to another.

Two words often understood as "impurity" are (in the qurʾānic vocalization) *najas* and *rijs*. *Najas* appears only a single time in Q 9:28: "O you who believe, polytheists *(al-mushrikūn)* are only [i.e. entirely] *najas;* do not let them draw near the sacred mosque after this, their year." Nothing here suggests contamination that is transferred to others; only that some quality of polytheism disqualifies one from attending the sacred mosque (see BELIEF AND UNBELIEF; POLYTHEISM AND ATHEISM). Nonetheless, the literature of qurʾānic commentary considers the possibility. According to exegetical traditions, Ibn ʿAbbās (d. ca. 67-8/686-8) maintained that *mushrikūn* were *najas* in their essence *(ʿayn)* like dogs or swine (see LAWFUL AND UNLAWFUL; DOG). And the Zaydīs reportedly held, as do some Imāmīs, that touching a polytheist *(mushrik)* requires ritual ablution (*wuḍūʾ,* Nīsābūrī, *Tafsīr,* x, 64; Qurṭubī, *Jāmiʿ,* viii, 98; see SHĪʿISM AND THE QURʾĀN). Yet the Prophet drank from *mushrik* vessels (Nīsābūrī, *Tafsīr,* x, 64). Moreover, nothing can make pork permissible for consumption *(ḥalāl)* but upon conversion to Islam, a *mushrik* ceases to be *najas*. It must be, as al-Ṭabarī (d. 310/923, *Tafsīr*, x, 105) suggests, that it is their dietary habits and omission of full ritual ablution *(ghusl)* that makes them deserving of the epithet for contamination or impurity *(najas)*.

The more common word in the Qurʾān is *rijs* — and this is surprising since the dominant words for ritually impermissible substances or acts in later legal literature are *(najis, najas* or *najāsa)*. *Rijs* occurs ten times in the qurʾānic text. The *locus classicus* for *rijs* as "contamination" is Q 5:90: "O you who believe, *al-khamr, al-maysar, al-anṣāb* and *al-azlām* (see INTOXICANTS; GAMBLING; DIVINATION) are entirely *rijsun*, and among the works of Satan (see DEVIL). Avoid it *(fa-jtanibūhu)*, that perhaps you might prosper." The verbs derived from the root *j-n-b* all convey, however, the sense of "separation, distinction from" in qurʾānic usage and so what is meant here is only that one should avoid these substances and practices. The basic meaning of the word, according to al-Nīsābūrī (d. mid eighth/fourteenth century; *Tafsīr*, vi, 23), is "an act that is repellent *(qabīḥ)*, disgusting *(al-qadhir)*." One commentarial tradition sees the *innamā* as governing the list of things to be prohibited so that it is only these items that are *rijs*, i.e. only wine, gambling, divining, etc. are *rijs* (Ṭabarī, *Tafsīr*, vii, 31). Al-Nīsābūrī (*Tafsīr*, vi, 23) and others differ. For them, wine *(khamr)* is "nothing but *rijs*." That is, under no circumstances can it be considered other than *rijs*.

Another passage often read as a reference to contamination is Q 6:145: "Say I do not find in what is revealed to me anything prohibited to eat except that it be carrion *(al-mayta*, see CARRION) or flowing *(masfūḥ)* blood (see BLOOD AND BLOOD CLOT) or the meat of swine — these are *rijs*... Whoever is compelled [to eat these things] while not desiring [to do so] nor in hostility, your Lord (q.v.) is forgiving, clement." It is not, therefore, that one is contaminated by contact with these items but that one is to avoid them. If there should be contact, no purification is necessary, no penance is to be performed (see also Q 22:30).

The underlying meaning of *rijs*, when not specifically contamination, is certainly "something worthy of avoidance" but the "why" of that avoidance is elusive (see Lane, 1037; Nīsābūrī, *Tafsīr*, vi, 23 for etymology). Some insight may be gained from consideration of the term in other contexts where the reference is not to substances or acts but is more metaphorical. Q 10:100 states: "And no soul will believe except by God's permission, and he places *al-rijs* upon those who do not reflect *(lā yaʿqilūn)*." The failure to use common sense, to reflect upon what one simply knows by virtue of living in the world, seems to result in *rijs*. Here the term must mean "repellent" or "being such as to cause avoidance." This meaning makes sense of other second-order usages such as Q 7:71: "[Hūd, q.v.] said '*rijs* and wrath *(ghaḍb*, see ANGER) from your Lord have befallen you.'" Those who have rejected Hūd have become objects of avoidance and wrath. Likewise Q 9:125: "As for those in whose hearts is a malady, repellence has been added to their repellence, and they shall die as unbelievers." It is clear then that *rijs* suggests something that evokes disgust, something that is repulsive.

Another domain often thought to reflect a notion of contamination is that of ritual purification. After urination and defecation, sexual intercourse, ejaculation (male and female), menstruation and parturition, one is ritually disabled until the appropriate ritual of purification is performed (see Q 4:43; 5:6). In these passages, however, (with one possible exception) there is no notion that the precluded *(junub)* person or the "affected" *(muḥdath)* person is contaminated or that the disability is contagious.

There is one suggestion that contamination by touch might be possible. Q 4:43, in the passage approving the "dry ablution" *(tayammum)* states: "And if you are ill, or on a journey, one of you comes from the privy or you have touched *(lamastum,* variant *lāmastum)* women, and you do not find water, then perform the dry-ablution [with] fine surface-soil and rub your faces and hands." The question turns on what is meant by "touching." The synonym for *lamastum* given in al-Ṭabarī (*Tafsīr,* v, 101) is *bāshartum,* the root meaning of which is "to touch skin to skin." Yet that term itself gives rise to substantial discussion, so it is clear that "touching" is exegetically significant. In one understanding, it is synecdochical and understood to mean conjugal relation *(jimāʿ)*. According to another, it is literal and means "any contact of the two skins" (Nīsābūrī, *Tafsīr,* v, 49). Al-Ṭabarī attributes these two positions to Arabs (q.v.), who understood it as conjugal relation, and to the *mawālī* (non-Arab converts to Islam), who interpret the term to mean "contact," respectively. Within the exegetical tradition, the contact position is attributed to Ibn Masʿūd (d. 32/652-3), Ibn ʿUmar (d. 73/693), al-Shaʿbī (d. ca. 110/728), al-Nakhaʿī (d. ca. 96/717) and al-Shāfiʿī (d. 204/820) and is justified by reference to Q 6:7: "So they could touch [the parchment book] with their hands" (with the root *l-m-s*). The sexual congress position is attributed to Ibn ʿAbbās, al-Ḥasan (d. 168/784-5), Mujāhid (d. 104/722), Qatāda (d. ca. 117/735), the Ḥanafīs and the Shīʿa (q.v.) and justified by analogy to Q 2:237: "If you divorce them before you have 'touched' them" (here the root is *m-s-s* not *l-m-s*) where touching clearly means "sexual intercourse" (Nīsābūrī, *Tafsīr,* v, 49-50; see MARRIAGE AND DIVORCE). Only in this qurʾānic passage does one find suggestion of contamination by contact with a woman. Yet, for the most part, the legal tradition rejected this literal reading and required at least "desire" or "pleasure" in the touching for one's purity to be "lifted" (see Qurṭubī, *Jāmiʿ,* v, 203f.).

The qurʾānic understanding that contamination or any repellent quality is not conveyed by transmission is confirmed in ḥadīth literature, for the most part, but is substantially modified in *fiqh,* particularly Shīʿī *fiqh* (see LAW AND THE QURʾĀN; ḤADĪTH AND THE QURʾĀN). Yet for those who chose to see Islamic ritual law as derivative of Jewish and Zoroastrian sources, this difference, between qurʾānic understanding of a repellent quality and the Jewish and Zoroastrian logics of pollution, constitutes a datum that must be explained (see SCRIPTURE AND THE QURʾĀN). See also PURITY AND IMPURITY; RITUAL PURITY; CLEANLINESS AND ABLUTION.

A. Kevin Reinhart

Bibliography
Primary: Nīsābūrī, *Tafsīr;* Ṭabarī, *Tafsīr;* Qurṭubī, *Jāmiʿ*.
Secondary: Izutsu, *Concepts,* 240-1; Lane; A. Kevin Reinhart, Impurity/No danger, in *History of religions* 30 (1990), 1-24; J.J. Rivlin, *Gesetz im Koran. Kultus und Ritus,* Jerusalem 1934, 66-7 on *rijs*.

Contemporary Critical Practices and the Qurʾān

Contemporary methodology operative in the study of the Qurʾān, especially in the West, and the philosophical and epistemological questions and problems related to the study of the Qurʾān in its function as the focal point of a religion and a religious tradition. See also POST-ENLIGHTMENT PREOCCUPATIONS OF QURʾĀNIC STUDY.

Introduction: The ranking of rational processes

Reason no longer offers the certainty it once did; only philosophers still adhere to the primacy of critical reflection in the implicitly or explicitly assumed hierarchy of approaches *(l'ordre des raisons)* in every cognitive construction. The social sciences continue to produce their own isolated critical approaches to knowledge, the result being a reduction of epistemological exchange and confrontation and the rise of what J. Derrida calls *teletechnoscientific reason,* a disjointed conglomerate that claims to be the only reliable form of thinking in current scholarly discourse. On the other hand, P. Bourdieu has recently presented a trenchant criticism of scholastic reason (in *Méditations pascaliennes*), which is nevertheless unlikely to elicit any fruitful response from the great figures of the scholarly world since it is the systematic spread of this very scholastic reason on which their reputation has been based and continues to depend.

Every scholar lives within the confines of a speciality which can become a private kingdom, and thus strives to establish certain aims which lack any real basis, in order to publicize assumptions of meaning *(effets de sens)* or representations of them. These, in turn, are presented under the guise of meaning or truth as established by a scientific method and as recognized by the community of scholars. According to J.F. Lyotard, "Scientific reason is not questioned according to the criterion of (cognitive) truth or falsehood on the message/referent axis, but according to its (pragmatical) performative abilities on the messenger/recipient axis" (*L'enthousiasme,* 15).

European modernity, at least since the eighteenth century, has left us with the impression that reason would finally be liberated from the constraints of dogmatism for the service of knowledge alone, once a radical separation between every church and the "neutral" state was accomplished. When this latter body is free to exercise an undisputed sovereignty, it does not, however, struggle with the same determination for such a radical separation between cognitive freedom and its own aims and rationality. This is not the place to explore this subject further; it is enough to recall now that in various Islamic contexts, reason multiplies the constraints which it had itself created for the sake of its initial independence in the face of the strict control of the state, a state which unilaterally proclaims itself the exclusive administrator of orthodox religious truth (q.v.).

Such are the two contexts in which the Qurʾān has been read, consulted and interpreted for fourteen centuries on the Muslim side and for some two centuries on the side of the modern West. This introduction of a hierarchy of approaches makes the debate on orientalism irrelevant as it has hitherto been conducted, i.e. apart from any preliminary critique, apart from scholastic reason (as defined above), and apart from recognition of the fact that cognitive reason has willingly accepted this utilitarian, pragmatic, teletechnoscientific reason. One must, however, remember two troublesome issues for the Western scholar of the Qurʾān who continues to be influenced by the tools and assumptions of a positivist and philological methodology: (1) With the exception of a handful of scholars who have had no lasting influence, all qurʾānic scholars have little regard for any methodological debate and reject, if they are not actually unaware of, questions of an epistemological nature. They are only sensitive to discussing the "facts" according to the meaning and in the cognitive framework which they themselves have chosen. (2) Apart from specialists who are themselves believers and bring their Jewish or Christian theological culture to bear on the question at hand, all who declare themselves agnostic, atheist or simply secular dodge the question of meaning in religious discourse and thus refuse to enter into a discussion of the content of faith (q.v.), not as a set of life rules to be internalized by every believer, but as a psycholinguistic, social and historical edifice. Hence the essential question about truth, for religious reason as well as that of the most critical philosphical kind, remains totally absent in the so-called scientific study of a corpus of texts of which the *raison d'être* — the ultimate goal to which all rhetorical and linguistic utterances bear witness — consists in providing for its immediate addressees, who have multiplied and succeeded one another throughout the centuries, the unique, absolute and intangible criterion of Truth as a True Being, a True Reality and a True Sense of Right *(al-Ḥaqq)*. Yet surely, this *Ḥaqq* has from the time it was first anounced orally between 610 and 632 C.E. until today developed in a way which history and cultural sociology must be willing to investigate and explain.

This is not a question of establishing the true meaning of texts as lived by the faithful, i.e. as sacred and revealed nor is it a matter of articulating the certitudes recorded in a long process of sacralization, transcendentalization, ontologization, spiritualization, etc., and systematized in the great products of theological, philosophical, legal or historiographical thought inherited from the Middle Ages. Rather, the task of the contemporary researcher is to problematize all systems which claim to produce meaning, all the forms, still existent or not, which offer meaning and assumptions of meaning. This is an essential distinction that encompasses many problems yet to be raised or, if they have been, only poorly or without full recognition. In the study of the Qurʾān and similar corpuses in other cultures — comparison must always be utilized — the scholar approaches the activity of the human spirit that most closely expresses its own utopian vision, its hopes, both those which are unfulfilled and those which recur, its struggle to push back the limits of its servitude and to attain the full exercise of its "will to know," combined with its critical and creative freedom. The theme in the case of the qurʾānic corpus and its vast historical development is to test the capacity of reason to decipher the mysteries which it has itself produced.

Despite this shared reference to a utopian vision, it is important not to lose sight of the fact that contemporary qurʾānic studies lag considerably behind biblical studies to which it must always be compared (see SCRIPTURE AND THE QURʾĀN). This lag could be said to reflect the different concerns that emerged in the historical development of societies in which the Qurʾān continues to play the role of ultimate and absolute reference point and in which it has never been replaced as the sole criterion for the definition and function of all true, legitimate and legal value. In the violent and passionate rejection of what political Islam calls "the West," the stakes lie less in the seizure of an ephemeral power than in the progress of the secular model of historical production which could ultimately render the "divine" model obsolete, as it has already done in the West. This point is important for any attempt to liberate the problematic of the Qurʾān from its isolation vis-à-vis the historical perspective of modernity as well as for any effort to address the religious problem, which has been at one and the same time appropriated by and disqualified by this political concern. The context is also essential for clarifying the strategy of mediating a solution and thus guiding the pedagogy of the reflective researcher *(chercheur-penseur)*.

During the years of struggle for political independence (1945-1970), one could have hoped that an opening toward modern historical criticism as shown in the Middle East and North Africa during the so-called

Renaissance (*Nahḍa*, 1830-1940), would have grown to incorporate subjects as taboo as qurʾānic studies, including the sacralised areas of law appropriated by the *sharīʿa* and its legal statutes and rulings (see LAW AND THE QURʾĀN), the corpus of ḥadīths (see ḤADĪTH AND THE QURʾĀN) which enjoy the status of fundamental source *(aṣl)* as defined by al-Shāfiʿī (d. 204/820). Certain historical events, however, altered this potential course, beginning with the 1979 Islamic revolution in Iran and its eventual global enlargement by so-called fundamentalist movements. This revived, in the already very complex and inadequately explored area of qurʾānic studies, the rather archaic combination of the violent and the sacred, a combination that was still able, with some effect, to bring its weight to bear upon the global civilization of disenchantment, desacralization and the supremacy of sciences over all dimensions of human reality. In order to enrich the questions of the social sciences and to radicalize their criticism in every area, including, of course, modernity, the reflective researcher must bear in mind the historical, sociological and psychological significance of the religious imagination. This is a reality which the assumptions of scientific socialism and militant secularism of the French kind believed it was possible to eradicate through teaching official atheism or through eliminating the concept of the religious event *(fait religieux)* from an educational system run by a state that self-proclaimed its neutrality. By agreeing to work within such assumptions, the social sciences have contributed to nourishing and even legitimizing recurrent wars between the forces, demographically in the majority, that support sacrality and sacralization and the so-called enlightened who support a rational process thought to be emancipatory. But this process actually has a hegemonic mission, since it continues to spread pragmatic truths while refusing to think philosophically about what is intolerable in relations between humans, cultures and civilizations (cf. Arkoun, *Les sciences sociales*).

Like Christians during the modernist crisis of the nineteenth century, Muslims have reacted — and still react — against earlier works marked by historicist-philologist positivism as well as against more recent research that is relatively free of the assumption of a triumphalist, even intolerant science. Under the pretext of not wanting to confuse different kinds of science, so-called pure researchers refuse to address the conflict between full-blown scientific reason and religious reason that is apparently vanquished intellectually or forced on the defensive despite its historical persistence. This refusal continues despite the many possible applications of an epistemological radicalization of the social sciences. These "pure" researchers steadfastly refuse to integrate theological reasoning — despite its popular persistence — into a methodological program for an epistemology of historical research *(épistémologie historique)* which could include all aspects and dimensions of reason and its products and in which relations between religious, philosophical and scientific reason could be examined. They also prefer simply to ignore even the mere suggestion of cooperation with a reflective researcher since he or she is dismissed as speculative and unable to respect particular evidence (which does, unfortunately, often happen) rather than as a rigorous academic committed to the establishment of facts. A necessary correction to this narrow perspective would mean moving toward the use of historical psychology, historical sociology and historical anthropology for vast territories of the past, long ignored by the historian interested in narration, description and taxonomy. The recently published work of

J. van Ess *(Theologie und Gesellschaft)* shows all the richness of which we have been deprived and points to what will potentially escape into the future.

As a rather marginal academic discipline, the history of religions is looked at askance by both theological authorities, guardians of orthodoxy, and by secular states which propagate a political "neutrality" yet to be adequately examined philosophically and anthropologically. Furthermore, this field remains uncertain of its precise scope since it spills into many other disciplines. The same uncertainty applies to its intended objects of study which largely involve the invisible, the untouchable, the unnamable, the supernatural, the miraculous, the mysterious, the sacred, the holy, hope, love, violence and so on, as well as its instruments, analytical framework and inevitable relation to other disciplines, themselves groping their way forward in the dark. There is another rarely mentioned fact about the history of religions: Specialists writing for their colleagues are fully aware of the academic constraints by which they will be judged and admitted to the profession or excluded from it, no less differently than theologians who must practice self-censorship in order to obtain the *imprimatur* of doctrinal authorities. In any case, the populace at large, long confined to the discourse of oral culture, does not appear in scholarly writing, although they are the most directly concerned addressee of this research and form by far the largest and most convinced bloc of consumers of systems of belief and non-belief which science has submitted to its examination. Medieval élites *(khāṣṣa)* already taught openly that the masses *(ʿawāmm)* should be kept away from scholarly debates. Today it is left to the scorned popularizers of knowledge to transmit to a large audience bits and pieces of a highly specialized science. The distinctive feature of religion, however, is that it is a source of inspiration, hope and legitimatization for all and first of all for those who have not received instruction in critical thought. In the case of the contemporary Muslim world, this observation bears considerably on qurʾānic studies.

Reading the Qurʾān today

As far as what is commonly called the Qurʾān is concerned, it must be said that this term has become so heavily laden by theological inquiry and the practical goals of secular approaches that it must be subjected to a preliminary deconstruction in order to make manifest levels of function and significance that have been sidestepped, suppressed or forgotten by pious tradition as well as by text-oriented philology. As is well-known, this situation has a long history, extending from the moment the Qurʾān was written down through its centuries of propagation in manuscript form until its modern-day dissemination in print, an historical process which has encouraged the rise of the clerical class to political and intellectual power. The present conceptual burden of the term Qurʾān is at odds with the social and cultural conditions prevailing at the time of the emergence and growth of that which the initial qurʾānic discourse calls *Qurʾān,* the celestial Text (*al-Kitāb,* see BOOK), recited as a faith event, aloud and before an audience. This annunciation can be called prophetic discourse and establishes an arena of communication between three grammatical persons: a speaker who articulates the discourse contained in the celestial Text; a first addressee, who transmits the message of annunciation as a faith event; and a second addressee, the people *(al-nās),* who constitute the group, large or small according to the circumstances, whose members are nevertheless all equal and free in their status as addressee. They are equal because they share the same discourse situation, i.e.

access to the same oral language used in the annunciation of the message. They are free because they respond immediately by assent, understanding, rejection, refutation or the demand for further explanation. More will be said about the crucial importance of the psycho-socio-linguistic analysis of what will henceforth be called prophetic discourse. (Justification will be given for the use of this qualification of "prophetic," which, historically, is strongly contested by the first addressee, after the adage that "no one is a prophet in his own country.") It must be remembered that all orientalist scholarship, in limiting itself to the curiosities of the task of a philological restoration of the text (grammar, morphology, lexicography, syntax) along with an historical reconstruction of the simple facts, has ignored the concepts of the structure of relations between persons (Benvéniste), of the discourse situation as conditioned by its context (as described by P. Zumptor for medieval literature by use of the term *orature* after the French *écriture,* "writing"), and of the dialectic between the powerful and the weak *(dialectique des puissances et des résidus)*. This last-mentioned encompasses the interaction between *orature* and *écriture,* knowledge of the structure of myth and critical historical knowledge, in other words the functional solidarity among 1) the centralizing program of state education, 2) *écriture,* 3) the scholarly milieu and the clerics who produce and manage it, and 4) orthodoxy. Thus, four dynamic socio-historical forces can be seen to be dialectically related to four other forces in the social arena which appear universally, as in Mecca (q.v.) and Medina (q.v.) at the time of the emergence of the qur'ānic event *(fait coranique)* no less than in the social milieu of the contemporary nation-state: 1) segmented society which defies uniformity, 2) *orature,* 3) culture which is called popular and disintegrates into populist culture in the contemporary megalopolis, and 4) heterodoxies. This interconnected conceptual framework allows an integration of all levels at which qur'ānic discourse functions — linguistic, social, anthropological, along with all historical periods — into the project of analysis and interpretation. This is demonstrated in a reading of Q 9, Sūrat al-Tawba (Arkoun).

One can still be grateful, in fairness to orientalist scholarship, for the efforts and achievements of such pioneers as J. Wellhausen, H. Grimme, T. Nöldeke, F. Schwally, G. Bergsträsser, O. Pretzl, I. Goldziher, T. Andrae, A. Guillaume, A. Jeffery, M. Bravmann, whose work has been continued by R. Paret, R. Blachère, H. Birkeland, R. Bell, W.M. Watt, J. Burton, J. Wansbrough, A.T. Welch, U. Rubin and so on. It should also be noted that for an area of studies which is so rich and vital, the names of those who really matter in this past century are quite few, as can be seen in bibliographies. The current generation seems promising, but the number and isolation of the researchers remain the same, along with the meager size of the projects and the less than considerable importance of the publications. Two additional remarks can elaborate these assessments:

(1) The question of an epistemological perspective — reductionist, scientist, positivist — that goes so far as to support, openly and aggressively, an atheism that does not acknowledge itself to be merely one simple doctrinal option, must be examined, especially where it concerns comparative history and the anthropological analysis of religion. This problem has to be addressed repeatedly and discussed in relation to every scholarly production concerning the religious event. (2) A scholar such as J. Van Ess, whose contribution to Islamic studies is exceptionally rich, represents another perspective, belonging to that

school which undertakes to censor itself, constantly and strictly, when it comes to the arena of faith, going so far as to respect the expression of this faith which proclaims itself to be orthodox by virtue of the sole fact of its sociological influence and political dominance. Against both perspectives, it must be emphasized that the deconstruction of every form of orthodoxy falsely rendered sacred by historical figures who happened to succeed politically is one of the most essential critical tasks for the social sciences. Within this context the following quotes from J. van Ess prove instructive: "I could have brought examples from the Muʿtazila (see MUʿTAZILĪS), but since they were considered to be heretics by the majority of Sunni Muslims afterward, I would have to reckon with the objection that they were ultimately not representative for Islam... He [i.e. Bishr al-Marīsī] is an interesting man, but, as in the case of the Muʿtazilites, I do not want to put the Islamic view of history upside down. This would be something for the Muslims themselves to do" (in Verbal inspiration? Language and revelation in classical Islamic theology, a lecture given on November 21, 1994 at the plenary session of the annual conference of the Middle Eastern Studies Association (MESA) and published in Wild, *Text,* 180-1). He adds, "As an historian and non-Muslim, I should not ask who was right, and who was wrong.... Indeed, whoever believed the recitation to be uncreated committed a sacrifice of intellect" (184-5). This is not the place to comment further on these two citations from the perspective of the necessary epistemological commitments of reason in the domain of religious studies in general and that of Islamic studies in particular. The possibility of securing such commitments and the way of defining this territory will be clarified in the remainder of this essay.

From the vantage point of a kind of research which is always accompanied by a critical return to procedures, a process of cutting and pasting, theoretical constructions, explanations and meaningful results, it can be concluded that the Qurʾān is only one among a number of events that have the same level of complexity and the same abundance of meanings. Others would be the Bible, the Gospels and founding texts of Buddhism and Hinduism, all of which have already known and may in the future know still more historical growth. It is necessary to ask what would finally serve to distinguish the religious corpus just mentioned from the vast Platonic and Aristotelian corpus with all its different forms in Islamic and later European contexts or from the corpus of the French Revolution or that of the October Revolution of 1917 (cf. the works of F. Furet). It is nevertheless clear that the invocation of a religious dimension, which can act, as a corrective, to remind us of the dangers of reductionist readings and the scholarship of cutting and pasting, ought not lead to any concession to dogmatic definitions as advanced by believers in the name of their sacred writings (which in fact are sacralized and sacralizing). The constructions of faith which aim to build and manage the heritage of symbols possessed by every community will be considered cultural manifestations and defining premises in the type of history produced with the attitude of the believer. There should be no question of screening these constructions of faith from historical research or from a critical assessment of the arguments of the authors who have defended them, the historical actors who have promoted them and the managers of orthodoxy who have perpetuated their point of view in scholastic traditions marked more or less by a dogmatic spirit. Belief is in itself a domain of human reality which has been either ignored or insufficiently integrated into larger undertakings of historical and philological research. Historical psychology, the discipline which ought to treat this subject, has only begun its first steps of exploration. Is it appropriate to fragment, under the pretext of inevitable specialization, this contiguous and indivisible domain which prophetic discourse has wrought and which believers perceive and express daily?

By way of concluding these introductory remarks, it will be helpful to ask whether scholarly experience as amassed by orientalist scholarship enables us to pass to a new phase of qurʾānic studies. What would then be the epistemological orientations, the methodological choices and the appropriate programs of this new stage? Such new fields of scholarly investigation of the qurʾānic event must obviously meet two requirements: (1) Many more Muslim reflective researchers should be urged to participate, by increasing the possibilities and places for the exchange and confrontation of thoughts, in order to make progress in what is bound to be a long-term enterprise with the ultimate goal, indeed, of comprehensive thinking and knowing *(la noèse et la gnoséologie);* (2) Room should be given to previous and contemporary scholarship of Muslim believers. But which scholarship? What positive knowledge, independent of theological requirements, can be derived from it? Will it be possible, from this heterogeneous but undivided reality that is the Qurʾān, the revealed word of God, to separate data that can be declared objective from the psychological burdens and the content of faith which believers attach to the Qurʾān in their daily use and which are still experienced as correct? Is it necessary to classify all Muslim (or Christian or Jewish...) discourse as prior or alien to the modern disposition towards reason, as merely documentation for psychological and historico-sociological inquiry? This would lead to the placement of a scientific goal, entirely artificial, next to the exuberant and effervescent production of history by the strong dialectical exchange between human faith (itself the fruit of the interaction between the social imagination, the imagined, reason and memory) and the forces of upheaval in what can be only partially expressed by our concepts of speech, discourse, text, Qurʾān, revealed word and so on.

I will attempt to answer these questions under the following subtitles: (1) Priorities and limits of historical-anthropological interpretation; (2) Linguistic, semiotic and literary interpretation; (3) Religious interpretation, (4) Final proposals.

Priorities and limits of historical-anthropological interpretation

The short list, given above, of pioneering researchers in the field of qurʾānic studies includes only orientalists. The choice to exclude Muslim authors is, in itself, enough to disqualify this study in the eyes of orthodox believers (by which is not meant Muslims in general since this generic name includes practising believers as well as the many individuals who make claims upon a culture, a sensitivity, a spirituality, in other words an Islamic ethos without confining their thought to the dogmatic enclosure of a single orthodoxy). Mention will be made of Islamic contribution to qurʾānic studies in the third part, though it is fitting to state here that no arbitrary boundary has been drawn. The epistemological criterion used here is open to debate provided that the essential distinction between the disposition of belief and that of critical reason be respected. While no claim can be made for the superiority of one over the other, there are important differences separating the two states of cognition in terms of function, choice, aims, interests and results. Furthermore, the confrontation between these two attitudes and their respective products is necessary for a fuller awareness of the dimensions of cognition.

The criterion is as follows: The Qurʾān as an object of research is a collection of initially oral utterances put into writing in historical conditions not yet elucidated. These utterances were then elevated, by the industry of generations of historical figures, to the status of a sacred book which preserves the transcendant word of God and serves as ultimate and inevitable point of reference for every act, every form of behavior and every thought of the faithful, who themselves are to be considered as communally interpreting this heritage. In this framework of study, a number of operative concepts and problems exist and still await a sufficiently objective, well-considered and inclusive elucidation so as to appeal not only to the community of reflective researchers but also to those believers who consider themselves practising and orthodox Muslims. This is a crucial point if one wants to overcome the arrogance of scientific reason which provides believers with no opportunity to speak and which interprets, cuts and pastes, categorizes and judges without actually elucidating the mechanisms, the omnipresence, the results and significance of belief for every human person. The task of the reflective researcher is to include in his or her field of investigation and analysis all that is said, experienced, constructed and emerges inside the dogmatic enclosure. To refuse today to enter these laboratories, so full of liveliness and significant events, which have become the societies remade by so-called religious revolutions, would deprive the social sciences of essential data to renew their theoretical positions and strategies of intervention.

It will be seen later how the fact and products of belief can be integrated into such scholarship while also submitting it to critical analysis of the most fruitful kind. In a spirit of equity, it is necessary to mention something of the still relevant achievements of orientalist scholarship. In *Lectures du Coran,* this author has presented three comparative tables which clarify the relations and differences between the Muslim approach as synthesized by al-Suyūṭī in his *Itqān fī ʿulūm al-Qurʾān,* the orientalist approach as summarized and followed by A.T. Welch *(Ḳurʾān)* and the approach, still in the process of elaboration, of the social sciences which are themselves subject to the ever evasive challenges of a comparative history of religions, conceived and written as an "anthropology of the past" and an "archaeology of daily life" (G. Duby, J. Le Goff, A. Dupront). Although not without problems, the theoretical project proposed by this last category of approach ought not to be too hastily reduced. For example, the synchronic linguistic exploration of qurʾānic discourse, combined with an anthropological analysis, has recently been used in an excellent monograph to be discussed later (Chabbi, *Le seigneur*). This third approach is made possible by the progress of the social sciences and by the accumulative achievements of orientalist scholarship.

The taboo that orthodoxy has always laid on qurʾānic studies was more easily lifted during the period of historical-philological positivism than it is today because the euphoria of positivist reasoning was boosted by colonial rule. Hence, the battle for a critical edition of the text of the Qurʾān, including most notably a chronological ranking of the sūras (see CHRONOLOGY AND THE QURʾĀN), is not as persistent as it was in the period between T. Nöldeke and R. Blachère. All the same, this initiative has lost nothing of its scientific relevance since it implies a more reliable historical reading less dependent on suppositions, hypotheses and the quest for the plausible. (Despite the trust she puts in her methods,

J. Chabbi cannot avoid writing in the conditional mood). Unless more incontrovertible manuscripts related to the history of the text are found, which is still possible, it seems better to draw the conclusion that an irreversible situation has been created by the systematic destruction of precious documents or by the lack of interest of people today in all that has become essential for modern historical knowledge.

This field of research does not seem to have broadened its horizons or inquiries, if one is to judge by three collections of articles bearing carefully chosen signatures: *Approaches to the history of the interpretation of the Qur'ān,* ed. Andrew Rippin, *Approaches to the Qur'ān,* ed. G.R. Hawting and Abdul-Kader A. Shareef, and *The Qur'ān as text,* already cited above, the title of which does not fulfill its promises, as its editor, S. Wild, has admitted. The articles in each volume seem to be limited to verifying the continuity of historicist problematics, philological procedures and peripheral curiosities. This syndrome, clarified by J. van Ess, is apparent in the work of the researchers who contribute to these collections, each of whom considers him or herself to be an expert in a well-defined domain but who is never a reflective researcher vis-à-vis an object of knowledge that demands precise intervention on all levels and manners of production and propagation of meaning and assumptions of meaning. This critique can be addressed to those involved in the collections under examination as well as to other interpretations, including those which circulate among the community interpreting its heritage *(la communauté interprétante)*.

The problem must be reiterated: We are dealing with a corpus of which the primary constitutive function of its linguistic articulation is to express the true meaning of human existence — the objective, ideal, intangible, insurmountable norms which have to be strictly observed to keep this existence in line with its true meaning. We are also dealing with secondary corpuses derived from the first, of which the linguistic articulation has, in its long history, functioned in a similar fashion (the *yaqūlu llāhu* of the exegetes and of current discourse or *jā'a fī l-ḥadīth*) to perpetuate, throughout the long course of history, the illusion of a lived continuity between the revealed norms and meanings and the accumulated interpretations and plans used by the living tradition of the community of believers. We are thus dealing with such an existential structure as translated into multiple, developing existential realities. Is the researcher permittted to sever systematically knowledge of marginal facts from the critique of prophetic discourse as a discourse of existentiation (the Arabic term, *ījād,* renders the causative function more explicit) which gives shape, content and orientation to the actual existence of the believers. This is the problem toward which the reflective researcher directs his or her sights, in reaction against the dominance of scholastic reason which imposes its manner of cutting and pasting the heritage, not on the basis of an intellectual authority — which would create a debt of meaning in its regard, but by the mechanisms of academic power which are intertwined with and dependent on the political philosophy of modern states, just as the clerics who create and guard religious orthodoxies, were enmeshed with these state powers before the secular revolution.

The concepts introduced here as well as those used previously are likely to alienate quite a number of readers or even researchers not familiar with the discourse used in the social sciences and in a Christian theology attentive to the challenges of the modern criticism of religious thought. Doubtlessly in deference to these pioneering theologians, J. van Ess leaves to

Muslims the responsibility of accomplishing the same theological tasks. There remains, however, an objection to this reticence on the epistemological and gnoseological level: The advances of critical thought, as brought to light by the example of their application to the Qurʾān, will certainly benefit from the conceptualization of thought and thinking as a general effort of the human spirit that can push back against the limits encountered by reductive critical analysis. In any event, it is important to recall the distinct absence of a prospective conceptual framework in the most recent and best informed writings on the Qurʾān and the Islamic tradition.

It is appropriate to say something now about J. Chabbi's contribution before analyzing it more fully later on. In brief, it is a welcome example of historical analysis of the Qurʾān which illustrates the possibility of crossing an epistemic and epistemological threshold in the progress towards the desired disposition of the reflective researcher. The author traces the insurmountable boundary between the normative code of the professional historian and the domain of the thought and knowledge of the believer, while still incorporating this methodologically separate domain into the field of historical inquiry. The result is real progress, not only in historical writing as such, but first and foremost in the elucidation of the linguistic and historical processes which generated this belief. The author works with a recognition that this belief has become the inexhaustible source and ever powerful force of all the combined efforts and mental projections for understanding an inaugural moment *(moment inaugurateur)* and its mythological, ideological, semantic and semiotic ramification and enlargement, as well as its intellectual, institutional and artistic creations which continue and become increasingly complex. By using anthropological categories such as myth and social imagination, the historian can, from the same critical analytic perspective, gather the diverse transformative dialectics reflected in the Meccan utterances of the Qurʾān, carefully restore them to their context, thus liberating them from the overly determined sense which subsequent religious readings have projected onto them. As such, one can retrace the inchoate manifestations of a supra-tribal rationality and the formation of a nascent conceptual framework, as expressed in the linguistic usage, belief and the account of the foundation of the defined social group *(nās, ʿashīra, qawm)* that was meant to be the addressee. One can see how this addressee gradually became the dialectical protagonist and the involuntary agent of an historical transformation which had been fought, refused and denied in Mecca before imposing itself in Medina through a doubly armed prophet who added the weapon of revelatory speech to that of military arms. The religious interpretation of these events, which historians and anthropologists seek to reconstruct by archaeological investigation, was later transformed into a conglomerate of actors in a vast and long-lasting foundation story — opponents in Mecca, helpers in Medina (the *kāfirūn, munāfiqūn,* vs. the *muʾminūn, muhājirūn* and *anṣār* of orthodox terminology; see OPPOSITION TO MUḤAMMAD; EMIGRANTS AND HELPERS; HYPOCRITES AND HYPOCRISY) — which also requires the same kind of archaeological investigation to distinguish between historical and sociological reality and the subsequent mythical enlargment of the religious imagination.

It is now becoming possible to see how one might step out of the scientist rigidity of the historical critical method which, since the nineteenth century, has imposed its judgments, chronological and thematic categories, divisions of reality and objects of study, etymologism and quest for origins and relations of ideas and accounts onto highly charged and creative contexts (e.g. the reduction of the Qurʾān to biblical and Hebraic sources to the detriment of its literary and spiritual creativity which transforms language and thought dynamically under the twofold horizon of fundamentally utopian thoughts and concrete action meant to actualize these thoughts in history). Yet J. Chabbi is not entirely successful in escaping all of these shortcomings despite the fact that she criticizes them sharply. For example, she was unsuccessful in clarifying the anthroplogical problems, like the tribal and political organization often used as key references for her impressionist interpretations, but not analyzed on the level required by her ambitious theorizations. Even in this enhanced scholarly environment, the philological concern is still unavoidable, but it can now be enriched by the contribution of linguistics so as to give place to the distinctive characteristics of the oral announcement *(l'énonciation orale)* in relation to written accounts *(énoncés écrits)* and to replace etymologism by the reconstruction of semantic fields and networks of language connotation. This is done through patient microanalysis which combines archaeological excavation (see ARCHAEOLOGY AND THE QURʾĀN) with vocabulary, ethno-linguistic inquiry and ecological, sociological, cultural and political recontextualization. All this must be attained by using sources known for their precariousness and insufficiency as well as disguise, selection, transfiguration, sublimation, transcendentalization, essentialization, sacralization, mythologization and, now today, gross ideologization. This is not the place to specify the significance for the historical method of this set of concepts, intentionally grouped together, which are often used to mark the substitution of a principle of interpretation which is careful to employ social dialectics and their effects on the relation between language and thought with a principle at once rigid, ignorant of these dialectics and with the tendency to turn developing ideas, contingent representations, the assumptions of truth, precarious power relations and functional or arbitrary categories into eternal essences, intangible substances, ontological and transcendent truths, and ethical and juridical norms immune to every human intervention.

The principle of interpretation for the qurʾānic text should be equally applied to all sources with the same set of requirements: the ḥadīth collections, the works of exegesis, the biographical literature, the expanding biblical-qurʾānic imagination in mystical experience, the *Isrāʾīliyyāt,* the lives of the prophets, the integration myths of symbolic founding figures, like Abraham (q.v.) in the pantheon and Arab rituals associated with the Kaʿba (q.v.). These rich sources can be reviewed and reinvested in an archaeological excavation, now writ large, where there is no question of quarreling over the sources or debating their authenticity and the truth of positive facts liberated from the superstitions of the straightjacket of legends, popular stories and the ramblings of a pious imagination. This is what historicism has long done, reinforced by dialectic materialism at a time when Marxist rhetoric made its prejudice of rationality prevail in all domains of knowledge. The great classical commentators are no longer consulted — as many orientalists have done and still continue to do — as reliable authorities in clearing up the semantic contents of qurʾānic vocabulary. All commentaries are treated as corpuses which must be read within the changing contexts of their production, reception and reproduction.

It will be useful to elaborate on Chabbi's monograph since it furnishes a relatively convincing illustration of both the methodological priority and the limits of the historical-anthropological approach applied to a corpus which lays the foundation of a religion. The limits are those which the historian imposes on himself in deciding when the work of scrutinizing and exploiting the documents is finished. One can see clearly that, regarding the question of contemporary critical practices and the Qurʾān, the historian is here caught within an extreme tension between two different attitudes of the human spirit: that of limiting knowledge to theoretical and practical pieces of information artificially constructed by scholarly disciplines or that of recognizing the reliable and potentially universal teaching of these disciplines while also creating space for a policy of hope, a concept that enables the integration of theological developments about the history of salvation, the quest for salvation and eschatological hope into historical psychology and religious sociology.

To clarify: If the present resources of historical inquiry are willing to concede, in accordance with a scientifically acceptable manner, that the Qurʾān, when viewed in the ecological, ethno-linguistic, sociological and political theater of tribal life (see TRIBES AND CLANS) in Mecca and Medina at the beginning of the seventh century C.E., cannot but change its cognitive status, a whole new field of work will be possible. This raises the question of whether a historian can do justice to two clearly different realms of cognition: 1) that of a Meccan Qurʾān restored to its concrete historical and linguistic reality as distinct from the Medinan corpus as well as from the universal corpus later imposed under the name of *muṣḥaf* (q.v.), and 2) that of this *muṣḥaf* which would be more aptly named the Closed Official Corpus (see COLLECTION OF THE QURʾĀN; CODICES OF THE QURʾĀN). It is this later corpus that the interpreting community has accepted and will continue to accept for the foreseeable future as a *tanzīl,* a revealed given *(donné révélé)* that abolishes — in interpretation and in experience, i.e. in the course of history — the status of the corpus as unveiled by historians.

One cannot dodge this question by saying that this later corpus is the concern of believers because it is the historian who uncovers the new status of belief to the extent that his or her achievements as a historian are recognized to be intellectually compelling. A first answer would consist in widening the same inquiry with the same deconstructive procedure to the entire history of societies in which this revealed given has been received, interpreted and translated into ethical, juridical, political, semantic, esthetic and spiritual codes. This author has proposed the concept of societies of the book-Book *(sociétés du Livre-livre),* including the Jewish and Christian examples, in order to integrate the revealed given into the productive forces of the history of these societies before it was disqualified, marginalized and even eliminated by scientific and political revolutions. It is possible that the historian's refusal — by leaving to the theologian and the philosopher a task lying within the scope of the historian's responsibility — to enlarge the working domain reflects a philosophical commitment to the *fait accompli* of the eighteenth century political revolutions in Europe and America. This would explain the difficulties of dialogue between historians, anthropologists, theologians and philosophers on these delicate subjects. This author has shown, with the example of the work of C. Cahen, that historians have until now not assumed the responsibilities that ensue from a historical-anthropological reading of the Meccan and Medinan Qurʾān (Arkoun, Transgresser, déplacer, dépasser, in *Arabica* 1996.1).

One should not forget that these battles

and debates take place within the historical trajectory of European thought as it has developed since the sixteenth century, i.e. with the first challenges to the medieval heritage by the Reformation and Renaissance. Within the Islamic context, these questions are still suppressed and considered unimagineable. One can see the disarray in the human spirit wherever there is a failure in the indispensable work, assigned to philosophy and anthropology, of taking charge of the domains of thought left in ruins by the social sciences which limit themselves to working on divided fragments of an undivided reality.

Linguistic, semiotic and literary interpretation

These approaches have produced far less foundational or innovative work than the historical approaches. Semiotics was in fashion in France between 1960 and 1980 with the support of A.J. Greimas and a number of his disciples. A relatively small number of doctoral theses on the Qurʾān have appeared in France during that period, but it has not been possible to publish any of them in contrast with studies on the Bible and the Gospels that have abounded and been published. Linguistic approaches to the Qurʾān, especially in the domain of discourse criticism, are not well represented either, despite the fact that studies of Arabic linguistic history have flourished especially during the last twenty years. One can see this paucity as clear proof of an intellectual timidity, itself nourished by the researcher's 'prudent' reluctance to study the Muslim sacred text. At the Sorbonne, many have preferred to renounce subjects which had aroused their intellectual curiosity but which also aroused their fears of rejection in their countries of origin. Among the few exceptions is C. Gilliot who has been willing to work on the common Islamic imagination as found in al-Ṭabarī's (d. 310/923) commentary, although limiting himself to the classical scholarly track in which he continues to make substantial contributions.

As for the literary approach, there is nothing in qurʾānic studies equivalent to N. Frye *(The great code)*, not to mention the abundant research which has enriched and renewed biblical studies. I have personally planned to treat the use of the metaphor in the Qurʾān in order to correct an intolerable shortcoming, one that has lasted since the medieval battles over accepting or totally rejecting the metaphorical dimension in the interpretation of God's word. A book by Ibn Qayyim al-Jawziyya (d. 751/1350), bearing the eloquent title, "Thunder Bolts Sent in Refutation of the Sectarian al-Jahmiyya and al-Muʿaṭṭila" *(al-Ṣawāʿiq al-mursala fī l-radd ʿalā al-Jahmiyya wa-l-Muʿaṭṭila)*, clearly sets out the stakes in the debate over the theology of revelation. I have not abandoned this rich project; but the terrain left to be cleared is immense and the few works available on this subject are largely irrelevant. Muslims are themselves scandalised at hearing of this shortcoming and refer with pride to al-Bāqillānī (d. 403/1013), al-Jurjānī (d. 471/1078), Fakhr al-Dīn al-Rāzī (d. 606/1210), al-Sakkākī (d. 629/1231) and to the immense *iʿjāz* literature of which the apologetic dimension still weighs heavily on contemporary works (e.g. Muṣṭafā Ṣādiq al-Rāfiʿī, Sayyid Quṭb, Muḥammad Shaḥrūr). These fail, however, to mention the current hostility to metaphor and the fact that the doctrine of the created Qurʾān (see CREATEDNESS OF THE QURʾĀN) has prevailed since the fourteenth century. For this reason, it is the literary approaches which triumph today. Studies of Arabic rhetoric and literary criticism are quick to scrutinize the positive and negative consequences of the influence exerted by theological tenets on linguistic, semiotic and literary approaches to the sacred text. Among the positive results is the possibility of enjoying, at one and the same time and with the profound attention of an undivided conscience, the spiritual emotion, ethical beauty and pleasure of the text, whether read or recited. It is one of the distinctive characteristics of prophetic discourse to bring together these three values — the true, the good and the beautiful — in order to draw the human subject more surely to the salvific utopia. This is exactly what Greek literature did before the intervention and victory of Aristotelian logocentrism. Additionally, there remains the simple fact that the foundational texts of religions never lose their initial status as oral announcement. Thus do the faithful identify with them through liturgical recitation, ritual conduct and quotations in current conversation (Graham, *Beyond;* see RECITATION OF THE QURʾĀN; RITUAL AND THE QURʾĀN; EVERYDAY LIFE, THE QURʾĀN IN).

It is therefore important to consider the possibilities of literary criticism itself lest religious discourse monopolize the methods and issues found in modern works. For example, beyond prophetic discourse, what status should be assigned to the immense corpus left by a figure like Ibn al-ʿArabī (d. 638/1240)? Religious and literary qualifications alone do not allow for an account of the exceptional richness and dimensions of such a written text, one for which the exact status has yet to be defined.

How to take up these scientific challenges? It is not enough to denounce the shortcomings of apology and the repression of innovation by the guardians of orthodoxy. To take one case, Naṣr Ḥāmid Abū Zayd, the first Muslim scholar to face the Arabic world directly by writing in Arabic while teaching at Cairo University, tried to break the many taboos which prohibit the application of the most relevant achievements of contemporary linguistics to the Qurʾān. Before him, Muḥammad Khalafallāh tried to apply literary criticism to narrative in the Qurʾān, and in spite of its modest scientific span, his essay caused a major upheaval. The works of Abū Zayd contain nothing revolutionary if one places them within the scholarly production of the last twenty years, since they explain quite straightforwardly the conditions necessary for applying the rules of defining and analysing a text to the Qurʾān *(Mafhūm al-naṣṣ)*. Once more, the violent reaction to attempts intending only to popularize knowledge long since widely accepted, underlines the area in contemporary Islamic thought of what cannot be and has not been thought.

The religious interpretation

The concept of an interpreting community leads to a wide range of possibilities for the use of speech that has become text and of a text that was laid down in the Closed Official Corpus but which is still invoked and experienced as speech. The range runs the gamut from the most learned exegesis to daily liturgical recitation and the spontaneous quoting of the text in current conversation, in controversy or at joyful or somber events. Qurʾānic studies has been chiefly interested in scholarly exegetical readings that offer historical information, cultural insights or grammatical and lexical explanations which could enrich the understanding of the text as given in the Closed Official Corpus. Insufficient account has been taken of the cognitive status of the many other religious approaches to the text as these are interpreted by and for the community. There are two major reasons for this: Firstly, all approaches and all appropriations are confined within a dogmatic enclosure; secondly, the great commentaries which were given authorization over the historical development of the living tradition function as orthodox corpuses of interpretation.

Not only are believing Muslims imprisoned in this dogmatic enclosure, orientalist scholarship has also long contented itself with transferring to European languages the exegetical orthodoxy of the dominant Sunnī Islam before doing the same with Shīʿī Islam (and that at a time when political events enabled political scientists to dispute the supremacy of expertise claimed by scholars of Islam). Those, for example, who attempted to tackle the question of the authenticity of the prophetic tradition have instead used this material to prop up artificially constructed historical argumentation. In so doing, they are careful to protect their scholarly status with certain rhetorical techniques: "according to Muslim tradition," "according to Muslim faith," etc., and thus does the dogmatic enclosure remain untouched and free to operate without restraint.

The term "dogmatic enclosure" applies to the totality of the articles of faith, representations, tenets and themes which allow a system of belief and unbelief (q.v.) to operate freely without any competing action from inside or outside. A strategy of refusal, consisting of an arsenal of discursive constraints and procedures, permits the protection and, if necessary, the mobilization of what is presumptuously called faith (q.v.). It is well known how scrupulously the profession of faith (*ʿaqīda*, see CREEDS) is translated and described, but no green light has ever been given to a deconstruction of the axioms, tenets and themes that hold together and establish the adventurous cohesion of every faith. The point is not to demonstrate the scientific validity or the irrationality of the articles of faith but rather to trace their genealogy from Nietzsche's perspective of the criticism of values as well as their psychological functions and decisive role in the construction and formation of every human subject. All this is a matter for historical psychology with its curiosity and inquiry which has, as previously mentioned, not yet been integrated into historical-anthropological methodology. A realization of this direction of research is greatly to be desired and could proceed by exploring the shared Islamic imagination as represented in the great corpuses of interpretation such as those of al-Ṭabarī, Fakhr al-Dīn al-Rāzī, Muḥammad al-Ṭāhir Ben ʿAshūr (d. 1867), and Muḥammad Ḥusayn Ṭabāṭabāʾī (d. 1980) amongst others. As long as faith and spirituality are the object of simple narrative and descriptive accounts — be it with the agnostic's cold distance (in the style of H. Laoust) or with the warm and exhorting empathy of the believer (in the style of J. Jomier or Kenneth Cragg) — qurʾānic studies and, more generally, the comparative history of religions will be unable to achieve the exhaustiveness and relevance expected of them.

The religious interpretation as applied to foundational texts is also the place where creativity of meaning, assumptions of meaning, representations and mythological or ideological construction emerge and erupt in accordance with the cultural contexts of different social groups. This is equally true for medieval approaches now considerd sacred and treated as obligatory classical reference works as well as for contemporary approaches. The functional relation between the Closed Official Corpus (including the ḥadīth collections), promoted to the rank of primordial foundational text, and the corpuses of interpretation to which the Closed Official Corpus gives rise remains the same whether these be religious corpuses, as in the societies of the book-Book, or secular corpuses, or those of modern political revolutions. The latter two categories, however, benefit from historical clarity and from tools of analysis which exclude any possibility of resorting explicitly, as does the first category, to mystery, the supernatural, transcendence and the miraculous, where the operation of sacralization, mythification, sublimation, transfiguration, ontologization and even mystification rests. Still, the historian has to determine the various forms of reason used (grammatical, theological, juridical, historiographical or philosophical reason) as well as the kind of rationality, imagination and modes of intervention and creative imagination, recognizing their diversity in figures such as al-Ḥallāj (d. 309/922), al-Tawḥīdī (d. 414/1023), Ibn al-ʿArabī (d. 638/1240), Mullā Ṣadra Shīrāzī (d. 1050/1604), Sayyid Quṭb (d. 1966), etc.

It is now possible to see in what way the integration of religious interpretation into the enlarged domain of the historian can enrich historical knowledge while also restricting speculative criticism of religious reason that, as demonstrated here, is only a modality of the reason of belief. At the same time, it has been shown that the various kinds of interpretation discussed here lead to the same acknowledgment, namely that the progress of qurʾānic studies has depended on the orientalist scholarship of the nineteenth century. (The term scholarship is used to underscore the orientalists' refusal to commit epistemologically their accumulated knowledge to a criticism of religious reason that would include all known examples in the societies of the book-Book). The refusal of the historian, anthropologist, sociologist, psychologist, literary critic and semiotician to identify and answer the challenges of prophetic discourse and the logical universe it generates, will lead finally to the degeneration of these disciplines themselves. As for Muslim scholarship, it continues to inflict upon itself limitations, mutilations and prohibitions that only accentuate the dependency and backwardness of qurʾānic studies. What it has produced since the nineteenth century has more of a documentary interest for a history of religious psychology and the enlargement of the imagination of religious discourse, especially in the domain of politics, than any intellectual and scientific merit which could enrich our knowledge of the qurʾānic event and of the Islamic event and, beyond those, of the religious event in general. The recently published volume by Muḥammad Shaḥrūr, "The Book and the Qurʾān" *(al-Kitāb wa-l-Qurʾān),* has had a success that bears witness to both the intolerable pressure of dogmatic control on qurʾānic studies and the limits within which every discourse with hopes of innovation must be pursued.

Final proposals

The project of publishing an *Encyclopaedia of the Qurʾān* that is conceived and realized with respect for the critical order of rational processes is long overdue. This delay confirms this article's position on the historical and epistemological discrepancy between philosophic and scientific reason, as practiced today in the West and elsewhere, and Islamic reason as it asserts itself in its positions on Islam as well as in political action, legal codes, educational systems and behaviors which encourage the traditional. As long as the Islamic logical universe continues to function within the dogmatic enclosure of its historical form as received since the thirteenth and fourteenth centuries, there will be a place for a parallel Islamic encyclopedia of Islam and, all the more, an Islamic encylopedia of the Qurʾān. The *Encyclopaedia of the Qurʾān* constitutes a basis of data that will undoubtedly, like every work of scholarship, be subject to discussions, additions and revisions. It will, however, be impossible to ignore, particularly by people who pursue the cognitive project of understanding the religious event in a universal way.

To sustain this project within that perspective, it would be helpful to conclude with the following proposals: It is necessary to open up the qurʾānic fact by situating it in a comparative approach not only within the three monotheistic religions but also within a historical anthropology of the religious event in its geo-historical and geo-cultural ambiance that can, for the time being, be qualified as Mediterranean. The historical phase of what historians explore under the name of the Near East should always be kept in sight, although not in order to rediscover so-called origins or to reconstruct linear relations of ideas, representations, linguistic forms and rituals of expression. The aim should be to deepen our knowledge of constituent elements common to the monotheistic religious conscience in its global historical genesis and manner of differentiation. This should include attention to inaugural moments and new departures from cultural codes that engender logical universes, dogmatic enclosures, societies of the book-Book and communities of election who have been promised salvation in contrast to anonymous groups destined to stray and be damned. In brief, it is a matter of deepening our knowledge of all these historical formations that the ethnographic view imprisons in so-called identities and encloses in alleged regions, traditions and cultures.

The concept of the Closed Official Corpus provides a good example of the comparative approach that will enable Muslim readers of the *Encyclopaedia of the Qurʾān* to better assess the stakes in a scientific problematization of the orthodox vocabulary inherited from a theological theory of values resistant to every critical examination. The Jewish and Christian traditions have similarly had a before and an after to what has been called the *fait accompli* of the Closed Official Corpus. Christians today are willing to read the apocryphal writings left out by the church between the fourth and the sixteenth centuries (cf. their publication in the *Pléiade* series by F. Bovon and P. Geoltrain). The results have not functioned in the same way before and after the triumph of a Closed Official Corpus in each tradition: Scholarly research without the burden of dogma creates more favorable conditions for historical re-readings of the texts that have been selected as sacred and thus untouchable. One can therefore understand why the concept of a Closed Official Corpus is more effective for a comparative history of the religious event in its prophetic trajectory.

Two more gaps are left that must be mentioned: The theological and philosophical attitudes of reason in the so-called societies of the book-Book should be the object of the same comparative historical approach within the perspective of a critical historical epistemology. Tackling such a task requires constant vigilance, not only to check the use of all conceptual frameworks which have been protected from the critique of deconstructionism but also to introduce and refine more inclusive concepts which are more productive from the perspective of a critique of religious reason beginning with its formulation by Jews, Christians and Muslims.

In that which concerns the Qurʾān more directly, it is clear that what is called for here is a protocol of interpretation that is free from both the dogmatic orthodox framework and the procedural disciplines of modern scientism which is, it must be admitted, no less constraining. It is an interpretation which wanders, in which every human, Muslim or non-Muslim, gives free rein to his or her own dynamic of associating ideas and representations, beginning from the freely chosen interpretation of a corpus of which the often imputed disorder, so often denounced, favors the freedom to wander. This approach is able to extricate itself definitively from every kind of arbitrary rhetoric, artificial and allegedly logical reconstruction, and delusive coherence later imposed by juridical, theological, apologetic, ideological and fantastic interpretations. One potential model here is, of course, the creative freedom of the likes of Ibn al-ʿArabī; but now the desired freedom is more subversive since it would include all forms and experiences of subversion that were ever attempted by mystics, poets, thinkers and artists.

M. Arkoun

Bibliography

The titles included in the text demonstrate more attention to the publications of the human and social sciences than to the literature of Islamic studies which I do not neglect, but which I consider to be known by the readers of this encyclopaedia. It is impossible to give here an ample and fully annotated bibliography of qurʾānic studies from the perspectives herein formulated. It would be necessary to include in such a list publications in Islamic languages, notably Arabic, Persian and Turkish. The programme of which I have just given a too brief overview will be more clearly defined and duly illustrated in my forthcoming *Lecture de la sourate* 9. It will also be noted that I have not evoked the essential contribution of J. Wansbrough. Discussions on his revolutionary positions have recently been relaunched in a rather redundant and all too brief fashion (see H. Berg, *Islamic origins reconsidered*). Wansbrough's scientific intervention finds its place in the framework I propose. It gives priority to methods of literary criticism which, like the historical-anthropological reading, lead to questions left to other disciplines and a level of reflection unimagineable in the current fundamentalist context. Within this context I would like to specify references briefly indicated in the text or which seem to me essential to the production of new works free from all the constraints of outdated knowledge or from condescending attitudes towards beliefs arbitrarily sacralized.

Primary: M. Ben ʿAshūr, *Tafsīr al-taḥrīr wa-l-tanwīr,* vols. 1-30, Tunis 1984 (this commentary, as well as those published since the nineteenth century — e.g. those of Ṭabāṭabāʾī and Sayyid Quṭub — should be presented as contemporary, not modern if by modern is meant the critical-historical framework of analysis and interpretation. It is easy to show that all of them depend on the classical exegesis more than on the modern approaches to religion as proposed by the social sciences. A good example of this epistemological posture which I support is given in the two following titles by P. Gisel. See also my essay, From inter-religious dialogue to the recognition of the religious phenomenon); Ibn Qayyim al-Jawziyya, *al-Ṣawāʿiq al-mursala fī l-radd ʿalā al-Jahmiyya wa-l-Muʿaṭṭila,* Cairo 1380/1960-1; Quṭb, *Ẓilāl;* Suyūṭī, *Itqān;* M.Ḥ. Ṭabāṭabāʾī, *al-Mīzān fī tafsīr al-Qurʾān,* 20 vols., Beirut 1971².

Secondary: M. Arkoun, *Les sciences sociales au défi de "l'islam,"* Paris 1998³; id., *Lectures* (a third edition is in preparation under the title *Critical introduction to Qurʾānic studies*, part of a larger project presented since 1984 in the first edition of *Pour une critique de la raison islamique*. New additions to this project are presented in the following volumes: *Qaḍāyā fī naqd al-ʿaql al-dīnī. Kayfa nafham al-islām al-yawm,* Beirut 1998; *al-Fikr al-uṣūlī wa-istiḥālat al-taʾṣīl,* Beirut 1999; *The unthought in contemporary Islamic thought,* London 2000, forthcoming; *Combats pour l'humanisme en contextes islamiques,* Paris 2000, forthcoming; *Penser l'islam aujourd'hui,* Paris 2000; id., *Lecture de la sourate 9,* forthcoming; M. Ayoub, *The Qurʾān and its interpreters,* New York, vol. 1, 1984; vol. 2, 1992 (other volumes are in preparation; this work has the merit of presenting Sunnī and Shīʿī commentary in the same volume, since a comparative study of both lines would shed light on the basic episteme underlying the hermeneutic activity in Islamic thought and would help introduce the study of the shared Islamic imagination); Meir M. Bar-Asher, *Scripture and exegesis in early Imāmī Shīʿism,* Leiden 1999; H. Berg (ed.), *Islamic origins reconsidered,* special issue of *Method and theory in the study of religion,* 9.1 (1997); id., *The development of exegesis in early Islam,* Richmond/Surrey 2000; I. Boullata (ed.), *Literary structures of religious meaning in the Qurʾān,* Richmond/Surrey 2000; P. Bourdieu, *Méditations pascaliennes,* Paris 1997; F. Bowie, *The anthopology of religion,* Oxford 2000; J. Chabbi, *Le seigneur des tribus. L'Islam de Mahomet,* Paris 1997; J. van Ess, Verbal inspiration? Language and revelation in classical Islamic theology, in Wild, *Text,* 180-1; id., *TG;* N. Frye, *The great code. The Bible and literature,* New York 1982; P. Gisel, *La théologie face aux sciences religieuses,* Geneva 1999; id. and P. Evrard (eds.), *La théologie en postmodernité,* Geneva 1996; Graham, *Beyond;* G.R. Hawting, *The idea of idolatry and the emergence of Islam. From polemic to history,* Cambridge 1999; id. and Shareef (eds.), *Approaches;* M. Lecker, *Muslims, Jews and pagans. Studies on early Islamic Medina,* Leiden, 1995 (an excellent monograph making the step towards a critical biography of the prophet Muḥammad in line with the methodology of the recent book of J. Le Goff, *Saint Louis,* Paris 1995); J.F. Lyotard, *L'enthousiasme. La critique kantienne de l'histoire,* Paris 1986; G. Makdisi, *Ibn ʿAqīl. Religion and culture in classical Islam,* Edinburgh 1997; Rippin, *Approaches;* id. (ed.), *The Qurʾān. Formative interpretation,* Brookfield (Vermont) 1999; N. Robinson, *Discovering the Qurʾān. A contemporary approach to a veiled text,* London 1996; G. Salame, *Des démocraties sans démocrates,* Paris 1994; M. Sharūr, *al-Kitāb wa-l-Qurʾān,* Damascus 1990; Wansbrough, *QS;* C. Versteegh, *Arabic grammar and qurʾānic exegesis in early Islam;* A.T. Welch, *al-Ḳurʾān,* in *EI²,* v, 400-29; Wild, *Text.*

Contracts and Alliances

Contract, a unilateral or bilateral agreement or promise to do or not to do a thing or a set of things; alliance, a relationship of solidarity and support to preserve and further the common interests of those participating in the relationship.

The concepts of a strictly legal contract or political alliance are not well articulated in the Qurʾān. That of a contract *(ʿaqd)* in the sense of a covenant (*ʿahd,* see COVENANT) between God and man does, however, appear frequently. The word *ʿahd* seems at times to be a virtual synonym of *ʿaqd* although the latter connotes more than the former a sense of bilateralism (Q 17:34). The use of *ʿahd* in the Qurʾān varies. In some passages it connotes a self-initiated commitment (as in Q 16:91) while in others it expresses a commitment of man toward God but a commitment imposed by God and accepted by man (as in Q 48:10). The commentators disagree as to the meaning of *ʿahd,* some arguing that it is God's commandment (see COMMANDMENTS) to his creation (q.v.) to live by the laws he revealed to them through his prophets and books (see BOOK; PROPHETS AND PROPHETHOOD). Failing to live by the law constitutes a breach of this commandment.

Other commentators advance a more limited definition of the term. The scope of *ʿahd,* they maintain, is confined to the People of the Book (q.v.). They breached it by rejecting Muḥammad and his message after having agreed to follow him once he appeared. According to a third group of commentators, apparently spearheaded by al-Zamakhsharī (d. 538/1144), *ʿahd* is the proof (q.v.) or set of proofs in favor of monotheism, proofs which God had implanted in the minds of disbelievers in the form of a commitment on their part, a commandment by which they should live.

In the majority of instances, the term *ʿahd* is used with a negative tenor, in the sense of breaching the commitment to God, a commitment of a binding nature that was also signified by the term *mīthāq* (Q 2:63; 4:90; see CHILDREN OF ISRAEL). The preservation or abandonment of the *ʿahd* demarcates the boundaries between belief and heresy, between believer *(muʾmin)* and disbeliever (*kāfir, fāsiq,* cf. Q 2:27-8, 100; 7:102; 33:23; see BELIEF AND UNBELIEF). The term also occurs in the sense of an alliance or a treaty between Muḥammad and one group or another of his contemporaries, such as the Meccan polytheists (see POLYTHEISM AND ATHEISM) and the People of the Book. Q 9:1 declares: "Freedom of obligation is proclaimed from God and his Messenger toward those of the idolaters with whom you made an alliance (or treaty)" (see also Q 9:7; 8:56; see IDOLATRY AND IDOLATERS). In other instances, *ʿahd* signifies personal commitment, such as in Q 17:34, "Come not near the wealth of the orphan (see ORPHANS) save with that which is better till he come to strength; and keep the commitment *(ʿahd)* for to the commitment [is attached] a responsibility."

The notion of alliance is preeminently expressed by the derivatives of the root *w-l-y*, especially the noun *walī* which appears in the Qurʾān over 85 times. It seems that in pre-Islamic Arabia, *walāʾ* (also known as *ḥilf*) represented a relationship of mutual support between two tribes or between particular individuals belonging to two tribes (see TRIBES AND CLANS; PRE-ISLAMIC ARABIA AND THE QURʾĀN). It also represented the admission of individuals into a clan or a tribe through an agreement with one of its members or with the tribe as a collectivity. The strength of such a relationship is reflected in the fact that once *walāʾ* is concluded the individuals on both sides would acquire equal rights, would inherit from each other and would be bound by the same set of obligations. From this perspective then *walāʾ* creates relationships that are equal in force to blood relationships (see KINSHIP; CLIENTS AND CLIENTAGE). But the term *walī* may designate a variety of relationships that include a more basic form of loyalty and support, relationships whose precise nature is not entirely clear. It is fair to say, however, that the relationship of *walāʾ* is nearly always understood to entail support. In numerous qurʾānic verses, the term *walī* appears conjoined with the word *naṣīr,* an ally, supporter or one aiding in achieving victory (Q 4:45, 75, 89, 123, 173; 33:17, 65).

A term that does not appear in the Qurʾān but which denoted significant relationships of tribal alliance was *ḥilf,* a compact into which various related and unrelated clans entered. The purpose of such alliances was to establish permanent peace among these clans, to unite them in war against common enemies, to consolidate their wealth (q.v.) to pay for blood money (q.v.; see also RETALIATION), to share pasturage, etc. Since these alliances strengthened tribal structures, which did not serve the cause of the new religion, the Prophet condemned them with his famous declaration: "There is no *ḥilf* in Islam."

In the Qurʾān, God is the true and, ultimately, only ally *(walī)* of the believers; those who swerve from the path of belief (see ASTRAY), especially apostates (see APOSTASY), are left without such an ally (Q 2:107; 9:74; 41:31). "And they have no protecting allies *(awliyāʾ)* to help them instead of God" (Q 42:46); "Besides God you have no protecting ally or supporter" (Q 2:107; 42:31). Entering into alliance with the People of the Book or with the Arab polytheists is considered particularly reprehensible, if not absolutely forbidden: "Do not take them as allies till they migrate in the path of God" (Q 4:89; see PATH OR WAY [OF GOD]); "O you who believe, choose not disbelievers for allies in place of believers" (Q 4:144); "O you who believe, take not the Jews and Christians for allies. They are allies of each other. He amongst you who takes them for allies is one of them" (5:51).

As mentioned earlier, the term *ʿahd* was considered virtually synonymous with *ʿaqd,* a word expressing notions of contractual obligation. The latter term makes an appearance only once in the Qurʾān (Q 5:1), in the plural form *ʿuqūd.* The form *ʿuqda* (lit. "knot"), however, in conjunction with the word *nikāḥ* appears twice in the sense of marriage contract (see MARRIAGE AND DIVORCE). Likewise, the verb *ʿaqada,* again used in the context of marriage, occurs twice.

The most general precept regarding obligations or contracts occurs in Q 5:1: "O you who believe, fulfill your contracts *(ʿuqūd).*" The term, Ibn Manẓūr reports (*Lisān al-ʿArab,* iii, 296-300, 311-5), was taken by some scholars to refer generally to *ʿuhūd* (pl. of *ʿahd*). Others understood it to connote the religious obligations imposed upon the believers. In commenting on this verse, al-Zajjāj (d. 311/923) construes it to have a double meaning; namely, the obligations that God imposed upon Muslims and those which Muslims imposed upon each other as elements of juridical contractual transactions. Thus, accordingly, the qurʾānic use of the root *ʿ-q-d* connotes both unilateral and bilateral obligations. When unilateral, they emanate from God and are directed toward Muslims; when bilateral, they are of human construction, although the principles upon which they are constructed are dictated by religion.

On the basis of Q 2:282, the Qurʾān was interpreted as having enjoined the writing down of obligations. This particular verse, however, pertains to the recording and attestation of debts (q.v.). It reads as follows:

O you who believe, when you contract a debt for a fixed term, record it in writing. Let a scribe record it in writing between you in (terms of) equity. No scribe should refuse to write as God had taught him, so let him write, and let him who incurred the debt dictate, and let him observe his duty to God his Lord, and diminish not thereof. But if he who owes the debt is of low understanding, or weak, or unable himself to dictate, then let the guardian of his interests dictate in [terms of] equity. And call to witness, from among your men, two witnesses. And if two men be not [available] then one man and two women, of such as you approve as witnesses, so that if one [woman] errs [through forgetfulness], the other will remember. And the witnesses shall not refuse when they are summoned (see WITNESSING AND TESTIFYING). Be not averse to writing down [the contract] whether it be small or great, with [record of] the term thereof. That is more equitable in the sight of God and more sure for testimony, and the best way of avoiding doubt between you; save only in the case when it is actual merchandise which you transfer among yourselves from hand to hand. In that case, it is no sin for you if you do not write it down. And have witnesses when you sell one to another, and let no harm be done to scribe or witness. If you do them harm, lo! It is a sin in you (see WRITING AND WRITING MATERIALS; SIN AND CRIME).

Despite the relative detail of this verse and the clarity of the prescription to write down contracts, Islamic law neither recognized the validity of written instruments nor elaborated a general, comprehensive theory of contracts and obligations. To be valid, it was required that an instrument be attested by witnesses. Thus it is by virtue of testimonial attestation that an instrument acquires validity. The fact of its being a written instrument did not, as a rule, bestow on it any validity. The Qurʾānic injunction to reduce contracts to writing reflected the legal practices of the Near East, both to the north and to the south of Mecca (q.v.) and Medina (q.v.). Why Islamic law — which developed primarily in the Fertile Crescent, Egypt and the Hijaz — broke away from this practice, even at the expense of ignoring a qurʾānic prescription, remains largely a mystery.

In classical and medieval Islamic law, several types of contract were recognized. The most common source of contractual obligations was primarily the *ʿaqd* in matters of pecuniary transactions. More specifically, the contract of sale (*bayʿ*, see SELLING AND BUYING) formed not only the archetype of contractual theory but also constituted the core of legal obligations. Commutative and other types of contracts stand on their own though they are nonetheless constructed on the contractual model of sale which otherwise includes barter and exchange. In the sale contract, strictly defined, the object sold is distinguished from the price and the value. And being bilateral, a contract requires offer *(ījāb)* and acceptance *(qabūl)*, both taking place in the same session in the presence of the contracting parties. It was generally required that offer and acceptance be expressly stated although the Mālikī school did fully recognize implied-in-fact contracts. The Qurʾān itself does not explicitly enjoin express offer and acceptance but it does acknowledge that the basis of contractual validity is mutual assent (Q 4:29).

Islamic law recognizes the right to rescision which is a unilateral right to cancel or ratify a contract of sale. The buyer has the right to rescind the contract at the time when he inspects the object purchased. The right to rescision arises if there is a defect in the object of sale. Deficiency is taken to be a cause for the reduction of the value and thus the price of the object, and reduction in price upsets the terms of the contract. This right, however, lapses if not exercised within a certain time limitation. And once it lapses, the sale would be considered complete and thus irrevocable. Similarly, once the time limitation on rescision has expired, it is assumed that the reciprocal taking of possession has gone into effect.

In addition to the narrowly defined contract of sale, Islamic law recognized a variety of other types of contracts. A special type was the *salam* which entailed the ordering of goods to be delivered later (assuming usually that they are custom-made) for a payment made immediately. Placing an order for a ship to be built, for instance, fell into this category. But because of the disparity between the time of payment and the delivery of goods, this type of contract came close to violating the prohibition on usury (*ribā*, see USURY). So did another, similar type of contract known as *nasīʾa* whereby goods are delivered immediately for a delayed payment.

An important type of contract is that of hire and lease which involves the sale of a usufruct. Two types of hire are distinguished, one for a period of time, the other to carry out a specific task. Marriage is also a type of contract under Islamic law and as such it involves offer, acceptance and the payment of a price, technically known as dower (*mahr*, see BRIDEWEALTH). The bridegroom concludes the contract with the legal guardian *(walī)* of the bride before two male witnesses or one man and two women. The *walī* is the nearest male relative, usually the father or older brother. The element of price in this contract is constituted by the dower which he pays to the bride instead of her guardian.

In the wake of the so-called legal reforms during the nineteenth and twentieth centuries, the law of obligations underwent various degrees of change, depending on the individual Muslim country in question. The most fundamental change occurred first in Egypt in 1949, when the Egyptian Civil Code became law through the efforts of ʿAbd al-Razzāq al-Sanhūrī. This code became in many important respects the model for the Syrian, Lebanese, Kuwaiti and Libyan reforms. With its appearance, a comprehensive and integrated text of legal obligations replaced the medieval law manuals, which lacked a unified theory of contracts. Furthermore, formal matters of wording and syntax, important in the medieval context, now become marginal if not obsolete. See also LAW AND THE QURʾĀN; BREAKING TRUSTS AND CONTRACTS.

Wael B. Hallaq

Bibliography

Primary: al-Ḥalabī, Muḥammad b. Ibrahīm, *Multaqā al-abḥur*, ed. Wahbī al-Albānī, 2 vols., Beirut 1989, i, 237f.; ii, 5-67, 157-69, 210-14; Ibn Kathīr, *Tafsīr;* Nawawī, *Taṣḥīḥ al-tanbīh*, 3 vols., Beirut 1996, iii, 85-94, 109-10, 177-92, 265-73; al-Qaffāl, M. al-Shāshī, *Ḥilyat al-ʿulamāʾ fī maʿrifat madhāhib al-fuqahāʾ*, 8 vols., Mecca 1988, iv, 5-402.
Secondary: Ch. Chehata, *Essai d'une théorie générale de l'obligation en droit musulman. i. Les sujets de l'obligation, avec une bibliographie, une méthodologie et un tableau général de la théorie de l'obligation en droit*

hanéfite, Cairo 1936; W.B. Hallaq, The use and abuse of evidence: The question of provincial and Roman influences on early Islamic law, in JAOS 110 (1989), 79-91; repr. in W. Hallaq, *Law and legal theory in classical and medieval Islam,* Aldershot/Hampshire 1995, ch. 9; J. Schacht, *An introduction to Islamic law,* Oxford 1964, 144-61; E. Tyan, Ḥilf, in *EI*², iii, 388-9.

Conversion

Spiritual and moral transformation attended by a sincere change of belief. The concept of conversion is represented in the Qurʾān by a group of teachings which together stress the importance of admitting God's lordship, accepting the guidance he gives, following the way he has established and conforming to his will (see BELIEF AND UNBELIEF; LORD; OBEDIENCE; ISLAM). It is essentially a matter of reverting to a norm perceptible to all and to which one is able to conform by one's own efforts. The initiative for the movement of restoration lies with God, though humankind has the ability to comply or not (see FREEDOM AND PREDESTINATION).

God has created all things primarily so that they should serve and worship (q.v.) him (e.g. Q 6:102; 16:48-50; 21:19-20; 64:1; see CREATION; SERVANT). Among them are humankind (Q 51:56) whose vocation is to seek God's help (Q 1:5) and thank him for the good he gives. But humans are weak and contentious (Q 2:30; 4:28; 16:4; see BLOODSHED; CORRUPTION) even though God has given them intelligence (Q 55:4), and they allow themselves to be seduced from their proper relationship with him (Q 20:121; 82:6-7; see DISOBEDIENCE; GRATITUDE AND INGRATITUDE). It is this fallibility that causes a slip from their true nature (Q 30:30; see FALL OF MAN) and which God in his mercy (q.v.) seeks to restore.

One of the commonest terms in the Qurʾān by which the notion of this restoration is expressed is guidance, *hudā*. It springs from the idea that the fundamental relationship entails that humans follow where God leads and in so doing fulfill their existence. But the term has rather more nuanced meanings than this basic depiction suggests. On the one hand, the Qurʾān makes clear that God's guidance enlightens (Q 24:35) and directs to the path of right action (Q 10:25) and that he provides signs (q.v.) to help along the way (Q 3:103). But this guidance is not made available to everyone. For on the other hand, some have fallen into error (q.v.; Q 7:30; 16:36) or even been cast aside by God (Q 4:88) and purposely willed by him to stray (Q 7:155; 7:178; see ASTRAY). Exactly why this should be is part of the divine mystery, for only God can give guidance (Q 7:43) and no one else, not even the Prophet (Q 2:272; 4:88; 28:56). A partial explanation, however, is provided by suggestions that humans have a crucial part to play for themselves, for God could have willed to guide all (Q 6:149; 13:31; 32:13) and he guides those who turn to him (Q 5:16; 13:27; 42:13). This is amplified by indications that he gives guidance to those who are already seeking it, *alladhīna htadaw hudān* (Q 19:76; cf. 47:17) and guides those who believe (Q 2:4-5).

The relationship between belief and guidance is made yet more explicit in references to those who have made a choice. God has shown the way to the grateful and the ungrateful (Q 76:3); however, he only guides those who believe (Q 64:11; 2:264). Believers who turn away from their belief can only be left to the consequences of their choice (Q 3:86; see FATE; DESTINY). Here the Qurʾān seems to suggest a subtle interplay between God's unbounded will to guide and the human ability to accept or reject. While humans are not left entirely to decide for themselves — because God's will is not to be resisted — the relationship does involve a measure of freedom, with the result that God's guidance is occasionally identifiable as forgiveness (q.v.) offered in order to bring back his willful creature to his way (Q 20:122-3).

This is the kind of awareness that is shown by Abū Ḥāmid al-Ghazālī (d. 505/1111) who tries to explain his recovery from the debilitating skepticism (see UNCERTAINTY) which struck him when he taught in Baghdad. Quoting Q 6:125, he relates that after a time God put light into his heart (q.v.) to give him clearer insights than he had obtained himself by the deductive methods that he had previously employed, implying that whereas his own faculties had led him into error, he was brought back to the truth by God's guidance. He readily admits that he is moved entirely by God in his new vocation of teaching the true knowledge and he asks God to guide him and through him to guide others (Ghazālī, *Munqidh,* 93, 159-60). It is clear from what al-Ghazālī says that he attributes the origins of his recovery wholly to God although the preparations he himself made for the conversion are detailed throughout his autobiographical account in his expositions of the weaknesses of the various sciences.

More or less the same dynamic is expressed in the less common notion that God admits *(adkhala)* humankind into the sphere of his mercy or into a place among the righteous. While he admits those whom he wills (Q 42:8; 48:25; cf. 110:2), he also allows to enter those who show their worth by good deeds (q.v.; Q 29:9; 45:30; cf. 9:99). The elaborate relationship of divine ordination and human qualification is intimated in the prayer of the prophet Solomon (Sulaymān, see SOLOMON) asking God to compel him to have gratitude and to act righteously and to admit him among his servants (Q 27:19). Human action and divine conduct are inseparable here, forming a partnership in which the responsibility for fulfilling God's expectations seems to be reciprocal.

The manner in which these terms are employed suggests that the act of conforming to God's way requires a conversion that is determined by God himself but also involves human initiative. The most intimate form of this relationship is denoted by the idea of returning to an initial position or restoring a lost condition, expressed by the verb *tāba* and its forms. In some instances this is used of humans alone and carries a strong element of repentance (Q 4:146; 9:11). But in other significant occurrences it is used of God, as when he turns to Adam and guides him (Q 20:122; see ADAM AND EVE), or when the three followers of Muḥammad who have failed in their duty try to run away until God turns to them to enable them to turn as well, (*thumma tāba ʿalayhim li-yatūbū* (Q 9:118; compare 9:117; see OPPOSITION TO MUḤAMMAD). The use of the same verb for both divine and human action here graphically portrays the way in which the fugitives' return is reciprocated by God's move to restore them. The same divine concern is shown in God's turning to those who believe (Q 33:73), suggesting that as soon as they signal their readiness, he too is ready to help them in their faith.

The accounts of how the theologian *(mutakallim)* Abū l-Ḥasan ʿAlī al-Ashʿarī (d. 324/936) abandoned the Muʿtazilī doctrines (see MUʿTAZILĪS; CREATEDNESS OF THE QURʾĀN) of his early years illustrate this cooperative action well. In most versions of the story of his conversion, he is first troubled by the insufficiency of the answers provided by speculative theology *(kalām)* and then, after praying to God, is guided in visions of the Prophet to accept traditional beliefs and to defend them with rational arguments (see EXEGESIS OF THE QURʾĀN: CLASSICAL AND MEDIEVAL). According to one version he publicly declares that he now embraces Islam and repents of his old ways, (*innī qad aslamtu l-sāʿa wa-innī tāʾib mimmā kuntu fī-hi,* Ibn ʿAsākir, *Tabyīn,* 40; also, R. McCarthy, *Theology of al-Ashʿarī,* 152). This conversion results from al-Ashʿarī's own preliminary efforts and God's guidance working together.

The same movement, though only with respect to human actors, is expressed in the verb *anāba,* which similarly suggests the motion of coming back to the same point. So humankind is enjoined to make this return (Q 31:15) and warned to do so before punishment is inflicted (Q 39:54; see CHASTISEMENT AND PUNISHMENT; PUNISHMENT STORIES; WARNING) though they only comply when in trouble and at other times ignore God's oneness (Q 39:8; see GOD AND HIS ATTRIBUTES). Human responsibility for making this move is emphasized in the forthright admonition to unbelievers: God leaves to stray those whom he wills but guides those who make the return (Q 13:27). Here again there is a hint that the action of God in guiding and that of humankind in accepting are interconnected. But if conversion consists in returning to the way that God has set and which humans are innately prepared to follow, there is still the necessity of actively pointing them to this way. The Qurʾān explains that the activity of calling humankind (see INVITATION), indicated by the verb *daʿā,* is undertaken both by God through clear signs (Q 2:221), and by the Prophet. Muḥammad is told to invite people (Q 7:193; 12:108; 28:87) with proper exhortation (Q 16:125) though, like Noah (q.v.) and other earlier messengers (cf. Q 71:7), he meets solid resistance (Q 23:73-5; 57:8; see MESSENGER; PROPHETS AND PROPHETHOOD). One reason for this is that God prevents those who have already ignored his signs from hearing and understanding (Q 18:57). And again we see an intimate relationship, this time between the Prophet's call, people's readiness to heed and God's ordaining the outcome. An obligation for individual Muslims and the community, the equivalent to the Prophet's calling, is striving, *jihād* (q.v.). While this term is often employed for fighting with arms, some uses suggest conduct that marks out believers. Such is the case when those who are called strive in God's way (see PATH OR WAY [OF GOD]) with person and possessions (e.g. Q 8:72; 49:15; 61:11), having been commanded to do this as part of the observance of faith, as though their conduct might attract others to imitate them.

This nexus of movements in which God and humankind seem engaged together achieves its end in the conforming of the individual to God's way. The Christian convert ʿAlī b. Rabban al-Ṭabarī (d. ca. 250/864) attests to this when he confesses that he was able to recognize the existence of one, eternal God through his own reason, though it was God who called *(daʿā)* him to exercise his reason and so escape from the error of unbelief (I.-A. Khalifé and W. Kutsch, *Radd,* 119). This is the true conversion, fulfilled in the action of bowing (see BOWING AND PROSTRATION) to God's will as expressed by the verb *aslama.* Its significance is perhaps most fully conveyed in Q 3:83 which proclaims that all things in heaven and earth surrender to God, whether obediently or not, and will return to him, indicating that God is the lord of all and that eventually nothing can remain indifferent to him. This receives endorsement elsewhere, e.g. where Muḥammad is told to say that God's is the only guidance and so humankind is commanded to surrender to him (Q 3:20; 6:71) and that there can be no help when punishment comes unless humankind surrenders to God (Q 39:54). There is a strong suggestion in such verses that the act of bowing and submitting results for reasonable creatures from an awareness of God and of the individual's status as subservient to him. Living indifferently to him is, therefore, unreasonable and fraught with obstacles, while living in harmonious conformity with his way brings self-enhancement.

The inference to be drawn is that conversion and return to the position for which creatures were ordained results from a rational acknowledgement of the relationship between the created order and the Creator. The prime example of this in the Qurʾān is the prophet Abraham (Ibrāhīm, see ABRAHAM) who, from the initial realization that idols cannot be objects of worship (see IDOLS AND IMAGES), engages in a process of deduction. From his observation of the changing condition of the natural world in which stars (q.v.), moon (q.v.) and sun (q.v.) can appear to be supreme until they decline and disappear, he deduces the existence of the one who made them all (Q 6:74-9; see COSMOLOGY IN THE QURʾĀN). The prophet himself works out the difference between the created and Creator but at the same time he is supported and guided in his growing understanding by God himself (Q 6:83).

It is salutary to be told in the Qurʾān that while the act of acknowledging God and submitting to him is in conformity with his will, it is not a cause for complacency as though those who had accomplished it have been able to do so through their own insight. For the very act itself results from God's guidance which he gives as a favor (Q 49:17; see BLESSING; POWER AND IMPOTENCE). Again, the human's return through reason to the appropriate position in relation to God is as much an act of God's care as the individual's efforts. See also ISLAM.

David Thomas

Bibliography
Primary: al-Ghazālī, Abū Ḥāmid Muḥammad, *al-Munqidh min al-ḍalāl,* ed. ʿA.-Ḥ. Maḥmūd, Cairo n.d.; Ibn ʿAsākir, *Tabyīn kadhib al-muftarī,* ed. Ḥ. al-Qudsī, Damascus 1928.
Secondary: T.W. Arnold, *The preaching of Islam. A history of the propagation of the Muslim faith,* London 1896; M.Gervers and R.J. Bikhazi (eds.), *Conversion and continuity. Indigenous Christian communities in Islamic lands, eighth to eighteenth centuries,* Toronto 1990; I.-A. Khalifé and W. Kutsch (eds.), ar-Radd ʿalā n-naṣārā de ʿAlī aṭ-Ṭabarī, in *Mélanges de l'Université Saint Joseph* 36 (1959), 115-48; N. Levtzion (ed.), *Conversion to Islam,* New York 1979; B. Lewis, *The Jews of Islam,* Princeton 1984; R.J. McCarthy, *The theology of al-Ashʿarī,* Beirut 1953 (contains a partial translation); W.M. Watt, Conversion in Islam at the time of the Prophet, in W.M. Watt, *Early Islam. Collected articles,* Edinburgh 1990.

Coral

The lime-skeleton of sea-creatures covered by animalcular polyps. Red coral *(Corallium rubrum),* which is particulary valued, is harvested from the depths of the sea and used in jewelry; moreover, it is supposed to possess curative power. The Arabic term for this coral, *marjān,* appears twice in the Qurʾān.

The two qurʾānic references to coral occur in Q 55 ("The Merciful," Sūrat al-Raḥmān; see GOD AND HIS ATTRIBUTES). Reflecting the name of the sūra, coral and pearls (*luʾluʾ,* see SOLOMON) are mentioned together in Q 55:22 as symbols of the mercy (q.v.) and benefits of God (see BLESSING): "He has loosed the two seas [fresh-water and salt-water] which meet. Between them is a barrier (q.v.) which they do not transgress. Which then of the benefits of your Lord will the two of you count false? From both come forth the pearl and the coral" (Q 55:19-22). (Q 35:12 contains a similar passage, but with no reference to any specific product: "... yet from each [of the two seas] you eat fresh meat, and bring forth adornment *(ḥilya)* to wear.") The second reference to coral is found in Q 55:58: "As if [in paradise] they [women of restrained glance] are jacinth and coral [i.e. like them in beauty]." In this passage, coral and jacinth (*yāqūt,* which term eventually came to denote a variety of minerals, most commonly referring to the colorless corundum) are used as attributes of modest women. They also symbolize the benefits of God in the next world (see REWARD AND PUNISHMENT).

Reliable Arabic commentaries on the Qurʾān like al-Ṭabarī's (d. 310/923) *Tafsīr,* al-Zamakhsharī's (d. 538/1144) *Kashshāf* or Ibn Kathīr's (d. 774/1373) *Tafsīr* refer to *marjān* not only as a precious red jewel, but provide several other connotations. The exegesis of Q 55:22 explains *marjān* to be a small pearl in opposition to the large one, the *luʾluʾ*. Commentary on Q 55:58 holds that jacinth serves as a symbol of pureness and coral as a symbol of beauty and glitter. Another interpretation of coral and jacinth offered by the commentators is that the lexemes refer to the transparent silk (q.v.) robes of the houris (q.v.) in paradise (q.v.) with their legs shining through.

As for the Arabic sources that do not deal with the Qurʾān, coral, which is classified as a mineral or a stone, is never found in the zoological works. An extensive description of coral that shows its resemblance to certain plants is offered by the Egyptian scholar al-Tīfāshī (d. 651/1253) in his work on mineralogy entitled *Azhār al-afkār.* Egypt (q.v.) was the center of the coral trade for centuries, as many varieties of coral are found in the Mediterranean Sea. See also MATERIAL CULTURE AND THE QURʾĀN.

Herbert Eisenstein

Bibliography

Primary: Ibn Kathīr, *Tafsīr;* Ṭabarī, *Tafsīr;* al-Tīfāshī, Aḥmad b. Yūsuf, *Kitāb Azhār al-afkār fī jawāhir al-aḥjār,* ed. M.Y. Ḥasan and M. Basyūnī Khafājī, Cairo 1977; Zamakhsharī, *Kashshāf.*

Secondary: A. Dietrich, Mardjān, in *EI²*, vi, 556-7; W. Heyd, *Histoire du commerce du Levant au Moyen-âge,* 2 vols., Leipzig 1885-6, Amsterdam 1959 (revised), ii, 609-10; Jeffery, *For. vocab.*, 261.

Corruption

Decay, depravity, impurity. The topic of corruption has two general references in the Qurʾān: (1) committing mischievous and depraved deeds that willfully subvert God's order and purposes (see DISOBEDIENCE); (2) perverting scripture (see SCRIPTURE AND THE QURʾĀN) so as to mislead and conceal its meanings. The first reference is most often expressed by the Arabic root *f-s-d,* occurring principally in late Meccan and Medinan passages, e.g. Q 2:251: "If God did not check one group of people by means of another, the earth (q.v.) would certainly have been corrupted" *(la-fasadati l-arḍ).* This root is very frequently paired with the phrase "in the land/earth," e.g. in the account of Cain's slaying of his brother Abel (see CAIN AND ABEL) in Q 5:32: "We decreed for the Children of Israel (q.v.) that if anyone killed a person — except for murder (q.v.; see also BLOODSHED) and corruption in the land *(fasād fī l-arḍ)* — it would be as if he had slain all the people." Punishment for "corruption in the land" is extremely severe ("execution, or crucifixion [q.v.], or the cutting off of hands and feet from opposite sides, or exile from the land; that is their disgrace in this world, and a heavy punishment is theirs in the hereafter," Q 5:33; see CHASTISEMENT AND PUNISHMENT; REWARD AND PUNISHMENT), unless the perpetrator sincerely repents in time (see REPENTANCE AND PENANCE). The sense that threads through such passages is that corruption and mischief are not only evil personal deeds but also expressions of fundamental hostility to and subversion of God's created order, an order which embraces both nature and justice (Q 26:151-2, 183; see JUSTICE AND INJUSTICE). A particularly pointed passage about the perpetrator of corruption is Q 2:204-5: "There is the type of individual whose speech about the life of this world delights you, and he calls God to witness what is in his heart (q.v.); yet he is the most contentious of opponents. When he turns away, his effort is to run about in the land sowing corruption in it *(yufsida fīhā)*, destroying crops and young livestock — God does not love corruption *(fasād)*."

Another root, occurring far less frequently than *f-s-d*, is chiefly found in Medinan passages: *kh-b-th*, as in Q 8:37, "that God may distinguish the corrupt *(khabīth)* from the good (*ṭayyib*, see GOOD AND EVIL), and put the corrupt one upon another, heap them together and cast them into hell (q.v.)." This root is dramatically displayed in Q 24:26, where both masculine and feminine forms are used: "Corrupt women *(al-khabīthāt)* are for corrupt men *(al-khabīthīn)*, and corrupt men for corrupt women." "Impure" is an alternative translation because the passage addresses the slandering of chaste women (see ADULTERY AND FORNICATION; CHASTITY). Humankind's proneness to corruption is an undesirable but inevitable consequence of their God-given freedom of action in the natural, moral and social realms (see FREEDOM AND PREDESTINATION).

The matter of distorting scripture is addressed in Medinan passages accusing Jews (see JEWS AND JUDAISM; MEDINA) of the practice, e.g. Q 4:46: "Some of those who are Jews shift *(yuḥarrifūna)* words from their proper places and say, 'We hear and disobey,' and 'Hear as one who hears not,' and *'rāʿinā'* [an insulting corruption of an Arabic phrase, *'rāʾinā,'* meaning "Please listen to us"], distorting with their tongues and slandering the religion." The corruption of scripture is not a major or sustained topic in the Qurʾān although it became an important and abiding theological as well as textual controversy in later relations between Muslims and the People of the Book (q.v.; see also POLEMICS AND POLEMICAL LANGUAGE; THEOLOGY AND THE QURʾĀN).

Frederick Mathewson Denny

Bibliography
ʿAbd al-Bāqī; J. Burton, The corruption of the scriptures, in *Occasional papers of the school of Abbasid studies* 4 (1992, 1994), 95-106; L. Gardet, Kawn wa-Fasād, in *EI²*, iv, 794-5; H.E. Kassis, *A concordance of the Qurʾān*, Berkeley 1983; H. Lazarus-Yafeh, Tarf, in *EI²*, x, 111-112 (see bibliography).

Corruption of Scripture see REVISION AND ALTERATION; PEOPLE OF THE BOOK; ABROGATION; CORRUPTION

Cosmogony see CREATION; COSMOLOGY IN THE QURʾĀN

Cosmography see COSMOLOGY IN THE QURʾĀN

Cosmology

Introduction

A divinely governed order of the universe and the place of humans within it. This qurʾānic understanding of cosmology is dramatized in diverse reports: the divine six-day-work of creation (q.v.; *khalq*) of the cosmos *(al-samāwāt wa-l-arḍ)*, of humankind *(insān)* and its habitat in nature (*nabāt al-arḍ;* see AGRICULTURE AND VEGETATION), of demons or spirits (*jinn*, q.v.) and the animal world (*al-ḍābba, al-anʿām,* see ANIMAL LIFE) as well as the resolution of created space on the day of doom (see JUDGMENT) — all occupy prominent roles in the Qurʾān. Additionally, the existence of humans on earth (q.v.), the ambiguity of their moral condition, the liability they bear to fall prey to the seduction exercised by a negative figure, Iblīs (Diabolos, see IBLIS; DEVIL) or al-Shayṭān (Satan) and the evil (*fasād;* see EVIL DEEDS; GOOD AND EVIL; CORRUPTION) they commit are all elaborated from an etiological orientation. All these issues may, however, be due to the peculiar genesis of the Qurʾān as viewed from two principally different perspectives. The Qurʾān first manifested itself as the immediate expression of the psychic-prophetic experience of Muḥammad himself, meant to be read out to his audience (*qurʾān);* only later, once being canonized (see COLLECTION OF THE QURʾĀN), did it become the binding document (*muṣḥaf,* q.v.) of a religion with social demands of its adherents, "the corporate confession of it in the inward possession of Islam and of Muslims" (Cragg, *Event*). In the latter context the cosmological recollections have served, as did the analogous accounts in the scriptures of the neighboring religions (see SCRIPTURE AND THE QURʾĀN), to explain a given world order and to justify particular rulings therein. To read them exclusively in a post-canonical context as etiological texts is, however, by no means the only way to look at them. One has to be aware that the status of a canon presupposes a fixed, indeed "frozen" corpus of equally ranked textual entities with no distinction regarding the function they held in the text as a *"qurʾān" in statu nascendi,* i.e. in that historically unique sequence of communications between a speaker and his audience, accompanying and at the same time documenting the historical process of the emergence of the early Muslim community (see COMMUNITY AND SOCIETY IN THE QURʾAN). The value of references to cosmology and of cosmogonic accounts in that process can be made clear only by observing their structural function within their particular context of discourse, i.e. their particular sūra.

Indeed, considered in the context of the emergence of a community, i.e. reflecting the process of a "canonization from below" of the successively publicized liturgical texts, the recollections of cosmogonic accounts assume a different value. They present themselves as new readings of a familiar narrative with the perspicuous tendency to demythologize it in certain substantial traits, though not without introducing new mythic elements meant to elevate contemporary developments onto a salvation-historical level (see MYTHIC AND LEGENDARY NARRATIVES). The qurʾānic cosmological recollections are presented to their listeners less as narrative accounts than as exhortations serving immediate theological rather than etiological aims: The creation of nature — flora and fauna — appears as a starting point of the divine interaction with humans, a "sign" *(āya)* of divine omnipotence and an instigation for human gratefulness *(shukr)*. The creation of human beings, moreover, framed in a divine deal with Iblīs, is presented as a challenge for the option of accepting divine guidance *(hudā)* and as an affirmation that the socio-religious antagonisms existing in the world of the addressees during the first transmission of the Qurʾān are nothing else than part of a divine plan of salvation (q.v.).

In order to give due attention to both perspectives, canonical and pre-canonical, evidence will be presented in this article, wherever possible, from two different angles: (1) a macro-structural perspective on the basis of the Qurʾān as canon, i.e.

presented in the form of a cumulative synopsis of qurʾānic references to cosmology; (2) a micro-structural perspective, by situating references into their communicational framework with a particular view to their various typological features such as situation of speech, context and referentiality.

The six-day work: Creation of the material world

Collecting the dispersed qurʾānic statements about the creation of the world into one comprehensive picture, an image in accord with more ancient Near Eastern lore emerges (for individual parallels see Speyer, *Erzählungen,* 4f.): God created the heavens (see HEAVEN) and the earth in six days (*khalaqa l-samāwāti wa-l-arḍa fī sittati ayyāmin,* Q 7:54, cf. 10:3; 11:7; 25:59; 32:3), not in jest (*wa-mā khalaqnā l-samāwāti wa-l-arḍa wa-mā baynahumā lāʿibīn,* Q 44:38-9, cf. 21:16), nor in vain (*a-fa-ḥasibtum annanā khalaqnākum ʿabathan,* Q 23:115; *wa-mā khalaqnā l-samāʾa wa-l-arḍa wa-mā baynahumā bāṭilan,* Q 38:27) but in truth and with a stated term (*illā bi-l-ḥaqqi wa-ajalin musamman,* Q 30:8; cf. 44:38). The heavens and earth were completed in two days (*khalaqa l-arḍa fī yawmayn,* Q 41:9), formed from an integrated disk-shaped mass which had to be split (*a-wa-lam yara lladhīna kafarū anna l-samāwāti wa-l-arḍa kānatā ratqan fa-fataqnāhumā,* Q 21:30). From smoke (*thumma stawā ilā l-samāʾi wahiya dukhānun,* Q 41:11f.) the seven heavens were created (*fa-qaḍāhunna sabʿa samāwātin fī yawmayn,* Q 41:12; cf. 23:17; 78:12) forming layers, one above the other (*ṭibāqan,* Q 67:3; cf. 71:14). In the seventh heaven or above it, where the angels praise God (*yusabiḥḥūna bi-ḥamdi rabbihim,* Q 40:7; cf. 39:75; 42:3; see ANGEL; PRAISE) and seek forgiveness (q.v.) for the believers (*yastaghfirūna li-lladhīna āmanū,* Q 40:7), the divine throne (*ʿarsh*) is located (see THRONE OF GOD), carried by angels (q.v.) (*alladhīna yaḥmilūna l-ʿarsha,* Q 40:7), who move in row after row (Q 89:22; cf. 37:1). The lowest heaven is adorned with lights (*wa-zayyannā l-samāʾa l-dunyā bi-maṣābīḥa,* Q 41:12): the sun and the moon (Q 71:16; 78:13), the stars (*bi-zīnati l-kawākib,* Q 37:6; cf. 67:5) and the constellations of the zodiac (*wa-laqad jaʿalnā fī l-samāʾi burūjan,* Q 15:16; cf. 25:61; 85:1). The sun (q.v.) which follows a regular path is considered to be subject to humans (*wa-sakhkhara lakumu l-shamsa wa-l-qamara dāʾibayni,* Q 14:33). Its course serves man to reckon the periods of time (*wa-jaʿalnā āyata l-nahāri mubṣiratan... li-taʿlamū ʿadada l-sinīna wa-l-ḥiṣāba,* Q 17:12; cf. 6:96-7; see DAY AND NIGHT; DAY, TIMES OF). As to the moon (q.v.), particular stations are decreed for it, again as a means at man's disposal for his chronological orientation (*wa-qaddarahu manāzila li-taʿlamū ʿadada l-sinīna wa-l-ḥisāba,* Q 10:5). Accordingly, the number of the months have been fixed at creation (*inna ʿiddata l-shuhūri ʿinda llāhi thnā ʿashara shahran fī kitābi llāhi yawma khalaqa l-samāwāti wa-l-arḍa,* Q 9:36). The stars serve to guide people in the darkness of the land and the sea (*wa-huwa lladhī jaʿala lakumu l-nujūma li-tahtadū bihā fī ẓulumāti l-barri wa-baḥri,* Q 6:97). The lowest heaven is also the assembling place of demons (*jinn, wa-laqad jaʿalnā fī l-samāʾi burūjan.../wa-ḥafiẓnāhā min kulli shayṭānin rajīm,* Q 15:16-7; cf. 21:33; 25:62; 67:5; 85:1), who attempt to listen to the heavenly councils in order to convey supernatural knowledge to privileged humans (*hal unabbiʾukum ʿalā man tanazzalu l-shayāṭīn,* Q 26:221). They are, however, chased away by shooting flames (*illā mani staraqa l-samʿa fa-atbaʿahu shihābun mubīn,* Q 15:18; cf. 37:6-10). God raised the vault of the heaven high (*rafaʿa samkahā fa-sawwāhā,* Q 79:28; *wa-l-samāʾa banaynāhā bi-aydin wa-innā la-mūsiʿūn,* Q 51:47) without support (*rafaʿa l-samāwāti bi-ghayri ʿamadin,* Q 13:2), keeping it from collapsing and falling down on the earth (*wa-yumsiku l-samāʾa an taqaʿa ʿalā l-arḍ,* Q 22:65). In accordance with ancient Near Eastern models the earth is viewed as being surrounded by waters separated by the creator through a barrier (*maraja l-baḥrayni... wa-jaʿala baynahumā barzakhan wa-ḥijran maḥjūran,* Q 25:53; cf. 27:61; 35:12; 55:19), which are themselves divided into two "oceans," the waters of one being fresh and sweet, those of the other being bitter (*hādhā ʿadhbun furātun wa-hādha milḥun ujājun,* Q 25:53; cf. 35:13).

God extinguishes the light (q.v.) of the day and introduces the night (see DARKNESS), as two of his signs (q.v.; *wa-jaʿalnā l-layla wa-l-nahāra āyatayni fa-maḥawnā āyata l-layli wa-jaʿalnā āyata l-nahāri mubṣiratan,* Q 17:12), alternating continuously (*innā fī khalqi l-samāwāti wa-l-arḍi wa-khtilāfi l-layli wa-l-nahāri... bi-mā yanfaʿu l-nāsa,* Q 2:164; cf. 3:26; 31:28; 35:14; 36:37; 39:7). In four days God furnished the creation of the earth with mountains, rivers and fruit-gardens (*wa-jaʿala fīhā rawāsiya min fawqihā wa-bāraka fīhā wa-qaddara fīhā aqwātaha fī arbaʿati ayyāmin sawāʾan lil-sāʾilīn,* Q 41:10; cf. 13:3-4; 15:19; 16:15-6; 27:61). From water (q.v.) he created the animals, some that creep on their bellies and others that walk on two or four feet (*wa-llāhu khalaqa kulla dābbatin min māʾin fa-minhum man yamshī ʿalā baṭnihi wa-minhum man yamshī ʿalā rijlayni wa-minhum man yamshī ʿalā arbaʿin,* Q 24:45). They have been created for the benefit and adornment of man (*wa-l-anʿāma khalaqahā lakum fīhā difʾun wa-manāfiʿu wa-minhā taʾkulūn,* Q 16:5). Man was elected to rule over the animals (*a-wa-lam yaraw annā khalaqnā lahum mimmā ʿamilat aydīnā anʿāman fa-hum lahā mālikun,* Q 36:71). No less was the sea created for the benefit of man, supplying him with food and ornaments to wear (*wa-huwa lladhī sakhkhara l-baḥra li-taʾkulū minhu laḥman ṭariyyan wa-tastakhrijū minhu ḥilyatan talbasūnahā,* Q 16:14; see CLOTHING).

Time in cosmological context

After the six-day work of creation (Q 7:54; 10:3; 11:7; 25:59; 32:4; 50:38; 57:4), that had neither tired nor wearied him (*wa-mā massanā min lughūb,* Q 50:38; *wa-lam yaʿya,* Q 46:33), God seated himself upon his divine throne (*thumma stawā ʿalā l-ʿarshi,* Q 7:54; 10:3; 13:2; 20:5; 25:59; 57:4) which extends over heavens and earth (*wasiʿa kursiyyuhu l-samāwāti wa-l-arḍa,* Q 2:255), to govern everything through his divine command (*yudabbiru l-amra,* Q 10:3). He is continuously occupied with maintaining his creation (*kulla yawmin huwa fī shaʾn,* Q 55:29) and does not rest (*lā taʾkhudhuhu sinnatun wa-lā nawm,* Q 2:255). This explicitly stated effortlessness and untiring activity (Böwering, Time) is in clear contrast to the human condition where sleep (q.v.) is part of the divinely ordained rhythm (*wa-jaʿalnā nawmakum subātan,* Q 78:9). God, moreover, plays an active role in man's sleep for "God takes the souls unto himself at the time of their death, and that which has not died in its sleep. He keeps those on whom he has decreed death, but looses the others till a stated term" (*Allāhu yatawaffā l-anfusa ḥīna mawtihā wa-llatī lam tamut fī manāmihā fa-yumsiku llatī qaḍā ʿalayhā l-mawta wa-yursilu l-ukhrā ilā ajalin musamman,* Q 39:42; see DEATH AND THE DEAD).

Still, God's undisrupted concern for the world is reflected in the rhythm of human interaction (see SOCIAL RELATIONS). Although the heptad as a measure for counting days must be assumed to have been known in ancient Arabia (see CALENDAR), the qurʾānic accounts of creation lack a cosmic etiology or a divine prototype for the concept of a six-day cycle of profane working days culminating in a sacred seventh day of rest, a concept so characteristic for the rhythm of life with Jews and Christians (see JEWS AND JUDAISM; CHRISTIANS AND CHRISTIANITY). A particular day of the week to be reserved for official services has been decreed in the Qurʾān (Q 62:9) but Friday was chosen for purely pragmatic and mundane reasons which lack any reference to cosmic contexts. Accordingly, not the whole day but only a particular period — the time until midday prayer — is reserved for religious purposes (see FRIDAY PRAYER), the rest being profane, a ruling that has given Islamic culture a distinct imprint of its own.

Even though no entire day of the week is held sacred, there are nonetheless particular times during the day which are considered to have a sacred character and are thus apt to be dedicated to communication with the divine, namely dawn (*fajr,* Q 89:1), afternoon (*ʿaṣr,* Q 106:1), sunset (*maghrib, qabla l-ghurūb,* Q 50:39), later evening (*ʿishāʾ,* Q 24:58; cf. Q 30:18 where *ʿashīyan* is used) and midday (*ẓuhr, ḥīna tuẓhirūn,* Q 30:18). Three of these prayer times (see PRAYER) coincide with Jewish practice and in the case of *maghrib,* the Hebrew *ʿerebh,* the analogy is even etymologically obvious. The two others are known as well in Christian monastic contexts (see MONASTICISM AND MONKS), for example, *ʿishāʿ,* reflecting the Greek *apodeipnon.* The Qurʾān knows about additional sacred times like the time when the day has reached its full light *(al-ḍuḥā),* a time marked by prayers in pre-Islamic times *(al-jāhiliyya)* and apparently also in the early years of the Muslim community (Q 91:1; 93:1). To be sure, the Qurʾān does not explicitly state that all these time periods bear a sacred character, but such can clearly be inferred from some particularly expressive verses which refer to these alone and to no other periods as significant in themselves. This relates to the early sūras where single oaths or oath clusters (see OATHS) refer to these periods (*wa-l-fajr/ wa-layālin ʿashr,* Q 89:1-2; *wa-l-ʿaṣr,* Q 103:1; *wa-l-ḍuḥā,* Q 93:1). It is worth noting (Neuwirth, Images) that all the sūras in which these oaths or oath clusters appear focus on the idea of the believer's intimate closeness to the divine speaker. The sūra texts thus unfold the inherent liturgical relevance implied in the sacred time evoked in their introductory oaths.

There are also longer cosmically determined periods of time which are deemed sacred *(ḥaram).* It is true that the holy months (*al-ashhuru l-ḥurum,* Q 9:5; see MONTHS) which were cherished in the *jāhiliyya* and during which no blood was to be shed (see BLOODSHED) — though reaffirmed in the Qurʾān — were already superseded in significance during qurʾānic development by two important cosmologically determined feast periods (see FESTIVALS AND COMMEMORATIVE DAYS), one inherited from pre-Islamic practice, the other newly institutionalized, namely the pilgrimage (q.v.) and the month of Ramaḍān (q.v.; *shahru ramaḍāna lladhī unzila fīhi l-qurʾān,* Q 2:185). Whereas the period of pilgrimage was to occupy only a number of days, the notion of a full holy month survived most vividly in Ramaḍān. This Muslim month of fasting (q.v.) was introduced as a cosmically defined sacred time early in the Medinan period (*fa-man shahida minkumu l-shahra fa-l-yaṣumhu... wa-li-tukmilū l-ʿiddata,* Q 2:185; SEE CHRONOLOGY AND THE QURʾĀN), its beginning and end discernible and definable only by the sighting *(ruʾyā)* of a cosmic sign, the appearance of the new moon *(hilāl),* as was the case for determining the beginning of the month of pilgrimage (*yasʾalūnaka ʿani l-ahillati qul hiya mawāqītu lil-nāsi wa-l-ḥajj,* Q 2:189). Similarly the exact period of daily fasting was defined by cosmic observations, the rising and the setting sun respectively. The qurʾānic ruling, however, refers to these cosmic aspects only obliquely, relying rather on a cultural criterion for the distinction between daylight and darkness, i.e., the possibility of distinguishing a white from a black thread. The reference is to a custom already in use in monotheistic contexts which presupposes a black-white garment used for prayer (*wa-kulū wa-shrabū ḥattā yatabayyana lakumu l-khayṭu l-abyaḍu mina l-khayṭi l-aswadi mina l-fajri thumma atimmū l-ṣiyāma ilā l-layli,* Q 2:187). Ramaḍān was marked from the outset by a particular affinity to liturgical practice, the divine response to human supplications uttered in that period being assured already in the Qurʾān itself (*wa-idhā saʾalaka ʿibādī ʿannī fa-innī qarībun ujību daʿwata ʾd-dāʿi idhā daʿāni fal-yastajībū lī,* Q 2:186; cf. *Isa* 55:6).

In accordance with a pre-Islamic custom, the first ten nights of the month of pilgrimage are also counted as exceptional as reflected in a qurʾānic oath (*wa-layālin ʿashr,* Q 89:2; see OATHS). This month, Dhū l-Ḥijja, had been — before the calendar became confused due to lax intercalations shortly before the event of the Qurʾān — the first month of the new year, a time in which ritual practices in support of the emergence of a new season (see SEASONS) had been essential. Though traces of ancient new year's practices are still recognizable in some qurʾānic pilgrimage rites (Wellhausen, *Reste*), the reform of the calendar, ordained through the Qurʾān, severed all relations of the pilgrimage with a seasonal festival. The necessity of adducing cosmic evidence for determining qurʾānically endorsed feasts, though interpreted explicitly as an act of obedience (q.v.) toward the divine legislator, still leaves a strong cosmic imprint on the character of Islamic feasts. This manifests itself not only in quantitative terms — cosmic observations alone are deemed valid as the criteria for the exact times of beginnings and ends — but in more general, aesthetic terms as well. The cosmic references engender a peculiar imagery which connects the idea of festiveness with that of the creation and the order of the cosmos, not as a merely sensual backdrop, adding emotional potential to the feasts, but in a more sober manner, as a communicated "sign" *(āya),* an invitation to humans to respond to the divine gift of creation by conveying gratefulness *(shukr)* and thus belief (see BELIEF AND UNBELIEF; BLESSING; GRATITUDE AND INGRATITUDE). So although an insistent iconoclasm cannot be denied, yet the impact of the Qurʾān — to use Kenneth Cragg's words — eloquently conserved that sense of the wonder of the natural order which inspires all religiosity, including so-called paganism, and told it in "the signs of God" as the grateful benediction of the divine unity suffused through the plural world (Cragg, *Event,* 24).

Space in cosmological context

The Qurʾān seems to reflect the Aristotelian-Ptolemaic model with the world *(al-dunyā)* as the lowest level in the center covered by seven homocentric spheres (*falak,* pl. *aflāk,* Q 21:33; 26:40). A closer look, however, provides traces of an older, ancient Near Eastern model of the world which is also reflected in Genesis 1:6 (*Allāhu lladhī khalaqa sabʿa samāwātin wa-min al-arḍi mithlahunna,* Q 65:12). Here, the world is viewed as not only covered by seven heavenly spheres but also as relying on as many layers of "earths." The whole structure is surrounded by waters, "oceans," separated by the creator through a barrier (*maraja l-baḥrayni yaltaqiyān/baynahumā barzakhun lā yabghiyān,* Q 55:19-20; cf. 25:53; see BARRIER; BARZAKH). The cryptic qurʾānic statement about the two oceans has engendered diverse interpretations, mostly attempts to vindicate the geocentric Aristotelean-Ptolemaic world view. Only al-Ṭabarī (d. 310/923) presents an interpretation in accordance with the qurʾānic evidence, the image of a world swimming in an ocean and being covered by another ocean above the highest heaven. Al-Ṭabarī (*Tafsīr,* xxvii, 75, ad

Q 55:19) states that the two oceans are located above the earth and around it respectively, the upper waters being fresh and sweet *(ʿadhbun furātun),* the lower salty and bitter *(milḥun ujājun).*

The metaphorical qurʾānic allusions to the all-encompassing dimensions of God's throne (*wasiʿa kursiyyuhu l-samāwāti wa-l-arḍ,* Q 2:255; *wa-huwa rabbu l-ʿarshi l-ʿaẓīm,* Q 9:129) were already taken literally by early exegetes who attempted to fit the two different designations for the throne image into a comprehensive scheme, *ʿarsh* thus figuring as the throne, *kursī* becoming the footstool underneath. Throne and footstool were imagined to be of a physical nature in the sense of celestial bodies located above the heavens and earths. The earthly observer, facing the footstool from below, thus finds himself in a dome-like hemisphere. Equally, the "overflowing ocean" (*wa-l-baḥri l-masjūr,* Q 52:6), introduced as an image of the overwhelming mono-mentality of creation under the sky, was claimed as a celestial phenomenon and explained as "the upper water under the throne." The assembled fragments of early cosmological theories agree that the space between the footstool or the whole throne and the earth is filled with water.

The inhabitants of the created world: humans and jinn

God created humans from dust (*wa-min āyātihi an khalaqakum min turābin,* Q 3:52; 30:20; 40:67; 45:11) or clay (q.v.; *wa-laqad khalaqnā l-insāna min sulālatin min ṭīn,* Q 23:12; cf. 6:2; 32:7; 37:11), potter's clay (*khalaqa l-insāna min ṣalṣālin ka-l-fakhkhār,* Q 55:14), fermented clay (*laqad khalaqnā l-insāna min ṣalṣālin min ḥamaʾin masnūn,* Q 15:26) in contradistinction to the demons which were created from smokeless fire (*wa-khalaqa l-jānna min mārijin min nār,* Q 55:15). He created, then proportioned and stabilized man (*alladhī khalaqaka fa-sawwāka fa-ʿadalaka,* Q 82:7), leading him through the various phases of his life (q.v.; *huwa lladhī khalaqakum min turābin thumma min nuṭfatin thumma min ʿalaqatin thumma yukhrijukum ṭiflan thumma li-tablughū ashuddakum thumma li-takūnū shuyūkhan,* Q 40:67), giving him the beautiful shape he intended (*wa-ṣawwarakum fa-aḥsana ṣuwarakum,* Q 64:3; cf. 7:10), supplying him with the sense of hearing and seeing (*wa-jaʿala lakumu l-samʿa wa-abṣāra wa-l-afʾida,* Q 32:9; see SEEING AND HEARING; EYES; EARS; HEARING AND DEAFNESS) and blowing his spirit (q.v.) into him (*wa-nafakha fīhi min rūḥihi,* Q 32.9, cf. 3:59; 40:68) or uttering the creational imperative "be" over him (*khalaqahu min turābin thumma qāla lahu "kun" fa-yakūn,* Q 3:59) while at once he fixed his death term (*thumma qaḍā ajalan wa-ajalun musamman ʿindahu,* Q 6:2). These stages of creation do not necessarily refer only to the mythical context of the creation of Adam (see ADAM AND EVE) but may perhaps apply as well to the empirically known process of human reproduction in which God takes an active part, forming the human being in the womb of the mother (*huwa lladhī yuṣawwirukum fī l-arḥāmi kayfa yashāʾu,* Q 3:6; see BIOLOGY AS THE CREATION AND STAGES OF LIFE).

Contrarily, *jinn* (pl. *jānn*) in general have been created from fire (*wa-khalaqa l-jānna min mārijin min nār,* Q 55:15; cf. 15:27). *Jinn* figure in the pre-qurʾānic world as familiar beings. They are known from desert life as mostly harmless demons manifesting themselves unexpectedly — often in the guise of an animal — in front of humans as a help (although sometimes as a trick). Alongside this ambivalent role, they also play a significant part as bearers of a faculty of communication crucial for the social life of *al-jāhiliyya,* acting as inspirers of supernatural knowledge to humans who thus become seers or poets (see POETRY AND POETS). A poet is supposed to be "possessed" by an inspiring spirit (i.e. to be *majnūn,* passive participle derived from *jinn*). This faculty of the *jinn* which contradicts monotheistic notions of inspiration is vehemently contested in the Qurʾān: Even the Prophet himself has to cleanse himself of the accusation of being inspired by *jinn* (*wa-mā ṣāḥibukum bi-majnūn,* Q 81:22; cf. 68:2, 51; 52:29; 37:36; 26:27; 15:6; see REVELATION AND INSPIRATION).

Among *jinn,* Iblīs (Q 2:34; 7:11; 15:31f.; 17:61; 18:50; 20:116; 26:95; 34:20; 38:74f.), whose name is derived from Greek "diabolos" (Jeffery, *For. vocab.,* 47f.), plays a prominent role in the Qurʾān. The noble substance from which he is created (fire, q.v.) induces him to claim superiority over man who is created from clay *(ṭīn)*. His double affiliation — on the one hand with *jinn,* as implied in Q 15:27f. and as one might infer from his occasional designation as *al-shayṭān* (Q 20:120; 36:60), and on the other hand with the angels, as evident from Q 15:30f. — suggests that the Qurʾān shares the notion developed in earlier Gnostic thought that both groups, demons and angels, are closely related. They become, however, clearly distinguishable in the Qurʾān when the function of inspiration is involved. The Prophet's own angelic intermediator (*qul man kāna ʿaduwwan li-Jibrīla fa-innahu nazzalahu ʿalā qalbika bi-idhni llāhi...,* Q 2:97; *innahu la-qawlu rasūlin karīm,* Q 69:40) is vehemently defended against the suspicion of belonging to the *jinn* as inspirers of poets (*wa-mā huwa bi-qawli shāʿir,* Q 69:41) or to be a *shayṭān* (*wa-mā huwa bi-qawli shayṭānin rajīm,* Q 81:25).

Descent of humans from paradise to earth

As known from the apocryphal "Life of Adam and Eve" and other pre-qurʾānic sources (for details, see Awn, *Tragedy*), though also found in the Qurʾān, God had announced his plan of creation to the angels (Q 2:28-31; 15:28-38). Man was to be the vicegerent of God on earth. When the angels contest the divine decree, God empowers Adam with the knowledge of the names of all things whereupon the angels accept to prostate themselves before him. Only Iblīs — figuring in the account as one of the angels — refuses, claiming to be created from nobler material than humans. Though condemning Iblīs for his disobedience (q.v.), God grants him his request to play an active role in humankind's destiny as the seducer who performs the task of testing humans until judgment day (Q 7:15-6).

After the creator has formed from Adam a wife for him, "from one soul" (*khalaqakum min nafsin wāḥidatin wa-khalaqa minhā zawjahā,* Q 4:1; cf. 7:189; 30:21; 39:6; 42:11), he lodges them in paradise (q.v.: *yā-Ādamu skun anta wa-zawjuka l-jannata,* Q 2:35; cf. 7:19; see GARDEN). He forbids them to taste from one particular tree (*wa-lā taqrabā hādhihi l-shajarata,* Q 2:35; cf. 7:19; see TREES), the tree of immortality (*shajarati l-khuldi wa-mulkin lā yablā,* Q 20:120), warning them about *al-shayṭān* (*yā-Ādamu inna hādhā ʿaduwwun laka wa-li-zawjika fa-lā yukhrijannakumā mina l-jannati fa-tashqayā,* Q 20:117), a figure identical to Iblīs but bearing in his function of the seducer the generic designation of *al-shayṭān,* i.e. a spirit closely related to the *jinn. Al-shayṭān* succeeds in seducing them with vain promises (Q 7:20-2) and induces them to eat from the forbidden tree. As a result they realize their nakedness and thus their sexuality (*fa-akalā minhā fa-badat lahumā sawʾatuhumā,* Q 20:121; cf. 7:22; also Bounfour, Sexe; see SEX AND SEXUALITY). Immediately they cover themselves with leaves. Overtaken by God, they have to descend from paradise to earth (*fa-qulnā hbiṭū,* Q 2:36) where they continue to live as mortals (*fīhā taḥyawna wa-fīhā tamūtūna wa-minhā tukhrajūn,* Q 7:25), but they do receive, after expressing repentance (*rabbanā alamnā anfusanā,* Q 7:23;

see REPENTANCE AND PENANCE), divine forgiveness (*fa-talaqqā Ādamu min rabbihi kalimātin fa-tāba ʿalayhi,* Q 2:37).

The episode is interpreted as an early covenant between God and Adam, a covenant which Adam and his offspring later forgot (*wa-laqad ʿahidnā ilā Ādama min qablu fa-nasiya wa-lam najid lahu ʿazman/... fa-qulnā yā-Ādamu inna hādhā ʿaduwwun laka...,* Q 20:115-7). The covenant in pre-existence is extended to humankind as a whole (*a-lam aʿhad ilaykum yā-banī Ādama an lā taʿbudū l-shayṭāna innahu lakum ʿaduwwun mubīn,* Q 36:60). In spite of man's liability to neglect it, Adam still figures as the first among the prophets with whom God entered into covenant and is the prototype of the vicegerent of God on earth, destined to reign in truth. The notion of a fatal sin committed by Adam and passed on to humankind does not exist in the Qurʾān (see FALL OF MAN).

The human habitat in space and time

Qurʾānic sections entailing narrative reports of the creation of the world (q.v.; Q 41:8-12) and of humans (Q 2:28-39; 7:10-34; 15:26-48; 17:61-5; 20:115-23; 38:71-85) are chronologically preceded by reminiscences of creation embedded in exhortations to give thanks to God, i.e. "signs of creation" *(āyāt)*. These mostly hymn-like appraisals of divine deeds, very frequent in the early sūras (Graham, Signs; Neuwirth, *Studien,* 192-6), that create the image of the world as a lodging for humans, as a tent granting them repose (*a-lam najʿali l-arḍa mihādan/wa-l-jibāla awtādan/wa-khalāqnākum azwājan/wa-jaʿalnā nawmakum subātan/wa-jaʿalnā l-layla libāsan/wa-jaʿalnā l-nahāra maʿāshan,* Q 78:6-11), are often clad in images familiar to the Psalms (compare, for instance, Q 55 with *Ps* 136). There is, however, the marked difference that while the psalmist praises God as the creator of a monumental cosmos and a paradisiacal dwelling for humans, in the qurʾānic case it is God who reminds them that his abundantly furnished habitat is both a gift demanding thanksgiving in return and a token for which account must be made.

It is obvious that the images used in the Qurʾān to depict the human habitat as divinely created and as divinely sustained are in striking opposition to the image of the heroic homelessness of human beings in the midst of threatening and invincible nature, as reflected in ancient Arabic poetry. Heroic man as depicted in the poetry of the pre-Islamic Arabia is not only charged with hardships to ensure the survival of his clan but also with existential achievements to ensure the honor of his tribe (see TRIBES AND CLANS). The human condition was understood to be governed by the anticipation of a person's *ajal,* his fated time, life being understood as governed by the inscrutable will of a dark, blind, semi-personal being, Fate (q.v.; *al-dahr*) from whose strong grip there was no escape (Izutsu, *God*). Humans thus find themselves in constant confrontation with *al-dahr,* a superior power which wastes his strength and eventually overwhelms him, if he himself does not forestall its blow by exposing himself to the worst dangers, thus inviting death itself to hit him before the appointed time. Contrary to that scenario, in the Qurʾān humans are not only provided for materially (Q 78:6-11), being accommodated in surroundings that sometimes reflects material abundance (*wa-l-arḍa waḍaʿahā li-l-anām/fīhā fākihatun wa-l-nakhlu dhātu l-akmām/wa-l-ḥabbu dhū l-ʿaṣfi wa-l-rayḥān/fa-bi-ayyi ālāʾi rabbikumā tukadhdhibān,* Q 55:10-13), but also spiritually since God takes the responsibility for their dignity by inviting them to accept his guidance. Nothing is left to an unpredictable fate, everything is measured in advance (*inna kulla shayʾin khalaqānhu bi-qadar,* Q 54:49).

The human being's approach to time, conceiving it as devastating, *al-ayyām* and even *al-layālī* — with the multiple meanings of darkness and fate — as wasting one's life away has thus been changed in value. Day has become the portion of time given to humans to strive for their livelihood (*wa-jaʿalnā l-nahāra maʿāshan,* Q 78:11) while nights are merely periods of repose to be spent in the familiar space of home and, moreover, conjugal company (*wa-khalaqnākum azwājan/wa-jaʿalnā nawmakum subātan/wa-jaʿalnā l-layla libāsan,* Q 78:8-10).

These presentations of an intact created space are not to be taken in isolation but are meant to hint at a concealed meaning. They are oriented toward an eschatological focus (see ESCHATOLOGY): God's absolute power to create *(khalq)* warrants his power to recreate (*khalq jadīd,* see POWER AND IMPOTENCE). The image drawn by the *āyāt* is therefore complemented by its reverse projection, the image of the dissolution of creation at the end of the days. These counter-accounts to the *āyāt,* the "eschatological scenarios" (Neuwirth, *Studien,* 190-1), present created space in the situation of its destruction. The eschatological events do not, however, mark the definite extinction of the created cosmos, but space — after passing the temporal limit of judgment — reappears under two contrasting images: the absolute negative, tormenting fire, hell (*jahannam,* see HELL; FIRE); and the absolute positive, the shady paradisiacal garden *(janna),* the representations of which occupy considerable space in the early sūras. The early verses about human accommodation on earth (*al-dunyā,* "the lower world") and in the hereafter (*al-ākhira,* "the last times"), though highly referential, only incidentally reflect the older scriptural narratives themselves. They are very often closely related to the liturgical recollections of ancient Near Eastern lore with their rich metaphoric resources such as the psalms (cf. Speyer, *Erzählungen,* 447-9; Neuwirth, Narrative; see METAPHOR; NARRATIVES) known from the practice of the monotheist groups adjacent to the early community — a fact scarcely astonishing in view of the liturgical character of the early sūras. It is only subsequently that later reminiscences of world creation, encountered in sūras that already serve primarily didactic ends, occur in the shape of sermon-like admonishments.

God and humans

The Qurʾān stresses again and again that humans, as such, are ambivalent creatures, being ungrateful (*qutila l-insānu mā akfarahu,* Q 80:17; cf. 22:46; 42:48; 43:15; see GRATITUDE AND INGRATITUDE) and stubborn (*inna l-insāna li-rabbihi la-kanūd,* Q 100:6), faint-hearted (*inna l-insāna khuliqa halūʿan,* Q 70:19), heavy (*laqad khalaqnā l-insāna fī kabad,* Q 90:4), unruly and willful (*inna l-insāna la-yaṭghā,* Q 96:6). This deficiency — as the context of the sūras in question shows — is due both to their shortsightedness and to their obligations to their creator (*a-yaḥsabu an lam yarahu aḥad,* Q 90:7; cf. 100:9f.). It is a defect anticipated by the angels who before the creation of Adam disapproved of God's plan to install humans as his deputies on earth arguing that they might cause corruption and shed blood (*qālū a-tajʿalu fīhā man yufsidu fīhā wa-yasfiku l-dimāʾ,* Q 2:30). Still, "humanity," through Adam, is a *khilāfa* (see caliph) of God. The centrality of humanity and its representational relationship to God can be seen as grounded in an ontological "community" (al-Azmeh, *Thought;* see COMMUNITY AND SOCIETY IN THE QURʾĀN). Although according to the Qurʾān human beings are not explicitly created in the image of God, they still share crucial faculties with God, primarily that of mercy (q.v.; *raḥma,* cf. e.g. *wa-huwa arḥamu l-rāḥimīn,* Q 12:92; and *fa-ammā l-yatīma fa-lā taqhar/*

wa-ammā l-sāʾila fa-lā tanhar, Q 93:9-10), the readiness to revise their positions and repent (*thumma yatūbūna min qarībin fa-ūlāʾika yatūbu llāhu ʿalayhim,* Q 4:17), to remain patient (*wa-laʾin ṣabartum la-huwa khayrun lil-ṣābirīn,* Q 16:126). If humans do not cope with the tasks imposed on them by God's primordial design, it still remains their destiny to take them upon themselves. As a creature the human being is surely subject to contradictory conditions, grandeur and wretchedness (*laqad khalaqnā l-insāna fī aḥsani taqwīm/thumma radadnāhu asfala sāfilīn,* Q 95:4-5). However, as the symbolic subtext of the sūra suggests, human time (q.v.) is not confined to the circular span of an individual's lifetime but has become linear, extending over a much longer period. Although human physical time does describe a circle from insignificant beginnings to its climax in adulthood and back to decrepitude, the significant, spiritual time of the human condition spans from primordial creation and subsequent divine revelation to humankind on the one hand, to the resolution of creation and the final, eschatological rendering of account on the other.

These images, in spite of their eschatological framework (see ESCHATOLOGY), are closely reminiscent of the psalms, not only implying an active, personal role on the side of God but also his faculty to work as an artisan who shapes humans like a potter shapes his forms (*khalaqa l-insāna min ṣalṣālin ka-l-fakhkhār,* Q 55:14), who used his own hands in creation (*mā manaʿaka an tasjuda li-mā khalaqtu bi-yadayya,* Q 38:75) and who certainly keeps everything under his supervision (*wa-ṣnaʿi l-fulka bi-aʿyuninā,* Q 11:37). These verses of the Qurʾān with their overtly anthropomorphic imagery, attributing to God not only power and will but also eyes (q.v.) and hands (q.v.) and most strikingly a stable location, a throne (*thumma stawā ʿalā l-ʿarshi,* Q 7:54), are apt to counterbalance the evidence of an absolute transcendence of God as suggested by the numerous verses about his extreme remoteness and exclusive power (see ANTHROPOMORPHISM). The notion of one particular God as the creator of the world, of course, had already been acknowledged in pre-Islamic Arabia but this association between creation and God had not always been necessarily firm and definite and thus could be taken to be of little relevance for created beings. It is exactly the awareness of human "creatureliness" (Isutzu, *God*), the acceptance of this particular descent of humankind, that forms the basis of an Islamic consciousness.

There is further evidence of a totally new scenario of mundane interaction: Social life appears not only to be based on God's providence, as though God were simply a substitute for the blind fate which overshadowed the *jāhilī* life (see AGE OF IGNORANCE), but also to be substantially new in nature. Human interaction is no longer confined to the human agents involved but has been extended to accommodate a new "mythic participant," — hierarchically more elevated than the human co-actors — who plays the role of a "stage director." He lends his hand to support his creatures in difficult ventures such as the exaction of blood revenge (see VENGEANCE) — previously a domain of the heroic individual (*faqad jaʿalnā li-waliyyihi sulṭānan falā yusrif fī l-qatli innahu kāna manṣūran,* Q 17:33) and relieves man of the burden of providing for his extended family in times of crisis; God's provision even works to eliminate the barbaric forms of self-preservation inherited from the *jāhiliyya,* such as infanticide (q.v.; Q 17:31, cf. 81:9). But God as the creator and preserver of his creatures is not only their co-actor, he is their preceptor as well: The mode of communicating the new knowledge about the personal divine-human relation itself claims to encompass the participation of the dominant new protagonist as it emerges as speech sent from on high. Insofar as this sender is at once an ever-present actor in the scenario of the new scripture-oriented interaction, communication as reflected in the Qurʾān decisively transcends all earlier analogies of superhuman transmission of knowledge, primarily the mode of soothsaying, *waḥy al-kahāna* (see SOOTHSAYERS).

Developments

The problem of evil and suffering (q.v.), the need to explain their existence, which does not arise in tribally oriented traditional religions, had to be introduced for pagan listeners of the qurʾānic message. The myth of the first sin or more precisely of human initiation in the notion of good and evil, is conveyed in a biblical context in the account of the first couple's tasting of the forbidden tree in the very beginning of the Judaeo-Christian scripture. As for the Qurʾān, the analogous account does not occupy a comparably prominent position. With regard to the early sūras, the divine creation of humans is often recollected, clad in hymn-like reminiscences of divine providence that appear in the context of short hymn-like verses (*qraʾ bismi rabbika lladhī khalaqa/khalaqa l-insāna min ʿalaq*, Q 96:1-2; *alladhī khalaqa fa-sawwā*, Q 87:2). These texts are not interested, however, in the dramatic circumstances of man's transition from a mythic orbit into that of lived reality. With the evolution of the polythematic sūra, i.e. with the transition of the Qurʾān from an oral to a written and thus scripture-oriented text and the accompanying process of a canonization from below (Neuwirth, Rezitationstext; see BOOK), a complex structure for the mythic drama emerges. The divine choice of the human being as God's elect and the ensuing election (q.v.) of a community is presented in six sūras; in later cases, it is complemented by the account of the first transgression. All cases, however, work to elucidate particular needs of the community. The complete set of structural elements are (1) a short introductory recollection of the creation of human beings or of the pact concluded between God and humankind. This is followed by (2) the drama in heaven: (a) God's announcement to the angels of Adam's creation, (b) their disapproval but (c) final acceptance of Adam's election, and (d) the deal concluded between God and Iblīs allowing for the testing of man by Iblīs/*al-shayṭān*. After its treatment in the first three sūra accounts, the deal story is finally followed by (3) the test of the first couple. It is, however, noteworthy that the canonized final text of the Qurʾān (*muṣḥaf*, q.v.) has placed a most elaborate and theologically relevant version of the comprehensive account in the first main part of the first long sūra though not the beginning of the corpus.

Sūra 15:26-48

The earliest testimony of the story occupies the central part of Q 15 (vv. 26-48). It is still confined to the drama of the deal in heaven (2 a, c, d). This simple type (i.e. without the test of the first couple) unfolds before the mythic backdrop of the creation of humans and *jinn* from diverse substances as stated in the programmatic verse Q 15:26, quoted almost exactly from the earlier Q 55:14-5 (*innā khalaqnā l-insāna min ṣalṣālin ka-l-fakhkhār wa-khalaqa l-jānna min mārijin min nār*, Q 15:26-7). This diversity of the elements of creation which did not produce immediate antagonisms between the two groups in Q 55, gains momentum in all the texts involving Iblīs. After creating the first human being from clay God invites the spirits — creatures generated from fire — to prostrate themselves before him (see BOWING AND PROSTRATION). Only Iblīs refuses — claiming to be of more noble origin than Adam. Accused of disobedience and cursed, he is nevertheless granted respite from punishment and authorized to set out to challenge his primordial rival, Adam, i.e. humankind, through seduction. God himself thus cedes part of his interaction with humankind to Iblīs, entitling him to test humans. He will, however, have no power over God's elected servants (*illā ʿibādaka minhumu l-mukhlaṣīn,* Q 15:40). Humans thus have the option of following guidance or giving way to seduction, which henceforth provides the criterion separating true believers and deluded disbelievers (see BELIEF AND UNBELIEF). It is the work of Iblīs that underlies the crisis reflected in the sūra, namely the schism of the Meccans into believers and unbelievers. Inasmuch as the agreement between God and Satan, concluded in pre-existence (for the type of this mythical story cf. Job), foresees that most of those put to the test by Iblīs/*al-shayṭān* will not resist seduction, it is only logical that the community of the first hearers of the Qurʾān *(ʿibādu llāhi mukhlaṣūn),* who have remained untouched by Iblīs, have to face a majority who insist on denying the message (see OPPOSITION TO MUḤAMMAD). The Meccan community and their opponents alike thus appear to have been preconceived as such in pre-existence. The focus of the argument is on the election of the group of actual listeners, the adherents of the qurʾānic message, who, though suffering social hardships, are divinely elected. The mythic narrative comes as a consolation (q.v.), serving to reaffirm for them the justice of their cause and to legitimate them as a religious community. Their status as a religious community is affirmed by the fact that the ensuing pericope addresses them (*nabbiʾ ʿibād,* Q 15:49) as the recipients of a divine message, including the exemplary story of previously beleaguered righteous believers. With such biblical predecessors of the Meccan community, who emerge from their struggle against calumny, prejudice, superstition and tradition, with manifest triumph, with their foes and hostile conspirators disowned and broken (Cragg, *Event,* 171), the sūra predicts success for those who endure.

Sūra 38:71-85

The second version of the simple type of the deal-story (Q 38:67-85) serves different ends. The pericope which differs in rhythm and rhyme from the preceding text may have been linked to it in order to supply a heavenly prototype (Q 38:69) for the ambivalent activity of arguing which appears as the leitmotiv of the whole sūra. Dispute is presented as the negative counterpart of the implementation of truth (*al-ḥukm bi-l-ḥaqq,* Q 38:22, 26; cf. 38:84; see DEBATE AND DISPUTATION). The central figure of the sūra is David (q.v.; Dāwūd), evoked as a prominent scriptural personification of the primordial deputy of God on earth, as divinely decreed (*yā-Dāwūdu inn jaʿalnāka khalīfatan fī l-arḍi fa-ḥkum bayna l-nāsi bi-l-ḥaqqi wa-lā tattabiʿi l-hawā fa-yuḍillaka ʿan sabīli llāhi,* Q 38:26). The episode relates that two numinous disputants (*wa-hal atāka nabaʾu l-khaṣmi.../idh dakhalū alā Dāwūda fa-faziʿa minhum qālū lā takhaf, khaṣmāni...,* Q 38:21-2) appear before David to enact a symbolical lawsuit thereby arousing his troubled conscience (*wa-ẓanna Dāwūdu annamā fattannāhu fa-staghfara rabbahu,* Q 38:24). The argument is about a case where truth was suppressed by rhetorical means (*wa-ʿazzanī fī l-khiṭāb,* Q 38:23), an inappropriate use of dispute. Dispute to avoid facing a truth is also practiced by those condemned to hell (*takhāṣumu ahli l-nār,* Q 38:64). But the primordial origin of arguing lies in the role played by Iblīs in the heavenly deal. It is true, the heavenly council (see COURT) itself is in dispute (*mā kāna lī min ʿilmin bi-l-malaʾi l-aʿlā idh yakhtaṣimūn,* Q 38:69), most probably an allusion to the angels' disapproval of the election of Adam as deputy of God and thus entitled to the obedience of the heavenly hosts (*wa-idh qāla rabbuka lil-malāʾikati innī jāʿilun fī l-arḍi khalīfatan fa-qālū a-tajʿalu fīhā man yufsidu fīhā,* Q 2:30). But all finally comply; only the pretentious Iblīs (*istakbara,* Q 38:74; see ARROGANCE) insists on the inferiority of humans to spirits, daring to dismiss God's argument of creating Adam with his own hands (*mā manaʿaka an tasjuda li-mā khalaqtu bi-yadayya,* Q 38:75) in view of his nobler substance. He is cursed (see CURSE) and driven from the heavens. Being granted, however, respite from punishment, he starts a new argument. He invokes God's omnipotence itself (*bi-ʿizzatika,* Q 38:82) in swearing to seduce all of Adam's offspring — again excluding explicitly the elected servants (Q 38:83; cf. 15:40). Against Iblīs' pathetic oath, God invokes the truth of his own word (*qāla fa-l-ḥaqqu wa-l-ḥaqqa aqūl,* Q 38:84) to attest to the firmness of his will to punish Iblīs and his followers, consigning them to hell. The pericope embedded in a section about reaffirmation of the community is — however close in content to that in Q 15 — distinguished from it by its far higher tension, being itself an enactment of a *takhāṣum,* a fierce argument. Arguing, in the sense disapproved by the ḥadīth (*inna abghaḍa l-nāsi ilā llāhi l-aladdu l-khaṣmi*) has its primordial origin in Iblīs' performance in the deal episode. The focus of the version presented in Q 38 is on the pretentiousness of Iblīs (*istakbara,* Q 38:74-5) who dares to argue with God, only to end up with the power to work seductive works (*la-ughwiyannahum,* Q 38:82) that fail next to God's true words (*al-ḥaqq,* Q 38:84). His is a merely rhetorical message devoid of truth and meant to lead to an illusive confidence in human self-sufficiency on the side of his followers.

Sūra 17:61-5

A further echo of the deal-story, again placed in the context of consolation in a crisis, is presented by a short pericope in Q 17:61-5. The passage is part of a vehement polemic (see POLEMIC AND POLEMICAL LANGUAGE) against unbelievers which entails admonitions to the community to remain patient with those who are obviously affected by Iblīs/*al-shayṭān* (*wa-qul li-ʿibādī yaqūlū llatī hiya aḥsanu inna l-shayṭāna yanzaghu baynahum inna l-shayṭāna kāna lil-insāni ʿaduwwan mubīnan,* Q 17:53). The isolation the community suffers thus follows from Iblīs' power over the majority of humankind (*la-aḥtanikanna dhurriyyatahu illā qalīlan,* Q 17:62), while it is at the same time proof of their being elected (*inna ʿibādī laysa laka ʿalayhim sulṭānun wa-kafā bi-rabbika wakīlan,* Q 17:65). The short recollection of the deal-narrative pinpoints the means of seduction introduced by *al-shayṭān,* particularly wealth and numerous offspring, those privileges of which the community's powerful opponents boast. The mythic story thus reveals them as most ambiguous commands, no more than divinely intended devices for testing. In the end, the essential remains the enactment of the human response to the offer of divine guidance.

Sūra 20:115-23

In the second type of the account, which focuses on the test (3) of the primordial couple, only allusion is made to the mythic deal (2) between God and Iblīs. This more complex narrative is presented in the final, consoling, section of Q 20 (vv. 115-23). The story is introduced (1) as a divine covenant (q.v.) with Adam. *Al-shayṭān,* obviously identical with Iblīs but introduced with his generic designation to underline his role as a malign force, seduces the first couple to taste from the tree of immortality (*shajaratu l-khuld,* Q 20:120). They comply — in spite of a divine warning (*yā-Ādamu inna hādhā ʿaduwwun laka wa-li-zawjika,* Q 20:117) — obviously from mere curiosity since God has reminded them that they do not lack anything by which to satisfy their hunger (*inna laka allā tajūʿa fīhā,* Q 20:118). What they actually gain from tasting the forbidden fruit is, however, not immortality but the awareness of their nakedness and their sexuality (Bounfour, Sexe). The hitherto unfelt desire to consume the fruit from the unknown tree is now followed by an equally novel desire to cover their bodies, a measure which God had declared to be superfluous (*inna laka allā tajūʿa fīhā wa-la taʿrā,* Q 20:118). Once the fruit is tasted, the awareness of individuality and thus the need of delimiting oneself from the surrounding world, of bearing a secret (see SECRETS) not to be exposed to outsiders, has been aroused: They cover themselves with leaves. The implications of their changing relationship towards the outer world are, however, fully elaborated. The transgression is, contrarily, viewed solely as demanding repentance. Accepted once again by God they are granted guidance. Though they have to descend from paradise, obviously understood as a demotion in status, they do not part without the divine promise that guidance will be offered to them later on to save them from going astray (q.v.). It is the awareness of this binding covenant between God and humankind which can only be disrupted by human forgetfulness (*qāla ka-dhālika atatka āyātunā fa-nasītahā wa-ka-dhālika l-yawma tunsā,* Q 20:126) that marks the dividing line between the community and the disbelievers. The community — and this is the message of the sūra — has become a people of a divine covenant (q.v.). It is noteworthy that this first version of the test-narrative displays a particular tendency to rid single narrative elements of their virtual mythic potency. Thus the act of tasting of the fruit deemed fatal in the biblical story as well as the desire to cover one's body, an experience marking the transition to a new stage of socialization, are both reduced in advance to a mere satisfaction of physical needs, God admonishing the first couple that they do not suffer from hunger nor from lack of clothing. The mythic significance of the acts, the momentum of their essential "firstness," has thus been lost and excluded.

Sūra 7:10-34

The third type of account, which is the most comprehensive account, entailing an introduction and both the deal- and the test-narratives (1, 2, 3), is presented in a pericope embedded in the polemical introductory section of Q 7 (vv. 10-34). It starts with an appeal (1) to the listeners — who are viewed as embodying Adam — to remember their creation and their accommodation in their earthly dwelling, presented as an ideal habitat, and to be accordingly grateful. The scenario then switches to the heavens (2) where Iblīs figures in his well-known role as a rebel refusing to prostrate himself before Adam; he is cursed but at his request granted a stay of punishment. Rather, he sets out to seduce humans to the vice of ingratitude — that particular human deficiency already lamented as prevailing among them in the introduction. The test story (3) again sets forth an appeal, addressed to Adam and his wife to enjoy the fruit of the garden except for one tree which they are to avoid. *Al-shayṭān,* eager to make them aware of their nakedness, whispers that the restriction has only been made to deny them the status of angels and eternal life. Arousing their curiosity and greed for a good withheld, he induces them to eat from the tree, thus causing their discovery of their nakedness. Again they hasten to cover themselves with leaves. The mischief cannot, however, remain hidden; God calls them to account, reminding them that they have been warned about *al-shayṭān* — an allusion to the earlier text Q 20:117 *(yā-Ādamu inna hādhā ʿaduwwun laka wa-li-zawjika fa-lā yukhrijannakuma mina l-jannati fa-tashqayā)*. They acknowledge their transgression and ask to be pardoned. Since the acceptance of the plea is already known from an earlier text (*thumma ijtabāhu rabbuhu fa-tāba ʿalayhi wa-hadā*, Q 20:122), the divine answer is confined to the decree that they have to leave paradise altogether to find their living on earth, destined moreover to be each other's enemies. Immortality is emphatically denied to them (*fīhā taḥyawna wa-fīhā tamūtūna*, Q 7:25) but death is not final in view of the central qurʾānic revelation, the promise of resurrection (*wa-minhā tukhrajūna*, Q 7:25). This account of both the election and the test of man, the fullest in the Qurʾān, functions as an etiological basis for an argument that is unfolded in the ensuing sermon. Humans are exhorted (see EXHORATIONS) to accept the custom of clothing as a divine grace calling for gratefulness, a social achievement to assure decency — which is only eclipsed in value by the allegorical cloth of humankind, the virtue of fear of God. They shall beware of *al-shayṭān* whose seduction brings about degradation in rank and humiliation through exposure. Further admonitions ensue regarding decent behavior in places of worship, while the upholders of coarse pagan customs are denounced as followers of *al-shayṭān*. The account, which is obviously understood to culminate in the primordial couple's shocking awareness of their nakedness, is thus put to the service of a reform concept, the plea for a less ostentatious pagan practice of ancient Arabian rites which were occasionally performed by naked worshipers.

Sūra 2:28-39

The fourth type (Q 2:28-39) presents yet a different selection of elements: It is characterized by a particularly elaborate prologue (2a) to the — shortly summarized — heavenly deal (2b), leading to the test story (3). The prologue, focusing on the newly developed design, serves to solve the enigma of God's demand of the angels to prostrate themselves before a figure other than himself. The pericope (Q 2:28-39) is part of a sūra which appears as a loose collection of diverse text units, thus making it difficult to judge the structural function of its single elements; the pericope may, however, be fruitfully juxtaposed to previous versions. With a prelude which recalls (1) the creation of humankind and the cosmos (Q 2:28-9) it continues with God's announcement that he is to establish a deputy on earth (*innī jāʿilun fī l-arḍi khalīfatan*, Q 2:30), a plan vehemently opposed by the angels who anticipate the moral ambivalence of human behavior in contrast to their own pure service of God (*wa-naḥnu nusabbiḥu bi-ḥamdika wa-nuqaddisu laka*, Q 2:30). In order for him to be superior to the angels Adam is endowed with the knowledge of the names of things and thus accepted. The angels refrain from further argument complying with God's knowledge of hidden truth (*a-lam aqul lakum innī aʿlamu ghayba l-samāwāti wa-l-arḍi*, Q 2:33; see HIDDEN AND THE HIDDEN). They prostrate themselves before God's elect with the now well-known exception of Iblīs whose ensuing "investiture" as seducer is now presupposed. In the second part of the narrative (3), Adam, whose future important role in the lower realm of the earth has already been disclosed to the listeners, has to go through the decisive change from a privileged but not self-responsible inhabitant of the garden to an active responsible agent on earth. The positive response to God's invitation to establish himself with his wife in the garden but to confine themselves to the share entrusted to them (*wa-kulā minhā raghadan ḥaythu shiʾtumā wa-lā taqrabā*..., Q 2:35) cannot therefore be lasting. Indeed, the ensuing transgression of the limits set in the divine offer is but the enactment of the transition demanded for the realization of the destined change. But the qurʾānic perspective is different: The blame is laid on *al-shayṭān* who is accused of having made them slip and thus of despoiling their enjoyment of the garden and the status they had held. They are ordered to descend to earth, inimical to each other (see ENEMY), where they will find a living place and provisional means of living. Their repentance and rehabilitation being known from the earlier texts, it is only fitting that Adam whose election as *khalīfatu llāh* on earth and whose endowment with knowledge constituted the beginning of the story, is honored in the end by a divine message (*fa-talaqqā Ādamu min rabbihi kalimātin*, Q 2:37) and promised guidance for his offspring. The pericope is strongly referential and relies on the listeners' knowledge of important details from earlier publicized pericopes. But the plot has by now changed its focus: It is no longer a consolation for the community of the elect confronted with followers of the seducer as in the earliest versions (type one), nor a lesson in obedience the neglect of which will result in shameful self-exposure and humiliating degradation from a noble status to a more burdensome one (type two), nor an argument for the implementation of new social norms (type three). Rather, it is obviously intended to be more universal by presenting the primordial exemplum for the endless coexistence of the positive option of divine guidance — to be implemented by the deputy of God on earth — and the negative option of following one's desire. Inclination towards the wrong choice has been already experienced by the first human being and is reflected in human behavior since then. The human being now established as the deputy of God on earth, the qurʾānic admonitions and recollections of examples acquire the momentum of this deputy's ethical project to be implemented on earth.

Summary: Some theological implications

The seemingly repetitive qurʾānic creation accounts clearly convey various messages. They share, however, the characteristic of a far-reaching emptiness of those mythical traits that in the biblical story serve to explain world order etiologically. Indeed, a kind of demystification has taken place. The first woman is neither compromised by a "secondary" origin from a rib of Adam, thus being degraded to comparatively inferior rank, nor does she play a fatal initiative role in the act of transgression that could win her the doubtful reputation of a seductress. Furthermore, the tasting of the food is not motivated by any alluring mystery that could arouse desire (the biblical *concupiscentia oculorum*); rather, the act is marginalized as essentially superfluous in view of the lack of hunger suffered by the inhabitants of the garden. Not even the sudden discovery of their nakedness as a shocking exposure is viewed as more than incidental mischief. The most significant role of Iblīs as a dialogical agent — bringing about the transformation of the human being from an obedient but not self-responsible creature to an active agent fit to take up his task on earth — remains unacknowledged in the Qurʾān. It is no surprise, then, that later exegetes in the Ṣūfī tradition have revised his image.

Iblīs becomes a tragic figure raised to the rank of the purest believer in the unrivalled uniqueness of his lord, whose refusal to prostate himself before Adam though an act of disobedience to God's command, becomes an act of faithfulness to God's will (Ḥallāj; Awn, *Tragedy*). It is noteworthy that determinist exegesis leads to similar conclusions: If God has decreed the role of Iblīs, how can Iblīs be blamed? The Qurʾān and mainstream exegesis, however, do not allow for such a moral rehabilitation of the figure. Still in the narrative, however, he alone retains a mythic dimension, posing an unsolved enigma. In view of the otherwise strikingly a-mythic reading of the ancient accounts in the Qurʾān it becomes all the more relevant that a mythic elevation of the community of believers has taken place, their emergence being foreshadowed in the deal concluded in pre-existence between God and Iblīs. It is in that sense that the community is anticipated, raised to the rank of God's elects, inaccessible to the machinations of Iblīs. The final growth of the account reached in Q 2:28-39 culminates in a combination of two election narratives, the universal election of Adam who is called upon to implement divine truth on earth and the historical election of the community to live up to the truth transmitted to them from the same source, is hardly purely accidental. At this advanced stage of the canonical process where the concept of a *khalīfatu llāh* on earth as an agent of God who is to reign in truth (already touched upon, but not yet unfolded in Q 38:26) constitutes the nucleus of a central qurʾānic design, could a more qualified personification of that divine design be imagined than that offered by the elect community?

A later, isolated verse, Q 33:72, presents a shorthand mythic image — familiar to other Near Eastern traditions as well (cf. Speyer, *Erzählungen*) — for the unique rank of man in the qurʾānic concept of cosmogony: "We offered the trust to the heavens and the earth and the mountains, but they refused to carry it and were afraid of it; and man carried it, verily man is sinful, very foolish" *(innā ʿaraḍnā l-amānata ʿalā l-samāwāti wa-l-arḍi wa-l-jibāli fa-abayna an yaḥmilnahā wa-ashfaqna minhā wa-ḥamalahā l-insānu innahu kāna ẓalūman jahūlan)*. Humans thus took upon themselves the challenge and the risk of falling prey to injustice and error (q.v.). Human consent to this privileged, yet dangerous stance within the venture of creation appears like a "fiat" to the order of a world that involves humans as serious partners from the beginning (Talbi, *L'homme*). The risk is, of course, mutual: Cragg (*Mind*, 142) has stressed, "there is an evident risk divinely taken at creation. Man was seen as a dubious proposition in the divine counsels — too frail to be trusted, too arrogant to be thus empowered, too liable to shed blood and corrupt the earth. In this qurʾānic myth of man-the-liability, history is seen as the sphere of the Satanic determination to prove the accusation valid and the divine risk discredited. The very theme of history is thus the question mark of human worth, albeit understood as a vital question-mark of divine wisdom and power. The wisdom of God is staked on the credibility of man as its supreme test and venture. The question of God is the question of man. The human is in this way the sphere in which the divine is either acknowledged or belied." See HISTORY AND THE QURʾĀN.

Angelika Neuwirth

Bibliography

A. Ambros, Gestaltung und Funktionen der Biosphäre im Koran, in *ZDMG* 140 (1990), 290-325; G.-C. Anawati, La notion de "péché originel" existe-t-elle dans l'Islam? in *SI* 31 (1970), 29-40; R. Arnaldez, Khalḳ, in *EI²*, iv, 980-8; A. al-Azmeh, *Arabic thought and Islamic societies*, London 1986; P.J. Awn, *Satan's tragedy and redemption. Iblis in Sufi psychology*, Leiden 1983;

A. Bounfour, Sexe, parole et culpabilité dans le recit coranique de l'origine, in *SI* 81 (1995), 43-65; G. Böwering, The concept of time in Islam, in *Proceedings of the American Philosophical Society* 141 (1997), 57; K. Cragg, *The event of the Qur'an. Islam in its scripture*, Oxford 1971, 1994; id., *The mind of the Qur'an*, London 1977; P. Crone and M. Hinds, *God's caliph. Religious authority in the first centuries of Islam*, Cambridge 1986; J. van Ess, Das begrenzte Paradies, in P. Salmon (ed.), *Mélanges d'Islamologie. Volume dédié à la mémoire de Armand Abel par ses collegues, ses élèves et ses amis*, Leiden 1974, 108-27; S.D. Goitein, Prayer in Islam, in S.D. Goitein (ed.), *Studies in Islamic history and institutions*, Leiden 1966, 73-89; W. Graham, "The winds to herald his mercy" and other "Signs for those of certain faith." Nature as token of God's sovereignty and grace in the Qurʾān, in Sang Hyun Lee et al. (eds.), *Faithful imagining. Essays in honor of Richard R. Niebuhr*, Atlanta 1995, 18-38; R. Grämlich, Der Urvertrag in der Koranauslegung (zu Sure 7:172-173), in *Der Islam* 60 (1983), 205-30; G. von Grunebaum, Observations on the Muslim concept of evil, in *SI* 31 (1970), 117-34; al-Ḥallāj, al-Ḥusayn b. Manṣūr, *Kitāb al-Ṭawāsīn*, ed. P. Nwyia, Beirut 1972; A. Heinen, *Islamic cosmology. A study of as-Suyūṭī's* Al-hayʾa as-sanīya fī l-hayʾa as-sunnīya *with a critical edition, translation, and commentary*, Beirut 1982; A. Neuwirth, Images and metaphors in the introductory sections of the Meccan *sūras*, in Hawting and Shareef, *Approaches*, 3-26; id., Vom Rezitationstext über die Liturgie zum Kanon. Zu Entstehung und Wiederauflösung der Surenkomposition im Verlauf der Entwicklung eines islamischen Kultus, in Wild, *Text*, 69-105; id., Qurʾānic literary structure revisited. Sūrat ar-Raḥmān between mythic account and decodation of myth, in S. Leder (ed.), *Fiction and fictionality in classical Arabic literature*, Halle 1999; R. Paret, Signification coranique de Ḫalīfa et d'autres derives de la racine Ḫalafa, in *SI* 31 (1970), 211-8; M. Talbi, *L'homme dans le Coran*, Paris 1970; K. Wagtendonk, *Fasting in the Koran*, Leiden 1968; W.M. Watt, God's caliph. Qur'anic interpretations and Umayyad claims, in C.E. Bosworth (ed.), *Iran and Islam*, Edinburgh 1971; J. Wellhausen, *Reste altarabischen Heidentums*, Berlin 1897², repr. 1927, 1961.

Courage

That quality of mind which enables one to meet danger and difficulties with resolve.

Although this notion is often invoked in the Qurʾān, especially in verses that describe the struggle of the Muslim community against their Meccan and pagan Arab foes (see OPPOSITION TO MUḤAMMAD; ARABS), it is usually expressed indirectly or descriptively. The words *shajāʿa*, *ḥamāsa* and *basāla* that commonly designate "courage," "bravery" or "valor" in pre-Islamic poetry and tribal lore are conspicuously absent from the qurʾānic text (see PRE-ISLAMIC ARABIA AND THE QURʾĀN). Qurʾānic terms such as *baʾs* (Q 48:16; 59:14; 27:33), *baṭsh* (Q 50:36), *ṣabr* and its derivatives (Q 3:142, 146; 2:153, 155; 8:46, 65; 19:65, etc.), *jihād* (q.v.) and its cognates (Q 3:142, 9:41,81, etc.), do not cover the same semantic field as the former three, although they do highlight some important aspects of the idea at hand.

The qurʾānic avoidance of the common pre-Islamic words for courage and bravery may be attributed to the radical transformation of the traditional bedouin (q.v.) tribal values following the advent of Islam (see TRIBES AND CLANS). Prominent among these values were *ḥamāsa*, *muruwwa*, and *ʿirḍ* which connoted, in addition to the dignity and power of a free tribesman, his "bravery in battle, patience in misfortune, persistence in seeking blood revenge [see RETALIATION; BLOOD MONEY; MURDER; VENGEANCE], protection (q.v.) of the weak, defiance of the strong" (Izutsu, *Concepts*, 27). More importantly, the word *ḥamāsa* implied the tribesman's readiness to defend valiantly the gods and religious customs of his tribe or tribal confederation, e.g. the *ḥums* and the *ḥilla* (Frantsouzoff, Processes; see IDOLATERS AND IDOLATRY; POLYTHEISM AND ATHEISM). Such connotations may have rendered it totally unacceptable from the Islamic viewpoint. After Islam had thoroughly revised these and other concepts to suit its overall value system, some of the terms that were intimately intertwined with the pre-Islamic bedouin mentality seem to have been consciously abandoned in favor of more neutral ones.

This Islamic revision of the old values and virtues did not necessarily entail a total and indiscriminate rejection of the pre-Islamic code of honor (q.v.) that praised courage and condemned cowardice. It is more appropriate to speak of a selective adaptation of this code to the central tenets of Islam. In the process of this adaptation, the thoughtless, impulsive bravery of the proud tribesman (see ARROGANCE) which often led to the senseless bloodshed (q.v.) and inhuman ferocity of tribal feuds was replaced with the idea of "a noble, well-disciplined courage with a lofty aim serving the cause of the right religion: courage 'in the way of God'" (Izutsu, *Concepts*, 85; see ISLAM; PATH OR WAY [OF GOD]). This type of courage is frequently invoked in the Qurʾān without, however, being described by such value-laden terms of the pre-Islamic past as *ḥamāsa, basāla, shajāʿa* and their derivatives. In the Qurʾān, the correct type of courage is consistently associated with the notions of *ḥilm* and *ṣabr*, which signify man's ability to "overcome his own blind passions and to remain tranquil and undisturbed" in the face of the gravest danger (Izutsu, *God*, 205) and to persevere in championing a religious cause (Izutsu, *Concepts*, 102). These virtues (see VIRTUE) are indispensable for the Muslim warrior on the battlefield (see EXPEDITIONS AND BATTLES; WAR). Therefore, they develop "quite naturally into the spirit of martyrdom, that is, the moral strength to undergo with amazing heroism death or any torment for the sake of one's own faith" (Izutsu, *Concepts*, 102; see MARTYR).

In the Qurʾān, these qualities are sometimes juxtaposed with the unpredictable, reckless behavior of the pagan Arab, who is quick to lose self-control and to succumb to fits of a destructive, blind rage. The contrast between the two types of behavior on the battlefield is thrown into relief in Q 48:26 which sets the senseless fierceness of the pagan inhabitants *(ḥamiyyat al-jāhiliyya)* of Mecca (q.v.; see AGE OF IGNORANCE) in opposition to the unshakable calmness and steadfast resignation of the Muslims, which they acquire through the Divine Presence (*sakīna*, see SECHINA) in their midst (cf. Q 9:26 and 40, where, in addition to the *sakīna*, God reinforces the believers with "the multitudes, or legions, [of angels?] you do not see"; see HIDDEN AND THE HIDDEN). Occasionally, the Muslims' unflagging allegiance to God's cause is presented in terms of a commercial deal between the two parties (see CONTRACTS AND ALLIANCES): "God has bought from the believers their souls and their possessions (see POSSESSION; WEALTH) as they will have the Garden (q.v.; see also PARADISE); they fight in the way of God, they kill and get killed; that is a promise binding upon God in the Torah (q.v.), and the Gospel (q.v.) and the Qurʾān; and who fulfills his covenant (q.v.) more truly than God?" (Q 9:111; see SELLING AND BUYING). The actions of the pagan warrior, on the other hand, are dictated primarily by his exaggerated sense of pride and independence, his obligations toward his kinsfolk (see KINSHIP) and his confidence of his superior physical strength, all of which constituted the bedouin code of honor.

The Qurʾān accentuates the disparity between the pagan and Muslim values by attributing the distinctive concepts of fear (q.v.) and honor to their respective carriers. While the pagan's haughty refusal to surrender to the will of any other person is dictated by his fear of tarnishing his personal honor, as dictated by the unwritten laws of the tribal society, the Qurʾān presents the Muslim as willingly bowing before the supreme authority and might of God (see BOWING AND PROSTRATION; AUTHORITY). Hence his only fear is to fail in his obligations toward his Lord, e.g. by withdrawing from battle or refusing to obey the commands of his Messenger (q.v.; see also DISOBEDIENCE). This pious fear (*khawf, taqwā,* see PIETY) strengthens the resolve of faithful Muslims in times of adversity, causing them to resign themselves to their destiny and to fight in the way of God to the bitter end (Q 3:172-5; cf. 9:81-3). Moreover, while pre-Islamic poetry (see POETRY AND POETS) usually celebrates individual courage, the Qurʾān emphasizes the collective spirit of its Islamic counterpart: "God loves those who fight in his way in ranks, as though they were a building well-compacted" (Q 61:4; see COMMUNITY AND SOCIETY; SOCIAL INTERACTIONS). In this context, the god-fearing attitude of the Muslim fighter which lies behind his inflexible determination to defend his faith is intimately linked to the central tenet of the Muslim religion, that is, the human being's unconditional submission to the will of God. In return God gives them "the reward of this world and the fairest reward of the world to come" (Q 3:148; see REWARD AND PUNISHMENT; BLESSING).

As for those who waver when confronted with a superior enemy force and who seek refuge in their homes due either to weakness or to the whisperings of Satan (see DEVIL; IBLĪS), they are threatened with "a grievous punishment" in the hereafter. The Qurʾān repeatedly condemns them as "the hypocrites and those in whose hearts is sickness" (Q 33:12; see HYPOCRITES AND HYPOCRISY). Boastful (see BOAST) and over-confident in times of peace (q.v.), they quickly panic and lose heart at the sight of the approaching enemy: "When fear comes upon them, you see them looking at you, their eyes rolling like one who swoons of death; but when the fear departs, they flay you with sharp tongues, covetous of the good things. Those have not believed" (Q 33:19). Since such people are interested primarily in the spoils of war (see BOOTY), they are prone to squabbling and mutual recriminations; they also routinely doubt the wisdom of the Prophet and the accuracy of his predictions (Q 3:149-52; see PROPHETS AND PROPHETHOOD; WISDOM; INFALLIBILITY). Their vacillation and opportunism are constantly juxtaposed with the moral strength and selfless heroism of the true believers who remain steadfast and unshakeable under any adversity or suffering: "They were true to their covenant with God; some of them have fulfilled their vow (q.v.) by death, and some are still awaiting, and they have not changed in the least" (Q 33:23).

In many verses, the trials and defeat in battle experienced by the Medinan community are depicted as divine tests that were meant to unmask the backsliders and separate them from the true believers. Although God unfailingly comes to his community's rescue with "legions you do not see," he wants the faithful to demonstrate their fidelity to his cause by exerting themselves in the struggle against their pagan foes (Q 3:140-2,154, 166; 47:4; see TRIAL). The valiant behavior of the Muslim warriors at Badr (q.v.) and Uḥud (q.v.) is prefigured by the feats of the faithful followers of the earlier prophets, e.g. those of Saul's (Ṭālūt; see SAUL) men against whom Samuel (q.v.) sent the superior army of Goliath (Jālūt; see GOLIATH) in an episode probably meant to inspire a similar unswerving loyalty in Muḥammad's own supporters following the defeat at Uḥud (Bell, *Commentary,* i, 52): "Said those who reckoned they should meet God, 'How often a little company has overcome a numerous company, by God's leave! And God is with the patient.' So when they went forth against Goliath and his hosts they said, 'Our Lord, pour out upon us patience, and make firm our feet, and give us aid against the people of the unbelievers!' And they routed them, by the leave of God!" (Q 2:249-50; see TRUST AND PATIENCE).

A large group of hortative verses appears to be explicitly designed to instill resolve in the Muslim warriors fighting against formidable odds. They urge the Prophet and his followers to "faint not, neither sorrow" (Q 3:139; cf. 4:104; 47:35), to "struggle for God as is his due" (Q 22:78; cf. 5:35; 9:41, 73, 86; 25:52; 66:9), and to "fight in the way of God" (Q 2:190, 244; cf. 2:193; 3:167; 4:76, 84; 5:24; 8:39; 9:12, 14, 29, 36, 123; 49:9). These and similar passages mostly pertain to the Muslim battles against pagan Arabs (al-Nakhla, Badr, Uḥud, Ḥunayn [q.v.], etc.). Often invoked in these contexts is the notion of *ṣabr,* "patience," that lies behind the Muslim fighter's "inflexible determination to persist in the face of unrelenting attacks of the enemy" (Izutsu, *Concepts,* 104). The frequency with which this notion is mentioned in "battle sūras" (Q 2:153-5; 3:142, 146, 150; 8:45, 65; 61:4) indicates its centrality to Muslim warfare. The concerted, disciplined war effort of the Muslim community is thus implicitly juxtaposed with the disorganized raiding expeditions of the pagan Arabs that quickly disintegrate when confronted with a stiff resistance or first reversals.

Verses pertaining to courage and heroism on the battlefield became objects of exegetical elaboration in later qurʾānic commentary *(tafsīr).* Muslim scholars sought to elucidate the socio-political context in which the particular verses were revealed in order to draw moral and ethical lessons (see OCCASIONS OF REVELATION; ETHICS IN THE QURʾĀN). In so doing, they often supported their exegesis by relevant ḥadīth enjoining martyrdom and bravery on the battlefield. Typical in this regard is Ibn Kathīr's (d. 774/1373) commentary on Q 3:143 in which he quotes the famous prophetic tradition: "Do not yearn for meeting your enemies; rather ask God for well-being. But if you meet them, be steadfast, and know that paradise is under the shadow of swords" (M. Ayoub, *The Qurʾān,* ii, 334). Al-Shawkānī (d. 1250/1832) explains Q 3:139 in the following manner: "God consoled the Muslims for the injuries and loss of life they suffered on the day of Uḥud. He urged them to fight steadfastly against their enemies and not give in to weakness and defeat. Then God informed them that they would prevail over their enemies with victory (q.v.) and conquest. God meant to say, 'You shall be uppermost over them and any other people after this battle'" (M. Ayoub, *The Qurʾān,* ii, 328). Ṣūfī commentators, on the other hand, sought to detach the "battle verses" from their historical context and infuse them with a spiritual, transcendent meaning (see ṢŪFISM AND THE QURʾĀN). As an example, one may quote a gloss on Q 3:141 by the Ṣūfī author al-Ḥasan al-Nīsābūrī (d. 728/1327). According to his interpretation, the pain and hardships suffered by Muslim warriors symbolize the "cleansing of their hearts (see HEART) of the darkness of unsalutary characteristics, illuminating them with lights of divine mysteries *(ghuyūb),* obliterating the attributes of unfaithfulness... and effacing the wicked marks of their characters. Thus they would be liberated from the prison of phantoms into the sacred realms of the spirits" (M. Ayoub, *The Qurʾān,* ii, 334).

Frequently, such interpretative explanations and conclusions evince the underlying religio-political agendas of the exegetes. Thus, in an effort to reproduce the devoted homogeneity and bold enthusiasm of the primitive community of Medina, Khārijī leaders often quoted "battle verses" to instill in their followers the spirit of self-denial and martyrdom that they attributed to the first Muslim heroes. Citing Q 9:111, the Khārijīs (q.v.) called themselves "vendors" *(shurāt)*, i.e. those who sold their lives and property to God in return for salvation (q.v.). Pro-ʿAlid and Shīʿī exegetes, for their part, use these verses in order to demonstrate the exceptional courage and loyalty to the Prophet shown by ʿAlī during the battles of Badr and Uḥud (see SHĪʿISM AND THE QURʾĀN; ʿALĪ B. ABĪ ṬĀLIB). Simultaneously, they tended to ascribe cowardice and wavering to some of the Companions (see COMPANIONS OF THE PROPHET), including ʿUthmān (q.v.) and to a lesser extent ʿUmar (q.v.), who are said to have fled from the battlefield leaving the Prophet face to face with his enemies. Conversely, Sunnī scholars sought to exonerate their rightly-guided Caliphs (see CALIPH) by offering various explanations on their behalf and by emphasizing Abū Bakr's unwavering commitment to the Prophet and the Muslim cause during these fateful encounters (M. Ayoub, *The Qurʾān*, ii, 311-3, 335-7, 339, 343, 354-5).

Alexander D. Knysh

Bibliography
Primary: Abū Tammām, *Dīwān*, 2 vols., n.p. 1331/1913; Ṭabarsī, *Majmaʿ*.
Secondary: M. Ayoub, *The Qurʾan and its interpreters*, 2 vols., Albany 1984-92, ii; S. Frantsouzoff, Ethnic and confessional processes in pre-Islamic Arabia (the religio-tribal communities of hums, hilla and tuls) [in Russian], in *Sovetskaya etnografiya* 3 (1986), 47-57; A. al-Ḥūfī, *al-Buṭūla wa-l-abṭāl*, Cairo 1967; id., *al-Jihād*, Cairo 1970; Izutsu, *Concepts*, ch. 5; id., *God*, ch. 8; V. Polosin, *A dictionary of the ʿAbs tribe* [in Russian], Moscow 1995; F. Rahman, *Major themes of the Qurʾān*, Minneapolis 1980, 28-31; M. Rodionov, *Muruwwa, ʿaṣabiyya, dīn:* Towards an interpretation of Near Eastern etiquette [in Russian], in *The etiquette of the west Asian peoples* [in Russian], Moscow 1988, 60-8; W.M. Watt, *The formative period of Islamic thought*, Edinburgh 1973.

Court

The celestial court of God as both divine ruler and judge. No qurʾānic wording directly corresponds to the concept of a celestial court but the idea is best approximated by the phrase *al-malaʾ al-aʿlā* which occurs only twice in the Qurʾān (Q 37:8; 38:69). Q 37:6-8 reads: "We have adorned the lowest heaven *(al-samāʾ al-dunyā)* with adornment, the planets, a security from every daring devil. They cannot listen to *al-malaʾ al-aʿlā;* they are pelted from every side." The Qurʾān contains many other scattered references to the celestial court of God, most containing only a few words or lines and offering too few specific details to form a clear picture of the court. This celestial court may be related to pre-Islamic pagan nature myths, which contain similar imagery and for which the sky is a central theme (cf. Bell, *Commentary*, ii, 149; P. Eichler, *Die Dschinn*, 30-1; see PRE-ISLAMIC ARABIA AND THE QURʾĀN; NATURAL WORLD AND THE QURʾĀN). The qurʾānic court consists of God and his angels (see ANGEL) with certain inanimate accoutrements, such as God's throne (e.g. Q 40:7; see THRONE OF GOD) and storehouses (e.g. Q 15:21-2). Mention of the court is mostly associated with either the creation (q.v.) or the last judgment (q.v.).

Among the ongoing purposes of the court is that it provides a place for the angels to sing God's praises and to ask forgiveness for the believers (Q 40:7-9). The angels' praises and supplications exalt God's majesty while also providing an authoritative model for the worship (q.v.) of God required of believers on earth (q.v.). Another purpose of the court is to serve as the locus from which God's commands are sent down to the earth (Q 32:5; cf. 16:2). The mediation of God's commands from the celestial court in the heavens, through angelic messengers, to the earth emphasizes the divine authority (q.v.) backing such commands (see MESSENGERS). When a decree of God goes forth, the devils try to steal a hearing of the court's conversations from the lowest heaven only to be pursued by meteors: "They cannot listen to *al-mala᾿ al-aʿlā;* they are pelted from every side, outcast and theirs is a perpetual torment; except for him who snatches a fragment and a piercing flame pursues him" (Q 37:8-10; cf. 72:8-10). Sometimes, the court takes on a military character as God sends down armies of angels to participate in certain earthly battles (Q 3:124-5; 8:9; see EXPEDITIONS AND BATTLES). The concept of God showering his bounty on earth from his storehouses may also be connected with the image of a regal court, although this does not appear to require angelic intermediaries (Q 15:21-2; see BLESSING).

The Qur᾿ān contains only general descriptions of the court's working; the account of the creation of Adam (see ADAM AND EVE) contains the sole mention of its being issued a specific commandment (Q 2:30-33). The other event of note in which the court participates is its assembling for God's final judgment (Q 2:210; 25:25; 78:38; 89:22) where the angels, prophets or others will not be permitted to intercede with God except by his permission (Q 20:109; 53:26; see INTERCESSION). On that day, certain angels will bear God's throne (Q 40:7; 69:17).

Although the qur᾿ānic references to the celestial court are brief, general and devoid of descriptive imagery, they still constitute a significant area of exegetical difficulty in Muslim religious literature and have become a major subject of debate between literalist and allegorical schools of interpretation (see EXEGESIS OF THE QUR᾿ĀN: CLASSICAL AND MEDIEVAL), the central issue being anthropomorphism (q.v.). On the one hand, the transmitters of ḥadīth *(ahl al-ḥadīth)* and those who, following Aḥmad b. Ḥanbal (d. 241/845), took a traditionalist approach to the interpretation of the Qur᾿ān, used a mass of prophetic traditions elaborating the qur᾿ānic verses on the court to support their insistence that the descriptions referred to actual identifiable objects and that God, in effect, had the likes of a royal court. On the other hand, most of the jurists *(ahl al-fiqh),* the specialists in speculative theology (the *mutakallimūn*) and the philosophers including al-Ghazālī (d. 505/1111) sought to de-emphasize or avoid such interpretations in favor of allegorical ones. Much debate was generated over God's location in the heavens and his ability to sit on a throne (cf. D. Gimaret, *Dieu a l'image de l'homme,* 66-9, 76-89). Most works of qur᾿ānic commentary, however, have no reticence about presenting both types of explanation side by side, especially as both sides — regardless of their opinion about the validity of a literal interpretation of the qur᾿ānic imagery — are agreed that the celestial court symbolizes God's dominion over the heavens and the earth (cf. Q 48:4, 7; 78:37). See also CREATEDNESS OF THE QUR᾿ĀN.

Khalid Yahya Blankinship

Bibliography
Primary: Abū l-Shaykh al-Iṣbahānī, *Kitāb al-ʿAẓama,* ed. R. al-Mubārakfūrī, 5 vols., Riyadh 1988 (discusses anthropomorphic ḥadīths); Ibn Abī Shaybah, *Kitāb al-ʿArsh wa-mā ruwiya fīhi,* ed. M. al-Ḥumūd, Cairo 1410/1990; Ibn Khuzayma, *Kitāb al-Tawḥīd wa-ithbāt ṣifāt al-rabb,* ed. M.M. Aʿẓamī, Cairo 1403/1982-3.
Secondary: Bell, *Commentary;* W.C. Chittick, *The Sufi path of knowledge. Ibn al-ʿArabi's metaphysics of imagination,* Albany 1989; P. Eichler, *Die Dschinn, Teufel und Engel im Koran,* Lucka in Thüringen 1928; R.M. Frank, *al-Ghazālī and the Asharite*

school, Durham 1978; D. Gimaret, *Dieu a l'image de l'homme. Les anthropomorphismes de la sunna et leur interpretation par les theologiens,* Paris 1997, 61-120; J.W. Morris, *The wisdom of the throne. An introduction to the philosophy of Mulla Sadra,* Princeton 1981; W.M. Watt (trans.), *Islamic creeds. A selection,* Edinburgh 1994.

Courtesy and Hospitality see HOSPITALITY AND COURTESY

Cousin see FAMILY

Covenant

An agreement between persons or parties; theologically, the promises of God offered to representatives of humanity as revealed in the scriptures. The Qurʾān employs two principal terms for the idea of covenant, *mīthāq* and *ʿahd,* using each in the singular. *ʿAqd,* the term that is used in Islamic law for the legal act of a contract, a will or other forms of bi- or unilateral declarations, has only a slim qurʾānic basis: Twice the cognate nominal form is used for the marriage contract, i.e. the "knot of marriage" (*ʿuqdat al-nikāḥ,* Q 2:235, 237; see MARRIAGE AND DIVORCE); once the plural, *ʿuqūd,* is employed, probably in reference to Muḥammad's treaty with the Meccans at al-Ḥudaybiya (q.v.; Q 5:1; cf. 9:1; see CONTRACTS AND ALLIANCES). Another cognate, *ʿaqīda,* which is the Arabic term for creed or article of faith (q.v.) and which is central to Islamic theology, does not appear at all in the Qurʾān (see CREEDS). The noun *mīthāq,* "agreement, covenant, contract," is found 25 times in the Qurʾān and is derived from *wathiqa* (constructed with *bi-*) "to place confidence in, depend on, trust in" and *wathuqa,* "to be firm, solid." *ʿAhd,* the term for commitment, obligation, pledge, or covenant, occurs 29 times in the Qurʾān. It is the infinitive *(maṣdar)* of *ʿahida,* "to entrust, empower, obligate," a verb that appears eleven times in the Qurʾān in its third verbal form, *ʿāhada,* "to make a covenant, to pledge oneself to," a meaning which stresses the bilateral aspect of covenant. Both terms are found frequently in sūras of the third Meccan and the Medinan periods of Muḥammad's qurʾānic proclamation (with the earlier term, *ʿahd,* already present in the second Meccan period and *mīthāq* appearing in the Medinan period; see CHRONOLOGY AND THE QURʾĀN) and are used interchangeably in the Qurʾān (compare Q 2:27 and Q 13:20, 25). These two terms are applied to political compacts and civil agreements as well as to the idea of a covenant between God and human beings (cf. A. Jeffery, Scripture, 119-121; see POLITICS AND THE QURʾĀN; LAW AND THE QURʾĀN). The political and civil uses are less frequent (for *ʿahd,* cf. Q 17:34; 23:8; 70:32; for *mīthāq,* cf. Q 4:90, 92; 8:72) with the compact between husband and wife termed once an inviolable covenant (*mīthāqan ghalīẓan,* Q 4:21). The principal qurʾānic signification of covenant, however, is God's enjoining a covenant upon human beings, particularly upon prophets and their followers (see PROPHETS AND PROPHETHOOD).

Underscoring God's unilateral imposition of the covenant, the Qurʾān prefers the phrase that God "took" or "enjoined" (*akhadhnā, akhadha llāh,* cf. Q 33:7, 3:81) the covenant *(mīthāq)* with Muḥammad (q.v.) and with other prophets such as Noah (q.v.), Abraham (q.v.), Moses (q.v.) and Jesus (q.v.). The same turn of phrase is used for God's covenant with the People of the Book (q.v.; Q 3:187), the Christians (*naṣārā,* Q 5:14; see CHRISTIANS AND CHRISTIANITY) and Muḥammad's following (Q 2:84; 57:8), whose loyal supporters keep the covenant (Q 13:20) while disloyal ones break it (Q 13:25; see EMIGRANTS AND HELPERS; OPPOSITION TO MUḤAMMAD). God's covenant *(mīthāq)* with the Children of Israel (q.v.), who broke the covenant made at Sinai (q.v.; Q 2:63, 83, 93; 4:154; 5:12, 70), is couched in an imagery that can be traced back to the biblical covenant *(berit/diathéke)* of the Pentateuch (cf. Horovitz, *KU,* 41, 51; Speyer, *Erzählungen,* 295-296; Wansbrough, *QS,* 8-12; see SCRIPTURE AND THE QURʾĀN). An intriguing reference to God's covenant is also found in Q 7:169 citing "the covenant of the book" (*mīthāq al-kitāb,* see BOOK) because it seems to imply that God separated the righteous from the damned prior to creation (see FREEDOM AND PREDESTINATION). Whether the qurʾānic "rope of God" (*ḥabl Allāh,* cf. Q 3:103, cf. 3:112) can be understood as an image of God's covenant depends in part on the interpretation of the parallel though cryptic phrase of "the most firm handle" *(al-ʿurwatu l-wuthqā,* cf. Q 2:256; 31:22; *wuthqā* and *mīthāq* are derived from the same triliteral Arabic root, *w-th-q).* The qurʾānic phrase of "holding on" to God's rope or to God himself (*iʿtaṣamū bi-llāh,* Q 4:146; cf. 4:175; *yaʿtaṣim,* Q 3:101), especially when paired with the duties of prayer (q.v.) and almsgiving (q.v.; Q 22:78), may refer to obligations pledged at the moment of entering the Muslim community in Medina (see COMMUNITY AND SOCIETY IN THE QURʾĀN). *Mawthiq,* a cognate form of *mīthāq,* is employed in reference to God as the guarantor of the pledge that Jacob (q.v.) takes from his sons promising Joseph's (q.v.) safe return (Q 12:66, 80).

In the Qurʾān, as F. Buhl has shown (Ḳurānexegese, 100-6), the notion of *ʿahd* generally implies a reciprocal obligation of two parties, yet frequently signifies the promise of God in the sense of a unilateral obligation (not unlike the pentateuchal *berit/diathéke*). This latter sense is contained in Q 20:115, "We made a covenant with Adam before *(la-qad ʿahidnā ilā Ādama min qablu),* but he forgot and we found no constancy in him." This crucial qurʾānic reference to God's covenant as *ʿahd* refers to that which Adam (see ADAM AND EVE) broke by eating from the tree of paradise when prompted by the whisperings of Satan (see FALL OF MAN). God also imposed a covenant on Adam's offspring (Q 36:60) obligating them not to serve Satan (see DEVIL). This covenant was broken by Israel through the idolatry of the calf (Q 20:86-9; cf. 7:102; see CALF OF GOLD). Furthermore, God concluded an *ʿahd* with Moses (cf. Q 7:134; cf. 43:49), voided his *ʿahd* for Abraham's progeny when they betrayed it (Q 2:124) and summoned the Children of Israel to fulfil the covenant so that he, God, might fulfil it (*wa-awfū bi-ʿahdī ūfi bi-ʿahdikum,* Q 2:40, perhaps the strongest bilateral declaration of covenant in the Qurʾān). Intercession (*shafāʿa,* see INTERCESSION) in the hereafter is only granted to one who has received the promise of the All-Merciful (*man ittakhadha ʿinda l-raḥmāni ʿahdan,* Q 19:87; cf. 19:78; 2:80). In their deceit, unbelievers among Muḥammad's followers pledge their willingness to give alms if they receive generously from God's abundance (Q 9:75; see BELIEF AND UNBELIEF; HYPOCRITES AND HYPOCRISY). Q 16:91 reminds the believers of the absolute obligation to fulfil the covenant of God into which they have entered *(wa-awfū bi-ʿahdi llāhi idhā ʿāhadtum).* In Q 9:1 and 54:43 the term *barāʾa* (originally, Aramaic *barīya*), seemingly reflecting the Hebrew *berit,* is mentioned in the meaning of God's "pact," and in Q 5:97 the Kaʿba (q.v.) is cited as the visible symbol of God's compact with humanity *(qiyāman lil-nās).* Furthermore, C. Luxenberg (*Die syro-aramäische Lesart des Koran,* 37-8) argues that the qurʾānic phrase *millat Ibrāhīm* (Q 6:161 and passim), understood on the basis of the Aramaic term underlying it (and the Syriac, *meltā,* "word"; cf. F. Buhl, Milla) implies the meaning of God's "covenant" with Abraham (cf. *Gen* 17:2).

On the qurʾānic evidence alone it cannot be demonstrated whether the entrance into Muḥammad's community was linked with a (ceremonial) compact between the neophyte and God (or the Prophet) or an oath of loyalty *(bayʿa)*. In Medina, however, Muḥammad required his followers to swear a solemn promise of allegiance or a pledge of loyalty (e.g. Q 33:15; 48:10; 60:12; *taḥta l-shajarati*, "under the tree," Q 48:18) prior to crucial moments of his cause. The term *ʿahd*, moreover, is used in the Islamic tradition for the treaty of protection (q.v.) the Christians of Najrān (q.v.) received from Muḥammad in exchange for their paying tribute (q.v.) after the ordeal of the *mubāhala* (mutual imprecation) had been averted (cf. Q 3:61, *thumma nabtahil*). For the qurʾānic significance of the oath *(qasam, yamīn)* as both God's oath and a human being's pledge to God, see OATHS; PLEDGE. For animal sacrifice connected to a pledge or a compact between two parties as a qurʾānic reflection of pre-Islamic Arab tribal custom, see SACRIFICE; CONSECRATION OF ANIMALS; PRE-ISLAMIC ARABIA AND THE QURʾĀN.

Early Islamic legal terminology used *ʿahd* (short for *kitāb al-ʿahd*) to signify a certificate of appointment to administrative office under the Umayyads while *mīthāq* denotes hostages given as a pledge of security (cf. E. Tyan, *Histoire*, 56-7; 180-1). The political language of *walī al-ʿahd*, the successor appointed by a ruler, and *ahl al-ʿahd*, non-Muslims with whom the Islamic state has entered into a treaty, also reflects post-qurʾānic usage. For the way in which Arab foreigners, non-Arab freedmen or converts to Islam became associated with the Arab tribal structure (see TRIBES AND CLANS) as kinsmen (see KINSHIP) by oath rather than birth, by way of *ʿahd* and through procedures known as compact or confederacy *(ḥilf)* or proximity of kinsmen or allies *(walāʾ)*, see CLIENTS AND CLIENTAGE and P. Crone, Mawlā.

Q 7:172 includes reference to neither *mīthāq* nor *ʿahd*, but nevertheless became the fulcrum of qurʾānic interpretation for the primordial covenant on the "Day of *Alastu*" (cf. Goldziher; Speyer, *Erzählungen*, 304-5; R. Gramlich, Urvertrag, 205-30) which anchors mystical speculations of Ṣūfism (Böwering, *Mystical*, 147-65; see ṢŪFISM AND THE QURʾĀN). God's servants professed monotheism as humanity's pledge in response to God's revelation in the event of a primordial covenant concluded at the dawn of creation. To God's question "Am I not your Lord?" *(alastu bi-rabbikum)* humanity answered with "Yes, we testify!" *(balā shahidnā)* thereby acknowledging God's oneness and sovereignty and instantiating the first conscious act of the human intellect (*ʿaql*, the source of knowledge by nature in antithesis to *naql*, tradition). Linked with the qurʾānic notions of "God-given nature" (*fiṭra*, Q 30:30) and baptism (*ṣibgha*, Q 2:138; cf. Jeffery, *For. vocab.*, 192; see BAPTISM), the covenant in pre-existence inspired theological controversies on the issue of predestination (cf. J. Van Ess, *Zwischen Ḥadīth*, 34-6, 105-7) and the infant's inborn nature *(anima naturaliter moslemica)* as expressed by the ḥadīth, "Every infant is born according to the *fiṭra* (*ʿalā l-fiṭra*, "on God's plan"); then his parents make him a Jew or a Christian or a Magian" (cf. D. Macdonald, *Religious attitude*, 243). The idea of a primordial covenant animated qurʾānic interpretation in both Sunnī and Shīʿī circles and contributed to the subtle insights of Islamic mysticism (cf. L. Massignon, Le jour, 86-92; U. Rubin, Pre-existence, 62-119; C. Schöck, *Adam*, 138-40, 166-9, 187-92). Lines of continuity between the qurʾānic covenant in pre-existence and the Judaeo-Christian (cf. J. Habermann, *Präexistenzaussagen*, 415-30) as well as the gnostic traditions (cf. I. Goldziher, Neuplatonische Elemente, 317-44) remain insufficiently studied. See also BREAKING TRUSTS AND CONTRACTS.

Gerhard Böwering

Bibliography
T. Andrae, *Die Person Muhammeds in Lehre und Glauben seiner Gemeinde,* Stockholm 1917; Böwering, *Mystical;* F. Buhl, Zur Ḳurānexegese, in *AO* 3 (1924), 98-108; P. Crone, Mawlā, in *EI*², vi, 874-82; id., Milla, in *EI*², vii, 61; J. van Ess, *Zwischen Ḥadīt und Theologie,* Berlin 1975; I. Goldziher, Neuplatonische and gnostische Elemente im Ḥadīt, in *ZA* 22 (1909), 317-44; E. Gräf, *Jagdbeute und Schlachttier im islamischen Recht,* Bonn 1959; R. Gramlich, Der Urvertrag in der Koranauslegung, in *Der Islam* 60 (1983), 205-30; J. Habermann, *Präexistenzaussagen im Neuen Testament,* Frankfurt 1990; Horovitz, *KU;* Jeffery, *For. vocab.;* id., The Qur'ān as scripture. Pts. 1-4, in *MW* 40 (1950), 41-55, 106-34, 185-206, 257-75; C. Luxenberg, *Die syro-aramäische Lesart des Koran,* Berlin 2000; D.B. Macdonald, *The religious attitude and life in Islam,* Chicago 1909; L. Massignon, Le "jour du covenant" *(yawm al-mīthāq),* in *Oriens* 15 (1962), 86-92; J. Pedersen, *Der Eid bei den Semiten,* Strassburg 1914; U. Rubin, Pre-existence and light, in *IOS* 5 (1975), 62-119; C. Schöck, *Adam im Islam,* Berlin 1993; Speyer, *Erzählungen;* E. Tyan, *Histoire de l'organisation judiciaire en pays d'Islam,* Leiden 1960² (revised); Wansbrough, *QS.*

Cow see ANIMAL LIFE

Coward see COURAGE

Cradle see JESUS

Createdness of the Qur'ān

A central issue in Muslim theological discussion that asks whether the Qur'ān was created by God or is, like him, eternal. The term creation *(khalq)* appears 48 times in the Qur'ān and designates the natural world and all existence as God's creation (q.v.). Instances of the perfect and imperfect tenses of the verb *(khalaqa, yakhluqu* and the passive *khuliqa, yukhlaqu)* appear over 200 times in reference to God's act of creation. God himself is referred to in the Qur'ān as the Creator *(khāliq)* twelve times, e.g. "There is no God but he, the creator of everything" (Q 6:102). The phrase *khalq al-Qur'ān,* often rendered as "createdness of the Qur'ān" or "creation of the Qur'ān (by God)," does not occur in the Qur'ān as such. Assertions that the Qur'ān was created appeared at the beginning of the second/eighth century and eventually came to be associated primarily with the heterodox theological school known as the Mu'tazila (see MU'TAZILĪS).

Introduction to the problem

The issue at hand does not conflict with the fact of the prophetic event, i.e. the revelation of the Qur'ān to Muḥammad at a particular point in history. Both proponents of and opponents to the theory of the createdness of the Qur'ān understand many qur'ānic verses as having been revealed in response to a particular situation in Muḥammad's life (see OCCASIONS OF REVELATION; REVELATION AND INSPIRATION). Both sides also acknowledge the role that Muslims in the generations after Muḥammad had in the collection and the ordering of the codices of the Qur'ān (see CODICES OF THE QUR'ĀN; COLLECTION OF THE QUR'ĀN). Nor did the discussion of "createdness" involve the status of the Qur'ān's existence prior to Muḥammad's receiving of the revelation or even its existence before the rest of creation. Rather, the debate over *khalq al-Qur'ān* focuses on the nature of the pre-existent prototype of the book (q.v.), which is known as *umm al-kitāb* (Mother of the Book, see HEAVENLY BOOK) or *lawḥ mahfūẓ* (Preserved Tablet [q.v.]). Both sides are agreed upon the existence of this heavenly prototype, but are in disagreement as to whether it is coeternal with God or contingent upon the will of God, and thus created and existing within a limited sphere of time (cf. van Ess, *TG*, iv, 625-7).

A legendary account of the origins of the assertion of the createdness of the Qur'ān that circulated among some Sunnī heresiographies traces it back through extreme Shī'ī revolutionaries to Ṭālūt, the son-in-law of a Jew, Labīd b. al-A'ṣām. Labīd is said to have tried to cast a magical spell on the Prophet (Ibn al-Athīr, *Kāmil*, 7:49; van Ess, *TG*, i, 442). This may be seen as a later orthodox attempt to depict the Mu'tazila and others who defended the doctrine as enemies of the Prophet Muḥammad as well as of the Qur'ān itself. Muslim heresiographers trace the first claims made by theologians *(mutakallimūn)* that the Qur'ān was created *(makhlūq)* by God and sent down to the Arabs in historical time to the last decade or so of the 'Abbāsid revolution that brought down Umayyad rule (ca. 120/738). In these tumultuous years of uprising and political conflict, inevitably religious in its articulation, two of the darker figures of early Muslim thought are named as proponents of the createdness of the Qur'ān: Ja'd b. Dirham (executed in 125/743) and Jahm b. Ṣafwān (killed in 128/745 while supporting the rebellion of al-Ḥārith b. Surayj).

Before the inquisition

Particular attention is paid to Jahm b. Ṣafwān in the heresiographical literature and especially among traditionalist opponents of the createdness of the Qur'ān such as 'Abdallāh b. 'Abd al-Raḥmān al-Dārimī (d. 255/869) and Aḥmad b. Ḥanbal (d. 241/855). In a heresiographical notice by Abū l-Ḥasan al-Ash'arī (d. 324/936), Jahm b. Ṣafwān is also accused of denying that heaven (q.v.) and hell (q.v.) are eternal (*Maqālāt*, 280, l. 4, 279, l. 2; see ESCHATOLOGY). Jahm's doctrine of God was founded on the strict assertion that God alone is eternal (see GOD AND HIS ATTRIBUTES). All else, including heaven and hell, and even the prototype of scripture — written on a heavenly Tablet, the Mother of the Book — is created. The strongest opponents of Jahm b. Ṣafwān and his followers, known as the Jahmiyya, were the Traditionalists *(muḥaddithūn)* led by Aḥmad b. Ḥanbal. The latter's refutation of Jahm is titled: *al-Radd 'alā l-Zanādiqa wa-l-Jahmiyya*, "Refutation of the deniers of our religion and the followers of Jahm." Jahm's followers lasted apparently until the fifth/eleventh century. W.M. Watt has warned that it is extremely difficult to identify those who are listed as members of the Jahmiyya except to conclude that they are enemies of the Ḥanbalīs (*Formative period*, 144-7; cf. van Ess, *TG*, ii, 507; v, 220, Text 19 d-e and W. Madelung, Origins, Nr. V, 506f. for a discussion on Jahm; a good summary is found in van Ess, *TG*, iv, 625-30). Nonetheless, the doctrine of the createdness of the Qur'ān seems to have found defenders after Jahm other than the Mu'tazila. The latter were, however, the most important in this debate. As a consequence of having to defend the assertion of the createdness of the Qur'ān, they developed a philosophy of language to support their claim that everything about the Qur'ān — paper, ink, organs of speech, memory, writing, sounds and phonemes — is a part of the phenomenal, created world.

One reason for Jahm's insistence that the Qur'ān was created was his strong denial of anthropomorphism (q.v.). According to Ibn Ḥanbal, Jahm held that "God has never spoken and does not speak" (Ibn Ḥanbal, *Radd*, 32). In the Qur'ān, Moses (q.v.) is presented as the only prophet to whom God spoke directly (from the fire, Q 20:10-48; cf. M. Seale, *Muslim theology*, 102-12 for an English translation of relevant passages from the *Radd*). Jahm held that God could not have a physical body like his creatures. Therefore God must create a speech (the Qurʾān) unlike his own speech which human ears can hear. Part of what was at issue in the ensuing debate between rationalist *mutakallimūn* on the one side and the traditionalist Ḥanbalīs and the Ashʿarīs on the other was the problem of God's attributes (*ṣifāt*, see GOD AND HIS ATTRIBUTES). Jahm promulgated a *theologia negativa* by declaring it possible for humans to say of God only what he is not. It followed that God's attributes such as his speech must be unlike the attribute of speech among God's creatures. During the three centuries after Jahm b. Ṣafwān, the Muʿtazila became the main, but not the exclusive, defenders of the doctrine of the createdness of the Qurʾān (which was not a monolithic position; cf. W. Madelung, Origins and van Ess, *TG*, iv, 620 for a discussion of the two prevalent views supporting *khalq al-Qurʾān*). They were opposed vigorously in the court of public opinion by traditionalists such as the popular Aḥmad b. Ḥanbal. Their chief theological opponents were the Ashʿarīs, who engaged the Muʿtazilī *mutakallimūn* on their own grounds of rational argumentation.

The inquisition and the Muʿtazilī doctrine

The dispute between those who defended the doctrine of the created Qurʾān and those who denied it was one among many such disputes in early Muslim thinking about the nature of God, his attributes and his revelation to humankind. It became a major fissure in Islamic religious doctrine when the caliph al-Maʾmūn (r. 198-218/813-33) made public affirmation of the created Qurʾān a requirement for judges (*qāḍīs*) during the last year of his reign (see W. Madelung, Origins). The inquisition (*miḥna*), as it was called, lasted some 16 years until finally reversed by the caliph al-Mutawwakil (r. 232-47/847-61) two years after he assumed the caliphate. Of the many judges and court-appointed witnesses in the service of the caliph (q.v.) and his provincial governors (not every province beyond Baghdad and its environs in Iraq paid much attention to al-Maʾmūn's decree), only two steadfastly refused to affirm the doctrine of the created Qurʾān, Aḥmad b. Ḥanbal and Muḥammad b. Nūḥ. The latter died on his way to prison, but Ibn Ḥanbal was imprisoned, beaten and subjected to theological interrogation and testing. Al-Maʾmūn's brother and successor, the caliph al-Muʿtaṣim (r. 218-27/833-42), was less adamant about promulgating the affirmation of the createdness of the Qurʾān and feared the public reaction gathering outside the prison in Baghdad where Aḥmad b. Ḥanbal was held. All along, Ibn Ḥanbal refused to affirm that the Qurʾān was created. After his release, he shunned public life and did not engage the issue when it cropped up again under the more aggressive inquisitional policies of al-Muʿtaṣim's son, the caliph al-Wāthiq (r. 227-32/842-7). Ibn Ḥanbal, nonetheless, is remembered as the victor over the Muʿtazilī doctrine of the created Qurʾān and, in reference to this particular doctrine, over the three caliphs who attempted to enforce it in Islamic public religious life (cf. van Ess, *TG*, iii, 446-508).

After the inquisition

The *miḥna* was not only a test of traditionalist beliefs about the Qurʾān. It was also a test of whether or not the caliphate had the authority to define and enforce religious doctrine. Politically, the *miḥna* and Ibn Ḥanbal's tenacious refusal to affirm the createdness of the Qurʾān constituted an important moment in the contest between the caliphate and the religious scholars (*ʿulamāʾ*) about the exercise of religious authority in early and medieval Islam (see EXEGESIS OF THE QURʾĀN: CLASSICAL AND MEDIEVAL). Theologically, the *miḥna* and the doctrine of *khalq al-Qur'ān* raised the question of whether divine revelation, "the Book" as the Qur'ān often refers to itself, was coeternal with God or a created vessel of communication from God to his creatures. Since the third/ninth century the majority of Muslims have condemned the Muʿtazilī doctrine of the created Qur-'ān by asserting that the Qur'ān is eternal. Historically, the orthodox Shīʿī rebuttal of the assertion of the createdness of the Qur'ān has been more guarded.

For example, even in the second/eighth century, the sixth Shīʿī *imām*, Jaʿfar al-Ṣādiq (d. 148/765), is said to have replied, when asked if the Qur'ān was the creator or the created, that it was neither. A great many early traditionalists such as Yaḥyā b. Yaḥyā al-Tamīmī (d. 226/840) asserted against the doctrine of the created Qur'ān that the Qur'ān is the speech (q.v.) of God. For the Muʿtazila, speech is phenomenal, that is, sounds and letters which come into being *(muḥdath)* in the world God creates. Speech is an attribute of God acting external to himself. Later Muʿtazila developed a sophisticated theory of language and linguistics based on the ontology and mechanics of speech. Whereas the Jahmiyya denied that God could speak on the grounds that this would constitute anthropomorphism — likening God to humans — the Muʿtazila accused their opponents of claiming that the Qur'ān was eternal, which was tantamount to implying that an entity other than God is coeternal with God, in other words, dualism. The unacceptability of dualism, referred to as *zandaqa* and *thanawiyya* in the heresiographical literature from the second/eighth century on, was as strong among traditionalists like Aḥmad b. Ḥanbal as it was among Muʿtazila.

In his super-commentary on Qāḍī ʿAbd al-Jabbār's (d. 414/1025) *Sharḥ al-uṣūl al-khamsa,* Aḥmad b. al-Ḥusayn b. Abī Hāshim, known as Mānkdīm (d. 425/1034), says that the Qāḍī classified the dispute about the createdness of the Qur'ān under the topic of divine justice (*al-ʿadl,* one of the five fundamentals of Muʿtazilī doctrine; see JUSTICE AND INJUSTICE) because the Qur'ān is one of God's acts (ʿAbd al-Jabbār, *Sharḥ,* 527). ʿAbd al-Jabbār identifies ʿAbdallāh b. Kullāb (d. 240/854) and those whom he terms the "mindless" *(al-ḥashwiyya)* Ḥanbalīs as holding that the Qur'ān is not created *(ghayr makhlūq)* and not produced *(lā muḥdath),* but that it is eternal with God. He states the Muʿtazilī doctrine of the createdness of the Qur'ān as follows:

> ... the Qur'ān is the speech of God and his revelation *(waḥy)*... it is created *(makhlūq)* and produced *(muḥdath).* God sent it down to his Prophet to be an emblem and evidence of [the latter's] prophethood. [God] made it an evidentiary proof *(dalāla)* so that we could have rules to which we could refer concerning what is permitted and what is forbidden (see LAWFUL AND UNLAWFUL).... Therefore, the Qur'ān is that which we hear and recite today. If it is not produced by God [in the present moment] it is attributed to him in reality, just as the poems we [might] recite today [can be] the poetry of Imru' al-Qays [a pre-Islamic poet] in reality, even though he is not producing them now [when we recite them] (ʿAbd al-Jabbār, *Sharḥ,* 528).

ʿAbd al-Jabbār's contemporary and opponent, the Ashʿarī Abū Bakr Muḥammad b. al-Ṭayyib b. al-Bāqillānī (d. 403/1013), replied to Muʿtazilī defenses of the createdness of the Qur'ān with arguments based on qur'ānic proof texts. Especially crucial was the passage from Q 16:40: "For to anything we (God) have willed, we say to it 'be' and thus it is," on which al-Bāqillānī builds several arguments to deny the createdness of the Qurʾān (Bāqillānī, *Tamhīd*, 237-57).

Several historians of Islamic thought in the twentieth century have also concluded that ʿAbd Allāh b. Kullāb, a contemporary of Ibn Ḥanbal and considered a forerunner or early exponent of many of the views held by al-Ashʿarī, was in fact the chief architect of the orthodox doctrine of the eternity of the Qurʾān (cf. van Ess, *TG*, vi, 411-2). W. Madelung (Origins) believes that the controversy over the createdness of the Qurʾān was not a critical public debate until al-Maʾmūn initiated the *miḥna*, and that Aḥmad b. Ḥanbal, not ʿAbdallāh b. Kullāb, added to the traditionalist denial of the createdness of the Qurʾān the claim that the Qurʾān is eternal *(qadīm)*. Taqī l-Dīn b. Taymiyya (d. 728/1328), the later theological critic of both Muʿtazilī and Ashʿarī theology *(kalām)* and reviver of Ḥanbalī traditionalist thought, also argued against the doctrine of the eternity of the Qurʾān on the grounds that the pious ancestors *(salaf)* had claimed only that it was the speech of God, not that it was eternal (*kalām Allāh;* Ibn Taymiyya, *Majmūʿa*, iii, 20 passim).

Conclusion

Although the Ashʿarī and traditionalist Sunnī doctrine of the eternity of the Qurʾān has prevailed down to the present, some modernist Muslims have challenged the Ashʿarī denial of the Muʿtazilī doctrine of the createdness of the Qurʾān. Muḥammad ʿAbduh (d. 1324/1906) did so in the late nineteenth century, although he removed his defense of the createdness of the Qurʾān after the publication of the first edition of *Risāla al-tawḥīd*, the work in which it appeared. More recently, revisionist modernist writers such as Mohammed Arkoun (*Rethinking Islam*, 6) have called for a return to the Muʿtazilī doctrine of the createdness of the Qurʾān. In the comparative study of religions, the dispute about the created versus the uncreated or eternal nature of the Qurʾān is a theological problem of the proportions of the ancient problem in Christian theology concerning the divine versus the human nature of Jesus Christ. In fact, as Trinitarian debates are attested within Christian circles at Baghdad contemporaneous with the Muslim discussion on the createdness of the Qurʾān, the formulation of the Christian doctrine of the Trinity (q.v.) and the Islamic debate on the createdness of the Qurʾān may have influenced one another (cf. H. Wolfson, *Philosophy*, 240-2; for a rebuttal of Wolfson's position, see van Ess, *TG*, iv, 625-7). See also THEOLOGY AND THE QURʾĀN.

Richard C. Martin

Bibliography
Primary: ʿAbd al-Jabbār, *al-Mughnī fī abwāb al-tawḥīd wa-l-ʿadl. vii. Khalq al-Qurʾān*, ed. Ibrāhīm al-Ibārī, Cairo 1380/1961; id., *Sharḥ al-uṣūl al-khamsa*, with the super-commentary by Aḥmad b. Ḥusayn b. Abī Hāshim known as Mānkdīm, ed. ʿAbd al-Karīm ʿUthmān, Cairo 1384/1965, 527-63; M. ʿAbduh, *Risālat al-tawḥīd*, Cairo 1315/1897; al-Ashʿarī, *Maqālāt al-islāmiyyīn*, ed. H. Ritter, Wiesbaden 1963; Ibn Ḥanbal, *al-Radd ʿala l-Zanādiqa wa-l-Jahmiyya*, ed. M.F. Shaqafa, n.p. 1967; Ibn Taymiyya, *Majmūʿat al-rasāʾil wa-l-masāʾil*, ed M. Rashīd Riḍā, 5 vols. in 2, Cairo 1976 (esp. vol. iii).
Secondary: M. Arkoun, *Rethinking Islam. Common questions, uncommon answers*, Boulder 1988; J. van Ess, Ibn Kullāb und die Miḥna, in *Oriens* 18-9 (1965-6), 97-142; id., *TG;* W. Madelung, The origins of the controversy concerning the creation of the Qurʾān, in W. Madelung, *Religious schools and sects in medieval Islam*, London 1985, Nr. V, 504-25; J. Nawas, *al-Maʾmūn. Miḥna and caliphate*, Ph.D. diss., Nijmegen 1992; W.M. Patton, *Aḥmad b. Ḥanbal and the* miḥna, Leiden 1897; M. Seale, *Muslim theology*, London 1964; W.M. Watt, Early discussions about the Qurʾān, in *MW* 40 (1950), 21-40, 96-105; id., *The formative*

period of Islamic thought, Edinburgh 1973; H.A. Wolfson, *Philosophy of the kalam,* London 1976.

Creation

God's origination of the universe and of humankind. In cultural traditions around the world, including the tradition of naturalistic evolution, creation stories serve to explain the nature of the human social and physical environment, to make sense of what befalls human beings and, often, to legitimate particular moral, political or ideological systems. One of the central themes in the Qurʾān is that reflection upon creation *(khalq)* ratifies God's peerless authority (q.v.) to command (see SOVEREIGNTY) and his unique prerogative to be worshipped (see WORSHIP). This, in turn, indicates that the proper response to him and to those who preach his revelation (see REVELATION AND INSPIRATION) is submission *(islām,* q.v.) to his will.

God as sole creator

The Qurʾān is insistent that God, Allāh, is the "creator *(badīʿ)* of the heavens and the earth" (Q 2:117; 6:101; cf. Q 2:54; 10:3; 12:101; 13:16; 21:56; 26:77-8; 35:1; 36:70; 39:46, 62; 40:62; 42:11; 46:3; 59:24; 64:2-3; 85:13; 91:5-6), which signifies that he is the creator of all things — the lowest, the highest and, implicitly, all that is in between.

Indeed, his being the creator is a central reason that he is deserving of worship (Q 2:21; 6:1, 80, 96; 7:10; 11:61, 118-9; 14:10, 32-4; 16:52, 80-1; 36:22; 39:6; 43:26-7; 56:57-62; 87:1-4) for the entire universe owes its existence to him. Moreover, in his role as creator as with other aspects of his nature, God has no partners, no helpers and thus no peers (see GOD AND HIS ATTRIBUTES). In fact, his uniqueness in this regard is recognized even by the Qurʾān's pagan opponents (Q 2:22, 164-5; 6:1, 14, 73, 80, 101-3; 7:54, 194; 10:32, 35, 69; 13:16; 16:17; 20:4; 25:3; 27:59-61, 64; 29:61; 30:27, 40; 31:11, 25; 32:4; 34:49; 35:3, 13, 40; 37:95-6; 39:38; 40:61-4; 41:9; 43:9, 87; 46:4; 52:35-6; 56:57-62) and therefore provides a point of common agreement from which theological debate can proceed. But, the Qurʾān says, the pagans fail to draw from their recognition of God as sole creator the appropriate conclusion, namely that he is uniquely worthy of worship: "Those upon whom they call besides God create nothing, and are themselves created" (Q 16:20; cf. Q 7:191; 25:2-3; see POLYTHEISM AND ATHEISM). "Those upon whom you call apart from God will never create a fly, even if they gathered together in order to do it. And if the fly should snatch something away from them, they would be unable to recover it from him. Weak is the petitioner, and weak is he who is petitioned" (Q 22:73; cf. 16:73; 25:2-3; see POWER AND IMPOTENCE).

The Qurʾān is not, however, content to assert merely that God created the universe at some definable point in the past. As opposed to deism or to certain readings of Newtonian physics, God continues to sustain the creation during every moment of its existence (Q 2:255). (As discussed below, this has implications for understanding precisely what the Qurʾān understands by creation). Accordingly, worship of him proceeds not merely from his gracious creative act in the past but from dependence upon him for existence at every instant of the present and the future. And in fact the Qurʾān is deeply impressed with the ongoing order of nature and summons all humankind to share in its admiration and to learn from it (Q 7:54-6; 24:43-4; 25:47-50, 53-4, 61, 62; 26:7; 29:19; 31:10; 35:13; see NATURAL WORLD AND THE QURʾĀN). It is, for instance, God who sends down water in rain and sends it coursing through rivers

(Q 6:6) — a power that would arouse particular attention in the aridity of Arabia.

God's purpose in creation

Creation had a divine purpose (Q 3:190-1; 15:85-6; 30:8) and was done "in truth" (Q 6:73; 29:44; 39:5; 44:39; 45:22). But that purpose is, in a sense, external to the deity who does not need a cosmos for himself. "We did not create heaven (q.v.) and earth (q.v.) and what is between them for sport. Had we wanted to adopt a pastime, we could have found it in ourself," says the God of the Qurʾān (Q 21:16-7; cf. Q 44:38). And since the creation and the cosmos itself are of a teleological character, those who believe (see BELIEF AND UNBELIEF) are not free to view the universe or even their own lives as pointless. "We did not create heaven and earth and what is between them for nothing. That is the thinking of those who disbelieve" (Q 38:27).

What was God's intention in creating the physical cosmos? On this point, the Qurʾān is unabashedly anthropocentric. God's purpose in the creation of the universe was focused on humanity. This is manifest, for example, in the fact that the universe is admirably designed to provide for human needs and wants (Q 2:22, 29; 10:67; 14:32-4; 16:5-8, 10-8, 80-1; 17:12; 20:54-5; 22:65; 23:17-22; 67:15; 78:6-13; 79:32-3). The Qurʾān offers its own version of what has come to be termed in cosmology the "cosmic anthropic principle." This beneficent, human-centered design characterizes not merely the arrangements on the earth where humans actually live. It extends beyond to the heavens: "He cleaves the dawn and makes the night for rest and the sun (q.v.) and the moon (q.v.) for reckoning. That is the decree of the Mighty, the Omniscient. He is the one who placed the stars for you, so that you might be guided in the darkness (q.v.) of land and sea" (Q 6:96-7; see COSMOLOGY IN THE QURʾĀN).

God did not, however, create the universe merely for the comfort and enjoyment of the human race. It is also arranged as a proving ground for them. "He it is who created the heavens and the earth in six days... in order to test you, which of you is best in conduct" (Q 11:7; cf. Q 18:7; 67:2; see TRIAL. The Qurʾān generally describes the creation of the universe as requiring the biblical six days [as at Q 7:54; 10:4; 11:7; 25:58-9; 32:4; 50:38; 57:4; but see 41:9-12]). "God made the heavens and the earth in truth, so that each soul (q.v.) could be rewarded for what it earned; they will not be wronged" (Q 45:22; see REWARD AND PUNISHMENT).

A qurʾānic natural theology

But the physical cosmos provides more than just necessities for survival and good things to enjoy; it is more than simply a place where humans can be tested and tried. It is a message to human beings that if heeded, will help them pass the divinely ordained test. It is, itself, a kind of revelation. Nature is constituted as it is "that you might remember" (Q 51:49). Thus undergirding the special revelation of the Qurʾān is a qurʾānically endorsed natural theology according to which serious and discerning minds can deduce much about the existence and character of God by contemplation of the cosmos (Q 10:6-7, 67; 13:2-4; 16:10-8, 65-9, 79; 17:12; 20:53-4; 24:41, 44-5; 25:61, 62; 29:44; 42:29; 55:1-15; 56:57-62; 71:14-20; 88:17-20). "Truly, in the creation of the heavens and the earth and the variation of night and day and in the ship (see SHIPS) that sails in the sea, carrying things useful to the people, and in the water (q.v.) that God sends down from the sky so that he enlivens the earth after its death and disperses every animal throughout it, and in the direction of the winds and of the subservient clouds between heaven and earth, there are signs *(āyāt)* for people who have intelligence" (Q 2:164; cf. 6:96-7; 45:3-5; see ANIMAL LIFE; AGRICULTURE AND VEGETATION; AIR AND WIND).

Significantly, the term used for the signs (q.v.) of the natural realm, *āyāt,* is the same Arabic word used to denote the individual verses (q.v.) of Islam's special revelation, the Qurʾān. Thus nature, properly viewed, becomes a revealed book (q.v.) very much like the Qurʾān is itself composed of individual signs or miracles (q.v.). (The identification of miracles as signs pointing to the divine recalls the equivalent usage of Greek *semeia* in the Gospel of John.) "Truly, in the creation of the heavens and the earth and the variation of night and day there are signs *(āyāt)* for those of understanding, those who remember God standing, sitting, and lying on their sides, and who contemplate the creation of the heavens and the earth: 'Our Lord, you did not create this for nothing!'" (Q 3:190-1; see PRAYER). "Have they not looked at the sky above them," the Qurʾān asks of the unbelievers, "how we have built it and adorned it without rifts? And the earth, how we spread it out and cast into it firmly-rooted mountains and scattered throughout it every delightful pair, as a sight and a reminder for every repentant worshiper?" (Q 50:6-8; cf. Q 67:2-5). Such passages imply that the ultimate condemnation of the pagan polytheists will be just even if they never heard the message of the Qurʾān itself because they had before them the book of nature and its clear testimony to the existence, beneficence and oneness of God.

The moral implications of God as sovereign and creator

Humanity has been divinely appointed to be God's vice-regent (see CALIPH) upon the earth (Q 2:30; the Qurʾān knows the story of the origin of the devil (q.v.), as when Iblīs (q.v.) failed to prostrate himself before the newly created Adam. See Q 2:30-4; 7:11-22; 15:26-35; 17:61-2; 18:51; 20:120; 38:75-86; see DISOBEDIENCE; BOWING AND PROSTRATION; ADAM AND EVE). In this respect, qurʾānic natural theology has ethical as well as purely theological implications (see ETHICS IN THE QURʾĀN). The universe has been organized into a cosmos rather than a chaos and humanity is accordingly warned to introduce no human disorder into the divinely ordained arrangement of the physical world: "Do not sow corruption *(lā tufsidū)* in the earth after its ordering *(baʿda iṣlāḥihā)*" (Q 7:56; see CORRUPTION). Moreover, humankind is admonished to read the signs (q.v.) of nature correctly: "Among his signs *(āyāt)* are night and day, the sun and the moon. Do not bow before sun and moon, but bow before God, who created them" (Q 41:37; cf. 6:75-9; see IDOLS AND IMAGES; IDOLATRY AND IDOLATERS). The symbols were not created for their own sake but are intended to point beyond themselves.

As the creator of all things God is obviously also the creator of humankind (Q 4:1; 6:2). In the intimate relationship between creator and creature he knows everything about human motivations, thoughts and acts; he is closer to each person than that individual's own jugular vein (Q 50:16; see ARTERY AND VEIN) and is therefore uniquely equipped both to understand and to judge.

God as absolutely free agent

The assertion that the creation of the heavens and earth was in some sense a greater achievement than the creation of man (Q 40:57; 79:27-30) does not imply that it was a more difficult act. For the Qurʾān stresses God's utter freedom in creation and the sublime effortlessness with which he acts (Q 4:133; 5:17; 14:19-20; 35:16-7; 42:49; 46:33; 50:38). The most dramatic qurʾānic assertion of divine creative power is the repeated declaration that God has merely to say, "'Be!' And it is" *(kun fa-yakūn,* at Q 3:47, 59; 6:73; 16:40; 19:35; 36:82; 40:68; 54:49-50). An uncritical reading might gloss such passages as promising material for the construction of a theory of creation from nothingness *(creatio ex nihilo)*. Indeed, verses containing this phrase or a variant thereof are commonly used to support such a concept. Usage of qurʾānic evidence alone, however, does not support the theory.

Origins of the doctrine of creatio ex nihilo
Although it is popularly regarded as a teaching of their canonical scriptures, the notion of creation from absolute nothingness appears to have developed relatively late in the history of Judaism and Christianity. The biblical terms that are generally rendered in English as "create" have their origins in the Hebrew terminology for handicrafts and the plastic arts. They primarily refer to mechanical actions such as cutting out or paring leather, molding something into shape or fabricating something, rather than to metaphysical origination (for which early Semitic thought almost certainly lacked the conceptual apparatus; metaphorical usage was a later development). Throughout the Hebrew Bible, the image recurs of God as a craftsman, a potter shaping a vessel from clay (q.v.) or a weaver at his loom (Isaiah 29:16; 40:22; 45:9; 51:13, 15-6; Psalms 74:13-7; 89:11; 90:2; Romans 9:20-3). Although it is very doubtful that a doctrine of creation from utter nothingness is to be found in either the Hebrew Bible or the Greek New Testament, by the early part of the third century of the common era *creatio ex nihilo* had become a fundamental doctrine of orthodox Christianity. Its near-universal adoption by Jews may have come still later.

Does the Qurʾān teach creatio ex nihilo?
In light of the widely-held misconceptions about the biblical attestation of creation out of nothingness, it appears necessary to examine whether such a concept appears in the Qurʾān. Traditional understandings to the contrary, it seems that it does not. In several of the passages where the phrase *kun fa-yakūn* occurs, *creatio ex nihilo* is excluded by the context. In no passages is absolute nothingness a necessary prerequisite for the effectiveness of God's creative act. The subject of Q 3:47, 3:59 and 19:35 is the virginal conception of Jesus (q.v.), whom, Q 3:59 affirms, God first created from dust, and *then* said to him "Be!" and he was *(kun fa-yakūn)*. This points to a striking characteristic of these passages: Q 2:117 typifies them in its assertion that God "decrees a matter *(amr)*" and *then* "says to it *(la-hu)* 'Be,' and it is" (compare Q 3:47; 40:68). Q 16:40 and 36:81-2 actually speak of a thing *(shayʾ)* to which God says "Be!" and it is *kun fa-yakūn,* (cf. Q 54:49-50; cf. 19:35; 40:68). There seems to be an underlying and pre-existing substrate to which the divine imperative is addressed as clearly is the case in the story of the Sabbath-breakers who are told "Be apes!" (*kūnū qiradatan,* Q 2:65; 7:166; see CURSE). The command *kun!* would therefore seem to be rather more determinative or constitutive than productive of something out of utter nothingness.

Indeed, a survey of the words used in the Qurʾān in connection with creation and an examination of the ways in which they are used, reveals little or no reason to suppose that any of them involves a creation from nothing. The great Andalusian jurist and philosopher Ibn Rushd (Averroës, d. 595/1198) appears to have been correct when he alleged that the theologians' adherence to creation from nothing rests upon an allegorical interpretation of the Qurʾān whose literal sense rather teaches a pre-existent matter which simply received the form given it in God's creative act. "For," as he observes, "it is not stated in scripture that God was existing with absolutely nothing else: A text to this effect is nowhere to be found" (Averroës, *On the harmony*, 56-7; see EXEGESIS OF THE QUR'ĀN: CLASSICAL AND MEDIEVAL).

The most common relevant qur'ānic terminolgy for creation involves the Arabic root *kh-l-q*. Its original meaning seems to have been associated, much like the creation-related vocabulary of the Hebrew Bible, with such things as working leather. The Qur'ān states that God created the heavens and the earth in six days (Q 7:54; 10:3; 11:7; 25:59; 32:4; 50:38; 57:4) and that humankind is also among his creations (as at Q 2:21; 6:94; 7:11; 26:184; 37:96; 41:21; cf. 5:18; 50:16; 51:56; 55:3; 56:57). An examination of the occurrences of the verb virtually rules out *creatio ex nihilo:* Thus Iblīs in particular (Q 7:12; 38:76) and the jinn (q.v.) in general (Q 15:27; 55:15) are created of fire *(nār)*. The human, on the other hand, is said to have been created from dust (*turāb*, Q 30:20; this is specifically stated of Adam and Jesus [q.v.] at Q 3:59), from the earth (*arḍ*, Q 20:55; see EARTH), from clay (*ṭīn*, Q 6:2; 7:12; 32:7; 38:71, 76; cf. 17:61), from sounding clay drawn from altered mud (*ṣalṣāl min ḥamā' masnūn*, Q 15:26, 28, 33), from an extraction of clay (*sulālat min ṭīn*, Q 23:12), from sticky clay (*ṭīn lāzib*, Q 37:11) and from sounding clay like earthenware (*ṣalṣāl ka-l-fakhkhār*, Q 55:14). God created man with his hands (*khalaqtu bi-yadayya*, Q 38:75-6) — recalling Jesus' "creation" of a bird from clay by the leave of God (Q 3:49; 5:110). See CLAY.

It is not only in the miraculous origination of Adam and Eve that the divine role of the creator is to be recognized. For, as noted above, God is actively involved in the ongoing order of the universe. Thus he is also the creator of men and women as manifested in the ordinary processes of human reproduction (Q 7:189; 16:4; 19:9; 23:78-9; 30:54; 35:11; 36:35; 39:6; 49:13; 53:32, 45; 67:23-4; 74:11-2; 76:2, 28; 82:6-8; 90:4; 92:3; 95:4-5) and in the natural succession of human generations (Q 2:21; 39:6). "He it is who forms you in the wombs as he pleases," says the Qur'ān. "There is no god but he" (Q 3:6). God's creative power is also at work in the everyday events of animal reproduction (Q 24:44-5; 36:36) and the propagation of plants (Q 6:95, 99; 13:4). The Qur'ān names yet other materials, besides clay and water, out of which the human body is created — materials which cannot have been involved in the origination of Adam and Eve (q.v.). It is produced from a single soul (*nafs*, Q 4:1; 7:189; 39:6) or from a male and a female (Q 49:13). It is created from a kind of water (Q 25:54, 77:20-2, 86:5-7) as were all animals (Q 24:45) — though this water is not to be confused with the primordial water from which Adam was taken. For the human body is created from a drop of sperm (*nuṭfa*, Q 16:4; 36:77; 76:2; 80:18-9; cf. Q 53:45-6; 86:5-7), "from an extract of contemptible fluid" (Q 32:8-9; cf. Q 77:20-2; 86:5-7). "We have created them, they know of what" (Q 70:39; this is reminiscent of the mishnaic injunction [Aboth 3:1] to "know whence thou art come." The Mishna's answer to this question, obviously designed to promote humility in humankind, is from a "putrid drop" *[tippah serukhah]*). Yet the human body is also created from a blood clot (*'alaq*, Q 96:2).

How are we to reconcile these varied and seemingly contradictory statements? It would seem that there is really no contradiction, for the Qur'ān affirms that human beings are created in stages (*aṭwār*, Q 71:14), obviously referring to the process of fetal development from conception through gestation to birth, a process which at every phase it ascribes to the creative agency of God. "He creates you in the wombs of your mothers, creation after creation in a three-fold gloom" (*khalqan min ba'di khalqin*, Q 39:6). The physical human body is made first from dust, then of a "drop," then of clotted blood, then of a morsel of partially formed flesh which turns into bones and covering skin and, finally, it becomes a man (*rajul*, Q 18:37; cf. 22:5; 23:12-4; 40:67; 75:37-9). In every case, the "creation" described occurs from pre-existing materials. See also BIRTH; BIOLOGY AS THE CREATION AND STAGES OF LIFE; BLOOD AND BLOOD CLOT.

Only two passages in the Qurʾān would seem to be susceptible to an interpretation indicative of *creatio ex nihilo*. Both occur in Q 19, "Mary" (Sūrat Maryam). When Zechariah (q.v.), a believer, expresses some doubt that he and Elizabeth should have a child at their advanced ages, the Lord (q.v.) replies, "That is easy for me, since I created you before, when you were not anything" (*wa-lam taku shayʾ*, Q 19:9). Later it is the unbelievers who express doubt when they question the possibility of bodily resurrection: "Man says, 'When I have died, shall I then be brought forth living?' Does man not remember that we created him before, when he was not anything?" (*wa-lam yaku shayʾ*, Q 19:66-7). But if these two passages teach *creatio ex nihilo*, they are the only qurʾānic passages that do so, which in turn suggests that they in fact do not propound such a concept. See also MARY.

There is no obligation, of course, to assume that the Qurʾān is a monolithic, totally consistent text, on this or any other matter. There is no *a priori* reason, however, to take the opposite position, i.e. to assume that the Qurʾān is inconsistent and self-contradictory. The situation must be evaluated on a case by case basis and, as will be clear, there is no compelling evidence contained within these two passages to imply that the Qurʾān contradicts itself on the issue of *creatio ex nihilo*. In the absence of such compelling evidence, it is reasonable to take this scripture as being internally consistent.

We know from Aristotle that the Platonists called preexistent matter "the non-existent" (*to mē on*, Aristotle, *Physics* 1.9.192a 6-7). More to the point, however, the early fourth century Syrian monastic writer Aphraates uses a similar argument to make precisely the same point as does the latter of the two passages in Q 19 — and Aphraates clearly does not intend to argue for *creatio ex nihilo*: "About this resurrection of the dead I shall instruct you, most dear one, to the best of my ability. God in the beginning created man; he molded him from dust and he raised him up. If, then, when man did not exist, he made him from nothing, how much easier is it for him now to raise him up like a seed sown in the earth" (cited by T. O'Shaughnessy, Creation from nothing, 278). What is involved here is creation not from absolute but from relative non-existence, from a condition when the human body did not exist as such but existed only potentially as dust or clay. It is God's ability to give life to inanimate matter both at birth and at the resurrection (q.v.) which is the ultimate proof of his power. *Creatio ex nihilo* is not the point at issue.

If *khalaqa* is associated with pre-existing material, the same is true of other words used qurʾānically in connection with God's creative activity. The root *j-ʿ-l*, for example, is used to describe God's creation of earth and sky (Q 40:64), of the constellations or zodiacal signs (Q 25:61), of darkness and light (i.e. night and day: Q 6:1; 10:67; 40:61), of the sun and the moon (Q 6:96). Indeed, it is very often used in precisely the same sense as *khalaqa* — as, for instance, when the Qurʾān states that every living thing, including particularly the posterity of Adam, has been made from a kind of water (Q 21:30; 32:8; see also Q 23:12-4, in which, when it is taken with other similar passages, *jaʿala* is synonymous with *khalaqa*). It is also used to refer to God's changing Sabbath-breakers into apes (Q 5:60), the transformation of what is on the earth into barren sterility (Q 18:8), the laying out of gardens (Q 36:34), the production of fire from a green tree (Q 36:80) and the divine dispensation of ships (q.v.) and of cattle for human usage (Q 43:12). It is a form of this root which is used when the Children of Israel (q.v.) demand of Moses (q.v.) that he "make" them a god like the gods of the idolaters (Q 7:138) — where presumably what is meant is the fashioning of a material idol (see CALF OF GOLD). Likewise it is the verb used by Pharaoh (q.v.) when he orders Hāmān (q.v.) and his servants to build him a tower out of fired clay bricks so that he may climb up to the god of Moses (Q 28:38).

Other verbs used in the Qurʾān seem to imply a similar pre-existent material, an *Urstoff,* out of which the universe was made. At the very least, there is nothing in them which would necessitate reading the Qurʾān as advocating *creatio ex nihilo.* Heaven, for example, of which it is repeatedly stated that God is the creator (using the root *kh-l-q* as at Q 65:12; 67:3; 71:15 and throughout the Qurʾān), is said to have been "built" as an "edifice" (both the noun and the verb are formed from the Arabic root letters *b-n-y,* Q 2:22; 40:64; 50:6; 51:47; 78:12; 79:27; 91:5). In another version of Pharaoh's order to Hāmān to build him a tower, *b-n-y* is used as a synonym of *jaʿala* (Q 40:36).

In the case of *badaʾa,* too — which is used as a synonym of *khalaqa* at Q 7:29 — there is no reason to infer, from the text as it stands, a creation out of nothing. In the passages relevant to the present concern, the root *b-d-ʾ* invariably serves as an inceptive helping verb, with the actual content relating to the creation being supplied by another root. (See, for example, Q 10:4, 34; 21:104; 27:64; 29:19-20; 30:11, 27; 32:7; 85:13 [by implication].)

The Arabic root *b-d-ʿ* (whose third radical differs from the root just discussed) occurs only four times in the Qurʾān. In two of the four occurrences of the root, God is simply declared to be the "creator of the heavens and the earth." Neither requires an understanding of *creatio ex nihilo.* In their third qurʾānic occurrence, the radicals appear in the eighth verbal form and are used to describe the allegedly unauthorized "invention" of monasticism by Christians (Q 57:27; see MONASTICISM AND MONKS; CHRISTIANS AND CHRISTIANITY). The fourth occurrence is in the form of the noun, innovation (*bidʿ,* Q 46:9). Admittedly, the latter two cases might be interpreted to support the concept of *creatio ex nihilo,* but there is nothing in the context to suggest that they should be so taken.

The Arabic root *b-r-ʾ,* cognate with the Hebrew verb of creation occurring at Genesis 1:1, is to be found almost solely (in the contexts which concern the present discussion) in the neutral meanings of "creator" (Q 2:54; 59:24) or "creature" (Q 98:6-7), where nothing is specified about the mode of creation. The one exception to this is Q 57:22, which speaks of misfortunes as foreordained before God brings them about. It is evident, however, that misfortunes in this life, whether earthquakes or diseases or war (q.v.), are "brought about" out of pre-existing matter or circumstances. Thus, again, nothing in the qurʾānic use of *baraʾa* compels an assumption of *creatio ex nihilo* and, indeed, what evidence the book does furnish would seem to militate against such an assumption.

Much the same can be said of the root *n-sh-ʾ* which, in its qurʾānic manifestation, essentially means "to cause something to grow." God produces gardens, for example (Q 6:141; 23:19), and he makes trees grow (Q 56:72). He also causes clouds to swell up, heavy with rain (*yunshi'u al-saḥāb al-thiqāl*, Q 13:12). Significantly, the root occasionally seems to be used as a synonym for *khalaqa* as at Q 36:77-9 and 29:19-20. God created humankind from a single soul (Q 6:98) or from the earth (Q 11:61; 53:32). Verbs derived from this root are also used to describe the raising up of a new human generation (Q 6:6, 133; 21:11; 23:31, 42; 28:45), the birth of a child (Q 23:14) and the development of sensory apparatus (Q 23:78). In none of these instances does a concept of *creatio ex nihilo* appear to play a role.

Protology and eschatology

A further clue to the qurʾānic doctrine of creation occurs in certain polemical passages (see POLEMIC AND POLEMICAL LANGUAGE) which might seem at first only marginally relevant. In accordance with the ancient notion of history as cyclical, almost every element of the traditional creation myths was taken up again in Judaeo-Christian apocalypticism, which taught that God would renew the world in a new creation or *palingenesia*. Not surprisingly, the same doctrine is abundantly attested in the Qurʾān where protology foretells eschatology (q.v.) and God's initial creation is a sign pointing forward to the resurrection at the end of time (see APOCALYPSE) as well as a demonstration of God's power actually to do it (Q 6:95; 7:29, 57; 10:55-6; 13:5; 16:70; 17:49-51, 98-9; 19:66-7; 20:55; 21:104; 22:5; 27:64; 29:19-20, 120; 30:11, 27; 31:28; 32:10; 36:76-8; 46:33; 50:2-11, 15; 53:45-6; 75:37-40; 86:5-8; cf. J. Bouman, *Gott und Mensch*, 252). God creates once and then he repeats the process to bring men before his tribunal at the day of judgment (Q 10:4; 30:11; 32:10; 46:33-4; see LAST JUDGMENT). Men will be "created" again when they are but bones and dust (Q 13:5; 17:49-51, 98-9; 32:10; 34:7; 36:77-82; see DEATH AND THE DEAD). "Were we wearied in the first creation," God asks, "that they should be in confusion about a new creation?" (Q 50:15). "Do they not see that God, who created the heavens and the earth and was not wearied in their creation, is able to give life to the dead?" (Q 46:33).

The nature of resurrection (q.v.) as a revivification of once animate, now inanimate, matter and the pointed comparisons to the initial creation (emphatically so at Q 22:5-6; 36:77-82; 75:37-40; 86:5-8) are significant in many ways. They sustain the view that the qurʾānic concept of creation was most likely conceived as the determination of pre-existent matter. They are also strikingly reminiscent of the argument advanced in a formative Jewish context at 2 Maccabees 7 — one of the most important documents for the study of the development of thinking in the Abrahamic traditions on the nature of creation (see also SCRIPTURE AND THE QURʾĀN). "When we are dust," exclaim Muḥammad's Meccan critics, "shall we indeed be in a new creation?" (Q 13:5; cf. 32:10; 34:7; see OPPOSITION TO MUḤAMMAD). "They say, 'When we are bones and fragments, shall we really be raised up again as a new creation?'" To this, Muḥammad is instructed to reply "'Be stones, or iron, or some creation yet more monstrous in your minds!' Then they will say, 'Who will bring us back?' Say: 'He who originated you the first time'" (Q 17:49-51). "Have they not seen that God, who created the heavens and the earth, is capable of creating the likes of them?" (Q 17:99; cf. 17:98).

Thus, while the Qurʾān forcefully asserts God's role as peerless creator of the universe and summons humanity to serve and to worship him on that account, it does not appear that a theory of *creatio ex nihilo* can be constructed on the basis of qurʾānic material alone. Rather, it is only with the development of the Islamic sciences, such as ḥadīth (reports of the sayings and the deeds of Muḥammad and his early followers), qurʾānic commentary *(tafsīr),* theology *(ʿilm al-kalām),* and philosophy *(falsafa)* that one finds extensive discussion about the divine act of creation from absolute nothingness (cf. R. Arnaldez, Khalḳ, esp. sec. III-VI; van Ess, *TG,* iv, 445-77 and "Schöpfung" in Index).

Daniel Carl Peterson

Bibliography
Primary: Averroës, *On the harmony of religion and philosophy,* trans. G.F. Hourani, London 1961.
Secondary: R. Arnaldez, Khalḳ, in *EI*², iv, 980-8; J. Bouman, *Gott und Mensch im Koran,* Darmstadt 1977, 11-38, 89-94, 252; van Ess, *TG;* J.A. Goldstein, The origins of the doctrine of creation ex nihilo, in *Journal of Jewish studies* 35 (1984), 127-35; G. May, *Schöpfung aus dem Nichts. Die Entstehung der Lehre von der Creatio Ex Nihilo,* Berlin 1978; J.D. McAuliffe, Fakhr al-Dīn al-Rāzī on God as al-Khāliq, in D. Burrell and B. McGinn (eds.), *God and creation. An ecumenical symposium,* Notre Dame 1990, 276-96 (examines creation in al-Rāzī's exegesis of the Qurʾān); K. Norman, Ex nihilo. The development of the doctrines of God and creation in early Christianity, in *BYU studies* 17 (1977), 291-318; T. O'Shaughnessy, *Creation and the teaching of the Qurʾān,* Rome 1985 (an updated expansion of his article); id., Creation from nothing and the teaching of the Qurʾān, in *ZDMG* 120 (1970), 274-80; D.C. Peterson, Does the Qurʾan teach creation *ex nihilo?* in J.M. Lundquist and S.D. Ricks (eds.), *By study and also by faith,* Salt Lake City 1990, 584-610; D. Winston, Creation ex nihilo revisited. A reply to Jonathan Goldstein, in *Journal of Jewish studies* 37 (1986), 88-91.

Creeds

Concise and authoritative formulae that provide a summation of the essentials of faith (q.v.). Professions of faith or creeds *(ʿaqāʾid,* sing. *ʿaqīda)* were formulated by individual scholars and by groups of scholars, yet there exists no standard or universally accepted Muslim creed. Rather, there are a variety of Islamic creeds, which vary substantially in length, contents and arrangement.

Although the Qurʾān does not proclaim any formal creed or compendium of faith, it does contain elements that form the basis for most creeds. First among these is the nature of God (see GOD AND HIS ATTRIBUTES), particularly his unity and unicity (e.g. Q 2:255; 27:26; 28:70, 112), although other attributes are sometimes included. The following are often singled out for special consideration: power (e.g. Q 2:20, 106, 109 etc.; see POWER AND IMPOTENCE), knowledge (e.g. Q 4:11, 17, 24 etc.; see KNOWLEDGE AND LEARNING), will (e.g. Q 3:40; 14:27; 22:18 etc.), life, including hearing (e.g. Q 2:181, 224; 3:34) and sight (e.g. Q 2:96, 110; 3:15; 4:58, 134), speech (Q 2:253; 4:164) and visibility (Q 75:22-3). Other themes include the prophetic mission of Muḥammad and earlier messengers (e.g. Q 4:136; 7:158; 8:1; 48:29; see PROPHETS AND PROPHETHOOD; MESSENGER) and eschatological matters, namely the day of resurrection *(yawm al-qiyāma,* e.g. Q 6:36; 50:41-2; 58:6, 18) following the annihilation of all creatures (e.g. Q 28:88) and preceding the last day or the day of judgment *(yawm al-dīn,* e.g. Q 37:20; 70:26; see ESCHATOLOGY; APOCALYPSE; LAST JUDGMENT; RESURRECTION). In some passages, the Qurʾān explicitly puts forth a credal prototype, such as that found at Q 4:136: "O believers, believe in God and his messenger, and the scripture (see BOOK) he has revealed to his messenger, and the scripture he revealed before. But he who believes not in God and his angels (see ANGEL) and his scriptures and his messengers and the last day, has wandered far away" (cf. Q 2:136, 285; 3:84; 57:7; see BELIEF AND UNBELIEF; ASTRAY; SCRIPTURE AND THE QURʾĀN).

The qurʾānic data constituting the necessary beliefs that determine the content of the Muslim faith were further supplemented by data from the sunna (q.v.).

Moreover, as a result of the controversies that developed during the earliest period of Islam and gave rise to the schisms within the Islamic community and various politico-religious traditions, other issues became relevant for consideration in any formulation of a credal proclamation of the tenets of the faith. These included the validity of the imāmate (see IMĀM), the nature of faith *(īmān)*, the conditions for salvation (q.v.), the question of God's predetermination of events and human responsibility for their actions (see FREEDOM AND PREDESTINATION) as well as the issue of the createdness versus the uncreatedness of the Qurʾān (see CREATEDNESS OF THE QURʾĀN). These issues, together with the conceptual elaboration of the qurʾānic data, were dealt with differently by various Muslim groups. Thus, professions of faith served not only to represent the faith of the community but were also meant to refute allegedly heterodox doctrines.

Although there are extant creeds from the second Islamic century (such as those of al-Awzāʿī, d. 157/774 and Sufyān al-Thawrī, d. 161/778; cf. Lālakāʾī, *Sharḥ*, i/ii, 170-5), most of the earliest creeds were formulated within the traditional, anti-rationalist camp, the adherents of which were hostile to speculative theology *(kalām)* and to esoteric interpretation by Ṣūfism (see ṢŪFISM AND THE QURʾĀN). Instead, they relied exclusively on the Qurʾān and the sunna in its apparent form. Professions of faith thus became a way for the adherents of orthodoxy to express their doctrine and to distance themselves from divergent groups. This applies in particular to the main representatives of orthodoxy, the Ḥanbalīs. Six creeds are attributed to the school's founder, Aḥmad b. Ḥanbal (d. 241/855; see Ibn Abī Yaʿlā, *Ṭabaqāt*, i, 24-36, 130-1, 241-6, 294-5, 311-3, 341-5; partial trans. in W.M. Watt, *Creeds*, 30-40; Lālakāʾī, *Sharḥ*, i/ii, 175-85, which contains a version of Ibn Ḥanbal's creed *(iʿtiqād)* as transmitted by his son, ʿAbdallāh, another rendition of which is found in J. Schacht, *Der Islam*, 36-7; cf. L. Massignon, *Recueil*, 213-4). Similar creeds are attributed to the disciples of Ibn Ḥanbal, notably his son ʿAbdallāh b. Aḥmad (d. 290/903) whose *Kitāb al-Sunna* (ed. A. b. Basyūnī Zaghlūl, Beirut 1994[2]) is one of the oldest extant Ḥanbalī creeds, and Muḥammad b. Idrīs Abū Ḥātim al-Rāzī (d. 277/890-1; see Ibn Abī Yaʿlā, *Ṭabaqāt*, i, 284-6). Another early creed is that of the famous compiler of the prophetic tradition, Muḥammad b. Ismāʿīl al-Bukhārī (d. 256/870; cf. Lālakāʾī, *Sharḥ*, i/ii, 193-7).

In the early Ḥanbalī creeds the importance of polemics often eclipses the enumeration of even the most central articles of faith, which are often missing. Moreover, these creeds frequently lack a logical arrangement. Among the Ḥanbalīs of the second half of the third/ninth century, mention should be made of Abū Bakr al-Khallāl (d. 311/922) who collected and classified in his *Kitāb al-Jāmiʿ*, partly extant in manuscript, the *responsa* of Ibn Ḥanbal on questions of law and dogmatics (cf. H. Laoust, al-Khallāl); and Abū Bakr al-Sijistānī (d. 316/928) who wrote, among other works, a short profession of faith in verse (see Ibn Abī Yaʿlā, *Ṭabaqāt*, ii, 53-4). One of the most significant Ḥanbalī creeds of this period was composed by the militant traditionalist Abū Muḥammad al-Barbahārī (d. 329/941) entitled *Kitāb al-Sunna* (see Ibn Abī Yaʿlā, *Ṭabaqāt*, ii, 18-44; H. Laoust, Les premières professions de foi, 22-5; C. Gilliot, Textes, in *MIDEO* 24). It is, above all, a polemic work denouncing the proliferation of blameworthy innovations *(bidʿa)*, condemning pernicious deviations resulting from a personal and arbitrary use of reason in the domain of religious beliefs and enjoining a return to the precepts of the "old religion" *(dīn ʿatīq)* of the first three caliphs. In his treatment of doctrinal issues such as the divine attributes and theodicy, al-Barbahārī reproduces data drawn from the Qurʾān and the sunna. His creed proved particularly influential for Ibn Baṭṭa al-ʿUkbarī (d. 387/997), who composed, among other works, two professions of faith belonging to the great tradition of Ḥanbalī polemics: the shorter version, *al-Ibāna al-saghīra* (cf. H. Laoust, *Profession d'Ibn Baṭṭa*) and the longer version, *al-Ibāna al-kubrā,* both of which have been published (cf. J. van Ess, Notizen, 130f.). Ibn Baṭṭa's creeds apparently influenced the various edicts issued between 408/1017 and 409/1018 by the ʿAbbāsid caliph al-Qādir (r. 381-422/991-1031), who wanted to make Ḥanbalism the official *credo* of the state. These edicts came to be known as the Qādirī Creed (*al-iʿtiqād al-qādirī,* cf. G. Makdisi, *Ibn ʿAqīl*, 8f.). However, despite its hostile attitude towards dogmatic theology, Ḥanbalism was not immune to its influence.

In contrast to former Ḥanbalī creeds, the dogmatic treatise of Abū Yaʿlā b. al-Farrāʾ (d. 458/1066), *Kitāb al-Muʿtamad,* is organized after contemporary treatises on *kalām*. Towards the end of the sixth/twelfth century and the beginning of the seventh/thirteenth century, Muwaffaq al-Dīn b. Qudāma (d. 620/1223) composed a short creed in traditional Ḥanbalī fashion, *Lumʿat al-iʿtiqād* (Brockelmann, *GAL,* i, 398; G. Anawati, Textes, in *MIDEO* 1, no. 22). Aḥmad b. Ḥamdān b. Shabīb al-Ḥarrānī (d. 695/1295) was also active in the seventh/thirteenth century. His creed, *Nihāyat al-mustadʿīn fī uṣūl al-dīn*, mentions the individual views of numerous former Ḥanbalī doctors (cf. J. van Ess, Notizen, 127-8). A century later, the neo-Ḥanbalī Ibn Taymiyya (d. 728/1328) wrote a number of creeds, among them the *ʿAqīda al-wāsiṭiyya* (cf. H. Laoust, *La profession de foi d'Ibn Taymiyya*) and the *ʿAqīda al-tadmuriyya* (cf. Wein, *Die islamische Glaubenslehre*). His student Ibn Qayyim al-Jawziyya (d. 751/1350-51) wrote a profession of faith in verse, the *Nūniyya* (published as *al-Kāfiyya al-shāfiyya fī l-intiṣār lil-firqa l-nājiyya,* Cairo 1901, 1920[2]; cf. Brockelmann, *GAL,* S ii, 128 no. 47), directed principally against the Jahmiyya and the Ittiḥādiyya. Much use of the work of Ibn Taymiyya was made by Muḥammad b. ʿAbd al-Wahhāb (d. 1206/1791) whose most significant writing, apart from several professions of faith, was his *Kitāb al-Tawḥīd* (found in his *Majmuʿat al-tawḥīd,* Cairo n.d., 21st treatise, 156-232; cf. H. Laoust, *Essai sur les doctrines sociales,* 514-24 and 615-24 for Laoust's French translation of this *ʿaqīda* and another Wahhābī creed).

To a lesser extent, the other legal schools have also developed creeds often attributed to their founders, although the authenticity of these attributions is not clear. Of Abū Ḥanīfa's (d. 150/767) own theological tracts, only two epistles addressed to a certain ʿUthmān al-Battī are extant (*Risālat Abī Ḥanīfa ilā ʿUthmān al-Battī,* in Abū Ḥanīfa, *al-ʿĀlim wa-l-mutaʿallim,* ed. M. Zāhid al-Kawtharī, Cairo 1949, 34-8). By contrast, *al-ʿĀlim wa-l-mutaʿallim* and *al-Fiqh al-absaṭ,* usually attributed to Abū Ḥanīfa, were composed by two of his students, Abū Muqātil al-Samarqandī (d. 208/823) and Abū Muṭīʿ al-Balkhī (d. 199/814) respectively (cf. U. Rudolph, *al-Māturīdī,* 30-78). Al-Balkhī's work is a collection of theological statements with commentary by Abū Ḥanīfa. One of the most prominent Ḥanafī creeds was composed towards the end of the third/ninth century by Abū l-Qāsim Isḥāq b. Muḥammad al-Ḥakīm al-Samarqandī (d. 342/953), *Radd ʿalā aṣḥāb al-ahwāʾ al-musammā Kitāb al-Sawād al-aʿẓam ʿalā madhhab al-īmām al-aʿẓam Abī Ḥanīfa (Refutation of those holding heretical views entitled the Book of the vast majority of people who follow the teaching of the worthy Imām Abū*

Ḥanīfa), which became known under the title *al-Sawād al-aʿẓam.* This creed, which al-Ḥakīm al-Samarqandī had been commissioned to write, won the formal approval of the Samanid ruler *(amīr)* Ismāʿīl b. Aḥmad (r. 279-95/892-907) and all the Ḥanafī doctors of Transoxania. The tract, translated into Persian and Turkish, served as the official creed under the Samanids and remained popular long after the fall of the dynasty (cf. U. Rudolph, *al-Māturīdī,* 106-31 for a summary of the tract; he gives a list of editions and translations on p. 374). The Ḥanafī jurist Abū l-Layth al-Samarqandī (d. 373/983) composed a short catechism, *ʿAqīdat al-uṣūl,* which became highly popular among Indonesian and Malayan Muslims (cf. Juynboll, Samarkandi's catechismus) and a manual of basic religious knowledge entitled *Bustān al-ʿārifīn.* In addition to these works, a commentary on the above-mentioned *al-Fiqh al-absaṭ* entitled *Sharḥ al-fiqh al-akbar* has been attributed to al-Samarqandī (H. Daiber, *Islamic concept of belief*). However, this attribution is disputed (cf. U. Rudolph, *al-Māturīdī,* 361-5).

Of the various professions of faith attributed to al-Shāfiʿī (d. 204/820) some *(al-Fiqh al-akbar fī l-tawḥīd* and *Waṣiyyat al-Shāfiʿī)* may give the impression that his theological thinking prefigured either Ashʿarism or, depending on who makes the claim, Ḥanbalism (Ibn Abī Yaʿlā, *Ṭabaqāt,* i, 283-4). However, these attributions are doubtful. For instance, later Shāfiʿī Ashʿarīs like Fakhr al-Dīn al-Rāzī (d. 606/1209) or al-Subkī (d. 771/1370) describe al-Shāfiʿī as having favored the exercise of speculative theology *(ʿilm al-kalām),* whereas according to traditionalist Shāfiʿīs, he is described as having been hostile to this discipline. Modern scholars usually consider both views to be retrospective projection (cf. Laoust, Šāfiʿī and Makdisi, Juridical Theology).

A profession of faith was also formulated by the historian and commentator on the Qurʾān, al-Ṭabarī (d. 310/923), who was the founder of a school of law which did not survive. Though his creed bears a strong resemblance to the traditional creeds of his time, al-Ṭabarī deviates to some extent from the orthodox doctrine regarding the question of the imāmate and that of the divine attributes. This was presumably the reason for the strong Ḥanbalī opposition he encountered (for the creed of al-Ṭabarī, cf. Gilliot, *Elt,* 60; Lālakāʾī, *Sharḥ,* i/ii, 206-9; D. Sourdel, Une profession; for creeds before al-Ṭabarī, cf. Gilliot, *Elt,* 208-10).

Although creeds were natural expressions of dogma for the orthodox, they are frequently encountered within other Muslim theological traditions. As the Māturīdiyya generally lagged behind the other *kalām* schools in methodological sophistication and systematization, professions of faith played a far more important role in expounding and elaborating the doctrine of al-Māturīdī (d. 333/944) than they did in the refinement of Ashʿarī doctrines. Most significant for the dissemination of Māturīdī dogma was a creed by Abū Ḥafṣ ʿUmar b. Muḥammad al-Nasafī (d. 537/1142; for *al-ʿAqāʾid al-nasafiyya,* see the second creed in W. Cureton, *Pillar;* D. Macdonald, *Development,* 308-15; J. Schacht, *Der Islam,* 81-7, no. 19; for Abū Ḥafs, see A. Wensinck, al-Nasafī, no. III). It was frequently versified and many commentaries and glosses were written on it, the best known by Saʿd al-Dīn al-Taftazānī (d. 792/1390; cf. C. Gilliot, Textes, in MIDEO 19, no. 49; the English translation of al-Taftazānī's commentary is E. Elder, *A commentary on the creed of Islam,* NY 1950; the best edition is that of Claude Salamé, Damascus 1974). ʿAlī b. ʿUthmān al-Ūshī (fl. 569/1173) composed another popular creed in verse, known as *al-Lāmiyya fī l-tawḥīd* or *Badʾ al-amālī* (cf. Brockelmann, GAL, i, 429; S i, 764). Numerous commentaries were written on it, some of them in Persian and Turkish. The most popular was *Ḍaw al-amālī* of ʿAlī al-Qārī (d. 1014/1605; cf. Brockelmann, GAL, S ii, 764, commentary no. 6). Other popular Māturīdī creeds were composed by Nūr al-Dīn al-Ṣābūnī al-Bukhārī (d. 580/1184) entitled *Kitāb al-Bidāya min al-kifāya fī l-hidāya* (ed. F. Khulayf, Cairo 1969, 180 p.) and by Abū l-Barakāt al-Nasafī (d. 710/1310; cf. W. Heffening, al-Nasafī, no. IV) entitled *ʿUmdat al-ʿaqīda li-ahl al-sunna* (ed. W. Cureton, *Pillar*). On this latter creed, in support of the creed of Abū Ḥafṣ al-Nasafī *(supra),* Abū l-Barakāt wrote a commentary entitled *Kitāb al-Iʿtimād fī l-iʿtiqād.*

Creeds were also frequently composed by Ashʿarī scholars. Al-Ashʿarī (d. 324/936) himself wrote a short creed, two versions of which are extant, in his *Ibāna* (9-13) and his *Maqālāt* (290-7; trans. W.M. Watt, *Creeds,* 41-7; R. McCarthy, *Theology,* 235f.). Later adherents of his school also composed numerous professions of faith. In contrast to the specialized and elaborate dogmatic treatises on Ashʿarī doctrine, these creeds were written for a wider audience with the purpose of attracting them to Ashʿarism. Examples are the *ʿAqīda* of al-Ustādh Abū Isḥāq al-Isfarāyinī (d. 418/1027; cf. R. Frank, al-Ustādh Abū Isḥāḳ); various creeds by Abū l-Qāsim al-Qushayrī (d. 465/1074) such as *al-Fuṣūl fī l-uṣūl* (for English translation, cf. R. Frank, Two short dogmatic works, [part 2] in *MIDEO* 16 (1983), 59-94), the *Lumaʿ fī l-iʿtiqād* (for English translation, cf. R. Frank, Two short dogmatic works, [part 1] in *MIDEO* 15 (1982), 53-74) and *al-Manẓūma,* an *ʿaqīda* in verse (ed. K. al-Samarrāʾī, in *Majallat al-majmaʿ al-ʿilmī l-ʿIrāqī,* 18 (1969), 284-6); *al-ʿAqīda al-niẓāmiyya* of Abū l-Maʿālī al-Juwaynī (d. 478/1085; cf. G. Anawati, Textes, in *MIDEO* 15, no. 13); a profession of faith by Abū l-Ḥāmid al-Ghazālī (d. 505/1111; trans. W.M. Watt, *Creeds,* 73-9); *al-ʿAqāʾid al-ʿaḍudiyya* of ʿAḍud al-Dīn al-Ījī (d. 756/1355; trans. W.M. Watt, *Creeds,* 86-9) as well as a number of popular creeds by Muḥammad b. Yūsuf al-Sanūsī (d. 891/1486 or 895/1490; cf. W.M. Watt, *Creeds,* 90-7).

Few if any creeds seem to have been formulated by the Muʿtazila (see MUʿTAZILĪS). However, a number of summaries of Muʿtazilī doctrine meant to serve as professions of faith are extant. Examples are the *Mukhtaṣar fī uṣūl al-dīn* (see *Rasāʾil,* i, 161-254) and the *Sharḥ al-uṣūl al-khamsa* by the Qāḍī ʿAbd al-Jabbār (d. 415/1025; cf. Gimaret, Les Uṣūl), who was the head of the disciples of Abū Hāshim ʿAbd al-Salām al-Jubbāʾī (d. 321/933), who are called in Arabic al-Bahshamiyya (cf. Shahrastānī, *Livre des religions,* 265-89). A further example is the *Minhāj fī uṣūl al-dīn* of Maḥmūd b. ʿUmar al-Zamakhsharī (d. 538/1144; (trans. Schmidtke, *A Muʿtazilite creed*), who was largely influenced by the views of the founder of the last innovative Muʿtazilī school, Abū l-Ḥusayn al-Baṣrī (d. 436/1044).

Countless professions of faith were composed by Imāmīs, not only by traditionalists like Ibn Bābawayh (d. 381/991; *Risālat al-iʿtiqādāt,* trans. A. Fyzee, *Shiʿite Creed*) but also by later Twelver Shīʿīs who were predominantly influenced by Muʿtazilism. Examples are the two popular creeds by the ʿAllāma al-Ḥillī (d. 726/1325), the *Bāb al-ḥādī ʿashar* (trans. W.M. Watt, *Creeds,* 98-105) and the *Risāla fī wājib al-iʿtiqād ʿalā jamīʿ al-ʿibād,* both of which received frequent and lengthy commentary; or the *Risāla tashtamilu ʿalā aqalli mā yajibu ʿalā l-mukallifīn min al-ʿilm bi-uṣūl al-dīn* by Ibn Abī Jumhūr al-Aḥsāʾī (d. after 904/1499; for further Imāmī creeds, see al-Tihrānī, *Dharīʿa,* ii, 224-9; xv, 281, 306). An example of an Ismāʿīlī creed is the *Tāj al-ʿaqāʾid* of

Sayyidnā ʿAlī b. Muḥammad al-Walīd (d. 612/1215; cf. Ivanov, *Creed*). Among the Ibāḍīs, professions of faith were written by Zakariyyāʾ Yaḥyā b. al-Khayr al-Jannāwunī (fifth/eleventh century; cf. Cuperly, Profession) and by Abū Ḥafṣ ʿAmr b. Jamīʿ (eighth/fourteenth-ninth/fifteenth century; cf. A. Motylinski, ʿAqīda). Concise overviews of the essentials of Islamic faith were also produced by Ṣūfīs (cf. W. Chittick, *Faith and Practice;* see SHĪʿISM AND THE QURʾĀN; ṢŪFISM AND THE QURʾĀN).

Sabine Schmidtke

Bibliography

Primary: al-Aḥsāʾī b. Abī Jumhūr, *Zād al-musāfirīn fī uṣūl al-dīn [= Risāla tashtamilu ʿalā aqalli mā yajibu ʿalā l-mukallafīn min al-ʿilm bi-uṣūl al-dīn],* ed. A. al-Kinānī, Beirut 1993; ʿAlī b. Muḥammad b. al-Walīd, *Tāj al-ʿaqāʾid wa-maʿdin al-fawāʾid,* ed. A. Tamer, Beirut 1967; al-Ashʿarī, Abū l-Ḥasan, *al-Ibāna ʿan uṣūl al-diyāna,* Hyderabad 1903; id., *Maqālāt al-islāmiyyīn,* ed. H. Ritter, Istanbul 1929-30; H. Daiber (ed. and trans.), *The Islamic concept of belief in the 4th/10th century. Abū l-Laiṯ as-Samarqandī's commentary on Abū Ḥanīfa (died* 150/767) al-Fiqh al-absaṭ, Tokyo 1995; A.A.A. Fyzee (trans.), *A Shiʾite creed. A translation of* Risālatu l-iʿtiqādāt *of Muḥammad b. ʿAlī Ibn Bābawayhi al-Qummī known as Shaykh Ṣadūq,* London 1942; Ḥasan al-Baṣrī, *Rasāʾil al-ʿadl wa-l-tawḥīd,* ed. M. ʿImāra, 2 vols., Cairo 1971; al-Ḥillī, Jamāl al-Dīn Ḥasan, *al-Bāb al-ḥādī ʿashar* (with the commentaries al-Miqdād al-Suyūrī, *al-Nāfiʿ yawm al-ḥashr* and Ibn Makhdūm, *Miftāḥ al-bāb*), ed. M. Muḥaqqiq, Tehran 1365/1986; id., *Risāla fī wājib al-iʿtiqād ʿalā jamīʿ al-ʿibād* (with al-Miqdād al-Suyūrī, *Iʿtimād fī sharḥ wājib al-iʿtiqād*), in *Kalimāt al-muḥaqqiqīn,* Tehran 1315/1897, 380-422; Ibn Abī Yaʿlā Abū l-Ḥusayn Muḥammad, *Ṭabaqāt al-Ḥanābila,* ed. Muḥammad Ḥāmid al-Fīqī, 2 vols., Cairo 1371/1952; Ibn Baṭṭa al-ʿUkbarī, *al-Ibāna l-kubrā [= al-Ibāna an sharʿiyyat al-firqati l-nājiyyati wa-mujānabat al-firaq al-madhmūma],* ed. R. Naʾsan Muʿṭī et al., 7 vols., Riyadh 1988-97; Ibn al-Farrāʾ, Abū Yaʿlā, *Kitāb al-Muʿtamad fī uṣūl al-dīn,* ed. Wadīʿ Zaydān Ḥaddād, Beirut 1974; Ibn Ḥanbal, *Kitāb al-Sunna,* Cairo 1349/1930; Ibn Taymiyya, al-ʿAqīda al-wāsiṭiyya, in id., *Majmūʿat al-rasāʾil al-kubrā,* 2 vols., Cairo 1323/1905, i, 387-406; H. Klopfer (ed. and trans.), *Das Dogma des Imām al-Ḥaramain al-Djuwaynī und sein Werk ʿAqīdat al-Nizāmīya,* Cairo 1958; al-Lālakāʾī, Hibat Allāh b. al-Ḥusayn b. Manṣūr al-Ṭabarī, *Sharḥ uṣūl iʿtiqād ahl al-sunna wa-l-jamāʿa,* ed. A. al-Ghāmirī, 9 vols. in 5, Riyadh 1997[5] (vol. 9 contains the first edition of *Karāmat awliyāʾ Allāh*); al-Qushayrī, *al-Manẓūma.* An ʿaqīda in verse, ed. K. al-Samarrāʾī, in *Majallat al-majmaʿ al-ʿilmī al-ʿIrāqī* 18 (1969), 284-6; al-Samarqandī, Abū l-Layth, *Kitāb Bustān al-ʿārifīn,* Beirut 1979; S. Schmidtke (ed. and trans.), *A Muʿtazilite creed of az-Zamaḫšarī (d. 538/1144) (al-Minhāǧ fī uṣūl al-dīn),* Stuttgart 1997; al-Shāfiʿī, Muḥammad b. Idrīs, *al-Fiqh al-akbar fī l-tawḥīd,* Cairo 1324/1906; id., *Waṣiyyat al-Shāfiʿī,* ed. Kern, in MSOS 13 (1910), 141-45; al-Tihrānī, Āghā Buzurg, *al-Dharīʿa ilā taṣānīf al-shīʿa,* 25 vols., Beirut 1403-6/1983-6.

Secondary: G. Anawati, Textes, in MIDEO 1 (1954), no. 22; id., Textes, in MIDEO 15 (1982), no. 13; E. Chaumont, Shāfiʿī, in *EI²,* ix, 181-5; W.C. Chittick, *Faith and practice in Islam. Three thirteenth century Sufi texts,* Albany 1992; P. Cuperly, Une profession de foi ibādite. La profession de foi d'Abū Zakariyyāʾ Yaḥyā ibn al-Ḫair al-Ǧannāwunī, in BEO 32-3 (1980-1), 21-54; W. Cureton (ed.), *Pillar of the creed of the Sunnites. Being a brief exposition of their principal tenets,* London 1843 (contains a creed of al-Nasafī); H. Daiber, The creed *(ʿaqīda)* of the Ḥanbalite Ibn Qudāma al-Maqdisī, in W. al-Qāḍī (ed.), *Studia Arabica et Islamica. Festschrift for Iḥsān ʿAbbās on his sixtieth birthday,* Beirut 1981, 105-25; E. Elder, *A commentary on the creed of Islam. Saʿd al-Dīn al-Taftazanī on the creed of Najm al-Dīn al-Nasafī,* New York 1950; J. van Ess, Biobibliographische Notizen zur islamischen Theologie, in WO 11 (1980), 122-34; id., Kritisches zum Fiqh akbar, in REI 54 (1986), 327-38; R.M. Frank, Two short dogmatic works of Abū l-Qāsim al-Qushayrī, in MIDEO 15 (1982), 53-74 and 16 (1983), 59-94; id., al-Ustādh Abū Isḥāḳ. An ʿaḳīda together with selected fragments, in MIDEO 19 (1989), 129-202; Gardet and Anawati, *Introduction,* 136-45; Gilliot, *Elt;* id., Textes, in MIDEO 19 (1989), no. 49; id., Textes, in MIDEO 24 (2000) no. 97; D. Gimaret, Les Uṣūl al-ḫamsa du Qāḍī ʿAbd al-Ǧabbār et leurs commentaires, in AI 15 (1979), 47-96; W. Heffening, al-Nasafī, in *EI²,* vii, 969, no. IV; W. Ivanov, *A creed of the Fatimids (A summary of the Tāju 'l-ʿaqāʾid, by Sayyidnā ʿAlī b. Muḥammad b. al-Walīd, ob. 612/1215),* Bombay 1936; A.W.T. Juynboll, Samarkandi's Catechismus opnieuw besproken, in *Bijdragen voor de Taal-, Land- en Volkenkunde van Nederlands Indie,* Ser. IV, 4 (1881), 267-84; H. Laoust, *Essai sur les doctrines sociales et politiques de Taki-d-Din Ahmad b. Taimiya,* Cairo 1939; id., Les premières professions de foi hanbalites, in *Mélanges Louis Massignon,* 3 vols.,

Damascus 1957, iii, 7-35; id., *La profession de foi d'Ibn Baṭṭa*, Damascus 1958; id., *La profession de foi d'Ibn Taymiyya. Texte, traduction et commentaire de la* Wāsiṭiyya, Paris 1986; id., *Šāfiʿī et le kalām* d'après Rāzī, in R. Arnaldez and S. van Riet (eds.), *Recherches d'islamologie. Recueil d'articles offert à Georges C. Anawati et Louis Gardet par leurs collègues et amis,* Louvain 1979, 389-401; G. Lecomte, La waṣiyya (testament spirituel) attribué à Abū Muḥammad ʿAbd Allāh b. Musim b. Qutayba, in *REI* 28 (1960), 73-92; D. Macdonald, *The development of Muslim theology, jurisprudence and constitutional theory,* London 1902, repr. 1985; W. Madelung, Sonstige religiöse Literatur, in *GAP,* ii, 379-83; G. Makdisi, *Ibn ʿAqīl et la résurgence de l'Islam traditionaliste au XIe siècle (Ve siècle de l'Hégire),* Damascus 1963; id., *Ibn ʿAqil. Religion and culture in classical Islam,* Edinburgh 1997; id., The juridical theology of Shāfiʿī. Origins and significance of *uṣūl al-fiqh,* in *SI* 59 (1984), 5-47; id. al-Khallāl, in *EI²,* iv, 989-90; L. Massignon, *Recueil de textes inédits concernant l'histoire de la mystique en pays d'Islam,* Paris 1929; R.J. McCarthy, *The theology of al-Ashʿarī,* Beirut 1953; A. de C. Motylinski, Lʾʿaqīda des Abadhites, in Algiers. Université. École supérieur des lettres, *Recueil de mémoires et de textes publiés en l'honneur du XIVe congrès d'orientalistes,* Alger 1905, 505-45; U. Rudolph, *al-Māturīdī und die sunnitische Theologie in Samarkand,* Leiden 1997; J. Schacht, *Der Islam. Mit Ausschluss des Qorʾans,* Tübingen 1931; D. Sourdel, Une profession de foi de l'historien al-Ṭabarī, in *REI* 36 (1968), 177-99; W.M. Watt, ʿAḳīda, in *EI²,* i, 332-6; id., Islamic creeds, in *ER,* iv, 150-53; id., *Islamic creeds. A selection,* Edinburgh 1994; C. Wein, *Die islamische Glaubenslehre (ʿaqīda) des Ibn Taimīya,* Ph.D. diss., Bonn 1973; A.J. Wensinck, *The Muslim creed. Its genesis and historical development,* Cambridge 1932, 1965²; id., al-Nasafī, in *EI²,* vii, 968-9, no. III.

Crescent see DAYS, TIMES OF

Crime see SIN AND CRIME

Criterion

A standard of judging. Among the many names used by Muslims for the Qurʾān, one of the most popular is *al-furqān,* usually translated "the Criterion." The word appears in the text seven times (Q 2:53, 185; 3:4; 8:29, 41; 21:48; 25:1) and is also one of the names given to Q 25. It has long been conjectured by Western scholars that the origin of *furqān* is the Aramaic/Syriac *purqāna* (salvation, deliverance, redemption; see FOREIGN VOCABULARY). Although a foreign origin has not been posited by the Muslim tradition, it has nonetheless been recognized that a simple derivation from the Arabic root letters *f-r-q* (to separate, distinguish) will not easily explain all the uses of *furqān*.

There seem to be two basic elements influencing qurʾānic usage of this term: a soteriological sense probably deriving from an Aramaic or Syriac origin and the notion of separation and discernment characteristic of the Arabic verb *faraqa*. When a sense of connection to revelation and scripture is added to these two factors, the resulting semantic field becomes quite complex (see REVELATION AND INSPIRATION; SCRIPTURE AND THE QURʾĀN). The aspect of salvation (q.v.) is clearest in Q 8:29: "O you who believe! If you fear God, he will create for you a *furqān,* acquit you of your evil-doing and forgive you (see FORGIVENESS)." Al-Ṭabarī (d. 310/923) notes that in this context authorities have interpreted the word variously as escape *(makhraj),* salvation *(najāt)* or separation/discernment (*faṣl,* cf. *Tafsīr,* ad loc.). Its use in connection with Moses (q.v.) and Aaron (q.v.) forms a conceptual link between salvation and scripture: "We granted to Moses the book (*al-kitāb,* see BOOK) and the *furqān*. Perhaps you might accept to be guided" (Q 2:53); "Indeed we granted to Moses and Aaron the *furqān* and a light and a reminder *(dhikr)* for the God-fearing" (Q 21:48; see PIETY). Since the career of Moses unites the roles of both liberator and deliverer of revelation, and since for the Qurʾān it is the latter role that is paramount, it is not difficult to see how the emphasis in the usage of this loanword might shift from salvation to revelation.

This dual emphasis is evident also in the career of the Prophet (see MUḤAMMAD): Q 8:41 refers to "what we revealed to our servant on the day of *al-furqān*, the day when the two armies met." The tradition universally recognizes this as referring to the battle of Badr (q.v.) and so links the revelation of the Qurʾān in the month of Ramaḍān (q.v.) with the divinely-granted victory of the Muslims over the Meccan forces (see CONQUEST; EXPEDITIONS AND BATTLES). In this verse the various levels of meaning in the word *furqān* can be seen to come together: God saves (Syr./Aram. *purqāna*) the smaller Muslim band from almost certain defeat and at this juncture a decisive break *(farq)* between Muslims and Meccans takes place. Furthermore, God's revelation in the Qurʾān is something by which right is distinguished *(faraqa)* from wrong and it is also what distinguishes *(faraqa)* Muslims from the unscriptured and from the recipients of earlier revelations (see PEOPLE OF THE BOOK). The sense that *al-furqān* refers to revelation is reinforced by the fact that it is used on all but one occasion with the verbs "to grant" *(atā)* and "to send down" *(nazzala/anzala)* — verbs most often, although not exclusively, connected with revelation. To the extent that the Qurʾān recognizes a need for salvation, the term *al-furqān* shows how it considers the salvific action of God to be the sending of prophetic guidance (see PROPHETS AND PROPHETHOOD).

Daniel Madigan

Bibliography
Primary: Ṭabarī, *Tafsīr*.
Secondary: Jeffery, *For. vocab.*, 225-9; R. Paret, Furḳān, in *EI²*, ii, 949-50, and authors cited there; Watt-Bell, *Introduction*, 145-7.

Criticism, Critical Theory see CONTEMPORARY CRITICAL PRACTICES

Cross see CRUCIFIXION

Crucifixion

Nailing or binding the hands and feet of a criminal to a cross of execution. The verb *ṣalaba*, "to crucify," occurs six times in the Qurʾān: twice in the root form and four times in the second verbal form. It is probably a Syriac loan word (see FOREIGN VOCABULARY).

Etymology and meaning

The verb "to crucify" *(ṣalaba)*, which occurs in the active voice at Q 4:157 and in the passive at Q 12:41, is a denominal verb from the noun *ṣalīb*, meaning a cross. This noun does not occur in the Qurʾān, although found in early poetry (see POETRY AND POETS). It is probably derived from *ṣᵉlībā*, the word for cross in Syriac. The precise meaning of the second form of the verb *(ṣallaba)*, which occurs at Q 5:33 in the passive voice and at Q 7:124, 20:71 and 26:49 in the active, is uncertain. J. Penrice assumes that it is causative (*Dictionary*, 85) but as the verb is denominal the first and second forms may be interchangeable. Other possibilities are that the second form is intensive ("to crucify with great violence") or numerically extensive ("to crucify in large numbers").

Crucifixion as a pre-Islamic punishment

Crucifixion was widely practiced in antiquity. Herodotus (fifth century B.C.E.) makes numerous references to its employment by the Persians and other classical authors testify to its currency amongst Indians, Assyrians, Celts, Carthaginians and Romans

(M. Hengel, *Crucifixion,* 4-5). According to the Gospels, when the Romans crucified Jesus they nailed him to a cross which had to be carried to the site of execution (e.g. *John* 19:17-23; 20:25). However, Paul equates crucifixion with hanging on a tree (*Gal* 3:13; cf. *Deut* 21:23).

In the Qurʾān, crucifixion is associated principally with ancient Egypt (q.v.). Joseph (q.v.) interprets the dream (see DREAMS AND SLEEP) of a fellow prisoner to mean that the latter will be crucified and birds will eat from his head (Q 12:41; cf. *Gen* 40:23, where Pharaoh's chief baker is hanged on a tree; see BREAD). Another instance occurs in reference to Moses (q.v.). When Pharaoh's magicians testify to their belief in the God of Moses, Pharaoh (q.v.) says that he will cut off their hands and feet on opposite sides and crucify them (Q 7:124; 20:71; 26:49). We are not given details of the procedure, although in one of these qurʾānic references, Pharaoh tells his magicians that he will crucify them "on the trunks of palm trees (q.v.)" (Q 20:71).

The non-crucifixion of Jesus

The Qurʾān takes the Jews to task for claiming that they killed Jesus (q.v.) and it states that they did not kill him or crucify him but that it appeared so to them (Q 4:157; see JEWS AND JUDAISM; CHRISTIANS AND CHRISTIANITY). According to the traditional Sunnī and Shīʿī commentators, God raised him alive to heaven, having first projected his likeness onto someone else whom the Jews crucified in the belief that he was Jesus. In support of this interpretation, they cite ḥadīths which state that Jesus will descend to kill the Antichrist (q.v.) before he dies (see APOCALYPSE; ESCHATOLOGY), as well as reports attributed to the early exegetes Ibn ʿAbbās (d. 68/686-8), Wahb b. Munabbih (d. 110 or 114 A.H.) and al-Suddī (d. ca. 127/745) which narrate how God outwitted the Jews (N. Robinson, *Christ in Islam,* 127-41, 171-2). Muslim rationalists were quick to point out the difficulties in the projection theory. Some of them proposed more credible alternatives, e.g. that the authorities, after failing to arrest Jesus, knowingly crucified another person and that the crowds were misled into thinking that the substitute was Jesus because they were kept at a distance and his appearance was disfigured by the ordeal (N. Robinson, *Christ in Islam,* 136-8, 172; see POLEMICS AND POLEMICAL LANGUAGE).

As some pre-Islamic texts such as the gnostic *Apocalypse of Peter* discovered at Nag Hammadi mention the crucifixion of a substitute, it is possible that the traditional commentators have interpreted this verse correctly. However, Christian apologists have long argued that Q 4:157 does not actually deny that Jesus was crucified, but rather, that it denies that it was the Jews who crucified him. This accords with the gospel accounts, which attribute his execution to the Romans (N. Robinson, *Christ in Islam,* 108-9). Christian apologists also draw attention to Q 3:55, which seems to imply that Jesus' death is in the past and to Q 3:169, which asserts that Muslim martyrs are alive with God. The Brethren of Purity (see BROTHER AND BROTHERHOOD) apparently accepted these arguments and adopted the view that Jesus' body was nailed to the cross but that his spirit was raised alive into God's presence (N. Robinson, *Christ in Islam,* 56).

M.Z. Khan's translation of Q 4:157 (… "those who have differed in the matter of his having been taken down alive from the cross are certainly in a state of doubt concerning it"…) gives the impression that the Arabic explicitly states that Jesus was taken down alive from the cross. However, as the Arabic reads: *wa-inna lladhīna khtalafū fīhi la-fī shakkin minhu,* a more literal translation would be along the lines of "those who have differed in it are certainly in a state of doubt concerning it." He also renders Q 2:72-5 so as to allude to the crucifixion. His rendition of Q 2:72-3, in particular, is at variance with the Arabic: "Call to mind also when you claimed to have brought about the death of a Personage [*wa-idh qataltum nafsan,* lit. "and when you killed a man"] and then differed among yourselves concerning it, and Allah would bring to mind that which you concealed. So We said: 'Test the crucial question by putting together other incidents relating to the affair and you will arrive at the truth.' Thus does Allah plan to preserve alive those considered dead [*kadhālika yuḥyi llāhu l-mawtā,* lit. "thus does God make the dead alive"] and shows you His Signs that you may understand." The interpretations conveyed in this translation, corresponding to the teaching of the Aḥmadiyya (q.v.), have no textual basis.

Crucifixion as a divinely-ordained punishment?
The traditional interpretation of Q 5:33 is that it prescribes crucifixion as one of four possible punishments for brigandage. The basis for this view is a ḥadīth which states that the verse *(āya)* was revealed when some people from the tribe of ʿUkl abused the Prophet's hospitality by killing a herdsman and stealing cattle (Bukhārī, *Ṣaḥīḥ,* viii, 201-2; see OCCASIONS OF REVELATION). Without mentioning this ḥadīth, M. Asad argues that the Qurʾān would hardly promulgate a divine law which advocated a punishment identical to that inflicted by Pharaoh, whose qurʾānic characterization is that of an enemy of God. Asad suggests that the *āya* is not a legal injunction, but rather a description of what the unbelievers were doing to each other in their perverseness (*The message,* 148-9; see CHASTISEMENT AND PUNISHMENT; BELIEF AND UNBELIEF; GRATITUDE AND INGRATITUDE; DISOBEDIENCE; LAW AND THE QURʾĀN).

Neal Robinson

Bibliography
Primary: K. Aland et al. (eds.), *The Greek New Testament,* London 1966; Bukhārī, *Ṣaḥīḥ;* M.Z. Khan, *The Quran. Arabic text with a new translation,* London 1971, 1981³ (rev. ed.); R. Kittel (ed.), *Biblica Hebraica,* Stuttgart 1937; J.M. Robinson, *The Nag Hammadi library in English,* Leiden 1977.
Secondary: M. Asad, *The message of the Qurʾān,* Gibraltar 1980; M. Hengel, *Crucifixion in the ancient world and the folly of the message of the cross,* London 1977; B.T. Lawson, The crucifixion of Jesus in the Qurʾān and qurʾānic commentary. A historical survey. Part II, in *Bulletin of the Henry Martyn Institute of Islamic Sciences* 10.3 (1991), 6-40; J. Penrice, *A dictionary and glossary of the Koran,* London 1873; repr. 1971; N. Robinson, *Christ in Islam and Christianity. The representation of Jesus in the Qurʾān and the classical Muslim commentaries,* London 1991; O. Spies, Über die Kreuzigung im Islam, in R. Thomas (ed.), *Religion und religionen. Festschrift für Gustav Mansching,* Bonn 1967, 143-56; F.E. Vogel, Ṣalb, in *EI²,* viii, 935-6; A.J. Wensinck and D. Thomas, Ṣalīb, in *EI²,* viii, 980-1.

Crusher see HELL

Crying see WEEPING

Cultivation see AGRICULTURE AND VEGETATION

Cups and Vessels

Hollow or concave receptacles for conveying food and drink. As with qurʾānic religious terminology, some of the Qurʾān's cultural vocabulary, such as the various lexemes for cups and vessels, are of non-Arabic origin (see FOREIGN VOCABULARY). As noted by Arthur Jeffery and others who have investigated the origins of foreign words in the Qurʾān, the borrowings came from other Semitic languages, such as Aramaic, Nabatean, Syriac, Ethiopian, as well as from Persian and Greek. Eleonore Haeuptner's study on material culture in the Qurʾān deals with the relationship between the references to material culture in the Qurʾān on the one hand — not so much focusing on specific vocabulary, but rather on general categories to which the terms belong — and pre-Islamic Arab culture on the other, as it is known from poetry and from other sources, such as ḥadīth and biographies (see PRE-ISLAMIC ARABIA AND THE QURʾĀN), presenting a panorama of the cultural environment of the Qurʾān. At least as important perhaps as the etymology of the material-cultural terms is the pattern of their occurrences. The enumeration of vessels presented below reveals such patterns with regards to certain lexemes. Some words are exclusively associated with specific contexts or certain stories and do not occur elsewhere. For example, *kaʾs, akwāb, abārīq,* and *qawārīr,* which are of diverse origins and all of which refer to various types of drinking vessels, occur only in descriptions of the pleasures of paradise (q.v.) whereas the words *ṣuwāʿ* and *siqāya,* which also translate as drinking vessels, are used only in Q 12 ("Joseph," Sūrat Yūsuf) where none of the previous paradisiacal vessels are mentioned. *Ṣiḥāf,* a kind of dish described as made from gold (q.v.) and "vessels" *(āniyya,* sing. *ināʾ),* which are described as made from silver, occur only in the context of descriptions of paradise. The word *zujāja,* like *qārūra,* is usually associated with a glass vessel, but the former is used only in the symbolic context of the oil lamp (q.v.) in the Light Verse (*āyat al-nūr,* Q 24:35; see also ANOINTING) whereas the latter is used only in a paradisiacal context. The following list of qurʾānic terms for vessels is arranged alphabetically. *Abārīq* (sing. *ibrīq*), ewer, jug: Like *kaʾs* and *akwāb,* the word *abārīq* is used in the context of paradise. It occurs only once and in the plural form (Q 56:18). *Akwāb* (sing. *kūb*), goblet: Like *kaʾs* the word is used in the context of paradisiacal drinks. In Q 43:71 the cups are golden, in Q 76:15 they are made of silver. In Q 56:18 the cup contains a wine that neither causes headache nor intoxicates (see INTOXICANTS). It occurs only in the plural form (Q 43:71; 56:18; 76:15; 88:14). *Āniyya min fiḍḍa,* silver vessels: Like *kaʾs* and *akwāb,* the term appears in the context of the pleasures of paradise (Q 76:15). *Dalw,* pail: It occurs only once, in Q 12 ("Joseph," Sūrat Yūsuf), which relates the story of Joseph (q.v.). Thrown by his brothers (see BROTHER AND BROTHERHOOD) into a well (see WELLS AND SPRINGS), Joseph was found by someone who was drawing water from the well with his pail (Q 12:19). *Jifān* (sing. *jafna*), basin: The word is used once, in the plural, to describe basins as large as troughs in King Solomon's (q.v.) palace (Q 34:13; see JINN; ART AND ARCHITECTURE AND THE QURʾĀN). *Kaʾs,* cup: The word occurs only in the singular, and in the context of the pleasures of paradise where the believers will be served in cups a drink (wine) from a paradisiacal well. In verse Q 76:5 the water in the cup is camphor-flavored (*kāfūr,* see CAMPHOR); in Q 76:17 the drink is ginger-flavored (*zanjabīl,* cf. Q 37:45; 56:18; 52:23; 76:5, 17; 78:34). *Qawārīr* (sing. *qārūra*), a glass vessel, perhaps a bottle: It is described as made of silver, which could still mean that it is a glass vessel, but comparable to or as shiny as silver. The word is used in the plural and in the context of paradisiacal delights; the believers will be served in such vessels as much as they like (Q 76:15-6; see BELIEF AND UNBELIEF). *Qudūr* (sing. *qidra*), cauldrons: The term occurs only once in the text and in the plural, referring to built-in cauldrons which the jinn made for King Solomon's palace (Q 34:13). *Mikyāl,* a measuring vessel: The word is used in the singular together with *mīzān* in the metaphorical sense of justice (Q 11:84-5; see WEIGHTS AND MEASURES; MEASUREMENT; METAPHOR). *Ṣiḥāf* (sing. *ṣaḥfa*), originally meaning a flat surface, in the Qurʾān the term refers to dishes. It occurs in the plural in the description of paradise, wherein the believers will be served in golden dishes (Q 43:71). *Siqāya,* drinking cup: The word is used in the singular, with two different meanings. At Q 12:70, Joseph places a cup *(siqāya)* in his youngest brother's saddlebag (see BENJAMIN). Used in the context of pilgrimage (q.v.) in Q 9:19, however, it means a water basin. *Ṣuwāʿ* (from *ṣāʿa, yaṣūʿu,* to measure), a drinking cup: The word is used once, as a synonym for *siqāya,* the cup which Joseph placed in his brother's bag. The *ṣuwāʿ* is described as a royal vessel (*ṣuwāʿ al-malik,* Q 12:72). *Zujāja,* glass vessel: The term occurs only once and in the singular, at Q 24:35 *(āyat al-nūr).* The lamp that symbolizes the divine light is described as including a *zujāja* or glass vessel, which contains the oil of an olive tree.

Conclusions about the significance of a qurʾānic lexeme cannot be drawn based solely upon its status as a "loan word" or an original Arabic term (see ARABS; BEDOUIN; ARABIC LANGUAGE; LANGUAGE AND STYLE OF THE QURʾĀN; LANGUAGE, CONCEPT OF). It is important to know the history of the presence of the term in the Arabic language and to determine whether its occurrence in the Qurʾān was an innovation. However, literature on material culture in the Qurʾān (see MATERIAL CULTURE AND THE QURʾĀN) remains particularly sparse.

Doris Behrens-Abouseif

Bibliography
ʿAbd al-Jalīl, ʿIsā, *al-Muṣḥaf al-muyassar,* Cairo 1399/ 1979; E. Haeuptner, *Koranische Hinweise auf die materielle Kultur der alten Araber,* Ph.D. diss., Tübingen 1966; Jeffery, *For. vocab.; Lisān al-ʿArab;* Paret; id., *Kommentar;* Suyūṭī, *Durr;* Ṭabarī, *Tafsīr; Tāj al-ʿarūs.*

Curse

A wish or prayer (q.v.) for misfortune or disaster to befall someone or something; with specific reference to God, the prediction or causation of misfortune; the expression of this invocation, prediction or causation or the result thereof. All of these significations are rendered in the Qurʾān by *laʿna,* "curse"; closely related is wrath (*ghaḍab,* see ANGER). Curses are often expressed by verbs with an optative sense, with "to curse, damn" *(laʿana)* appearing most frequently. Other verses which may be read as curses are: "May God fight against them!" (Q 9:30; 63:4), "May their hands be tied and may they be cursed for what they have said!" (Q 5:64), "May the hands [i.e. the power] of Abū Lahab (q.v.) perish, and may he perish as well!" (Q 111:1). The passive *qutila* ("may he be killed!") occurs five times (Q 51:10; 74:19, 20; 80:17; 85:4). The accusative absolute understood to modify a suppressed verb may also express a curse: "May perdition befall them *(fa-taʿsan lahum)* and may [God] make their actions vain!" (Q 47:8); "May the denizens of hellfire be far removed [from mercy]!" (*fa-suḥqan li-aṣḥābi l-saʿīr,* Q 67:11; see HELL; FIRE); "May the wrongdoing folk be far removed!" (*fa-buʿdan lil-qawmi l-ẓālimīn,* Q 23:41; cf. 11:44, 60, 68, 95; 23:44; see PUNISHMENT STORIES). A curse is created by inversion of the greeting "Welcome!": "May you not be welcome!" (*lā marḥaban bikum,* Q 38:60). The noun *wayl,* "woe, misfortune," appears in such frequent curses as "Woe to the deniers on that day!" (e.g. ten times in Q 77; see LAST JUDGMENT).

The act of cursing is most often performed by God. God has cursed Satan

(Q 4:118; see DEVIL), enemies of the faith such as unbelievers, apostates, hypocrites and those who conceal God's signs (q.v.; Q 2:88, 159; 3:8; 9:6; 33:64; see BELIEF AND UNBELIEF; ASTRAY; APOSTASY; HYPOCRITES AND HYPOCRISY; IDOLATERS AND IDOLATRY) as well as perpetrators of specific legal infractions such as Sabbath breakers, murderers and those who accuse innocent women of adultery (Q 4:47, 93; 24:23; see BOUNDARIES AND PRECEPTS; MURDER; BLOODSHED; ADULTERY AND FORNICATION). The curse of God is sometimes associated solely with eternal damnation (e.g. Q 4:93; 33:64; 48:6) while other passages imply that it has two distinct effects: damnation in the afterlife and destruction in this world (Q 11 passim; see CHASTISEMENT AND PUNISHMENT; REWARD AND PUNISHMENT). God's curse renders hypocrites blind and deaf (Q 47:23) and turns those who have incurred his wrath into apes and pigs (cf. Q 5:60). Those who are cursed by God are doomed and will find no one to help them (Q 4:52; see FATE; DESTINY). The curses of angels and people may reinforce those of God (Q 2:159, 161). Nations curse their predecessors for leading them astray and causing their doom to hell (Q 7:38). Earlier prophets including Noah (q.v.), Moses (q.v.) and Jesus (q.v.) cursed the stubborn opponents among their peoples for refusing to accept the Lord's messages (Q 5:78; 10:88; 71:24-8; see DISOBEDIENCE; GRATITUDE AND INGRATITUDE; OPPOSITION TO MUḤAMMAD).

An oath often contains a conditional curse upon oneself as with *liʿān*, whereby a husband who has no witnesses other than himself swears four times that his wife has committed adultery and his wife swears her innocence, each invoking God's curse if he or she is lying (Q 24:6-9; see MARRIAGE AND DIVORCE; LAW AND THE QURʾĀN; OATHS). As a means to settle a dispute concerning the nature of Jesus as divine or human, Q 3:61 proposes a technique of mutual cursing known as *mubāhala*, wherein the assembled disputants each present their case, then pray humbly (i.e. to God; *ibtahala*) and, finally, invoke the curse of God upon those who lie. This incident, which apparently was never actually carried out, is said to have been occasioned by a Christological debate between the Prophet and a deputation from the Christian Balḥārith b. Kaʿb of Najrān (q.v.) in 10/632 (see POLEMICS AND POLEMICAL LANGUAGE; CHRISTIANS AND CHRISTIANITY; DEBATE AND DISPUTATION). See also BLESSING.

Devin J. Stewart

Bibliography

R. Brunschvig, Bayyina in *EI²*, i, 1150-1151; L. Massignon, La mubāhala de Médine et l'hyperdulie de Fāṭima, in *Opera minora*, Beirut 1963, i, 550f.; J. Pederson, Ḳasam, *EI²*, iv, 687-690; J. Schacht, Liʿān, in *EI²*, v, 730-2; W. Schmucker, Mubāhala, in *EI²*, vi, 276-7; R. Strothman, Die Mūbahala in Tradition und Liturgie, in *Der Islam* 33 (1958), 5f.

Custom

see SUNNA; TRADITION AND CUSTOM

D

Dahr see FATE

Damnation see LAST JUDGMENT

Dance see ṢŪFISM AND THE QURʾĀN

Dār al-Ḥarb see COMMUNITY AND SOCIETY IN THE QURʾĀN

Dār al-Islām see COMMUNITY AND SOCIETY IN THE QURʾĀN

Darkness

The absence of light (q.v.). In the Qurʾān, darkness is almost always evoked within the semantic field of the term unbelief (*kufr,* see BELIEF AND UNBELIEF) as a metaphorical expression descriptive of the spiritual state of the unbeliever *(kāfir)*. It is expressed by the word *ẓulumāt* (the plural of *ẓulma/ẓuluma*) attested 23 times in the text. The fourth verbal form, which means to become or to make dark (*aẓlama,* Q 2:20) and its active participle *muẓlim* (Q 10:27; cf. 36:37), account for the only other qurʾānic references to darkness. Finally, the elative form *(aẓlam),* where it occurs, is not directly related to darkness semantically, but rather to injustice (see JUSTICE AND INJUSTICE), arrogance (q.v.), unbelief, etc. *(ẓulm)*.

As its antonym, light *(nūr),* stands for faith (q.v.; *īmān*), darkness is inextricably associated with the concepts of error (q.v.) or straying from truth (*ḍalāla,* see ASTRAY), perfidy *(nifāq),* and unbelief *(kufr)*. Going astray, open or hidden breach of faith and concealment of the truth (q.v.) plunge human beings into the darkness of doubt (see UNCERTAINTY), delusion and ultimately faithlessness. In two powerful sequential similes, the hypocritical dissenters (*munāfiqūn,* see HYPOCRITES AND HYPOCRISY) are likened first to those who have lit a fire which has gone out and left them in total darkness so that they cannot see and then to those who are caught in a rainstorm at night, paralyzed by fear and darkness, ironically able to take a few steps only in the light provided by the lightening of which they are terrified (Q 2:17-20). The unbelievers, by contrast, are totally blind and cannot be compared to "those with sight *(baṣīr),*" i.e. the believers (Q 13:16; 35:19-20). The parallelism here between the antonym pairs of light-darkness and seeing-blindness is unmistakable. The commentators take the obvious step and superimpose the pair *īmān-kufr* onto the other two. This move also suggests an answer to the question of why darkness is always expressed in the plural: Right guidance is singular and integral while error is multiple (e.g. Bayḍāwī, *Anwār,* i, 292, ad Q 6:1).

Even the more straightforward usage of the term as in the expression "the darknesses of the land and of the sea" (Q 6:63, 97; 27:63), which the commentators regularly gloss as difficulties attendant on travel by land and sea, preserves the core metaphorical connotation of straying from the proper course. The only exception to this pattern is in Q 39:6 where the "three darknesses" enveloping the fetus are decoded as the belly, the womb, and the placenta by the commentators (e.g. Ṭabarī, *Tafsīr,* x, 615-6; see BIOLOGY AS THE STAGES AND CREATION OF LIFE; BLOOD AND BLOOD CLOT). The commentary tradition cites the crying out of Dhū l-Nūn (see JONAH) in the darkness (Q 21:87) as another exception to the general metaphorical interpretation of darkness by interpreting *ẓulumāt* here as physical darkness (of the fish's belly, of the sea, of the night, e.g. Ṭabarī, *Tafsīr,* ix, 76-7); yet the verse is patently about Jonah's temporary spiritual deviation and his subsequent return to the truth, making a metaphorical understanding of the term difficult to rule out. Finally, it is noteworthy that *ẓulumāt* is not found in semantic proximity to the important qur'ānic pair, day and night (q.v.).

Ahmet T. Karamustafa

Bibliography
Bayḍāwī, *Anwār,* 2 vols., Beirut 1408/1988;
Ṭabarī, *Tafsīr,* 12 vols., Beirut 1412/1992.

Date Palm

Phoenix dactylifera, a widely-cultivated tree of great economic importance in the Middle East: *nakhl* (collective noun), *nakhīl* (plural), and *nakhla (nomen unitatis)*. These forms appear in the Qur'ān a total of nineteen times.

The date palm is mentioned in two general contexts. The first is as one of the signs (q.v.) of God's munificence towards his creation, occurring often with the olive and the grape, e.g. Q 6:99; 16:11; 80:29. The second is in a metaphorical sense, likening God's punishment of sin (see SIN, MAJOR AND MINOR; CHASTISEMENT AND PUNISHMENT) to the "uprooted trunks of palm trees," as in Q 54:20 and Q 69:7. Both contexts underline the great importance of the palm tree in its various species to agriculture and human subsistence throughout the Middle East (see AGRICULTURE AND VEGETATION).

This is confirmed by the unusually large number of terms in the Qur'ān which are related to the plant, more in fact than to any other. Of the following almost all are single references, some used in a figurative or metaphorical sense: *līna,* a kind of palm tree (Q 59:5); *masad,* the fibers growing at the roots of the palm branches, used for making rope (Q 111:5); *nawā,* the date stone (Q 6:95); *haḍīm,* palm spathe (Q 26:148); *dusur* (sing. *disār*), the palm fiber cord traditionally used in Arabian shipbuilding to bind the planks of the hull together (Q 54:13); *akmām* (sing. *kumm*), the calyx of the flowers, the date bud (Q 41:47; 55:11); *qiṭmīr,* the thin skin around a date stone (Q 35:13); *qinwān,* said by al-Ṭabarī (d. 310/923) to be the fruit stalks and fruit of the palm when ripe (Q 6:99); *naqīr,* the groove in a date stone (Q 4:53, 124); *jidh'* (pl. *judhū'*), the palm trunk (Q 19:23, 25; 20:71); *'urjūn,* the dry date stalk (Q 36:39); *janā,* fresh ripe dates (Q 55:54); *a'jāz* (sing. *'ajuz*), trunks of the palm tree (Q 54:20, 69:7); *ṭal',* the spadix of the palm (Q 50:10); *ṣarīm,* dates cut from the tree (Q 68:20).

Two remarkable references may also be

noted. In Q 19:23-5 Mary (q.v.) seeks the cooling shelter of a palm tree and then is fed by its nourishing fruit *(ruṭab),* while painfully awaiting the imminent birth of her child. And in Q 16:67 there is a mention of the fruit of palms and grapes used to make an intoxicating drink and a "good substance." Attention is directed to these products as a sign of God. Commentators agreed that these verses were later abrogated by the verses prohibiting the use of alcohol (see INTOXICANTS; ABROGATION).

In a ḥadīth attributed to the Prophet, the date palm is said to be the most blessed of trees just as Muslims are the most blessed community of humankind (see COMMUNITY AND SOCIETY IN THE QURʾĀN). This saying appears to have derived from the widespread notion in Iraq that the date palm occupies in the plant kingdom the same rank as the human being among the animals. The date palm was honored with the epithet of "Adam's sister" (Ibn Waḥshiyya [fl. late third/ninth century], *al-Filāḥa al-nabaṭiyya,* ii, 1339). In another tradition, the Prophet recommended eating seven *ʿajwa* (the best variety of dates grown in Medina, called *umm al-tamr,* "the mother of dates") in the morning to counteract the effects of poison and other ills throughout the day. The Prophet is said to have enjoyed *ḥays,* a mixture of pitted dates, clarified butter and dried curd, vigorously kneaded together into a paste and shaped into mouth-sized portions. Finally, dates could be used to pay off a grower's debts (Bukhārī, *Ṣaḥīḥ, K. Aṭʿima* for all references; see DEBT).

In Ibn Waḥshiyya's *Nabatean agriculture (al-Filāḥa al-nabaṭiyya)* the date is judged to be more useful than the olive. It was more widely cultivated than the olive and the tree and its fruit were put to numerous uses. The consumption of dates was seen as the cause of the supposed longevity of Arabs and was said to provide protection against ulcers and tumors. Wine, vinegar and syrup could be produced from the fruit. Palm fronds were used to make doors, beds, floor coverings and tents. (Indeed, down to the present day, houses constructed of palm fronds are found in certain coastal areas of Oman). Palm fiber was woven to make shrouds for the dead, plates, baskets, trays and jar covers. The wood of the trunks could be burned or used as a building material. The first mosque (q.v.) in the city of Medina (q.v.) was constructed of palm trees. See also FOOD AND DRINK.

David Waines

Bibliography
Primary: Ibn Waḥshiyya, *al-Filāḥa al-nabaṭiyya,* ed. and trans. T. Fahd, *L'agriculture nabateenne. Traduction en arabe attribuée a Abū Bakr Aḥmad b. ʿAlī al-Kasdānī, Ibn Waḥshiyya,* 2 vols., Damascus 1993-5.
Secondary: P. Costa, The *tarqbah:* a traditional date processing plant of Oman, in *Quaderni di Studi Arabi* 5-6 (1987-8), 167-88; R.B. Serjeant, A maqāmah on palm-protection, in *JNES* 40 (1981), 307-22; M. Vanhove, The making of palm vinegar at al-Hiswah (near Aden) and some other crafts related to palm trees, in *New Arabian Studies* 2 (1997), 175-85; F. Viré, Nakhl, in *EI²*, vii, 923-4.

Dates see DATE PALM

Dating see CALENDAR

Daughters see CHILDREN

Daughters of God see POLYTHEISM AND ATHEISM; IDOLS AND IMAGES; IDOLATRY AND IDOLATERS; PRE-ISLAMIC ARABIA AND THE QURʾĀN

David

The Israelite king, mentioned sixteen times in the Qurʾān. David (Dāwūd) appears in the Qurʾān as a link in the chain of prophets who preceded Muḥammad (Q 4:163; 6:84). Although he is not one of the law giving prophets *(ulū al-ʿazm),* he is far from a marginal figure.

David in the Qurʾān

David was the recipient of a written divine book of psalms (q.v.; Q 4:163; 17:55). Mountains and birds obeyed him in praising God (Q 21:79; 34:10). He killed Goliath (q.v.; Jālūt) and God granted him kingship (*mulk,* see KINGS AND RULERS) after Saul (q.v.; Ṭālūt) and wisdom (q.v.; *ḥikma,* Q 2:251), sometimes explained as the gift of prophecy (e.g. Ṭabarī, *Taʾrīkh,* i, 559). God also gave David and his son Solomon (q.v.) "knowledge" (*ʿilm,* Q 27:15), which in this case is sometimes understood to be the ability to comprehend the language of the birds and animals (see KNOWLEDGE AND LEARNING). He was appointed a deputy of God on the earth *(khalīfa fī l-arḍ,* Q 38:26; see CALIPH), a title given only to him and to Adam (see ADAM AND EVE). David cursed the unbelievers among the Children of Israel (q.v.; Q 5:78). Exegetes commonly connect this verse with Q 7:166: "Be you apes, miserably slinking!" (e.g. Ṭabarsī, *Majmaʿ,* iii, 231). He was given the ability to distinguish between truth (q.v.) and falsehood when dispensing justice (*faṣl al-khiṭāb,* Q 38:20; see JUSTICE AND INJUSTICE; DECISION). God softened iron for him and instructed him to make coats of mail (Q 21:80; 34:10-1) to provide for his livelihood. David thought that God was putting him to the test (see TRIAL). Then he prayed and repented and God forgave him (Q 38:24-5; see FORGIVENESS; REPENTANCE AND PENANCE). A divine forgiveness that commentators have linked to the biblical story of Bathsheba and Uriah (Ṭabarī, *Tafsīr,* ad Q 38:24) yet unlike the Hebrew Bible, the Qurʾān does not explicitly mention anything about Uriah, Bathsheba or the other wives of David or about Absalom or his other sons, with the exception of Solomon. There is also no mention of his stay in Hebron and Jerusalem (q.v.) and his conflicts with the Philistines.

Sūrat Ṣād (Q 38) is also called "the sūra of David" (Hibat Allāh b. Salāma, *Nāsikh,* 262). Exegetes explain that since David prostrated when asking God to forgive him, Muḥammad was ordered to imitate him and to perform a prostration when reading this sūra (Bukhārī, *Ṣaḥīḥ,* vi, 155; see BOWING AND PROSTRATION).

David in qurʾānic exegesis and the stories of prophets

The need to explain some cryptic allusions in the Qurʾān opened the door to the abundant and readily available Jewish and Christian legends about David (see MYTHIC AND LEGENDARY NARRATIVES). In particular, homiletic interpretations of the scriptures (*midrash,* see SCRIPTURE AND THE QURʾĀN) and pious Jewish legends *(haggada)* were to figure prominently in the exegesis of the Qurʾān and in the nascent literature of the "stories of prophets" *(qiṣaṣ al-anbiyāʾ).* An early collector, Wahb b. Munabbih (d. 110/728 or 114/732), played an important role as a source for traditions about David.

The image of David in later exegesis closely parallels that in the Jewish sources (e.g. the Books of Chronicles, the *mishna,* the *talmud* and the *haggada*), where he is represented as completely purified of all sins. Such traditions were compatible with the Islamic doctrine of infallibility of prophets which developed in the second/eighth and third/ninth centuries (see IMPECCABILITY AND INFALLIBILITY) and Muslim authors followed this lead. For example, in the Muslim tradition Bathsheba was engaged to Uriah, not married to him. David asked for her hand and her parents preferred him, the king, to Uriah, the warrior. Other versions of the story maintain that Bathsheba was divorced or widowed and Uriah was resurrected for a moment to tell David that he forgave him, not for sending him to his death, but for marrying his widow. God pardoned David (Sibṭ b. al-Jawzī, *Mirʾāt al-zamān,* i, 484-5). Muslim story-tellers *(quṣṣāṣ,* sing. *qāṣṣ)* accepted these legends and rejected the older image of David from the Book of Samuel and Kings, where he is charged with adultery and murder. Further, it seems that such a total change in the attitude towards David (and other biblical figures) in the Jewish sources is one of the bases for the qurʾānic accusation that the Jews had falsified the Bible (Q 2:75; 4:46; 5:13, 41; see CORRUPTION).

The image of David varies in different currents of Islam. The canonical Sunnī ḥadīth collections, which were compiled in the third/ninth century (see ḤADĪTH AND THE QURʾĀN), strengthened opposition to the use of traditions from Jewish sources *(Isrāʾīliyyāt)* by neglecting all the above-mentioned stories. In these sources David is represented largely by his prayers, fasts, songs and handiwork. On the other hand, the Shīʿī tradition insisted on the complete infallibility of David and blamed the Sunnīs for the accounts which portray him as less than perfect (Majlisī, *Biḥār,* xiv, 26). Finally, the Ṣūfīs made David a symbol of asceticism, circulating his pious prayers and utterances and the legends dealing with his repentance. He became a supreme example of devotion (Mojtabāʾī, Dāwūd in *EIr,* vii, 161-2). Accounts concerning David also form an integral part of every book celebrating the importance and sanctity of Jerusalem *(faḍāʾil bayt al-maqdis).* See also PROPHETS AND PROPHETHOOD.

Isaac Hasson

Bibliography

Primary: ʿAbdallāh b. al-Mubārak, *Kitāb al-Zuhd,* ed. Ḥ.R. al-Aʿẓamī, Beirut n.d., 161-4; Aḥmad b. Ḥanbal, *al-Zuhd,* Cairo 1987, 111-2, 114, 134; R.G. Khoury, *Wahb b. Munabbih* (*Codices arabici antiqui* i), Wiesbaden 1972 (with bibliography); id., *Les légendes prophétiques dans l'Islam depuis le Ier jusqu'au IIIe siècle de l'hégire* (*Codices arabici antiqui* iii), Wiesbaden 1978, 157-74; Hibat Allāh b. Salāma, *al-Nāsikh wa-l-mansūkh* (in the margin of Wāḥidī, *Asbāb*), Cairo 1316/1898-9, 262; Ibn Qudāma al-Maqdisī, *Kitāb al-Tawwābīn,* ed. ʿA.Q. Arnāʾūṭ, Beirut 1974; Majlisī, *Biḥār al-anwār,* Beirut 1983, xiv, 1-64; lxxiv, 39-44; Muqātil, *Tafsīr,* i, 423; ii, 87-8, 639-43; iii, 87-8, 298-9, 525-6; Sibṭ Ibn al-Jawzī, *Mirʾāt,* i, 472-92; Suyūṭī, *Durr,* vii, 148-76; Ṭabarī, *Tafsīr,* v, 360-76; Ṭabarsī, *Majmaʿ.*

Secondary: A. Geiger, *Judaism and Islam,* Madras 1898, 144-5; E. Margoliouth, *The convicted in the Bible, cleared from guilt in the Talmud and Midrash* (Hebrew), London 1949, 60-7; F.A. Mojtabāʾī, Dāwūd, in *Encyclopedia Iranica,* vii, 161-2; R. Paret, Dāwūd, in *EI²,* ii, 182; Y. Zakovitch, *David. From shepherd to Messiah* (Hebrew), Jerusalem 1995 (see especially Annex A by A. Shinʾan, 181-99).

Daʿwa see INVITATION

Dawn see DAY, TIMES OF

Day and Night

Alternation between light (q.v.) and darkness (q.v.) due to the rotation of the earth upon its axis. The numerous references in the Qurʾān to day and night *(al-nahār wa-l-layl)* fall under four general themes. First, the phenomenon of day and night itself, or aspects of it, is frequently presented as a sign (*āya,* see SIGNS), lesson *(ʿibra)* or expression of God's mercy (q.v.) for the wise to note and remember. The other related aspects of the phenomenon of day and night include their alteration *(ikhtilāf),* succession, covering up one by the other and stripping off one from the other *(yūliju, yaqlibu, yaghshā, yaslukhu).* As signs or proofs of God, the darkness of the night and the brightness of the day are called to witness against unbelievers (see BELIEF AND UNBELIEF). Second, the Qurʾān repeatedly affirms that together with such natural phenomena as the heavens (see HEAVEN), earth (q.v.), sea, clouds and wind (see AIR AND WIND), God subjugates *(yusakhkhir)* the night and day for the service of humankind (see NATURAL WORLD AND THE QUR'ĀN; CREATION). Thus, the night has been created as a time for rest, sleep, covering up and concealment *(maskan, manām, subāt, libās, sarmad, mustakhfā)* while the day exists for seeing, rising, walking freely and seeking one's livelihood *(mubṣir, nushūr, sārib, ma'āsh, ibtighā')*. The alteration of night and day also enables people to compute years and numbers (Q 17:12; Qurṭubī, *Jāmi'*, viii, 227-8; see CALENDAR; NUMBERS AND ENUMERATION). The third theme is the precise manner in which God creates day and night (Q 39:5) so that each has a prescribed measure (Q 73:20) and does not transgress the orbit of the other (Q 36:40). Interpretations of Q 73:20 often maintain that only God knows the exact measures of day and night whereas humans need to investigate and exercise their judgment to estimate these measures (Qurṭubī, *Jāmi'*, xix, 53). Finally, there are several references to praying and singing the praise (q.v.) of God during the night and day or parts thereof. Moreover, the Qur'ān enjoins people to pray at the "watches of the night" *(min ānā'i l-layl)* and the "ends of the day" *(aṭrāf al-nahār,* Q 20:130); this, according to many interpreters, is a reference to the sunset *(maghrib)* and evening *('ishā')* prayers (Qurṭubī, *Jāmi'*, xi, 261; see PRAYER).

Qur'ānic references, in addition to various mundane concerns, gave rise to an elaborate mathematical tradition of calculating the exact length of day and night and of determining the times of prayer relative to their beginning and duration. Two systems were used for measuring the length of the hours of the night and day. In the system of equal hours, one daylight hour is equal in length to one night hour and the whole day is divided into twenty-four equal parts. In the system of unequal hours, however, the arc of daylight and the arc of the night are each divided into twelve equal parts; thus, one daylight hour generally differs from a night hour while the total number of each of the daylight hours and the night hours is always twelve. While this and other topics were already treated in pre-Islamic astronomy, there are some subjects unique to the Islamic astronomical tradition which received no equivalent attention in earlier traditions (see COSMOLOGY AND THE QUR'ĀN; SCIENCE AND THE QUR'ĀN). One such subject is the elaborate discussion of dawn and twilight which originated in the need to determine the morning and evening prayers commencing after dawn and sunset, respectively. Many works of Islamic astronomy include chapters on dawn and twilight and provide exact mathematical methods for their determination (see DAY, TIMES OF).

A. Dallal

Bibliography
Primary: Qurṭubī, *Jāmi'*.
Secondary: E.S. Kennedy, al-Bīrūnī on the Muslim times of prayer, in E.S. Kennedy et al. (eds.), *Studies in the Islamic exact sciences,* Beirut 1983, 299-310 (see also the sections on planetary and lunar visibility [140-163] and on rising times, daylight lengths and the duration of dawn and twilight [253-310]); D.A. King, Some early Islamic tables for determining lunar crescent visibility, in D. King and G. Saliba (eds.), *From deferent to equant. A volume of studies in the history of science in the ancient and medieval Near East in honor of E.S. Kennedy,* New York 1987, 185-225; G. Saliba, The height of the atmosphere according to Mu'ayyad al-Dīn al-'Urḍī, Quṭb al-Dīn al-Shīrāzī and Ibn Mu'ādh, in D. King and G. Saliba (eds.), *From deferent to equant. A volume of studies in the history of science in the ancient and medieval Near East in honor of E.S. Kennedy,* New York 1987, 445-65.

Day of Judgment

see LAST JUDGMENT

Day, Times of

Day *(yawm)* together with the corresponding terms night *(layl)* and daytime *(nahār),* as well as the regular intervals of the day and parts or particular times of the day. Such apparently familiar concepts actually have considerable importance in the Qurʾān. Five sūras are named for times of day or daily natural phenomena: "The Dawn" (al-Fajr, Q 89); "The Night" (al-Layl, Q 92); "The Forenoon" (al-Ḍuḥā, Q 93); "The (late) Afternoon" (al-ʿAṣr, Q 103) and "The Daybreak" (al-Falaq, Q 113). Times of day serve as a framework for the events of the history of revelation and sometimes determine rules of worship, i.e. ritual as opposed to the actions of everyday life. They are also used metaphorically and can assume a supernatural dimension in formulas of evocation. Understanding such uses can offer much insight into the intellectual and emotional sensibilities of Islam.

The entire day

The full day is called *yawm*. To express the full period of twenty-four hours, the Qurʾān usually employs "night and daytime" *(layl wa-nahār)* or, figuratively, "evening and morning." An entire day is the period from sunset to sunset. The night makes up its first half, starting immediately after sunset at dusk (Q 17:78; Ibn al-Sikkīt, *Kanz,* 51). The understanding of night as the naturally more immediate portion of the full day is reflected in the Islamic calculation of the twelve months (Q 9:36) according to the lunar phases (see CALENDAR) and the notion that the daytime is somehow derived from night (Q 36:37). This seems to have already been common practice among the Arabs in pre-Islamic times (cf. Fischer, "Tag und Nacht," 741; see PRE-ISLAMIC ARABIA AND THE QURʾĀN) as it was in much of the ancient world. According to Pliny in his *Naturalis historia* (cf. Orelli, Tag, 312), the earliest Hebrews and the Athenians counted the entire day from sunset to sunset (cf. "evening-morning," *Dan* 8:14; "night-day," *2 Cor* 11:25; see also Day and Night, in *Encyclopedia Judaica*), while the Babylonians counted from morning to morning, and the Egyptians and the Romans from midnight to midnight. The proto-Semitic sequence "day-night" *(*yawm-*laylay)* has been substantiated, with **yawm,* originally designating daytime, but eventually coming to mean the entire day (Fischer, "Tag und Nacht," 753-5). The simple fact that the qurʾānic reference to sun (q.v.) always precedes that to the moon (q.v.), when the two occur in sequence (eighteen times except Q 71:16), is possibly due to this proto-Semitic understanding of the day (Fischer, "Tag und Nacht," 745-6).

The indication of a period of time by days, as can be seen in Western translations of the Qurʾān, is often expressed in terms of nights (*layl,* less frequently *layl,* pl. *layālin,* see Q 2:51 [but cf. *Exod* 34:28]; Q 7:142; 19:10; cf. also Q 89:2 and *Luke* 1:20 without indication of time). This method of counting can also be found in ḥadīth (e.g. Muslim, *Ṣaḥīḥ,* no. 584). The reference to God's creation of heaven (q.v.) and earth (q.v.) in six days (*ayyām,* Q 7:54) has a biblical parallel (*Exod* 20:11). In Q 69:7, *yawm* indicates not the entire day, but daytime (Paret, *Koran,* 405).

"Day" *(yawm)* occurs 378 time as a noun, mostly in the singular, but also in the dual (Q 2:203; 41:9, 12) and as an adverb of time (*al-yawma,* "on the day [of judgment]" or "today"; *yawma,* "the day when," cf. Watt-Bell, *Introduction,* 79-80; *yawman,* "on a [certain] day"). The plural *(ayyām)* appears 27 times; and the temporal adverb "on that day/time" *(yawmaʾidhin)* 69 times. Generally, *yawm* describes a definite day, an event or a certain date. In what follows, the specific connotations of the word will be given.

(a) In eschatology (q.v.): The day of judgment (see LAST JUDGMENT) is expressed in several ways in the Qurʾān, each beginning with the word "day," as in the day of doom (*yawm al-dīn,* e.g. Q 1:4; 13 times); the day of resurrection (*yawm al-qiyāma,* e.g. Q 2:85; 70 times; cf. Rosenthal, The "Time," 13-4); the last day (*al-yawm al-ākhir,* e.g. Q 2:8; 38 times); a mighty/dreadful day (*yawm ʿaẓīm,* Q 6:15; 10 times); a great day (*yawm kabīr,* Q 11:3); a painful day (*yawm alīm,* Q 11:26; 43:65); an encompassing day (*yawm muḥīṭ,* Q 11:84); a tempestuous day (*yawm ʿāṣif,* Q 14:18); a day wherein shall be neither bargaining nor befriending (*yawm lā bayʿun fīhi wa-lā khullatun wa-la shafāʿatun,* Q 2:254; *yawm lā bayʿun fīhi wa la-khilālun,* Q 14:31); the day of the time appointed (*yawm al-waqt al-maʿlūm,* Q 15:38; 38:81; see DEATH AND THE DEAD); an appointed day (*yawm maʿlūm,* Q 56:50); the day of (painful) distress (*yawm al-ḥasra,* Q 19:39); a disastrous day (*yawm ʿaqīm,* Q 22:55); the day of victory (*yawm al-fatḥ,* Q 32:29); the day of decision (*yawm al-faṣl,* Q 37:21, 6 times; see DECISION); the day of reckoning (*yawm al-ḥisāb,* Q 38:16, 26, 53; 40:27); the day of the encounter (*yawm al-talāqi,* Q 40:15); day of the imminent doom (*yawm al-azifa,* Q 40:18); the day of [disaster for] the factions [of unbelievers] (*yawm al-aḥzāb,* Q 40:30); the day of invocation (*yawm al-tanādi,* Q 40:32; cf. 41:47); the day of gathering (*yawm al-jamʿ,* Q 42:7; 64:9); the day of the threat (*yawm al-waʿīd,* Q 50:20); the day of eternity (*yawm al-khulūd,* Q 50:34); the day of coming forth (from the grave; *yawm al-khurūj,* Q 50:42); a hard day (*yawm ʿasir/ʿasīr,* Q 54:8; 74:9); the day of advantage (of believers over unbelievers; *yawm al-taghābun,* Q 64:9; see BELIEF AND UNBELIEF); a gloomy and wrathful day (*yawm ʿabūs qamṭarīr,* Q 76:10); a burdensome day (*yawm thaqīl,* Q 76:27); and the promised day (*al-yawm al-mawʿūd,* Q 85:2).

(b) In the history of revelation (see REVELATION AND INSPIRATION): The ʿĀd (q.v.) were killed "on a day of constant calamity" (*fī yawmi naḥsin mustamirrin,* Q 54:19); Moses (q.v.) set the feast day (*yawm al-zīna,* Q 20:59); Lot (q.v.) spoke about the final judgment in terms of a fierce day (*yawm ʿaṣīb,* Q 11:77; cf. Paret, *Kommentar,* 238-9 on Q 11:69-83); the magicians of Pharaoh (q.v.) were gathered on an appointed day (*yawm maʿlūm,* Q 26:38; cf. Paret, *Kommentar,* 170 on Q 7:113-4); and on an appointed day the Thamūd (q.v.) were given a sign (Q 26:155).

(c) In early Islamic history: the day of decision/salvation (*yawm al-furqān,* Q 8:41; probably in reference to the battle of Badr [q.v.]; cf. Paret, *Kommentar,* 19 on Q 2:53 and 187, Q 8:29 and the literature given there on *al-furqān;* see also CRITERION; SALVATION); and the day of Ḥunayn (q.v.; Q 9:25, in reference to the battle of Ḥunayn; cf. Buhl, *Das Leben,* 311-3).

(d) In religious and everyday life: the day of congregation (*yawm al-jumʿa,* Q 62:9; see FRIDAY PRAYER); the Jewish Sabbath (q.v.; *yawm sabtihim,* Q 7:163; 16:124); the day of the greater pilgrimage (*yawm al-ḥajj al-akbar,* Q 9:3, probably in reference to the major day of the pilgrimage [q.v.] on the ninth/tenth Dhū l-Ḥijja; cf. Paret, *Kommentar,* 195 ad Q 9:3; but noted differently by Bell, Muḥammad's pilgrimage, 233-44); the day of the harvest (*yawm al-ḥaṣād,* Q 6:141); and a day of privation (*fī yawmin dhī masghaba,* Q 90:14).

The particular times of a day: the night and daytime

The times of a day and their terminology reflect the natural cycle of darkness (q.v.) and light (q.v.; Q 2:187) and the position of the sun (Q 25:45) and moon, God having created "the sun and moon [as a medium] for reckoning [time]" (Q 6:96; 55:5). A mathematical-chronometrical division of the day (as the Babylonian system of hours, minutes and seconds) is not encountered in the Qurʾān.

The word "hour" *(sāʿa)* is mentioned several times. It does not, however, describe a timed or calculated hour but rather an indefinite shorter period or particular time of the day. Thus we find the hour of difficulty (*sāʿat al-ʿusra,* Q 9:117); the hour of judgment (Q 6:31, 40; 7:187; 12:107; 15:85; 18:21, 36; 19:75; 20:15; 21:49; 22:1, 7, 55; 25:11; 30:12, 14, 55; 31:34; 33:63; 34:3, 30; 40:46, 59; 41:47, 50; 42:17, 18; 43:61, 66, 85; 45:27, 32; 47:18; 54:1, 46; 79:42) where God's order comes to pass in "a twinkling of the eye or less" (Q 16:77); the period until the last judgment will not be extended "by a single hour" (Q 7:34; 10:49; 16:61); and after the resurrection people will feel as if they had not tarried but "an hour," long enough to "mutually recognize one another" (Q 10:45; 46:35; also Q 30:55). It should be added that the manner in which time is partitioned "by a strip of the night" (*bi-qiṭʿin min al-layl,* Q 11:81; 10: 27; 15:65) remains vague.

The corresponding terms "night and daytime" (*al-layl wa-l-nahār,* cf. Pellat, Layl and nahār) often express — in addition to amounting to an entire day (e.g. Q 34:18) — reiteration, regularity or unqualified continuation of an action or a procedure. One should, therefore, "constantly" give alms (from one's wealth; Q 2:274; see ALMSGIVING); to God belongs "whatsoever inhabits the night and the day," i.e. all things (Q 6:13); and God's command is to be expected "at any time" (Q 10:24); one should glorify the Lord "continuously" (Q 21:20), etc.

God subjected "the night and the daytime" to the benefit of humankind (Q 7:54; 14:33; 16:12). Their creation as a pair (Q 17:22; 21:33) and their permanent and mutual succession (Q 24:44) are signs of God's omnipotence (e.g. Q 2:164). "God [alone] determines [the extent and goal of] night and daytime" (Q 73:20). Here again, night precedes daytime (Q 2:164; 3:190; 10:6; 23:80; 25:62; 45:5) and retreats before it (Q 74:33). However, night covers daytime [then again] (Q 7:54; 1313), since both night and daytime are made to enter into one another (Q 3:27; 21:61; 31:29; 35:13), and to become wrapped together (Q 39:5). Like all celestial phenomena night and daytime follow divinely ordained rules: "The [following] night will never outstrip the daytime" (Q 36:40) although "it [daytime] is in haste to follow it (Q 7:54). The night "conceals" the sunlight (Q 91:4), "enshrouding [everything with darkness]" (Q 92:1).

Night implies quietness, tranquillity (Q 93:2) and security. It is "a garment [in which you can swathe yourself] and [it offers you] sleep for rest" (Q 25:47; 78:9). Darkness can also imply helplessness: "Their faces were covered with [and unprotected like] strips of night shadowy" (Q 10:27). Important events in the history of revelation occur at night: The Qurʾān is revealed in "a blessed night" (Q 44:3), the Night of Power (q.v.; *laylat al-qadr*), which "is better than a thousand months" (Q 97:1-3); Muḥammad is taken at night on his journey from Mecca to the Farther Mosque in (Jerusalem and to) heaven (Q 17:1; see ASCENSION); Muḥammad's opponents seem to have tried to discredit him by claiming that writings of the ancients were dictated to him at dawn and early in the evening (Q 25:5; see ILLITERACY); and the night gives to the god-fearing protection from Pharaoh (q.v.; Q 44:23).

Morning, conversely, implies freshness and pristineness (e.g. the root *b-k-r* from which is derived not only early morning *[bukra],* but also virgins *[abkār],* Q 56:36; 66:5). At this time, the normal work of the day is described as beginning (Q 68:21-2, 25) and important events such as battles (Q 3:121) are prepared. Also a decreed punishment came upon the people in the early morning (Q 54:38; see CHASTISEMENT AND PUNISHMENT) as did the wind which killed the ʿĀd (Q 69:7; see AIR AND WIND). In the daytime everything is clearly visible (Q 10:67; 17:12; 27:86; 40:61) and obvious (Q 13:10). It is the time when one becomes active again (Q 25:47). It is the time of action (Q 6:60), created so that people might earn their living (Q 78:11) and seek the bounty of the Lord (Q 17:12; see BLESSING).

In early Mekkan sūras (see CHRONOLOGY AND THE QURʾĀN), certain times of the day frequently occur as basic elements in formulaic evocation, contributing to the hymnal tenor of the given sūra, as in Q 74:33, "[I swear] by the... night when it retreats and the dawn when it is white"; Q 81:17, "by the night swarming"; Q 81:17-18, "by the dawn sighing"; Q 92:1, "by the night enshrouding"; Q 89:4, "by the night when it journeys on"; and Q 93:1,"by the sun and his morning brightness"; etc. (see Günther, Tag und Tageszeiten, 54-5). This special way of evoking a time of the day seems somehow to record "the liturgical experience of the recipient of the revelation." It seems to keep present the perception of light and dark accompanying certain exercises of worship and thus to 'capture' this powerful experience for later generations of worshippers (Neuwirth, Zur Relevanz, 21). It is interesting to note in passing that the emphasis here is on the time of twilight, i.e. the impressive period of transition from dark to light and *vice versa* as known in the Middle East. However, the last part of the night, i.e. the time of morning twilight, seems to be of particular importance in this regard. This observation is confirmed by two epithets of God: "lord of the daybreak" (*rabb al-falaq,* Q 113:1) and "the one who splits the sky into dawn" (*fāliq al-iṣbāḥ,* Q 6:96).

Divine service, rules of religious and everyday life

The ritual prayer (q.v.; *ṣalāt*), including its five appointed times (*mīqāt,* pl. *mawāqīt,* cf. Wensinck, Mīḳāt) was standardized only after the death of the Prophet in ḥadīth and in works on jurisprudence *(fiqh).* The Qurʾān only generally mentions times of day for (a) prayer and (b) glorification of God *(tasbīḥ).* This led Muslim and non-Muslim commentators to differing interpretations of qurʾānic information on the times of prayer (e.g. Paret, *Kommentar,* 305 on Q 17:78-9; Watt-Bell, *Introduction,* 163; "the middle prayer" [*al-ṣalāt al-wusṭā,* Q 2:238], which gives no indication of time).

(a) "And perform the prayer *(ṣalāt)* at the two ends of the day and nigh of the night" (Q 11:114, i.e. the morning prayer at dawn *(ṣalāt al-ṣubḥ* or *ṣalāt al-fajr),* the afternoon prayer at the beginning of sunset *(ṣalāt al-ẓuhr* or *ṣalāt al-ʿaṣr),* and the evening prayer immediately after sunset *(ṣalāt al-maghrib).* "Perform the prayer at the sinking of the sun to the darkening of the night, and the recital of [the Qurʾān at] dawn" (*qurʾān al-fajr,* Q 17:78). Some authorities interpret the time of "the sinking of the sun" to start from the point of the sun's culmination (at noon) and thus include four canonical prayers, i.e. *al-ẓuhr, al-ʿaṣr, al-maghrib, al-ʿishāʾ*. Then, the fifth canonical prayer, *ṣalāt al-ṣubḥ,* would be represented by *qurʾān al-fajr* (cf. Paret, *Kommentar,* 305-6 on Q 17:78-80).

(b) God should be remembered, glorified and praised in the morning and evening (e.g. Q 7:205; 33:41; 48:9) when all who are in the heavens and the earth bow to him (Q 13:15; 24:36; also 38:18; 41:38; see BOWING AND PROSTRATION; GLORY; PRAISE). Early sūras call to "remember the name of your Lord at dawn and in the evening and part of the night... and magnify him through the long night" (Q 76:26; also 73:2); or "in the night, and at the declining of the stars" (Q 52:49). Among the People of the Book (q.v.), there is a standing *(qāʾim)* community "that recites God's signs [at certain times] of the night..." (Q 3:113). To "keep vigil a part of the night" is a supererogatory work and will be rewarded in the next world (Q 17:79; see REWARD AND PUNISHMENT). Further utterances, however, state that the "first part of night is heavier in tread, more upright in speech" (Q 73:6) and that eating, drinking and sexual intercourse are permitted on the nights of Ramaḍān (q.v.) "until [the early morning when] the white thread appears clearly to you [in distinction] from a black thread" (Q 2:187).

The times of the day in chronological order

The "night" (*layl,* 93 times; *layla,* 8 times; pl. *layāl,* 4 times) is the first, dark half of the full day. It starts with the "evening twilight" (*shafaq,* Q 84:16; defined as "the first moment of the night," *li-awwal sāʿa min al-layl* [Hamadhānī, *Alfāẓ,* 287]; cf. Pellat, Layl and nahār, 709). Furthermore, the beginning of the night is described as "a darkening [at the beginning] of the night" (*ghasaq al-layl,* Q 17:78) or the "nigh of the night" (*zulafan min al-layl,* Q 11:114; see DAY AND NIGHT).

The "late, dark evening" *(ʿashī, ʿashiyya)* corresponds to the period "from the time when the sun starts to disappear until it completely sets" (Qurṭubī, *Jāmiʿ,* vi, 82, ad Q 3:41). It marks the "end of the bright day" (*Jalālayn,* 54, ad Q 3:41). It occurs as *ʿashiyyatan* (Q 79:46); *bi-l-ʿashī* (Q 38:31); *bi-l-ʿashī wa-l-ibkār* (Q 3:41; 40:55); *bi-l-ʿashī wa-l-ishrāq* (Q 38:18); *ʿashiyyan wa-ḥīna tuẓhirūna* (Q 30:18); *ʿashiyyatan aw ḍuḥāhā* (Q 79:46); and, in a different sequence, *bi-l-ghadāti wa-l-ʿashī* (Q 6:52; 18:28); *ghuduwwan wa-ʿashiyyan* (Q 40:46); *bukratan wa-ʿashiyyan* (Q 19:11, 62). The term *ʿishāʾ,* however, is used both as a synonym for *ʿashī* and in designation of a time following it (Hamadhānī, *Alfāẓ,* 287). It foreshadows the beginning of darkness (q.v.); see *ʿishāʾan* (Q 12:16) and *ṣalāt al-ʿishāʾ* (Q 24:58).

"The night when it journeys forth" (*wa-l-layli idhā yasri,* Q 89:4) is one of several metaphorical utterances which denote the end of the night (see METAPHOR). Similarly, at "the setting of stars" (*idbār al-nujūm,* Q 52:49) can mean not only the very early morning but also, more generally, the day (cf. Paret, *Kommentar,* 460 ad Q 52:48-9; 456 ad Q 50:39-4). The short period directly before daybreak is referred to by a term best translated as "the breaking of morning" (*saḥar,* Q 54:34; pl. *asḥār,* Q 3:17; 51:18; cf. Mustafa, Morgenanbruch, 113). The "daybreak" *(falaq)* itself designates the time when dark and light split (lord of the daybreak, *rabb al-falaq,* Q 113:1; and cleaver of the daybreak, *fāliq al-iṣbāḥ,* Q 6:96).

Daytime (*nahār,* 57 times; *nahāran,* three times) is the second half of the full day. It starts with the opening or "face of daytime" (*wajh al-nahār,* Q 3:72). In this sense, also used are the "[rising of] dawn, morning twilight" (*maṭlaʿ al-fajr,* Q 97:5; *fajr,* Q 2:187; 17:28 [two times]; 24:58; 89:1) and the period "before sunrise" (*qabla ṭulūʿi l-shams,* Q 20:130; 50:39).

The "[early] morning" *(ibkār)* indicates the time "before sunrise" (Hamadhānī, *Alfāẓ,* 287), "the end of the night" (Ibn Kathīr, *Tafsīr,* iv, 134 ad Q 40:55) and "the beginning of the bright day" (*Jalālayn,* 54 ad Q 3:41). It is the counterpart of the late evening (*bi-l-ʿashī wa-l-ibkār,* Q 3:41; 40:55). Another word for morning, *bukra,* is also used in this sense; it is also given as a counterpart to both the early evening in which daylight still appears (*bukratan, bukratan wa-aṣīlan,* Q 25:5; 33:42; 48:9; 54:38; 76:25) and the late evening when daylight is gone (*bukratan wa-ʿashiyyan,* Q 19:11, 62). The period of "sunrise" (*ishrāq,* cf. *bi-l-ʿashī wa-l-ishrāq,* Q 38:18; *mushriqīn,* Q 15:73; 26:60) is also called "the sun, when it [rises]" (*al-shams idhā ṭalaʿat,* Q 18:17) or "the sun rising" (*al-shams bāzighatan,* Q 6:78).

The "[early bright] morning" *(ghadāh, ghuduww)* generally relates to the time "after sunrise" (Hamadhānī, *Alfāẓ,* 287). We find it as *bi-l-ghadāt (wa-l-ʿashī), ghuduww (an wa-ʿashiyyan),* Q 6:52; 18:28; 34:12;

40:46; *bi-l-ghudū wa-l-aṣāl,* Q 7:205; 13:15; 24:36; "breakfast," *ghadā',* Q 18:62; *ghadā,* Q 3:121; 68:22, 25. Both "the dawning of morning" (*iṣbāḥ,* Q 6:96) and "morning" *(ṣubḥ, ṣabāḥ)* designate the "first hour of the daytime (before sunrise)" (Hamadhānī, *Alfāẓ,* 287; see *ṣubḥ,* Q 11:81; 74:34; 81:18; 100:3; *ṣabāḥ,* Q 37:177; *ṣabbaḥahum bukratan,* Q 54:38; *aṣbaḥa,* Q 7:78, 91; 11:67, 94; 18:40, 41, 42, 45; 28:18, 37, 82; 30:17; 46:25; 67:30; 68:20; *muṣbiḥīna,* Q 15:66, 83; 37:137; 68:17, 21). The time when the Lord "has stretched out the shadow" (*madda l-ẓilla,* Q 25:45), again, refers to early morning.

The "completely bright morning, or forenoon" (*ḍuḥā,* Q 7:98; 20:59; 79:29, 46; 91:1; 93:1) follows *al-ghadāh* (Hamadhānī, *Alfāẓ,* 287), represents the "first part of the daytime [after sunrise] or daytime itself" (*Jalālayn,* 567 ad Q 93:1), but also means "sunlight" (*wa-l-shamsi wa-ḍuḥāhā,* Q 91:1). This time is followed by the "heat of the noon" (*ẓahīra,* Q 24:58; see also "in your noontide hour," *ḥīna tuẓhirūna,* Q 30:18).

The "later afternoon" (*'aṣr,* Q 103:1) generally indicates the period from before sunset until the sky is red with the glow of the setting sun (Hamadhānī, *Alfāẓ,* 287). It is also described, however, as "the period... between the sinking of the sun [after passing its culmination, *zawāl*] and sunset" (*Jalālayn,* 572 ad Q 103:1). The period of the "return" home in the evening (*rawāḥ,* Q 34:12) seems to precede (Hamadhānī, *Alfāẓ,* 287) the "late afternoon" or "early bright evening" (*aṣīl,* Q 25:5; 33:42; 48:9; 76:25; pl. *āṣāl* Q 7:205; 13:15; 24:36). The latter determines the "end of the daytime" (*Jalālayn,* 382 ad Q 33:42; Ibn Kathīr, *Tafsīr,* iv, 298 ad Q 48:9) and is explained as being a synonym for both *'ashī* (Qurṭubī, *Jāmi',* vi, 267 ad Q 48:9) and *masā'* (Ibn Kathīr, *Tafsīr,* iii, 818 ad Q 33:42). Its counterpart is the "early morning" *(bukra).*

The time of *aṣīl* is followed by the "evening" (*masā',* Hamadhānī, *Alfāẓ,* 287): "in your evening hour and in your morning hour" (*ḥīna tumsūna wa-ḥīna tuṣbiḥūna,* Q 30:17).

Apart from this, the time "before sunset" (*qabla l-ghurūb,* Q 50:39) appears to precede the period of the "sinking of the sun [against the horizon]" (*dulūk al-shams,* Q 17:78), although the latter can designate both (a) the time starting with noon, when the sun has passed its zenith and, probably originally, (b) the time of the bright evening, directly before sunset.

Sebastian Günther

Bibliography

Primary: al-Hamadhānī, 'Abd al-Raḥmān b. 'Īsā, *Kitāb al-Alfāẓ al-kitābiyya,* ed. L. Cheikho, Beirut 1885, 284-7 *(al-nahār);* 287-91 *(al-layl);* Ibn Kathīr, *Tafsīr,* ed. 'Alī Shīrī al-Dimashqī, 4 vols., Beirut ca. 1989; Ibn al-Sikkīt, Abū Yūsuf Ya'qūb b. Isḥāq, *Kanz al-ḥuffāẓ. Kitāb Tahdhīb al-alfāẓ,* ed. L. Cheikho, Beirut 1896-8, 405-27 (chapters *al-layl* and *al-nahār*); *Jalālayn,* ed. 'Abd al-Raḥīm Muḥammad, Cairo 1355/1936; Muslim, *Ṣaḥīḥ;* Qurṭūbī, *Jāmi',* 24 vols., Beirut 1405-14/1985-93.

Secondary: R. Bell, Muḥammad's pilgrimage proclamation, in *JRAS* (1937), 233-44; Fr. Buhl, *Das Leben Muhammeds,* Leipzig 1930, 311-3; Day and Night, in *Encyclopedia Judaica,* Jerusalem n.d., ii, 1374-6; A. Fischer, "Tag und Nacht" im Arabischen und die semitische Tagesberechnung, in *Abhandlung der Philosophisch-Historischen Klasse der Königlichen Sächsischen Gesellschaft der Wissenschaften,* Leipzig 1909, vol. xxvii, 789-758; S. Günther, Tag und Tageszeiten im Qur'ān, in *Erlesenes. Hallesche Beiträge zur Orientwissenschaft* 25 (1998), 47-68; L. Ideler, *Handbuch der mathematischen und technischen Chronologie. Aus den Quellen bearbeitet,* 2 vols., Berlin 1825, vol. i; A.H. Mustafa, Morgenanbruch in den nordwestsemitischen Sprachen, in *Hallesche Beiträge zur Orientwissenschaft* 13/14 (1990), 113-6; A. Neuwirth, Zur Relevanz der einleitenden Schwurserien für die Suren der frühmekkanischen Zeit, in U. Tworuschka (ed.), *Gottes ist der Orient, Gottes ist der Okzident. Festschrift für Abdoljavad Falaturi zum 65. Geburtstag,* Vienna 1991, 3-39; V. Orelli, Tag bei den Hebräern, in *Realenzyklopädie für protestantische Theologie und Kirche,* Leipzig 1907[3], ixx, 312-3; Paret, *Kommentar,* 1985[3]; id., *Der Koran. Übersetzung,* 1985[4]; Ch. Pellat, Layl an d nahār, in *EI²,* v, 707-10; F. Rosenthal, The "Time" of Muslim historians and Muslim mystics, in *JSAI* 19 (1995), 5-35; A.J. Wensinck, Ṣalāt, in *EI¹,* viii, 96-105; id., Mīḳāt, in *EI¹,* v, 492-3.

Days of God

A literal translation of the Arabic expression *ayyām Allāh*. The expression assumes its fuller significance in analogy to the phrase *ayyām al-ʿarab,* i.e. battles of Arab tribes in the pre-Islamic era (see PRE-ISLAMIC ARABIA AND THE QURʾĀN), leading to the more appropriate translation, "battles of God." The phrase *ayyām Allāh* occurs twice in the Qurʾān.

The first occurrence is Q 14:5 (Sūrat Ibrāhīm), which reflects God's retribution — grace and reward for believers and punishment for unbelievers (see REWARD AND PUNISHMENT; CHASTISEMENT AND PUNISHMENT). More specifically, *ayyām Allāh* in Q 14:5 refers to the signs God sent through Moses (q.v.) for distinguishing between belief and unbelief (q.v.). Apart from this explicit injunction to Moses in Q 14:5, exegetes identified this and following verses with the ill omens that befell the peoples of ʿĀd (q.v.) and Thamūd (q.v.) for rejecting God's revelations (see PUNISHMENT STORIES).

The second occurrence of *ayyām Allāh* is Q 45:14 (Sūrat al-Jāthiyya, "The Hobbling"), the only verse revealed at Medina of this otherwise Meccan sūra (see CHRONOLOGY AND THE QURʾĀN). The verse, which urges believers to forgive those who do not look ahead to *ayyām Allāh* but who will ultimately receive their due in the final abode, i.e. hell (q.v.), was eventually abrogated (see ABROGATION). Indeed, the Qurʾān repeatedly commands the believers to fight against unbelievers — thus contravening the injunction for forgiveness in the verse just cited.

The specific qurʾānic locus of the abrogation of Q 45:14 is uncertain. Whereas some consider it to be the ninth sūra (Sūrat al-Tawba, "Repentance") in its entirety, others restrict this function to Q 9:5 alone (since it specifically calls for violence against unbelievers, it is known as the verse of the sword, *āyat al-sayf*). Other authorities link it to either Q 9:5 or 9:36, or both. Further, a minority view considers Q 22:39 (Sūrat al-Ḥajj, "The Pilgrimage") as an alternative. Finally, there are exegetes who argue that Q 8 (Sūrat al-Anfāl, "The Spoils") is acting in conjunction with Q 9. Reference to Sūrat al-Anfāl — a sūra revealed shortly after the battle of Badr (q.v.) — constitutes a direct link to that battle and as such forms the basis for the analogy touched upon earlier between *ayyām Allāh* and *ayyām al-ʿarab*. The Muslim victory at Badr highlighted God's support of the believers and gave them a flawless rationale for setting themselves apart from unbelievers. Since Badr reflects in essence a battle between good and evil (q.v.), there is logic to the claim of those who point to Sūrat al-Anfāl as the sūra which abrogates Q 45:14, a verse that initially called for the forgiveness of those who are not part of God's religion. See also EXPEDITIONS AND BATTLES; WAR.

John A. Nawas

Bibliography

Primary: Abū Ḥayyān, *Baḥr,* ed. ʿA.A. ʿAbd al-Wujūd and ʿA.M. Muʿawwaḍ, 8 vols., Beirut 1993, v, 394-5; Ṭabarī, *Tafsīr,* vii, 416-8; xi, 256-7.
Secondary: Horowitz, *KU,* 22; T. Nagel, *Medinensische Einschübe in mekkanischen Suren,* Göttingen 1995, 78; Paret, *Kommentar,* 267; W.M. Watt, *Companion to the Qurʾān,* London 1967, 124, 226.

Deadly Sins see SIN, MAJOR AND MINOR

Death and the Dead

The end of life (q.v.). The following aspects of the qurʾānic depiction of death *(mawt, wafāt)* and the dead *(al-mawtā)* shall be addressed here: various qurʾānic descriptions of attitudes towards death on the part of both believers and unbelievers (see BELIEF AND UNBELIEF); the main themes connected with death which occur in the Qurʾān, ordered according to Bell's chronology; distinctive features of qurʾānic statements about death; and, finally, a sketch of the qurʾānic vision of death and its meaning.

Attitudes of believers and unbelievers

The Qurʾān, especially in its Medinan parts, takes the human fear of death for granted. Death is the great enemy of humankind which overtakes *(adraka)* even those who seek refuge in lofty towers (Q 4:78). Dying is a physical and spiritual event of great importance that only happens under divine authority and by divine decree. Death — whether natural or in battle — loses its terror for the true believer: "... my life and my death belong to God..." (Q 6:162). Three passages containing the prayers of those known to be believers depict them as requesting that God allow them to die *(tawaffā)* as just men or "surrenderers" to God's will *(muslimūn*, Q 7:126; cf. Q 3:193; 12:101). In short, death need be feared only by those who have led evil lives (see EVIL DEEDS). Those who have given witness of their belief by dying as martyrs (in battle; see MARTYR) should be thought of not as dead but as living (Q 2:154; 3:169). One passage promises immediate passage (lit. gathering *[tuḥsharūna]*) to God for those who die "in the way of God," (*fī sabīl Allāh*, Q 3:157-8; see PATH OR WAY [OF GOD]).

An unbeliever, however, clings to this life and believes death to be the inevitable result of fate *(dahr)*. Unbelievers who do not believe in the resurrection (q.v.) are only concerned with life in this world (*dunyā*, Q 6:29; 23:37). They think their life is splendid but deceive themselves and are deceived by Iblīs (q.v.; Q 15:39; see DEVIL); they should rather be called "dead" already. They have reason to fear doubly: to fear death itself and to fear retribution; when they are punished it will be too late to repent (see REWARD AND PUNISHMENT; REPENTANCE AND PENANCE). The Qurʾān vividly describes the last moments of their lives (Q 6:93; 33:19; 47:20; 56:83) and their agony (Q 50:19). Angels of death stretch out their hands and speak to them while they are dying (Q 6:93). Those attached to this world flee death in vain. One text, however, describes how in a particular case God had pity on thousands of people who, threatened by death, left their houses (Q 2:243).

Main themes of death

Following T. O'Shaughnessy (*Muhammad's thoughts on death*, the only monograph on the subject), one can organize the various qurʾānic themes of death according to Bell's chronology of the revelation of the Qurʾān (see CHRONOLOGY AND THE QURʾĀN). In the Meccan period, death is first used metaphorically in "sign passages," texts speaking of God's providence: He brings to life dead land (i.e. waste land) by sending rain; in seeds he gives life to what has been considered dead (see AGRICULTURE AND VEGETATION). Very soon those who refuse to believe in God and his judgment (see LAST JUDGMENT) are also considered to be "dead." Inability to recognize God's bounty (see BLESSING) and his control over life and death is presented as a spiritual death. In a further development hell (q.v.) is called a "second" or "living" death, reserved for those who have entered into their "first" death as unbelievers. In the face of skeptics in Mecca and Medina who maintain that there is only one (i.e. the first physical) death, the Qurʾān asserts this second death as well for the unbelievers.

The question "When I am dead, shall I be brought out alive?" (Q 19:66) elicits lengthy responses. The imagery of the earlier "sign passages" referring to God's providence is combined here with the theme of the resurrection which testifies to God's supreme power over life and death. The resurrection represents the final restoration and re-commencement of the human race as it was at the beginning, at the pristine moment of creation (q.v.). It is God who brings to life and causes to die, who raises the dead as a new act of life-giving creation and who brings the faithful back to him in paradise (q.v.). This power of God is the decisive argument in the Qur'ān for belief in God (see POWER AND IMPOTENCE).

In the Medinan period these themes all receive further elaboration in various ways. Here, however, the stress is on God's omnipotence and his control of anything that has to do with life and death, the ultimate proof being the resurrection which is viewed as a second creation. God's causing objects to penetrate *(walaja)* one another and then to come forth *(kharaja)* from one another also illustrates his omnipotence. Yet, most important is the fact that he has power *(qādir* or *qadīr)* to bring the dead to life. In former times, God returned the dead to life in this world: He raised some of the dead from among the followers of Moses (q.v.; Q 2:55-6) and gave leave to Jesus (q.v.) to bring the dead to life (Q 3:49; 5:110). God differs from all living beings in that he does not die; he is the Living One *(al-ḥayy,* Q 25:58; see GOD AND HIS ATTRIBUTES). By his capacity to create life God distinguishes himself from the idols which are themselves created and simply dead (Q 16:20-1; see IDOLS AND IMAGES).

The appointed term *(ajal)* of human life also receives emphasis in Medina. God determines *(qaddara)* a human's life span at his birth (see FATE; FREEDOM AND PREDESTINATION). At death God executes *(qaḍā)* this predetermined will for each person and takes him or her to himself *(tawaffā)*. Consequently, human life and death are presented as subject to God's direct authority.

It is no accident that notions of God's omnipotence and the human being's predetermined life are stressed in the Medinan years of war (see WAR; EXPEDITIONS AND BATTLES; OPPOSITION TO MUḤAMMAD). The same holds for a third theme, that of fear (q.v.) of death, which is found almost exclusively in the verses of this period. All 48 qur'ānic passages treating it are Medinan. These texts include explicit references to Muḥammad's own foreseeable death as well as to the deaths of earlier prophets (see PROPHETS AND PROPHETHOOD). Moreover, they affirm God's providence and protection (q.v.) of every believer. Typically, even more than before, they insist that humans should not cling to this passing life but instead prepare for the everlasting life in the hereafter. They should commit their lives to causes connected with God; those who fight in *jihād* (q.v.), for instance, make proper use of their life "in the way of God." In *jihād,* the fear of death is absent, at least consciously. In this period the theme of violent death, whether of those committed to the cause of Islam or of innocent people, is a matter of particular concern (see MURDER; BLOODSHED).

Distinct features of the qur'ānic treatment of death

The presentation of death in the Qur'ān, while resembling that of other religious systems, also has its own distinctive traits. For the Arabs of the pre-Islamic period, for instance, death came about through the (sometimes sudden) entrance of fate *(dahr)* into a human's life (see PRE-ISLAMIC ARABIA AND THE QUR'ĀN). They saw death basically as the soul's (q.v.) departure from the body, either in a bloody fashion (in case of a violent death) or by escaping from the nose at the final breath (in case of natural death). The survivors had the duty to see to a correct burial and to exact vengeance (q.v.; in case of a violent death), to ensure peace for the departed soul, which would be forced to wander otherwise, and to maintain the honor of the tribe (see TRIBES AND CLANS). In ancient times a certain cult of the dead may have existed, with offerings and sacrifices. A real man would show no fear of death and the survivors would glorify the departed (see COURAGE).

In the Qurʾān it is not *dahr* but God who decides the appointed time *(ajal)* of each individual and who causes the person to die *(amāta);* human beings can only mortally wound *(qatala)* someone but it is God who causes that person to die. The last act in a person's life is thus an act of God.

The relation to death is a key issue for two reasons. First, it implies a relation to life and the freedom to decide what to do with it. Second, in the qurʾānic view any attitude to death implies an attitude to God, either of belief or unbelief. In the qurʾānic view, life and death have been instruments of God's providence to humankind from the very beginning. This theocentric view of death implies a radical contingency of human beings as well as of the world in which they live and to which they should no longer attach themselves. The way of life of the ancient Arabs is declared to have been ignorance (*jāhiliyya*, see AGE OF IGNORANCE). Life itself comes about through God's blowing something of his spirit (*rūḥ*, see SPIRIT) into Adam's form (Q 15:29; 32:9; 38:72; see ADAM AND EVE). This *rūḥ* is thus the principle of life which leaves the body at the moment of death. The fact that it originates in God has important implications. First of all, life is a gift apportioned by God; this also means that it is forbidden to kill someone (for instance, out of revenge) except after due process of law (see BLOOD MONEY; RETALIATION). Second, the community of the faithful replaces the older kinship (q.v.) and tribal community organized along blood relationships (see COMMUNITY AND SOCIETY IN THE QURʾĀN). Third, every believer is individually responsible for his life, thought and action. The ancient glorification of the dead gives way to a humble appeal to God to show mercy (q.v.) on the dead. The Qurʾān suggests the continued existence of the *rūḥ* after it has left the body in death but leaves unspecified the period between the grave and later resurrection (see BARZAKH). In the new Islamic theocentric framework, it is no longer the exact moment of death but the allotted term of life as man's testing period (see TRIAL) that is important. Islam brings a profound change not only in the visible customs of life but also in the way in which one can and does understand one's own life. Human life is not the individual's property but a divine gift to be used in God's service (*ʿibāda*, see SERVANT) or to be dedicated to a divine cause or to God himself. God is seen as creator of all that is and as the source of all life: "... everything perishes except his countenance..." (Q 28:88).

Thus, with Islam, death is no longer the end of life, but only the end of the appointed period *(ajal)* in which humans are tested in the world. Human existence has been extended to eternity and death becomes a merely transitional phase during which the *rūḥ*, the principle of life, provisionally remains separated from the disintegrating body. In other words, death has been designed as a part of creation and is put to use to attain creation's aim; God wants human life — understood as service *(ʿibāda)* to him — not to end but to receive eternity in paradise.

In a broader context the qurʾānic message thus follows very much the tradition of the Near Eastern prophetic religions from Zoroastrianism and the oldest prophets of Israel onwards, all of whom call people to choose between the new life which they offer and the old life linked to by-gone conditions, ways of life and ideas, which they consider to be in the realm of death. Different prophetic religions, including Christianity, have given different descriptions of what may be called the old dispensation in the light of their particular message of renewal. They proclaim God as a fundamentally liberating force.

In this context the Qurʾān distinguishes itself first by its proclamation of the God of providence, liberating human beings from the curse of *dahr* by causing them to rise again as a new creation. After humankind has been haunted by fear of *dahr* and death, *dahr* is nullified and death is brought under God's omnipotence. Additionally, the Qurʾān distinguishes itself from other prophetic messages by calling specifically for action in this world in the dedicated service of God. It shares the general framework of resurrection and judgment (q.v.) known since Zoroaster and shares with the Akkadian and the Israelite religions the idea of a gloomy abode for the deceased. There is a striking parallelism between the qurʾānic and Syriac emphasis on the inevitability of death and the consequences humans should thereby draw regarding their eternal destiny (q.v.), ending in parallel descriptions of the terrors of hell as the destiny of unbelievers. In the case of the Qurʾān, however, this preaching did not lead to monastic asceticism (see MONASTICISM AND MONKS) as in Eastern Christianity but to a particular form of "inner-worldly" asceticism (q.v.).

Two facts are worth noting. First, this kind of "Weberian" attitude produced an outburst of energy which was invested in worldly enterprises of a military, political and economic nature. The qurʾānic view of life and death undoubtedly contributed to the mobilization of many in this sense. Second, in Islam as in other prophetic religions, God was proclaimed to be the force which brings about a decisive change from death to life. Where unbelief was seen as chaotic since it did not recognize the providence and rule of God in this world, belief was held to lead to the establishment of God's rule through a particular ordering of this world by means of a law considered to have been revealed and to be contained, at least in essentials, in the Qurʾān.

The qurʾānic vision of death; its meaning

Throughout the Qurʾān the issue of death is apparent, explicitly in the numerous verses and implicitly as an inescapable human condition, which the Qurʾān's preaching continuously notes. Though the descriptions of resurrection and final judgment have attracted much scholarly attention, the subject of death — with the exception of T. O'Shaughnessy's study — has been strangely neglected. For the Near East at the time of Muḥammad, death was a problem, solutions for which were sought in ascetic orientations and movements. There is reason to assume that this was also the case among bedouin Arabs (see BEDOUIN; ARABS) and townspeople in Arabia, for whom it was the impersonal, law-like and fatal *dahr* that brought man's life to an end (Q 45:24).

If the Qurʾān maintains that the moment of death is inescapably determined, this is no longer the work of the power or law of fate, but has been established, as the moment of birth, by God. The vision broadens still further through the idea that God alone can conquer death. This conquest shows his omnipotence and his divinity; idols cannot rival him. The final delivery from death by fate *(dahr)* happens through the anticipated resurrection. From the second Meccan period onwards, there is a qurʾānic triad of concepts that constantly reappears: God, life/death and resurrection. The last is primarily a deliverance of humankind from the condition of death, for the sake of a new creation, a gift of restoration. The judgment may be positive for some, negative for others; common to all, whether they like it or not, is that they are brought to life again. Only God is able to restore the creation after the temporary condition of death.

Life and death — like God and humankind or this world and the hereafter — are absolutely opposed to each other in the Qur'ān, but a shift in meaning is discernible. The terms no longer signify the natural contrast between what is alive and what is not, but indicate the opposition between two states that are metaphysical rather than physical, religious rather than empirical. On the one hand there are those who reject belief in one God, in Muḥammad as a prophet and in the Qur'ān, its preaching and prescriptions as revelation (see REVELATION AND INSPIRATION). Since unbelief is viewed as a kind of death, these people, seen as attached to this world and imprisoned by it, are considered to be "dead." On the other hand, those who believe in God and the resurrection as well as in Muḥammad and the revelation are thereby considered to be oriented towards eternal life, as "living." In the Qur'ān the natural opposition between life and death merges into the spiritual one between belief and disbelief.

This vision of death is part of the broader qur'ānic vision of the purpose of God's creation of humans to whom he has assigned a final destiny. As a created being, the human should live in his Creator's service (*'ibāda*). To carry out his task, he disposes of his natural faculties, his reason and the revelation provided in the Qur'ān. As a logical consequence, once he has accomplished this *'ibāda* in the course of the lifetime allotted to him, he will be with God forever. Human life has an eternal destiny and the earthly phase of this life is essentially a test of human submission to God. Death in this perspective is simply the end of a testing period and a threshold which must necessarily be passed. Those who fail the test will simply not reach their destiny. Normally, life stretches from birth to paradise; abnormally, it extends from birth to hell. The message which emerges from this vision is clear. Humans are warned (see WARNING) and called not to attach themselves to this life or to delude themselves with rewards that are of a transient nature. They should turn to God and take care to live as God's servants and hence prepare for the real life of the hereafter.

The Qur'ānic view of death and the attitude and actions which derive from it signify a complete shift from what may be called the "natural" as well as the "secular" view of life. As in other prophetic religions, life and death are simply a testing ground of human beings' basic intentions regarding eternity and, in the case of the Qur'ān, the human willingness to put one's life entirely at God's disposal. The result may be not only an inner life of faith (q.v.) and piety (q.v.) but also an extraordinary mobilization of life forces for action — communal or individual — in this world. The Qur'ān's message on the subject can be seen as a liberation from the confines of death, for which humans are grateful to God (see GRATITUDE AND INGRATITUDE). Or is the very concept of God in prophetic religions perhaps born from the experience of a conquest of and a liberation from death — whatever the concept has meant in particular contexts?

Jacques Waardenburg

Bibliography

M. Abdesselem, Mawt, in *EI²*, vi, 910-1; R. Bell, *The Qur'ān translated, with a critical re-arrangement of the surahs,* 2 vols., Edinburgh 1937-9; J. Bowker, *The meanings of death,* Cambridge 1991; E. Gräf, Auffassungen vom Tod im Rahmen islamischer Anthropologie, in J. Schwartländer (ed.), *Der*

Mensch und sein Tod, Göttingen 1976, 126-45; T.E. Homerin, Echos of a thirsty owl. Death and the afterlife in pre-Islamic Arabic poetry, in *JNES* 44 (1985), 165-84; J.H. Marks and R.M. Good (eds.), *Love and death in the ancient Near East. Essays in honor of M.H. Pope,* Guilford 1987; T. O'Shaughnessy, *Muhammad's thoughts on death,* Leiden 1969; H. Reintjes-Anwari, Der Tod aus islamischer Sicht, in C. von Barloewen (ed.), *Der Tod in den Weltkulturen und Weltreligionen,* München 1996, 169-200; J.I. Smith and Y.Y. Haddad., *The Islamic understanding of death and resurrection,* Albany 1981; J. Waardenburg, 'Leben verlieren' oder 'Leben gewinnen' als Alternative in prophetischen Religionen, in G. Stephenson (ed.), *Leben und Tod in den Religionen. Symbol und Wirklichkeit,* Darmstadt 1980, 36-60.

Death Penalty see BOUNDARIES AND PRECEPTS

Debate and Disputation

An oppositional mode of discourse and a formal process of argumentation. References to the activities of disputation and debate are associated with several qur'ānic verbs in their various forms. Terminology pertinent to the process of argumentation occurs throughout the Qur'ān and the importance of such forensic activities as proving, explaining and making manifest is repeatedly stressed. Demonstrable proof (q.v.) and convincing argumentation are represented as indispensable elements of conveying the divine message and actual or anticipated opponents are a prominent feature of much qur'ānic discourse. Further, the qur'ānic text frames and focuses upon striking scenes of debate: Satan (Iblīs, see DEVIL) argues with God about his superiority over humans (Q 15:30-3; 7:11-2; 17:61; 38:73-6); Abraham (q.v.) and Noah (q.v.) dispute with the unbelievers among the people to whom they are sent as do such other prophets as Hūd (q.v.), Ṣāliḥ (q.v.) and Shu'ayb (q.v.). Lengthy pericopes report the exchanges of Moses (q.v.) and Pharaoh (q.v.). Even the famous parable of the two gardens (see GARDEN) in Q 18 (Sūrat al-Kahf, "The Cave") is cast in the form of a debate.

As just stated, the Qur'ān uses several terms to designate the multiple modes of oppositional discourse. Of these *jadala* in its various forms is central. While Arabic lexicographers give "to twist firmly" or "to make strong and compact" as the base meaning of this verb, they also note the more frequent use of those forms of the verb that can denote reciprocal speech acts such as debates, disputations, altercations, arguments, quarrels, etc. (*Tāj al-'arūs,* vii, 253-5; see also DIALOGUES). Extra-qur'ānic attestation of *jadala* and its cognates, with connotations of debate and confrontation, can be gathered from a range of early sources such as the verses of al-Kumayt b. Zayd (d. 126/743) and Dāwūd b. Salm (d. ca. 132/750).

In the Qur'ān *jadala* and its cognates occur 29 times, with the first use in Q 2:197 and the last in Q 58:1. This latter sūra, which is entitled Sūrat al-Mujādala ("She Who Disputes"), is the only sūra to carry a form of the triliteral Arabic root *j-d-l* as its title. The first use of a form of *jadala* in the Qur'ān is an imperative, as are four other occurrences (Q 4:107; 16:125; 22:68; 29:46). All but one of these is, like the first, a negative imperative prohibiting disputation. The initial mention, in Q 2:197, groups disputation *(jidāl)* with obscenity *(rafath)* and wickedness *(fusūq)* as forms of behavior prohibited during the pilgrimage (q.v.) and the majority of the other uses in this category are also negative imperatives.

Descriptive and interrogative uses of *jadala* and its cognates constitute a larger category. Q 4:109 raises the issue of disputation on behalf of the soul (q.v.) on the day of resurrection (q.v.) by asking, "You have disputed on their behalf in this present life, but who will dispute with God on their behalf *(fa-man yujādilu llāha ʿanhum)* on the day of resurrection?" Q 16:111 speaks of the "day when every soul shall come debating on its own behalf *(tujādilu ʿan nafsihā)* and every soul (q.v.) will be recompensed for what it has done and they will not be wronged." A quasi-judicial eschatology (q.v.) is evoked by this vocabulary. If debate can constitute part of the process of human accountability, then the individual's pleading may take the form of self- or mediated representation.

Yet this eschatological possibility captures only a small proportion of the descriptive and interrogative uses of *jadala* forms. In most cases disputation is portrayed as deliberate disavowal of God's "signs" (q.v.). A prominent example of this is Q 6:25 which insists, "Were they to see every one of the signs, they would not believe in them, even to the extent that when they come to you, they dispute with you *(yujādilūnaka)* [and] those who do not believe say, 'These are nothing but the tales of the ancients.'" Again, Q 13:12-3 contends, "He is the one who shows you the lightning, [arousing] both fear and hope, and raises the clouds heavy [with rain]. Thunder extols his praise (q.v.), as do the angels with awe. He sends thunderbolts, striking by them whom he wishes. Yet they dispute about God *(wa-hum yujādilūna fī llāhi)*." There is a persistent rhetorical structure that emerges in these qurʾānic references to debate: Messengers (see MESSENGER) have been sent, the truth (q.v.) has been given, parables have been struck and "signs" made manifest but still people dispute (cf. Q 8:6; 18:54, 56; 31:20). This connection of debate with "signs" is pervasive. Multiple mentions of such phrases as "those who dispute about the signs of God" *(alladhīna yujādilūna fī āyāti llāhi,* Q 40:56; cf. 42:35; 40:69) and "the only ones who dispute about the signs of God are those who disbelieve" *(mā yujādilu fī āyāti llāhi illā lladhīna kafarū,* Q 40:4; cf. 40:35) reinforce the linkage of disputation and God's "signs." In every instance this linkage is connected with condemnation and rebuke.

Rebuke also characterizes the reference to ignorantly disputing about God himself. Q 22:3, 8; 31:20 contain the phrase, "There are people who dispute about God without knowledge *(wa-mina l-nāsi man yujādilu fī llāhi bi-ghayri ʿilmin)*." The first time this accusation occurs, Q 22:3, it is connected with devils or with behavior prompted by devils. "Those who dispute about God without knowledge" are characterized as following "every willful devil" *(kulla shayṭānin murīdin)* while Q 6:121 states, "Truly the devils prompt their friends to debate with you *(li-yujādilūkum)*. If you obey them, you are polytheists."

A final note should be made of a category of statements which associates *jadala* with the prophets, sometimes directly, sometimes tangentially. These would include the brief pericope in Q 43:57-8: "When the son of Mary (q.v.) is cited as an example *(mathal),* your people turn away from it [the example]. They say, 'Are our gods better or is he?' They cite it to you only in debate *(jadal)*. Indeed they are a contentious people *(qawmun khaṣimūn)*." (Cf. Q 18:54 — with its similar tagline — where the provision of another "example" provokes dispute.) At Q 43:57-8 Jesus' (q.v.) association with disputation is somewhat tangential. A more immediate connection between prophets and disputation is found in those instances where the prophets themselves argue. In Q 7:71, Hūd challenges his people: "Atrocity and anger have fallen on you from your Lord; would you dispute with me about names *(tujādilūnanī fī asmāʾ)* that you and your fathers have assigned for which God has sent down no authorization?" The figure of Noah is particularly associated with disputation. In

Q 11:32 Noah's people charge: "Noah, you have debated with us and prolonged our disputation *(qad jādaltanā fa-aktharta jidālanā)*. Now, if you are truthful, bring upon us what you threatened." Perhaps most striking are Abraham's debates with God himself: "When fear had left Abraham and the good news [of Isaac's (q.v.) conception] came to him, he was disputing with us *(yujādilunā)* concerning the people of Lot (q.v.)" (Q 11:74; cf. *Gen* 18:23-32). The classical exegetical tradition (see EXEGESIS OF THE QURʾĀN, CLASSICAL AND MEDIEVAL) also regularly understood Abraham to be debating the messengers *(rusul)* mentioned in Q 11:69. Of course, with Muḥammad himself the topos of prophets who debate and dispute reaches its fullest exemplification (see OPPOSITION TO MUḤAMMAD; PROPHETS AND PROPHETHOOD). Disputation, recollected and anticipated, drives the rhetorical engine of the Qurʾān. Instances of this are too numerous to catalog but at least one should be mentioned since it is captured by the title of a sūra. This is Muḥammad's exchange in Q 58:1 with the eponymous "disputatious woman" *(mujādila)*. The literature dealing with the circumstance under which this verse was revealed (*sabab al-nuzūl*, see OCCASIONS OF REVELATION) asserts virtually unanimously its exegetical association with the wife of Aws b. al-Ṣāmit, who was complaining that her husband had unjustly divorced her. (For representative accounts and for variations of her name, e.g. Khawla bt. Thaʿlaba, see Ṭabarī, *Tafsīr*, xxviii, 1-6.)

There are other qurʾānic terms relevant to this topic such as the vocabulary related to *ikhtaṣama* and *nāzaʿa*, both meaning "to argue or dispute," that can be grouped in the same way as the *jadala* category. These include the strong negative imperative of Q 50:28, "Do not dispute in my presence when I have already set the threat before you *(lā takhtaṣimū ladayya wa-qad qaddamtu ilaykum bi-l-waʿīd)*," and other occurrences that maintain the connection of debate and disputation with eschatological events (Q 36:49; 38:64; 39:31), with the rejection of "signs" (cf. Q 22:19) and with the denigration or disregard of messengers (Q 26:96-7; 27:45; cf. 3:44). The nearly synonymous nature of this vocabulary is evidenced by paired usage in passages like Q 4:105-7 and Q 43:58 (forms of the Arabic roots *j-d-l* and *kh-ṣ-m*) and Q 22:67-8 (forms of the Arabic roots *j-d-l* and *n-z-ʿ*). Taken together the qurʾānic vocabulary associated with this topic demonstrates that, in the overwhelming majority of cases, debate and disputation are assessed negatively. The activity of oppositional discourse is associated with human ignorance or with satanic insinuation or with human insolence, as when individuals are unwilling to recognize the probative value of God's "signs." Although Abraham was permitted to debate with God about the people of Lot, other qurʾānic scenarios depict prophets whose people dispute with them as a form of rejection. While there are exceptions such as the eschatological possibility in Q 16:111, the human propensity to debate and dispute generally elicits qurʾānic condemnation. In fact, Q 18:54 laments that "more than anything, humans are disputatious *(wa-kāna l-insānu akthara shayʾin jadalan)*."

Yet a keen awareness of that very propensity emerges in those verses describing how one should deal with disputation that express an etiquette of oppositional discourse. Q 22:68 advises: "If they dispute with you *(wa-in jādalūka)*, then say, 'God knows best what you are doing.'" Even more explicit is Q 16:125 with its encouragement to "summon to the way of your Lord (q.v.) with wisdom and fine exhortation (see EXHORTATIONS) and debate with them in the better way *(wa-jādilhum bi-llatī hiya aḥsanu)*."

This latter verse emerged in post-qurʾānic

literature as a frequently cited justification for the use of disputation as a powerful tool in fields such as law (see LAW AND THE QURʾĀN) and theology (see THEOLOGY AND THE QURʾĀN). With the assimilation of Greek dialectic as a major mode of intellectual engagement, classical Muslim scholars began to discuss scenes of debate and disputation in the Qurʾān from the perspective of these refined rhetorical tools. As indicated above, they were able to point to many instances of this within the textual narrative but they were also cognizant of the frequent qurʾānic denunciation of the human propensity to argue, disagree and contradict. Consequently, in the classical Islamic treatises devoted to such topics as logic and jurisprudential theory it became common to enumerate the qurʾānic texts where disputation is censured or, less frequently, praised. This commonplace of commendable/reprehensible disputation — the usual pair of Arabic adjectives is *maḥmūd* and *madhmūm* — can be found in the works of many authors. Some examples are Isḥāq b. Ibrāhīm's (fl. third/ninth century) *al-Burhān fī wujūh al-bayān*, Ibn Fūrak's (d. 406/1015) *Mujarrad maqālāt al-Ashʿarī*, the *Kāfiyya fī l-jadal* attributed to Imām al-Ḥaramayn ʿAbd al-Malik al-Juwaynī (d. 478/1085; but see D. Gimaret, *La doctrine d'al-Ashaʿrī*, 183, n. 2), Sulaymān b. Khalaf al-Bājī's (d. 474/1081) *al-Minhāj fī tartīb al-ḥijāj*, Ibn Ḥazm's (d. 456/1064) *al-Iḥkām fī uṣūl al-aḥkām*, Ibn al-Ḥanbalī's (d. 634/1236) *Istikhrāj al-jidāl min al-Qurʾān al-karīm*, Najm al-Dīn al-Ṭūfī's (d. 716/1316) *ʿAlam al-jadhal fī ʿilm al-jadal*. Finally, the most noted of the works on the traditional disciplines of qurʾānic study (q.v.) include debate *(jadal)* among their long list of contents. Al-Zarkashī (d. 793/1391) included a section on the subject in his *Burhān* as did al-Suyūṭī (d. 911/1505) in his *Itqān*. See also RHETORIC OF THE QURʾĀN.

Jane Dammen McAuliffe

Bibliography

Primary: al-Bājī, *al-Minhāj fī tartīb al-ḥijāj*, ed. A.M. Turkī, Paris 1978; Ibn Fūrak, *Muǧarrad maqālāt al-Ašʿarī. Exposé de la doctrine d'al-Ašarī*, ed. D. Gimaret, Beirut 1987; Ibn al-Ḥanbalī, *Kitāb Aqyisat al-nabī al-muṣṭafā Muḥammad*, ed. A.Ḥ. Jābir and ʿA.A. al-Khaṭīb, Beirut 1415/1994; Ibn Ḥazm, *al-Iḥkām fī uṣūl al-aḥkām*, Beirut 1987/1407; Ibn al-Jawzī, *Zād;* Ibn Qutayba, *Kitāb al-Maʿānī al-kabīr*, 3 vols. in 2, Hyderabad 1368/1949; Isḥāq b. Ibrāhīm, *al-Burhān fī wujūh al-bayān*, ed. A. Maṭlūb and Kh. al-Ḥadīthī, Baghdad 1387/1967; Pseudo-al-Juwaynī, *al-Kāfiyya fī l-jadal*, ed. F.Ḥ. Maḥmūd, Cairo 1399/1969; Suyūṭī, *Itqān*, iv, 52-7; Ṭabarī, *Tafsīr; Tāj al-ʿarūs*, Cairo 1306-7; al-Ṭūfī, *ʿAlam al-jadhal fī ʿilm al-jadal*, ed. W. Heinrichs, Wiesbaden 1987; Zamakhsharī, *Kashshāf;* Zarkashī, *Burhān*, ii, 24-7.
Secondary: M. Abū Zahra, *Taʾrīkh al-jadal*, Cairo 1980; Ẓ. b. ʿA. al-Almaʿī, *Manāhij al-jadal fī l-Qurʾān al-karīm*, Beirut 1400/1980; D. Gimaret, Un document majeur pour l'histoire du kalām. Le *Muǧarrad maqālāt al-Ašʿarī* d'Ibn Fūrak, in *Arabica* 32 (1985), 185-218; W. Heinrichs, Ǧadal bei aṭ-Ṭūfī. Einer Interpretation seiner Beispielsammlung, in *ZDMG, Suppl.* 3.1, Wiesbaden 1977, 463-73; M. al-Kattānī, *Jadal al-ʿaql wa-l-naql fī manāhij al-tafkīr al-Islāmī*, Beirut 1412/1992; G. Makdisi, Dialect and disputation. The relation between the texts of Qirqisani and Ibn ʿAqil, in P. Salmon (ed.), *Mélanges d'islamologie. Volume dédié à la mémoire de Armand Abel*, 3 vols., Leiden 1974-78, i, 201-6; J.D. McAuliffe, Debate with them in the better way. The construction of a qurʾānic commonplace, in B. Embaló et al. (eds.), *Myths, historical archetypes and symbolic figures in Arabic literature*, Beirut 1999, 163-88; L. Miller, *Islamic disputation theory. A study of the development of dialectic in Islam from the tenth through fourteenth centuries*, Ph.D. diss., Princeton 1984; Ḥ. al-Sharqāwī, *al-Jadal fī l-Qurʾān*, Alexandria 1986; A.M. Turki, Argument d'authorité, preuve rationnelle et absence de prevues dans la méthodologie juridique musulmane, in *SI* 42 (1976), 59-91.

Debt

A financial obligation due to another. The qurʾānic expression for debt is the Arabic word *dayn*. Two places in the Qurʾān, both Medinan chapters, deal with the matter of debts. At Q 2:282, the longest verse in the Qurʾān, detailed instructions are given for the actual handling of debts. All debts, be they large or small, in the form of loans or deferred payment for goods received, are to be recorded in writing. The only exception to this is "local business transactions" involving nearly immediate exchange. Recognizing the paucity of literacy (q.v.) in first/seventh century Arabia, the Qurʾān instructs the literate minority to serve as recorders in cases where the parties to a debt are illiterate. Recognizing also the tribal structure of the society, literate persons are forbidden to refuse to record a debt whenever they are petitioned to do so; and they are commanded to discharge this duty with accuracy and without prejudice to either party, i.e. regardless of clan- or tribe-affiliation (see TRIBES AND CLANS; CHEATING). Debtors, not creditors, are to dictate to recorders. If a debtor is mentally or physically incapable, a representative is to dictate on his or her behalf. In addition to being recorded, debts are to be validated by witnesses, preferably two males or, if that is not possible, one male and two females. (As an aside, it is on the basis of this verse that the jurists have developed the more general rule that one male equals two female witnesses in a court of law [see LAW AND THE QURʾĀN; WITNESSING AND TESTIFYING]). Both male and female witnesses must be morally upright. Here again, regardless of clan- or tribe-affiliation, individuals are commanded not to refuse to serve as witnesses nor to refuse to come forth and testify to what they witnessed whenever petitioned to do so. Finally, in circumstances such as journeys where there is no access to scribes to record the transaction, debtors are instructed to offer collateral to their creditors. This, however, is not obligatory and those who contract debts without collateral are commanded not to betray the trust placed in them.

The second passage that deals with debts is in the fourth sūra, entitled "Women" (Sūrat al-Nisāʾ; see WOMEN AND THE QURʾĀN). In a series of appendages to verses outlining the shares of inheritance the stipulation is added that any debts contracted by the deceased prior to death are to be excluded from the shares distributed to his or her heirs (cf. Q 4:11-2). The shares of inheritance (q.v.), in other words, are to be computed *after* any and all debts have been settled even if these should exhaust the entire estate.

The Qurʾān mentions no legal sanctions to be applied to those who fail or refuse to pay their debts. The matter is referred rather to the *forum internum* as the Qurʾān bids debtors to be conscious of God in their financial dealings (see ECONOMICS). Islamic law, however, subsequently developed elaborate rules on bankruptcy and related matters (cf. A. Delcambre, Dayn). See also CONTRACTS AND ALLIANCES; BREAKING TRUSTS AND CONTRACTS.

Sherman A. Jackson

Bibliography
Primary: ʿAbd al-Bāqī, Cairo 1407/1987, ad Q 2:282; 4:11-2; Ibn Kathīr, *Mukhtaṣar tafsīr Ibn Kathīr,* 3 vols., Beirut 1402/1982, ad Q 2:282; 4:11-2; Ṣābūnī, *Tafsīr,* 3 vols., Beirut 1402/1982⁴, ad Q 2:282; 4:11-2; Shawkānī, *Tafsīr,* ad Q 2:282; 4:11-2; Ṭabarī, *Tafsīr,* Cairo 1388/1968³, ad Q 2:282; 4:11-2.
Secondary: A. Delcambre, Dayn, in *EI²,* Supp. fasc. 3-4, 207; Ṣubḥī Maḥmaṣānī, *al-Naẓarriyya al-ʿāmma lil-mūjabāt wa-l-ʿuqūd,* Beirut 1948.

Decadence see EVIL DEEDS; INTOXICANTS

Decalogue see COMMANDMENTS

Deceit see TRICK

Decision

In the qurʾānic context, a divine decree reflecting omniscience and omnipotence. The notion of decision in the Qurʾān is related to the concept of God as the creator, the king and the judge whose decisions —

decrees, judgments and sentences — represent his supreme wisdom (q.v.) and power (see POWER AND IMPOTENCE). These decisions emerge in both the initial and the final phase of all acts and events. Through them God creates inanimate objects and human beings (see CREATION), rules over the life of his creatures, which he brings to their final end on the day of judgment (see LAST JUDGMENT).

There is, however, no unique term in the Qurʾān which speaks in general to this conception of decision. The terms which convey the idea — namely *ḥukm, faṣl,* and *qaḍāʾ* — can function interchangeably (e.g. Q 4:65; 6:57; 27:78; 42:21). There are, however, significant semantic differences between the three terms and the frequency with which they occur also varies.

The most ubiquitous of the terms, *ḥukm,* which is best translated as judgment (q.v.), is historically related to pre-Islamic judges *(ḥakam,* pl. *ḥukkām)* who exercised justice in ancient Arabia (see PRE-ISLAMIC ARABIA AND THE QURʾĀN). Lexically, it is associated with wisdom *(ḥikma)* and authority *(ḥukm, ḥukūma)* embodied in two of the most beautiful names of God (*al-asmāʾ al-ḥusnā,* see GOD AND HIS ATTRIBUTES): al-Ḥakam, "the Judge," and al-Ḥakīm, "the Wise." The term *ḥukm* already occurs in early Meccan sūras (see CHRONOLOGY AND THE QURʾĀN) in the juxtaposition of the human judgments of the pagan Arabs (see AGE OF IGNORANCE) next to divine judgment (Q 5:50). God is described as "the most just of judges" (*aḥkam al-ḥākimīn,* Q 11:45; 95:8) and "the best of judges" (*khayr al-ḥākimīn,* Q 7:87; 10:109; 12:80). Of the three stages of existence of humans and the world — creation, life history and resurrection (q.v.) — *ḥukm* is overwhelmingly related to the second and the third, since it appears in only one qurʾānic passage in the context of creation (Q 13:41; see DEATH AND THE DEAD; ESCHATOLOGY). *Ḥukm* is also used in discussions about the prophetic authority to judge individuals with the help of scriptures (see BOOK), wherein special emphasis is given to Muḥammad and the Qurʾān, which is called "the Arabic code" (*ḥukm ʿarabī,* Q 13:37). Moses (q.v.), David (q.v.) and Jesus (q.v.) are also mentioned in this context, together with the Torah (q.v.; Q 5:44) and the Gospel (q.v.; Q 5:47).

The term *faṣl,* which is translated variously as cut, division, separation, differentiation and judgment, and which appears the least frequently of the three qurʾānic terms for decision, resembles *ḥukm* in its usage. It refers to the last judgment (Q 22:17; 60:3) and gives an early name for it, "the day of separation" (*yawm al-faṣl,* Q 37:21; 44:40; 77:13, 14, 38; 78:17), which is later replaced with "the day of judgment" (*yawm al-dīn,* as in Q 1:4). It is etymologically related to the biblical Hebrew idiom as well as to a qurʾānic epithet of God, "the best of arbiters" (*khayr al-fāṣilīn,* Q 6:57). It is also associated with the notion that the revealed word, speech or utterance is the basis of the judgment of prophets (Q 6:57; 42:21; 86:13; see PROPHETS AND PROPHETHOOD; REVELATION AND INSPIRATION).

The third term, *qaḍāʾ,* which has the sense of decree, order or final judgment, is opposed to the previous two in many respects. First, it never occurs in the early Meccan sūras. Secondly, it rarely conveys the idea of a human judgment (with the exception of Q 10:71 and 20:72). Thirdly, the term usually implies God's pre-existent decision to undertake creation (q.v.; *kun fa-yakūn,* Q 2:117; 3:47; 19:35; 40:68) as well as the pre-ordained life-span *(ajal)* of human life (Q 6:2; 10:11; see FATE), approximating the meaning of *qadar,* i.e. the Lord's eternal universal decision concerning his creatures which he has determined for them from their creation (see FREEDOM AND PREDESTINATION). The main issues which Muslim theology (see THEOLOGY AND THE QURʾĀN) discussed in connection with *qaḍāʾ* included the following: determinism; the essence of the Prophet's mission; "acquisition" *(kasb* or *iktisāb),* i.e. the way in which humans acquire the acts determined and created for them by God (see ANTHROPOMORPHISM; MUʿTAZILA); the relationship between justice (see JUSTICE AND INJUSTICE) and mercy (q.v.) at the last judgment and the role of intercession (q.v.).

Dmitry V. Frolov

Bibliography
Primary: al-Ashʿarī, Abū l-Ḥasan, *Risāla ilā ahl al-thaghr,* Medina/Beirut 1988 (for an account of relevant theological topics, cf. esp. expositions of the Muslim creed); Ibn Ḥazm, *Milal;* Ibn Kathīr, *Tafsīr,* ad loc.; *Jalālayn; Lisān al-ʿArab,* xii, 14-5 *(ḥukm);* xi, 521-4 *(faṣl);* xv, 186-9 *(qaḍāʾ);* Shahrastānī, *Milal;* Suyūṭī, *Durr;* Ṭabarī, *Tafsīr,* ad loc.; Zamakhsharī, *Kashshāf.*
Secondary: Gardet and Anawati, *Introduction,* especially pp. 37-8, 151-2, 257-8; Izutsu, *God* (see indices); Gy. Káldy Nagy, Ḳaḍāʾ, in *EI²,* iv, 364-5; A.J. Wensinck, *The Muslim creed,* Cambridge 1932.

Decoration see MATERIAL CULTURE AND THE QURʾĀN

Deed Scroll see RECORD OF HUMAN ACTIONS; BOOK

Deeds see ETHICS IN THE QURʾĀN; EVIL DEEDS; GOOD DEEDS

Defamation see LIE; OPPOSITION TO MUḤAMMAD

Deferral

The qurʾānic concept of postponement or delay in God's punishment. It was this concept, derived from the single occurrence of this word in conjunction with the decision-making character of God at Q 9:106, that formed the basis of the doctrine of a number of different groups of early Muslims usually called Murjiʾīs *(murjiʾa,* see CREEDS; THEOLOGY AND THE QURʾĀN).

The concept of deferral *(irjāʾ)* is derived from the fourth form of the Arabic root *r-j-ʾ,* uniquely used in connection with God's judgment (q.v.) at Q 9:106 (the fourth form is also used at Q 33:51 but in reference to the Prophet's choice of spouses; see WIVES OF THE PROPHET). The word means to "delay" or "postpone" and refers to a group whose ultimate fate is postponed. With this definition, the verse could be translated: "There are others for whom God's command is deferred *(murjawna),* whether he will punish them or forgive them; for God is knowing, wise." Some commentators read the word as *murjaʾūnā* from the same root and with the same meaning while others derive the word from the root *r-j-w,* meaning "to hope" or "to anticipate," rendering the translation: "There are others who are made to hope for God's command...." This reading, however, contradicts the historical understanding of Q 9:106 (see OCCASIONS OF REVELATION).

The context of Q 9:106 is usually understood to involve the defection of some of Muḥammad's putative supporters in the expedition to Tabūk (see EXPEDITIONS AND BATTLES). There were those who were said to receive punishment twice, meaning in this world and the next (see REWARD AND PUNISHMENT), whereas those whose actions were considered a mixture of good and bad and who acknowledged their bad deeds (see GOOD AND EVIL) were offered the hope of God's forgiveness (q.v.; Q 9:101-2). The third group, those of Q 9:106, who had not repented but were not in either of the other groups, had their judgment deferred (see REPENTANCE AND PENANCE). After Muḥammad's death, various doctrinal and political positions arose around the issues of sin and punishment (see SIN, MAJOR AND MINOR). The Khārijīs (q.v.) held that anyone who committed a grave sin had also committed apostasy (q.v.) and was condemned to hell (q.v.). They had emerged from a group of adherents to the fourth caliph (q.v.), ʿAlī (see ʿALĪ B. ABĪ ṬĀLIB), whose soldiers parted ways with him over the issue of arbitration during the battle of Ṣiffīn (q.v.). They held that ʿAlī and his Umayyad opponents were guilty of such a sin and were thus not to be followed. In opposition to the Khārijite position, some argued that these Muslims belonged to the category of those for whom God's judgment was deferred, and they too thus refrained from making a categorical judgment. From this also developed the notion that faith (q.v.) was sufficient to make one a Muslim, even if his or her works were not perfect (see WORK; GOOD DEEDS; EVIL DEEDS). As Islam spread into Khurāsān and Transoxania, the Murjiʾīs became supporters of unity among all Muslims and were thus in opposition to Shīʿīs as well as Khārijīs in disputes about legitimate rule as well as the definition of a good Muslim, the Shīʿīs holding as illegitimate the rule of the caliphs Abū Bakr (q.v.; r. 11-13/632-4), ʿUmar (q.v.; r. 13-23/634-44) and ʿUthmān (q.v.; r. 23-35/644-56). While the Murjiʾīs split into a number of factions, Murjiʾism became identified with support of converts to Islam, in opposition to some Umayyad policies, and Murjiʾīs became the champions of the converted non-Arab Muslims, the *mawālī*. The famous jurist Abū Ḥanīfa (81-150/700-760) held moderate Murjiʾī beliefs and many scholars see the origins of later Sunnism in moderate Murjiʾism.

Gordon Darnell Newby

Bibliography

Primary: Ibn Isḥāq, *Sīra;* Shahrastānī, *Milal;* Ṭabarī, *Taʾrīkh.*

Secondary: J. van Ess, *Frühe muʿtazilitische Häresiographie,* Beirut 1971; J. Givoni, *The Murjiʾa and the theological school of Abu Hanifa. A historical and theological study,* Ph.D. diss., Edinburgh 1977; M.I. Ibrāhīm, *Muʿjām al-alfāẓ wa-l-aʿlām al-qurʾāniyya,* Cairo 1969; W. Madelung, Murdjiʾa, in *EI²*, vii, 605-7; id., *Religious trends in early Islamic Iran,* New York 1988; W.M. Watt, *Free will and predestination in early Islam,* London 1948; id., *Islamic philosophy and theology,* Edinburgh 1987; A.J. Wensinck, *The Muslim creed,* Cambridge 1932; id., al-Murdjiʾa, in *The shorter encyclopaedia of Islam,* Leiden 1974, 412.

Defilement see PURITY AND IMPURITY

Deities see POLYTHEISM AND ATHEISM; IDOLS AND IMAGES; IDOLATRY AND IDOLATERS

Deliverance

Throughout the Qurʾān, but especially in later Meccan sūras, various forms of deliverance *(najjā/anjā, anqadha, waqā)* illustrate God's saving power (see POWER AND IMPOTENCE; SALVATION). God typically speaks in the divine plural, recalling specific settings in which he had acted on behalf of either the prophets or their people. Many of the references occur in the context of Muḥammad's efforts to counteract Meccan opposition (see OPPOSITION TO MUḤAMMAD).

Prominent among the beneficiaries of divine deliverance are the prophets (see PROPHETS AND PROPHETHOOD), several of whom God rescues from the treacherous designs of those who reject their message (see MESSENGER). Moses (q.v.), Noah (q.v.) and Lot (q.v.) appear most often in this connection, their deliverance usually linked to that of the believers among their peoples. God rescues Moses (Q 14:6; 20:40, 65), the people of Israel (Q 2:49; 10:86; 20:80; 44:30; see CHILDREN OF ISRAEL) and Moses' brother Aaron (q.v.; Q 37:115) from the evil designs of Pharaoh (q.v.). The ḥadīth attribute the cause for fasting (q.v.) on ʿĀshūrāʾ (the voluntary fast-day observed on the tenth of Muḥarram) to that rescue *(al-Ḥadīth al-sharīf,* Bukhārī 3145 and parallels, *najjā)*. Earlier in his career, Moses begs deliverance from the angry throng pursuing him after his murder of the Egyptian (Q 28:21; also 28:25). Pharaoh's wife, Āsiya, becomes the paradigm of the believer whom God saves in the very home of the arch-unbeliever (Q 66:11); but God accepts even Pharaoh's conversion as the sea engulfs him (Q 10:92). See BELIEF AND UNBELIEF.

Noah's escape from the clutches of unbelievers appears frequently (Q 7:64; 10:73; 21:76; 23:28; 26:118). Several texts (Q 10:22-3; 17:67; 29:65; 31:32) speak of God rescuing sea travelers from storms, only to have them return to idolatry once safely on land. One such text (Q 36:43) comes immediately after a reference to Noah's ark (q.v.), emphasizing that only God's power saves from death (see DEATH AND THE DEAD). For that verse, some exegetes gloss *anqadha* with *najjā* (Ṭabarī, *Tafsīr,* x, 446; Bayḍāwī, *Anwār,* ii, 283; Abū Ḥayyān, *Baḥr,* viii, 324); other exegetes elaborate and identify deliverance as purification (see PURITY AND IMPURITY) from all that is loathsome (Ibn al-Jawzī, *Zād,* vi, 282), and compare drowning to eternal punishment (Qurtubī, *Jāmiʿ,* xv, 25; see REWARD AND PUNISHMENT). Lot and his family (Q 21:74; 26:169-70; 37:134), with the exception of his unbelieving wife (Q 29:32), merit deliverance, once in explicit association with Abraham (Q 21:71). God rescues all three of the pre-Islamic Arabian prophets: Hūd (q.v.), Shuʿayb (q.v.), and Ṣāliḥ (q.v.; Q 11:58, 94, 66; 41:18).

Though references to the deliverance of Muḥammad's people are scarce (Q 6:63-4), some texts refer to God protecting believers, either in general or as nameless individuals, from apocalyptic or eschatological disasters (see APOCALYPSE; ESCHATOLOGY) such as the fire of hell (q.v.; Q 52:18 which uses *waqā* in the sense of "deliver"; Q 70:14 *[anjā];* Q 3:103; 39:19 *[anqadha]*), fearsome wind (Q 58:23, often associated with the destruction of Hūd's [q.v.] people, the ʿĀd [q.v.]) or the evil of the last day (Q 39:61; 76:11; 10:103; see LAST JUDGMENT). The ḥadīth speak of the deliverance of individuals from the fire more often than the Qurʾān. For example, among the three kinds of people who experience the sweetness of faith (q.v.) are those who, once God has delivered them *(anqadha)* from unbelief, would rather be thrown into hell (q.v.) than revert to unbelief *(kufr, al-Ḥadīth al-sharīf,* Bukhārī 20; Muslim 60; Ibn Ḥanbal 11563; Tirmidhī 2548; Ibn Māja 4023; Nasāʾī 4902 and parallels; a similar theme is found in Ibn Ḥanbal 8051, 13467 and parallels). God alone is the unprotected protector *(wa-huwa yujīru wa-lā yujār ʿalayhi,* Q 23:88) whose deliverance and forgiveness (q.v.) await all who heed the prophets (Q 46:31; see also Q 67:28 and 72:22 on denial of deliverance).

John Renard

Bibliography
Abū Ḥayyān, *Baḥr;* Bayḍāwī, *Anwār; al-Ḥadīth al-sharīf,* CD-ROM, Version 1.1, Cairo 1995; Ibn al-Jawzī, *Zād;* Qurtubī, *Jāmiʿ;* Ṭabarī, *Tafsīr.*

Demons

see DEVIL; SPIRITUAL BEINGS

Deobandis

The name given to Muslim scholars *(ʿulamāʾ)* associated with the Indo-Pakistani reformist movement centered in the religious school *(dār al-ʿulūm)* of Deoband, a country town some ninety miles northeast of Delhi. Founded in 1867, the school was a pioneering effort to transmit the religious sciences by organizing staff and instruction on the model of British colonial schools (see TRADITIONAL DISCIPLINES OF QURʾĀNIC

STUDY). The goal of the school was to preserve the teachings of the faith (q.v.) in a period of non-Muslim rule and considerable social change by holding Muslims to a standard of correct individual practice. Central to that goal was the creation of a class of formally trained and popularly supported religious scholars (*ʿulamā,* see SCHOLAR) who served as imams (see IMĀM), guardians and trustees of mosques (see MOSQUE) and tombs, preachers, muftis, spiritual guides, writers and publishers of religious works. The school's curriculum has included study of the art of reciting the Qurʾān (*tajwīd, qirāʾāt,* see RECITATION OF THE QURʾĀN), of translation (*tarjama,* see TRANSLATION OF THE QURʾĀN) and of qurʾānic commentary (*tafsīr* and *uṣūl-i tafsīr* such as *Jalālayn;* Shāh Walī Allāh, *al-Fawz al-kabīr;* al-Bayḍāwī, *Anwār;* and Ibn Kathīr, *Tafsīr;* see EXEGESIS OF THE QURʾĀN: CLASSICAL AND MEDIEVAL). At its first centenary in 1967, Deoband counted almost 10,000 graduates including several hundred from foreign countries. Hundreds of Deobandi schools, moreover, have been founded across the Indian sub-continent.

The early Deobandis were associated with a shift in emphasis from the rational sciences *(al-ʿulūm al-ʿaqliyya)* to the revealed or traditional sciences *(al-ʿulūm al-naqliyya)* of Qurʾān and, above all, ḥadīth. In this they followed their forebear, Shāh Walī Allāh Dihlavī (1702-63) whose qurʾānic commentary stressing the clear meaning of the Qurʾān was highly influential and whose translation of the Qurʾān into Persian stimulated further translations into Urdu, among them two produced by his sons. They have also been firmly committed to the Ḥanafī legal tradition (see LAW AND THE QURʾĀN). The Deobandis were among those *ʿulamāʾ* who took advantage of the newly available lithographic presses to disseminate sacred texts and vernacular materials widely. The scholar and revered spiritual guide, Mawlānā Ashraf ʿAlī Thānavī (1864-1943), one of the most influential Deobandis of this century, is an important example of the school's qurʾānic scholars. He was an accomplished reciter *(qāriʾ)* of the Qurʾān, enjoyed the prestige of those who knew the holy text by heart *(ḥāfiẓ),* was esteemed for his natural voice in recitation and authored many works on *tajwīd.* He translated the Qurʾān into excellent and accurate Urdu and prepared a twelve-volume commentary, *Tafsīr bayān al-Qurʾān,* with citations from ḥadīth to elucidate matters of law and Ṣūfism (see ṢŪFISM AND THE QURʾĀN).

Deobandi devotion to the Qurʾān was not merely scholarly. When Rashīd Aḥmad Gangōhī (1829-1905), for example, read the Qurʾān alone at night, his biographer wrote, he would be overcome with joy or shake in terror as he read of God's mercy (q.v.) or his wrath (see ANGER). The Deobandis also used sections of the Qurʾān for *ʿamaliyyāt,* i.e. prescriptions of certain prayers and readings intended to secure particular concrete goals. Indeed another of Ashraf ʿAlī Thānavī's books was the *Aʿmāl-i qurʾānī,* intended to save common people from undertaking illegitimate works *(aʿmāl).*

The central school, as well as Deobandi schools throughout the sub-continent, continue to teach many students. The apolitical strand within the school's teaching has taken shape for many in the widespread, now trans-national, pietist movement known since the 1920s as Tablīghī Jamāʿat; the movement has particularly cherished the popular writings of Mawlānā Muḥammad Zakariyyā Kandhalavī (1897-1982), among them the *Faḍāʾil-i Qurʾān* (1930) and its discussion of forty ḥadīth.

Barbara D. Metcalf

Bibliography
ʿAbd al-Rashīd Arshad, *Bīs Bar'ē Musalmān,* Sahiwal 1969 (a compendium of detailed biographical information about leading Indian Muslim scholars of the twentieth century, most of them Deobandis including Ashraf ʿAlī Thānavī); P. Hardy, *The Muslims of British India,* Cambridge 1972 (an excellent survey, providing a good context for specific educational and political movements); B.D. Metcalf, *Islamic revival in British India. Deoband 1860-1900,* Princeton 1982 (a study of Deoband in its early decades based on institutional records, government records, biographies, memoirs, diaries, tracts, letters and *fatāwā*; it also includes an overview of other movements of the period: that of the Ahl-i Ḥadīth, the Barelwis, the Nadwatu l-ʿUlamāʾ and Aligarh); Muḥammad Ṭayyib Qāriʾ, *Dār al-ʿulūm dēōband kīṣad sālah zindagī,* Deoband 1965 (an extremely valuable study of the school, including detailed information on curriculum, written by a revered scholar and qurʾānic reciter *(qāriʾ)* as well as rector of the school and grandson of one of its eminent founders).

Depravity see EVIL

Desert see GEOGRAPHY IN THE QURʾĀN

Design see COSMOLOGY IN THE QURʾĀN

Desire see WISH AND DESIRE

Despair

The loss of hope. Rendered in Arabic by the following five different roots: *y-ʾ-s, q-n-ṭ, b-ʾ-s, b-l-s, w-h-n.* Loss of hope in God's mercy (q.v.) is the chief cause of despair in the Qurʾān which contrasts human responses in good times with feelings that can prevail in dire straits. Human beings consider bounty to be the result of their own doing, but when they encounter difficulties, they assume God is to blame and give up (Q 11:9; 17:83; 41:49; 57:23; see 30:49, 42:28 for the converse). In fact, human beings often cause their own sense of desperation through evil deeds (q.v.; Q 30:36; 47:35). A ḥadīth says that God "laughs at the despair of his servants," amused at humanity's insecurity about something so infinitely certain as the divine mercy (*al-Ḥadīth al-sharīf,* Ibn Māja 177, Ibn Ḥanbal 15598, 15612).

Prophets (see PROPHETS AND PROPHETHOOD) must maintain courage (q.v.) while striving in the way of God (Q 3:146; see PATH OR WAY [OF GOD]) amongst unbelieving peoples (Q 12:110) though they may be tempted to despair of God's largess for themselves as Abraham (q.v.) did when he doubted that the birth of a son would come to pass (Q 15:55, 56). Joseph (q.v.) tells Benjamin (q.v.) not to lose heart at the actions of their brothers (Q 12:60), and God instructs Noah (q.v.) to rise above rejection and build the ark (q.v.; Q 11:36). Conversely, a prophet's enemies (q.v.) may despair when they fail to undermine the divine message (Q 5:3). Joseph's brothers lose hope of persuading Joseph not to detain the falsely accused Benjamin (Q 12:80). Ironically, Jacob (q.v.) later encourages his sons to return to Egypt (q.v.) to ask about Joseph, so as not to despair of God's mercy as unbelievers do (Q 12:87; see BELIEF AND UNBELIEF).

All who reject God's signs (q.v.) despair of divine deliverance (q.v.) and of a life hereafter (Q 29:23; 60:13; see REWARD AND PUNISHMENT). After death (see DEATH AND THE DEAD) the burden of their deeds will mire them in hopelessness (Q 43:75), for none will intercede for them (Q 30:12; see INTERCESSION). Distracted by every whim, the spiritually petulant expect blessing (q.v.) without consequence, unable to cope with the ethical demands of God-given success (Q 23:77), while people of faith (q.v.) do not lose heart (Q 3:139). A ḥadīth says: "No believer who knows the punishment God has in store aspires to heaven; and no unbeliever who knows the extent of

God's mercy despairs *(q-n-ṭ)* of paradise" *(al-Ḥadīth al-sharīf,* Tirmidhī 3465; Muslim 4948; Ibn Ḥanbal 8063, 8799, 9890).

For sinners, trust in God's forgiveness is a struggle (q.v.; Q 39:53). Ibn Kathīr (d. 774/1373; *Tafsīr,* iv, 65-6) provides an excursus on ḥadīth about counteracting despair with the certainty of divine forgiveness; al-Ṭabarī (d. 310/923; *Tafsīr,* xi, 14) and Ibn al-Jawzī (d. 597/1200; *Zād,* vii, 59) gloss *q-n-ṭ* with *y-ʾ-s;* the Muʿtazilite al-Zamakhsharī (d. 538/1144; *Kashshāf,* iv, 130-1) emphasizes that God forgives *all* sin since he is impervious and "does not care," i.e. is not affected by the sins of his creatures. God seeks to bring the heedless back through bounty, only to see them regress into hopelessness at the merest hint of accountability (Q 6:44). Ṣūfī authors also develop the theme. Abū Ṭālib al-Makkī (d. 386/996) quotes Q 39:53 in his section on hope *(rajāʾ, Qūt,* i, 375); Abū Saʿīd al-Kharrāz (d. 286/899) glosses *rajāʾ* as " 'despair *(yaʾs)* of all that God has marked with the stamp of nothingness,' that is, all that is not God" and interprets the "truth of longing" *(ṣidq al-raghba)* as despairing *(qunūṭ)* of lust and covetousness (Nwyia, *Exégèse,* 280-1; see ṢŪFISM AND THE QURʾĀN).

John Renard

Bibliography
Primary: *al-Ḥadīth al-sharīf,* Version 1.1, CD-ROM, Sakhr Software 1995; Abū Ṭālib al-Makkī, *Qūt al-qulūb,* 2 vols., Beirut 1997; Ṭabarī, *Tafsīr,* 12 vols., Beirut 1992; Zamakhsharī, *Kashshāf;* Ibn al-Jawzī, *Zād;* Ibn Kathīr, *Tafsīr.*
Secondary: Nwyia, *Exégèse;* Wensinck, *Concordance.*

Destiny

The predetermined course of events in general and of human actions and eternal fate in particular, a condition foreordained by divine will or human will, a real or imaginary impersonal power or agency. From the first Islamic centuries, the question of the agency of human works and eternal destiny was a widely discussed controversy among Muslim theologians — whether they are ordained by God's decree or whether they are executed by man himself (see FREEDOM AND PREDESTINATION; ANTHROPOMORPHISM; DECISION). Both determinists and non-determinists made reference to the Qurʾān in support of their respective views with scriptural proofs (see THEOLOGY AND THE QURʾĀN).

In the Qurʾān, deterministic and non-deterministic sayings stand side by side. The qurʾānic concept of the last judgment (q.v.) when God will demand individual reckoning from each human being clearly presupposes man's individual liberty and responsibility for his actions in this world and his destiny in the hereafter (e.g. Q 3:161, 182; 4:110-2; 18:29-31; 36:54; 45:24-37; 53:33-41, 56-62; 99:1-8). All that a person has done in this world is recorded in his or her individual record book *(al-kitāb)* throughout life (see RECORD OF HUMAN ACTIONS). When the day of judgment comes, the acts of everyone in this world are shown to the individual by God (e.g. Q 6:59; 10:61-5; 17:13-4, 71-2; 34:3; 36:12; 39:69-70; 45:28-9; 83:7-24). God is considered an impartial judge. He objectively evaluates that which the individual has done in this world. The objective character of the judgment is allegorically expressed by the metaphor of scales (e.g. Q 7:8-9; 21:47; 23:101-5; 101:4-11; see ESCHATOLOGY). Without the freedom to choose one's actions, personal responsibility for conduct on the day of judgment would be meaningless. Free choice is also expressly stated in those passages where God is said not to lead astray (q.v.) except if one chooses to disobey (e.g. Q 7:28; 11:101; see DISOBEDIENCE). Similarly, God cannot effectively guide those who are not willing to receive his guidance (e.g. Q 16:104).

In contrast, other passages of the Qurʾān emphasize God's omnipotence and omniscience and human responsibility appears completely eclipsed. Here, human destiny is said to depend on the will of God. He is the originator of belief and unbelief (q.v.), he guides or leads astray as he pleases. Whomsoever God desires to guide, he opens his heart (q.v.) to Islam (q.v.); whomsoever he desires to lead astray, he hardens his heart, narrow, tight, as if forced to climb to heaven unaided. So God lays abomination upon those who believe not (Q 6:125; see also Q 2:6-7; 7:177-9; 9:51; 10:98-103; 11:118; 13:27; 14:27; 16:35-40; 16:93; 18:17; 24:21; 32:12-4; 76:27-31; 81:27-9). God's omniscience furthermore includes foreknowledge of all future events which are laid down in the clear book *(kitāb mubīn)* or heavenly book (*umm al-kitāb*, see BOOK). In contrast to the record book, *kitāb* here refers to a book of destiny that contains everything that God knows (e.g. Q 6:38; 11:6; 13:38-43; 15:4; 17:58; 20:51-5; 22:70; 27:75; 35:11; 57:22-3). The idea of predetermination is also conveyed by the concept of fixed terms *(ajal)* set by God in his governing of the world and denoting, at least in some instances, the time of death (Q 3:145; 10:49; 11:3; 15:4; 39:42; 63:10-11; see DEATH AND THE DEAD).

In other passages a combination of determinist and non-determinist outlooks is found. In the following verses, for instance, the idea of a book of account seems to be confused with the idea of destiny or fate fastened on man's neck: "Around each man's neck we have hung his ledger *(ṭāʾir)* of deeds and on the day of resurrection we will present it as a book spread out [and say]: 'Read your ledger; this day you are sufficient to take your own account'" (Q 17:13-4; see also Q 22:67-72; 27:71-5; 34:1-5; 53:33-62; see RECORD OF HUMAN ACTIONS; RESURRECTION).

It has been argued (Blachère, Paret) that the discrepancies of the Qurʾān on the issue of human destiny are to be explained in terms of chronological development. During his early period, when the Prophet demanded repentance in the face of impending judgment (see REPENTANCE AND PENANCE), he assumed freedom of choice and responsibility on the part of his hearers. The opposition he encountered, however, called for an explanation which was found in the idea of predestination; the unbelief of his hearers must be due to the will of God (see OPPOSITION TO MUḤAMMAD). This explanation also served as a practical source of comfort for the Prophet who was thus freed from personal responsibility for the unbelievers. Other scholars (Rahbar, Räisänen) have argued that the determinist passages should be interpreted in the light of non-determinist sayings and attempted to show that there are no predestinarian teachings at all in the Qurʾān. In their view, the idea of human responsibility and of judgment according to deeds is so fundamental in the Qurʾān that it predominates even where the language has a predestinarian coloring. Nagel and Jomier do not see a contradiction in the two standpoints as found throughout the Qurʾān, but rather understand them to result from and stand in subordination to the notion of the divine who is both supreme judge and omnipotent, bountiful creator and preserver of his creation (see GOD AND HIS ATTRIBUTES; CREATION). Whenever emphasis is placed on God as the supreme judge over his creation, man's freedom and responsibility is implied. Whenever God is referred to as omnipotent, bountiful creator and preserver of his creation the deterministic standpoint is included (see POWER AND IMPOTENCE). It should also be mentioned that the Qurʾān, a text designed to call people to faith (q.v.), had no intention of precise theological harmony, but stands on the force of its rhetoric, much of which involves contrasting language to evoke a response in its hearers (see RHETORIC OF THE QURʾĀN).

Sabine Schmidtke

Bibliography
R. Blachère, *Le problème de Mahomet. Essai de biographie critique du fondateur de l'Islam,* Paris 1952; L. Gardet, *Dieu et la destinée de l'homme,* Paris 1967; J. Jomier, La tout-puissance de Dieu et les créatures dans le Coran, in *MIDEO* 16 (1983), 31-58; Nagel; R. Paret, *Mohammed und der Koran. Geschichte und Verkündigung des arabischen Propheten,* Stuttgart 1957, 1980⁵ (rev. ed.); id., Der Koran und die Prädestination, in *OLZ* 58 (1963), 117-21; D. Rahbar, *God of justice. A study in the ethical doctrine of the Qurʾān,* Leiden 1960; H. Räisänen, *The idea of divine hardening. A comparative study of the notion of divine hardening, leading astray and inciting to evil in the Bible and the Qurʾān,* Helsinki 1976; H. Ringgren, *Studies in Arabian fatalism,* Uppsala, Wiesbaden 1955; W.M. Watt, *Free will and predestination in early Islam,* London 1948.

Destroyed Cities and Peoples see PUNISHMENT STORIES

Determinism see FREEDOM AND PREDESTINATION

Devil

The fallen angel (q.v.) or jinn (q.v.) known by two names in the Qurʾān, Iblīs (q.v.) and Shayṭān. The ambiguities present in the English word "devil" (themselves a result of early Christian translation activities; see Jeffrey Burton Russell, *The devil. Perceptions of evil from antiquity to primitive Christianity,* Ithaca 1977) are precisely those reflected in the Qurʾān, such that the heritage of the Greek demon "accuser" and the Hebrew "adversary" are brought together in one character.

The word *shayṭān* is used 70 times in the Qurʾān in the singular form, including six times in the indefinite (Q 4:117; 15:17; 22:3; 37:7; 43:36; 81:25), plus 18 times in the plural, *shayāṭīn,* which is always definite. Etymologically, the word is related to the Hebrew *sāṭān;* and the passage of the word into Arabic is not clear, although it is usually thought to have come into Arabic through Christian languages (especially Ethiopic; see FOREIGN VOCABULARY). A recent study of early Qurʾān manuscripts has suggested another reason for the particular form of the Arabic word: The pronunciation of the word may be due to a misunderstanding of early Arabic orthography (see CALLIGRAPHY). The word was originally to be pronounced *sāṭān* or *shāṭān,* and the first long *a* of the word was written with a *yāʾ,* contrary to the rules of later orthography which does not allow *yāʾ* to represent *ā* in the middle of a word (but only at the end). The loss of understanding of that orthography then resulted in the pronunciation *shayṭān* (see Gerd-R. Puin, Neue Wege der Koranforschung, in *Universität des Saarlandes Magazin Forschung* 1 (1999), p. 40).

Iblīs, on the other hand, is used only 11 times in the Qurʾān, always as a proper name. The general consensus is that the word is derived from the Greek *diabolos.* Arab tradition connects the word to the verbal sense of *ublisa* meaning "he was rendered without hope," a reference to Iblīs' fate of being cursed and sentenced to punishment by God (see Jeffery, *For. vocab.,* 47-8, with a full bibliography). That sense of the verbal root is itself present in Q 30:12: "On the day when the hour will arrive the guilty will be in despair," and also Q 6:44, 23:77, and 43:75, with the same sense of the punishment of the evil doers (see CHASTISEMENT AND PUNISHMENT); in

Q 30:49 people are in despair (q.v.) over the difficulties of life. In none of those cases, however, does the figure of Iblīs actually enter into the picture.

The name Iblīs figures mainly in the stories of the creation of Adam (see ADAM AND EVE) and the subsequent fall of the devil (the context of nine of the instances of the name is the "bowing" before Adam). When the angels were ordered to bow before the first man Adam (see BOWING AND PROSTRATION), Iblīs refused (Q 2:34; 7:11; 15:31; 17:61; 18:50; 20:116; 38:74-5; see COSMOLOGY IN THE QUR'ĀN), citing the human's creation from clay as the reason (e.g. Q 15:33: "I am not going to bow to man whom You have created from clay of moulded mud"). God then curses Iblīs, calling him "accursed," *rajīm* (Q 15:34; 38:77, lit. "stoned," also used in reference to al-Shayṭān and the *shayāṭīn* and symbolically as "accursed" but meant literally in the rituals of the pilgrimage [q.v.; *ḥajj*]; see the commentary *(tafsīr)* tradition on the *isti'ādha* [the statement said before reciting the Qur'ān, "I seek refuge with God from Satan, the accursed"], e.g. Ṭabarī, *Tafsīr,* i, 111-13, trans. J. Cooper, *The commentary on the Qur'ān by Abū Ja'far Muḥammad b. Jarīr al-Ṭabarī,* Oxford 1987, 46-7). God orders Iblīs "out" (of paradise presumably; Q 15:34; 38:77) but the punishment promised to him (unspecified but cf. Q 26:94-5: "they will be thrown into it [hell, q.v.], they and the perverse, and the hosts of Iblīs") is delayed until the judgment day (see LAST JUDGMENT), as a result of Iblīs's plea. Iblīs is given the power to lead astray (q.v.) those who are not followers of the true God (Q 15: 39-40; 34:20-1). The name al-Shayṭān, however, is used in speaking of Iblīs' first act of temptation, when he tempts Adam and Eve to eat of the "tree of immortality" (Q 20:120-3; see also 7:20-2; see FALL OF MAN).

Al-Shayṭān's role in scripture extends well beyond this one myth (see MYTHIC AND LEGENDARY NARRATIVES), however, while the figure of Iblīs is confined to it. Iblīs may be characterized, then, as the one who is proud and disobedient (see DISOBEDIENCE; ARROGANCE), while al-Shayṭān is the tempter, and it is in that role that the emphasis falls within other sections of the Qur'ān when al-Shayṭān is mentioned. It is notable that the two names, Iblīs and al-Shayṭān, are used within the same narrative (Q 2:30-9; 7:11-25; 20:116-23) in such a manner as to discount a simple blending of separate myths related to these two names; rather, the narrative appears integrated and the change in name is best interpreted to suggest that Iblīs gained the name al-Shayṭān after his disobedience, which is how the Muslim tradition has frequently understood it.

The details of the story of the fall of the devil are very similar to those found in Jewish and especially Christian apocryphal literature (and quite distinct from the sketchy story found in the biblical text itself; see SCRIPTURE AND THE QUR'ĀN). The idea of the angels worshipping Adam and of the devil's refusal is found in the *Life of Adam and Eve* (written no later than 400 C.E.; see the introduction and translation by M.D. Johnston, in James H. Charlesworth, *The Old Testament Pseudepigrapha,* Garden City, NJ 1985, vol. 2, 249-95, esp. *Vita* 12:1-16:3) and the *Questions of Bartholomew* (likely third century C.E. in its original form) explains, among many details similar to the qur'ānic story, that the devil's refusal to bow was based on the objection that his essence was of fire (q.v.) as opposed to Adam's clay (q.v.; see the introduction and translation by F. Scheidweiler and W. Schneemelcher in W. Schneelmelcher (ed.), *New Testament Apocrypha,* vol. 1, *Gospels and related writings,* trans. R.M. Wilson, Louisville 1991, 537-53, esp. 4:54).

It is thus to al-Shayṭān that most of what

have become the traditional characteristics of the devil are ascribed. He has the ability to cause fear (Q 3:175), cause people to slip (Q 2:36; 3:155), lead astray (Q 4:60), precipitate enmity and hatred (Q 5:91), make people forget (Q 6:68; 12:42; 18:63), tempt (Q 7:27; 47:25), and provoke strife (Q 17:53). He is described as a comrade to unbelievers (Q 4:38), a manifest foe (Q 7:22, 17:53, 43:62), an enemy (Q 12:5). Guile (Q 4:76), defilement (Q 8:11) and abomination (Q 5:90) are associated with him. The image of evil (see EVIL DEEDS) as a "path," like that of righteousness, is conveyed in Q 7:16-7, "Said [the devil], 'Now, for Your putting me out, I will sit in ambush for them on Your straight path. Then I will assault them from in front and from behind, from their right and their left.'" Al-Shayṭān also is spoken of as "taking steps" and his followers take steps towards him (Q 2:168, 208; 6:142; 24:21; see also 4:83). He is seen as an influence towards a number of specific as well as more general sins (see SIN, MAJOR AND MINOR), actions which take people away from God. Among his tools to do this are several vocal attributes: He calls (Q 31:21), simply speaks (Q 14:22; 59:16), promises (Q 2:268), and whispers (Q 7:20; 20:120; see also 50:16; 104:4-5). The attributes, "the deluder" (*gharūr,* Q 3:33; 35:5; 57:14) and "the one who slinks or sneaks around" (*khannās,* Q 114:4) have particularly stuck with al-Shayṭān, such that they have even been used on occasion as proper names for particularly evil people.

The proper name al-Shayṭān may be distinguished from the qur'ānic plural usage *shayāṭīn* which is often thought to reflect Arabian notions of devils (although it is used in a sense which is not unknown within the biblical tradition as in the "adversaries" of 1 *Sam* 29:4). These "devils" can be humans or jinn (Q 6:112) and come in varying ranks (see SPIRITUAL BEINGS). The word is used to refer to the hosts of evil (Q 2:102; 6:121), the evil leaders among humans (e.g. Q 2:14) and mischievous spirits very similar to jinn (Q 6:71; 21:82). They are the friends of the unbelievers (Q 7:27), they make evil suggestions (Q 23:97) and they were believed by Muḥammad's opponents to be the source of his inspiration (Q 26:210, 221; see OPPOSITION TO MUḤAMMAD).

In exegetical material and other literature reflecting more popular images, especially those associated with Ṣūfism, the qur'ānic predominance of the evil influence of al-Shayṭān on humans becomes overtaken by the personality of Iblīs, ultimately reaching the point of mystical meditation on the "disobedience of Iblīs." This results from Iblīs's ascetic, worshipping nature (his refusal to bow down to Adam is an indication of how serious he took the command to worship God alone) and because of his personality which reflects human ambiguity and complexity (see ṢŪFISM AND THE QUR'ĀN). By no means is al-Shayṭān neglected, however, although the two names do become separated to some degree in later Islamic thought, such that al-Shayṭān is the force of malevolence (see GOOD AND EVIL) and Iblīs more of a symbolic figure of human failings.

A good deal of discussion has taken place over the original nature of Iblīs (and, thus, al-Shayṭān). One statement in the Qur'ān suggest that he was a jinn (Q 18:50, "They bowed themselves save Iblīs; he was one of the jinn"); and yet he was among the angels when they were commanded to bow to Adam. Resolving this apparent inconsistency consumed many pages in classical Muslim writing and continues to vex polemicists today. The problem revolves around an understanding of the nature of the angels and the jinn. The angels were considered incapable of disobedience; being sinless and able only to follow God's will, they are unable to have offspring, and they were said to have been created from light (q.v.). The Qurʾān clearly indicates, however, that Iblīs was one of the jinn, that the jinn were made from fire (Q 55:15, "He created the jinn of a smokeless fire"), and that he has offspring (Q 18:50, "What, do you take him [Iblīs] and his seed to be your friends apart from Me while they are an enemy to you?"). To resolve the problem, many solutions were put forth, and they are gathered together in works such as al-Ṭabarī's (d. 310/923) *History* and most Qurʾān commentaries (mainly when dealing with Q 2:34). One line of thought affirms Iblīs's angelic nature. The suggestion is made that jinn was a tribal or clan name of some of the angels (perhaps of the cultivators who lived on earth). The word jinn was also said to be derived from *janna,* paradise (q.v.) or garden (q.v.), and the jinn are a special class of angels in charge of access to paradise. In fact, Iblīs's downfall was the result of his pride (q.v.) at being in charge of everything between heaven and earth. On the other hand, some argued for Iblīs as a member of a distinct class of creation, the jinn. One story recounts that Iblīs was a jinn who was captured by the angels when young and raised by them. This was the result of a battle between the two groups. Among the many reports on the subject, al-Ṭabarī states, "God created the angels on Wednesday, he created the jinn on Thursday, and he created Adam on Friday.... Some jinn disbelieved, and the angels went down to them on earth to fight them. Thus, bloodshed (q.v.) and corruption (q.v.) came into being on earth." (Ṭabarī, *Taʾrīkh,* i, 82, trans. Rosenthal, 253) and "the angels used to fight the jinn and Iblīs was taken captive. He was young and used to worship together with the angels" (i, 85, trans. 256). Popular imagination wound these and other such narrative fragments into an imaginative story to reconcile the various qurʾānic elements, although no consensus was truly reached as to the nature or origin of Iblīs.

Andrew Rippin

Bibliography
Primary: Ṭabarī, *Taʾrīkh,* i, esp. 78-86, trans. F. Rosenthal, *The history of al-Ṭabarī,* volume 1, *General introduction and from the creation to the flood,* Albany 1989, 249-57.
Secondary: H. Algar, "Eblīs" in *Encyclopaedia Iranica,* vol. 7, fasc. 6; P.J. Awn, *Satan's tragedy and redemption. Iblīs in Sufi psychology,* Leiden 1983 (the fullest treatment of the devil in Islam, especially pp. 18-56 on qurʾānic commentaries and ḥadīth); E. Beck, Iblis und Mensch, Satan und Adam. Der Werdegang einer koranischen Erzählung, in *Muséon* 89 (1976), 195-244; J. Chabbi, *Le seigneur des tribus. L'islam de Mahomet,* Paris 1997, 185-211; A. Eichler, *Die Dschinn, Teufel und Engel im Koran,* Leipzig 1928; F. Rahman, *Major themes of the Qurʾān,* Minneapolis and Chicago 1980, 121-31; H. Speyer, *Die biblischen Erzählungen im Qoran,* Gräfenhainichen 1931, esp. pp. 54-60; A.T. Welch, Allah and other supernatural beings. The emergence of the Qurʾānic doctrine of *tawḥīd,* in *Journal of the American Academy of Religion* (thematic issue) 47 (1979), 733-58.

Dhikr see PRAYER

Dhimma see PEOPLE OF THE BOOK

Dhū l-Kifl

An enigmatic figure, whose name appears in the Qurʾān in two places: "And [remember] Ismāʿīl (see ISHMAEL) and Idrīs (q.v.) and Dhū l-Kifl, all of them were patient" (Q 21:85); "And call to mind Ismāʿīl and Alyasaʿ and Dhū l-Kifl and all of the best" (Q 38:48).

In some exegetical works, it is held that Dhū l-Kifl was a prophet since he is mentioned alongside other prophets (see PROPHETS AND PROPHETHOOD). Most exegetes, however, deny his prophethood, confining themselves to repeating the qurʾānic statement that he belonged to those who were patient and the best.

A person named Dhū l-Kifl is unknown to the Bible (q.v.). One starting point for fleshing out this figure is the meaning of the root *k-f-l:* to nourish, to take care of, to oblige oneself *(kafala);* to entrust *(kaffala);* to vouch for, to guarantee, to engage oneself *(takaffala);* portion *(kifl,* also *naṣīb,* i.e. "share," sc. of felicity, *ḥaẓẓ);* the double and more *(ḍiʿf),* sc. of doing good works and of recompense (Azharī, *Tahdhīb,* x, 250-3; *Lisān al-ʿArab,* xiv, 107-10; see GOOD DEEDS).

Many stories are told in exegetical literature *(tafsīr)* and extra-scriptural tales *(qiṣaṣ)* to explain the name. While G. Vajda styles these stories "edifying," they do have a theological meaning. Ibn al-Jawzī (d. 597/1200; *Zād,* ad Q 21:85) tells, on the transmission of Muḥammad b. al-Sāʾib (d. 146/763), the story of Dhū l-Kifl's rescue of a hundred prophets threatened with death by an ungodly king and his care for them, which recalls the biblical story of Obadiah and Jezebel (*1 Kings* 18:4). Another story, in which Dhū l-Kifl promises a pious man who performed a hundred prayers (*ṣalāt,* see PRAYER) every day to do the same after the latter's death, first appears in ʿAbd al-Razzāq al-Ṣanʿānī (d. 211/827; *Tafsīr,* ii, 25), on the transmission of Abū Mūsā al-Ashʿarī (d. ca. 42/662; a prominent *ṣaḥābī,* see COMPANIONS OF THE PROPHET) and is based on *kifl* meaning "the double and more." The story of Dhū l-Kifl's kindness to a prostitute illustrates the meaning of *kifl* as "portion, delight" *(naṣīb, ḥaẓẓ)*: There, he solicits her with money, but overcomes the temptation and, having promised never again to sin, dies the same night (Thaʿlabī, *Qiṣaṣ,* 232; Shawkānī, *Tafsīr,* iii, 425f.). He was rewarded by eternal delight in paradise (q.v.; see REWARD AND PUNISHMENT). An example of Dhū l-Kifl's trust in God and belief in the freedom of the will (see FREEDOM AND PREDESTINATION) is the popular story of his appointment to succeed to the office of a prophet or king of the Israelites, on condition of committing himself *(takaffala)* to fast during the day, to remain awake at night and to act as a judge without becoming angered. The devil's efforts at making him angry produce no effect (Sufyān al-Thawrī, *Tafsīr,* 161f.; Suyūṭī, *Durr,* iv, 595f.). The story of Dhū l-Kifl acting as bailsman *(kafīl)* on behalf of the heathen king Kanʿān is an example of divinely conferred prophetic authority: Dhū l-Kifl converts the king and gives him a letter in which he guarantess God's obligation to reward the king *(al-kafīl ʿalā llāh li-Kanʿān)* with paradise (Fasawī, *Badʾ l-khalq,* 71-4, in three different versions; see also Ṭarafī, *Qiṣaṣ al-anbiyāʾ,* 239-41; Qurṭubī, *Jāmiʿ,* xi, 217, has all six stories).

Much in these stories reminds one of biblical tales of prophets and other heroes, especially the Elijah (q.v.) and Elisha (q.v.) cycle (*1 Kings,* 17; *2 Kings* 13) and Moses' (q.v.) appointment of Joshua as his successor (*Num* 27,16-23). Accordingly, Dhū l-Kifl has been numbered among the prophets by identifying him as Elijah, Joshua or Zechariah (Zamakhsharī, *Kashshāf,* iii, 581; Rāzī, *Tafsīr,* xxii, 183; Bayḍāwī, *Anwār,* ii, 77; Shawkānī, *Tafsīr,* iii, 425). His identification as Zechariah (q.v.) is possibly based on Q 3:37, *wa-kaffalahā Zakariyyā,* "and he entrusted her [Mary] to the care of Zechariah."

According to al-Ṭabarī (*Taʾrīkh,* i, 364), God called Bishr, the son of Job (q.v.), to prophethood after his father's death, naming him Dhū l-Kifl; he converted the Rūm (Thaʿlabī, *Qiṣaṣ,* 145; see BYZANTINES). When identified as Elisha (perhaps in recollection of *2 Kings* 2:9, "Let me inherit a double share of your spirit"), Dhū l-Kifl is said to be a cousin of the biblical and qurʾānic Elisha (Bayḍāwī, *Anwār,* ii, 314), a brother of the latter (Burūsawī, *Tafsīr,* iii,

368) or Elisha, the son of Akhṭūb or Yakhṭūb (Ṭabarsī, *Majma'*, vii, 107).

Heribert Busse

Bibliography
Primary: 'Abd al-Razzāq, *Tafsīr;* Azharī, Abū l-Manṣūr Muḥammad b. Aḥmad, *Tahdhīb al-lugha,* ed. 'Abd al-Salām Muḥammad Hārūn and Muḥammad 'Alī al-Najjār, 15 vols., Cairo 1964, x, 250-3; Bayḍāwī, *Anwār;* Burūsawī, *Tafsīr rūḥ al-bayān,* 10 vols., Istanbul, 1911-28; Fasawī, 'Umāra b. Wathīma, *Kitāb Bad' l-khalq wa-qiṣaṣ al-anbiyā',* ed. R.G. Khoury, Wiesbaden 1978; Ibn al-Jawzī, *Zād; Lisān al-'Arab,* xiv, 107-10; Qurṭubī, *Jāmi';* Rāzī, *Tafsīr,* Beirut 1411/1990; Shawkānī, *Tafsīr;* Sufyān al-Thawrī, *Tafsīr;* Suyūṭī, *Durr;* Ṭabarī, *Ta'rīkh;* Ṭabarsī, *Majma';* Ṭarafī, Muḥammad b. Aḥmad, *Qiṣaṣ al-anbiyā',* ed. R. Tottoli, Naples 1996; Tha'labī, *Qiṣaṣ;* Zamakhsharī, *Kashshāf.*
Secondary: Bell, *Commentary,* i, 555 (suggests Dhū l-Kifl to be Tobit, *kifl* meaning "deposit"); I. Goldziher, Dhu l-Kifl, in *EI¹*, i, 962-3; R. Tottoli, The *Qiṣaṣ al-anbiyā'* of Ibn Muṭarrif al-Ṭarafī (d. 454/1062). Stories of the prophets from al-Andalus, in *Qanṭara* 19 (1998), 131-60; G. Vajda, Dhu l-Kifl, in *EI²*, ii, 242 (with bibliography of secondary literature, to which has to be added Paret, *Kommentar,* 422, ad Q 38:48).

Dhū l-Nūn see JONAH

Dhū l-Qarnayn see ALEXANDER

Dialectic and Debate see DEBATE AND DISPUTATION

Dialects

Different forms of the Arabic language (q.v.). Commentators on the language of the Qur'ān, both medieval and modern, often turn to dialectal material as a relevant source for understanding the contents and linguistic background of the sacred text (see EXEGESIS OF THE QUR'ĀN). Already in the earliest sources treating of dialectal forms (dating back to the end of the second/eighth century), which were produced within the context of qur'ānic exegesis and the description of the Arabic language, the word *lugha* denotes not only language variants but also dialectal forms, i.e. the particular form of Arabic used in a region or by an ethnic (tribal or super-tribal) group (pace Hadj-Salah, Lugha). Kinberg's index of al-Farrā''s (d. 207/822) *Ma'ānī l-Qur'ān* lists 25 groups with their own forms of the language (i.e. *lugha, kalām*): Azd 'Ummān, Banū Asad, Tamīm, Tamīm wa-Bakr, Tamīm wa-Rabī'a, 'Ulyā Tamīm wa-Suflā Qays, Tihāma, Ahl al-Ḥijāz, Ahl al-Ḥijāz wa-Ahl al-'Āliya, Banū l-Ḥārith b. Ka'b, Ḥaḍramawt, Ahl al-Ḥawrān, Salīm, al-Ṭā'iyyūna, Banū 'Uqayl, 'Ukal, al-'Āliya, Banū 'Āmir, Quraysh, Qays, Kinda, Najd, al-Anṣār, Hudhayl, and Ahl al-Yaman, also called *lugha yamaniyya* (Kinberg, *Lexicon,* 744-53; see TRIBES AND CLANS). For all that, it should be noted that these early sources tend to refer to a vague notion of *lugha* without any further attribution. Al-Farrā', for instance, states in his discussion of Q 1:7 on the alternative expression *'alayhum* for *'alayhim: wa-humā lughatāni li-kull lugha madhhab fī l-'arabiyya,* "... they are two modes of expression, each one of which belongs to an accepted custom in Arabic" (Farrā', *Ma'ānī,* i, 5). Likewise, in his discussion of Q 2:61, al-Farrā' (*Ma'ānī,* i, 41) identifies the use of "corn" (*fūm,* variant reading "garlic") as an archaic usage of the language *(lugha qadīma).* The very obscure *lughat man qāla akalūnī l-barāghīth,* "the *lugha* of those saying 'The fleas devoured me,'" is Sībawayhi's (d. ca. 180/796) recurring label for what we would define as a structure in which the verb (which should be in the feminine singular form, but is in the masculine plural) agrees with its subject in number (for the analysis of the Arab grammarians, see Levin, What is meant).

Sībawayhi does not define the group following this usage, but Abū ʿUbayda (d. 209/824-5) ascribes the label and the personal use of this structure as it occurs in Q 3:113 and in 5:71 to one Abū ʿAmr al-Hudhalī, i.e. a person from Hudhayl (*Majāz*).

It is instructive that the early commentators do not identify the language of the Qurʾān as purely Ḥijāzī. For example, in Q 25:18, "They were a corrupt people" (*wa-kānū qawman būran*), the meaning of *būr* is identified with the better known term for "corrupt" (*fāsid*) in "the language of the Azd of ʿUmmān" (*lughat Azd ʿUmmān*) as opposed to the common speech of the Arabs in general (*kalām al-ʿarab*), in which it means "nothing" (*lā shayʾ*). There is, however, a tendency to prefer Ḥijāzī variants, especially when they are faithful to the orthography of the canonical text, e.g. the reading *fa-ajāʾahā* of Ahl al-Ḥijāz and al-ʿĀliya at Q 19:23 is considered "qurʾānic" whereas Tamīm's *ashāʾa* is called "another language not valid in the book (i.e. the Qurʾān)" (*lugha ukhrā lā taṣluḥu fī l-kitāb*). Indication of dialectal peculiarities offered early scholars a means by which to explain variations in qurʾānic readings such as the Ḥijāzī *mathulāt* and the Tamīmi *muthlāt* in Q 13:6 and, likewise, *ṣaduqāt* and *ṣudqāt* in Q 4:4 (see READINGS OF THE QURʾĀN).

The study of dialectal forms serves also to explain the linguistic peculiarities of the Qurʾān, for instance, the four occurrences of "They fear not meeting us [God]" (*lā yarjūna liqāʾanā*, Q 10:7, 11, 15; 25:21) in which the verb seems to mean "to be afraid of," and not the usual rendering, "to wish." A Tihāmī use of *rajā* in this sense is offered as explanation by al-Farrāʾ (*Maʿānī*, ii, 265). Even more interesting is the attempt, regrettably missing in the otherwise useful study of Burton (Linguistic errors), to recruit dialectal study for a convincing solution of the dialectal variant in "These two men are sorcerers" (*inna hādhāni la-sāḥirāni*, Q 20:63). Al-Farrāʾ (*Maʿānī*, ii, 183-4) explains the unexpected use of the nominative *hādhāni* (instead of the accusative *hādhayni*) on the basis of information received from a "most reliable" informant with Asad affiliation (literally, "most eloquent," in the sense of an accurate and natural instinctive sense for language peculiarities) who states that the tribe of Ḥārith b. Kaʿb has an uninflected dual case-ending *-ā(ni)* as well as an uninflected relative dual *alladhāni*. In the same context, al-Farrāʾ (*Maʿānī, ii,* 184) mentions another dialectal peculiarity concerning the *iʿrāb* (i.e. desinential inflection) of *alladhūna* as attested by the tribe of Kināna. A similar attempt is made by Abū Zayd according to al-Akhfash's (d. ca. 221/835) report in his *Maʿānī l-Qurʾān*, who identifies the dialectal form in question as a shift of all *-ay* to *ā* (e.g. *ʿalayka* > *ʿalāka*) and attributes its distribution to the tribe of Balḥārith (see Talmon, *Arabic grammar*). Could it be that this mode of utilizing dialectal data in the service of qurʾānic exegesis created the dogma which is formulated as "The Qurʾān has been revealed in seven dialectal versions" (*nazala l-Qurʾān bi-sabʿ lughāt*)? Similarly, al-Farrāʾ contends that *hayta* in Q 12:23, "Come, she said, take me [lit. I'm yours]" (*qālat hayta laka*) is a way of expressing oneself peculiar to the people of Ḥawrān which had been adopted by the Meccans (*Maʿānī*, ii, 40: *innahā lugha li-ahl Ḥawrān saqaṭat ilā Makka fa-takallamū bihā*) whereas "the Medinans read *hīta*," (*wa-ahl al-Madīna yaqraʾūna hīta*). This, it can be argued, is indicative of the thesis, developed later, that the virtues of the Meccan dialect in the Prophet's days comprised the virtues of all other dialects.

Modern scholarship on the relations between the dialects of old Arabia and their relation to qurʾānic language reached its peak in the 1940s with the studies of Koffler (Reste altarabische Dialekte) and Rabin *(Ancient west Arabian)*. A revision of their findings is a desideratum, considering the abundance of first hand information about the old philologists' original studies on these data (see GRAMMAR AND THE QUR'ĀN). Mention should also be made of Nöldeke's careful treatment of the question of dialectal features in the Qur'ān, particularly two exemplary cases. First (*Neue Beiträge*, 21), he identifies the qur'ānic negative particle *in* as a dialectal form of Mecca and Medina on the basis of later citations of local speech as recorded in al-Ṭabarī's *History*, Ibn Hishām's biography of the Prophet *(Sīra)* and in parallel passages. In the same study, he suggests Jarīr's use of *lawlā* to be a case of qur'ānic influence and notes the editor's change to *hallā* whereas *lawlā* was current in Mecca and possibly in Medina. A generally more skeptical attitude towards Arab philologists' identification of dialectal features, notably the indication of a Ḥijāzī-Tamīmī dichotomy, is also expressed by Nöldeke (*Neue Beiträge*, 3f.).

Rafael Talmon

Bibliography
Primary: Abū 'Ubayda, *Majāz;* Akhfash, *Ma'ānī*, ed. 'Abd al-Amīr Ward, 2 vols., Beirut 1985 and H.M. Qurra'a, 2 vols., Cairo 1990; Farrā', *Ma'ānī*.
Secondary: J. Burton, Linguistic errors in the Qur'ān, in *JSS* 33 (1988), 181-96; A. Hadj-Salah, Lugha, in *EI²*, v, 803-6; N. Kinberg, *A lexicon of al-Farrā''s terminology in his Qur'ān commentary*, Leiden 1996; H. Koffler, Reste altarabischer Dialekte, in *WZKM* 47 (1940), 48 (1941), 49 (1942); A. Levin, What is meant by *'akalūnī l-barāghīthu?* in *JSAI* 12 (1989), 40-65; Th. Nöldeke, *Neue Beiträge zur Semitischen Sprachwissenschaft*, Strasbourg 1910, 1-5, 5-23; Ch. Rabin, *Ancient west Arabian*, London 1951; R. Talmon, *Arabic grammar in its formative age:* Kitāb al-'Ayn *and its attribution to Ḫalīl b. Aḥmad*, Leiden 1997.

Dialogues

Conversations between two or more persons. Dialogue is an important and frequently occurring feature of qur'ānic style. Direct speech, in fact, predominates in many sūras while narration (see NARRATIVES) occupies relatively little space.

Of the four periods into which the qur'ānic sūras are usually divided (three Meccan and one Medinan; see CHRONOLOGY AND THE QUR'ĀN), the second and third Meccan periods are especially rich in dialogue. The lack of dialogue in the sūras from the early period may be explained by the fact that, throughout the first Meccan period, the Quraysh (q.v.) ignored or ridiculed Muḥammad's message (see OPPOSITION TO MUḤAMMAD). When, however, Muḥammad began to gain followers and pose a challenge to their supremacy, they began to take his presence seriously by raising questions about the tenets of Islam and doubts about its validity. In other words, as they entered into a "dialogue" with the Prophet, their questions and doubts were increasingly addressed in the Qur'ān. The criticisms made by the Quraysh, which began in the second Meccan period, continued into the third, thus providing an explanation for the Qur'ān's frequent use of dialogue in these two periods. In the Medinan period, dialogue was to become less frequent since the establishment of an Islamic state in Medina created a situation in which recourse to dialogue was less likely. Consequently, the absence of dialogue in certain periods is as significant as its presence in others.

Using the criteria of speaker and content, qur'ānic dialogues can be divided into five types. (1) Probably the most common dialogue is that between a prophet and the nation to which he is sent: A prophet presents his message to his nation, which usually responds by ignoring or rejecting it (see

PROPHETS AND PROPHETHOOD). Q 26 contains a series of such dialogues involving the following prophets: Abraham (q.v.; Q 26:69-82), Noah (q.v.; Q 26:105-18), ʿĀd (q.v.; Q 26:123-38), Ṣāliḥ (q.v.; Q 26:141-56), Lot (q.v.; Q 26:160-9), and Shuʿayb (q.v.; Q 26:176-88). (2) Another common example of qurʾānic dialogue is one which takes place between God and prophets. Here, a prophet is charged with a mission (see MESSENGER), a certain demand is made by a prophet and God responds, or a prophet is given an insight into divine acts (see IMPECCABILITY AND INFALLIBILITY). Examples are Q 2:260, where Abraham demands to know how God will resurrect the dead; Q 7:143, in which Moses (q.v.) demands to see God; and Q 28:29-35, where Moses, commanded by God to go to Pharaoh (q.v.), expresses his fear that Pharaoh will have him killed. (3) A number of dialogues are situated in the hereafter: In Q 74:40-7 the people of heaven (q.v.) and the people of hell (q.v.) converse; in Q 7:38-9 the people of hell curse one another; and in Q 34:31-3 the wicked leaders and their followers indulge in recriminations. (4) In some dialogues the speakers consult with each other about some important matter: In Q 12:8-10 Joseph's (q.v.) jealous brothers (see BROTHER AND BROTHERHOOD) discuss ways to get rid of Joseph and enjoy their father's love and affection, while in Q 27:29-35 the Queen of Sheba (see BILQĪS) solicits her courtiers' views on the appropriate response to Solomon's (q.v.) letter. (5) In some passages, only one side of the dialogue is related: In Q 2:34-9 God addresses first Satan (see IBLĪS; DEVIL) and then Adam and Eve (q.v.), and in Q 31:12-9 Luqmān (q.v.), a wise man of ancient Arabia, gives advice to his son.

Certain features mark the structure of qurʾānic dialogues. The onset of a dialogue may be signaled by a short phrase like *idh/wa-idh* + verb ("Recall the time when such-and-such an event occurred") as in Q 2:30-3, which reports the conversation between God and angels (see ANGEL) at the time of Adam's creation (q.v.) or Q 5:20-5, where the Israelites (see CHILDREN OF ISRAEL) refuse to enter Palestine when commanded to do so by Moses. Two other phrases serve the same function *fa-lammā* + verb + *qāla* ("When such-and-such a thing happened, so-and-so said," cf. Q 10:76), and *hal atāka ḥadīthu fulānin* ("Has the report about so-and-so reached you?" e.g. Q 20:9; 51:24-8; cf. 38:21-4).

Sometimes one dialogue blends seamlessly with another. In Q 26:10-7, God commands Moses and Aaron (q.v.) to confront Pharaoh, and at Q 26:17 God asks Moses and Aaron to tell Pharaoh that he must let the Israelites leave Egypt (q.v.). Although the speaker in this verse is God, the following verse, Q 26:18, opens with Pharaoh's response to the demand while addressing Moses — and thus starting a new dialogue. It is assumed that Moses repeated the demand before Pharaoh but since this is not explicitly stated, verse 17 serves as a connecting link between the two dialogues since it belongs to both. Another example is Q 12:80-2, where Joseph's brothers — while still in Egypt — deliberate on how to break the news to Jacob (q.v.) of Benjamin's (q.v.) detention in Egypt. They agree to inform Jacob that Benjamin was taken into custody as punishment for theft and that other members of the caravan may be asked to verify this (Q 12:82). Since the very next verse reports Jacob's skepticism about their statement, it must be assumed that the brothers, on their return from Egypt, repeated the content of Q 12:82. Dialogues like these impart continuity to the narrative by "splicing" two passages. This point calls for further comment.

The importance of dialogue in qurʾānic narrative can be judged from the fact that in some sūras it acts almost as an organizing principle. For example, Q 12 (Sūrat

Yūsuf), which has 111 verses, is conceived in terms of a series of dialogues: Joseph and Jacob (Q 12:4-6); Joseph's brothers (Q 12:8-10); the brothers and Jacob (Q 12:11-4, 16-8); Potiphar's wife and Joseph (Q 12:23); Potiphar's wife, Joseph, the wise observer and Potiphar (Q 12:25-9); Potiphar's wife, the Egyptian ladies and Joseph (Q 12:31-3); Joseph and his two prison-mates (Q 12:36-42); the king and his courtiers (Q 12:43-4); the butler and Joseph (Q 12:46-9); the king, the Egyptian ladies and Potiphar's wife (Q 12:51); the king and Joseph (Q 12:54-5); Joseph and his brothers (Q 12:58-61); the brothers, and Jacob (Q 12:63-7); the brothers, Joseph's men and Joseph (Q 12:70-9); the brothers among themselves (Q 12:80-2); the brothers and Jacob (Q 12:83-7); the brothers and Joseph (Q 12:88-93); Jacob and his neighbors (Q 12:94-5); and the brothers and Jacob (Q 12:96-8). It is thus through dialogue that the plot of the story advances. Even in the narrative portions of the sūra, direct speech occurs in the form of a comment, exclamation or aside (e.g. Q 12:19, 30, 62, 77). A detailed study of the sūras of the second and third Meccan periods is likely to highlight the role of dialogue in establishing continuity and coherence in the qurʾānic text.

Qurʾānic dialogues illustrate major themes of scripture. A statement of the themes may precede or follow the dialogues. Q 2:257 says that God is the friend and supporter of the believers and leads them out of darkness (q.v.) into light (q.v.) whereas the *ṭāghūt*, "those who rebel (against God)," are the friends of the unbelievers and lead them out of light into darkness (see BELIEF AND UNBELIEF; REBELLION). This statement is followed by three short dialogues: between Abraham and the king of his time, usually identified as Nimrod (q.v.); between God and a certain man whom God had caused to die for one hundred years and then brought back to life; and between God and Abraham. Taken together, these dialogues explain how the believers are strengthened in their faith by God and the unbelievers are led further astray (q.v.) by the *ṭāghūt*. Q 5:32, where the law of vengeance or retaliation (*qiṣāṣ*, see BLOODSHED; RETALIATION) is stated, is immediately preceded by a dialogue between Cain and Abel (q.v.). Q 37 (Sūrat al-Ṣāffāt, "Those ranged in ranks") underscores the theme of the unity of prophecy and people's unwillingness to accept it readily through a series of dialogues between prophets and their nations in which a number of prophets present essentially the same message to their nations who frequently respond to it negatively. Finally, the Qurʾān emphasizes that prophets, though chosen individuals, are nonetheless human and do not make any claims to divinity nor should they be considered as such. In illustration of this, Moses, when commanded by God to go to Pharaoh, shows fear and reservation with words which any other mortal might have spoken (Q 26:12-4). Similarly, when angels visit Lot in the guise of young boys, he is approached by his people, who demand that the boys be handed over to them. Lot feels helpless and utters, as would any other, a cry of pain: "I wish I had the power to confront you or could seek some powerful support" (Q 11:80).

The Qurʾān uses dialogue to portray character, as well, such as that of the prophets. A study of the dialogues of Abraham and Moses reveals interesting differences between them. Abraham has a sense of humor and would even play a practical joke on his opponents. In Q 21:62-7 he smashes all the idols (see IDOLS AND IMAGES) in the temple save one, and when questioned by the indignant priests, he tells them with tongue in cheek that it was the work of the chief idol, whom he had spared: "Ask them," he says curtly, referring to the broken idols, "if they can speak." In this way he plays upon the foolishness of deifying inanimate, powerless things. The dialogue illustrates Abraham's characteristic use of irony and satire (see LANGUAGE AND STYLE OF THE QUR'ĀN) to defeat his opponents in a debate (see DEBATE AND DISPUTATION). Just before destroying the idols, he engages in a mock dialogue with them, asking them ironically why they are not eating the food placed before them and why they are not speaking (Q 37:91-2). Moses, on the other hand, has a serious temperament and is also quick to anger. On returning from Mount Sinai he learns that the Israelites have started worshipping a calf in his absence (see CALF OF GOLD). Without stopping to investigate the matter, he rebukes Aaron for his failure to prevent the calf-worship. Aaron addresses him with the words "Son of my mother," which show Aaron's humility and his love for his brother (Q 7:150). In Q 26 Moses goes on a sea voyage to meet a certain individual whom the Qur'ān calls one of God's servants but whom tradition has identified as Khiḍr (see KHĀḌIR/KHIḌR). Khiḍr is supposed to initiate Moses into certain mysteries. In the course of the journey Khiḍr makes a hole in a boat, kills a young man and repairs a wall. Moses, who has promised to remain silent until addressed by Khiḍr, is unable to contain himself on any of these occasions. The dialogue which ensues between the two after each outburst demonstrates well Moses' impetuous nature. In Q 12 the characters of Joseph and many other figures are revealed through dialogue. When, for example, Joseph informs Jacob about his dream (see DREAMS AND SLEEP), he says: "My dear father, I have seen eleven stars and the sun and the moon — I have seen them bowing down before me!" (Q 12:4). The repetition of "I have seen" *(ra'aytu),* signifying as it does a certain hesitation on Joseph's part, is significant, for it provides insight into Joseph's character: Being modest, he is reluctant to relate a dream in which he receives homage from the heavenly bodies. His hesitation may also be due to the fact that he already knows the interpretation of the dream and feels that he may appear presumptuous by relating the dream. Only direct speech could delineate character with such subtle force. Similarly, only dialogue could have revealed Joseph's tactfulness in his attempt, while imprisoned, to convert his two fellow inmates (see PRISONERS) to his religion: When the butler and the baker (see BREAD) approach him for an interpretation of their dreams, he assures them that they will have the interpretation very soon; with this delay tactic, he proceeds to acquaint them with his own monotheistic belief.

Dialogue represents one of the ways in which the Qur'ān differs from pre-Islamic Arabic literature, which primarily exists only in the form of poetry. Essentially the impassioned utterance of the individual soul, pre-Islamic Arabic poetry (see AGE OF IGNORANCE; POETRY AND POETS; PRE-ISLAMIC ARABIA AND THE QUR'ĀN) makes very little use of dialogue whereas the Qur'ān — which presents a program of social action within a framework of struggle — reflects, through dialogue, the interaction between the Muslim and non-Muslim communities of Arabia on the one hand and among the members of the Muslim community itself on the other. Dialogue is inevitably interactive and social, and given the Qur'ān's overt and strong social dimension (see COMMUNITY AND SOCIETY IN THE QUR'ĀN), its frequent use in the Qur'ān is understandable. At the same time, use of dialogue makes the Qur'ān stylistically akin to the Bible, where dialogue is very prominent (see SCRIPTURE AND THE QUR'ĀN).

Mustansir Mir

Bibliography
R. Bell, *Introduction to the Qurʾān,* Edinburgh 1953; ʿA. al-Khaṭīb, *al-Qaṣaṣ al-qurʾānī. Fī manṭūqihī wa-mafhūmihī,* Egypt 1965; M. Mir, Dialogue in the Qurʾān, in *Religion and literature* 24 (1992), 1-22; S. Quṭb, *al-Taṣwīr al-fannī fī l-Qurʾān,* n.p. 1963.

Difficult Passages

Seemingly contradictory verses in the Qurʾān. Although qurʾānic scholars frequently used the word *mushkil* in its more usual sense of "difficult to understand" in reference to verses (q.v.) and individual vocabulary items in the Qurʾān, as a technical term *(mushkil al-Qurʾān)* it refers specifically to the apparently contradictory passages within the holy text. In this application, the term "difficult" may have been somewhat euphemistic. The analogous term in the study of the reports of the utterances and actions ascribed to the Prophet — where the possibility of genuine contradiction, at least among unauthentic reports, was admitted — was called "contradictory ḥadīth" *(ikhtilāf* — or *mukhtalif al-ḥadīth).*

The avowed aim of those who treated the difficult passages was nothing less than confirming the divine origin of the Qurʾān by vindicating Q 4:82: "If it [i.e. the Qurʾān] had been from someone other than God, they would have found much contradiction *(ikhtilāf)* in it." The Cairene expert in qurʾānic commentary as well as several other religious disciplines, al-Zarkashī (d. 794/1392), stated this bluntly: "Sometimes a beginner comes across something which he mistakenly believes to be a contradiction — and it is not one — so [the putative contradiction] needs to be eliminated" (*Burhān,* ii, 45). The range of difficult passages would seem to cover some of the same territory as that of the abrogating and abrogated verses (*al-nāsikh wa-l-mansūkh,* see ABROGATION) and at least one author regarded abrogation as a component of the broader study of apparently contradictory verses (al-Kāfījī, *Taysīr,* 228-35). In practice, classical Muslim scholars gave much more attention to the supposed instances of abrogation than to the other apparently contradictory verses, which deal largely with such matters as the creation (q.v.) of the universe, the nature of God (see GOD AND HIS ATTRIBUTES) and eschatological events (see ESCHATOLOGY), in other words, subjects to which the mechanism of abrogation could not be readily applied.

It appears that in the earliest times, Muslim attitudes about the validity of commentary on the difficult passages varied considerably, paralleling in some respects those regarding the "ambiguous verses" (*mutashābihāt,* see AMBIGUOUS). In one report, the early commentator Ibn ʿAbbās (d. ca. 68/687) is said to have refused discussion of the apparent qurʾānic contradictions (Suyūṭī, *Itqān,* iii, 83); in others he speaks volubly about them. Similarly, it remains unclear who undertook this criticism of the Qurʾān by pointing out its alleged inconsistencies. Those who harmonized the apparent contradictions were defending the faith against non-Muslim attacks (e.g. a Jew; Suyūṭī, *Itqān,* iii, 83) and even intra-communal criticism (cf. the title in Ibn al-Nadīm of the contribution of Quṭrub Muḥammad b. al-Mustanīr [d. 206/821]: *Regarding the verses of Qurʾān which the heretics question [Fīmā saʾala ʿanhu al-mulḥidūn min āyi l-Qurʾān], Fihrist,* ed. R. Tajaddud, 41). On the other hand, it is argued that the fact of the Qurʾān's revelation in a hostile environment encouraged the Prophet's enemies to claim inconsistency and contradiction (Zarkashī, *Burhān,* ii, 46). In fact, most of the examples of apparent contradictions cited in the various manuals are often trivial (e.g. the alleged objection that phrases like, "Indeed, God *was [kāna]* all-hearing, all-seeing," mean that he is no longer all-hearing, etc.) or concern matters of which humans can have no certain knowledge (e.g. whether the earth was created first [Q 41:9-11] or the heavens [Q 79:27-30]). Despite its immense theoretical importance, the discipline of difficult passages never seems to have been widely cultivated. In fact, most modern works ignore it. Furthermore, the arguments produced to eliminate the apparent contradictions, while important for a systematic presentation of the faith, usually offer little to inter-confessional polemic. As the passage quoted above from al-Zarkashī suggests, it would seem that the real reason for a scholar to study the difficult passages was to equip himself to silence the conundrums posed by students in elementary classes on qurʾānic commentary.

Eerik Dickinson

Bibliography
Ibn Qutayba, *Taʾwīl mushkil al-Qurʾān,* ed. S.A. Ṣaqr, Cairo 1393/1973², 65-85; al-Kāfījī, *al-Taysīr fī qawāʿid ʿilm al-tafsīr,* ed. N. al-Maṭrūdī, Beirut 1410/1990; Suyūṭī, *Itqān,* iii, 79-89; Ṭāshkubrīzāda, *Miftāḥ al-saʿāda,* ed. K.K. Bakr and ʿAbd al-Wahhāb Abū Nūr, 4 vols., Cairo 1968, ii, 445; Zarkashī, *Burhān,* ii, 45-67.

Dīn see RELIGION; LAST JUDGMENT

Disciple see APOSTLE

Disobedience

Transgression of or failure to comply with God's commands (see COMMANDMENTS). Disobedience, of which both angels (see ANGEL) and humans are capable, appears in a variety of forms in the Qurʾān. The Arabic root corresponding most directly to disobedience is *ʿ-ṣ-y* (e.g. Q 20:121, "And Adam disobeyed his lord"), which appears 32 times in the Qurʾān, and is translated variously as to disobey, to rebel, to resist, to flinch or to flout. Other roots reflecting different nuances of disobedience — such as sin (*kh-ṭ-ʾ,* 22 times in the Qurʾān; e.g. Q 4:92, 112; 12:29; also *j-n-ḥ,* 25 times, and *dh-n-b,* 27 times; see SIN AND CRIME), fault (*ʾ-th-m,* 35 times) and transgression *(ʿudwān)* of the limits sanctioned by God (*ḥudūd allāh,* see BOUNDARIES AND PRECEPTS) — also appear in the Qurʾān. Disobedience often appears in conjunction with the denial of God's signs (q.v.) or miracles (see MIRACLE), which leads one to go astray (*ghawā,* Q 20:121; see ASTRAY) and to transgress specified limits (*iʿtadā,* cf. Q 2:61; 3:112; 5:78).

The Qurʾān distinguishes between the disobedient and the obedient (see OBEDIENCE). Two verses serve as reminders of the fact that the angels are always obedient, even those in charge of hell (q.v.) "do not disobey God in what he commands them" (Q 66:6). Abraham (q.v.) admits to his father that "Satan (see DEVIL) is a rebel against the All-Merciful" (Q 19:44). However, human beings are the only creatures required to show proof (q.v.) of their obedience (various forms of the root *ṭ-w-ʿ,* "to obey, be obedient," appear 76 times in the Qurʾān). Nevertheless, for many different reasons, humans do disobey God.

Various peoples disobey the messengers (see MESSENGER) sent by God for their guidance. Noah (q.v.) states this in his supplication: "My Lord! Lo! They have disobeyed me" (Q 71:21). The people of ʿĀd (q.v.) act no better with regard to the prophet Hūd (q.v.; cf. Q 11:59-60). As for Abraham (q.v.), he was obliged to say: "Whoever follows me belongs to me, and whoever disobeys me, but You are indeed all-forgiving" (Q 14:36). Aaron (q.v.), Pharaoh (q.v.) and the Children of Israel (*Banū Isrāʾīl,* see CHILDREN OF ISRAEL) all disobey Moses (q.v.). The latter reproaches his brother concerning the golden calf (see CALF OF GOLD): "O Aaron! What held you back when you saw that they had gone astray, that you did not follow me? Have you then disobeyed my order?" (Q 20:92-3). Pharaoh himself repeatedly refuses to obey Moses: "Pharaoh disobeyed the messenger" (Q 73:16); "He denied and disobeyed" (Q 79:21). Similarly, after the disaster which befell him in the midst of the sea, he is told: "What! Now! When hitherto you have disobeyed and been of the wrong-doers!" (Q 10:91). So Pharaoh, like others who "disobeyed the messenger of their Lord" (Q 69:10), is condemned (see PUNISHMENT STORIES). Moses' people experienced humiliation, wretchedness and the wrath (see ANGER) of God because, to use ʿA. Yūsuf ʿAlī's rendition of Q 2:61, "they rejected faith, slew God's messengers and went on transgressing." Twice the Children of Israel are reported to have said, "We hear and we disobey" (*samiʿnā wa-ʿaṣaynā,* Q 2:93; 4:46), for (again, according to ʿA. Yūsuf ʿAlī's rendition) "the calf is the symbol of disobedience, rebellion (q.v.), want of faith (q.v.)." Moses, however, was an example of obedience, saying to his anonymous guide and spiritual leader: "God willing, you shall find me patient, nor shall I disobey you in anything" (Q 18:69). Another model of obedience is John, son of Zechariah (q.v.), for he "was not arrogant or rebellious" (Q 19:14).

Muḥammad, just like the previous prophets, experienced rejection by his own people (see OPPOSITION TO MUḤAMMAD). Q 4:42 reads: "Those who disbelieved and disobeyed the messenger will wish that they were level with the ground." In fact, God said to the Prophet: "If they [your kinsfolk] disobey you, say: 'Lo! I am innocent of what they do!'" (Q 26:216). The Qurʾān cites the battle of Uḥud (q.v.; see BATTLES AND EXPEDITIONS) as a particular instance of the disobedience of Muḥammad's followers: "When... you disobeyed after he had shown you that for which you longed!" (Q 3:152). So the followers of Muḥammad must not disobey because "[God] has made detestable to you disbelief, wickedness and disobedience" (Q 49:7; see BELIEF AND UNBELIEF). Indeed, women are mentioned as taking the oath of allegiance to Muḥammad so that, among other things, "they will not disobey you in what is right" (Q 60:12; see WOMEN AND THE QURʾĀN). Q 58:8-9 summarizes the qurʾānic position on disobedience: Regarding hypocrites (see HYPOCRITES AND HYPOCRISY), Q 58:8 states, "Did you not see those who were forbidden to hold secret counsels... and now conspire together for sin, transgression and disobedience toward the messenger." Q 58:9 then reads, "O believers! When you hold secret counsel, do it not for sin, transgression and disobedience toward the messenger; but do it for righteousness and piety (q.v.); and fear God." Jews (see JEWS AND JUDAISM), who are identified as disbelieving in the revelations of God, are described as having incurred the wrath of God (see ANGER) "because they were rebellious and used to transgress" (Q 3:112). This disobedience had also been denounced by the messengers before Muḥammad: "They were cursed by the tongue of David (q.v.), and of Jesus (q.v.), son of Mary (q.v.), because they disobeyed and used to transgress" (Q 5:78).

To disobey his messengers is to disobey God himself, a truth asserted on three occasions, each of which implies various consequences: "Whoever disobeys God and his messenger" and "transgresses his limits, he will make him enter fire (q.v.)" (Q 4:14); "he verily goes astray in error (q.v.) manifest" (Q 33:36); "his is the fire of hell" (Q 72:23). It is the disobedience towards God which is the most serious infraction. This, indeed, was Adam's (see ADAM AND EVE) sin: "And Adam disobeyed his Lord, so went astray" (Q 20:121). Herein lies the central theme expressed by the messengers of God: In no way was God to be disobeyed. Sent to the Thamūd (q.v.), Ṣāliḥ (q.v.) expressed this fear in his own way: "Who will save me from God if I disobey Him?" (Q 11:63). Muḥammad likewise expresses this fear: "If I were to disobey my Lord, I should myself fear retribution of an awful day" (Q 10:15). He is actually commanded to express such a fear on two occasions: "Say: I would verily, if I disobeyed my Lord, fear retribution of an awful day" (Q 6:15; 39:13; see REWARD AND PUNISHMENT).

These, then, are the types of disobedience which appear in the Qurʾān: Those who disobey the messengers are really disobeying him who sent them. One interpretation of the prophetic mission is that the prophets obey God's law and beg God that they might in no way be rebellious *(ʿaṣī)* to his will (see PROPHETS AND PROPHETHOOD). Does not the fear of God *(taqwā)* consist in obeying his commands *(awāmir)?* If obedience to God's commands is the proper response in gratitude for his benificence, is not disobedience, then, the highest form of ingratitude? See GRATITUDE AND INGRATITUDE; SIN, MAJOR AND MINOR.

Maurice Borrmans

Bibliography
ʿA.Y. ʿAlī, *The glorious Qurʾān*, 1934; Arberry; Pickthall; L. Gardet, *Dieu et la destinée de l'homme*, Paris 1967, 85-6.

Dissension

Partisan quarreling which, in the Qurʾān, denotes religious sectarianism. The qurʾānic concept of dissension is expressed by the Arabic terms *ikhtilāf* or *tafarruq*, both of which carry a pejorative sense. According to Q 2:213 and 10:19, humankind started its existence on earth as a united religious community. The nature of this primordial religion is not specified in the Qurʾān; in exegetical literature it is described as "the religion of truth" *(dīn al-ḥaqq)*, sometimes explicitly equated with Islam. The dissension that set in later and resulted in the disruption of this unity is seen as a negative development, which God wanted to rectify by sending prophets to preach and warn (see PROPHETS AND PROPHETHOOD; WARNER). Dissension is reported to have been rampant between Jews and Christians who denounced each other's religion (Q 2:113; see JEWS AND JUDAISM; CHRISTIANS AND CHRISTIANITY). Dissension within each of these two scriptuary communities (see PEOPLE OF THE BOOK) was also recorded: Some believed in the revelation they received and some rejected it (Q 2:253). The Qurʾān instructs Muslims not to follow the example of the scriptuaries but rather to guard their own unity (Q 3:103, 105). Religious dissension is thus perceived as a negative phenomenon; nevertheless, God did not use his power to unify all humanity in one religious community and saved from dissension only those to whom he showed mercy (q.v.; Q 11:117-8; see COMMUNITY AND SOCIETY IN THE QURʾĀN).

Attitudes to dissension in the ḥadīth vary (see ḤADĪTH AND THE QURʾĀN). Prior to his death, the Prophet intended to write a document that — according to some interpretations — would have prevented later dissension among Muslims. He is also reported to have said that "Unity is tantamount to (divine) mercy while dissension is torment" *(al-jamāʿa raḥma wa-l-furqa ʿadhāb*, Ibn Ḥanbal, *Musnad*, iv, 278, 375). The Companion of the Prophet, Ḥudhayfa b. al-Yamān, advocated the codification of the Qurʾān to save Muslims from the dissension that plagued Jews and Christians (Bukhārī, *Ṣaḥīḥ, Faḍāʾil al-Qurʾān*, 3, iii, 393;

see THE COLLECTION OF THE QUR'ĀN). Given the failure to achieve this ideal of unity, however, a ḥadīth offers the gloomy prospect of the division of the Muslim community into 73 sects, only one of which will merit paradise (q.v.; Dārimī, *Sunan,* ii, 158).

In support of the opposing view is the well-known tradition which maintains that "dissension among my Companions (or in my community) is (divine) mercy" *(ihktilāfu aṣḥābī/ummatī raḥma)*. Diversity among the Companions of the Prophet (q.v.) is implied and legitimized in a tradition that states: "My Companions are like the stars: Whichever one [of them] you follow, you will find the straight path" *(aṣḥābī ka-l-nujūm bi-ayyihim iqtadaytum ihtadaytum)*. Such diversity was seen as minimizing the danger of deviations from the prophetic sunna (q.v.). Similarly, the Umayyad ʿUmar b. ʿAbd al-ʿAzīz (r. 99/717-101/720) gave legitimacy to the diverse views of the religious scholars *(ʿulamāʾ)* in various areas of the Muslim state and refused to impose a unified code on all (Dārimī, *Sunan,* i, 122). The Shāfiʿī jurist al-Dimashqī (fl. eighth/fourteenth century) wrote in the introduction to his *Raḥmat al-umma fī ikhtilāf al-aʾimma* that the scholars "dissented while exerting themselves in the search of truth and their dissension was mercy for the people" *(fa-khtalafū bi-shiddat ijtihādihim fī ṭalab al-ḥaqq wa-kāna ikhtilāfuhum raḥmatan lil-khalq)*.

Traditions with a sympathetic view of dissension were not included in the canonical collections of ḥadīth. They were relegated to compilations of lesser authority or to compilations dedicated to traditions considered "fabricated" *(mawḍūʿ)* by the Muslim mainstream. Conversely, traditions advocating unity found their way into the more authoritative compilations. This is an indication of the importance attributed by mainstream Islam to the unity of religious belief. Nevertheless, the idea of dissension was accepted in jurisprudential literature, where differences of opinion between schools of law and individual jurists became a permanent fact of life (for a survey of relevant literature, see J. Schacht, Ikhtilāf; see LAW AND THE QUR'ĀN; CREEDS). In an attempt to find theological justification for the existence of dissension amongst Muslims, some scholars have argued that without religious dissension the world would cease to be a place of trial (q.v.), in which people must choose the right way; there would be no need of *ijtihād* and the *ʿulamāʾ* would loose their prestige *(faḍīla)* as arbiters of the law.

Political dissension in the Muslim community is referred to as "strife" *(fitna)*, sometimes equated with *ikhtilāf* (see Ibn Ḥanbal, *Musnad,* ii, 345; v, 292). Al-Bukhārī (d. 256/870; *Ṣaḥīḥ, Maghāzī,* 12, iii, 70) mentions two such moments of strife in early Muslim history: the assassination of ʿUthmān (q.v.) and the battle of Ḥarra (see L. Veccia Vaglieri, al-Ḥarra). The struggle between ʿAlī (see ʿALĪ B. ABĪ ṬĀLIB) and Muʿāwiya and other internal disputes among the Muslims are also considered to be strife which threatened the unity of the Muslim community (see also REBELLION).

Yohanan Friedmann

Bibliography

Primary: Bukhārī, *Ṣaḥīḥ;* Dārimī, *Sunan,* Medina 1966; Dhahabī, *Mīzān al-iʿtidāl,* ed. ʿA.M. al-Bijāwī, nos. 1511, 2299; al-Dimashqī (al-ʿUthmānī), Abū ʿAbdallāh Muḥammad, *Raḥmat al-umma fī ikhtilāf al-aʾimma,* Cairo 1300/1883, 2; al-Fattanī, Muḥammad al-Ṭāhir b. Aḥmad al-Hindī, *Tadhkirat al-mawḍūʿāt,* Beirut n.d., 90-1; Ibn Ḥanbal, *Musnad;* Ismāʿīl b. Muḥammad al-Jarrāḥī, *Kashf al-khafāʾ wa-muzīl al-ilbās ʿammā shtahara min al-aḥādīth ʿalā alsinat al-nās,* Beirut 1351 AH, i, 132, no. 381 (for *aṣḥābī ka-l-nujūm bi-ayyihim iqtadaytum ihtadaytum*); al-Khaṭṭābī, Ḥamd b. Muḥammad, *Aʿlām al-ḥadīth fī sharḥ Ṣaḥīḥ al-Bukhārī,* Mecca 1988-, i, 217-2 (for *ihktilāfu ummatī raḥma;* I am indebted to V. Tokatli for this reference); Murtaḍā al-Zabīdī, *Itḥāf al-sāda al-muttaqīn bi-sharḥ asrār Iḥyāʾ ʿulūm al-dīn,* 10 vols., Cairo 1311/1894, i, 204-6;

al-Muttaqī al-Hindī, *Kanz al-ʿummāl,* 18 vols., Aleppo 1969-1984, x, 136 (no. 28686). Secondary: van Ess, *TG,* iv, 654-60; L. Gardet, Fitna, in *EI²,* ii, 930-1; I. Goldziher, *The Ẓahiris,* trans. and ed. W. Behn, Leiden 1971, 89-102; G.H.A. Juynboll, Muslim's introduction to his *Ṣaḥīḥ,* translated and annotated with an excursus on the chronology of *fitna* and *bidʿa,* in *JSAI* 5 (1984), 303-8; R. Paret, Innerislamischer Pluralismus, in U. Haarman and P. Bachmann (eds.), *Die islamische Welt zwischen Mittelalter und Neuzeit. Festschrift für Hans Robert Römer zum 65. Geburtstag,* Beirut 1979, 523-9; J. Schacht, Ikhtilāf, in *EI²,* iii, 1061-2; id., *The origins of Muhammadan jurisprudence,* Oxford 1950, 95-7; R. Sellheim, *Der zweite Bürgerkrieg im Islam (680-692),* Wiesbaden 1970; L. Veccia Vaglieri, al-Ḥarra, in *EI²,* iii, 226-7.

Dissimulation

The action of concealing one's religious convictions when divulgence would bring danger or death, called *taqiyya* in Arabic. Two qurʾānic verses seem to allow Muslims to conceal their true convictions in case of danger, i.e. Q 3:28 and 40:28 (cf. Q 16:106). The two main terms found in these verses for tactical dissimulation or mental concealment in matters of faith are *taqiyya,* literally "care" or "fear" (from the same root *w-q-y* come *tattaqū* and *tuqātan* in Q 3:28) and *kitmān,* literally "the act of concealing or hiding" (from *k-t-m,* cf. *yaktumu* in Q 40:28).

The first Muslims to have practiced *taqiyya* seem to be the ʿAlid Kaysāniyya (Qummī, *Kitāb al-Maqālāt,* 22) and the Khārijīs (q.v.) except for the Azāriqa sub-sect who considered *taqiyya* illicit (Shahrastānī, *Milal,* 379). Another Khārijī sub-sect, the Najadāt, used it both in word and deed, the Ṣufriyya only in speech (Shahrastānī, *Milal,* 379, 413; Goldziher, Das Prinzip, 217/63). Among the Khārijīs in general, dissimulation was used in the context of *jihād* (q.v.) against non-Khārijīs while the Kaysānīs practiced it within the context of their esoteric teachings. All such sects designated regions outside their community as "the abode of dissimulation" (*dār al-taqiyya,* but the Azāriqa used "the abode of unbelief" (*dār al-kufr,* see BELIEF AND UNBELIEF) while referring to their own milieu as "the abode of openness" (*dār al-ʿalāniyya,* Qummī, *Maqālat,* 22; Ashʿarī, *Maqālāt,* 97f., 111, 120; Baghdādī, *Farq,* 108).

Although *taqiyya* is known to have been practiced by Sunnī Muslims in particular political situations (Meyer, Anlass und Anwendungsbereich, 47f.; Kohlberg, Taqiyya in Shīʿī theology, 361-2, n. 89), dissimulation has remained closely linked to the Shīʿīs (with the exception of the Zaydīs; see SHĪʿĪSM AND THE QURʾĀN) since the classical period. The origin of the practice most likely derives from the Shīʿī doctrine of associating *(tawallī)* with ʿAlī (see ʿALĪ B. ABĪ ṬĀLIB) and disassociating *(tabarrī)* from the first three caliphs, in particular the first two, Abū Bakr (q.v.) and ʿUmar (q.v.; Ashʿarī, *Maqālāt,* 17; Shahrastānī, *Milal,* 435). Later *taqiyya* would be more precisely applied to the concealment of particular religious beliefs, divulgence of which ran the risk of putting believers and especially their leader, the Imām (q.v.), in danger. Qarmāṭīs and later Ismāʿīlīs use it frequently (Daftary, *The Ismāʿīlīs*), but the notion and practice of *taqiyya* became an article of faith with important doctrinal developments only amongst the Twelver Shīʿa (Kohlberg, Imāmī-Shīʿī views; id., Taqiyya).

Taqiyya in Twelver Shīʿism is usually compared to the theological concept of *badāʾ,* i.e. change in God's decisions (see DECISION) or will. It is with this connotation that it became the principal accusation against the Twelver Shīʿa, reproached for hiding their erroneous and contradictory views under the guise of dissimulation (Nawbakhtī, *Firaq,* 52; Shahrastānī, *Milal,* 469).

In addition to the above-mentioned verses, the Twelver Shīʿa used other qurʾānic passages to legitimize their practice of dissimulation — called by them *taqiyya, kitmān* or *khabʾ* — such as Q 2:61, 4:83, 16:106 or 41:34 (Kohlberg, Imāmī-Shīʿī views, 396b; id., Taqiyya, 352). In Kohlberg's analysis, the concept underwent development in Twelver Shīʿism (Kohlberg, Taqiyya), allowing us to distinguish two kinds of *taqiyya:* (1) a "prudential *taqiyya*" which especially characterized the Shīʿa (q.v.) during the Umayyad period, when most made use of armed revolt against caliphal authority (q.v.; see CALIPH; REBELLION) and (2) a "non-prudential *taqiyya*" which took shape primarily after the drama of Karbalāʾ. This second form of dissimulation arose along with the Shīʿī shift towards quietism and the corresponding attempt to elaborate esoteric doctrines in justification of their positions, especially from the time of the imāmates of Muḥammad al-Bāqir (d. 114/732 or 119/737) and Jaʿfar al-Ṣādiq (d. 148/765).

Though Shīʿī law considers dissimulation unnecessary as far as less significant articles of faith are concerned (Kohlberg, Imāmī-Shīʿī views, 399b-400a), *taqiyya* nonetheless remains a canonical duty for fundamental points of doctrine (Amir-Moezzi, *Le guide divin,* 310-2). In many traditions attributed to the Imāms, Twelver Shīʿī teachings are presented as esoteric and hidden knowledge (see HIDDEN AND THE HIDDEN), a secret (see SECRETS) that must be concealed and protected from unworthy people (Amir-Moezzi, *Le Guide divin,* 143; 174-199). Generally, the Shīʿa present their doctrines as a secret, esoteric dimension of Islam in accordance with the tradition that "all things have a secret, the secret of Islam is Shīʿism" (*li-kulli shayʾ sirrun sirru l-Islām al-shīʿa,* Kulaynī, *Rawḍa,* ii, 14; Amir-Moezzi, Du droit à la théologie, 38-40). A special form of dissimulation, which seems to have been elaborated ever since it found its way into the oldest sources, is the technique of attributing writings to Jābir b. Ḥayyān (fl. second/eighth century), called *tabdīd al-ʿilm* (lit. "dispersion of knowledge") which consist of fragmentary esoteric teachings dispersed in the most unexpected places throughout the corpus attributed to this figure (Amir-Moezzi, *Le guide divin,* index, s.v.). Moreover, the *ẓāhir/bāṭin* (manifest/hidden) complex is at work in every level of reality, and each doctrinal system or religious science is composed of many levels, from the most apparent and obvious to the most secret. In other words, both exoteric and esoteric cosmogonies exist as well as exoteric (obvious) and esoteric (secret) qurʾānic exegesis (see EXEGESIS OF THE QURʾĀN: CLASSICAL AND MEDIEVAL), an exoteric and esoteric theology (see THEOLOGY AND THE QURʾĀN), a divulged and secret law (see LAW AND THE QURʾĀN) and so forth (Amir-Moezzi, Du droit à la théologie).

It is well-known that dissimulation and secrecy tend to be natural practices of minority movements. Notions like protection of the secret *(ḥifẓ al-sirr),* dissimulation *(katm* or *kitmān),* deception (i.e. making something ambiguous, *talbīs*), hiding the real state of one's conviction *(ikhfāʾ al-ḥāl)* all constitute important characteristics in occult sciences as well as in Ṣūfī (especially *malāmatī*) circles (see ṢŪFISM AND THE QURʾĀN), in philosophical teachings or in mystical poetry, especially in Persian (Suhrawardī, *ʿAwārif,* 72; Hujwīrī, *Kashf,* 500-1; ʿAfīfī, *Malāmatiyya,* 89, 117; Shaybī, *Taqiyya,* 20f.). In Persian literature, for instance, poets constantly refer to "the affair of al-Ḥallāj," the famous mystic who was brutally tortured and executed in 309/922 and to his divulgence of the secret *par excellence,* i.e. the utterance of the celebrated *shaṭḥ* (ecstatic exclamation): "I am the

Truth" *(anā l-ḥaqq)*. The greatest Persian mystical poets, like ʿAṭṭār (d. 627/1230), ʿIrāqī (d. 688/1289) or Ḥāfiẓ (d. 792/1390), often make allusion to the "the crucified one of Baghdad" (i.e. al-Ḥallāj, d. 309/922) and call authentically inspired individuals "people of the secret" *(ahl-e rāz*, Khorramshāhī, *Ḥāfiẓ Nāmeh)*.

Mohammad Ali Amir-Moezzi

Bibliography
Primary: al-Ashʿarī, Abū l-Ḥasan ʿAlī b. Ismāʿīl, *Maqālāt al-islāmiyyīn wa-khtilāf al-muṣallīn*, ed. H. Ritter, Wiesbaden 1382/1963²; Baghdādī, *Farq*, ed. M. ʿAbd al-Ḥamīd, Cairo; Hujwīrī, *Kashf al-maḥjūb* (in Persian), ed. Jukovski, Teheran 1399/1979; Kulaynī, Abū Jaʿfar Muḥammad b. Yaʿqūb, *al-Rawḍa min al-Kāfī*, ed. H. Rasūlī Maḥallātī, Tehran 1389/1969; Nawbakhtī, Abū Muḥammad al-Ḥasan b. Mūsā, *Firaq al-shīʿa*, ed. H. Ritter, Istanbul 1931; Qummī, Saʿd b. ʿAbdallāh, *Kitāb al-Maqālāt wa-l-firaq*, ed. M.J. Mashkūr, Tehran 1963; Shahrastānī, *Milal*, trans. D. Gimaret and G. Monnot, *Livre des religions et des sectes*, vol. 1, Louvain 1986; Suhrawardī, Abū Ḥafs ʿUmar b. Muḥammad b. ʿAlī, *Kitāb ʿAwārif al-maʿārif*, Beirut 1966.
Secondary: A.A. ʿAfīfī, *Al-Malāmatiyya wa-l-taṣawwuf wa-ahl al-futuwwa*, Cairo 1945; M.A. Amir-Moezzi, *Le guide divin dans le shiʿisme originel*, Paris 1992; id., Du droit à la théologie. Les niveaux de réalité dans le shiʿisme duodécimain, in *L'esprit et la nature, Actes du Colloque de Paris (11-12 mai 1996), Cahiers du Groupe d'Études Spirituelles Comparées* 5 (1997), 37-63; F. Daftary, *The Ismāʿīlīs. Their history and doctrines*, Cambridge 1990; I. Goldziher, Das Prinzip der *Takijja* im Islam, in *ZDMG* 60 (1906), 213-26 (= *Gesammelte Schriften*, ed. J. de Somogyi, Hildesheim 1967-70, v, 59-72); B. Khorramshāhī, *Ḥāfiẓ Nāmeh* (in Persian), Tehran 1987; E. Kohlberg, Some Imāmī-Shīʿī views on *taqiyya*, in *JAOS* 95 (1975), 395-402 (= *Belief and law in Imāmī Shīʿism*, Aldershot 1991, iii); id., Taqiyya in Shīʿī theology and religion, in H.G. Kippenberg and G.G. Stroumsa (eds.), *Secrecy and concealment. Studies in the history of Mediterranean and Near Eastern religions*, Leiden 1995, 345-80; E. Meyer, Anlass und Anwendungsbereich der Taqiyya, in *Der Islam* 57 (1980), 246-80; K.M. al-Shaybī, al-Taqiyya uṣūluhā wa-taṭawwuruhā, in *Revue de la faculté des lettres de l'Université d'Alexandrie*, 16 (1962-3), 14-40; R. Strothmann-[Moktar Djebeli], Taḳiyya, in *EI²*, x, 134-6.

Divination

The art of foretelling the future or discovering hidden knowledge through augury or omen (see OMENS). In Q 52:29 and 69:42, God reassures his messenger (q.v.) that he is not a *kāhin* (i.e. a soothsayer; see SOOTHSAYERS); in Q 36:69 and 69:41, Muḥammad is told that his message is not poetry (see POETRY AND POETS). Such verses, along with others (e.g. Q 21:5 and 52:30) mean to demonstrate that Muḥammad is neither poet nor magician (*sāḥir, siḥr*, see MAGIC, PROHIBITION OF), nor possessed by a demon (*majnūn, masḥūr*, see INSANITY). Whereas these last qualifications were applied to all previous messengers, only the terms *kāhin* (i.e. soothsayer) and *shāʿir* (i.e. poet) were used as a label for Muḥammad. This is related to the fact that these two categories played an important role in the pagan society of pre-Islamic Arabia (see PRE-ISLAMIC ARABIA AND THE QURʾĀN). In preaching to the members of this society, Muḥammad made use, at the very beginning of the revelation, of the rhythmic and oracular style then common (see RHYMED PROSE). His opponents took this as a pretext to reduce his message to the level of the rhymed prose (q.v.; *sajʿ*) of the soothsayers and/or the *rajaz* (end-rhyme) of the poets (cf. Fahd, Sadjʿ; see OPPOSITION TO MUḤAMMAD).

The Prophet of Islam was born in an era in which divination *(kihāna)* continued to form one of the rare manifestations of the divine in an Arab society in which religiosity, as it had been practised in the past, had reached a critical point, if it had not actually begun to fossilize (cf. Fahd, *Le panthéon*, intro.). Thus, the *kāhin*, with his various attributes (cf. Fahd, *La divination*, 91-129), continued to exist, although with nothing of his former prestige and prosperity (which may be concluded from the great number of divinities in the Meccan pantheon; see KAʿBA). The absence of other designations in the Qurʾān differentiating the *kāhin*'s functions is another indication of the collapse of a religious, cultural and social framework in the face of calls for the renewal of outdated religious and social concepts which no longer resonated with the society and its predominantly commercial activities and orientation. The *kāhin* was, in the eyes of Muḥammad's contemporaries, already scorned and despised, and thus calling Muḥammad a *kāhin* was a clear attempt to minimize his role and attack the revelation itself. Since his craft was limited to a traditional knowledge, the *kāhin* was confined to a less significant role than he had had in ancient society. The decline of religious thought and the cult in central Arabia in the fifth and sixth centuries C.E. reduced the *kāhin* to a mere charlatan, magician or even searcher of lost objects and camels (see CAMEL). More privatized forms of faith gradually replaced public acts of devotion in which the rites of pilgrimage (q.v.) remained the sole manifestation of community feeling. The development of individual conscience favored the adoption of new ideas; these found inspiration in the monotheist environment of the surrounding countries through which Meccan trading caravans used to travel (see CARAVAN). Such developments contributed to the depreciation of the surviving elements of the *jāhiliyya* (i.e. pre-Islamic times and customs; see AGE OF IGNORANCE) while opening a venue for the new horizons of enlightened spirits, such as poets, "monotheists" (*ḥanīf*, q.v.), preachers *(khaṭīb)* and sages.

In an effort to comfort his messenger (see CONSOLATION), always inclined to doubt his vocation, God asks him to tell his fellow tribesmen that his message cannot be compared to that of a *kāhin,* "It is the speech of a noble messenger. It is not the speech of a poet (little do you believe) nor the speech of a soothsayer (little do you remember), a sending down [i.e. revelation] from the Lord (q.v.) of all worlds" (Q 69:40-3). Another Meccan sūra (Q 52:29-34; see CHRONOLOGY AND THE QURʾĀN) emphasizes the same assertion even more forcefully: "Therefore remind [them]! By your Lord's blessing (q.v.) you are not a soothsayer, nor possessed. Or do they say, 'He is a poet for whom we await fate's (q.v.) uncertainty' [particularly times of war]?.... Or do their intellects [*aḥlām,* lit. dreams of an evil origin; see DREAMS AND SLEEP] bid them do this? Or are they an insolent people? Or do they say: 'He has invented it?' Nay, but they do not believe. Then let them bring a discourse like it, if they speak truly" (a listing of all God's works — beyond human capacity — follows). This sūra reflects the objections raised by Muḥammad's adversaries. The most relevant, so they believed, was the comparison of his first revelations to the prophecies of the soothsayers *(kuhhān,* pl. of *kāhin)* and to the trance of possessed poets. The Qurʾān underscores the following response to these objections (Q 81:22-5): "Your companion *(ṣāḥibukum)* is not possessed; he truly saw him [i.e. God] on the clear horizon; he does not hold back [what he knows] of the unseen (see HIDDEN AND THE HIDDEN). And it is not the word of an accursed satan (see DEVIL; CURSE)." The accusation levelled at Muḥammad was apparently based on observed practices. In their ecstatic manifestations, the ancient soothsayers used a more elevated style than that of common language. Prophetic and divinatory language is characterized by its rhythm, the structure of the sentence, the balanced use of verbs, a vocabulary full of imagery and the use of uncommon terms. This is called by the Qurʾān *zukhruf al-qawl,* "the adornment of speech," which sought to mislead and seduce people *(ghurūran)*. Arabs were (and remain) very sensitive to the melody of rhythm and the magic of the word. The first schism in

Islam (*ridda,* see APOSTASY), the return to paganism by the Yemenite tribes of the Madhḥij in the year 11/632, was instigated by Dhū l-Ḥimār ʿAbhala b. Kaʿb, nicknamed al-Aswad (i.e. the black one), a soothsayer, conjurer and magician, who "charmed the hearts of those who heard him speak" (Ṭabarī, *Taʾrīkh,* i, 1851-80). The second schism, led by Musaylima al-Kadhdhāb (see MUSAYLIMA AND PSEUDO-PROPHETS), also arose in response to the seductive powers of his oratory style (Ṭabarī, *Taʾrīkh,* i, 1929-57).

Muḥammad's opinion about soothsayers and divination illustrates his belief, particularly prior to his prophetic vocation, that they offered a means by which the mysteries of God might be unveiled. When asked about the *kuhhān,* Muḥammad is said to have replied: "They are nothing." Those with him remarked that these soothsayers nevertheless predicted events that came to pass. The Prophet replied: "The true part of what they say comes from the jinn (q.v.) who, like chickens, cackle it into the ears of the one into whose service he is placed, while they mix with it more than a hundred lies" (Bukhārī, for reference see Fahd, Nubuwwa). A ḥadīth reported by Anas b. Mālik (Wensinck, *Concordance,* ii, 26, s.v. *khurāfa*) confirms that the Prophet put great faith in revelations by jinn. This ḥadīth concerns a man by the name of Khurāfa from the tribe of ʿUdhra who was abducted by the jinn; he listened to their reports from the sky and passed them on to the inhabitants of earth (q.v.).

In other words, Muḥammad acknowledged that the *kāhin* received his knowledge from a spirit through possession *(majnūn),* i.e. a personal relationship with a jinn who observes from the sky events below and relays this information to his confidant(s). When the Qurʾān was revealed to Muḥammad, the angels (q.v.) were said to have been charged with guarding the sky by firing shooting-stars at the jinn in order to prevent their spying (Q 15:15-8; cf. 41:12; 67:5; Ibn Isḥāq, *Sīra,* 129f.; Ibn Saʿd, *Ṭabaqāt,* i, 1, 110).

The constant assertion that there is to be no divination after the Islamic prophecy *(lā kihāna baʿd al-nubuwwa)* was not accompanied by any negative assessment of a message transmitted by a jinn or *shayṭān* (see DEVIL). Though there is no talk in Islam of soothsayers, *kihāna* was never formally prohibited by the Qurʾān or even the sunna (q.v.). Two matters are, however, forbidden: first, consultation of a *kāhin* and belief in what he says, since this is tantamount to denying the revelation made to Muḥammad (Wensinck, *Concordance,* iv, 196); secondly, earning money as a *kāhin* or alloting a salary for this activity (Wensinck, *Concordance,* i, 505). Nowhere in the Qurʾān can one find a prohibition analogous to the one in Leviticus 19:3: "Do not turn to mediums or wizards; do not seek them out, to be defiled by them." It seems, however, that such a prohibition was not altogether absent; in fact, it is related on the authority of Wahb b. Munabbih (d. 114/732) that God revealed to Mūsā b. Manassa b. Yūsuf and his people the following: "I have nothing to do with whoever practices magic or consults a magician, with whoever practices soothsaying or consults a soothsayer and with whoever draws omens from birds or whoever lets anyone do so… Let he who sincerely believes in me trust in me sincerely…" (Ibn Qutayba, *ʿUyūn,* ii, 263; cf. *Lev* 20:6).

The Prophet's reluctance to condemn divination outright can be related to the overall conception of prophecy and medium (i.e. supernatural agency) of his day (see PROPHETS AND PROPHETHOOD). Since prophecy was considered an extension of divination and an indication of a superior state of being, it was only normal that certain pre-Islamic ideas and prophetic processes should have carried over into the young Islamic community. This explains the fact that the role of mediums, angels, demons and jinn remained prominent in the notion of inspiration as conceived by early Islam (see Fahd, *La divination*, 63f., 68f.; id., Kihāna, Nubuwwa; see also REVELATION AND INSPIRATION).

In conclusion, it can be stated that vestiges of ancient Semitic concepts appear in both the Qurʾān and the ḥadīth, including the recognition of a strong relationship between the seer and the divine: Knowledge of the seer originates in divinity and no incompatibility exists between the craft of the seer and divine inspiration; only the origin of the message, its nature and its content make it different.

T. Fahd

Bibliography
Primary: Bukhārī, *Ṣaḥīḥ;* Ibn Isḥāq, *Sīra;* Ibn Qutayba, Abū Muḥammad ʿAbdallāh b. Muslim, *ʿUyūn al-akhbār,* 4 vols., Cairo, 1925-1930; Ibn Saʿd, *Ṭabaqāt;* Ṭabarī, *Taʾrīkh.*
Secondary: T. Fahd, *La divination arabe. Études religieuses, sociologiques et folkloriques sur le milieu natif de l'Islam,* Leiden 1966; Paris 1987²; id., *Le panthéon de l'arabie centrale à la veille de l'hégire,* Paris 1968; id., Anges, démons et djinns en Islam, in *Sources Orientales,* viii, Paris 1971, 155-213 (Ital. trans. in *Méditerranée,* Rome 1994, 129-80); id., La connaissance de l'inconnaissable et l'obtention de l'impossible dans la pensée mantique et magique de l'Islam, in *BEO* 44 (1992), 33-44; id., Kihāna, in *EI²,* v, 99-101; id., Nubuwwa, in *EI²,* viii, 93-7; id., Sadjʿ, in *EI²,* viii, 732-4; J.-G. Heintz (ed.), *Oracles et prophéties dans l'antiquité. Actes du Colloque de Strasbourg (15-17 juin 1995),* Paris 1997 (see, among others, T. Fahd, De l'oracle à la prophétie en Arabie, 231-41; R.G. Khoury, Poésie et prophétie en Arabie. Convergences et luttes, 243-58); Wensinck, *Concordance.*

Divisions of the Qurʾān see FORM AND STRUCTURE OF THE QURʾĀN

Divisions of the Qurʾān for Recitation see RECITATION, THE ART OF

Divorce see MARRIAGE AND DIVORCE

Djinn see JINN

Dog

A carnivorous domesticated mammal, the dog *(kalb)* is mentioned twice in the Qurʾān, once in a generic sense and once in reference to the dog of the Men of the Cave (q.v.). Islamic law considers the animal unclean (see PURITY AND IMPURITY), and although this cannot be inferred from the qurʾānic references, it is evident in the exegetical literature (see EXEGESIS OF THE QURʾĀN). That dogs were not entirely shunned may be seen in Q 5:4, which declares permissible eating that which has been killed by "beasts of prey trained as hounds." It has been taken to mean any beasts (even birds) of prey, but the adjective "trained as hounds" *(mukallabīn),* is a derivation of *kalb,* indicating the importance of the hunting dog. However, the occasion for this revelation (see OCCASIONS OF REVELATION) is said to have been an order of the Prophet to kill all the dogs in Medina (q.v.), for the angel Gabriel (q.v.) would not enter a house in which there was a dog.

In Q 7:176, the dog is used in a simile in reference to the unbeliever or apostate (see APOSTASY): "So his likeness is as the likeness of a dog: If you attack it, it lolls its tongue out; if you leave it, it lolls its tongue out. That is that people's likeness who accuse our signs (q.v.) of being lies." Sometimes this is considered to refer to the biblical figure Balaam. The simile implies the thoughtlessness of the dog, but exegetes often claimed that the dog represents the most base of creatures, distinguished by the "weakness of its heart (q.v.)."

The story of the Men of the Cave (Q 18:9-26) contains two references to a dog, here presented as the companion of the Sleepers. The believers sleep, and "their dog stretches out its paws on the threshold" (Q 18:18). Utterance of this verse (or of Q 55:33), it is claimed, will stop a dog from attacking (al-Damīrī, ii, 265). More enigmatic is Q 18:22: "[Some] will say: They were three, their dog the fourth, and [some] say: Five, their dog the sixth, guessing at random; and [some] say: Seven, and their dog the eighth." Narrative details on the appearance and name of the animal, as well as its relation to the Sleepers, are described variously, but more esoteric interpretations, even from the most conservative commentators, have been inspired by the place of the dog in the parable. It is said to follow their religion, and in one common tradition, the men try to drive the dog away, but it miraculously speaks, telling them that it is the most beloved of God and will watch over them. The fact of its presence among them is proof of its exalted status, and it will be the only dog to enter paradise (q.v.). L. Massignon cites Ismāʿīlī explanations in which the dog is the spiritual instructor of the Sleepers or Salmān Pāk, accompanying the Seven Imams (Les sept dormants, 72-3). In other versions the dog is a human or the reincarnation of a human, or some other animal. There seems to have been a desire to see it as a human, perhaps as the owner of the dog, and a variant reading to this effect is attributed to Jaʿfar al-Ṣādiq (d. 148/765; *kālibuhum* instead of *kalbuhum*), but as pointed out by al-Ṭūsī (d. 459/1066), this variant is difficult to reconcile with "stretching its paws/arms on the threshold" (*Tibyān*, v, 30).

Bruce Fudge

Bibliography
Primary: In addition to the exegetical tradition for the relevant verses, see al-Damīrī, *Ḥayāt al-ḥayawān al-kubrā*, Beirut n.d., 242-72, esp. 249-65; al-Jāḥiẓ, *Kitāb al-Ḥayawān*, ed. ʿA.S.M. Hārūn, Cairo n.d., ii, 15-7, 187-90; iii 43-4; al-Rummānī, *al-Nukat*, 76, ad Q 7:176).
Secondary: I. Goldziher, Islamisme et parsisme, in *Actes du premier Congrès International d'Histoire de Religions*, Paris 1900, 135-8 (early Muslim attitudes towards dogs), also published in J. Desomogyi (ed.), *Gesammelte Schriften*, Hildesheim 1967-73, iv, 248-51; L. Massignon, Les sept dormants d'Éphèse *(ahl al-kahf)* en islam et chrétienté, in *REI* 12 (1954), 61-110, esp. 72-3; R. Paret, Aṣḥāb al-kahf, in *EI*², i, 691; F. Viré, Kalb, in *EI*², 489-92.

Donkey see ANIMAL LIFE

Doubt see UNCERTAINTY

Dower/Dowry see BRIDEWEALTH

Dreams see DREAMS AND SLEEP; SLEEP

Dreams and Sleep

Visions (q.v.) seen while asleep which convey a message or meaning of some import. Four different terms denote dreams in the Qurʾān. The word *ruʾyā* appears six times (Q 12:5, 43, 100; 17:60; 37:105; 48:27); the word *manām* appears four times, twice meaning sleep (q.v.; Q 30:23; 39:42) and twice meaning dream (Q 8:43; 37:102); *bushrā*, which means good tidings (see GOOD NEWS), is interpreted once to mean a dream (Q 10:64). All three words signify good dreams. For bad dreams the Qurʾān uses *ḥulm*. This word occurs twice, both times in the expression *aḍghāth aḥlām*, meaning "confused dreams" (Q 12:44; 21:5). Of the ten references, six deal with biblical figures: four with Joseph (q.v.; Q 12:5, 43, 44, 100) and two with Abraham (q.v.; Q 37:102, 105); the other references deal with matters relating to central Islamic issues.

In their remarks on verses that mention dreams, most qurʾānic commentators adduce ḥadīth sayings of the kind found in the canonical ḥadīth collections (see ḤADĪTH AND THE QURʾĀN). These sayings deal with the authority (q.v.) of dreams and their usage as a means of legitimization. (For a characterization of the nature of dreams in the ḥadīth collections, see *Manām,* Introduction, 36.) In citing these sayings, the exegetical works *(tafsīr)* associate the qurʾānic dreams with the general Islamic attitude toward dreams as expressed in the ḥadīth. The ḥadīth contributes to this association by referring to qurʾānic dreams and citing relevant qurʾānic verses in its dream chapters (for example Bukhārī, *Ṣaḥīḥ, Bāb al-taʿbīr, Bāb ruʾyā al-ṣāliḥīn*). The same occurs in other sources that dedicate special chapters to dreams, using qurʾānic dreams to support their interest in the topic of dreams (for example Abū l-Qāsim al-Qushayrī, *Risāla;* cf. the examination of *bushrā* below).

Some commentators suggest that qurʾānic dreams be classified according to their fulfillment and clarity. Al-Rāzī (d. 606/1210; *Tafsīr,* xxvi, 157), for example, mentions three classes: (1) dreams in which the message or description becomes reality, such as the message in Muḥammad's dream in Ḥudaybiya (q.v.), foretelling the conquest of Mecca (q.v.; Q 48:27); (2) dreams in which the message is fulfilled in the opposite way, e.g. Abraham's dream, where the message was to sacrifice a son but the reality was the sacrifice of a lamb (Q 37:102-5; see ISAAC; ISHMAEL); (3) dreams that need interpretation to be understood, exemplified by the four dreams in Sūrat Yūsuf (Q 12).

The remainder of this article is devoted to an examination of qurʾānic verses that allude to dreams (with a translation of the verses), a summary of the relevant *tafsīr* sections as well as an analysis of their applicability to the ḥadīth.

Abraham's dream

Q 37:102-5 reads: "And when [his son] was old enough to walk with him, he said, 'My son, I see in a dream *(manām)* that I shall sacrifice (q.v.) you; consider, what do you think?' He said, 'My father, do as you are commanded; you shall find me, God willing, one of the steadfast.' When they had surrendered, and he flung him upon his brow, we called unto him, 'Abraham, you have confirmed the vision *(ruʾyā)*'..." Exegetical commentaries on these verses add details to complete the account and raise a few questions about the content and process of Abraham's dream. Through such details and questions, the status of dreams in Islamic thought, not necessarily in the Qurʾān, was articulated.

Several commentators mention that when Abraham was informed about the future birth of his child, he took an oath (see OATHS) that he would sacrifice the child to God. In a dream he was reminded of that oath (Muqātil, *Tafsīr,* iii, 615; Rāzī, *Tafsīr,* xxvi, 153; Qurṭubī, *Jāmiʿ,* xv, 102; Suyūṭī, *Durr,* v, 307). Exegesis (see EXEGESIS OF THE QURʾĀN: CLASSICAL AND MEDIEVAL) further reports that Abraham saw the dream three nights in a row. In the morning after the first night, Abraham thought about the dream and wondered whether it was from God or from Satan (see DEVIL). The next night he had the same dream and then he knew that the message was from God. By the third night, Abraham was ready to sacrifice his son (Rāzī, *Tafsīr,* xxvi, 153; Baghawī, *Maʿālim,* iv, 569; Qurṭubī, *Jāmiʿ,* xv, 101-2; Suyūṭī, *Durr,* v, 308). Abraham's hesitation is understood to be in disagreement with the ḥadīth that states that prophets' dreams *(ruʾyā)* are equal to revelation (*waḥy,* Suyūṭī, *Durr,* v, 305; cf. Joseph's dream below). If dreams have the authority of revelation, Abraham should not have hesitated. Furthermore, the Qurʾān narrates that Abraham consulted his son about the sacrifice *(fa-nẓur mādhā tarā)*. This, in the eyes of some commentators, constitutes a contradiction: If dreams are authoritative, as indicated by the ḥadīth, why did this dream not elicit Abraham's immediate trust and certitude (see TRUST AND PATIENCE)? On the other hand, if the dream does not supply decisive proof of its reliability, which may explain the hesitation, how did it happen that Abraham decided to sacrifice his son after all? Al-Rāzī's (d. 606/1210) (*Tafsīr,* xxvi, 153) answer to both questions is that Abraham hesitated with regard to the dream *(ruʾyā)* but was reassured by a clear revelation *(al-waḥy al-ṣarīkh)*.

Attention should be given to the terminology used by al-Rāzī: Although the verse itself uses the word *manām,* the commentator refers to the word *ruʾyā* without indicating whether it was a synonym for *manām* or not. When dealing with *ruʾyā,* he also refers to *waḥy*. The difference between the two may be associated with the ḥadīth that defines dreams as part of prophecy (see Abū Hājir Zaghlūl, *Mawsūʿa,* v, 156; Kinberg, Literal dreams, 283-4, and n. 12; Qurṭubī, ad Joseph's dream, below). Al-Rāzī, when explaining how Abraham made the decision, puts *ruʾyā* and *waḥy* in a hierarchy, in which the latter authorizes the former.

The *tafsīr* emphasizes that Abraham was so determined about what he was going to do that the efforts of Satan to change his mind were in vain (Baghawī, *Maʿālim,* iv, 570; Suyūṭī, *Durr,* v, 306-7). Abraham made all the preparations and when he was about to sacrifice his son, a voice was heard, complimenting him for trusting the dream (*ruʾyā,* Q 37:105). This, according to al-Rāzī, indicates Abraham's awareness of the fact that the message delivered in his dream was obligatory. This does not mean, however, that the command was actually carried out (Rāzī, *Tafsīr,* xxvi, 156). Following this argument, al-Rāzī classifies this dream among those in which the message is fulfilled in an opposite way (id., 157).

Dreams related to Joseph

In Sūrat Yūsuf (Q 12) there are four dreams that are symbolic and require interpretation. As such they fit the third category of dreams mentioned above. In the beginning of the sūra (Q 12:3), Joseph tells his father that he dreamt he had seen eleven stars, the sun (q.v.) and the moon (q.v.), all bowing down before him (cf. *Gen* 37:4-6; see BOWING AND PROSTRATION). Later in the sūra we read about the dreams of the two men who met Joseph in prison. One saw himself pressing grapes, the other saw himself carrying bread (q.v.) on his head while birds were picking at it. Joseph interpreted the dreams to mean that the first man will pour wine for his king and the other will be crucified (Q 35-41; cf. *Gen* 40:5-19; see CRUCIFIXION). Verse 12:43 tells of Pharaoh's (q.v.) dream about the seven fat cows eating the seven lean ones and about the seven green and seven withered ears of corn. Pharaoh's counselors could not interpret the dream and defined it as *adghāth aḥlām,* "confused dreams" (Q 12:44). Joseph interprets the symbols as standing for seven good years that will be devoured by seven bad years (Q 12:47-9). Toward the end of the sūra Joseph's dream, mentioned at the outset of the sūra, is fulfilled with the arrival of his family to Egypt: "And he lifted his father and mother upon the throne and they fell down prostrate before him. 'See, father,' he said, 'this is the interpretation of my vision of long ago; my Lord (q.v.) has made it true'" (Q 12:100).

As in the case of Abraham's dream, here too exegesis contributes to the understanding of the status of dreams in Islam. While dealing with the verse that cites Jacob's (q.v.) advice to Joseph not to tell his dream to his brothers (Q 12:5), most commentators focus on the prophetic nature of this dream and elaborate on the relationship between prophecy and dreams. Al-Wāḥidī (d. 468/1076; *Wasīṭ*, ii, 600), for example, explains that Joseph was a prophet and states that prophets' dreams *(ruʾyā)* are equal to revelation (*waḥy*, cf. Abraham's dream above). Jacob knew that his sons, Joseph's brothers, would understand the meaning of the dream and would try to do away with Joseph. Thus he advised him not to tell them his dream.

For the same verse, al-Qurṭubī (d. 671/1272) adduces some of the ḥadīth sayings that actually underscore the reliability of dreams such as the one which defines dreams as part of prophecy (the 26th, 40th, 44th, 46th, 49th, 50th part of prophecy, *Jāmiʿ*, ix, 122-4; cf. Abraham's dream above; see REVELATION AND INSPIRATION; PROPHETS AND PROPHETHOOD). He further examines the qualities of dreams as truth-holders (see TRUTH), as prophecies that come true, and compares different kinds of dreams and different times of dreaming (Qurṭubī, *Jāmiʿ*, 125-9). He ends his commentary with the presentation of Joseph as a prophet and as the best dream-interpreter on earth (id., 129, ad v. 6). In his commentary on the verses dealing with Joseph's interpretation of the dreams of the two men in prison (Q 12:35-42), al-Qurṭubī raises a question concerning the actualization of dreams according to their interpretation: When the dreamer tells the truth, his dream will be fulfilled according to its interpretation. The process is different when the dreamer lies. In this case, only the interpretation of a prophet will be carried out. This is the way to understand Joseph's words: "The matter is decided whereon you enquire" (Q 12:41). Al-Qurṭubī explains that when Joseph interpreted the dream of the doomed man, the latter denied having the dream. To that Joseph answered, "Whether you saw it or not, 'the matter is decided whereon you enquire'" (Qurṭubī, *Jāmiʿ*, ix, 193). The question of the fulfillment of dreams is raised again by al-Qurṭubī when dealing with the number of years that passed from the time Joseph had his dream as a boy until he met his family in Egypt as a hero (Q 12:100). Forty years, as stated by al-Qurṭubī, is the longest time that can pass from the time the dream occurred until its actualization (id., 264 ad Q 12:100).

Al-Qurṭubī's elaboration conveys the exegetical inclination to consider qurʾānic dreams an integral part of the literature of dream interpretation *(taʿbīr)*. An examination of the *taʿbīr* literature shows that although it also manifests that it has been influenced by foreign cultures such as Babylonian (Bland, Muhammedan science, 119; Fahd, The dream, 351), Greek (Bland, Muhammedan science, 123-4; Fahd, The dream, 248; Somogyi, Interpretation, 2) and Jewish (Kister, Interpretation, 99-101). The literature on oneiromancy is, however, Islamic in nature: A basic requirement imposed on every Muslim dream-interpreter is a thorough knowledge of the tradition of qurʾānic commentary *(tafsīr)* from which many ways of interpretation derive (Bland, Muhammedan science, 132). Qurʾānic verses are also often cited in *taʿbīr* works and are frequently used as means of interpretation (id., 122; Kister, Interpretation, 90, 91; Somogyi, Interpretation, 15-8). Joseph appears in *taʿbīr* books in illustration of methods of interpretation (Bland, Muhammedan science, 125). Certain parts of the Qurʾān are considered protectors against bad dreams (id., 129-30) and verses heard or seen in dreams are interpreted according to the nature of the sūra in which they occur (id., 143).

More qurʾānic references to dreams deal

with issues taken from the biography of Muḥammad (see SĪRA AND THE QURʾĀN) and contribute to the establishment of basic elements of Islamic belief related to good tidings about the next world *(bushrā),* the battle of Badr, the conquest of Mecca, the nocturnal journey of the Prophet (see ASCENSION) and the accusation against Muḥammad of being inspired by *aḍghāth aḥlām,* "confused dreams" (see OPPOSITION TO MUḤAMMAD).

Bushrā

Q 10:62-4 reads: "Surely God's friends — no fear shall be on them, neither shall they sorrow. Those who believe, and are godfearing — for them is good tidings in the present life and in the world to come. There is no changing the words of God; that is the mighty triumph." Several definitions of "good tidings" *(bushrā)* are adduced in the commentary on this verse, among which "dream" *(ruʾyā)* is one. Dreams are the good tidings in the present world; the gardens of Eden (*jannāt Adan* (see GARDEN)) are the good tidings of the next world (Ṭabarsī, *Majmaʿ,* iii, 70). Apart from commentary, this verse is often adduced as an opening to examination of dreams. For example, al-Qushayrī begins the chapter about dreams in his *Risāla* with this verse in order to legitimize the interest Islam has in dreams (Qushayrī, *Risāla, Bāb ruʾyā al-qawm,* 304). Al-Qushayrī further develops the legitimization of dreams by adducing a set of prophetic sayings that denote the special value of this medium.

Similar traditions also appear in exegetical works. Al-Suyūṭī (d. 911/1505), in his commentary on this verse, cites a variety of sayings defining dreams as a part of prophecy that has ceased to exist (*Durr,* iii, 337-9; Ibn ʿAṭiyya, *Muḥarrar,* iii, 129). Kāshānī (d. after 1091/1680), on the same verse, quotes a few Shīʿite traditions to demonstrate the way in which the good tidings are delivered. Such is the one transmitted by ʿAyyāshī (d. early fourth/tenth) on the authority of Abū Jaʿfar al-Bāqir (the sixth Shīʿī Imām, d. 114/733): When a man is about to die, the angel of death comforts him by telling him that his hopes will be fulfilled and that none of his fears will materialize to hurt him. Then the angel (q.v.) opens a door facing the gardens of Eden and lets the man see his future abode (see GARDEN); there he sees the Prophet and ʿAlī (see ʿALĪ B. ABĪ ṬĀLIB) and Ḥasan and Ḥusayn (Kāshānī, *Ṣāfī,* ii, 410; see FAMILY OF THE PROPHET; SHĪʿISM AND THE QURʾĀN). Visions of paradise (q.v.) and descriptions of rewards in the next world are the most common motifs in the literature of dreams (see REWARD AND PUNISHMENT). By using these motifs, and by referring to ḥadīth sayings that legitimize the usage of dreams, commentators try to anchor dream literature in the Qurʾān.

The battle of Badr

Q 8:43 reads: "When God showed them to you [Muḥammad] in your dream *(manām)* as few; and had he shown them as many you would have lost heart, and quarrelled about the matter; but God saved [you]; he knows the thoughts in the breasts." Some commentators report that before the battle of Badr (q.v.), Muḥammad had a dream in which he saw the enemy to be few in number. Upon divulging the dream, the people were encouraged and declared that their Prophet's dream revealed the truth. In the battlefield, God, to fulfill Muḥammad's dream, decreased the number of infidels in the eyes of the believers (Muqātil, *Tafsīr,* ii, 117; Abū l-Layth al-Samarqandī, *Tafsīr,* ii, 20; cf. Rāzī, *Tafsīr,* xv, 174). This verse should be read together with Q 3:13 which states that the victory of the believers at Badr became possible through a divine sign *(āya)* which had caused a deceptive change in the number. Thus, if Q 8:43

deals with a preliminary, revealing dream, Q 3:13 describes some kind of apparition (q.v.) that took place on the battlefield in the fulfillment of the dream.

The conquest of Mecca

Q 48:27 reads: "God has indeed fulfilled the vision *(ru'yā)*. He vouchsafed to his messenger truly: 'You shall enter the holy mosque (q.v.), if God wills, in security, your heads shaved, your hair cut short, not fearing.' He knew what you knew not, and gave you a victory beforehand." Of the three groups of dreams presented above, this verse is used to demonstrate the first kind, where the message or description is fulfilled and becomes a part of reality.

In explaining the background to the verse, commentators emphasize that the verse alludes to a dream which the Prophet had before he went to Ḥudaybiya. In the dream, he saw the believers entering the holy mosque. The believers were pleased to hear the dream, believing that they would enter Mecca (q.v.) that same year. When this did not happen, the so-called hypocrites (*munāfiqūn*, see HYPOCRITES AND HYPOCRISY) became doubtful. The verse was revealed to encourage believers and to certify the trustworthiness of the dream (see OCCASIONS OF REVELATION), namely the future entrance into Mecca (Muqātil, *Tafsīr*, iv, 76; Ṭabarsī, *Majma'*, iv, 78; Shawkānī, *Tafsīr*, v, 55; Rāzī, *Tafsīr*, xxviii, 104. See also Bukhārī, *Ṣaḥīḥ*, *Bāb al-ta'bīr*, *Bāb ru'yā al-ṣāliḥīn*).

God's promise to fulfill the dream ("You shall enter the holy mosque") seems to contradict the addition "if God wills." Exegesis suggests several ways to settle the contradiction, all of which convey a need, almost an obligation, to interpret the verse in a manner that does not contradict the idea of dreams as truth-holders or, as stated by al-Qurṭubī, as "means to deliver revelations to prophets" (*Jāmi'*, xvi, 290).

The nocturnal journey of the Prophet

Q 17:60 reads: "And when we said to you, 'Surely your Lord encompasses humankind,' and we made the vision *(ru'yā)*, that we showed you, an ordeal *(fitna)* for humankind and [also] the tree cursed in the Qur'ān; and we frighten them, but it only increases them in great insolence." Exegetical literature offers various occasions to which the *ru'yā* in this verse may refer: One is the ascension (q.v.; *isrā'*), mentioned in the first verse of the same sūra. In this case, *ru'yā* (dream) might mean *ru'yat 'ayn*, "physical seeing in wakefulness" and the cursed tree *(al-shajara al-mal'ūna)* is the *zaqūm* (Ṭabarsī, *Majma'*, iv (xv), 66; Suyūṭī, *Durr*, iv, 210; Shawkānī, *Tafsīr*, iii, 240; Ibn 'Aṭiyya, *Muḥarrar*, iii, 467, 468; see TREES). The reference could also be to Muḥammad's dream regarding the conquest of Mecca (Q 48:27; Ṭabarsī, *Majma'*, iv [xv], 66; Shawkānī, *Tafsīr*, iii, 240; Ālūsī, *Rūḥ*, viii, 107; Ibn 'Aṭiyya, *Muḥarrar*, iii, 468) or to the dream in which the Prophet saw monkeys climbing his pulpit *(minbar)*, interpreted as being the Umayyad caliphs. According to the last interpretation, the cursed tree alludes to the Umayyad dynasty (Ṭabarsī, *Majma'*, iv (xv), 66; Suyūṭī, *Durr*, iv, 211; Shawkānī, *Tafsīr*, iii, 240; Ālūsī, *Rūḥ*, viii, 107; Kāshānī, *Ṣāfī*, iii, 200; Ibn 'Aṭiyya, *Muḥarrar*, iii, 468).

Unlike the other references discussed above, the exegesis on this verse does not examine the dream as a medium which reveals a future event but rather raises a question as to the circumstances under which the dream could cause *fitna*, "ordeal, insolence, dissension (q.v.)." Performing the ascension *(isrā')* through a dream would not cause *fitna* (Ibn 'Aṭiyya, *Muḥarrar*, iii, 468). Only physical ascension could be considered a miracle, the acceptance of which requires profound belief and as such puts people to the test. Following this line, attention should be given to the exceptional usage of *ruʾyā* in this verse. It means physical seeing rather than dreaming and indicates wakefulness rather than sleep (see SEEING AND HEARING). If that *ruʾyā* refers to the dream Muḥammad had before the conquest of Mecca, *fitna* could be the outcome of the disappointment of the people who did not witness the immediate fulfillment of the dream (see "The conquest of Mecca" above).

Aḍghāth aḥlām

Dreams of this category are defined as frightful nightmares, deceptive dreams or dreams with a meaning that cannot be interpreted (Qurṭubī, *Jāmiʿ*, xi, 270). In the case of Pharaoh, the counselors did not know how to interpret his dream and named it *aḍghāth aḥlām* (Q 12:44). In Q 21:5 the term refers to the Qurʾān brought by Muḥammad and was used by those who doubted his mission. Although not elaborated in the *tafsīr*, the difference between the term *aḍghāth aḥlām* and *ruʾyā/manām* can be easily perceived. The latter are considered part of prophecy, of divine origin, revealing the future (see *Bushrā* above), they hold the truth (see Muḥammad's dream before the conquest of Mecca, mentioned above) and have the authority to lead people and instruct them on how to act (see Abraham's dream, and all the dreams in Sūrat Yūsuf, mentioned above). *Aḍghāth aḥlām,* on the other hand, are represented as misleading lies, stories inspired by demons and, as such, invalid. By comparing the negative features of *aḍghāth aḥlām,* the value and weight of *ruʾyā* and *manām* become prominent. This differentiation also appears in the ḥadīth literature, expressed in a widespread saying "*ruʾyā* is from God and *ḥulm* is from Satan" (*al-ruʾyā min Allāh wa-l-ḥulm min al-shayṭān,* for a reference to different versions of this ḥadīth, see Abū Hājir Zaghlūl, *Mawsūʿa,* v, 157).

Conclusions

Of all the references to dreams examined above, only in Sūrat Yūsuf do we come across dream narratives (q.v.). In all other cases, the term "dream" is mentioned but nothing is said about the content of the dream, the reason for it or its background (*asbāb al-nuzūl*; see OCCASIONS OF REVELATION); these are elaborated in the exegetical literature. This observation allows us to say that — except for the dreams in Sūrat Yūsuf — the Qurʾān does not contain narratives of dreams. The examination of dreams in the exegetical literature reflects the concerns of later times, when dreams had already gained a special status in Islam.

The legitimization of the usage of dreams, established in the ḥadīth, was set to justify the special role dreams began to play in the nascent Islamic community that had lost its Prophet. People's search for the authority of dreams increased after the death of the Prophet, when prophecy came to an end (see Kinberg, Literal dreams, 283, and n. 12; also Von Grünebaum, Cultural function, 7). As part of prophecy, dreams were perceived as vehicles through which transcendental information could reach the believers. This created a special interest in dreams and, due to the trust people had in them, they began to function in a way similar to that of the ḥadīth, especially that of edifying ḥadīth (for further details see Kinberg, Literal dreams, 283-92 [Dreams as a functional parallel to ḥadīth]). The Qurʾān naturally was not in need of this kind of dream. The exegetical literature, nevertheless, tried to relate ḥadīth and Qurʾān.

The same can be said of the relationship between qurʾānic dreams and *taʿbīr* literature, the interpretation of dreams. Exegesis, whenever applicable, dealt with the way in which the interpretation of dreams operated and the circumstances under which they could be fulfilled. *Taʿbīr* books, which developed into a distinct genre (for details see *Manām,* Introduction, 43-6), referred to the Qurʾān and used its verses as a means of interpretation. Nonetheless, were it not for the contribution of *tafsīr,* no qurʾānic verse would have been associated with the *taʿbīr* literature.

Leah Kinberg

Bibliography

Primary: Abū Hājir Zaghlūl (ed.), *Mawsūʿat aṭrāf al-ḥadīth,* Beirut 1989; Abū l-Layth al-Samarqandī, *Tafsīr;* Bukhārī, *Ṣaḥīḥ;* Ālūsī, *Rūḥ;* Baghawī, *Maʿālim;* Ibn ʿAṭiyya, *Muḥarrar;* Kāshānī, *Ṣāfī; Manām,* see below Kinberg, *Morality;* Muqātil, *Tafsīr;* Qurṭubī, *Jāmiʿ;* Qushayrī, Abū l-Qāsim, *al-Risāla al-Qushayriyya,* Beirut 1987; Rāzī, *Tafsīr;* Shawkānī, *Tafsīr;* Suyūṭī, *Durr;* Ṭabarsī, *Majmaʿ;* Wāḥidī, *Wasīṭ.*
Secondary: N. Bland, On the Muhammedan science of *taʿbīr* or interpretation of dreams, in JRAS (1856), 118-79; T. Fahd, Les procédés oniromantiques, in id., *La divination arabe,* Leiden 1966, 247-367; id., The dream in medieval Islamic society, in G.E. von Grünebaum and R. Callois (eds.), *The dream and human societies,* Berkeley 1966, 351-63; G.E. von Grünebaum, The cultural function of the dream as illustrated by classical Islam, in *The dream and human societies,* 3-21; L. Kinberg, Literal dreams and prophetic *ḥadīṯ* in classical Islam. A comparison of two ways of legitimation, in *Der Islam* (1993), 279-300; id., *Morality in the guise of dreams. Ibn Abī al-Dunyā's* K. al-Manām (a critical edition with introduction), Leiden 1994 *(= Manām),* and see the bibliography there; M.J. Kister, The interpretation of dreams. An unknown manuscript of Ibn Qutaybah's *ʿIbārat al-ruʾyā,* in IOS 4 (1974), 67-103; J. de Somogyi, The interpretation of dreams in ad-Damīrī's *Ḥayāt al-ḥayawān,* in JRAS (1940), 1-20.

Dress

see CLOTHING

Drink

see FOOD AND DRINK

Drowning

Death by suffocation under water. Alongside warnings about the day of judgment on which individuals will receive their reckoning (see LAST JUDGMENT; APOCALYPSE; ESCHATOLOGY), the Qurʾān also recounts instances of God's judgments against entire communities in former times. Due to their corruption (q.v.), God had destroyed these once powerful peoples, as stated in Q 29:40: "And we seized [and punished] each for its crime. We sent a hail of stones against some; others were overtaken by an awful cry; some we had the earth (q.v.) swallow up; while still others we drowned! Surely God did not wrong them; rather they had wronged themselves." Such drownings *(gharaq, aghraq, mughraq)* occur approximately twenty times in the Qurʾān and almost always in explicit reference to either the story of Noah (q.v.) and the flood or to the destruction of Pharaoh (q.v.) and his army in pursuit of Moses (q.v.) and the Children of Israel (q.v.). Both accounts depict people who are intransigent in their evil ways (see EVIL DEEDS) and deny the messengers sent by God to warn them of his impending judgment (see MESSENGER; WARNER): "When the folk of Noah called the messengers liars, we drowned them and made them a sign for humanity. We have prepared a painful punishment for oppressors!" (Q 25:37; cf. 10:90; 11:37, 43; 23:27; 36:43; 44:24; 71:25). Thus, and at times in nearly identical language, the Qurʾān describes God's deliverance (q.v.) of Noah and Moses as well as his punishment of their enemies by drowning: "And we saved Moses and all of those with him, then we drowned the others. In that is a sign, but most do not believe" (Q 26:65-7; cf. 26:119-21; also 2:50; 7:64, 136; 8:54; 17:103; 21:77). Far from being random acts of nature (see NATURAL WORLD AND THE QURʾĀN), these drownings result from the flood of forty days and the parting of the Red Sea and as such they are miraculous in nature (see MIRACLE). Due to their miraculous nature, these and similar events are meant both to underscore God's justice (see JUSTICE AND INJUSTICE) and, equally important, to serve as a sign (*āya*, see SIGNS) for later generations (q.v.), that they might take heed and follow God guidance for humanity as revealed by his prophets (see PROPHETS AND PROPHETHOOD): "So when they angered us, we took vengeance (q.v.) and drowned them all, and so we made them a precedent and an example for those to come" (Q 43:55-6; also see 17:69; 25:37). See also CHASTISEMENT AND PUNISHMENT; PUNISHMENT STORIES; ANGER.

Th. Emil Homerin

Bibliography
Primary: ʿAbd al-Bāqī; Qushayrī, *Laṭāʾif*, iii, 370-1; Quṭb, *Ẓilāl*, Beirut 1393-4/1973-4; 1407/1987[13] (rev. ed.), v, 2599, 2735-6, 3194; Rāzī, *Tafsīr*, Cairo 1352/1933, xxiv, 140-1; xxv, 67; xxvii, 217; Ṭabarī, *Tafsīr*, Cairo 1373-77/1954-7, ixx, 51-5, 57; xx, 96-7; xxv, 50-51.
Secondary: F. Rahman, *Major themes of the Qurʾān*, Chicago 1980.

Druzes

A religio-ethnic community and offshoot of the Shīʿī Ismāʿīlī branch of Islam. The Druze *(durzī*, pl. *durūz)* trace their origins to early eleventh-century Fāṭimid Cairo and the reign of the Ismāʿīlī Imām-Caliph al-Ḥākim bi-Amr Allāh (r. 386/996-411/1021). The Druze faith or doctrine *(madhhab)* is based on 111 "Epistles of Wisdom" *(rasāʾil al-ḥikma)* written during the brief period of its propagation, 408/1017-435/1043. Three centuries later these epistles were collected into six books by ʿĪsā al-Tanūkhī. His organization of these epistles constitutes the Druze Canon (14 in Book I, 25 in Book II, 15 in Book III, 13 in Book IV, 7 in Book V and 36 in Book VI; epistle 50 is addressed to Tanūkhī, himself. With the exception of eleven epistles whose authorship is unknown, all others bear the name of one of the three founders of the faith: Ḥamza b. ʿAlī al-Zawzanī (d. after 411/1021), known as the guide of the believers *(hādī l-mustajībīn)*, nos. 5-35 (although bearing no author's name, the style of Epistles 5, 7, 8 and 11 indicate his authorship); Ismāʿīl b. Muḥammad al-Tamīmī, second in rank, nos. 36-40; and Bahāʾ al-Dīn al-Muqtanā (d. after 434/1032), whom Ḥamza called the mouthpiece of the believers (lit. tongue of the unitarians, *lisān al-muwaḥḥidīn*) on account of his skill in articulating the faith, nos. 42-111. The founders called themselves and their followers unitarians *(mūwaḥḥidūn)* and their doctrine unitarianism *(daʿwat al-tawḥīd)*. Both terms appear on almost every page of the Druze Canon, where the epistles quote, either in full or in part or sometimes even with a single word, more than 250 verses from the Qurʾān to corroborate *tawḥīd* or to refute tenets inconsistent with Druze doctrine (Book I quotes 109 qurʾānic verses, Book II 58, Book III 30, Book V 60, Books IV and VI 4 each). For Ḥamza (epistle 6), the Qurʾān as revelation has seven forms *(unzila ʿalā sabʿat ṣunūf)*, one part of which is *nāsikh* (abrogating), the other *mansūkh* (abrogated), and seven readings *(quriʾa bi-sabʿat aḥruf)*. See ABROGATION; READINGS OF THE QURʾĀN.

From Ismāʿīlism to Daʿwat al-tawḥīd

Shīʿī Ismāʿīlī precepts and beliefs grew out of those of the Shīʿa Imāmiyya (see SHĪʿISM AND THE QURʾĀN) in the second half of the third/ninth century. Disagreement over the identity of the legitimate imāms led to divergence in doctrine (see CREEDS; DISSENSION), which soon set the Ismāʿīlīs apart as an independent sect. Ismāʿīlism achieved its most brilliant success in North Africa when in 297/909 it became the religion of the Fāṭimid state that soon conquered Egypt in 360/969. After the establishment of this state, Ismāʿīlī theologians instilled in the followers of the sect messianic expectations of the coming of the *mahdī* (the divinely guided figure destined to usher in the eschatological age of justice; see ESCHATOLOGY), personified eventually in the Fāṭimīd Imām-Caliph (see IMĀM; CALIPH). Some orthodox Ismāʿīlīs were eager to see the messianic promise fulfilled during their own lifetime and thus were described as extremists *(ghulāt)*. Such messianic hopes reached their peak in 386/996 when, after almost a century and five Fāṭimid caliphs, al-Ḥākim bi-Amr Allāh ascended the throne. In 408/1017 Fāṭimid Ismāʿīlī missionaries *(duʿāt,* sing. *dāʿī)* claimed that al-Ḥākim was not only of divine nature but that he was the long-awaited *mahdī*. It is at this point that tradition locates the origin of the Druze religious sect.

The most radical change introduced by Druzism was the abolishment of a hereditary system of the Imāmate; after the divine manifestation in al-Ḥākim, the Ismāʿīlī messianic belief in the coming *mahdī* was replaced by the definitive triumph of unitarianism. The Druze belief is based on the idea that human beings, bound by their physical nature, possess a faculty of comprehension which is correspondingly bound by space and time and thus incapable of conceiving the essence of the divine *(lāhūt)*. God can be understood only within the limits of our own comprehension: Like an image in a mirror, the divine appears in human form *(nāsūt)*. *Lāhūt* and *nāsūt* are based on an interpretation of qurʾānic verses. For example: "Say: 'Who is the lord *(rabb)* of the heavens and earth?' Say: 'Allāh'" (Q 13:16). The qurʾānic terms *rabb* and Allāh are interpreted by Ḥamza (epistle 10) as the "*Lāhūt* of our lord... who cannot be defined and described." The *nāsūt* does not signify an incarnation of God (see ANTHROPOMORPHISM) but an image through which God brings himself closer to human understanding. Al-Tamīmī (epistle 36) bases the form of *nāsūt* on the Qurʾān: "Like a mirage in a desert which the thirsty takes to be water, until when he comes to it, he finds it to be nothing, discovering instead God beside him" (Q 24:39). Al-Ḥākim was the penultimate manifestation of the *lāhūt* in the *nāsūt* form, completing the cycle of unitarian messages. Throughout the Epistles of the Druze Canon, there is a strong emphasis on the unitarian concept, and warning is given against taking the *nāsūt* image for the divine itself: "God is unique, eternal, without a beginning, and abiding without end. He is beyond the comprehension of human understanding. Thus, he cannot be defined by words or attributes distinct from his essence. He has no body or spirit."

Tawḥīḍ

Druze doctrine follows Ismāʿīlism in its distinction between formal revelation and esoteric interpretation (see REVELATION AND INSPIRATION) but adds a third element in its call to apply, above all else, the heart and mind to deep devotion to God, not to rules and rituals. Those who follow either the exoteric *(tanzīl)* or esoteric *(taʾwīl)* approach to interpreting scripture (see EXEGESIS OF THE QURʾĀN: CLASSICAL AND MEDIEVAL) remain dependent on intermediaries and can thus never reach true belief in God *(tawḥīd)*. True unitarians have no need for such mediation when it comes to worship. They are exempt from the performance of ritual obligations (*daʿāʾim taklīfiyya* or *al-takālīf al-sharʿiyya,* see RITUAL AND THE QURʾĀN) which they view as a form of punishment God has set aside for non-*muwaḥḥidūn* (see CHASTISEMENT AND PUNISHMENT). In place of the seven ritual obligations or pillars *(daʿāʾim taklīfiyya),* the Druze faith substitutes seven unitarian principles: (1) truthfulness, (2) mutual aid, (3) disassociation from unbelievers, (4) renunciation of belief inconsistent with *tawḥīd*, (5) belief that the unitarian doctrine was preached in every age, (6) content resignation to all God's actions and (7) submission to God's will. Al-Tamīmī (epistle 37) considers *daʿāʾim taklīfiyya* to be fire (q.v.) which scorches those who practice the ritual obligations, as the Qurʾān describes: "The fire will scorch their faces" (Q 23:104).

Thus early Ismāʿīlism was articulated around the notion of the superiority of the esoteric *(bāṭin)* over the exoteric *(ẓāhir)* and *taʾwil* over *tanzīl*, with the accompanying conclusion that outward ritual acts are God's punishment for non-Ismāʿīlīs, i.e. *tawḥīd* replaces *tanzīl* and *tāʾwīl*. In this, Druze doctrine differs from the Shīʿī and Ismāʿīlī approaches as well as the Sunnī emphasis on the sacred law *(sharīʿa)*. The writers of the Druze Canon took pains to ground their unique position in the Qurʾān through allegorical interpretation of qurʾānic verses which are invariably quoted to explain the principle of the unitarian doctrine as the third or middle doctrine *(maslak)* to which, according to al-Tamīmī (epistle 38), the Q 57:13 refers: "Between them will be a wall with a door: The inner side *(bāṭinuhu)* will contain mercy, and the outer side in front *(wa-ẓāhiruhu min qablihi)* the punishment." The three doctrines are perceived as three stages of the religious faith: "Islam *(ẓāhir)* is the door to faith *(īmān*, i.e. inner faith, *bāṭin)* and *īmān* is the door to the ultimate goal *(tawḥīd)*, the highest stage of the religion" (epistle 9). Al-Tamīmī (epistle 38) distinguishes these stages by quoting Q 20:55 in the following way: "'From it did we create you,' i.e. from *ẓāhir*, 'into it do we bring you again,' i.e. to *bāṭin*, 'and from it do we bring you forth another time,' i.e. by setting the *muwaḥḥidūn* apart from *ẓāhir* and *bāṭin* and bringing them to the middle doctrine of *al-tawḥīd*." There are three corresponding ranks of believers: *ahl al-ẓāhir*, i.e. Muslims *(al-muslimūn)*; *ahl al-bāṭin*, i.e. Believers *(al-muʾminūn)*; and *ahl al-raḥma*, i.e. Unitarians *(al-muwaḥḥidūn)*.

Ethics

While the Epistles provide a general framework for morality (see ETHICS IN THE QURʾĀN), the influence of Ṣūfism (see ṢŪFISM AND THE QURʾĀN) comes to the fore in the many mystical principles to which Druze sheikhs adhere in their overall demeanor (*maslak*, lit. way, path, course), i.e. the way they eat, dress and pray and in their attitude towards others (see FOOD AND DRINK; CLOTHING; PRAYER; SOCIAL RELATIONS). Interesting is the way Bahāʾ al-Dīn deals with qurʾānic references to issues such as marriage *(nikāh)* which, according to him, contradict one another. This contradiction is explained by the existence of abrogating *(nāsikh)* and abrogated *(mansūkh)* verses. Accepting the *nāsikh* but viewing *mansūkh* as an addition to the qurʾānic revelation, Bahāʾ al-Dīn (epistle 71) considers that only what is true, i.e. non-contradictory, in the Qurʾān comes from God. Epistle 25 grants women complete equality with men (see FEMINISM AND THE QURʾĀN; WOMEN AND THE QURʾĀN) in what concerns marriage and divorce (q.v.) as well as inheritance rights (where Islamic law normally makes a distinction between sons and daughters; see INHERITANCE). Four epistles (8, 18, 83 and 84) are addressed to female unitarians *(al-muwaḥḥidāt)* and extol the values of purity (*ṭahāra*, see PURITY AND IMPURITY) and good conduct. Furthermore, women have full access to the Canon and take part in religious meetings.

al-Amīr al-Sayyid al-Tanūkhī

Al-Amīr al-Sayyid Jamāl al-Dīn ʿAbdallāh al-Tanūkhī (820/1417-884/1479) is revered almost as highly as the propagators of the faith themselves. Al-Amīr al-Sayyid devoted his life to the study of the Arabic language, logic, poetry, history and, above all, the Qurʾān and the Druze Canon. His legacy includes fourteen volumes with commentary on the Epistles, theology and ethics, with the aim of creating unity in the exegesis of the Canon which guides the Druze sages *(ʿuqqāl)* until today. The moral principles articulated by al-Sayyid and his elaboration of "the lawful and the prohibited" (*al-ḥalāl wa-l-ḥarām,* see LAWFUL AND UNLAWFUL) soon became the elementary code on which Druze came to rely in their everyday life and in the rules of their newly-established religious courts.

Modern times

Until the end of the Ottoman era in 1918, the Druze were able to preserve their traditional characteristics as a close-knit ethno-religious community. In modern times an emerging generation of intellectuals has begun to search for ways to combine Islam and Arab nationalism in order to unite all the various Muslim sects. They now emphasize the Islamic character of the Druze "school" *(madhhab)* and turn to the Qurʾān, in addition to the Druze Canon, in order to demonstrate that their *madhhab* represented one among several autonomous Muslim doctrines. This work is often the result of personal efforts of interpretation and thus frequently adds new Islamic elements and incorporate beliefs current among the Druze at large (*juhhāl,* lit. the ignorants), whose role in the formation of the Druze faith has increased with the rise of modernization and consequent diminishment of the numbers of *ʿuqqāl.*

At the close of the twentieth century, the Druze numbered about one million and are geographically dispersed over Syria, Lebanon, Jordan and Israel/Palestine. Emigration mainly from Syria and Lebanon has created small pockets of Druze populations in the American continents, Australia and West Africa. Thus, socio-economic and political changes, including growing secularization, are reshaping the life of the community as a whole.

Kais M. Firro

Bibliography

Manuscripts (see below Firro, 1992): Ashrafānī, ʿAbd al-Malik, *ʿUmdat al-ʿārifīn; al-Kathīf wa-l-laṭīf; al-Munfarid bi-dhātihi; Rasāʾil al-ḥikma* (The Druze Canon); Tanūkhī, Sayyid ʿAbdallāh, *Sharḥ* (of Three Epistles of the Druze Canon); Taqī l-Dīn, Zayn al-Dīn ʿAbd al-Ghaffār, *Majrā l-zamān.*

Primary: Antākī, Yaḥyā b. Saʿīd, *Tāʾrīkh Yaḥyā b. Saʿīd al-Antākī,* ed. L. Cheikho, B. Carra de Vaux and H. Zayyat, Beirut/Paris 1909; Ibn Sabāṭ, Ḥamza, *Sidq al-akhbār. Tāʾrīkh Ibn Sabāṭ,* ed. ʿU.ʿA. Tadmurī, Tripoli, Lebanon 1993; Ibn Yaḥyā, Ṣāliḥ, *Tāʾrīkh Bayrūt,* ed. L. Cheikho, Beirut 1927; Kirmānī, Ḥamīd al-Dīn Aḥmad b. ʿAlī, *Rāḥat al-ʿaql,* ed. M. Ghālib, Beirut 1983; id., *al-Risāla al-wāʿiẓa,* ed. M.K. Ḥusayn, Cairo 1952.

Secondary: N. Abu Izzeddin, *The Druzes. A new study of their history, faith and society,* Leiden 1984; S. Assaad, *The reign of al-Hakim bi Amr Allah, 996-1021. A political study,* Beirut 1974; D. Brayer, The origin of the Druze religion, in *Der Islam* 52 (1975), 47-84, 239-261 and 53 (1976), 5-27; S. De Sacy, *Exposé de la religion des Druzes,* Paris 1838; Amsterdam 1964²; K. Firro, *A history of the Druzes,* Leiden 1992; id., *The Druzes in the Jewish state. A brief history,* Leiden 1999; P. Hitti, *The origin of the Druze people and religion,* New York 1928; M. Hodgson, al-Darazi and Hamza in the origin of the Druze religion, in *JAOS* 82 (1962), 5-20; S. Makarem, *Aḍwāʾ ʿalā maslak al-tawḥīd,* Beirut 1966; id., *Maslak al-tawḥīd,* Beirut 1980; ʿA. Najjār, *Madhhab al-durūz wa-l-tawḥīd,* Cairo 1965; ʿA. Nuwayhid, *Sīrat al-Amīr al-Sayyid Jamāl al-Dīn ʿAbdallāh al-Tanūkhī,* Beirut 1975; A. Taliʿ, *Aṣl al-muwaḥḥidīn al-durūz,* Beirut n.d.

Dunyā see WORLD; LIFE